SURPRISING RHYMING

THE ALTERNATIVE RHYMING DICTIONARY TO INSPIRE RHYMES PEOPLE MAY NOT EXPECT TO HEAR

Edited by:
BRIAN OLIVER

Published by Big **6** Publishing
www.thehitformula.com

COPYRIGHT © 2018 by Brian Oliver
The moral right of the author has been asserted.
All rights reserved.

No part of this publication may be reproduced, stored in or introduced into a retrieval system, or transmitted, in any form or by any means, electronic, mechanical, photocopying, recording or otherwise, without the prior permission in writing of the copyright owner, except in the case of brief excerpts or quotations embodied in published articles and reviews. Nor shall this publication be otherwise circulated in any form of binding or cover other than that in which it is published and without a similar condition, including this condition, being imposed on the subsequent purchaser.

Limit of Liability/Disclaimer of Warranty
The publisher and the author make no representations or warranties with respect to the accuracy or completeness of the contents of this work and specifically disclaim all warranties, including without limitation warranties of fitness for a particular purpose. No warranty may be created or extended by sales or promotional materials. The advice contained herein may not be suitable for every situation. This work is sold with the understanding that the publisher and the author are not engaged in rendering legal, accounting or other professional services. If professional assistance is required, the services of a competent professional person should be sought. Neither the publisher nor the author shall be liable for damages arising herefrom.

Published by Big **6** Publishing
www.thehitformula.com

ISBN-13: 978-1986114547
ISBN-10: 1986114546

Cover photo: Aliko Sunawang, www.pixabay.com

ABOUT THE EDITOR

Brian Oliver is a highly experienced music publisher, songwriter, musician and music consultant who has been involved in the music industry for over 25 years.

As a publisher, he has worked on the songs of legendary writers such as Neil Diamond, Janis Ian, Albert Hammond, James Taylor, Chip Taylor and Gilbert O'Sullivan, as well as bands like The Stranglers, Spandau Ballet and The Shadows, and leading film and TV composer Colin Towns. He has also been a consultant to major companies such as Universal Music, Warner Music and BMG.

He is the author of the five-star rated book, *How [Not] to Write a Hit Song! 101 Common Mistakes to Avoid If You Want Songwriting Success*. This much-praised book takes a close look at the essential elements consistently found in the structure, melodies and lyrics of all hit songs. It highlights the most common errors made when these key components are built into a song—so that new songwriters can try to avoid such mistakes in their own songs (you'll find more information on Page 623 of this book).

He is also the author of *How [Not] to Write Great Lyrics! 40 Common Mistakes to Avoid When Writing Lyrics for Your Songs*. Written in an easy, non-technical style, the book identifies the most frequent causes of lyric writing problems and aims to help aspiring songwriters steer clear of the many traps they can easily fall into when writing lyrics. From how to prevent common errors in the basic construction of their lyrics ... to the perils of making bad choices when it comes to titles, opening lines, lyrical hooks, verb selection, clichés, rhyming patterns, and many other issues.

* * *

TABLE OF CONTENTS

INTRODUCTION 7

SURPRISING YOUR AUDIENCE 11

HOW TO USE THIS BOOK 15

PART ONE: 'A' 19

PART TWO: 'E' 121

PART THREE: 'I' 325

PART FOUR: 'O' 433

PART FIVE: 'U' 571

OTHER BOOKS BY BRIAN OLIVER 623

INTRODUCTION

THE CONCEPT of this book was inspired by a PBS *News Hour* interview with Stephen Sondheim that I saw a few years ago. When the interviewer, Jeffrey Brown, asked the legendary Broadway composer and lyricist about the importance of rhyme, Sondheim told him:

> "One of the uses of rhyme is not only to focus the [listener's] attention on the word, but to strengthen what you're saying...The ears expect certain rhymes, so you want to fool them because one of the things you want to do is surprise an audience."

But how can writers follow Sondheim's advice and consistently come up with rhymes that will take people by surprise?

A standard rhyming dictionary can certainly be a powerful tool to help writers discover possible rhyming mates, but most dictionaries concentrate on 'perfect' rhymes in which the stressed vowels and any succeeding consonants are always identical (such as: *great/late*, *dutiful/beautiful*, *believe/conceive* or *skylight/highlight*). From my own experience as a music publisher, this can still lead to fairly predictable results because, in most cases, only exact rhymes are listed.

I found myself wondering: what if writers had access to a new kind of rhyming dictionary, one that focused on 'imperfect' rhymes instead of being limited to 'true' rhymes? What if writers were able to gain creative inspiration from an alternative rhyming guide crammed with thousands of unexpected 'false' or 'near' rhymes that could fool a listener's ears, just as Sondheim advocated?

And that's how the idea for *Surprising Rhyming* began ...

Of course, some songwriters and poets fear that using any kind of rhyming dictionary will somehow make them less of a creative writer—like a painter who has to rely on a paint-by-numbers kit to create a great piece of art. In practice, though, successful writers across many different genres recommend using a rhyming dictionary as a valuable brainstorming tool.

In the PBS interview, Stephen Sondheim revealed that he always uses a "well-thumbed" rhyming dictionary and a 1946 edition of *Roget's Thesaurus*. "Trick rhymes you have to think up yourself," he said. "But to rhyme 'bay', do you know how many dozens of words there are for that? You can't think them all up yourself! And looking down the list will give you ideas."

At the other end of the creative spectrum, rapper Eminem has also admitted that he frequently turns to a rhyming dictionary for inspiration. In a CNN interview, he revealed that he often spends hours studying a dictionary to create lists of words for his rhymes.

Another acclaimed songwriter who believes in keeping a rhyming dictionary handy is Jimmy Webb, whose platinum-selling songs include 'Up, Up and Away', 'By the Time I Get to Phoenix', 'Wichita Lineman' and 'MacArthur Park'. "If a rhyme scheme is stubborn and difficult to complete," says Webb, "a dictionary may suggest another word that is more easily and naturally rhymed."

Although *Surprising Rhyming* does include perfect rhymes, its main purpose is to deliver thousands of off-the-wall rhymes designed to take your rhyming options a step further. It aims to help you become more adventurous in your writing by giving you suggestions for rhymes that are less predictable and therefore free of the usual clichés.

In this book, 'surprising' rhymes are typically formed by words with similar but not identical sounds (such as *rain/blame* or *day/late*, rather than perfect rhymes like *rain/pain* or *day/lay*). In most instances, either the vowel segments are different while the consonants are identical, or vice versa.

Most significantly, though, the 'surprising' rhymes listed on these pages are based on an analysis of thousands of 'near' rhymes that have actually been used by some of the world's greatest and most influential songwriters and lyricists. They include: Chuck Berry, David Bowie, Sara Bareilles, James Bay, Leonard Cohen, Bob Dylan, Sia Furler, Hozier, Jay-Z, Billy Joel, Carole King, Michael Kiwanuka, John Lennon, Lorde, John Mayer, Joni Mitchell, Paul McCartney, Van Morrison, Bonnie McKee, Randy Newman, Dolly Parton, Christina Perri, Katy Perry, Ed Sheeran, Paul Simon, Stephen Sondheim, Taylor Swift, Cat Stevens, Bernie Taupin, James Taylor, Jimmy Webb, Lucinda Williams, Stevie Wonder ... and many more.

While our researchers found that *girl/world* and *love/enough* were two of the 'false' rhyming mates used most frequently by these acclaimed writers, many of them have inserted some highly inventive 'imperfect' rhymes into their rhyming patterns.

For example, Chuck Berry managed to rhyme 'trouble' and 'struggle' in his classic song 'Promised Land', while Ed Sheeran's songs have featured imaginative rhymes like *fellas/jealous* and *disastrous/pastures*. Meanwhile, Eminem achieved the seemingly impossible in his 1999 song 'Brain Damage' by rhyming the notoriously difficult word 'orange' with 'door hinge' and 'four-inch'!

Many writers have found that breaking rhyming rules in this way can be very liberating, especially when it has the effect of drawing listeners' ears closer to the rest of the song or poem.

Our research also found that the art of rhyming in song lyrics and poetry has changed significantly in recent years, not least because of the influence of hip-hop on the construction of rhyming schemes. Rap and hip-hop use more rhymes than any other genre.

One noticeable impact of this is that rhymes no longer only tend to appear at the end of a line as a kind of punctuation mark. Instead, we're now seeing much greater use of internal rhymes and compound rhymes (rhymes that contain two or more syllables). And it's increasingly common for several words that rhyme to appear in the same sentence.

This means many writers now face the challenge of having to come up with a much greater number of rhymes for each song or poem. That's why this book is designed to give you a bigger choice of potential rhyming words. It provides a rich collection of thousands of surprising rhymes in addition to many of the regular rhymes that appear in traditional rhyming dictionaries.

Surprising Rhyming doesn't include profanities and contains only a few proper nouns. It largely focuses on action verbs, vivid verbs, adjectives, adverbs and nouns that describe action, setting or senses. We've also omitted words which, in our view, are unlikely to be used in emotive creative writing, such as complex technical, medical, legal or scientific terms.

However, we have included many new words that have been added to leading dictionaries in recent years—such as 'photobomb', 'bitcoin', 'bootylicious' and 'twerking'.

Of course, there are now websites that offer rhyming solutions. But, unlike the computer algorithms that drive these sites, the rhymes suggested in this book are based on **human** writers' ear for pitch, rhythm and sense—and, most importantly, the similarity in *sound* between words, rather than their spelling.

Most rhymes listed here are broken down into one-, two- or three-syllable words (and occasionally four syllables). The processes that power online rhyming sites often can't tell the difference between one-syllable words and multi-syllable words that contain stressed and unstressed syllables. And automated rhyming systems have no appreciation of the emotional context of lyrics or poetry. That's why online sources can end up offering some pretty clumsy suggestions!

This book can't hope to help you come up with trick rhymes or clever compounds like Rakim's groundbreaking *righteous/might just* in 1987, or flashes of genius such as Bob Dylan's pairing of 'kiddin' you' and 'didn't you' in 'Like a Rolling Stone' in 1965. But I hope it will help you be more creatively courageous in your approach to rhyming ... and thus avoid the worn-out, clichéd rhymes that we've all heard countless times before.

So, challenge yourself and make your rhymes less predictable.

Surprise your audience ...

Brian Oliver
May 2018

SURPRISING YOUR AUDIENCE
by Brian Oliver

"The most difficult thing to do with writing a song is finding a phrase that you haven't heard before."
—Ed Sheeran

AS A MUSIC PUBLISHER I have listened to thousands of demos by aspiring songwriters and, despite always hoping to discover a fresh new talent, I've ended up feeling disappointed because I found I could predict what the next rhyme was going to be on almost every line.

Inexperienced writers often weaken a potentially good song by going for the easiest and most obvious rhyme, or by using the same rhyme sound too many times in a row.

This simply makes the lyrics sound boring, monotonous and colorless.

It's not enough to simply go through the alphabet trying to think of words that rhyme—irrespective of whether the chosen word helps to underpin the meaning of your song and drive the story forward. This lazy approach usually results in worn-out, clichéd rhymes that we've all heard countless times before.

Lyrics don't always have to rhyme, of course, but rhyming is a mnemonic device that assists the memory and makes it easier for people to remember a song. Rhyming also plays an important part in giving a lyric a sense of form and symmetry.

"In a couplet, the first rhyme is like a question to which the second rhyme is an answer," explains James Fenton, a former Professor of Poetry at Oxford University. "In most quatrains [four-line verses], space is created between the rhyme that poses the question and the rhyme that gives the answer ... it's like a pleasure deferred."

Historically, many pop songs in the rock era have featured 'perfect' rhymes where a one-syllable word is rhymed with another one-syllable word (such as 'kiss' and 'miss'), or where two words have the same spelling in the last syllable (such as 'love and 'above').

But perfect rhymes tend to get tedious. And many of the cleverest perfect rhymes have been used so many times over the years that they've now become clichés.

Hit songwriting is more sophisticated these days, and publishers and A&R reps have much higher expectations of lyricists. So, if you have a rhyme in your head, ask yourself if you've heard it before. If it sounds too familiar, try finding another way of saying it—perhaps by using a metaphor rather than just a literal rhyme, or an off-the-wall 'imperfect' rhyme.

Sometimes, simply putting an unexpected adjective or a visual descriptor (like Homer's "rosy-fingered dawn" and "wine-dark sea") in front of a clichéd rhyming noun can surprise the listener and make the cliché sound less familiar.

You can often create a much greater impact by rhyming words that don't have the same combination of letters but sound similar (such as 'clown' and 'around', or 'made' and 'late'). This is because lyrics are meant for the ears, so how words *sound* is more important than how they're written. It's the similarity between the sound of the syllables (for example, 'rougher' and 'suffer') that creates the rhyme and engages the listener, rather than the words themselves.

"Rhyming doesn't have to be exact anymore," Bob Dylan told Paul Zollo of *American Songwriter* magazine in a 2012 interview. "It gives you a thrill to rhyme something and you think, 'Well, that's never been rhymed before'. Nobody's going to care if you rhyme 'represent' with 'ferment', you know. Nobody's gonna care."

Dylan once admitted to *Rolling Stone* magazine that he stunned himself when he wrote the first two lines of 'Like a Rolling Stone' and rhymed "kiddin' you" with "didn't you". "It just about knocked me out," he said.

In fact, many established songwriters now try to steer clear of perfect rhymes because they've recognized that rhymes that are too exact can sometimes limit the expression of true emotion. Using imperfect rhymes to create word pictures—or to convey what you want to say more accurately—can often be much more effective than pure rhymes.

With imperfect rhymes (also referred to as false-rhymes, half-rhymes, slant-rhymes or near-rhymes), the vowel sounds are identical, but the consonants that follow or precede those vowel sounds are different and don't match. For example: 'forever' and 'together', 'time' and 'mind', or 'make' and 'fate'. The matching vowels are enough to make the rhyme work.

When people hear the word 'man', for example, they will naturally expect to hear something like 'can' or 'ran' as the rhyme. If you unexpectedly slip in a rhyme that has an extra consonant at the end (for example, the word 'stand'), they may listen more closely to hear what comes next.

Unpredictable rhymes can also be created by varying the rhyme sounds in your choice of words. For example, a single-sound rhyme in a multi-syllable word (such as 'indicate' and 'celebrate' or 'fingernail' and 'fairy tale'), You can also use double-sound rhymes ('walking' and 'talking'), or triple-sound rhymes ('addiction' and 'prediction').

Instead of rhyming a noun with a noun, or a verb with a verb, you can also create an unexpected rhyme by pairing different parts of speech, such as a noun and an adjective (for example, 'guess' and 'pointless').

Many experienced writers feel that using imperfect rhymes gives them greater freedom and flexibility to create word pictures. It also provides an ingenious way to avoid employing rhyming clichés or rhymes that are too obvious. For example, in her award-winning 2013 song 'Brave' (co-written with Jack Antonoff), Sara Bareilles rhymes 'outcast' with 'backlash', 'inside' with 'sunlight', 'there' with 'stared', and 'run' with 'tongue'.

Imperfect rhymes have always been used in hip-hop in conjunction with assonance (the repetition of vowel sounds to create internal rhyming within lyric lines). In one section of his 1992 song 'N.Y. State of Mind', rapper Nas manages to rhyme the word 'prosperous' with the words 'dangerous', 'blamin' us' and 'hostages'.

If you study the latest chart hits and compare where the rhymes are positioned—and what kind of rhymes are being used—you're likely to find much looser (and more conversational) 'near rhymes' placed in the *middle* of the lines in the verse, instead of at the end of each line (which is the traditional approach).

This is partly due to the influence of hip-hop since the late 1980s. Run DMC's classic 1986 album *Raising Hell* is credited with paving the way for much greater use of mid-line rhymes rather than relying on end rhymes. Although internal rhymes had been used previously, they had never been employed so consistently over a whole album as on *Raising Hell*.

An internal rhyming pattern involves repeating vowels and consonants (and combinations of both) within each individual line. A good example of this is Phil Lynott's classic Thin Lizzy song 'With Love' which includes the line: "I must confess that in my quest I felt depressed and restless".

Using mid-line rhymes in this way helps to build the lyrical rhythm and can strengthen the forward motion of the verse.

You can surprise listeners by having your internal rhyme fall on the second or third syllable of a multi-syllable word instead of at the end—for example, by putting the rhyme on the syllable that is stressed most strongly in normal speech (such as 'unach<u>iev</u>able' and 'bel<u>iev</u>able').

You can also rhyme a multi-syllable word with a word that only has one syllable (such as 'sublime' and 'time').

In 1987, acclaimed hip-hop lyricist Rakim pioneered the multi-syllabic approach to rhyming with compound rhymes that paired one word with two words, such as 'righteous' and 'might just'. It was a style (since adopted by other rappers) that introduced a rapid, continuous, rhythmic flow, based on deeply-woven rhyme structures that incorporated internal rhymes.

Today, Eminem tends to fill his songs with more internal rhymes than anyone else in contemporary pop. He once told *Rolling Stone* magazine: "Even as a kid, I always wanted the most words to rhyme. If I saw a word like 'transcendalistic tendencies', I would write it out on a piece of paper and underneath I'd line a word up with each syllable. Even if it didn't make sense, that's the kind of drill I would do."

Consistency is essential when it comes to creating impactful rhyming schemes. For example, if you use internal rhymes in the first verse, you should put them in the same place in the subsequent verses in order to maintain the kind of symmetry that listeners like to hear.

And even when you're using a rhyming dictionary, don't always go for the most obvious rhyme word. By digging deeper, you can often discover rhymes that inspire new themes or fresh ideas that can take your lyrics in a more exciting (and less predictable) direction.

© Brian Oliver, 2018

* * *

This article is based on an extract from Brian Oliver's book:

"HOW [NOT] TO WRITE GREAT LYRICS!
40 Common Mistakes to Avoid
When Writing Lyrics for Your Songs"

The book is available as a paperback or an eBook from Amazon, Apple's iTunes Store, Barnes & Noble and Kobo Books.

* * *

HOW TO USE THIS BOOK

THE RHYMES listed in this book are all based on the *sound* of a word, not the spelling. And because the sound of any word is formed by the vowels it contains, the 'surprising rhyming' suggestions on these pages are basically words that share similar or approximate vowel sounds.

In most cases, the sound of the primary or dominant vowel in each word is the sound that is rhymed, rather than any secondary vowels or the consonants that follow or precede the vowels. In the word "late", for example, "ay" is the primary vowel sound. In the two-sound word "dated" or the three-sound word "created", or the four-sound word "cultivated", "ay" is still the dominant vowel for rhyming purposes.

So, when you're trying to find a rhyming mate, you must first identify the primary vowel sound in the word you're looking to rhyme.

That's why this book is split into five parts based on the main vowel letters: A, E, I, O, U.

Because there is no single sound for each of these vowel letters, the five sections are broken down into the following sub-vowels:

Part 1: A = "ar", "at", "ay".

Part 2: E = "ee", "er", "eer", "eh".

Part 3: I = "i" (as in "it") and "iy" (as in "eye").

Part 4: O = "oe", "or", "oy", "ow", "oo", "o" (as in "hot").

Part 5: U = "uh" (as in "up"), "urr".

Each of these sub-vowel sections contains deeper variations of the basic sub-vowel sound. For example, in the 'A' section (Part 1), you'll see that "ar" is further divided into more than 20 different sub-sets such as "arge", "arch", "ard" and "arf".

To make it easier and quicker to find these variations in each sub-vowel section, they are identified with the aid of familiar words that give an approximation of the dominant vowel sound. Under "ar", for example, you'll find sub-sets described like this: "--arge" *(as in "large")*, "--arch" *(as in "march")*, "--ard" *(as in "hard")* and "--arf" *(as in "scarf")*.

Within each sub-vowel section, the numerous sound variations are further split into two categories: (1) perfect (or 'true') rhymes and (2) our suggested 'surprising rhymes' which are either imperfect rhymes (also known as false-rhymes, half-rhymes, slant-rhymes or near-rhymes) or augmented rhymes.

To help speed up the process of finding an appropriate rhyme, the suggested rhyme words in each deep sub-section are listed **alphabetically** by the first letter of the word.

In addition, this book mostly arranges rhyme suggestions by the number of syllables in each word. The symbol **[1]** indicates one-syllable words; **[2]** shows two-syllable words; **[3]** lists three-syllable words, and **[4]** indicates four-syllable words.

HOW TO FIND A RHYME

STEP 1. Begin by isolating the **dominant vowel sound** in the word you want to rhyme. If your word is 'soon', for example, the primary sound is "oo". If your word is 'scatter', the dominant sound is "at". If your word is 'unbelievable', the dominant sound is "ee".

If a word contains more than one strong vowel sound that could be rhymed (such as 'heartache'), the ending rhyme (e.g. the "ay" sound in 'heartache') is, in most cases, the dominant sound.

Please note that the entries in this guide mostly relate to pronunciation in Standard English. While there are likely to be regional or international variations in the way some English words are spoken, if you pronounce a word in a certain way you should be able to find rhymes that match your pronunciation. This book also flags up words that have different spellings in U.S. and Standard English.

STEP 2. Go to the **Table of Contents** and find the vowel letter and sub-vowel sound that match the dominant vowel sound of your word. For example, in the case of 'soon' (with the dominant sound of "oo"), you would go to the vowel letter 'O' (Part 4) and the sub-vowel section "oo".

If you're trying to rhyme the word 'scatter' (with the dominant sound of "at"), you would search the Table of Contents for 'A' (Part 1) and the sub-vowel section "at".

For 'unbelievable' (with the dominant sound of "ee"), go to 'E' (Part 2) and the sub-vowel section "ee".

To find rhymes for the "ake" sound in 'heartache', go to 'A' (Part 1) and the sub-vowel section "ay".

STEP 3. When you've found the relevant **sub-vowel section** for your key word, you'll see there are many variations of the sound that you're trying to rhyme. Look for the one that is the best match for your word.

For example, if you were trying to find a rhyming mate for the word 'soon' under the "oo" section in Part 4, you'll see a list of more than 40 different kinds of "oo" sounds. Look for the "oo" variation that is a good fit for your word. In this case, it would be **4.6.33 "--oon" (as in "moon")**.

For the word 'scatter', you'll find over 100 variations of the "at" sound listed in Part 1. The best match will be in **1.2.99 "--atter" (as in "matter")**.

Similarly, if you wanted to find a word that rhymes with 'unbelievable' in the "ee" section of Part 2, you'll find there are about 90 varieties of "ee" sounds to choose from. The best match will be in **2.1.70 "--eevable" (as in "believable")**.

You'll find about 100 options for the double-sound word 'heartache' in the "ay" section of Part 1. The most appropriate sound match will be under **1.3.24 "--ake" (as in "fake")**.

STEP 4. When you've found the best sound match for your key word, you'll see the rhyme suggestions are itemized in alphabetical order in two separate sections: **Perfect (or 'true') rhymes** and, below that, our suggested **Alternative rhymes** (under the sub-heading: 'SURPRISING RHYMING').

As mentioned earlier, the words are mostly arranged according to the number of syllables they contain, denoted by the symbols: **[1]**, **[2]**, **[3]**, **[4]**.

If you see your key word on the list of Perfect rhymes, then you'll know you're in the right place to find a suitable 'surprising' rhyme mate.

STEP 5. You can either look for a rhyme for your key word in the Perfect rhymes section, or you can search for a less predictable rhyme in the 'SURPRISING' list (such as *soon/wound, soon/zoom,* or *soon/ doomed*).

You don't always have to rhyme words that contain exactly the same number of syllables. Rhyming a one-syllable word with a multi-syllable word (such as *gone/everyone* or *gone/photobomb*) can be an effective device.

Unpredictable rhymes can also be created by varying the rhyme sounds in your choice of words—for example by using a single-sound rhyme in a multi-syllable word (such as 'hesitate' and 'imitate' or 'fairytale' and 'setting sail'). In his hit song 'Perfect', Ed Sheeran rhymes 'deserve this' with 'perfect'. You can also use double-sound rhymes ('crooning' and 'swooning'), or triple-sound rhymes ('rational' and 'national').

You may find extra inspiration by pairing a one-syllable word (like 'soon') with a two- or three-syllable word from the 'SURPRISING' list. For example, in the **4.6.33** section you'll find suggestions such as: *soon/perfume, soon/presume,* or *soon/rendezvous*.

Using augmented (or 'additive') rhymes can also surprise your audience. When listeners hear the first word in a pair of rhymes, they expect to hear a perfect mating of sounds in the end rhyme (such as *soon/moon*). In augmented rhymes, the second rhyme mate is extended by an additional consonant sound after the vowel (such as *soon/marooned, man/stand* or *soul/gold*). Another example from Ed Sheeran's 'Perfect' is the augmented rhyme: *slow/own*.

For writers, an augmented rhyme can help to extend your rhyming possibilities and reduce the risk of clichés. For listeners, it can be a very satisfying substitute for a perfect rhyme.

It can sometimes be less satisfying, though, if you put the longer word first (such as *unfold/go* or *pursued/who*). This is known as a diminished rhyme. When the sound of the rhyme mate (without the consonant) is smaller, it may be less pleasing to the ear because it creates an imbalance that affects listeners' subconscious desire for symmetry.

You can also create unexpected rhymes by pairing different parts of speech. Instead of rhyming a noun with a noun, or a verb with a verb, try partnering a noun and an adjective, or a verb and an adverb. For example: *guess/pointless, seen/supreme, rain/complain,* or *bread/regret.* Coupling different parts of speech is considered a superior rhyme.

And don't always go for the most obvious rhyme. By digging deeper into the list of suggested rhymes in this book, you may discover sound pairings that inspire new themes or fresh ideas that can take your lyrics or poetry in a more exciting (and less predictable) direction.

* * *

PART 1

'A'

1.1 "ar" sounds..Index on Page 20
1.2 "at" sounds..Index on Page 20
1.3 "ay" sounds ....Index on Page 22

1.1 "ar"

1.1.1 "--ar" (as in "star") ... 25
1.1.2 "--arge" (as in "large") ... 25
1.1.3 "--arch" (as in "march") ... 26
1.1.4 "--ard" (as in "hard") ... 26
1.1.5 "--arder" (as in "harder") ... 26
1.1.6 "--arded" (as in "guarded") ... 27
1.1.7 "--arf" (as in "scarf") ... 27
1.1.8 "--ark" (as in "bark") ... 27
1.1.9 "--arked" (as in "parked") ... 28
1.1.10 "--arker" (as in "darker") ... 28
1.1.11 "--arm" (as in "harm") ... 29
1.1.12 "--armed" (as in "alarmed") ... 29
1.1.13 "--arming" (as in "charming") ... 29
1.1.14 "--arma" (as in "drama") ... 29
1.1.15 "--arn" (as in "barn") ... 30
1.1.16 "--arnished" (as in "tarnished") ... 30
1.1.17 "--ana" (as in "nirvana") ... 30
1.1.18 "--arp" (as in "sharp") ... 31
1.1.19 "--art" (as in "heart") ... 31
1.1.20 "--arted" (as in "started") ... 32
1.1.21 "--arting" (as in "starting") ... 32
1.1.22 "--arter" (as in "smarter") ... 32
1.1.23 "--arling" (as in "darling") ... 32

1.2 "at"

1.2.1 "--at" (as in "that") ... 33
1.2.2 "--ab" (as in "stab") ... 33
1.2.3 "--abbed" (as in "stabbed") ... 34
1.2.4 "--abby" (as in "shabby") ... 34
1.2.5 "--abble" (as in "scrabble") ... 34
1.2.6 "--ack" (as in "back") ... 34
1.2.7 "--act" (as in "fact") ... 35
1.2.8 "--acker" (as in "hacker") ... 36
1.2.9 "--acking" (as in "backing") ... 36
1.2.10 "--ackle" (as in "crackle") ... 37
1.2.11 "--action" (as in "attraction") ... 37
1.2.12 "--acted" (as in "attracted") ... 37
1.2.13 "--active" (as in "attractive") ... 38
1.2.14 "--ad" (as in "glad") ... 38
1.2.15 "--adder" (as in "sadder") ... 38
1.2.16 "--addy" (as in "daddy") ... 39
1.2.17 "--addle" (as in "saddle") ... 39
1.2.18 "--addled" (as in "saddled") ... 39
1.2.19 "--adly" (as in "badly") ... 39
1.2.20 "--aff" as in "laugh") ... 40
1.2.21 "--aft" (as in "laughed") ... 40

1.2.22 "--affle" (as in "baffle") 40
1.2.23 "--after" (as in "after") 41
1.2.24 "--ag" (as in "bag") 41
1.2.25 "--agged" (as in "wagged") 42
1.2.26 "--agger" (as in "dagger") 42
1.2.27 "--aggy" (as in "shaggy") 43
1.2.28 "--aggle" (as in "haggle") 43
1.2.29 "--ahl" (as in "pal") 43
1.2.30 "--al" (as in "normal") 43
1.2.31 "--alice" (as in "malice") 44
1.2.32 "--allow" (as in "shallow") 44
1.2.33 "--allying" (as in "rallying") 44
1.2.34 "--am" (as in "jam") 45
1.2.35 "--ammed" (as in "jammed") 45
1.2.36 "--amp" (as in "lamp") 46
1.2.37 "--amble" (as in "gamble") 46
1.2.38 "--ambler" (as in "gambler") 47
1.2.39 "--ambling" (as in "gambling") 47
1.2.40 "--ambles" (as in "gambles") 47
1.2.41 "--ammer" (as in "hammer") 47
1.2.42 "--amming" (as in "jamming") 48
1.2.43 "--amper" (as in "pamper") 48
1.2.44 "--ampering" (as in "hampering") 48
1.2.45 "--amping" (as in "stamping") 48
1.2.46 "--an" (as in "man") 49
1.2.47 "--and" (as in "hand") 50
1.2.48 "--ang" (as in "bang") 50
1.2.49 "--anged" (as in "banged") 51
1.2.50 "--angle" (as in "bangle") 51
1.2.51 "--ank" (as in "thank") 52
1.2.52 "--anking" (as in "thanking") 52
1.2.53 "--anker" (as in "banker") 53
1.2.54 "--ance" (as in "chance") 53
1.2.55 "--anced" (as in "chanced") 54
1.2.56 "--ant" (as in "pant") 54
1.2.57 "--anter" (as in "banter") 55
1.2.58 "--antic" (as in "frantic") 55
1.2.59 "--anting" (as in "panting") 56
1.2.60 "--anded" (as in "handed") 56
1.2.61 "--ander" (as in "grander") 56
1.2.62 "--andy" (as in "handy") 57
1.2.63 "--anding" (as in "standing") 57
1.2.64 "--anner" (as in "banner") 57
1.2.65 "--anic" (as in "panic") 57
1.2.66 "--anning" (as in "scanning") 58
1.2.67 "--ancer" (as in "dancer") 58
1.2.68 "--ancy" (as in "fancy") 58

1.2.69 "--arnt" (as in "can't") 59
1.2.70 "--ap" (as in "trap") 59
1.2.71 "--apped" (as in "trapped") 60
1.2.72 "--apper" (as in "rapper") 60
1.2.73 "--appy" (as in "happy") 61
1.2.74 "--apping" (as in "clapping") 61
1.2.75 "--appier" (as in "happier") 61
1.2.76 "--appiest" (as in "happiest") 62
1.2.77 "--arrow" (as in "narrow") 62
1.2.78 "--arrying" (as in "carrying") 62
1.2.79 "--ass" (as in "class") 62
1.2.80 "--ash" (as in "crash") 63
1.2.81 "--ashed" (as in "smashed") 63
1.2.82 "--ask" (as in "mask") 63
1.2.83 "--asp" (as in "grasp") 64
1.2.84 "--ast" (as in "fast") 64
1.2.85 "--asses" (as in "passes") 65
1.2.86 "--asher" (as in "smasher") 65
1.2.87 "--ashes" (as in "crashes") 65
1.2.88 "--ashing" (as in "splashing") 66
1.2.89 "--asket" (as in "basket") 66
1.2.90 "--asted" (as in "blasted") 66
1.2.91 "--aster" (as in "faster") 66
1.2.92 "--astic" (as in "plastic") 67
1.2.93 "--asting" (as in "lasting") 67
1.2.94 "--ashional" (as in "rational") 67
1.2.95 "--ath" (as in "path") 68
1.2.96 "--atted" (as in "chatted") 68
1.2.97 "--attic" (as in "ecstatic") 68
1.2.98 "--attle" (as in "rattle") 69
1.2.99 "--atter" (as in "matter") 69
1.2.100 "--atterer" (as in "flatterer") 69
1.2.101 "--attering" (as in "flattering") 69
1.2.102 "--atch" (as in "catch") 70
1.2.103 "--atcher" (as in "catcher") 70
1.2.104 "--atches" (as in "patches") 70
1.2.105 "--atching" (as in "scratching") 71
1.2.106 "--atched" (as in scratched") 71
1.2.107 "--atchable" (as in "catchable") 71
1.2.108 "--ax" (as in "tax") 72

1.3 "ay"

1.3.1 "--ay" (as in "day") 72
1.3.2 "--aby" (as in "baby") 74
1.3.3 "--able" (as in "table") 74
1.3.4 "--abled" (as in "cabled") 74
1.3.5 "--abling" as in "enabling") 74
1.3.6 "--ace" (as in "place") 75

1.3.7 "--aced" (as in "taste") ... 75
1.3.8 "--acer" (as in "racer") ... 75
1.3.9 "--acing" (as in "facing") ... 76
1.3.10 "--aceless" (as in "faceless") ... 76
1.3.11 "--asted" (as in "tasted") ... 76
1.3.12 "--ade" (as in "aid") ... 77
1.3.13 "--aded" (as in "faded") ... 78
1.3.14 "--aider" (as in "raider") ... 78
1.3.15 "--ading" (as in "fading") ... 79
1.3.16 "--ady" (as in "lady") ... 79
1.3.17 "--afe" (as in "safe") ... 80
1.3.18 "--aig" (as in "vague") ... 81
1.3.19 "--age" (as in "page") ... 81
1.3.20 "--aged" (as in "raged") ... 82
1.3.21 "--ages" (as in "pages") ... 83
1.3.22 "--ageing" (as in "raging") ... 83
1.3.23 "--ageous" (as in "courageous") ... 83
1.3.24 "--ake" (as in "fake") ... 84
1.3.25 "--aked" (as in "baked") ... 84
1.3.26 "--aken" (as in "shaken") ... 85
1.3.27 "--aker" (as in "baker") ... 86
1.3.28 "--aking" (as in "waking") ... 86
1.3.29 "--akable" (as in "breakable") ... 87
1.3.30 "--ale" (as in "nail") ... 87
1.3.31 "--ailed" (as in "nailed") ... 88
1.3.32 "--ailing" (as in "sailing") ... 88
1.3.33 "--ailer" (as in "jailer") ... 89
1.3.34 "--ailest" (as in "palest") ... 89
1.3.35 "--aily" (as in "daily") ... 89
1.3.36 "--aim" (as in "fame") ... 89
1.3.37 "--aimer" (as in "gamer") ... 91
1.3.38 "--aimed" (as in "blamed") ... 91
1.3.39 "--aiming" (as in "shaming") ... 92
1.3.40 "--aimful" (as in "shameful") ... 92
1.3.41 "--aimless" (as in "nameless") ... 92
1.3.42 "--ain" (as in "rain") ... 93
1.3.43 "--aining" (as in "raining") ... 94
1.3.44 "--ained" (as in "chained") ... 94
1.3.45 "--ainful" (as in "painful") ... 95
1.3.46 "--ainger" (as in "danger") ... 96
1.3.47 "--ainless" (as in "painless") ... 96
1.3.48 "--ainly" (as in "mainly") ... 96
1.3.49 "--ainted" (as in "tainted") ... 96
1.3.50 "--ainy" (as in "rainy") ... 96
1.3.51 "--ainge" (as in "strange") ... 97
1.3.52 "--ainging" (as in "changing") ... 97
1.3.53 "--ainment" (as in "attainment") ... 98
1.3.54 "--aint" (as in "paint") ... 98

1.3.55 "--ainfully" (as in "painfully") ... 98
1.3.56 "--ape" (as in "grape") ... 99
1.3.57 "--aped" (as in "shaped") ... 99
1.3.58 "--aper" (as in "paper") ... 100
1.3.59 "--aping" (as in "shaping") ... 101
1.3.60 "--air" (as in "care") ... 101
1.3.61 "--aired" (as in "scared") ... 101
1.3.62 "--airest" (as in "fairest") ... 102
1.3.63 "--airful" (as in "careful") ... 102
1.3.64 "--airing" (as in "caring") ... 102
1.3.65 "--airless" (as in "careless") ... 102
1.3.66 "--airly" (as in "fairly") ... 103
1.3.67 "--airness" (as in "fairness") ... 103
1.3.68 "--airy" (as in "scary") ... 103
1.3.69 "--airable" as in "bearable") ... 103
1.3.70 "--aringly (as in "daringly") ... 104
1.3.71 "--asing" (as in "chasing") ... 104
1.3.72 "--ate" (as in "date") ... 104
1.3.73 "--ated" (as in "dated") ... 105
1.3.74 "--ayter" (as in "later") ... 106
1.3.75 "---aying" (as in "praying") ... 106
1.3.76 "--ating" (as in "dating") ... 107
1.3.77 "--atefully" (as in "fatefully") ... 108
1.3.78 "---ayve" (as in "save") ... 108
1.3.79 "--aved" (as in "saved") ... 108
1.3.80 "--ayver" (as in "braver") ... 109
1.3.81 "--ayvery" (as in "bravery") ... 109
1.3.82 "--ayvering" (as in wavering") ... 109
1.3.83 "--avy" (as in "navy") ... 110
1.3.84 "--aving" (as in "waving") ... 110
1.3.85 "--aze" (as in "haze") ... 111
1.3.86 "--azed" (as in "dazed") ... 112
1.3.87 "--azen" (as in "brazen") ... 113
1.3.88 "--azer" (as in "razor") ... 113
1.3.89 "--azy (as in "crazy") ... 114
1.3.90 "--azing" (as in "amazing") ... 114
1.3.91 "--ayable" (as in "payable") ... 115
1.3.92 "--ayday" as in "payday") ... 115
1.3.93 "--ayer" (as in "player") ... 116
1.3.94 "--ayshul" (as in "facial") ... 116
1.3.95 "--ayshun" (as in "persuasion") ... 116
1.3.96 "--ayshus" (as in "gracious") ... 117
1.3.97 "--ayty" (as in "eighty") ... 117
1.3.98 "--aytime" (as in "daytime") ... 117
1.3.99 "--aytly" (as in "lately") ... 118
1.3.100 "--ayven" (as in "raven") ... 118

1.1. "ar"

1.1.1 "--ar" (as in "star")
[1] are, ah, baa, bah, bar, bra, blah, car, char, czar, dah, far, ha, hah, jar, la, ma, mar, noir, pa, par, scar, spa, spar, star, tar, tsar, yah.
[2] afar, aha, ajar, bazaar, bête noire, bizarre, boxcar, boudoir, bourgeois, catarrh, caviar, cha-cha, chamois, char, cigar, co-star, crossbar, crowbar, doodah, éclat, faux pas, film noir, foie gras, fracas, gaga, guitar, grandma, grandpa, ha-ha, hoopla, hurrah, hussar, jaguar, Kasbah, mama, memoir, nightjar, nougat, oompah, papa, polestar, pulsar, quasar, radar, railcar, rollbar, sandbar, sang-froid, sidebar, sidecar, sitar, savoir, so far, sonar, streetcar, stock-car, sunstar, tartare, tow-bar, tramcar.
[3] aide-mémoire, avatar, au revoir, baccarat, cablecar, café-noir, caviar, comme çi comme ça, coup d'état, handlebar, heelbar, indycar, je ne sais quoi, la-di-da, lodestar, Mardi Gras, ménage à trois, megastar, minibar, objet d'art, railroad car, registrar, repertoire, reservoir, seminar, Shangri-La, shooting-star, superstar, tra-la-la.

SURPRISING RHYMING:
[1] Barred, card, charred, guard, hard, jarred, lard, marred, scarred, shard, sparred, starred, tarred, yard.
Arc, ark, bark, dark, hark, lark, narc, mark, park, quark, shark, spark, stark.
Art, cart, chart, dart, harp, heart, mart, part, sharp, smart, start, tart.
[2] Backyard, barnyard, bollard, bombard, charade, courtyard, discard, disbarred, die-hard, façade, farmyard, flashcard, graveyard, ill-starred, junkyard, lifeguard, placard, postcard, regard, rock-hard, safeguard, scorecard, timecard, unscarred, vanguard.
Apart, depart, dustcart, faintheart, flowchart, impart, kick-start, Mozart, outsmart, rampart, re-start, sweetheart, teacart, go-kart, upstart, wallchart.
Ballpark, benchmark, birthmark, car park, bookmark, earmark, embark, hallmark, landmark, loan shark, monarch, postmark, remark, skatepark, skylark, trademark.
[3] Avant-garde, bodyguard, boulevard, disregard, promenade.
A la carte, apple tart, counterpart, heart-to-heart, torn apart.
Disembark, fingermark, matriarch, patriarch, watermark.

1.1.2 "--arge" (as in "large")
[1] barge, charge, large, raj, sarge.
[2] at large, barrage, corsage, collage, discharge, dressage, enlarge, garage, massage, mirage, montage, surcharge.
[3] camouflage, cover charge, espionage, entourage, fuselage, overcharge, sabotage, turbocharge, undercharge.

SURPRISING RHYMING:
[1] Barged, charged.
Arch, march, starch.
Art, cart, chart, dart, heart, mart, part, smart, start, tart.
Arc, ark, bark, clerk, dark, hark, lark, mark, narc, nark, park, shark, spark, stark.
Carp, harp, sharp, tarp, cardsharp.
Are, ah, baa, bah, bar, bra, blah, car, char, czar, dah, far, ha, hah, jar, la, ma, pa, par, scar, spa, spar, star, tar, tsar, yah.
[2] Discharged, enlarged, garaged, massaged, surcharged.
Apart, depart, dustcart, faintheart, flowchart, impart, kick-start, Mozart, outsmart, rampart, re-start, sweetheart, teacart, go-kart, upstart, wallchart.
Ballpark, benchmark, birthmark, car park, bookmark, earmark, embark, hallmark, landmark, loan shark, monarch, postmark, remark, skatepark, skylark, trademark.
Afar, aha, ajar, bazaar, bête noire, bizarre, boxcar, boudoir, bourgeois, catarrh, caviar, cha-cha, chamois, char, cigar, co-star, crossbar, crowbar, doodah, éclat, faux pas, film noir, foie gras, fracas, gaga, guitar, grandma, grandpa, ha-ha, hoopla, hurrah, hussar, jaguar, Kasbah, mama, memoir, nightjar, nougat, oompah, papa, polestar, pulsar, quasar, radar, railcar, rollbar, sandbar, sang-froid, sidebar, sidecar, sitar, savoir, so far, sonar, streetcar, stock-car, sunstar, tartare, tow-bar, tramcar.

[3] **Camouflaged**, overcharged, sabotaged, turbocharged.
Aide-mémoire, avatar, au revoir, baccarat, cablecar, café-noir, caviar, comme çi comme ça, coup d'état, handlebar, heelbar, indycar, je ne sais quoi, la-di-da, lodestar, lone star, Mardi Gras, ménage à trois, megastar, minibar, objet d'art, railroad car, registrar, repertoire, reservoir, rouge et noir, seminar, shooting-star, superstar, tra-la-la.

1.1.3 "--arch" (as in "march")
[1] arch, larch, march, starch.
[2] frogmarch, overarch.

SURPRISING RHYMING:
[1] **Arched**, marched, starched.
Barge, charge, large, raj, sarge.
Card, guard, hard, lard, shard, sparred, starred, yard.
[2] **At large**, barrage, corsage, collage, discharge, dressage, enlarge, garage, massage, mirage, montage, surcharge.
[3] **Camouflage**, cover charge, espionage, entourage, fuselage, overcharge, sabotage, turbocharge, undercharge.

1.1.4 "--ard" (as in "hard")
[1] bard, barred, card, charred, guard, hard, jarred, lard, marred, scarred, shard, sparred, starred, tarred, yard.
[2] backyard, barnyard, bollard, bombard, charade, courtyard, discard, disbarred, die-hard, façade, farmyard, flashcard, graveyard, ill-starred, junkyard, lifeguard, placard, postcard, regard, rock-hard, safeguard, scorecard, timecard, unscarred, vanguard.
[3] avant-garde, bodyguard, boulevard, disregard, promenade.

SURPRISING RHYMING:
[1] **Are**, ah, baa, bah, bar, bra, blah, car, char, czar, dah, far, ha, hah, jar, la, ma, mar, noir, pa, par, scar, spa, spar, star, tar, tsar.
Art, cart, chart, dart, heart, mart, part, smart, start, tart.
Arc, ark, bark, clerk, dark, hark, lark, mark, narc, nark, park, shark, spark, stark.
Calf, graph, half, laugh, scarf, staff.
Arm, balm, calm, charm, farm, harm, ma'am, palm, psalm, qualm.
Carp, harp, sharp, tarp, cardsharp.
[2] **Afar**, aha, ajar, bazaar, bête noire, bizarre, boxcar, boudoir, bourgeois, caviar, cha-cha, chamois, char, cigar, co-star, crossbar, crowbar, doodah, faux pas, film noir, fracas, gaga, guitar, grandma, grandpa, ha-ha, hoopla, hurrah, hussar, jaguar, mama, memoir, nightjar, nougat, oompah, papa, polestar, radar, railcar, rollbar, sandbar, sang-froid, sidebar, sidecar, sitar, savoir, so far, sonar, streetcar, stock-car, tramcar.
Apart, depart, dustcart, faintheart, flowchart, impart, kick-start, Mozart, outsmart, re-start, sweetheart, go-kart, upstart, wallchart.
Ballpark, benchmark, birthmark, car park, bookmark, earmark, embark, hallmark, landmark, loan shark, monarch, postmark, remark, skatepark, skylark, trademark.
Alarm, becalm, disarm, firearm, forearm, rearm, schoolmarm.
[3] **Aide-mémoire**, avatar, au revoir, baccarat, boulevard, cablecar, café-noir, caviar, comme çi comme ça, coup d'état, handlebar, heelbar, indycar, je ne sais quoi, la-di-da, lodestar, Mardi Gras, ménage à trois, megastar, minibar, objet d'art, registrar, repertoire, reservoir, seminar, Shangri-La, shooting-star, superstar, tra-la-la.
A la carte, apple tart, counterpart, heart-to-heart, torn apart.
Disembark, fingermark, matriarch, meadowlark, patriarch, watermark.
Autograph, choreograph, epitaph, paragraph, photograph, polygraph, telegraph.

1.1.5 "--arder" (as in "harder")
[2] ardour/ardor (U.S.), harder, larder.
[3] armada, enchilada, lambada, piña colada.

SURPRISING RHYMING:
[2] **Barter**, charter, charger, darter, garter, larger, martyr, sharper, smarter, starter.

Armour/armor (U.S.), calmer, charmer, drama, farmer, karma, lama, llama, mama.
Darker, marker, sparker, starker.
[3] Bookmarker, cantata, chipolata, departure, go-karter, hereafter, kick-starter, persona non-grata, piña colada, sonata, strata, thereafter.
Disarmer, embalmer, pyjama/pajama (U.S.), snake-charmer.
[4] Dalai Lama, docudrama, melodrama, panorama, psychodrama.

1.1.6 "--arded" (as in "guarded")
[2] carded, guarded, larded.
[3] bombarded, discarded, disregarded, regarded, retarded, safeguarded.

SURPRISING RHYMING
[2] **Carted**, charted, darted, hearted, parted, smarted, started.
[3] **Cold-hearted**, departed, downhearted, fainthearted, good-hearted, hard-hearted, heavy-hearted, imparted, kick-started, kind-hearted, light-hearted, lion-hearted, outsmarted, soft-hearted, stout-hearted, tender-hearted, true-hearted, uncharted, warm-hearted, weak-hearted, wholehearted.

1.1.7 "--arf" (as in "scarf")
[1] calf, graph, half, laugh, scarf, staff.
[2] behalf, giraffe, headscarf, mooncalf.
[3] autograph, choreograph, epitaph, paragraph, photograph, polygraph, telegraph.

SURPRISING RHYMING:
[1] **Are**, ah, baa, bah, bar, bra, blah, car, char, czar, dah, far, ha, hah, jar, la, ma, mar, noir, pa, par, scar, spa, spar, star, tar, tsar.
Art, cart, chart, dart, heart, mart, part, smart, start, tart.
Arc, ark, bark, clerk, dark, hark, lark, mark, narc, nark, park, shark, spark, stark.
Carp, harp, sharp, tarp, cardsharp.
Bath, hearth, path.
[2] **Afar**, aha, ajar, bazaar, bête noire, bizarre, boxcar, boudoir, bourgeois, caviar, cha-cha, chamois, cigar, co-star, crossbar, crowbar, doodah, faux pas, film noir, foie gras, fracas, gaga, guitar, grandma, grandpa, ha-ha, hoopla, hurrah, hussar, jaguar, Kasbah, mama, memoir, nougat, oompah, papa, polestar, radar, railcar, sandbar, sang-froid, sidebar, sidecar, sitar, savoir, so far, sonar, streetcar, stock-car, tow-bar, tramcar.
[2] **Apart**, depart, faintheart, flowchart, impart, kick-start, Mozart, outsmart, re-start, sweetheart, teacart, go-kart, upstart, wallchart.
Ballpark, benchmark, birthmark, car park, bookmark, embark, hallmark, landmark, loan shark, monarch, pockmark, postmark, remark, salesclerk, skatepark, skylark, trademark.
Warpath, towpath, footpath.
[3] **Aide-mémoire**, avatar, au revoir, baccarat, boulevard, cablecar, café-noir, caviar, comme çi comme ça, coup d'état, handlebar, heelbar, indycar, je ne sais quoi, la-di-da, lodestar, Mardi Gras, ménage à trois, megastar, minibar, objet d'art, railroad car, registrar, repertoire, reservoir, seminar, Shangri-La, shooting-star, superstar, tra-la-la.
A la carte, apple tart, counterpart, heart-to-heart, torn apart.
Disembark, fingermark, matriarch, meadowlark, patriarch, watermark.

1.1.8 "--ark" (as in "bark")
[1] arc, ark, bark, clerk, dark, hark, lark, mark, narc, nark, park, shark, spark, stark.
[2] ballpark, benchmark, birthmark, car park, bookmark, earmark, embark, hallmark, landmark, loan shark, monarch, pockmark, postmark, remark, salesclerk, skatepark, skylark, tidemark, trademark.
[3] disembark, fingermark, matriarch, meadowlark, patriarch, watermark.

SURPRISING RHYMING:
[1] **Arced**, barked, harked, larked, marked, parked, sparked.
Are, ah, baa, bah, bar, bra, blah, car, char, czar, dah, far, ha, hah, jar, la, ma, mar, noir, pa, par, scar, spa, spar, star, tar, tsar.
Art, cart, chart, dart, heart, mart, part, smart, start, tart.

Barred, card, charred, guard, hard, jarred, lard, marred, scarred, shard, sparred, starred, tarred, yard.
Calf, graph, half, laugh, scarf, staff.
Arm, balm, calm, charm, farm, harm, ma'am, palm, psalm, qualm.
Carp, harp, sharp, tarp, cardsharp.
[2] **Afar**, aha, ajar, bazaar, bête noire, bizarre, boxcar, boudoir, bourgeois, caviar, cha-cha, chamois, char, cigar, co-star, crossbar, crowbar, doodah, faux pas, film noir, fracas, gaga, guitar, grandma, grandpa, ha-ha, hoopla, hurrah, hussar, jaguar, mama, memoir, nightjar, nougat, oompah, papa, polestar, radar, railcar, rollbar, sandbar, sang-froid, sidebar, sidecar, sitar, savoir, so far, sonar, streetcar, stock-car, tramcar.
Apart, depart, dustcart, faintheart, impart, kick-start, Mozart, outsmart, rampart, re-start, sweetheart, go-kart, upstart, wallchart.
Backyard, barnyard, bollard, bombard, charade, courtyard, discard, disbarred, die-hard, façade, farmyard, flashcard, graveyard, ill-starred, junkyard, lifeguard, placard, postcard, regard, rock-hard, safeguard, scorecard, stockyard, timecard, unscarred, vanguard.
Behalf, giraffe, headscarf, mooncalf.
Alarm, becalm, disarm, firearm, forearm, rearm, schoolmarm, yardarm.
[3] **Avatar**, au revoir, baccarat, boulevard, cablecar, café-noir, caviar, comme çi comme ça, coup d'état, handlebar, heelbar, indycar, je ne sais quoi, la-di-da, lodestar, Mardi Gras, ménage à trois, megastar, minibar, objet d'art, railroad car, registrar, repertoire, reservoir, seminar, Shangri-La, shooting-star, superstar, tra-la-la.
A la carte, apple tart, counterpart, heart-to-heart, torn apart.
Avant-garde, bodyguard, boulevard, disregard, promenade.
Autograph, choreograph, epitaph, paragraph, photograph, polygraph, telegraph.

1.1.9 "--arked" (as in "parked")
[1] arced, barked, harked, marked, narked, parked, sparked.
[2] benchmarked, birthmarked, bookmarked, earmarked, embarked, pockmarked, postmarked, remarked, trademarked.
[3] disembarked, watermarked.

SURPRISING RHYMING:
[1] **Are**, bar, bra, car, far, jar, noir, scar, star.
Art, cart, chart, dart, heart, mart, part, smart, start, tart.
Carp, harp, sharp, tarp, cardsharp.
Barred, card, charred, guard, hard, jarred, lard, marred, scarred, shard, sparred, starred, tarred, yard.
[2] **Apart**, depart, dustcart, faintheart, flowchart, impart, kick-start, rampart, re-start, sweetheart, teacart, go-kart, upstart, wallchart.
Afar, aha, ajar, bazaar, bête noire, bizarre, boxcar, boudoir, bourgeois, caviar, cha-cha, chamois, cigar, co-star, crossbar, crowbar, doodah, éclat, faux pas, film noir, fracas, gaga, guitar, grandma, grandpa, ha-ha, hoopla, hurrah, hussar, jaguar, mama, memoir, nightjar, nougat, oompah, papa, polestar, radar, railcar, rollbar, sandbar, sang-froid, sidebar, sidecar, sitar, savoir, so far, sonar, streetcar, stock-car, tow-bar, tramcar.
[3] **A la carte**, apple tart, counterpart, heart-to-heart.
Aide-mémoire, avatar, au revoir, baccarat, cablecar, café-noir, caviar, comme çi comme ça, coup d'état, handlebar, je ne sais quoi, la-di-da, lodestar, Mardi Gras, ménage à trois, megastar, minibar, objet d'art, railroad car, repertoire, reservoir, shooting-star, superstar.

1.1.10 "--arker" (as in "darker")
barker, bookmarker, darker, larker, marker, parker, sparker, starker.

SURPRISING RHYMING:
[2] **Barter**, charter, garter, martyr, sharper, smarter, starter, strata.
Ardour/ardor (U.S.), harder, larder.
After, grafter, laughter, rafter.
[3] **Armada**, enchilada, hereafter, lambada, piña colada, thereafter.
Cantata, departure, enchilada, lambada, persona non-grata, piña colada, sonata.

*

1.1.11 "--arm" (as in "harm")
[1] arm, balm, calm, charm, farm, harm, ma'am, palm, psalm, qualm.
[2] alarm, becalm, disarm, firearm, forearm, rearm, schoolmarm, yardarm.

SURPRISING RHYMING:
[1] **Armed**, calmed, charmed, farmed, harmed, palmed.
Are, bar, barn, bra, car, darn far, jar, noir, scar, star, yarn.
Barred, card, charred, guard, hard, jarred, lard, marred, scarred, shard, sparred, starred, tarred, yard.
[2] **Alarmed**, becalmed, disarmed, rearmed, unarmed, unharmed.
Afar, aha, ajar, bazaar, bête noire, bizarre, boxcar, boudoir, bourgeois, caviar, cha-cha, chamois, cigar, co-star, crossbar, crowbar, éclat, faux pas, film noir, fracas, gaga, guitar, grandma, grandpa. hoopla, hurrah, hussar, jaguar, mama, memoir, nougat, papa, polestar, pulsar, quasar, radar, railcar, sandbar, sang-froid, sidebar, sidecar, sitar, savoir, so far, sonar, streetcar, stock-car, tow-bar, tramcar.
Backyard, barnyard, bollard, bombard, charade, courtyard, discard, disbarred, die-hard, façade, farmyard, flashcard, graveyard, ill-starred, junkyard, lifeguard, placard, postcard, regard, rock-hard, safeguard, scorecard, stockyard, timecard, unscarred, vanguard.
[3] **Aide-mémoire**, avatar, au revoir, baccarat, cablecar, café-noir, caviar, comme çi comme ça, coup d'état, handlebar, je ne sais quoi, lodestar, Mardi Gras, ménage à trois, megastar, minibar, railroad car, registrar, repertoire, reservoir, shooting-star, superstar.
Avant-garde, bodyguard, boulevard, disregard, promenade.

1.1.12 "--armed" (as in "alarmed")
[1] armed, calmed, charmed, farmed, harmed, palmed.
[2] alarmed, becalmed, disarmed, rearmed, unarmed, unharmed.

SURPRISING RHYMING:
[1] **Arm**, balm, barn, calm, charm, darn(ed), farm, harm, ma'am, palm, psalm, qualm.
Bard, barred, card, charred, guard, hard, jarred, lard, marred, scarred, shard, sparred, starred, tarred, yard.
[2] **Alarm**, becalm, disarm, firearm, forearm, rearm, schoolmarm.
Afar, aha, ajar, bazaar, bête noire, bizarre, boxcar, boudoir, bourgeois, caviar, cha-cha, chamois, cigar, co-star, crossbar, crowbar, éclat, faux pas, film noir, fracas, gaga, guitar, grandma, grandpa. hoopla, hurrah, hussar, jaguar, mama, memoir, nougat, papa, polestar, pulsar, quasar, radar, railcar, sandbar, sang-froid, sidebar, sidecar, sitar, savoir, so far, sonar, streetcar, stock-car, tow-bar, tramcar.
Backyard, barnyard, bollard, bombard, charade, courtyard, discard, disbarred, die-hard, façade, farmyard, flashcard, graveyard, ill-starred, junkyard, lifeguard, placard, postcard, regard, rock-hard, safeguard, scorecard, stockyard, timecard, unscarred, vanguard.
Apart, depart, dustcart, faintheart, flowchart, impart, kick-start, Mozart, outsmart, rampart, re-start, sweetheart, teacart, go-kart, upstart, wallchart.
[3] **Aide-mémoire**, avatar, au revoir, baccarat, cablecar, café-noir, caviar, comme çi comme ça, coup d'état, handlebar, je ne sais quoi, lodestar, Mardi Gras, ménage à trois, megastar, minibar, railroad car, registrar, repertoire, reservoir, shooting-star, superstar.
Avant-garde, bodyguard, boulevard, disregard, promenade.

1.1.13 "--arming" (as in "charming")
arming, alarming, calming, charming, disarming, farming, harming.

SURPRISING RHYMING
[2] **Darling**, gnarling, marling, starling.
Carting, charting, darting, guarding, parting, smarting, starting.
Barring, carving, charging, enlarging, jarring, marring, marking, scarring, starring.
[3] **Departing**, kick-starting, outsmarting, re-starting, self-starting, sweethearting.
Bombarding, penny-farthing, regarding, safeguarding, self-regarding.

1.1.14 "--arma" (as in "drama")
[2] armour/armor (U.S.), calmer, charmer, drama, farmer, karma, lama, llama, mama.

[3] disarmer, embalmer, pyjama/pajama (U.S.), snake-charmer.
[4] Dalai Lama, docudrama, melodrama, panorama, psychodrama.

SURPRISING RHYMING:
[2] **Ardour/ardor** (U.S.), harder, larder.
Afar, aha, ajar, bazaar, bête noire, bizarre, boxcar, boudoir, bourgeois, caviar, cha-cha, chamois, cigar, co-star, crossbar, crowbar, éclat, faux pas, film noir, fracas, gaga, guitar, grandma, grandpa. hoopla, hurrah, jaguar, mama, memoir, nougat, papa, polestar, pulsar, quasar, radar, railcar, sandbar, sang-froid, sidebar, sidecar, sitar, savoir, so far, sonar, streetcar, stock-car, tow-bar, tramcar.
Barter, charter, darter, garter, martyr, smarter, starter, strata.
Barker, darker, marker, parker, sharper, sparker, starker.
[3] **Armada**, enchilada, lambada, piña colada.
Avatar, au revoir, baccarat, cablecar, café-noir, caviar, comme çi comme ça, coup d'état, handlebar, je ne sais quoi, la-di-da, lodestar, Mardi Gras, ménage à trois, megastar, minibar, objet d'art, railroad car, repertoire, reservoir, shooting-star, superstar, tra-la-la.
Banana, cabana, darner, garner, gymkhana, iguana, manana, nirvana, piranha, sultana.

1.1.15 "--arn" (as in "barn")
autobahn, barn, darn, yarn.

SURPRISING RHYMING:
[1] **Are**, bar, bra, car, char, czar, far, jar, ma, noir, pa, scar, spa, star, tar, tsar.
Arm, balm, calm, charm, farm, harm, ma'am, palm, psalm, qualm.
[2] **Afar**, aha, ajar, bazaar, bête noire, bizarre, boxcar, boudoir, bourgeois, caviar, cha-cha, chamois, cigar, co-star, crossbar, crowbar, éclat, faux pas, film noir, fracas, gaga, guitar, grandma, grandpa. hoopla, hurrah, jaguar, mama, memoir, nougat, papa, polestar, pulsar, quasar, radar, railcar, sandbar, sang-froid, sidebar, sidecar, sitar, savoir, so far, sonar, streetcar, stock-car, tow-bar, tramcar.
Alarm, becalm, disarm, firearm, forearm, rearm, schoolmarm.
[3] **Avatar**, au revoir, baccarat, cablecar, café-noir, caviar, comme çi comme ça, coup d'état, handlebar, je ne sais quoi, la-di-da, lodestar, Mardi Gras, ménage à trois, megastar, minibar, objet d'art, railroad car, repertoire, reservoir, shooting-star, superstar.

1.1.16 "--arnished" (as in "tarnished")
[2] garnished, tarnished, varnished.

SURPRISING RHYMING:
[1] **Bitch**, ditch, glitch, hitch, itch, kitsch, pitch, rich, snitch, stitch, switch, twitch, which, witch.
Bitched, ditched, hitched, itched, pitched, snitched, stitched, switched, twitched.
Dish, fish, squish, swish, this, wish.
Cyst, fist, kissed, list, missed, mist, tryst, twist, whist, wrist.
[2] **Bewitched**, enriched, unhitched, re-stitched, unstitched.
Anguish, blueish, brownish, devilfish, feverish, goldfish, greenish, jellyfish, reddish, selfish, shellfish, starfish, yellowish.
Artist, assist, consist, dismissed, enlist, exist, insist, persist, resist, subsist, wish-list.
Farthest, greatest, harvest.
[3] **Activist**, alarmist, anarchist, atheist, analyst, botanist, catalyst, columnist, communist, egotist, exorcist, fatalist, hobbyist, humourist/humorist(U.S.), hypnotist, idealist, journalist, lobbyist, moralist, motorist, novelist, optimist, organist, pacifist, pessimist, pre-exist, publicist, realist socialist, soloist, specialist, strategist, terrorist.

1.1.17 "--ana" (as in "nirvana")
[3] banana, cabana, darner, garner, gymkhana, iguana, manana, nirvana, piranha.

SURPRISING RHYMING:
[2] **Armour/armor** (U.S.), calmer, charmer, drama, farmer, karma, lama, llama, mama.
Ardour/ardor (U.S.), harder, larder.

Barter, carter, charter, darter, garter, martyr, smarter, starter, strata.
Barker, bookmarker, darker, marker, sharper, starker.
Barger, charger, enlarger, larger, massager.
[3] **Disarmer**, embalmer, pyjama/pajama (U.S.), snake-charmer.
Armada, enchilada, lambada, piña colada.
[4] **Dalai Lama**, docudrama, melodrama, panorama, psychodrama.

1.1.18 "--arp" (as in "sharp")
carp, harp, sharp, tarp, cardsharp.

SURPRISING RHYMING:
[1] **Are**, bar, bra, car, char, czar, far, jar, ma, noir, pa, scar, spa, star, tar, tsar.
Art, cart, chart, dart, heart, mart, part, smart, start, tart.
Barred, card, charred, guard, hard, marred, scarred, shard, sparred, starred, yard.
[2] **Afar**, aha, ajar, bazaar, bête noire, bizarre, boxcar, boudoir, bourgeois, caviar, cha-cha, chamois, cigar, co-star, crossbar, crowbar, éclat, faux pas, film noir, fracas, gaga, guitar, grandma, grandpa. hoopla, hurrah, jaguar, mama, memoir, nougat, papa, polestar, pulsar, quasar, radar, railcar, sandbar, sang-froid, sidebar, sidecar, sitar, savoir, so far, sonar, streetcar, stock-car, tow-bar, tramcar.
Apart, depart, dustcart, faintheart, flowchart, impart, kick-start, Mozart, outsmart, rampart, re-start, sweetheart, teacart, go-kart, upstart, wallchart.
Backyard, barnyard, bollard, bombard, charade, courtyard, discard, disbarred, die-hard, façade, farmyard, flashcard, graveyard, ill-starred, junkyard, lifeguard, placard, postcard, regard, rock-hard, safeguard, scorecard, timecard, unscarred, vanguard.
[3] **Avatar**, au revoir, baccarat, cablecar, café-noir, caviar, comme çi comme ça, coup d'état, handlebar, je ne sais quoi, la-di-da, lodestar, Mardi Gras, ménage à trois, megastar, minibar, objet d'art, railroad car, repertoire, reservoir, shooting-star, superstar.
A la carte, apple tart, counterpart, heart-to-heart, torn apart.
Avant-garde, bodyguard, boulevard, disregard, promenade.

1.1.19 "--art" (as in "heart")
[1] art, cart, chart, dart, heart, mart, part, smart, start, tart.
[2] apart, depart, dustcart, faintheart, flowchart, impart, kick-start, Mozart, outsmart, rampart, re-start, sweetheart, teacart, go-kart, upstart, wallchart.
[3] a la carte, apple tart, counterpart, heart-to-heart, torn apart.

SURPRISING RHYMING:
[1] **Are**, bar, bra, car, char, czar, far, jar, ma, noir, pa, scar, spa, star, tar, tsar.
Arc, ark, bark, clerk, dark, hark, lark, mark, narc, nark, park, shark, spark, stark.
Carp, harp, sharp, tarp, cardsharp.
Barred, card, charred, guard, hard, marred, scarred, shard, sparred, starred, yard.
Arm, balm, calm, charm, farm, harm, ma'am, palm, psalm, qualm.
Calf, graph, half, laugh, scarf, staff.
[2] **Afar**, aha, ajar, bazaar, bête noire, bizarre, boxcar, boudoir, bourgeois, caviar, cha-cha, chamois, cigar, co-star, crossbar, crowbar, éclat, faux pas, film noir, fracas, gaga, guitar, grandma, grandpa. hoopla, hurrah, jaguar, mama, memoir, nougat, papa, polestar, pulsar, quasar, radar, railcar, sandbar, sang-froid, sidebar, sidecar, sitar, savoir, so far, sonar, streetcar, stock-car, tow-bar, tramcar.
[2] **Ballpark**, benchmark, birthmark, car park, bookmark, earmark, embark, hallmark, landmark, loan shark, monarch, postmark, remark, skatepark, skylark, trademark.
Backyard, barnyard, bollard, bombard, charade, courtyard, discard, disbarred, die-hard, façade, farmyard, flashcard, graveyard, ill-starred, junkyard, lifeguard, placard, postcard, regard, rock-hard, safeguard, scorecard, timecard, unscarred, vanguard.
Alarm, becalm, disarm, firearm, forearm, rearm, schoolmarm.
Behalf, giraffe, headscarf, mooncalf.
[3] **Avatar**, au revoir, baccarat, cablecar, café-noir, caviar, comme çi comme ça, coup d'état, handlebar, je ne sais quoi, la-di-da, lodestar, Mardi Gras, ménage à trois, megastar, minibar, objet d'art, railroad car, repertoire, reservoir, shooting-star, superstar.
Avant-garde, bodyguard, boulevard, disregard, promenade.
Disembark, fingermark, matriarch, patriarch, watermark.

Autograph, choreograph, epitaph, paragraph, photograph, polygraph, telegraph.

1.1.20 "--arted" (as in "started")
[2] carted, charted, darted, hearted, parted, smarted, started.
[3] departed, cold-hearted, downhearted, fainthearted, good-hearted, hard-hearted, heavy-hearted, imparted, kick-started, kind-hearted, light-hearted, lion-hearted, outsmarted, soft-hearted, stout-hearted, tender-hearted, true-hearted, uncharted, warm-hearted, weak-hearted, whole-hearted.

SURPRISING RHYMING
[2] **Carded**, guarded, larded.
Arty, hearty, illuminati, karate, party.
Carpet, scarlet, starlet, target.
Market, hypermarket, supermarket.
[3] **Bombarded**, discarded, disregarded, regarded, safeguarded.

1.1.21 "--arting" (as in "starting")
[2] carting, charting, darting, parting, smarting, starting.
[3] departing, imparting, kick-starting, outsmarting, re-starting, self-starting, sweethearting.

SURPRISING RHYMING:
[2] **Arming**, alarming, calming, charming, darning, farming, harming.
Barring, carving, guarding, jarring, marring, scarring, starring.
Arcing, barking, harking, larking, marking, parking, sparking.
Darling, gnarling, marling, starling.
[3] **Benchmarking**, bookmarking, disembarking, earmarking, embarking, remarking.
Bombarding, discarding, disregarding, regarding, safeguarding.

1.1.22 "--arter" (as in "smarter")
[2] barter, charter, garter, martyr, smarter, starter, strata, tartar.

SURPRISING RHYMING:
[2] **After**, grafter, laughter, rafter.
Ardour/ardor (U.S.), harder, larder.
Barker, darker, larker, marker, parker, sharper, sparker, starker.
Capture, pasture, rapture, recapture, enrapture.
Armour/armor (U.S.), calmer, charmer, drama, farmer, karma, llama, mama.
[3] **Armada**, cantata, chipolata, departure, enchilada, enchanter, hereafter, lambada, persona non-grata, piña colada, sonata, thereafter.
Disarmer, embalmer, pyjama/pajama (U.S.), snake-charmer.
[4] **Dalai Lama**, docudrama, melodrama, panorama, psychodrama.

1.1.23 "--arling" (as in "darling")
[2] darling, gnarling, marling, starling.

SURPRISING RHYMING:
[2] **Arming**, calming, charming, darning, farming, harming.
Carting, charting, darting, guarding, parting, smarting, starting.
Barring, carving, charging, co-starring, jarring, marring, scarring, starring.
[3] **Alarming**, disarming, discarding.
Departing, imparting, kick-starting, outsmarting, re-starting, self-starting, sweethearting.
Bombarding, penny-farthing, regarding, safeguarding, self-regarding.

* * *

1.2 "at"

1.2.1 "--at" (as in "that")
[1] at, bat, brat, cat, chat, drat, fat, flat, frat, gnat, hat, mat, matte, pat, prat, rat, sat, scat, slat, spat, splat, sprat, stat, tat, that, vat.
[2] backchat, bearcat, bobcat, brickbat, chitchat, combat, doormat, fat cat, format, full-fat, hard hat, hellcat, high-hat, howzat, polecat, rat-tat, sun hat, that's that, tomcat, top hat, whereat, wildcat, wombat.
[3] acrobat, aristocrat, autocrat, automat, baseball bat, bureaucrat, copycat, cricket bat, democrat, diplomat, habitat, kitty cat, lariat, laundromat, pitapat, plutocrat, pussycat, scaredy-cat, tabby cat, technocrat, that's that, thermostat, tit-for-tat.

SURPRISING RHYMING:
[1] **Act**, fact, pact, tact, tract.
Ad, add, bad, cad, clad, dad, fad, glad, grad, had, lad, mad, pad, plaid, sad, tad.
App, cap, chap, clap, crap, flap, gap, knap, lap, map, nap, pap, rap, sap, scrap, slap, snap, strap, tap, trap, wrap, yap.
Back, black, crack, fact, flak, hack, jack, knack, lack, mac, pack, plaque, quack, rack, sack, shack, slack, smack, snack, stack, tack, track, whack, yak.
Bath, laugh, math, path, wrath.
Blast, cast, caste, fast, last, mast, massed, past, passed, vast.
[2] **Abstract**, attract, compact, contact, contract, detract, distract, enact, exact, extract, impact, intact, play act, ransacked, react, retract, sidetracked, subtract, unpacked.
Aghast, amassed, at last, breakfast, broadcast, contrast, downcast, forecast, gymnast, harassed, hold fast, fly-past, miscast, outcast, outlast, outclassed, steadfast, surpassed.
Backslap, flat-cap, icecap, kneecap, flip-flap, mishap, nightcap, redcap, recap, whitecap.
Entrap, footpath, madcap, mantrap, roadmap, stopgap, uncap, warpath.
[3] **Artefact**, counteract, inexact, interact, matter-of-fact, overact, overreact, re-enact.
Counterblast, flabbergast, heavy-clad, myriad, overcast, undergrad, unsurpassed.

1.2.2 "--ab" (as in "stab")
[1] blab, cab, crab, dab, drab, fab, flab, gab, grab, jab, nab, scab, slab, stab, tab.
[2] kebab, minicab, prefab, rehab, screen-grab, smash and grab, taxicab, vocab.

SURPRISING RHYMING:
[1] **Ad**, add, bad, bade, cad, clad, dad, fad, gad, glad, grad, had, have, lad, mad, pad, plaid, sad, shad, tad, trad.
App, bap, cap, chap, clap, crap, flap, gap, lap, knap, map, nap, pap, rap, sap, scrap, slap, snap, strap, tap, trap, wrap, yap, zap.
At, bat, brat, cat, chat, drat, fat, flat, frat, gnat, hat, mat, matte, pat, prat, rat, sat, scat, slat, spat, splat, sprat, stat, tat, that, vat.
Bag, blag, brag, crag, drag, fag, flag, gag, hag, jag, lag, mag, nag, rag, sag, slag, snag, stag, swag, tag, wag, zag.
[2] **Footpad**, grandad, helipad, iron-clad, ivy-clad, jihad, keypad, kneepad, launchpad, myriad, nomad, notepad, scratchpad, sketchpad, triad, touchpad, unclad, undergrad.
Backslap, bitmap, bootstrap, catnap, cold snap, deathtrap, firetrap, giftwrap, handclap, hubcap, icecap, kidnap, kneecap, madcap, mantrap, mishap, mousetrap, nightcap, recap, roadmap, snowcap, speed trap, stopgap, suntrap, unwrap, watchstrap, whitecap.
Backchat, bearcat, bobcat, brickbat, chitchat, combat, doormat, fat cat, format, full-fat, hard hat, hellcat, high-hat, howzat, polecat, tomcat, top hat, whereat, wildcat, wombat.
Beanbag, bumbag, chinwag, dog-tag, fleabag, gasbag, gulag, handbag, jetlag, kitbag, mailbag, moneybag, nosebag, postbag, punchbag, ragbag, ragtag, ratbag, saddlebag, sandbag, scallywag/scalawag(U.S.), scumbag, tea-bag, washbag, windbag, zigzag.
[3] **Acrobat**, aristocrat, autocrat, automat, baseball bat, bureaucrat, copycat, cricket bat, democrat, diplomat, habitat, kitty cat, lariat, laundromat, pitapat, plutocrat, pussycat, scaredy-cat, tabby cat, technocrat, that's that, thermostat, thunderclap, tit-for-tat.
Autograph, belly laugh, better half, cenotaph, choreograph, epitaph, lithograph, paragraph, phonograph, photograph, polygraph, telegraph.

1.2.3 "--abbed" (as in "stabbed")
[1] blabbed, dabbed, gabbed, grabbed, jabbed, nabbed, slabbed, stabbed, tabbed.

SURPRISING RHYMING:
[1] **Ad**, add, bad, bade, cad, clad, dad, fad, gad, glad, grad, had, have, lad, mad, pad, plaid, sad, shad, tad, trad.
Bagged, blagged, bragged, dragged, flagged, gagged, jagged, lagged, nagged, ragged, sagged, snagged, tagged, wagged, zagged.
Aft, craft, daft, draft, draught, graft, laughed, raft, shaft, staffed.
Capped, clap, flapped, lapped, knapped, mapped, napped, rapped, sapped, scrapped, slapped, snapped, strapped, tapped, trapped, wrapped, yapped, zapped.
At, bat, brat, cat, chat, drat, fat, flat, frat, gnat, hat, mat, matte, pat, prat, rat, sat, scat, slat, spat, splat, sprat, stat, tat, that, vat.
[2] **Debagged**, dog-tagged, handbagged, jetlagged, sandbagged, zigzagged.
Footpad, grandad, helipad, iron-clad, ivy-clad, jihad, keypad, kneepad, launchpad, myriad, nomad, notepad, scratchpad, sketchpad, triad, touchpad, unclad, undergrad.
Backslapped, catnapped, entrapped, flip-flapped, giftwrapped, handclapped, ice-capped, kidnapped, kneecapped, recapped, snowcapped, uncapped, unsnapped, unwrapped.
Backchat, bearcat, bobcat, brickbat, chitchat, combat, doormat, fat cat, format, full-fat, hard hat, hellcat, high-hat, howzat, polecat, tomcat, top hat, whereat, wildcat, wombat.
Beanbag, bumbag, chinwag, dog-tag, fleabag, gasbag, gulag, handbag, jetlag, kitbag, mailbag, moneybag, nosebag, postbag, punchbag, ragbag, ragtag, ratbag, saddlebag, sandbag, scallywag/scalawag(U.S.), scumbag, tea-bag, washbag, windbag, zigzag.
scallywag/scalawag(U.S.), scumbag, tea-bag, washbag, wigwag, windbag, zigzag.
[3] **Handicapped**, overlapped, photomapped.
Acrobat, aristocrat, autocrat, automat, baseball bat, bureaucrat, copycat, cricket bat, democrat, diplomat, habitat, kitty cat, lariat, laundromat, pitapat, plutocrat, pussycat, scaredy-cat, tabby cat, technocrat, that's that, thermostat, tit-for-tat.

1.2.4 "--abby" (as in "shabby")
[2] abbey, blabby, cabby, crabby, flabby, gabby, scabby, shabby.

SURPRISING RHYMING:
[2] **Baddy,** caddy, daddy, faddy, laddie, paddy, sugar daddy.
Baggy, craggy, naggy, raggy, saggy, scraggy, shaggy, swaggy.
Chappie, crappy, flappy, happy, nappy, pappy, sappy, scrappy, slap-happy, snappy, unhappy, yappy, zappy.
Alley, carry, dally, dilly-dally, galley, marry, pally, rally, reveille, sally, tally, valley.
Badly, gladly, madly, sadly.
Habit, rabbit, cohabit, inhabit.

1.2.5 "--abble" (as in "scrabble")
[2] babble, dabble, rabble, scrabble.

SURPRISING RHYMING:
[2] **Bedraggle**, gaggle, haggle, paddle, saddle, skedaddle, straddle, straggle, waggle.
Baffle, battle, cattle, chattel, embattle, prattle, raffle, rattle, snaffle, tattle, tittle-tattle.
Apple, chapel, dapple, grapple.
Cackle, crackle, hackle, jackal, shackle, tackle.
Bedazzle, castle, dazzle, frazzle, hassle, razzle, tassel.
Gavel, gravel, raffle, ravel, travel, unravel.
Amble, bramble, gamble, preamble, ramble, scramble, shamble, unscramble.
Angle, bangle, dangle, jangle, mangle, spangle, strangle, tangle, wangle, wrangle.
Candle, handle, manhandle, mishandle, sandal, scandal, vandal.

1.2.6 "--ack" (as in "back")
[1] back, black, crack, flak, hack, jack, knack, lack, mac, Mach, pack, plaque, quack, rack, sack, shack, slack, smack, snack, stack, tack, thwack, track, vac, whack, wrack.
[2] aback, attack, backpack, backtrack, bareback, blackjack, blowback, Blu-Tack,

bootblack, bushwhack, callback, cheapjack, clawback, cognac, comeback, cutback, drawback, fallback, feedback, fightback, flapjack, flashback, fullback, greenback, hardback, hatchback, haystack, hijack, holdback, horseback, kayak, kickback, knapsack, knick-knack, mudpack, Muzak, outback, payback, pitchblack, playback, Prozac, racetrack, ransack, rollback, rucksack, setback, sidetrack, skyjack, slingback, smokestack, softback, soundtrack, splashback, switchback, tailback, tarmac, talkback, throwback, ticktack, tic-tac, tieback, unpack, way back, wingback, wisecrack.
[3] almanac, anorak, bivouac, bric-a-brac, cardiac, chimney stack, crackerjack, cul-de-sac, haversack, lumberjack, maniac, paddywhack, paperback, pickaback, piggyback, quarterback, razorback, saddleback, union jack, zodiac.
[4+] amnesiac, egomaniac, hypochondriac, insomniac, kleptomaniac, megalomaniac.

SURPRISING RHYMING:
[1] Act, backed, cracked, fact, lacked, packed, pact, quacked, racked, tacked, tact, tracked, tract, whacked, wracked.
Ask, bask, cask, flask, mask, task, unmask.
At, bat, brat, cat, chat, drat, fat, flat, frat, gnat, hat, mat, matte, pat, prat, rat, sat, scat, slat, spat, splat, sprat, stat, tat, that, vat.
App, cap, chap, clap, crap, flap, gap, lap, map, nap, pap, rap, sap, scrap, slap, snap, strap, tap, trap, wrap, yap, zap.
Bag, blag, brag, crag, drag, fag, flag, gag, hag, jag, lag, mag, nag, rag, sag, slag, snag, stag, swag, tag, wag, zag.
Blast, cast, fast, last, mast, massed, past, passed, vast.
[2] Abstract, attract, compact, contact, contract, detract, distract, enact, exact, extract, impact, intact, play act, ransacked, react, retract, sidetracked, subtract, unpacked.
Backchat, bearcat, bobcat, brickbat, chitchat, combat, doormat, fat cat, format, full-fat, hard hat, hellcat, high-hat, howzat, polecat, tomcat, top hat, whereat, wildcat, wombat.
Backslap, bitmap, bootstrap, catnap, cold snap, deathtrap, firetrap, giftwrap, handclap, hubcap, icecap, kidnap, kneecap, madcap, mantrap, mishap, mousetrap, nightcap, recap, roadmap, snowcap, speed trap, stopgap, suntrap, unwrap, watchstrap, whitecap.
Beanbag, bumbag, chinwag, dog-tag, fleabag, gasbag, gulag, handbag, jetlag, kitbag, mailbag, moneybag, nosebag, postbag, punchbag, ragbag, ragtag, ratbag, saddlebag, sandbag, scallywag/scalawag(U.S.), scumbag, tea-bag, washbag, windbag, zigzag.
Aghast, at last, breakfast, broadcast, contrast, die-cast, downcast, gymnast, harassed, hold fast, fly-past, miscast, outcast, outlast, outclassed, steadfast, surpassed, typecast.
[3] Artefact, cataract, counteract, inexact, interact, matter-of-fact, overact, overreact.
Acrobat, aristocrat, autocrat, automat, baseball bat, bureaucrat, copycat, cricket bat, democrat, diplomat, habitat, laundromat, pitapat, plutocrat, pussycat, scaredy-cat, tabby cat, technocrat, that's that, thermostat, tit-for-tat.
Handicap, overlap, photomap, thunderclap
Flabbergast, overcast, telecast, unsurpassed.
Aftermath, bloodbath, footpath, psychopath, sociopath, towpath, warpath.

1.2.7 "--act" (as in "fact")
[1] act, fact, pact, tact, tract.
[2] abstract, attract, compact, contact, contract, detract, distract, enact, exact, extract, hump-backed, hunchbacked, impact, intact, play act, protract, ransacked, react, redact, retract, sidetracked, subtract, transact, unpacked.
[3] artefact, counteract, inexact, interact, matter-of-fact, overact, overreact, re-enact.

SURPRISING RHYMING:
[1] Back, black, clack, crack, flak, hack, jack, knack, lack, mac, Mach, pack, plaque, quack, rack, sack, shack, slack, smack, snack, stack, tack, thwack, track, whack.
Backed, cracked, lacked, packed, racked, tacked, tracked, tract, whacked, wracked.
At, bat, brat, cat, chat, drat, fat, flat, frat, gnat, hat, mat, matte, pat, prat, rat, sat, scat, slat, spat, splat, sprat, stat, tat, that, vat.
Blast, cast, caste, fast, last, mast, massed, past, passed, vast.
Aft, craft, daft, draft, draught, gaffed, graft, laughed, raft, shaft, staffed, waft.
[2] Aback, attack, backpack, backtrack, bareback, blackjack, blowback, bootblack, bushwhack, callback, cheapjack, claw back, cognac, comeback, cutback, drawback,

fallback, feedback, fightback, flapjack, flashback, greenback, hatchback, haystack, hijack, holdback, horseback, kayak, kickback, knapsack, knick-knack, mudpack, Muzak, outback, payback, pitch black, playback, Prozac, racetrack, ransack, rollback, rucksack, setback, sidetrack, skyjack, slingback, smokestack, soundtrack, splashback, switchback, tailback, tarmac, talkback, throwback, tieback, unpack, way back, wingback, wisecrack.
Abstract, attract, compact, contact, contract, detract, distract, enact, exact, extract, impact, intact, play act, ransacked, react, retract, sidetracked, subtract, unpacked.
Backchat, bearcat, bobcat, brickbat, chitchat, combat, doormat, fat cat, format, full-fat, hard hat, hellcat, high-hat, howzat, polecat, tomcat, top hat, wheat, wildcat, wombat.
Aghast, at last, breakfast, broadcast, contrast, die-cast, downcast, gymnast, harassed, hold fast, fly-past, miscast, outcast, outlast, outclassed, steadfast, surpassed, typecast.
Aircraft, backdraft, handcraft, life-raft, redraft, spacecraft, stagecraft, unstaffed, witchcraft.
[3] Almanac, anorak, bivouac, bric-a-brac, cardiac, chimney stack, cul-de-sac, lumberjack, maniac, paperback, pickaback, piggyback, quarterback, union jack, zodiac.
Acrobat, aristocrat, autocrat, automat, baseball bat, bureaucrat, copycat, cricket bat, democrat, diplomat, habitat, kitty cat, laundromat, pitapat, plutocrat, pussycat, scaredy-cat, tabby cat, technocrat, that's that, thermostat, tit-for-tat.
Handicraft, hovercraft, needlecraft, overdraft, overstaffed, understaffed.

1.2.8 "--acker" (as in "hacker")
[2] backer, blacker, clacker, cracker, hacker, knacker, lacquer, packer, sacker, slacker, smacker, stacker, tacker, tracker, whacker.
[3] attacker, bushwhacker, firecracker, hijacker, lipsmacker, nutcracker, ransacker.

SURPRISING RHYMING:
[2] **Anchor**, banker, blanker, canker, flanker, franker, hanker, pranker, rancour/rancor (U.S.), spanker, tanker, thanker, yanker.
Batter, chatter, clatter, fatter, flatter, hatter, latter, matter, natter, patter, platter, regatta, scatter, shatter, smatter, spatter, splatter.
Clapper, crapper, dapper, flapper, mapper, napper, rapper, sapper, scrapper, slapper, snapper, tapper, trapper, wrapper, yapper.
Bagger, blagger, bragger, carpetbagger, dagger, dragger, flagger, gagger, lagger, nagger, snagger, stagger, swagger, wagger.
Adder, bladder, gladder, ladder, madder, sadder, stepladder.
Clamour/clamor (U.S.), crammer, enamour/enamor (U.S.), glamour/glamor (U.S.), grammar, hammer, jammer, mamma, programmer, rammer, slammer, sledgehammer, spammer, stammer, windjammer, yammer.
Blabber, drabber, grabber, jabber, stabber.
Blaster, caster, castor, faster, master, pastor, plaster, vaster.
After, crafter, dafter, drafter, grafter, hereafter, laughter, rafter, thereafter.
Actor, adaptor, attractor, captor, chapter, contractor, extractor, factor, raptor, tractor.

1.2.9 "--acking" (as in "backing")
[2] backing, blacking, clacking, cracking, fracking, hacking, lacking, packing, quacking, racking, sacking, smacking, snacking, stacking, tracking, whacking, wracking.
[3] attacking, backtracking, ransacking, unpacking.

SURPRISING RHYMING:
[2] **Cackling**, crackling, shackling, tackling.
Batting, chatting, combatting, formatting, matting, patting, scatting.
Capping, chapping, clapping, flapping, kidnapping/kidnaping (U.S.), lapping, mapping, napping, overlapping, rapping, scrapping, slapping, snapping, strapping, tapping, trapping, wrapping, yapping.
Bragging, carpetbagging, dragging, flagging, lagging, nagging, snagging, wagging.
Blabbing, cabbing, dabbing, grabbing, jabbing, nabbing, stabbing.
Banning, caravanning, fanning, manning, planning, scanning, spanning, tanning.
Asking, axing, basking, faxing, masking, maxing, tasking, taxing, unmasking, waxing.
Blasting, casting, clasping, fasting, gasping, grasping, lasting, rasping.
Banking, blanking, clanking, cranking, ranking, spanking, tanking, thanking, yanking.

[3] **Acting**, attracting, contacting, contracting, detracting, distracting, enacting, exacting, extracting, impacting, overacting, play acting, ransacking, reacting, retracting, subtracting.
Breakfasting, broadcasting, contrasting, everlasting, forecasting, outlasting.
Decanting, enchanting, implanting, recanting, supplanting, transplanting.
[4] **Interacting**, overacting, overreacting, re-enacting.

1.2.10 "--ackle" (as in "crackle")
[2] cackle, crackle, hackle, jackal, shackle, tackle.
[3] barnacle, coracle, debacle, manacle, miracle, obstacle, oracle, pinnacle, ramshackle, spectacle, tabernacle, unshackle.

SURPRISING RHYMING:
[2] **Battle**, cattle, chattel, embattle, prattle, rattle, tattle, tittle-tattle.
Bedraggle, draggle, gaggle, haggle, straggle, waggle.
Addle, babble, dabble, paddle, rabble, saddle, scrabble, skedaddle, straddle, unsaddle.
Apple, chapel, dapple, grapple.
Axle, bedazzle, castle, dazzle, hassle, rascal, razzle, tassel, vassal.
Baffle, gavel, gravel, raffle, ravel, snaffle, travel, unravel.

1.2.11 "--action" (as in "attraction")
[2] action, faction, fraction, traction.
[3] abstraction, all-action, attraction, contraction, detraction, diffraction, distraction, extraction, inaction, proaction, protraction, reaction, redaction, refraction, retraction, subtraction, traction, transaction.
[4] counteraction, dissatisfaction, interaction, retroaction, satisfaction, stupefaction.

SURPRISING RHYMING:
[2] **Ashen**, fashion, compassion, imagine, passion, ration.
Fasten, flaxen, klaxon, relaxing, Saxon, waxen.
Caption, contraption, expansion, mansion, sanction.
Bashing, cashing, clashing, crashing, dashing, earbashing, flashing, gatecrashing, mashing, rehashing, slashing, smashing, splashing, stashing, thrashing, trashing.
Batching, catching, hatching, matching, patching, scratching, snatching, thatching.

1.2.12 "--acted" (as in "attracted")
[3] abstracted, acted, attracted, compacted, contacted, contracted, detracted, diffracted, distracted, enacted, exacted, extracted, impacted, protracted, reacted, redacted, refracted, retracted, subtracted, transacted.
[4] interacted, counteracted, overreacted, play-acted, re-enacted, subcontracted.

SURPRISING RHYMING:
[2] **Bracket**, jacket, packet, racket.
Acid, placid, rancid, rapid.
Crafted, drafted, grafted, rafted, shafted, wafted.
Atlantis, lattice, practice, practise, malpractice.
Carted, charted, darted, hearted, karted, parted, started.
Banded, branded, candid, candied, handed, landed, sanded, stranded.
Chanted, granted, panted, planted, ranted.
Batted, chatted, fatted, formatted, hatted, matted, patted, platted.
[3] **Active**, attractive, hyperactive, interactive, overactive, radioactive, reactive, unattractive.
Downhearted, good-hearted, hard-hearted, heavy-hearted, imparted, kick-started, kind-hearted, light-hearted, lion-hearted, outsmarted, push-started, uncharted, wholehearted.
Backhanded, barehanded, blackhanded, cack-handed, commanded, demanded, disbanded, expanded, heavy-handed, highhanded, left-handed, light-handed, offhanded, one-handed, red-handed, remanded, right-handed, shorthanded, single-handed, two-handed, unbranded, underhanded, unhanded.
Bombastic, drastic, dynastic, elastic, enthusiastic, fantastic, gymnastic, monastic, plastic, sarcastic, scholastic.

1.2.13 "--active" (as in "attractive")

active, abstractive, attractive, detractive, distractive, hyperactive, inactive, interactive, overactive, radioactive, reactive, refractive, subtractive, unattractive.

SURPRISING RHYMING:
[2] **Antic**, attic, frantic, static.
Atlantis, blasted, fasted, lasted, lattice, practice, practise, malpractice, taxes.
[3] **Acted**, attracted, compacted, contacted, contracted, detracted, diffracted, distracted, enacted, extracted, impacted, protracted, reacted, redacted, retracted, subtracted.
Acting, attracting, compacting, contacting, detracting, distracting, enacting, exacting, extracting, impacting, play acting, ransacking, reacting, redacting, retracting, subtracting.
Contrasted, forecasted, outlasted, three-masted.
Drastic, elastic, enthusiastic, fantastic, gymnastic, monastic, plastic, sarcastic.
Aquatic, asthmatic, chromatic, climatic, dogmatic, dramatic, ecstatic, emphatic, erratic, fanatic, phlegmatic, pneumatic, pragmatic, rheumatic, schematic, stigmatic, traumatic.
Captive, combative, massive, passive, impassive, seductive.
[4] **Interacted**, counteracted, overreacted, play-acted, re-enacted..
Acrobatic, aerobatic, aristocratic, aromatic, autocratic, automatic, bureaucratic, charismatic, cinematic, democratic, diplomatic, enigmatic, melodramatic, operatic, problematic, psychosomatic, symptomatic, systematic, thermostatic.

1.2.14 "--ad" (as in "glad")

[1] ad, add, bad, bade, cad, clad, dad, fad, gad, glad, grad, had, lad, mad, pad, plaid, sad, shad, tad, trad.
[2] footpad, forbade, grandad, heavy-clad, helipad, iron-clad, ivy-clad, jihad, keypad, kneepad, launchpad, myriad, nomad, notepad, scratchpad, sketchpad, triad, touchpad, unclad, undergrad, winter-clad.

SURPRISING RHYMING:
[1] **At**, bat, brat, cat, chat, drat, fat, flat, frat, gnat, hat, mat, matte, pat, prat, rat, sat, scat, slat, spat, splat, sprat, stat, tat, that, vat.
Blab, cab, crab, dab, drab, fab, flab, gab, grab, jab, lab, nab, scab, slab, stab, tab.
Bag, blag, brag, crag, drag, fag, flag, gag, hag, jag, lag, mag, nag, rag, sag, slag, snag, stag, swag, tag, wag, zag.
[2] **Backchat**, bearcat, bobcat, brickbat, chitchat, combat, doormat, fat cat, format, full-fat, hard hat, hellcat, high-hat, howzat, polecat, tomcat, top hat, wildcat, wombat.
Confab, kebab, minicab, prefab, rehab, screen-grab, smash and grab, taxicab, vocab.
Beanbag, bumbag, chinwag, dog-tag, fleabag, gasbag, gulag, handbag, jetlag, kitbag, mailbag, moneybag, nosebag, postbag, punchbag, ragbag, ragtag, ratbag, saddlebag, sandbag, scallywag/scalawag(U.S.), scumbag, tea-bag, washbag, windbag, zigzag.
[3] **Acrobat**, aristocrat, baseball bat, bureaucrat, copycat, democrat, diplomat, habitat, laundromat, pussycat, scaredy-cat, tabby cat, technocrat, that's that, thermostat, tit-for-tat.
Autograph, belly laugh, better half, cenotaph, choreograph, epitaph, lithograph, paragraph, phonograph, photograph, polygraph, telegraph.

1.2.15 "--adder" (as in "sadder")

[2] adder, bladder, gladder, ladder, madder, sadder, stepladder.

SURPRISING RHYMING:
[2] **Bagger**, blagger, bragger, carpetbagger, dagger, dragger, flagger, gagger, lagger, nagger, snagger, stagger, swagger.
Banner, fanner, manna, manner, manor, nana, planner, scanner, spanner, tanner.
Blabber, drabber, grabber, jabber, stabber.
Clamour/clamor (U.S.), crammer, enamour/enamor (U.S.), glamour/glamor (U.S.), grammar, hammer, jammer, mamma, programmer, rammer, slammer, sledgehammer, spammer, stammer, windjammer, yammer.
Banger, clanger, ganger, gangbanger, hanger, hangar, haranguer, rang her, twanger.
Answer, cancer, chancer, dancer, glancer, lancer, prancer.
After, crafter, dafter, drafter, grafter, hereafter, laughter, rafter, thereafter.

Clapper, dapper, flapper, napper, rapper, scrapper, slapper, snapper, trapper, wrapper.
Backer, blacker, cracker, hacker, knacker, lacquer, packer, sacker, slacker, smacker, stacker, tacker, tracker, whacker.
[3] Bandanna, caravanner, hosanna, Pollyanna, savannah
Backslapper, entrapper, hand-clapper, kidnapper, whippersnapper, wiretapper.
Attacker, bushwhacker, firecracker, hijacker, lipsmacker, nutcracker.

1.2.16 "--addy" (as in "daddy")
[2] baddy, caddy, daddy, faddy, laddie, paddy, sugar daddy.

SURPRISING RHYMING:
[2] **Abbey,** badly, cabby, crabby, flabby, gladly, madly, sadly, scabby, shabby.
Baggy, carry, craggy, harry, marry, naggy, parry, raggy, saggy, scraggy, shaggy.
Chappie, crappy, happy, nappy, pappy, scrappy, slap-happy, snappy, unhappy, zappy.
Alley, dally, galley, pally, rally, reveille, sally, tally, valley.
Chatty, fatty, scatty, classy, sassy, Grammy, mammy, granny, savvy, wacky.
Habit, rabbit, cohabit, inhabit.

1.2.17 "--addle" (as in "saddle")
[2] addle, paddle, saddle, skedaddle, straddle, unsaddle.

SURPRISING RHYMING:
[2] **Addled,** paddled, saddled, straddled.
Babble, bedraggle, dabble, gaggle, haggle, rabble, scrabble, straggle, waggle.
Apple, chapel, dapple, grapple.
Battle, cattle, chattel, embattle, prattle, rattle, tattle, tittle-tattle.
Baffle, gavel, gravel, raffle, ravel, snaffle, travel, unravel.
Bedazzle, castle, dazzle, frazzle, hassle, razzle, tassel.
Cackle, crackle, hackle, jackal, shackle, tackle.
Candle, handle, manhandle, mishandle, sandal, scandal, vandal.
Amble, bramble, gamble, preamble, ramble, scramble, shamble, unscramble.
Angle, bangle, dangle, jangle, mangle, spangle, strangle, tangle, wangle, wrangle.

1.2.18 "--addled" (as in "saddled")
[2] addled, paddled, saddled, straddled, unsaddled.

SURPRISING RHYMING:
[2] **Addle,** paddle, saddle, skedaddle, straddle, unsaddle.
Bedraggled, dabbled, dappled, grappled, haggled, scrabbled, straggled, waggled.
Bedazzled, dazzled, frazzled, hassled.
Baffled, graveled, raffled, raveled, snaffled, travelled, unraveled.
Battled, cackled, crackled, embattled, prattled, rattled, shackled, tackled.
Manhandled, mishandled, panhandled.
Ambled, gambled, rambled, scrambled, shambled, unscrambled.
Angled, bangled, dangled, jangled, spangled, strangled, tangled, wangled, wrangled.

1.2.19 "--adly" (as in "badly")
[2] badly, gladly, madly, sadly.

SURPRISING RHYMING:
[2] **Bandy,** brandy, candy, dandy, handy, randy, sandy, shandy.
Alley, dally, galley, pally, rally, reveille, tally, valley.
Baddy, caddy, daddy, faddy, laddie, paddy, sugar daddy.
Abbey, blabby, cabby, crabby, flabby, gabby, scabby, shabby, shabbily, tabby.
Baggy, craggy, naggy, raggy, saggy, scraggy, shaggy.
Acne, flatly, lastly, nasty, steadfastly, vastly.
Chatty, fatty, scatty, classy, sassy, Grammy, mammy, granny, savvy, wacky.
Chappie, crappy, flappy, happy, happily, nappy, pappy, sappy, scrappy, slap-happy, snappy, unhappy, yappy, zappy.

1.2.20 "--aff" as in "laugh"
[1] caff, calf, chaff, daff, faff, gaff, gaffe, graph, half, laugh, naff, staff
[2] behalf, carafe, decaf, flagstaff, giraffe, horselaugh, mooncalf, riffraff
[3] autograph, bellylaugh, better half, cenotaph, choreograph, epitaph, paragraph, phonograph, photograph, polygraph, telegraph.

SURPRISING RHYMING:
[1] **Aft,** craft, daft, draft, draught, gaffed, graft, laughed, raft, shaft, staffed, waft.
Bath, hath, have, math, path, wrath.
Ash, bash, brash, cache, cash, clash, crash, dash, flash, gash, gnash, hash, lash, mash, pash, rash, sash, slash, smash, splash, stash, 'tache, thrash, trash.
[2] **Aircraft,** backdraft, life-raft, redraft, spacecraft, stagecraft, unstaffed, witchcraft.
Aftermath, birdbath, bloodbath, footpath, osteopath, psychopath, towpath, warpath.
Backlash, earbash, eyelash, gatecrash, goulash, mishmash, moustache/mustache (U.S.), newsflash, panache, rehash, slapdash, whiplash.
[3] **Handicraft,** hovercraft, needlecraft, overdraft, overstaffed, understaffed.

1.2.21 "--aft" (as in "laughed")
[1] aft, craft, daft, draft, draught, gaffed, graft, laughed, raft, shaft, staffed, waft.
[2] aircraft, backdraft, folk-craft, handcraft, life-raft, redraft, spacecraft, stagecraft, unstaffed, witchcraft, woodcraft.
[3] handicraft, hovercraft, needlecraft, overdraft, overstaffed, understaffed.

SURPRISING RHYMING:
[1] **Caff,** calf, chaff, daff, faff, gaff, gaffe, graph, half, laugh, naff, staff
Bath, hath, have, math, path, wrath.
At, act, bat, brat, cat, chat, drat, fact, fat, flat, frat, gnat, hat, mat, matte, pact, pat, prat, rat, sat, scat, slat, spat, splat, sprat, stat, tact, tat, that, tract. vat.
App, bap, cap, chap, clap, crap, flap, gap, lap, knap, map, nap, pap, rap, sap, scrap, slap, snap, strap, tap, trap, wrap, yap, zap.
Blast, cast, caste, fast, last, mast, massed, past, passed, vast.
Bashed, cashed, clashed, crashed, dashed, flashed, gashed, gnashed, hashed, lashed, mashed, sashed, slashed, smashed, splashed, stashed, thrashed, trashed.
[2] **Behalf,** carafe, decaf, giraffe, horselaugh, mooncalf, riffraff
Aghast, at last, breakfast, broadcast, contrast, die-cast, downcast, gymnast, harassed, hold fast, fly-past, miscast, outcast, outlast, outclassed, steadfast, surpassed, typecast.
Backchat, bearcat, bobcat, brickbat, chitchat, combat, doormat, fat cat, format, full-fat, hard hat, hellcat, high-hat, howzat, polecat, tomcat, top hat, whereat, wildcat, wombat.
Backslap, bitmap, bootstrap, catnap, cold snap, deathtrap, firetrap, giftwrap, handclap, hubcap, icecap, kidnap, kneecap, madcap, mantrap, mishap, mousetrap, nightcap, recap, roadmap, snowcap, speed trap, stopgap, suntrap, unwrap, watchstrap, whitecap.
Abstract, attract, compact, contact, contract, detract, distract, enact, exact, extract, impact, intact, play act, ransacked, react, retract, sidetracked, subtract, unpacked.
[3] **Autograph,** belly laugh, better half, cenotaph, choreograph, epitaph, paragraph, phonograph, photograph, polygraph, telegraph.
Abashed, gatecrashed, moustached/mustached (U.S.), rehashed.
Aftermath, birdbath, bloodbath, footpath, osteopath, psychopath, towpath, warpath.
Acrobat, aristocrat, baseball bat, bureaucrat, copycat, democrat, diplomat, habitat, laundromat, pussycat, scaredy-cat, tabby cat, technocrat, that's that, thermostat, tit-for-tat.
Artefact, counteract, inexact, interact, matter-of-fact, overact, overreact, re-enact.
Handicap, overlap, photomap, thunderclap

1.2.22 "--affle" (as in "baffle")
[2] baffle, raffle, snaffle.

SURPRISING RHYMING:
[2] **Baffled,** gavel, gravel, raffled, ravel, snaffled, travel, travelled, unravel, unraveled
Addle(d), paddle(d), saddle(d), skedaddle(d), straddle(d), unsaddle(d).
Babble, barrel, carol, dabble, rabble, scrabble.

Bedraggle, gaggle, haggle, raggle-taggle, straggle, waggle.
Candle, handle, manhandle, mishandle, sandal, scandal, vandal.
Apple, chapel, dapple, grapple.
Basil, bedazzle, castle, dazzle, frazzle, hassle, razzle, razzle-dazzle, tassel.
Cackle, crackle, hackle, jackal, shackle, tackle.
Battle, cattle, chattel, embattle, prattle, rattle, tattle, tittle-tattle.
Amble, camel, gamble, mammal, preamble, ramble, scramble, shamble, unscramble.
Angle, bangle, dangle, jangle, mangle, spangle, strangle, tangle, wangle, wrangle.

1.2.23 "--after" (as in "after")
after, crafter, dafter, drafter, grafter, hereafter, laughter, rafter, thereafter, whereafter.

SURPRISING RHYMING:
[2] **Capture**, departure, enrapture, fracture, manufacture, pasture, rapture, recapture.
Farther, father, forefather, grandfather, lather, rather.
Answer, cancer, chancer, dancer, glancer, lancer, prancer.
Blaster, caster, castor, faster, master, pastor, plaster, vaster.
Actor, adaptor, attractor, captor, chapter, contractor, extractor, factor, raptor, tractor.
Batter, clatter, fatter, flatter, hatter, latter, matter, natter, patter, platter, regatta, scatter, shatter, smatter, spatter, splatter.
Catcher, hatcher, matcher, scratcher, snatcher, stature, thatcher.
Clapper, dapper, flapper, grappa, mapper, napper, rapper, sapper, scrapper, slapper, snapper, tapper, trapper, wrapper, yapper.
Adder, bladder, gladder, ladder, madder, sadder, stepladder.
[3] **Bandmaster**, broadcaster, choirmaster, disaster, forecaster, grandmaster, headmaster, newscaster, quizmaster, ringmaster, schoolmaster, spymaster, taskmaster.
Baby-snatcher, backscratcher, body-snatcher, cradle-snatcher, dogcatcher, flycatcher.

1.2.24 "--ag" (as in "bag")
[1] bag, blag, brag, crag, drag, fag, flag, gag, hag, jag, lag, mag, nag, rag, sag, scag, scrag, shag, slag, snag, stag, swag, tag, wag, zag.
[2] beanbag, bumbag, chinwag, debag, dishrag, dog-tag, fleabag, gasbag, growbag, gulag, handbag, jetlag, kitbag, luggage tag, mailbag, moneybag, nosebag, postbag, punchbag, ragbag, ragtag, ratbag, saddlebag, sandbag, scallywag/scalawag(U.S.), scumbag, tea-bag, washbag, wigwag, windbag, zigzag.

SURPRISING RHYMING:
[1] **Bagged**, blagged, bragged, dragged, flagged, gagged, jagged, lagged, nagged, ragged, sagged, snagged, tagged, wagged, zagged.
Blab, cab, crab, dab, drab, fab, flab, gab, grab, jab, lab, nab, scab, slab, stab, tab.
Add, bad, bade, cad, clad, dad, fad, glad, had, lad, mad, pad, plaid, sad, tad, trad.
App, cap, chap, clap, crap, flap, gap, knap, lap, map, nap, pap, rap, sap, scrap, slap, snap, strap, tap, trap, wrap, yap.
Back, black, crack, flak, hack, jack, knack, lack, mac, Mach, pack, plaque, quack, rack, sack, shack, slack, smack, snack, stack, tack, thwack, track, vac, whack, wrack.
Ant, scant, pant, rant.
Bank, blank, clank, crank, dank, drank, flank, franc, frank, hank, lank, plank, prank, rank, sank, shank, shrank, spank, stank, swank, tank, thank, yank.
[2] **Debagged**, dog-tagged, handbagged, jetlagged, sandbagged, zigzagged.
Confab, kebab, minicab, prefab, rehab, screen-grab, smash and grab, taxicab, vocab.
Grandad, heavy-clad, helipad, iron-clad, ivy-clad, jihad, keypad, kneepad, launchpad, myriad, nomad, notepad, scratchpad, sketchpad, triad, touchpad, unclad, undergrad.
Aback, attack, backpack, backtrack, bareback, blackjack, blowback, bootblack, bushwhack, callback, cheapjack, claw back, cognac, comeback, cutback, drawback, fallback, feedback, fightback, flapjack, flashback, greenback, hatchback, haystack, hijack, holdback, horseback, kayak, kickback, knapsack, knick-knack, mudpack, Muzak, outback, payback, pitch black, playback, Prozac, racetrack, ransack, rollback, rucksack, setback, sidetrack, skyjack, slingback, smokestack, soundtrack, splashback, switchback, tailback, tarmac, talkback, throwback, tieback, unpack, way back, wingback, wisecrack.

[3] **Almanac**, anorak, bivouac, bric-a-brac, cardiac, chimney stack, crackerjack, cul-de-sac, haversack, lumberjack, maniac, paddywhack, paperback, pickaback, piggyback, quarterback, razorback, saddleback, union jack, zodiac.

1.2.25 "--agged" (as in "wagged")
[1] bagged, blagged, bragged, dragged, flagged, gagged, jagged, lagged, nagged, ragged, sagged, snagged, tagged, wagged, zagged.
[2] debagged, dog-tagged, handbagged, jetlagged, sandbagged, zigzagged.

SURPRISING RHYMING:
[1] **Bag**, blag, brag, crag, drag, fag, flag, gag, hag, jag, lag, mag, nag, rag, sag, slag, snag, stag, swag, tag, wag, zag.
Blabbed, dabbed, grabbed, jabbed, nabbed, scabbed, slabbed, stabbed, tabbed.
Add, bad, bade, cad, clad, dad, fad, glad, had, lad, mad, pad, plaid, sad, tad, trad.
Aft, craft, daft, draft, draught, gaffed, graft, laughed, raft, shaft, staffed, waft.
And, band, banned, bland, brand, canned, fanned, gland, grand, hand, land, manned, panned, planned, sand, scanned, spanned, stand, strand, tanned.
Blab, cab, crab, dab, drab, fab, flab, gab, grab, jab, lab, nab, scab, slab, stab, tab.
At, bat, brat, cat, chat, drat, fat, flat, frat, gnat, hat, mat, matte, pat, prat, rat, sat, scat, slat, spat, splat, sprat, stat, tat, that, vat.
[2] **Grandad**, helipad, iron-clad, ivy-clad, jihad, keypad, kneepad, launchpad, myriad, nomad, notepad, scratchpad, sketchpad, triad, touchpad, unclad, undergrad.
Beanbag bumbag, chinwag, dog-tag, fleabag, gasbag, gulag, handbag, jetlag, kitbag, mailbag, moneybag, nosebag, postbag, punchbag, ragbag, ragtag, ratbag, saddlebag, sandbag, scallywag/scalawag(U.S.), scumbag, tea-bag, washbag, windbag, zigzag.
Backslapped, catnapped, entrapped, flip-flapped, giftwrapped, handclapped, ice-capped, kidnapped, kneecapped, recapped, snowcapped, uncapped, unsnapped, unwrapped.
Abstract, attract, compact, contact, contract, detract, distract, enact, exact, extract, impact, intact, play act, ransacked, react, retract, sidetracked, subtract, unpacked.
Kebab, minicab, prefab, rehab, screen-grab, smash and grab, taxicab, vocab.
[3] **Acrobat**, aristocrat, autocrat, automat, baseball bat, bureaucrat, copycat, cricket bat, democrat, diplomat, habitat, kitty cat, lariat, laundromat, pitapat, plutocrat, pussycat, scaredy-cat, tabby cat, technocrat, that's that, thermostat, tit-for-tat.

1.2.26 "--agger" (as in "dagger")
[2] bagger, blagger, bragger, carpetbagger, dagger, dragger, flagger, gagger, jagger, lagger, nagger, snagger, stagger, swagger, wagger.

SURPRISING RHYMING:
[2] **Adder**, bladder, gladder, ladder, madder, sadder, stepladder.
Clamour/clamor (U.S.), crammer, enamour/enamor (U.S.), gamma, glamour/glamor (U.S.), grammar, hammer, jammer, mamma, programmer, rammer, slammer, sledgehammer, spammer, stammer, windjammer, yammer.
Blabber, drabber, grabber, jabber, stabber.
Batter, chatter, clatter, fatter, flatter, hatter, latter, matter, natter, patter, platter, regatta, scatter, shatter, smatter, spatter, splatter.
Banner, fanner, manna, manner, manor, nana, planner, scanner, spanner, tanner.
Banger, clanger, ganger, gangbanger, hanger, hangar, haranguer, rang her, twanger.
Clapper, crapper, dapper, flapper, mapper, napper, rapper, sapper, scrapper, slapper, snapper, tapper, trapper, wrapper, yapper.
Backer, blacker, clacker, cracker, hacker, knacker, lacquer, packer, sacker, slacker, smacker, stacker, tacker, tracker, whacker.
Blaster, caster, castor, faster, master, pastor, plaster, vaster.
After, crafter, dafter, drafter, grafter, hereafter, laughter, rafter.
[3] **Bandanna**, caravanner, hosanna, Pollyanna, savannah
Backslapper, entrapper, hand-clapper, kidnapper, whippersnapper, wiretapper.
Attacker, bushwhacker, firecracker, hijacker, lipsmacker, maraca, nutcracker, ransacker.
Advancer, enhancer, romancer.

*

1.2.27 "--aggy" (as in "shaggy")
[2] baggy, braggy, craggy, naggy, raggy, saggy, scraggy, shaggy, swaggy, waggy.

SURPRISING RHYMING:
[2] **Abbey**, blabby, cabby, crabby, flabby, gabby, scabby, shabby.
Baddy, caddy, daddy, faddy, laddie, paddy, sugar daddy.
Chappie, crappy, flappy, happy, nappy, pappy, scrappy, slap-happy, snappy, unhappy.
Classy, sassy, Grammy, jammy, mammy, savvy, wacky.
Carry, harry, marry, parry, tarry.
Alley, dally, dilly-dally, galley, pally, rally, reveille, sally, tally, valley.
Badly, gladly, madly, sadly.
Bandy, brandy, candy, dandy, granny, handy, jim-dandy, modus operandi, randy, sandy, shandy.
Auntie, panty, scanty, shanty, vigilante.

1.2.28 "--aggle" (as in "haggle")
[2] bedraggle, draggle, gaggle, haggle, straggle, waggle.

SURPRISING RHYMING:
[2] **Babble**, dabble, paddle, rabble, saddle, scrabble, skedaddle, straddle, unsaddle.
Baffle, gavel, gravel, raffle, ravel, snaffle, travel, unravel.
Cackle, crackle, hackle, jackal, shackle, tackle.
Battle, cattle, chattel, embattle, prattle, rattle, tattle, tittle-tattle.
Apple, chapel, dapple, grapple.
Bedazzle, castle, dazzle, frazzle, hassle, razzle, tassel.
Amble, bramble, gamble, preamble, ramble, scramble, shamble, unscramble.
Angle, bangle, dangle, jangle, mangle, spangle, strangle, tangle, wangle, wrangle.
Candle, handle, manhandle, mishandle, sandal, scandal, vandal.

1.2.29 "--ahl" (as in "pal")
[1] gal, mall, pal, shall.
[2] banal, cabal, canal, chorale, corral, decal, et al, locale, morale, pen pal, timbale.
[3] chaparral, entente cordiale, femme fatale, musical, pastoral, rationale.

SURPRISING RHYMING:
[3] **National**, passional, rational.
Actual, animal, biblical, cannibal, capital, carnival, casual, classical, comical, cynical, decimal, digital, ethical, festival, fractional, genial, graphical, hospital, integral, interval, logical, lyrical, madrigal, magical, manual, marital, medical, menial, mineral, minimal, musical, mystical, mythical, national, natural, notional, physical, pivotal, practical, principal, punctual, radical, rational, regional, rhythmical, seasonal, serial, several, sexual, tactical, technical, topical, tropical, typical, usual, vertical, virtual, visual.
[4] **Emotional**, international, irrational, multinational, promotional.
Additional, confessional, conventional, exceptional, intentional, traditional, three-dimensional, two-dimensional, conditional, nutritional.

1.2.30 "--al" (as in "normal")
[2] dismal, fiscal, formal, local, mammal, moral, normal, primal, signal, vocal.
[3] abnormal, abysmal, actual, admiral, aerial, animal, autumnal, biblical, bilingual, cannibal, capital, carnival, casual, cerebral, chemical, classical, clinical, comical, communal, cynical, decimal, digital, ethical, festival, genial, hospital, informal, integral, interval, logical, lyrical, madrigal, magical, manual, marital, medical, menial, mineral, minimal, musical, mystical, mythical, national, nautical, optical, optimal, orbital, paranormal, physical, pivotal, practical, principal, punctual, radical, rascal, rational, regional, rhythmical, seasonal, serial, several, sexual, skeletal, stoical, tactical, technical, topical, tragical, tropical, typical, usual, vertical, virtual, visual, whimsical.
[4] botanical, conventional, diagonal, fanatical, fantastical, grammatical, impractical, international, ironical, irrational, mechanical, millennial, multinational, octagonal, perennial, sabbatical, satirical, tyrannical.

SURPRISING RHYMING:
[3] **Article**, bicycle, circle, chronicle, cubicle, encircle, follicle, icicle, miracle, particle, pinnacle, Popsicle, tricycle, vehicle.
Barnacle, debacle, manacle, obstacle, oracle, sparkle, spectacle, unshackle.
Affable, capable, changeable, danceable, fallible, fashionable, feasible, flammable, gullible, laughable, legible, liable, miserable, payable, playable, pliable, tangible, viable.
[4] **Achievable**, adaptable, agreeable, amiable, amenable, attachable, available, believable, compatible, conceivable, considerable, degradable, deniable, detachable, discernible, dishonourable/dishonorable (U.S.), expandable, explainable, foreseeable, inaudible, infallible, inflatable, inflammable, implacable, incapable, incomparable, incredible, inedible, inexorable, infallible, insatiable, inseparable, insufferable, intolerable, invaluable, programmable, reclaimable, redeemable, reliable, retrievable, returnable, sustainable, unfavourable/unfavorable (U.S.), unflappable, unspeakable, variable.
[5] **Disagreeable**, inconceivable, irretrievable, unattainable, unavailable, unbelievable, undeniable, unexplainable, unforeseeable.

1.2.31 "--alice" (as in "malice")
[2] chalice, malice, palace.

SURPRISING RHYMING:
[1] **Bliss**, diss, hiss, kiss, miss, piss, sis, 'tis, this.
Dissed, fist, gist, hissed, kissed, list, midst, missed, mist, pissed, tryst, twist, wrist.
[2] **Badness**, madness, regardless, sadness.
Classless, darkness, dismiss, heartless, jaundice, office, remiss, surface.
Atlantis, anguish, flourish, lattice, nourish, practice, practise, malpractice.
Chances, dances, glances, prances, stances, trances.
Batches, catches, hatches, latches, matches, patches, scratches, snatches.
Ashes, bashes, caches, cashes, catch us, clashes, crashes, dashes, flashes, gashes, lashes, rashes, sashes, slashes, smashes, splashes, stashes, thrashes.
Asses, axes, axis, classes, faxes, gases, glasses, lasses, masses, passes, taxes.
[3] **Attaches**, detaches, dispatches, mismatches, relaxes, rematches, unlatches.
Cowardice, emphasis, genesis, liquorice/licorice (U.S.), nemesis, prejudice, reminisce.

1.2.32 "--allow" (as in "shallow")
[2] aloe, allow, callow, fallow, hallow, mallow, marshmallow, sallow, shallow, tallow.

SURPRISING RHYMING:
[2] **Aggro**, afro, arrow, alto, barrow, farrow, harrow, marrow, narrow, sparrow, tarot.
Follow, gallows, hallows, mallows, marshmallows, rainbow, shadow, swallow, wallow.
Avow, bow-wow, endow, eyebrow, highbrow, somehow.
[3] **Anyhow**, Apollo, buffalo, disallow, disavow, fiasco, foreshadow, piano, wheelbarrow.

1.2.33 "--allying" (as in "rallying")
[3] dallying, dilly-dallying, rallying, shillyshallying, tallying.

SURPRISING RHYMING:
[2] **Angling**, dangling, jangling, mangling, paneling, spangling, strangling, tangling, wangling, wrangling.
Cackling, crackling, hackling, shackling, tackling.
Ambling, gambling, rambling, scrambling, shambling.
Handling, manhandling, mishandling, panhandling.
Babbling, dabbling, gaggling, haggling, straggling, waggling.
Paddling, saddling, skedaddling, straddling, unsaddling.
Raffling, raveling, travelling, unravelling.
Bedazzling, dazzling, frazzling, razzling.
Battling, grappling, prattling, rattling.
Hampering, pampering, scampering, tampering.
[3] **Carrying**, harrying, marrying, parrying, tarrying.

*

1.2.34 "--am" (as in "jam")
[1] am, bam, clam, cram, dam, damn, dram, femme, flam, glam, gram, ham, jam, jamb, lam, lamb, ma'am, mam, pram, ram, scam, scram, sham, slam, Spam, swam, tram, wham, yam.
[2] exam, flimflam, goddam, logjam, madam, pro-am, programme/program (U.S.), slow jam, wigwam, whim-wham.
[3] ad nauseam, anagram, cardiogram, centigram, diagram, diaphragm, epigram, hologram, kilogram, kissogram, mammogram, milligram, monogram, phonogram, radiogram, stereogram, telegram.

SURPRISING RHYMING:
[1] Clammed, crammed, dammed, damned, glammed, jammed, rammed, scammed, scrammed, shammed, slammed, spammed, whammed.
An, ban, bran, can, clan, fan, flan, gran, man, nan, pan, plan, ran, scan, scran, span, stan, tan, than, van, vin.
And, band, banned, bland, brand, canned, fanned, gland, grand, hand, land, manned, panned, planned, sand, scanned, spanned, stand, strand, tanned.
Bang, clang, dang, fang, gang, hang, pang, prang, rang, sang, slang, sprang, tang, thang, twang, whang.
Amp, camp, champ, clamp, cramp, damp, lamp, ramp, scamp, stamp, tramp, vamp.
[2] Flimflammed, goddammed, logjammed, programmed/programed.
Adman, airman, ape man, bagman, bandman, barman, Batman, bedpan, began, birdman, boatman, brakeman, can-can, caveman, Chopin, churchman, clansman, craftsman, crewman, cyan, deadpan, divan, dustpan, élan, fireman, footman, freeman, freshman, game plan, guardsman, gunman, hangman, headman, he-man, henchman, horseman, huntsman, iceman, jazzman, kaftan, layman, lineman, madman, mailman, marksman, milkman, odd man, oilcan, oilman, outran, Pac-man, ploughman/plowman (U.S.), postman, ragman, salesman, sampan, sandman, seaman, sedan, shaman, showman, songman, spaceman, spokesman, sportsman, statesman, stockman, suntan, swagman, swordsman, taxman, trashcan, watchman, woman, woodsman, yachtsman.
Bandstand, broadband, clubland, command, deckhand, demand, disband, dreamland, expand, farmhand, farmland, firebrand, firsthand, freehand, gangland, grandstand, grassland, handstand, headband, headland, homeland, inland, lampstand, left-hand, longhand, lowland, mainland, marshland, moorland, newsstand, nightstand, offhand, quicksand, remand, right-hand, shorthand, showband, stagehand, suntanned, sweatband, unmanned, wasteland, waveband, withstand, woodland, wristband.
Boomerang, chain-gang, charabanc, gangbang, harangue, meringue, mustang, overhang, pressgang, shebang, whizz-bang.
[3] African, also-ran, artisan, caravan, cardigan, clergyman, countryman, courtesan, dairyman, fisherman, ferryman, frontiersman, gentleman, guardian, highwayman, hooligan, merchantman, middleman, parmesan, partisan, policeman, repairman, ruffian, signalman, spick-and-span, superman, talisman, tallyman, thespian.
Beforehand, borderland, contraband, fatherland, fairyland, misunderstand, motherland, no-man's-land, overland, reprimand, secondhand, underhand, understand, upper hand, wonderland.

1.2.35 "--ammed" (as in "jammed")
[1] clammed, crammed, dammed, damned, glammed, jammed, rammed, scammed, scrammed, slammed, spammed, whammed.
[2] flimflammed, goddammed, logjammed, programmed/programed.

SURPRISING RHYMING:
[1] Am, bam, clam, cram, dam, damn, dram, femme, flam, glam, ham, jam, lam, lamb, ma'am, mam, pram, ram, scam, scram, sham, slam, Spam, swam, tram, wham.
And, band, banned, bland, brand, canned, fanned, gland, grand, hand, land, manned, panned, planned, sand, scanned, spanned, stand, strand, tanned.
Banged, clanged, fanged, hanged, panged, pranged, twanged.
[2] Exam, flimflam, goddam, logjam, madam, pro-am, programme/program (U.S.), slow jam, wigwam, whim-wham.

Armband, Bandstand, broadband, clubland, command, deckhand, demand, disband, dreamland, expand, farmhand, farmland, firebrand, firsthand, freehand, gangland, grandstand, grassland, handstand, headband, headland, homeland, inland, lampstand, left-hand, longhand, lowland, mainland, marshland, moorland, newsstand, nightstand, offhand, quicksand, remand, right-hand, shorthand, showband, stagehand, suntanned, sweatband, unmanned, wasteland, waveband, withstand, woodland, wristband.
Boomeranged, gangbanged, harangued, pressganged.
[3] **Beforehand**, borderland, contraband, fatherland, fairyland, hinterland, misunderstand, motherland, no-man's-land, overland, reprimand, secondhand, underhand, understand, upper hand, wonderland.
Anagram, diagram, hologram, kilogram, kissogram, milligram, phonogram, telegram.

1.2.36 "--amp" (as in "lamp")

[1] amp, camp, champ, clamp, cramp, damp, lamp, ramp, scamp, stamp, tramp, vamp.
[2] blowlamp, decamp, encamp, headlamp, revamp, spotlamp, streetlamp, sunlamp, unclamp, wheelclamp.

SURPRISING RHYMING:
[1] **Camped**, clamped, cramped, damped, lamped, ramped, stamped, tamped, vamped.
Ant, scant, pant, rant.
Am, bam, clam, cram, dam, damn, dram, femme, flam, glam, ham, jam, lam, lamb, ma'am, mam, pram, ram, scam, scram, sham, slam, Spam, swam, tram, wham.
Clammed, crammed, dammed, damned, glammed, jammed, rammed, scammed, scrammed, slammed, spammed, whammed.
Bang, dang, fang, gang, hang, pang, prang, rang, sang, slang, sprang, tang, twang.
Bank, blank, clank, crank, dank, drank, flank, franc, frank, hank, lank, plank, prank, rank, sank, shank, shrank, spank, stank, swank, tank, thank, yank.
An, ban, bran, can, clan, fan, flan, gran, man, nan, pan, plan, ran, scan, scran, span, stan, tan, than, van, vin.
App, bap, cap, chap, clap, crap, flap, gap, lap, knap, map, nap, pap, rap, sap, scrap, slap, snap, strap, tap, trap, wrap, yap, zap.
[2] **Descant**, encamped, gallant, recant, revamped, unclamped, wheel-clamped.
Exam, flimflam, goddam, logjam, madam, pro-am, programme/program (U.S.), slow jam, wigwam, whim-wham.
Boomerang, chain-gang, charabanc, harangue, mustang, overhang, shebang, whizz-bang.
Antitank, databank, fishtank, foodbank, gangplank, hand-crank, mudbank, outflank, outrank, piggybank, pointblank, riverbank, sandbank, savings bank, think tank.
Adman, airman, ape man, bagman, bandman, barman, Batman, bedpan, began, birdman, boatman, brakeman, can-can, caveman, Chopin, churchman, clansman, craftsman, crewman, cyan, deadpan, divan, dustpan, élan, fireman, footman, freeman, freshman, game plan, guardsman, gunman, hangman, headman, he-man, henchman, horseman, huntsman, iceman, jazzman, kaftan, layman, lineman, madman, mailman, marksman, milkman, odd man, oilcan, oilman, outran, Pac-man, ploughman/plowman (U.S.), postman, ragman, salesman, sampan, sandman, seaman, sedan, shaman, showman, songman, spaceman, spokesman, sportsman, statesman, stockman, suntan, swagman, swordsman, taxman, trashcan, watchman, woman, woodsman, yachtsman.
[3] **Anagram**, diagram, hologram, kilogram, kissogram, milligram, phonogram, telegram.

1.2.37 "--amble" (as in "gamble")

[2] amble, bramble, gamble, preamble, ramble, scramble, shamble, unscramble.

SURPRISING RHYMING:
[2] **Angle**, bangle, dangle, jangle, panel, spangle, strangle, tangle, wangle, wrangle.
Candle, handle, manhandle, mishandle, sandal, scandal, vandal.
Bedraggle, draggle, gaggle, haggle, straggle, waggle.
Babble, dabble, paddle, rabble, saddle, scrabble, skedaddle, straddle, unsaddle.
Baffle, gavel, gravel, raffle, ravel, snaffle, travel, unravel.
Apple, battle, chapel, cattle, chattel, embattle, grapple, rattle, tattle, tittle-tattle.
Bedazzle, castle, dazzle, frazzle, hassle, razzle, tassel.

1.2.38 "--ambler" (as in "gambler")
[2] ambler, brambler, gambler, rambler, scrambler.

SURPRISING RHYMING:
[1] **Angler,** dangler, jangler, strangler, wangler, wrangler.
Blander, candour/candor (U.S.), dander, gander, grander, panda, pander, slander.
Banter, canter, chanter, granter, grantor, planter, ranter, Santa, scanter.
Camper, clamper, damper, hamper, pamper, scamper, stamper, tamper, tramper.
Answer, chancer, dancer, glancer, lancer, prancer.
After, crafter, dafter, drafter, grafter, hereafter, laughter, rafter, thereafter, traveler.
Actor, adaptor, captor, chapter, contractor, extractor, factor, raptor, redactor, tractor.
Handler, paddler, saddler, straddler.
[3] **Backhander,** bystander, commander, coriander, demander, expander, gerrymander, jacaranda, left-hander, meander, memoranda, outlander, philander, propaganda, right-hander, salamander, veranda.
Advancer, enhancer, romancer.

1.2.39 "--ambling" (as in "gambling")
[2] ambling, brambling, gambling, rambling, scrambling, shambling.

SURPRISING RHYMING:
[2] **Angling,** dangling, jangling, strangling, tangling, wangling, wrangling.
Handling, manhandling, mishandling, panhandling.
Babbling, dabbling, gaggling, haggling, straggling, waggling.
Paddling, saddling, skedaddling, straddling, unsaddling.
Bedazzling, baffling, dazzling, frazzling, razzling.
Battling, grappling, prattling, rattling, raffling, snaffling.
Raffling, raveling, travelling, unravelling.

1.2.40 "--ambles" (as in "gambles")
[2] ambles, brambles, gambles, rambles, scrambles, shambles.

SURPRISING RHYMING:
[2] **Angles,** bangles, dangles, jangles, spangles, strangles, tangles, wangles, wrangles.
Candles, handles, manhandles, sandals, scandals, vandals.
Paddles, saddles, skedaddles, straddles, unsaddles.
Baffles, gavels, battles, chattels, raffles, rattles, ravels, travels, unravels.
Cackles, crackles, hackles, jackals, shackles, tackles.
Apples, chapels, grapples.
Bedazzles, castles, dazzles, hassles, tassels, vassals.

1.2.41 "--ammer" (as in "hammer")
[2] clamour/clamor (U.S.), crammer, enamour/enamor (U.S.), gamma, glamour/glamor (U.S.), grammar, hammer, jammer, mamma, programmer, rammer, slammer, sledgehammer, spammer, stammer, windjammer, yammer.

SURPRISING RHYMING:
[2] **Banner,** fanner, manna, manner, manor, nana, planner, scanner, spanner, tanner.
Banger, clanger, ganger, gangbanger, hanger, hangar, haranguer, rang her, twanger.
Bagger, blagger, bragger, carpetbagger, dagger, gagger, nagger, stagger, swagger.
Batter, chatter, clatter, fatter, flatter, hatter, latter, matter, natter, patter, platter, regatta, scatter, shatter, smatter, spatter, splatter.
Clapper, dapper, flapper, napper, rapper, sapper, scrapper, slapper, snapper, tapper, trapper, wrapper, yapper.
Blabber, drabber, gladder, grabber, jabber, ladder, madder, sadder, stabber, stepladder.
Cracker, hacker, knacker, lacquer, packer, sacker, slacker, smacker, stacker, tracker.
[3] **Bandanna,** caravanner, hosanna, Pollyanna, savannah
Backslapper, hand-clapper, kidnapper, whippersnapper, wiretapper.
Attacker, bushwhacker, firecracker, hijacker, lipsmacker, maraca, nutcracker, ransacker.

47

1.2.42 "--amming" (as in "jamming")
[2] clamming, cramming, damning, damming, jamming, programming, ramming, shamming, slamming, spamming, whamming.

SURPRISING RHYMING:
[2] **Banning**, caravanning, fanning, manning, planning, scanning, spanning, tanning.
Blabbing, cabbing, dabbing, grabbing, jabbing, nabbing, stabbing.
Batting, chatting, combatting, formatting, matting, patting.
Clapping, flapping, kidnapping/kidnaping (U.S.), lapping, mapping, napping, overlapping, rapping, scrapping, slapping, snapping, strapping, tapping, trapping, wrapping, yapping.
Bragging, carpetbagging, dragging, flagging, lagging, nagging, snagging, wagging.
Banging, clanging, hanging, haranguing, overhanging, twanging.
Ambling, gambling, rambling, scrambling, shambling.
Camping, clamping, damping, stamping, tramping, ramping, vamping.
Branding, handing, landing, sanding, standing, stranding.
[3] **Commanding**, crash-landing, demanding, disbanding, expanding, freestanding, outstanding, remanding, upstanding, withstanding.
[4] **Misunderstanding**, notwithstanding, understanding.

1.2.43 "--amper" (as in "pamper")
[2] camper, clamper, damper, hamper, pamper, scamper, stamper, tamper.

SURPRISING RHYMING:
[2] **Banter**, canter, cantor, chanter, granter, grantor, planter, ranter, Santa, scanter.
Angler, dangler, gambler, jangler, rambler, scrambler, strangler, wangler, wrangler.
Blander, candour/candor (U.S.), dander, gander, grander, handler, lander, panda, pander, sander, slander, stander.
Answer, chancer, dancer, glancer, lancer, prancer.
Banner, fanner, manna, manner, manor, nana, planner, scanner, spanner, tanner.
Clamour/clamor (U.S.), crammer, enamour/enamor (U.S.), glamour/glamor (U.S.), grammar, hammer, jammer, mamma, programmer, rammer, slammer, sledgehammer, spammer, stammer, windjammer.
Banger, clanger, gangbanger, hanger, hangar, haranguer, twanger.
Actor, adaptor, captor, chapter, contractor, extractor, factor, raptor, redactor, tractor.
Anchor, banker, blanker, flanker, franker, hanker, pranker, rancour/rancor (U.S.), spanker, tanker, thanker.
Bragger, carpetbagger, dagger, dragger, flagger, gagger, nagger, stagger, swagger.
Clapper, dapper, flapper, napper, rapper, scrapper, slapper, snapper, trapper, wrapper.
[3] **Backhander**, bystander, commander, demander, expander, gerrymander, left-hander, meander, outlander, philander, propaganda, right-hander, romancer, veranda.

1.2.44 "--ampering" (as in "hampering")
[3] hampering, pampering, scampering, tampering.

SURPRISING RHYMING:
[3] **Angering**, clamouring/clamoring (U.S.), hammering, stammering.
Battering, chattering, flattering, gathering, scattering, shattering, smattering, spattering.
Camping, clamping, damping, stamping, tamping, tramping, ramping, vamping.
Cackling, crackling, shackling, tackling.
Ambling, gambling, rambling, scrambling, shambling.
Angling, dangling, jangling, strangling, tangling, wangling, wrangling.
Handling, manhandling, mishandling, panhandling, pandering, slandering.
Anchoring, answering, bantering, blabbering, capturing, hankering, jabbering, meandering, philandering, staggering, swaggering.
Carrying, harrying, marrying, parrying, tarrying.

1.2.45 "--amping" (as in "stamping")
[2] camping, clamping, damping, stamping, tamping, tramping, ramping, vamping.

48

SURPRISING RHYMING:
[2] **Branding**, handing, landing, sanding, standing, stranding.
Banking, blanking, cranking, flanking, ranking, spanking, tanking, thanking, yanking.
Chanting, granting, panting, planting, ranting, slanting.
Banging, clanging, hanging, haranguing, overhanging, twanging.
Cramming, damning, damming, jamming, programming, ramming, shamming, slamming, spamming, whamming.
Clapping, flapping, kidnapping/kidnaping (U.S.), lapping, mapping, napping, overlapping, rapping, scrapping, slapping, snapping, strapping, tapping, trapping, wrapping, yapping.
Blasting, casting, fasting, lasting.
Blabbing, dabbing, grabbing, jabbing, nabbing, stabbing.
Bragging, carpetbagging, dragging, flagging, lagging, nagging, snagging, wagging.
[3] **Hampering**, pampering, scampering, tampering.
Commanding, crashlanding, demanding, disbanding, enchanting, expanding, freestanding, hardstanding, outstanding, upstanding, withstanding.
Broadcasting, contrasting, die-casting, everlasting, forecasting, outlasting, typecasting.
[4] **Misunderstanding**, notwithstanding, understanding.

1.2.46 "--an" (as in "man")

[1] an, ban, bran, can, clan, fan, flan, gran, man, nan, pan, plan, ran, scan, scran, span, stan, tan, than, van, vin.
[2] adman, airman, ape man, bagman, bandman, barman, Batman, bedpan, began, birdman, boatman, brakeman, can-can, caveman, Chopin, churchman, clansman, craftsman, crewman, cyan, deadpan, divan, dustpan, élan, fireman, footman, freeman, freshman, game plan, guardsman, gunman, hangman, headman, he-man, henchman, horseman, huntsman, iceman, jazzman, kaftan, layman, lineman, madman, mailman, marksman, milkman, odd man, oilcan, oilman, outran, Pac-man, ploughman/plowman (U.S.), postman, ragman, salesman, sampan, sandman, seaman, sedan, shaman, showman, songman, spaceman, spokesman, sportsman, statesman, stockman, suntan, swagman, swordsman, taxman, trashcan, watchman, woman, woodsman, yachtsman.
[3] African, alderman, also-ran, artisan, caravan, cardigan, catamaran, clergyman, countryman, courtesan, dairyman, fisherman, ferryman, frontiersman, gentleman, guardian, highwayman, hooligan, lesbian, longshoreman, marzipan, merchantman, middleman, midshipman, nobleman, orangutan, partisan, policeman, repairman, rifleman, ruffian, signalman, spick-and-span, superman, talisman, tallyman, thespian.

SURPRISING RHYMING:
[1] **Am,** bam, clam, cram, dam, damn, dram, femme, flam, glam, ham, jam, lam, lamb, ma'am, mam, pram, ram, scam, scram, sham, slam, Spam, swam, tram, wham.
Crammed, dammed, damned, glammed, jammed, rammed, scammed, scrammed, slammed, spammed, whammed.
And, band, banned, bland, brand, canned, fanned, gland, grand, hand, land, manned, panned, planned, sand, scanned, spanned, stand, strand, tanned.
Bang, clang, fang, gang, hang, pang, prang, rang, sang, slang, sprang, tang, twang.
Amp, camp, champ, clamp, cramp, damp, lamp, ramp, scamp, stamp, tramp, vamp.
[2] **Exam**, flimflam, goddam, logjam, madam, pro-am, programme/program (U.S.), slow jam, wigwam, whim-wham.
Flimflammed, goddammed, logjammed, programmed/programed.
Bandstand, broadband, clubland, command, deckhand, demand, disband, dreamland, expand, farmhand, farmland, firebrand, firsthand, freehand, gangland, grandstand, grassland, handstand, headband, headland, homeland, inland, lampstand, left-hand, longhand, lowland, mainland, marshland, moorland, newsstand, nightstand, offhand, quicksand, remand, right-hand, shorthand, showband, stagehand, suntanned, sweatband, unmanned, wasteland, waveband, withstand, woodland, wristband.
Boomerang, chain-gang, charabanc, harangue, mustang, overhang, shebang, whizz-bang.
[3] **Anagram**, diagram, hologram, kilogram, kissogram, milligram, phonogram, telegram.
Beforehand, borderland, contraband, fatherland, fairyland, hinterland, misunderstand, motherland, no-man's-land, overland, reprimand, secondhand, underhand, understand, upper hand, wonderland.

1.2.47 "--and" (as in "hand")
[1] and, band, banned, bland, brand, canned, fanned, gland, grand, hand, land, manned, panned, planned, sand, scanned, spanned, stand, strand, tanned.
[2] armband, backhand, bandstand, broadband, chargehand, clubland, command, deckhand, demand, disband, dreamland, expand, farmhand, farmland, firebrand, firsthand, forehand, freehand, gangland, grandstand, grassland, handstand, headband, headland, homeland, inland, lampstand, left-hand, longhand, lowland, mainland, marshland, moorland, neckband, newsstand, nightstand, offhand, quicksand, remand, right-hand, shorthand, showband, stagehand, suntanned, sweatband, unmanned, unplanned, upland, waistband, wasteland, waveband, withstand, woodland, wristband.
[3] ampersand, beforehand, borderland, contraband, countermand, fatherland, fairyland, hinterland, misunderstand, motherland, no-man's-land, overhand, overland, reprimand, secondhand, underhand, understand, upper hand, wonderland.

SURPRISING RHYMING:
[1] **An**, ban, bran, can, clan, fan, flan, gran, man, nan, pan, plan, ran, scan, scran, span, stan, tan, than, van, vin.
Am, bam, clam, cram, dam, damn, dram, femme, flam, glam, ham, jam, lam, lamb, ma'am, mam, pram, ram, scam, scram, sham, slam, Spam, swam, tram, wham.
Crammed, dammed, damned, glammed, jammed, rammed, scammed, scrammed, slammed, spammed, whammed.
Bang, clang, fang, gang, hang, pang, prang, rang, sang, slang, sprang, tang, twang.
Banged, clanged, fanged, hanged, panged, pranged, twanged.
Amp, camp, champ, clamp, cramp, damp, lamp, ramp, scamp, stamp, tramp, vamp.
[2] **Adman**, airman, ape man, bagman, bandman, barman, Batman, bedpan, began, birdman, boatman, brakeman, can-can, caveman, Chopin, churchman, clansman, craftsman, crewman, cyan, deadpan, divan, dustpan, élan, fireman, footman, freeman, freshman, game plan, guardsman, gunman, hangman, headman, he-man, henchman, horseman, huntsman, iceman, jazzman, kaftan, layman, lineman, madman, mailman, marksman, milkman, odd man, oilcan, oilman, outran, Pac-man, ploughman/plowman (U.S.), postman, ragman, salesman, sampan, sandman, seaman, sedan, shaman, showman, songman, spaceman, spokesman, sportsman, statesman, stockman, suntan, swagman, swordsman, taxman, trashcan, watchman, woman, woodsman, yachtsman.
Boomerang(ed), chain-gang, harangue(d), pressgang(ed), shebang, whizz-bang.
Exam, flimflam, grand-slam, logjam, madam, programme/program (U.S.), wigwam.
Flimflammed, goddammed, logjammed, programmed/programed.
[3] **African**, also-ran, artisan, caravan, cardigan, clergyman, countryman, courtesan, dairyman, fisherman, ferryman, frontiersman, gentleman, guardian, highwayman, hooligan, merchantman, middleman, parmesan, partisan, policeman, repairman, ruffian, signalman, spick-and-span, superman, talisman, tallyman, thespian.
Anagram, diagram, hologram, kilogram, kissogram, milligram, phonogram, telegram.
Arrogant, confidant, covenant, dissonant, dominant, elegant, elephant, emigrant, gallivant, hesitant, ignorant, immigrant, important, informant, irritant, jubilant, militant, radiant, relevant, stimulant, sycophant, tolerant, triumphant, vigilant.

1.2.48 "--ang" (as in "bang")
[1] bang, clang, dang, fang, gang, hang, pang, prang, rang, sang, slang, sprang, tang, thang, twang, whang.
[2] boomerang, chain-gang, charabanc, gangbang, harangue, meringue, mustang, overhang, pressgang, shebang, whizz-bang.

SURPRISING RHYMING:
[1] **Banged**, clanged, fanged, hanged, panged, pranged, twanged.
An, ban, bran, can, clan, fan, flan, gran, man, nan, pan, plan, ran, scan, scran, span, stan, tan, than, van, vin.
Am, bam, clam, cram, dam, damn, dram, femme, flam, glam, gram, ham, jam, lam, lamb, ma'am, mam, pram, ram, scam, scram, sham, slam, spam, swam, tram, wham.
Crammed, damned, glammed, jammed, rammed, scammed, slammed, spammed.

And, band, banned, bland, brand, canned, fanned, grand, hand, land, manned, panned, planned, sand, scanned, spanned, stand, strand, tanned.
[2] Boomeranged, gangbanged, harangued, pressganged.
Adman, airman, ape man, bagman, bandman, barman, Batman, bedpan, began, birdman, boatman, brakeman, can-can, caveman, Chopin, churchman, clansman, craftsman, crewman, cyan, deadpan, divan, dustpan, élan, fireman, footman, freeman, freshman, game plan, guardsman, gunman, hangman, headman, he-man, henchman, horseman, huntsman, iceman, jazzman, kaftan, layman, lineman, madman, mailman, marksman, milkman, odd man, oilcan, oilman, outran, Pac-man, ploughman/plowman (U.S.), postman, ragman, salesman, sampan, sandman, seaman, sedan, shaman, showman, songman, spaceman, spokesman, sportsman, statesman, stockman, suntan, swagman, swordsman, taxman, trashcan, watchman, woman, woodsman, yachtsman.
Exam, goddam, logjam, madam, programme/program (U.S.), slow jam, wigwam.
Armband, Bandstand, broadband, clubland, command, deckhand, demand, disband, dreamland, expand, farmhand, farmland, firebrand, firsthand, freehand, gangland, grandstand, grassland, handstand, headband, headland, homeland, inland, lampstand, left-hand, longhand, lowland, mainland, marshland, moorland, newsstand, nightstand, offhand, quicksand, remand, right-hand, shorthand, showband, stagehand, suntanned, sweatband, unmanned, wasteland, waveband, withstand, woodland, wristband.
Flimflammed, goddammed, logjammed, programmed/programed..
[3] African, also-ran, artisan, caravan, cardigan, clergyman, countryman, courtesan, dairyman, fisherman, ferryman, frontiersman, gentleman, guardian, highwayman, hooligan, merchantman, middleman, parmesan, partisan, policeman, repairman, ruffian, signalman, spick-and-span, superman, talisman, tallyman, thespian.
Beforehand, borderland, contraband, fatherland, fairyland, hinterland, misunderstand, motherland, no-man's-land, overland, reprimand, secondhand, underhand, understand, upper hand, wonderland.
Anagram, diagram, hologram, kilogram, kissogram, milligram, phonogram, telegram.

1.2.49 "--anged" (as in "banged")
[1] banged, clanged, danged, fanged, hanged, panged, pranged, twanged, whanged.
[2] boomeranged, gangbanged, harangued, pressganged.

SURPRISING RHYMING:
[1] Bang, clang, dang, fang, gang, hang, pang, prang, rang, sang, slang, sprang, tang, thang, twang, whang.
And, band, banned, bland, brand, canned, fanned, grand, hand, land, manned, panned, planned, sand, scanned, spanned, stand, strand, tanned.
Clammed, crammed, dammed, damned, glammed, jammed, rammed, scammed, scrammed, slammed, spammed, whammed.
[2] Boomerang, chain-gang, harangue, mustang, overhang, shebang, whizz-bang.
Bandstand, broadband, clubland, command, deckhand, demand, disband, dreamland, expand, farmhand, farmland, firebrand, firsthand, freehand, gangland, grandstand, grassland, handstand, headband, headland, homeland, inland, lampstand, left-hand, longhand, lowland, mainland, marshland, moorland, newsstand, nightstand, offhand, quicksand, remand, right-hand, shorthand, showband, stagehand, suntanned, sweatband, unmanned, wasteland, waveband, withstand, woodland, wristband.
Goddammed, logjammed, programmed/programed (U.S.).
[3] Beforehand, borderland, contraband, fatherland, fairyland, hinterland, misunderstand, motherland, no-man's-land, overland, reprimand, secondhand, underhand, understand, upper hand, wonderland.

1.2.50 "--angle" (as in "bangle")
[2] angle, bangle, dangle, jangle, mangle, spangle, strangle, tangle, wangle, wrangle.
[3] bespangle, disentangle, entangle, fandangle, pentangle, quadrangle, rectangle, right-angle, triangle, untangle, wide-angle.

SURPRISING RHYMING:
[2] Candle, handle, manhandle, mishandle, sandal, scandal, vandal.
Amble, gamble, preamble, ramble, scramble, shamble, unscramble.

Apple, battle, chapel, cattle, chattel, embattle, grapple, rattle, tattle, tittle-tattle.
Actual, casual, manual, rascal, sexual, virtual, visual.
Babble, dabble, paddle, rabble, saddle, scrabble, skedaddle, straddle, unsaddle.
Baffle, gavel, gravel, raffle, ravel, snaffle, travel, unravel.
Bedazzle, castle, dazzle, frazzle, hassle, razzle, tassel.

1.2.51 "--ank" (as in "thank")
[1] bank, blank, clank, crank, dank, drank, flank, franc, frank, hank, lank, plank, prank, rank, sank, shank, shrank, spank, stank, swank, tank, thank, yank.
[2] antitank, databank, fishtank, foodbank, gangplank, hand-crank, mudbank, outflank, outrank, piggybank, pointblank, riverbank, sandbank, savings bank, think tank.

SURPRISING RHYMING:
[1] **Ant**, banked, blanked, clanked, cranked, flanked, outflanked, outranked, pant, ranked, rant, scant, spanked, swanked, tanked, thanked, yanked.
Amp, camp, champ, clamp, cramp, damp, lamp, ramp, scamp, stamp, tramp, vamp.
Act, fact, pact, tact, tract.
Bang, clang, fang, gang, hang, pang, prang, rang, sang, slang, sprang, tang, twang.
[2] **Blowlamp**, encamp, headlamp, revamp, streetlamp, sunlamp, unclamp, wheelclamp.
Decant, descant, gallant, recant.
Boomerang, chain-gang, charabanc, harangue, mustang, overhang, shebang, whizz-bang.
Abstract, attract, compact, contact, contract, detract, distract, enact, exact, extract, impact, intact, play act, ransacked, react, retract, sidetracked, subtract, unpacked.
[3] **Arrogant**, confidant, covenant, dissonant, dominant, elegant, elephant, emigrant, gallivant, hesitant, ignorant, immigrant, important, informant, irritant, jubilant, radiant, registrant, relevant, stimulant, sycophant, tolerant, triumphant, vigilant.

1.2.52 "--anking" (as in "thanking")
[2] banking, blanking, clanking, cranking, flanking, franking, ranking, spanking, tanking, thanking, yanking.

SURPRISING RHYMING:
[2] **Chanting**, granting, panting, planting, ranting, slanting.
Camping, clamping, damping, stamping, tramping, vamping.
Banging, clanging, hanging, haranguing, overhanging, twanging.
Angling, dangling, jangling, spangling, strangling, tangling, wangling, wrangling.
Handling, manhandling, mishandling, panhandling.
Paddling, saddling, skedaddling, straddling, unsaddling.
Babbling, battling, dabbling, gaggling, grappling, haggling, rattling, straggling, waggling.
Bedazzling, baffling, dazzling, frazzling.
Backing, blacking, clacking, cracking, fracking, hacking, lacking, packing, quacking, racking, sacking, smacking, snacking, stacking, tracking, whacking, wracking.
Banning, caravanning, fanning, manning, panning, planning, scanning, spanning.
Branding, handing, landing, sanding, standing, stranding.
Asking, axing, basking, faxing, masking, maxing, tasking, taxing, unmasking, waxing.
Batting, chatting, combatting, formatting, matting, patting, scatting.
Capping, clapping, flapping, kidnapping, lapping, mapping, napping, overlapping, rapping, scrapping, slapping, snapping, strapping, tapping, trapping, wrapping, yapping.
Bragging, carpetbagging, dragging, flagging, lagging, nagging, snagging, wagging.
Blabbing, cabbing, dabbing, grabbing, jabbing, nabbing, stabbing.
[3] **Decanting**, enchanting, implanting, recanting, supplanting, transplanting.
Commanding, crashlanding, demanding, disbanding, expanding, freestanding, outstanding, withstanding.
Acting, attracting, contacting, contracting, detracting, distracting, enacting, exacting, extracting, impacting, overacting, play acting, ransacking, reacting, redacting, retracting.
[4] **Interacting**, overacting, overreacting, re-enacting.
Misunderstanding, notwithstanding, understanding.

*

1.2.53 "--anker" (as in "banker")

[2] anchor, banker, blanker, canker, flanker, franker, hanker, pranker, rancour/rancor (U.S.), spanker, tanker, thanker.

SURPRISING RHYMING:
[2] **Banter**, canter, cantor, chanter, granter, grantor, planter, ranter, Santa, scanter.
Actor, adaptor, captor, chapter, contractor, extractor, factor, raptor, redactor, tractor.
Camper, clamper, damper, hamper, pamper, scamper, stamper, tamper, vamper.
Angler, dangler, jangler, strangler, tangler, wangler, wrangler.
Blander, candour/candor (U.S.), dander, gander, grander, panda, pander, slander.
Banner, fanner, manna, manner, manor, nana, planner, scanner, spanner, tanner.
Backer, blacker, cracker, hacker, knacker, packer, slacker, smacker, stacker, tracker.
Clamour/clamor (U.S.), crammer, enamour/enamor (U.S.), glamour/glamor (U.S.), grammar, hammer, jammer, mamma, programmer, rammer, slammer, sledgehammer, spammer, stammer, windjammer.
Banger, clanger, ganger, gangbanger, hanger, hangar, haranguer.
Batter, clatter, fatter, flatter, latter, matter, natter, patter, platter, regatta, scatter, shatter, smatter, spatter, splatter.
Dapper, flapper, napper, rapper, scrapper, slapper, snapper, trapper, wrapper, yapper.
Bragger, carpetbagger, dagger, nagger, snagger, stagger, swagger.
Blaster, caster, castor, faster, master, pastor, plaster, vaster.
[3] **Decanter**, enchanter, tam-o'-shanter, transplanter.
Attacker, bushwhacker, firecracker, hijacker, lipsmacker, maraca, nutcracker, ransacker.

1.2.54 "--ance" (as in "chance")

REGULAR:
[1] chance, dance, France, glance, lance, manse, prance, stance, trance.
[2] advance, askance, balance, brilliance, distance, enhance, entrance, expanse, finance, fragrance, freelance, grievance, guidance, hindrance, instance, mischance, nuance, nuisance, penance, perchance, pittance, presence, riddance, romance, science, séance, semblance, sentence, square dance, tap-dance, vengeance.
[3] aberrance, abeyance, acceptance, accordance, acquaintance, adherence, admittance, allegiance, allowance, ambulance, annoyance, appearance, arrogance, ascendance, assistance, assonance, assurance, attendance, audience, avoidance, brilliance, circumstance, clairvoyance, clearance, coherence, coincidence, comeuppance, compliance, confidence, connivance, consonance, continence, conveyance, countenance, dalliance, defiance, deliverance, deviance, dissonance, disturbance, dominance, elegance, encumbrance, endurance, expedience, experience, extravagance, exuberance, flamboyance, furtherance, happenstance, ignorance, importance, inheritance, insurance, intelligence, interference, jubilance, maintenance, misguidance, negligence, nonchalance, obedience, occurrence, performance, perseverance, prominence, providence, radiance, relevance, reliance, reluctance, remembrance, remittance, Renaissance, repentance, resistance, resonance, substance, sufferance, subsidence, sustenance, temperance, tolerance, underpants, utterance, variance, vigilance.

SURPRISING RHYMING:
[1] **Chanced**, danced, glanced, lanced, pranced.
Bans, cans, clans, fans, flans, pans, plans, scans, spans, tans, vans.
Bands, brands, hands, lands, sands, stands, strands.
Clams, crams, hams, jams, lambs, prams, rams, scams, shams, slams, spams, trams.
Ants, aunts, grants, pants, plants, rants.
Catch, hatch(ed), latch(ed), match(ed), patch(ed), scratch(ed), snatch(ed), thatch(ed).
Ash, bash, brash, cache, cash, clash, crash, dash, flash, gash, gnash, hash, lash, mash, rash, sash, slash, smash, splash, stash, 'tache, thrash, trash.
Blast, cast, caste, fast, last, mast, massed, past, passed, vast.
Ass, brass, class, crass, gas, glass, grass, lass, mass, pass, sass.
[2] **Advanced**, enhanced, entranced, financed, romanced.

Exams, programmes/programs (U.S.), wigwams.
Bedpans, divans, dustpans, game plans, kaftans, sedans, suntans, trash cans.
Bandstands, commands, deckhands, demands, disbands, expands, farmhands, farmlands, grasslands, handstands, headbands, headlands, homelands, lowlands, marshlands, moorlands, newsstands, nightstands, showbands, stagehands, uplands, waistbands, wastelands, wavebands, wetlands, withstands, woodlands, wristbands.
Attach, detach, dispatch, eyepatch, knee patch, mismatch, outmatch, rematch, unlatch.
Attached, detached, dispatched, mismatched, unlatched, unmatched.
Backlash, eyelash, gatecrash, mishmash, moustache/mustache (U.S.), newsflash, panache, rehash, slapdash, whiplash.
Aghast, at last, broadcast, contrast, downcast, harassed, miscast, outcast, outlast, outclassed, steadfast, surpassed, typecast.
Alas, badass, bluegrass, compass, crevasse, en masse, eyeglass, first class, fracas, harass, hourglass, impasse, jackass, kick-ass, Midas, morass, outclass, reclass, smart-ass, spyglass, stained glass, surpass, teargas, trespass, volte-face, world class.
[3] Africans, also-rans, artisans, caravans, cardigans, catamarans, courtesans, guardians, hooligans, orangutans, partisans, ruffians, thespians.
Anagrams, diagrams, holograms, kilograms, kissograms, milligrams, telegrams.
Alias, bonny lass, coup-de-grace, gravitas, looking glass, masterclass, middle-class, overpass, pancreas, underclass, underpass, upper-class, weatherglass, working class.

1.2.55 "--anced" (as in "chanced")
[1] chanced, danced, glanced, lanced, pranced.
[2] advanced, enhanced, entranced, financed, romanced.

SURPRISING RHYMING:
[1] **Chance,** dance, France, glance, lance, prance, stance, trance.
Bans, cans, clans, fans, flans, grans, pans, plans, scans, spans, tans, vans.
Bands, brands, hands, lands, sands, stands, strands.
Clams, crams, dams, drams, grams, hams, jams, lambs, prams, rams, scams, hams, slams, spams, trams.
Ants, aunts, grants, pants, plants, rants.
Blast, cast, fast, last, mast, massed, past, passed, vast.
Ass, brass, class, crass, gas, glass, grass, lass, mass, pass, sass.
[2] **Advance,** balance, brilliance, distance, enhance, entrance, expanse, finance, fragrance, freelance, grievance, guidance, hindrance, instance, nuance, nuisance, penance, pittance, presence, riddance, romance, science, séance, semblance, sentence, square dance, tap-dance.
Exams, programmes/programs (U.S.), wigwams.
Bedpans, divans, dustpans, game plans, kaftans, sedans, suntans, trash cans.
Bandstands, commands, deckhands, demands, disbands, expands, farmhands, farmlands, grasslands, handstands, headbands, headlands, homelands, lowlands, marshlands, moorlands, newsstands, nightstands, showbands, stagehands, uplands, waistbands, wastelands, wavebands, wetlands, withstands, woodlands, wristbands.
Attached, detached, dispatched, mismatched, unlatched, unmatched.
Aghast, at last, broadcast, contrast, downcast, harassed, miscast, outcast, outlast, outclassed, steadfast, surpassed, typecast.
Gatecrashed, mishmashed, moustached/mustached (U.S.), rehashed.
[3] **Africans,** also-rans, artisans, caravans, cardigans, catamarans, courtesans, guardians, hooligans, orangutans, partisans, ruffians, thespians.
Anagrams, diagrams, holograms, kilograms, kissograms, milligrams, telegrams.

1.2.56 "--ant" (as in "pant")
[1] ant, aunt, chant, grant, plant, pant, rant, scant, slant.
[2] decant, descant, eggplant, enchant, gallant, houseplant, implant, pendant, recant, supplant, transplant.
[3] applicant, arrogant, confidant, covenant, debutante, dominant, elegant, elephant, emigrant, gallivant, hesitant, ignorant, immigrant, important, informant, irritant, jubilant, nonchalant, radiant, relevant, stimulant, sycophant, tolerant, triumphant, vigilant.

SURPRISING RHYMING:
[1] **Amp**, camp, champ, clamp, cramp, damp, lamp, ramp, stamp, tramp, vamp.
And, band, banned, bland, brand, canned, fanned, grand, hand, land, manned, panned, planned, sand, scanned, spanned, stand, strand, tanned.
Crammed, dammed, damned, glammed, jammed, rammed, scammed, scrammed, slammed, spammed, whammed.
Bang, clang, fang, gang, hang, pang, prang, rang, sang, slang, sprang, tang, twang.
Bank, blank, crank, dank, drank, flank, franc, frank, hank, lank, plank, prank, rank, sank, shank, shrank, spank, stank, swank, tank, thank, yank.
Chance, dance, France, glance, lance, prance, stance, trance.
[2] **Abstract**, attract, compact, contact, contract, detract, distract, enact, exact, extract, impact, intact, play act, ransacked, react, retract, sidetracked, subtract, unpacked.
Blowlamp, decamp, encamp, headlamp, revamp, streetlamp, sunlamp, unclamp.
Bandstand, broadband, clubland, command, deckhand, demand, disband, dreamland, expand, farmhand, farmland, firebrand, firsthand, freehand, gangland, grandstand, grassland, handstand, headband, headland, homeland, inland, lampstand, left-hand, longhand, lowland, mainland, marshland, moorland, newsstand, nightstand, offhand, quicksand, remand, right-hand, shorthand, showband, stagehand, suntanned, sweatband, unmanned, wasteland, waveband, withstand, woodland, wristband.
Goddammed, logjammed, programmed/programed (U.S.).
Boomerang, chain-gang, charabanc, harangue, mustang, overhang, shebang, whizz-bang.
Databank, fishtank, foodbank, gangplank, mudbank, outflank, outrank, piggybank, pointblank, riverbank, sandbank, savings bank, think tank.
[3] **Beforehand**, borderland, contraband, fatherland, fairyland, hinterland, misunderstand, motherland, no-man's-land, overland, reprimand, secondhand, underhand, understand, upper hand, wonderland.

1.2.57 "--anter" (as in "banter")
[2] banter, canter, cantor, chanter, granter, grantor, planter, ranter, Santa, scanter.
[3] decanter, enchanter, tam-o'-shanter, transplanter.

SURPRISING RHYMING:
[2] **Anchor**, banker, blanker, franker, hanker, rancour/rancor (U.S.), spanker, tanker.
Actor, adaptor, captor, chapter, contractor, extractor, factor, raptor, redactor, tractor.
After, crafter, dafter, drafter, grafter, hereafter, laughter, rafter, thereafter, traveler.
Blander, candour/candor (U.S.), dander, gander, grander, pander, slander, stander.
Camper, clamper, damper, hamper, pamper, scamper, stamper, tamper, tramper.
Angler, dangler, jangler, strangler, tangler, wangler, wrangler.
Answer, chancer, dancer, glancer, lancer, prancer.
Anger, banger, clanger, hanger, hangar, haranguer, rang her, twanger.
[3] **Backhander**, bystander, commander, demander, left-hander, meander, outlander, philander, propaganda, right-hander, veranda.
Advancer, enhancer, romancer.

1.2.58 "--antic" (as in "frantic")
antic, Atlantic, frantic, gigantic, pedantic, romantic, sycophantic, transatlantic, unromantic.

SURPRISING RHYMING:
[2] **Manic**, mechanic, messianic, oceanic, organic, panic, satanic, titanic, volcanic.
Attic, classic, drastic, graphic, magic, plastic, static, traffic, tragic.
Bandit, granite, habit, inhabit, jacket, packet, planet, rabbit, racket, transit.
Active, attractive, hyperactive, inactive, interactive, overactive, radioactive, reactive.
[3] **Bombastic**, drastic, dynastic, elastic, enthusiastic, fantastic, gymnastic, monastic, plastic, sarcastic, scholastic.
Aquatic, asthmatic, chromatic, climatic, dogmatic, dramatic, ecstatic, emphatic, erratic, fanatic, phlegmatic, pneumatic, pragmatic, rheumatic, schematic, stigmatic, traumatic.
Acted, attracted, contacted, detracted, distracted, enacted, exacted, extracted, impacted, protracted, reacted, redacted, refracted, retracted, subtracted, transacted.
Captive, combative, massive, passive, impassive, seductive.

[4] Acrobatic, aerobatic, aristocratic, aromatic, autocratic, automatic, bureaucratic, charismatic, cinematic, democratic, diplomatic, enigmatic, melodramatic, operatic, problematic, psychosomatic, symptomatic, systematic, thermostatic.
Interacted, counteracted, overreacted, play-acted, re-enacted.

1.2.59 "--anting" (as in "panting")
[2] chanting, granting, panting, planting, ranting, slanting.
[3] decanting, enchanting, implanting, recanting, supplanting, transplanting.

SURPRISING RHYMING:
[2] **Camping**, clamping, damping, stamping, tramping, ramping, vamping.
Branding, handing, landing, sanding, standing, stranding.
Banking, clanking, cranking, flanking, ranking, spanking, tanking, thanking, yanking.
Banging, clanging, hanging, haranguing, overhanging, twanging.
Ambling, angling, dangling, gambling, jangling, rambling, scrambling, shambling, strangling, tangling, wangling, wrangling.
Cramming, damning, damming, jamming, programming, ramming, shamming, slamming, spamming, whamming.
Clapping, flapping, kidnapping/kidnaping (U.S.), lapping, mapping, napping, overlapping, rapping, scrapping, slapping, snapping, strapping, tapping, trapping, wrapping, yapping.
Blabbing, cabbing, dabbing, grabbing, jabbing, nabbing, stabbing.
Bragging, carpetbagging, dragging, flagging, lagging, nagging, snagging, wagging.
[3] **Demanding**, expanding, freestanding, outstanding, remanding, withstanding.
[4] **Misunderstanding**, notwithstanding, understanding.

1.2.60 "--anded" (as in "handed")
[2] banded, branded, candid, candied, handed, landed, sanded, stranded.
[3] backhanded, barehanded, blackhanded, cack-handed, commanded, demanded, disbanded, expanded, heavy-handed, highhanded, left-handed, light-handed, offhanded, one-handed, red-handed, remanded, right-handed, shorthanded, single-handed, two-handed, unbranded, underhanded, unhanded.

SURPRISING RHYMING:
[2] **Chanted**, granted, panted, planted, ranted.
Acted, crafted, drafted, grafted, rafted, shafted, wafted.
Ahead, blockhead, bloodshed, bobsled, bonehead, bullhead, co-ed, crossbred, deadhead, drop dead, forehead, highbred, homebred, homestead, hotbed, hothead, inbred, instead, misled, purebred, redhead, spearhead, well-fed, widespread.
[3] **Attracted**, contacted, distracted, enacted, impacted, reacted, redacted, retracted.
Downhearted, good-hearted, hard-hearted, heavy-hearted, imparted, kick-started, kind-hearted, light-hearted, lion-hearted, outsmarted, push-started, uncharted, wholehearted.
[4] **Interacted**, counteracted, overreacted, play-acted, re-enacted.

1.2.61 "--ander" (as in "grander")
[2] blander, candour/candor (U.S.), dander, gander, grander, lander, panda, pander, sander, slander, stander.
[3] backhander, bystander, commander, coriander, demander, expander, gerrymander, left-hander, meander, outlander, philander, propaganda, right-hander, veranda.

SURPRISING RHYMING:
[2] **Banter**, canter, cantor, chanter, granter, planter, ranter, Santa.
Camper, clamper, damper, hamper, pamper, scamper, stamper, tamper, tramper.
Angler, dangler, gambler, jangler, rambler, scrambler, strangler, wangler, wrangler.
Answer, chancer, dancer, glancer, lancer, prancer.
Banner, manna, manner, manor, nana, planner, scanner, spanner, tanner.
Clamour/clamor (U.S.), crammer, enamour/enamor (U.S.), glamour/glamor (U.S.), grammar, hammer, jammer, mamma, programmer, rammer, slammer, sledgehammer, spammer, stammer, windjammer.
Anchor, banker, hanker, rancour/rancor (U.S.), spanker, tanker, thanker.

1.2.62 "--andy" (as in "handy")
bandy, brandy, candy, dandy, handy, jim-dandy, modus operandi, randy, sandy, shandy.

SURPRISING RHYMING:
[2] **Anti**, auntie, panty, scanty, shanty, vigilante.
Cranky, hanky, hanky-panky, lanky, swanky, Yankee.
Baddy, caddy, daddy, faddy, laddie, paddy, sugar daddy.
Badly, gladly, madly, sadly.
Abbey, blabby, cabby, crabby, flabby, gabby, scabby, shabby.
Baggy, craggy, naggy, raggy, saggy, scraggy, shaggy, snaggy, swaggy, waggy.
Chappie, happy, nappy, pappy, scrappy, slap-happy, snappy, unhappy, yappy, zappy.
[3] **Alchemy**, bigamy, blasphemy, bonhomie, enemy, excuse me, infamy, tsunami.
Burgundy, C.O.D, comedy, custody, dogsbody, embody, fool-hardy, jeopardy, melody, nobody, parody, Ph.D., raggedy, remedy, rhapsody, somebody, subsidy, tragedy.
Buoyancy, captaincy, chancy, constancy, fancy, fragrancy, flagrancy, flippancy, infancy, poignancy, pregnancy, stagnancy, tenancy, truancy, vacancy, vagrancy, vibrancy.

1.2.63 "--anding" (as in "standing")
[2] branding, handing, landing, sanding, standing, stranding.
[3] commanding, crashlanding, demanding, disbanding, expanding, freestanding, hardstanding, outstanding, remanding, unhanding, upstanding, withstanding.
[4] misunderstanding, notwithstanding, understanding.

SURPRISING RHYMING:
[2] **Handling**, manhandling, mishandling, panhandling.
Paddling, saddling, skedaddling, straddling, unsaddling.
Banning, caravanning, manning, panning, planning, scanning, spanning, tanning.
Angling, dangling, gambling, jangling, rambling, scrambling, shambling, spangling, strangling, tangling, wangling, wrangling.
Babbling, baffling, dabbling, dazzling, gaggling, haggling, straggling, waggling.
Cackling, crackling, hackling, shackling, tackling.
Battling, grappling, prattling, rattling, travelling, unravelling.
Banking, cranking, flanking, franking, ranking, spanking, tanking, thanking, yanking.

1.2.64 "--anner" (as in "banner")
[2] banner, fanner, manna, manner, manor, nana, planner, scanner, spanner, tanner.
[3] bandanna, caravanner, hosanna, Pollyanna, savannah

SURPRISING RHYMING:
[2] **Clamour/clamor** (U.S.), crammer, enamour/enamor (U.S.), glamour/glamor (U.S.), grammar, hammer, jammer, mamma, programmer, rammer, slammer, sledgehammer, spammer, stammer, windjammer.
Banger, clanger, ganger, gangbanger, hanger, hangar, haranguer, rang her, twanger.
Bragger, carpetbagger, dagger, lagger, nagger, stagger, swagger.
Blabber, drabber, gladder, grabber, ladder, madder, sadder, stabber, stepladder.
Backer, cracker, hacker, knacker, lacquer, slacker, smacker, stacker, tracker, whacker.
Clapper, dapper, flapper, napper, rapper, scrapper, slapper, snapper, trapper, wrapper.
Batter, fatter, flatter, latter, matter, natter, patter, scatter, shatter, spatter, splatter.
[3] **Attacker**, firecracker, hijacker, lipsmacker, maraca, nutcracker, ransacker, regatta.

1.2.65 "--anic" (as in "panic")
botanic, manic, mechanic, messianic, oceanic, organic, panic, satanic, titanic, volcanic.

SURPRISING RHYMING:
[2] **Antic**, Atlantic, frantic, gigantic, romantic, sycophantic, transatlantic, unromantic.
Attic, classic, drastic, graphic, magic, plastic, static, traffic, tragic.
Bracket, jacket, packet, racket.
Bandit, granite, habit, inhabit, planet, rabbit, transit.

57

Banded, branded, candid, candied, handed, landed, sanded, stranded.
[3] **Aquatic**, asthmatic, barbaric, dogmatic, dramatic, dynamic, ecstatic, emphatic, erratic, fanatic, metallic, pragmatic, rheumatic, sporadic, stigmatic, traumatic.
Bombastic, elastic, enthusiastic, fantastic, gymnastic, monastic, sarcastic, scholastic.
[4] **Acrobatic**, aristocratic, aromatic, automatic, bureaucratic, charismatic, cinematic, democratic, diplomatic, emblematic, enigmatic, melodramatic, operatic, panoramic, plutocratic, problematic, psychosomatic, symptomatic, systematic, thermostatic.

1.2.66 "--anning" (as in "scanning")
[2] banning, canning, caravanning, fanning, manning, panning, planning, scanning, spanning, tanning.

SURPRISING RHYMING:
[2] **Cramming**, damning, damming, jamming, programming, ramming, shamming, slamming, spamming, whamming.
Banging, clanging, hanging, haranguing, overhanging, pranging, twanging.
Blabbing, cabbing, dabbing, grabbing, jabbing, nabbing, stabbing.
Batting, chatting, combatting, formatting, matting, patting, scatting.
Capping, clapping, flapping, kidnapping/kidnaping (U.S.), lapping, mapping, napping, overlapping, rapping, scrapping, slapping, snapping, strapping, trapping, wrapping.
Bragging, carpetbagging, dragging, flagging, lagging, nagging, snagging, wagging.
Ambling, gambling, rambling, scrambling, shambling.
Camping, clamping, damping, stamping, ramping, vamping.
Branding, chanting, granting, handing, landing, panting, planting, ranting, standing.
[3] **Commanding**, demanding, disbanding, expanding, freestanding, outstanding, upstanding, withstanding.
Decanting, enchanting, implanting, recanting, transplanting.
[4] **Misunderstanding**, notwithstanding, understanding.

1.2.67 "--ancer" (as in "dancer")
[2] answer, cancer, chancer, dancer, glancer, lancer, prancer.
[3] advancer, enhancer, entrancer, romancer.

SURPRISING RHYMING:
[2] **Banter**, canter, cantor, chanter, granter, grantor, planter, ranter, Santa, scanter.
Blaster, caster, castor, faster, master, pastor, plaster, vaster.
Catcher, hatcher, matcher, scratcher, snatcher, stature, thatcher.
Capture, departure, enrapture, fracture, manufacture, pasture, rapture, recapture.
Brasher, crasher, dasher, flasher, gatecrasher, haberdasher, masher, rasher, slasher, smasher, stasher, thrasher.
Banner, fanner, manna, manner, manor, nana, planner, scanner, spanner, tanner.
Angler, dangler, gambler, jangler, rambler, scrambler, strangler, wangler, wrangler.
Blander, candour/candor (U.S.), dander, gander, grander, panda, pander, slander.
Actor, adaptor, captor, chapter, contractor, extractor, factor, raptor, redactor, tractor.
Anchor, banker, blanker, hanker, rancour/rancor (U.S.), spanker, tanker, thanker.
Camper, clamper, damper, hamper, pamper, scamper, stamper, tamper, tramper.
[3] **Bandmaster**, broadcaster, choirmaster, disaster, forecaster, grandmaster, headmaster, newscaster, paymaster, postmaster, quizmaster, ringmaster, schoolmaster, scoutmaster, spymaster, taskmaster, telecaster.
Back-scratcher, body-snatcher, cradle-snatcher, dispatcher, dogcatcher, flycatcher.
Backhander, bystander, commander, demander, left-hander, meander, outlander, propaganda, right-hander, veranda.

1.2.68 "--ancy" (as in "fancy")
[3] buoyancy, captaincy, chancy, constancy, fancy, fragrancy, flagrancy, flippancy, infancy, poignancy, pregnancy, tenancy, truancy, vacancy, vagrancy, vibrancy.
[4] accountancy, ascendancy, consultancy, deviancy, discordancy, discrepancy, expectancy, extravagancy, flamboyancy, hesitancy, malignancy, militancy, occupancy, radiancy, redundancy, sycophancy.

SURPRISING RHYMING:
[2] **Brandy**, candy, dandy, handy, jim-dandy, modus operandi, randy, sandy, shandy.
Alley, carry, dally, galley, marry, pally, parry. rally, reveille, tally, valley.
Abbey, blabby, cabby, crabby, flabby, scabby, shabby.
Baddy, badly, caddy, daddy, faddy, gladly, laddie, madly, sadly, sugar daddy.
Chappie, happy, nappy, pappy, scrappy, slap-happy, snappy, unhappy, yappy, zappy.
[3] **Ecstasy**, embassy, fantasy, galaxy, jealousy, piracy, privacy.
Agency, fluency, frequency, legacy, regency.
[4] **Accuracy**, aristocracy, bureaucracy, celibacy, conspiracy, delicacy, democracy, diplomacy, hypocrisy, immediacy, intimacy, intricacy, legitimacy, literacy, lunacy, numeracy, pharmacy, supremacy.
Clemency, consistency, contingency, currency, deficiency, dependency, despondency, emergency, expediency, leniency, presidency, residency, transparency, urgency.

1.2.69 "--arnt" (as in "can't")

[1] aren't, aunt, can't, chant, grant, plant, shan't, slant.
[2] détente, eggplant, enchant, houseplant, implant, replant, supplant, transplant.
[3] debutante, nonchalant.

SURPRISING RHYMING:
[1] **Arced**, barked, harked, larked, marked, parked, sparked.
Chance(d), dance(d), France, glance(d), lance(d), prance(d), stance, trance.
Arc, ark, bark, dark, hark, lark, mark, marque, narc, park, quark, shark, spark, stark.
Ass, brass, class, glass, grass, pass.
Blast, cast, caste, fast, last, mast, past, vast.
[2] **Advance(d)**, askance, enhance(d), entranced, freelance, mischance, nuance, perchance, romance(d), séance, square dance, tap-dance(d).
Bluegrass, bypass, crevasse, en masse, eyeglass, first class, hourglass, impasse, outclass, smart-arse, spyglass, stained glass, surpass, trespass, wine glass, world class.
Aghast, at last, broadcast, contrast, downcast, fly-past, forecast, gymnast, half-mast, hold fast, miscast, newscast, outcast, steadfast, surpassed, typecast.
[3] **Disembark**, matriarch, question-mark, tiger shark, trailer park, watermark.
Coup-de-grace, looking glass, masterclass, middle-class, overpass, underclass, underpass, upper-class, weatherglass, working class.

1.2.70 "--ap" (as in "trap")

[1] app, bap, cap, chap, clap, crap, flap, gap, lap, knap, map, nap, pap, rap, sap, scrap, slap, snap, strap, tap, trap, wrap, yap, zap.
[2] backslap, bitmap, bootstrap, catnap, claptrap, deathtrap, entrap, firetrap, flat-cap, flip-flap, flytrap, foolscap, giftwrap, handclap, hubcap, icecap, kidnap, kneecap, madcap, mantrap, mishap, mousetrap, mudflap, nightcap, recap, redcap, roadmap, snowcap, stopgap, suntrap, toecap, uncap, unsnap, unwrap, watchstrap, whitecap.
[3] handicap, overlap, photomap, thunderclap

SURPRISING RHYMING:
[1] **Capped**, clap, flapped, lapped, knapped, mapped, napped, rapped, sapped, scrapped, slapped, snapped, strapped, tapped, trapped, wrapped, yapped, zapped.
At, act, bat, brat, cat, chat, drat, fact, fat, flat, frat, gnat, hat, mat, matte, pact, pat, prat, rat, sat, scat, slat, spat, splat, sprat, stat, tact, tat, that, vat.
Back, black, clack, claque, crack, flak, hack, jack, knack, lack, mac, pack, plaque, quack, rack, sack, shack, slack, smack, snack, stack, tack, thwack, track, whack.
Asp, clasp, gasp, grasp, rasp.
Blab, cab, crab, dab, drab, fab, flab, gab, grab, jab, lab, nab, scab, slab, stab, tab.
[2] **Backslapped**, catnapped, entrapped, flip-flapped, giftwrapped, handclapped, ice-capped, kidnapped, kneecapped, recapped, snowcapped, uncapped, unwrapped.
Backchat, bearcat, bobcat, brickbat, chitchat, combat, doormat, fat cat, format, full-fat, hard hat, hellcat, high-hat, howzat, polecat, tomcat, top hat, whereat, wildcat, wombat.
Aback, attack, backpack, backtrack, bareback, blackjack, blowback, bootblack,

bushwhack, callback, cheapjack, claw back, cognac, comeback, cutback, drawback, fallback, feedback, fightback, flapjack, flashback, greenback, hatchback, haystack, hijack, holdback, horseback, kayak, kickback, knapsack, knick-knack, mudpack, Muzak, outback, payback, pitch black, playback, Prozac, racetrack, ransack, rollback, rucksack, setback, sidetrack, skyjack, slingback, smokestack, soundtrack, splashback, switchback, tailback, tarmac, talkback, throwback, tieback, unpack, way back, wingback, wisecrack.
Abstract, attract, compact, contact, contract, detract, distract, enact, exact, extract, impact, intact, play act, ransacked, react, retract, sidetracked, subtract, unpacked.
[3] Acrobat, aristocrat, baseball bat, bureaucrat, copycat, democrat, diplomat, habitat, laundromat, pussycat, scaredy-cat, tabby cat, technocrat, that's that, thermostat, tit-for-tat.
Almanac, anorak, bivouac, bric-a-brac, cardiac, chimney stack, cul-de-sac, lumberjack, maniac, paperback, pickaback, piggyback, quarterback, union jack, zodiac.
Artefact, counteract, inexact, interact, matter-of-fact, overact, overreact, re-enact.

1.2.71 "--apped" (as in "trapped")
[1] capped, clap, flapped, lapped, knapped, mapped, napped, rapped, sapped, scrapped, slapped, snapped, strapped, tapped, trapped, wrapped, yapped, zapped.
[2] backslapped, catnapped, entrapped, flip-flapped, giftwrapped, handclapped, ice-capped, kidnapped, kneecapped, recapped, snowcapped, uncapped, unwrapped.
[3] handicapped, overlapped, photomapped.

SURPRISING RHYMING:
[1] **App**, bap, cap, chap, clap, crap, flap, gap, knap, map, nap, pap, rap, sap, scrap, slap, snap, strap, tap, trap, wrap, yap, zap.
At, act, bat, brat, cat, chat, drat, fact, fat, flat, frat, gnat, hat, mat, matte, pact, pat, prat, rat, sat, scat, slat, spat, splat, sprat, stat, tact, tat, that, vat.
Back, black, clack, claque, crack, flak, hack, jack, knack, lack, mac, pack, plaque, quack, rack, sack, shack, slack, smack, snack, stack, tack, thwack, track, whack.
Asp, clasp, gasp, grasp, rasp.
[2] **Backslap,** bitmap, bootstrap, catnap, cold snap, deathtrap, firetrap, giftwrap, handclap, hubcap, icecap, kidnap, kneecap, madcap, mantrap, mishap, mousetrap, nightcap, recap, roadmap, snowcap, speed trap, stopgap, suntrap, unwrap, watchstrap.
Backchat, bearcat, bobcat, brickbat, chitchat, combat, doormat, fat cat, format, full-fat, hard hat, hellcat, high-hat, howzat, polecat, tomcat, top hat, whereat, wildcat, wombat.
Aback, attack, backpack, backtrack, bareback, blackjack, blowback, bootblack, bushwhack, callback, cheapjack, claw back, cognac, comeback, cutback, drawback, fallback, feedback, fightback, flapjack, flashback, greenback, hatchback, haystack, hijack, holdback, horseback, kayak, kickback, knapsack, knick-knack, mudpack, Muzak, outback, payback, pitch black, playback, Prozac, racetrack, ransack, rollback, rucksack, setback, sidetrack, skyjack, slingback, smokestack, soundtrack, splashback, switchback, tailback, tarmac, talkback, throwback, tieback, unpack, way back, wingback, wisecrack.
Abstract, attract, compact, contact, contract, detract, distract, enact, exact, extract, impact, intact, play act, ransacked, react, retract, sidetracked, subtract, unpacked.
[3] **Handicap,** overlap, photomap, thunderclap
Acrobat, aristocrat, baseball bat, bureaucrat, copycat, democrat, diplomat, habitat, laundromat, pussycat, scaredy-cat, tabby cat, technocrat, that's that, thermostat, tit-for-tat.
Almanac, anorak, bivouac, bric-a-brac, cardiac, chimney stack, cul-de-sac, lumberjack, maniac, paperback, pickaback, piggyback, quarterback, union jack, zodiac.
Artefact, counteract, inexact, interact, matter-of-fact, overact, overreact, re-enact.

1.2.72 "--apper" (as in "rapper")
[2] clapper, crapper, dapper, flapper, grappa, napper, rapper, scrapper, slapper, snapper, trapper, wrapper, yapper.
[3] backslapper, entrapper, hand-clapper, kidnapper, whippersnapper, wiretapper.

SURPRISING RHYMING:
[2] **Actor**, adaptor, captor, chapter, contractor, extractor, factor, redactor, tractor.
Batter, chatter, clatter, fatter, flatter, hatter, latter, matter, natter, patter, platter, regatta, scatter, shatter, smatter, spatter, splatter.
Capture, departure, enrapture, fracture, manufacture, pasture, rapture, recapture.

Blaster, caster, castor, faster, master, pastor, plaster, vaster.
Anchor, banker, franker, hanker, rancour/rancor (U.S.), spanker, tanker, thanker.
Blabber, drabber, grabber, jabber, stabber.
Backer, cracker, hacker, knacker, lacquer, packer, slacker, smacker, stacker, tracker.
After, dafter, drafter, grafter, hereafter, laughter, rafter, thereafter.
Bragger, carpetbagger, dagger, dragger, flagger, gagger, nagger, stagger, swagger.
Banner, fanner, manna, manner, manor, nana, planner, scanner, spanner, tanner.
Clamour/clamor (U.S.), crammer, enamour/enamor (U.S.), glamour/glamor (U.S.), grammar, hammer, jammer, mamma, programmer, rammer, slammer, sledgehammer, spammer, stammer, windjammer, yammer.
Banger, clanger, ganger, gangbanger, hanger, hangar, haranguer, rang her, twanger.
[3] **Attacker**, bushwhacker, firecracker, hijacker, lipsmacker, nutcracker, ransacker.
Back-scratcher, body-snatcher, cradle-snatcher, dispatcher, dogcatcher, flycatcher.

1.2.73 "--appy" (as in "happy")
[2] chappie, crappy, flappy, happy, nappy, pappy, sappy, scrappy, slap-happy, snappy, unhappy, yappy, zappy.

SURPRISING RHYMING:
[2] **Batty**, chatty, fatty, scatty, classy, sassy, Grammy, mammy, granny, savvy, wacky.
Abbey, blabby, cabby, crabby, flabby, scabby, shabby.
Flatly, lastly, nasty, steadfastly, vastly.
Brandy, candy, dandy, handy, jim-dandy, modus operandi, randy, sandy, shandy.
Habit, rabbit, cohabit, inhabit.
Cranky, hanky, hanky-panky, lanky, swanky, Yankee.
Classy, sassy, Grammy, mammy, savvy, wacky.
Anti, auntie, panty, scanty, shanty, vigilante.
Baddy, caddy, daddy, faddy, laddie, paddy, sugar daddy.
Baggy, braggy, craggy, naggy, raggy, saggy, scraggy, shaggy, swaggy, waggy.
Alley, dally, galley, pally, rally, reveille, tally, valley.
Carry, harry, marry, parry, tarry.
Badly, gladly, madly, sadly.
[3] **Abstractly**, compactly, exactly, matter-of-factly.

1.2.74 "--apping" (as in "clapping")
[2] capping, chapping, clapping, flapping, napping, mapping, kidnapping/kidnaping (U.S.), lapping, overlapping, rapping, scrapping, slapping, snapping, strapping, tapping, trapping, wrapping, yapping.

SURPRISING RHYMING:
[2] **Batting**, chatting, combatting, formatting, matting, patting.
Backing, cracking, hacking, lacking, packing, quacking, racking, sacking, smacking, snacking, stacking, tracking, whacking.
Catching, hatching, latching, matching, patching, scratching, snatching, thatching.
Bragging, carpetbagging, dragging, flagging, lagging, nagging, snagging, wagging.
Blabbing, dabbing, grabbing, jabbing, nabbing, stabbing.
Asking, basking, clasping, gasping, grasping, masking, rasping, tasking, unmasking.
Cramming, damning, jamming, programming, ramming, shamming, slamming, spamming, whamming.
Banking, blanking, clanking, cranking, ranking, spanking, tanking, thanking, yanking.
Chanting, granting, panting, planting, ranting, slanting.
[3] **Acting**, attacking, attracting, contacting, contracting, detracting, distracting, enacting, extracting, impacting, overacting, play acting, ransacking, reacting, redacting, retracting.
Attaching, back-scratching, detaching, dispatching, mismatching, re-matching, unlatching.

1.2.75 "--appier" (as in "happier")
[3] happier, scrappier, snappier

SURPRISING RHYMING:
[3] **Batterer**, chatterer, clatterer, flatterer, natterer, shatterer.
Barrier, carrier, farrier, harrier, marrier
Baggier, craggier, shaggier, waggier.
Classier, sassier, wackier.

1.2.76 "--appiest" (as in "happiest")
[3] happiest, scrappiest, snappiest.

SURPRISING RHYMING:
[2] **Abreast**, addressed, arrest, behest, bequest, caressed, contest, depressed, detest, digest, digressed, distressed, divest, expressed, headrest, inquest, invest, Midwest, molest, northwest, oppressed, possessed, progressed, repressed, request, southwest, suggest, suppressed, transgressed, undressed, unrest.
[3] **Chattiest**, classiest, nastiest, sassiest, scattiest, wackiest.
Crankiest, dandiest, fanciest, giddiest, handiest, lankiest, shabbiest, swankiest.
Dispossessed, effervesced, happiness, interest, manifest, readdressed, reassessed, repossessed, self-possessed.

1.2.77 "--arrow" (as in "narrow")
[2] arrow, barrow, farrow, harrow, marrow, narrow, sparrow, tarot, wheelbarrow.

SURPRISING RHYMING:
[2] **Afro,** aggro, aloe, allow, alto, callow, hallow, mallow, marshmallow, sallow, shallow.
Crossbow, follow, gallows, hallows, hobo, lasso, mallows, marshmallows, oboe, rainbow, salvo, shadow, swallow, wallow.
Bureau, chateau, escrow, hedgerow, outgrow, plateau, scarecrow, sorrow, tiptoe.
Avow, bow-wow, endow, eyebrow, highbrow, somehow.
[3] **Anyhow**, disallow, disavow.
Apollo, bungalow, diablo, dynamo, Eskimo, fiasco, foreshadow, gigolo, overflow, piano.

1.2.78 "--arrying" (as in "carrying")
[3] carrying, harrying, marrying, parrying, tarrying.

SURPRISING RHYMING:
[3] **Dallying**, dilly-dallying, rallying, shillyshallying, tallying.
Hampering, pampering, scampering, tampering.
Angering, clamouring/clamoring (U.S.), hammering, stammering.
Battering, chattering, clattering, flattering, gathering, scattering, shattering, smattering.
Anchoring, answering, bantering, blabbering, capturing, hankering, jabbering, meandering, philandering, staggering, swaggering.

1.2.79 "--ass" (as in "class")
[1] ass, bass, brass, class, crass, gas, glass, grass, lass, mass, pass, sass.
[2] alas, amass, badass, bluegrass, bypass, compass, crevasse, en masse, eyeglass, first class, fracas, harass, hourglass, impasse, jackass, kick-ass, Midas, morass, outclass, reclass, smart-ass, spyglass, stained glass, surpass, teargas, terrace, trespass, volte-face, wine glass, world class.
[3] alias, bonny lass, coup-de-grace, gravitas, looking glass, masterclass, middle-class, overpass, pancreas, underclass, underpass, upper-class, weatherglass, working class.

SURPRISING RHYMING:
[1] **Blast**, cast, caste, fast, last, mast, massed, past, passed, vast.
Asp, clasp, gasp, grasp, rasp.
Ash, bash, brash, cache, cash, clash, crash, dash, flash, gash, gnash, hash, lash, mash, rash, sash, slash, smash, splash, stash, 'tache, thrash, trash.
Ask, bask, cask, flask, mask, task, unmask.
[2] **Aghast**, at last, breakfast, broadcast, contrast, downcast, gymnast, harassed, hold fast, fly-past, miscast, outcast, outlast, outclassed, steadfast, surpassed, typecast.

Abash, backlash, earbash, eyelash, gatecrash, goulash, mishmash, moustache/mustache (U.S.), newsflash, panache, rehash, slapdash, whiplash
[3] **Flabbergast**, overcast, telecast, unsurpassed.

1.2.80 "--ash" (as in "crash")
[1] ash, bash, brash, cache, cash, clash, crash, dash, flash, gash, gnash, hash, lash, mash, rash, sash, slash, smash, splash, stash, tache, thrash, trash.
[2] abash, backlash, earbash, eyelash, gatecrash, goulash, mishmash, moustache/mustache (U.S.), newsflash, panache, rehash, slapdash, whiplash
[3] balderdash, pebbledash, thunderflash

SURPRISING RHYMING:
[1] **Bashed**, cashed, clashed, crashed, dashed, flashed, gashed, gnashed, hashed, lashed, mashed, sashed, slashed, smashed, splashed, stashed, thrashed, trashed.
Ass, brass, class, crass, gas, glass, grass, lass, mass, pass, sass.
Blast, cast, fast, last, mast, massed, past, passed, vast.
Batch, catch, hatch, latch, match, patch, scratch, snatch, thatch.
[2] **Abashed**, gatecrashed, moustached/mustached (U.S.), rehashed.
Alas, badass, bluegrass, bypass, compass, crevasse, en masse, eyeglass, first class, fracas, harass, hourglass, impasse, jackass, kick-ass, Midas, morass, outclass, smart-ass, spyglass, stained glass, surpass, teargas, trespass, volte-face, world class.
Attach, detach, dispatch, eyepatch, knee patch, mismatch, unlatch.
Aghast, at last, breakfast, broadcast, contrast, die-cast, downcast, gymnast, harassed, hold fast, fly-past, miscast, outcast, outlast, outclassed, steadfast, surpassed, typecast.
[3] **Alias**, bonny lass, coup-de-grace, gravitas, looking glass, masterclass, middle-class, overpass, pancreas, underclass, underpass, upper-class, weatherglass, working class.

1.2.81 "--ashed" (as in "smashed")
[1] bashed, cashed, clashed, crashed, dashed, flashed, gashed, gnashed, hashed, lashed, mashed, sashed, slashed, smashed, splashed, stashed, thrashed, trashed.
[2] abashed, gatecrashed, moustached/mustached (U.S.), rehashed.

SURPRISING RHYMING:
[1] **Ash**, bash, brash, cache, cash, clash, crash, dash, flash, gash, gnash, hash, lash, mash, rash, sash, slash, smash, splash, stash, 'tache, thrash, trash.
Ass, brass, class, crass, gas, glass, grass, lass, mass, pass, sass.
Blast, cast, caste, fast, last, mast, massed, past, passed, vast.
Batch, catch, hatch(ed), latch(ed), match(ed), patch(ed), scratch(ed), snatch(ed), thatch.
[2] **Backlash**, earbash, eyelash, gatecrash, mishmash, moustache/mustache (U.S.), newsflash, panache, rehash, slapdash, whiplash.
Alas, badass, bluegrass, bypass, compass, crevasse, en masse, eyeglass, first class, fracas, harass, hourglass, impasse, jackass, kick-ass, Midas, morass, outclass, smart-ass, spyglass, stained glass, surpass, teargas, trespass, volte-face, world class.
Attached, detached, dispatched.
Aghast, at last, breakfast, broadcast, contrast, downcast, gymnast, harassed, hold fast, fly-past, miscast, outcast, outlast, outclassed, steadfast, surpassed, typecast.

1.2.82 "--ask" (as in "mask")
[1] ask, bask, cask, flask, mask, task, unmask.

SURPRISING RHYMING:
[1] **Blast**, cast, caste, fast, gassed, last, mast, massed, past, passed, vast.
Ass, brass, class, crass, gas, glass, grass, lass, mass, pass, sass.
Asp, clasp, gasp, grasp, rasp.
Back, black, crack, flak, hack, jack, knack, lack, mac, pack, plaque, quack, rack, sack, shack, slack, smack, snack, stack, tack, thwack, track, whack, wrack, yak.
[2] **Aghast**, at last, breakfast, broadcast, contrast, downcast, gymnast, harassed, hold fast, fly-past, miscast, outcast, outlast, outclassed, steadfast, surpassed, typecast.
Alas, badass, bluegrass, bypass, compass, crevasse, en masse, eyeglass, first class,

fracas, harass, hourglass, impasse, jackass, kick-ass, Midas, morass, outclass, smart-ass, spyglass, stained glass, surpass, teargas, trespass, volte-face, world class.
Aback, attack, backpack, backtrack, bareback, blackjack, blowback, bootblack, bushwhack, callback, cheapjack, claw back, cognac, comeback, cutback, drawback, fallback, feedback, fightback, flapjack, flashback, greenback, hatchback, haystack, hijack, holdback, horseback, kayak, kickback, knapsack, knick-knack, mudpack, Muzak, outback, payback, pitch black, playback, Prozac, racetrack, ransack, rollback, rucksack, setback, sidetrack, skyjack, slingback, smokestack, soundtrack, splashback, switchback, tailback, tarmac, talkback, throwback, tieback, unpack, way back, wisecrack.

1.2.83 "--asp" (as in "grasp")
[1] asp, clasp, gasp, grasp, rasp.

SURPRISING RHYMING:
[1] **Blast**, cast, fast, last, mast, massed, past, passed, vast.
Ask, bask, cask, flask, mask, task, unmask.
Ass, brass, class, crass, gas, glass, grass, lass, mass, pass, sass.
App, cap, chap, clap, crap, flap, gap, knap, lap, map, nap, pap, rap, sap, scrap, slap, snap, strap, tap, trap, wrap, yap.
[2] **Aghast**, at last, breakfast, broadcast, contrast, downcast, gymnast, harassed, hold fast, fly-past, miscast, outcast, outlast, outclassed, steadfast, surpassed, typecast.
Alas, badass, bluegrass, bypass, compass, crevasse, en masse, eyeglass, first class, fracas, harass, hourglass, impasse, jackass, kick-ass, Midas, morass, outclass, smart-ass, spyglass, stained glass, surpass, teargas, trespass, volte-face, world class.
Backslap, flat-cap, icecap, kneecap, flip-flap, mishap, nightcap, redcap, recap.
Entrap, madcap, mantrap, roadmap, stopgap, uncap.

1.2.84 "--ast" (as in "fast")
[1] blast, cast, caste, fast, gassed, last, mast, massed, past, passed, vast.
[2] aghast, amassed, at last, ballast, bombast, breakfast, broadcast, contrast, die-cast, downcast, fly-past, forecast, gymnast, harassed, half-mast, hold fast, mainmast, miscast, newscast, outcast, outclassed, outlast, precast, repast, steadfast, surpassed, typecast.
[3] counterblast, flabbergast, overcast, telecast, unsurpassed.

SURPRISING RHYMING:
[1] **Ass**, brass, clasp, class, crass, gas, gasp, glass, grass, grasp, lass, mass, pass.
Ask, bask, cask, flask, mask, task, unmask.
Craft, daft, draft, draught, graft, laughed, raft, shaft, staffed, waft.
Ash, bash, brash, cache, cash, clash, crash, dash, flash, gash, gnash, hash, lash, mash, rash, sash, slash, smash, splash, stash, 'tache, thrash, trash.
Bashed, cashed, clashed, crashed, dashed, flashed, gashed, gnashed, lashed, mashed, sashed, slashed, smashed, splashed, stashed, thrashed, trashed.
Axe/ax (U.S.), backs, cracks, fax, flax, hacks, lacks, lax, max, packs, pax, racks, sacks, sax, slacks, snacks, stacks, Stax, tacks, tracks, tax, thwacks, wax, whacks.
Back, black, crack, flak, hack, knack, lack, mac, pack, plaque, quack, rack, sack, shack, slack, smack, snack, stack, tack, thwack, track, whack, wrack, yak.
[2] **Abashed**, gatecrashed, moustached/mustached (U.S.), rehashed.
Alas, badass, bluegrass, bypass, compass, crevasse, en masse, eyeglass, first class, fracas, harass, hourglass, impasse, jackass, kick-ass, Midas, morass, outclass, smart-ass, spyglass, stained glass, surpass, teargas, trespass, volte-face, world class.
Backlash, earbash, eyelash, gatecrash, mishmash, moustache/mustache (U.S.), newsflash, panache, rehash, slapdash, whiplash.
Aircraft, backdraft, life-raft, spacecraft, stagecraft, unstaffed, witchcraft, woodcraft.
Aback, attack, backpack, backtrack, bareback, blackjack, bushwhack, callback, cheapjack, claw back, cognac, comeback, cutback, drawback, fallback, feedback, fightback, flapjack, flashback, greenback, hatchback, haystack, hijack, holdback, horseback, kayak, kickback, knick-knack, mudpack, Muzak, outback, payback, pitch black, playback, Prozac, racetrack, ransack, rucksack, setback, sidetrack, skyjack, smokestack, soundtrack, tailback, tarmac, talkback, throwback, unpack, wisecrack.

Anthrax, backtracks, battleaxe/battleax (U.S.), beeswax, climax, earwax, greenbacks, haystacks, parallax, pickaxe/ pickax (U.S.), poleaxe, ransacks, relax, syntax.
Advance, balance, brilliance, distance, enhance, entrance, expanse, finance, fragrance, grievance, guidance, hindrance, instance, nuance, nuisance, penance, pittance, presence, riddance, romance, science, séance, sentence, square dance, tap-dance.
[3] Alias, bonny lass, coup-de-grace, gravitas, looking glass, masterclass, middle-class, overpass, underclass, underpass, upper-class, weatherglass, working class.
Handicraft, hovercraft, needlecraft, overdraft, overstaffed.
Anti-climax, income tax, Filofax, jumping jacks, parallax, railtracks, wisecracks.

1.2.85 "--asses" (as in "passes")
[2] asses, classes, gases, glasses, grasses, lasses, masses, passes
[3] amasses, bad-asses, eyeglasses, harasses, hourglasses, molasses, outclasses, spyglasses, sunglasses, surpasses.

SURPRISING RHYMING:
[2] **Ashes**, bashes, caches, cashes, catch us, clashes, crashes, dashes, flashes, gashes, lashes, rashes, sashes, slashes, smashes, splashes, stashes, thrashes.
Axes, axis, faxes, flaxes, relaxes, saxes, taxes, waxes.
Chances, dances, glances, lances, prances, stances, trances.
Batches, catches, hatches, matches, patches, scratches, snatches.
Chalice, malice, massive, palace, passive, impassive.
[3] Eyelashes, moustaches/mustaches (U.S.), rehashes.
Attaches, detaches, dispatches, eyepatches, mismatches, rematches, unlatches.
Advances, balances, circumstances, distances, enhances, entrances, expanses, finances, fragrances, grievances, nuisances, romances, séances.

1.2.86 "--asher" (as in "smasher")
[2] basher, brasher, casher, clasher, crasher, dasher, flasher, gatecrasher, haberdasher, lasher, masher, rasher, slasher, smasher, splasher, stasher, thrasher.

SURPRISING RHYMING:
[2] **Catcher**, matcher, scratcher, snatcher, stature, thatcher.
Answer, cancer, chancer, dancer, glancer, lancer, prancer.
Blaster, caster, faster, master, pastor, plaster, vaster.
Capture, departure, enrapture, fracture, manufacture, pasture, rapture, recapture.
Batter, chatter, clatter, fatter, flatter, latter, matter, natter, patter, platter, regatta, scatter, shatter, smatter, spatter, splatter.
After, dafter, drafter, grafter, hereafter, laughter, rafter, thereafter.
[3] Back-scratcher, dispatcher, dogcatcher, flycatcher.
Broadcaster, choirmaster, disaster, forecaster, grandmaster, headmaster, newscaster, paymaster, postmaster, quizmaster, ringmaster, schoolmaster, scoutmaster, spymaster.
Advancer, enhancer, romancer.
[4] Baby-snatcher, body-snatcher, cradle-snatcher.

1.2.87 "--ashes" (as in "crashes")
[2] ashes, bashes, caches, cashes, clashes, crashes, dashes, flashes, gashes, lashes, rashes, sashes, smashes, splashes, thrashes.
[3] abashes, backlashes, eyelashes, moustaches/mustaches (U.S.), rehashes.

SURPRISING RHYMING:
[2] **Asses**, classes, gases, glasses, grasses, lasses, masses, passes.
Batches, catches, hatches, matches, patches, scratches, snatches.
Axes, axis, climaxes, faxes, flaxes, relaxes, saxes, taxes, waxes.
Chances, dances, glances, prances, stances, trances.
Anguish, chalice, malice, massive, nourish, palace, passive, impassive.
[3] Attaches, detaches, dispatches, eyepatches, mismatches, rematches, unlatches.
Distances, enhances, finances, fragrances, grievances, nuisances, romances, séances.
Bad-asses, eyeglasses, harasses, outclasses, spyglasses, sunglasses, surpasses.

1.2.88 "--ashing" (as in "splashing")
[2] bashing, cashing, clashing, crashing, dashing, flashing, hashing, lashing, mashing, smashing, splashing, thrashing, tongue-lashing.

SURPRISING RHYMING:
[2] **Catching**, hatching, latching, matching, patching, scratching, snatching, thatching.
Ashen, fashion, compassion, imagine, passion, ration.
Action, dancing, fraction, glancing, lancing, prancing, trancing.
Blasting, casting, clasping, fasting, gasping, grasping, lasting, rasping.
Caption, contraption, expansion, mansion, sanction.
Asking, axing, basking, masking, maxing, tasking, taxing, unmasking.
Batting, chatting, combatting, formatting, matting, patting, scatting.
Clapping, flapping, kidnapping, lapping, mapping, napping, overlapping, rapping, scrapping, slapping, snapping, strapping, tapping, trapping, wrapping, yapping.
[3] **Breakfasting**, broadcasting, contrasting, everlasting, miscasting, newscasting, outlasting, passing, romancing, surpassing, typecasting.
Attaching, back-scratching, detaching, dispatching, mismatching, re-matching.
All-action, attraction, distraction, extraction, inaction, reaction, retraction, relaxing.

1.2.89 "--asket" (as in "basket")
[2] basket, breadbasket, casket, gasket.

SURPRISING RHYMING:
[2] **Acid**, blasted, fasted, fastest, lasted, placid, rancid, rapid.
Blanket, bracket, gadget, jacket, magnet, packet, racket, straitjacket.
Asking, basking, masking, tasking, unmasking.
Attic, classic, drastic, graphic, magic, plastic, static, traffic, tragic.
[3] **Drastic**, elastic, enthusiastic, fantastic, gymnastic, monastic, sarcastic, scholastic.

1.2.90 "--asted" (as in "blasted")
[2] blasted, fasted, lasted, masted.
[3] bombasted, contrasted, forecasted, outlasted.

SURPRISING RHYMING:
[2] **Basket**, breadbasket, casket, gasket.
Atlantis, lattice, practice, practise, malpractice, taxes.
Active, attractive, detractive, distractive, hyperactive, inactive, interactive, overactive, radioactive, reactive, subtractive, unattractive.
Acted, crafted, drafted, grafted, placid, rafted, rapid, shafted, wafted.
Chanted, granted, panted, planted, ranted.
Ashes, bashes, caches, clashes, crashes, dashes, flashes, gashes, lashes, sashes, smashes, splashes, stashes, thrashes.
Asses, classes, gases, glasses, grasses, lasses, masses, passes.
[3] **Drastic**, elastic, enthusiastic, fantastic, gymnastic, monastic, sarcastic, scholastic.
Attracted, contacted, distracted, impacted, protracted, reacted, redacted.

1.2.91 "--aster" (as in "faster")
[2] blaster, caster, castor, faster, master, pastor, plaster, vaster.
[3] bandmaster, broadcaster, choirmaster, disaster, forecaster, grandmaster, headmaster, newscaster, paymaster, postmaster, quizmaster, ringmaster, schoolmaster, scoutmaster, spymaster, taskmaster, telecaster.

SURPRISING RHYMING:
[2] **Catcher**, hatcher, matcher, scratcher, snatcher, stature, thatcher.
Capture, departure, enrapture, fracture, manufacture, pasture, rapture, recapture.
Basher, brasher, crasher, dasher, flasher, gatecrasher, haberdasher, masher, rasher, slasher, smasher, stasher, thrasher.
Answer, chancer, dancer, gangster, glancer, prancer.
After, dafter, drafter, grafter, hereafter, laughter, rafter, thereafter.

Actor, adaptor, captor, chapter, contractor, extractor, factor, raptor, redactor, tractor.
[3+] Back-scratcher, body-snatcher, cradle-snatcher, dispatcher, dogcatcher, flycatcher.
Advancer, enhancer, romancer.

1.2.92 "--astic" (as in "plastic")
bombastic, drastic, dynastic, elastic, enthusiastic, fantastic, gymnastic, monastic, plastic, sarcastic, scholastic.

SURPRISING RHYMING:
[2] Manic, mechanic, messianic, oceanic, organic, panic, satanic, titanic, volcanic.
Attic, classic, fabric, lovesick, magic, matchstick, slapstick, static, traffic, tragic.
Bracket, jacket, packet, racket.
Bandit, granite, habit, inhabit, planet, rabbit, transit.
Active, attractive, hyperactive, interactive, overactive, radioactive, reactive, unattractive.
Antic, Atlantic, carsick, frantic, gigantic, romantic, sycophantic, transatlantic, unromantic.
Basket, blasted, casket, fasted, gasket, lasted.
[3] Anarchic, aquatic, asthmatic, climatic, dogmatic, dramatic, ecstatic, emphatic, erratic, fanatic, Jurassic, nostalgic, pragmatic, stigmatic, traumatic.
Bombasted, contrasted, forecasted, outlasted, three-masted.
[4] Acrobatic, aerobatic, aristocratic, aromatic, automatic, bureaucratic, charismatic, cinematic, democratic, diplomatic, enigmatic, melodramatic, operatic, problematic, psychosomatic, symptomatic, systematic..
Acted, attracted, contacted, distracted, reacted, redacted, retracted, subtracted.

1.2.93 "--asting" (as in "lasting")
[2] blasting, casting, fasting, lasting.
[3] breakfasting, broadcasting, contrasting, everlasting, forecasting, outlasting.

SURPRISING RHYMING:
[2] Asking, basking, masking, tasking, unmasking.
Clasping, gasping, grasping, rasping.
Catching, hatching, latching, matching, patching, scratching, snatching, thatching.
Clashing, crashing, dashing, flashing, mashing, slashing, smashing, splashing, thrashing.
Chancing, dancing, glancing, lancing, prancing, trancing.
Clapping, flapping, kidnapping/kidnaping (U.S.), lapping, mapping, napping, overlapping, rapping, scrapping, slapping, snapping, strapping, tapping, trapping, wrapping, yapping.
Backing, blacking, cracking, hacking, lacking, packing, sacking, smacking, snacking, stacking, tracking, whacking, wracking.
Chanting, granting, panting, planting, ranting, slanting.
[3] Drastic, elastic, enthusiastic, fantastic, gymnastic, monastic, plastic, sarcastic.
Attaching, back-scratching, detaching, dispatching, mismatching, re-matching.
Earbashing, gatecrashing, mishmashing, rehashing.
Advancing, balancing, enhancing, financing, freelancing, romancing, tap-dancing.
Acting, attracting, contacting, contracting, detracting, distracting, enacting, exacting, extracting, impacting, play acting, ransacking, reacting, redacting, retracting, subtracting.
Enchanting, implanting, recanting, supplanting, transplanting.

1.2.94 "--ashional" (as in "rational")
[3] national, passional, rational.
[4] international, irrational, multinational.

SURPRISING RHYMING:
[3] Actual, animal, cannibal, capital, carnival, casual, classical, comical, cynical, digital, ethical, festival, genial, graphical, hospital, integral, interval, logical, lyrical, madrigal, magical, manual, marital, medical, menial, mineral, minimal, musical, mystical, mythical, natural, pastoral, physical, pivotal, practical, principal, punctual, radical, seasonal, serial, several, sexual, topical, tragical, tropical, typical, usual, vertical, virtual, visual.
Affable, capable, changeable, danceable, fallible, fashionable, feasible, flammable, laughable, liable, miserable, pliable, tangible, touchable, untouchable, viable, valuable.

[4] Additional, conventional, exceptional, emotional, intentional, notional, traditional, three-dimensional, two-dimensional, conditional, nutritional, promotional.
Confessional, inspirational, occasional, sensational, unconventional, unintentional.
Botanical, diagonal, fanatical, fantastical, grammatical, impractical, international, ironical, irrational, mechanical, millennial, multinational, perennial, sabbatical, satirical, tyrannical.

1.2.95 "--ath" (as in "path")
[1] bath, hath, math, path, wrath.
[2] aftermath, bird-bath, bloodbath, eye-bath, footpath, mudbath, osteopath, psychopath, sociopath, towpath, warpath.

SURPRISING RHYMING:
[1] **Caff**, chaff, daff, faff, gaff, gaffe, graph, half, laugh, naff, staff
Ash, bash, brash, cache, cash, clash, crash, dash, flash, gash, gnash, hash, lash, mash, rash, sash, slash, smash, splash, stash, 'tache, thrash, trash.
Aft, craft, daft, draft, draught, gaffed, graft, laughed, raft, shaft, staffed, waft.
Ass, brass, class, crass, gas, glass, grass, lass, mass, pass, sass.
Bashed, cashed, clashed, crashed, dashed, flashed, gashed, gnashed, hashed, lashed, mashed, sashed, slashed, smashed, splashed, stashed, thrashed, trashed.
Blast, cast, caste, fast, last, mast, massed, past, passed, vast.
Aghast, at last, breakfast, broadcast, contrast, downcast, gymnast, harassed, hold fast, fly-past, miscast, outcast, outlast, outclassed, steadfast, surpassed, typecast.
[2] **Behalf,** carafe, decaf, giraffe, horselaugh, mooncalf, riffraff.
Backlash, earbash, eyelash, gatecrash, mishmash, moustache/mustache (U.S.), newsflash, panache, rehash, slapdash, whiplash.
Aircraft, backdraft, life-raft, spacecraft, stagecraft, unstaffed, witchcraft, woodcraft.
Alas, badass, bluegrass, bypass, compass, crevasse, en masse, eyeglass, first class, fracas, harass, hourglass, impasse, jackass, kick-ass, Midas, morass, outclass, smart-ass, spyglass, stained glass, surpass, teargas, trespass, volte-face, world class.
[3] **Autograph**, belly laugh, better half, choreograph, epitaph, paragraph, phonograph, photograph, polygraph, telegraph.

1.2.96 "--atted" (as in "chatted")
[2] batted, chatted, fatted, formatted, hatted, matted, patted, platted.

SURPRISING RHYMING:
[2] **Attic**, classic, drastic, graphic, jacket, magic, plastic, racket, static, traffic, tragic.
Bandit, co-habit, granite, habit, inhabit, planet, rabbit, transit.
Banded, branded, candid, handed, landed, stranded.
Acid, added, chanted, granted, panted, planted, placid, rancid, ranted, rapid.
Crafted, drafted, grafted, rafted, shafted, wafted.
[3] **Aquatic**, asthmatic, barbaric, ceramic, dogmatic, dramatic, dynamic, ecstatic, emphatic, erratic, fanatic, metallic, pragmatic, sporadic, traumatic.
Active, attractive, hyperactive, interactive, overactive, radioactive, reactive, unattractive.
Acted, attracted, contacted, distracted, extracted, impacted, reacted, redacted, retracted.
Downhearted, good-hearted, hard-hearted, imparted, kick-started, kind-hearted, light-hearted, lion-hearted, outsmarted, push-started, uncharted, wholehearted.
Backhanded, commanded, demanded, disbanded, expanded, heavy-handed, highhanded, left-handed, light-handed, one-handed, red-handed, remanded, right-handed, shorthanded, single-handed, two-handed, unbranded, underhanded, unhanded.
[4] **Interacted**, overreacted, play-acted, re-enacted.

1.2.97 "--attic" (as in "ecstatic")
[2] attic, static.
[3] aquatic, asthmatic, chromatic, climatic, dogmatic, dramatic, ecstatic, emphatic, erratic, fanatic, phlegmatic, pragmatic, rheumatic, schematic, stigmatic, traumatic.
[4] acrobatic, aerobatic, aristocratic, aromatic, automatic, bureaucratic, charismatic, cinematic, democratic, diplomatic, enigmatic, melodramatic, operatic, problematic, psychosomatic, symptomatic, systematic, thermostatic.

SURPRISING RHYMING:
[2] **Bracket**, jacket, packet, racket.
Antic, Atlantic, frantic, gigantic, pedantic, romantic, transatlantic, unromantic.
Classic, drastic, fabric, lovesick, magic, matchstick, slapstick, plastic, traffic, tragic.
Manic, mechanic, messianic, oceanic, organic, panic, satanic, titanic, volcanic.
Bandit, granite, habit, inhabit, planet, rabbit, transit.
Acid, blasted, crafted, drafted, grafted, lasted, placid, rancid, rapid, shafted, wafted.
Chatted, formatted, hatted, matted, patted, platted.
Basket, breadbasket, casket, gasket.
[3] **Acted**, attracted, contacted, distracted, enacted, extracted, impacted, protracted, reacted, redacted, retracted, subtracted, transacted.
Drastic, elastic, enthusiastic, fantastic, gymnastic, monastic, plastic, sarcastic.
[4] **Interacted**, counteracted, overreacted, play-acted, re-enacted.

1.2.98 "--attle" (as in "rattle")
[2] battle, cattle, chattel, embattle, prattle, rattle, tattle, tittle-tattle.

SURPRISING RHYMING:
[2] **Apple**, chapel, dapple, grapple.
Cackle, crackle, hackle, jackal, shackle, tackle.
Bedraggle, draggle, gaggle, haggle, straggle, waggle.
Barrel, carol, apparel.
Babble, dabble, paddle, rabble, saddle, scrabble, skedaddle, straddle, unsaddle.
Baffle, gavel, gravel, raffle, ravel, snaffle, travel, unravel.
Bedazzle, castle, dazzle, frazzle, hassle, razzle, tassel.
Angle, bangle, dangle, jangle, mangle, spangle, strangle, tangle, wangle, wrangle.
Amble, camel, channel, gamble, mammal, mantle, ramble, scramble, unscramble.

1.2.99 "--atter" (as in "matter")
[2] batter, chatter, clatter, fatter, flatter, hatter, latter, matter, natter, patter, platter, ratter, regatta, scatter, shatter, smatter, spatter, splatter.

SURPRISING RHYMING:
[2] **Backer**, cracker, hacker, knacker, lacquer, slacker, smacker, stacker, tracker.
Clapper, dapper, flapper, napper, rapper, scrapper, slapper, snapper, trapper, wrapper.
Actor, adaptor, captor, chapter, contractor, extractor, factor, raptor, redactor, tractor.
Anchor, banker, franker, hanker, rancour/rancor (U.S.), spanker, tanker, thanker.
Bragger, carpetbagger, dagger, dragger, flagger, gagger, nagger, stagger, swagger.
Banner, manna, manner, manor, nana, planner, scanner, spanner, tanner.
Catcher, hatcher, matcher, scratcher, snatcher, stature.
Camper, damper, hamper, pamper, scamper, stamper.
Capture, departure, enrapture, fracture, manufacture, pasture, rapture, recapture.
Faster, master, pastor, plaster, vaster.
After, dafter, drafter, grafter, hereafter, laughter, rafter, thereafter.
Adder, bladder, gladder, ladder, madder, sadder, stepladder.
[3] **Backslapper**, entrapper, hand-clapper, kidnapper, whippersnapper, wiretapper.
Attacker, bushwhacker, firecracker, hijacker, lipsmacker, nutcracker.

1.2.100 "--atterer" (as in "flatterer")
[3] batterer, chatterer, clatterer, flatterer, natterer, scatterer, shatterer, splatterer.

SURPRISING RHYMING:
[3] **Gatherer**, panderer, slanderer, philanderer, manufacturer.
Barrier, carrier, classier, farrier, harrier, marrier, sassier.
Baggier, craggier, saggier, shaggier, wackier, waggier.

1.2.101 "--attering" (as in "flattering")
[3] battering, chattering, clattering, flattering, pattering, scattering, shattering, smattering, spattering.

SURPRISING RHYMING:
[3] **Angering**, clamouring/clamoring (U.S.), hammering, stammering.
Hampering, pampering, scampering, tampering.
Anchoring, answering, blabbering, capturing, gathering, hankering, jabbering, meandering, philandering, staggering, swaggering.
Carrying, harrying, marrying, parrying, tarrying.
Handling, manhandling, mishandling, pandering, slandering.
Bedazzling, baffling, dazzling, frazzling, razzling.

1.2.102 "--atch" (as in "catch")
[1] batch, catch, hatch, latch, match, patch, scratch, snatch.
[2] attach, crosshatch, detach, dispatch, eyepatch, knee patch, mismatch, outmatch, rematch, thatch, unlatch.

SURPRISING RHYMING:
[1] **Badge**, hatched, latched, matched, patched, scratched, snatched, thatched.
Ash, bash, brash, cache, cash, clash, crash, dash, flash, gash, gnash, hash, lash, mash, rash, sash, slash, smash, splash, stash, 'tache, thrash, trash.
Axe/ax (U.S.), backs, cracks, fax, flax, hacks, lacks, lax, max, packs, racks, sacks, sax, slacks, snacks, stacks, Stax, tacks, tracks, tax, thwacks, wax, whacks, yaks.
Ask, asp, bask, cask, clasp, flask, gasp, grasp, mask, rasp, task, unmask.
Blast, cast, caste, fast, last, mast, massed, past, passed, vast.
[2] **Attached**, detached, dispatched, mismatched.
Backlash, earbash, eyelash, gatecrash, mishmash, moustache/mustache (U.S.), newsflash, panache, rehash, slapdash, whiplash.
Attract, compact, contact, contract, detract, distract, enact, exact, extract, impact, intact, play act, ransacked, react, redact, retract, sidetracked, subtract, unpacked.
Anthrax, backtracks, battleaxe/battleax (U.S.), beeswax, climax, earwax, greenbacks, haystacks, parallax, pickaxe/ pickax (U.S.), poleaxe, ransacks, relax, syntax.
Aghast, at last, breakfast, broadcast, contrast, downcast, gymnast, harassed, hold fast, fly-past, miscast, outcast, outlast, outclassed, steadfast, surpassed, typecast.
[3] **Anti-climax,** income tax, Filofax, jumping jacks, railtracks, wisecracks.
Counterblast, flabbergast, overcast, telecast, unsurpassed.

1.2.103 "--atcher" (as in "catcher")
[2] catcher, hatcher, matcher, patcher, scratcher, snatcher, stature, thatcher.
[3+] back-scratcher, body-snatcher, cradle-snatcher, dispatcher, dogcatcher, flycatcher.

SURPRISING RHYMING:
[2] **Capture**, enrapture, fracture, manufacture, pasture, rapture, recapture.
Blaster, caster, faster, master, pastor, plaster, vaster.
Answer, cancer, chancer, dancer, glancer, lancer, prancer.
After, crafter, dafter, grafter, hereafter, laughter, rafter.
Actor, adaptor, captor, chapter, contractor, extractor, factor, raptor, redactor, tractor.
Brasher, clasher, crasher, dasher, flasher, gatecrasher, haberdasher, lasher, masher, rasher, slasher, smasher, stasher, thrasher.
Banter, canter, cantor, chanter, granter, planter, ranter, Santa.
Camper, damper, gambler, hamper, pamper, rambler, scamper, stamper, tamper.
[3] **Broadcaster**, choirmaster, disaster, forecaster, grandmaster, headmaster, newscaster, postmaster, quizmaster, ringmaster, schoolmaster, spymaster, taskmaster.
Advancer, enhancer, entrancer, romancer.

1.2.104 "--atches" (as in "patches")
[2] batches, catches, hatches, latches, matches, patches, scratches, snatches.
[3] attaches, detaches, dispatches, eyepatches, mismatches, rematches, unlatches.

SURPRISING RHYMING:
[2] **Axes**, axis, climaxes, faxes, relaxes, saxes, taxes, waxes.
Chances, dances, glances, prances, stances, trances.

Ashes, bashes, caches, clashes, crashes, dashes, flashes, gashes, lashes, slashes, smashes, splashes, stashes, thrashes.
Asses, classes, glasses, grasses, lasses, masses, passes.
[3] Advances, balances, distances, enhances, entrances, expanses, finances, fragrances, grievances, nuisances, romances, séances.
Backlashes, eyelashes, moustaches/mustaches (U.S.), rehashes.
Bad-asses, eyeglasses, harasses, outclasses, spyglasses, sunglasses, surpasses.

1.2.105 "--atching" (as in "scratching")
[2] catching, hatching, latching, matching, patching, scratching, snatching, thatching.
[3] attaching, back-scratching, detaching, dispatching, mismatching, re-matching.

SURPRISING RHYMING:
[2] **Clashing**, crashing, dashing, flashing, lashing, mashing, slashing, smashing, splashing, thrashing, tongue-lashing.
Badging, cadging, chancing, dancing, glancing, lancing, prancing, trancing.
Backing, cracking, hacking, lacking, packing, quacking, racking, sacking, smacking, snacking, stacking, tracking, whacking, wracking.
Asking, axing, basking, faxing, masking, maxing, tasking, taxing, unmasking.
Blasting, clasping, casting, fasting, gasping, grasping, lasting, rasping.
Clapping, flapping, kidnapping/kidnaping (U.S.), mapping, napping, overlapping, rapping, scrapping, slapping, snapping, strapping, tapping, trapping, wrapping, yapping.
[3] **Earbashing,** gatecrashing, mishmashing, rehashing.
Advancing, enhancing, financing, freelancing, romancing, sentencing, tap-dancing.
Attacking, ransacking, unpacking.
Acting, attracting, contacting, distracting, enacting, impacting, play acting, ransacking, reacting, redacting, relaxing, retracting, subtracting.
Amassing, breakfasting, broadcasting, contrasting, everlasting, forecasting, newscasting, outlasting, typecasting.
[4] **Interacting**, overacting, overreacting, re-enacting.

1.2.106 "--atched" (as in scratched")
[1] batched, hatched, latched, matched, patched, scratched, snatched, thatched.
[2] attached, detached, dispatched, mismatched, unlatched, unmatched.

SURPRISING RHYMING:
[1] **Batch**, catch, hatch, latch, match, patch, scratch, snatch.
Axed, faxed, laxed, maxed, taxed, waxed.
Clashed, crashed, dashed, flashed, gashed, gnashed, lashed, mashed, slashed, smashed, splashed, stashed, thrashed, trashed.
Asked, basked, clasped, gasped, grasped, masked, tasked, unmasked, rasped.
Blast, cast, caste, fast, last, mast, massed, past, passed, vast.
Act, fact, pact, tact, tract.
[2] **Attach**, detach, dispatch, eyepatch, knee patch, mismatch, rematch, unlatch.
Climaxed, poleaxed, relaxed.
Abashed, backlashed, gatecrashed, rehashed, whiplashed.
Abstract, attract, compact, contact, contract, detract, distract, enact, exact, extract, impact, intact, play act, ransacked, react, retract, sidetracked, subtract, unpacked.
Aghast, at last, breakfast, broadcast, contrast, downcast, gymnast, harassed, hold fast, fly-past, miscast, outcast, outlast, outclassed, steadfast, surpassed, typecast.
[3] **Artefact**, counteract, inexact, interact, matter-of-fact, overact, overreact, re-enact.
Anti-climax, income tax, Filofax, jumping jacks, parallax, railtracks, wisecracks.

1.2.107 "--atchable" (as in "catchable")
[3] catchable, hatchable, matchable, patchable, scratchable, snatchable.
[4] attachable, detachable.

SURPRISING RHYMING:
[3] **Actual**, animal, cannibal, capital, carnival, casual, classical, comical, cynical, digital,

ethical, festival, genial, graphical, hospital, integral, interval, logical, lyrical, madrigal, magical, manual, marital, medical, menial, mineral, minimal, musical, mystical, mythical, natural, pastoral, physical, pivotal, practical, principal, punctual, radical, seasonal, serial, several, sexual, topical, tragical, tropical, typical, usual, vertical, virtual, visual.
Affable, capable, danceable, fallible, fashionable, flammable, gullible, laughable, legible, liable, miserable, payable, pliable, tangible, touchable, untouchable, viable, valuable.
[4] Achievable, agreeable, amiable, amenable, available, believable, compatible, conceivable, considerable, deniable, disagreeable, dishonourable/dishonorable (U.S.), explainable, foreseeable, inaudible, inconceivable, infallible, inflatable, inflammable, incapable, incomparable, incredible, indiscernible, inedible, infallible, irretrievable, insatiable, inseparable, insufferable, intangible, intolerable, invaluable, nonreturnable, programmable, reclaimable, redeemable, reliable, retrievable, sustainable, unassailable, unattainable, unavailable, unbelievable, undeniable, unexplainable, unflappable, unfavourable/unfavorable (U.S.), unforeseeable, unspeakable, untraceable, variable.
Conventional, fanatical, fantastical, impractical, international, ironical, irrational, mechanical, millennial, multinational, octagonal, perennial, sabbatical, satirical, tyrannical.

1.2.108 "--ax" (as in "tax")
[1] axe/ax (U.S.), backs, cracks, fax, flax, hacks, jacks, lacks, lax, max, packs, pax, racks, sacks, sax, slacks, snacks, stacks, Stax, tacks, tracks, tax, wax, whacks, .
[2] anthrax, backtracks, battleaxe/battleax (U.S.), beeswax, climax, earwax, greenbacks, haystacks, parallax, pickaxe/pickax (U.S.), poleaxe, ransacks, relax, syntax.
[3] anti-climax, income tax, Filofax, jumping jacks, parallax, railtracks, wisecracks.

SURPRISING RHYMING:
[1] **Axed**, faxed, laxed, maxed, poleaxed, relaxed, taxed, waxed.
Backs, cracks, hacks, jacks, knacks, lacks, macs, packs, plaques, quacks, racks, sacks, shacks, slacks, smacks, snacks, stacks, tacks, thwacks, tracks, whacks, yaks.
Acts, facts, pacts, tracts.
Batch, catch, hatch, latch, match, patch, scratch, snatch, thatch.
Bashed, cashed, clashed, crashed, dashed, flashed, gashed, gnashed, hashed, lashed, mashed, sashed, slashed, smashed, splashed, stashed, thrashed, trashed.
Ask, bask, cask, flask, mask, task, unmask.
Blast, cast, caste, fast, last, mast, massed, past, passed, vast.
[2] **Attacks**, backpacks, backtracks, cutbacks, drawbacks, flapjacks, flashbacks, greenbacks, hardbacks, hatchbacks, haystacks, hijacks, holdbacks, hunchbacks, kayaks, kickbacks, knapsacks, knick-knacks, mudpacks, paybacks, playbacks, racetracks, ransacks, rucksacks, setbacks, sidetracks, skyjacks, slingbacks, smokestacks, softbacks, soundtracks, switchbacks, tailbacks, throwbacks, tiebacks, unpacks, wisecracks.
Attracts, contacts, contracts, detracts, distracts, extracts, impacts, reacts, redacts.
Attach, detach, dispatch, eyepatch, knee patch, mismatch, outmatch, rematch, unlatch.
Abashed, gatecrashed, moustached/mustached (U.S.), rehashed.
[3] **Almanacs**, anoraks, chimney stacks, cul-de-sacs, haversacks, lumberjacks, maniacs, paperbacks, quarterbacks, razorbacks, saddlebacks, union jacks, zodiacs.
Artefacts, cataracts, interacts, overacts, overreacts, re-enacts.

* * *

1.3 "ay"

1.3.1 "--ay" (as in "day")
[1] bay, clay, day, eh, fray, gay, gray/grey, hay, hey, lay, may, pay, play, pray, prey, ray, say, slay, sleigh, spray, stay, stray, sway, they, tray, way, weigh, yea.
[2] affray, airplay, airway, allay, archway, array, ashtray, astray, au fait, away, ballet, beret, betray, birthday, blasé, bobsleigh, bouquet, bray, byway, Broadway, buffet, cachet, café, chalet, cliché, convey, coupé, croquet, decay, deejay, delay, dismay, display, doomsday, doorway, downplay, driveway, duvet, entrée, essay, fair play, fairway, foreplay, forte, foyer, Friday, freeway, gangway, gateway, gilet, gourmet, hairspray, halfway, hallway, headway, hearsay, heyday, highway, hombre, hooray, horseplay, hurray, inlay, in-tray, latte, lamé, mainstay, mayday, melee, midday, midway,

mislay, Monday, obey, okay, olé, one day, outlay, outplay, outstay, outweigh, padre, part-way, passé, pathway, payday, portray, prepay, railway, reggae, relay, repay, replay, risqué, roadway, rosé, runway, sachet, sashay, screenplay, segue, sickbay, soirée, someday, some way, stairway, subway, sundae, Sunday, survey, Thursday, today, touché, toupée, Tuesday, two-way, waylay, weekday, wordplay, x-ray.
[3] a.k.a., A-OK, alleyway, anyway, attaché, awayday, breakaway, cabaret, café au lait, castaway, Christmas Day, cinéma-vérité, croupier, disarray, disobey, everyday, exposé, expressway, faraway, fiancé, flyaway, giveaway, getaway, hideaway, holiday, interplay, matinée, Milky Way, motorway, negligee, overlay, overplay, passageway, protégé, ricochet, résumé, runaway, Saturday, stowaway, straightaway, takeaway, tearaway, throwaway, underplay, walk away, wedding day, Wednesday, working day, yesterday.

SURPRISING RHYMING:
[1] Ate, crate, date, grate, great, hate, late.
Aid, blade, fade, glade, grade, jade, laid, made, paid, plague, played, shade, sprayed, stayed, strayed, suede, vague, wade, weighed.
Aim, blame, came, claim, fame, flame, frame, game, name, shame, tame, babe.
Bait, eight, fate, fête, freight, gate, mate, plate, rate, skate, slate, spate, state, straight, trait, wait, weight.
Brain, cane, chain, drain, feign, gain, grain, lane, main, mane, pain, pane, plain, plane, rain, reign, rein, sane, slain, sprain, stain, strain, train, twain, vain, vein, wane.
Brave, cave, chafe, safe, save, wave, waif.
Ace, daze, faze, gaze, haze, phase, place, raise.
Drape, gape, grape, scrape, shape, tape, vape.
[2] Berate, deflate, elate, escape, inflate, landscape, lightweight, locate, magnate, mutate, relate, soulmate, stagnate, stalemate, template, translate.
Abstain, again, airplane, arcane, attain, birdbrain, bloodstain, butane, campaign, champagne, chowmein, complain, constrain, contain, detain, disdain, domain, explain, humane, inane, lamebrain, maintain, methane, migraine, mundane, obtain, octane, ordain, profane, propane, refrain, remain, retain, sustain, terrain, urbane.
Acclaim, aflame, became, exclaim, inflame, nickname, proclaim.
Afraid, arcade, away, betrayed, blockade, brain fade, cascade, charade, conveyed, crusade, decayed, degrade, delayed, dismayed, evade, handmade, homemade, invade, nightshade, obeyed, parade, persuade, relayed, repaid, self-made, surveyed, today.
Await, birth rate, cheapskate, checkmate, classmate, create, debate, dictate, estate, fixate, flat-mate, frustrate, gyrate, irate, jailbait, migrate, narrate, ornate, outdate, placate, playmate, portrait, pulsate, sedate, update, vacate, vibrate.
[3] Activate, advocate, aggravate, aggregate, agitate, alienate, allocate, alternate, animate, automate, calculate, candidate, captivate, celebrate, circulate, complicate, consecrate, concentrate, confiscate, congregate, consummate, contemplate, correlate, culminate, cultivate, decorate, dedicate, delegate, demonstrate, designate, desolate, devastate, deviate, dislocate, dominate, duplicate, educate, elevate, emigrate, emulate, escalate, estimate, excavate, fabricate, fascinate, fluctuate, formulate, generate, graduate, gravitate, heavyweight, hesitate, hibernate, hyphenate, illustrate, imitate, implicate, incubate, indicate, infiltrate, innovate, instigate, insulate, integrate, interstate, intimate, intricate, inundate, irrigate, irritate, isolate, legislate, levitate, liberate, liquidate, litigate, lubricate, magistrate, meditate, moderate, motivate, navigate, operate, orchestrate, overrate, overstate, overweight, paperweight, penetrate, percolate, permeate, perpetuate, pollinate, populate, procreate, propagate, punctuate, radiate, recreate, regulate, reinstate, relegate, relocate, renovate, salivate, segregate, separate, simulate, situate, speculate, stimulate, stipulate, syndicate, syncopate, terminate, tête-à-tête, tolerate, underrate, understate, underweight, validate, ventilate, vindicate, violate.
Entertain, inhumane, overcame, scatterbrain, sugar cane, windowpane, weathervane.
Barricade, cavalcade, centigrade, disarray(ed), escapade, lemonade, masquerade, overpaid, readymade, renegade, ricochet(ed), serenade, unafraid.
[4] Accelerate, accommodate, alienate, alleviate, anticipate, authenticate, collaborate, communicate, concentrate, congratulate, contaminate, cooperate, corroborate, deteriorate, elaborate, eradicate, evaporate, exaggerate, exonerate, hallucinate, impersonate, infuriate, initiate, humiliate, intimidate, investigate, invigorate, necessitate, negotiate, orientate, participate, recuperate, refrigerate, remunerate, reverberate.

1.3.2 "--aby" (as in "baby")
[2] baby, crybaby, maybe.

SURPRISING RHYMING:
[2] **Amaze me**, crazy, daily, daisy, eighty, faded, gaily, Haiti, hazy, lady, lazy, matey, safety, shady, weighty.
Achy, flaky, quaky, shaky.
[3] **Humanely**, insanely, landlady, milady, mundanely, ungainly, urbanely.

1.3.3 "--able" (as in "table")
[2] able, cable, fable, gable, label, sable, stable, table.
[3] disable, enable, payable, timetable, turntable, unable, unstable.
[4] available, unavailable.

SURPRISING RHYMING:
[2] **Cabled**, fabled, gabled, labeled, stabled, stapled, tabled.
Blameful, careful, changeful, disdainful, disgraceful, distasteful, fatal, fateful, faithful, graceful, grateful, hateful, playful, shameful, unfaithful, ungrateful, wakeful.
Angel, baneful, gainful, naval, navel, painful.
Maple, papal, PayPal, staple.
Facial, glacial, hazel, nasal, naval, navel, palatial, racial, reappraisal, special, spatial.
Bagel, cradle, ladle.
Craven, graven, haven, raven, shaven.
[3] **Enabled**, disabled, mislabeled, unlabeled.
Betrayal, portrayal.
Blamable, breakable, claimable, drainable, fakeable, makeable, shakable.
[4] **Mistakable**, unbreakable, unshakeable, unmistakable.
Insatiable, payable, playable, swayable, unsayable.
Appraisal, interracial, multiracial, reappraisal, witch hazel.

1.3.4 "--abled" (as in "cabled")
[2] cabled, fabled, gabled, labeled, stabled, tabled.
[3] disabled, enabled, mislabeled, unlabeled.

SURPRISING RHYMING:
[2] **Able,** cable, fable, gable, label, sable, stable, stapled, table.
Blameful, disgraceful, distasteful, fatal, fateful, faithful, graceful, grateful, hateful, playful, shameful, unfaithful, ungrateful, wakeful.
Angel, baneful, gainful, naval, navel, painful.
Cradled, ladled, laid-up, made up, paid up.
[3] **Betrayal**, disable, enable, payable, portrayal, timetable, turntable, unable, unstable.

1.3.5 "--abling" (as in "enabling")
[2] cabling, stabling, tabling.
[3] disabling, enabling, labeling.

SURPRISING RHYMING:
[2] **Aiding**, cradling, fading, grading, ladling, raiding, trading, shading, wading.
Bracing, casing, chasing, facing, lacing, pacing, placing, racing, spacing, tracing.
Ageing, caging, gauging, paging, raging, staging, waging.
Aiming, blaming, claiming, flaming, framing, gaming, naming, shaming, taming.
Aping, draping, gaping, scraping, shaping, taping.
[3] **Debasing**, defacing, embracing, erasing, escaping, horseracing, interfacing, landscaping, misplacing, replacing, reshaping, self-effacing, unlacing.
Degrading, invading, parading, crusading, persuading, cascading, evading, dissuading.
Engaging, enraging, outraging, rampaging, upstaging.
Acclaiming, defaming, disclaiming, explaining, exclaiming, inflaming, nicknaming, proclaiming, reclaiming, remaining, renaming.

*

1.3.6 "--ace" (as in "place")
[1] ace, base, bass, brace, case, chase, face, grace, lace, mace, pace, place, plaice, race, space, trace, vase, ways.
[2] apace, backspace, birthplace, bookcase, bootlace, briefcase, coalface, debase, deface, disgrace, displace, efface, embrace, encase, erase, fireplace, first place, grimace, misplace, nutcase, outpace, paleface, rat-race, replace, retrace, shoelace, showcase, someplace, staircase, suitcase, typeface, unlace, workplace, workspace.
[3] angel face, anyplace, baby face, commonplace, database, everyplace, headcase, hiding place, interface, interlace, in-your-face, marketplace, meeting place, nutcase, packing case, paperchase, pillowcase, resting place, steeplechase.

SURPRISING RHYMING:
[1] **Based**, braced, cased, chased, chaste, faced, haste, laced, paced, paste, placed, raced, spaced, taste, traced, waist, waste.
Blaze, craze, days, daze, faze, gaze, glaze, graze, haze, laze, maze, pays, phase, phrase, praise, raise, stays, ways.
Blazed, crazed, dazed, fazed, gazed, glazed, grazed, lazed, phased, praised, raised.
Date, fate, gate, great, hate, late, plate, shape, skate, straight, wait, wake, wakes.
[2] **Ablaze**, always, amaze, anyways, appraise, cafés, catchphrase, edgeways, erase, Fridays, leastways, liaise, malaise, Mondays, sideways, stargaze, Sundays, Tuesdays, Thursdays, Wednesdays, Saturdays, nowadays.
Aftertaste, angel-faced, baby-faced, barefaced, embraced, encased, erased, fast-paced, red-faced, replaced, shamefaced, strait-laced, toothpaste, two-faced, untraced.
[3] **Celebrate**, dominate, evaluate, hesitate, negotiate, tolerate.

1.3.7 "--aced" (as in "taste")
[1] based, braced, cased, chaste, chased, faced, graced, haste, laced, paste, paced, placed, raced, spaced, taste, traced, waste, waist.
[2] barefaced, debased, encased, embraced, erased, fast-paced, red-faced, replaced, shamefaced, strait-laced, toothpaste, two-faced, unplaced, untraced.
[3] aftertaste, angel-faced, baby-faced, dirty-faced, freckle-faced, interlaced.

SURPRISING RHYMING:
[1] **Ace**, base, bass, brace, case, chase, face, grace, lace, mace, pace, place, plaice, race, space, trace, vase.
Crazed, days, daze, gaze, glaze, graze, haze, laze, maze, pays, phase, phrase, praise, raise, stays, ways.
Date, fate, gate, great, hate, late, plate, straight, wait, wakes.
[2] **Ablaze**, always, amaze, anyways, appraise, cafés, catchphrase, dazed, edgeways, erase, leastways, liaise, longways, Mondays, places, sideways, stargaze, Sundays.
Await, celebrate, dominate, evaluate, hesitate, mistake, negotiate.
Backspace, birthplace, bookcase, briefcase, coalface, debase, deface, disgrace, embrace, erase, fireplace, grimace, headcase, misplace, nutcase, outpace, paleface, rat-race, replace, retrace, showcase, someplace, staircase, suitcase, unlace, workplace.
[3] **Angel face**, anyplace, baby face, commonplace, database, everyplace, headcase, hiding place, interface, interlace, interspace, in-your-face, marketplace, meeting place, nowadays, nutcase, packing case, paperchase, pillowcase, resting place, steeplechase.

1.3.8 "--acer" (as in "racer")
[2] acer, bracer, chaser, facer, lacer, mesa, pacer, placer, racer, spacer, tracer.
[3] defacer, disgracer, embracer, encase, eraser, horse-racer, replacer, steeplechaser.

SURPRISING RHYMING:
[2] **Blazer**, gazer, glazer, grazer, laser, razor.
Caper, paper, scraper, shaper, vapour/vapor (U.S.).
Cater, crater, data, freighter, greater, hater, later, skater, straighter, traitor, waiter.
Fader, grader, raider, trader, wader.
[3] **Appraiser**, crazier, hellraiser, lazier, stargazer, trailblazer.
Creator, curator, equator, narrator, spectator, translator.

Crusader, dissuader, evader, invader, persuader, upgrader.
Escaper, notepaper, newspaper, sandpaper, skyscraper, wallpaper.
[4+] Commentator, figure-skater, masquerader, percolator, serenader, undertaker.

1.3.9 "--acing" (as in "facing")
{2} bracing, casing, chasing, facing, lacing, pacing, placing, racing, spacing, tracing.
[3] debasing, defacing, displacing, effacing, embracing, encasing, erasing, horseracing, interfacing, misplacing, replacing, self-effacing, unlacing.

SURPRISING RHYMING:
[2] **Baiting**, dating, grating, hating, mating, rating, skating, slating, stating, waiting.
Aching, baking, braking, breaking, faking, making, quaking, shaking, taking, waking.
Aiding, braiding, fading, grading, raiding, shading, trading, wading.
Blazing, erasing, fazing, gazing, glazing, grazing, hazing, lazing, phasing, phrasing, praising, raising.
Aping, draping, gaping, scraping, shaping, taping.
Braving, craving, paving, raving, shaving, saving, slaving, waiving, waving.
[3] **Abating**, awaiting, backdating, berating, creating, debating, deflating, dictating, frustrating, gyrating, hydrating, inflating, locating, migrating, narrating, placating, pulsating, relating, rotating, stagnating, translating, updating, vacating, vibrating.
Amazing, appraising, double-glazing, fundraising, hellraising, stargazing, trailblazing.
Awaking, backbreaking, bookmaking, breathtaking, dressmaking, earthshaking, forsaking, heartbreaking, lovemaking, matchmaking, mistaking, partaking, painstaking, peacemaking, troublemaking, undertaking, unmaking, watchmaking.
Behaving, depraving, engraving, enslaving, lifesaving, time-saving.
Cascading, crusading, degrading, dissuading, evading, invading, parading, persuading.
Escaping, landscaping, reshaping, skyscraping.
[4] **Calculating**, deviating, fascinating, fluctuating, graduating, humiliating, infiltrating, infuriating, initiating, insinuating, mediating, misbehaving, nauseating, navigating, penetrating, punctuating, radiating, recreating, unabating, underrating, understating.
[5] **Abbreviating**, alleviating, appreciating, associating, differentiating, discriminating, evacuating, negotiating, retaliating, substantiating.

1.3.10 "--aceless" (as in "faceless")
[2] baseless, faceless, graceless, placeless, traceless

SURPRISING RHYMING:
[2] **Address**, breathless, caress, confess, de-stress, distress, express, finesse, I guess, impress, obsess, oppress, princess, reckless, restless, sweetness, undress, weakness.
Aimless, brainless, famous, frailest, nameless, painless, palest, stalest, stainless.
[3] **Baroness**, convalesce, dispossess, effervesce, forgiveness, loneliness, nonetheless, reassess, repossess, promises, shepherdess, SOS, stewardess, thoughtfulness.

1.3.11 "--asted" (as in "tasted")
[2] basted, pasted, tasted, waisted, wasted

SURPRISING RHYMING:
[2] **Aided**, bladed, braided, faded, graded, jaded, raided, shaded, traded, waded.
Bacon, shaken, taken, waken.
Dated, fated, hated, mated, rated, stated, waited.
[3] **Abated**, awaited, belated, berated, checkmated, created, debated, deflated, elated, frustrated, ill-fated, inflated, instated, outdated, postdated, predated, related, x-rated.
Blockaded, cascaded, crusaded, degraded, dissuaded, downgraded, evaded, invaded, paraded, persuaded, unaided.
Forsaken, mistaken.
[4] **Elevated**, evaluated, fascinated, gravitated, insinuated, reinstated, saturated, underrated, understated, unrelated.
Barricaded, masqueraded, serenaded.

*

1.3.12 "--ade" (as in "aid")

[1] aid, blade, fade, glade, grade, jade, laid, made, maid, paid, played, prayed, raid, shade, spade, sprayed, stayed, strayed, suede, they'd, wade, weighed.

[2] afraid, arcade, away, barmaid, betrayed, blockade, brain fade, bridesmaid, cascade, charade, conveyed, crusade, decayed, degrade, delayed, dismayed, downgrade, evade, grenade, handmade, homemade, invade, lampshade, man-made, mermaid, nightshade, nursemaid, obeyed, parade, persuade, prepaid, ram raid, relayed, repaid, self-made, surveyed, today, unmade, unpaid.

[3] barricade, cavalcade, centigrade, colonnade, disarray, disarrayed, escapade, lemonade, marmalade, masquerade, not afraid, overpaid, razor blade, readymade, renegade, ricocheted, serenade, tailor-made, unafraid, underpaid.

SURPRISING RHYMING:

[1] Ape, cape, crepe, drape, gape, grape, scrape, shape, tape, vape.
Ate, bait, crate, date, eight, fate, fête, freight, gate, gait, great, grate, hate, late, mate, plate, rate, skate, slate, spate, state, strait, straight, trait, weight, wait.
Aim(ed), blame(d), came, claim(ed), fame(d), flame(d), frame(d), game, lame, name(d), same, shame(d), tame(d), vain, vein.
Bay, clay, day, eh, fray, gay, gray/grey, hay, hey, lay, may, pay, play, pray, prey, ray, say, slay, sleigh, spray, stay, stray, sway, they, tray, way, weigh, yea.
Brain, cane, chain, crane, drain, feign, gain, lain, lane, main, mane, pain, pane, plain, plane, rain, reign, rein, sane, slain, sprain, stain, strain, train, twain, vain, vein, wane.
Brave, cave, crave, fave, gave, grave, pave, rave, save, shave, slave, they've, wave.
Blaze, craze, days, daze, faze, gaze, glaze, graze, haze, laze, maze, maize, phase, phrase, praise, raise, stays, vase, ways.

[2] Abate, await, berate, birth rate, cheapskate, checkmate, classmate, create, debate, deflate, dictate, estate, fixate, flat-mate, frustrate, helpmate, inflate, irate, jailbait, lightweight, locate, migrate, narrate, ornate, outdate, placate, playmate, portrait, pulsate, relate, rotate, sedate, soulmate, stagnate, stalemate, translate, update, vacate, vibrate.
Abstain, again, airplane, arcane, attain, birdbrain, bloodstain, campaign, champagne, complain, constrain, contain, detain, domain, explain, humane, lamebrain, maintain, migraine, mundane, obtain, profane, refrain, remain(s), retain, sustain, terrain, urbane..
Acclaim, aflame, became, defame, disclaim, disdain, endgame, exclaim, inflame, nickname, proclaim, reclaim, rename, surname, unnamed.
Airplay, array, ashtray, astray, au fait, away, ballet, beret, betray, birthday, blasé, bouquet, byway, Broadway, buffet, cachet, café, chalet, cliché, convey, coupé, croquet, decay, deejay, delay, dismay, display, doomsday, doorway, downplay, driveway, duvet, entrée, essay, fair play, foreplay, forte, foyer, Friday, freeway, gangway, gateway, gourmet, hairspray, halfway, hallway, headway, hearsay, heyday, highway, hombre, hooray, horseplay, hurray, inlay, latte, lamé, mayday, melee, midday, midway, mislay, Monday, obey, okay, olé, outlay, outstay, outweigh, padre, part-way, passé, payday, portray, railway, reggae, repay, replay, risqué, roadway, rosé, runway, sachet, sashay, screenplay, segue, soirée, someday, stairway, straightaway, subway, Sunday, survey, Thursday, today, touché, toupée, Tuesday, two-way, weekday, wordplay, x-ray.
Escape, landscape, red tape, reshape, shipshape.
Behave, brainwave, deprave, engrave, enslave, forgave, heatwave.
Ablaze, always, amaze, catchphrase, erase, liaise, malaise, sideways, stargaze.

[3] Activate, aggravate, alienate, allocate, animate, automate, captivate, celebrate, circulate, complicate, consecrate, concentrate, confiscate, congregate, consummate, contemplate, cultivate, decorate, dedicate, demonstrate, desolate, devastate, deviate, discriminate, dominate, duplicate, educate, elevate, eliminate, emigrate, emulate, escalate, estimate, exterminate, fascinate, fluctuate, generate, graduate, gravitate, heavyweight, hesitate, hibernate, illuminate, illustrate, imitate, implicate, infiltrate, innovate, instigate, interstate, intimate, intricate, inundate, irritate, isolate, liberate, magistrate, mediate, meditate, moderate, motivate, navigate, operate, orchestrate, overstate, overweight, paperweight, penetrate, percolate, procreate, radiate, regulate, relocate, renovate, segregate, separate, simulate, situate, speculate, stimulate, stipulate, suffocate, syncopate, terminate, tête-à-tête, tolerate, underrate, violate.
Aftershave, microwave, misbehave.

A.k.a., A-OK, alleyway, anyway, anyway, attaché, awayday, breakaway, cabaret, café au lait, castaway, Christmas Day, croupier, disarray, disobey, everyday, exposé, expressway, faraway, fiancé, flyaway, giveaway, getaway, hideaway, holiday, interplay, matinée, Milky Way, motorway, negligee, overlay, overplay, passageway, protégé, ricochet, résumé, runaway, Saturday, stowaway, straightaway, takeaway, tearaway, throwaway, underplay, walk away, wedding day, Wednesday, working day, yesterday.
Cityscape, sellotape, ticker tape.
Aeroplane, ascertain, counterclaim, entertain, hurricane, inhumane, overcame, preordain, scatterbrain, windowpane, weathervane.
[4] Accelerate, accommodate, alienate, alleviate, anticipate, associate, authenticate, certificate, collaborate, communicate, concentrate, congratulate, contaminate, cooperate, corroborate, deteriorate, elaborate, eradicate, evaporate, exaggerate, exasperate, exonerate, hallucinate, humiliate, impersonate, infuriate, intimidate, invigorate, investigate, negotiate, participate, recuperate, refrigerate, reverberate.

1.3.13 "--aded" (as in "faded")
[2] aided, bladed, braided, faded, graded, jaded, raided, shaded, traded, waded.
[3] blockaded, cascaded, crusaded, degraded, dissuaded, downgraded, evaded, invaded, paraded, persuaded, unaided, unbraided.
[4] barricaded, masqueraded, serenaded.

SURPRISING RHYMING:
[2] **Aching**, baking, braking, breaking, faking, making, quaking, shaking, snaking, taken, taking, waking.
Baby, lady, maybe, shady.
Fainted, painted, sainted, tainted.
Dated, fated, gated, grated, hated, mated, rated, sated, stated, waited, weighted.
Birthday, deejay, doomsday, Friday, heyday, mayday, midday, Monday, one day, padre, payday, someday, sundae, Sunday, Thursday, today, Tuesday, weekday.
Braving, craving, paving, raving, saving, shaving, slaving, waiving, waving.
Craven, graven, haven, raven, shaven.
Crazy, daily, daisy, gaily, glazy, hazy, lazy, mazy, ukulele.
[3] **Abated**, awaited, belated, berated, created, debated, deflated, elated, fixated, frustrated, gyrated, hydrated, ill-fated, inflated, outdated, postdated, related, x-rated.
Acquainted, awaken, forsaken, mistaken, safe-haven, unshaven
Crybaby, landlady, milady, stir-crazy.
Bookcases, embraces, erases, headcases, nutcases, replaces, showcases, suitcases..
Behaving, clean-shaven, depraving, engraving, lifesaving, time-saving, unshaven.
[4] **Antiquated**, calculated, celebrated, complicated, cultivated, dedicated, dehydrated, educated, elevated, elongated, fascinated, hyphenated, medicated, perforated, reinstated, saturated, simulated, underrated, understated.
[5] **Dilapidated**, evaluated, exaggerated, infatuated, opinionated, sophisticated.

1.3.14 "--aider" (as in "raider")
[2] fader, raider, trader, wader.
[3] blockader, crusader, degrader, dissuader, evader, first-aider, invader, persuader.
[4] masquerader, rollerblader, serenader.

SURPRISING RHYMING:
[2] **Acre**, baker, breaker, faker, maker, nature, shaker, taker, waker.
Blazer, chaser, eraser, gazer, grazer, laser, nature, racer, raiser, razor, Taser, tracer.
Braver, favour/favor (U.S.), flavour/flavor (U.S.), raver, saver, savour/savor (U.S.), shaver.
Cater, crater, data, dater, greater, hater, later, skater, slater, traitor, waiter.
Changer, danger, manger, ranger, stranger.
Frailer, jailer, paler, sailor, staler, trailer, tailor, wailer, whaler.
Greyer/grayer (U.S.), layer, mayor, payer, player, prayer, slayer, stayer, strayer.
[3] **Abseiler**, blackmailer, exhaler, inhaler, loudhailer, regaler, retailer, wholesaler.
Arranger, endanger, exchanger, shortchanger.
Bookmaker, caretaker, dressmaker, heartbreaker, icebreaker, lawbreaker, matchmaker, mischief-maker, muckraker, peacemaker, shoemaker, troublemaker, undertaker..

Creator, curator, dictator, equator, freighter, narrator, rotator, spectator, translator.
Defacer, embracer, eraser, fundraiser, hellraiser, horse-racer, stargazer, trailblazer.
Depraver, disfavour/disfavor (U.S.), engraver, lifesaver, timesaver.
Remainder, remainer, retainer.
[4+] Accelerator, agitator, alligator, animator, aviator, calculator, collaborator, commentator, decorator, educator, elevator, escalator, generator, gladiator, illustrator, imitator, impersonator, indicator, instigator, interrogator, investigator, liberator, mediator, negotiator, operator, percolator, perpetrator, refrigerator, speculator, terminator, ventilator.

1.3.15 "--ading" (as in "fading")
[2] aiding, grading, fading, raiding, trading, braiding, shading, wading.
[3] degrading, invading, blockading, parading, crusading, pervading, persuading, cascading, evading, dissuading, unfading.

SURPRISING RHYMING:
[2] **Aching**, baking, braking, breaking, faking, shaking, snaking, taking, waking.
Ailing, failing, hailing, jailing, mailing, nailing, railing, sailing, tailing, trailing, wailing.
Aiming, blaming, claiming, flaming, framing, gaming, naming, shaming, taming.
Aping, baiting, draping, gaping, grating, making, quaking, scraping, shaping, taping.
Blazing, erasing, fazing, gazing, grazing, hazing, lazing, liaising, praising, raising.
Braving, craving, paving, raving, saving, shaving, waiving, waving.
Caring, daring, faring, flaring, glaring, scaring, staring, swearing.
Changing, dating, hating, ranging, skating, slating, stating, waiting.
[3] **Abating**, backdating, berating, dictating, frustrating, locating, migrating, narrating, placating, postdating, updating.
Exclaiming, inflaming, nicknaming, proclaiming, reclaiming, renaming.
Amazing, appraising, fundraising, hellraising, stargazing, trailblazing.
Availing, entailing, exhaling, impaling, inhaling, prevailing, regaling, retailing, unveiling.
Awaiting, creating, debating, deflating, gyrating, inflating, pulsating, relating, rotating, stagnating, translating, vacating, vibrating.
Awaking, backbreaking, breathtaking, earthshaking, forsaking, heartbreaking, lovemaking, matchmaking, mistaking, partaking, painstaking, peacemaking, troublemaking.
Behaving, depraving, engraving, enslaving, lifesaving, time-saving.
Blackmailing, curtailing, detailing, unfailing.
Declaring, despairing, hardwearing, impairing, repairing, seafaring, uncaring, wayfaring.
Exchanging, shortchanging, unchanging.
Escaping, landscaping, reshaping, skyscraping.
[4] **Calculating**, deviating, fascinating, graduating, humiliating, infuriating, insinuating, mediating, nauseating, penetrating, radiating, recreating, understating, undertaking.
[5] **Abbreviating**, alleviating, appreciating, associating, depreciating, discriminating, evacuating, negotiating, perpetuating, retaliating, substantiating.

1.3.16 "--ady" (as in "lady")
[2] lady, shady.
[3] landlady, milady.

SURPRISING RHYMING:
[2] **Baby**, crybaby, daily, gaily, maybe, ukulele.
Aided, faded, graded, jaded, raided, shaded, traded, waded.
Bacon, shaken, taken, waken.
Ailing, failing, hailing, jailing, mailing, nailing, sailing, tailing, trailing.
Mainly, plainly, sanely, vainly.
Brainy, grainy, miscellany, rainy, zany.
Barely, dairy, fairy, fairly, hairy, prairie, rarely, scary, squarely, unfairly, vary, wary.
Dated, fated, gated, grated, hated, mated, plated, rated, sated, stated, waited.
Baiting, dating, grating, hating, mating, rating, skating, slating, stating, waiting.
Gravy, hazy, lazy, mazy, navy, stir-crazy, oops-a-daisy, upsy-daisy, wavy.
Blazing, erasing, fazing, gazing, lazing, liaising, phasing, phrasing, praising, raising.
Eighty, Haiti, hate me, matey, safety, weighty.
Greatly, innately, irately, lately, ornately, sedately, stately, straightly.

[3] Cascaded, degraded, dissuaded, evaded, invaded, paraded, persuaded, unaided.
Availing, blackmailing, curtailing, detailing, entailing, exhaling, inhaling, prevailing, regaling, retailing, unfailing, unveiling.
Humanely, insanely, mundanely, ungainly, urbanely.
Canary, contrary, rosemary, unwary.
Abated, awaited, belated, berated, created, debated, deflated, elated, frustrated, ill-fated, inflated, instated, outdated, postdated, predated, related, x-rated.
Awaiting, berating, creating, debating, dictating, frustrating, locating, migrating, narrating, placating, pulsating, relating, stagnating, translating, updating, vacating.
Amazing, appraising, fundraising, hellraising, self-raising, stargazing, trailblazing.
[4] Barricaded, Godforsaken, masqueraded, serenaded.
Antiquated, calculated, celebrated, complicated, cultivated, dedicated, dehydrated, educated, elevated, elongated, fascinated, hyphenated, medicated, reinstated, saturated, simulated, underrated, understated, unrelated.
Fascinating, graduating, humiliating, infuriating, initiating, insinuating, mediating, nauseating, penetrating, radiating, recreating, underrating, understating.
[5] Dilapidated, evaluated, exaggerated, infatuated, insinuated, opinionated, sophisticated.
Abbreviating, alleviating, appreciating, associating, depreciating, differentiating, discriminating, evacuating, negotiating, perpetuating, retaliating, substantiating.

1.3.17 "--afe" (as in "safe")
chafe, safe, strafe, unsafe, waif.

SURPRISING RHYMING:
[1] Ape, cape, drape, gape, grape, scrape, shape, tape, vape.
Ate, bait, crate, date, eight, fate, fête, freight, gate, great, grate, hate, late, mate, plate, rate, skate, slate, spate, state, straight, trait, weight, wait.
Aid, blade, fade, glade, grade, jade, laid, made, maid, paid, played, prayed, raid, shade, spade, sprayed, stayed, strayed, suede, they'd, vague, wade, weighed.
Ace, base, bass, brace, case, chase, face, grace, lace, mace, pace, place, race, space, trace, vase, way.
Ache, bake, brake, break, cake, fake, flake, lake, make, quake, sake, shake, sheik, snake, stake, steak, take, wake.
Ain't, faint, paint, quaint, saint.
Bay, clay, day, gay, gray/grey, hay, hey, lay, may, pay, play, pray, prey, ray, say, slay, sleigh, spray, stay, stray, sway, they, tray, way, weigh, yea.
Brave, cave, crave, fave, gave, grave, pave, rave, save, shave, slave, they've, wave.
Braved, caved, craved, paved, raved, saved, shaved, slaved, waved.
Based, braced, cased, chaste, chased, faced, graced, haste, laced, paste, paced, placed, raced, spaced, taste, traced, waste, waist.
[2] Behave, brainwave, deprave, engrave, enslave, forgave, heatwave.
Airplay, array, astray, away, ballet, beret, betray, birthday, blasé, bouquet, roadway, buffet, café, chalet, cliché, convey, coupé, decay, deejay, delay, dismay, display, doomsday, doorway, downplay, driveway, duvet, fair play, foreplay, forte, foyer, Friday, freeway, gangway, gateway, gourmet, hairspray, halfway, hallway, headway, hearsay, heyday, highway, hombre, hooray, horseplay, hurray, inlay, latté, lamé, mainstay, mayday, melee, midday, midway, mislay, Monday, obey, okay, olé, one day, outlay, outplay, outstay, outweigh, padre, part-way, passé, pathway, payday, portray, railway, reggae, relay, repay, replay, ricochet, risqué, roadway, rosé, runway, sachet, sashay, screenplay, segue, soirée, someday, some way, stairway, subway, Sunday, sunray, survey, Thursday, today, touché, toupée, Tuesday, two-way, waylay, weekday, x-ray.
Birthplace, bookcase, deface, disgrace, displace, embrace, erase, fireplace, first place, misplace, nutcase, outpace, paleface, rat-race, replace, retrace, shoelace, showcase, someplace, staircase, suitcase, typeface, unlace, wheelbase, workplace, workspace.
Barefaced, embraced, erased, fast-paced, replaced, red-faced, shamefaced, strait-laced, toothpaste, two-faced.
Awake, backache, beefcake, beefsteak, cheesecake, cornflake, cupcake, daybreak, earache, earthquake, firebreak, footbrake, forsake, fruitcake, handshake, headache, heartache, heartbreak, jailbreak, keepsake, milkshake, mistake, moonquake, namesake, opaque, outbreak, outtake, pancake, snowflake, toothache, windbreak.

Acquaint, complaint, constraint, greasepaint, restraint, war-paint.
Amazed, behaved, depraved, engraved, enslaved, erased, rephrased, stargazed.

1.3.18 "--aig" (as in "vague")
plague, vague.

SURPRISING RHYMING:
[1] **Bay**, clay, day, eh, fray, gay, gray/grey, hay, hey, lay, may, pay, play, pray, prey, ray, say, slay, sleigh, spray, stay, stray, sway, they, tray, way, weigh, yea.
Aid, blade, fade, glade, grade, jade, laid, made, maid, paid, played, prayed, raid, shade, spade, sprayed, stayed, strayed, suede, they'd, wade, weighed.
Ache, bake, brake, break, cake, fake, lake, make, quake, sake, shake, sheik, snake, stake, steak, take, wake.
Ale, bale, bail, fail, frail, gale, grail, hail, jail, male, mail, nail, pale, rail, sale, sail, scale, snail, stale, tale, tail, they'll, trail, vale, veil, whale, wail.
Brain, cane, chain, drain, feign, gain, grain, lain, lane, main, pain, plain, plane, rain, reign, rein, sane, slain, sprain, stain, strain, train, vain, vein, wane.
Ain't, faint, paint, quaint, saint, taint.
Ate, bait, crate, date, eight, fate, fête, freight, gate, great, hate, late, mate, plate, rate, skate, slate, spate, state, straight, trait, weight, wait.
Brave, cave, crave, fave, gave, grave, pave, rave, save, shave, slave, they've, wave.
Blazed, crazed, dazed, fazed, gazed, glazed, lazed, phased, phrased, praised, raised.
[2] **Afraid**, arcade, barmaid, betrayed, brain fade, bridesmaid, cascade, charade, crusade, decayed, degrade, delayed, dismayed, evade, grenade, handmade, homemade, invade, man-made, mermaid, nightshade, nursemaid, obeyed, parade, persuade, ram raid, repaid, self-made, surveyed, today, unpaid.
Behave, brainwave, deprave, engrave, enslave, forgave, heatwave.
Airplay, array, astray, away, ballet, beret, betray, birthday, blasé, bouquet, roadway, buffet, café, chalet, cliché, convey, coupé, decay, deejay, delay, dismay, display, doomsday, doorway, downplay, driveway, duvet, fair play, foreplay, forte, foyer, Friday, freeway, gangway, gateway, gourmet, hairspray, halfway, hallway, headway, hearsay, heyday, highway, hombre, hooray, horseplay, hurray, inlay, latté, lamé, mainstay, mayday, melee, midday, midway, mislay, Monday, obey, okay, olé, one day, outlay, outplay, outstay, outweigh, padre, part-way, passé, pathway, payday, portray, railway, reggae, relay, repay, replay, ricochet, risqué, roadway, rosé, runway, sachet, sashay, screenplay, segue, soirée, someday, some way, stairway, subway, Sunday, sunray, survey, Thursday, today, touché, toupée, Tuesday, two-way, waylay, weekday, x-ray.
Abstain, again, airplane, arcane, attain, birdbrain, bloodstain, campaign, champagne, complain, constrain, contain, detain, domain, explain, humane, lamebrain, maintain, migraine, mundane, obtain, profane, refrain, remain(s), retain, sustain, terrain, urbane.

1.3.19 "--age" (as in "page")
[1] age, cage, gage, gauge, page, rage, sage, stage, wage.
[2] assuage, backstage, birdcage, engage, enrage, greengage, offstage, onstage, outrage, rampage, ribcage, space-age, teenage, underage, upstage.
[3] disengage.

SURPRISING RHYMING:
[1] **Aged,** caged, change, gauged, paged, raged, range, staged, strange, waged.
Ate, bait, crate, date, eight, fate, fête, freight, gate, great, grate, hate, late, mate, plate, rate, skate, slate, spate, state, straight, trait, weight, wait.
Bay, clay, day, eh, fray, gay, gray/grey, hay, hey, lay, may, pay, play, pray, prey, ray, say, slay, sleigh, spray, stay, stray, sway, they, tray, way, weigh, yea.
Braved, craved, paved, raved, saved, shaved, slaved, waved.
Blazed, crazed, dazed, fazed, gazed, hazed, lazed, phased, phrased, praised, raised.
Aid, blade, fade, grade, jade, laid, made, maid, paid, played, prayed, raid, shade, spade, sprayed, stayed, strayed, suede, they'd, wade, weighed.
Ailed, baled, failed, hailed, jailed, mailed, nailed, sailed, tailed, trailed, veiled, wailed.
Braced, chaste, chased, faced, graced, haste, laced, paste, paced, placed, raced, spaced, taste, traced, waste, waist.

Brain, cane, chain, crane, drain, feign, gain, grain, lain, lane, main, pain, pane, plain, plane, rain, reign, rein, sane, slain, sprain, stain, strain, train, twain, vain, vein, wane.
[2] **Engaged**, enraged, outraged, rampaged, upstaged.
Await, berate, cheapskate, checkmate, classmate, create, debate, deflate, dictate, fixate, flat-mate, frustrate, gyrate, inflate, innate, irate, jailbait, lightweight, locate, migrate, narrate, ornate, placate, playmate, portrait, pulsate, relate, sedate, soulmate, stagnate, stalemate, translate, update, vacate, vibrate.
Airplay, array, astray, away, ballet, beret, betray, birthday, blasé, bouquet, roadway, buffet, café, chalet, cliché, convey, coupé, decay, deejay, delay, dismay, display, doomsday, doorway, downplay, driveway, duvet, fair play, foreplay, forte, foyer, Friday, freeway, gangway, gateway, gourmet, hairspray, halfway, hallway, headway, hearsay, heyday, highway, hombre, hooray, horseplay, hurray, inlay, latté, lamé, mainstay, mayday, melee, midday, midway, mislay, Monday, obey, okay, olé, one day, outlay, outplay, outstay, outweigh, padre, part-way, passé, pathway, payday, portray, railway, reggae, relay, repay, replay, ricochet, risqué, roadway, rosé, runway, sachet, sashay, screenplay, segue, soirée, someday, some way, stairway, subway, Sunday, sunray, survey, Thursday, today, touché, toupée, Tuesday, two-way, waylay, weekday, x-ray.
Behave(d), depraved, engrave(d), enslave(d), unpaved, unshaved.
Amazed, appraised, erased, liaised, rephrased, stargazed.
Arrange, deranged, estrange, exchange, short-change.
Afraid, arcade, barmaid, betrayed, brain fade, bridesmaid, cascade, charade, crusade, decayed, degrade, delayed, dismayed, evade, grenade, handmade, homemade, invade, man-made, mermaid, nightshade, nursemaid, obeyed, parade, persuade, ram raid, repaid, self-made, surveyed, today, unpaid.
Abstain, again, airplane, arcane, attain, birdbrain, bloodstain, campaign, champagne, complain, constrain, contain, detain, domain, explain, humane, lamebrain, maintain, migraine, mundane, obtain, profane, refrain, remain(s), retain, sustain, terrain, urbane.
[3] **Disengaged**, misbehaved.
Aftertaste, angel-faced, baby-faced, dirty-faced, freckle-faced.

1.3.20 "--aged" (as in "raged")
[1] aged, caged, gauged, paged, raged, staged, waged.
[2] engaged, enraged, outraged, rampaged, unassuaged, unengaged, upstaged.

SURPRISING RHYMING:
[1] **Age**, cage, change, gauge, page, rage, range, stage, strange, wage.
Based, braced, cased, chaste, chased, faced, graced, haste, laced, paste, paced, placed, raced, spaced, taste, traced, waste, waist.
Aid, blade, fade, grade, jade, laid, made, maid, paid, played, prayed, raid, shade, spade, sprayed, stayed, strayed, suede, they'd, vague, wade, weighed.
Ate, bait, crate, date, eight, fate, fête, freight, gate, great, grate, hate, late, mate, plate, rate, skate, slate, spate, state, strait, straight, trait, weight, wait.
Aimed, blamed, claimed, famed, framed, maimed, named, shamed, tamed.
Braved, craved, paved, raved, saved, shaved, slaved, waved.
Blazed, crazed, dazed, fazed, gazed, glazed, lazed, phased, phrased, praised, raised.
Brain, cane, chain, drain, feign, gain, grain, lain, lane, main, pain, pane, plain, plane, rain, reign, rein, sane, slain, sprain, stain, strain, train, vain, vein, wane.
[2] **Engage**, enrage, outrage, rampage,, upstage.
Arranged, deranged, estranged, exchanged, short-changed.
Amazed, appraised, erased, liaised, rephrased, reappraised, stargazed.
Barefaced, embraced, erased, fast-paced, red-faced, replaced, shamefaced, strait-laced, toothpaste, two-faced.
Afraid, barmaid, betrayed, brain fade, bridesmaid, cascade, charade, crusade, decayed, degrade, delayed, dismayed, evade, handmade, homemade, invade, man-made, mermaid, nightshade, nursemaid, obeyed, parade, persuade, ram raid, self-made, today.
Ashamed, exclaimed, nicknamed, proclaimed, reclaimed, renamed.
Abate, await, berate, birth rate, cheapskate, checkmate, classmate, create, debate, deflate, dictate, estate, fixate, flat-mate, frustrate, helpmate, inflate, irate, jailbait, lightweight, locate, migrate, narrate, ornate, outdate, placate, playmate, portrait, pulsate, relate, rotate, sedate, soulmate, stagnate, stalemate, translate, update, vacate, vibrate.

Behaved, depraved, engraved, enslaved, unpaved, unshaved.
Abstain, again, airplane, arcane, attain, birdbrain, bloodstain, campaign, champagne, complain, constrain, contain, detain, domain, explain, humane, lamebrain, maintain, migraine, mundane, obtain, profane, refrain, remain(s), retain, sustain, terrain, urbane.
[3] **Aftertaste**, angel-faced, baby-faced, dirty-faced, freckle-faced.
Cavalcade, centigrade, disarrayed, escapade, lemonade, marmalade, masquerade, overpaid, razor blade, readymade, renegade, ricocheted, serenade, tailor-made, unafraid.
Interchange, part-exchanged, pre-arranged, rearranged.

1.3.21 "--ages" (as in "pages")
[2] ages, cages, gauges, pages, rages, stages, wages.
[3] engages, enrages, outrages, rampages.

SURPRISING RHYMING:
[2] **Audacious**, curvaceous, flirtatious, gracious, mendacious, pugnacious, sagacious, spacious, ostentatious, pugnacious, tenacious, ungracious, vexatious, vivacious.
Baseless, faceless, graceless, placeless, traceless, status.
Aimless, blameless, famous, frailest, frameless, graceless, grayness/greyness, nameless, palest, plainness, sameness, shameless, tameless, tameness.
Brainless, nameless, painless, rainless, spontaneous, stainless.
Breathless, I guess, princess, recess, reckless, restless, sweetness, weakness.
Arranges, changes, exchanges, ranges, part-exchanges, rearranges.
[3] **Advantageous**, contagious, courageous, outrageous.

1.3.22 "--ageing" (as in "raging")
[2] ageing, caging, gauging, paging, raging, staging, waging.
[3] assuaging, engaging, enraging, outraging, rampaging, upstaging.

SURPRISING RHYMING:
[2] **Changing**, ranging.
Aiding, grading, fading, raiding, trading, braiding, shading, wading.
Aching, baking, braking, breaking, faking, making, quaking, shaking, taking, waking.
Ailing, failing, jailing, mailing, nailing, railing, sailing, tailing, trailing, veiling, wailing.
Explaining, feigning, gaining, raining, reigning, staining, straining, training, waning.
Aping, draping, gaping, scraping, shaping, taping.
Baiting, dating, grating, hating, mating, skating, slating, stating, waiting, weighting.
Braving, craving, paving, raving, saving, shaving, slaving, waiving, waving.
Blazing, fazing, gazing, hazing, lazing, phasing, phrasing, praising, raising.
[3] **Arranging**, exchanging, rearranging, shortchanging, unchanging.
Degrading, invading, parading, crusading, persuading, cascading, evading, dissuading.
Awaking, backbreaking, breathtaking, earthshaking, forsaking, heartbreaking, lovemaking, matchmaking, mistaking, painstaking, peacemaking, troublemaking, undertaking.
Blackmailing, curtailing, entailing, exhaling, inhaling, prevailing, unfailing, unveiling.
Abstaining, complaining, containing, detaining, entertaining, maintaining, obtaining.
Escaping, landscaping, reshaping, skyscraping.
Awaiting, berating, creating, debating, deflating, frustrating, locating, migrating, narrating, placating, pulsating, relating, stagnating, updating, vacating, vibrating.
Behaving, engraving, enslaving, lifesaving, time-saving.
Amazing, appraising, erasing, fundraising, hellraising, stargazing, trailblazing.
[4] **Fascinating**, humiliating, infuriating, initiating, insinuating, nauseating, navigating, penetrating, punctuating, radiating, recreating, unabating, underrating, understating.
[5] **Abbreviating**, alleviating, appreciating, associating, depreciating, differentiating, discriminating, evacuating, negotiating, perpetuating, retaliating, substantiating.

1.3.23 "--ageous" (as in "courageous")
[3] advantageous, contagious, courageous, outrageous, rampageous.

SURPRISING RHYMING:
[2] **Ages**, cages, gauges, pages, rages, stages, wages.

Audacious, curvaceous, flirtatious, gracious, mendacious, pugnacious, sagacious, spacious, ostentatious, pugnacious, tenacious, ungracious, vexatious, vivacious.
Baseless, faceless, graceless, placeless, traceless, status.
Aimless, blameless, famous, frailest, frameless, graceless, grayness/greyness, nameless, palest, plainness, sameness, shameless, tameless, tameness.
Brainless, nameless, painless, rainless, spontaneous, stainless.
Breathless, princess, recess, reckless, restless, sweetness, weakness.
Arranges, changes, exchanges, ranges, part-exchanges.
[3] **Engages**, enrages, outrages, rampages.

1.3.24 "--ake" (as in "fake")
[1] ache, bake, brake, break, cake, fake, flake, lake, make, quake, rake, sake, shake, sheik, snake, stake, steak, take, wake.
[2] awake, backache, beefcake, beefsteak, cheesecake, cornflake, cupcake, daybreak, earache, earthquake, firebreak, footbrake, forsake, fruitcake, grubstake, handbrake, handshake, headache, heartache, heartbreak, intake, jailbreak, keepsake, milkshake, mistake, moonquake, muckrake, namesake, opaque, outbreak, outtake, pancake, partake, retake, snowflake, sunbake, sweepstake, toothache, uptake, windbreak.
[3] bellyache, overtake, rattlesnake, stomachache, undertake, wide-awake.

SURPRISING RHYMING:
[1] **Ate**, bait, crate, date, eight, fate, fête, freight, gate, great, grate, hate, late, mate, plate, rate, skate, slate, spate, state, strait, straight, trait, weight, wait.
Ace, base, bass, brace, case, chase, face, grace, lace, pace, place, plaice, race, space, trace, vase, ways.
Ape, cape, drape, gape, grape, nape, scrape, shape, tape, vape.
Aid, blade, fade, glade, grade, jade, laid, made, maid, paid, played, prayed, raid, shade, spade, sprayed, stayed, strayed, suede, they'd, vague, wade, weighed.
[2] **Abate**, await, berate, birth rate, cheapskate, checkmate, classmate, create, debate, deflate, dictate, estate, fixate, flat-mate, frustrate, helpmate, inflate, irate, jailbait, lightweight, locate, migrate, narrate, ornate, outdate, placate, playmate, portrait, pulsate, relate, rotate, sedate, soulmate, stagnate, stalemate, translate, update, vacate, vibrate.
Awaken, heartbreaking, mistaken, shaken.
Birthplace, bookcase, deface, disgrace, embrace, erase, fireplace, misplace, nutcase, outpace, rat-race, replace, retrace, showcase, someplace, staircase, suitcase, workplace.
Afraid, betrayed, brain fade, bridesmaid, cascade, charade, crusade, decayed, degrade, delayed, dismayed, evade, handmade, homemade, invade, man-made, mermaid, nightshade, nursemaid, obeyed, parade, persuade, ram raid, self-made, today.
Escape, landscape, red tape, reshape, shipshape.
[3] **Activate**, aggravate, alienate, allocate, animate, automate, captivate, celebrate, circulate, complicate, consecrate, concentrate, confiscate, congregate, consummate, contemplate, cultivate, decorate, dedicate, demonstrate, desolate, devastate, deviate, discriminate, dominate, duplicate, educate, elevate, eliminate, emigrate, emulate, escalate, estimate, exterminate, fascinate, fluctuate, generate, graduate, gravitate, heavyweight, hesitate, hibernate, illuminate, illustrate, imitate, implicate, infiltrate, innovate, instigate, interstate, intimate, intricate, inundate, irritate, isolate, liberate, magistrate, mediate, meditate, moderate, motivate, navigate, operate, orchestrate, overstate, overweight, paperweight, penetrate, percolate, procreate, radiate, regulate, relocate, renovate, segregate, separate, simulate, situate, speculate, stimulate, stipulate, suffocate, syncopate, terminate, tête-à-tête, tolerate, underrate, violate.
Barricade, cavalcade, centigrade, colonnade, disarrayed, escapade, lemonade, marmalade, masquerade, not afraid, overpaid, razor blade, readymade, renegade, ricochet, ricocheted, serenade, tailor-made, unafraid, underpaid.

1.3.25 "--aked" (as in "baked")
ached, baked, braked, faked, flaked, half-baked, quaked, raked, snaked, sunbaked.

SURPRISING RHYMING:
[1] **Ape(d)**, cape(d), drape(d), gape(d), scrape(d), shape(d), tape(d), vape(d).
Ain't, faint, feint, paint, quaint, saint, taint.

Ate, bait, crate, date, eight, fate, fête, freight, gate, gait, great, grate, hate, late, mate, plate, rate, skate, slate, spate, state, strait, straight, trait, weight, wait.
Brained, caned, chained, drained, feigned, gained, pained, rained, reigned, sprained, stained, strained, trained, waned.
[2] Escape(d), landscape(d), red tape, reshape(d), shipshape.
Acquaint, complaint, constraint, greasepaint, restraint, war-paint.
Abate, await, berate, birth rate, cheapskate, checkmate, classmate, create, debate, deflate, dictate, estate, fixate, flat-mate, frustrate, helpmate, inflate, irate, jailbait, lightweight, locate, migrate, narrate, ornate, outdate, placate, playmate, portrait, pulsate, relate, rotate, sedate, soulmate, stagnate, stalemate, translate, update, vacate, vibrate.
[3] Activate, aggravate, alienate, allocate, animate, automate, captivate, celebrate, circulate, complicate, consecrate, concentrate, confiscate, congregate, consummate, contemplate, cultivate, decorate, dedicate, demonstrate, desolate, devastate, deviate, discriminate, dominate, duplicate, educate, elevate, eliminate, emigrate, emulate, escalate, estimate, exterminate, fascinate, fluctuate, generate, graduate, gravitate, heavyweight, hesitate, hibernate, illuminate, illustrate, imitate, implicate, infiltrate, innovate, instigate, interstate, intimate, intricate, inundate, irritate, isolate, liberate, magistrate, mediate, meditate, moderate, motivate, navigate, operate, orchestrate, overstate, overweight, paperweight, penetrate, percolate, procreate, radiate, regulate, relocate, renovate, segregate, separate, simulate, situate, speculate, stimulate, stipulate, suffocate, syncopate, terminate, tête-à-tête, tolerate, underrate, violate.
[4] Accelerate, accommodate, alienate, alleviate, anticipate, associate, authenticate, certificate, collaborate, communicate, concentrate, congratulate, contaminate, cooperate, corroborate, deteriorate, elaborate, eradicate, evaporate, exaggerate, exasperate, exonerate, hallucinate, humiliate, impersonate, infuriate, intimidate, invigorate, investigate, negotiate, participate, recuperate, refrigerate, reverberate.

1.3.26 "--aken" (as in "shaken")
[2] bacon, shaken, taken, waken.
[3] awaken, forsaken, mistaken, unshaken, untaken, wind-shaken.
[4] godforsaken, overtaken, undertaken.

SURPRISING RHYMING:
[2] Aching, breaking, faking, making, quaking, shaking, taking, waking.
Dating, hating, mating, rating, skating, slating, stating, waiting.
Aping, draping, gaping, scraping, shaping, taping.
Brazen, changing, craven, haven, nation, raisin, station.
Blazing, fazing, gazing, lazing, phasing, phrasing, praising, raising.
Ailing, failing, hailing, jailing, mailing, nailing, sailing, tailing, trailing, veiling, wailing.
Braving, craving, paving, raving, saving, shaving, slaving, waiving, waving.
[3] Backbreaking, breathtaking, earthshaking, forsaking, heartbreaking, lovemaking, matchmaking, mistaking, painstaking, peacemaking, troublemaking, undertaking.
Escaping, landscaping, reshaping, skyscraping.
Creation, damnation, duration, elation, fixation, flirtation, foundation, frustration, invasion, location, migration, narration, occasion, ovation, persuasion, quotation, relation, salvation, sensation, starvation, taxation, temptation, translation, vacation, vibration.
Fascinating, graduating, humiliating, infuriating, insinuating, mediating, nauseating, navigating, penetrating, punctuating, radiating, recreating, underrating, understating.
Blackmailing, curtailing, detailing, entailing, exhaling, inhaling, prevailing, unveiling.
Amazing, clean-shaven, erasing, fundraising, hellraising, stargazing, trailblazing.
Awaiting, berating, creating, debating, dictating, frustrating, locating, migrating, narrating, placating, pulsating, relating, stagnating, translating, updating, vacating.
Behaving, depraving, engraving, enslaving, lifesaving, time-saving.

[4] **Aberration**, accusation, admiration, adoration, adulation, aggravation, allegation, altercation, animation, aspiration, cancellation, celebration, combination, compensation, complication, concentration, condemnation, confirmation, confrontation, congregation, conservation, consolation, constellation, contemplation, conversation, decoration, dedication, degradation, demonstration, deprivation, desolation, desperation, destination, devastation, education, emigration, excitation, exclamation, expectation, explanation, exploitation, fascination, generation, graduation, imitation, immigration, implication, incarnation, inclination, indication, indignation, information, innovation, inspiration, invitation, irritation, isolation, jubilation, liberation, limitation, meditation, moderation, motivation, obligation, observation, occupation, operation, palpitation, penetration, perspiration, preparation, presentation, preservation, provocation, publication, recreation, relaxation, reputation, reservation, resignation, revelation, scintillation, separation, situation, speculation, stimulation, stipulation, syncopation, titillation, transformation, transportation, trepidation, vaccination, valuation, violation, vindication.
[5] **Acceleration**, accommodation, alienation, annihilation, anticipation, appreciation, civilization, collaboration, communication, congratulations, consideration, cooperation, cross-examination, determination, discrimination, elimination, evacuation, evaluation, exaggeration, exhilaration, humiliation, imagination, infatuation, interrogation, interpretation, intoxication, investigation, justification, manipulation, multiplication, negotiation, organization, participation, qualification, realization, recommendation, reconciliation, recrimination, reincarnation, retaliation, reverberation, sophistication.
Appreciating, discriminating, negotiating, perpetuating, retaliating, substantiating.

1.3.27 "--aker" (as in "baker")
[2] acre, baker, breaker, faker, maker, shaker, taker, waker
[3] bookmaker, caretaker, dressmaker, heartbreaker, icebreaker, lawbreaker, lawmaker, matchmaker, mischief-maker, muckraker, peacemaker, saltshaker, shoemaker, strikebreaker, troublemaker, undertaker, watchmaker.

SURPRISING RHYMING:
[2] **Caper**, draper, gaper, paper, scraper, shaper, taper, vaper, vapour/vapor (U.S.).
Fader, raider, trader, wader.
Cater, crater, data, dater, greater, hater, later, skater, traitor, waiter.
Braver, craver, favour/favor (U.S.), flavour/flavor (U.S.), raver, saver, savour/savor (U.S.), shaver, waiver, waver.
Blazer, gazer, grazer, hazer, laser, raiser, razor, Taser.
[3] **Escaper**, notepaper, newspaper, skyscraper, wallpaper.
Blockader, crusader, evader, first-aider, invader, persuader.
Creator, curator, debater, dictator, equator, freighter, narrator, spectator, translator.
Disfavour/disfavor (U.S.), engraver, enslaver, lifesaver, timesaver.
Appraiser, eraser, fundraiser, hellraiser, stargazer, trailblazer.
[4] **Accelerator**, agitator, alligator, animator, aviator, calculator, collaborator, commentator, decorator, educator, elevator, escalator, generator, gladiator, illustrator, imitator, impersonator, indicator, instigator, interrogator, investigator, liberator, mediator, negotiator, operator, percolator, perpetrator, refrigerator, speculator, terminator, ventilator.
Masquerader, rollerblader, serenader.

1.3.28 "--aking" (as in "waking")
[2] aching, baking, braking, breaking, faking, making, quaking, shaking, taking, waking.
[3] awaking, backbreaking, bookmaking, breathtaking, dressmaking, earthshaking, forsaking, heartbreaking, lovemaking, matchmaking, mistaking, partaking, painstaking, peacemaking, troublemaking, undertaking, unmaking.

SURPRISING RHYMING:
[2] **Dating**, grating, hating, mating, rating, skating, slating, stating, waiting, weighting.
Aiding, changing, grading, fading, raiding, trading, shading, wading.
Braving, craving, paving, raving, saving, shaving, slaving, waiving, waving, wavering.
Aping, draping, gaping, scraping, shaping, taping.
Aiming, blaming, claiming, flaming, framing, gaming, naming, shaming, taming.
Ailing, failing, hailing, jailing, mailing, nailing, sailing, tailing, trailing, veiling, wailing.

Blazing, fazing, gazing, hazing, lazing, phasing, phrasing, praising, raising.
Caning, chaining, craning, draining, feigning, gaining, paining, raining, reigning, reining, spraining, staining, straining, training, waning.
[3] Awaiting, backdating, berating, creating, debating, deflating, dictating, frustrating, locating, migrating, narrating, placating, pulsating, relating, stagnating, translating, updating, vacating, vibrating.
Degrading, invading, parading, pervading, persuading, cascading, evading, dissuading.
Favouring/favoring (U.S.), flavouring/flavoring (U.S.), savouring/savoring (U.S.)
Behaving, engraving, enslaving, lifesaving, time-saving.
Escaping, landscaping, reshaping, skyscraping.
Explaining, exclaiming, inflaming, nicknaming, proclaiming, reclaiming, remaining.
Blackmailing, curtailing, entailing, exhaling, inhaling, prevailing, unfailing, unveiling.
Amazing, appraising, erasing, fundraising, hellraising, stargazing, trailblazing.
Abstaining, attaining, campaigning, complaining, constraining, containing, detaining, entertaining, maintaining, obtaining, refraining, retaining, sustaining.
[4] Calculating, fascinating, graduating, humiliating, infuriating, insinuating, mediating, nauseating, navigating, penetrating, punctuating, radiating, recreating, understating.
[5] Alleviating, appreciating, depreciating, discriminating, evacuating, retaliating.

1.3.29 "--akable" (as in "breakable")
[3] breakable, fakeable, makeable, shakable.
[4] mistakable, unbreakable, unshakeable, unmistakable.

SURPRISING RHYMING:
[3] Capable, changeable, payable, playable, swayable, shapeable, traceable, weighable.
Curable, durable, deniable, liable, pliable, viable, reliable.
Edible, credible, beddable, sensible.
Bicycle, carnival, classical, cynical, digital, electrical, festival, hospital, icicle, logical, magical, marital, musical, mythical, pinnacle, principal, radical, rhythmical, theatrical, tricycle, typical, vehicle, whimsical.
Fantastical, practical, tactical,
Mystical, physical, quizzical.
Aerial, genial, menial, trivial.
Actual, annual, casual, eventual, factual, gradual, manual, punctual, ritual, virtual.
Comical, critical, ethical, lyrical, miracle, mythical, sceptical/skeptical, spectacle, vertical.
[4] Amiable, attainable, capable, conventional, deniable, erasable, explainable, insatiable, obtainable, remarkable, unattainable, unobtainable, unstoppable, variable.
Available, debatable, degradable, incapable, inescapable, irreplaceable, replaceable.
Dislikable, impeccable, remarkable, retractable, unspeakable.
Compatible, impossible, responsible.
Delectable, detectable, inflexible, predictable, respectable, uncomfortable.
Disposable, forgivable, implausible, impossible, inflexible.
Commendable, dependable, expendable, inedible, incredible, formidable.
Acceptable, perceptible, susceptible.
Agreeable, foreseeable.
Applicable, explicable, inexplicable.
Endurable, incurable, insurable
Forgettable, regrettable, unforgettable.
Historical, hysterical, illogical, identical, poetical, political, rhetorical, satirical.
Celestial, conspiratorial, memorial, millennial, proverbial, secretarial.
[5] Analytical, astronomical, chronological, diabolical, economical, hypocritical, mythological, psychological, technological.

1.3.30 "--ale" (as in "nail")
[1] ail, ale, bale, bail, dale, fail, flail, frail, gale, grail, hail, jail, male, mail, nail, pale, rail, sale, sail, scale, shale, snail, stale, tale, tail, they'll, trail, vale, veil, whale, wail.
[2] abseil, assail, avail, bobtail, blackmail, cocktail, curtail, derail, detail, doornail, dovetail, entail, exhale, female, guardrail, handrail, hangnail, hightail, impale, inhale, pigtail, prevail, regale, resale, retail, tall tale, telltale, thumbnail, toenail, travail, unveil.
[3] fairytale, fingernail, monorail, nightingale, holy grail, ponytail.

SURPRISING RHYMING:
[1] Ailed, baled, bailed, failed, flailed, hailed, jailed, mailed, nailed, paled, sailed, scaled, tailed, trailed, veiled, wailed.
Bay, clay, day, eh, fray, gay, gray/grey, hay, hey, lay, may, pay, play, pray, prey, ray, say, slay, sleigh, spray, stay, stray, sway, they, tray, way, weigh, yea.
Brained, caned, chained, drained, feigned, gained, pained, rained, reigned, sprained, stained, strained, trained, waned.
[2] Blackmailed, curtailed, derailed, detailed, dovetailed, entailed, exhaled, hightailed, impaled, inhaled, pigtailed, prevailed, regaled, retailed, unveiled.
Airplay, array, astray, away, ballet, beret, betray, birthday, blasé, bouquet, roadway, buffet, café, chalet, cliché, convey, coupé, decay, deejay, delay, dismay, display, doomsday, doorway, downplay, driveway, duvet, fair play, foreplay, forte, foyer, Friday, freeway, gangway, gateway, gourmet, hairspray, halfway, hallway, headway, hearsay, heyday, highway, hombre, hooray, horseplay, hurray, inlay, latté, lamé, mainstay, mayday, melee, midday, midway, mislay, Monday, obey, okay, olé, one day, outlay, outplay, outstay, outweigh, padre, part-way, passé, pathway, payday, portray, railway, reggae, relay, repay, replay, ricochet, risqué, roadway, rosé, runway, sachet, sashay, screenplay, segue, soirée, someday, some way, stairway, subway, Sunday, sunray, survey, Thursday, today, touché, toupée, Tuesday, two-way, waylay, weekday, x-ray.
Attained, birdbrained, bloodstained, complained, contained, detained, explained, lamebrained, maintained, obtained, refrained, remained, restrained, retained, sustained.

1.3.31 "--ailed" (as in "nailed")
[1] ailed, baled, bailed, failed, hailed, jailed, mailed, nailed, paled, railed, sailed, scaled, tailed, trailed, veiled, wailed.
[2] abseiled, availed, blackmailed, curtailed, derailed, detailed, dovetailed, hightailed, entailed, exhaled, impaled, inhaled, pigtailed, prevailed, regaled, unveiled.

SURPRISING RHYMING:
[1] Ail, ale, bale, bail, dale, fail, flail, frail, gale, grail, hail, jail, male, mail, nail, pale, rail, sale, sail, scale, shale, snail, stale, tale, tail, they'll, trail, vale, veil, whale, wail.
Brained, caned, chained, drained, feigned, gained, pained, rained, reigned, sprained, stained, strained, trained, waned.
[2] Blackmail, cocktail, curtail, derail, detail, entail, exhale, female, guardrail, handrail, hightail, impale, inhale, pigtail, prevail, resale, tall tale, telltale, thumbnail, unveil.
[3] Fairytale, fingernail, monorail, nightingale, holy grail, ponytail.

1.3.32 "--ailing" (as in "sailing")
[2] ailing, failing, flailing, hailing, jailing, mailing, nailing, paling, railing, sailing, scaling, tailing, trailing, veiling, wailing, whaling.
[3] availing, blackmailing, curtailing, detailing, dovetailing, entailing, exhaling, impaling, inhaling, prevailing, regaling, retailing, unfailing, unveiling, wholesaling.

SURPRISING RHYMING:
[2] Fading, raiding, trading, wading.
Dating, grating, hating, skating, waiting.
Braving, craving, paving, raving, saving, shaving, waiving, waving.
Laying, paying, playing, praying, slaying, staying, spraying.
Blazing, erasing, gazing, grazing, hazing, lazing, praising, raising.
[3] Blockading, degrading, dissuading, evading, first-aiding, invading, persuading.
Escaping, creating, debating, dictating, equating, locating, narrating, spectating, translating, vibrating.
Depraving, engraving, enslaving, lifesaving, timesaving.
Betraying, conveying, delaying, displaying, portraying, soothsaying, taxpaying.
Appraising, fundraising, hellraising, stargazing, trailblazing.
[4] Masquerading, rollerblading, serenading.

Accelerating, agitating, animating, calculating, collaborating, decorating, demonstrating, detonating, educating, elevating, escalating, excavating, exterminating, generating, illustrating, imitating, impersonating, indicating, instigating, interrogating, investigating, liberating, mediating, moderating, negotiating, percolating, perpetrating, radiating, simulating, speculating, stimulating, terminating, ventilating, violating.

1.3.33 "--ailer" (as in "jailer")
[2] frailer, jailer, mailer, paler, sailor, staler, trailer, tailor, scaler, wailer, whaler.
[3] abseiler, blackmailer, exhale, inhaler, loudhailer, regaler, retailer, wholesaler.

SURPRISING RHYMING:
[2] **Fader**, raider, trader, wader.
Caper, draper, paper, scraper, shaper, taper, vaper, vapour/vapor.
Cater, crater, data, dater, grater, greater, hater, later, skater, slater, traitor, waiter.
Braver, caver, craver, favour/favor (U.S.), flavour/flavor (U.S.), graver, paver, raver, saver, savour/savor (U.S.), shaver, slaver, quaver, waiver, waver.
Greyer/grayer (U.S.), layer, mayor, payer, player, prayer, slayer, stayer, sprayer.
Blazer, eraser, gazer, glazer, grazer, hazer, laser, praiser, raiser, razor, Taser.
[3] **Blockader**, crusader, degrader, dissuader, evader, first-aider, invader, persuader.
Escaper, flypaper, notepaper, newspaper, sandpaper, skyscraper, wallpaper.
Creator, curator, dictator, equator, narrator, rotator, spectator, translator, vibrator.
Disfavour/disfavor (U.S.), engraver, enslaver, lifesaver, timesaver.
Appraiser, fundraiser, hellraiser, stargazer, trailblazer.
[4] **Masquerader**, rollerblader, serenader.
Accelerator, agitator, alligator, animator, aviator, calculator, collaborator, commentator, decorator, educator, elevator, escalator, generator, gladiator, illustrator, imitator, impersonator, indicator, instigator, interrogator, investigator, liberator, mediator, negotiator, operator, percolator, perpetrator, refrigerator, speculator, terminator, ventilator.

1.3.34 "--ailest" (as in "palest")
[2] frailest, palest, stalest.

SURPRISING RHYMING:
[1] **Best**, blessed, breast, chest, crest, dressed, guest, jest, nest, pest, quest, rest, test, vest, west, wrest, zest.
[2] **Abreast**, armrest, bequest, conquest, contest, digest, divest, footrest, headrest, northwest, protest, road test, unrest, southwest, suggest.
Addressed, confessed, depressed, digressed, duress, impressed, obsessed, oppressed, princess, progress, protest, success, well-dressed.
[3] **Manifest**, overdressed, second-best, self-confessed, self-possessed, unimpressed.

1.3.35 "--aily" (as in "daily")
[2] daily, gaily, ukulele.

SURPRISING RHYMING:
[2] **Baby**, crybaby, lady, maybe, milady, shady.
Brainy, grainy, mainly, miscellany, plainly, rainy, sanely, vainly, zany.
Airy, dairy, fairy, hairy, prairie, scary, vary, wary.
Glazy, gravy, hazy, lazy, mazy, navy, wavy.
Greatly, innately, irately, lately, ornately, sedately, stately, straightly.
[3] **Humanely**, insanely, mundanely, profanely, ungainly, urbanely.
Airy-fairy, canary, contrary, stir-crazy, oops-a-daisy, unwary, upsy-daisy.

1.3.36 "--aim" (as in "fame")
[1] aim, blame, came, claim, fame, flame, frame, game, lame, maim, name, named, same, shame, tame, vain, vein.
[2] acclaim, aflame, became, defame, disclaim, doorframe,, endgame, exclaim, inflame, nickname, proclaim, reclaim, rename, surname.
[3] counterclaim, overcame.

SURPRISING RHYMING:
[1] **Brain**, cane, chain, drain, explain, feign, gain, grain, lain, lane, main, pain, pane, plain, plane, rain, reign, rein, sane, slain, sprain, stain, strain, train, vain, vein, wane.
Aid, blade, fade, glade, grade, jade, laid, made, maid, paid, played, prayed, raid, shade, spade, sprayed, stayed, strayed, suede, they'd, wade, weighed.
Ape, cape, crepe, drape, gape, grape, scrape, shape, tape, vape.
Ate, bait, crate, date, eight, fate, fête, freight, gate, gait, grate, great, hate, late, mate, plate, rate, skate, slate, spate, state, strait, straight, trait, weight, wait.
Bay, clay, day, eh, fray, gay, gray/grey, hay, hey, lay, may, pay, play, pray, prey, ray, say, slay, sleigh, spray, stay, stray, sway, they, tray, way, weigh, yea.
[2] **Again**, arcane, campaign, champagne, detain, domain, humane, inane, lamebrain, migraine, mundane, obtain, octane, ordain, profane, propane, refrain, retain, terrain.
Abstain, airplane, attain, birdbrain, bloodstain, complain, constrain, contain, disdain, explain, maintain, remain, sustain, urbane.
Abate, await, berate, birth rate, cheapskate, checkmate, classmate, create, debate, deflate, dictate, estate, fixate, flat-mate, frustrate, helpmate, inflate, irate, jailbait, lightweight, locate, migrate, narrate, ornate, outdate, placate, playmate, portrait, pulsate, relate, rotate, sedate, soulmate, stagnate, stalemate, translate, update, vacate, vibrate.
Airplay, array, astray, away, ballet, beret, betray, birthday, blasé, bouquet, roadway, buffet, café, chalet, cliché, convey, coupé, decay, deejay, delay, dismay, display, doomsday, doorway, downplay, driveway, duvet, fair play, foreplay, forte, foyer, Friday, freeway, gangway, gateway, gourmet, hairspray, halfway, hallway, headway, hearsay, heyday, highway, hombre, hooray, horseplay, hurray, inlay, latté, lamé, mainstay, mayday, melee, midday, midway, mislay, Monday, obey, okay, olé, one day, outlay, outplay, outstay, outweigh, padre, part-way, passé, pathway, payday, portray, railway, reggae, relay, repay, replay, ricochet, risqué, roadway, rosé, runway, sachet, sashay, screenplay, segue, soirée, someday, some way, stairway, subway, Sunday, sunray, survey, Thursday, today, touché, toupée, Tuesday, two-way, waylay, weekday, x-ray.
Afraid, betrayed, brain fade, bridesmaid, cascade, charade, crusade, decayed, degrade, delayed, dismayed, evade, handmade, homemade, invade, man-made, mermaid, nightshade, nursemaid, obeyed, parade, persuade, ram raid, self-made, today.
[3] **Activate**, aggravate, alienate, allocate, animate, automate, captivate, celebrate, circulate, complicate, consecrate, concentrate, confiscate, congregate, consummate, contemplate, cultivate, decorate, dedicate, demonstrate, desolate, devastate, deviate, discriminate, dominate, duplicate, educate, elevate, eliminate, emigrate, emulate, escalate, estimate, exterminate, fascinate, fluctuate, generate, graduate, gravitate, heavyweight, hesitate, hibernate, illuminate, illustrate, imitate, implicate, infiltrate, innovate, instigate, interstate, intimate, intricate, inundate, irritate, isolate, liberate, magistrate, mediate, meditate, moderate, motivate, navigate, operate, orchestrate, overstate, overweight, paperweight, penetrate, percolate, procreate, radiate, regulate, relocate, renovate, segregate, separate, simulate, situate, speculate, stimulate, stipulate, suffocate, syncopate, terminate, tête-à-tête, tolerate, underrate, violate.
A.k.a., A-OK, alleyway, anyway, attaché, awayday, breakaway, cabaret, café au lait, castaway, Christmas Day, croupier, disarray, disobey, everyday, exposé, expressway, faraway, fiancé, flyaway, giveaway, getaway, hideaway, holiday, interplay, matinée, Milky Way, motorway, negligee, overlay, overplay, passageway, protégé, ricochet, résumé, runaway, Saturday, stowaway, straightaway, takeaway, tearaway, throwaway, underplay, walk away, wedding day, Wednesday, working day, yesterday.
Ascertain, entertain, inhumane, scatterbrain, sugar cane, weathervane, windowpane.
Barricade, cavalcade, centigrade, colonnade, disarrayed, escapade, lemonade, marmalade, masquerade, not afraid, overpaid, razor blade, readymade, renegade, ricocheted, serenade, tailor-made, unafraid, underpaid.
[4] **Accelerate**, accommodate, alienate, alleviate, anticipate, collaborate, communicate, concentrate, congratulate, contaminate, cooperate, corroborate, deteriorate, elaborate, eradicate, evaporate, exaggerate, hallucinate, humiliate, infuriate, intimidate, invigorate, investigate, negotiate, participate, recuperate, refrigerate, reverberate.

1.3.37 "--aimer" (as in "gamer")
aimer, disclaimer, exclaimer, framer, gamer, proclaimer, shamer, tamer.

SURPRISING RHYMING:
[2] **Drainer**, entertainer, explainer, feigner, gainer, plainer, saner, trainer, vainer.
Changer, danger, manger, ranger, stranger.
Frailer, jailer, mailer, paler, sailor, staler, trailer, tailor, scaler, wailer, whaler.
Caper, draper, paper, scraper, shaper, taper, vaper, vapour/vapor(U.S.).
Cater, crater, data, dater, grater, greater, hater, later, skater, slater, traitor, waiter.
Braver, craver, favour/favor (U.S.), flavour/flavor (U.S.), graver, paver, raver, saver, savour/savor (U.S.), shaver, waiver, waver.
Blazer, eraser, gazer, glazer, grazer, laser, raiser, razor, Taser.
Greyer/grayer (U.S.), layer, mayor, payer, player, prayer, slayer, stayer, sprayer.
Acre, baker, breaker, faker, maker, nature, shaker, taker, waker.
[3] **Abstainer**, campaigner, complainer, container, detainer, retainer.
Arranger, endanger, exchanger, shortchanger.
Blackmailer, exhale, inhaler, loudhailer, regaler, retailer, wholesaler.
Blockader, crusader, evader, first-aider, invader, persuader.
Escaper, notepaper, newspaper, sandpaper, skyscraper, wallpaper.
Creator, curator, debater, dictator, equator, narrator, rotator, spectator, translator.
Depraver, disfavour/disfavor (U.S.), engraver, lifesaver, timesaver.
Betrayer, delayer, displayer, portrayer, purveyor, soothsayer, surveyor, taxpayer.
Appraiser, fundraiser, hellraiser, stargazer, trailblazer.
Bookmaker, caretaker, dressmaker, heartbreaker, icebreaker, lawbreaker, matchmaker, mischief-maker, muckraker, peacemaker, troublemaker, undertaker, watchmaker.
[4+] **Accelerator**, agitator, alligator, animator, aviator, calculator, collaborator, commentator, decorator, educator, elevator, escalator, generator, gladiator, illustrator, imitator, impersonator, indicator, instigator, interrogator, investigator, liberator, mediator, negotiator, operator, percolator, perpetrator, refrigerator, speculator, terminator, ventilator.
Masquerader, rollerblader, serenader.

1.3.38 "--aimed" (as in "blamed")
[1] aimed, blamed, claimed, famed, framed, maimed, named, shamed, tamed.
[2] acclaimed, ashamed, defamed, disclaimed, exclaimed, nicknamed, proclaimed, reclaimed, renamed, unnamed.

SURPRISING RHYMING:
[1] **Brained**, caned, chained, drained, feigned, gained, pained, planed, rained, reigned, sprained, stained, strained, trained, waned.
Aim, blame, claim, fame, frame, maim, name, shame, tame.
Brain, cane, chain, drain, feign, gain, grain, lain, lane, main, pain, pane, plain, plane, rain, reign, rein, sane, slain, sprain, stain, strain, train, vain, vein, wane.
Ain't, faint, feint, paint, quaint, saint, taint.
Bay, clay, day, eh, fray, gay, gray/grey, hay, hey, lay, may, pay, play, pray, prey, ray, say, slay, sleigh, spray, stay, stray, sway, they, tray, way, weigh, yea.
[2] **Abstain**, again, airplane, arcane, attain, birdbrain, bloodstain, champagne, complain, constrain, contain, detain, domain, explain, humane, lamebrain, maintain, migraine, mundane, obtain, profane, refrain, remain(s), retain, sustain, terrain, urbane.
Abstained, arraigned, attained, birdbrained, bloodstained, complained, constrained, contained, detained, explained, lamebrained, maintained, obtained, ordained, refrained, regained, remained, restrained, retained, sustained, unchained.
Acquaint, complaint, constraint, greasepaint, repaint, restraint, spray-paint, war-paint.
Airplay, array, astray, away, ballet, beret, betray, birthday, blasé, bouquet, roadway, buffet, café, chalet, cliché, convey, coupé, decay, deejay, delay, dismay, display, doomsday, doorway, downplay, driveway, duvet, fair play, foreplay, forte, foyer, Friday, freeway, gangway, gateway, gourmet, hairspray, halfway, hallway, headway, hearsay, heyday, highway, hombre, hooray, horseplay, hurray, inlay, latté, lamé, mainstay, mayday, melee, midday, midway, mislay, Monday, obey, okay, olé, one day, outlay, outplay, outstay, outweigh, padre, part-way, passé, pathway, payday, portray, railway,

reggae, relay, repay, replay, ricochet, risqué, roadway, rosé, runway, sachet, sashay, screenplay, segue, soirée, someday, some way, stairway, subway, Sunday, sunray, survey, Thursday, today, touché, toupée, Tuesday, two-way, waylay, weekday, x-ray.
[3] Ascertain(ed), entertain(ed), hurricane, inhumane, scatterbrain(ed), weathervane.
A.k.a., A-OK, alleyway, anyway, attaché, awayday, breakaway, cabaret, café au lait, castaway, Christmas Day, croupier, disarray, disobey, everyday, exposé, expressway, faraway, fiancé, flyaway, giveaway, getaway, hideaway, holiday, interplay, matinée, Milky Way, motorway, negligee, overlay, overplay, passageway, protégé, ricochet, résumé, runaway, Saturday, stowaway, straightaway, takeaway, tearaway, throwaway, underplay, walk away, wedding day, Wednesday, working day, yesterday.

1.3.39 "--aiming" (as in "shaming")
[2] aiming, blaming, claiming, flaming, framing, gaming, naming, shaming, taming.
[3] acclaiming, defaming, disclaiming, exclaiming, inflaming, nicknaming, proclaiming, reclaiming, renaming.

SURPRISING RHYMING:
[2] **Caning**, chaining, craning, draining, feigning, gaining, paining, raining, reigning, reining, spraining, staining, straining, training, waning.
Aiding, grading, fading, raiding, trading, braiding, shading, wading.
Ailing, failing, hailing, jailing, mailing, nailing, sailing, tailing, trailing, veiling, wailing.
Dating, hating, mating, rating, skating, slating, stating, waiting, weighting.
Braving, caving, craving, paving, raving, saving, shaving, slaving, waiving, waving.
Blazing, fazing, gazing, hazing, grazing, lazing, phasing, phrasing, praising, raising.
Ageing, raging, staging, waging.
[3] **Abstaining**, attaining, bloodstaining, complaining, constraining, containing, detaining, explaining, maintaining, obtaining, ordaining, refraining, remaining, retaining, sustaining.
Degrading, invading, parading, persuading, cascading, evading, dissuading, unfading.
Blackmailing, curtailing, detailing, exhaling, inhaling, regaling, unfailing, unveiling.
Abating, awaiting, backdating, berating, creating, debating, deflating, dictating, frustrating, locating, migrating, narrating, placating, pulsating, relating, stagnating, translating, updating, vacating, vibrating.
Behaving, depraving, engraving, enslaving, lifesaving, misbehaving, time-saving.
Amazing, appraising, erasing, fundraising, hellraising, stargazing, trailblazing.
[4] **Fascinating**, entertaining, fluctuating, graduating, humiliating, infuriating, insinuating, mediating, nauseating, penetrating, punctuating, radiating, recreating, underrating.
[5] **Appreciating**, discriminating, evacuating, perpetuating, retaliating, substantiating.

1.3.40 "--aimful" (as in "shameful")
[2] aimful, shameful, blameful.

SURPRISING RHYMING:
[2] **Baneful**, gainful, painful.
Changeful, fateful, faithful, graceful, grateful, hateful, playful, wakeful.
[3] **Disdainful**, disgraceful, distasteful, unfaithful, ungrateful.

1.3.41 "--aimless" (as in "nameless")
[2] aimless, blameless, frameless, nameless, shameless, tameless.

SURPRISING RHYMING:
[2] **Brainless**, famous, painless, plainness, sameness, stainless, tameness.
Audacious, contagious, curvaceous, flirtatious, gracious, mendacious, pugnacious, spacious, ostentatious, pugnacious, spontaneous, tenacious, vivacious, voracious.
Breathless, faceless, palest, princess, reckless, restless, status, sweetness, weakness.
Bareness, fairness, rareness.
[3] **Advantageous**, courageous, outrageous, rampageous.
Awareness, unfairness.
Acquiesce, S.O.S., convalesce, nonetheless, nevertheless.

*

1.3.42 "--ain" (as in "rain")

[1] brain, cane, chain, crane, drain, feign, gain, grain, lain, lane, main, mane, pain, pane, plain, plane, rain, reign, rein, sane, slain, sprain, stain, strain, train, twain, vain, vane, vein, wane.

[2] abstain, again, airplane, arcane, attain, birdbrain, bloodstain, butane, campaign, champagne, chowmein, complain, constrain, contain, detain, disdain, domain, explain, humane, inane, insane, lamebrain, maintain, methane, migraine, mundane, obtain, octane, ordain, profane, propane, refrain, remain, retain, sustain, terrain, urbane.

[3] aeroplane, ascertain, entertain, hurricane, inhumane, novocaine, preordain, scatterbrain, sugar cane, windowpane, weathervane.

SURPRISING RHYMING:
[1] **Aim**, blame, came, claim, fame, flame, frame, game, name, same, shame, tame.
Bay, clay, day, eh, fray, gay, gray/grey, hay, hey, lay, may, pay, play, pray, prey, ray, say, slay, sleigh, spray, stay, stray, sway, they, tray, way, weigh, yea.
Aid, blade, fade, glade, grade, jade, laid, made, maid, paid, played, prayed, raid, shade, spade, sprayed, stayed, strayed, suede, they'd, wade, weighed.
Ape, cape, drape, gape, grape, nape, scrape, shape, tape, vape.
Ate, bait, crate, date, eight, fate, fête, freight, gate, gait, great, grate, hate, late, mate, plate, rate, skate, slate, spate, state, strait, straight, trait, weight, wait.
Change, range, strange.
[2] **Acclaim**, became, defame, disclaim, doorframe, endgame, exclaim, inflame, nickname, proclaim, reclaim, rename, surname, unnamed.
Airplay, array, astray, away, ballet, beret, betray, birthday, blasé, bouquet, roadway, buffet, café, chalet, cliché, convey, coupé, decay, deejay, delay, dismay, display, doomsday, doorway, downplay, driveway, duvet, fair play, foreplay, forte, foyer, Friday, freeway, gangway, gateway, gourmet, hairspray, halfway, hallway, headway, hearsay, heyday, highway, hombre, hooray, horseplay, hurray, inlay, latté, lamé, mainstay, mayday, melee, midday, midway, mislay, Monday, obey, okay, olé, one day, outlay, outplay, outstay, outweigh, padre, part-way, passé, pathway, payday, portray, railway, reggae, relay, repay, replay, ricochet, risqué, roadway, rosé, runway, sachet, sashay, screenplay, segue, soirée, someday, some way, stairway, subway, Sunday, sunray, survey, Thursday, today, touché, toupée, Tuesday, two-way, waylay, weekday, x-ray.
Afraid, betrayed, brain fade, bridesmaid, cascade, charade, crusade, decayed, degrade, delayed, dismayed, evade, handmade, homemade, invade, man-made, mermaid, nightshade, nursemaid, obeyed, parade, persuade, ram raid, self-made, today.
Abate, await, berate, birth rate, cheapskate, checkmate, classmate, create, debate, deflate, dictate, estate, fixate, flat-mate, frustrate, helpmate, inflate, irate, jailbait, lightweight, locate, migrate, narrate, ornate, outdate, placate, playmate, portrait, pulsate, relate, rotate, sedate, soulmate, stagnate, stalemate, translate, update, vacate, vibrate.
Arrange, derange, estrange, exchange, short-change.
[3] **A.k.a.**, A-OK, alleyway, anyway, attaché, awayday, breakaway, cabaret, café au lait, castaway, Christmas Day, croupier, disarray, disobey, everyday, exposé, expressway, faraway, fiancé, flyaway, giveaway, getaway, hideaway, holiday, interplay, matinée, Milky Way, motorway, negligee, overlay, overplay, passageway, protégé, ricochet, résumé, runaway, Saturday, stowaway, straightaway, takeaway, tearaway, throwaway, underplay, walk away, wedding day, Wednesday, working day, yesterday.
Barricade, cavalcade, centigrade, colonnade, disarrayed, escapade, lemonade, marmalade, masquerade, not afraid, overcame, overpaid, razor blade, readymade, renegade, ricocheted, serenade, tailor-made, unafraid, underpaid.
Activate, aggravate, alienate, allocate, animate, automate, captivate, celebrate, circulate, complicate, consecrate, concentrate, confiscate, congregate, consummate, contemplate, cultivate, decorate, dedicate, demonstrate, desolate, devastate, deviate, discriminate, dominate, duplicate, educate, elevate, eliminate, emigrate, emulate, escalate, estimate, exterminate, fascinate, fluctuate, generate, graduate, gravitate, heavyweight, hesitate, hibernate, illuminate, illustrate, imitate, implicate, infiltrate, innovate, instigate, interstate, intimate, intricate, inundate, irritate, isolate, liberate, magistrate, mediate, meditate, moderate, motivate, navigate, operate, orchestrate, overstate, overweight, paperweight, penetrate, percolate, procreate, radiate, regulate, relocate, renovate, segregate, separate, simulate, situate, speculate, stimulate, stipulate,

suffocate, syncopate, terminate, tête-à-tête, tolerate, underrate, violate.
Interchange, part-exchange, pre-arrange, rearrange.
[4] Accelerate, accommodate, alienate, alleviate, anticipate, associate, authenticate, certificate, collaborate, communicate, concentrate, congratulate, contaminate, cooperate, corroborate, deteriorate, elaborate, eradicate, evaporate, exaggerate, exasperate, exonerate, hallucinate, humiliate, impersonate, infuriate, intimidate, invigorate, investigate, negotiate, participate, recuperate, refrigerate, reverberate.

1.3.43 "--aining" (as in "raining")
[2] caning, chaining, craning, draining, explaining, feigning, gaining, paining, planing, raining, reigning, reining, spraining, staining, straining, training, waning.
[3] abstaining, attaining, bloodstaining, campaigning, complaining, constraining, containing, detaining, maintaining, obtaining, refraining, remaining, retaining, sustaining.
[4] ascertaining, entertaining.

SURPRISING RHYMING:
[2] **Aiming**, blaming, claiming, flaming, framing, gaming, naming, shaming, taming.
Greying/graying (U.S.), laying, paying, playing, praying, saying, slaying, spraying, staying, straying, swaying, way-in, weighing.
Aiding, fading, grading, raiding, shading, stayed in, wading.
Aping, draping, gaping, scraping, shaping, taping.
Dating, hating, late-in, mating, rating, skating, slating, stating, straight-in, waiting.
[3] **Acclaiming**, defaming, disclaiming, exclaiming, inflaming, proclaiming, reclaiming.
Allaying, betraying, conveying, decaying, deejaying, delaying, dismaying, displaying, downplaying, mislaying, obeying, okaying, outplaying, outstaying, outweighing, portraying, repaying, replaying, sashaying, x-raying.
Cascading, crusading, degrading, downgrading, evading, invading, parading, persuading.
Escaping, landscaping, reshaping.
Awaiting, berating, creating, debating, dictating, fixating, frustrating, narrating, placating, pulsating, relating, stagnating, translating, updating, vacating, vibrating.
[4] **Barricading**, masquerading, serenading.
Disobeying, holidaying, overplaying, ricocheting, underplaying.
Activating, aggravating, alienating, allocating, alternating, animating, captivating, celebrating, circulating, complicating, concentrating, confiscating, congregating, consummating, contemplating, decorating, devastating, discriminating, dominating, educating, eliminating, emigrating, emulating, escalating, estimating, fascinating, fluctuating, generating, graduating, hesitating, hibernating, illustrating, imitating, implicating, indicating, instigating, irritating, levitating, liberating, mediating, meditating, moderating, motivating, orchestrating, overstating, penetrating, percolating, recreating, replicating, segregating, separating, speculating, stimulating, stipulating, suffocating, syncopating, tolerating, understating, vindicating, violating.
[5] **Accelerating**, alienating, alleviating, anticipating, collaborating, communicating, congratulating, contaminating, cooperating, deteriorating, elaborating, exaggerating, exasperating, hallucinating, humiliating, impersonating, infuriating, intimidating, invigorating, investigating, participating, recuperating, refrigerating, reverberating.

1.3.44 "--ained" (as in "chained")
[1] brained, caned, chained, drained, feigned, gained, pained, planed, rained, reigned, sprained, stained, strained, trained, waned.
[2] abstained, arraigned, attained, birdbrained, bloodstained, campaigned, complained, constrained, contained, detained, disdained, explained, lamebrained, maintained, obtained, refrained, regained, remained, restrained, retained, sustained, unchained.
[3] ascertained, entertained, preordained, scatterbrained.

SURPRISING RHYMING:
[1] **Brain**, cane, chain, drain, explain, feign, gain, grain, lain, lane, main, mane, pain, pane, plain, plane, rain, reign, rein, sane, slain, sprain, stain, strain, train, vain, wane.
Aim(ed), blame(d), came, claim(ed), fame(d), flame, frame(d), game, name(d), same, shame(d), tame(d), vain, vein.
Arrange, change, exchange, range, strange.

Bay, clay, day, eh, fray, gay, gray/grey, hay, hey, lay, may, pay, play, pray, prey, ray, say, slay, sleigh, spray, stay, stray, sway, they, tray, way, weigh, yea.
Aid, blade, fade, glade, grade, jade, laid, made, maid, paid, played, prayed, raid, shade, spade, sprayed, stayed, strayed, suede, they'd, wade, weighed.
Ape, cape, drape, gape, grape, nape, scrape, shape, tape, vape.
Ate, bait, crate, date, eight, fate, fête, freight, gate, gait, great, grate, hate, late, mate, plate, rate, skate, slate, spate, state, strait, straight, trait, weight, wait.
[2] Abstain, again, airplane, arcane, attain, birdbrain, bloodstain, campaign, champagne, complain, constrain, contain, detain, domain, explain, humane, lamebrain, maintain, migraine, mundane, obtain, profane, refrain, remain, retain, sustain, terrain.
Acclaim, became, endgame, exclaim, inflame, nickname, proclaim, reclaim, rename.
Airplay, array, astray, away, ballet, beret, betray, birthday, blasé, bouquet, roadway, buffet, café, chalet, cliché, convey, coupé, decay, deejay, delay, dismay, display, doomsday, doorway, downplay, driveway, duvet, fair play, foreplay, forte, foyer, Friday, freeway, gangway, gateway, gourmet, hairspray, halfway, hallway, headway, hearsay, heyday, highway, hombre, hooray, horseplay, hurray, inlay, latté, lamé, mainstay, mayday, melee, midday, midway, mislay, Monday, obey, okay, olé, one day, outlay, outplay, outstay, outweigh, padre, part-way, passé, pathway, payday, portray, railway, reggae, relay, repay, replay, ricochet, risqué, roadway, rosé, runway, sachet, sashay, screenplay, segue, soirée, someday, some way, stairway, subway, Sunday, sunray, survey, Thursday, today, touché, toupée, Tuesday, two-way, waylay, weekday, x-ray.
Afraid, betrayed, brain fade, bridesmaid, cascade, charade, crusade, decayed, degrade, delayed, dismayed, evade, handmade, homemade, invade, man-made, mermaid, nightshade, nursemaid, obeyed, parade, persuade, ram raid, self-made, today.
Escape, landscape, red tape, reshape, shipshape.
Abate, await, berate, birth rate, cheapskate, checkmate, classmate, create, debate, deflate, dictate, estate, fixate, flat-mate, frustrate, helpmate, inflate, irate, jailbait, lightweight, locate, migrate, narrate, ornate, outdate, placate, playmate, portrait, pulsate, relate, rotate, sedate, soulmate, stagnate, stalemate, translate, update, vacate, vibrate.
[3] Entertain, hurricane, inhumane, scatterbrain, sugar cane, windowpane, weathervane.
Counterclaim, overcame.
A.k.a., A-OK, alleyway, anyway, attaché, awayday, breakaway, cabaret, café au lait, castaway, Christmas Day, croupier, disarray, disobey, everyday, exposé, expressway, faraway, fiancé, flyaway, giveaway, getaway, hideaway, holiday, interplay, matinée, Milky Way, motorway, negligee, overlay, overplay, passageway, protégé, ricochet, résumé, runaway, Saturday, stowaway, straightaway, takeaway, tearaway, throwaway, underplay, walk away, wedding day, Wednesday, working day, yesterday.
Barricade, cavalcade, centigrade, colonnade, disarrayed, escapade, lemonade, marmalade, masquerade, not afraid, razor blade, readymade, renegade, ricocheted, serenade, tailor-made, unafraid, underpaid.
Activate, aggravate, alienate, allocate, animate, automate, captivate, celebrate, circulate, complicate, consecrate, concentrate, confiscate, congregate, consummate, contemplate, cultivate, decorate, dedicate, demonstrate, desolate, devastate, deviate, discriminate, dominate, duplicate, educate, elevate, eliminate, emigrate, emulate, escalate, estimate, exterminate, fascinate, fluctuate, generate, graduate, gravitate, heavyweight, hesitate, hibernate, illuminate, illustrate, imitate, implicate, infiltrate, innovate, instigate, interstate, intimate, intricate, inundate, irritate, isolate, liberate, magistrate, mediate, meditate, moderate, motivate, navigate, operate, orchestrate, overstate, overweight, paperweight, penetrate, percolate, procreate, radiate, regulate, relocate, renovate, segregate, separate, simulate, situate, speculate, stimulate, stipulate, suffocate, syncopate, terminate, tête-à-tête, tolerate, underrate, violate.

1.3.45 "--ainful" (as in "painful")
baneful, gainful, painful, disdainful.

SURPRISING RHYMING:
Blameful, careful, changeful, disgraceful, distasteful, fateful, faithful, graceful, grateful, hateful, playful, shameful, unfaithful, ungrateful, wakeful.

1.3.46 "--ainger" (as in "danger")
[2] changer, danger, manger, ranger, stranger.
[3] arranger, endanger, exchanger, shortchanger.

SURPRISING RHYMING:
[2] **Acre**, baker, breaker, faker, maker, shaker, taker, waker.
Fainter, painter, quainter.
Fader, raider, trader, wader.
Frailer, jailer, mailer, paler, sailor, staler, trailer, tailor, wailer.
Chaser, embracer, eraser, facer, lacer, mesa, nature, pacer, racer, tracer.
[3] **Heartbreaker**, icebreaker, lawbreaker, lawmaker, matchmaker, mischief-maker, muckraker, peacemaker, saltshaker, shoemaker, troublemaker, undertaker, watchmaker.
Crusader, degrader, dissuader, evader, first-aider, invader, persuader, teenager.
[4] **Masquerader**, rollerblader, serenader.

1.3.47 "--ainless" (as in "painless")
[2] brainless, chainless, grainless, painless, rainless, stainless.

SURPRISING RHYMING:
[2] **Aimless**, blameless, frameless, graceless, greyness/grayness (U.S.), nameless, plainness, sameness, shameless, tameless, tameness.
Baseless, faceless, graceless, placeless, traceless.

1.3.48 "--ainly" (as in "mainly")
[2] gainly, mainly, plainly, sanely, vainly.
[3] humanely, insanely, mundanely, profanely, ungainly, urbanely.

SURPRISING RHYMING:
[2] **Daily**, gaily, gamely, lamely, namely, tamely.
Brainy, grainy, rainy, zany.
Greatly, lady, lately, shady, shapely, stately.
Dairy, fairy, hairy, prairie, vary, wary.
[3] **Irately**, innately, ornately, sedately.
Airy-fairy, canary, contrary, unwary.

1.3.49 "--ainted" (as in "tainted")
acquainted, fainted, repainted, painted, sainted, tainted.

SURPRISING RHYMING:
[2] **Aided**, bladed, braided, faded, graded, jaded, raided, shaded, traded, waded.
Dated, fated, gated, hated, mated, rated, sated, stated, waited, weighted.
[3] **Cascaded**, degraded, dissuaded, downgraded, evaded, invaded, paraded, persuaded, unaided.
Abated, awaited, belated, berated, checkmated, created, debated, deflated, elated, frustrated, ill-fated, outdated, postdated, related, stalemated, truncated, X-rated.
[4] **Barricaded**, masqueraded, serenaded.
Antiquated, celebrated, complicated, cultivated, dedicated, educated, elevated, fascinated, medicated, saturated, underrated, understated, unrelated, venerated.
[5] **Dilapidated**, evaluated, exaggerated, infatuated, insinuated, opinionated, sophisticated.

1.3.50 "--ainy" (as in "rainy")
[2] brainy, grainy, miscellany, rainy, zany.

SURPRISING RHYMING:
[2] **Daily**, gaily, gamely, gainly, mainly, namely, plainly, sanely, tamely, ukulele, vainly.
Greatly, innately, irately, lately, ornately, sedately, stately.
Baby, crybaby, lady, maybe, shady.
[3] **Humanely**, insanely, mundanely, ungainly, urbanely.

1.3.51 "--ainge" (as in "strange")
[1] change, range, strange.
[2] arrange, derange, estrange, exchange, short-change.
[3] interchange, part-exchange, pre-arrange, rearrange.

SURPRISING RHYMING:
[1] **Changed**, ranged.
Age, cage, gage, gauge, page, rage, sage, stage, wage.
Brain, cane, chain, drain, feign, gain, grain, lain, lane, main, mane, pain, pane, plain, plane, rain, reign, rein, sane, slain, sprain, stain, strain, train, vain, vane, vein, wane.
[2] **Arranged**, deranged, estranged, exchanged, short-changed.
Backstage, birdcage, engage, enrage, offstage, onstage, outrage, rampage, ribcage, space-age, teenage, underage, upstage.
Assuaged, engaged, enraged, outraged, rampaged, unassuaged, unengaged, upstaged.
Abstain, again, airplane, arcane, attain, birdbrain, bloodstain, campaign, champagne, complain, constrain, contain, detain, domain, explain, humane, lamebrain, maintain, migraine, mundane, obtain, profane, refrain, remain(s), retain, sustain, terrain, urbane.
[3] **Disengaged**, part-exchanged, pre-arranged, rearranged.
Entertain, hurricane, inhumane, scatterbrain, sugar cane, windowpane, weathervane.

1.3.52 "--ainging" (as in "changing")
[2] changing, ranging.
[3] arranging, deranging, estranging, exchanging, shortchanging, unchanging.
[4] part-exchanging, pre-arranging, rearranging.

SURPRISING RHYMING:
[2] **Ageing**, changeling, gauging, paging, raging, staging, waging.
Aiding, grading, fading, raiding, trading, shading, wading.
Dating, fainting, hating, mating, painting, skating, slating, stating, tainting, waiting.
Caning, chaining, craning, draining, explaining, feigning, gaining, paining, raining, reigning, reining, spraining, staining, straining, training, waning.
Braving, caving, craving, paving, raving, saving, shaving, slaving, waiving, waving.
Blazing, fazing, gazing, grazing, hazing, lazing, phasing, phrasing, praising, raising.
Basing, bracing, chasing, facing, lacing, pacing, placing, racing, spacing, tracing.
Ailing, failing, hailing, jailing, mailing, nailing, sailing, tailing, trailing, veiling, wailing.
Aiming, blaming, claiming, flaming, framing, gaming, naming, shaming, taming.
Aching, baking, braking, breaking, faking, making, quaking, shaking, taking, waking.
Bathing, plaything, scathing.
Graying/greying (U.S.), laying, paying, playing, praying, preying, saying, slaying, spraying, staying, straying, swaying, weighing.
[3] **Assuaging**, engaging, enraging, rampaging, upstaging.
Degrading, invading, blockading, parading, persuading, cascading, evading, dissuading.
Awaiting, berating, creating, debating, dictating, frustrating, migrating, narrating, placating, pulsating, relating, stagnating, translating, updating, vacating, vibrating.
Abstaining, attaining, bloodstaining, campaigning, complaining, containing, detaining, explaining, maintaining, obtaining, refraining, remaining, retaining, sustaining.
Behaving, depraving, engraving, enslaving, lifesaving, time-saving.
Blackmailing, curtailing, entailing, exhaling, inhaling, prevailing, unfailing, unveiling.
Amazing, appraising, erasing, fundraising, hellraising, stargazing, trailblazing.
Defacing, displacing, embracing, erasing, misplacing, replacing, retracing, showcasing.
Defaming, exclaiming, inflaming, nicknaming, proclaiming, reclaiming, renaming.
Awaking, backbreaking, breathtaking, earthshaking, forsaking, heartbreaking, lovemaking, matchmaking, mistaking, painstaking, peacemaking, troublemaking, undertaking.
Anything, enabling, labeling.
Betraying, decaying, deejaying, delaying, dismaying, disobeying, displaying, downplaying, holidaying, obeying, outweighing, overpaying, overstaying, portraying, relaying, replaying, ricocheting, sashaying, soothsaying, x-raying.
[4] **Fascinating**, graduating, humiliating, infuriating, initiating, insinuating, mediating, nauseating, navigating, penetrating, radiating, recreating, underrating, understating.

[5] **Abbreviating**, alleviating, appreciating, associating, discriminating, evacuating, negotiating, perpetuating, retaliating, substantiating.

1.3.53 "--ainment" (as in "attainment")
[3] arraignment, attainment, containment, detainment, entertainment, ordainment.

SURPRISING RHYMING:
[2] **Ailment**, amazement, basement, blatant, claimant, flagrant, fragrant, latent, patent, patient, payment, pavement, placement, statement, vagrant.
[3] **Abatement**, adjacent, arrangement, complacent, displacement, engagement, escapement, impatient, reinstatement, repayment, replacement, understatement.

1.3.54 "--aint" (as in "paint")
[1] ain't, faint, feint, paint, quaint, saint, taint.
[2] acquaint, complaint, constraint, greasepaint, repaint, restraint, spray-paint, war-paint.

SURPRISING RHYMING:
[1] **Brain**, cane(d), chain(ed), drain(ed), feign(ed), gain(ed), lain, lane, main, mane, pain(ed), pane, plain, plane, rain(ed), reign(ed), rein, sane, slain, sprain(ed), stain(ed), strain(ed), train(ed), vain, vein, wane(d).
Aim, blame, came, claim, fame, flame, frame, game, name, same, shame, tame, vain.
Aimed, blamed, claimed, famed, flamed, framed, named, shamed, tamed, veined.
Ate, bait, crate, date, eight, fate, fête, freight, gate, gait, great, grate, hate, late, mate, plate, rate, skate, slate, spate, state, strait, straight, trait, weight, wait.
[2] **Abstain**, again, airplane, arcane, attain, birdbrain, bloodstain, campaign, champagne, complain, constrain, contain, detain, domain, explain, humane, lamebrain, maintain, migraine, mundane, obtain, profane, refrain, remain(s), retain, sustain, terrain.
Abstained, arraigned, attained, birdbrained, bloodstained, complained, constrained, contained, detained, explained, lamebrained, maintained, obtained, refrained, regained, remained, restrained, retained, sustained, unchained.
Acclaim, became, endgame, exclaim, inflame, nickname, proclaim, reclaim, surname.
Abate, await, berate, birth rate, cheapskate, checkmate, classmate, create, debate, deflate, dictate, estate, fixate, flat-mate, frustrate, helpmate, inflate, irate, jailbait, lightweight, locate, migrate, narrate, ornate, outdate, placate, playmate, portrait, pulsate, relate, rotate, sedate, soulmate, stagnate, stalemate, translate, update, vacate, vibrate.
[3] **Entertain**, hurricane, inhumane, overcame, scatterbrain, windowpane, weathervane.
Activate, aggravate, alienate, allocate, animate, automate, captivate, celebrate, circulate, complicate, consecrate, concentrate, confiscate, congregate, consummate, contemplate, cultivate, decorate, dedicate, demonstrate, desolate, devastate, deviate, discriminate, dominate, duplicate, educate, elevate, eliminate, emigrate, emulate, escalate, estimate, exterminate, fascinate, fluctuate, generate, graduate, gravitate, heavyweight, hesitate, hibernate, illuminate, illustrate, imitate, implicate, infiltrate, innovate, instigate, interstate, intimate, intricate, inundate, irritate, isolate, liberate, magistrate, mediate, meditate, moderate, motivate, navigate, operate, orchestrate, overstate, overweight, paperweight, penetrate, percolate, procreate, radiate, regulate, relocate, renovate, segregate, separate, simulate, situate, speculate, stimulate, stipulate, suffocate, syncopate, terminate, tête-à-tête, tolerate, underrate, violate.
[4] **Accelerate**, accommodate, alienate, alleviate, anticipate, associate, authenticate, certificate, collaborate, communicate, concentrate, congratulate, contaminate, cooperate, corroborate, deteriorate, elaborate, eradicate, evaporate, exaggerate, exasperate, exonerate, hallucinate, humiliate, impersonate, infuriate, intimidate, invigorate, investigate, negotiate, participate, recuperate, refrigerate, reverberate.

1.3.55 "--ainfully" (as in "painfully")
banefully, gainfully, painfully, disdainfully.

SURPRISING RHYMING:
Delightfully, eventually, faithfully, fatefully, finally, gracefully, gratefully, hatefully, respectfully, tastefully, wastefully.

1.3.56 "--ape" (as in "grape")
[1] ape, cape, crepe, drape, gape, grape, nape, scrape, shape, tape, vape.
[2] escape, landscape, red tape, reshape, shipshape.
[3] cityscape, sellotape, ticker tape.

SURPRISING RHYMING:
[1] **Ate**, bait, crate, date, eight, fate, fête, freight, gate, gait, great, grate, hate, late, mate, plate, rate, skate, slate, spate, state, strait, straight, trait, weight, wait.
Ache, bake, brake, break, cake, fake, flake, lake, make, quake, rake, sake, shake, sheik, snake, stake, steak, take, wake.
Aid, blade, fade, glade, grade, jade, laid, made, maid, paid, played, prayed, raid, shade, spade, sprayed, stayed, strayed, suede, they'd, wade, weighed.
[2] **Abate**, await, berate, birth rate, cheapskate, checkmate, classmate, create, debate, deflate, dictate, estate, fixate, flat-mate, frustrate, helpmate, inflate, irate, jailbait, lightweight, locate, migrate, narrate, ornate, outdate, placate, playmate, portrait, pulsate, relate, rotate, sedate, soulmate, stagnate, stalemate, translate, update, vacate, vibrate.
Awake, backache, beefcake, beefsteak, cheesecake, cornflake, cupcake, daybreak, earache, earthquake, firebreak, footbrake, forsake, fruitcake, grubstake, handbrake, handshake, headache, heartache, heartbreak, jailbreak, keepsake, milkshake, mistake, moonquake, muckrake, namesake, opaque, outbreak, outtake, pancake, partake, snowflake, sunbake, sweepstake, toothache, unmake, uptake, windbreak.
Afraid, betrayed, brain fade, bridesmaid, cascade, charade, crusade, decayed, degrade, delayed, dismayed, evade, handmade, homemade, invade, man-made, mermaid, nightshade, nursemaid, obeyed, parade, persuade, ram raid, self-made, today.
[3] **Activate**, aggravate, alienate, allocate, animate, automate, captivate, celebrate, circulate, complicate, consecrate, concentrate, confiscate, congregate, consummate, contemplate, cultivate, decorate, dedicate, demonstrate, desolate, devastate, deviate, discriminate, dominate, duplicate, educate, elevate, eliminate, emigrate, emulate, escalate, estimate, exterminate, fascinate, fluctuate, generate, graduate, gravitate, heavyweight, hesitate, hibernate, illuminate, illustrate, imitate, implicate, infiltrate, innovate, instigate, interstate, intimate, intricate, inundate, irritate, isolate, liberate, magistrate, mediate, meditate, moderate, motivate, navigate, operate, orchestrate, overstate, overweight, paperweight, penetrate, percolate, procreate, radiate, regulate, relocate, renovate, segregate, separate, simulate, situate, speculate, stimulate, stipulate, suffocate, syncopate, terminate, tête-à-tête, tolerate, underrate, violate.
Overtake, rattlesnake, stomachache, undertake, wide-awake.
Barricade, cavalcade, centigrade, colonnade, disarrayed, escapade, lemonade, marmalade, masquerade, not afraid, overpaid, razor blade, readymade, renegade, ricochet, ricocheted, serenade, tailor-made, unafraid, underpaid.
[4] **Accelerate**, accommodate, alienate, alleviate, anticipate, associate, authenticate, certificate, collaborate, communicate, concentrate, congratulate, contaminate, cooperate, corroborate, deteriorate, elaborate, eradicate, evaporate, exaggerate, exasperate, exonerate, hallucinate, humiliate, impersonate, infuriate, intimidate, invigorate, investigate, negotiate, participate, recuperate, refrigerate, reverberate.

1.3.57 "--aped" (as in "shaped")
[1] aped, caped, draped, gaped, scraped, shaped, taped, vaped.
[2] escaped, reshaped.
[3] sellotaped, videotaped.

SURPRISING RHYMING:
[1] **Ape**, cape, drape, gape, grape, scrape, shape, tape, vape.
[2] **Abate**, await, berate, birth rate, cheapskate, checkmate, classmate, create, debate, deflate, dictate, estate, fixate, flat-mate, frustrate, helpmate, inflate, irate, jailbait, lightweight, locate, migrate, narrate, ornate, outdate, placate, playmate, portrait, pulsate, relate, rotate, sedate, soulmate, stagnate, stalemate, translate, update, vacate, vibrate.
Awake, backache, beefcake, beefsteak, cheesecake, cornflake, cupcake, daybreak, earache, earthquake, firebreak, footbrake, forsake, fruitcake, grubstake, handbrake,

handshake, headache, heartache, heartbreak, jailbreak, keepsake, milkshake, mistake, moonquake, muckrake, namesake, opaque, outbreak, outtake, pancake, partake, snowflake, sunbake, sweepstake, toothache, unmake, uptake, windbreak.
Afraid, betrayed, brain fade, bridesmaid, cascade, charade, crusade, decayed, degrade, delayed, dismayed, evade, handmade, homemade, invade, man-made, mermaid, nightshade, nursemaid, obeyed, parade, persuade, ram raid, self-made, today.
[3] Activate, aggravate, alienate, allocate, animate, automate, captivate, celebrate, circulate, complicate, consecrate, concentrate, confiscate, congregate, consummate, contemplate, cultivate, decorate, dedicate, demonstrate, desolate, devastate, deviate, discriminate, dominate, duplicate, educate, elevate, eliminate, emigrate, emulate, escalate, estimate, exterminate, fascinate, fluctuate, generate, graduate, gravitate, heavyweight, hesitate, hibernate, illuminate, illustrate, imitate, implicate, infiltrate, innovate, instigate, interstate, intimate, intricate, inundate, irritate, isolate, liberate, magistrate, mediate, meditate, moderate, motivate, navigate, operate, orchestrate, overstate, overweight, paperweight, penetrate, percolate, procreate, radiate, regulate, relocate, renovate, segregate, separate, simulate, situate, speculate, stimulate, stipulate, suffocate, syncopate, terminate, tête-à-tête, tolerate, underrate, violate.
Overtake, rattlesnake, stomachache, undertake, wide-awake.
Barricade, cavalcade, centigrade, colonnade, disarrayed, escapade, lemonade, marmalade, masquerade, not afraid, overpaid, razor blade, readymade, renegade, ricocheted, serenade, tailor-made, unafraid.
[4] Accelerate, accommodate, alienate, alleviate, anticipate, associate, authenticate, certificate, collaborate, communicate, concentrate, congratulate, contaminate, cooperate, corroborate, deteriorate, elaborate, eradicate, evaporate, exaggerate, exasperate, exonerate, hallucinate, humiliate, impersonate, infuriate, intimidate, invigorate, investigate, negotiate, participate, recuperate, refrigerate, reverberate.

1.3.58 "--aper" (as in "paper")
[2] caper, draper, gaper, paper, scraper, shaper, taper, vaper, vapour/vapor (U.S.).
[3] escaper, flypaper, notepaper, newspaper, sandpaper, skyscraper, wallpaper.

SURPRISING RHYMING:
[2] **Cater,** crater, data, dater, grater, greater, hater, later, skater, slater, traitor, waiter.
Acre, baker, breaker, faker, maker, nature, shaker, taker, waker.
Blazer, chaser, eraser, gazer, laser, mesa, nature, pacer, placer, praiser, racer, raiser, razor, spacer, tracer, Taser.
Fader, raider, trader, wader.
Changer, danger, manger, ranger, stranger.
Frailer, jailer, mailer, paler, sailor, staler, trailer, tailor, scaler, wailer, whaler.
Greyer/grayer (U.S.), layer, mayor, payer, player, prayer, stayer, strayer, sprayer.
Braver, craver, favour/favor (U.S.), flavour/flavor (U.S.), graver, paver, raver, saver, savour/savor (U.S.), shaver, waiver, waver.
[3] Creator, curator, debater, dictator, equator, narrator, rotator, spectator, translator.
Bookmaker, caretaker, dressmaker, heartbreaker, icebreaker, lawbreaker, lawmaker, matchmaker, mischief-maker, muckraker, peacemaker, saltshaker, shoemaker, strikebreaker, troublemaker, undertaker, watchmaker.
Fundraiser, hellraiser, stargazer, trailblazer.
Crusader, degrader, dissuader, evader, first-aider, invader, persuader.
Arranger, endanger, exchanger, shortchanger.
Abseiler, blackmailer, exhale, inhaler, loudhailer, regaler, retailer, wholesaler.
Betrayer, bricklayer, delayer, displayer, portrayer, purveyor, soothsayer, taxpayer.
Defacer, embracer, eraser, horse-racer, misplacer, replacer, retracer, steeplechaser.
Depraver, disfavour/disfavor (U.S.), engraver, lifesaver, timesaver.
Container, remainder, remainer, retainer.
[4+] Accelerator, agitator, alligator, animator, aviator, calculator, collaborator, commentator, decorator, educator, elevator, escalator, generator, gladiator, illustrator, imitator, impersonator, indicator, instigator, interrogator, investigator, liberator, mediator, negotiator, operator, percolator, perpetrator, refrigerator, speculator, terminator, ventilator.
Masquerader, rollerblader, serenader.

1.3.59 "--aping" (as in "shaping")
[2] aping, draping, gaping, scraping, shaping, taping.
[3] escaping, landscaping, reshaping, skyscraping.

SURPRISING RHYMING:
[2] **Dating**, grating, hating, skating, slating, waiting.
Aching, baking, breaking, faking, making, raking, shaking, staking, taking, waking.
Blazing, erasing, gazing, grazing, lazing, praising, phrasing, raising.
Fading, raiding, trading, wading.
Jailing, mailing, sailing, trailing, scaling, wailing, whaling.
Laying, paying, playing, praying, slaying, staying, straying, weighing.
Bracing, changing, chasing, facing, pacing, placing, racing, ranging, spacing, tracing.
Braving, craving, paving, raving, saving, shaving, waiving, waving.
[3] **Creating**, curating, debating, dictating, locating, narrating, spectating, vibrating.
Bookmaking, caretaking, dressmaking, forsaking, heartbreaking, icebreaking, lawbreaking, lawmaking, matchmaking, mischief-making, muckraking, painstaking, peacemaking, troublemaking, undertaking.
Appraising, fundraising, hellraising, stargazing, trailblazing.
Crusading, degrading, dissuading, evading, first-aiding, invading, persuading.
Arranging, containing, exchanging, remaining, retaining, shortchanging.
Abseiling, blackmailing, exhaling, inhaling, regaling, retailing.
Betraying, bricklaying, conveying, delaying, displaying, portraying, soothsaying.
Defacing, embracing, encasing, erasing, horse-racing, misplacing, replacing, retracing.
Depraving, engraving, enslaving, lifesaving, timesaving.
[4+] **Accelerating**, agitating, animating, calculating, collaborating, decorating, delegating, demonstrating, educating, escalating, generating, illustrating, imitating, impersonating, indicating, instigating, interrogating, investigating, liberating, mediating, moderating, percolating, perpetrating, radiating, simulating, speculating, stimulating, violating.
Masquerading, rollerblading, serenading.

1.3.60 "--air" (as in "care")
[1] air, bear, bare, blare, care, chair, dare, fare, fair, flair, flare, glare, hair, hare, heir, lair, mare, ne're, pair, pare, pear, prayer, rare, scare, share, snare, spare, square, stair, stare, swear, tear, there, their, they're, where, ware, wear, yeah.
[2] affair, airfare, armchair, au pair, aware, beware, bugbear, childcare, compare, compère, deckchair, declare, despair, éclair, elsewhere, ensnare, fanfare, footwear, forbear, funfair, glassware, hardware, haircare, impair, knitwear, longhair, mayor, menswear, mid-air, mohair, neckwear, nightmare, nightwear, nowhere, outstare, prayer, premiere, prepare, pushchair, repair, shorthair, skincare, software, somewhere, swimwear, threadbare, timeshare, unfair, warfare, welfare, wheelchair.
[3] aftercare, anywhere, billionaire, cafetière, charge d'affaires, chemin de fer, debonair, disrepair, everywhere, kitchenware, Medicare, millionaire, open-air, overbear, pied-a-terre, questionnaire, ready-to-wear, rocking chair, savoir-faire, solitaire, tableware, thoroughfare, unaware, underwear, well-aware.

SURPRISING RHYMING:
[1] **Aired**, bared, blared, cared, dared, fared, flared, glared, laird, paired, scared, shared, snared, spared, squared, stared.
[2] **Blonde-haired**, compared, compèred, declared, despaired, ensnared, gray-haired/grey-haired, impaired, longhaired, prepared, red-haired, repaired, shorthaired.
[3] **Open-aired**, unprepared, unimpaired.

1.3.61 "--aired" (as in "scared")
[1] aired, bared, blared, cared, dared, fared, flared, glared, paired, scared, shared, snared, spared, squared, stared.
[2] blonde-haired, compared, compèred, declared, despaired, grey-haired/gray-haired, ensnared, impaired, longhaired, prepared, red-haired, repaired, shorthaired.
[3] open-aired, unprepared, unimpaired.

SURPRISING RHYMING:
[1] **Air**, bear, bare, blare, care, chair, dare, fare, fair, flair, flare, glare, hair, hare, heir, lair, mare, ne're, pair, pare, pear, prayer, rare, scare, share, snare, spare, square, stair, stare, swear, tear, there, their, they're, where, ware, wear, yeah.
[2] **Affair**, airfare, armchair, au pair, aware, beware, bugbear, childcare, compare, compère, deckchair, declare, despair, elsewhere, ensnare, fanfare, footwear, funfair, glassware, hardware, haircare, impair, knitwear, longhair, mayor, menswear, mid-air, mohair, nightmare, nowhere, prayer, premiere, prepare, pushchair, repair, shorthair, skincare, software, somewhere, swimwear, threadbare, timeshare, unfair, warfare, welfare, wheelchair.
[3] **Aftercare**, anywhere, billionaire, cafetière, charge d'affaires, chemin de fer, debonair, disrepair, everywhere, kitchenware, Medicare, millionaire, open-air, overbear, pied-a-terre, questionnaire, ready-to-wear, rocking chair, savoir-faire, solitaire, tableware, thoroughfare, unaware, underwear, well-aware.

1.3.62 "--airest" (as in "fairest")
[2] barest, fairest, rarest.

SURPRISING RHYMING:
[1] **Best**, blessed, breast, chest, crest, dressed, guest, jest, nest, pest, quest, rest, test, vest, west, wrest, zest.
[2] **Airless**, careless, fairness, hairless, heirless, stairless.
Baseless, faceless, graceless, placeless, traceless.
Abreast, armrest, bequest, conquest, contest, digest, divest, headrest, northwest, protest, unrest, southwest, suggest.
Addressed, confessed, depressed, digressed, duress, impressed, obsessed, oppressed, princess, progress, protest, success, well-dressed.
[3] **Awareness**, manifest, overdressed, second-best, self-addressed, self-confessed, self-possessed, unaddressed, unfairness, unimpressed.

1.3.63 "--airful" (as in "careful")
careful, prayerful, overcareful.

SURPRISING RHYMING:
[2] **Blameful**, disgraceful, fateful, faithful, gainful, graceful, grateful, hateful, painful, playful, shameful, wakeful.
[3] **Disdainful**, distasteful, unfaithful, ungrateful.

1.3.64 "--airing" (as in "caring")
[2] airing, bearing, blaring, caring, daring, faring, flaring, glaring, pairing, raring, scaring, sharing, snaring, sparing, staring, swearing, tearing, wearing.
[3] declaring, despairing, impairing, repairing, seafaring, time-sharing, wayfaring.

SURPRISING RHYMING:
[2] **Blazing**, fazing, gazing, grazing, hazing, lazing, phasing, phrasing, praising, raising.
Favouring/favoring (U.S.), flavouring/flavoring (U.S.), savouring/savoring (U.S.), wavering.
Changing, gee-string, keyring, offspring, ranging.
[3] **Amazing**, appraising, erasing, fundraising, hellraising, stargazing, trailblazing.
Arranging, deranging, estranging, exchanging, shortchanging, unchanging.

1.3.65 "--airless" (as in "careless")
[2] airless, careless, hairless, heirless, stairless.

SURPRISING RHYMING:
[2] **Awareness**, fairness, heiress.
Faceless, faithless, tasteless.
Aimless, blameless, brainless, nameless, painless, plainness, sameness, shameless, stainless, tameness.
Access, address, confess, distress, duress, excess, express, impress, largesse,

noblesse, obsess, possess, princess, process, progress, solace, success, unless.
Endless, friendless, necklace, reckless, selfless.
Greatness, lateness, paleness, waitress.
[3] **Acquiesce**, S.O.S., convalesce, nonetheless, nevertheless.

1.3.66 "--airly" (as in "fairly")
[2] barely, fairly, rarely, squarely, unfairly.

SURPRISING RHYMING:
[2] **Carefree**, dairy, fairy, hairy, prairie, scary, vary, wary.
[3] **Airy-fairy**, canary, contrary, unwary.

1.3.67 "--airness" (as in "fairness")
awareness, bareness, fairness, rareness, unfairness.

SURPRISING RHYMING:
[1] **Best**, bless, blessed, breast, chest, crest, dressed, guest, jest, nest, pest, quest, rest, stressed, test, vest, west, wrest, zest.
[2] **Barest**, fairest, rarest.
Airless, careless, greatness, hairless, heiress, heirless, stairless.
Abreast, armrest, bequest, conquest, contest, digest, divest, footrest, headrest, northwest, protest, request, road test, southwest, suggest, unrest.
Addressed, confessed, depressed, digressed, duress, expressed, impressed, obsessed, oppressed, princess, possessed, progress, protest, success, well-dressed.
[3] **Manifest**, overdressed, second-best, self-addressed, self-confessed, self-possessed, unaddressed, unexpressed, unimpressed.
Acquiesce, S.O.S., convalesce, nonetheless, nevertheless.
Bitterness, slenderness, tenderness, togetherness, wilderness.

1.3.68 "--airy" (as in "scary")
[2] airy, dairy, fairy, hairy, prairie, scary, vary, wary.
[3] airy-fairy, canary, contrary, rosemary, unwary.

SURPRISING RHYMING:
[2] **Barely**, fairly, rarely, squarely, unfairly.
Carefree, guarantee, jamboree, marquee.
Brainy, grainy, miscellany, rainy, zany.
Gainly, mainly, plainly, sanely, vainly.
Daily, gaily, ukulele.
Greatly, innately, irately, lately, ornately, sedately, stately.
Baby, crybaby, lady, maybe, shady.
Crazy, daisy, hazy, lazy, pastry.
[3] **Humanely**, insanely, mundanely, ungainly, urbanely.
Stir-crazy, oops-a-daisy, upsy-daisy.

1.3.69 "--airable" (as in "bearable")
bearable, comparable, shareable, tearable, wearable, unbearable, repairable, untearable, unwearable.

SURPRISING RHYMING:
Aerial, fallible, gullible, horrible, interval, proverbial, regrettable, respectable, terrible.
Breakable, debatable, mistakeable, unbreakable, unmistakable, unshakeable.
Available, capable, incapable, inescapable, saleable, sailable, unavailable, unassailable.
Attainable, explainable, obtainable.
Agreeable, foreseeable, disagreeable, unforeseeable.
Beddable, credible, edible, incredible.
Commendable, dependable, expendable, mendable, recommendable.
Identifiable, justifiable, notifiable.
Eventual, gradual, sensual, casual, visual, virtual, mutual, punctual, sexual.

Casual, continual, conventional, eventual, gradual, memorial, mutual, perpetual, pictorial, sensual, sexual, unusual, usual, virtual, visual.

1.3.70 "--aringly (as in "daringly")
blaringly, caringly, daringly, despairingly, flaringly, glaringly, sparingly, uncaringly.

SURPRISING RHYMING:
[3] **Carefully**, faithfully, gracefully, painfully, playfully, shamefully, wakefully, wastefully.
Achingly, quakingly, snakingly, takingly.
Fatefully, gratefully, hatefully.
[4] **Amazingly**, breathtakingly, earthshakingly, frustratingly, heartbreakingly, painstakingly.
Degradingly, disgracefully, distastefully, eventually, finally, reassuringly, respectfully, tastefully, unfailingly, unfaithfully.

1.3.71 "--asing" (as in "chasing")
[1] bracing, casing, chasing, facing, lacing, pacing, placing, racing, spacing, tracing.
[2] backspacing, debasing, defacing, disgracing, displacing, effacing, embracing, encasing, erasing, horse-racing, misplacing, outpacing, replacing, retracing, showcasing.
[3] interfacing, steeplechasing.

SURPRISING RHYMING:
[2] **Blazing**, gazing, grazing, lazing, praising, phrasing, raising.
Fading, raiding, trading, wading.
Jailing, mailing, paling, sailing, trailing, scaling, wailing, whaling.
Laying, paying, playing, praying, slaying, staying, straying, weighing.
Braving, craving, paving, raving, saving, shaving, waiving, waving.
[3] **Appraising**, fundraising, hellraising, stargazing, trailblazing.
Crusading, degrading, dissuading, evading, first-aiding, invading, persuading.
Abseiling, blackmailing, exhaling, inhaling, regaling, retailing.
Betraying, conveying, delaying, displaying, portraying, purveying, soothsaying, taxpaying.
Depraving, engraving, enslaving, lifesaving, timesaving.
Creating, curating, debating, dictating, locating, narrating, rotating, spectating, vibrating.
[4+] **Accelerating**, agitating, animating, calculating, collaborating, decorating, delegating, demonstrating, educating, escalating, generating, illustrating, imitating, impersonating, indicating, instigating, interrogating, investigating, liberating, mediating, moderating, percolating, perpetrating, radiating, simulating, speculating, stimulating, violating.
Masquerading, rollerblading, serenading.

1.3.72 "--ate" (as in "date")
[1] ate, bait, crate, date, eight, fate, fête, freight, gate, gait, great, grate, hate, late, mate, plate, rate, skate, slate, spate, state, strait, straight, trait, weight, wait.
[2] abate, airfreight, await, be late, berate, birth rate, cheapskate, checkmate, classmate, collate, create, debate, deflate, dictate, elate, estate, fixate, flat-mate, frustrate, gyrate, helpmate, inflate, innate, instate, irate, jailbait, lightweight, locate, magnate, migrate, mutate, narrate, ornate, outdate, placate, playmate, portrait, postdate, predate, pulsate, rebate, relate, rotate, sedate, soulmate, stagnate, stalemate, template, translate, update, vacate, vibrate.
[3] abdicate, activate, adulate, advocate, aggravate, aggregate, agitate, alienate, allocate, alternate, animate, automate, calculate, candidate, captivate, celebrate, circulate, complicate, consecrate, concentrate, confiscate, congregate, consummate, contemplate, correlate, culminate, cultivate, decorate, dedicate, delegate, demonstrate, designate, desolate, devastate, deviate, discriminate, dislocate, dominate, duplicate, educate, elevate, eliminate, emigrate, emulate, escalate, estimate, excavate, exterminate, extricate, fabricate, fascinate, fluctuate, formulate, generate, graduate, granulate, gravitate, heavyweight, hesitate, hibernate, hyphenate, illuminate, illustrate, imitate, implicate, incubate, indicate, infiltrate, innovate, instigate, insulate, integrate, interstate, intimate, intricate, inundate, irrigate, irritate, isolate, legislate, levitate, liberate, liquidate, litigate, lubricate, magistrate, mediate, meditate, moderate, motivate, navigate, obligate, operate, orchestrate, overrate, overstate, overweight, paperweight, penetrate,

percolate, permeate, perpetuate, pollinate, populate, procreate, propagate, punctuate, radiate, re-create, regulate, reinstate, relegate, relocate, renovate, replicate, salivate, saturate, segregate, separate, simulate, situate, speculate, stimulate, stipulate, suffocate, syncopate, syndicate, terminate, tête-à-tête, tolerate, triplicate, underrate, understate, underweight, validate, ventilate, vindicate, violate.
[4] accelerate, accommodate, alienate, alleviate, anticipate, associate, authenticate, certificate, collaborate, communicate, concentrate, congratulate, contaminate, cooperate, coordinate, corroborate, depreciate, deteriorate, elaborate, eradicate, evaporate, exaggerate, exasperate, exonerate, facilitate, hallucinate, humiliate, impersonate, infuriate, initiate, infatuate, intimidate, invigorate, investigate, necessitate, negotiate, orientate, participate, recuperate, refrigerate, remunerate, reverberate.

SURPRISING RHYMING:
[1] **Bay**, clay, day, eh, fray, gay, gray/grey, hay, hey, lay, may, pay, play, pray, prey, ray, say, slay, sleigh, spray, stay, stray, sway, they, tray, way, weigh, yea.
Aid, blade, fade, glade, grade, jade, laid, made, maid, paid, played, prayed, raid, shade, spade, sprayed, stayed, strayed, suede, they'd, wade, weighed.
Aim, blame, came, claim, fame, flame, frame, game, name, same, shame, tame, vain.
Ape, cape, drape, gape, grape, nape, scrape, shape, tape, vape.
Brain, cane, chain, drain, feign, gain, grain, lain, lane, main, mane, pain, pane, plain, plane, rain, reign, rein, sane, slain, sprain, stain, strain, train, vain, vane, vein, wane.
[2] **Airplay**, array, astray, away, ballet, beret, betray, birthday, blasé, bouquet, roadway, buffet, café, chalet, cliché, convey, coupé, decay, deejay, delay, dismay, display, doomsday, doorway, downplay, driveway, duvet, fair play, foreplay, forte, foyer, Friday, freeway, gangway, gateway, gourmet, hairspray, halfway, hallway, headway, hearsay, heyday, highway, hombre, hooray, horseplay, hurray, inlay, latté, lamé, mainstay, mayday, melee, midday, midway, mislay, Monday, obey, okay, olé, one day, outlay, outplay, outstay, outweigh, padre, part-way, passé, pathway, payday, portray, railway, reggae, relay, repay, replay, ricochet, risqué, roadway, rosé, runway, sachet, sashay, screenplay, segue, soirée, someday, some way, stairway, subway, Sunday, sunray, survey, Thursday, today, touché, toupée, Tuesday, two-way, weekday, x-ray.
Afraid, betrayed, brain fade, bridesmaid, cascade, charade, crusade, decayed, degrade, delayed, dismayed, evade, handmade, homemade, invade, man-made, mermaid, nightshade, nursemaid, obeyed, parade, persuade, ram raid, self-made, today.
Acclaim, became, disclaim, endgame, exclaim, inflame, nickname, proclaim, surname.
Escape, landscape, red tape, reshape, shipshape.
Abstain, again, airplane, arcane, attain, birdbrain, bloodstain, campaign, champagne, complain, constrain, contain, detain, domain, explain, humane, lamebrain, maintain, migraine, mundane, obtain, profane, refrain, remain(s), retain, sustain, terrain, urbane.
[3] **A.k.a**., A-OK, alleyway, anyway, attaché, awayday, breakaway, cabaret, café au lait, castaway, Christmas Day, croupier, disarray, disobey, everyday, exposé, expressway, faraway, fiancé, flyaway, giveaway, getaway, hideaway, holiday, interplay, matinée, Milky Way, motorway, negligee, overlay, overplay, passageway, protégé, ricochet, résumé, runaway, Saturday, stowaway, straightaway, takeaway, tearaway, throwaway, underplay, walk away, wedding day, Wednesday, working day, yesterday.
Cavalcade, centigrade, disarrayed, escapade, lemonade, marmalade, masquerade, not afraid, overpaid, razor blade, readymade, renegade, ricocheted, serenade, tailor-made.
Aeroplane, ascertain, entertain, hurricane, inhumane, novocaine, preordain, scatterbrain, sugar cane, windowpane, weathervane.

1.3.73 "--ated" (as in "dated")
[2] bated, baited, crated, dated, fated, gated, gaited, grated, hated, mated, plated, rated, sated, stated, waited, weighted.
[3] abated, awaited, belated, berated, checkmated, created, cremated, debated, deflated, elated, frustrated, gyrated, hydrated, ill-fated, inflated, instated, outdated, postdated, predated, related, stalemated, truncated, X-rated.
[4] antiquated, calculated, celebrated, complicated, cultivated, dedicated, dehydrated, educated, elevated, elongated, fascinated, gravitated, hyphenated, medicated, perforated, reinstated, saturated, simulated, unabated, underrated, understated, unrelated, venerated.

[5] coordinated, dilapidated, evaluated, exaggerated, incorporated, infatuated, insinuated, opinionated, premeditated, sophisticated, unmitigated.

SURPRISING RHYMING:
[1] **Bed**, dead, fed, head, lead, led, fled, sled, sped, red, read, bread, bred, dread, spread, shred, tread, thread, said, shed, stead, wed.
[2] **Aided**, faded, graded, jaded, raided, shaded, spaded, waded.
Airhead, co-ed, deathbed, instead, misled, well-fed, well-read.
[3] **Cascaded**, degraded, downgraded, evaded, invaded, paraded, persuaded.
Figurehead, go-ahead, loggerhead, letterhead, overhead.
[4] **Barricaded**, cavalcaded, masqueraded, serenaded.

1.3.74 "--ayter" (as in "later")
[2] cater, crater, data, dater, grater, greater, hater, later, skater, slater, traitor, waiter.
[3] collator, creator, curator, debater, dictator, equator, freighter, gyrator, locator, narrator, rotator, spectator, translator, vibrator.
[4+] accelerator, agitator, alligator, animator, aviator, calculator, collaborator, commentator, coordinator, decorator, delegator, demonstrator, detonator, educator, elevator, escalator, excavator, exterminator, generator, gladiator, illustrator, imitator, impersonator, incinerator, incubator, indicator, instigator, interrogator, investigator, liberator, liquidator, mediator, moderator, navigator, negotiator, operator, percolator, perpetrator, radiator, refrigerator, regulator, speculator, stimulator, terminator, violator.

SURPRISING RHYMING:
[2] **Blazer**, chaser, gazer, laser, nature, pacer, placer, praiser, racer, razor, tracer.
Caper, paper, scraper, shaper, vapour/vapor (U.S.).
Fader, grader, raider, trader, wader.
Acre, baker, breaker, faker, maker, nature, shaker, taker.
[3] **Embracer**, eraser, hellraiser, horse-racer, replacer, stargazer, trailblazer.
Crusader, dissuader, evader, invader, persuader, serenader.
Escaper, notepaper, newspaper, sandpaper, skyscraper, wallpaper.
Bookmaker, caretaker, heartbreaker, icebreaker, lawbreaker, lawmaker, matchmaker, mischief-maker, muckraker, peacemaker, risk-taker, troublemaker, watchmaker.
[4+] **Commentator**, figure-skater, illustrator, masquerader, percolator, undertaker.

1.3.75 "---aying" (as in "praying")
[2] baying, fraying, graying/greying), laying, neighing, paying, playing, praying, preying, saying, slaying, sleighing, spraying, staying, straying, swaying, weighing.
[3] betraying, conveying, crocheting, decaying, deejaying, delaying, dismaying, disobeying, displaying, downplaying, holidaying, obeying, outplaying, outweighing, overpaying, overstaying, portraying, relaying, replaying, respraying, ricocheting, prepaying, sashaying, soothsaying, surveying, x-raying.

SURPRISING RHYMING:
[2] **Ailing**, failing, hailing, jailing, mailing, nailing, sailing, tailing, trailing, veiling, wailing.
Aiming, blaming, claiming, flaming, framing, gaming, naming, shaming, taming.
Braving, craving, paving, raving, saving, shaving, waiving, waving.
Aiding, grading, fading, raiding, trading, braiding, shading, wading.
Blazing, erasing, fazing, gazing, lazing, phasing, phrasing, praising, raising.
Dating, hating, skating, slating, stating, waiting, weighting.
Aching, baking, braking, breaking, faking, making, quaking, shaking, taking, waking.
[3] **Degrading**, invading, parading, persuading, cascading, evading, dissuading.
Blackmailing, curtailing, exhaling, inhaling, prevailing, regaling, unfailing, unveiling.
Behaving, depraving, engraving, enslaving, lifesaving, time-saving.
Amazing, appraising, fundraising, hellraising, stargazing, trailblazing.
Abating, berating, dictating, frustrating, locating, migrating, narrating, placating, updating.
Acclaiming, exclaiming, inflaming, nicknaming, proclaiming, reclaiming, renaming.
Awaking, backbreaking, breathtaking, earthshaking, forsaking, heartbreaking, lovemaking, matchmaking, mistaking, partaking, peacemaking, troublemaking.
Awaiting, creating, debating, pulsating, relating, stagnating, vacating, vibrating.

Escaping, landscaping, reshaping, skyscraping.
[4] Fascinating, graduating, humiliating, infuriating, insinuating, mediating, nauseating, penetrating, punctuating, radiating, recreating, underrating, understating, undertaking.
[5] Abbreviating, alleviating, appreciating, associating, discriminating, evacuating, negotiating, perpetuating, retaliating, substantiating.

1.3.76 "--ating" (as in "dating")
[2] baiting, dating, hating, mating, rating, skating, slating, stating, waiting, weighting.
[3] abating, awaiting, backdating, berating, collating, creating, debating, deflating, dictating, frustrating, gyrating, hydrating, inflating, locating, migrating, mutating, narrating, placating, pulsating, relating, stagnating, translating, updating, vacating, vibrating.
[4] abdicating, activating, advocating, aggravating, agitating, alienating, allocating, alternating, animating, automating, calculating, captivating, celebrating, circulating, complicating, consecrating, concentrating, confiscating, congregating, consummating, contemplating, correlating, culminating, cultivating, decorating, dedicating, delegating, demonstrating, designating, devastating, deviating, discriminating, dislocating, dominating, duplicating, educating, elevating, eliminating, emigrating, emulating, escalating, estimating, excavating, exterminating, extricating, fabricating, fascinating, fluctuating, formulating, generating, graduating, granulating, gravitating, hesitating, hibernating, hyphenating, illuminating, illustrating, imitating, implicating, incubating, indicating, infiltrating, innovating, instigating, insulating, integrating, intimating, inundating, irrigating, irritating, isolating, legislating, levitating, liberating, liquidating, litigating, lubricating, mediating, meditating, moderating, motivating, navigating, obligating, operating, orchestrating, overrating, overstating, penetrating, percolating, permeating, perpetuating, populating, procreating, punctuating, radiating, re-creating, regulating, reinstating, relegating, relocating, renovating, replicating, saturating, segregating, separating, simulating, situating, speculating, stimulating, stipulating, suffocating, syncopating, terminating, tolerating, underrating, understating, validating, vindicating, violating.
[5] abbreviating, accelerating, accommodating, alienating, alleviating, anticipating, , appreciating, associating, authenticating, collaborating, communicating, concentrating, congratulating, contaminating, cooperating, coordinating, corroborating, depreciating, deteriorating, discriminating, elaborating, eradicating, evacuating, evaporating, exaggerating, exasperating, exonerating, facilitating, hallucinating, humiliating, impersonating, infuriating, initiating, infatuating, intimidating, invigorating, investigating, necessitating, negotiating, orientating, participating, perpetuating, recuperating, refrigerating, remunerating, retaliating, reverberating, substantiating.

SURPRISING RHYMING:
[2] **Greying/graying** (U.S.), laying, paying, playing, praying, preying, saying, slaying, spraying, straying, swaying, weigh-in.
Aiding, fading, grading, raiding, shading, stayed in, wading.
Aiming, blaming, claiming, flaming, framing, gaming, naming, shaming, taming.
Aping, draping, gaping, scraping, shaping, taping.
Blazing, fazing, gazing, grazing, hazing, lazing, phasing, phrasing, praising, raising.
Chaining, draining, explaining, feigning, gaining, raining, reigning, remaining, spraining, staining, straining, waning.
Braving, craving, paving, raving, saving, shaving, slaving, waiving, waving.
[3] **Betraying**, conveying, decaying, deejaying, delaying, dismaying, displaying, downplaying, mislaying, obeying, okaying, outplaying, outstaying, outweighing, portraying, relaying, repaying, replaying, sashaying, surveying, waylaying, x-raying.
Cascading, degrading, downgrading, evading, invading, parading, persuading.
Acclaiming, exclaiming, inflaming, nicknaming, proclaiming, reclaiming, renaming.
Escaping, landscaping, reshaping.
Amazing, appraising, erasing, fundraising, hellraising, stargazing, trailblazing.
Abstaining, complaining, constraining, containing, detaining, explaining, maintaining, obtaining, refraining, remaining, retaining, sustaining.
Behaving, engraving, enslaving, lifesaving, time-saving.
[4] **Disobeying**, holidaying, overplaying, ricocheting, underplaying.
Barricading, cavalcading, entertaining, masquerading, serenading.

1.3.77 "--atefully" (as in "fatefully")
fatefully, gratefully, hatefully.

SURPRISING RHYMING:
Carefully, faithfully, gainfully, gracefully, painfully, playfully, shamefully, wastefully.
Blaringly, caringly, daringly, flaringly, glaringly, sparingly.
Delightfully, despairingly, disdainfully, disgracefully, distastefully, eventually, finally, reassuringly, respectfully, tastefully, unfaithfully.

1.3.78 "--ayve" (as in "save")
[1] brave, cave, crave, fave, gave, grave, knave, pave, rave, save, shave, slave, stave, they've, waive, wave.
[2] behave, brainwave, concave, deprave, engrave, enslave, forgave, heatwave.
[3] aftershave, microwave, misbehave.

SURPRISING RHYMING:
[1] **Aid**, blade, fade, glade, grade, jade, laid, made, maid, paid, played, prayed, raid, shade, spade, sprayed, stayed, strayed, suede, they'd, wade, weighed.
Bay, clay, day, eh, fray, gay, grey/gray (U.S.), hay, hey, lay, may, pay, play, pray, prey, ray, say, slay, sleigh, spray, stay, stray, sway, they, tray, way, weigh, yea.
Brain, cane, chain, drain, feign, gain, grain, lain, lane, main, mane, pain, pane, plain, plane, rain, reign, rein, sane, slain, sprain, stain, strain, train, vain, vane, vein, wane.
Aim, blame, came, claim, fame, flame, frame, game, name, same, shame, tame, vain.
Bathe, faith, lathe, safe, scathe, sunbathe, swathe, vague, waif.
[2] **Afraid**, betrayed, brain fade, bridesmaid, cascade, charade, crusade, decayed, degrade, delayed, dismayed, evade, handmade, homemade, invade, man-made, mermaid, nightshade, nursemaid, obeyed, parade, persuade, ram raid, self-made, today.
Airplay, array, astray, away, ballet, beret, betray, birthday, blasé, bouquet, roadway, buffet, café, chalet, cliché, convey, coupé, decay, deejay, delay, dismay, display, doomsday, doorway, downplay, driveway, duvet, fair play, foreplay, forte, foyer, Friday, freeway, gangway, gateway, gourmet, hairspray, halfway, hallway, headway, hearsay, heyday, highway, hombre, hooray, horseplay, hurray, inlay, latté, lamé, mainstay, mayday, melee, midday, midway, mislay, Monday, obey, okay, olé, one day, outlay, outplay, outstay, outweigh, padre, part-way, passé, pathway, payday, portray, railway, reggae, relay, repay, replay, ricochet, risqué, roadway, rosé, runway, sachet, sashay, screenplay, segue, soirée, someday, some way, stairway, subway, Sunday, sunray, survey, Thursday, today, touché, toupée, Tuesday, two-way, waylay, weekday, x-ray.
Abstain, again, airplane, arcane, attain, birdbrain, bloodstain, campaign, champagne, complain, constrain, contain, detain, domain, explain, humane, lamebrain, maintain, migraine, mundane, obtain, profane, refrain, remain(s), retain, sustain, terrain, urbane.
Acclaim, became, endgame, exclaim, inflame, nickname, proclaim, reclaim, surname.
[3] **Barricade**, cavalcade, centigrade, disarrayed, escapade, lemonade, marmalade, masquerade, not afraid, overpaid, razor blade, readymade, renegade, ricocheted, serenade, tailor-made, unafraid.
A.k.a., A-OK, alleyway, anyway, attaché, awayday, breakaway, cabaret, café au lait, castaway, Christmas Day, croupier, disarray, disobey, everyday, exposé, expressway, faraway, fiancé, flyaway, giveaway, getaway, hideaway, holiday, interplay, matinée, Milky Way, motorway, negligee, overlay, overplay, passageway, protégé, ricochet, résumé, runaway, Saturday, stowaway, straightaway, takeaway, tearaway, throwaway, underplay, walk away, wedding day, Wednesday, working day, yesterday.
Ascertain, entertain, hurricane, inhumane, overcame, scatterbrain, windowpane.

1.3.79 "--ayved" (as in "saved")
[1] braved, caved, craved, paved, raved, saved, shaved, slaved, waved.
[2] behaved, depraved, engraved, enslaved, repaved, unpaved, unshaved.
[3] microwaved, misbehaved.

SURPRISING RHYMING:
[1] **Brave**, crave, fave, gave, grave, pave, rave, save, shave, slave, they've, wave.
Aid, blade, fade, glade, grade, jade, laid, made, maid, paid, played, prayed, raid, shade, spade, sprayed, stayed, strayed, suede, they'd, vague, wade, weighed.
Chained, drained, gained, pained, rained, reigned, sprained, stained, strained, waned.
Aimed, blamed, claimed, famed, flamed, framed, named, shamed, tamed.
Bathed, scathed, sunbathed, swathed, unscathed.
[2] **Behave**, brainwave, concave, deprave, engrave, enslave, forgave, heatwave.
Afraid, betrayed, brain fade, bridesmaid, cascade, charade, crusade, decayed, degrade, delayed, dismayed, evade, handmade, homemade, invade, man-made, mermaid, nightshade, nursemaid, obeyed, parade, persuade, ram raid, self-made, today.
Abstained, arraigned, attained, birdbrained, bloodstained, complained, contained, detained, entertained, explained, lamebrained, maintained, obtained, refrained, regained, remained, restrained, retained, sustained, unchained.
Acclaimed, exclaimed, inflamed, nicknamed, proclaimed, reclaimed, renamed, unnamed.
[3] **Aftershave**, microwave, misbehave.
Cavalcade, centigrade, colonnade, disarrayed, disobeyed, holidayed, escapade, lemonade, marmalade, masquerade, not afraid, overpaid, overplayed, razor blade, readymade, renegade, ricocheted, serenade, tailor-made, unafraid, underpaid.

1.3.80 "--ayver" (as in "braver")
[2] braver, craver, favour/favor (U.S.), flavour/flavor (U.S.), graver, paver, raver, saver, savour/savor (U.S.), shaver, slaver, quaver, waiver, waver.
[3] disfavour/disfavor (U.S.), engraver, enslaver, lifesaver, timesaver.

SURPRISING RHYMING:
[2] **Bather**, safer, sunbather, wafer
Greyer/grayer (U.S.), payer, player, slayer, sprayer.
Entertainer, explainer, feigner, gainer, plainer, saner, trainer, vainer.
Aimer, blamer, claimer, framer, gamer, shamer, tamer.
Changer, danger, manger, ranger, stranger.
[3] **Arranger**, endanger, exchanger, life-changer.
Betrayer, crusader, evader, first-aider, invader, persuader.
Behaviour/behavior (U.S.), misbehaviour/misbehavior (U.S.), saviour/savior (U.S.).
Abstainer, campaigner, complainer, container, disclaimer, proclaimer, remainer, retainer.
[4] **Masquerader**, serenader.

1.3.81 "--avery" (as in "bravery")
bravery, knavery, savoury/savory (U.S.), slavery, unsavoury/unsavory (U.S.).

SURPRISING RHYMING:
[2] **Baby**, cagey, daily, lady, lazy, maybe, shady, stagy.
Diary, enquiry, fiery, inquiry, memory, papery.
Gamely, lamely, mainly, namely, tamely, vainly.
Faintly, lately, patiently, patently, saintly, stately.
[3] **Aviary**, bakery, fakery, flowery, gracefully, misery, neighbourly/neighborly (U.S.), poetry, stationery, stationary, vacancy, variety, priority.
[4] **Eventually**, generally, hyperbole, naturally, usually.

1.3.82 "--avering" (as in wavering")
[3] favouring/favoring (U.S.), flavouring/flavoring (U.S.), savouring/savoring (U.S.), quavering, wavering.

SURPRISING RHYMING:
[3] **Despairing**, hardwearing, repairing, seafaring, time-sharing, uncaring, wayfaring.
Catering, layering, papering, tailoring, tapering, varying, waitering.
Dangering, endangering, disfavouring/disfavoring (U.S.), neighbouring/neighboring (U.S.),
Amazing, appraising, fundraising, hellraising, stargazing, trailblazing.

*

1.3.83 "--avy" (as in "navy")
[2] gravy, navy, wavy.

SURPRISING RHYMING:
[2] **Baby**, crybaby, shady, lady, maybe.
Glazy, hazy, lazy, mazy.
Airy, carefree, dairy, fairy, hairy, prairie, scary, vary, wary.
Greatly, irately, lately, ornately, sedately, shapely, stately.
Brainy, grainy, mainly, marquee, plainly, rainy, sanely, vainly, zany.
Achy, flaky, quaky, shaky.
Daily, gaily, ukulele.
Eighty, Haiti, hate me, matey, safety, weighty.
[3] **Bravery**, knavery, savoury/savory (U.S.), slavery, unsavoury/unsavory (U.S.).
Humanely, insanely, mundanely, profanely, ungainly, urbanely.
Guarantee, jamboree, melody, urgency.
Stir-crazy, oops-a-daisy, upsy-daisy.

1.3.84 "--aving" (as in "waving")
[2] braving, caving, craving, paving, raving, saving, shaving, slaving, waiving, waving.
[3] behaving, depraving, engraving, enslaving, lifesaving, misbehaving, time-saving.

SURPRISING RHYMING:
[2] **Aiding**, grading, fading, raiding, trading, shading, wading.
Ailing, failing, hailing, jailing, mailing, nailing, sailing, tailing, trailing, veiling, wailing.
Aiming, blaming, claiming, flaming, framing, gaming, naming, shaming, taming.
Blazing, fazing, gazing, grazing, hazing, lazing, phasing, phrasing, praising, raising.
Caning, chaining, draining, feigning, gaining, raining, reigning, reining, spraining, staining, straining, training, waning.
Aching, baking, braking, breaking, faking, making, quaking, shaking, taking, waking.
Dating, grating, hating, mating, rating, skating, slating, stating, waiting, weighting.
[3] **Degrading**, invading, blockading, parading, crusading, pervading, persuading, cascading, evading, dissuading, unfading.
Blackmailing, entailing, exhaling, inhaling, prevailing, regaling, unfailing, unveiling.
Acclaiming, exclaiming, inflaming, nicknaming, proclaiming, reclaiming, renaming.
Amazing, appraising, erasing, fundraising, hellraising, stargazing, trailblazing.
Abstaining, attaining, bloodstaining, campaigning, complaining, constraining, containing, detaining, explaining, maintaining, obtaining, refraining, remaining, retaining, sustaining.
Awaking, backbreaking, breathtaking, earthshaking, forsaking, heartbreaking, lovemaking, matchmaking, mistaking, partaking, painstaking, peacemaking, troublemaking, undertaking.
Awaiting, berating, creating, debating, dictating, frustrating, migrating, narrating, placating, pulsating, relating, stagnating, translating, updating, vacating, vibrating.
[4] **Abdicating**, activating, aggravating, alienating, allocating, animating, automating, captivating, celebrating, circulating, complicating, concentrating, confiscating, congregating, consummating, contemplating, cultivating, decorating, dedicating, demonstrating, devastating, deviating, discriminating, dominating, duplicating, educating, elevating, eliminating, emigrating, emulating, entertaining, escalating, estimating, excavating, fabricating, fascinating, fluctuating, generating, graduating, hesitating, hibernating, illuminating, illustrating, imitating, implicating, indicating, instigating, integrating, intimating, inundating, irritating, isolating, liberating, liquidating, litigating, lubricating, mediating, meditating, moderating, motivating, navigating, orchestrating, overstating, penetrating, percolating, radiating, recreating, regulating, relocating, renovating, segregating, separating, simulating, speculating, stimulating, stipulating, suffocating, syncopating, syndicating, terminating, tolerating, vindicating, violating.
[5] **Abbreviating**, accelerating, alienating, alleviating, anticipating, appreciating, collaborating, communicating, concentrating, congratulating, cooperating, deteriorating, discriminating, elaborating, evaporating, exaggerating, exasperating, hallucinating, humiliating, impersonating, infuriating, intimidating, invigorating, investigating, participating, perpetuating, recuperating, retaliating, reverberating, substantiating.

*

1.3.85 "--aze" (as in "haze")
[1] blaze, craze, days, daze, faze, gaze, glaze, graze, haze, laze, maze, maize, phase, phrase, praise, raise, stays, vase, ways.
[2] ablaze, always, amaze, appraise, catchphrase, erase, malaise, sideways, stargaze.
[3] hollandaise, mayonnaise, nowadays, paraphrase, reappraise.

SURPRISING RHYMING:
[1] Blazed, crazed, dazed, fazed, gazed, glazed, grazed, hazed, lazed, phased, phrased, praised, raised.
Bay, clay, day, eh, fray, gay, gray/grey, hay, hey, lay, may, pay, play, pray, prey, ray, say, slay, sleigh, spray, stay, stray, sway, they, tray, way, weigh, yea.
Ace, base, bass, brace, case, chase, face, grace, lace, mace, pace, place, plaice, race, space, trace, vase, ways.
Based, braced, cased, chaste, chased, faced, graced, haste, laced, paste, paced, placed, raced, spaced, taste, traced, waste, waist.
Brave, crave, fave, gave, grave, pave, rave, save, shave, slave, they've, waive, wave.
Age, cage, change, gage, gauge, page, rage, range, sage, stage, strange, wage.
Chafe, safe, strafe, unsafe, waif.
Ate, bait, crate, date, eight, fate, fête, freight, gate, gait, great, grate, hate, late, mate, plate, rate, skate, slate, spate, state, strait, straight, trait, weight, wait.
[2] Amazed, appraised, erased, liaised, reappraised, stargazed.
Birthplace, bookcase, bootlace, briefcase, coalface, deface, disgrace, embrace, erase, fireplace, grimace, misplace, nutcase, rat-race, replace, retrace, shoelace, showcase, someplace, staircase, suitcase, typeface, unlace, workplace, workspace.
Barefaced, embraced, erased, fast-paced, red-faced, replaced, shamefaced, strait-laced, toothpaste, two-faced, untraced.
Behave, brainwave, deprave, engrave, enslave, forgave, heatwave.
Backstage, birdcage, engage, enrage, offstage, onstage, outrage, rampage, ribcage, space-age, teenage, underage, upstage.
Arrange, derange, estrange, exchange, short-change.
Airplay, array, astray, away, ballet, beret, betray, birthday, blasé, bouquet, roadway, buffet, café, chalet, cliché, convey, coupé, decay, deejay, delay, dismay, display, doomsday, doorway, downplay, driveway, duvet, fair play, foreplay, forte, foyer, Friday, freeway, gangway, gateway, gourmet, hairspray, halfway, hallway, headway, hearsay, heyday, highway, hombre, hooray, horseplay, hurray, inlay, latté, lamé, mainstay, mayday, melee, midday, midway, mislay, Monday, obey, okay, olé, one day, outlay, outplay, outstay, outweigh, padre, part-way, passé, pathway, payday, portray, railway, reggae, relay, repay, replay, ricochet, risqué, roadway, rosé, runway, sachet, sashay, screenplay, segue, soirée, someday, some way, stairway, subway, Sunday, sunray, survey, Thursday, today, touché, toupée, Tuesday, two-way, waylay, weekday, x-ray.
Abate, await, berate, birth rate, cheapskate, checkmate, classmate, create, debate, deflate, dictate, estate, fixate, flat-mate, frustrate, helpmate, inflate, irate, jailbait, lightweight, locate, migrate, narrate, ornate, outdate, placate, playmate, portrait, pulsate, relate, rotate, sedate, soulmate, stagnate, stalemate, translate, update, vacate, vibrate.
[3] Disengage, paraphrase, reappraised.
A.k.a., A-OK, alleyway, anyway, attaché, awayday, breakaway, cabaret, café au lait, castaway, Christmas Day, croupier, disarray, disobey, everyday, exposé, expressway, faraway, fiancé, flyaway, giveaway, getaway, hideaway, holiday, interplay, matinée, Milky Way, motorway, negligee, overlay, overplay, passageway, protégé, ricochet, résumé, runaway, Saturday, stowaway, straightaway, takeaway, tearaway, throwaway, underplay, walk away, wedding day, Wednesday, working day, yesterday.
Angel face, anyplace, baby face, commonplace, database, headcase, hiding place, interface, in-your-face, meeting place, nutcase, paperchase, pillowcase, steeplechase.
Aftertaste, angel-faced, baby-faced, dirty-faced, freckle-faced.
Interchange, part-exchange, pre-arrange, rearrange.
Aftershave, microwave, misbehave.
Activate, aggravate, alienate, allocate, animate, automate, captivate, celebrate, circulate, complicate, consecrate, concentrate, confiscate, congregate, consummate, contemplate, cultivate, decorate, dedicate, demonstrate, desolate, devastate, deviate, discriminate, dominate, duplicate, educate, elevate, eliminate, emigrate, emulate,

escalate, estimate, fascinate, fluctuate, generate, graduate, gravitate, heavyweight, hesitate, hibernate, illuminate, illustrate, imitate, implicate, infiltrate, innovate, instigate, interstate, intimate, intricate, inundate, irritate, isolate, liberate, magistrate, mediate, meditate, moderate, motivate, navigate, operate, orchestrate, overstate, overweight, paperweight, penetrate, percolate, procreate, radiate, regulate, relocate, renovate, segregate, separate, simulate, situate, speculate, stimulate, stipulate, suffocate, syncopate, terminate, tête-à-tête, tolerate, underrate, violate.
[4] **Accelerate**, accommodate, alienate, alleviate, anticipate, associate, authenticate, certificate, collaborate, communicate, concentrate, congratulate, contaminate, cooperate, corroborate, deteriorate, elaborate, eradicate, evaporate, exaggerate, exasperate, exonerate, hallucinate, humiliate, impersonate, infuriate, intimidate, invigorate, investigate, negotiate, participate, recuperate, refrigerate, reverberate.

1.3.86 "--azed" (as in "dazed")
[1] blazed, crazed, dazed, fazed, gazed, glazed, grazed, hazed, lazed, phased, phrased, praised, raised.
[2] amazed, appraised, erased, liaised, rephrased, stargazed.
[3] paraphrased, reappraised.

SURPRISING RHYMING:
[1] **Blaze**, craze, days, daze, faze, gaze, glaze, graze, haze, laze, maze, maize, phase, phrase, praise, raise, stays, vase, ways.
Frayed, laid, made, paid, played, prayed, preyed, sprayed, stayed, strayed, swayed, they'd, weighed.
Chased, chaste, faced, graced, haste, laced, paced, paste, placed, raced, spaced, taste, traced, waist, waste.
Braved, craved, paved, raved, saved, shaved, slaved, they've, waived, waved.
Aged, caged, changed, gauged, paged, raged, ranged, staged, strange, waged.
Ate, bait, crate, date, eight, fate, fête, freight, gate, gait, great, grate, hate, late, mate, plate, rate, skate, slate, spate, state, strait, straight, trait, weight, wait.
[2] **Ablaze**, always, amaze, appraise, catchphrase, erase, malaise, sideways, stargaze.
Barefaced, disgraced, embraced, erased, fast-paced, misplaced, red-faced, replaced, retraced, shamefaced, showcased, staircase, strait-laced, suitcase, toothpaste, two-faced.
Behaved, depraved, engraved, enslaved, forgave.
Backstage, birdcage, engage, enrage, offstage, onstage, outrage, rampage, ribcage, space-age, teenage, underage, upstage.
Arranged, deranged, estranged, exchanged, short-changed.
Afraid, betrayed, brain fade, bridesmaid, cascade, charade, crusade, decayed, degrade, delayed, dismayed, evade, handmade, homemade, invade, man-made, mermaid, nightshade, nursemaid, obeyed, parade, persuade, ram raid, self-made, today.
Await, cheapskate, checkmate, classmate, create, debate, dictate, fixate, flat-mate, irate, jailbait, lightweight, locate, migrate, narrate, ornate, placate, playmate, portrait, pulsate, relate, sedate, soulmate, stagnate, stalemate, translate, update, vacate, vibrate.
[3] AKA, A-OK, alleyway, anyway, attaché, awayday, breakaway, cabaret, café au lait, castaway, Christmas Day, croupier, disarray, disobey, everyday, exposé, expressway, faraway, fiancé, flyaway, giveaway, getaway, hideaway, holiday, interplay, matinée, Milky Way, motorway, negligee, overlay, overplay, passageway, protégé, ricochet, résumé, runaway, Saturday, stowaway, straightaway, takeaway, tearaway, throwaway, underplay, walk away, wedding day, Wednesday, working day, yesterday.
Angel face, anyplace, baby face, commonplace, database, headcase, hiding place, interface, in-your-face, meeting place, nutcase, paperchase, pillowcase, steeplechase.
Aftertaste, angel-faced, baby-faced, dirty-faced, freckle-faced.
Disengaged, part-exchanged, pre-arranged, rearranged.
Aftershave, microwave, misbehave.
Activate, aggravate, alienate, allocate, animate, automate, captivate, celebrate, circulate, complicate, consecrate, concentrate, confiscate, congregate, consummate, contemplate, cultivate, decorate, dedicate, demonstrate, desolate, devastate, deviate, discriminate, dominate, duplicate, educate, elevate, eliminate, emigrate, emulate, escalate, estimate, fascinate, fluctuate, generate, graduate, gravitate, heavyweight, hesitate, hibernate, illuminate, illustrate, imitate, implicate, infiltrate, innovate, instigate,

112

interstate, intimate, intricate, inundate, irritate, isolate, liberate, magistrate, mediate, meditate, moderate, motivate, navigate, operate, orchestrate, overstate, overweight, paperweight, penetrate, percolate, procreate, radiate, regulate, relocate, renovate, segregate, separate, simulate, situate, speculate, stimulate, stipulate, suffocate, syncopate, terminate, tête-à-tête, tolerate, underrate, violate.
[4] **Accelerate**, accommodate, alienate, alleviate, anticipate, associate, authenticate, certificate, collaborate, communicate, concentrate, congratulate, contaminate, cooperate, corroborate, deteriorate, elaborate, eradicate, evaporate, exaggerate, exasperate, exonerate, hallucinate, humiliate, impersonate, infuriate, intimidate, invigorate, investigate, negotiate, participate, recuperate, refrigerate, reverberate.

1.3.87 "--azen" (as in "brazen")
[2] brazen, emblazon, liaison, raisin.

SURPRISING RHYMING:
[2] **Basin**, chasten, hasten, nation, station, washbasin.
Bacon, shaken, taken, waken.
Craven, graven, haven, raven, shaven.
[3] **Creation**, clean-shaven, damnation, duration, elation, fixation, flirtation, frustration, invasion, location, migration, narration, occasion, ovation, persuasion, quotation, relation, salvation, sensation, starvation, temptation, translation, unshaven, vacation, vibration.
Awaken, forsaken, mistaken, unshaken, untaken.
[4] **Aberration**, accusation, admiration, adoration, adulation, aggravation, allegation, altercation, animation, aspiration, cancellation, celebration, combination, compensation, complication, concentration, condemnation, confirmation, confrontation, congregation, conservation, consolation, constellation, contemplation, conversation, decoration, dedication, degradation, demonstration, deprivation, desolation, desperation, destination, devastation, education, emigration, excitation, exclamation, expectation, explanation, exploitation, fascination, generation, graduation, imitation, immigration, implication, incarnation, inclination, indication, indignation, information, innovation, inspiration, invitation, irritation, isolation, jubilation, liberation, limitation, meditation, moderation, motivation, obligation, observation, occupation, operation, palpitation, penetration, perspiration, preparation, presentation, preservation, provocation, publication, recreation, relaxation, reputation, reservation, resignation, revelation, scintillation, separation, situation, speculation, stimulation, stipulation, syncopation, titillation, transformation, transportation, trepidation, vaccination, valuation, violation, vindication.
[5] **Acceleration**, accommodation, alienation, annihilation, anticipation, appreciation, civilization, collaboration, communication, congratulations, consideration, cooperation, cross-examination, determination, discrimination, elimination, evacuation, evaluation, exaggeration, exhilaration, humiliation, imagination, infatuation, interrogation, interpretation, intoxication, investigation, justification, manipulation, multiplication, negotiation, organization, participation, qualification, realization, recommendation, reconciliation, recrimination, reincarnation, retaliation, reverberation, sophistication.

1.3.88 "--azer" (as in "razor")
[2] blazer, eraser, gazer, glazer, grazer, hazer, laser, praiser, raiser, razor, Taser.
[3] appraiser, fundraiser, hellraiser, stargazer, trailblazer.

SURPRISING RHYMING:
[2] **Chaser**, fascia, geisha, glacier, mesa, nature, pacer, placer, racer, spacer, tracer.
Braver, fader, favour/favor (U.S.), flavour/flavor (U.S.), grader, graver, raider, raver, saver, savour/savor (U.S.), shaver, quaver, wader, waiver, waver.
Caper, paper, scraper, shaper, vapour/vapor (U.S.).
Cater, crater, data, dater, greater, hater, later, skater, traitor, waiter.
Changer, danger, manger, ranger, stranger.
Acre, baker, breaker, faker, maker, nature, shaker, taker.
Greyer/grayer (U.S.), layer, mayor, payer, player, prayer, slayer, stayer, prayer.
Frailer, jailer, mailer, paler, sailor, staler, trailer, tailor, wailer.
[3] **Embracer**, eraser, horse-racer, misplacer, replacer, retracer, steeplechaser.
Crusader, engraver, evader, invader, life-saver, persuader, serenader, timesaver.

Arranger, endanger, exchanger, shortchanger.
Escaper, notepaper, newspaper, sandpaper, skyscraper, wallpaper.
Betrayer, bricklayer, delayer, displayer, portrayer, purveyor, soothsayer, taxpayer.
Bookmaker, caretaker, heartbreaker, icebreaker, lawbreaker, lawmaker, matchmaker, mischief-maker, muckraker, peacemaker, risk-taker, troublemaker, undertaker.
Creator, curator, dictator, equator, freighter, narrator, spectator, translator.
Abseiler, blackmailer, exhale, inhaler, loudhailer, retailer, wholesaler.
Abstainer, campaigner, complainer, container, entertainer, retainer.
[4+] Accelerator, agitator, alligator, animator, aviator, calculator, collaborator, commentator, decorator, educator, elevator, escalator, generator, gladiator, illustrator, imitator, impersonator, indicator, instigator, interrogator, investigator, liberator, mediator, negotiator, operator, percolator, perpetrator, refrigerator, speculator, terminator, ventilator.

1.3.89 "--azy (as in "crazy")
crazy, daisy, glazy, hazy, lazy, mazy, oops-a-daisy, stir-crazy.

SURPRISING RHYMING:
[2] Baby, lady, maybe, shady.
Daily, gaily, mainly, plainly, sanely, ukulele, vainly.
Brainy, grainy, miscellany, rainy, zany.
Gravy, greatly, innately, irately, lately, navy, ornately, sedately, stately, wavy.
Blazing, gazing, grazing, lazing, phasing, phrasing, praising, raising.
Airy, dairy, fairy, hairy, prairie, scary, vary, wary.
[3] Amazing, appraising, erasing, fundraising, hellraising, stargazing, trailblazing.
Humanely, insanely, mundanely, profanely, ungainly, urbanely.
Airy-fairy, canary, contrary, rosemary, unwary.
Stir-crazy, oops-a-daisy, upsy-daisy.

1.3.90 "--azing" (as in "amazing")
[2] blazing, fazing, gazing, grazing, hazing, lazing, phasing, phrasing, praising, raising.
[3] amazing, appraising, erasing, fundraising, hellraising, liaising, stargazing, trailblazing.
[4] paraphrasing, reappraising.

SURPRISING RHYMING:
[2] Chasing, facing, gracing, lacing, pacing, placing, racing, spacing, tasting, tracing.
Ageing, caging, changing, gauging, paging, raging, ranging, staging, waging.
Braving, craving, paving, raving, saving, shaving, slaving, strafing, waiving, waving.
Dating, grating, hating, mating, plating, rating, skating, slating, stating, waiting.
Aiding, grading, fading, raiding, trading, braiding, shading, wading.
Ailing, failing, hailing, jailing, mailing, nailing, sailing, tailing, trailing, veiling, wailing.
Aiming, blaming, claiming, flaming, framing, gaming, naming, shaming, taming.
Chaining, feigning, gaining, raining, reigning, staining, straining, training, waning.
Aping, draping, gaping, scraping, shaping, taping.
[3] Embracing, erasing, misplacing, outpacing, replacing, retracing, showcasing.
Behaving, depraving, engraving, enslaving.
Arranging, engaging, enraging, exchanging, rampaging, short-changing, upstaging.
Betraying, decaying, deejaying, delaying, dismaying, displaying, downplaying, mislaying, obeying, okaying, outplaying, outstaying, outweighing, portraying, sashaying, x-raying.
Awaiting, berating, creating, debating, dictating, frustrating, migrating, narrating, placating, pulsating, relating, stagnating, translating, updating, vacating, vibrating.
Degrading, invading, parading, persuading, cascading, evading, dissuading, unfading.
Blackmailing, curtailing, entailing, exhaling, inhaling, prevailing, unfailing, unveiling.
Exclaiming, inflaming, nicknaming, proclaiming, reclaiming, renaming.
Abstaining, attaining, complaining, constraining, containing, detaining, explaining, maintaining, obtaining, refraining, remaining, retaining, sustaining.
Escaping, landscaping, reshaping, skyscraping.
[4] Disengaging, interchanging, paraphrasing, part-exchanging, reappraising, rearranging..
Disobeying, holidaying, overlaying, overplaying, ricocheting.
Ascertaining, entertaining, microwaving, misbehaving.

Activating, aggravating, alienating, allocating, animating, automating, captivating, celebrating, circulating, complicating, concentrating, confiscating, congregating, consummating, contemplating, cultivating, decorating, dedicating, demonstrating, devastating, deviating, discriminating, dominating, duplicating, educating, elevating, eliminating, emigrating, emulating, entertaining, escalating, estimating, excavating, fabricating, fascinating, fluctuating, generating, graduating, hesitating, hibernating, illuminating, illustrating, imitating, implicating, indicating, instigating, integrating, intimating, inundating, irritating, isolating, liberating, liquidating, litigating, lubricating, mediating, meditating, moderating, motivating, navigating, orchestrating, overstating, penetrating, percolating, radiating, recreating, regulating, relocating, renovating, segregating, separating, simulating, speculating, stimulating, stipulating, suffocating, syncopating, syndicating, terminating, tolerating, vindicating, violating.
[5] **Accelerating**, agitating, animating, calculating, collaborating, decorating, delegating, demonstrating, educating, escalating, generating, illustrating, imitating, impersonating, indicating, instigating, interrogating, investigating, liberating, mediating, moderating, percolating, perpetrating, radiating, simulating, speculating, stimulating, violating.

1.3.91 "--ayable" (as in "payable")
payable, playable, repayable, swayable, unplayable, weighable.

SURPRISING RHYMING:
[3] **Bailable**, blamable, cannibal, capable, eatable, edible, gradable, laughable, liable, readable, stainable, traceable.
[4] **Amiable**, available, conveyable, degradable, explainable, inflatable, incapable, insatiable, untraceable, variable.
Reclaimable, sustainable, unassailable, unattainable, unavailable, unexplainable, unfavourable/unfavorable (U.S.).

1.3.92 "--ayday" (as in "payday")
awayday, heyday, mayday, payday.

SURPRISING RHYMING:
[2] **Airplay**, array, astray, away, ballet, beret, betray, birthday, blasé, bouquet, roadway, buffet, café, chalet, cliché, convey, coupé, decay, deejay, delay, dismay, display, doomsday, doorway, downplay, driveway, duvet, fair play, foreplay, forte, foyer, Friday, freeway, gangway, gateway, gourmet, hairspray, halfway, hallway, headway, hearsay, heyday, highway, hombre, hooray, horseplay, hurray, inlay, latté, lamé, mainstay, mayday, melee, midday, midway, mislay, Monday, obey, okay, olé, one day, outlay, outplay, outstay, outweigh, padre, part-way, passé, pathway, payday, portray, railway, reggae, relay, repay, replay, ricochet, risqué, roadway, rosé, runway, sachet, sashay, screenplay, segue, soirée, someday, some way, stairway, subway, Sunday, sunray, survey, Thursday, today, touché, toupée, Tuesday, two-way, weekday, x-ray.
Berate, lightweight, locate, relate, soulmate, stagnate, stalemate, template, translate.
Abstain, again, airplane, arcane, attain, birdbrain, bloodstain, campaign, champagne, complain, constrain, contain, detain, domain, explain, humane, lamebrain, maintain, migraine, mundane, obtain, profane, refrain, remain(s), retain, sustain, terrain, urbane.
Became, exclaim, inflame, nickname, proclaim.
Afraid, betrayed, brain fade, bridesmaid, cascade, charade, crusade, decayed, degrade, delayed, dismayed, evade, handmade, homemade, invade, man-made, mermaid, nightshade, nursemaid, obeyed, parade, persuade, ram raid, self-made, today.
Await, cheapskate, checkmate, classmate, create, debate, dictate, estate, fixate, flat-mate, frustrate, irate, jailbait, migrate, narrate, ornate, outdate, placate, playmate, portrait, pulsate, sedate, update, vacate, vibrate.
[3] **A.k.a.**, A-OK, alleyway, anyway, attaché, awayday, breakaway, cabaret, café au lait, castaway, Christmas Day, croupier, disarray, disobey, everyday, exposé, expressway, faraway, fiancé, flyaway, giveaway, getaway, hideaway, holiday, interplay, matinée, Milky Way, motorway, negligee, overlay, overplay, passageway, protégé, ricochet, résumé, runaway, Saturday, stowaway, straightaway, takeaway, tearaway, throwaway, underplay, walk away, wedding day, Wednesday, working day, yesterday.

Barricade, cavalcade, centigrade, escapade, lemonade, masquerade, overpaid, readymade, renegade, ricocheted, serenade, unafraid.

1.3.93 "--ayer" (as in "player")
[2] greyer/grayer (U.S.), layer, mayor, payer, player, prayer, slayer, stayer, sprayer.
[3] betrayer, delayer, displayer, portrayer, purveyor, soothsayer, surveyor, taxpayer.

SURPRISING RHYMING:
[2] **Fader**, raider, trader, wader.
Frailer, jailer, mailer, paler, sailor, staler, trailer, tailor, wailer, whaler.
Caper, paper, scraper, shaper, taper, vaper, vapour/vapor (U.S.).
Cater, crater, data, dater, grater, greater, hater, later, skater, slater, traitor, waiter.
Braver, craver, favour/favor (U.S.), flavour/flavor (U.S.), raver, saver, savour/savor (U.S.), shaver, waiver, waver.
Blazer, eraser, gazer, grazer, laser, raiser, razor, Taser.
[3] **Blockader**, crusader, degrader, dissuader, evader, first-aider, invader, persuader.
Blackmailer, inhaler, lifesaver, loudhailer, regaler, retailer, timesaver, wholesaler.
Escaper, flypaper, notepaper, newspaper, sandpaper, skyscraper, wallpaper.
Creator, curator, debater, dictator, equator, freighter, narrator, spectator, translator.
Betrayer, delayer, displayer, portrayer, purveyor, soothsayer, surveyor, taxpayer.
Appraiser, fundraiser, hellraiser, stargazer, trailblazer.
[4] **Masquerader**, rollerblader, serenader.
Accelerator, agitator, alligator, animator, aviator, calculator, collaborator, commentator, decorator, educator, elevator, escalator, generator, gladiator, illustrator, imitator, impersonator, indicator, instigator, interrogator, investigator, liberator, mediator, negotiator, operator, percolator, perpetrator, refrigerator, speculator, terminator, ventilator.

1.3.94 "--ayshul" (as in "facial")
facial, glacial, racial, spatial, palatial, interracial, multiracial.

SURPRISING RHYMING:
[2] **Angel**, blameful, careful, changeful, fatal, fateful, faithful, gainful, graceful, grateful, hateful, naval, navel, painful, playful, shameful, wakeful.
Able, bagel, cable, cradle, fable, gable, label, ladle, maple, sable, stable, staple, table.
Appraisal, hazel, nasal, natal, naval, navel.
[3] **Disdainful**, disgraceful, distasteful, unfaithful, ungrateful.
Disabled, enabled, mislabeled, timetable, turntable, unable, unlabeled, unstable.

1.3.95 "--ayshun" (as in "persuasion")
[2] Asian, nation, station.
[3] abrasion, causation, cessation, creation, cremation, crustacean, damnation, deflation, dictation, dissuasion, donation, duration, elation, equation, evasion, fixation, flirtation, flotation, formation, foundation, frustration, gestation, gyration, inflation, invasion, location, meditation, migration, mutation, narration, notation, occasion, oration, ovation, persuasion, plantation, probation, pulsation, quotation, radiation, relation, salvation, sedation, sensation, starvation, taxation, temptation, translation, vacation, vibration.
[4] aberration, accusation, admiration, adoration, adulation, aggravation, allegation, altercation, animation, aspiration, cancellation, celebration, combination, compensation, complication, concentration, condemnation, confirmation, confrontation, congregation, conservation, consolation, constellation, contemplation, conversation, decoration, dedication, degradation, demonstration, deprivation, desolation, desperation, destination, devastation, education, emigration, excitation, exclamation, expectation, explanation, exploitation, fascination, generation, graduation, imitation, immigration, implication, incarnation, inclination, indication, indignation, information, innovation, inspiration, invitation, irritation, isolation, jubilation, liberation, limitation, meditation, moderation, motivation, obligation, observation, occupation, operation, palpitation, penetration, perspiration, preparation, presentation, preservation, provocation,

publication, recreation, relaxation, reputation, reservation, resignation, revelation, scintillation, separation, situation, speculation, stimulation, stipulation, syncopation, titillation, transformation, transportation, trepidation, vaccination, valuation, violation, vindication.
[5] abbreviation, acceleration, accommodation, accumulation, affiliation, alienation, annihilation, anticipation, appreciation, association, capitulation, civilization, classification, collaboration, communication, conciliation, congratulation, consideration, contamination, continuation, cooperation, cross-examination, determination, deterioration, discrimination, dramatization, elimination, emancipation, eradication, evacuation, evaluation, exaggeration, examination, exasperation, exhilaration, gesticulation, humiliation, identification, imagination, impersonation, indoctrination, infatuation, initiation, interrogation, interpretation, intoxication, investigation, justification, manipulation, modification, multiplication, negotiation, notification, organization, participation, preoccupation, qualification, ramification, realization, recommendation, reconciliation, recrimination, refrigeration, reincarnation, repudiation, retaliation, reverberation, sophistication, telecommunication, verification.

SURPRISING RHYMING:
[2] **Caveman**, layman, Satan, salesman, spaceman, statesman, straighten, vegan.
Apron, bacon, matron, patron.
Question, suggestion, digestion.
Laden, maiden, shaken, taken, waken.
Basin, chasten, hasten, mason, washbasin.
[3] **Forsaken**, unshaken, mistaken, awaken, godforsaken, overtaken, undertaken.
Contagion, misshapen, unshapen.

1.3.96 "--ayshus" (as in "gracious")
[2] audacious, curvaceous, flirtatious, gracious, mendacious, pugnacious, sagacious, spacious, ostentatious, pugnacious, tenacious, ungracious, vexatious, vivacious.

SURPRISING RHYMING:
[2] **Baseless**, faceless, graceless, traceless, status.
Aimless, blameless, famous, frailest, frameless, graceless, grayness/greyness, nameless, palest, plainness, sameness, shameless, tameless, tameness.
Brainless, nameless, painless, rainless, spontaneous, stainless.
Breathless, princess, reckless, restless, sweetness, weakness.
[3] **Awareness**, bareness, fairness, rareness, unfairness.
Ambitious, auspicious, avaricious, capricious, fictitious, judicious, malicious, pretentious.

1.3.97 "--ayty" (as in "eighty")
[2] eighty, Haiti, matey, weighty.

SURPRISING RHYMING:
[2] **Chastely**, greatly, hasty, lately, safety, stately, tasty, pasty, overhasty.
Dainty, faintly, frailty, safely, saintly, quaintly.
Bravely, gravely, gravy, vaguely, gamely, insanely, lamely, mainly, namely, navy, plainly, shapely, strangely, tamely, vainly, wavy.
Ably, baby, crybaby, lady, maybe, shady.
Crazy, daily, daisy, faded, gaily, hazy, lacy, lazy, mazy, racy, shady, ukulele.
[3] **Humanely**, insanely, mundanely, ungainly, urbanely.
Desolately, innately, irately, ornately, sedately.

1.3. 98 "--aytime" (as in "daytime")
[2] daytime, playtime.

SURPRISING RHYMING:
[1] **Chime(d)**, climb(ed), crime, dime, grime, I'm, lime, mime(d), prime(d), rhyme(d), slime, timed.
Align, fine, line, mine, nine, pine, shrine, shine, sign, spine, swine, vine, whine, wine.

Blind, find, fined, grind, kind, lined, mind, mined, pined, signed, whined, wined.
Bide, bride, chide, cried, died, dried, dyed, eyed, glide, guide, hide, I'd, lied, pried, pride, ride, sighed, side, slide, snide, spied, stride, tide, tied, tried, wide.
[2] Bedtime, full-time, half-time, lifetime, longtime, maritime, meantime, nighttime, paradigm, part-time, pastime, peacetime, ragtime, sometime, springtime, sublime.
Airline, align, alpine, assign, benign, canine, combine, confine, consign, deadline, decline, define, design, divine, enshrine, entwine, feline, goldmine, headline, hemline, incline, moonshine, outshine, recline, red wine, refine, resign, sunshine, turbine.
Aligned, behind, combined, declined, defined, designed, entwined, inclined, maligned, mankind, reclined, refined, resigned, unkind, unwind.
Abide, aside, astride, bedside, beside, broadside, black-eyed, blue-eyed, brown-eyed, child bride, cock-eyed, confide, cowhide, decide, denied, divide, downside, green-eyed, hawk-eyed, high tide, hillside, inside, lakeside, low tide, offside, outside, preside, provide, rawhide, red-eyed, reside, seaside, subside, tie-dyed, tongue-tied, topside, untied, untried, upside, wayside, wide-eyed, worldwide, Yuletide.
[3] Anytime, pantomime, summertime, wintertime, overtime.
Alkaline, auld lang syne, concubine, intertwine, realign, underline, undermine, valentine.
Colour/color blind, intertwined, mastermind, redesigned, underlined, unsigned.
Amplified, beautified, bona fide, coincide, countryside, crucified, cyanide, dignified, dry-eyed, eagle-eyed, evil-eyed, falsified, fireside, glorified, goggle-eyed, gratified, homicide, justified, magnified, modified, mountainside, multiplied, mystified, nationwide, notified, nullified, occupied, oceanside, qualified, pacified, pie-eyed, petrified, purified, rectified, riverside, satisfied, specified, stupefied, suicide, terrified, testified, underside, waterside.

1.3.99 "--aytly" (as in "lately")
[2] greatly, innately, irately, lately, ornately, sedately, stately.

SURPRISING RHYMING:
[2] Eighty, Haiti, hate me, matey, safety, weighty.
Baby, crybaby, lady, maybe, shady.
Amaze me, crazy, daily, daisy, faded, gaily, glazy, hazy, lazy, mazy, pastry.
Brainy, grainy, mainly, plainly, rainy, sanely, vainly, zany.
Daily, gaily, gravy, navy, ukulele, wavy.
Barely, dairy, fairy, fairly, hairy, prairie, rarely, scary, squarely, unfairly, vary, wary.
Carefree, guarantee, jamboree, marquee.
[3] Humanely, insanely, mundanely, ungainly, urbanely.
Airy-fairy, canary, contrary, rosemary, unwary.
Stir-crazy, oops-a-daisy, upsy-daisy.

1.3.100 "--ayven" (as in "raven")
[2] craven, graven, haven, raven, shaven.
[3] clean-shaven, smooth-shaven, unshaven, misbehavin'.

SURPRISING RHYMING:
[2] Asian, nation, station.
Caveman, layman, Satan, salesman, shaman, spaceman, statesman, straighten, vegan.
Bacon, apron, matron, patron, shaken, taken, waken.
Brazen, emblazon, laden, liaison, maiden, raisin.
[3] Creation, damnation, duration, elation, fixation, flirtation, foundation, frustration, invasion, location, migration, narration, occasion, ovation, persuasion, quotation, relation, salvation, sensation, starvation, taxation, temptation, translation, vacation, vibration.
Awaken, forsaken, mistaken, unshaken, untaken.
[4] Godforsaken, overtaken, undertaken.
Aberration, accusation, admiration, adoration, adulation, aggravation, allegation, altercation, animation, aspiration, cancellation, celebration, combination, compensation, complication, concentration, condemnation, confirmation, confrontation, congregation, conservation, consolation, constellation, contemplation, conversation, decoration, dedication, degradation, demonstration, deprivation, desolation, desperation, destination, devastation, education, emigration, excitation, exclamation, expectation, explanation, exploitation, fascination, generation, graduation, imitation, immigration, implication,

incarnation, inclination, indication, indignation, information, innovation, inspiration, invitation, irritation, isolation, jubilation, liberation, limitation, meditation, moderation, motivation, obligation, observation, occupation, operation, palpitation, penetration, perspiration, preparation, presentation, preservation, provocation, publication, recreation, relaxation, reputation, reservation, resignation, revelation, scintillation, separation, situation, speculation, stimulation, stipulation, syncopation, titillation, transformation, transportation, trepidation, vaccination, valuation, violation, vindication.
[5] **Acceleration**, accommodation, alienation, annihilation, anticipation, appreciation, civilization, collaboration, communication, congratulations, consideration, cooperation, cross-examination, determination, discrimination, elimination, evacuation, evaluation, exaggeration, exhilaration, humiliation, imagination, infatuation, interrogation, interpretation, intoxication, investigation, justification, manipulation, multiplication, negotiation, organization, participation, qualification, realization, recommendation, reconciliation, recrimination, reincarnation, retaliation, reverberation, sophistication.

* * *

PART 2

'E'

2.1 "ee" sounds ....Index on Page 122
2.2 "er" sounds ....Index on Page 123
2.3 "eer" sounds ....Index on Page 127
2.4 "eh" sounds ....Index on Page 128

2.1 "ee"

2.1.1 "--bee" (as in "bee") 131
2.1.2 "--dee" (as in "melody") 134
2.1.3 "--fee" (as in "coffee") 137
2.1.4 "--gee" (as in "allergy") 140
2.1.5 "--kee" (as in "key") 142
2.1.6 "--lee" (as in "flee") 145
2.1.7 "--me" (as in "me") 148
2.1.8 "--nee" (as in "knee") 151
2.1.9 "--pee" (as in "recipe") 154
2.1.10 "--ree" (as in "free") 157
2.1.11 "--see" (as in "fantasy") 160
2.1.12 "--tee" (as in "certainty") 163
2.1.13 "--thee" (as in "sympathy") 166
2.1.14 "--vee" (as in "envy") 169
2.1.15 "--we" (as in "snowy") 172
2.1.16 "--zee" (as in "easy") 175
2.1.17 "--ablee" (as in "probably") 175
2.1.18 "--eech" (as in "reach") 177
2.1.19 "--eed" (as in "greed") 178
2.1.20 "--eeded" (as in "needed") 179
2.1.21 "--eeder" (as in "leader") 179
2.1.22 "--eedy" (as in "greedy") 179
2.1.23 "--eeding" (as in "needing") 180
2.1.24 "--eediest" (as in "greediest") 180
2.1.25 "--eef" (as in "thief") 181
2.1.26 "--eek" (as in "cheek") 182
2.1.27 "--eeked" (as in "sneaked") 183
2.1.28 "--eeker" (as in "seeker") 184
2.1.29 "--eeking" (as in "seeking") 184
2.1.30 "--eekly" (as in "weekly") 184
2.1.31 "--eel" (as in "feel") 185
2.1.32 "--eeled" (as in "sealed") 185
2.1.33 "--eelded" (as in "shielded") 185
2.1.34 "--eelding" (as in "shielding") 185
2.1.35 "--eeler" (as in "healer") 186
2.1.36 "--eeling" (as in "feeling") 186
2.1.37 "--eem" (as in "seem") 187
2.1.38 "--eemed" (as in "seemed") 187
2.1.39 "--eemer" (as in "dreamer") 188
2.1.40 "--eemy" (as in "dreamy") 188
2.1.41 "--eeming" (as in "dreaming") 188
2.1.42 "--een" (as in "been") 189
2.1.43 "--eened" (as in "leaned") 189
2.1.44 "--eena" (as in "greener") 190
2.1.45 "--eenest" (as in "greenest") 190
2.1.46 "--eening" (as in "meaning") 190

2.1.47 "--eep" (as in "keep") 191
2.1.48 "--eeped" (as in "reaped") 191
2.1.49 "--eeper" (as in "deeper") 192
2.1.50 "--eepee" (as in "weepy") 192
2.1.51 "--eeping" (as in "sleeping") 193
2.1.52 "--eeple" (as in "steeple") 193
2.1.53 "--eer" (as in "cheer") 193
2.1.54 "--eered" (as in "steered") 194
2.1.55 "--eerence" (as in "appearance") 194
2.1.56 "--eerest" (as in "dearest") 194
2.1.57 "--eerful" (as in "cheerful") 194
2.1.58 "--eery" (as in "weary") 195
2.1.59 "--earring" (as in "fearing") 195
2.1.60 "--earless" (as in "fearless") 196
2.1.61 "--eerly" (as in "nearly") 196
2.1.62 "--eece" (as in "peace") 197
2.1.63 "--eest" (as in "east") 197
2.1.64 "--eet" (as in "feet") 198
2.1.65 "--eeter (as in "cheater") 199
2.1.66 "--eeted" (as in "tweeted") 199
2.1.67 "--eeth" (as in "teeth") 199
2.1.68 "--eev" (as in "leave") 200
2.1.69 "--eeved" (as in "believed") 201
2.1.70 "--eevable" (as in "believable") 201
2.1.71 "--eeze" (as in "please") 202
2.1.72 "--eecher" (as in "teacher") 202
2.1.73 "--eeching" (as in "teaching") 203
2.1.74 "--eezer" (as in "teaser") 203
2.1.75 "--eeing" (as in "being") 204
2.1.76 "--eeces" (as in "pieces") 204
2.1.77 "--eezily" (as in "easily") 204
2.1.78 "--eeable" (as in "agreeable") 205
2.1.79 "--eerfully" (as in "tearfully") 205
2.1.80 "--eezable" (as in "squeezable") 206
2.1.81 "--eezingly" (as in "teasingly") 206
2.1.82 "--urlee" (as in "early") 206
2.1.83 "--ollee" (as in "holly") 207
2.1.84 "--allee" (as in "valley") 207
2.1.85 "--unnee" (as in "funny") 207
2.1.86 "--oppee" (as in "copy") 208
2.1.87 "--ittee" (as in "pretty") 208
2.1.88 "--ilitee" (as in "ability") 209
2.1.89 "--aritee" (as in "charity") 209

2.2 "er"

2.2.1 "--acker" (as in "hacker") 210
2.2.2 "--actor" (as in "tractor") 210
2.2.3 "--acer" (as in "racer") 211

2.2.4 "--azer" (as in "razor") 211
2.2.5 "--adder" (as in "sadder") 212
2.2.6 "--after" (as in "after") 212
2.2.7 "--agger" (as in "dagger") 213
2.2.8 "--ainter" (as in "painter") 213
2.2.9 "--airer" (as in "fairer") 214
2.2.10 "--aider" (as in "raider") 214
2.2.11 "--ailer" (as in "jailer") 215
2.2.12 "--aimer" (as in "gamer") 215
2.2.13 "--ainger" (as in "danger") 216
2.2.14 "--amper" (as in "pamper") 216
2.2.15 "--amber" (as in "clamber") 216
2.2.16 "--ambler" (as in "gambler") 217
2.2.17 "--ammer" (as in "hammer") 217
2.2.18 "--anner" (as in "banner") 217
2.2.19 "--ancer" (as in "dancer") 218
2.2.20 "--ander" (as in "grander") 218
2.2.21 "--anker" (as in "banker") 219
2.2.22 "--anter" (as in "banter") 219
2.2.23 "--apper" (as in "rapper") 219
2.2.24 "--arber" (as in "barber") 220
2.2.25 "--archer" (as in "marcher") 220
2.2.26 "--arder" (as in "harder") 220
2.2.27 "--arger" (as in "larger") 221
2.2.28 "--arker" (as in "darker") 221
2.2.29 "--armer" (as in "charmer") 221
2.2.30 "--arner" (as in "banana") 222
2.2.31 "--arper" (as in "sharper") 222
2.2.32 "--arter" (as in "smarter") 222
2.2.33 "--aster" (as in "faster") 223
2.2.34 "--asher" (as in "smasher") 223
2.2.35 "--atcher" (as in "catcher") 223
2.2.36 "--atter" (as in "shatter") 224
2.2.37 "--atterer" (as in "scatterer") 224
2.2.38 "--ayer" (as in "player") 224
2.2.39 "--ayker (as in "taker") 225
2.2.40 "--ayper" (as in "paper") 225
2.2.41 "--ayter" (as in "later") 226
2.2.42 "--ayver" (as in "saver") 226
2.2.43 "--edder" (as in "shredder") 227
2.2.44 "--eecher" (as in "teacher") 227
2.2.45 "--eeder" (as in "leader") 228
2.2.46 "--eeger" (as in "eager") 228
2.2.47 "--eeker" (as in "seeker") 229
2.2.48 "--eeler" (as in "healer") 229
2.2.49 "--eemer" (as in "dreamer") 230
2.2.50 "--eener" (as in "greener") 230
2.2.51 "--eeper" (as in "keeper") 231

2.2.52 "--eeter" (as in "sweeter") 231
2.2.53 "--eever" (as in "leaver") 232
2.2.54 "--eezer" (as in "teaser") 232
2.2.55 "--easure" (as in "treasure") 233
2.2.56 "--eller" (as in "cellar") 233
2.2.57 "--elthier" (as in "wealthier") 233
2.2.58 "--ember" (as in "remember") 234
2.2.59 "--ender" (as in "tender") 234
2.2.60 "--enser" (as in "censor") 234
2.2.61 "--enter" (as in "enter") 235
2.2.62 "--esser" (as in "lesser") 235
2.2.63 "--ester" (as in "protester") 235
2.2.64 "--etter" (as in "better") 235
2.2.65 "--ether" (as in "weather") 236
2.2.66 "--ever" (as in "never") 236
2.2.67 "--ibbler" (as in "nibbler) 236
2.2.68 "--iber" (as in "briber") 236
2.2.69 "--icer" (as in "nicer") 237
2.2.70 "--icker" (as in "kicker") 237
2.2.71 "--ider" (as in "spider") 237
2.2.72 "--ier" (as in "liar") 238
2.2.73 "--ieter" (as in "quieter") 238
2.2.74 "--iffer (as in "differ") 238
2.2.75 "--ifter" (as in "drifter") 238
2.2.76 "--iyger" (as in "tiger") 239
2.2.77 "--igger" (as in "bigger") 239
2.2.78 "--iggler" (as in "giggler") 239
2.2.79 "--iler" (as in "smiler") 240
2.2.80 "--iller" (as in "thriller") 240
2.2.81 "--illder" (as in "builder") 240
2.2.82 "--imer" (as in "climber") 240
2.2.83 "--imber" (as in "timber") 241
2.2.84 "--immer" (as in "swimmer") 241
2.2.85 "--imper" (as in "whimper") 241
2.2.86 "--inder" (as in "kinder") 242
2.2.87 "--iner" (as in "finer") 242
2.2.88 "--inger" (as in "singer") 243
2.2.89 "--inister" (as in "sinister") 243
2.2.90 "--inker" (as in "thinker") 243
2.2.91 "--inner" (as in "dinner") 243
2.2.92 "--inter" (as in "winter") 244
2.2.93 "--iper" (as in "wiper") 244
2.2.94 "--ipper" (as in "slipper") 244
2.2.95 "--iter" (as in "writer") 245
2.2.96 "--iver" (as in "driver") 245
2.2.97 "--isser" (as in "kisser") 245
2.2.98 "--isher" (as in "wisher") 246
2.2.99 "--ister" (as in "sister") 246

2.2.100 "--iskier" (as in "riskier") 246
2.2.101 "--itcher" (as in "richer") 246
2.2.102 "--itter" (as in "bitter") 247
2.2.103 "--ivver" (as in "river") 247
2.2.104 "--ixer" (as in "mixer") 247
2.2.105 "--izer" (as in "wiser") 248
2.2.106 "--izzier" (as in "dizzier") 248
2.2.107 "--oater" (as in "voter") 248
2.2.108 "--obber" (as in "robber") 249
2.2.109 "--obbler" (as in "cobbler") 249
2.2.110 "--ocer" (as in "grocer") 249
2.2.111 "--ocker" (as in "rocker") 250
2.2.112 "--odder" (as in "fodder") 250
2.2.113 "--oder" (as in "loader") 250
2.2.114 "--offer" (as in "offer") 250
2.2.115 "--ogger" (as in "blogger") 251
2.2.116 "--ohwer" (as in "slower") 251
2.2.117 "--oiler" (as in "boiler") 252
2.2.118 "--oker" (as in "joker") 252
2.2.119 "--olar" (as in "polar") 252
2.2.120 "--older" (as in "colder") 253
2.2.121 "--ollar" (as in "collar") 253
2.2.122 "--olter" (as in "falter") 253
2.2.123 "--omer" (as in "aroma") 253
2.2.124 "--onder" (as in "wander") 254
2.2.125 "--ooker" (as in "cooker") 254
2.2.126 "--opper" (as in "bopper") 254
2.2.127 "--oper" (as in "no-hoper") 255
2.2.128 "--ora" (as in "aura") 255
2.2.129 "--order" (as in "border") 255
2.2.130 "--orker" (as in "walker") 256
2.2.131 "--orler" (as in "trawler") 256
2.2.132 "--ormer" (as in "warmer") 256
2.2.133 "--orner" (as in "corner") 257
2.2.134 "--orter" (as in "daughter") 257
2.2.135 "--osser" (as in "embosser") 257
2.2.136 "--otter" (as in "hotter") 257
2.2.137 "--ounder" (as in "rounder") 258
2.2.138 "--outer" (as in "shouter") 258
2.2.139 "--over" (as in "rover") 258
2.2.140 "--owner" (as in "loner") 259
2.2.141 "--oyer" (as in "destroyer") 259
2.2.142 "--owder" (as in "powder") 259
2.2.143 "--owser" (as in "browser") 259
2.2.144 "--ower" (as in "flower") 260
2.2.145 "--owler" (as in "prowler") 260
2.2.146 "--oxer" (as in "boxer") 260
2.2.147 "--ozer" (as in "composer") 260

2.2.148 "--ooder" (as in "intruder") ... 261
2.2.149 "--ooer" (as in "fewer") ... 261
2.2.150 "--ooler" (as in "cooler") ... 262
2.2.151 "--oomer" (as in "boomer") ... 262
2.2.152 "--ooner" (as in "sooner") ... 262
2.2.153 "--ooper" (as in "super") ... 262
2.2.154 "--oorer" (as in "poorer") ... 263
2.2.155 "--ooter" (as in "computer") ... 263
2.2.156 "--oover" (as in "remover") ... 263
2.2.157 "--oozer" (as in "loser") ... 264
2.2.158 "--uffer" (as in "suffer") ... 264
2.2.159 "--ugger" (as in "sugar") ... 264
2.2.160 "--uggler" (as in "juggler") ... 265
2.2.161 "--ukker" (as in "trucker") ... 265
2.2.162 "--uller" (as in "duller") ... 265
2.2.163 "--ummer" (as in "summer") ... 265
2.2.164 "--umber" (as in "number") ... 266
2.2.165 "--umbler" (as in "tumbler") ... 266
2.2.166 "--umper" (as in "jumper") ... 266
2.2.167 "--unner" (as in "runner") ... 266
2.2.168 "--under" (as in "under") ... 267
2.2.169 "--unger" (as in "younger") ... 267
2.2.170 "--unter" (as in "hunter") ... 267
2.2.171 "--upper" (as in "supper") ... 268
2.2.172 "--urcher" (as in "searcher") ... 268
2.2.173 "--urder" (as in "murder") ... 268
2.2.174 "--urger" (as in "merger") ... 268
2.2.175 "--urker" (as in "worker") ... 268
2.2.176 "--urmer" (as in "firmer") ... 269
2.2.177 "--urner" (as in "earner") ... 269
2.2.178 "--urser" (as in "vice versa") ... 269
2.2.179 "--urver" (as in "observer") ... 269
2.2.180 "--utter" (as in "butter") ... 270
2.2.181 "--usher" (as in "usher") ... 270
2.2.182 "--uster" (as in "buster") ... 270
2.2.183 "--uvver" (as in "lover") ... 270
2.2.184 "--uther" (as in "mother") ... 271

2.3 "eer"

2.3.1 "--eer" (as in "cheer") ... 271
2.3.2 "--eered" (as in "steered") ... 271
2.3.3 "--eerence" (as in "appearance") ... 272
2.3.4 "--eerest" (as in "dearest") ... 272
2.3.5 "--eerful" (as in "cheerful") ... 272
2.3.6 "--eerfully" (as in "tearfully") ... 272
2.3.7 "--eery" (as in "weary") ... 273
2.3.8 "--earring" (as in "fearing") ... 274
2.3.9 "--earless" (as in "fearless") ... 274

2.3.10 "--eerly" (as in "nearly") 274

2.4 "eh"

2.4.1 "--easure" (as in "treasure") 275
2.4.2 "--ebble" (as in "pebble") 275
2.4.3 "--eck" (as in "neck") 276
2.4.4 "--ecking" (as in "wrecking") 276
2.4.5 "--ecks" (as in "checks") 277
2.4.6 "--ect" (as in "checked") 277
2.4.7 "--ects" (as in "reflects") 278
2.4.8 "--eckless" (as in "necklace") 279
2.4.9 "--ection" (as in "affection") 279
2.4.10 "--ected" (as in "affected") 279
2.4.11 "--ector" (as in "collector") 280
2.4.12 "--ecting" (as in "affecting") 281
2.4.13 "--ective" (as in "reflective") 281
2.4.14 "--ed" (as in "bed") 282
2.4.15 "--edge" (as in "ledge") 283
2.4.16 "--edged" (as in "pledged") 283
2.4.17 "--edded" (as in "threaded") 283
2.4.18 "--edder" (as in "shredder") 284
2.4.19 "--edding" (as in "wedding") 284
2.4.20 "--eddly" (as in "medley") 285
2.4.21 "--eddline" (as in "headline") 285
2.4.22 "--eddlock" (as in "deadlock") 285
2.4.23 "--edges" (as in "pledges") 286
2.4.24 "--edging" (as in "hedging") 286
2.4.25 "--edible" (as in "edible") 287
2.4.26 "--edicate" (as in "dedicate") 287
2.4.27 "--eddily" (as in "readily") 287
2.4.28 "--eff" (as in "chef") 288
2.4.29 "--efference" (as in "preference") 288
2.4.30 "--egg" (as in "beg") 289
2.4.31 "--egging" (as in "begging") 289
2.4.32 "--ell" (as in "tell") 290
2.4.33 "--eld" (as in "held") 290
2.4.34 "--elf" (as in "self") 290
2.4.35 "--elm" (as in "realm") 290
2.4.36 "--elp" (as in "help") 291
2.4.37 "--elt" (as in "belt") 291
2.4.38 "--elth" (as in "health") 291
2.4.39 "--elve" (as in "shelve") 292
2.4.40 "--elves" (as in "shelves") 292
2.4. 41 "--eller" (as in "cellar") 292
2.4.42 "--elling" (as in "telling") 293
2.4.43 "--ello" (as in "hello") 293
2.4.44 "--elted" (as in "melted") 294
2.4.45 "--elting" (as in "melting") 294

2.4.46 "--eltering" (as in "sheltering") 295
2.4.47 "--elthier" (as in "wealthier") 295
2.4.48 "--ellously" (as in "jealously") 295
2.4.49 "--ember" (as in "remember") 296
2.4.50 "--em" (as in "them") 296
2.4.51 "--empt" (as in "tempt") 297
2.4.52 "--en" (as in "when") 297
2.4.53 "--end" (as in "send") 298
2.4.54 "--ench" (as in "clench") 298
2.4.55 "--ence" (as in "fence") 299
2.4.56 "--enced" (as in "commenced") 300
2.4.57 "--ent" (as in "went") 300
2.4.58 "--ended" (as in "ended") 301
2.4.59 "--endent" (as in "dependent") 302
2.4.60 "--ender" (as in "tender") 302
2.4.61 "--ending" (as in "sending") 302
2.4.62 "--enser" (as in "censor") 303
2.4.63 "--ential" (as in "essential") 304
2.4.64 "--ention" (as in "mention") 304
2.4.65 "--encing" (as in "commencing") 304
2.4.66 "--ensive" (as in "expensive") 305
2.4.67 "--ented" (as in "scented") 305
2.4.68 "--enter" (as in "enter") 306
2.4.69 "--endable" (as in "mendable") 306
2.4.70 "--enderest" (as in "tenderest") 306
2.4.71 "--entering" (as in "entering") 307
2.4.72 "--ep" (as in "step") 307
2.4.73 "--ept" (as in "slept") 307
2.4.74 "--eption" (as in "deception") 308
2.4.75 "--erry" (as in "very") 308
2.4.76 "--erries" (as in "berries") 309
2.4.77 "--ess" (as in "dress") 309
2.4.78 "--esk" (as in "desk") 310
2.4.79 "--est" (as in "best") 310
2.4.80 "--estion" (as in "question") 311
2.4.81 "--escent" (as in "crescent") 311
2.4.82 "--esser" (as in "lesser") 312
2.4.83 "--esses" (as in "caresses") 312
2.4.84 "--ession" (as in "confession") 313
2.4.85 "--essing" (as in "caressing") 313
2.4.86 "--essive" (as in "impressive") 314
2.4.87 "--ested" (as in "rested") 314
2.4.88 "--ester" (as in "protester") 315
2.4.89 "--esting" (as in "resting") 315
2.4.90 "--esents" (as in "presents") 316
2.4.91 "--esidents" (as in "presidents") 316
2.4.92 "--et" (as in "bet") 317
2.4.93 "--eth" (as in "breath") 317

2.4.94 "--etching" (as in "fetching") 318
2.4.95 "--etch" (as in "sketch") 318
2.4.96 "--etched" (as in "stretched") 318
2.4.97 "--etted" (as in "regretted") 319
2.4.98 "--etter" (as in "better") 319
2.4.99 "--ether" (as in "weather") 319
2.4.100 "--ethered" (as in "weathered") 320
2.4.101 "--etty" (as in "petty") 320
2.4.102 "--ettic" (as in "poetic") 320
2.4.103 "--etting" (as in "getting") 321
2.4.104 "--ettal" (as in "metal") 321
2.4.105 "--ethery" (as in "feathery") 321
2.4.106 "--ever" (as in "never") 322
2.4.107 "--everence" (as in "reverence") 322
2.4.108 "--evity" (as in "levity") 322
2.4.109 "--ext" (as in "next") 323

* * *

2.1 "ee"

2.1.1 "--bee" (as in "bee")
[1] be, bee.
[2] abbey, baby, bobby, busby, cabby, chubby, crabby, derby, flabby, Frisbee, gabby hobby, grubby, hubby, lobby, maybe, ruby, scabby, shabby, snobby, would-be, zombie.
[3] bumblebee, honeybee, namby-pamby, wallaby, wannabe.

SURPRISING RHYMING:
[1] **Brie,** fee, flea, flee, free, gee, glee, he, key, knee, lee, me, pea, pee, sea, see, spree, tee, tea, the, thee, three, tree, twee, we, wee, whee, zee.
Beam, cream, deem, dream, gleam, meme, ream, scheme, scream, seam, seem, steam, stream, team, teem, theme.
[2] **Agree,** angry, beery, belfry, berry, bleary, blurry, boundary, bury, carefree, carry, cheery, cherry, country, curry, dairy, dearie, debris, degree, dowry, dreary, dust-free, eerie, entry, esprit, every, fairy, ferry, fiery, flowery, flurry, furry, fury, gentry, germ-free, glory, gory, Grand Prix, gumtree, hairy, hoary, hurry, hungry, jury, laundry, leery, lorry, marry, merry, paltry, pantry, parry, pastry, poultry, powdery, prairie, quandary, quarry, query, scary, scot-free, sentry, sorry, starry, storey, story, sultry, tawdry, teary, theory, treachery, vary, very, vestry, wary, weary, wintry, wiry, worry.
Bumpy, chappie, chippy, chirpy, crappie, creepy, crispy, dippy, dopey, drippy, droopy, dumpy, flappy, frumpy, green pea, grippy, groupie, grumpy, happy, hippie, humpy, jumpy, lippy, loopy, lumpy, nappy, nippy, pappy, peppy, plummy, preppy, pulpy, puppy, raspy, ropy, sappy, scampi, scrappy, scrummy, scrumpy, skimpy, sleepy, slippy, snappy, snippy, snoopy, soapy, soupy, stripy, stumpy, swampy, sweetpea, teepee, trippy, vampy, weepy, whippy, whoopee, wimpy, wispy, yuppie, zappy, zippy.
Bitty, city, ditty, gritty, pity, pretty, witty.
Baddy, bawdy, beady, bloody, body, brandy, buddy, caddie, candy, cloudy, daddy, dandy, dowdy, foodie, gaudy, giddy, greedy, handy, hardy, heady, hoodie, howdy, kiddie, laddie, lady, MD, midi, moody, mouldy/moldy (U.S.), muddy, needy, nerdy, oldie, randy, ready, roadie, rowdy, sandy, seedy, shady, shandy, shoddy, speedy, steady, study, sturdy, tardy, teddy, tidy, trendy, tweedy, weedy, windy, woody, wordy.
Beefy, coffee, comfy, daffy, fluffy, goofy, huffy, iffy, jiffy, leafy, puffy, scruffy, selfie, sniffy, stuffy, toffee, toughie, trophy.
Army, balmy, barmy, blimey, chamois, chummy, clammy, creamy, crummy, dreamy, dummy, Emmy, foamy, gimme, gleamy, gloomy, Grammy, grimy, gummy, hammy, homey, jammy, lemme, limey, mammy, me, mommy, mummy, plummy, roomy, samey, scrummy, seamy, slimy, slummy, smarmy, stormy, tummy, whammy, wormy, yummy.
Acne, any, beanie, blarney, bonny, bony, brainy, brawny, briny, brownie, canny, chimney, cine, cockney, corny, cranny, crony,
Disney, genie, grainy, granny, greeny, guinea, hinny, horny, journey, kidney, knee, loony, many, meanie, mini, nanny, ninny, penny, phoney/phony (U.S.), pony, puny, queenie, rainy, sarnie, scrawny, shinny, shiny, skinny, spinney, stony, teeny, thorny, tinny, tiny, townie, trainee, tranny, tweeny, uni, weeny, whinny, whiny, zany.
Budgie, cagey, clergy, dingy, dodgy, edgy, gee, gee-gee, grungy, gungy, mangy, orgy, podgy, pudgy, rangy, sludgy, smudgy, spongy, squeegee, squidgy, stagy, stingy, stodgy, veggie, wedgie, whingy.
Achy, baccy, balky, beaky, bookie, brickie, bulky, car key, chalky, cheeky, chunky, cliquey, clunky, cocky, cookie, corky, creaky, crikey, croaky, dinky, donkey, door key, ducky, dusky, flaky, flunkey, folkie, folky, freaky, frisky, funky, gawky, hanky, hickey, hockey, hokey, hookey, hunky, husky, icky, inky, jerky, jockey, jokey, junkie, key, karaoke, khaki, kinky, lackey, lanky, latchkey, leaky, lucky, marquee, mickey, milky, murky, monkey, mucky, musky, narky, nooky, passkey, peaky, perky, pesky, picky, pinkie, pinky, plucky, pokey, porky, psyche, punky, quaky, quickie, quirky, reeky, risky, rocky, rookie, shaky, sickie, silky, ski, slinky, smoky, snaky, sneaky, sparky, spiky, spooky, squeaky, sticky, stinky, stocky, streaky, sulky, swanky, tacky, talkie, techie, tricky, turkey, turnkey, wacky, whiskey/whisky, wonky, Yankee, yucky.
Ably, amply, aptly, barley, beastly, belly, bobbly, bubbly, bully, chili, chilly, cleanly,

131

comely, coolie, coolly, costly, coyly, crackly, crawly, crinkly, crumbly, crumply, cuddly, daily, dally, dangly, deadly, deathly, deli, dimly, dimply, doily, drily, drizzly, dully, duly, earthly, elderly, fiddly, filly, fitly, flatly, fleshly, freckly, friendly, frilly, fully, gaily, gangly, ghastly, ghostly, giggly, goalie, godly, goodly, googly, gristly, grizzly, grumbly, hilly, hotly, holy, hourly, husbandly, hyperbole, idly, jelly, jangly, jiggly, jingly, jowly, kindly, kingly, knobbly, likely, lily, lively, lonely, lordly, lovely, lowly, madly, manly, medley, monthly, mostly, motley, muesli, muscly, newly, niggly, nightly, oddly, oily, only, orderly, paisley, parley, pebbly, pimply, poorly, portly, prickly, priestly, princely, purply, queenly, really, rumbly, sadly, saintly, scribbly, seemly, shapely, shyly, sickly, silly, slightly, slyly, smiley, smelly, snarly, sparkly, spindly, sprightly, squiggly, stately, steely, stiffly, straggly, sully, surely, tangly, telly, tickly, timely, tingly, tinkly, trembly, trimly, trolley, truly, twiddly, twinkly, ugly, volley, waffly, wally, weakly, weekly, welly, wetly, wheelie, wifely, wiggly, wily, wobbly, woolly, worldly, wriggly, wrinkly, wryly, yearly.
Bossy, bouncy, brassy, chassis, classy, curtsy, Dixie, dressy, emcee, fancy, fleecy, folksy, footsie, foresee, foxy, fussy, glassy, glitzy, glossy, grassy, greasy, gutsy, gypsy, horsey, hussy, saucy, icy, kissy, lacy, lassie, look-see, maxi, mercy, messy, missy, mousy, pacey, pixie, posse, pricey, juicy, prissy, proxy, pussy, racy, ritzy, sassy, schmaltzy, sexy, sightsee, sissy, spacey, specie, spicy, taxi, tipsy, tootsie, waxy.
Anti, arty, auntie, batty, beastie, bitty, catty, chatty, city, crafty, cruelty, dainty, ditty, draughty/drafty (U.S.), eighty, fatty, fifty, frailty, goatee, gritty, guilty, hasty, hearty, hefty, jetty, lefty, matey, meaty, minty, misty, nasty, nifty, party, pasty, petit, petty, pity, plenty, pretty, QT, safety, scanty, settee, shanty/chanty (U.S.), shifty, sixty, sweaty, sweetie, swiftie, tarty, tatty, tasty, thrifty, treaty, twenty, twisty, weighty, witty, yeti.
Breathy, earthy, filthy, frothy, healthy, lengthy, mouthy, pithy, smithy, smoothie, stealthy, swarthy, toothy, wealthy, worthy.
Bevvy, Chevy, curvy, envy, gravy, groovy, heavy, ivy, levee, levy, lovey, luvvy, movie, navy, nervy, savvy, skivvy, wavy.
Blowy, bluey, chewy, dewy, doughy, ennui, gluey, gooey, hooey, peewee, phooey, screwy, showy, snowy.
Burly, curly, early, girlie, hurly-burly, surly, swirly, twirly, whirly.
Brolly, collie, dolly, folly, golly, holly, jolly, lolly, trolley, volley, wally.
Alley, dally, galley, pally, rally, reveille, sally, tally, valley.
Bunny, funny, gunny, honey, money, runny, sonny, sunny.
Choppy, copy, floppy, jalopy, poppy, sloppy, soppy, stroppy.
[3] Ancestry, archery, artistry, bakery, battery, bigotry, binary, blackberry, blubbery, blueberry, blustery, brasserie, bravery, brewery, bribery, burglary, calorie, carpentry, carvery, cavalry, celery, century, chemistry, chicory, chivalry, Christmas tree, colliery, contrary, devilry, diary, dietary, disagree, dithery, doddery, drudgery, dungaree, duty-free, eatery, enquiry, estuary, expiry, factory, fakery, feathery, filigree, finery, fishery, flattery, fluttery, forestry, forgery, gallery, geometry, gimmickry, glittery, greenery, grocery, history, imagery, injury, inquiry, ivory, jamboree, jewellery/jewelry (U.S.), jittery, leathery, lingerie, lottery, luxury, memory, mercury, misery, momentary, monastery, mystery, nursery, obituary, obligatory, pageantry, pedigree, perjury, pillory, pleasantry, poetry, pottery, primary, priory, quivery, referee, revelry, reverie, rivalry, robbery, rockery, rosary, rubbery, salary, sanctuary, savagery, savory, scenery, sensory, shimmery, shivery, silvery, slavery, slippery, sorcery, sugary, surgery, tapestry, thundery, treachery, trickery, victory, wintery, wizardry.
Aromatherapy, gossipy, photocopy, recipe, slap-happy, syrupy, therapy, unhappy.
Burgundy, chickadee, COD, comedy, custody, dogsbody, embody, fool-hardy, jeopardy, malady, melody, nobody, parody, perfidy, Ph.D., raggedy, remedy, rhapsody, somebody, subsidy, tragedy.
Alchemy, bigamy, blasphemy, blossomy, bonhomie, enemy, excuse me, infamy, pastrami, salami, sesame, tsunami.
Agony, attorney, balcony, baloney, bikini, botany, colony, company, cottony, cushiony, destiny, ebony, felony, gluttony, halfpenny, harmony, Houdini, irony, larceny, litany, martini, mutiny, satiny, scrutiny, symphony, tiffany, timpani, trainee, tyranny, villainy.
Allergy, effigy, elegy, emoji, energy, eulogy, lethargy, liturgy, ology, prodigy, refugee, strategy, synergy, trilogy.
Actually, brotherly, easterly, elderly, equally, fatherly, finally, formally, formerly, gingerly, gravelly, leisurely, masterly, miserly, motherly, naturally, neighbourly/neighborly (U.S.),

normally, northerly, orderly, overly, partially, properly, scholarly, sisterly, southerly, specially, thoroughly, usually, utterly, virtually, westerly.
Committee, gravity, nitty-gritty, responsibility, sanity, self-pity.
Anarchy, finicky, garlicky, gimmicky, headachy, malarkey, monarchy, panicky, plasticky.
Assembly, bimonthly, biweekly, bodily, comradely, cowardly, dastardly, directly, easterly, family, finale, fleur-de-lis, fortnightly, heavenly, hillbilly, homily, icily, jubilee, laggardly, maidenly, matronly, panoply, plug-ugly, quarterly, rascally, readily, reveille, simile, slovenly, soldierly, ungainly, unruly, user-friendly, wizardly, womanly.
Actressy, agency, bankruptcy, blatancy, bourgeoisie, buoyancy, Christmassy, clemency, courtesy, currency, decency, divorcee, ecstasy, embassy, fallacy, fantasy, fluency, galaxy, heresy, infancy, jealousy, legacy, licensee, leniency, lunacy, odyssey, oversee, papacy, pharmacy, piracy, policy, potency, pregnancy, primacy, privacy, prophecy, regency, secrecy, tendency, Tennessee, truancy, undersea, urgency, vacancy.
Absentee, amnesty, brevity, casualty, cavity, certainty, charity, chastity, clarity, committee, confetti, crotchety, crudity, deity, density, deputy, devotee, dignity, dynasty, enmity, entity, fidgety, gaiety, graffiti, gravity, guarantee, honesty, invitee, karate, laity, levity, liberty, machete, majesty, modesty, nudity, oddity, parity, penalty, piety, poverty, property, puberty, purity, quality, repartee, rickety, sanctity, sanctuary, seventy, sovereignty, spaghetti, specialty, three-sixty, trinity, unity, uppity, vanity, velvety.
Apathy, empathy, newsworthy, noteworthy, praiseworthy, roadworthy, seaworthy, sympathy, trustworthy, unhealthy, unworthy.
Anchovy, c'est la vie, eau-de-vie, lovey-dovey, top-heavy, topsy-turvy, vis-à-vis.
Billowy, chop suey, echoey, shadowy, yellowy, willowy.
Freezingly, pleasingly, teasingly, wheezingly.
[4] Accessory, adultery, artillery, cautionary, cemetery, compulsory, confectionery, conciliatory, constabulary, contemporary, customary, debauchery, delivery, dictionary, directory, discovery, distillery, elementary, embroidery, explanatory, exploratory, hunky-dory, idolatry, imaginary, incendiary, infirmary, inflammatory, judiciary, laboratory, legendary, literary, machinery, mandatory, mercenary, military, missionary, necessary, ordinary, patisserie, perfumery, preliminary, psychiatry, publicity, reactionary, recovery, secretary, secondary, simplicity, skullduggery, solitary, stationary, stationery, temporary, territory, tomfoolery, upholstery, visionary, vocabulary.
Anybody, busybody, everybody, fuddy-duddy, hurdy-gurdy, oldie worlde, understudy.
Academy, anatomy, astronomy, economy, epitome, origami.
Aborigine, accompany, acrimony, alimony, cacophony, ceremony, epiphany, hootenanny, ignominy, macaroni, mahogany, matrimony, minestrone, monotony, pepperoni, teeny-weeny, telephony, testimony.
Apostrophe, biography, catastrophe, choreography, geography, philosophy, photography.
Analogy, anthology, apology, archeology, astrology, biology, cardiology, chronology, ecology, geology, ideology, mythology, psychology, technology, theology, zoology.
Ability, agility, civility, facility, fertility, fragility, futility, hostility, humility, mobility, nobility, responsibility, stability, tranquillity/tranquility (U.S.), utility, versatility, virility, volatility.
Especially, eventually, initially, incidentally, melancholy, monopoly, occasionally, officially, originally, personally, universally, unmannerly.
Absolutely, anomaly, creepy-crawly, curmudgeonly, dilly-dally, eco-friendly, facsimile, fait accompli, gentlemanly, holy-moly, hurly-burly, immediately, melancholy, monopoly, rockabilly, roly-poly, shilly-shally, softly-softly, ukulele, underbelly, willy-nilly, yellow-belly.
Accuracy, ascendancy, complacency, consistency, conspiracy, contingency, controversy, deficiency, delicacy, diplomacy, discrepancy, efficiency, emergency, hypocrisy, idiocy, intimacy, intricacy, itsy-bitsy, paparazzi, presidency, prima facie, proficiency, radiancy, redundancy, relentlessly, sufficiency, supremacy, transparency.
Absurdity, affinity, amenity, anxiety, barbarity, calamity, cognoscenti, community, conformity, credulity, difficulty, dilettante, divinity, enormity, equality, eternity, fatality, fidelity, fifty-fifty, fraternity, frivolity, glitterati, heredity, hilarity, humanity, humidity, immunity, impunity, indemnity, infinity, infirmity, intercity, literati, maternity, modernity, morality, nitty-gritty, obscenity, profanity, proximity, reality, senility, serenity, sobriety, solemnity, virility, stupidity, twenty-twenty, variety, vicinity, vigilante, virginity, vulgarity.
[5] Anniversary, beneficiary, camaraderie, complementary, complimentary, contradictory, directory, documentary, evolutionary, revolutionary, rudimentary, supplementary.
Ambiguity, anonymity, continuity, familiarity, femininity, impropriety, ingenuity,

irregularity, liability, masculinity, notoriety, opportunity, peculiarity, popularity, regularity, serendipity, similarity, solidarity, spontaneity, uniformity, versatility, viability, volatility.

2.1.2 "--dee" (as in "melody")

[2] baddy, bandy, bawdy, beady, bloody, body, brandy, buddy, caddie, candy, cloudy, daddy, dandy, diddy, dowdy, foodie, gaudy, giddy, greedy, handy, hardy, heady, hoodie, howdy, kiddie, laddie, lardy, lady, MD, midi, moody, mouldy/moldy (U.S.), muddy, needy, nerdy, oldie, randy, ready, roadie, rowdy, sandy, seedy, shady, shandy, shoddy, speedy, steady, study, sturdy, tardy, teddy, tidy, trendy, tweedy, windy, wordy.
[3] burgundy, chickadee, COD, comedy, custody, dogsbody, fool-hardy, jeopardy, malady, melody, nobody, parody, perfidy, Ph.D., raggedy, remedy, rhapsody, somebody, subsidy, tragedy, .
[4] anybody, busybody, everybody, fuddy-duddy, higgledy-piggledy, hurdy-gurdy, oldie worlde, oven-ready, understudy.

SURPRISING RHYMING:
[1] **Be**, bee, fee, flea, flee, gee, glee, he, key, knee, me, pea, pee, sea, see, ski, tee, tea, the, thee, twee, we, wee, whee, zee.
Brie, free, re, spree, three, tree.
Beam, cream, deem, dream, gleam, meme, ream, scheme, scream, seam, seem, steam, stream, team, teem, theme.
[2] **Abbey**, baby, bobby, busby, cabby, chubby, crabby, derby, flabby, Frisbee, gabby hobby, grubby, hubby, lobby, maybe, ruby, scabby, shabby, snobby, would-be, zombie.
Agree, angry, beery, belfry, berry, bleary, blurry, boundary, bury, carefree, carry, cheery, cherry, country, curry, dairy, dearie, debris, degree, dowry, dreary, dust-free, eerie, entry, esprit, every, fairy, ferry, fiery, flowery, flurry, furry, fury, gentry, germ-free, glory, gory, Grand Prix, gumtree, hairy, hoary, hurry, hungry, jury, laundry, leery, lorry, marry, merry, paltry, pantry, parry, pastry, poultry, powdery, prairie, quandary, quarry, query, scary, scot-free, sentry, sorry, starry, storey, story, sultry, tawdry, teary, theory, treachery, vary, very, vestry, wary, weary, wintry, wiry, worry.
Bumpy, chappie, chippy, chirpy, clippie, crappie, creepy, crispy, dippy, dopey, drippy, droopy, dumpy, flappy, frumpy, grippy, groupie, grumpy, happy, hippie, humpy, jumpy, lippy, loopy, lumpy, nappy, nippy, pappy, peppy, plummy, preppy, pulpy, puppy, raspy, ropy, sappy, scampi, scrappy, scrummy, scrumpy, skimpy, sleepy, slippy, snappy, snippy, snoopy, soapy, soupy, stripy, stumpy, swampy, sweetpea, teepee, trippy, vampy, weepy, whippy, whoopee, wimpy, wispy, yuppie, zappy, zippy.
Bitty, city, ditty, gritty, pity, pretty, witty.
Beefy, coffee, comfy, daffy, fluffy, goofy, huffy, iffy, jiffy, leafy, puffy, scruffy, selfie, sniffy, stuffy, toffee, toughie, trophy.
Army, balmy, barmy, blimey, chamois, chummy, clammy, creamy, crummy, dreamy, dummy, Emmy, foamy, gimme, gleamy, gloomy, Grammy, grimy, gummy, hammy, homey, jammy, lemme, limey, mammy, me, mommy, mummy, plummy, roomy, samey, scrummy, seamy, slimy, slummy, smarmy, stormy, tummy, whammy, wormy, yummy.
Acne, any, beanie, blarney, bonny, bony, brainy, brawny, briny, brownie, canny, chimney, cine, cockney, corny, cranny, crony, Disney, genie, grainy, granny, guinea, hinny, horny, journey, knee, loony, many, meanie, mini, nanny, ninny, penny, pony, phoney/phony (U.S.), puny, queenie, rainy, sarnie, scrawny, shiny, skinny, stony, teeny, thorny, tinny, tiny, townie, trainee, tranny, tweeny, uni, weeny, whiny, zany.
Budgie, cagey, clergy, dingy, dodgy, edgy, gee, gee-gee, grungy, gungy, mangy, orgy, sludgy, smudgy, spongy, squeegee, squidgy, stagy, stingy, stodgy, veggie, whingy.
Achy, baccy, balky, beaky, bookie, brickie, bulky, car key, chalky, cheeky, chunky, cliquey, clunky, cocky, cookie, corky, creaky, crikey, croaky, dinky, donkey, door key, ducky, dusky, flaky, flunkey, folkie, folky, freaky, frisky, funky, gawky, hanky, hickey, hockey, hokey, hookey, hunky, husky, icky, inky, jerky, jockey, jokey, junkie, key, karaoke, khaki, kinky, lackey, lanky, latchkey, leaky, lucky, marquee, mickey, milky, murky, monkey, mucky, musky, narky, nooky, passkey, peaky, perky, pesky, picky, pinkie, pinky, plucky, pokey, porky, psyche, punky, quaky, quickie, quirky, reeky, risky, rocky, rookie, shaky, sickie, silky, ski, slinky, smoky, snaky, sneaky, sparky, spiky, spooky, squeaky, sticky, stinky, stocky, streaky, sulky, swanky, tacky, talkie, techie, tricky, turkey, turnkey, wacky, whiskey/whisky, wonky, Yankee, yucky.

Ably, amply, aptly, barley, beastly, belly, bobbly, bubbly, bully, chili, chilly, cleanly, comely, coolie, coolly, costly, coyly, crackly, crawly, crinkly, crumbly, crumply, cuddly, daily, dally, dangly, deadly, deathly, deli, dimly, dimply, doily, drily, drizzly, dully, duly, earthly, elderly, fiddly, filly, fitly, flatly, fleshly, freckly, friendly, frilly, fully, gaily, gangly, ghastly, ghostly, giggly, goalie, godly, goodly, googly, gristly, grizzly, grumbly, hilly, hotly, holy, hourly, husbandly, hyperbole, idly, jelly, jangly, jiggly, jingly, jowly, kindly, kingly, knobbly, likely, lily, lively, lonely, lordly, lovely, lowly, madly, manly, medley, monthly, mostly, motley, muesli, muscly, newly, niggly, nightly, oddly, oily, only, orderly, paisley, parley, pebbly, pimply, poorly, portly, prickly, priestly, princely, purply, queenly, really, rumbly, sadly, saintly, scribbly, seemly, shapely, shyly, sickly, silly, slightly, slyly, smiley, smelly, snarly, sparkly, spindly, sprightly, squiggly, stately, steely, stiffly, straggly, sully, surely, tangly, telly, tickly, timely, tingly, tinkly, trembly, trimly, trolley, truly, twiddly, twinkly, ugly, volley, waffly, wally, weakly, weekly, welly, wetly, wheelie, wifely, wiggly, wily, wobbly, woolly, worldly, wriggly, wrinkly, wryly, yearly.
Bossy, bouncy, brassy, chassis, classy, curtsy, Dixie, dressy, emcee, fancy, fleecy, folksy, footsie, foresee, foxy, fussy, glassy, glitzy, glossy, grassy, greasy, gutsy, gypsy, horsey, hussy, saucy, icy, kissy, lacy, lassie, look-see, maxi, mercy, messy, missy, mousy, pacey, pixie, posse, pricey, juicy, prissy, proxy, pussy, racy, ritzy, sassy, schmaltzy, sexy, sightsee, sissy, spacey, specie, spicy, taxi, tipsy, tootsie, waxy.
Anti, arty, auntie, batty, beastie, bitty, catty, chatty, city, crafty, cruelty, dainty, ditty, draughty/drafty (U.S.), eighty, fatty, fifty, frailty, goatee, gritty, guilty, hasty, hearty, hefty, jetty, lefty, matey, meaty, minty, misty, nasty, nifty, party, pasty, petit, petty, pity, plenty, pretty, QT, safety, scanty, settee, shanty/chanty (U.S.), shifty, sixty, sweaty, sweetie, swiftie, tarty, tatty, tasty, thrifty, treaty, twenty, twisty, weighty, witty, yeti.
Breathy, earthy, filthy, frothy, healthy, lengthy, mouthy, smithy, smoothie, stealthy, swarthy, toothy, wealthy, worthy.
Bevvy, Chevy, curvy, envy, gravy, groovy, heavy, ivy, levee, lovey, luvvy, movie, navy, nervy, savvy, scurvy, skivvy, spivvy, wavy.
Blowy, chewy, dewy, doughy, gluey, gooey, hooey, phooey, screwy, showy, snowy.
Burly, curly, early, girlie, hurly-burly, surly, swirly, twirly, whirly.
Brolly, collie, dolly, folly, golly, holly, jolly, lolly, trolley, volley, wally.
Alley, dally, dilly-dally, galley, pally, rally, reveille, sally, tally, valley.
Bunny, funny, gunny, honey, money, runny, sonny, sunny, tunny.
Choppy, copy, floppy, jalopy, poppy, sloppy, soppy, stroppy.
[3] Bumblebee, honeybee, namby-pamby, wallaby, wannabe.
Ancestry, archery, artistry, bakery, battery, bigotry, binary, blackberry, blubbery, blueberry, blustery, brasserie, bravery, brewery, bribery, burglary, calorie, carpentry, carvery, cavalry, celery, century, chemistry, chicory, chivalry, Christmas tree, colliery, contrary, devilry, diary, dietary, disagree, dithery, doddery, drudgery, dungaree, duty-free, eatery, enquiry, estuary, expiry, factory, fakery, feathery, filigree, finery, fishery, flattery, fluttery, forestry, forgery, gallery, geometry, gimmickry, glittery, greenery, grocery, history, imagery, injury, inquiry, ivory, jamboree, jewellery/jewelry (U.S.), jittery, leathery, lingerie, lottery, luxury, memory, mercury, misery, momentary, monastery, mystery, nursery, obituary, obligatory, pageantry, pedigree, perjury, pillory, pleasantry, poetry, pottery, primary, priory, quivery, referee, revelry, reverie, rivalry, robbery, rockery, rosary, rubbery, salary, sanctuary, savagery, savory, scenery, sensory, shimmery, shivery, silvery, slavery, slippery, sorcery, sugary, surgery, tapestry, thundery, treachery, trickery, victory, wintery, wizardry.
Aromatherapy, gossipy, photocopy, recipe, slap-happy, syrupy, therapy, unhappy.
Alchemy, bigamy, blasphemy, blossomy, bonhomie, enemy, excuse me, infamy, pastrami, salami, sesame, tsunami.
Agony, attorney, balcony, baloney, bikini, botany, colony, company, cottony, cushiony, destiny, ebony, felony, gluttony, halfpenny, harmony, Houdini, irony, larceny, litany, martini, mutiny, satiny, scrutiny, symphony, tiffany, timpani, trainee, tyranny, villainy.
Allergy, effigy, elegy, emoji, energy, eulogy, lethargy, prodigy, refugee, strategy, synergy, trilogy.
Actually, broccoli, brotherly, easterly, elderly, equally, fatherly, finally, formally, formerly, gingerly, gravelly, leisurely, masterly, miserly, motherly, naturally, neighbourly/neighborly (U.S.), normally, northerly, orderly, overly, partially, properly, rascally, scholarly, sisterly, specially, thoroughly, usually, utterly, virtually, westerly.

Committee, gravity, nitty-gritty, responsibility, sanity, self-pity.
Anarchy, finicky, garlicky, gimmicky, headachy, hierarchy, malarkey, master key, monarchy, panicky, plasticky.
Assembly, bimonthly, biweekly, bodily, cowardly, dastardly, directly, easterly, family, finale, fleur-de-lis, fortnightly, frizzly, heavenly, hillbilly, homily, icily, jubilee, laggardly, maidenly, mannerly, matronly, panoply, plug-ugly, quarterly, rascally, readily, reveille, simile, slovenly, soldierly, ungainly, unruly, user-friendly, wizardly, womanly.
Actressy, agency, autopsy, bankruptcy, blatancy, bourgeoisie, buoyancy, Christmassy, clemency, courtesy, currency, decency, divorcee, ecstasy, embassy, fallacy, fantasy, fluency, galaxy, heresy, infancy, jealousy, legacy, leniency, lunacy, odyssey, oversee, pharmacy, piracy, policy, potency, pregnancy, primacy, privacy, prophecy, regency, secrecy, tendency, Tennessee, truancy, undersea, urgency, vacancy.
Absentee, amnesty, brevity, casualty, certainty, charity, chastity, clarity, committee, confetti, crotchety, crudity, density, deputy, devotee, dignity, dynasty, enmity, entity, fidgety, gaiety/gayety (U.S.), graffiti, gravity, guarantee, honesty, karate, levity, liberty, machete, majesty, modesty, nudity, oddity, parity, penalty, piety, poverty, probity, property, puberty, purity, quality, repartee, rickety, sanctity, sanctuary, scarcity, seventy, sovereignty, spaghetti, specialty, three-sixty, trinity, unity, uppity, vanity, velvety.
Apathy, empathy, newsworthy, noteworthy, praiseworthy, roadworthy, seaworthy, sympathy, trustworthy, unhealthy, unworthy.
Anchovy, c'est la vie, eau-de-vie, lovey-dovey, top-heavy, topsy-turvy, vis-à-vis.
Billowy, chop suey, echoey, shadowy, yellowy, willowy.
Freezingly, pleasingly, teasingly, wheezingly.
[4] Accessory, adultery, artillery, cautionary, cemetery, compulsory, confectionery, conciliatory, constabulary, contemporary, customary, debauchery, delivery, dictionary, directory, discovery, distillery, elementary, embroidery, explanatory, exploratory, hunky-dory, idolatry, imaginary, incendiary, infirmary, inflammatory, judiciary, laboratory, legendary, literary, machinery, mandatory, mercenary, military, missionary, necessary, ordinary, patisserie, perfumery, preliminary, psychiatry, publicity, reactionary, recovery, secretary, secondary, simplicity, skullduggery, solitary, stationary, stationery, temporary, territory, tomfoolery, upholstery, visionary, vocabulary.
Academy, anatomy, astronomy, economy, epitome, origami.
Aborigine, accompany, acrimony, alimony, cacophony, ceremony, epiphany, hootenanny, ignominy, macaroni, mahogany, matrimony, minestrone, monotony, pepperoni, teeny-weeny, telephony, testimony.
Apostrophe, atrophy, biography, cardiography, catastrophe, choreography, geography, philosophy, photography.
Analogy, anthology, apology, archeology, astrology, biology, cardiology, chronology, ecology, geology, ideology, mythology, psychology, technology, theology, zoology.
Ability, agility, fertility, fragility, futility, hostility, humility, liability, mobility, nobility, responsibility, stability, tranquillity/tranquility (U.S.), versatility, viability, virility, volatility.
Especially, eventually, initially, incidentally, melancholy, monopoly, occasionally, officially, originally, personally, universally, unmannerly.
Hanky-panky, happy-go-lucky, hokey-cokey, okey-dokey, wakey-wakey, walkie-talkie.
Absolutely, anomaly, creepy-crawly, curmudgeonly, dilly-dally, eco-friendly, facsimile, fait accompli, gentlemanly, holy-moly, hurly-burly, immediately, melancholy, monopoly, rockabilly, roly-poly, shilly-shally, softly-softly, tagliatelle, ukulele, willy-nilly, yellow-belly.
Accuracy, ascendancy, complacency, consistency, conspiracy, contingency, controversy, deficiency, delicacy, diplomacy, discrepancy, efficiency, emergency, flamboyancy, hypocrisy, idiocy, intimacy, intricacy, itsy-bitsy, paparazzi, presidency, prima facie, radiancy, redundancy, relentlessly, sufficiency, supremacy, transparency.
Absurdity, affinity, amenity, anxiety, barbarity, calamity, cognoscenti, community, conformity, credulity, difficulty, dilettante, enormity, equality, eternity, fatality, fidelity, fifty-fifty, fraternity, frivolity, glitterati, heredity, hilarity, humanity, humidity, immunity, impunity, indemnity, infinity, intercity, literati, maternity, modernity, morality, nitty-gritty, obscenity, profanity, reality, senility, serenity, sobriety, solemnity, virility, stupidity, timidity, totality, twenty-twenty, variety, vicinity, vigilante, virginity, vulgarity.
Antipathy, telepathy.
[5] Anniversary, beneficiary, camaraderie, complementary, complimentary, contradictory, directory, documentary, evolutionary, revolutionary, rudimentary, supplementary.

136

Ambiguity, anonymity, continuity, familiarity, femininity, impropriety, ingenuity, irregularity, liability, masculinity, notoriety, opportunity, peculiarity, popularity, regularity, serendipity, similarity, solidarity, spontaneity, uniformity, versatility, viability, volatility.

2.1.3 "--fee" (as in "coffee")
[2] beefy, chuffy, coffee, comfy, daffy, fee, fluffy, goofy, huffy, iffy, jiffy, leafy, puffy, scruffy, selfie, sniffy, stiffy, stuffy, toffee, toughie, trophy, whiffy.
[4] apostrophe, atrophy, biography, catastrophe, choreography, geography, philosophy, photography.

SURPRISING RHYMING:
[1] **Be**, bee, fee, flea, flee, gee, glee, he, key, knee, me, pea, pee, sea, see, tee, tea, the, thee, twee, we, wee, whee, zee.
Brie, free, re, spree, three, tree.
Beam, cream, deem, dream, gleam, meme, ream, scheme, scream, seam, seem, steam, stream, team, teem, theme.
[2] **Baddy**, bawdy, beady, bloody, body, brandy, buddy, caddie, candy, cloudy, daddy, dandy, dowdy, foodie, gaudy, giddy, greedy, handy, hardy, heady, hoodie, howdy, kiddie, laddie, lady, MD, midi, moody, mouldy/moldy (U.S.), muddy, needy, nerdy, oldie, randy, ready, roadie, rowdy, sandy, seedy, shady, shandy, shoddy, speedy, steady, study, sturdy, tardy, teddy, tidy, trendy, tweedy, weedy, windy, woody, wordy.
Abbey, baby, bobby, busby, cabby, chubby, crabby, derby, flabby, Frisbee, gabby hobby, grubby, hubby, lobby, maybe, ruby, scabby, shabby, snobby, would-be, zombie.
Agree, angry, beery, belfry, berry, bleary, blurry, boundary, bury, carefree, carry, cheery, cherry, country, curry, dairy, dearie, debris, degree, dowry, dreary, dust-free, eerie, entry, esprit, every, fairy, ferry, fiery, flowery, flurry, furry, fury, gentry, germ-free, glory, gory, Grand Prix, gumtree, hairy, hoary, hurry, hungry, jury, laundry, leery, lorry, marry, merry, paltry, pantry, parry, pastry, poultry, powdery, prairie, quandary, quarry, query, scary, scot-free, sentry, sorry, starry, storey, story, sultry, tawdry, teary, theory, treachery, vary, very, vestry, wary, weary, wintry, wiry, worry.
Bumpy, chappie, chippy, chirpy, clippie, crappie, creepy, crispy, dippy, dopey, drippy, droopy, dumpy, flappy, frumpy, grippy, groupie, grumpy, happy, hippie, humpy, jumpy, lippy, loopy, lumpy, nappy, nippy, pappy, peppy, plummy, preppy, pulpy, puppy, raspy, ropy, sappy, scampi, scrappy, scrummy, scrumpy, skimpy, sleepy, slippy, snappy, snippy, snoopy, soapy, soupy, stripy, stumpy, swampy, sweetpea, teepee, trippy, vampy, weepy, whippy, whoopee, wimpy, wispy, yuppie, zappy, zippy.
Bitty, city, ditty, gritty, pity, pretty, witty.
Acme, army, balmy, barmy, beamy, blimey, chamois, chummy, clammy, creamy, crummy, dreamy, dummy, Emmy, foamy, gammy, gimme, gleamy, gloomy, Grammy, grimy, gummy, hammy, homey, jammy, jimmy, lemme, limey, mammy, me, mommy, mummy, palmy, plummy, roomy, rummy, samey, scummy, scrummy, seamy, slimy, slummy, smarmy, stormy, tummy, whammy, wormy, yummy.
Army, balmy, barmy, blimey, chamois, chummy, clammy, creamy, crummy, dreamy, dummy, Emmy, foamy, gammy, gimme, gleamy, gloomy, Grammy, grimy, gummy, hammy, homey, jammy, lemme, limey, mammy, me, mommy, mummy, plummy, roomy, samey, scrummy, seamy, slimy, slummy, smarmy, stormy, tummy, whammy, wormy, yummy.
Budgie, cagey, clergy, dingy, dodgy, edgy, gee, gee-gee, grungy, gungy, mangy, orgy, sludgy, smudgy, spongy, squeegee, squidgy, stagy, stingy, stodgy, veggie, whingy.
Achy, baccy, balky, beaky, bookie, brickie, bulky, car key, chalky, cheeky, chunky, cliquey, clunky, cocky, cookie, corky, creaky, crikey, croaky, dinky, donkey, door key, ducky, dusky, flaky, flunkey, folkie, folky, freaky, frisky, funky, gawky, hanky, hickey, hockey, hokey, hookey, hunky, husky, icky, inky, jerky, jockey, jokey, junkie, key, karaoke, khaki, kinky, lackey, lanky, latchkey, leaky, lucky, marquee, mickey, milky, murky, monkey, mucky, musky, narky, nooky, passkey, peaky, perky, pesky, picky, pinkie, pinky, plucky, pokey, porky, psyche, punky, quaky, quickie, quirky, reeky, risky, rocky, rookie, shaky, sickie, silky, ski, slinky, smoky, snaky, sneaky, sparky, spiky, spooky, squeaky, sticky, stinky, stocky, streaky, sulky, swanky, tacky, talkie, techie, tricky, turkey, turnkey, wacky, whiskey/whisky, wonky, Yankee, yucky.
Ably, amply, aptly, barley, beastly, belly, bobbly, bubbly, bully, chili, chilly, cleanly, comely, coolie, coolly, costly, coyly, crackly, crawly, crinkly, crumbly, crumply, cuddly,

daily, dally, dangly, deadly, deathly, deli, dimly, dimply, doily, drily, drizzly, dully, duly, earthly, elderly, fiddly, filly, fitly, flatly, fleshly, freckly, friendly, frilly, fully, gaily, gangly, ghastly, ghostly, giggly, goalie, godly, goodly, googly, gristly, grizzly, grumbly, hilly, hotly, holy, hourly, husbandly, hyperbole, idly, jelly, jangly, jiggly, jingly, jowly, kindly, kingly, knobbly, likely, lily, lively, lonely, lordly, lovely, lowly, madly, manly, medley, monthly, mostly, motley, muesli, muscly, newly, niggly, nightly, oddly, oily, only, orderly, paisley, parley, pebbly, pimply, poorly, portly, prickly, priestly, princely, purply, queenly, really, rumbly, sadly, saintly, scribbly, seemly, shapely, shyly, sickly, silly, slightly, slyly, smiley, smelly, snarly, sparkly, spindly, sprightly, squiggly, stately, steely, stiffly, straggly, sully, surely, telly, tickly, timely, tingly, tinkly, trembly, trimly, trolley, truly, twinkly, ugly, volley, waffly, wally, weakly, weekly, welly, wetly, wheelie, wifely, wiggly, wily, wobbly, woolly, worldly, wriggly, wrinkly, wryly, yearly.
Bossy, bouncy, brassy, chassis, classy, curtsy, Dixie, dressy, emcee, fancy, fleecy, folksy, footsie, foresee, foxy, fussy, glassy, glitzy, glossy, grassy, greasy, gutsy, gypsy, horsey, hussy, saucy, icy, kissy, lacy, lassie, look-see, maxi, mercy, messy, missy, mousy, pacey, pixie, posse, pricey, juicy, prissy, proxy, pussy, racy, ritzy, sassy, schmaltzy, sexy, sightsee, sissy, spacey, specie, spicy, taxi, tipsy, tootsie, waxy.
Anti, arty, auntie, batty, beastie, bitty, catty, chatty, city, crafty, cruelty, dainty, ditty, draughty/drafty (U.S.), eighty, fatty, fifty, frailty, goatee, gritty, guilty, hasty, hearty, hefty, jetty, lefty, matey, meaty, minty, misty, nasty, nifty, party, pasty, petit, petty, pity, plenty, pretty, QT, safety, scanty, settee, shanty/chanty (U.S.), shifty, sixty, sweaty, sweetie, swiftie, tarty, tatty, tasty, thrifty, treaty, twenty, twisty, weighty, witty, yeti.
Breathy, earthy, filthy, frothy, healthy, lengthy, mouthy, smithy, smoothie, stealthy, swarthy, toothy, wealthy, worthy.
Bevvy, Chevy, curvy, envy, gravy, groovy, heavy, ivy, levee, levy, lovey, luvvy, movie, navy, nervy, savvy, skivvy, spivvy, wavy.
Blowy, bluey, chewy, dewy, doughy, ennui, gluey, gooey, hooey, peewee, phooey, screwy, showy, snowy.
Burly, curly, early, girlie, hurly-burly, surly, swirly, twirly, whirly.
Brolly, collie, dolly, folly, golly, holly, jolly, lolly, trolley, volley, wally.
Alley, dally, galley, pally, rally, reveille, sally, tally, valley.
Bunny, funny, gunny, honey, money, runny, sonny, sunny.
Choppy, copy, floppy, jalopy, poppy, sloppy, soppy, stroppy.
[3] Bumblebee, honeybee, namby-pamby, wallaby, wannabe.
Burgundy, chickadee, COD, comedy, custody, dogsbody, embody, fool-hardy, jeopardy, melody, nobody, parody, Ph.D., raggedy, remedy, rhapsody, somebody, tragedy.
Ancestry, archery, artistry, bakery, battery, bigotry, binary, blackberry, blubbery, blueberry, blustery, brasserie, bravery, brewery, bribery, burglary, calorie, carpentry, carvery, cavalry, celery, century, chemistry, chicory, chivalry, Christmas tree, colliery, contrary, devilry, diary, dietary, disagree, dithery, doddery, drudgery, dungaree, duty-free, eatery, enquiry, estuary, expiry, factory, fakery, feathery, filigree, finery, fishery, flattery, fluttery, forestry, forgery, gallery, geometry, gimmickry, glittery, greenery, grocery, history, imagery, injury, inquiry, ivory, jamboree, jewellery/jewelry (U.S.), jittery, leathery, lingerie, lottery, luxury, memory, mercury, misery, momentary, monastery, mystery, nursery, obituary, obligatory, pageantry, pedigree, perjury, pillory, pleasantry, poetry, pottery, primary, priory, quivery, referee, revelry, reverie, rivalry, robbery, rockery, rosary, rubbery, salary, sanctuary, savagery, savory, scenery, sensory, shimmery, shivery, silvery, slavery, slippery, sorcery, sugary, surgery, tapestry, thundery, treachery, trickery, victory, wintery, wizardry.
Aromatherapy, gossipy, photocopy, recipe, slap-happy, syrupy, therapy, unhappy.
Alchemy, bigamy, blasphemy, blossomy, bonhomie, enemy, infamy, sesame, tsunami.
Agony, attorney, balcony, baloney, bikini, botany, colony, company, cottony, cushiony, destiny, ebony, felony, gluttony, halfpenny, harmony, Houdini, irony, larceny, litany, martini, mutiny, satiny, scrutiny, symphony, tiffany, timpani, trainee, tyranny, villainy.
Allergy, effigy, emoji, energy, eulogy, lethargy, refugee, strategy, synergy, trilogy.
Actually, brotherly, easterly, elderly, equally, fatherly, finally, formally, formerly, gingerly, gravelly, leisurely, miserly, motherly, naturally, neighbourly/neighborly (U.S.), normally, northerly, orderly, partially, properly, scholarly, sisterly, southerly, specially, thoroughly, usually, utterly, virtually, westerly.
Committee, gravity, nitty-gritty, responsibility, sanity, self-pity.

Anarchy, finicky, garlicky, gimmicky, headachy, malarkey, monarchy, panicky, plasticky.
Assembly, bimonthly, biweekly, bodily, comradely, cowardly, dastardly, directly, easterly, family, finale, fleur-de-lis, fortnightly, heavenly, hillbilly, homily, icily, jubilee, laggardly, maidenly, mannerly, matronly, panoply, plug-ugly, quarterly, readily, reveille, simile, slovenly, ungainly, unruly, user-friendly, wizardly, womanly.
Actressy, agency, autopsy, bankruptcy, blatancy, bourgeoisie, buoyancy, Christmassy, clemency, courtesy, currency, decency, divorcee, ecstasy, embassy, fallacy, fantasy, fluency, galaxy, heresy, infancy, jealousy, legacy, leniency, lunacy, odyssey, oversee, pharmacy, piracy, policy, potency, pregnancy, primacy, privacy, prophecy, regency, secrecy, tendency, Tennessee, truancy, undersea, urgency, vacancy.
Absentee, amnesty, brevity, casualty, certainty, charity, chastity, clarity, committee, confetti, crotchety, crudity, density, deputy, devotee, dignity, dynasty, enmity, entity, fidgety, gaiety/gayety (U.S.), graffiti, gravity, guarantee, honesty, karate, levity, liberty, machete, majesty, modesty, nudity, oddity, parity, penalty, piety, poverty, probity, property, puberty, purity, quality, repartee, rickety, sanctity, sanctuary, scarcity, seventy, sovereignty, spaghetti, specialty, three-sixty, trinity, unity, uppity, vanity, velvety.
Apathy, empathy, newsworthy, noteworthy, praiseworthy, roadworthy, seaworthy, sympathy, trustworthy, unhealthy, unworthy.
Anchovy, c'est la vie, eau-de-vie, lovey-dovey, top-heavy, topsy-turvy, vis-à-vis.
Billowy, chop suey, echoey, shadowy, yellowy, willowy.
Freezingly, pleasingly, teasingly, wheezingly.
[4] Anybody, busybody, everybody, fuddy-duddy, hurdy-gurdy, oldie worlde, understudy.
Accessory, adultery, artillery, cautionary, cemetery, compulsory, confectionery, conciliatory, constabulary, contemporary, customary, debauchery, delivery, dictionary, directory, discovery, distillery, elementary, embroidery, explanatory, exploratory, hunky-dory, idolatry, imaginary, incendiary, infirmary, inflammatory, judiciary, laboratory, legendary, literary, machinery, mandatory, mercenary, military, missionary, necessary, ordinary, patisserie, perfumery, preliminary, psychiatry, publicity, reactionary, recovery, secretary, secondary, simplicity, skullduggery, solitary, stationary, stationery, temporary, territory, tomfoolery, upholstery, visionary, vocabulary.
Academy, anatomy, astronomy, economy, epitome, origami.
Accompany, acrimony, alimony, cacophony, ceremony, epiphany, hootenanny, ignominy, mahogany, matrimony, monotony, teeny-weeny, telephony, testimony.
Analogy, anthology, apology, archeology, astrology, biology, cardiology, chronology, ecology, geology, ideology, mythology, psychology, technology, theology, zoology.
Ability, agility, fertility, fragility, futility, hostility, humility, liability, mobility, nobility, responsibility, stability, tranquillity/tranquility (U.S.), versatility, viability, virility, volatility.
Especially, eventually, initially, incidentally, melancholy, monopoly, occasionally, officially, originally, personally, universally, unmannerly.
Hanky-panky, happy-go-lucky, hokey-cokey, okey-dokey, wakey-wakey, walkie-talkie.
Absolutely, anomaly, creepy-crawly, curmudgeonly, dilly-dally, eco-friendly, facsimile, fait accompli, gentlemanly, holy-moly, hurly-burly, immediately, melancholy, monopoly, rockabilly, roly-poly, shilly-shally, softly-softly, ukulele, underbelly, willy-nilly, yellow-belly.
Accuracy, ascendancy, complacency, consistency, conspiracy, contingency, controversy, deficiency, delicacy, diplomacy, discrepancy, efficiency, emergency, flamboyancy, hypocrisy, idiocy, intimacy, intricacy, itsy-bitsy, paparazzi, presidency, prima facie, proficiency, redundancy, relentlessly, sufficiency, supremacy, transparency.
Absurdity, affinity, amenity, anxiety, barbarity, calamity, cognoscenti, community, conformity, credulity, difficulty, dilettante, enormity, equality, eternity, fatality, fidelity, fifty-fifty, fraternity, frivolity, glitterati, heredity, hilarity, humanity, humidity, immunity, impunity, indemnity, infinity, intercity, literati, maternity, modernity, morality, nitty-gritty, obscenity, profanity, reality, senility, serenity, sobriety, solemnity, virility, stupidity, timidity, totality, twenty-twenty, variety, vicinity, vigilante, virginity, vulgarity.
Antipathy, telepathy.
[5] Anniversary, beneficiary, camaraderie, complementary, complimentary, contradictory, directory, documentary, evolutionary, revolutionary, rudimentary, supplementary.
Ambiguity, anonymity, continuity, familiarity, femininity, impropriety, ingenuity, irregularity, liability, masculinity, notoriety, opportunity, peculiarity, popularity, regularity, serendipity, similarity, solidarity, spontaneity, uniformity, versatility, viability, volatility.

*

2.1.4 "--gee" (as in "allergy")

[2] budgie, bulgy, cagey, clergy, dingy, dodgy, edgy, gee, gee-gee, grungy, gungy, mangy, orgy, podgy, pudgy, rangy, sludgy, smudgy, spongy, squeegee, squidgy, stagy, stingy, stodgy, veggie, whingy.
[3] allergy, effigy, elegy, emoji, energy, eulogy, lethargy, liturgy, ology, prodigy, refugee, strategy, synergy, trilogy.
[4] analogy, anthology, apology, archeology, astrology, biology, cardiology, chronology, ecology, geology, ideology, mythology, psychology, technology, theology, zoology.

SURPRISING RHYMING:
[1] **Be**, bee, fee, flea, flee, gee, glee, he, key, knee, me, pea, pee, sea, see, ski, tee, tea, the, thee, twee, we, wee, whee, zee.
Brie, free, re, spree, three, tree.
Beam, cream, deem, dream, gleam, meme, ream, scheme, scream, seam, seem, steam, stream, team, teem, theme.
[2] **Baddy**, bawdy, beady, bloody, body, brandy, buddy, caddie, candy, cloudy, daddy, dandy, dowdy, foodie, gaudy, giddy, greedy, handy, hardy, heady, hoodie, howdy, kiddie, laddie, lady, MD, midi, moody, mouldy/moldy (U.S.), muddy, needy, nerdy, oldie, randy, ready, roadie, rowdy, sandy, seedy, shady, shandy, shoddy, speedy, steady, study, sturdy, tardy, teddy, tidy, trendy, tweedy, weedy, windy, woody, wordy.
Abbey, baby, bobby, busby, cabby, chubby, crabby, derby, flabby, Frisbee, gabby, hobby, grubby, hubby, lobby, maybe, ruby, scabby, shabby, snobby, would-be, zombie.
Agree, angry, beery, belfry, berry, bleary, blurry, boundary, bury, carefree, carry, cheery, cherry, country, curry, dairy, dearie, debris, degree, dowry, dreary, dust-free, eerie, entry, esprit, every, fairy, ferry, fiery, flowery, flurry, furry, fury, gentry, germ-free, glory, gory, Grand Prix, gumtree, hairy, hoary, hurry, hungry, jury, laundry, leery, lorry, marry, merry, paltry, pantry, parry, pastry, poultry, powdery, prairie, quandary, quarry, query, scary, scot-free, sentry, sorry, starry, storey, story, sultry, tawdry, teary, theory, treachery, vary, very, vestry, wary, weary, wintry, wiry, worry.
Bumpy, chappie, chippy, chirpy, clippie, crappie, creepy, crispy, dippy, dopey, drippy, droopy, dumpy, flappy, frumpy, grippy, groupie, grumpy, happy, hippie, humpy, jumpy, lippy, loopy, lumpy, nappy, nippy, pappy, peppy, plummy, preppy, pulpy, puppy, raspy, ropy, sappy, scampi, scrappy, scrummy, scrumpy, skimpy, sleepy, slippy, snappy, snippy, snoopy, soapy, soupy, stripy, stumpy, swampy, sweetpea, teepee, trippy, vampy, weepy, whippy, whoopee, wimpy, wispy, yuppie, zappy, zippy.
Bitty, city, ditty, gritty, pity, pretty, witty.
Army, balmy, barmy, blimey, chamois, chummy, clammy, creamy, crummy, dreamy, dummy, Emmy, foamy, gimme, gleamy, gloomy, Grammy, grimy, gummy, hammy, homey, jammy, lemme, limey, mammy, me, mommy, mummy, plummy, roomy, samey, scrummy, seamy, slimy, slummy, smarmy, stormy, tummy, whammy, wormy, yummy.
Acne, any, beanie, blarney, bonny, bony, brainy, brawny, briny, brownie, canny, chimney, cine, cockney, corny, cranny, crony, Disney, genie, grainy, granny, guinea, hinny, horny, journey, knee, loony, many, meanie, mini, nanny, ninny, penny, pony, phoney/phony (U.S.), puny, queenie, rainy, sarnie, scrawny, shiny, skinny, stony, teeny, thorny, tinny, tiny, townie, trainee, tranny, tweeny, uni, weeny, whiny, zany.
Achy, baccy, balky, beaky, bookie, brickie, bulky, car key, chalky, cheeky, chunky, cliquey, clunky, cocky, cookie, corky, creaky, crikey, croaky, dinky, donkey, door key, ducky, dusky, flaky, flunkey, folkie, folky, freaky, frisky, funky, gawky, hanky, hickey, hockey, hokey, hookey, hunky, husky, icky, inky, jerky, jockey, jokey, junkie, key, karaoke, khaki, kinky, lackey, lanky, latchkey, leaky, lucky, marquee, mickey, milky, murky, monkey, mucky, musky, narky, nooky, passkey, peaky, perky, pesky, picky, pinkie, pinky, plucky, pokey, porky, psyche, punky, quaky, quickie, quirky, reeky, risky, rocky, rookie, shaky, sickie, silky, ski, slinky, smoky, snaky, sneaky, sparky, spiky, spooky, squeaky, sticky, stinky, stocky, streaky, sulky, swanky, tacky, talkie, techie, tricky, turkey, turnkey, wacky, whiskey/whisky, wonky, Yankee, yucky.
Ably, amply, aptly, barley, beastly, belly, bobbly, bubbly, bully, chili, chilly, cleanly, comely, coolie, coolly, costly, coyly, crackly, crawly, crinkly, crumbly, crumply, cuddly, daily, dally, dangly, deadly, deathly, deli, dimly, dimply, doily, drily, drizzly, dully, duly, earthly, elderly, fiddly, filly, fitly, flatly, fleshly, freckly, friendly, frilly, fully, gaily, gangly, ghastly, ghostly, giggly, goalie, godly, goodly, googly, gristly, grizzly, grumbly, hilly,

hotly, holy, hourly, husbandly, hyperbole, idly, jelly, jangly, jiggly, jingly, jowly, kindly, kingly, knobbly, likely, lily, lively, lonely, lordly, lovely, lowly, madly, manly, medley, monthly, mostly, motley, muesli, muscly, newly, niggly, nightly, oddly, oily, only, orderly, paisley, parley, pebbly, pimply, poorly, portly, prickly, priestly, princely, purply, queenly, really, rumbly, sadly, saintly, scribbly, seemly, shapely, shyly, sickly, silly, slightly, slyly, smiley, smelly, snarly, sparkly, spindly, sprightly, squiggly, stately, steely, stiffly, straggly, sully, surely, telly, tickly, timely, tingly, tinkly, trembly, trimly, trolley, truly, twinkly, ugly, volley, waffly, wally, weakly, weekly, welly, wetly, wheelie, wifely, wiggly, wily, wobbly, woolly, worldly, wriggly, wrinkly, wryly, yearly.
Bossy, bouncy, brassy, chassis, classy, curtsy, Dixie, dressy, emcee, fancy, fleecy, folksy, footsie, foresee, foxy, fussy, glassy, glitzy, glossy, grassy, greasy, gutsy, gypsy, horsey, hussy, saucy, icy, kissy, lacy, lassie, look-see, maxi, mercy, messy, missy, mousy, pacey, pixie, posse, pricey, prissy, proxy, pussy, racy, ritzy, sassy, schmaltzy, sexy, sightsee, sissy, spacey, specie, spicy, taxi, tipsy, tootsie, waxy.
Anti, arty, auntie, batty, beastie, bitty, catty, chatty, city, crafty, cruelty, dainty, ditty, draughty/drafty (U.S.), eighty, fatty, fifty, frailty, goatee, gritty, guilty, hasty, hearty, hefty, jetty, lefty, matey, meaty, minty, misty, nasty, nifty, party, pasty, petit, petty, pity, plenty, pretty, QT, safety, scanty, settee, shanty/chanty (U.S.), shifty, sixty, sweaty, sweetie, swiftie, tarty, tatty, tasty, thrifty, treaty, twenty, twisty, weighty, witty, yeti.
Beefy, coffee, comfy, daffy, fee, fluffy, goofy, huffy, iffy, jiffy, leafy, puffy, scruffy, selfie, sniffy, stuffy, toffee, toughie, trophy.
Breathy, earthy, filthy, frothy, healthy, lengthy, mouthy, pithy, smithy, smoothie, stealthy, swarthy, toothy, wealthy, worthy.
Bevvy, Chevy, curvy, envy, gravy, groovy, heavy, ivy, levee, levy, lovey, luvvy, movie, navy, nervy, savvy, skivvy, spivvy, wavy.
Blowy, chewy, dewy, doughy, gluey, gooey, hooey, phooey, screwy, showy, snowy.
Burly, curly, early, girlie, hurly-burly, surly, swirly, twirly, whirly.
Brolly, collie, dolly, folly, golly, holly, jolly, lolly, trolley, volley, wally.
Alley, dally, galley, pally, rally, reveille, sally, tally, valley.
Bunny, funny, gunny, honey, money, runny, sonny, sunny.
Choppy, copy, floppy, jalopy, poppy, sloppy, soppy, stroppy.
[3] Bumblebee, honeybee, namby-pamby, wallaby, wannabe.
Burgundy, chickadee, COD, comedy, custody, dogsbody, embody, fool-hardy, jeopardy, melody, nobody, parody, Ph.D., raggedy, remedy, rhapsody, somebody, tragedy.
Ancestry, archery, artistry, bakery, battery, bigotry, binary, blackberry, blubbery, blueberry, blustery, brasserie, bravery, brewery, bribery, burglary, calorie, carpentry, carvery, cavalry, celery, century, chemistry, chicory, chivalry, Christmas tree, colliery, contrary, devilry, diary, dietary, disagree, dithery, doddery, drudgery, dungaree, duty-free, eatery, enquiry, estuary, expiry, factory, fakery, feathery, filigree, finery, fishery, flattery, fluttery, forestry, forgery, gallery, geometry, gimmickry, glittery, greenery, grocery, history, imagery, injury, inquiry, ivory, jamboree, jewellery/jewelry (U.S.), jittery, leathery, lingerie, lottery, luxury, memory, mercury, misery, momentary, monastery, mystery, nursery, obituary, obligatory, pageantry, pedigree, perjury, pillory, pleasantry, poetry, pottery, primary, priory, quivery, referee, revelry, reverie, rivalry, robbery, rockery, rosary, rubbery, salary, sanctuary, savagery, savory, scenery, sensory, shimmery, shivery, silvery, slavery, slippery, sorcery, sugary, surgery, tapestry, thundery, treachery, trickery, victory, wintery, wizardry.
Aromatherapy, gossipy, photocopy, recipe, slap-happy, syrupy, therapy, unhappy.
Alchemy, bigamy, blasphemy, blossomy, bonhomie, enemy, infamy, sesame, tsunami.
Agony, attorney, balcony, baloney, bikini, botany, colony, company, cottony, cushiony, destiny, ebony, felony, gluttony, halfpenny, harmony, Houdini, irony, larceny, litany, martini, mutiny, satiny, scrutiny, symphony, tiffany, timpani, trainee, tyranny, villainy.
Actually, brotherly, easterly, elderly, equally, fatherly, finally, formally, formerly, gingerly, gravelly, leisurely, masterly, miserly, naturally, neighbourly/neighborly (U.S.), normally, northerly, orderly, partially, properly, rascally, scholarly, sisterly, southerly, specially, thoroughly, usually, utterly, virtually, westerly.
Committee, gravity, nitty-gritty, responsibility, sanity, self-pity.
Anarchy, finicky, garlicky, gimmicky, headachy, malarkey, monarchy, panicky, plasticky.
Assembly, beggarly, bimonthly, biweekly, bodily, comradely, cowardly, dastardly, directly, easterly, family, finale, fleur-de-lis, fortnightly, heavenly, hillbilly, homily,

141

icily, jubilee, maidenly, mannerly, matronly, plug-ugly, quarterly, rascally, readily, reveille, simile, slovenly, soldierly, ungainly, unruly, user-friendly, wizardly, womanly.
Actressy, agency, autopsy, bankruptcy, blatancy, bourgeoisie, buoyancy, Christmassy, clemency, courtesy, currency, decency, divorcee, ecstasy, embassy, fallacy, fantasy, fluency, galaxy, heresy, infancy, jealousy, legacy, leniency, lunacy, odyssey, oversee, pharmacy, piracy, policy, potency, pregnancy, primacy, privacy, prophecy, regency, secrecy, tendency, Tennessee, truancy, undersea, urgency, vacancy.
Absentee, amnesty, brevity, casualty, certainty, charity, chastity, clarity, committee, confetti, crotchety, crudity, density, deputy, devotee, dignity, dynasty, enmity, entity, fidgety, gaiety/gayety (U.S.), graffiti, gravity, guarantee, honesty, karate, levity, liberty, machete, majesty, modesty, nudity, oddity, parity, penalty, piety, poverty, probity, property, puberty, purity, quality, repartee, rickety, sanctity, sanctuary, scarcity, seventy, sovereignty, spaghetti, specialty, three-sixty, trinity, unity, uppity, vanity, velvety.
Apathy, empathy, newsworthy, noteworthy, praiseworthy, roadworthy, seaworthy, sympathy, trustworthy, unhealthy, unworthy.
Anchovy, c'est la vie, eau-de-vie, lovey-dovey, top-heavy, topsy-turvy, vis-à-vis.
Billowy, chop suey, echoey, shadowy, yellowy, willowy.
Freezingly, pleasingly, teasingly, wheezingly.
[4] **Anybody**, busybody, everybody, fuddy-duddy, hurdy-gurdy, oldie worlde, understudy.
Accessory, adultery, artillery, cautionary, cemetery, compulsory, confectionery, conciliatory, constabulary, contemporary, customary, debauchery, delivery, dictionary, directory, discovery, distillery, elementary, embroidery, explanatory, exploratory, hunky-dory, idolatry, imaginary, incendiary, infirmary, inflammatory, judiciary, laboratory, legendary, literary, machinery, mandatory, mercenary, military, missionary, necessary, ordinary, patisserie, perfumery, preliminary, psychiatry, publicity, reactionary, recovery, secretary, secondary, simplicity, skullduggery, solitary, stationary, stationery, temporary, territory, tomfoolery, upholstery, visionary, vocabulary.
Apostrophe, biography, catastrophe, choreography, geography, philosophy, photography.
Academy, anatomy, astronomy, economy, epitome, origami.
Accompany, acrimony, alimony, cacophony, ceremony, epiphany, hootenanny, ignominy, mahogany, matrimony, monotony, teeny-weeny, telephony, testimony.
Ability, agility, fertility, fragility, futility, hostility, humility, liability, mobility, nobility, responsibility, stability, tranquillity/tranquility (U.S.), versatility, viability, virility, volatility.
Especially, eventually, initially, incidentally, melancholy, monopoly, occasionally, officially, originally, personally, universally, unmannerly.
Hanky-panky, happy-go-lucky, hokey-cokey, okey-dokey, wakey-wakey, walkie-talkie.
Absolutely, anomaly, creepy-crawly, curmudgeonly, dilly-dally, eco-friendly, facsimile, fait accompli, gentlemanly, holy-moly, hurly-burly, immediately, melancholy, monopoly, rockabilly, roly-poly, shilly-shally, softly-softly, ukulele, underbelly, willy-nilly, yellow-belly.
Accuracy, complacency, consistency, conspiracy, contingency, controversy, delicacy, diplomacy, discrepancy, efficiency, emergency, flamboyancy, hypocrisy, idiocy, intimacy, intricacy, paparazzi, presidency, redundancy, sufficiency, supremacy, transparency.
Absurdity, affinity, amenity, anxiety, barbarity, calamity, cognoscenti, community, conformity, credulity, difficulty, dilettante, enormity, equality, eternity, fatality, fidelity, fifty-fifty, fraternity, frivolity, glitterati, heredity, hilarity, humanity, humidity, immunity, impunity, indemnity, infinity, intercity, literati, maternity, modernity, morality, nitty-gritty, obscenity, profanity, reality, senility, serenity, sobriety, solemnity, virility, stupidity, timidity, totality, twenty-twenty, variety, vicinity, vigilante, virginity, vulgarity.
[5] **Anniversary**, beneficiary, camaraderie, complementary, complimentary, contradictory, directory, documentary, evolutionary, revolutionary, rudimentary, supplementary.
Ambiguity, anonymity, continuity, familiarity, femininity, impropriety, ingenuity, irregularity, masculinity, notoriety, opportunity, peculiarity, popularity, regularity, responsibility, serendipity, similarity, solidarity, spontaneity, versatility, viability, volatility.

2.1.5 "--kee" (as in "key")
[2] achy, baccy, balky, beaky, bookie, brickie, bulky, car key, chalky, cheeky, chunky, cliquey, clunky, cocky, cookie, corky, creaky, crikey, croaky, dinky, donkey, door key, ducky, dusky, flaky, flunkey, folkie, folky, freaky, frisky, funky, gawky, hanky, hickey, hockey, hokey, hookey, hunky, husky, icky, inky, jerky, jockey, jokey, junkie, key, karaoke, khaki, kinky, lackey, lanky, latchkey, leaky, lucky, marquee, mickey, milky,

142

murky, monkey, mucky, musky, narky, nooky, passkey, peaky, perky, pesky, picky, pinkie, pinky, plucky, pokey, porky, psyche, punky, quaky, quickie, quirky, reeky, risky, rocky, rookie, shaky, sickie, silky, ski, sleeky, slinky, smoky, snaky, sneaky, sparky, spiky, spooky, squeaky, sticky, stinky, stocky, streaky, sulky, swanky, tacky, talkie, techie, tricky, turkey, turnkey, wacky, whiskey/whisky, wonky, Yankee, yucky.
[3] anarchy, finicky, garlicky, gimmicky, headachy, hierarchy, malarkey, monarchy, panicky, plasticky.
[4] hanky-panky, happy-go-lucky, hokey-cokey, okey-dokey, wakey-wakey, walkie-talkie.

SURPRISING RHYMING:
[1] **Be**, bee, fee, flea, flee, gee, glee, he, key, knee, me, pea, pee, sea, see, tee, tea, the, thee, twee, we, wee, whee, zee.
Brie, free, re, spree, three, tree.
Beam, cream, deem, dream, gleam, meme, ream, scheme, scream, seam, seem, steam, stream, team, teem, theme.
[2] **Baddy**, bawdy, beady, bloody, body, brandy, buddy, caddie, candy, cloudy, daddy, dandy, dowdy, foodie, gaudy, giddy, greedy, handy, hardy, heady, hoodie, howdy, kiddie, laddie, lady, MD, midi, moody, mouldy/moldy (U.S.), muddy, needy, nerdy, oldie, randy, ready, roadie, rowdy, sandy, seedy, shady, shandy, shoddy, speedy, steady, study, sturdy, tardy, teddy, tidy, trendy, tweedy, weedy, windy, woody, wordy.
Abbey, baby, bobby, busby, cabby, chubby, crabby, derby, flabby, Frisbee, gabby hobby, grubby, hubby, lobby, maybe, ruby, scabby, shabby, snobby, would-be, zombie.
Agree, angry, beery, belfry, berry, bleary, blurry, boundary, bury, carefree, carry, cheery, cherry, country, curry, dairy, dearie, debris, degree, dowry, dreary, dust-free, eerie, entry, esprit, every, fairy, ferry, fiery, flowery, flurry, furry, fury, gentry, germ-free, glory, gory, Grand Prix, gumtree, hairy, hoary, hurry, hungry, jury, laundry, leery, lorry, marry, merry, paltry, pantry, parry, pastry, poultry, powdery, prairie, quandary, quarry, query, scary, scot-free, sentry, sorry, starry, storey, story, sultry, tawdry, teary, theory, treachery, vary, very, vestry, wary, weary, wintry, wiry, worry.
Bumpy, chappie, chippy, chirpy, clippie, crappie, creepy, crispy, dippy, dopey, drippy, droopy, dumpy, flappy, frumpy, grippy, groupie, grumpy, happy, hippie, humpy, jumpy, lippy, loopy, lumpy, nappy, nippy, pappy, peppy, plummy, preppy, pulpy, puppy, raspy, ropy, sappy, scampi, scrappy, scrummy, scrumpy, skimpy, sleepy, slippy, snappy, snippy, snoopy, soapy, soupy, stripy, stumpy, swampy, sweetpea, teepee, trippy, vampy, weepy, whippy, whoopee, wimpy, wispy, yuppie, zappy, zippy.
Bitty, city, ditty, gritty, pity, pretty, witty.
Army, balmy, barmy, blimey, chamois, chummy, clammy, creamy, crummy, dreamy, dummy, Emmy, foamy, gimme, gleamy, gloomy, Grammy, grimy, gummy, hammy, homey, jammy, lemme, limey, mammy, me, mommy, mummy, plummy, roomy, samey, scrummy, seamy, slimy, slummy, smarmy, stormy, tummy, whammy, wormy, yummy.
Acne, any, beanie, blarney, bonny, bony, brainy, brawny, briny, brownie, canny, chimney, cine, cockney, corny, cranny, crony, Disney, genie, grainy, granny, guinea, hinny, horny, journey, knee, loony, many, meanie, mini, nanny, ninny, penny, pony, phoney/phony (U.S.), puny, queenie, rainy, sarnie, scrawny, shiny, skinny, stony, teeny, thorny, tinny, tiny, townie, trainee, tranny, tweeny, uni, weeny, whiny, zany.
Budgie, cagey, clergy, dingy, dodgy, edgy, gee, grungy, gungy, mangy, orgy, sludgy, smudgy, spongy, squeegee, squidgy, stagy, stingy, stodgy, veggie, whingy.
Ably, amply, aptly, barley, beastly, belly, bobbly, bubbly, bully, chili, chilly, cleanly, comely, coolie, coolly, costly, coyly, crackly, crawly, crinkly, crumbly, crumply, cuddly, daily, dally, dangly, deadly, deathly, deli, dimly, dimply, doily, drily, drizzly, dully, duly, earthly, elderly, fiddly, filly, fitly, flatly, fleshly, freckly, friendly, frilly, fully, gaily, gangly, ghastly, ghostly, giggly, goalie, godly, goodly, googly, gristly, grizzly, grumbly, hilly, hotly, holy, hourly, husbandly, hyperbole, idly, jelly, jangly, jiggly, jingly, jowly, kindly, kingly, knobbly, likely, lily, lively, lonely, lordly, lovely, lowly, madly, manly, medley, monthly, mostly, motley, muesli, muscly, newly, niggly, nightly, oddly, oily, only, orderly, paisley, parley, pebbly, pimply, poorly, portly, prickly, priestly, princely, purply, queenly, really, rumbly, sadly, saintly, scribbly, seemly, shapely, shyly, sickly, silly, slightly, slyly, smiley, smelly, snarly, sparkly, spindly, sprightly, squiggly, stately, steely, stiffly, straggly, sully, surely, telly, tickly, timely, tingly, tinkly, trembly, trimly, trolley, truly, twinkly, ugly, volley, waffly, wally, weakly, weekly, welly, wetly, wheelie, wifely,

wiggly, wily, wobbly, woolly, worldly, wriggly, wrinkly, wryly, yearly.
Bossy, bouncy, brassy, chassis, classy, curtsy, Dixie, dressy, emcee, fancy, fleecy, folksy, footsie, foresee, foxy, fussy, glassy, glitzy, glossy, grassy, greasy, gutsy, gypsy, horsey, hussy, saucy, icy, kissy, lacy, lassie, look-see, maxi, mercy, messy, missy, mousy, pacey, pixie, posse, pricey, juicy, prissy, proxy, pussy, racy, ritzy, sassy, schmaltzy, sexy, sightsee, sissy, spacey, specie, spicy, taxi, tipsy, tootsie, waxy.
Anti, arty, auntie, batty, beastie, bitty, catty, chatty, city, crafty, cruelty, dainty, ditty, draughty/drafty (U.S.), eighty, fatty, fifty, frailty, goatee, gritty, guilty, hasty, hearty, hefty, jetty, lefty, matey, meaty, minty, misty, nasty, nifty, party, pasty, petit, petty, pity, plenty, pretty, QT, safety, scanty, settee, shanty/chanty (U.S.), shifty, sixty, sweaty, sweetie, swiftie, tarty, tatty, tasty, thrifty, treaty, twenty, twisty, weighty, witty, yeti.
Beefy, coffee, comfy, fluffy, goofy, huffy, iffy, jiffy, leafy, puffy, scruffy, selfie, sniffy, stiffy, stuffy, toffee, toughie, trophy.
Breathy, earthy, filthy, frothy, healthy, lengthy, mouthy, smithy, smoothie, stealthy, swarthy, toothy, wealthy, worthy.
Bevvy, Chevy, curvy, envy, gravy, groovy, heavy, ivy, levee, lovey, luvvy, movie, navy, nervy, savvy, scurvy, wavy.
Blowy, chewy, dewy, doughy, gluey, gooey, hooey, phooey, screwy, showy, snowy.
Burly, curly, early, girlie, hurly-burly, surly, swirly, twirly, whirly.
Brolly, collie, dolly, folly, golly, holly, jolly, lolly, trolley, volley, wally.
Alley, dally, galley, pally, rally, reveille, sally, tally, valley.
Bunny, funny, gunny, honey, money, runny, sonny, sunny.
Choppy, copy, floppy, jalopy, poppy, sloppy, soppy, stroppy.
[3] Bumblebee, honeybee, namby-pamby, wallaby, wannabe.
Burgundy, chickadee, COD, comedy, custody, dogsbody, embody, fool-hardy, jeopardy, melody, nobody, parody, Ph.D., raggedy, remedy, rhapsody, somebody, tragedy.
Ancestry, archery, artistry, bakery, battery, bigotry, binary, blackberry, blubbery, blueberry, blustery, brasserie, bravery, brewery, bribery, burglary, calorie, carpentry, carvery, cavalry, celery, century, chemistry, chicory, chivalry, Christmas tree, colliery, contrary, devilry, diary, dietary, disagree, dithery, doddery, drudgery, dungaree, duty-free, eatery, enquiry, estuary, expiry, factory, fakery, feathery, filigree, finery, fishery, flattery, fluttery, forestry, forgery, gallery, geometry, gimmickry, glittery, greenery, grocery, history, imagery, injury, inquiry, ivory, jamboree, jewellery/jewelry (U.S.), jittery, leathery, lingerie, lottery, luxury, memory, mercury, misery, momentary, monastery, mystery, nursery, obituary, obligatory, pageantry, pedigree, perjury, pillory, pleasantry, poetry, pottery, primary, priory, quivery, referee, revelry, reverie, rivalry, robbery, rockery, rosary, rubbery, salary, sanctuary, savagery, savory, scenery, sensory, shimmery, shivery, silvery, slavery, slippery, sorcery, sugary, surgery, tapestry, thundery, treachery, trickery, victory, wintery, wizardry.
Aromatherapy, gossipy, photocopy, recipe, slap-happy, syrupy, therapy, unhappy.
Alchemy, bigamy, blasphemy, blossomy, bonhomie, enemy, infamy, sesame, tsunami.
Agony, attorney, balcony, baloney, bikini, botany, colony, company, cottony, cushiony, destiny, ebony, felony, gluttony, halfpenny, harmony, Houdini, irony, larceny, litany, martini, mutiny, satiny, scrutiny, symphony, tiffany, timpani, trainee, tyranny, villainy.
Actually, brotherly, easterly, elderly, equally, fatherly, finally, formally, formerly, gingerly, gravelly, leisurely, masterly, miserly, naturally, neighbourly/neighborly (U.S.), normally, northerly, orderly, overly, partially, properly, scholarly, sisterly, southerly, specially, thoroughly, usually, utterly, virtually, westerly.
Committee, gravity, nitty-gritty, responsibility, sanity, self-pity.
Allergy, effigy, emoji, energy, eulogy, lethargy, refugee, strategy, synergy, trilogy.
Assembly, bimonthly, biweekly, bodily, comradely, cowardly, dastardly, directly, easterly, family, finale, fleur-de-lis, fortnightly, heavenly, hillbilly, homily, icily, jubilee, laggardly, mannerly, matronly, plug-ugly, quarterly, readily, reveille, simile, slovenly, soldierly, ungainly, unruly, user-friendly, wizardly, womanly.
Actressy, agency, autopsy, bankruptcy, blatancy, bourgeoisie, buoyancy, Christmassy, clemency, courtesy, currency, decency, divorcee, ecstasy, embassy, fallacy, fantasy, fluency, galaxy, heresy, infancy, jealousy, legacy, leniency, lunacy, odyssey, oversee, pharmacy, piracy, policy, potency, pregnancy, primacy, privacy, prophecy, regency, secrecy, tendency, Tennessee, truancy, undersea, urgency, vacancy.
Absentee, amnesty, brevity, casualty, certainty, charity, chastity, clarity, committee,

144

confetti, crotchety, crudity, density, deputy, devotee, dignity, dynasty, enmity, entity, fidgety, gaiety/gayety (U.S.), graffiti, gravity, guarantee, honesty, karate, levity, liberty, machete, majesty, modesty, nudity, oddity, parity, penalty, piety, poverty, probity, property, puberty, purity, quality, repartee, rickety, sanctity, sanctuary, scarcity, seventy, sovereignty, spaghetti, specialty, three-sixty, trinity, unity, uppity, vanity, velvety.
Apathy, empathy, newsworthy, noteworthy, praiseworthy, roadworthy, seaworthy, sympathy, trustworthy, unhealthy, unworthy.
Anchovy, c'est la vie, eau-de-vie, lovey-dovey, topsy-turvy, vis-à-vis.
Billowy, chop suey, echoey, shadowy, yellowy, willowy.
Freezingly, pleasingly, teasingly, wheezingly.
[4] Anybody, busybody, everybody, fuddy-duddy, hurdy-gurdy, oldie worlde, understudy.
Accessory, adultery, artillery, cautionary, cemetery, compulsory, confectionery, conciliatory, constabulary, contemporary, customary, debauchery, delivery, dictionary, directory, discovery, distillery, elementary, embroidery, explanatory, exploratory, hunky-dory, idolatry, imaginary, incendiary, infirmary, inflammatory, judiciary, laboratory, legendary, literary, machinery, mandatory, mercenary, military, missionary, necessary, ordinary, patisserie, perfumery, preliminary, psychiatry, publicity, reactionary, recovery, secretary, secondary, simplicity, skullduggery, solitary, stationary, stationery, temporary, territory, tomfoolery, upholstery, visionary, vocabulary.
Apostrophe, biography, catastrophe, choreography, geography, philosophy, photography.
Academy, anatomy, astronomy, economy, epitome, origami.
Analogy, anthology, apology, archeology, astrology, biology, cardiology, chronology, ecology, geology, ideology, mythology, psychology, technology, theology, zoology.
Accompany, acrimony, alimony, cacophony, ceremony, epiphany, hootenanny, ignominy, matrimony, monotony, pepperoni, teeny-weeny, telephony, testimony.
Ability, agility, fertility, fragility, futility, hostility, humility, liability, mobility, nobility, responsibility, stability, tranquillity/tranquility (U.S.), versatility, viability, virility, volatility.
Especially, eventually, initially, incidentally, melancholy, monopoly, occasionally, officially, originally, personally, universally, unmannerly.
Absolutely, creepy-crawly, curmudgeonly, dilly-dally, eco-friendly, facsimile, fait accompli, gentlemanly, holy-moly, hurly-burly, immediately, melancholy, monopoly, rockabilly, roly-poly, shilly-shally, softly-softly, ukulele, underbelly, willy-nilly, yellow-belly.
Accuracy, complacency, consistency, conspiracy, contingency, controversy, delicacy, diplomacy, discrepancy, efficiency, emergency, flamboyancy, hypocrisy, idiocy, intimacy, intricacy, paparazzi, presidency, redundancy, sufficiency, supremacy, transparency.
Absurdity, affinity, amenity, anxiety, barbarity, calamity, cognoscenti, community, conformity, credulity, difficulty, dilettante, enormity, equality, eternity, fatality, fidelity, fifty-fifty, fraternity, frivolity, glitterati, heredity, hilarity, humanity, humidity, immunity, impunity, indemnity, infinity, intercity, literati, maternity, modernity, morality, nitty-gritty, obscenity, profanity, reality, senility, serenity, sobriety, solemnity, virility, stupidity, timidity, totality, twenty-twenty, variety, vicinity, vigilante, virginity, vulgarity.
[5] Anniversary, beneficiary, camaraderie, complementary, complimentary, contradictory, directory, documentary, evolutionary, revolutionary, rudimentary, supplementary.
Ambiguity, anonymity, continuity, familiarity, femininity, impropriety, ingenuity, irregularity, liability, masculinity, notoriety, opportunity, peculiarity, popularity, regularity, responsibility, serendipity, similarity, solidarity, spontaneity, versatility, viability, volatility.

2.1.6 "--lee" (as in "flee")
[1] flea, flee, glee, lee.
[2] ably, alley, amply, aptly, bailey, barley, beastly, belly, bobbly, brolly, bubbly, bully, burly, chili, chill, clerkly, cleanly, collie, comely, coolie, coolly, costly, courtly, coyly, crackly, crawly, crinkly, crumbly, crumply, cuddly, curly, daily, dally, dangly, deadly, deathly, deli, dilly, dimly, dimply, doily, dolly, drily, drizzly, dully, duly, early, earthly, elderly, fatly, fiddly, filly, fitly, flatly, fleshly, folly, freckly, friendly, frilly, fully, gaily, galley, gangly, ghastly, ghostly, giggly, girlie, gnarly, goalie, godly, golly, goodly, googly, gristly, grizzly, grumbly, gulley, gully, hilly, holly, hotly, holy, hourly, husbandly, hyperbole, idly, jelly, jangly, jiggly, jingly, jolly, jowly, kindly, kingly, knobbly, likely, lily, lively, lolly, lonely, lordly, lovely, lowly, madly, manly, medley, monthly, mostly, motley, muesli, newly, niggly, nightly, oddly, oily, only, orderly, paisley, pally, parley, pearly, pebbly, pimply, poorly, portly, prickly, priestly, princely, pulley, purply, queenly, rally,

rawly, really, redly, ripply, rumly, rumbly, sadly, saintly, sally, scaly, scraggly, scrawly, scribbly, seemly, shapely, shelly, shyly, shingly, sickly, silly, slightly, slyly, smiley, smelly, snarly, sniffly, spangly, sparkly, spindly, sprightly, squally, squiggly, squirrelly, stately, steely, stiffly, stilly, straggly, sully, surely, surly, swirly, tally, tangly, telly, termly, tickly, tiddly, timely, tingly, tinkly, trebly, trembly, trimly, trolley, truly, twinkly, twirly, ugly, valley, volley, waffly, wally, wanly, weakly, weekly, welly, wheelie, wifely, wiggly, willy, wily, wobbly, woolly, worldly, wriggly, wrinkly, wryly, yearly.
[3] assembly, beggarly, bimonthly, biweekly, blackguardly, bodily, broccoli, brotherly, comradely, cowardly, dastardly, directly, easterly, family, fatherly, finale, fleur-de-lis, fortnightly, frizzly, gingerly, gravelly, heavenly, hillbilly, homily, icily, jubilee, laggardly, leisurely, maidenly, mannerly, masterly, matronly, miserly, motherly, neighbourly/neighborly (U.S.), northerly, panoply, plug-ugly, quarterly, rascally, readily, reveille, scholarly, simile, sisterly, slovenly, southerly, ungainly, unruly, user-friendly, westerly, wizardly, womanly.
[4] absolutely, anomaly, creepy-crawly, curmudgeonly, eco-friendly, facsimile, fait accompli, gentlemanly, holy-moly, hurly-burly, immediately, melancholy, monopoly, piccalilli, ravioli, rockabilly, roly-poly, shilly-shally, softly-softly, tagliatelle, ukulele, underbelly, willy-nilly, yellow-belly.

SURPRISING RHYMING:
[1] **Be**, bee, fee, flea, flee, gee, glee, he, key, knee, me, pea, pee, sea, see, tee, tea, the, thee, twee, we, wee, whee, zee.
Brie, free, re, spree, three, tree.
Beam, cream, deem, dream, gleam, meme, ream, scheme, scream, seam, seem, steam, stream, team, teem, theme.
[2] **Baddy**, bawdy, beady, bloody, body, brandy, buddy, caddie, candy, cloudy, daddy, dandy, dowdy, foodie, gaudy, giddy, greedy, handy, hardy, heady, hoodie, howdy, kiddie, laddie, lady, MD, midi, moody, mouldy/moldy (U.S.), muddy, needy, nerdy, oldie, randy, ready, roadie, rowdy, sandy, seedy, shady, shandy, shoddy, speedy, steady, study, sturdy, tardy, teddy, tidy, trendy, tweedy, weedy, windy, woody, wordy.
Abbey, baby, bobby, busby, cabby, chubby, crabby, derby, flabby, Frisbee, gabby, grubby, hobby, hubby, lobby, maybe, ruby, scabby, shabby, snobby, would-be, zombie.
Agree, angry, beery, belfry, berry, bleary, blurry, boundary, bury, carefree, carry, cheery, cherry, country, curry, dairy, dearie, debris, degree, dowry, dreary, dust-free, eerie, entry, esprit, every, fairy, ferry, fiery, flowery, flurry, furry, fury, gentry, germ-free, glory, gory, Grand Prix, gumtree, hairy, hoary, hurry, hungry, jury, laundry, leery, lorry, marry, merry, paltry, pantry, parry, pastry, poultry, powdery, prairie, quandary, quarry, query, scary, scot-free, sentry, sorry, starry, storey, story, sultry, tawdry, teary, theory, treachery, vary, very, vestry, wary, weary, wintry, wiry, worry.
Bumpy, chappie, chippy, chirpy, clippie, crappie, creepy, crispy, dippy, dopey, drippy, droopy, dumpy, flappy, frumpy, grippy, groupie, grumpy, happy, hippie, humpy, jumpy, lippy, loopy, lumpy, nappy, nippy, pappy, peppy, plummy, preppy, pulpy, puppy, raspy, ropy, sappy, scampi, scrappy, scrummy, scrumpy, skimpy, sleepy, slippy, snappy, snippy, snoopy, soapy, soupy, stripy, stumpy, swampy, sweetpea, teepee, trippy, vampy, weepy, whippy, whoopee, wimpy, wispy, yuppie, zappy, zippy.
Bitty, city, ditty, gritty, pity, pretty, witty.
Achy, baccy, balky, beaky, bookie, brickie, bulky, car key, chalky, cheeky, chunky, cliquey, clunky, cocky, cookie, corky, creaky, crikey, croaky, dinky, donkey, door key, ducky, dusky, flaky, flunkey, folkie, folky, freaky, frisky, funky, gawky, hanky, hickey, hockey, hokey, hookey, hunky, husky, icky, inky, jerky, jockey, jokey, junkie, key, karaoke, khaki, kinky, lackey, lanky, latchkey, leaky, lucky, marquee, mickey, milky, murky, monkey, mucky, musky, narky, nooky, passkey, peaky, perky, pesky, picky, pinkie, pinky, plucky, pokey, porky, psyche, punky, quaky, quickie, quirky, reeky, risky, rocky, rookie, shaky, sickie, silky, ski, slinky, smoky, snaky, sneaky, sparky, spiky, spooky, squeaky, sticky, stinky, stocky, streaky, sulky, swanky, tacky, talkie, techie, tricky, turkey, turnkey, wacky, whiskey/whisky, wonky, Yankee, yucky.
Army, balmy, barmy, blimey, chamois, chummy, clammy, creamy, crummy, dreamy, dummy, Emmy, foamy, gimme, gleamy, gloomy, Grammy, grimy, gummy, hammy, homey, lemme, limey, mammy, me, mommy, mummy, plummy, roomy, samey, scrummy, seamy, slimy, slummy, smarmy, stormy, tummy, whammy, wormy, yummy.

Acne, any, beanie, blarney, bonny, bony, brainy, brawny, briny, brownie, canny, chimney, cine, cockney, corny, cranny, crony, Disney, genie, grainy, granny, guinea, hinny, horny, journey, knee, loony, many, meanie, mini, nanny, ninny, penny, pony, phoney/phony (U.S.), puny, queenie, rainy, sarnie, scrawny, shiny, skinny, stony, teeny, thorny, tinny, tiny, townie, trainee, tranny, tweeny, uni, weeny, whiny, zany.
Budgie, bulgy, cagey, clergy, dingy, dodgy, edgy, grungy, gungy, mangy, orgy, rangy, smudgy, spongy, squeegee, squidgy, stagy, stingy, stodgy, veggie, wedgie, whingy.
Bossy, bouncy, brassy, chassis, classy, curtsy, Dixie, dressy, emcee, fancy, fleecy, folksy, footsie, foresee, foxy, fussy, glassy, glitzy, glossy, grassy, greasy, gutsy, gypsy, horsey, hussy, saucy, icy, kissy, lacy, lassie, look-see, maxi, mercy, messy, missy, mousy, pacey, pixie, posse, pricey, juicy, prissy, proxy, pussy, racy, ritzy, sassy, schmaltzy, sexy, sightsee, sissy, spacey, specie, spicy, taxi, tipsy, tootsie, waxy.
Anti, arty, auntie, batty, beastie, bitty, catty, chatty, city, crafty, cruelty, dainty, ditty, draughty/drafty (U.S.), eighty, fatty, fifty, frailty, goatee, gritty, guilty, hasty, hearty, hefty, jetty, lefty, matey, meaty, minty, misty, nasty, nifty, party, pasty, petit, petty, pity, plenty, pretty, QT, safety, scanty, settee, shanty/chanty (U.S.), shifty, sixty, sweaty, sweetie, swiftie, tarty, tatty, tasty, thrifty, treaty, twenty, twisty, weighty, witty, yeti.
Beefy, coffee, comfy, stuffy, toffee, toughie, trophy.
Breathy, earthy, filthy, frothy, healthy, lengthy, mouthy, pithy, smoothie, stealthy, swarthy, toothy, wealthy, worthy.
Bevvy, Chevy, curvy, envy, gravy, groovy, heavy, ivy, levee, levy, lovey, luvvy, movie, navy, nervy, savvy, skivvy, spivvy, wavy.
Blowy, chewy, dewy, doughy, gluey, gooey, hooey, phooey, screwy, showy, snowy.
Burly, curly, early, girlie, hurly-burly, surly, swirly, whirly.
Brolly, collie, dolly, folly, golly, holly, jolly, lolly, trolley, volley, wally.
Alley, dally, galley, pally, rally, reveille, sally, tally, valley.
Bunny, funny, gunny, honey, money, runny, sonny, sunny.
Choppy, copy, floppy, jalopy, poppy, sloppy, soppy, stroppy.
[3] **Bumblebee**, honeybee, namby-pamby, wallaby, wannabe.
Burgundy, chickadee, COD, comedy, custody, dogsbody, embody, fool-hardy, jeopardy, melody, nobody, parody, Ph.D., raggedy, remedy, rhapsody, somebody, tragedy.
Ancestry, archery, artistry, bakery, battery, bigotry, binary, blackberry, blubbery, blueberry, blustery, brasserie, bravery, brewery, bribery, burglary, calorie, carpentry, carvery, cavalry, celery, century, chemistry, chicory, chivalry, Christmas tree, colliery, contrary, devilry, diary, dietary, disagree, dithery, doddery, drudgery, dungaree, duty-free, eatery, enquiry, estuary, expiry, factory, fakery, feathery, filigree, finery, fishery, flattery, fluttery, forestry, forgery, gallery, geometry, gimmickry, glittery, greenery, grocery, history, imagery, injury, inquiry, ivory, jamboree, jewellery/jewelry (U.S.), jittery, leathery, lingerie, lottery, luxury, memory, mercury, misery, momentary, monastery, mystery, nursery, obituary, obligatory, pageantry, pedigree, perjury, pillory, pleasantry, poetry, pottery, primary, priory, quivery, referee, revelry, reverie, rivalry, robbery, rockery, rosary, rubbery, salary, sanctuary, savagery, savory, scenery, sensory, shimmery, shivery, silvery, slavery, slippery, sorcery, sugary, surgery, tapestry, thundery, treachery, trickery, victory, wintery, wizardry.
Aromatherapy, gossipy, photocopy, recipe, slap-happy, syrupy, therapy, unhappy.
Alchemy, bigamy, blasphemy, blossomy, bonhomie, enemy, infamy, sesame, tsunami.
Anarchy, finicky, garlicky, gimmicky, headachy, malarkey, monarchy, panicky, plasticky.
Agony, attorney, balcony, baloney, bikini, botany, colony, company, cottony, cushiony, destiny, ebony, felony, gluttony, halfpenny, harmony, Houdini, irony, larceny, litany, martini, mutiny, satiny, scrutiny, symphony, tiffany, timpani, trainee, tyranny, villainy.
Actually, brotherly, easterly, elderly, equally, fatherly, finally, formally, formerly, gingerly, gravelly, leisurely, masterly, miserly, naturally, neighbourly/neighborly (U.S.), normally, northerly, orderly, overly, partially, properly, scholarly, sisterly, southerly, specially, thoroughly, usually, utterly, virtually, westerly.
Committee, gravity, nitty-gritty, responsibility, sanity, self-pity.
Allergy, effigy, emoji, energy, eulogy, lethargy, refugee, strategy, synergy, trilogy.
Actressy, agency, autopsy, bankruptcy, blatancy, bourgeoisie, buoyancy, Christmassy, clemency, courtesy, currency, decency, divorcee, ecstasy, embassy, fallacy, fantasy, fluency, galaxy, heresy, infancy, jealousy, legacy, leniency, lunacy, odyssey, oversee, pharmacy, piracy, policy, potency, pregnancy, primacy, privacy, prophecy, regency,

147

secrecy, tendency, Tennessee, truancy, undersea, urgency, vacancy.
Absentee, amnesty, brevity, casualty, certainty, charity, chastity, clarity, committee, confetti, crotchety, crudity, density, deputy, devotee, dignity, dynasty, enmity, entity, fidgety, gaiety/gayety (U.S.), graffiti, gravity, guarantee, honesty, karate, levity, liberty, machete, majesty, modesty, nudity, oddity, parity, penalty, piety, poverty, probity, property, puberty, purity, quality, repartee, rickety, sanctity, sanctuary, scarcity, seventy, sovereignty, spaghetti, specialty, three-sixty, trinity, unity, uppity, vanity, velvety.
Apathy, empathy, newsworthy, noteworthy, praiseworthy, roadworthy, seaworthy, sympathy, trustworthy, unhealthy, unworthy.
Anchovy, c'est la vie, eau-de-vie, lovey-dovey, top-heavy, topsy-turvy, vis-à-vis.
Billowy, chop suey, echoey, shadowy, yellowy, willowy.
Freezingly, pleasingly, teasingly, wheezingly.
[4] Anybody, busybody, everybody, fuddy-duddy, hurdy-gurdy, oldie worlde, understudy.
Accessory, adultery, artillery, cautionary, cemetery, compulsory, confectionery, conciliatory, constabulary, contemporary, customary, debauchery, delivery, dictionary, directory, discovery, distillery, elementary, embroidery, explanatory, exploratory, hunky-dory, idolatry, imaginary, incendiary, infirmary, inflammatory, judiciary, laboratory, legendary, literary, machinery, mandatory, mercenary, military, missionary, necessary, ordinary, patisserie, perfumery, preliminary, psychiatry, publicity, reactionary, recovery, secretary, secondary, simplicity, skullduggery, solitary, stationary, stationery, temporary, territory, tomfoolery, upholstery, visionary, vocabulary.
Apostrophe, biography, catastrophe, choreography, geography, philosophy, photography.
Academy, anatomy, astronomy, economy, epitome, origami.
Hanky-panky, happy-go-lucky, hokey-cokey, okey-dokey, wakey-wakey, walkie-talkie.
Analogy, anthology, apology, archeology, astrology, biology, cardiology, chronology, ecology, geology, ideology, mythology, psychology, technology, theology, zoology.
Accompany, acrimony, alimony, cacophony, ceremony, epiphany, hootenanny, ignominy, matrimony, monotony, pepperoni, teeny-weeny, telephony, testimony.
Ability, agility, fertility, fragility, futility, hostility, humility, liability, mobility, nobility, responsibility, stability, tranquillity/tranquility (U.S.), versatility, viability, virility, volatility.
Especially, eventually, initially, incidentally, melancholy, monopoly, occasionally, officially, originally, personally, universally, unmannerly.
Accuracy, complacency, consistency, conspiracy, contingency, controversy, delicacy, diplomacy, discrepancy, efficiency, emergency, flamboyancy, hypocrisy, idiocy, intimacy, intricacy, paparazzi, presidency, redundancy, sufficiency, supremacy, transparency.
Absurdity, affinity, amenity, anxiety, barbarity, calamity, cognoscenti, community, conformity, credulity, difficulty, dilettante, enormity, equality, eternity, fatality, fidelity, fifty-fifty, fraternity, frivolity, glitterati, heredity, hilarity, humanity, humidity, immunity, impunity, indemnity, infinity, intercity, literati, maternity, modernity, morality, nitty-gritty, obscenity, profanity, reality, senility, serenity, sobriety, solemnity, virility, stupidity, timidity, totality, twenty-twenty, variety, vicinity, vigilante, virginity, vulgarity.
[5] Anniversary, beneficiary, camaraderie, complementary, complimentary, contradictory, directory, documentary, evolutionary, revolutionary, rudimentary, supplementary.
Ambiguity, anonymity, continuity, familiarity, femininity, impropriety, ingenuity, irregularity, liability, masculinity, notoriety, opportunity, peculiarity, popularity, regularity, serendipity, similarity, solidarity, spontaneity, uniformity, versatility, viability, volatility.

2.1.7 "--mee" (as in "me")

[2] acme, army, balmy, barmy, beamy, blimey, chamois, chummy, clammy, creamy, crummy, dreamy, dummy, Emmy, foamy, gammy, gimme, gleamy, gloomy, Grammy, grimy, gummy, hammy, homey, jammy, jimmy, lemme, limey, mammy, me, mommy, mummy, palmy, plummy, roomy, rummy, samey, scummy, scrummy, seamy, shammy, shimmy, slimy, slummy, smarmy, stormy, tummy, whammy, wormy, yummy.
[3] alchemy, bigamy, blasphemy, blossomy, bonhomie, enemy, excuse me, infamy, pastrami, salami, sesame, tsunami.
[4] academy, anatomy, astronomy, economy, epitome, origami.

SURPRISING RHYMING:
[1] Be, bee, fee, flea, flee, gee, glee, he, key, knee, pea, pee, sea, see, tee, tea, the, thee, twee, we, wee, whee, zee.

Brie, free, re, spree, three, tree.
Beam, cream, deem, dream, gleam, meme, ream, scheme, scream, seam, seem, steam, stream, team, teem, theme.
[2] Baddy, bawdy, beady, bloody, body, brandy, buddy, caddie, candy, cloudy, daddy, dandy, dowdy, foodie, gaudy, giddy, greedy, handy, hardy, heady, hoodie, howdy, kiddie, laddie, lady, MD, midi, moody, mouldy/moldy (U.S.), muddy, needy, nerdy, oldie, randy, ready, roadie, rowdy, sandy, seedy, shady, shandy, shoddy, speedy, steady, study, sturdy, tardy, teddy, tidy, trendy, tweedy, weedy, windy, woody, wordy.
Abbey, baby, bobby, busby, cabby, chubby, crabby, derby, flabby, Frisbee, gabby hobby, grubby, hubby, lobby, maybe, ruby, scabby, shabby, snobby, would-be, zombie.
Ably, amply, aptly, barley, beastly, belly, bobbly, bubbly, bully, chili, chilly, cleanly, comely, coolie, coolly, costly, coyly, crackly, crawly, crinkly, crumbly, crumply, cuddly, daily, dally, dangly, deadly, deathly, deli, dimly, dimply, doily, drily, drizzly, dully, duly, earthly, elderly, fiddly, filly, fitly, flatly, fleshly, freckly, friendly, frilly, fully, gaily, gangly, ghastly, ghostly, giggly, goalie, godly, goodly, googly, gristly, grizzly, grumbly, hilly, hotly, holy, hourly, husbandly, hyperbole, idly, jelly, jangly, jiggly, jingly, jowly, kindly, kingly, knobbly, likely, lily, lively, lonely, lordly, lovely, lowly, madly, manly, medley, monthly, mostly, motley, muesli, muscly, newly, niggly, nightly, oddly, oily, only, orderly, paisley, parley, pebbly, pimply, poorly, portly, prickly, priestly, princely, purply, queenly, really, rumbly, sadly, saintly, scribbly, seemly, shapely, shyly, sickly, silly, slightly, slyly, smiley, smelly, snarly, sparkly, spindly, sprightly, squiggly, stately, steely, stiffly, straggly, sully, surely, telly, tickly, timely, tingly, tinkly, trembly, trimly, trolley, truly, twinkly, ugly, volley, waffly, wally, weakly, weekly, welly, wetly, wheelie, wifely, wiggly, wily, wobbly, woolly, worldly, wriggly, wrinkly, wryly, yearly.
Agree, angry, beery, belfry, berry, bleary, blurry, boundary, bury, carefree, carry, cheery, cherry, country, curry, dairy, dearie, debris, degree, dowry, dreary, dust-free, eerie, entry, esprit, every, fairy, ferry, fiery, flowery, flurry, furry, fury, gentry, germ-free, glory, gory, Grand Prix, gumtree, hairy, hoary, hurry, hungry, jury, laundry, leery, lorry, marry, merry, paltry, pantry, parry, pastry, poultry, powdery, prairie, quandary, quarry, query, scary, scot-free, sentry, sorry, starry, storey, story, sultry, tawdry, teary, theory, treachery, vary, very, vestry, wary, weary, wintry, wiry, worry.
Bumpy, chappie, chippy, chirpy, clippie, crappie, creepy, crispy, dippy, dopey, drippy, droopy, dumpy, flappy, frumpy, grippy, groupie, grumpy, happy, hippie, humpy, jumpy, lippy, loopy, lumpy, nappy, nippy, pappy, peppy, plummy, preppy, pulpy, puppy, raspy, ropy, sappy, scampi, scrappy, scrummy, scrumpy, skimpy, sleepy, slippy, snappy, snippy, snoopy, soapy, soupy, stripy, stumpy, swampy, sweetpea, teepee, trippy, vampy, weepy, whippy, whoopee, wimpy, wispy, yuppie, zappy, zippy.
Bitty, city, ditty, gritty, pity, pretty, witty.
Achy, baccy, balky, beaky, bookie, brickie, bulky, car key, chalky, cheeky, chunky, cliquey, clunky, cocky, cookie, corky, creaky, crikey, croaky, dinky, donkey, door key, ducky, dusky, flaky, flunkey, folkie, folky, freaky, frisky, funky, gawky, hanky, hickey, hockey, hokey, hookey, hunky, husky, icky, inky, jerky, jockey, jokey, junkie, key, karaoke, khaki, kinky, lackey, lanky, latchkey, leaky, lucky, marquee, mickey, milky, murky, monkey, mucky, musky, narky, nooky, passkey, peaky, perky, pesky, picky, pinkie, pinky, plucky, pokey, porky, psyche, punky, quaky, quickie, quirky, reeky, risky, rocky, rookie, shaky, sickie, silky, ski, slinky, smoky, snaky, sneaky, sparky, spiky, spooky, squeaky, sticky, stinky, stocky, streaky, sulky, swanky, tacky, talkie, techie, tricky, turkey, wacky, whiskey/whisky, wonky, Yankee, yucky.
Acne, any, beanie, blarney, bonny, bony, brainy, brawny, briny, brownie, canny, chimney, cine, cockney, corny, cranny, crony, Disney, genie, grainy, granny, guinea, hinny, horny, journey, knee, loony, many, meanie, mini, nanny, ninny, penny, pony, phoney/phony (U.S.), puny, queenie, rainy, sarnie, scrawny, shiny, skinny, stony, teeny, thorny, tinny, tiny, townie, trainee, tranny, tweeny, uni, weeny, whiny, zany.
Budgie, bulgy, cagey, clergy, dingy, dodgy, edgy, grungy, gungy, mangy, orgy, smudgy, spongy, squeegee, squidgy, stagy, stingy, stodgy, veggie, wedgie, whingy.
Bossy, bouncy, brassy, chassis, classy, curtsy, Dixie, dressy, emcee, fancy, fleecy, folksy, footsie, foresee, foxy, fussy, glassy, glitzy, glossy, grassy, greasy, gutsy, gypsy, horsey, hussy, saucy, icy, kissy, lacy, lassie, look-see, maxi, mercy, messy, missy, mousy, pacey, pixie, posse, pricey, prissy, proxy, pussy, racy, ritzy, sassy, schmaltzy, sexy, sightsee, sissy, spacey, specie, spicy, taxi, tipsy, tootsie, waxy.

Anti, arty, auntie, batty, beastie, bitty, catty, chatty, city, crafty, cruelty, dainty, ditty, draughty/drafty (U.S.), eighty, fatty, fifty, frailty, goatee, gritty, guilty, hasty, hearty, hefty, jetty, lefty, matey, meaty, minty, misty, nasty, nifty, party, pasty, petit, petty, pity, plenty, pretty, QT, safety, scanty, settee, shanty/chanty (U.S.), shifty, sixty, sweaty, sweetie, swiftie, tarty, tatty, tasty, thrifty, treaty, twenty, twisty, weighty, witty, yeti.
Beefy, coffee, comfy, fluffy, goofy, huffy, iffy, jiffy, leafy, puffy, scruffy, selfie, sniffy, stiffy, stuffy, toffee, toughie, trophy.
Breathy, earthy, filthy, frothy, healthy, lengthy, mouthy, pithy, smithy, smoothie, stealthy, swarthy, toothy, wealthy, worthy.
Bevvy, Chevy, curvy, envy, gravy, groovy, heavy, ivy, levee, levy, lovey, luvvy, movie, navy, nervy, savvy, skivvy, spivvy, wavy.
Blowy, bluey, chewy, dewy, doughy, ennui, gluey, gooey, hooey, peewee, phooey, screwy, showy, snowy.
Burly, curly, early, girlie, hurly-burly, surly, swirly, twirly, whirly.
Brolly, collie, dolly, folly, golly, holly, jolly, lolly, trolley, volley, wally.
Alley, dally, dilly-dally, galley, pally, rally, reveille, sally, tally, valley.
Bunny, funny, gunny, honey, money, runny, sonny, sunny, tunny.
Choppy, copy, floppy, jalopy, poppy, sloppy, soppy, stroppy.
Airstream, blaspheme, daydream, downstream, extreme, ice-cream, jet stream, light-beam, mainstream, moonbeam, redeem, regime, self-esteem, slipstream, supreme.
[3] **Bumblebee**, honeybee, namby-pamby, wallaby, wannabe.
Burgundy, chickadee, COD, comedy, custody, dogsbody, embody, fool-hardy, jeopardy, melody, nobody, parody, Ph.D., raggedy, remedy, rhapsody, somebody, tragedy.
Ancestry, archery, artistry, bakery, battery, bigotry, binary, blackberry, blubbery, blueberry, blustery, brasserie, bravery, brewery, bribery, burglary, calorie, carpentry, carvery, cavalry, celery, century, chemistry, chicory, chivalry, Christmas tree, colliery, contrary, devilry, diary, dietary, disagree, dithery, doddery, drudgery, dungaree, duty-free, eatery, enquiry, estuary, expiry, factory, fakery, feathery, filigree, finery, fishery, flattery, fluttery, forestry, forgery, gallery, geometry, gimmickry, glittery, greenery, grocery, history, imagery, injury, inquiry, ivory, jamboree, jewellery/jewelry (U.S.), jittery, leathery, lingerie, lottery, luxury, memory, mercury, misery, momentary, monastery, mystery, nursery, obituary, obligatory, pageantry, pedigree, perjury, pillory, pleasantry, poetry, pottery, primary, priory, quivery, referee, revelry, reverie, rivalry, robbery, rockery, rosary, rubbery, salary, sanctuary, savagery, savory, scenery, sensory, shimmery, shivery, silvery, slavery, slippery, sorcery, sugary, surgery, tapestry, thundery, treachery, trickery, victory, wintery, wizardry.
Aromatherapy, gossipy, photocopy, recipe, slap-happy, syrupy, therapy, unhappy.
Assembly, bimonthly, biweekly, bodily, comradely, cowardly, dastardly, directly, easterly, family, finale, fleur-de-lis, fortnightly, heavenly, hillbilly, homily, icily, jubilee, laggardly, maidenly, mannerly, matronly, plug-ugly, quarterly, readily, reveille, simile, slovenly, ungainly, unruly, user-friendly, wizardly, womanly.
Anarchy, finicky, garlicky, gimmicky, headachy, malarkey, monarchy, panicky, plasticky.
Agony, attorney, balcony, baloney, bikini, botany, colony, company, cottony, cushiony, destiny, ebony, felony, gluttony, halfpenny, harmony, Houdini, irony, larceny, litany, martini, mutiny, satiny, scrutiny, symphony, tiffany, timpani, trainee, tyranny, villainy.
Actually, brotherly, easterly, elderly, equally, fatherly, finally, formally, formerly, gingerly, gravelly, leisurely, masterly, miserly, naturally, neighbourly/neighborly (U.S.), normally, northerly, orderly, overly, partially, properly, scholarly, sisterly, southerly, specially, thoroughly, usually, utterly, virtually, westerly.
Committee, gravity, nitty-gritty, responsibility, sanity, self-pity.
Allergy, effigy, emoji, energy, eulogy, lethargy, refugee, strategy, synergy, trilogy.
Actress, agency, autopsy, bankruptcy, blatancy, bourgeoisie, buoyancy, Christmassy, clemency, courtesy, currency, decency, divorcee, ecstasy, embassy, fallacy, fantasy, fluency, galaxy, heresy, infancy, jealousy, legacy, leniency, lunacy, odyssey, oversee, pharmacy, piracy, policy, potency, pregnancy, primacy, privacy, prophecy, regency, secrecy, tendency, Tennessee, truancy, undersea, urgency, vacancy.
Absentee, amnesty, brevity, casualty, certainty, charity, chastity, clarity, committee, confetti, crotchety, crudity, density, deputy, devotee, dignity, dynasty, enmity, entity, fidgety, gaiety/gayety (U.S.), graffiti, gravity, guarantee, honesty, karate, levity, liberty, machete, majesty, modesty, nudity, oddity, parity, penalty, piety, poverty, probity,

property, puberty, purity, quality, repartee, rickety, sanctity, sanctuary, scarcity, seventy, sovereignty, spaghetti, specialty, three-sixty, trinity, unity, uppity, vanity, velvety.
Apathy, empathy, newsworthy, noteworthy, praiseworthy, roadworthy, seaworthy, sympathy, trustworthy, unworthy.
Anchovy, c'est la vie, eau-de-vie, lovey-dovey, top-heavy, topsy-turvy, vis-à-vis.
Billowy, chop suey, echoey, shadowy, yellowy, willowy.
Freezingly, pleasingly, teasingly, wheezingly.
[4] Anybody, busybody, everybody, fuddy-duddy, hurdy-gurdy, oldie worlde, understudy.
Accessory, adultery, artillery, cautionary, cemetery, compulsory, confectionery, conciliatory, constabulary, contemporary, customary, debauchery, delivery, dictionary, directory, discovery, distillery, elementary, embroidery, explanatory, exploratory, hunky-dory, idolatry, imaginary, incendiary, infirmary, inflammatory, judiciary, laboratory, legendary, literary, machinery, mandatory, mercenary, military, missionary, necessary, ordinary, patisserie, perfumery, preliminary, psychiatry, publicity, reactionary, recovery, secretary, secondary, simplicity, skullduggery, solitary, stationary, stationery, temporary, territory, tomfoolery, upholstery, visionary, vocabulary.
Apostrophe, biography, catastrophe, choreography, geography, philosophy, photography.
Absolutely, anomaly, creepy-crawly, curmudgeonly, dilly-dally, eco-friendly, facsimile, fait accompli, gentlemanly, holy-moly, hurly-burly, immediately, melancholy, monopoly, rockabilly, roly-poly, shilly-shally, softly-softly, ukulele, underbelly, willy-nilly, yellow-belly.
Hanky-panky, happy-go-lucky, hokey-cokey, okey-dokey, wakey-wakey, walkie-talkie.
Analogy, anthology, apology, archeology, astrology, biology, cardiology, chronology, ecology, geology, ideology, mythology, psychology, technology, theology, zoology.
Accompany, acrimony, alimony, cacophony, ceremony, epiphany, hootenanny, matrimony, minestrone, monotony, pepperoni, teeny-weeny, telephony, testimony.
Ability, agility, fertility, fragility, futility, hostility, humility, liability, mobility, nobility, responsibility, stability, tranquillity/tranquility (U.S.), versatility, viability, virility, volatility.
Especially, eventually, initially, incidentally, melancholy, monopoly, occasionally, officially, originally, personally, universally, unmannerly.
Accuracy, complacency, consistency, conspiracy, contingency, controversy, delicacy, diplomacy, discrepancy, efficiency, emergency, flamboyancy, hypocrisy, idiocy, intimacy, intricacy, paparazzi, presidency, redundancy, sufficiency, supremacy, transparency.
Absurdity, affinity, amenity, anxiety, barbarity, calamity, cognoscenti, community, conformity, credulity, difficulty, dilettante, enormity, equality, eternity, fatality, fidelity, fifty-fifty, fraternity, frivolity, glitterati, heredity, hilarity, humanity, humidity, immunity, impunity, indemnity, infinity, intercity, literati, maternity, modernity, morality, nitty-gritty, obscenity, profanity, reality, senility, serenity, sobriety, solemnity, virility, stupidity, timidity, totality, twenty-twenty, variety, vicinity, vigilante, virginity, vulgarity.
[5] Anniversary, beneficiary, camaraderie, complementary, complimentary, contradictory, directory, documentary, evolutionary, revolutionary, rudimentary, supplementary.
Ambiguity, anonymity, continuity, familiarity, femininity, impropriety, ingenuity, irregularity, liability, masculinity, notoriety, opportunity, peculiarity, popularity, regularity, responsibility, serendipity, similarity, solidarity, spontaneity, versatility, viability, volatility.

2.1.8 "--nee" (as in "knee")

[2] acne, any, beanie, blarney, bonny, bony, brainy, brawny, briny, brownie, bunny, canny, chimney, cine, cockney, corny, cranny, crony, Disney, funny, genie, grainy, granny, guinea, hinny, honey, horny, journey, kidney, knee, loony, many, meanie, mini, money, nanny, ninny, penny, phoney/phony (U.S.), pony, puny, queenie, rainy, runny, sarnie, scrawny, shinny, shiny, skinny, sonny, spinney, stony, sunny, teeny, thorny, tinny, tiny, townie, trainee, tranny, tweeny, uni, weeny, whinny, whiny, zany.
[3] agony, attorney, balcony, baloney, bikini, botany, cartoony, catchpenny, colony, company, cottony, cushiony, destiny, detainee, ebony, felony, gluttony, halfpenny, harmony, Houdini, irony, larceny, lemony, litany, martini, mountainy, mutiny, nominee, pinchpenny, satiny, scrutiny, sunshiny, symphony, tiffany, timpani, trainee, tyranny, villainy.
[4] Aborigine, accompany, acrimony, alimony, cacophony, ceremony, epiphany, hootenanny, ignominy, macaroni, mahogany, matrimony, minestrone, monotony, pepperoni, teeny-weeny, telephony, testimony.

SURPRISING RHYMING:
[1] **Be**, bee, fee, flea, flee, gee, glee, he, key, knee, me, pea, pee, sea, see, tee, tea, the, thee, twee, we, wee, whee, zee.
Brie, free, re, spree, three, tree.
Beam, cream, deem, dream, gleam, meme, ream, scheme, scream, seam, seem, steam, stream, team, teem, theme.
[2] **Baddy**, bawdy, beady, bloody, body, brandy, buddy, caddie, candy, cloudy, daddy, dandy, dowdy, foodie, gaudy, giddy, greedy, handy, hardy, heady, hoodie, howdy, kiddie, laddie, lady, MD, midi, moody, mouldy/moldy (U.S.), muddy, needy, nerdy, oldie, randy, ready, roadie, rowdy, sandy, seedy, shady, shandy, shoddy, speedy, steady, study, sturdy, tardy, teddy, tidy, trendy, tweedy, weedy, windy, woody, wordy.
Abbey, baby, cabby, chubby, derby, flabby, Frisbee, hobby, grubby, hubby, lobby, maybe, ruby, shabby, snobby, would-be, zombie.
Ably, amply, aptly, barley, beastly, belly, bobbly, bubbly, bully, chili, chilly, cleanly, comely, coolie, coolly, costly, coyly, crackly, crawly, crinkly, crumbly, crumply, cuddly, daily, dally, dangly, deadly, deathly, deli, dimly, dimply, doily, drily, drizzly, dully, duly, earthly, elderly, fiddly, filly, fitly, flatly, fleshly, freckly, friendly, frilly, fully, gaily, gangly, ghastly, ghostly, giggly, goalie, godly, goodly, googly, gristly, grizzly, grumbly, hilly, hotly, holy, hourly, husbandly, hyperbole, idly, jelly, jangly, jiggly, jingly, jowly, kindly, kingly, knobbly, likely, lily, lively, lonely, lordly, lovely, lowly, madly, manly, medley, monthly, mostly, motley, muesli, muscly, newly, niggly, nightly, oddly, oily, only, orderly, paisley, parley, pebbly, pimply, poorly, portly, prickly, priestly, princely, purply, queenly, really, rumbly, sadly, saintly, scribbly, seemly, shapely, shyly, sickly, silly, slightly, slyly, smiley, smelly, snarly, sparkly, spindly, sprightly, squiggly, stately, steely, stiffly, straggly, sully, surely, telly, tickly, timely, tingly, tinkly, trembly, trimly, trolley, truly, twinkly, ugly, volley, waffly, wally, weakly, weekly, welly, wetly, wheelie, wifely, wiggly, wily, wobbly, woolly, worldly, wriggly, wrinkly, wryly, yearly.
Agree, angry, beery, belfry, berry, bleary, blurry, boundary, bury, carefree, carry, cheery, cherry, country, curry, dairy, dearie, debris, degree, dowry, dreary, dust-free, eerie, entry, esprit, every, fairy, ferry, fiery, flowery, flurry, furry, fury, gentry, germ-free, glory, gory, Grand Prix, gumtree, hairy, hoary, hurry, hungry, jury, laundry, leery, lorry, marry, merry, paltry, pantry, parry, pastry, poultry, powdery, prairie, quandary, quarry, query, scary, scot-free, sentry, sorry, starry, storey, story, sultry, tawdry, teary, theory, treachery, vary, very, vestry, wary, weary, wintry, wiry, worry.
Bumpy, chappie, chippy, chirpy, clippie, crappie, creepy, crispy, dippy, dopey, drippy, droopy, dumpy, flappy, frumpy, grippy, groupie, grumpy, happy, hippie, humpy, jumpy, lippy, loopy, lumpy, nappy, nippy, pappy, peppy, plummy, preppy, pulpy, puppy, raspy, ropy, sappy, scampi, scrappy, scrummy, scrumpy, skimpy, sleepy, slippy, snappy, snippy, snoopy, soapy, soupy, stripy, stumpy, swampy, sweetpea, teepee, trippy, vampy, weepy, whippy, whoopee, wimpy, wispy, yuppie, zappy, zippy.
Bitty, city, ditty, gritty, pity, pretty, witty.
Army, balmy, barmy, blimey, chamois, chummy, clammy, creamy, crummy, dreamy, dummy, Emmy, foamy, gimme, gleamy, gloomy, Grammy, grimy, gummy, hammy, homey, jammy, lemme, limey, mammy, me, mommy, mummy, plummy, roomy, samey, scrummy, seamy, slimy, slummy, smarmy, stormy, tummy, whammy, wormy, yummy.
Achy, baccy, balky, beaky, bookie, brickie, bulky, car key, chalky, cheeky, chunky, cliquey, clunky, cocky, cookie, corky, creaky, crikey, croaky, dinky, donkey, door key, ducky, dusky, flaky, flunkey, folkie, folky, freaky, frisky, funky, gawky, hanky, hickey, hockey, hokey, hookey, hunky, husky, icky, inky, jerky, jockey, jokey, junkie, key, karaoke, khaki, kinky, lackey, lanky, latchkey, leaky, lucky, marquee, mickey, milky, murky, monkey, mucky, musky, narky, nooky, passkey, peaky, perky, pesky, picky, pinkie, pinky, plucky, pokey, porky, psyche, punky, quaky, quickie, quirky, reeky, risky, rocky, rookie, shaky, sickie, silky, ski, slinky, smoky, snaky, sneaky, sparky, spiky, spooky, squeaky, sticky, stinky, stocky, streaky, sulky, swanky, tacky, talkie, techie, tricky, turkey, wacky, whiskey/whisky, wonky, Yankee, yucky.
Budgie, bulgy, cagey, clergy, dingy, dodgy, edgy, grungy, gungy, mangy, orgy, smudgy, spongy, squeegee, squidgy, stagy, stingy, stodgy, veggie, wedgie, whingy.
Bossy, bouncy, brassy, chassis, classy, curtsy, Dixie, dressy, emcee, fancy, fleecy, folksy, footsie, foresee, foxy, fussy, glassy, glitzy, glossy, grassy, greasy, gutsy, gypsy, horsey, hussy, saucy, icy, kissy, lacy, lassie, look-see, maxi, mercy, messy, missy,

152

mousy, pacey, pixie, posse, pricey, juicy, prissy, proxy, pussy, racy, ritzy, sassy, schmaltzy, sexy, sightsee, sissy, spacey, specie, spicy, taxi, tipsy, tootsie, waxy.
Anti, arty, auntie, batty, beastie, bitty, catty, chatty, city, crafty, cruelty, dainty, ditty, draughty/drafty (U.S.), eighty, fatty, fifty, frailty, goatee, gritty, guilty, hasty, hearty, hefty, jetty, lefty, matey, meaty, minty, misty, nasty, nifty, party, pasty, petit, petty, pity, plenty, pretty, QT, safety, scanty, settee, shanty/chanty (U.S.), shifty, sixty, sweaty, sweetie, swiftie, tarty, tatty, tasty, thrifty, treaty, twenty, twisty, weighty, witty, yeti.
Beefy, coffee, comfy, fluffy, goofy, huffy, iffy, jiffy, leafy, puffy, scruffy, selfie, sniffy, stiffy, stuffy, toffee, toughie, trophy.
Breathy, earthy, filthy, frothy, healthy, lengthy, mouthy, pithy, smoothie, stealthy, swarthy, toothy, wealthy, worthy.
Bevvy, Chevy, curvy, envy, gravy, groovy, heavy, ivy, levee, levy, lovey, luvvy, movie, navy, nervy, savvy, skivvy, wavy.
Blowy, chewy, dewy, doughy, gluey, gooey, hooey, phooey, screwy, showy, snowy.
Burly, curly, early, girlie, hurly-burly, surly, swirly, twirly, whirly
Brolly, collie, dolly, folly, golly, holly, jolly, lolly, trolley, volley, wally.
Alley, dally, galley, pally, rally, reveille, sally, tally, valley.
Bunny, funny, gunny, honey, money, runny, sonny, sunny.
Choppy, copy, floppy, jalopy, poppy, sloppy, soppy, stroppy.
[3] Bumblebee, honeybee, namby-pamby, wallaby, wannabe.
Burgundy, chickadee, COD, comedy, custody, dogsbody, fool-hardy, jeopardy, malady, melody, nobody, parody, Ph.D., raggedy, remedy, rhapsody, somebody, tragedy.
Ancestry, archery, artistry, bakery, battery, bigotry, binary, blackberry, blubbery, blueberry, blustery, brasserie, bravery, brewery, bribery, burglary, calorie, carpentry, carvery, cavalry, celery, century, chemistry, chicory, chivalry, Christmas tree, colliery, contrary, devilry, diary, dietary, disagree, dithery, doddery, drudgery, dungaree, duty-free, eatery, enquiry, estuary, expiry, factory, fakery, feathery, filigree, finery, fishery, flattery, fluttery, forestry, forgery, gallery, geometry, gimmickry, glittery, greenery, grocery, history, imagery, injury, inquiry, ivory, jamboree, jewellery/jewelry (U.S.), jittery, leathery, lingerie, lottery, luxury, memory, mercury, misery, momentary, monastery, mystery, nursery, obituary, obligatory, pageantry, pedigree, perjury, pillory, pleasantry, poetry, pottery, primary, priory, quivery, referee, revelry, reverie, rivalry, robbery, rockery, rosary, rubbery, salary, sanctuary, savagery, savory, scenery, sensory, shimmery, shivery, silvery, slavery, slippery, sorcery, sugary, surgery, tapestry, thundery, treachery, trickery, victory, wintery, wizardry.
Aromatherapy, gossipy, photocopy, recipe, slap-happy, syrupy, therapy, unhappy.
Assembly, bimonthly, biweekly, bodily, comradely, cowardly, dastardly, directly, easterly, family, finale, fleur-de-lis, fortnightly, heavenly, hillbilly, homily, icily, jubilee, laggardly, mannerly, matronly, plug-ugly, quarterly, readily, reveille, simile, slovenly, soldierly, ungainly, unruly, user-friendly, wizardly, womanly.
Alchemy, bigamy, blasphemy, blossomy, bonhomie, enemy, infamy, sesame, tsunami.
Anarchy, finicky, garlicky, gimmicky, headachy, malarkey, monarchy, panicky, plasticky.
Actually, brotherly, easterly, elderly, equally, fatherly, finally, formally, formerly, gingerly, leisurely, masterly, miserly, motherly, naturally, neighbourly/neighborly (U.S.), normally, northerly, orderly, overly, partially, properly, scholarly, sisterly, southerly, specially, thoroughly, usually, utterly, virtually, westerly.
Committee, gravity, nitty-gritty, responsibility, sanity, self-pity.
Allergy, effigy, emoji, energy, eulogy, lethargy, refugee, strategy, synergy, trilogy.
Actressy, agency, autopsy, bankruptcy, blatancy, bourgeoisie, buoyancy, Christmassy, clemency, courtesy, currency, decency, divorcee, ecstasy, embassy, fallacy, fantasy, fluency, galaxy, heresy, infancy, jealousy, legacy, leniency, lunacy, odyssey, oversee, pharmacy, piracy, policy, potency, pregnancy, primacy, privacy, prophecy, regency, secrecy, tendency, Tennessee, truancy, undersea, urgency, vacancy.
Absentee, amnesty, brevity, casualty, certainty, charity, chastity, clarity, committee, confetti, crotchety, crudity, density, deputy, devotee, dignity, dynasty, enmity, entity, fidgety, gaiety/gayety (U.S.), graffiti, gravity, guarantee, honesty, karate, levity, liberty, machete, majesty, modesty, nudity, oddity, parity, penalty, piety, poverty, probity, property, puberty, purity, quality, repartee, rickety, sanctity, sanctuary, scarcity, seventy, sovereignty, spaghetti, specialty, three-sixty, trinity, unity, uppity, vanity, velvety.
Apathy, empathy, newsworthy, noteworthy, praiseworthy, roadworthy, seaworthy,

sympathy, trustworthy, unhealthy, unworthy.
Anchovy, c'est la vie, eau-de-vie, lovey-dovey, top-heavy, topsy-turvy, vis-à-vis.
Billowy, chop suey, echoey, shadowy, yellowy, willowy.
Freezingly, pleasingly, teasingly, wheezingly.
[4] Anybody, busybody, everybody, fuddy-duddy, hurdy-gurdy, oldie worlde, understudy.
Accessory, adultery, artillery, cautionary, cemetery, compulsory, confectionery, conciliatory, constabulary, contemporary, customary, debauchery, delivery, dictionary, directory, discovery, distillery, elementary, embroidery, explanatory, exploratory, hunky-dory, idolatry, imaginary, incendiary, infirmary, inflammatory, judiciary, laboratory, legendary, literary, machinery, mandatory, mercenary, military, missionary, necessary, ordinary, patisserie, perfumery, preliminary, psychiatry, publicity, reactionary, recovery, secretary, secondary, simplicity, skullduggery, solitary, stationary, stationery, temporary, territory, tomfoolery, upholstery, visionary, vocabulary.
Academy, anatomy, astronomy, economy, epitome, origami.
Apostrophe, biography, catastrophe, choreography, geography, philosophy, photography.
Absolutely, anomaly, creepy-crawly, curmudgeonly, dilly-dally, eco-friendly, facsimile, fait accompli, gentlemanly, holy-moly, hurly-burly, immediately, melancholy, monopoly, rockabilly, roly-poly, shilly-shally, softly-softly, ukulele, underbelly, willy-nilly, yellow-belly.
Hanky-panky, happy-go-lucky, hokey-cokey, okey-dokey, wakey-wakey, walkie-talkie.
Analogy, anthology, apology, archeology, astrology, biology, cardiology, chronology, ecology, geology, ideology, mythology, psychology, technology, theology, zoology.
Ability, agility, civility, fertility, fragility, futility, hostility, humility, mobility, nobility, stability, tranquillity/tranquility (U.S.), utility, virility.
Especially, eventually, initially, incidentally, melancholy, monopoly, occasionally, officially, originally, personally, universally.
Accuracy, complacency, consistency, conspiracy, contingency, controversy, delicacy, diplomacy, discrepancy, efficiency, emergency, flamboyancy, hypocrisy, idiocy, intimacy, intricacy, paparazzi, presidency, redundancy, sufficiency, supremacy, transparency.
Absurdity, affinity, amenity, anxiety, barbarity, calamity, cognoscenti, community, conformity, credulity, difficulty, dilettante, enormity, equality, eternity, fatality, fidelity, fifty-fifty, fraternity, frivolity, glitterati, heredity, hilarity, humanity, humidity, immunity, impunity, indemnity, infinity, intercity, literati, maternity, modernity, morality, nitty-gritty, obscenity, profanity, reality, senility, serenity, sobriety, solemnity, virility, stupidity, timidity, totality, twenty-twenty, variety, vicinity, vigilante, virginity, vulgarity.
[5] Anniversary, beneficiary, camaraderie, complementary, complimentary, contradictory, directory, documentary, evolutionary, revolutionary, rudimentary, supplementary.
Ambiguity, anonymity, continuity, familiarity, femininity, impropriety, ingenuity, irregularity, liability, masculinity, notoriety, opportunity, peculiarity, popularity, regularity, responsibility, serendipity, similarity, solidarity, spontaneity, versatility, viability, volatility.

2.1.9 "--pee" (as in "recipe")

[2] bumpy, chappie, chippy, chirpy, choppy, clippie, clumpy, copy, crappie, creepy, crispy, dippy, dopey, drippy, droopy, dumpy, flappy, floppy, frumpy, green pea, grippy, groupie, grumpy, happy, hippie, humpy, jumpy, lippy, loopy, lumpy, nappy, nippy, pappy, pea, pee, peppy, plummy, poppy, preppy, pulpy, puppy, raspy, ropy, sappy, scampi, scrappy, scrummy, scrumpy, skimpy, sleepy, slippy, sloppy, snappy, snippy, snoopy, soapy, soppy, soupy, stripy, stroppy, stumpy, swampy, sweetpea, teepee, trippy, vampy, weepy, whippy, whoopee, wimpy, wispy, yuppie, zappy, zippy.
[3+] aromatherapy, canopy, escapee, gossipy, jalopy, photocopy, recipe, slap-happy, syrupy/syrupy, therapy, unhappy.

SURPRISING RHYMING:
[1] **Be**, bee, fee, flea, flee, gee, glee, he, key, knee, me, sea, see, tee, tea, the, thee, twee, we, wee, whee, zee.
Brie, free, re, spree, three, tree.
Beam, cream, deem, dream, gleam, meme, ream, scheme, scream, seam, seem, steam, stream, team, teem, theme.
[2] **Baddy**, bawdy, beady, bloody, body, brandy, buddy, caddie, candy, cloudy, daddy, dandy, dowdy, foodie, gaudy, giddy, greedy, handy, hardy, heady, hoodie, howdy,

kiddie, laddie, lady, MD, midi, moody, mouldy/moldy (U.S.), muddy, needy, nerdy, oldie, randy, ready, roadie, rowdy, sandy, seedy, shady, shandy, shoddy, speedy, steady, study, sturdy, tardy, teddy, tidy, trendy, tweedy, weedy, windy, woody, wordy.
Abbey, baby, bobby, busby, cabby, chubby, crabby, derby, flabby, Frisbee, gabby hobby, grubby, hubby, lobby, maybe, ruby, scabby, shabby, snobby, would-be, zombie.
Ably, amply, aptly, barley, beastly, belly, bobbly, bubbly, bully, chili, chilly, cleanly, comely, coolie, coolly, costly, coyly, crackly, crawly, crinkly, crumbly, crumply, cuddly, daily, dally, dangly, deadly, deathly, deli, dimly, dimply, doily, drily, drizzly, dully, duly, earthly, elderly, fiddly, filly, fitly, flatly, fleshly, freckly, friendly, frilly, fully, gaily, gangly, ghastly, ghostly, giggly, goalie, godly, goodly, googly, gristly, grizzly, grumbly, hilly, hotly, holy, hourly, husbandly, hyperbole, idly, jelly, jangly, jiggly, jingly, jowly, kindly, kingly, knobbly, likely, lily, lively, lonely, lordly, lovely, lowly, madly, manly, medley, monthly, mostly, motley, muesli, muscly, newly, niggly, nightly, oddly, oily, only, orderly, paisley, parley, pebbly, pimply, poorly, portly, prickly, priestly, princely, purply, queenly, really, rumbly, sadly, saintly, scribbly, seemly, shapely, shyly, sickly, silly, slightly, slyly, smiley, smelly, snarly, sparkly, spindly, sprightly, squiggly, stately, steely, stiffly, straggly, sully, surely, telly, tickly, timely, tingly, tinkly, trembly, trimly, trolley, truly, twinkly, ugly, volley, waffly, wally, weakly, weekly, welly, wetly, wheelie, wifely, wiggly, wily, wobbly, woolly, worldly, wriggly, wrinkly, wryly, yearly.
Agree, angry, beery, belfry, berry, bleary, blurry, boundary, bury, carefree, carry, cheery, cherry, country, curry, dairy, dearie, debris, degree, dowry, dreary, dust-free, eerie, entry, esprit, every, fairy, ferry, fiery, flowery, flurry, furry, fury, gentry, germ-free, glory, gory, Grand Prix, gumtree, hairy, hoary, hurry, hungry, jury, laundry, leery, lorry, marry, merry, paltry, pantry, parry, pastry, poultry, powdery, prairie, quandary, quarry, query, scary, scot-free, sentry, sorry, starry, storey, story, sultry, tawdry, teary, theory, treachery, vary, very, vestry, wary, weary, wintry, wiry, worry.
Bitty, city, ditty, gritty, pity, pretty, witty.
Army, balmy, barmy, blimey, chamois, chummy, clammy, creamy, crummy, dreamy, dummy, Emmy, foamy, gimme, gleamy, gloomy, Grammy, grimy, gummy, hammy, homey, lemme, limey, mammy, me, mommy, mummy, plummy, roomy, samey, scrummy, seamy, slimy, slummy, smarmy, stormy, tummy, whammy, wormy, yummy.
Achy, baccy, balky, beaky, bookie, brickie, bulky, car key, chalky, cheeky, chunky, cliquey, clunky, cocky, cookie, corky, creaky, crikey, croaky, dinky, donkey, door key, ducky, dusky, flaky, flunkey, folkie, folky, freaky, frisky, funky, gawky, hanky, hickey, hockey, hokey, hookey, hunky, husky, icky, inky, jerky, jockey, jokey, junkie, key, karaoke, khaki, kinky, lackey, lanky, latchkey, leaky, lucky, marquee, mickey, milky, murky, monkey, mucky, musky, narky, nooky, passkey, peaky, perky, pesky, picky, pinkie, pinky, plucky, pokey, porky, psyche, punky, quaky, quickie, quirky, reeky, risky, rocky, rookie, shaky, sickie, silky, ski, slinky, smoky, snaky, sneaky, sparky, spiky, spooky, squeaky, sticky, stinky, stocky, streaky, sulky, swanky, tacky, talkie, techie, tricky, turkey, wacky, whiskey/whisky, wonky, Yankee, yucky.
Acne, any, beanie, blarney, bonny, bony, brainy, brawny, briny, brownie, canny, chimney, cine, cockney, corny, cranny, crony, Disney, genie, grainy, granny, guinea, hinny, horny, journey, knee, loony, many, meanie, mini, nanny, ninny, penny, pony, phoney/phony (U.S.), puny, queenie, rainy, sarnie, scrawny, shiny, skinny, stony, teeny, thorny, tinny, tiny, townie, trainee, tranny, tweeny, uni, weeny, whiny, zany.
Budgie, bulgy, cagey, clergy, dingy, dodgy, edgy, grungy, gungy, mangy, orgy, smudgy, spongy, squeegee, squidgy, stagy, stingy, stodgy, veggie, wedgie, whingy.
Bossy, bouncy, brassy, chassis, classy, curtsy, Dixie, dressy, emcee, fancy, fleecy, folksy, footsie, foresee, foxy, fussy, glassy, glitzy, glossy, grassy, greasy, gutsy, gypsy, horsey, hussy, saucy, icy, kissy, lacy, lassie, look-see, maxi, mercy, messy, missy, mousy, pacey, pixie, posse, pricey, prissy, proxy, pussy, racy, ritzy, sassy, schmaltzy, sexy, sightsee, sissy, spacey, specie, spicy, taxi, tipsy, tootsie, waxy.
Anti, arty, auntie, batty, beastie, bitty, catty, chatty, city, crafty, cruelty, dainty, ditty, draughty/drafty (U.S.), eighty, fatty, fifty, frailty, goatee, gritty, guilty, hasty, hearty, hefty, jetty, lefty, matey, meaty, minty, misty, nasty, nifty, party, pasty, petit, petty, pity, plenty, pretty, QT, safety, scanty, settee, shanty/chanty (U.S.), shifty, sixty, sweaty, sweetie, swiftie, tarty, tatty, tasty, thrifty, treaty, twenty, twisty, weighty, witty, yeti.
Beefy, coffee, comfy, fluffy, goofy, huffy, iffy, jiffy, leafy, puffy, scruffy, selfie, sniffy, stiffy, stuffy, toffee, toughie, trophy.

Breathy, earthy, filthy, frothy, healthy, lengthy, smoothie, stealthy, toothy, wealthy, worthy.
Bevvy, Chevy, curvy, envy, gravy, groovy, heavy, ivy, levee, levy, lovey, luvvy, movie, navy, nervy, savvy, skivvy, spivvy, wavy.
Blowy, chewy, dewy, doughy, gluey, gooey, hooey, phooey, screwy, showy, snowy.
Burly, curly, early, girlie, hurly-burly, surly, swirly, twirly, whirly.
Brolly, collie, dolly, folly, golly, holly, jolly, lolly, trolley, volley, wally.
Alley, dally, dilly-dally, galley, pally, rally, reveille, sally, tally, valley.
Bunny, funny, gunny, honey, money, runny, sonny, sunny, tunny.
Choppy, copy, floppy, jalopy, poppy, sloppy, soppy, stroppy.
[3] **Bumblebee**, honeybee, namby-pamby, wallaby, wannabe.
Burgundy, chickadee, COD, comedy, custody, dogsbody, fool-hardy, jeopardy, malady, melody, nobody, parody, Ph.D., raggedy, remedy, rhapsody, somebody, tragedy.
Agony, attorney, balcony, baloney, bikini, botany, colony, company, cottony, cushiony, destiny, ebony, felony, gluttony, halfpenny, harmony, Houdini, irony, larceny, litany, martini, mutiny, satiny, scrutiny, symphony, tiffany, timpani, trainee, tyranny, villainy.
Ancestry, archery, artistry, bakery, battery, bigotry, binary, blackberry, blubbery, blueberry, blustery, brasserie, bravery, brewery, bribery, burglary, calorie, carpentry, carvery, cavalry, celery, century, chemistry, chicory, chivalry, Christmas tree, colliery, contrary, devilry, diary, dietary, disagree, dithery, doddery, drudgery, dungaree, duty-free, eatery, enquiry, estuary, expiry, factory, fakery, feathery, filigree, finery, fishery, flattery, fluttery, forestry, forgery, gallery, geometry, gimmickry, glittery, greenery, grocery, history, imagery, injury, inquiry, ivory, jamboree, jewellery/jewelry (U.S.), jittery, leathery, lingerie, lottery, luxury, memory, mercury, misery, momentary, monastery, mystery, nursery, obituary, obligatory, pageantry, pedigree, perjury, pillory, pleasantry, poetry, pottery, primary, priory, quivery, referee, revelry, reverie, rivalry, robbery, rockery, rosary, rubbery, salary, sanctuary, savagery, savory, scenery, sensory, shimmery, shivery, silvery, slavery, slippery, sorcery, sugary, surgery, tapestry, thundery, treachery, trickery, victory, wintery, wizardry.
Assembly, bimonthly, biweekly, bodily, comradely, cowardly, dastardly, directly, easterly, family, finale, fleur-de-lis, fortnightly, heavenly, hillbilly, homily, icily, jubilee, laggardly, maidenly, mannerly, matronly, panoply, plug-ugly, quarterly, readily, reveille, simile, slovenly, ungainly, unruly, user-friendly, wizardly, womanly.
Alchemy, bigamy, blasphemy, blossomy, bonhomie, enemy, infamy, sesame, tsunami.
Anarchy, finicky, garlicky, gimmicky, headachy, malarkey, monarchy, panicky, plasticky.
Actually, brotherly, easterly, elderly, equally, fatherly, finally, formally, formerly, gingerly, leisurely, masterly, miserly, motherly, naturally, neighbourly/neighborly (U.S.), normally, northerly, orderly, overly, partially, properly, scholarly, sisterly, southerly, specially, thoroughly, usually, utterly, virtually, westerly.
Committee, gravity, nitty-gritty, responsibility, sanity, self-pity.
Allergy, effigy, emoji, energy, eulogy, lethargy, refugee, strategy, synergy, trilogy.
Actressy, agency, autopsy, bankruptcy, blatancy, bourgeoisie, buoyancy, Christmassy, clemency, courtesy, currency, decency, divorcee, ecstasy, embassy, fallacy, fantasy, fluency, galaxy, heresy, infancy, jealousy, legacy, leniency, lunacy, odyssey, oversee, pharmacy, piracy, policy, potency, pregnancy, primacy, privacy, prophecy, regency, secrecy, tendency, Tennessee, truancy, undersea, urgency, vacancy.
Absentee, amnesty, brevity, casualty, certainty, charity, chastity, clarity, committee, confetti, crotchety, crudity, density, deputy, devotee, dignity, dynasty, enmity, entity, fidgety, gaiety/gayety (U.S.), graffiti, gravity, guarantee, honesty, karate, levity, liberty, machete, majesty, modesty, nudity, oddity, parity, penalty, piety, poverty, probity, property, puberty, purity, quality, repartee, rickety, sanctity, sanctuary, scarcity, seventy, sovereignty, spaghetti, specialty, three-sixty, trinity, unity, uppity, vanity, velvety.
Apathy, empathy, newsworthy, noteworthy, praiseworthy, roadworthy, seaworthy, sympathy, trustworthy, unhealthy, unworthy.
Anchovy, c'est la vie, eau-de-vie, lovey-dovey, top-heavy, topsy-turvy, vis-à-vis.
Billowy, chop suey, echoey, shadowy, yellowy, willowy.
Freezingly, pleasingly, teasingly, wheezingly.
[4] **Anybody**, busybody, everybody, fuddy-duddy, hurdy-gurdy, oldie worlde, understudy.
Accessory, adultery, artillery, cautionary, cemetery, compulsory, confectionery,

conciliatory, constabulary, contemporary, customary, debauchery, delivery, dictionary, directory, discovery, distillery, elementary, embroidery, explanatory, exploratory, hunky-dory, idolatry, imaginary, incendiary, infirmary, inflammatory, judiciary, laboratory, legendary, literary, machinery, mandatory, mercenary, military, missionary, necessary, ordinary, patisserie, perfumery, preliminary, psychiatry, publicity, reactionary, recovery, secretary, secondary, simplicity, skullduggery, solitary, stationary, stationery, temporary, territory, tomfoolery, upholstery, visionary, vocabulary.
Academy, anatomy, astronomy, economy, epitome, origami.
Accompany, acrimony, alimony, cacophony, ceremony, epiphany, hootenanny, ignominy, matrimony, monotony, pepperoni, teeny-weeny, telephony, testimony.
Apostrophe, biography, catastrophe, choreography, geography, philosophy, photography.
Absolutely, anomaly, creepy-crawly, curmudgeonly, dilly-dally, eco-friendly, facsimile, fait accompli, gentlemanly, holy-moly, hurly-burly, immediately, melancholy, monopoly, rockabilly, roly-poly, shilly-shally, softly-softly, ukulele, underbelly, willy-nilly, yellow-belly.
Hanky-panky, happy-go-lucky, hokey-cokey, okey-dokey, wakey-wakey, walkie-talkie.
Analogy, anthology, apology, archeology, astrology, biology, cardiology, chronology, ecology, geology, ideology, mythology, psychology, technology, theology, zoology.
Ability, agility, civility, fertility, fragility, futility, hostility, humility, mobility, nobility, stability, tranquillity/tranquility (U.S.), utility, virility.
Especially, eventually, initially, incidentally, melancholy, monopoly, occasionally, officially, originally, personally, universally.
Accuracy, complacency, consistency, conspiracy, contingency, controversy, delicacy, diplomacy, discrepancy, efficiency, emergency, flamboyancy, hypocrisy, idiocy, intimacy, intricacy, paparazzi, presidency, redundancy, sufficiency, supremacy, transparency.
Absurdity, affinity, amenity, anxiety, barbarity, calamity, cognoscenti, community, conformity, credulity, difficulty, dilettante, enormity, equality, eternity, fatality, fidelity, fifty-fifty, fraternity, frivolity, glitterati, heredity, hilarity, humanity, humidity, immunity, impunity, indemnity, infinity, intercity, literati, maternity, modernity, morality, nitty-gritty, obscenity, profanity, reality, senility, serenity, sobriety, solemnity, virility, stupidity, telepathy, timidity, totality, twenty-twenty, variety, vicinity, vigilante, virginity, vulgarity.
[5] Anniversary, beneficiary, camaraderie, complementary, complimentary, contradictory, directory, documentary, evolutionary, revolutionary, rudimentary, supplementary.
Ambiguity, anonymity, continuity, familiarity, femininity, impropriety, ingenuity, irregularity, liability, masculinity, notoriety, opportunity, peculiarity, popularity, regularity, responsibility, serendipity, similarity, solidarity, spontaneity, uniformity, versatility.

2.1.10 "--ree" (as in "free")
[1] brie, free, re, spree, three, tree.
[2] agree, airy, angry, beery, belfry, berry, bleary, blurry, boundary, bury, carefree, carry, cheery, cherry, country, curry, dairy, dearie, debris, degree, dowry, dreary, dust-free, eerie, entry, esprit, every, eyrie/aerie, fairy, ferry, fiery, floury, flowery, flurry, foundry, furry, fury, gentry, germ-free, glory, gory, Grand Prix, gumtree, hairy, hoary, hurry, hungry, jury, laundry, leery, lorry, marry, merry, paltry, pantry, parry, pastry, pinetree, poultry, powdery, prairie, quandary, quarry, query, scary, scot-free, sentry, shoetree, Siri, sorry, starry, storey, story, sultry, sundry, surrey, tawdry, teary, theory, treachery, unfree, vary, very, vestry, wary, weary, wintry, wiry, witchery, worry.
[3] ancestry, archery, armory, artery, artistry, bakery, balladry, battery, bigotry, binary, blackberry, blubbery, blueberry, blustery, boundary, brasserie, bravery, brewery, bribery, burglary, butchery, buttery, calorie, canary, cannery, carpentry, carvery, cavalry, celery, century, chemistry, chicory, chivalry, Christmas tree, colliery, commentary, compadre, contrary, cookery, cranberry, cursory, cutlery, dentistry, devilry, diary, dietary, disagree, dithery, doddery, drapery, drudgery, dungaree, duty-free, eatery, enquiry, estuary, expiry, factory, fakery, falconry, fancy-free, feathery, filigree, finery, fishery, flattery, fluttery, forestry, forgery, friary, furore, gadgetry, gallantry, gallery, geometry, gimmickry, gingery, glittery, glossary, greenery, grocery, heathery, hickory, history, husbandry, imagery, industry, infantry, injury, inquiry, ivory, jamboree, jewelry/jewellery, jittery, leathery, library, lingerie, livery, lottery, luxury, mastery, memory, menagerie, mercury, mimicry, ministry, misery, mockery, momentary, monastery, mortuary, mulberry, mystery, notary, nursery, obituary, obligatory, pageantry, palmistry, pedigree, peppery, perjury, pillory, pleasantry, poetry, pottery, potpourri, predatory, primary, priory, prudery,

puppetry, quackery, quivery, raspberry, referee, registry, revelry, reverie, ribaldry, rivalry, robbery, rockery, rocketry, rookery, rosary, rotary, rubbery, salary, sanctuary, savagery, savory, scenery, sensory, shimmery, shivery, shrubbery, shuddery, signatory, silvery, slavery, slippery, slithery, snobbery, sorcery, spidery, strawberry, sugary, summary, surgery, symmetry, tandoori, tapestry, thievery, thuggery, thundery, treachery, treasury, trickery, victory, voluntary, watery, weaponry, wintery, wizardry, zealotry.
[4] accessory, adultery, adversary, advisory, allegory, ancillary, arbitrary, artillery, auxiliary, aviary, category, cautionary, cemetery, centenary, compulsory, confectionery, conciliatory, constabulary, contemporary, culinary, customary, debauchery, derisory, dictionary, discovery, discretionary, distillery, elementary, embroidery, exemplary, explanatory, exploratory, huckleberry, hunky-dory, idolatry, illusory, imaginary, incendiary, infirmary, inflammatory, jiggery-pokery, judiciary, laboratory, legendary, literary, luminary, machinery, mandatory, mercenary, migratory, military, missionary, multistorey, necessary, ordinary, patisserie, perfunctory, perfumery, periphery, preliminary, proprietary, psychiatry, reactionary, recovery, secretary, secondary, skullduggery, solitary, stationary, stationery, statutory, subsidiary, temporary, territory, tomfoolery, upholstery, visionary, vocabulary.
[5] anniversary, beneficiary, camaraderie, complementary, complimentary, contradictory, directory, documentary, evolutionary, revolutionary, rudimentary, supplementary.

SURPRISING RHYMING:
[1] **Be**, bee, fee, flea, flee, gee, glee, he, key, knee, me, pea, pee, sea, see, tee, tea, the, thee, twee, we, wee, whee, zee.
Beam, cream, deem, dream, gleam, meme, ream, scheme, scream, seam, seem, steam, stream, team, teem, theme.
[2] **Baddy**, bawdy, beady, bloody, body, brandy, buddy, caddie, candy, cloudy, daddy, dandy, dowdy, foodie, gaudy, giddy, greedy, handy, hardy, heady, hoodie, howdy, kiddie, laddie, lady, MD, midi, moody, mouldy/moldy (U.S.), muddy, needy, nerdy, oldie, randy, ready, roadie, rowdy, sandy, seedy, shady, shandy, shoddy, speedy, steady, study, sturdy, tardy, teddy, tidy, trendy, tweedy, weedy, windy, woody, wordy.
Abbey, baby, bobby, busby, cabby, chubby, crabby, derby, flabby, Frisbee, gabby, hobby, grubby, hubby, lobby, maybe, ruby, scabby, shabby, snobby, would-be, zombie.
Ably, amply, aptly, barley, beastly, belly, bobbly, bubbly, bully, chili, chilly, cleanly, comely, coolie, coolly, costly, coyly, crackly, crawly, crinkly, crumbly, crumply, cuddly, daily, dally, dangly, deadly, deathly, deli, dimly, dimply, doily, drily, drizzly, dully, duly, earthly, elderly, fiddly, filly, fitly, flatly, fleshly, freckly, friendly, frilly, fully, gaily, gangly, ghastly, ghostly, giggly, goalie, godly, goodly, googly, gristly, grizzly, grumbly, hilly, hotly, holy, hourly, husbandly, hyperbole, idly, jelly, jangly, jiggly, jingly, jowly, kindly, kingly, knobbly, likely, lily, lively, lonely, lordly, lovely, lowly, madly, manly, medley, monthly, mostly, motley, muesli, muscly, newly, niggly, nightly, oddly, oily, only, orderly, paisley, parley, pebbly, pimply, poorly, portly, prickly, priestly, princely, purply, queenly, really, rumbly, sadly, saintly, scribbly, seemly, shapely, shyly, sickly, silly, slightly, slyly, smiley, smelly, snarly, sparkly, spindly, sprightly, squiggly, stately, steely, stiffly, straggly, sully, surely, telly, tickly, timely, tingly, tinkly, trembly, trimly, trolley, truly, twinkly, ugly, volley, waffly, wally, weakly, weekly, welly, wetly, wheelie, wifely, wiggly, wily, wobbly, woolly, worldly, wriggly, wrinkly, wryly, yearly.
Bitty, city, ditty, gritty, pity, pretty, witty.
Bumpy, chappie, chippy, chirpy, clippie, crappie, creepy, crispy, dippy, dopey, drippy, droopy, dumpy, flappy, frumpy, grippy, groupie, grumpy, happy, hippie, humpy, jumpy, lippy, loopy, lumpy, nappy, nippy, pappy, peppy, plummy, preppy, pulpy, puppy, raspy, ropy, sappy, scampi, scrappy, scrummy, scrumpy, skimpy, sleepy, slippy, snappy, snippy, snoopy, soapy, soupy, stripy, stumpy, swampy, sweetpea, teepee, trippy, vampy, weepy, whippy, whoopee, wimpy, wispy, yuppie, zappy, zippy.
Army, balmy, barmy, blimey, chamois, chummy, clammy, creamy, crummy, dreamy, dummy, Emmy, foamy, gimme, gleamy, gloomy, Grammy, grimy, gummy, hammy, homey, jammy, lemme, limey, mammy, me, mommy, mummy, plummy, roomy, samey, scrummy, seamy, slimy, slummy, smarmy, stormy, tummy, whammy, wormy, yummy.
Achy, baccy, balky, beaky, bookie, brickie, bulky, car key, chalky, cheeky, chunky, cliquey, clunky, cocky, cookie, corky, creaky, crikey, croaky, dinky, donkey, door key, ducky, dusky, flaky, flunkey, folkie, folky, freaky, frisky, funky, gawky, hanky, hickey, hockey, hokey, hookey, hunky, husky, icky, inky, jerky, jockey, jokey, junkie, key,

karaoke, khaki, kinky, lackey, lanky, latchkey, leaky, lucky, marquee, mickey, milky, murky, monkey, mucky, musky, narky, nooky, passkey, peaky, perky, pesky, picky, pinkie, pinky, plucky, pokey, porky, psyche, punky, quaky, quickie, quirky, reeky, risky, rocky, rookie, shaky, sickie, silky, ski, slinky, smoky, snaky, sneaky, sparky, spiky, spooky, squeaky, sticky, stinky, stocky, streaky, sulky, swanky, tacky, talkie, techie, tricky, turkey, wacky, whiskey/whisky, wonky, Yankee, yucky.
Acne, any, beanie, blarney, bonny, bony, brainy, brawny, briny, brownie, canny, chimney, cine, cockney, corny, cranny, crony, Disney, genie, grainy, granny, guinea, hinny, horny, journey, knee, loony, many, meanie, mini, nanny, ninny, penny, pony, phoney/phony (U.S.), puny, queenie, rainy, sarnie, scrawny, shiny, skinny, stony, teeny, thorny, tinny, tiny, townie, trainee, tranny, tweeny, uni, weeny, whiny, zany.
Budgie, bulgy, cagey, clergy, dingy, dodgy, edgy, grungy, gungy, mangy, orgy, smudgy, spongy, squeegee, squidgy, stagy, stingy, stodgy, veggie, wedgie, whingy.
Bossy, bouncy, brassy, chassis, classy, curtsy, Dixie, dressy, emcee, fancy, fleecy, folksy, footsie, foresee, foxy, fussy, glassy, glitzy, glossy, grassy, greasy, gutsy, gypsy, horsey, hussy, saucy, icy, kissy, lacy, lassie, look-see, maxi, mercy, messy, missy, mousy, pacey, pixie, posse, pricey, juicy, prissy, proxy, pussy, racy, ritzy, sassy, schmaltzy, sexy, sightsee, sissy, spacey, specie, spicy, taxi, tipsy, tootsie, waxy.
Anti, arty, auntie, batty, beastie, bitty, catty, chatty, city, crafty, cruelty, dainty, ditty, draughty/drafty (U.S.), eighty, fatty, fifty, frailty, goatee, gritty, guilty, hasty, hearty, hefty, jetty, lefty, matey, meaty, minty, misty, nasty, nifty, party, pasty, petit, petty, pity, plenty, pretty, QT, safety, scanty, settee, shanty/chanty (U.S.), shifty, sixty, sweaty, sweetie, swiftie, tarty, tatty, tasty, thrifty, treaty, twenty, twisty, weighty, witty, yeti.
Beefy, coffee, comfy, fluffy, goofy, huffy, iffy, jiffy, leafy, puffy, scruffy, selfie, sniffy, stiffy, stuffy, toffee, toughie, trophy.
Breathy, earthy, filthy, frothy, healthy, lengthy, mouthy, pithy, smithy, smoothie, stealthy, swarthy, toothy, wealthy, worthy.
Bevvy, Chevy, curvy, envy, gravy, groovy, heavy, ivy, levee, levy, lovey, luvvy, movie, navy, nervy, savvy, skivvy, spivvy, wavy.
Blowy, chewy, dewy, doughy, gluey, gooey, hooey, phooey, screwy, showy, snowy.
Burly, curly, early, girlie, hurly-burly, surly, swirly, twirly, whirly.
Brolly, collie, dolly, folly, golly, holly, jolly, lolly, trolley, volley, wally.
Alley, dally, dilly-dally, galley, pally, rally, reveille, sally, tally, valley.
Bunny, funny, gunny, honey, money, runny, sonny, sunny, tunny.
Choppy, copy, floppy, jalopy, poppy, sloppy, soppy, stroppy.
[3] Bumblebee, honeybee, namby-pamby, wallaby, wannabe.
Burgundy, chickadee, COD, comedy, custody, dogsbody, fool-hardy, jeopardy, malady, melody, nobody, parody, Ph.D., raggedy, remedy, rhapsody, somebody, tragedy.
Agony, attorney, balcony, baloney, bikini, botany, colony, company, cottony, cushiony, destiny, ebony, felony, gluttony, halfpenny, harmony, Houdini, irony, larceny, litany, martini, mutiny, satiny, scrutiny, symphony, tiffany, timpani, trainee, tyranny, villainy.
Assembly, bimonthly, biweekly, bodily, comradely, cowardly, dastardly, directly, easterly, family, finale, fleur-de-lis, fortnightly, frizzly, heavenly, hillbilly, homily, icily, jubilee, laggardly, maidenly, mannerly, matronly, panoply, plug-ugly, quarterly, readily, reveille, simile, slovenly, ungainly, unruly, user-friendly, wizardly, womanly.
Aromatherapy, gossipy, photocopy, recipe, slap-happy, syrupy, therapy, unhappy.
Alchemy, bigamy, blasphemy, blossomy, bonhomie, enemy, infamy, sesame, tsunami.
Anarchy, finicky, garlicky, gimmicky, headachy, malarkey, monarchy, panicky, plasticky.
Actually, brotherly, easterly, elderly, equally, fatherly, finally, formally, formerly, gingerly, leisurely, masterly, miserly, motherly, naturally, neighbourly/neighborly (U.S.), normally, northerly, orderly, overly, partially, properly, scholarly, sisterly, southerly, specially, thoroughly, usually, utterly, virtually, westerly.
Committee, gravity, nitty-gritty, responsibility, sanity, self-pity.
Allergy, effigy, emoji, energy, eulogy, lethargy, refugee, strategy, synergy, trilogy.
Actress, agency, autopsy, bankruptcy, blatancy, bourgeoisie, buoyancy, Christmassy, clemency, courtesy, currency, decency, divorcee, ecstasy, embassy, fallacy, fantasy, fluency, galaxy, heresy, infancy, jealousy, legacy, leniency, lunacy, odyssey, oversee, pharmacy, piracy, policy, potency, pregnancy, primacy, privacy, prophecy, regency, secrecy, tendency, Tennessee, truancy, undersea, urgency, vacancy.

Absentee, amnesty, brevity, casualty, certainty, charity, chastity, clarity, committee, confetti, crotchety, crudity, density, deputy, devotee, dignity, dynasty, enmity, entity, fidgety, gaiety/gayety (U.S.), graffiti, gravity, guarantee, honesty, karate, levity, liberty, machete, majesty, modesty, nudity, oddity, parity, penalty, piety, poverty, probity, property, puberty, purity, quality, repartee, rickety, sanctity, sanctuary, scarcity, seventy, sovereignty, spaghetti, specialty, three-sixty, trinity, unity, uppity, vanity, velvety.
Apathy, empathy, newsworthy, noteworthy, praiseworthy, roadworthy, seaworthy, sympathy, trustworthy, unhealthy, unworthy.
Anchovy, c'est la vie, eau-de-vie, lovey-dovey, top-heavy, topsy-turvy, vis-à-vis.
Billowy, chop suey, echoey, shadowy, yellowy, willowy.
Freezingly, pleasingly, teasingly, wheezingly.
[4] Anybody, busybody, everybody, fuddy-duddy, hurdy-gurdy, oldie worlde, understudy.
Academy, anatomy, astronomy, economy, epitome, origami.
Accompany, acrimony, alimony, cacophony, ceremony, epiphany, hootenanny, ignominy, matrimony, monotony, pepperoni, teeny-weeny, telephony, testimony.
Apostrophe, biography, catastrophe, choreography, geography, philosophy, photography.
Absolutely, anomaly, creepy-crawly, curmudgeonly, dilly-dally, eco-friendly, facsimile, fait accompli, gentlemanly, holy-moly, hurly-burly, immediately, melancholy, monopoly, rockabilly, roly-poly, shilly-shally, softly-softly, ukulele, underbelly, willy-nilly, yellow-belly.
Hanky-panky, happy-go-lucky, hokey-cokey, okey-dokey, wakey-wakey, walkie-talkie.
Analogy, anthology, apology, archeology, astrology, biology, cardiology, chronology, ecology, geology, ideology, mythology, psychology, technology, theology, zoology.
Ability, agility, civility, fertility, fragility, futility, hostility, humility, mobility, nobility, stability, tranquillity/tranquility (U.S.), utility, virility.
Especially, eventually, initially, incidentally, melancholy, monopoly, occasionally, officially, originally, personally, universally.
Accuracy, complacency, consistency, conspiracy, contingency, controversy, delicacy, diplomacy, discrepancy, efficiency, emergency, flamboyancy, hypocrisy, idiocy, intimacy, intricacy, paparazzi, presidency, redundancy, sufficiency, supremacy, transparency.
Absurdity, affinity, amenity, anxiety, barbarity, calamity, cognoscenti, community, conformity, credulity, difficulty, dilettante, enormity, equality, eternity, fatality, fidelity, fifty-fifty, fraternity, frivolity, glitterati, heredity, hilarity, humanity, humidity, immunity, impunity, indemnity, infinity, intercity, literati, maternity, modernity, morality, nitty-gritty, obscenity, profanity, reality, senility, serenity, sobriety, solemnity, virility, stupidity, timidity, totality, twenty-twenty, variety, vicinity, vigilante, virginity, vulgarity.
[5] Ambiguity, anonymity, continuity, familiarity, femininity, impropriety, ingenuity, irregularity, liability, masculinity, notoriety, opportunity, peculiarity, popularity, regularity, responsibility, serendipity, similarity, solidarity, spontaneity, versatility, viability, volatility.

2.1.11 "--see" (as in "fantasy")

[1] sea, see.
[2] bossy, bouncy, brassy, chancy, chassis, classy, curtsy, Dixie, dressy, emcee, fancy, fleecy, folksy, footsie, foresee, foxy, fussy, glassy, glitzy, glossy, grassy, greasy, gutsy, gypsy, horsey, hussy, saucy, icy, kissy, lacy, lassie, look-see, maxi, mercy, messy, missy, mousy, pacey, pixie, posse, precis, pricey, juicy, prissy, proxy, pussy, racy, ritzy, sassy, schmaltzy, sexy, sightsee, spacey, specie, spicy, taxi, tipsy, waxy.
[3] actressy, addressee, agency, autopsy, bankruptcy, blatancy, bourgeoisie, buoyancy, Christmassy, clemency, cogency, courtesy, currency, decency, divorcee, ecstasy, embassy, fallacy, fantasy, fluency, franchisee, galaxy, heresy, Holy See, infancy, jealousy, legacy, leprosy, licensee, leniency, lunacy, odyssey, oversee, papacy, pharmacy, piracy, policy, potency, pregnancy, primacy, privacy, prophecy, regency, secrecy, stagnancy, tendency, Tennessee, truancy, undersea, urgency, vacancy.
[4] accuracy, ascendancy, complacency, consistency, conspiracy, contingency, controversy, deficiency, delicacy, diplomacy, discrepancy, efficiency, emergency, hypocrisy, idiocy, intimacy, intricacy, itsy-bitsy, paparazzi, presidency, prima facie, proficiency, radiancy, redundancy, relentlessly, sufficiency, supremacy, transparency.

SURPRISING RHYMING:
[1] **Be**, bee, fee, flea, flee, gee, glee, he, key, knee, me, sea, see, tee, tea, the, thee, twee, we, wee, whee, zee.

Brie, free, re, spree, three, tree.
Beam, cream, deem, dream, gleam, meme, ream, scheme, scream, seam, seem, steam, stream, team, teem, theme.
[2] Agree, angry, beery, belfry, berry, bleary, blurry, boundary, bury, carefree, carry, cheery, cherry, country, curry, dairy, dearie, debris, degree, dowry, dreary, dust-free, eerie, entry, esprit, every, fairy, ferry, fiery, flowery, flurry, furry, fury, gentry, germ-free, glory, gory, Grand Prix, gumtree, hairy, hoary, hurry, hungry, jury, laundry, leery, lorry, marry, merry, paltry, pantry, parry, pastry, poultry, powdery, prairie, quandary, quarry, query, scary, scot-free, sentry, sorry, starry, storey, story, sultry, tawdry, teary, theory, treachery, vary, very, vestry, wary, weary, wintry, wiry, worry.
Baddy, bawdy, beady, bloody, body, brandy, buddy, caddie, candy, cloudy, daddy, dandy, dowdy, foodie, gaudy, giddy, greedy, handy, hardy, heady, hoodie, howdy, kiddie, laddie, lady, MD, midi, moody, mouldy/moldy (U.S.), muddy, needy, nerdy, oldie, randy, ready, roadie, rowdy, sandy, seedy, shady, shandy, shoddy, speedy, steady, study, sturdy, tardy, teddy, tidy, trendy, tweedy, weedy, windy, woody, wordy.
Abbey, baby, bobby, busby, cabby, chubby, crabby, derby, flabby, Frisbee, gabby, hobby, grubby, hubby, lobby, maybe, ruby, scabby, shabby, snobby, would-be, zombie.
Ably, amply, aptly, barley, beastly, belly, bobbly, bubbly, bully, chili, chilly, cleanly, comely, coolie, coolly, costly, coyly, crackly, crawly, crinkly, crumbly, crumply, cuddly, daily, dally, dangly, deadly, deathly, deli, dimly, dimply, doily, drily, drizzly, dully, duly, earthly, elderly, fiddly, filly, fitly, flatly, fleshly, freckly, friendly, frilly, fully, gaily, gangly, ghastly, ghostly, giggly, goalie, godly, goodly, googly, gristly, grizzly, grumbly, hilly, hotly, holy, hourly, husbandly, hyperbole, idly, jelly, jangly, jiggly, jingly, jowly, kindly, kingly, knobbly, likely, lily, lively, lonely, lordly, lovely, lowly, madly, manly, medley, monthly, mostly, motley, muesli, muscly, newly, niggly, nightly, oddly, oily, only, orderly, paisley, parley, pebbly, pimply, poorly, portly, prickly, priestly, princely, purply, queenly, really, rumbly, sadly, saintly, scribbly, seemly, shapely, shyly, sickly, silly, slightly, slyly, smiley, smelly, snarly, sparkly, spindly, sprightly, squiggly, stately, steely, stiffly, straggly, sully, surely, telly, tickly, timely, tingly, tinkly, trembly, trimly, trolley, truly, twinkly, ugly, volley, waffly, wally, weakly, weekly, welly, wetly, wheelie, wifely, wiggly, wily, wobbly, woolly, worldly, wriggly, wryly, yearly.
Bitty, city, ditty, gritty, pity, pretty, witty.
Bumpy, chappie, chippy, chirpy, clippie, crappie, creepy, crispy, dippy, dopey, drippy, droopy, dumpy, flappy, frumpy, grippy, groupie, grumpy, happy, hippie, humpy, jumpy, lippy, loopy, lumpy, nappy, nippy, pappy, peppy, plummy, preppy, pulpy, puppy, raspy, ropy, sappy, scampi, scrappy, scrummy, scrumpy, skimpy, sleepy, slippy, snappy, snippy, snoopy, soapy, soupy, stripy, stumpy, swampy, sweetpea, teepee, trippy, vampy, weepy, whippy, whoopee, wimpy, wispy, yuppie, zappy, zippy.
Army, balmy, barmy, blimey, chamois, chummy, clammy, creamy, crummy, dreamy, dummy, Emmy, foamy, gimme, gleamy, gloomy, Grammy, grimy, gummy, hammy, homey, jammy, lemme, limey, mammy, me, mommy, mummy, plummy, roomy, samey, scrummy, seamy, slimy, slummy, smarmy, stormy, tummy, whammy, wormy, yummy.
Achy, baccy, balky, beaky, bookie, brickie, bulky, car key, chalky, cheeky, chunky, cliquey, clunky, cocky, cookie, corky, creaky, crikey, croaky, dinky, donkey, door key, ducky, dusky, flaky, flunkey, folkie, folky, freaky, frisky, funky, gawky, hanky, hickey, hockey, hokey, hookey, hunky, husky, icky, inky, jerky, jockey, jokey, junkie, key, karaoke, khaki, kinky, lackey, lanky, latchkey, leaky, lucky, marquee, mickey, milky, murky, monkey, mucky, musky, narky, nooky, passkey, peaky, perky, pesky, picky, pinkie, pinky, plucky, pokey, porky, psyche, punky, quaky, quickie, quirky, reeky, risky, rocky, rookie, shaky, sickie, silky, ski, slinky, smoky, snaky, sneaky, sparky, spiky, spooky, squeaky, sticky, stinky, stocky, streaky, sulky, swanky, tacky, talkie, techie, tricky, turkey, wacky, whiskey/whisky, wonky, Yankee, yucky.
Acne, any, beanie, blarney, bonny, bony, brainy, brawny, briny, brownie, canny, chimney, cine, cockney, corny, cranny, crony, Disney, genie, grainy, granny, guinea, hinny, horny, journey, knee, loony, many, meanie, mini, nanny, ninny, penny, pony, phoney/phony (U.S.), puny, queenie, rainy, sarnie, scrawny, shiny, skinny, stony, teeny, thorny, tinny, tiny, townie, trainee, tranny, tweeny, uni, weeny, whiny, zany.
Budgie, bulgy, cagey, clergy, dingy, dodgy, edgy, grungy, gungy, mangy, orgy, smudgy, spongy, squeegee, squidgy, stagy, stingy, stodgy, veggie, wedgie, whingy.
Anti, arty, auntie, batty, beastie, bitty, catty, chatty, city, crafty, cruelty, dainty, ditty,

draughty/drafty (U.S.), eighty, fatty, fifty, frailty, goatee, gritty, guilty, hasty, hearty, hefty, jetty, lefty, matey, meaty, minty, misty, nasty, nifty, party, pasty, petit, petty, pity, plenty, pretty, QT, safety, scanty, settee, shanty/chanty (U.S.), shifty, sixty, sweaty, sweetie, swiftie, tarty, tatty, tasty, thrifty, treaty, twenty, twisty, weighty, witty, yeti.
Beefy, coffee, comfy, fluffy, goofy, huffy, iffy, jiffy, leafy, puffy, scruffy, selfie, sniffy, stiffy, stuffy, toffee, toughie, trophy.
Breathy, earthy, filthy, frothy, healthy, lengthy, mouthy, smithy, smoothie, stealthy, swarthy, toothy, wealthy, worthy.
Bevvy, Chevy, curvy, envy, gravy, groovy, heavy, ivy, levee, levy, lovey, luvvy, movie, navy, nervy, savvy, skivvy, spivvy, wavy.
Blowy, chewy, dewy, doughy, gluey, gooey, hooey, phooey, screwy, showy, snowy.
Burly, curly, early, girlie, hurly-burly, surly, swirly, twirly, whirly.
Brolly, collie, dolly, folly, golly, holly, jolly, lolly, trolley, volley, wally.
Alley, dally, galley, pally, rally, reveille, sally, tally, valley.
Bunny, funny, honey, money, runny, sonny, sunny, tunny.
Choppy, copy, floppy, jalopy, poppy, sloppy, soppy, stroppy.
[3] Ancestry, archery, artistry, bakery, battery, bigotry, binary, blackberry, blubbery, blueberry, blustery, brasserie, bravery, brewery, bribery, burglary, calorie, carpentry, carvery, cavalry, celery, century, chemistry, chicory, chivalry, Christmas tree, colliery, contrary, devilry, diary, dietary, disagree, dithery, doddery, drudgery, dungaree, duty-free, eatery, enquiry, estuary, expiry, factory, fakery, feathery, filigree, finery, fishery, flattery, fluttery, forestry, forgery, gallery, geometry, gimmickry, glittery, greenery, grocery, history, imagery, injury, inquiry, ivory, jamboree, jewellery/jewelry (U.S.), jittery, leathery, lingerie, lottery, luxury, memory, mercury, misery, momentary, monastery, mystery, nursery, obituary, obligatory, pageantry, pedigree, perjury, pillory, pleasantry, poetry, pottery, primary, priory, quivery, referee, revelry, reverie, rivalry, robbery, rockery, rosary, rubbery, salary, sanctuary, savagery, savory, scenery, sensory, shimmery, shivery, silvery, slavery, slippery, sorcery, sugary, surgery, tapestry, thundery, treachery, trickery, victory, wintery, wizardry.
Bumblebee, honeybee, namby-pamby, wallaby, wannabe.
Burgundy, chickadee, COD, comedy, custody, dogsbody, fool-hardy, jeopardy, malady, melody, nobody, parody, Ph.D., raggedy, remedy, rhapsody, somebody, tragedy.
Agony, attorney, balcony, baloney, bikini, botany, colony, company, cottony, cushiony, destiny, ebony, felony, gluttony, halfpenny, harmony, Houdini, irony, larceny, litany, martini, mutiny, satiny, scrutiny, symphony, tiffany, timpani, trainee, tyranny, villainy.
Assembly, bimonthly, biweekly, bodily, comradely, cowardly, dastardly, directly, easterly, family, finale, fleur-de-lis, fortnightly, heavenly, hillbilly, homily, icily, jubilee, laggardly, maidenly, mannerly, matronly, panoply, plug-ugly, quarterly, readily, reveille, simile, slovenly, ungainly, unruly, user-friendly, wizardly, womanly.
Aromatherapy, gossipy, photocopy, recipe, slap-happy, syrupy, therapy, unhappy.
Alchemy, bigamy, blasphemy, blossomy, bonhomie, enemy, infamy, sesame, tsunami.
Anarchy, finicky, garlicky, gimmicky, headachy, malarkey, monarchy, panicky, plasticky.
Actually, brotherly, easterly, elderly, equally, fatherly, finally, formally, formerly, gingerly, leisurely, masterly, miserly, motherly, naturally, neighbourly/neighborly (U.S.), normally, northerly, orderly, overly, partially, properly, rascally, scholarly, signally, sisterly, southerly, specially, thoroughly, usually, utterly, virtually, westerly.
Committee, gravity, nitty-gritty, responsibility, sanity, self-pity.
Allergy, effigy, emoji, energy, eulogy, lethargy, refugee, strategy, synergy, trilogy.
Absentee, amnesty, brevity, casualty, certainty, charity, chastity, clarity, committee, confetti, crotchety, crudity, density, deputy, devotee, dignity, dynasty, enmity, entity, fidgety, gaiety/gayety (U.S.), graffiti, gravity, guarantee, honesty, karate, levity, liberty, machete, majesty, modesty, nudity, oddity, parity, penalty, piety, poverty, probity, property, puberty, purity, quality, repartee, rickety, sanctity, sanctuary, scarcity, seventy, sovereignty, spaghetti, specialty, three-sixty, trinity, unity, uppity, vanity, velvety.
Apathy, empathy, newsworthy, noteworthy, praiseworthy, roadworthy, seaworthy, sympathy, trustworthy, unhealthy, unworthy.
Anchovy, c'est la vie, eau-de-vie, lovey-dovey, top-heavy, topsy-turvy, vis-à-vis.
Billowy, chop suey, echoey, shadowy, yellowy, willowy.
Freezingly, pleasingly, teasingly, wheezingly.
[4] Anybody, busybody, everybody, fuddy-duddy, hurdy-gurdy, oldie worlde, understudy.

162

Accessory, adultery, artillery, cautionary, cemetery, compulsory, confectionery, conciliatory, constabulary, contemporary, customary, debauchery, delivery, dictionary, directory, discovery, distillery, elementary, embroidery, explanatory, exploratory, hunky-dory, idolatry, imaginary, incendiary, infirmary, inflammatory, judiciary, laboratory, legendary, literary, machinery, mandatory, mercenary, military, missionary, necessary, ordinary, patisserie, perfumery, preliminary, psychiatry, publicity, reactionary, recovery, secretary, secondary, simplicity, skullduggery, solitary, stationary, stationery, temporary, territory, tomfoolery, upholstery, visionary, vocabulary.
Academy, anatomy, astronomy, economy, epitome, origami.
Accompany, acrimony, alimony, cacophony, ceremony, epiphany, hootenanny, ignominy, matrimony, monotony, pepperoni, teeny-weeny, telephony, testimony.
Apostrophe, biography, catastrophe, choreography, geography, philosophy, photography.
Absolutely, anomaly, creepy-crawly, curmudgeonly, dilly-dally, eco-friendly, facsimile, fait accompli, gentlemanly, holy-moly, hurly-burly, immediately, melancholy, monopoly, rockabilly, roly-poly, shilly-shally, softly-softly, ukulele, underbelly, willy-nilly, yellow-belly.
Hanky-panky, happy-go-lucky, hokey-cokey, okey-dokey, wakey-wakey, walkie-talkie.
Analogy, anthology, apology, archeology, astrology, biology, cardiology, chronology, ecology, geology, ideology, mythology, psychology, technology, theology, zoology.
Ability, agility, fertility, fragility, futility, hostility, humility, liability, mobility, nobility, responsibility, stability, tranquillity/tranquility (U.S.), versatility, viability, virility, volatility.
Especially, eventually, initially, incidentally, melancholy, monopoly, occasionally, officially, originally, personally, universally, unmannerly.
Antipathy, telepathy.
Absurdity, affinity, amenity, anxiety, barbarity, calamity, cognoscenti, community, conformity, credulity, difficulty, dilettante, enormity, equality, eternity, fatality, fidelity, fifty-fifty, fraternity, frivolity, glitterati, heredity, hilarity, humanity, humidity, immunity, impunity, indemnity, infinity, intercity, literati, maternity, modernity, morality, nitty-gritty, obscenity, profanity, reality, senility, serenity, sobriety, solemnity, virility, stupidity, timidity, totality, twenty-twenty, variety, vicinity, vigilante, virginity, vulgarity.
[5] Ambiguity, anonymity, continuity, familiarity, femininity, impropriety, ingenuity, liability, masculinity, notoriety, opportunity, peculiarity, popularity, regularity, responsibility, serendipity, similarity, solidarity, spontaneity, versatility, volatility.
Anniversary, beneficiary, camaraderie, complementary, complimentary, contradictory, documentary, evolutionary, intermediary, revolutionary, rudimentary, supplementary.

2.1.12 "--tee" (as in "certainty")

[1] tee, tea.
[2] anti, arty, auntie, batty, beastie, bitty, bootee, catty, chatty, chesty, chitty, city, crafty, cruelty, dainty, ditty, draftee, draughty/drafty, eighty, fatty, fifty, flinty, frailty, goatee, gritty, guilty, hasty, hearty, hefty, high tea, jetty, kitty, lefty, matey, meaty, minty, misty, nasty, nicety, nifty, party, pasty, petit, petty, pity, plenty, pretty, ratty, QT, safety, scanty, scatty, settee, shanty/chanty, shifty, sixty, sweaty, sweetie, tarty, tatty, tasty, thrifty, treaty, trustee, twenty, twisty, weighty, witty, yeti, zesty.
[3] absentee, amity, amnesty, amputee, appointee, brevity, casualty, cavity, certainty, charity, chastity , clarity, committee, confetti, crotchety, crudity, deity, density, deportee, deputy, devotee, dignity, dynasty, enmity, entity, faculty, fidgety, gaiety/gayety, graffiti, gravity, guarantee, honesty, invitee, karate, laity, levity, liberty, machete, majesty, modesty, nudity, oddity, parity, penalty, piety, poverty, probity, property, puberty, purity, quality, repartee, rickety, sanctity, sanctuary, seventy, snippety, sovereignty, spaghetti, sparsity, specialty, three-sixty, trinity, unity, uppity, vanity, velvety, warranty.
[4] ability, absurdity, acidity, affinity, agility, amenity, annuity, anxiety, barbarity, calamity, civility, cognoscenti, commodity, community, conformity, credulity, difficulty, dilettante, divinity, enormity, equality, eternity, facility, fatality, fertility, fidelity, fifty-fifty, fragility, fraternity, frivolity, futility, glitterati, gratuity, heredity, hilarity, hostility, humanity, humidity, humility, immunity, impunity, indemnity, infinity, infirmity, intercity, literati, maternity, mobility, modernity, morality, nitty-gritty, nobility, obscenity, profanity, proximity, reality, senility, serenity, sobriety, solemnity, stability, virility, stupidity, timidity, totality, tranquillity/tranquility (U.S.), twenty-twenty, utility, variety, vicinity, vigilante, virginity, virility, vulgarity.
[5] ambiguity, anonymity, Christianity, continuity, familiarity, femininity, impropriety,

ingenuity, irregularity, liability, masculinity, notoriety, opportunity, peculiarity, popularity, regularity, serendipity, similarity, spontaneity, uniformity, versatility, viability, volatility.

SURPRISING RHYMING:
[1] **Be**, bee, fee, flea, flee, gee, glee, he, key, knee, me, pea, pee, sea, see, tee, tea, the, thee, twee, we, wee, whee.
Brie, free, re, spree, three, tree.
Beam, cream, deem, dream, gleam, meme, ream, scheme, scream, seam, seem, steam, stream, team, teem, theme.
[2] **Agree**, angry, beery, belfry, berry, bleary, blurry, boundary, bury, carefree, carry, cheery, cherry, country, curry, dairy, dearie, debris, degree, dowry, dreary, dust-free, eerie, entry, esprit, every, fairy, ferry, fiery, flowery, flurry, furry, fury, gentry, germ-free, glory, gory, Grand Prix, gumtree, hairy, hoary, hurry, hungry, jury, laundry, leery, lorry, marry, merry, paltry, pantry, parry, pastry, poultry, powdery, prairie, quandary, quarry, query, scary, scot-free, sentry, sorry, starry, storey, story, sultry, tawdry, teary, theory, treachery, vary, very, vestry, wary, weary, wintry, wiry, worry.
Baddy, bawdy, beady, bloody, body, brandy, buddy, caddie, candy, cloudy, daddy, dandy, dowdy, foodie, gaudy, giddy, greedy, handy, hardy, heady, hoodie, howdy, kiddie, laddie, lady, MD, midi, moody, mouldy/moldy (U.S.), muddy, needy, nerdy, oldie, randy, ready, roadie, rowdy, sandy, seedy, shady, shandy, shoddy, speedy, steady, study, sturdy, tardy, teddy, tidy, trendy, tweedy, weedy, windy, woody, wordy.
Abbey, baby, bobby, busby, cabby, chubby, crabby, derby, flabby, Frisbee, gabby hobby, grubby, hubby, lobby, maybe, ruby, scabby, shabby, snobby, would-be, zombie.
Ably, amply, aptly, barley, beastly, belly, bobbly, bubbly, bully, chili, chilly, cleanly, comely, coolie, coolly, costly, coyly, crackly, crawly, crinkly, crumbly, crumply, cuddly, daily, dally, dangly, deadly, deathly, deli, dimly, dimply, doily, drily, drizzly, dully, duly, earthly, elderly, fiddly, filly, fitly, flatly, fleshly, freckly, friendly, frilly, fully, gaily, gangly, ghastly, ghostly, giggly, goalie, godly, goodly, googly, gristly, grizzly, grumbly, hilly, hotly, holy, hourly, husbandly, hyperbole, idly, jelly, jangly, jiggly, jingly, jowly, kindly, kingly, knobbly, likely, lily, lively, lonely, lordly, lovely, lowly, madly, manly, medley, monthly, mostly, motley, muesli, muscly, newly, niggly, nightly, oddly, oily, only, orderly, paisley, parley, pebbly, pimply, poorly, portly, prickly, priestly, princely, purply, queenly, really, rumbly, sadly, saintly, scribbly, seemly, shapely, shyly, sickly, silly, slightly, slyly, smiley, smelly, snarly, sparkly, spindly, sprightly, squiggly, stately, steely, stiffly, straggly, sully, surely, telly, tickly, timely, tingly, tinkly, trembly, trimly, trolley, truly, twinkly, ugly, volley, waffly, wally, weakly, weekly, welly, wetly, wheelie, wifely, wiggly, wily, wobbly, woolly, worldly, wriggly, wrinkly, wryly, yearly.
Bitty, city, ditty, gritty, pity, pretty, witty.
Bossy, bouncy, brassy, chassis, classy, curtsy, Dixie, dressy, emcee, fancy, fleecy, folksy, footsie, foresee, foxy, fussy, glassy, glitzy, glossy, grassy, greasy, gutsy, gypsy, horsey, hussy, saucy, icy, kissy, lacy, lassie, look-see, maxi, mercy, messy, missy, mousy, pacey, pixie, posse, pricey, juicy, prissy, proxy, pussy, racy, ritzy, sassy, schmaltzy, sexy, sightsee, sissy, spacey, specie, spicy, taxi, tipsy, tootsie, waxy.
Bumpy, chappie, chippy, chirpy, clippie, crappie, creepy, crispy, dippy, dopey, drippy, droopy, dumpy, flappy, frumpy, grippy, groupie, grumpy, happy, hippie, humpy, jumpy, lippy, loopy, lumpy, nappy, nippy, pappy, peppy, plummy, preppy, pulpy, puppy, raspy, ropy, sappy, scampi, scrappy, scrummy, scrumpy, skimpy, sleepy, slippy, snappy, snippy, snoopy, soapy, soupy, stripy, stumpy, swampy, sweetpea, teepee, trippy, vampy, weepy, whippy, whoopee, wimpy, wispy, yuppie, zappy, zippy.
Army, balmy, barmy, blimey, chamois, chummy, clammy, creamy, crummy, dreamy, dummy, Emmy, foamy, gimme, gleamy, gloomy, Grammy, grimy, gummy, hammy, homey, lemme, limey, mammy, me, mommy, mummy, plummy, roomy, samey, scrummy, seamy, slimy, slummy, smarmy, stormy, tummy, whammy, wormy, yummy.
Achy, baccy, balky, beaky, bookie, brickie, bulky, car key, chalky, cheeky, chunky, cliquey, clunky, cocky, cookie, corky, creaky, crikey, croaky, dinky, donkey, door key, ducky, dusky, flaky, flunkey, folkie, folky, freaky, frisky, funky, gawky, hanky, hickey, hockey, hokey, hookey, hunky, husky, icky, inky, jerky, jockey, jokey, junkie, key, karaoke, khaki, kinky, lackey, lanky, latchkey, leaky, lucky, marquee, mickey, milky, murky, monkey, mucky, musky, narky, nooky, passkey, peaky, perky, pesky, picky, pinkie, pinky, plucky, pokey, porky, psyche, punky, quaky, quickie, quirky, reeky, risky,

164

rocky, rookie, shaky, sickie, silky, ski, slinky, smoky, snaky, sneaky, sparky, spiky, spooky, squeaky, sticky, stinky, stocky, streaky, sulky, swanky, tacky, talkie, techie, tricky, turkey, wacky, whiskey/whisky, wonky, Yankee, yucky.
Acne, any, beanie, blarney, bonny, bony, brainy, brawny, briny, brownie, canny, chimney, cine, cockney, corny, cranny, crony, Disney, genie, grainy, granny, guinea, hinny, horny, journey, knee, loony, many, meanie, mini, nanny, ninny, penny, pony, phoney/phony (U.S.), puny, queenie, rainy, sarnie, scrawny, shiny, skinny, stony, teeny, thorny, tinny, tiny, townie, trainee, tranny, tweeny, uni, weeny, whiny, zany.
Budgie, bulgy, cagey, clergy, dingy, dodgy, edgy, gee, grungy, gungy, mangy, orgy, smudgy, spongy, squeegee, squidgy, stagy, stingy, stodgy, veggie, wedgie, whingy.
Beefy, coffee, comfy, fluffy, goofy, huffy, iffy, jiffy, leafy, puffy, scruffy, selfie, sniffy, stiffy, stuffy, toffee, toughie, trophy.
Breathy, earthy, filthy, frothy, healthy, lengthy, mouthy, pithy, smithy, smoothie, stealthy, swarthy, toothy, wealthy, worthy.
Bevvy, Chevy, curvy, envy, gravy, groovy, heavy, ivy, levee, levy, lovey, luvvy, movie, navy, nervy, savvy, skivvy, spivvy, wavy.
Blowy, chewy, dewy, doughy, gluey, gooey, hooey, phooey, screwy, showy, snowy.
Burly, curly, early, girlie, hurly-burly, surly, swirly, twirly, whirly.
Brolly, collie, dolly, folly, golly, holly, jolly, lolly, trolley, volley, wally.
Alley, dally, dilly-dally, galley, pally, rally, reveille, sally, tally, valley.
Bunny, funny, gunny, honey, money, runny, sonny, sunny, tunny.
Choppy, copy, floppy, jalopy, poppy, sloppy, soppy, stroppy.
[3] Ancestry, archery, artistry, bakery, battery, bigotry, binary, blackberry, blubbery, blueberry, blustery, brasserie, bravery, brewery, bribery, burglary, calorie, carpentry, carvery, cavalry, celery, century, chemistry, chicory, chivalry, Christmas tree, colliery, contrary, devilry, diary, dietary, disagree, dithery, doddery, drudgery, dungaree, duty-free, eatery, enquiry, estuary, expiry, factory, fakery, feathery, filigree, finery, fishery, flattery, fluttery, forestry, forgery, gallery, geometry, gimmickry, glittery, greenery, grocery, history, imagery, injury, inquiry, ivory, jamboree, jewellery/jewelry (U.S.), jittery, leathery, lingerie, lottery, luxury, memory, mercury, misery, momentary, monastery, mystery, nursery, obituary, obligatory, pageantry, pedigree, perjury, pillory, pleasantry, poetry, pottery, primary, priory, quivery, referee, revelry, reverie, rivalry, robbery, rockery, rosary, rubbery, salary, sanctuary, savagery, savory, scenery, sensory, shimmery, shivery, silvery, slavery, slippery, sorcery, sugary, surgery, tapestry, thundery, treachery, trickery, victory, wintery, wizardry.
Bumblebee, honeybee, namby-pamby, wallaby, wannabe.
Actressy, agency, autopsy, bankruptcy, blatancy, bourgeoisie, buoyancy, Christmassy, clemency, courtesy, currency, decency, divorcee, ecstasy, embassy, fallacy, fantasy, fluency, galaxy, heresy, infancy, jealousy, legacy, leniency, lunacy, odyssey, oversee, pharmacy, piracy, policy, potency, pregnancy, primacy, privacy, prophecy, regency, secrecy, tendency, Tennessee, truancy, undersea, urgency, vacancy.
Burgundy, chickadee, COD, comedy, custody, dogsbody, fool-hardy, jeopardy, malady, melody, nobody, parody, Ph.D., raggedy, remedy, rhapsody, somebody, tragedy.
Agony, attorney, balcony, baloney, bikini, botany, colony, company, cottony, cushiony, destiny, ebony, felony, gluttony, halfpenny, harmony, Houdini, irony, larceny, litany, martini, mutiny, satiny, scrutiny, symphony, tiffany, timpani, trainee, tyranny, villainy.
Assembly, bimonthly, biweekly, bodily, comradely, cowardly, dastardly, directly, easterly, family, finale, fleur-de-lis, fortnightly, heavenly, hillbilly, homily, icily, jubilee, laggardly, maidenly, mannerly, matronly, panoply, plug-ugly, quarterly, readily, reveille, simile, slovenly, ungainly, unruly, user-friendly, wizardly, womanly.
Aromatherapy, gossipy, photocopy, recipe, slap-happy, syrupy, therapy, unhappy.
Alchemy, bigamy, blasphemy, blossomy, bonhomie, enemy, infamy, sesame, tsunami.
Anarchy, finicky, garlicky, gimmicky, headachy, malarkey, monarchy, panicky, plasticky.
Actually, brotherly, easterly, elderly, equally, fatherly, finally, formally, formerly, gingerly, leisurely, masterly, miserly, motherly, naturally, neighbourly/neighborly (U.S.), normally, northerly, orderly, overly, partially, properly, rascally, scholarly, signally, sisterly, southerly, specially, thoroughly, usually, utterly, virtually, westerly.
Committee, gravity, nitty-gritty, responsibility, sanity, self-pity.
Allergy, effigy, emoji, energy, eulogy, lethargy, refugee, strategy, synergy, trilogy.
Apathy, empathy, newsworthy, noteworthy, praiseworthy, roadworthy, seaworthy,

sympathy, trustworthy, unhealthy, unworthy.
Anchovy, c'est la vie, eau-de-vie, lovey-dovey, top-heavy, topsy-turvy, vis-à-vis.
Billowy, chop suey, echoey, shadowy, yellowy, willowy.
Freezingly, pleasingly, teasingly, wheezingly.
[4] **Anybody**, busybody, everybody, fuddy-duddy, hurdy-gurdy, oldie worlde, understudy.
Accessory, adultery, adversary, advisory, allegory, ancillary, arbitrary, artillery, auxiliary, aviary, category, adultery, artillery, cautionary, cemetery, compulsory, confectionery, conciliatory, constabulary, contemporary, customary, debauchery, delivery, dictionary, directory, discovery, distillery, elementary, embroidery, explanatory, exploratory, hunky-dory, idolatry, imaginary, incendiary, infirmary, inflammatory, judiciary, laboratory, legendary, literary, machinery, mandatory, mercenary, military, missionary, necessary, ordinary, patisserie, perfumery, preliminary, psychiatry, publicity, reactionary, recovery, secretary, secondary, simplicity, skullduggery, solitary, stationary, stationery, temporary, territory, tomfoolery, upholstery, visionary, vocabulary.
Academy, anatomy, astronomy, economy, epitome, origami.
Accuracy, complacency, consistency, conspiracy, contingency, controversy, delicacy, diplomacy, discrepancy, efficiency, emergency, flamboyancy, hypocrisy, idiocy, intimacy, intricacy, paparazzi, presidency, redundancy, sufficiency, supremacy, transparency.
Accompany, acrimony, alimony, cacophony, ceremony, epiphany, hootenanny, ignominy, matrimony, monotony, pepperoni, teeny-weeny, telephony, testimony.
Apostrophe, biography, catastrophe, choreography, geography, philosophy, photography.
Absolutely, anomaly, creepy-crawly, curmudgeonly, dilly-dally, eco-friendly, facsimile, fait accompli, gentlemanly, holy-moly, hurly-burly, immediately, melancholy, monopoly, rockabilly, roly-poly, shilly-shally, softly-softly, ukulele, underbelly, willy-nilly, yellow-belly.
Hanky-panky, happy-go-lucky, hokey-cokey, okey-dokey, wakey-wakey, walkie-talkie.
Analogy, anthology, apology, archeology, astrology, biology, cardiology, chronology, ecology, geology, ideology, mythology, psychology, technology, theology, zoology.
Especially, eventually, initially, incidentally, melancholy, monopoly, occasionally, officially, originally, personally, universally, unmannerly.
Antipathy, telepathy.
[5] **Anniversary**, beneficiary, camaraderie, complementary, complimentary, contradictory, documentary, evolutionary, intermediary, revolutionary, rudimentary, supplementary.

2.1.13 "--thee" (as in "sympathy")
[1] the, thee.
[2] breathy, earthy, filthy, frothy, healthy, lengthy, mouthy, pithy, smithy, smoothie, stealthy, swarthy, toothy, wealthy, worthy.
[3] airworthy, apathy, empathy, newsworthy, noteworthy, praiseworthy, roadworthy, seaworthy, sympathy, trustworthy, unhealthy, unworthy.
[4] antipathy, telepathy.

SURPRISING RHYMING:
[1] **Be**, bee, fee, flea, flee, gee, glee, he, key, knee, me, pea, pee, sea, see, tee, tea, the, thee, twee, we, wee, whee, zee.
Brie, free, re, spree, three, tree.
[2] **Agree**, angry, beery, belfry, berry, bleary, blurry, boundary, bury, carefree, carry, cheery, cherry, country, curry, dairy, dearie, debris, degree, dowry, dreary, dust-free, eerie, entry, esprit, every, fairy, ferry, fiery, flowery, flurry, furry, fury, gentry, germ-free, glory, gory, Grand Prix, gumtree, hairy, hoary, hurry, hungry, jury, laundry, leery, lorry, marry, merry, paltry, pantry, parry, pastry, poultry, powdery, prairie, quandary, quarry, query, scary, scot-free, sentry, sorry, starry, storey, story, sultry, tawdry, teary, theory, treachery, vary, very, vestry, wary, weary, wintry, wiry, worry.
Baddy, bawdy, beady, bloody, body, brandy, buddy, caddie, candy, cloudy, daddy, dandy, dowdy, foodie, gaudy, giddy, greedy, handy, hardy, heady, hoodie, howdy, kiddie, laddie, lady, MD, midi, moody, mouldy/moldy (U.S.), muddy, needy, nerdy, oldie, randy, ready, roadie, rowdy, sandy, seedy, shady, shandy, shoddy, speedy, steady, study, sturdy, tardy, teddy, tidy, trendy, tweedy, weedy, windy, woody, wordy.
Abbey, baby, bobby, busby, cabby, chubby, crabby, derby, flabby, Frisbee, gabby, hobby, grubby, hubby, lobby, maybe, ruby, scabby, shabby, snobby, would-be, zombie.
Ably, amply, aptly, barley, beastly, belly, bobbly, bubbly, bully, chili, chilly, cleanly,

166

comely, coolie, coolly, costly, coyly, crackly, crawly, crinkly, crumbly, crumply, cuddly, daily, dally, dangly, deadly, deathly, deli, dimly, dimply, doily, drily, drizzly, dully, duly, earthly, elderly, fiddly, filly, fitly, flatly, fleshly, freckly, friendly, frilly, fully, gaily, gangly, ghastly, ghostly, giggly, goalie, godly, goodly, googly, gristly, grizzly, grumbly, hilly, hotly, holy, hourly, husbandly, hyperbole, idly, jelly, jangly, jiggly, jingly, jowly, kindly, kingly, knobbly, likely, lily, lively, lonely, lordly, lovely, lowly, madly, manly, medley, monthly, mostly, motley, muesli, muscly, newly, niggly, nightly, oddly, oily, only, orderly, paisley, parley, pebbly, pimply, poorly, portly, prickly, priestly, princely, purply, queenly, really, rumbly, sadly, saintly, scribbly, seemly, shapely, shyly, sickly, silly, slightly, slyly, smiley, smelly, snarly, sparkly, spindly, sprightly, squiggly, stately, steely, stiffly, straggly, sully, surely, telly, tickly, timely, tingly, tinkly, trembly, trimly, trolley, truly, twinkly, ugly, volley, waffly, wally, weakly, weekly, welly, wetly, wheelie, wifely, wiggly, wily, wobbly, woolly, worldly, wriggly, wrinkly, wryly, yearly.
Bitty, city, ditty, gritty, pity, pretty, witty.
Anti, arty, auntie, batty, beastie, bitty, catty, chatty, city, crafty, cruelty, dainty, ditty, draughty/drafty (U.S.), eighty, fatty, fifty, frailty, goatee, gritty, guilty, hasty, hearty, hefty, jetty, lefty, matey, meaty, minty, misty, nasty, nifty, party, pasty, petit, petty, pity, plenty, pretty, QT, safety, scanty, settee, shanty/chanty (U.S.), shifty, sixty, sweaty, sweetie, swiftie, tarty, tatty, tasty, thrifty, treaty, twenty, twisty, weighty, witty, yeti.
Bossy, bouncy, brassy, chassis, classy, curtsy, Dixie, dressy, emcee, fancy, fleecy, folksy, footsie, foresee, foxy, fussy, glassy, glitzy, glossy, grassy, greasy, gutsy, gypsy, horsey, hussy, saucy, icy, kissy, lacy, lassie, look-see, maxi, mercy, messy, missy, mousy, pacey, pixie, posse, pricey, prissy, proxy, pussy, racy, ritzy, sassy, schmaltzy, sexy, sightsee, sissy, spacey, specie, spicy, taxi, tipsy, tootsie, waxy.
Bumpy, chappie, chippy, chirpy, clippie, crappie, creepy, crispy, dippy, dopey, drippy, droopy, dumpy, flappy, frumpy, grippy, groupie, grumpy, happy, hippie, humpy, jumpy, lippy, loopy, lumpy, nappy, nippy, pappy, peppy, plummy, preppy, pulpy, puppy, raspy, ropy, sappy, scampi, scrappy, scrummy, scrumpy, skimpy, sleepy, slippy, snappy, snippy, snoopy, soapy, soupy, stripy, stumpy, swampy, sweetpea, teepee, trippy, vampy, weepy, whippy, whoopee, wimpy, wispy, yuppie, zappy, zippy.
Army, balmy, barmy, blimey, chamois, chummy, clammy, creamy, crummy, dreamy, dummy, Emmy, foamy, gimme, gleamy, gloomy, Grammy, grimy, gummy, hammy, homey, jammy, lemme, limey, mammy, me, mommy, mummy, plummy, roomy, samey, scrummy, seamy, slimy, slummy, smarmy, stormy, tummy, whammy, wormy, yummy.
Achy, baccy, balky, beaky, bookie, brickie, bulky, car key, chalky, cheeky, chunky, cliquey, clunky, cocky, cookie, corky, creaky, crikey, croaky, dinky, donkey, door key, ducky, dusky, flaky, flunkey, folkie, folky, freaky, frisky, funky, gawky, hanky, hickey, hockey, hokey, hookey, hunky, husky, icky, inky, jerky, jockey, jokey, junkie, key, karaoke, khaki, kinky, lackey, lanky, latchkey, leaky, lucky, marquee, mickey, milky, murky, monkey, mucky, musky, narky, nooky, passkey, peaky, perky, pesky, picky, pinkie, pinky, plucky, pokey, porky, psyche, punky, quaky, quickie, quirky, reeky, risky, rocky, rookie, shaky, sickie, silky, ski, slinky, smoky, snaky, sneaky, sparky, spiky, spooky, squeaky, sticky, stinky, stocky, streaky, sulky, swanky, tacky, talkie, techie, tricky, turkey, wacky, whiskey/whisky, wonky, Yankee, yucky.
Acne, any, beanie, blarney, bonny, bony, brainy, brawny, briny, brownie, canny, chimney, cine, cockney, corny, cranny, crony, Disney, genie, grainy, granny, guinea, hinny, horny, journey, knee, loony, many, meanie, mini, nanny, ninny, penny, pony, phoney/phony (U.S.), puny, queenie, rainy, sarnie, scrawny, shiny, skinny, stony, teeny, thorny, tinny, tiny, townie, trainee, tranny, tweeny, uni, weeny, whiny, zany.
Budgie, cagey, clergy, dingy, dodgy, edgy, gee, grungy, gungy, mangy, orgy, sludgy, smudgy, spongy, squeegee, squidgy, stagy, stingy, stodgy, veggie, whingy.
Beefy, coffee, comfy, fluffy, goofy, huffy, iffy, jiffy, leafy, puffy, scruffy, selfie, sniffy, stiffy, stuffy, toffee, toughie, trophy.
Breathy, earthy, filthy, frothy, healthy, lengthy, mouthy, pithy, smithy, smoothie, stealthy, swarthy, toothy, wealthy, worthy.
Bevvy, Chevy, curvy, envy, gravy, groovy, heavy, ivy, levee, levy, lovey, luvvy, movie, navy, nervy, savvy, skivvy, spivvy, wavy.
Blowy, chewy, dewy, doughy, gluey, gooey, hooey, phooey, screwy, showy, snowy.
Burly, curly, early, girlie, hurly-burly, surly, swirly, twirly, whirly.
Brolly, collie, dolly, folly, golly, holly, jolly, lolly, trolley, volley, wally.

Alley, dally, galley, pally, rally, reveille, sally, tally, valley.
Bunny, funny, honey, money, runny, sonny, sunny, tunny.
Choppy, copy, floppy, jalopy, poppy, sloppy, soppy, stroppy.
[3] Absentee, amnesty, brevity, casualty, certainty, charity, chastity, clarity, committee, confetti, crotchety, crudity, density, deputy, devotee, dignity, dynasty, enmity, entity, fidgety, gaiety/gayety (U.S.), graffiti, gravity, guarantee, honesty, karate, levity, liberty, machete, majesty, modesty, nudity, oddity, parity, penalty, piety, poverty, probity, property, puberty, purity, quality, repartee, rickety, sanctity, sanctuary, scarcity, seventy, sovereignty, spaghetti, specialty, three-sixty, trinity, unity, uppity, vanity, velvety.
Ancestry, archery, artistry, bakery, battery, bigotry, binary, blackberry, blubbery, blueberry, blustery, brasserie, bravery, brewery, bribery, burglary, calorie, carpentry, carvery, cavalry, celery, century, chemistry, chicory, chivalry, Christmas tree, colliery, contrary, devilry, diary, dietary, disagree, dithery, doddery, drudgery, dungaree, duty-free, eatery, enquiry, estuary, expiry, factory, fakery, feathery, filigree, finery, fishery, flattery, fluttery, forestry, forgery, gallery, geometry, gimmickry, glittery, greenery, grocery, history, imagery, injury, inquiry, ivory, jamboree, jewellery/jewelry (U.S.), jittery, leathery, lingerie, lottery, luxury, memory, mercury, misery, momentary, monastery, mystery, nursery, obituary, obligatory, pageantry, pedigree, perjury, pillory, pleasantry, poetry, pottery, primary, priory, quivery, referee, revelry, reverie, rivalry, robbery, rockery, rosary, rubbery, salary, sanctuary, savagery, savory, scenery, sensory, shimmery, shivery, silvery, slavery, slippery, sorcery, sugary, surgery, tapestry, thundery, treachery, trickery, victory, wintery, wizardry.
Bumblebee, honeybee, namby-pamby, wallaby, wannabe.
Actressy, agency, autopsy, bankruptcy, blatancy, bourgeoisie, buoyancy, Christmassy, clemency, courtesy, currency, decency, divorcee, ecstasy, embassy, fallacy, fantasy, fluency, galaxy, heresy, infancy, jealousy, legacy, leniency, lunacy, odyssey, oversee, pharmacy, piracy, policy, potency, pregnancy, primacy, privacy, prophecy, regency, secrecy, tendency, Tennessee, truancy, undersea, urgency, vacancy.
Burgundy, chickadee, COD, comedy, custody, dogsbody, fool-hardy, jeopardy, malady, melody, nobody, parody, Ph.D., raggedy, remedy, rhapsody, somebody, tragedy.
Agony, attorney, balcony, baloney, bikini, botany, colony, company, cottony, cushiony, destiny, ebony, felony, gluttony, halfpenny, harmony, Houdini, irony, larceny, litany, martini, mutiny, satiny, scrutiny, symphony, tiffany, timpani, trainee, tyranny, villainy.
Assembly, beggarly, bimonthly, biweekly, bodily, comradely, cowardly, dastardly, directly, easterly, family, finale, fleur-de-lis, fortnightly, frizzly, heavenly, hillbilly, homily, icily, jubilee, laggardly, maidenly, matronly, panoply, plug-ugly, quarterly, readily, reveille, simile, slovenly, ungainly, unruly, user-friendly, wizardly, womanly.
Aromatherapy, gossipy, photocopy, recipe, slap-happy, syrupy, therapy, unhappy.
Alchemy, bigamy, blasphemy, blossomy, bonhomie, enemy, infamy, sesame, tsunami.
Anarchy, finicky, garlicky, gimmicky, headachy, malarkey, monarchy, panicky, plasticky.
Actually, brotherly, easterly, elderly, equally, fatherly, finally, formally, formerly, gingerly, leisurely, masterly, miserly, motherly, naturally, neighbourly/neighborly (U.S.), normally, northerly, orderly, overly, partially, properly, scholarly, sisterly, southerly, specially, thoroughly, usually, utterly, virtually, westerly.
Committee, gravity, nitty-gritty, responsibility, sanity, self-pity.
Allergy, effigy, emoji, energy, eulogy, lethargy, refugee, strategy, synergy, trilogy.
Apathy, empathy, newsworthy, noteworthy, praiseworthy, roadworthy, seaworthy, sympathy, trustworthy, unhealthy, unworthy.
Anchovy, c'est la vie, eau-de-vie, lovey-dovey, top-heavy, topsy-turvy, vis-à-vis.
Billowy, chop suey, echoey, shadowy, yellowy, willowy.
Freezingly, pleasingly, teasingly, wheezingly.
[4] Ability, agility, fertility, fragility, futility, hostility, humility, liability, mobility, nobility, responsibility, stability, tranquillity/tranquility (U.S.), versatility, viability, virility, volatility.
Anybody, busybody, everybody, fuddy-duddy, hurdy-gurdy, oldie worlde, understudy.
Accessory, adultery, artillery, cautionary, cemetery, compulsory, confectionery, conciliatory, constabulary, contemporary, customary, debauchery, delivery, dictionary, directory, discovery, distillery, elementary, embroidery, explanatory, exploratory, hunky-dory, idolatry, imaginary, incendiary, infirmary, inflammatory, judiciary, laboratory, legendary, literary, machinery, mandatory, mercenary, military, missionary, necessary, ordinary, patisserie, perfumery, preliminary, psychiatry, publicity, reactionary, recovery,

168

secretary, secondary, simplicity, skullduggery, solitary, stationary, stationery, temporary, territory, tomfoolery, upholstery, visionary, vocabulary.
Academy, anatomy, astronomy, economy, epitome, origami.
Accuracy, complacency, consistency, conspiracy, contingency, controversy, delicacy, diplomacy, discrepancy, efficiency, emergency, flamboyancy, hypocrisy, idiocy, intimacy, intricacy, paparazzi, presidency, redundancy, sufficiency, supremacy, transparency.
Absurdity, affinity, amenity, anxiety, barbarity, calamity, cognoscenti, community, conformity, credulity, difficulty, dilettante, enormity, equality, eternity, fatality, fidelity, fifty-fifty, fraternity, frivolity, glitterati, heredity, hilarity, humanity, humidity, immunity, impunity, indemnity, infinity, intercity, literaty, maternity, modernity, morality, nitty-gritty, obscenity, profanity, reality, senility, serenity, sobriety, solemnity, virility, stupidity, timidity, totality, twenty-twenty, variety, vicinity, vigilante, virginity, vulgarity.
Accompany, acrimony, alimony, cacophony, ceremony, epiphany, hootenanny, ignominy, matrimony, monotony, pepperoni, teeny-weeny, telephony, testimony.
Apostrophe, biography, catastrophe, choreography, geography, philosophy, photography.
Absolutely, anomaly, creepy-crawly, curmudgeonly, dilly-dally, eco-friendly, facsimile, fait accompli, gentlemanly, holy-moly, hurly-burly, immediately, melancholy, monopoly, rockabilly, roly-poly, shilly-shally, softly-softly, ukulele, underbelly, willy-nilly, yellow-belly.
Hanky-panky, happy-go-lucky, hokey-cokey, okey-dokey, wakey-wakey, walkie-talkie.
Analogy, anthology, apology, archeology, astrology, biology, cardiology, chronology, ecology, geology, ideology, mythology, psychology, technology, theology, zoology.
Especially, eventually, initially, incidentally, melancholy, monopoly, occasionally, officially, originally, personally, universally, unmannerly.
[5] Anniversary, beneficiary, camaraderie, complementary, complimentary, contradictory, directory, documentary, evolutionary, revolutionary, rudimentary, supplementary.
Ambiguity, anonymity, Christianity, continuity, familiarity, femininity, impropriety, ingenuity, liability, masculinity, notoriety, opportunity, peculiarity, popularity, regularity, responsibility, serendipity, similarity, solidarity, spontaneity, usability, versatility, volatility.

2.1.14 "--vee" (as in "envy")
[2] bevvy, Chevy, curvy, envy, gravy, groovy, heavy, ivy, levee, levy, lovey, luvvy, movie, navy, navvy, nervy, privy, savvy, scurvy, skivvy, spivvy, wavy.
[3] anchovy, c'est la vie, eau-de-vie, lovey-dovey, top-heavy, topsy-turvy, vis-à-vis.

SURPRISING RHYMING:
[1] **Be**, bee, fee, flea, flee, gee, glee, he, key, knee, me, pea, pee, sea, see, tee, tea, the, thee, twee, we, wee, whee, zee.
Brie, free, re, spree, three, tree.
Beam, cream, deem, dream, gleam, meme, ream, scheme, scream, seam, seem, steam, stream, team, teem, theme.
[2] **Agree**, angry, beery, belfry, berry, bleary, blurry, boundary, bury, carefree, carry, cheery, cherry, country, curry, dairy, dearie, debris, degree, dowry, dreary, dust-free, eerie, entry, esprit, every, fairy, ferry, fiery, flowery, flurry, furry, fury, gentry, germ-free, glory, gory, Grand Prix, gumtree, hairy, hoary, hurry, hungry, jury, laundry, leery, lorry, marry, merry, paltry, pantry, parry, pastry, poultry, powdery, prairie, quandary, quarry, query, scary, scot-free, sentry, sorry, starry, storey, story, sultry, tawdry, teary, theory, treachery, vary, very, vestry, wary, weary, wintry, wiry, worry.
Breathy, earthy, filthy, frothy, healthy, lengthy, mouthy, smithy, smoothie, stealthy, swarthy, toothy, wealthy, worthy.
Baddy, bawdy, beady, bloody, body, brandy, buddy, caddie, candy, cloudy, daddy, dandy, dowdy, foodie, gaudy, giddy, greedy, handy, hardy, heady, hoodie, howdy, kiddie, laddie, lady, MD, midi, moody, mouldy/moldy (U.S.), muddy, needy, nerdy, oldie, randy, ready, roadie, rowdy, sandy, seedy, shady, shandy, shoddy, speedy, steady, study, sturdy, tardy, teddy, tidy, trendy, tweedy, weedy, windy, woody, wordy.
Abbey, baby, bobby, busby, cabby, chubby, crabby, derby, flabby, Frisbee, gabby hobby, grubby, hubby, lobby, maybe, ruby, scabby, shabby, snobby, would-be, zombie.
Ably, amply, aptly, barley, beastly, belly, bobbly, bubbly, bully, chili, chilly, cleanly, comely, coolie, coolly, costly, coyly, crackly, crawly, crinkly, crumbly, crumply, cuddly, daily, dally, dangly, deadly, deathly, deli, dimly, dimply, doily, drily, drizzly, dully, duly,

earthly, elderly, fiddly, filly, fitly, flatly, fleshly, freckly, friendly, frilly, fully, gaily, gangly, ghastly, ghostly, giggly, goalie, godly, goodly, googly, gristly, grizzly, grumbly, hilly, hotly, holy, hourly, husbandly, hyperbole, idly, jelly, jangly, jiggly, jingly, jowly, kindly, kingly, knobbly, likely, lily, lively, lonely, lordly, lovely, lowly, madly, manly, medley, monthly, mostly, motley, muesli, muscly, newly, niggly, nightly, oddly, oily, only, orderly, paisley, parley, pebbly, pimply, poorly, portly, prickly, priestly, princely, purply, queenly, really, rumbly, sadly, saintly, scribbly, seemly, shapely, shyly, sickly, silly, slightly, slyly, smiley, smelly, snarly, sparkly, spindly, sprightly, squiggly, stately, steely, stiffly, straggly, sully, surely, telly, tickly, timely, tingly, tinkly, trembly, trimly, trolley, truly, twinkly, ugly, volley, waffly, wally, weakly, weekly, welly, wetly, wheelie, wifely, wiggly, wily, wobbly, woolly, worldly, wriggly, wrinkly, wryly, yearly.
Bitty, city, ditty, gritty, pity, pretty, witty.
Anti, arty, auntie, batty, beastie, bitty, catty, chatty, city, crafty, cruelty, dainty, ditty, draughty/drafty (U.S.), eighty, fatty, fifty, frailty, goatee, gritty, guilty, hasty, hearty, hefty, jetty, lefty, matey, meaty, minty, misty, nasty, nifty, party, pasty, petit, petty, pity, plenty, pretty, QT, safety, scanty, settee, shanty/chanty (U.S.), shifty, sixty, sweaty, sweetie, tarty, tatty, tasty, thrifty, treaty, twenty, twisty, weighty, witty, yeti.
Bossy, bouncy, brassy, chassis, classy, curtsy, Dixie, dressy, emcee, fancy, fleecy, folksy, footsie, foresee, foxy, fussy, glassy, glitzy, glossy, grassy, greasy, gutsy, gypsy, horsey, hussy, saucy, icy, kissy, lacy, lassie, look-see, maxi, mercy, messy, missy, mousy, pacey, pixie, posse, pricey, prissy, proxy, pussy, racy, ritzy, sassy, schmaltzy, sexy, sightsee, sissy, spacey, spicy, taxi, tipsy, tootsie, waxy.
Bumpy, chappie, chippy, chirpy, clippie, crappie, creepy, crispy, dippy, dopey, drippy, droopy, dumpy, flappy, frumpy, grippy, groupie, grumpy, happy, hippie, humpy, jumpy, lippy, loopy, lumpy, nappy, nippy, pappy, peppy, plummy, preppy, pulpy, puppy, raspy, ropy, sappy, scampi, scrappy, scrummy, scrumpy, skimpy, sleepy, slippy, snappy, snippy, snoopy, soapy, soupy, stripy, stumpy, swampy, sweetpea, teepee, trippy, vampy, weepy, whippy, whoopee, wimpy, wispy, yuppie, zappy, zippy.
Army, balmy, barmy, blimey, chamois, chummy, clammy, creamy, crummy, dreamy, dummy, Emmy, foamy, gimme, gleamy, gloomy, Grammy, grimy, gummy, hammy, homey, jammy, lemme, limey, mammy, me, mommy, mummy, plummy, roomy, samey, scrummy, seamy, slimy, slummy, smarmy, stormy, tummy, whammy, wormy, yummy.
Achy, baccy, balky, beaky, bookie, brickie, bulky, car key, chalky, cheeky, chunky, cliquey, clunky, cocky, cookie, corky, creaky, crikey, croaky, dinky, donkey, door key, ducky, dusky, flaky, flunkey, folkie, folky, freaky, frisky, funky, gawky, hanky, hickey, hockey, hokey, hookey, hunky, husky, icky, inky, jerky, jockey, jokey, junkie, key, karaoke, khaki, kinky, lackey, lanky, latchkey, leaky, lucky, marquee, mickey, milky, murky, monkey, mucky, musky, narky, nooky, passkey, peaky, perky, pesky, picky, pinkie, pinky, plucky, pokey, porky, psyche, punky, quaky, quickie, quirky, reeky, risky, rocky, rookie, shaky, sickie, silky, ski, slinky, smoky, snaky, sneaky, sparky, spiky, spooky, squeaky, sticky, stinky, stocky, streaky, sulky, swanky, tacky, talkie, techie, tricky, turkey, wacky, whiskey/whisky, wonky, Yankee, yucky.
Acne, any, beanie, blarney, bonny, bony, brainy, brawny, briny, brownie, canny, chimney, cine, cockney, corny, cranny, crony, Disney, genie, grainy, granny, guinea, hinny, horny, journey, knee, loony, many, meanie, mini, nanny, ninny, penny, pony, phoney/phony (U.S.), puny, queenie, rainy, sarnie, scrawny, shiny, skinny, stony, teeny, thorny, tinny, tiny, townie, trainee, tranny, tweeny, uni, weeny, whiny, zany.
Budgie, cagey, clergy, dingy, dodgy, edgy, gee, grungy, gungy, mangy, orgy, sludgy, smudgy, spongy, squeegee, squidgy, stagy, stingy, stodgy, veggie, whingy.
Beefy, coffee, comfy, daffy, fee, fluffy, goofy, huffy, iffy, jiffy, leafy, puffy, scruffy, selfie, sniffy, stuffy, toffee, toughie, trophy.
Breathy, earthy, filthy, frothy, healthy, lengthy, mouthy, smithy, smoothie, stealthy, swarthy, toothy, wealthy, worthy.
Blowy, chewy, dewy, doughy, gluey, gooey, hooey, phooey, screwy, showy, snowy.
Burly, curly, early, girlie, hurly-burly, surly, swirly, twirly, whirly.
Brolly, collie, dolly, folly, golly, holly, jolly, lolly, trolley, volley, wally.
Alley, dally, galley, pally, rally, reveille, sally, tally, valley.
Bunny, funny, gunny, honey, money, runny, sonny, sunny.
Choppy, copy, floppy, jalopy, poppy, sloppy, soppy, stroppy.

[3] **Absentee**, amnesty, brevity, casualty, certainty, charity, chastity, clarity, committee, confetti, crotchety, crudity, density, deputy, devotee, dignity, dynasty, enmity, entity, fidgety, gaiety/gayety (U.S.), graffiti, gravity, guarantee, honesty, karate, levity, liberty, machete, majesty, modesty, nudity, oddity, parity, penalty, piety, poverty, probity, property, puberty, purity, quality, repartee, rickety, sanctity, sanctuary, scarcity, seventy, sovereignty, spaghetti, specialty, three-sixty, trinity, unity, uppity, vanity, velvety.
Apathy, empathy, newsworthy, noteworthy, praiseworthy, roadworthy, seaworthy, sympathy, trustworthy, unworthy.
Ancestry, archery, artistry, bakery, battery, bigotry, binary, blackberry, blubbery, blueberry, blustery, brasserie, bravery, brewery, bribery, burglary, calorie, carpentry, carvery, cavalry, celery, century, chemistry, chicory, chivalry, Christmas tree, colliery, contrary, devilry, diary, dietary, disagree, dithery, doddery, drudgery, dungaree, duty-free, eatery, enquiry, estuary, expiry, factory, fakery, feathery, filigree, finery, fishery, flattery, fluttery, forestry, forgery, gallery, geometry, gimmickry, glittery, greenery, grocery, history, imagery, injury, inquiry, ivory, jamboree, jewellery/jewelry (U.S.), jittery, leathery, lingerie, lottery, luxury, memory, mercury, misery, momentary, monastery, mystery, nursery, obituary, obligatory, pageantry, pedigree, perjury, pillory, pleasantry, poetry, pottery, primary, priory, quivery, referee, revelry, reverie, rivalry, robbery, rockery, rosary, rubbery, salary, sanctuary, savagery, savory, scenery, sensory, shimmery, shivery, silvery, slavery, slippery, sorcery, sugary, surgery, tapestry, thundery, treachery, trickery, victory, wintery, wizardry.
Bumblebee, honeybee, namby-pamby, wallaby, wannabe.
Actressy, agency, autopsy, bankruptcy, blatancy, bourgeoisie, buoyancy, Christmassy, clemency, courtesy, currency, decency, divorcee, ecstasy, embassy, fallacy, fantasy, fluency, galaxy, heresy, infancy, jealousy, legacy, leniency, lunacy, odyssey, oversee, pharmacy, piracy, policy, potency, pregnancy, primacy, privacy, prophecy, regency, secrecy, tendency, Tennessee, truancy, undersea, urgency, vacancy.
Burgundy, chickadee, COD, comedy, custody, dogsbody, fool-hardy, jeopardy, malady, melody, nobody, parody, Ph.D., raggedy, remedy, rhapsody, somebody, tragedy.
Agony, attorney, balcony, baloney, bikini, botany, colony, company, cottony, cushiony, destiny, ebony, felony, gluttony, halfpenny, harmony, Houdini, irony, larceny, litany, martini, mutiny, satiny, scrutiny, symphony, tiffany, timpani, trainee, tyranny, villainy.
Assembly, bimonthly, biweekly, bodily, comradely, cowardly, dastardly, directly, easterly, family, finale, fleur-de-lis, fortnightly, heavenly, hillbilly, homily, icily, jubilee, maidenly, mannerly, matronly, panoply, plug-ugly, quarterly, rascally, readily, reveille, simile, slovenly, ungainly, unruly, user-friendly, wizardly, womanly.
Aromatherapy, gossipy, photocopy, recipe, slap-happy, syrupy, therapy, unhappy.
Alchemy, bigamy, blasphemy, blossomy, bonhomie, enemy, infamy, sesame, tsunami.
Anarchy, finicky, garlicky, gimmicky, headachy, malarkey, monarchy, panicky, plasticky.
Actually, brotherly, easterly, elderly, equally, fatherly, finally, formally, formerly, gingerly, leisurely, masterly, miserly, motherly, naturally, neighbourly/neighborly (U.S.), normally, northerly, orderly, overly, partially, properly, scholarly, sisterly, southerly, specially, thoroughly, usually, utterly, virtually, westerly.
Committee, gravity, nitty-gritty, responsibility, sanity, self-pity.
Allergy, effigy, emoji, energy, eulogy, lethargy, refugee, strategy, synergy, trilogy.
Apathy, empathy, newsworthy, noteworthy, praiseworthy, roadworthy, seaworthy, sympathy, trustworthy, unhealthy, unworthy.
Billowy, chop suey, echoey, shadowy, yellowy, willowy.
Freezingly, pleasingly, teasingly, wheezingly.
[4] **Ability**, agility, fertility, fragility, futility, hostility, humility, liability, mobility, nobility, responsibility, stability, tranquillity/tranquility (U.S.), versatility, viability, virility, volatility.
Anybody, busybody, everybody, fuddy-duddy, hurdy-gurdy, oldie worlde, understudy.
Accessory, adultery, artillery, cautionary, cemetery, compulsory, confectionery, conciliatory, constabulary, contemporary, customary, debauchery, delivery, dictionary, directory, discovery, distillery, elementary, embroidery, explanatory, exploratory, hunky-dory, idolatry, imaginary, incendiary, infirmary, inflammatory, judiciary, laboratory, legendary, literary, machinery, mandatory, mercenary, military, missionary, necessary, ordinary, patisserie, perfumery, preliminary, psychiatry, publicity, reactionary, recovery, secretary, secondary, simplicity, skullduggery, solitary, stationary, stationery, temporary, territory, tomfoolery, upholstery, visionary, vocabulary.

Academy, anatomy, astronomy, economy, epitome, origami.
Accuracy, complacency, consistency, conspiracy, contingency, controversy, delicacy, diplomacy, discrepancy, efficiency, emergency, flamboyancy, hypocrisy, idiocy, intimacy, intricacy, paparazzi, presidency, redundancy, sufficiency, supremacy, transparency.
Absurdity, affinity, amenity, anxiety, barbarity, calamity, cognoscenti, community, conformity, credulity, difficulty, dilettante, enormity, equality, eternity, fatality, fidelity, fifty-fifty, fraternity, frivolity, glitterati, heredity, hilarity, humanity, humidity, immunity, impunity, indemnity, infinity, intercity, literati, maternity, modernity, morality, nitty-gritty, obscenity, profanity, reality, senility, serenity, sobriety, solemnity, virility, stupidity, timidity, totality, twenty-twenty, variety, vicinity, vigilante, virginity, vulgarity.
Accompany, acrimony, alimony, cacophony, ceremony, epiphany, hootenanny, ignominy, matrimony, monotony, pepperoni, teeny-weeny, telephony, testimony.
Apostrophe, biography, catastrophe, choreography, geography, philosophy, photography.
Absolutely, anomaly, creepy-crawly, curmudgeonly, dilly-dally, eco-friendly, facsimile, fait accompli, gentlemanly, holy-moly, hurly-burly, immediately, melancholy, monopoly, rockabilly, roly-poly, shilly-shally, softly-softly, ukulele, underbelly, willy-nilly, yellow-belly.
Hanky-panky, happy-go-lucky, hokey-cokey, okey-dokey, wakey-wakey, walkie-talkie.
Analogy, anthology, apology, archeology, astrology, biology, cardiology, chronology, ecology, geology, ideology, mythology, psychology, technology, theology, zoology.
Especially, eventually, initially, incidentally, melancholy, monopoly, occasionally, officially, originally, personally, universally, unmannerly.
Antipathy, telepathy.
[5] Anniversary, beneficiary, camaraderie, complementary, complimentary, contradictory, directory, documentary, evolutionary, revolutionary, rudimentary, supplementary.
Ambiguity, anonymity, continuity, familiarity, femininity, impropriety, ingenuity, irregularity, liability, masculinity, notoriety, opportunity, peculiarity, popularity, regularity, responsibility, serendipity, similarity, solidarity, spontaneity, versatility, viability, volatility.

2.1.15 "--we" (as in "snowy")
[1] oui, twee, we, wee, whee.
[2] blowy, chewy, dewy, doughy, gluey, gooey, hooey, phooey, screwy, showy, snowy.
[3] billowy, chop suey, echoey, pillowy, shadowy, yellowy, willowy.

SURPRISING RHYMING:
[1] **Be,** bee, fee, flea, flee, gee, glee, he, key, knee, me, pea, pee, sea, see, tee, tea, the, thee, twee, we, wee, whee, zee.
Brie, free, re, spree, three, tree.
Beam, cream, deem, dream, gleam, meme, ream, scheme, scream, seam, seem, steam, stream, team, teem, theme.
[2] **Agree,** angry, beery, belfry, berry, bleary, blurry, boundary, bury, carefree, carry, cheery, cherry, country, curry, dairy, dearie, debris, degree, dowry, dreary, dust-free, eerie, entry, esprit, every, fairy, ferry, fiery, flowery, flurry, furry, fury, gentry, germ-free, glory, gory, Grand Prix, gumtree, hairy, hoary, hurry, hungry, jury, laundry, leery, lorry, marry, merry, paltry, pantry, parry, pastry, poultry, powdery, prairie, quandary, quarry, query, scary, scot-free, sentry, sorry, starry, storey, story, sultry, tawdry, teary, theory, treachery, vary, very, vestry, wary, weary, wintry, wiry, worry.
Breathy, earthy, filthy, frothy, healthy, lengthy, mouthy, smithy, smoothie, stealthy, swarthy, toothy, wealthy, worthy.
Bevvy, Chevy, curvy, envy, gravy, groovy, heavy, ivy, levee, levy, lovey, luvvy, movie, navy, nervy, savvy, skivvy, spivvy, wavy.
Baddy, bawdy, beady, bloody, body, brandy, buddy, caddie, candy, cloudy, daddy, dandy, dowdy, foodie, gaudy, giddy, greedy, handy, hardy, heady, hoodie, howdy, kiddie, laddie, lady, MD, midi, moody, mouldy/moldy (U.S.), muddy, needy, nerdy, oldie, randy, ready, roadie, rowdy, sandy, seedy, shady, shandy, shoddy, speedy, steady, study, sturdy, tardy, teddy, tidy, trendy, tweedy, weedy, windy, woody, wordy.
Abbey, baby, cabby, chubby, derby, flabby, Frisbee, hobby, grubby, hubby, lobby, maybe, ruby, shabby, snobby, would-be, zombie.
Ably, amply, aptly, barley, beastly, belly, bobbly, bubbly, bully, chili, chilly, cleanly, comely, coolie, coolly, costly, coyly, crackly, crawly, crinkly, crumbly, crumply, cuddly, daily, dally, dangly, deadly, deathly, deli, dimly, dimply, doily, drily, drizzly, dully, duly,

172

earthly, elderly, fiddly, filly, fitly, flatly, fleshly, freckly, friendly, frilly, fully, gaily, gangly, ghastly, ghostly, giggly, goalie, godly, goodly, googly, gristly, grizzly, grumbly, hilly, hotly, holy, hourly, husbandly, hyperbole, idly, jelly, jangly, jiggly, jingly, jowly, kindly, kingly, knobbly, likely, lily, lively, lonely, lordly, lovely, lowly, madly, manly, medley, monthly, mostly, motley, muesli, muscly, newly, niggly, nightly, oddly, oily, only, orderly, paisley, parley, pebbly, pimply, poorly, portly, prickly, priestly, princely, purply, queenly, really, rumbly, sadly, saintly, scribbly, seemly, shapely, shyly, sickly, silly, slightly, slyly, smiley, smelly, snarly, sparkly, spindly, sprightly, squiggly, stately, steely, stiffly, straggly, sully, surely, telly, tickly, timely, tingly, tinkly, trembly, trimly, trolley, truly, twinkly, ugly, volley, waffly, wally, weakly, weekly, welly, wetly, wheelie, wifely, wiggly, wily, wobbly, woolly, worldly, wriggly, wrinkly, wryly, yearly.
Bitty, city, ditty, gritty, pity, pretty, witty.
Anti, arty, auntie, batty, beastie, bitty, catty, chatty, city, crafty, cruelty, dainty, ditty, draughty/drafty (U.S.), eighty, fatty, fifty, frailty, goatee, gritty, guilty, hasty, hearty, hefty, jetty, lefty, matey, meaty, minty, misty, nasty, nifty, party, pasty, petit, petty, pity, plenty, pretty, QT, safety, scanty, settee, shanty/chanty (U.S.), shifty, sixty, sweaty, sweetie, tarty, tatty, tasty, thrifty, treaty, twenty, twisty, weighty, witty, yeti.
Bossy, bouncy, brassy, chassis, classy, curtsy, Dixie, dressy, emcee, fancy, fleecy, folksy, footsie, foresee, foxy, fussy, glassy, glitzy, glossy, grassy, greasy, gutsy, gypsy, horsey, hussy, saucy, icy, kissy, lacy, lassie, look-see, maxi, mercy, messy, missy, mousy, pacey, pixie, posse, pricey, juicy, prissy, proxy, pussy, racy, ritzy, sassy, schmaltzy, sexy, sightsee, sissy, spacey, spicy, taxi, tipsy, tootsie, waxy.
Bumpy, chappie, chippy, chirpy, clippie, crappie, creepy, crispy, dippy, dopey, drippy, droopy, dumpy, flappy, frumpy, grippy, groupie, grumpy, happy, hippie, humpy, jumpy, lippy, loopy, lumpy, nappy, nippy, pappy, peppy, plummy, preppy, pulpy, puppy, raspy, ropy, sappy, scampi, scrappy, scrummy, scrumpy, skimpy, sleepy, slippy, snappy, snippy, snoopy, soapy, soupy, stripy, stumpy, swampy, sweetpea, teepee, trippy, vampy, weepy, whippy, whoopee, wimpy, wispy, yuppie, zappy, zippy.
Army, balmy, barmy, blimey, chamois, chummy, clammy, creamy, crummy, dreamy, dummy, Emmy, foamy, gimme, gleamy, gloomy, Grammy, grimy, gummy, hammy, homey, jammy, lemme, limey, mammy, me, mommy, mummy, plummy, roomy, samey, scrummy, seamy, slimy, slummy, smarmy, stormy, tummy, whammy, wormy, yummy.
Achy, baccy, balky, beaky, bookie, brickie, bulky, car key, chalky, cheeky, chunky, cliquey, clunky, cocky, cookie, corky, creaky, crikey, croaky, dinky, donkey, door key, ducky, dusky, flaky, flunkey, folkie, folky, freaky, frisky, funky, gawky, hanky, hickey, hockey, hokey, hookey, hunky, husky, icky, inky, jerky, jockey, jokey, junkie, key, karaoke, khaki, kinky, lackey, lanky, latchkey, leaky, lucky, marquee, mickey, milky, murky, monkey, mucky, musky, narky, nooky, passkey, peaky, perky, pesky, picky, pinkie, pinky, plucky, pokey, porky, psyche, punky, quaky, quickie, quirky, reeky, risky, rocky, rookie, shaky, sickie, silky, ski, slinky, smoky, snaky, sneaky, sparky, spiky, spooky, squeaky, sticky, stinky, stocky, streaky, sulky, swanky, tacky, talkie, techie, tricky, turkey, wacky, whiskey/whisky, wonky, Yankee, yucky.
Acne, any, beanie, blarney, bonny, bony, brainy, brawny, briny, brownie, canny, chimney, cine, cockney, corny, cranny, crony, Disney, genie, grainy, granny, guinea, hinny, horny, journey, knee, loony, many, meanie, mini, nanny, ninny, penny, pony, phoney/phony (U.S.), puny, queenie, rainy, sarnie, scrawny, shiny, skinny, stony, teeny, thorny, tinny, tiny, townie, trainee, tranny, tweeny, uni, weeny, whiny, zany.
Budgie, cagey, clergy, dingy, dodgy, edgy, gee, grungy, gungy, mangy, orgy, sludgy, smudgy, spongy, squeegee, squidgy, stagy, stingy, stodgy, veggie, whingy.
Beefy, coffee, comfy, daffy, fee, fluffy, goofy, huffy, iffy, jiffy, leafy, puffy, scruffy, selfie, sniffy, stuffy, toffee, toughie, trophy.
Breathy, earthy, filthy, frothy, healthy, lengthy, mouthy, pithy, smoothie, stealthy, swarthy, toothy, wealthy, worthy.
Bevvy, Chevy, curvy, envy, gravy, groovy, heavy, ivy, levee, levy, lovey, luvvy, movie, navy, nervy, savvy, skivvy, wavy.
Burly, curly, early, girlie, hurly-burly, surly, swirly, twirly, whirly.
Brolly, collie, dolly, folly, golly, holly, jolly, lolly, trolley, volley, wally.
Alley, dally, galley, pally, rally, reveille, sally, tally, valley.
Bunny, funny, gunny, honey, money, runny, sonny, sunny.
Choppy, copy, floppy, jalopy, poppy, sloppy, soppy, stroppy.

173

[3] Absentee, amnesty, brevity, casualty, certainty, charity, chastity, clarity, committee, confetti, crotchety, crudity, density, deputy, devotee, dignity, dynasty, enmity, entity, fidgety, gaiety/gayety (U.S.), graffiti, gravity, guarantee, honesty, karate, levity, liberty, machete, majesty, modesty, nudity, oddity, parity, penalty, piety, poverty, probity, property, puberty, purity, quality, repartee, rickety, sanctity, sanctuary, scarcity, seventy, sovereignty, spaghetti, specialty, three-sixty, trinity, unity, uppity, vanity, velvety.
Apathy, empathy, newsworthy, noteworthy, praiseworthy, roadworthy, seaworthy, sympathy, trustworthy, unhealthy, unworthy.
Anchovy, c'est la vie, eau-de-vie, lovey-dovey, top-heavy, topsy-turvy, vis-à-vis.
Ancestry, archery, artistry, bakery, battery, bigotry, binary, blackberry, blubbery, blueberry, blustery, brasserie, bravery, brewery, bribery, burglary, calorie, carpentry, carvery, cavalry, celery, century, chemistry, chicory, chivalry, Christmas tree, colliery, contrary, devilry, diary, dietary, disagree, dithery, doddery, drudgery, dungaree, duty-free, eatery, enquiry, estuary, expiry, factory, fakery, feathery, filigree, finery, fishery, flattery, fluttery, forestry, forgery, gallery, geometry, gimmickry, glittery, greenery, grocery, history, imagery, injury, inquiry, ivory, jamboree, jewellery/jewelry (U.S.), jittery, leathery, lingerie, lottery, luxury, memory, mercury, misery, momentary, monastery, mystery, nursery, obituary, obligatory, pageantry, pedigree, perjury, pillory, pleasantry, poetry, pottery, primary, priory, quivery, referee, revelry, reverie, rivalry, robbery, rockery, rosary, rubbery, salary, sanctuary, savagery, savory, scenery, sensory, shimmery, shivery, silvery, slavery, slippery, sorcery, sugary, surgery, tapestry, thundery, treachery, trickery, victory, wintery, wizardry.
Bumblebee, honeybee, namby-pamby, wallaby, wannabe.
Actressy, agency, autopsy, bankruptcy, blatancy, bourgeoisie, buoyancy, Christmassy, clemency, courtesy, currency, decency, divorcee, ecstasy, embassy, fallacy, fantasy, fluency, galaxy, heresy, infancy, jealousy, legacy, leniency, lunacy, odyssey, oversee, pharmacy, piracy, policy, potency, pregnancy, primacy, privacy, prophecy, regency, secrecy, tendency, Tennessee, truancy, undersea, urgency, vacancy.
Burgundy, chickadee, COD, comedy, custody, dogsbody, fool-hardy, jeopardy, malady, melody, nobody, parody, Ph.D., raggedy, remedy, rhapsody, somebody, tragedy.
Agony, attorney, balcony, baloney, bikini, botany, colony, company, cottony, cushiony, destiny, ebony, felony, gluttony, halfpenny, harmony, Houdini, irony, larceny, litany, martini, mutiny, satiny, scrutiny, symphony, tiffany, timpani, trainee, tyranny, villainy.
Assembly, bimonthly, biweekly, bodily, comradely, cowardly, dastardly, directly, easterly, family, finale, fleur-de-lis, fortnightly, heavenly, hillbilly, homily, icily, jubilee, laggardly, maidenly, mannerly, matronly, panoply, plug-ugly, quarterly, readily, reveille, simile, slovenly, ungainly, unruly, user-friendly, wizardly, womanly.
Aromatherapy, gossipy, photocopy, recipe, slap-happy, syrupy, therapy, unhappy.
Alchemy, bigamy, blasphemy, blossomy, bonhomie, enemy, infamy, sesame, tsunami.
Anarchy, finicky, garlicky, gimmicky, headachy, malarkey, monarchy, panicky, plasticky.
Actually, brotherly, easterly, elderly, equally, fatherly, finally, formally, formerly, gingerly, leisurely, masterly, miserly, motherly, naturally, neighbourly/neighborly (U.S.), normally, northerly, orderly, overly, partially, properly, scholarly, sisterly, southerly, specially, thoroughly, usually, utterly, virtually, westerly.
Committee, gravity, nitty-gritty, responsibility, sanity, self-pity.
Allergy, effigy, emoji, energy, eulogy, lethargy, refugee, strategy, synergy, trilogy.
Apathy, empathy, newsworthy, noteworthy, praiseworthy, roadworthy, seaworthy, sympathy, trustworthy, unhealthy, unworthy.
Anchovy, c'est la vie, eau-de-vie, lovey-dovey, top-heavy, topsy-turvy, vis-à-vis.
Freezingly, pleasingly, teasingly, wheezingly.
[4] Ability, agility, fertility, fragility, futility, hostility, humility, liability, mobility, nobility, responsibility, stability, tranquillity/tranquility (U.S.), versatility, viability, virility, volatility.
Anybody, busybody, everybody, fuddy-duddy, hurdy-gurdy, oldie worlde, understudy.
Accessory, adultery, artillery, cautionary, cemetery, compulsory, confectionery, conciliatory, constabulary, contemporary, customary, delivery, dictionary, directory, discovery, distillery, elementary, embroidery, explanatory, exploratory, hunky-dory, idolatry, imaginary, incendiary, infirmary, inflammatory, judiciary, legendary, literary, machinery, mercenary, military, missionary, necessary, ordinary, patisserie, perfumery, preliminary, publicity, reactionary, recovery, secretary, secondary, simplicity, skullduggery, solitary, stationary, stationery, temporary, territory, visionary, vocabulary.

174

Academy, anatomy, astronomy, economy, epitome, origami.
Accuracy, complacency, consistency, conspiracy, contingency, controversy, delicacy, diplomacy, discrepancy, efficiency, emergency, flamboyancy, hypocrisy, idiocy, intimacy, intricacy, paparazzi, presidency, redundancy, sufficiency, supremacy, transparency.
Absurdity, affinity, amenity, anxiety, barbarity, calamity, cognoscenti, community, conformity, credulity, difficulty, dilettante, enormity, equality, eternity, fatality, fidelity, fifty-fifty, fraternity, frivolity, glitterati, heredity, hilarity, humanity, humidity, immunity, impunity, indemnity, infinity, intercity, literati, maternity, modernity, morality, nitty-gritty, obscenity, profanity, reality, senility, serenity, sobriety, solemnity, virility, stupidity, timidity, totality, twenty-twenty, variety, vicinity, vigilante, virginity, vulgarity.
Accompany, acrimony, alimony, cacophony, ceremony, epiphany, hootenanny, ignominy, matrimony, monotony, pepperoni, teeny-weeny, telephony, testimony.
Apostrophe, biography, catastrophe, choreography, geography, philosophy, photography.
Absolutely, anomaly, creepy-crawly, curmudgeonly, dilly-dally, eco-friendly, facsimile, fait accompli, gentlemanly, holy-moly, hurly-burly, immediately, melancholy, monopoly, rockabilly, roly-poly, shilly-shally, softly-softly, ukulele, underbelly, willy-nilly, yellow-belly
Hanky-panky, happy-go-lucky, okey-dokey, wakey-wakey.
Analogy, anthology, apology, archeology, astrology, biology, cardiology, chronology, ecology, geology, ideology, mythology, psychology, technology, theology, zoology.
Especially, eventually, initially, incidentally, melancholy, monopoly, occasionally, officially, originally, personally, universally, unmannerly.
Antipathy, telepathy.
[5] **Anniversary**, beneficiary, camaraderie, complementary, complimentary, contradictory, directory, documentary, evolutionary, revolutionary, rudimentary, supplementary.
Ambiguity, anonymity, Christianity, continuity, familiarity, femininity, impropriety, ingenuity, irregularity, liability, masculinity, notoriety, opportunity, peculiarity, popularity, regularity, responsibility, serendipity, similarity, solidarity, spontaneity, versatility, volatility.

2.1.16 "--zee" (as in "easy")
breezy, cheesy, easy, easy-peasy, greasy, sleazy, squeezy, uneasy, wheezy, a-to-zee.

SURPRISING RHYMING:
[1] **Sea**, see.
[2] **Bossy**, bouncy, brassy, chassis, classy, curtsy, Dixie, dressy, emcee, fancy, fleecy, folksy, footsie, foresee, foxy, fussy, glassy, glitzy, glossy, grassy, greasy, gutsy, gypsy, horsey, hussy, saucy, icy, kissy, lacy, lassie, look-see, maxi, mercy, messy, missy, mousy, pacey, pixie, posse, pricey, juicy, prissy, proxy, pussy, racy, ritzy, sassy, schmaltzy, sexy, sightsee, sissy, spacey, spicy, taxi, tipsy, tootsie, waxy.
[3] **Actressy**, agency, autopsy, bankruptcy, blatancy, bourgeoisie, buoyancy, Christmassy, clemency, courtesy, currency, decency, divorcee, ecstasy, embassy, fallacy, fantasy, fluency, galaxy, heresy, infancy, jealousy, legacy, leniency, lunacy, odyssey, oversee, pharmacy, piracy, policy, potency, pregnancy, primacy, privacy, prophecy, regency, secrecy, tendency, truancy, undersea, urgency, vacancy.
[4] **Accuracy**, complacency, consistency, conspiracy, contingency, controversy, delicacy, diplomacy, discrepancy, efficiency, emergency, flamboyancy, hypocrisy, idiocy, intimacy, intricacy, paparazzi, presidency, redundancy, sufficiency, supremacy, transparency.

2.1.17 "--ablee" (as in "probably")
[3] affably, bearably, capably, culpably, curably, durably, enjoyably, notably, probably, palpably, sizably, suitably, variably, viably.
[4] achievably, admirably, advisably, amiably, answerably, applicably, arguably, believably, charitably, commendably, comparably, conceivably, controllably, creditably, debatably, deniably, dependably, disputably, endurably, enviably, excitably, explicably, fashionably, favourably/favorably (U.S.), forgettably, forgivably, formidably, honourably/honorably (U.S.), hospitably, incapably, incurably, irritably, inscrutably, lamentably, measurably, memorably, miserably, pleasurably, preferably, profitably, questionably, reasonably, regrettably, reliably, remarkably, reputably, retrievably, seasonably, tolerably, unbearably, unsuitably, venerably, vulnerably.
[5] certifiably, considerably, dishonourably/dishonorably (U.S.), excusably, identifiably, impressionably, inadvisably, incomparably, inconceivably, inconsiderably, inconsolably,

175

indescribably, indisputably, indomitably, inescapably, inexcusably, inexplicably, inexorably, inextricably, inevitably, inhospitably, inimitably, irrefutably, irreplaceably, irretrievably, inseparably, insufferably, intolerably, justifiably, recognizably, unaccountably, unbelievably, uncontrollably, undeniably, understandably, unfavourably/unfavorably (U.S.), unforgettably, unprofitably, unreliably, unreasonably, verifiably.

SURPRISING RHYMING:
[2] **Badly**, gladly, madly, sadly.
[3] **Audibly**, credibly, feasibly, forcibly, flexibly, gullibly, horribly, laudably, movably, plausibly, possibly, risibly, sensibly, tangibly, terribly, visibly, wallaby, wannabe, wobbly.
Battery, bigotry, binary, boundary, burglary, cavalry, chivalry, commentary, contrary, diary, disagree, estuary, fakery, flattery, gallantry, infantry, library, luxury, memory, misery, mockery, momentary, mystery, obligatory, pageantry, primary, rivalry, robbery, sanctuary, savagery, snobbery, strawberry, sugary, treachery, voluntary, wizardry.
Canopy, gossipy, recipe, syrupy, therapy, unhappy.
Burgundy, comedy, custody, embody, fool-hardy, jeopardy, malady, melody, nobody, parody, raggedy, remedy, rhapsody, somebody, subsidy, tragedy.
Alchemy, bigamy, blasphemy, enemy, infamy, sesame, tsunami.
Agony, attorney, balcony, botany, colony, company, destiny, ebony, harmony, litany, symphony, timpani, tyranny, villainy.
Actually, bodily, equally, finally, formally, homily, naturally, normally, partially, sloppily, specially, usually, virtually.
Anarchy, hierarchy, malarkey, monarchy.
Cowardly, dastardly, family, finale, rascally, scholarly, womanly.
Buoyancy, Christmassy, ecstasy, embassy, fallacy, fantasy, galaxy, infancy, legacy, lunacy, pharmacy, piracy, privacy, urgency, vacancy.
Casualty, cavity, charity, clarity, dynasty, guarantee, majesty, parity, penalty, quality, sanctuary, specialty, warranty.
Apathy, empathy, sympathy.
[4] **Acceptably**, accessibly, addictively, defensibly, discernibly, immovably, impossibly, improbably, incredibly, invincibly, invisibly, noticeably, perceptibly, susceptibly.
Dismissively, expressively, negatively, permissively, submissively.
Academy, anatomy, astronomy, autonomy, economy, epitome, gastronomy, origami.
Apostrophe, biography, catastrophe, choreography, geography, philosophy, photography.
Ability, agility, fertility, fragility, futility, hostility, humility, liability, mobility, nobility, responsibility, stability, tranquillity/tranquility (U.S.), versatility, viability, virility, volatility.
Accessory, adultery, artillery, cautionary, cemetery, compulsory, confectionery, conciliatory, constabulary, contemporary, customary, debauchery, delivery, dictionary, directory, discovery, distillery, elementary, embroidery, explanatory, exploratory, hunky-dory, idolatry, imaginary, incendiary, infirmary, inflammatory, judiciary, laboratory, legendary, literary, machinery, mandatory, mercenary, military, missionary, necessary, ordinary, patisserie, perfumery, preliminary, psychiatry, publicity, reactionary, recovery, secretary, secondary, simplicity, skullduggery, solitary, stationary, stationery, temporary, territory, tomfoolery, upholstery, visionary, vocabulary.
Accompany, cacophony, epiphany, mahogany, monotony, telepathy.
Especially, eventually, initially, monopoly, occasionally, officially, originally, personally.
Accuracy, ascendancy, complacency, consistency, conspiracy, delicacy, diplomacy, discrepancy, efficiency, emergency, flamboyancy, intimacy, redundancy, supremacy.
Absurdity, acidity, affinity, amenity, annuity, anxiety, barbarity, calamity, cognoscenti, commodity, community, conformity, credulity, difficulty, dilettante, divinity, enormity, equality, eternity, fatality, fidelity, fifty-fifty, fraternity, frivolity, glitterati, gratuity, heredity, hilarity, humanity, humidity, immunity, impunity, indemnity, infinity, infirmity, intercity, literati, maternity, modernity, morality, nitty-gritty, obscenity, profanity, proximity, reality, senility, serenity, sobriety, solemnity, virility, stupidity, timidity, tonality, totality, twenty-twenty, variety, vicinity, vigilante, virginity, vulgarity.
Anxiety, barbarity, calamity, eternity, facility, fragility, fraternity, frivolity, futility, glitterati, hilarity, humanity, totality, variety, vulgarity.
[5] **Imperceptibly**, inadmissibly, incomprehensibly, indefensibly, indiscernibly, indispensably, irrepressibly, reprehensibly, unacceptably.
Apprehensively, comprehensively.

Ambiguity, anonymity, continuity, familiarity, femininity, impropriety, ingenuity, irregularity, liability, masculinity, notoriety, opportunity, peculiarity, popularity, regularity, responsibility, serendipity, similarity, solidarity, spontaneity, versatility, viability, volatility.
Anniversary, beneficiary, camaraderie, complementary, complimentary, contradictory, documentary, evolutionary, intermediary, revolutionary, rudimentary, supplementary.

2.1.18 "--eech" (as in "reach")
[1] beach, beech, bleach, breach, breech, each, leach, leech, peach, preach, reach, screech, speech, teach.
[2] beseech, impeach, outreach.

SURPRISING RHYMING:
[1] **Be**, bee, fee, flea, flee, gee, glee, he, key, knee, me, sea, see, tee, tea, the, thee, twee, we, wee, whee, zee.
Brie, free, re, spree, three, tree.
Beat(s), beet, bleat, cheat, cleat, eat, feat, feet, fleet, greet, heat, meat, meet, neat, peat, pleat, seat, sheet, skeet, sleet, street, suite, sweet, teat, treat, tweet, wheat.
Beef, belief, brief, chief, fief, grief, leaf, reef, sheaf, thief.
Bleed, breed, cede, creed, deed, feed, freed, greed, he'd, heed, keyed, knead, kneed, lead, mead, need, plead, read, reed, seed, she'd, speed, steed, tweed, we'd, weed.
Beak, bleak, cheek, chic, clique, creak, creek, eke, freak, geek, leak, leek, meek, peak, peek, pique, reek, seek, sheik, shriek, sleek, sneak, speak, streak, squeak, teak, tweak, weak, week, wreak.
Beast, cease(d), crease(d), east, feast, fleece(d), grease(d), least, niece, peace, piece(d), piste, priest, yeast.
Beep, bleep, cheep, cheap, creep, deep, heap, jeep, keep, leap, peep, reap, seep, sheep, sleep, steep, sweep, weep.
Heath, 'neath, sheath, teeth, wreath.
Eve, grieve, heave, leave, sleeve, thieve, weave, we've.
Breeze, cheese, ease, fees, freeze, frieze, he's, jeez, keys, knees, please, sees, seize, she's, sleaze, sneeze, squeeze, teas, tease, tees, these, trees, tweeze, wheeze.
[2] **Debrief**, fig leaf, flyleaf, mischief, motif, relief, tea leaf.
Agreed, airspeed, birdseed, concede, chickweed, crossbreed, decreed, exceed, flaxseed, Godspeed, handfeed, hayseed, impede, inbreed, indeed, knock-kneed, linseed, lip-read, milkweed, misdeed, mislead, misread, nosebleed, pokeweed, precede, proceed, recede, re-read, seaweed, sight-read, spoon-feed, stampede, succeed.
Antique, boutique, critique, midweek, mystique, oblique, physique, technique, unique.
Apiece, caprice, cassis, decease, decrease, hairpiece, increase, mouthpiece, neckpiece, obese, police, release, sublease, timepiece, two-piece, valise.
Asleep, chimney sweep, oversleep, scrapheap, skin-deep, upkeep.
Artiste, decreased, deceased, increased, northeast, policed, released, southeast.
Beneath, bequeath, eyeteeth, underneath.
Achieve, aggrieve, believe, bereave, conceive, deceive, naïve, perceive, receive, relieve, reprieve, retrieve, shirtsleeve, upheave.
Appease, Aries, chemise, deep-freeze, degrees, disease, herpes, Pisces, reprise, species, striptease, trapeze, unease, valise.
[3] **Bittersweet**, easy street, incomplete, indiscreet, obsolete, overeat, overheat.
Aperitif, disbelief, handkerchief, misbelief, overleaf.
Aniseed, centipede, chickenfeed, disagreed, filigreed, guaranteed, intercede, millipede, overfeed, pedigreed, proofread, refereed, supersede, tumbleweed.
Hide-and-seek, technospeak, tongue-in-cheek.
Centerpiece/centerpiece, mantelpiece, masterpiece, predecease, unreleased.
Disbelieve, interleave, interweave, make-believe, misconceive, overachieve, preconceive, reconceive, semibreve, underachieve.
Achilles, antifreeze, emojis, enemies, expertise, guarantees, Hercules, indices, journalese, manganese, melodies, overseas.
Burgundy, chickadee, COD, comedy, custody, dogsbody, fool-hardy, jeopardy, malady, melody, nobody, parody, Ph.D., raggedy, remedy, rhapsody, somebody, tragedy.
Allergy, effigy, emoji, energy, eulogy, lethargy, refugee, strategy, synergy, trilogy.

2.1.19 "--eed" (as in "greed")
[1] bead, bleed, breed, cede, creed, deed, feed, freed, greed, he'd, heed, keyed, knead, kneed, lead, mead, need, peed, plead, read, reed, seed, she'd, speed, steed, treed, tweed, we'd, weed.
[2] agreed, airspeed, birdseed, concede, chickweed, crossbreed, decreed, exceed, flaxseed, Godspeed, handfeed, hayseed, impede, inbreed, indeed, knock-kneed, linseed, lip-read, milkweed, misdeed, mislead, misread, nosebleed, precede, proceed, rapeseed, recede, re-read, seaweed, secede, sight-read, spoon-feed, stampede, succeed.
[3] aniseed, centipede, chickenfeed, cottonseed, disagreed, filigreed, guaranteed, intercede, millipede, overfeed, pedigreed, proofread, refereed, supersede, tumbleweed.

SURPRISING RHYMING:
[1] **Be**, bee, fee, flea, flee, gee, glee, he, key, knee, me, sea, see, tee, tea, the, thee, twee, we, wee, whee, zee.
Brie, free, re, spree, three, tree.
Beat, beats, beet, bleat, cheat, cleat, eat, feat, feet, fleet, greet, heat, meat, meet, neat, peat, pleat, seat, sheet, skeet, sleet, street, suite, sweet, treat, tweet, wheat.
Beef, belief, brief, chief, fief, grief, leaf, reef, sheaf, thief.
Beak, bleak, cheek, chic, clique, creak, creek, eke, freak, geek, leak, leek, meek, peak, peek, pique, reek, seek, sheik, shriek, sleek, sneak, speak, streak, squeak, teak, tweak, weak, week.
Beast, cease(d), crease(d), east, feast, fleece(d), grease(d), least, niece, peace, piece(d), piste, priest, yeast.
Beep, bleep, cheep, cheap, creep, deep, heap, jeep, keep, leap, peep, reap, seep, sheep, sleep, steep, sweep, weep.
Heath, 'neath, sheath, teeth, wreath.
Eve, grieve, heave, leave, sleeve, thieve, weave, we've.
Breeze, cheese, ease, fees, freeze, frieze, he's, jeez, keys, knees, please, sees, seize, she's, sleaze, sneeze, squeeze, teas, tease, tees, these, trees, tweeze, wheeze.
Beach, bleach, breach, each, leech, peach, preach, reach, screech, speech, teach.
[2] **Athlete**, backbeat, backstreet, breakbeat, broadsheet, browbeat, compete, complete, conceit, concrete, deadbeat, deceit, defeat, delete, deplete, discreet, discrete, downbeat, drumbeat, dustsheet, effete, elite, entreat, excrete, flysheet, heartbeat, maltreat, mistreat, mincemeat, offbeat, petite, receipt, reheat, repeat, reseat, retreat, secrete, spreadsheet, sweetmeat, time sheet, upbeat, unseat.
Beneath, bequeath, debrief, eyeteeth, fig leaf, mischief, motif, relief, underneath..
Antique, boutique, critique, midweek, mystique, oblique, physique, technique, unique.
Apiece, caprice, cassis, decease, decrease, hairpiece, increase, mouthpiece, neckpiece, obese, police, release, sublease, timepiece, two-piece, valise.
Asleep, chimney sweep, oversleep, scrapheap, skin-deep, upkeep.
Artiste, decreased, deceased, increased, northeast, policed, released, southeast.
Achieve, aggrieve, believe, conceive, deceive, naïve, perceive, receive, relieve, reprieve, retrieve, shirtsleeve, upheave.
Appease, Aries, chemise, deep-freeze, degrees, disease, displease, herpes, Pisces, reprise, species, striptease, trapeze, unease, unfreeze, valise.
[3] **Bittersweet**, easy street, incomplete, indiscreet, obsolete, overeat, overheat.
Aperitif, disbelief, handkerchief, misbelief, overleaf.
Hide-and-seek, technospeak, tongue-in-cheek.
Centerpiece/centerpiece, mantelpiece, masterpiece, predecease, unreleased.
Disbelieve, make-believe, misconceive, overachieve, preconceive, underachieve.
Achilles, antifreeze, emojis, enemies, expertise, Hercules, melodies, overseas.
Burgundy, chickadee, COD, comedy, custody, dogsbody, fool-hardy, jeopardy, malady, melody, nobody, parody, Ph.D., raggedy, remedy, rhapsody, somebody, tragedy.
Allergy, effigy, emoji, energy, eulogy, lethargy, refugee, strategy, synergy, trilogy.
Actressy, agency, autopsy, bankruptcy, blatancy, bourgeoisie, buoyancy, Christmassy, clemency, courtesy, currency, decency, divorcee, ecstasy, embassy, fallacy, fantasy, fluency, galaxy, heresy, infancy, jealousy, legacy, leniency, lunacy, odyssey, oversee, pharmacy, piracy, policy, potency, pregnancy, primacy, privacy, prophecy, regency, secrecy, tendency, Tennessee, truancy, undersea, urgency, vacancy.

Absentee, amnesty, brevity, casualty, certainty, charity, chastity, clarity, committee, confetti, crotchety, crudity, density, deputy, devotee, dignity, dynasty, enmity, entity, fidgety, gaiety/gayety (U.S.), graffiti, gravity, guarantee, honesty, karate, levity, liberty, machete, majesty, modesty, nudity, oddity, parity, penalty, piety, poverty, probity, property, puberty, purity, quality, repartee, rickety, sanctity, sanctuary, scarcity, seventy, sovereignty, spaghetti, specialty, three-sixty, trinity, unity, uppity, vanity, velvety.

2.1.20 "--eeded" (as in "needed")
[2] beaded, ceded, deeded, heeded, needed, pleaded, seeded, tweeded, weeded.
[3] acceded, conceded, exceeded, impeded, preceded, proceeded, receded, stampeded, succeeded, unheeded, unneeded, unweeded.
[4] interceded, superseded.

SURPRISING RHYMING:
[2] **Bleated**, cheated, cleated, greeted, heated, meted, pleated, seated, sheeted, treated, tweeted.
Fielded, shielded, wielded, yielded.
[3] **Beat it**, competed, completed, conceited, defeated, deleted, depleted, entreated, excreted, mistreated, preheated, reheated, repeated, reseated, retreated, secreted, undefeated, unheated.

2.1.21 "--eeder" (as in "leader")
[2] bleeder, breeder, cedar, feeder, heeder, leader, pleader, reader, speeder, weeder.
[3] bandleader, cheerleader, conceder, corrida, lip-reader, mind-reader, misleader, newsreader, ringleader, stampeder.

SURPRISING RHYMING:
[2] **Beeper**, bleeper, cheaper, creeper, deeper, keeper, leaper, peeper, reaper, sleeper, steeper, sweeper, weeper.
Beaker, bleaker, eureka, leaker, meeker, peeker, seeker, sleeker, sneaker, speaker, streaker, squeaker, tikka, weaker, wreaker.
Dealer, feeler, healer, heeler, kneeler, peeler, sealer, spieler, stealer, squealer, wheeler.
Beamer, creamer, dreamer, prima, reamer, schemer, screamer, steamer, streamer.
Cleaner, gleaner, greener, keener, leaner, meaner, screener.
Beezer, Caesar, Deezer, freezer, geezer, geyser, Mona Lisa, squeezer, teaser, visa.
Creature, feature, preacher, reacher, screecher, teacher.
[3] **Barkeeper**, beekeeper, bookkeeper, gamekeeper, gatekeeper, goalkeeper, housekeeper, innkeeper, peacekeeper, shopkeeper, storekeeper, timekeeper, zookeeper.
Appealer, enfant terrible, faith-healer, tequila, wheeler-dealer.
Arena, blasphemer, cantina, czarina/tsarina, daydreamer, demeanour/demeanor (U.S.), hyena, marina, redeemer, subpoena.
[4] **Ballerina**, concertina, misdemeanour/misdemeanor (U.S.).

2.1.22 "--eedy" (as in "greedy")
[2] beady, greedy, needy, reedy, seedy, speedy, tweedy, weedy.

SURPRISING RHYMING:
[1] **Be**, bee, fee, flea, flee, gee, glee, he, key, knee, me, sea, see, tee, tea, the, thee, twee, we, wee, whee, zee.
Brie, free, spree, three, tree.
[2] **Creamy**, dreamy, gleamy, seamy, steamy.
Beanie, cleanly, genie, greeny, meanie, queenie, teeny, tweeny, weeny.
Cheapie, creepy, sleepy, specie, squeegee, teepee, weepy, yippee.
Bleary, cheery, clearly, dearly, dreary, eerie, leery, merely, nearly, query, theory, weary.
Beaky, cheeky, cliquey, creaky, freaky, leaky, peaky, reeky, sneaky, squeaky, streaky.
Beefy, easy, fleecy, greasy, leafy, specie.
Beastly, beastie, freely, guilty, meaty, priestly, really, seemly, steely, sweetie, wieldy.
Bleakly, meekly, sleekly, weakly, weekly.
[3] **Burgundy**, chickadee, COD, comedy, custody, dogsbody, fool-hardy, jeopardy,

malady, melody, nobody, parody, Ph.D., remedy, rhapsody, somebody, tragedy.
Absentee, amnesty, brevity, casualty, certainty, charity, chastity, clarity, committee, confetti, crotchety, crudity, density, deputy, devotee, dignity, dynasty, enmity, entity, fidgety, gaiety/gayety (U.S.), graffiti, gravity, guarantee, honesty, karate, levity, liberty, machete, majesty, modesty, nudity, oddity, parity, penalty, piety, poverty, probity, property, puberty, purity, quality, repartee, rickety, sanctity, sanctuary, scarcity, seventy, sovereignty, spaghetti, specialty, three-sixty, trinity, unity, uppity, vanity, velvety.
Austerely, cavalierly, insincerely, severely, sincerely.
[4] **Anybody**, busybody, everybody, fuddy-duddy, hurdy-gurdy, oldie worlde, understudy.
Ability, agility, fertility, fragility, futility, hostility, humility, liability, mobility, nobility, responsibility, stability, tranquillity/tranquility (U.S.), versatility, viability, virility, volatility.

2.1.23 "--eeding" (as in "needing")
[2] bleeding, breeding, ceding, feeding, heeding, kneading, leading, needing, pleading, reading, seeding, speeding, weeding.
[3] conceding, cross-breeding, exceeding, impeding, inbreeding, misleading, misreading, preceding, proceeding, receding, re-reading, re-seeding, seceding, sight-reading, stampeding, succeeding.
[4] interbreeding, interceding, overfeeding, proofreading, superseding.

SURPRISING RHYMING:
[2] **Being**, fleeing, freeing, keying, kneeing, seeing, teeing.
Beating, bleating, cheating, eating, fleeting, greeting, heating, meeting, treating, tweeting.
Creaking, freaking, leaking, peeking, reeking, seeking, shrieking, sneaking, speaking, streaking, squeaking, tweaking, wreaking.
Ceasing, creasing, feasting, fleecing, greasing, leasing, piecing.
Breezing, easing, freezing, pleasing, seizing, sneezing, squeezing, teasing, wheezing.
Beeping, bleeping, cheeping, creeping, heaping, keeping, leaping, peeping, reaping, seeping, sleeping, sweeping, weeping.
Grieving, heaving, leaving, thieving, weaving.
Beaching, bleaching, breaching, breeching, preaching, reaching, screeching, teaching.
[3] **Browbeating**, competing, completing, concreting, deceiving, defeating, deleting, depleting, heart beating, maltreating, mistreating, reheating, repeating, retreating.
Appeasing, decreasing, increasing, policing, releasing.
Achieving, believing, conceiving, debriefing, deceiving, displeasing, perceiving, receiving, relieving, reprieving, reprising, retrieving.
[4] **Disbelieving**, interweaving, make-believing, misconceiving, overachieving, overeating, overheating, preconceiving, underachieving.

2.1.24 "--eediest" (as in "greediest")
[3] beadiest, greediest, neediest, seediest, speediest.

SURPRISING RHYMING:
[1] **Best**, blessed, breast, chest, crest, dressed, guest, guessed, jest, messed, nest, pest, quest, stressed, test, vest, west, zest.
[2] **Abreast**, addressed, arrest, attest, Beau Geste, behest, bequest, caressed, compressed, contest, depressed, detest, digest, digressed, distressed, divest, expressed, footrest, headrest, ingest, inquest, invest, Midwest, molest, northwest, oppressed, possessed, progressed, recessed, repressed, request, southwest, suggest, suppressed, transgressed, undressed, unrest.
[3] **Angriest**, cheeriest, dreariest, eeriest, furious, glorious, grittiest, hairiest, hungriest, merriest, prettiest, scariest, sorriest, weariest, wittiest.
Bumpiest, chirpiest, creepiest, crispiest, crummiest, droopiest, frumpiest, grumpiest, happiest, nippiest, skimpiest, snappiest.
Bloodiest, cloudiest, gaudiest, handiest, moodiest, mouldiest/moldiest (U.S.), muddiest, rowdiest, sandiest, shoddiest, steadiest, sturdiest, tidiest, trendiest, windiest.
Beefiest, comfiest, fluffiest, goofiest, leafiest, scruffiest, stuffiest.
Balmiest, barmiest, creamiest, crummiest, gloomiest, roomiest, seamiest, slimiest, smarmiest, stormiest.

Bonniest, boniest, brainiest, canniest, corniest, dingiest, dodgiest, genius, grainiest, rainiest, scrawniest, shiniest, skinniest, stingiest, tiniest, zaniest.
Bulkiest, chalkiest, cheekiest, creakiest, croakiest, flakiest, freakiest, friskiest, funkiest, hunkiest, huskiest, kinkiest, lankiest, leakiest, luckiest, milkiest, murkiest, perkiest, pluckiest, quirkiest, riskiest, rockiest, shakiest, silkiest, slinkiest, smokiest, sneakiest, spookiest, squeakiest, stickiest, stockiest, swankiest, trickiest, wackiest.
Bubbliest, chilliest, costliest, crinkliest, crumbliest, cuddliest, deadliest, friendliest, frilliest, grizzliest, holiest, kindliest, likeliest, liveliest, loneliest, loveliest, lowliest, oiliest, prickliest, silliest, smelliest, ugliest, wiliest, wobbliest.
Bossiest, classiest, fanciest, fussiest, glitziest, glossiest, greasiest, gutsiest, sauciest, messiest, juiciest, ritziest, sexiest, spiciest.
Craftiest, daintiest, draughtiest/draftiest (U.S.), grittiest, meatiest, nastiest, pettiest, prettiest, shiftiest, sweatiest, tartiest, tastiest, thriftiest, wittiest.
Earthiest, filthiest, frothiest, healthiest, lengthiest, wealthiest.
Chewiest, grooviest, heaviest, screwiest, snowiest.
Burliest, curliest, earliest, funniest, sunniest, surliest.
Dispossessed, effervesced, interest, manifest, reassessed, self-possessed.
Baroness, convalesce, dispossess, effervesce, nonetheless, overstress, poetess, reassess, repossess, shepherdess, stewardess.
Breeziest, cheesiest, easiest, greasiest, sleaziest, wheeziest.

2.1.25 "--eef" (as in "thief")
[1] beef, belief, brief, chief, fief, grief, leaf, reef, sheaf, thief.
[2] broadleaf, debrief, fig leaf, flyleaf, mischief, motif, relief, tea leaf.
[3] aperitif, disbelief, handkerchief, misbelief, overleaf.

SURPRISING RHYMING:
[1] **Be**, bee, fee, flea, flee, gee, glee, he, key, knee, me, sea, see, tee, tea, the, thee, twee, we, wee, whee, zee.
Brie, free, re, spree, three, tree.
Beat, beats, beet, bleat, cheat, cleat, eat, feat, feet, fleet, greet, heat, meat, meet, neat, peat, pleat, seat, sheet, skeet, sleet, street, suite, sweet, treat, tweet, wheat.
Bleed, breed, cede, creed, deed, feed, freed, greed, he'd, heed, keyed, knead, kneed, lead, mead, need, plead, read, reed, seed, she'd, speed, steed, tweed, we'd, weed.
Beak, bleak, cheek, chic, clique, creak, creek, eke, freak, geek, leak, meek, peak, peek, pique, reek, seek, sheik, shriek, sleek, sneak, speak, streak, squeak, teak, tweak, weak, week, wreak.
Cease, crease, fleece, geese, grease, lease, niece, peace, piece.
Beep, bleep, cheep, cheap, creep, deep, heap, jeep, keep, leap, peep, reap, seep, sheep, sleep, steep, sweep, weep.
Beast, ceased, east, feast, fleeced, greased, least, leased, pieced, piste, priest, yeast.
Heath, 'neath, sheath, teeth, wreath.
Eve, grieve, heave, leave, sleeve, thieve, weave, we've.
Breeze, cheese, ease, fees, freeze, frieze, he's, jeez, keys, knees, please, sees, seize, she's, sleaze, sneeze, squeeze, teas, tease, tees, these, trees, tweeze, wheeze.
Beach, beech, bleach, breach, breech, each, leach, leech, peach, preach, reach, screech, speech, teach.
[2] **Athlete**, backbeat, backstreet, breakbeat, broadsheet, browbeat, buckwheat, compete, complete, conceit, concrete, deadbeat, deceit, defeat, delete, deplete, discreet, discrete, downbeat, drumbeat, dustsheet, effete, elite, entreat, excrete, flysheet, groundsheet, heartbeat, maltreat, mincemeat, mistreat, offbeat, petite, receipt, reheat, repeat, reseat, retreat, secrete, spreadsheet, sweetmeat, time sheet, upbeat.
Agreed, airspeed, birdseed, concede, chickweed, crossbreed, decreed, exceed, flaxseed, Godspeed, handfeed, hayseed, impede, inbreed, indeed, knock-kneed, linseed, lip-read, milkweed, misdeed, mislead, misread, nosebleed, precede, proceed, recede, re-read, seaweed, secede, sight-read, spoon-feed, stampede, succeed.
Antique, boutique, critique, midweek, mystique, oblique, physique, technique, unique.
Apiece, caprice, cassis, decease, decrease, hairpiece, increase, mouthpiece, neckpiece, obese, police, release, sublease, timepiece, two-piece, valise.
Asleep, chimney sweep, oversleep, scrapheap, skin-deep, upkeep.

Artiste, decreased, deceased, increased, northeast, policed, released, southeast.
Beneath, bequeath, eyeteeth, underneath.
Achieve, aggrieve, believe, bereave, conceive, deceive, naïve, perceive, receive, relieve, reprieve, retrieve, shirtsleeve.
Appease, Aries, chemise, deep-freeze, degrees, disease, displease, herpes, Pisces, reprise, species, striptease, trapeze, unease, unfreeze, valise.
[3] **Bittersweet**, easy street, incomplete, indiscreet, obsolete, overeat, overheat.
Aniseed, centipede, chickenfeed, cottonseed, disagreed, filigreed, guaranteed, interbreed, intercede, overfeed, pedigreed, proofread, refereed, supersede, tumbleweed.
Hide-and-seek, technospeak, tongue-in-cheek.
Centerpiece/centerpiece (U.S.), mantelpiece, masterpiece, predecease, unreleased.
Disbelieve, make-believe, misconceive, overachieve, preconceive, underachieve.
Achilles, antifreeze, emojis, enemies, expertise, guarantees, Hercules, indices, journalese, legalese, melodies, overseas.
Burgundy, chickadee, COD, comedy, custody, dogsbody, fool-hardy, jeopardy, malady, melody, nobody, parody, Ph.D., raggedy, remedy, rhapsody, somebody, tragedy.
Allergy, effigy, emoji, energy, eulogy, lethargy, refugee, strategy, synergy, trilogy.
Actressy, agency, autopsy, bankruptcy, blatancy, bourgeoisie, buoyancy, Christmassy, clemency, courtesy, currency, decency, divorcee, ecstasy, embassy, fallacy, fantasy, fluency, galaxy, heresy, infancy, jealousy, legacy, leniency, lunacy, odyssey, oversee, pharmacy, piracy, policy, potency, pregnancy, primacy, privacy, prophecy, regency, secrecy, tendency, Tennessee, truancy, undersea, urgency, vacancy.
Absentee, amnesty, brevity, casualty, certainty, charity, chastity, clarity, committee, confetti, crotchety, crudity, density, deputy, devotee, dignity, dynasty, enmity, entity, fidgety, gaiety/gayety (U.S.), graffiti, gravity, guarantee, honesty, karate, levity, liberty, machete, majesty, modesty, nudity, oddity, parity, penalty, piety, poverty, probity, property, puberty, purity, quality, repartee, rickety, sanctity, sanctuary, scarcity, seventy, sovereignty, spaghetti, specialty, three-sixty, trinity, unity, uppity, vanity, velvety.

2.1.26 "--eek" (as in "cheek")
[1] beak, bleak, cheek, chic, clique, creak, creek, eke, freak, geek, leak, leek, meek, peak, peek, pique, reek, seek, sheik, shriek, sleek, sneak, speak, streak, squeak, teak, tweak, weak, week, wreak.
[2] antique, boutique, critique, midweek, mystique, oblique, physique, pipsqueak, technique, unique.
[3] hide-and-seek, technospeak, tongue-in-cheek.

SURPRISING RHYMING:
[1] **Be**, bee, fee, flea, flee, gee, glee, he, key, knee, me, sea, see, tee, tea, the, thee, twee, we, wee, whee, zee.
Brie, free, re, spree, three, tree.
Beat, beats, beet, bleat, cheat, cleat, eat, feat, feet, fleet, greet, heat, meat, meet, neat, peat, pleat, seat, sheet, skeet, sleet, street, suite, sweet, treat, tweet, wheat.
Bleed, breed, cede, creed, deed, feed, freed, greed, he'd, heed, keyed, knead, kneed, lead, mead, need, plead, read, reed, seed, she'd, speed, steed, tweed, we'd, weed.
Cease, crease, fleece, geese, grease, lease, niece, peace, piece.
Beep, bleep, cheep, cheap, creep, deep, heap, jeep, keep, leap, peep, reap, seep, sheep, sleep, steep, sweep, weep.
Beef, belief, brief, chief, fief, grief, leaf, reef, sheaf, thief.
Beast, ceased, east, feast, fleeced, greased, least, leased, pieced, piste, priest, yeast.
Heath, 'neath, sheath, teeth, wreath.
Eve, grieve, heave, leave, peeve, sleeve, thieve, weave, we've.
Breeze, cheese, ease, fees, freeze, frieze, he's, jeez, keys, knees, please, sees, seize, she's, sleaze, sneeze, squeeze, teas, tease, tees, these, trees, tweeze, wheeze.
Beach, beech, bleach, breach, breech, each, leach, leech, peach, preach, reach, screech, speech, teach.
[2] **Athlete**, backbeat, backstreet, breakbeat, broadsheet, browbeat, buckwheat, compete, complete, conceit, concrete, deadbeat, deceit, defeat, delete, deplete, discreet, discrete, downbeat, drumbeat, dustsheet, effete, elite, entreat, excrete, flysheet, groundsheet, heartbeat, maltreat, mincemeat, mistreat, offbeat, petite, receipt,

reheat, repeat, reseat, retreat, secrete, spreadsheet, sweetmeat, time sheet, upbeat.
Agreed, airspeed, birdseed, concede, decreed, exceed, Godspeed, handfeed, impede, indeed, knock-kneed, lip-read, misdeed, mislead, misread, nosebleed, precede, proceed, recede, seaweed, sight-read, spoon-feed, stampede, succeed.
Apiece, caprice, cassis, decease, decrease, hairpiece, increase, mouthpiece, obese, police, release, sublease, timepiece, two-piece, valise.
Asleep, chimney sweep, oversleep, scrapheap, skin-deep, upkeep.
Artiste, decreased, deceased, increased, northeast, policed, released, southeast.
Beneath, bequeath, eyeteeth, underneath.
Debrief, fig leaf, flyleaf, mischief, motif, relief, tea leaf.
Achieve, aggrieve, believe, bereave, conceive, deceive, naïve, perceive, receive, relieve, reprieve, retrieve, shirtsleeve, upheave.
Appease, Aries, chemise, deep-freeze, degrees, disease, displease, herpes, Pisces, reprise, species, striptease, trapeze, unease, unfreeze, valise.
[3] **Bittersweet**, easy street, incomplete, indiscreet, obsolete, overeat, overheat.
Aniseed, centipede, chickenfeed, cottonseed, disagreed, filigreed, guaranteed, interbreed, intercede, millipede, overfeed, proofread, refereed, supersede, tumbleweed.
Centerpiece/centerpiece, frontispiece, mantelpiece, masterpiece, unreleased.
Disbelieve, interleave, interweave, make-believe, misconceive, overachieve, preconceive, reconceive, semibreve, underachieve.
Aperitif, disbelief, handkerchief, misbelief, overleaf.
Achilles, antifreeze, emojis, enemies, expertise, guarantees, Hercules, indices, legalese, manganese, melodies, overseas.
Burgundy, chickadee, COD, comedy, custody, dogsbody, fool-hardy, jeopardy, malady, melody, nobody, parody, Ph.D., raggedy, remedy, rhapsody, somebody, tragedy.
Allergy, effigy, emoji, energy, eulogy, lethargy, refugee, strategy, synergy, trilogy.
Actressy, agency, autopsy, bankruptcy, blatancy, bourgeoisie, buoyancy, Christmassy, clemency, courtesy, currency, decency, divorcee, ecstasy, embassy, fallacy, fantasy, fluency, galaxy, heresy, infancy, jealousy, legacy, leniency, lunacy, odyssey, oversee, pharmacy, piracy, policy, potency, pregnancy, primacy, privacy, prophecy, regency, secrecy, tendency, Tennessee, truancy, undersea, urgency, vacancy.
Absentee, amnesty, brevity, casualty, certainty, charity, chastity, clarity, committee, confetti, crotchety, crudity, density, deputy, devotee, dignity, dynasty, enmity, entity, fidgety, gaiety/gayety (U.S.), graffiti, gravity, guarantee, honesty, karate, levity, liberty, machete, majesty, modesty, nudity, oddity, parity, penalty, piety, poverty, probity, property, puberty, purity, quality, repartee, rickety, sanctity, sanctuary, scarcity, seventy, sovereignty, spaghetti, specialty, three-sixty, trinity, unity, uppity, vanity, velvety.

2.1.27 "--eeked" (as in "sneaked")
[1] cheeked, creaked, eked, freaked, leaked, peaked, peeked, piqued, reeked, shrieked, sneaked, streaked, squeaked, tweaked, wreaked.
[2] antiqued, eagle-beaked, pink-cheeked, red-cheeked, rosy-cheeked.

SURPRISING RHYMING:
[1] **Beat**, beats, beet, bleat, cheat, cleat, eat, feat, feet, fleet, greet, heat, meat, meet, neat, peat, pleat, seat, sheet, skeet, sleet, street, suite, sweet, treat, tweet, wheat.
Bleed, breed, cede, creed, deed, feed, freed, greed, he'd, heed, keyed, knead, kneed, lead, mead, need, plead, read, reed, seed, she'd, speed, steed, tweed, we'd, weed.
Beep, bleep, cheep, cheap, creep, deep, heap, jeep, keep, leap, peep, reap, seep, sheep, sleep, steep, sweep, weep.
Beast, ceased, east, feast, fleeced, greased, least, leased, pieced, piste, priest, yeast.
[2] **Athlete**, backbeat, backstreet, breakbeat, broadsheet, browbeat, buckwheat, compete, complete, conceit, concrete, deadbeat, deceit, defeat, delete, deplete, discreet, discrete, downbeat, drumbeat, dustsheet, effete, elite, entreat, excrete, flysheet, groundsheet, heartbeat, maltreat, mincemeat, mistreat, offbeat, petite, receipt, reheat, repeat, reseat, retreat, secrete, spreadsheet, sweetmeat, time sheet, upbeat.
Agreed, airspeed, birdseed, concede, decreed, exceed, Godspeed, handfeed, impede, indeed, knock-kneed, lip-read, misdeed, mislead, misread, nosebleed, precede, proceed, recede, seaweed, sight-read, spoon-feed, stampede, succeed.
Asleep, chimney sweep, oversleep, scrapheap, skin-deep, upkeep.

Artiste, decreased, deceased, increased, policed, released.
[3] **Bittersweet**, easy street, incomplete, indiscreet, obsolete, overeat, overheat.
Aniseed, centipede, chickenfeed, disagreed, filigreed, guaranteed, intercede, millipede, overfeed, pedigreed, proofread, refereed, supersede, tumbleweed.

2.1.28 "--eeker" (as in "seeker")
[2] beaker, bleaker, leaker, meeker, peeker, seeker, shrieker, sleeker, sneaker, speaker, streaker, squeaker, tikka, tweaker, weaker, wreaker.
[3] eureka, loudspeaker.

SURPRISING RHYMING:
[2] **Bleeder**, breeder, cedar, feeder, heeder, leader, pleader, reader, seeder, speeder.
Beeper, bleeper, cheaper, creeper, deeper, keeper, leaper, peeper, reaper, sleeper, steeper, sweeper, weeper.
Beezer, Caesar, Deezer, easer, freezer, geezer, geyser, pleaser, sneezer, squeezer, teaser, tweezer, visa, wheezer.
Dealer, feeler, healer, heeler, kneeler, peeler, sealer, spieler, stealer, squealer, wheeler.
Cleaner, gleaner, greener, keener, leaner, meaner, screener, serener, weaner, wiener.
Beamer, creamer, dreamer, prima, schemer, screamer, steamer, streamer.
[3] **Bandleader**, cheerleader, corrida, lip-reader, mind-reader, misleader, newsreader, ringleader, stampeder, succeeder.
Barkeeper, beekeeper, bookkeeper, doorkeeper, gamekeeper, gatekeeper, goalkeeper, housekeeper, innkeeper, peacekeeper, shopkeeper, storekeeper, timekeeper, wicketkeeper, zookeeper.
Appeaser, blasphemer, daydreamer, displeaser, Mona Lisa.
Appealer, enfant terrible, faith-healer, tequila, wheeler-dealer.
Arena, cantina, czarina/tsarina, demeanour/demeanor (U.S.), hyena, marina, redeemer.
[4] **Disbeliever**, interweaver, make-believer, misconceiver, overachiever, underachiever.
Ballerina, concertina, misdemeanour/misdemeanor (U.S.).

2.1.29 "--eeking" (as in "seeking")
[2] creaking, eking, freaking, leaking, peaking, peeking, reeking, seeking, self-seeking, shrieking, sleeking, sneaking, speaking, streaking, squeaking, tweaking, wreaking.

SURPRISING RHYMING:
[2] **Beeping**, bleeping, cheeping, creeping, heaping, keeping, leaping, peeping, reaping, seeping, sleeping, sweeping, weeping.
Beating, bleating, cheating, eating, fleeting, greeting, heating, meeting, seating, sheeting, treating, tweeting.
Bleeding, breeding, feeding, heeding, leading, needing, pleading, reading, speeding.
Beaming, creaming, dreaming, scheming, screaming, steaming, streaming.
Cleaning, demeaning, gleaning, greening, leaning, meaning, screening, weaning.
Ceiling, dealing, feeling, healing, kneeling, pealing, peeling, reeling, sealing, stealing, squealing, wheeling.
Beaching, bleaching, breaching, breeching, preaching, reaching, screeching, teaching.
Breezing, easing, freezing, pleasing, seizing, sneezing, squeezing, teasing, wheezing.
[3] **Browbeating**, competing, completing, concreting, deceiving, defeating, deleting, depleting, heart beating, maltreating, mistreating, reheating, repeating, retreating.
Appealing, revealing, self-sealing, wheeler-dealing.
Appeasing, blaspheming, daydreaming, decreasing, increasing, policing, releasing.
Achieving, believing, conceiving, deceiving, displeasing, perceiving, receiving, redeeming, relieving, reprieving, reprising, retrieving.

2.1.30 "--eekly" (as in "weekly")
[2] bleakly, meekly, sleekly, weakly, weekly.
[3] biweekly, obliquely, triweekly, uniquely.

SURPRISING RHYMING:
[2] **Clearly**, dearly, freely, merely, nearly, queerly, really, yearly.

Cleanly, keenly, leanly, queenly, seemly.
Cheaply, deeply, steeply.
[3] Austerely, cavalierly, insincerely, severely, sincerely.
Completely, concretely, discreetly, discretely, incompletely, indiscreetly.
Obscenely, pristinely, routinely, serenely.
[4] Ability, agility, fertility, fragility, futility, hostility, humility, liability, mobility, nobility, responsibility, stability, tranquillity/tranquility (U.S.), versatility, viability, virility, volatility.

2.1.31 "--eel" (as in "feel")

[1] deal, eel, feel, heal, heel, he'll, keel, kneel, meal, peal, peel, real, reel, seal, she'll, steal, steel, spiel, squeal, teal, they'll, veal, we'll, wheel, zeal.
[2] appeal, cartwheel, conceal, congeal, cornmeal, flywheel, freewheel, genteel, ideal, newsreel, oatmeal, ordeal, piecemeal, repeal, reveal, spiel, unreal, unseal.
[3] automobile, glockenspiel, imbecile, paddle-wheel, snowmobile, steering wheel.

SURPRISING RHYMING:
[1] Field, healed, heeled, keeled, kneeled, pealed, peeled, sealed, shield, steeled, squealed, wheeled, wield, yield.
[2] Afield, airfield, appealed, congealed, cornfield, freewheeled, gumshield, infield, midfield, minefield, oilfield, outfield, repealed, revealed, unpeeled, unsealed, upfield, well-heeled, windshield.
[3] Battlefield, unconcealed, unrepealed, unrevealed.

2.1.32 "--eeled" (as in "sealed")

[1] field, healed, heeled, keeled, kneeled, pealed, peeled, sealed, shield, steeled, squealed, wheeled, wield, yield.
[2] afield, airfield, appealed, congealed, cornfield, freewheeled, gumshield, infield, midfield, minefield, oilfield, outfield, repealed, revealed, unpeeled, unsealed, upfield, well-heeled, windshield.
[3] battlefield, chesterfield, unconcealed, unrepealed, unrevealed.

SURPRISING RHYMING:
[1] Deal, eel, feel, heal, heel, he'll, keel, kneel, meal, peal, peel, real, reel, seal, she'll, steal, steel, spiel, squeal, teal, they'll, veal, we'll, wheel, zeal.
[2] Appeal, cartwheel, chenille, conceal, congeal, flywheel, freewheel, genteel, ideal, newsreel, oatmeal, ordeal, piecemeal, repeal, reveal, spiel, unreal, unseal, wholemeal.
[3] Automobile, glockenspiel, goldenseal, imbecile, paddle-wheel, snowmobile, steering wheel, unideal, unreal.

2.1.33 "--eelded" (as in "shielded")

[2] fielded, shielded, wielded, yielded.

SURPRISING RHYMING:
[2] Beaded, ceded, deeded, heeded, needed, pleaded, seeded, weeded.
Bleated, cheated, greeted, heated, meted, pleated, seated, sheeted, treated, tweeted.
Agreed it, beat it, eat it, tweet it, read it.
[3] Acceded, conceded, exceeded, impeded, preceded, proceeded, receded, stampeded, succeeded, unheeded, unneeded.
Competed, completed, conceited, defeated, deleted, depleted, entreated, excreted, mistreated, preheated, reheated, repeated, reseated, retreated, secreted, undefeated, unheated, unseated.

2.1.34 "--eelding" (as in "shielding")

[2] fielding, shielding, wielding, yielding.

SURPRISING RHYMING:
[2] Ceiling, dealing, feeling, healing, kneeling, pealing, peeling, reeling, sealing, stealing, squealing, wheeling.
Bleeding, breeding, feeding, heeding, leading, needing, pleading, reading, speeding.

Beaming, creaming, dreaming, scheming, screaming, streaming.
Cleaning, greening, keening, leaning, meaning, screening, weaning.
Beating, bleating, cheating, eating, fleeting, greeting, heating, meeting, pleating, seating, sheeting, treating, tweeting.
Creaking, freaking, leaking, peeking, reeking, seeking, shrieking, sneaking, speaking, streaking, squeaking, tweaking, wreaking.
Ceasing, creasing, feasting, fleecing, greasing, leasing, piecing.
Beeping, bleeping, cheeping, creeping, heaping, keeping, leaping, peeping, reaping, seeping, sleeping, sweeping, weeping.
Grieving, heaving, leaving, nearing, thieving, weaving.
Breezing, easing, freezing, pleasing, seizing, sneezing, squeezing, teasing, wheezing.
Beaching, bleaching, preaching, reaching, screeching, teaching.
[3] **Appealing**, revealing, self-sealing, wheeler-dealing.
Adhering, appearing, disappearing, endearing, God-fearing, veneering.
Convening, demeaning, dry-cleaning, overweening, spring-cleaning, well-meaning.
Conceding, cross-breeding, exceeding, impeding, misleading, misreading, preceding, proceeding, receding, re-reading, sight-reading, stampeding, succeeding, unheeding.
Browbeating, competing, completing, concreting, deceiving, defeating, deleting, depleting, heart beating, maltreating, mistreating, reheating, repeating, retreating.
Appeasing, decreasing, increasing, policing, releasing.
Achieving, believing, conceiving, debriefing, deceiving, displeasing, perceiving, receiving, relieving, reprieving, reprising, retrieving.

2.1.35 "--eeler" (as in "healer")
[2] dealer, feeler, healer, kneeler, peeler, reeler, sealer, spieler, stealer, squealer.
[3] appealer, concealer, enfant terrible, faith-healer, revealer, tequila, wheeler-dealer.

SURPRISING RHYMING:
[2] **Beaver**, cleaver, griever, heaver, leaver, weaver.
Bleeder, breeder, cedar, feeder, heeder, leader, pleader, reader, seeder, speeder.
Caesar, Deezer, easer, freezer, geezer, geyser, pleaser, sneezer, squeezer, teaser, tweezer, visa, wheezer.
Beamer, creamer, dreamer, prima, schemer, steamer, streamer.
Cleaner, greener, keener, leaner, meaner, screener, serener.
Cheerer, clearer, dearer, nearer, queerer, severer, shearer, sincerer.
Beeper, bleeper, cheaper, creeper, deeper, keeper, leaper, peeper, reaper, sleeper, steeper, sweeper, weeper.
Creature, feature, freer, preacher, screecher, teacher, schoolteacher.
Beaker, bleaker, leaker, meeker, peeker, seeker, sleeker, sneaker, speaker, streaker, squeaker, tikka, weaker, wreaker.
[3] **Achiever**, believer, deceiver, perceiver, receiver, reliever, retriever, school-leaver.
Bandleader, cheerleader, corrida, lip-reader, mind-reader, misleader, newsreader, ringleader, stampeder, succeeder.
Appealer, enfant terrible, eureka, faith-healer, tequila, wheeler-dealer.
Appeaser, blasphemer, daydreamer, displeaser, Mona Lisa.
Arena, cantina, czarina/tsarina, demeanour/demeanor (U.S.), hyena, marina, redeemer.
[4] **Disbeliever**, make-believer, overachiever, underachiever.
Ballerina, concertina, misdemeanour/misdemeanor (U.S.).

2.1.36 "--eeling" (as in "feeling")
[2] ceiling, dealing, feeling, healing, kneeling, pealing, peeling, reeling, sealing, stealing, squealing, wheeling.
[3] appealing, concealing, congealing, repealing, revealing, unfeeling.

SURPRISING RHYMING:
[2] **Fielding**, shielding, wielding, yielding.
Agreeing, being, fleeing, freeing, seeing, skiing, teeing.
Grieving, heaving, leaving, thieving, weaving.
Cheering, clearing, earring, fearing, hearing, jeering, leering, nearing, peering, rearing, sneering, spearing, steering, veering.

Bleeding, breeding, feeding, heeding, leading, needing, pleading, reading, speeding.
Beaming, dreaming, scheming, screaming, steaming, streaming.
Cleaning, keening, leaning, meaning, screening, weaning.
Beating, bleating, cheating, eating, fleeting, greeting, heating, meeting, seating, sheeting, treating, tweeting.
Beeping, bleeping, creeping, heaping, keeping, leaping, peeping, piecing, reaping, seeping, sleeping, sweeping, weeping.
Breezing, ceasing, easing, feasting, fleecing, freezing, greasing, pleasing, seizing, sneezing, squeezing, teasing, tweezing, wheezing.
Beaching, bleaching, breaching, breeching, preaching, reaching, screeching, teaching.
Creaking, freaking, leaking, peeking, reeking, seeking, shrieking, sneaking, speaking, streaking, squeaking, tweaking, wreaking.
[3] **Decreeing**, farseeing, foreseeing, human being, sightseeing, unseeing, well-being.
Achieving, believing, conceiving, deceiving, displeasing, perceiving, receiving, relieving, reprieving, reprising, retrieving.
Adhering, appearing, disappearing, endearing, God-fearing, veneering.
Demeaning, dry-cleaning, overweening, re-convening, spring-cleaning, well-meaning.
Conceding, cross-breeding, exceeding, impeding, misleading, misreading, preceding, proceeding, receding, re-reading, sight-reading, stampeding, succeeding, unheeding.
Browbeating, competing, completing, deceiving, defeating, deleting, depleting, heart beating, maltreating, mistreating, reheating, repeating, retreating.
Appeasing, decreasing, increasing, policing, releasing.
[4] **Disbelieving**, make-believing, misconceiving, overachieving, self-deceiving.

2.1.37 "--eem" (as in "seem")
[1] beam, bream, cream, deem, dream, gleam, meme, scheme, scream, seam, seem, steam, team, teem, theme.
[2] airstream, blaspheme, crossbeam, daydream, downstream, esteem, extreme, ice-cream, jet stream, light-beam, mainstream, millstream, moonbeam, redeem, regime, self-esteem, slipstream, sunbeam, supreme, upstream.

SURPRISING RHYMING:
[1] **Beamed**, creamed, deemed, dreamed, gleamed, schemed, screamed, seemed, steamed, streamed, teamed, teemed, themed.
Bean, been, clean, dean, gene, glean, green, keen, lean, mean, preen, queen, scene, screen, seen, sheen, spleen, teen, ween.
Be, bee, fee, flea, flee, gee, glee, he, key, knee, me, sea, see, tee, tea, the, thee, twee, we, wee, whee, zee.
Brie, free, re, spree, three, tree.
[2] **Beguine**, between, caffeine, canteen, codeine, colleen, convene, cuisine, daydream, demean, eighteen, fanzine, fifteen, foreseen, fourteen, has-been, hygiene, kerosene, machine, marine, May Queen, morphine, nineteen, obscene, pea-green, pristine, protein, ravine, redeemed, routine, sardine, sea-green, serene, sixteen, smokescreen, spring-clean, thirteen, unclean, umpteen, unseen, vaccine, widescreen, windscreen.
[3] **Contravene(d)**, crimplene, evergreen, figurine, gasoline, go-between, guillotine, Halloween, in-between, intervene(d), jellybean, kerosene, libertine, limousine, magazine, margarine, nectarine, nicotine, overseen, quarantine, saccharine, seventeen, submarine, tambourine, tangerine, trampoline, unforeseen, Vaseline, wintergreen, wolverine.

2.1.38 "--eemed" (as in "seemed")
[1] beamed, creamed, deemed, dreamed, gleamed, reamed, schemed, screamed, seamed, seemed, steamed, streamed, teamed, teemed, themed.
[2] blasphemed, daydreamed, esteemed, redeemed.

SURPRISING RHYMING:
[1] **Beam**, cream, deem, dream, gleam, meme, scheme, scream, seam, seem, steam, stream, team, teem, theme.
Bean, been, clean, dean, gene, glean, green, keen, lean, mean, preen, queen, scene, screen, seen, sheen, spleen, teen.

Be, bee, fee, flea, flee, gee, glee, he, key, knee, me, sea, see, tee, tea, the, thee, twee, we, wee, whee, zee.
Brie, free, re, spree, three, tree.
Cleaned, fiend, gleaned, keened, leaned, preened, queened, screened, weaned.
[2] **Airstream**, blaspheme, crossbeam, daydream, downstream, esteem, extreme, ice-cream, jet stream, light-beam, mainstream, millstream, moonbeam, redeem, regime, self-esteem, slipstream, sunbeam, supreme, upstream.
Beguine, between, caffeine, canteen, codeine, colleen, convene, cuisine, daydream, demean, eighteen, fanzine, fifteen, foreseen, fourteen, has-been, hygiene, kerosene, machine, marine, May Queen, morphine, nineteen, obscene, pea-green, pristine, protein, ravine, redeemed, routine, sardine, sea-green, serene, sixteen, smokescreen, spring-clean, thirteen, unclean, umpteen, unseen, vaccine, widescreen, windscreen.
Archfiend, careened, convened, demeaned, spring-cleaned.
[3] **Contravene(d)**, evergreen, figurine, gasoline, go-between, guillotine(d), Halloween, in-between, intervene(d), jellybean, kerosene, libertine, limousine, magazine, margarine, nectarine, nicotine, overseen, quarantine(d), saccharine, seventeen, submarine, tambourine, tangerine, trampoline(d), unforeseen, Vaseline, wintergreen, wolverine.
[4] **Aquamarine**, polystyrene.

2.1.39 "--eemer" (as in "dreamer")
[2] beamer, creamer, dreamer, prima, reamer, schemer, screamer, steamer, streamer.
[3] blasphemer, daydreamer, redeemer.

SURPRISING RHYMING:
[2] **Cleaner**, gleaner, greener, keener, leaner, meaner.
Dealer, feeler, healer, heeler, kneeler, peeler, sealer, stealer, squealer, wheeler.
Beeper, bleeper, cheaper, creeper, deeper, keeper, leaper, peeper, reaper, sleeper, steeper, sweeper, weeper.
Bleeder, breeder, cedar, feeder, heeder, leader, pleader, reader, seeder, speeder.
Caesar, Deezer, easer, freezer, geezer, geyser, pleaser, sneezer, squeezer, teaser, tweezer, visa, wheezer.
[3] **Arena**, cantina, czarina/tsarina, demeanour/demeanor (U.S.), hyena, marina.
Bandleader, cheerleader, conceder, lip-reader, mind-reader, misleader, newsreader, ringleader, stampeder, succeeder.
Achiever, believer, deceiver, receiver, retriever, school-leaver.
Enfant terrible, faith-healer, revealer, tequila, wheeler-dealer.
[4] **Disbeliever**, make-believer, overachiever, underachiever.
Ballerina, concertina, misdemeanour/misdemeanor (U.S.).

2.1.40 "--eemy" (as in "dreamy")
[2] creamy, dreamy, gleamy, seamy, screamy, steamy.

SURPRISING RHYMING:
[1] **Be**, bee, fee, gee, he, key, knee, me, sea, see, tee, tea, the, thee, twee, we, wee, whee, zee.
[2] **Beanie**, genie, greenie, meanie, queenie, teeny, teensy, tweeny, weeny, weenie.
Beady, beefy, greedy, leafy, needy, seedy, speedy, tweedy, weedy.
Bleary, cheery, dreary, eerie, freely, leery, query, teary, theory, weary.
Breezy, cheesy, easy, greasy, sleazy, squeezy, uneasy, wheezy.
Cheapie, creepy, recipe, sleepy, sweetpea, teepee, weepy.
Cheeky, cliquey, creaky, freaky, leaky, sneaky, squeaky, streaky, weakly, weekly.
Beastly, cleanly, really, seemly, steely, wheelie.
[3] **Bumblebee**, comedy, honeybee, Houdini, wallaby, wannabe.

2.1.41 "--eeming" (as in "dreaming")
[2] beaming, creaming, deeming, dreaming, gleaming, reaming, scheming, screaming, seaming, seeming, steaming, streaming, teaming, teeming.
[3] blaspheming, daydreaming, redeeming.

SURPRISING RHYMING:
[2] **Cleaning**, gleaning, leaning, meaning, screening, weaning.
Breathing, grieving, leaving, seething, teething, thieving, weaving.
Ceiling, dealing, feeling, healing, kneeling, pealing, peeling, reeling, sealing, stealing, squealing, wheeling.
Bleeding, breeding, feeding, heeding, leading, needing, pleading, reading, speeding.
Beating, bleating, cheating, eating, fleeting, greeting, heating, meeting, pleating, seating, sheeting, treating, tweeting.
Cheering, clearing, earring, fearing, gearing, hearing, jeering, leering, nearing, peering, rearing, searing, shearing, sneering, spearing, steering, tearing, veering.
Creaking, freaking, leaking, peaking, peeking, reeking, seeking, shrieking, sneaking, speaking, streaking, squeaking, tweaking.
Beeping, bleeping, cheeping, creeping, heaping, keeping, leaping, peeping, reaping, seeping, sleeping, sweeping, weeping.
Ceasing, creasing, feasting, fleecing, greasing, leasing, piecing.
Breezing, easing, freezing, pleasing, seizing, sneezing, squeezing, teasing, wheezing.
[3] **Demeaning**, dry-cleaning, overweening, re-convening, spring-cleaning, well-meaning.
Achieving, believing, conceiving, deceiving, displeasing, perceiving, receiving, relieving, reprieving, reprising, retrieving.
Conceding, exceeding, impeding, inbreeding, misleading, misreading, preceding, proceeding, receding, stampeding, succeeding.
Appealing, appeasing, decreasing, increasing, policing, releasing, revealing.
Adhering, appearing, disappearing, endearing, God-fearing, veneering.
Browbeating, competing, completing, defeating, deleting, mistreating, repeating, retreating.

2.1.42 "--een" (as in "been")
[1] bean, been, clean, dean, gene, glean, green, keen, lean, lien, mean, preen, queen, scene, screen, seen, sheen, spleen, teen, wean, ween.
[2] beguine, benzene, between, caffeine, canteen, careen, codeine, colleen, convene, cuisine, demean, eighteen, fanzine, fifteen, foreseen, fourteen, has-been, hygiene, kerosene, machine, marine, May Queen, morphine, nineteen, obscene, pea-green, pristine, protein, ravine, routine, sardine, sea-green, serene, sixteen, smokescreen, spring-clean, thirteen, unclean, umpteen, unseen, vaccine, widescreen, windscreen.
[3] contravene, crimplene, dopamine, evergreen, figurine, gabardine, gasoline, go-between, guillotine, Halloween, in-between, intervene, jellybean, kerosene, libertine, limousine, magazine, margarine, mezzanine, nectarine, nicotine, overseen, peregrine, polythene, quarantine, saccharine, serpentine, seventeen, submarine, tambourine, tangerine, trampoline, TV screen, unforeseen, Vaseline, wintergreen, wolverine.
[4] aquamarine, polystyrene.

SURPRISING RHYMING:
[1] **Be**, bee, fee, flea, flee, gee, glee, he, key, knee, me, sea, see, tee, tea, the, thee, twee, we, wee, whee, zee.
Brie, free, re, spree, three, tree.
Cleaned, fiend, gleaned, keened, leaned, preened, queened, screened, weaned.
Beam(ed), cream(ed), deem(ed), dream(ed), gleam(ed), meme, ream, scheme(d), scream(ed), seam, seem(ed), steam(ed), stream(ed), team(ed), teem(ed), theme(d).
[2] **Airstream**, blaspheme, crossbeam, daydream, downstream, esteem, extreme, ice-cream, jet stream, light-beam, mainstream, millstream, moonbeam, redeem, regime, self-esteem, slipstream, sunbeam, supreme, upstream.
Convened, demeaned, machined, spring-cleaned.
[4] **Ability**, agility, fertility, fragility, futility, gravity, hostility, humility, mobility, nobility, sanity, self-pity, stability, tranquility, utility, virility.
[5] **Edibility**, liability, responsibility, usability, versatility, viability, volatility.

2.1.43 "--eened" (as in "leaned")
[1] cleaned, fiend, gleaned, keened, leaned, preened, queened, screened, weaned.
[2] archfiend, careened, convened, demeaned, machined, spring-cleaned, trampolined.
[3] contravened, guillotined, intervened, quarantined.

SURPRISING RHYMING:
[1] **Beamed**, creamed, deemed, dreamed, gleamed, schemed, screamed, seemed, steamed, streamed, teamed, teemed, themed.
Bead, bleed, breed, cede, creed, deed, feed, freed, greed, he'd, heed, keyed, kneed, lead, mead, need, plead, read, reed, seed, she'd, speed, steed, tweed, we'd.
Cleaved, grieved, heaved, peeved, sleeved, thieved.
[2] **Blasphemed**, daydreamed, esteemed, redeemed.
Agreed, airspeed, birdseed, concede, decreed, exceed, Godspeed, handfeed, impede, indeed, knock-kneed, lip-read, misdeed, mislead, misread, nosebleed, precede, proceed, recede, seaweed, sight-read, spoon-feed, stampede, succeed.
Achieved, aggrieved, believed, bereaved, conceived, deceived, perceived, received, relieved, reprieved, retrieved.
[3] **Aniseed**, centipede, chickenfeed, disagreed, filigreed, guaranteed, intercede, millipede, overfeed, pedigreed, proofread, refereed, supersede, tumbleweed.
Disbelieved, misconceived, overachieved, preconceived.

2.1.44 "--eena" (as in "greener")
[2] cleaner, gleaner, greener, keener, leaner, meaner, screener, serener, weaner.
[3] arena, cantina, czarina/tsarina, demeanour/demeanor (.U.S.), hyena, marina.
[4] ballerina, concertina, misdemeanour/misdemeanor (U.S.), signorina.

SURPRISING RHYMING:
[2] **Beamer**, dreamer, prima, schemer, screamer, steamer, streamer.
Dealer, feeler, healer, heeler, kneeler, peeler, sealer, stealer, squealer, wheeler.
Bleeder, breeder, cedar, feeder, heeder, leader, pleader, reader, seeder, speeder.
Deezer, easer, freezer, geezer, pleaser, sneezer, squeezer, teaser, tweezer, visa.
Beeper, bleeper, cheaper, creeper, deeper, keeper, leaper, peeper, reaper, sleeper, steeper, sweeper, weeper.
[3] **Blasphemer**, daydreamer, redeemer.
Bandleader, cheerleader, conceder, lip-reader, mind-reader, misleader, newsreader, ringleader, stampeder, succeeder.
Achiever, appeaser, believer, deceiver, Mona Lisa, receiver, retriever, school-leaver.
Enfant terrible, faith-healer, revealer, tequila, wheeler-dealer.
[4] **Disbeliever**, interweaver, make-believer, misconceiver, overachiever, underachiever.
Ballerina, concertina, misdemeanour/misdemeanor (U.S.).

2.1.45 "--eenest" (as in "greenest")
[2] cleanest, greenest, keenest, leanest, meanest.

SURPRISING RHYMING:
[1] **Best**, blessed, breast, chest, crest, dressed, guest, guessed, jest, messed, nest, pest, quest, stressed, test, vest, west, zest.
[2] **Clearest**, dearest, merest, nearest, queerest, severest, sincerest.
Cheerless, earless, fearless, gearless, idealess, peerless, tearless.
Cheapest, deepest, steepest.
Abreast, addressed, arrest, attest, Beau Geste, behest, bequest, caressed, contest, depressed, detest, digest, digressed, distressed, divest, expressed, headrest, inquest, invest, Midwest, molest, northwest, oppressed, possessed, progressed, recessed, repressed, request, southwest, suggest, suppressed, transgressed, undressed, unrest.
[3] **Dispossessed**, effervesced, interest, manifest, reassessed, self-possessed.

2.1.46 "--eening" (as in "meaning")
[2] cleaning, greening, keening, leaning, meaning, screening, weaning.
[3] careening, convening, demeaning, dry-cleaning, machining, overweening, spring-cleaning, well-meaning.

SURPRISING RHYMING:
[2] **Beaming**, dreaming, scheming, screaming, steaming, streaming.

Being, fleeing, freeing, keying, kneeing, seeing, teeing.
Ceiling, dealing, feeling, healing, kneeling, pealing, peeling, reeling, stealing, squealing.
Bleeding, breeding, feeding, heeding, leading, needing, pleading, reading, speeding.
Evening, grieving, heaving, leaving, thieving, weaving.
Beating, bleating, cheating, eating, fleeting, greeting, heating, meeting, seating, sheeting, treating, tweeting.
Fielding, shielding, wielding, yielding.
Cheering, clearing, earring, fearing, gearing, hearing, jeering, leering, nearing, peering, sneering, steering, tearing, veering.
Beeping, bleeping, cheeping, creeping, heaping, keeping, leaping, peeping, reaping, seeping, sleeping, sweeping, weeping.
Breezing, easing, freezing, pleasing, seizing, sneezing, squeezing, teasing, wheezing.
[3] **Blaspheming**, daydreaming, redeeming, reasoning, seasoning.
Agreeing, being, fleeing, freeing, seeing, skiing, teeing.
Achieving, believing, conceiving, debriefing, deceiving, displeasing, perceiving, receiving, relieving, reprieving, reprising, retrieving.
Appealing, revealing, self-sealing, wheeler-dealing.
Adhering, appearing, disappearing, endearing, God-fearing.
Browbeating, competing, completing, concreting, deceiving, defeating, deleting, depleting, excreting, heart beating, maltreating, mistreating, reheating, repeating, reseating, retreating, secreting.
[4] **Disbelieving**, make-believing, misconceiving, overachieving, preconceiving, self-deceiving, underachieving.

2.1.47 "--eep" (as in "keep")
[1] beep, bleep, cheep, cheap, creep, deep, heap, jeep, keep, leap, peep, reap, seep, sheep, sleep, steep, sweep, weep.
[2] asleep, bo-peep, chimney sweep, oversleep, scrapheap, skin-deep, upkeep.

SURPRISING RHYMING:
[1] **Beak**, bleak, cheek, chic, clique, creak, creek, eke, freak, geek, leak, leek, meek, peak, peek, pique, reek, seek, sheik, shriek, sleek, sneak, speak, streak, squeak, teak, tweak, weak, week.
Beat, beet, bleat, cheat, cleat, eat, feat, feet, fleet, greet, heat, meat, meet, neat, peat, pleat, seat, sheet, skeet, sleet, street, suite, sweet, teat, treat, tweet, wheat.
Be, bee, fee, flea, flee, gee, glee, he, key, knee, me, sea, see, tee, tea, the, thee, twee, we, wee, whee, zee.
Breathe, heath, 'neath, sheath, teeth, wreath.
[2] **Antique**, boutique, critique, midweek, mystique, oblique, physique, pipsqueak, technique, unique.
Athlete, backbeat, backstreet, breakbeat, broadsheet, browbeat, compete, complete, conceit, concrete, deadbeat, deceit, defeat, delete, deplete, discreet, discrete, downbeat, drumbeat, effete, elite, heartbeat, maltreat, mistreat, offbeat, petite, receipt, reheat, repeat, reseat, retreat, secrete, spreadsheet, time sheet, upbeat, worksheet.
Beneath, bequeath, eyeteeth, underneath.
[3] **Hide-and-seek**, technospeak, tongue-in-cheek.
Bittersweet, easy street, incomplete, indiscreet, obsolete, overeat, overheat.

2.1.48 "--eeped" (as in "reaped")
[1] beeped, bleeped, cheeped, heaped, leaped, peeped, reaped, seeped, steeped.

SURPRISING RHYMING:
[1] **Creaked**, eked, freaked, leaked, peaked, peeked, piqued, reeked, shrieked, sneaked, streaked, squeaked, tweaked, wreaked.
Beep, bleep, cheep, cheap, creep, deep, heap, jeep, keep, leap, peep, reap, seep, sheep, sleep, steep, sweep, weep.
Beat, beet, bleat, cheat, cleat, eat, feat, feet, fleet, greet, heat, meat, meet, neat, peat, pleat, seat, sheet, skeet, sleet, street, suite, sweet, teat, treat, tweet, wheat.

Beak, bleak, cheek, chic, clique, creak, eke, freak, geek, leak, leek, meek, peak, peek, pique, reek, seek, sheik, shriek, sleek, sneak, speak, streak, squeak, teak, tweak, week, wreak.
[2] **Asleep**, chimney sweep, scrapheap, skin-deep, upkeep.
Athlete, backbeat, backstreet, breakbeat, broadsheet, browbeat, compete, complete, conceit, concrete, deadbeat, deceit, defeat, delete, deplete, discreet, discrete, downbeat, drumbeat, effete, elite, heartbeat, maltreat, mistreat, offbeat, petite, receipt, reheat, repeat, reseat, retreat, secrete, spreadsheet, time sheet, upbeat, worksheet.
Antique, boutique, critique, midweek, mystique, oblique, physique, technique, unique.
Antiqued, pink-cheeked, red-cheeked, rosy-cheeked.
[3] **Bittersweet**, easy street, incomplete, indiscreet, obsolete, overeat, overheat.
Hide-and-seek, technospeak, tongue-in-cheek.

2.1.49 "--eeper" (as in "deeper")
[2] beeper, bleeper, cheaper, creeper, deeper, keeper, leaper, peeper, reaper, sleeper, steeper, sweeper, weeper.
[3] barkeeper, beekeeper, bookkeeper, doorkeeper, gamekeeper, gatekeeper, goalkeeper, housekeeper, innkeeper, peacekeeper, shopkeeper, storekeeper, timekeeper, wicketkeeper, zookeeper.

SURPRISING RHYMING:
[2] **Beater**, bleater, cheater, eater, fleeter, greeter, heater, neater, pleater, seater, sheeter, sweeter, treater, tweeter.
Beaker, bleaker, leaker, meeker, seeker, shrieker, sleeker, sneaker, speaker, streaker, squeaker, tikka, weaker, wreaker.
Bleeder, breeder, cedar, feeder, leader, pleader, reader, speeder.
Beamer, dreamer, prima, schemer, screamer, steamer, streamer.
Caesar, Deezer, freezer, geezer, geyser, Mona Lisa, squeezer, teaser, visa.
Creature, feature, preacher, screecher, teacher, schoolteacher.
Cleaner, gleaner, greener, keener, leaner, meaner, screener, serener, weaner.
Dealer, feeler, healer, heeler, kneeler, peeler, sealer, stealer, squealer, wheeler.
Beaver, cleaver, griever, heaver, leaver, weaver.
[3] **Eureka**, loudspeaker.
Browbeater, completer, defeater, heartbeater, maltreater, mistreater, repeater, retreater.
Bandleader, cheerleader, corrida, lip-reader, mind-reader, misleader, newsreader, ringleader, stampeder.
Appealer, concealer, enfant terrible, faith-healer, revealer, tequila, wheeler-dealer.
Achiever, believer, deceiver, receiver, retriever, school-leaver.

2.1.50 "--eepee" (as in "weepy")
[2] cheapie, creepy, rupee, sleepy, sweetpea, tepee, weepy, yippee.

SURPRISING RHYMING:
[1] **Be**, bee, fee, flea, flee, gee, glee, he, key, knee, me, sea, see, tee, tea, the, thee, twee, we, wee, whee, zee.
Brie, free, spree, three, tree.
[2] **Beaky**, cheeky, cliquey, creaky, freaky, leaky, peaky, reeky, sleeky, sneaky, squeaky, streaky, weakly, weekly.
Beastie, guilty, meaty, sweetie, treaty.
Beady, greedy, needy, reedy, seedy, speedy, tweedy, weedy.
Beanie, creamy, dreamy, gleamy, genie, meanie, queenie, screamy, steamy, teeny, teensy, tweeny, weeny.
Bleary, cheery, clearly, dearly, dreary, eerie, merely, nearly, query, teary, theory, weary, yearly.
Beefy, breezy, cheesy, easy, fleecy, greasy, leafy, sleazy, squeezy, uneasy, wheezy.
Bleakly, meekly, sleekly, weakly, weekly.
[3] **Comedy**, custody, melody, nobody, parody, Ph.D., remedy, rhapsody, somebody, subsidy, tragedy.
Charity, dignity, graffiti, gravity, piety, purity, quality, sanctity, sanity, scarcity, sparsity, three-sixty, trinity, unity, uppity.

Completely, concretely, discreetly, indiscreetly, recipe.
[4] Ability, agility, fertility, fragility, futility, hostility, humility, liability, mobility, nobility, responsibility, stability, tranquillity/tranquility (U.S.), versatility, viability, virility, volatility.

2.1.51 "--eeping" (as in "sleeping")
[2] beeping, bleeping, cheeping, creeping, heaping, keeping, leaping, peeping, reaping, seeping, sleeping, steeping, sweeping, weeping.
[3] bookkeeping, housekeeping, oversleeping, safekeeping, timekeeping, upkeeping.

SURPRISING RHYMING:
[2] Beating, bleating, cheating, eating, fleeting, greeting, heating, meeting, seating, sheeting, treating, tweeting.
Bleeding, breeding, feeding, heeding, leading, needing, pleading, reading, speeding.
Creaking, freaking, leaking, peeking, reeking, seeking, shrieking, sneaking, speaking, streaking, squeaking, tweaking, wreaking.
Beaming, dreaming, scheming, screaming, steaming, streaming.
Cleaning, gleaning, greening, leaning, meaning, screening, weaning.
Breezing, easing, freezing, pleasing, seizing, sneezing, squeezing, teasing, wheezing.
Being, fleeing, freeing, seeing, skiing, teeing, treeing.
[3] Browbeating, competing, completing, concreting, deceiving, defeating, deleting, depleting, heart beating, maltreating, mistreating, reheating, repeating, retreating.
Conceding, exceeding, impeding, misleading, misreading, preceding, proceeding, receding, re-reading, sight-reading, stampeding, succeeding, unheeding.
Blaspheming, daydreaming, demeaning, redeeming.
Agreeing, decreeing, foreseeing, sightseeing, unseeing, well-being.
Appeasing, decreasing, increasing, policing, releasing, subleasing.

2.1.52 "--eeple" (as in "steeple")
[2] people, steeple, townspeople.

SURPRISING RHYMING:
[2] Cheerful, earful, fearful, feral, spheral, tearful.
Beetle, equal, evil, primeval, retrieval, sequel, unequal, upheaval.
Eagle, feeble, legal, needle, regal, illegal, seagull, wheedle.
Easel, diesel, gleeful, lethal, needful, peaceful, teasel, weasel.
[3] Beautiful, eatable, beatable, logical, unbeatable, repeatable.
Amenable, feasible, genial, meaningful, menial, deceitful.
Eventful, resentful, uneventful.
[4] Achievable, agreeable, believable, conceivable, foreseeable, disagreeable, irretrievable, medieval, retrievable, unbelievable, unforeseeable, inconceivable.

2.1.53 "--eer" (as in "cheer")
[1] beer, cheer, clear, dear, deer, ear, fear, gear, hear, here, jeer, leer, mere, near, peer, pier, queer, rear, seer, sear, shear, sheer, smear, sneer, spear, sphere, steer, tear, tears, tier, veer, weir, we're, year.
[2] adhere, appear, arrears, austere, besmear, brassiere, career, cashier, cashmere, cohere, endear, footgear, frontier, headgear, premier, midyear, mishear, nadir, reindeer, revere, severe, Shakespeare, sincere, unclear, veneer.
[3] atmosphere, auctioneer, brigadier, buccaneer, cavalier, chandelier, commandeer, disappear, domineer, engineer, financier, ginger beer, gondolier, hemisphere, idea, insincere, interfere, mountaineer, musketeer, overhear, persevere, pioneer, profiteer, puppeteer, racketeer, reappear, rocketeer, souvenir, stratosphere, volunteer, yesteryear.

SURPRISING RHYMING:
[1] Beard, cheered, cleared, feared, geared, jeered, leered, peered, reared, sheared, sneered, steered, teared, tiered, veered, weird.
[2] Adhered, appeared, endeared, lop-eared, revered, veneered.
[3] Commandeered, disappeared, domineered, engineered, interfered, mountaineered, persevered, pioneered, privateered, profiteered, reappeared, volunteered.

2.1.54 "--eered" (as in "steered")
[1] beard, cheered, cleared, feared, geared, jeered, leered, neared, peered, reared, seared, sheared, sheered, smeared, sneered, steered, teared, tiered, veered, weird.
[2] adhered, appeared, careered, cashiered, endeared, lop-eared, revered, veneered.
[3] commandeered, disappeared, domineered, engineered, interfered, mountaineered, persevered, pioneered, privateered, profiteered, reappeared, volunteered.

SURPRISING RHYMING:
[1] **Beer**, blear, cheer, clear, dear, deer, ear, fear, gear, hear, here, jeer, leer, mere, near, peer, pier, queer, rear, seer, sear, shear, sheer, smear, sneer, spear, sphere, steer, tear, tears, tier, veer, weir, we're, year.
[2] **Adhere**, appear, austere, career, cashier, cashmere, endear, footgear, frontier, headgear, premier, midyear, mishear, nadir, reindeer, revere, severe, Shakespeare, sincere, unclear, veneer.
[3] **Atmosphere**, auctioneer, balladeer, brigadier, buccaneer, cavalier, chandelier, commandeer, disappear, domineer, engineer, ginger beer, gondolier, hemisphere, idea, insincere, interfere, mountaineer, musketeer, overhear, persevere, pioneer, puppeteer, racketeer, reappear, rocketeer, souvenir, stratosphere, volunteer, yesteryear.

2.1.55 "--eerence" (as in "appearance")
[3] appearance, adherence, clearance, coherence, disappearance, incoherence, interference, non-appearance, perseverance, reappearance.

SURPRISING RHYMING:
Allegiance, antecedence, competence, circumstance, convenience, credence, endurance, high-maintenance, impedance, inconvenience, maintenance, malfeasance, obedience, patience, precedence, reassurance, sequence, tea-dance.

2.1.56 "--eerest" (as in "dearest")
[2] clearest, dearest, merest, nearest, queerest, severest, sheerest, sincerest.

SURPRISING RHYMING:
[1] **Best**, blessed, breast, chest, crest, dressed, guest, guessed, jest, messed, nest, pest, quest, stressed, test, vest, west, zest.
[2] **Behest**, bequest, caressed, depressed, detest, recessed, refreshed, repressed, request.
Cheerless, earless, fearless, gearless, idealess, peerless, tearless.
Cheapest, cleanest, deepest, greenest, keenest, leanest, meanest, steepest.
Dreamless, fleetest, neatest, seamless, sweetest, unreleased.
Decent, needn't, adherent, coherent.
[3] **Defeatist**, elitist, extremist, graffitist, hygienist, idealist, realist, strategist, surrealist.
Dispossessed, effervesced, interest, manifest, reassessed, repossessed, self-possessed.

2.1.57 "--eerful" (as in "cheerful")
[2] cheerful, earful, fearful, tearful.

SURPRISING RHYMING:
[2] **People**, steeple, townspeople.
Beetle, deceitful, evil, gleeful, lethal, medieval, needful, primeval, retrieval, upheaval.
Eagle, feeble, legal, needle, regal, illegal, seagull, wheedle.
Easel, diesel, merciful, peaceful, teasel, weasel.
Equal, sequel, treacle, unequal.
[3] **Eatable**, beatable, unbeatable, repeatable.
Amenable, feasible, genial, meaningful, menial, deceitful.
Enfeeble, peaceable, readable, redeemable, unreadable.
Reachable, teachable, impeachable, unspeakable, unteachable.
[4] **Agreeable**, foreseeable, disagreeable, unforeseeable.
Achievable, believable, conceivable, unbelievable, irretrievable, inconceivable.

Reasonable, seasonable, unreasonable.
Cereal, serial, venereal, funereal, imperial, arterial, material, bacterial, ethereal.

2.1.58 "--eery" (as in "weary")
[2] beery, bleary, carefree, cheery, dearie, degree, dreary, eerie, eyrie/aerie, leery, query, teary, theory, smeary, weary.

SURPRISING RHYMING:
[1] **Fee**, gee, he, key, knee, me, sea, see, tee, tea, the, thee, twee, we, whee, zee.
Brie, flea, flee, free, glee, lee, spree, three, tree.
[2] **Carefree**, degree, dust-free, freebie, Frisbee.
Clearly, dearly, merely, nearly, queerly, yearly.
Creepy, sleepy, sweetpea, teepee, weepy.
Creamy, dreamy, gleamy, seamy, screamy, steamy.
Beady, freely, greedy, needy, reedy, seedy, speedy, sweetie, treaty, tweedy, weedy.
Beefy, coffee, leafy, toffee.
Beanie, genie, greeny, meanie, queenie, teeny, tweeny, weeny.
Cheeky, marquee, reeky, sleeky, sneaky, squeaky, streaky, whiskey/whisky, Yankee.
Bleakly, meekly, sleekly, weakly, weekly.
Cleanly, seemly, queenly, seemly, steely, wheelie.
Easy, breezy, fleecy, foresee, look-see, queasy, sightsee, specie.
[3] **Ancestry**, archery, artistry, bakery, battery, bigotry, binary, blackberry, blubbery, blueberry, blustery, brasserie, bravery, brewery, bribery, burglary, calorie, carpentry, carvery, cavalry, celery, century, chemistry, chicory, chivalry, Christmas tree, colliery, contrary, devilry, diary, dietary, disagree, dithery, doddery, drudgery, dungaree, duty-free, eatery, enquiry, estuary, expiry, factory, fakery, feathery, filigree, finery, fishery, flattery, fluttery, forestry, forgery, gallery, geometry, gimmickry, glittery, greenery, grocery, history, imagery, injury, inquiry, ivory, jamboree, jewellery/jewelry (U.S.), jittery, leathery, lingerie, lottery, luxury, memory, mercury, misery, momentary, monastery, mystery, nursery, obituary, obligatory, pageantry, pedigree, perjury, pillory, pleasantry, poetry, pottery, primary, priory, quivery, referee, revelry, reverie, rivalry, robbery, rockery, rosary, rubbery, salary, sanctuary, savagery, savory, scenery, sensory, shimmery, shivery, silvery, slavery, slippery, sorcery, sugary, surgery, tapestry, thundery, treachery, trickery, victory, wintery, wizardry.
Austerely, cavalierly, insincerely, severely, sincerely.
[4] **Accessory**, adultery, artillery, cautionary, cemetery, compulsory, confectionery, conciliatory, constabulary, contemporary, customary, debauchery, delivery, dictionary, directory, discovery, distillery, elementary, embroidery, explanatory, exploratory, hunky-dory, idolatry, imaginary, incendiary, infirmary, inflammatory, judiciary, laboratory, legendary, literary, machinery, mandatory, mercenary, military, missionary, necessary, ordinary, patisserie, perfumery, preliminary, psychiatry, publicity, reactionary, recovery, secretary, secondary, simplicity, skullduggery, solitary, stationary, stationery, temporary, territory, tomfoolery, upholstery, visionary, vocabulary.

2.1.59 "--earring" (as in "fearing")
[2] cheering, clearing, earring, fearing, gearing, hearing, jeering, leering, nearing, peering, rearing, searing, shearing, sneering, spearing, steering, tearing, veering.
[3] adhering, appearing, besmearing, disappearing, endearing, God-fearing, veneering.
[4] auctioneering, electioneering, engineering, mountaineering, orienteering, volunteering.

SURPRISING RHYMING:
[2] **Cleaning**, keening, leaning, meaning, screening, weaning.
Fielding, shielding, wielding, yielding.
Grieving, heaving, leaving, thieving, weaving.
Being, fleeing, freeing, seeing, skiing, teeing, treeing.
Ceiling, dealing, feeling, healing, kneeling, pealing, peeling, reeling, stealing, squealing.
Bleeding, breeding, feeding, heeding, leading, needing, pleading, reading, speeding.
Beaming, dreaming, scheming, screaming, steaming, streaming.
Beating, bleating, cheating, eating, fleeting, greeting, heating, meeting, pleating, seating, sheeting, treating, tweeting.

Creaking, freaking, leaking, peeking, reeking, seeking, shrieking, sneaking, speaking, streaking, squeaking, tweaking, wreaking.
Beeping, bleeping, cheeping, creeping, heaping, keeping, leaping, peeping, reaping, seeping, sleeping, sweeping, weeping.
Ceasing, creasing, feasting, fleecing, greasing, leasing, piecing.
Breezing, easing, freezing, pleasing, seizing, sneezing, squeezing, teasing, wheezing.
[3] **Appealing**, revealing, self-sealing, wheeler-dealing.
Demeaning, dry-cleaning, overweening, re-convening, spring-cleaning, well-meaning.
Conceding, exceeding, impeding, misleading, misreading, preceding, proceeding, receding, sight-reading, stampeding, succeeding, unheeding.
Browbeating, competing, completing, concreting, deceiving, defeating, deleting, depleting, heart beating, maltreating, mistreating, reheating, repeating, retreating.
Appeasing, decreasing, increasing, policing, releasing, subleasing.
Achieving, believing, conceiving, debriefing, deceiving, displeasing, perceiving, receiving, relieving, reprieving, reprising, retrieving.

2.1.60 "--earless" (as in "fearless")
[2] cheerless, earless, fearless, gearless, idealess, peerless, tearless.

SURPRISING RHYMING:
[1] **Best**, blessed, breast, chest, crest, dressed, guest, guessed, jest, messed, nest, pest, quest, stressed, test, vest, west, zest.
[2] **Clearest**, dearest, merest, nearest, queerest, sheerest, sincerest.
Cleanest, greenest, keenest, leanest, meanest.
Cheapest, deepest, steepest.
Abreast, addressed, arrest, attest, Beau Geste, behest, bequest, caressed, compressed, contest, depressed, detest, digest, digressed, distressed, expressed, inquest, invest, molest, oppressed, possessed, progressed, recessed, refreshed, repressed, request, suggest, suppressed, transgressed, undressed, unless, unrest.

2.1.61 "--eerly" (as in "nearly")
[2] clearly, dearly, merely, nearly, queerly, yearly.
[3] austerely, cavalierly, insincerely, severely, sincerely.

SURPRISING RHYMING:
[2] **Foresee**, greasy, look-see, maxi, mercy, sightsee, specie, tipsy.
Bleary, carefree, cheery, debris, dreary, eerie, esprit, hairy, hungry, leery, quarry, query, storey, story, sultry, teary, theory, weary.
Greedy, needy, reedy, seedy, speedy.
Freebie, maybe, ruby, would-be, zombie.
Ably, beastly, cleanly, early, earthly, freely, friendly, likely, lowly, medley, mostly, muesli, newly, nightly, oily, paisley, priestly, really, seemly, steely, truly, weakly, weekly, wheelie, yearly.
Creepy, hippie, sleepy, teepee, weepy.
Beamy, creamy, dreamy, gimme, gleamy, seamy.
Achy, beaky, car key, cheeky, cliquey, creaky, freaky, karaoke, leaky, psyche, reeky, risky, sleeky, sneaky, squeaky, streaky.
Acne, any, Disney, genie, meanie, queenie, teeny, tweeny, weeny.
Gritty, guilty, meaty, misty, pity, pretty, sweetie, tasty, treaty.
[3] **Ancestry**, archery, artistry, bakery, battery, bigotry, binary, blackberry, blubbery, blueberry, blustery, brasserie, bravery, brewery, bribery, burglary, calorie, carpentry, carvery, cavalry, celery, century, chemistry, chicory, chivalry, Christmas tree, colliery, contrary, devilry, diary, dietary, disagree, dithery, doddery, drudgery, dungaree, duty-free, eatery, enquiry, estuary, expiry, factory, fakery, feathery, filigree, finery, fishery, flattery, fluttery, forestry, forgery, gallery, geometry, gimmickry, glittery, greenery, grocery, history, imagery, injury, inquiry, ivory, jamboree, jewellery/jewelry (U.S.), jittery, leathery, lingerie, lottery, luxury, memory, mercury, misery, momentary, monastery,

196

mystery, nursery, obituary, obligatory, pageantry, pedigree, perjury, pillory, pleasantry, poetry, pottery, primary, priory, quivery, referee, revelry, reverie, rivalry, robbery, rockery, rosary, rubbery, salary, sanctuary, savagery, savory, scenery, sensory, shimmery, shivery, silvery, slavery, slippery, sorcery, sugary, surgery, tapestry, thundery, treachery, trickery, victory, wintery, wizardry.
Courtesy, currency, decency, heresy, leniency, odyssey, oversee, prophecy, secrecy.
Cheerily, drearily, eerily, merrily, warily, wearily.
Comedy, remedy, gravity, recipe, sanity.
Alchemy, blasphemy, enemy, infamy, sesame.
Actually, broccoli, brotherly, easterly, equally, fatherly, leisurely.
Certainty, charity, clarity, deputy, dignity, graffiti, gravity, guarantee, honesty, liberty, poverty, quality, sanctity, unity, vanity, velvety.
Anchovy, c'est la vie, eau-de-vie, vis-à-vis.

2.1.62 "--eece" (as in "peace")

[1] cease, crease, fleece, geese, grease, lease, niece, peace, piece.
[2] apiece, caprice, cassis, decease, decrease, hairpiece, increase, mouthpiece, neckpiece, obese, police, release, sublease, timepiece, two-piece, valise.
[3] centrepiece/centerpiece (U.S.), mantelpiece, masterpiece, predecease.

SURPRISING RHYMING:
[1] **Beast**, ceased, creased, east, feast, fleeced, greased, least, piste, priest, yeast.
Breathe, breeze, cheese, ease, fees, freeze, frieze, he's, jeez, keys, knees, please, seas, sees, seize, she's, sleaze, sneeze, squeeze, teas, tease, tees, these, trees, tweeze, wheeze.
Beat, beet, bleat, cheat, cleat, eat, feat, feet, fleet, greet, heat, meat, meet, neat, peat, pleat, seat, sheet, skeet, sleet, street, suite, sweet, teat, treat, tweet, wheat.
Bleed, breed, cede, creed, deed, feed, freed, greed, he'd, heed, keyed, knead, kneed, lead, mead, need, plead, read, reed, seed, she'd, speed, steed, tweed, we'd, weed.
Beep, bleep, cheep, cheap, creep, deep, heap, jeep, keep, leap, peep, reap, seep, sheep, sleep, steep, sweep, weep.
[2] **Artiste**, decreased, deceased, increased, northeast, policed, released, southeast.
Appease, Aries, chemise, deep-freeze, degrees, disease, displease, herpes, Pisces, reprise, species, striptease, trapeze, unease, unfreeze, valise.
Athlete, backbeat, backstreet, breakbeat, broadsheet, browbeat, compete, complete, conceit, concrete, deadbeat, deceit, defeat, delete, deplete, discreet, discrete, downbeat, drumbeat, effete, elite, heartbeat, maltreat, mistreat, offbeat, petite, receipt, reheat, repeat, reseat, retreat, secrete, spreadsheet, time sheet, upbeat, worksheet.
Agreed, airspeed, birdseed, concede, decreed, exceed, Godspeed, handfeed, impede, indeed, knock-kneed, lip-read, misdeed, mislead, misread, nosebleed, precede, proceed, recede, seaweed, sight-read, spoon-feed, stampede, succeed.
Asleep, bo-peep, scrapheap, skin-deep, upkeep.
[3] **Achilles**, antifreeze, emojis, enemies, expertise, guarantees, Hercules, journalese, legalese, manganese, melodies, overseas.
Bittersweet, easy street, incomplete, indiscreet, obsolete, overeat, overheat, unreleased.
Aniseed, centipede, chickenfeed, disagreed, filigreed, guaranteed, intercede, millipede, overfeed, pedigreed, proofread, refereed, supersede, tumbleweed.
[4] **Abilities**, agilities, analyses, antipodes, diabetes, diagnoses, eccentricities, facilities, fragilities, hostilities, hypotheses, neuroses, synopses, utilities.

2.1.63 "--eest" (as in "east")

[1] beast, ceased, creased, east, feast, fleeced, greased, least, leased, piste, priest.
[2] artiste, decreased, deceased, increased, northeast, policed, released, southeast.
[3] arriviste, unreleased.

SURPRISING RHYMING:
[1] **Cease**, crease, fleece, geese, grease, niece, peace, piece.
Beat, beet, bleat, cheat, cleat, eat, feat, feet, fleet, greet, heat, meat, meet, neat, peat, pleat, seat, sheet, skeet, sleet, street, suite, sweet, teat, treat, tweet, wheat.

Bleed, breed, cede, creed, deed, feed, freed, greed, he'd, heed, keyed, knead, kneed, lead, mead, need, plead, read, reed, seed, she'd, speed, steed, tweed, we'd, weed.
Beep, bleep, cheep, cheap, creep, deep, heap, jeep, keep, leap, peep, reap, seep, sheep, sleep, steep, sweep, weep.
Breathe, breeze, cheese, ease, fees, freeze, frieze, he's, jeez, keys, knees, please, seas, sees, seize, she's, sleaze, sneeze, squeeze, teas, tease, tees, these, trees, tweeze, wheeze.
[2] Apiece, cassis, decease, decrease, hairpiece, increase, mouthpiece, obese, police, release, timepiece, two-piece, valise.
Appease, Aries, chemise, deep-freeze, degrees, disease, displease, herpes, Pisces, reprise, species, striptease, trapeze, unease.
Athlete, backbeat, backstreet, breakbeat, broadsheet, browbeat, compete, complete, conceit, concrete, deadbeat, deceit, defeat, delete, deplete, discreet, discrete, downbeat, drumbeat, effete, elite, heartbeat, maltreat, mistreat, offbeat, petite, receipt, reheat, repeat, reseat, retreat, secrete, spreadsheet, time sheet, upbeat, worksheet.
Agreed, airspeed, birdseed, concede, decreed, exceed, Godspeed, handfeed, impede, indeed, knock-kneed, lip-read, misdeed, mislead, misread, nosebleed, precede, proceed, recede, seaweed, sight-read, spoon-feed, stampede, succeed.
Asleep, bo-peep, scrapheap, skin-deep, upkeep.
[3] Centerpiece/centerpiece, mantelpiece, masterpiece, predecease.
Achilles, antifreeze, emojis, enemies, expertise, guarantees, Hercules, journalese, legalese, manganese, melodies, overseas.
Bittersweet, easy street, incomplete, indiscreet, obsolete, overeat, overheat, unreleased.
Aniseed, centipede, chickenfeed, disagreed, filigreed, guaranteed, intercede, millipede, overfeed, pedigreed, proofread, refereed, supersede, tumbleweed.
[4] Abilities, agilities, analyses, antipodes, diabetes, diagnoses, eccentricities, fragilities, hostilities, hypotheses, neuroses, synopses.

2.1.64 "--eet" (as in "feet")
[1] beat, beet, bleat, cheat, cleat, eat, feat, feet, fleet, greet, heat, meat, meet, neat, peat, pleat, seat, sheet, skeet, sleet, street, suite, sweet, teat, treat, tweet, wheat.
[2] athlete, backbeat, backstreet, breakbeat, broadsheet, browbeat, buckwheat, compete, complete, conceit, concrete, deadbeat, deceit, defeat, delete, deplete, discreet, discrete, downbeat, drumbeat, dustsheet, effete, elite, entreat, excrete, flysheet, groundsheet, heartbeat, maltreat, mincemeat, mistreat, offbeat, petite, receipt, reheat, repeat, reseat, retreat, secrete, spreadsheet, sweetmeat, time sheet, upbeat, unseat, unsweet, worksheet.
[3] balance sheet, bittersweet, easy street, incomplete, indiscreet, obsolete, overeat, overheat, parakeet, tout de suite, window seat.

SURPRISING RHYMING:
[1] Bleed, breed, creed, deed, feed, freed, greed, he'd, heed, keyed, knead, kneed, lead, mead, need, plead, read, reed, seed, she'd, speed, steed, tweed, we'd, weed.
Beep, bleep, cheep, cheap, creep, deep, heap, jeep, keep, leap, peep, reap, seep, sheep, sleep, steep, sweep, weep.
Beeped, bleeped, cheeped, heaped, leaped, peeped, reaped, seeped, steeped.
Beak, bleak, cheek, chic, clique, creak, creek, eke, freak, geek, leak, leek, meek, peak, peek, pique, reek, seek, sheik, shriek, sleek, sneak, speak, streak, squeak, teak, tweak, weak, week.
Creaked, eked, freaked, leaked, peaked, peeked, piqued, reeked, shrieked, sneaked, streaked, squeaked, tweaked, wreaked.
Heath, 'neath, sheath, teeth, wreath.
Beach, beech, bleach, breach, breech, each, leach, leech, peach, preach, reach, screech, speech, teach.
Be, bee, brie, fee, flea, flee, free, gee, glee, he, key, knee, me, sea, see, spree, tee, tea, the, thee, three, tree, twee, we, wee, whee, zee.
[2] Agreed, airspeed, birdseed, concede, decreed, exceed, Godspeed, handfeed, impede, indeed, knock-kneed, lip-read, misdeed, mislead, misread, nosebleed, precede, proceed, recede, seaweed, sight-read, spoon-feed, stampede, succeed.
Asleep, bo-peep, scrapheap, skin-deep, upkeep.

Antique, boutique, critique, mean streak, midweek, mystique, oblique, physique, pipsqueak, technique, unique.
Beneath, bequeath, eyeteeth, underneath.
[3] Aniseed, centipede, chickenfeed, disagreed, filigreed, guaranteed, intercede, millipede, overfeed, pedigreed, proofread, refereed, supersede, tumbleweed.
Hide-and-seek, technospeak, tongue-in-cheek.

2.1.65 "--eeter (as in "cheater")
[2] beater, bleater, cheater, eater, fleeter, greeter, heater, litre/liter (U.S.), metre/meter, neater, pleater, seater, sheeter, sweeter, teeter, treater, tweeter.
[3] anteater, beefeater, browbeater, completer, defeater, drumbeater, eggbeater, heartbeater, maltreater, mistreater, repeater, retreater, windcheater.
[4] Centimetre/centimeter (U.S.), kilometer, millimetre/millimeter (U.S.).

SURPRISING RHYMING:
[2] **Beeper**, bleeper, cheaper, creeper, deeper, keeper, leaper, peeper, reaper, sleeper, steeper, sweeper, weeper.
Beaker, bleaker, eureka, leaker, meeker, seeker, shrieker, sleeker, sneaker, speaker, streaker, squeaker, tikka, weaker, wreaker.
Bleeder, breeder, cedar, feeder, heeder, leader, pleader, reader, seeder, speeder.
Beamer, dreamer, prima, schemer, screamer, steamer, streamer.
Caesar, Deezer, freezer, geezer, geyser, Mona Lisa, squeezer, teaser, visa.
Creature, feature, preacher, teacher, schoolteacher.
Cleaner, gleaner, greener, keener, leaner, meaner, screener, serener, weaner, wiener.
Dealer, feeler, healer, heeler, kneeler, peeler, sealer, stealer, squealer, wheeler.
Beaver, cleaver, griever, heaver, leaver, weaver.
[3] **Barkeeper**, beekeeper, bookkeeper, doorkeeper, gamekeeper, gatekeeper, goalkeeper, housekeeper, innkeeper, peacekeeper, shopkeeper, storekeeper, timekeeper, wicketkeeper, zookeeper.
Bandleader, cheerleader, conceder, lip-reader, mind-reader, misleader, newsreader, ringleader, stampeder, succeeder.
Enfant terrible, faith-healer, revealer, tequila, wheeler-dealer.
Achiever, believer, deceiver, receiver, retriever, school-leaver.

2.1.66 "--eeted" (as in "tweeted")
[2] bleated, cheated, greeted, heated, meted, pleated, seated, treated, tweeted.
[3] competed, completed, conceited, defeated, deleted, depleted, entreated, mistreated, preheated, reheated, repeated, reseated, retreated, undefeated, unheated, unseated.

SURPRISING RHYMING:
[2] **Beaded**, ceded, heeded, needed, pleaded, seeded, weeded.
Agreed it, beat it, eat it, immediate, tweet it, read it.
Fielded, shielded, wielded, yielded.
[3] **Acceded**, conceded, exceeded, impeded, preceded, proceeded, receded, stampeded, succeeded, unheeded, unneeded, unweeded.
[4] **Interceded**, superseded.

22.1.67 "--eeth" (as in "teeth")
[1] heath, 'neath, sheath, teeth, wreath.
[2] beneath, bequeath, eyeteeth, underneath.

SURPRISING RHYMING:
[1] **Beef**, belief, brief, chief, grief, leaf, reef, sheaf, thief.
Cease, crease, fleece, geese, grease, lease, niece, peace, piece.
Beat, beet, bleat, cheat, cleat, eat, feat, feet, fleet, greet, heat, meat, meet, neat, peat, pleat, seat, sheet, skeet, sleet, street, suite, sweet, teat, treat, tweet, wheat.
Bleed, breed, cede, creed, deed, feed, freed, greed, he'd, heed, keyed, knead, kneed, lead, mead, need, plead, read, reed, seed, she'd, speed, steed, tweed, we'd, weed.

Beep(ed), bleep(ed), cheep(ed), cheap, creep, deep, heap(ed), jeep, keep, leap(ed), peep(ed), reap(ed), seep(ed), sheep, sleep, steep(ed), sweep, weep(ed).
Beak, bleak, cheek, chic, clique, creak, creek, eke, freak, geek, leak, leek, meek, peak, peek, pique, reek, seek, sheik, shriek, sleek, sneak, speak, streak, squeak, teak, tweak, weak, week.
Creaked, eked, freaked, leaked, peaked, peeked, piqued, reeked, shrieked, sneaked, streaked, squeaked, tweaked, wreaked.
Beach, beech, bleach, breach, breech, each, leach, leech, peach, preach, reach, screech, speech, teach.
Be, bee, brie, fee, flea, flee, free, gee, glee, he, key, knee, me, sea, see, spree, tee, tea, the, thee, three, tree, twee, we, wee, whee, zee.
[2] Debrief, fig leaf, flyleaf, mischief, motif, relief, tea leaf.
Apiece, caprice, cassis, decease, decrease, hairpiece, increase, mouthpiece, obese, police, release, sublease, timepiece, two-piece, valise.
Appease, Aries, chemise, deep-freeze, degrees, disease, displease, herpes, Pisces, reprise, species, striptease, trapeze, unease, unfreeze, valise.
Athlete, backbeat, backstreet, breakbeat, broadsheet, browbeat, compete, complete, conceit, concrete, deadbeat, deceit, defeat, delete, deplete, discreet, discrete, downbeat, drumbeat, effete, elite, heartbeat, maltreat, mistreat, offbeat, petite, receipt, reheat, repeat, reseat, retreat, secrete, spreadsheet, time sheet, upbeat, worksheet.
Agreed, airspeed, birdseed, concede, decreed, exceed, Godspeed, handfeed, impede, indeed, knock-kneed, lip-read, misdeed, mislead, misread, nosebleed, precede, proceed, recede, seaweed, sight-read, spoon-feed, stampede, succeed.
Asleep, bo-peep, scrapheap, skin-deep, upkeep.
Antique, boutique, critique, mean streak, midweek, mystique, oblique, physique, pipsqueak, technique, unique.
[3] Aperitif, disbelief, handkerchief, misbelief, overleaf.
Aniseed, centipede, chickenfeed, disagreed, filigreed, guaranteed, intercede, millipede, overfeed, pedigreed, proofread, refereed, supersede, tumbleweed.
Hide-and-seek, technospeak, tongue-in-cheek.
Centerpiece/centerpiece, mantelpiece, masterpiece, predecease.
Achilles, antifreeze, emojis, enemies, expertise, guarantees, Hercules, journalese, legalese, manganese, melodies, overseas.
Bittersweet, easy street, incomplete, indiscreet, obsolete, overeat, overheat, unreleased.
[4] Abilities, agilities, analyses, antipodes, diabetes, diagnoses, eccentricities, facilities, fragilities, hostilities, hypotheses, neuroses, synopses, utilities.

2.1.68 "--eev" (as in "leave")

[1] cleave, eve, grieve, heave, leave, peeve, sleeve, thieve, weave, we've.
[2] achieve, aggrieve, believe, bereave, conceive, deceive, naïve, perceive, receive, relieve, reprieve, retrieve, reweave, shirtsleeve, upheave.
[3] disbelieve, interleave, interweave, make-believe, misconceive, overachieve, preconceive, reconceive, semibreve, underachieve.

SURPRISING RHYMING:
[1] Cleaved, grieved, heaved, peeved, sleeved, thieved.
Beef, belief, brief, chief, fief, grief, leaf, reef, sheaf, thief.
Breeze, cheese, ease, fees, freeze, frieze, he's, jeez, keys, knees, please, sees, seize, she's, sleaze, sneeze, squeeze, teas, tease, tees, these, trees, tweeze, wheeze.
Bead, bleed, breed, cede, creed, deed, feed, freed, greed, he'd, heed, keyed, knead, kneed, lead, mead, need, peed, plead, read, reed, seed, she'd, speed, steed, treed, tweed, we'd, weed.
Be, bee, brie, fee, flea, flee, free, gee, glee, he, key, knee, me, sea, see, spree, tee, tea, the, thee, three, tree, twee, we, wee, whee, zee.
[2] Achieved, aggrieved, believed, bereaved, conceived, deceived, perceived, received, relieved, reprieved, retrieved, upheaved.
Debrief, fig leaf, flyleaf, mischief, motif, relief, tea leaf.
Appease, Aries, chemise, deep-freeze, degrees, disease, displease, herpes, Pisces, reprise, species, striptease, trapeze, unease, unfreeze, valise.

Agreed, airspeed, birdseed, concede, decreed, exceed, Godspeed, handfeed, impede, indeed, knock-kneed, lip-read, misdeed, mislead, misread, nosebleed, precede, proceed, recede, seaweed, sight-read, spoon-feed, stampede, succeed.
[3] **Disbelieved**, make-believe, misconceived, overachieved, preconceived, underachieved.
Aperitif, disbelief, handkerchief, misbelief, overleaf.
Achilles, antifreeze, emojis, enemies, expertise, Hercules, melodies, overseas.
Aniseed, centipede, chickenfeed, disagreed, filigreed, guaranteed, intercede, millipede, overfeed, pedigreed, proofread, refereed, supersede, tumbleweed.
Absentee, amnesty, brevity, casualty, certainty, charity, chastity, clarity, committee, confetti, crotchety, crudity, density, deputy, devotee, dignity, dynasty, enmity, entity, fidgety, gaiety/gayety (U.S.), graffiti, gravity, guarantee, honesty, karate, levity, liberty, machete, majesty, modesty, nudity, oddity, parity, penalty, piety, poverty, probity, property, puberty, purity, quality, repartee, rickety, sanctity, sanctuary, scarcity, seventy, sovereignty, spaghetti, specialty, three-sixty, trinity, unity, uppity, vanity, velvety.

2.1.69 "--eeved" (as in "believed")
[1] cleaved, grieved, heaved, peeved, sleeved, thieved.
[2] achieved, aggrieved, believed, bereaved, conceived, deceived, perceived, received, relieved, reprieved, retrieved.
[3] disbelieved, interleaved, misconceived, overachieved, preconceived, reconceived, unconceived, underachieved, unperceived.

SURPRISING RHYMING:
[1] **Grieve**, heave, leave, peeve, sleeve, thieve, weave, we've.
Beef, belief, brief, chief, fief, grief, leaf, reef, sheaf, thief.
Breeze, cheese, ease, fees, freeze, frieze, he's, jeez, keys, knees, please, sees, seize, she's, sleaze, sneeze, squeeze, teas, tease, tees, these, trees, tweeze, wheeze.
Bleed, breed, cede, creed, deed, feed, freed, greed, he'd, heed, keyed, knead, kneed, lead, mead, need, plead, read, reed, seed, she'd, speed, steed, tweed, we'd, weed.
Be, bee, brie, fee, flea, flee, free, gee, glee, he, key, knee, me, sea, see, spree, tee, tea, the, thee, three, tree, twee, we, wee, whee, zee.
[2] **Achieve**, aggrieve, believe, bereave, conceive, deceive, naïve, perceive, receive, relieve, reprieve, retrieve, shirtsleeve, upheave.
Debrief, fig leaf, flyleaf, mischief, motif, relief, tea leaf.
Appease, Aries, chemise, deep-freeze, degrees, disease, displease, herpes, Pisces, reprise, species, striptease, trapeze, unease.
Agreed, airspeed, birdseed, concede, decreed, exceed, Godspeed, handfeed, impede, indeed, knock-kneed, lip-read, misdeed, mislead, misread, nosebleed, precede, proceed, recede, seaweed, sight-read, spoon-feed, stampede, succeed.
[3] **Disbelieve**, make-believe, misconceive, overachieve, preconceive, underachieve.
Aperitif, disbelief, handkerchief, misbelief, overleaf.
Achilles, antifreeze, emojis, enemies, expertise, Hercules, melodies, overseas.
Aniseed, centipede, chickenfeed, disagreed, filigreed, guaranteed, intercede, millipede, overfeed, pedigreed, proofread, refereed, supersede, tumbleweed.
Absentee, amnesty, brevity, casualty, certainty, charity, chastity, clarity, committee, confetti, crotchety, crudity, density, deputy, devotee, dignity, dynasty, enmity, entity, fidgety, gaiety/gayety (U.S.), graffiti, gravity, guarantee, honesty, karate, levity, liberty, machete, majesty, modesty, nudity, oddity, parity, penalty, piety, poverty, probity, property, puberty, purity, quality, repartee, rickety, sanctity, sanctuary, scarcity, seventy, sovereignty, spaghetti, specialty, three-sixty, trinity, unity, uppity, vanity, velvety.

2.1.70 "--eevable" (as in "believable")
[4] achievable, believable, retrievable, conceivable, unbelievable, inconceivable.

SURPRISING RHYMING:
[2] **Cheerful**, earful, fearful, tearful.
Beetle, equal, evil, people, sequel, steeple, unequal, weevil.
Eagle, feeble, legal, needle, regal, illegal, seagull, wheedle.
Easel, diesel, peaceful, weasel.

Gleeful, heedful, lethal, needful.
[3] **Beatable**, eatable, readable, repeatable, unbeatable.
Feasible, freezable, peaceable, pleasable, squeezable, teasable.
Deceitful, genial, meaningful, menial, upheaval, primeval, retrieval.
Reachable, teachable, impeachable, unteachable.
[4] **Agreeable**, foreseeable, disagreeable, unforeseeable, medieval.
Amenable, irredeemable, unreadable, unspeakable.
Reasonable, seasonable, unreasonable, unseasonable.
Funereal, imperial, arterial, material, bacterial, ethereal.

2.1.71 "--eeze" (as in "please")
[1] breeze, cheese, ease, fees, freeze, frieze, he's, jeez, keys, knees, please, seas, sees, seize, she's, sleaze, sneeze, squeeze, teas, tease, tees, these, trees, wheeze.
[2] appease, Aries, chemise, deep-freeze, degrees, disease, displease, herpes, Pisces, reprise, species, striptease, trapeze, unease, unfreeze, valise.
[3] Achilles, antifreeze, emojis, enemies, expertise, guarantees, Hercules, indices, journalese, legalese, manganese, melodies, overseas.
[4] abilities, agilities, analyses, antipodes, diabetes, diagnoses, eccentricities, facilities, fragilities, hostilities, hypotheses, neuroses, synopses, utilities.

SURPRISING RHYMING:
[1] **Breezed**, eased, pleased, seized, sneezed, squeezed, teased, wheezed.
Cease, crease, fleece, geese, grease, lease, niece, peace, piece.
Beast, ceased, creased, east, feast, fleeced, greased, least, pieced, piste, priest.
Heath, 'neath, sheath, teeth, wreath.
Grieve, heave, leave, leaves, peeve, sleeve, thieve, weave, we've.
Beads, bleeds, breeds, creeds, deeds, feeds, freed, greed, he'd, heeds, keyed, kneed, leads, needs, pleads, reads, seeds, she'd, speeds, steeds, tweeds, we'd, weeds.
Beef, belief, brief, chief, fief, grief, leaf, reef, sheaf, thief.
Be, bee, brie, fee, flea, flee, free, gee, glee, he, key, knee, me, sea, see, spree, tee, tea, the, thee, three, tree, twee, we, wee, whee, zee.
[2] **Apiece**, decease, decrease, hairpiece, increase, mouthpiece, obese, police, release, timepiece, two-piece, valise.
Appeased, decreased, deceased, diseased, displeased, increased, northeast, policed, released, reprised, southeast, subleased, uncreased.
Beneath, bequeath, eyeteeth, underneath.
Achieve, aggrieve, believe, bereave, conceive, deceive, naïve, perceive, receive, relieve, reprieve, retrieve, shirtsleeve, upheave.
Agreed, airspeed, birdseed, concede, decreed, exceed, Godspeed, handfeed, impede, indeed, knock-kneed, lip-read, misdeed, mislead, misread, nosebleed, precede, proceed, recede, seaweed, sight-read, spoon-feed, stampede, succeed.
Debrief, fig leaf, flyleaf, mischief, motif, relief, tea leaf.
[3] **Centerpiece**/centerpiece, mantelpiece, masterpiece, predecease, unreleased.
Disbelieve, make-believe, misconceive, overachieve, preconceive, underachieve.
Aperitif, disbelief, handkerchief, misbelief, overleaf.
Aniseed, centipede, chickenfeed, disagreed, filigreed, guaranteed, intercede, millipede, overfeed, pedigreed, proofread, refereed, supersede, tumbleweed.
Agency, autopsy, bankruptcy, bourgeoisie, buoyancy, Christmassy, clemency, cogency, courtesy, currency, decency, divorcee, ecstasy, embassy, endorsee, envy, fallacy, fantasy, fluency, franchisee, galaxy, heresy, Holy See, jealousy, legacy, leniency, lunacy, odyssey, oversee, pharmacy, piracy, policy, potency, pregnancy, privacy, prophecy, regency, sanity, secrecy, tendency, truancy, undersea, urgency, vacancy.

2.1.72 "--eecher" (as in "teacher")
[2] bleacher, breacher, creature, feature, preacher, reacher, screecher, teacher.

SURPRISING RHYMING:
[2] **Beeper**, bleeper, cheaper, creeper, deeper, keeper, leaper, peeper, reaper, sleeper, steeper, sweeper, weeper.
Bleeder, breeder, cedar, feeder, heeder, leader, pleader, reader, speeder, weeder.

Beaker, bleaker, leaker, meeker, peeker, seeker, shrieker, sleeker, sneaker, speaker, streaker, squeaker, tikka, tweaker, weaker.
Dealer, feeler, healer, heeler, kneeler, peeler, sealer, spieler, stealer, squealer.
Beamer, creamer, dreamer, prima, reamer, schemer, screamer, steamer, streamer.
Cleaner, greener, keener, leaner, meaner, screener, serener.
Caesar, Deezer, freezer, geezer, geyser, Mona Lisa, squeezer, teaser, visa.
[3] **Beekeeper**, bookkeeper, eureka, gamekeeper, gatekeeper, goalkeeper, housekeeper, innkeeper, loudspeaker, peacekeeper, storekeeper, timekeeper, zookeeper.
Bandleader, cheerleader, conceder, corrida, lip-reader, mind-reader, misleader, newsreader, ringleader, stampeder, succeeder.
Enfant terrible, faith-healer, revealer, tequila, wheeler-dealer.
Arena, blasphemer, cantina, czarina/tsarina, daydreamer, demeanour/demeanor (U.S.), hyena, marina, redeemer.
[4] **Ballerina**, concertina, misdemeanour/misdemeanor (U.S.), signorina.

2.1.73 "--eeching" (as in "teaching")

[2] beaching, bleaching, breaching, I Ching, preaching, reaching, screeching, teaching.
[3] beseeching, far-reaching, impeaching, outreaching.

SURPRISING RHYMING:
[2] **Beeping**, bleeping, creeping, keeping, leaping, peeping, reaping, sleeping, sweeping, weeping.
Bleeding, breeding, feeding, heeding, leading, pleading, reading, speeding, weeding.
Leaking, peeking, seeking, shrieking, sneaking, speaking, streaking, squeaking, tweaking, wreaking.
Dealing, feeling, healing, heeling, kneeling, peeling, sealing, spieling, stealing, squealing, wheeling.
Beaming, dreaming, scheming, screaming, steaming, streaming.
Cleaning, gleaning, greening, leaning, meaning, screening, weaning.
Breezing, ceasing, freezing, seizing, squeezing, teasing, wheezing.
[3] **Barkeeping**, beekeeping, bookkeeping, game-keeping, gatekeeping, goalkeeping, housekeeping, innkeeping, peacekeeping, storekeeping, timekeeping, zookeeping.
Bandleading, cheerleading, conceding, lip-reading, mind-reading, misleading, stampeding, succeeding.
Appealing, concealing, faith-healing, revealing
Blaspheming, daydreaming, demeaning, redeeming.

2.1.74 "--eezer" (as in "teaser")

[2] beezer, Caesar, Deezer, easer, freezer, geezer, geyser, pleaser, sneezer, squeezer, teaser, tweezer, visa, wheezer.
[3] appeaser, displeaser, Mona Lisa.

SURPRISING RHYMING:
[2] **Beaver**, cleaver, griever, heaver, leaver, weaver.
Bleeder, breeder, cedar, feeder, leader, pleader, reader, speeder.
Dealer, feeler, healer, heeler, kneeler, stealer, squealer, wheeler.
Creature, feature, preacher, screecher, teacher, schoolteacher.
Beamer, dreamer, prima, schemer, screamer, steamer, streamer.
Cleaner, greener, keener, leaner, meaner, screener, serener.
Cheerer, clearer, dearer, nearer, queerer, severer, shearer, sheerer.
[3] **Achiever**, believer, deceiver, perceiver, receiver, reliever, retriever, school-leaver.
Bandleader, cheerleader, lip-reader, mind-reader, newsreader, ringleader, succeeder.
Enfant terrible, faith-healer, revealer, tequila, wheeler-dealer.
Arena, blasphemer, cantina, czarina/tsarina, daydreamer, demeanour/demeanor (U.S.), hyena, marina, redeemer.
[4] **Disbeliever**, interweaver, make-believer, misconceiver, overachiever, underachiever.
Ballerina, concertina, misdemeanour/misdemeanor (U.S.).

*

2.1.75 "--eeing" (as in "being")
[2] agreeing, being, fleeing, freeing, seeing, skiing, teeing, treeing.
[3] decreeing, farseeing, foreseeing, human being, sightseeing, unseeing, well-being.

SURPRISING RHYMING:
[2] **Ceiling**, dealing, feeling, healing, kneeling, pealing, peeling, reeling, sealing, stealing, squealing, wheeling.
Cheering, clearing, earring, fearing, gearing, hearing, jeering, leering, nearing, peering, rearing, searing, shearing, sneering, spearing, steering, tearing, veering.
Bleeding, breeding, feeding, heeding, leading, needing, pleading, reading, speeding.
Beaming, dreaming, scheming, screaming, steaming, streaming.
Cleaning, greening, keening, leaning, meaning, screening, weaning.
Beating, bleating, cheating, eating, fleeting, greeting, heating, meeting, pleating, seating, sheeting, treating, tweeting.
Creaking, freaking, leaking, peaking, peeking, reeking, seeking, shrieking, sneaking, speaking, streaking, squeaking, tweaking.
Ceasing, creasing, feasting, fleecing, greasing, leasing, piecing.
Beeping, bleeping, cheeping, creeping, heaping, keeping, leaping, peeping, reaping, seeping, sleeping, sweeping, weeping.
Beefing, briefing, grieving, heaving, leafing, leaving, thieving, weaving.
Breezing, easing, freezing, pleasing, seizing, sneezing, squeezing, teasing, wheezing.
Beaching, bleaching, preaching, reaching, screeching, teaching.
[3] **Appealing**, revealing, self-sealing, wheeler-dealing.
Adhering, appearing, disappearing, endearing, God-fearing, veneering.
Demeaning, dry-cleaning, overweening, re-convening, spring-cleaning, well-meaning.
Conceding, exceeding, impeding, inbreeding, misleading, misreading, preceding, proceeding, receding, seceding, sight-reading, stampeding, succeeding, unheeding.
Browbeating, competing, completing, concreting, deceiving, defeating, deleting, depleting, heart beating, maltreating, mistreating, reheating, repeating, retreating.
Appeasing, decreasing, increasing, policing, releasing, subleasing.
Achieving, believing, conceiving, debriefing, deceiving, displeasing, perceiving, receiving, relieving, reprieving, reprising, retrieving.
Bookkeeping, gamekeeping, goalkeeping, housekeeping, oversleeping, peacekeeping, safekeeping, shop-keeping, timekeeping.
[4] **Disbelieving**, make-believing, overachieving, self-deceiving, underachieving.

2.1.76 "--eeces" (as in "pieces")
[2] ceases, creases, fleeces, greases, leases, nieces, pieces, pleases.
[3] caprices, decreases, increases, releases, subleases, valises.

SURPRISING RHYMING:
[2] **Breezes**, cheeses, eases, Eighties, Fifties, Forties, freezes, Nineties, Noughties, pleases, seizes, Sixties, sneezes, squeezes, teases, Thirties, Twenties, wheezes.
He says, she says, todays, today's.
Fact is, that is, he is, she is
Appease, Aries, chemise, deep-freeze, degrees, disease, displease, herpes, Pisces, reprise, species, striptease, trapeze, unease, unfreeze, valise.
Cheerless, dreamless, fearless, gearless, idealess, neatest, peerless, seamless, sweetest, tearless.
[3] **Achilles**, antifreeze, emojis, enemies, expertise, Hercules, melodies, overseas.
Appeases, diseases, displeases, reprises.

2.1.77 "--eezily" (as in "easily")
[3] breezily, cheesily, easily, queasily, sleazily, uneasily, wheezily.

SURPRISING RHYMING:
[3] **Actressy**, agency, autopsy, bankruptcy, blatancy, bourgeoisie, buoyancy, Christmassy, clemency, courtesy, currency, decency, divorcee, ecstasy, embassy,

fallacy, fantasy, fluency, galaxy, heresy, infancy, jealousy, legacy, leniency, lunacy, odyssey, oversee, pharmacy, piracy, policy, potency, pregnancy, privacy, prophecy, regency, secrecy, tendency, Tennessee, truancy, undersea, urgency, vacancy.
Freezingly, pleasingly, teasingly, wheezingly.
Ancestry, archery, artistry, bakery, battery, bigotry, binary, blackberry, blubbery, blueberry, blustery, brasserie, bravery, brewery, bribery, burglary, calorie, carpentry, carvery, cavalry, celery, century, chemistry, chicory, chivalry, Christmas tree, colliery, contrary, devilry, diary, dietary, disagree, dithery, doddery, drudgery, dungaree, duty-free, eatery, enquiry, estuary, expiry, factory, fakery, feathery, filigree, finery, fishery, flattery, fluttery, forestry, forgery, gallery, geometry, gimmickry, glittery, greenery, grocery, history, imagery, injury, inquiry, ivory, jamboree, jewellery/jewelry (U.S.), jittery, leathery, lingerie, lottery, luxury, memory, mercury, misery, momentary, monastery, mystery, nursery, obituary, obligatory, pageantry, pedigree, perjury, pillory, pleasantry, poetry, pottery, primary, priory, quivery, referee, revelry, reverie, rivalry, robbery, rockery, rosary, rubbery, salary, sanctuary, savagery, savory, scenery, sensory, shimmery, shivery, silvery, slavery, slippery, sorcery, sugary, surgery, tapestry, thundery, treachery, trickery, victory, wintery, wizardry.
Canopy, escapee, gossipy, recipe, syrupy, therapy, unhappy.
Burgundy, chickadee, COD, comedy, custody, dogsbody, fool-hardy, jeopardy, malady, melody, nobody, parody, Ph.D., raggedy, remedy, rhapsody, somebody, tragedy.
Alchemy, bigamy, blasphemy, blossomy, bonhomie, enemy, infamy, sesame, tsunami.
Agony, attorney, balcony, baloney, bikini, botany, colony, company, cottony, cushiony, destiny, ebony, felony, gluttony, halfpenny, harmony, Houdini, irony, larceny, litany, martini, mutiny, satiny, scrutiny, symphony, tiffany, timpani, trainee, tyranny, villainy.
Allergy, effigy, emoji, energy, eulogy, lethargy, refugee, strategy, synergy, trilogy.
Actually, bodily, brotherly, cowardly, dastardly, directly, easterly, elderly, equally, family, fatherly, finally, finale, fleur-de-lis, formally, formerly, fortnightly, gingerly, happily, heavenly, homily, icily, jubilee, leisurely, masterly, matronly, miserly, motherly, naturally, neighbourly/neighborly (U.S.), normally, northerly, orderly, overly, partially, properly, rascally, readily, reveille, scholarly, simile, sisterly, slovenly, southerly, specially, thoroughly, ungainly, unruly, usually, utterly, virtually, westerly wizardly, womanly.
Amnesty, casualty, certainty, chastity, confetti, density, deputy, devotee, dignity, dynasty, entity, faculty, fidgety, graffiti, gravity, guarantee, honesty, karate, liberty, majesty, modesty, nudity, oddity, penalty, piety, poverty, property, puberty, purity, quality, repartee, rickety, sanctity, sanctuary, sanity, scarcity, seventy, sovereignty, spaghetti, specialty, trinity, unity, uppity, vanity, velvety, warranty.
Apathy, empathy, sympathy, trustworthy, unhealthy, unworthy.
C'est la vie, eau-de-vie, shadowy, vis-à-vis, yellowy, willowy.

2.1.78 "--eeable" (as in "agreeable")
[4] agreeable, foreseeable, disagreeable, unforeseeable.

SURPRISING RHYMING:
[2] Cheerful, earful, fearful, tearful.
[3] Feasible, genial, meaningful, menial, reachable, readable.
Beautiful, beatable, eatable, unbeatable, readable, repeatable.
Eventful, resentful, uneventful.
[4] Achievable, amenable, believable, conceivable,
inconceivable, retrievable, irretrievable, unbelievable.
Amenable, irredeemable, redeemable, unreadable, unspeakable.

2.1.79 "--eerfully" (as in "tearfully")
[3] cheerfully, fearfully, tearfully.

SURPRISING RHYMING:
[3] Gleefully, lethally, peacefully, sympathy.
Freezingly, pleasingly, teasingly, wheezingly.
Easterly, equally, happily, heavenly, leisurely, misery, readily, neighbourly/neighborly (U.S.), simile, specially, thoroughly, virtually.
Comedy, jeopardy, melody, nobody, remedy, rhapsody, tragedy.

Bravery, brewery, century, chemistry, diary, duty-free, eatery, enquiry, feathery, filigree, greenery, jewelry/jewellery, memory, misery, mystery, pedigree, perjury, pillory, pleasantry, poetry, quivery, referee, reverie, scenery, sensory, treachery, wintery.
Courtesy, decency, divorcee, ecstasy, fantasy, jealousy, leniency, lunacy, odyssey, privacy, prophecy, secrecy, urgency, vacancy.
Agony, bikini, company, destiny, ebony, felony, harmony, martini, mutiny, scrutiny, symphony, tyranny, villainy.
Casualty, certainty, charity, clarity, dignity, fidgety, graffiti, gravity, honesty, liberty, modesty, poverty, property, quality, sanctuary, sanity, scarcity, unity, vanity, velvety.

2.1.80 "--eezable" (as in "squeezable")
[3] feasible, freezable, peaceable, pleasable, seizable, squeezable, teasable.

SURPRISING RHYMING:
[3] **Feedable**, leadable, readable, unreadable.
Impeachable, possible, reachable, teachable, unteachable.
Beatable, eatable, repeatable, unbeatable.
[4] **Achievable**, available, believable, retrievable, conceivable, unbelievable, inconceivable, irresistible, irretrievable.
Agreeable, foreseeable, disagreeable, unforeseeable.
Reasonable, seasonable, unreasonable, unseasonable.
Amenable, irredeemable, redeemable, unreadable, unspeakable.
Amiable, doable, enviable, renewable, variable, viewable.
Acceptable, imperceptible, irresistible, perceptible, predictable, resistible, susceptible, unacceptable.
Delectable, detectable, erasable, inflexible, predictable, respectable, unspeakable.

2.1.81 "--eezingly" (as in "teasingly")
[3] freezingly, pleasingly, teasingly, wheezingly.

SURPRISING RHYMING:
Appealingly, believingly, deceivingly, decreasingly, demeaningly, endearingly, exceedingly, fleetingly, gleamingly, grievingly, increasingly, misleadingly, pleadingly, reassuringly, revealingly, seemingly, sneeringly, sweepingly.

2.1.82 "--urlee" (as in "early")
[2] burly, curly, early, girlie, hurley, hurly-burly, pearly, surly, swirly, twirly, whirly.

SURPRISING RHYMING:
[2] **Blurry**, curry, flurry, furry, germ-free, gumtree, hurry, hungry, jury, sultry, sundry, surrey, teary, theory, worry.
Bubbly, bully, crumbly, crumply, cuddly, dully, duly, earthly, fully, grumbly, lovely, monthly, newly, poorly, pulley, purply, rumbly, surely, termly, truly, ugly, worldly.
Bumpy, droopy, dumpy, frumpy, grumpy, humpy, jumpy, lumpy, puppy, whoopee.
Budgie, bulgy, clergy, grungy, gungy, sludgy, smudgy, spongy.
Chunky, clunky, dusky, flunkey, funky, hunky, husky, jerky, junkie, lucky, murky, monkey, musky, perky, plucky, punky, quirky, rookie, sulky, turkey, turnkey, yucky.
Chummy, dreamy, dummy, gummy, mummy, tummy, yummy.
Curtsy, fussy, gutsy, hussy, look-see, mercy, pussy.
[3] **Allergy**, effigy, emoji, energy, eulogy, lethargy, refugee, strategy, synergy, trilogy.
Brotherly, cowardly, dastardly, directly, easterly, family, fatherly, fleur-de-lis, gingerly, jubilee, laggardly, leisurely, mannerly, masterly, motherly, neighbourly/neighborly (U.S.), northerly, quarterly, scholarly, sisterly, soldierly, southerly, westerly, wizardly, womanly.
Ancestry, archery, artistry, bakery, battery, bigotry, binary, blackberry, blubbery, blueberry, blustery, brasserie, bravery, brewery, bribery, burglary, calorie, carpentry, carvery, cavalry, celery, century, chemistry, chicory, chivalry, Christmas tree, colliery, contrary, devilry, diary, dietary, disagree, dithery, doddery, drudgery, dungaree, duty-free, eatery, enquiry, estuary, expiry, factory, fakery, feathery, filigree, finery, fishery,

flattery, fluttery, forestry, forgery, gallery, geometry, gimmickry, glittery, greenery, grocery, history, imagery, injury, inquiry, ivory, jamboree, jewellery/jewelry (U.S.), jittery, leathery, lingerie, lottery, luxury, memory, mercury, misery, momentary, monastery, mystery, nursery, obituary, obligatory, pageantry, pedigree, perjury, pillory, pleasantry, poetry, pottery, primary, priory, quivery, referee, revelry, reverie, rivalry, robbery, rockery, rosary, rubbery, salary, sanctuary, savagery, savory, scenery, sensory, shimmery, shivery, silvery, slavery, slippery, sorcery, sugary, surgery, tapestry, thundery, treachery, trickery, victory, wintery, wizardry.

2.1.83 "--ollee" (as in "holly")
[2] brolly, collie, dolly, folly, golly, holly, jolly, lolly, trolley, volley, wally.
[4] melancholy, monopoly.

SURPRISING RHYMING:
[2] **Bobby**, body, gaudy, hobby, lobby, shoddy, snobby, zombie.
Glory, gory, lorry, quarry, sorry.
Bonny, bony, brawny, corny, horny, mommy, phoney/phony (U.S.), pony, scrawny, stony, stormy, thorny.
Bossy, foresee, foxy, glossy, horsey, saucy, posse, proxy.
Coffee, frothy, toffee.
Blowy, doughy, showy, snowy.
Choppy, copy, floppy, jalopy, poppy, sloppy, soppy, stroppy.
Corky, door key, gawky, hockey, jockey, rocky, smoky, stocky.
[4] **Anybody**, busybody, everybody, nobody, photocopy, somebody.
Hunky-dory, statutory, territory, transitory.
Alimony, ceremony, macaroni, matrimony, minestrone, pepperoni.

2.1.84 "--allee (as in "valley")
[2] alley, dally, dilly-dally, finale, galley, pally, rally, reveille, sally, tally, valley.

SURPRISING RHYMING:
[1] **Be**, Be, bee, brie, fee, flea, flee, free, gee, glee, he, key, knee, me, sea, see, spree, tee, tea, the, thee, three, tree, twee, we, wee, whee, zee.
[2] **Baddy**, bandy, brandy, caddie, caddy, candy, daddy, dandy, handy, hardy, laddie, sandy, tardy.
Abbey, cabby, crabby, flabby, savvy, scabby, shabby.
Angry, carry, marry, pantry, parry, starry.
Chappie, crappy, happy, nappy, sappy, scrappy, snappy, zappy.
Hanky, khaki, lanky, sparky, swanky, tacky, wacky, Yankee.
Army, balmy, barmy, clammy, Grammy, hammy, jammy, mammy, smarmy, whammy.
Acne, canny, cranny, granny, nanny, tranny.
Brassy, chancy, chassis, classy, fancy, glassy, grassy, lassie, maxi, sassy, taxi, waxy.
Anti, arty, auntie, batty, catty, chatty, draughty/drafty, fatty, hearty, karate, nasty, party, ratty, scatty, tarty.
Amply, aptly, barley, dangly, flatly, gangly, ghastly, gnarly, golly, jangly, lolly,
Madly, manly, sadly, sally, snarly, sparkly, straggly, tangly.
[4] **Anybody**, busybody, everybody, namby-pamby, solitary, origami, paparazzi.

2.1.85 "--unnee" (as in "funny")
[2] bunny, dunny, funny, gunny, honey, money, runny, sonny, sunny, tunny.

SURPRISING RHYMING:
[1] **Be**, bee, brie, fee, flea, flee, free, gee, glee, he, key, knee, me, sea, see, spree, tee, tea, the, three, tree, twee, we, wee.
[2] **Chubby**, grubby, hubby, would-be.
Curry, flurry, furry, hurry, hungry, lorry, scurry, surrey, worry.
Bumpy, dumpy, grumpy, humpy, jumpy, lumpy, puppy, yuppie.
Bloody, buddy, hoodie, muddy, study, sturdy, woodie.
Comfy, fluffy, huffy, puffy, selfie, scruffy, stuffy, toughie.

Chummy, crummy, dummy, mummy, plummy, rummy, scrummy, tummy, yummy.
Bookie, chunky, clunky, cookie, ducky, dusky, flunkey, funky, hunky, husky, junkie, lucky, monkey, mucky, musky, nooky, plucky, punky, rookie, sulky, turkey, yucky.
Bubbly, bully, comely, crumbly, crumply, cuddly, dully, fully, grumbly, gulley, gully, monthly, pulley, rumbly, sully, ugly, woolly.
Fussy, gutsy, hussy, pussy, tootsie.
Burly, curly, early, girlie, hurly-burly, surly, swirly, twirly, whirly.
[3] **Destiny**, harmony, lemony, rhapsody, symphony, somebody, tyranny, villainy.
Allergy, effigy, elegy, emoji, energy, eulogy, lethargy, tragedy.
Brotherly, cowardly, elderly, equally, family, fatherly, finally, formally, formerly, gingerly, leisurely, masterly, miserly, motherly, neighbourly/neighborly (U.S.), normally, northerly, orderly, properly, sisterly, southerly, specially, usually, utterly, virtually, westerly.
Jealousy, odyssey, prophecy, secrecy, truancy, urgency.
Charity, chastity, clarity, deputy, dignity, dynasty, gravity, guarantee, honesty, liberty, modesty, penalty, piety, poverty, purity, quality, sanctity, sanctuary, sanity, seventy, unity, vanity, velvety.
Antipathy, apathy, empathy, sympathy, telepathy.
[4] **Anybody**, busybody, everybody, fuddy-duddy, hurdy-gurdy, lovey-dovey, understudy.
Accessory, adultery, advisory, cautionary, compulsory, debauchery, derisory, discovery, distillery, elementary, idolatry, illusory, imaginary, legendary, ordinary, patisserie, perfunctory, perfumery, psychiatry, reactionary, recovery, tomfoolery, visionary.
Analogy, anomaly, anthology, apology, astrology, biology, ecology, geology, ideology, mythology, psychology, technology, theology.
Ability, agility, facility, fertility, fragility, futility, hostility, humility, mobility, nobility, stability, tranquillity/tranquility (U.S.), utility, virility.

2.1.86 "--oppee" (as in "copy")

[2] choppy, copy, floppy, jalopy, photocopy, poppy, sloppy, soppy, stroppy.

SURPRISING RHYMING:
[2] **Coffee**, frothy, toffee.
Bossy, foresee, foxy, glossy, horsey, saucy, posse, proxy.
Body, gaudy, shoddy, squaddie.
Bobby, hobby, lobby, snobby, zombie.
Bonny, brawny, corny, mommy, phoney/phony (U.S.), pony, scrawny, stony, stormy.
Brolly, collie, dolly, folly, golly, holly, jolly, lolly, trolley, volley, wally.
[3] **Chicory**, cursory, factory, hickory, history, ivory, memory, savory, sensory, vapory, victory, Glory, lorry, sorry, story, worry.
[4] **Anybody**, busybody, everybody, dogsbody, nobody, somebody.
Analogy, anomaly, anthology, apology, astrology, biology, ecology, geology, ideology, mythology, psychology, technology, theology.

2.1.87 "--ittee" (as in "pretty")

[2] bitty, chitty, city, ditty, gritty, kitty, pity, pretty, witty.
[3] committee, gravity, nudity, oddity, quality, sanity, self-pity, vanity.
[4] ability, agility, anxiety, calamity, equality, eternity, fertility, fidelity, fragility, futility, hostility, humanity, humility, nitty-gritty, humidity, mobility, notoriety, responsibility, sobriety, society, stability, stupidity, tranquillity/tranquility (U.S.), variety, virility.

SURPRISING RHYMING:
[2] **Chippy**, clippie, crispy, drippy, grippy, hippie, lippy, nippy, slippy, trippy, zippy.
Brickie, hickey, icky, mickey, milky, picky, pinkie, pinky, quickie, sickie, silky, slinky, sticky, tricky, whiskey/whisky.
Diddy, giddy, kiddie, midi.
Busy, dizzy, Dixie, fizzy, frizzy, glitzy, kissy, missy, prissy, ritzy, tizzy.
Filly, fifty, frilly, hilly, hillbilly, silly, willy, rockabilly.
Fifty, fifty-fifty, iffy, jiffy, sniffy, stiffy, pithy, smithy.
Guilty, minty, misty, nasty, nicety, nifty, shifty, sixty, swiftie, thrifty.
Cine, gimme, lemme, mini, ninny, shinny, skinny, tinny, whinny.

2.1.88 "--ilitee" (as in "ability")
[4] ability, agility, civility, facility, fertility, fragility, futility, hostility, humility, mobility, nobility, stability, tranquillity/tranquility (U.S.), utility, virility.
[5] edibility, liability, responsibility, usability, versatility, viability, volatility.

SURPRISING RHYMING:
[2] **Bitty**, chitty, city, ditty, gritty, kitty, pity, pretty, witty.
[3] **Burgundy**, COD, comedy, custody, dogsbody, fool-hardy, jeopardy, malady, melody, nobody, parody, Ph.D., raggedy, remedy, rhapsody, somebody, tragedy.
Amnesty, casualty, certainty, chastity, confetti, density, deputy, devotee, dignity, dynasty, entity, faculty, fidgety, graffiti, gravity, guarantee, honesty, karate, liberty, majesty, modesty, nudity, oddity, penalty, piety, poverty, property, puberty, purity, quality, repartee, rickety, sanctity, sanctuary, sanity, scarcity, seventy, sovereignty, spaghetti, specialty, trinity, unity, uppity, vanity, velvety, warranty.
Allergy, effigy, emoji, energy, eulogy, lethargy, refugee, strategy, synergy, trilogy.
Bodily, family, fleur-de-lis, heavenly, homily, icily, jubilee, melancholy, miserly, readily.
Mimicry, ministry, misery, priory, reverie.
Gossipy, recipe, slap-happy, syrupy, therapy, unhappy.
[4] **Absurdity**, affinity, amenity, anxiety, barbarity, calamity, cognoscenti, community, conformity, credulity, difficulty, dilettante, enormity, equality, eternity, fatality, fidelity, fifty-fifty, fraternity, frivolity, glitterati, heredity, hilarity, humanity, humidity, immunity, impunity, indemnity, infinity, intercity, literati, maternity, modernity, morality, nitty-gritty, obscenity, profanity, reality, senility, serenity, sobriety, solemnity, stupidity, timidity, totality, twenty-twenty, variety, vicinity, vigilante, virginity, vulgarity.
[5] **Ambiguity**, anonymity, continuity, familiarity, femininity, impropriety, ingenuity, irregularity, liability, masculinity, notoriety, opportunity, peculiarity, popularity, regularity, responsibility, serendipity, similarity, solidarity, spontaneity, versatility, viability, volatility.

2.1.89 "--aritee" (as in "charity")
[3] charity, clarity, parity.
[4] barbarity, hilarity, polarity, vulgarity.
[5] familiarity, irregularity, jocularity, peculiarity, popularity, regularity, similarity, solidarity.

SURPRISING RHYMING:
[3] **Amnesty**, casualty, certainty, chastity, confetti, density, deputy, devotee, dignity, dynasty, entity, faculty, fidgety, graffiti, gravity, guarantee, honesty, karate, liberty, majesty, modesty, nudity, oddity, penalty, piety, poverty, property, puberty, purity, quality, repartee, rickety, sanctity, sanctuary, sanity, scarcity, seventy, sovereignty, spaghetti, specialty, trinity, unity, uppity, vanity, velvety, warranty.
Bodily, family, fleur-de-lis, heavenly, homily, icily, jubilee, melancholy, miserly, readily.
Comedy, custody, jeopardy, melody, nobody, parody, perfidy, raggedy, remedy, rhapsody, somebody, subsidy, tragedy.
Agony, balcony, company, destiny, harmony, Houdini, irony, mutiny, symphony, tiffany, timpani, tyranny, villainy.
Ancestry, archery, artistry, bakery, battery, bigotry, binary, blackberry, blubbery, blueberry, blustery, brasserie, bravery, brewery, bribery, burglary, calorie, carpentry, carvery, cavalry, celery, century, chemistry, chicory, chivalry, Christmas tree, colliery, contrary, devilry, diary, dietary, disagree, dithery, doddery, drudgery, dungaree, duty-free, eatery, enquiry, estuary, expiry, factory, fakery, feathery, filigree, finery, fishery, flattery, fluttery, forestry, forgery, gallery, geometry, gimmickry, glittery, greenery, grocery, history, imagery, injury, inquiry, ivory, jamboree, jewellery/jewelry (U.S.), jittery, leathery, lingerie, lottery, luxury, memory, mercury, misery, momentary, monastery, mystery, nursery, obituary, obligatory, pageantry, pedigree, perjury, pillory, pleasantry, poetry, pottery, primary, priory, quivery, referee, revelry, reverie, rivalry, robbery, rockery, rosary, rubbery, salary, sanctuary, savagery, savory, scenery, sensory, shimmery, shivery, silvery, slavery, slippery, sorcery, sugary, surgery, tapestry, thundery, treachery, trickery, victory, wintery, wizardry.
[4] **Ability**, agility, fertility, fragility, futility, hostility, humility, liability, mobility, nobility, responsibility, stability, tranquillity/tranquility (U.S.), versatility, viability, virility, volatility.

209

Absurdity, affinity, amenity, anxiety, barbarity, calamity, cognoscenti, community, conformity, credulity, difficulty, dilettante, enormity, equality, eternity, fatality, fidelity, fifty-fifty, fraternity, frivolity, glitterati, heredity, hilarity, humanity, humidity, immunity, impunity, indemnity, infinity, intercity, literati, maternity, modernity, morality, nitty-gritty, obscenity, profanity, reality, senility, serenity, sobriety, solemnity, virility, stupidity, timidity, totality, twenty-twenty, variety, vicinity, vigilante, virginity, vulgarity.
[5] Ambiguity, anonymity, continuity, familiarity, femininity, impropriety, ingenuity, irregularity, liability, masculinity, notoriety, opportunity, peculiarity, popularity, regularity, responsibility, serendipity, similarity, solidarity, spontaneity, versatility, viability, volatility.

2.2 "er"

2.2.1 "--acker" (as in "hacker")
[2] backer, blacker, clacker, cracker, hacker, knacker, lacquer, packer, quacker, racker, sacker, slacker, smacker, snacker, stacker, tracker, whacker.
[3] attacker, backpacker, bushwhacker, firecracker, hijacker, linebacker, lipsmacker, maraca, nutcracker, ransacker, repacker, safecracker, skyjacker, unpacker, wisecracker.

SURPRISING RHYMING:
[2] **Anchor**, banker, blanker, canker, Casablanca, clanker, flanker, franker, hanker, pranker, rancour/rancor (U.S.), ranker, spanker, tanker, thanker, up-anchor, yanker.
Actor, batter, chatter, clatter, factor, fatter, flatter, hatter, latter, matter, natter, patter, platter, scatter, shatter, smatter, spatter, splatter, tractor, yatter.
Banter, canter, chanter, granter, grantor, mantra, panter, planter, ranter, scanter, Santa.
Clapper, dapper, flapper, grappa, lapper, napper, rapper, scrapper, slapper, snapper, strapper, tapper, trapper, wrapper, yapper.
Bagger, blagger, bragger, carpetbagger, dagger, dragger, flagger, gagger, lagger, nagger, snagger, stagger, swagger, zigzagger.
Banner, canner, fanner, hosanna, manna, manner, manor, nana/nanna, panner, planner, scanner, spanner, tanner.
Anger, blander, candour/candor (U.S.), dander, gander, grander, pander, slander.
Camper, clamper, damper, hamper, pamper, scamper, stamper, tamper, tramper.
Catcher, hatcher, latcher, matcher, patcher, scratcher, snatcher, stature, thatcher.
Clamour/clamor (U.S.), crammer, gamma, glamour/glamor (U.S.), grammar, hammer, jammer, mamma, rammer, shammer, slammer, spammer, stammer.
Basher, brasher, casher, clasher, crasher, dasher, flasher, gasher, gate-crasher, lasher, masher, rasher, slasher, smasher, splasher, stasher, thrasher.
[3] **Benefactor**, chiropractor, contractor, enactor, extractor, hereafter, protractor, reactor, redactor, refractor, retractor, subcontractor.
Antimatter, decanter, enchanter, pitter-patter, regatta, supplanter, transplanter.
Backslapper, entrapper, hand-clapper, handicapper, kidnapper, knee-capper, recapper, whippersnapper, wiretapper.
Alabaster, bandmaster, broadcaster, choirmaster, disaster, forecaster, flabbergaster, grandmaster, headmaster, newscaster, paymaster, postmaster, quartermaster, quizmaster, ringmaster, schoolmaster, spymaster, stationmaster, taskmaster.
Bandanna, caravanner, savannah.
Enamour/enamor (U.S.), programmer, sledgehammer, windjammer.
Backhander, bystander, commander, coriander, demander, disbander, expander, inlander, jacaranda, left-hander, meander, memoranda, oleander, outlander, philander, propaganda, remander, right-hander, understander, veranda.

2.2.2 "--actor" (as in "tractor")
[2] actor, factor, tractor.
[3] abstractor, attractor, benefactor, chiropractor, compactor, contractor, enactor, exactor, extractor, protractor, reactor, redactor, refractor, retractor, subcontractor.

SURPRISING RHYMING:
[2] **Cracker**, hacker, knacker, lacquer, sacker, slacker, smacker, snacker, tracker.
Catcher, hatcher, latcher, matcher, patcher, scratcher, snatcher, stature, thatcher.

After, crafter, dafter, drafter, grafter, laughter, rafter.
Anchor, banker, blanker, canker, Casablanca, clanker, flanker, franker, hanker, pranker, rancour/rancor (U.S.), ranker, spanker, tanker, thanker, up-anchor, yanker.
Banter, canter, chanter, granter, grantor, mantra, panter, planter, ranter, scanter, Santa.
Batter, chatter, clatter, fatter, flatter, hatter, latter, matter, natter, patter, platter, scatter, shatter, smatter, spatter, splatter, yatter.
Clapper, dapper, flapper, grappa, lapper, napper, rapper, sapper, scrapper, slapper, snapper, strapper, trapper, wrapper, yapper.
Camper, damper, hamper, pamper, scamper, stamper, tamper.
Answer, cancer, chancer, dancer, glancer, lancer, prancer.
Bagger, blagger, bragger, carpetbagger, dagger, dragger, flagger, gagger, lagger, nagger, snagger, stagger, swagger, zigzagger.
Clamour/clamor (U.S.), crammer, gamma, glamour/glamor (U.S.), grammar, hammer, jammer, mamma, rammer, shammer, slammer, spammer, stammer.
[3] **Attacker**, backpacker, bushwhacker, firecracker, hijacker, linebacker, lipsmacker, maraca, nutcracker, ransacker, repacker, safecracker, skyjacker, unpacker, wisecracker.
Back-scratcher, body-snatcher, cradle-snatcher, dispatcher, dogcatcher, flycatcher.
Alabaster, bandmaster, broadcaster, choirmaster, disaster, forecaster, flabbergaster, grandmaster, headmaster, newscaster, paymaster, postmaster, quartermaster, quizmaster, ringmaster, schoolmaster, spymaster, stationmaster, taskmaster.
Backslapper, entrapper, hand-clapper, kidnapper, knee-capper, recapper, whippersnapper, wiretapper.
Backhander, bystander, commander, demander, expander, left-hander, meander, memoranda, outlander, philander, propaganda, right-hander, understander, veranda.

2.2.3 "--acer" (as in "racer")
[2] acer, bracer, chaser, facer, lacer, mesa, pacer, placer, racer, spacer, tracer.
[3] embracer, encaser, eraser, horse-racer, misplacer, replacer, retracer, steeplechaser.

SURPRISING RHYMING:
[2] **Blazer**, gazer, grazer, laser, phraser, praiser, razor, tazer.
Caper, gaper, paper, scraper, shaper, taper, vapour/vapor (U.S.).
Cater, crater, data, dater, greater, hater, later, skater, slater, straighter, traitor, waiter.
Braver, favour/favor (U.S.), flavour/flavor (U.S.), raver, saver, savour/savor (U.S.), shaver.
Frailer, hailer, jailer, mailer, nailer, paler, sailor, staler, trailer, tailor.
Aimer, claimer, disclaimer, exclaimer, framer, gamer, proclaimer, shamer, tamer.
Changer, danger, manger, ranger, stranger.
Greyer/grayer (U.S.), layer, mayor, payer, player, prayer, slayer, stayer, strayer.
[3] **Appraiser**, eraser, fundraiser, impresa, stargazer, trail-blazer.
Escaper, notepaper, newspaper, sandpaper, skyscraper, wallpaper.
Creator, curator, debater, dictator, dumbwaiter, equator, narrator, negator, peseta, rotator, spectator, translator.
Disfavour/disfavor (U.S.), engraver, lifesaver, timesaver.
Abseiler, blackmailer, exhaler, inhaler, loudhailer, regaler, retailer, wholesaler.
Arranger, endanger, exchanger, moneychanger, shortchanger.
Betrayer, bill-payer, bricklayer, conveyor, delayer, displayer, gainsayer, obeyer, portrayer, purveyor, record player, soothsayer, surveyor, taxpayer.
[4] **Abdicator**, agitator, alligator, aviator, animator, calculator, captivator, celebrator, commentator, decorator, demonstrator, educator, elevator, escalator, figure-skater, generator, gladiator, hesitater, illustrator, imitator, indicator, innovator, instigator, liberator, mediator, moderator, motivator, operator, orchestrater, percolator, perpetrator, radiator, simulator, speculator, terminator, violator.
[5] **Accelerator**, collaborator, impersonator, incinerator, interrogator, investigator, negotiator, refrigerator, resuscitator, ventilator.

2.2.4 "--azer" (as in "razor")
[2] blazer, gazer, glazer, grazer, hazer, laser, phraser, praiser, raiser, razor, tazer.
[3] appraiser, eraser, fundraiser, impresa, stargazer, trail-blazer.

SURPRISING RHYMING:
[2] **Bracer**, chaser, mesa, pacer, placer, racer, spacer, tracer.
Braver, favour/favor (U.S.), flavour/flavor (U.S.), raver, saver, savour/savor (U.S.), shaver.
Greyer/grayer (U.S.), layer, mayor, payer, player, prayer, slayer, stayer, strayer.
Caper, gaper, paper, scraper, shaper, taper, vapour/vapor (U.S.).
Cater, crater, data, dater, greater, hater, later, skater, straighter, traitor, waiter.
Frailer, jailer, paler, sailor, staler, trailer, tailor, wailer, whaler.
Defamer, disclaimer, exclaimer, framer, gamer, proclaimer, shamer, tamer.
Changer, danger, manger, ranger, stranger.
[3] **Embracer**, encaser, eraser, horse-racer, misplacer, replacer, retracer, steeplechaser.
Disfavour/disfavor (U.S.), engraver, enslaver, lifesaver, semiquaver, timesaver.
Betrayer, delayer, displayer, obeyer, portrayer, record player, soothsayer, taxpayer.
Escaper, flypaper, notepaper, newspaper, sandpaper, skyscraper, wallpaper.
Creator, curator, debater, dictator, equator, frustrater, narrator, spectator, translator.
Abseiler, blackmailer, exhaler, inhaler, loudhailer, regaler, retailer.
Arranger, endanger, exchanger, moneychanger, shortchanger.
[4] **Abdicator**, agitator, alligator, aviator, animator, calculator, captivator, celebrator, commentator, decorator, demonstrator, educator, elevator, escalator, figure-skater, generator, gladiator, hesitater, illustrator, imitator, indicator, innovator, instigator, liberator, mediator, moderator, motivator, operator, orchestrater, percolator, perpetrator, radiator, simulator, speculator, terminator, violator.
[5] **Accelerator**, collaborator, impersonator, incinerator, interrogator, investigator, negotiator, refrigerator, resuscitator, ventilator.

2.2.5 "--adder" (as in "sadder")
[2] adder, bladder, gladder, sadder, ladder, madder, step-ladder.

SURPRISING RHYMING:
[2] **Banner**, hosanna, manna, manner, manor, nana/nanna, planner, scanner, spanner.
Anger, blander, candour/candor (U.S.), dander, gander, grander, pander, slander.
Bagger, blagger, bragger, carpetbagger, dagger, dragger, flagger, gagger, lagger, nagger, snagger, stagger, swagger, zigzagger.
Clamour/clamor (U.S.), crammer, gamma, glamour/glamor (U.S.), grammar, hammer, jammer, mamma, rammer, shammer, slammer, spammer, stammer.
Camper, clamper, damper, hamper, pamper, scamper, stamper, tamper, tramper.
Banter, canter, chanter, granter, grantor, mantra, panter, planter, ranter, scanter, Santa.
Answer, cancer, chancer, dancer, glancer, lancer, prancer.
After, crafter, dafter, drafter, grafter, laughter, rafter.
Barker, darker, larker, marker, parka, parker, sparker, starker.
Backer, blacker, cracker, hacker, knacker, slacker, smacker, snacker, stacker, tracker.
[3] **Backhander**, bystander, commander, demander, expander, left-hander, meander, memoranda, outlander, philander, propaganda, right-hander, understander, veranda.
Enamour/enamor (U.S.), programmer, sledgehammer, windjammer.
Decanter, enchanter, supplanter, transplanter.
Advancer, enhancer, entrancer, romancer.
Bookmarker, moussaka, nosy-parker, postmarker,
Attacker, backpacker, bushwhacker, firecracker, hijacker, linebacker, lipsmacker, nutcracker, safecracker,, skyjacker, wisecracker.

2.2.6 "--after" (as in "after")
[2] after, crafter, dafter, drafter, grafter, laughter, rafter.
[3] hereafter, thereafter, whereafter.

SURPRISING RHYMING:
[2] **Anger**, blander, candour/candor (U.S.), dander, gander, grander, pander, slander.
Adder, bladder, gladder, sadder, ladder, madder, step-ladder.
Blaster, caster, castor, faster, master, pasta, pastor, plaster, vaster.
Amber, camber, clamber, mamba, samba, timbre.
Answer, cancer, chancer, dancer, glancer, lancer, prancer.
Ambler, brambler, gambler, rambler, scrambler, shambler.

212

Banner, canner, fanner, hosanna, manna, manner, manor, nana/nanna, panner, planner, scanner, spanner, tanner.
Banter, canter, chanter, granter, grantor, mantra, panter, planter, ranter, scanter, Santa.
Clamour/clamor (U.S.), crammer, gamma, glamour/glamor (U.S.), grammar, hammer, jammer, mamma, rammer, shammer, slammer, spammer, stammer.
Actor, factor, tractor.
Camper, damper, hamper, pamper, scamper, stamper, tamper.
[3] **Benefactor**, chiropractor, compactor, contractor, enactor, exactor, extractor, protractor, reactor, redactor, refractor, retractor, subcontractor.
Backhander, bystander, commander, demander, expander, left-hander, meander, memoranda, outlander, philander, propaganda, right-hander, understander, veranda.

2.2.7 "--agger" (as in "dagger")
[2] bagger, blagger, bragger, carpetbagger, dagger, dragger, flagger, gagger, jagger, lagger, nagger, snagger, stagger, swagger, zigzagger.

SURPRISING RHYMING:
[2] **Adder**, bladder, gladder, sadder, ladder, madder, step-ladder.
Anger, blander, candour/candor (U.S.), dander, gander, grander, pander, slander.
Banner, hosanna, manna, manner, manor, nana/nanna, planner, scanner, spanner.
Batter, chatter, clatter, fatter, flatter, hatter, latter, matter, natter, patter, platter, scatter, shatter, smatter, spatter, splatter, yatter.
Backer, blacker, cracker, hacker, knacker, slacker, smacker, snacker, stacker, tracker.
Clapper, dapper, flapper, napper, rapper, scrapper, slapper, snapper, trapper, wrapper.
Actor, factor, tractor.
Answer, cancer, chancer, dancer, glancer, lancer, prancer.
Clamour/clamor (U.S.), gamma, glamour/glamor (U.S.), grammar, hammer, jammer, mamma, rammer, slammer, spammer, stammer.
[3] **Backhander,** bystander, commander, demander, expander, left-hander, meander, memoranda, outlander, philander, propaganda, right-hander, understander, veranda.
Attacker, backpacker, bushwhacker, firecracker, hijacker, linebacker, lipsmacker, nutcracker, safecracker, skyjacker, wisecracker.
Backslapper, entrapper, hand-clapper, handicapper, kidnapper, knee-capper, whippersnapper, wiretapper.

2.2.8 "--ainter" (as in "painter")
[2] fainter, painter, quainter.

SURPRISING RHYMING:
[2] **Cater**, crater, data, dater, greater, hater, later, skater, straighter, traitor, waiter.
Braver, favour/favor (U.S.), flavour/flavor (U.S.), raver, saver, savour/savor (U.S.), shaver.
Frailer, jailer, paler, sailor, staler, trailer, tailor, wailer, whaler.
Aimer, defamer, disclaimer, exclaimer, framer, gamer, proclaimer, shamer, tamer.
Changer, danger, manger, ranger, stranger.
Chaser, facer, pacer, placer, racer, spacer, tracer.
Blazer, gazer, grazer, laser, phraser, praiser, raiser, razor, tazer.
[3] **Creator**, curator, debater, dictator, equator, frustrater, narrator, spectator, translator.
Crusader, degrader, dissuader, evader, first-aider, invader, masquerader, parader, persuader, ram-raider, rollerblader, serenader.
Disfavour/disfavor (U.S.), engraver, lifesaver, timesaver.
Abseiler, blackmailer, exhaler, inhaler, loudhailer, regaler, retailer, wholesaler.
Arranger, endanger, exchanger, moneychanger, shortchanger.
Embracer, eraser, horse-racer, misplacer, replacer, retracer, steeplechaser.
Appraiser, eraser, fundraiser, impresa, stargazer, trail-blazer.
[4] **Abdicator**, agitator, alligator, aviator, animator, calculator, captivator, celebrator, commentator, decorator, demonstrator, educator, elevator, escalator, figure-skater, generator, gladiator, hesitater, illustrator, imitator, indicator, innovator, instigator, liberator, mediator, moderator, motivator, operator, orchestrater, percolator, perpetrator, radiator, simulator, speculator, terminator, violator.

[5] **Accelerator**, collaborator, impersonator, incinerator, interrogator, investigator, negotiator, refrigerator, resuscitator, ventilator.

2.2.9 "--airer" (as in "fairer")

[2] airer, bearer, carer, darer, fairer, rarer, scarer, sharer, share her, snarer, sparer, squarer, starer, swearer, tearer, wearer.
[3] cause célèbre, declarer, despairer, pallbearer, preparer, repairer, seafarer, sword-bearer, torch-bearer, wayfarer.

SURPRISING RHYMING:
[2] **Frailer**, jailer, paler, sailor, staler, trailer, tailor, wailer, whaler.
Aimer, defamer, disclaimer, exclaimer, framer, gamer, proclaimer, shamer, tamer.
Changer, danger, manger, ranger, stranger.
Bracer, chaser, facer, pacer, placer, racer, spacer, tracer.
Blazer, gazer, grazer, laser, phraser, praiser, raiser, razor, tazer.
Cater, crater, data, dater, greater, hater, later, skater, slater, straighter, traitor, waiter.
[3] **Creator**, curator, debater, dictator, equator, frustrater, narrator, spectator, translator.
Aider, crusader, degrader, dissuader, evader, first-aider, invader, masquerader, parader, persuader, ram-raider, rollerblader, serenader, wader.
Abseiler, blackmailer, exhaler, inhaler, loudhailer, regaler, retailer.
Arranger, endanger, exchanger, moneychanger, shortchanger.
Embracer, encaser, eraser, horse-racer, misplacer, replacer, retracer, steeplechaser.
Appraiser, eraser, fundraiser, impresa, stargazer, trail-blazer.
[4] **Agitator**, alligator, aviator, animator, calculator, captivator, celebrator, commentator, decorator, demonstrator, educator, elevator, escalator, figure-skater, generator, gladiator, hesitater, illustrator, imitator, indicator, innovator, instigator, liberator, mediator, moderator, motivator, operator, orchestrater, percolator, perpetrator, radiator, simulator, speculator, terminator, violator.
[5] **Accelerator**, collaborator, impersonator, incinerator, interrogator, investigator, negotiator, refrigerator, resuscitator, ventilator.

2.2.10 "--aider" (as in "raider")

aider, blockader, crusader, degrader, dissuader, evader, fader, first-aider, grader, invader, masquerader, parader, persuader, raider, ram-raider, rollerblader, serenader, trader, upgrader, wader.

SURPRISING RHYMING:
[2] **Greyer/grayer (U.S.)**, layer, mayor, payer, player, prayer, slayer, stayer, strayer.
Fainter, painter, quainter.
Caper, gaper, paper, scraper, shaper, taper, vapour/vapor (U.S.).
Cater, crater, data, dater, greater, hater, later, skater, slater, straighter, traitor, waiter.
Braver, favour/favor (U.S.), flavour/flavor (U.S.), raver, saver, savour/savor (U.S.), shaver.
Frailer, jailer, paler, sailor, staler, trailer, tailor, wailer, whaler.
Disclaimer, exclaimer, framer, gamer, proclaimer, shamer, tamer.
Changer, danger, manger, ranger, stranger.
[3] **Container**, remainder, remainer, retainer.
Betrayer, delayer, displayer, portrayer, purveyor, record player, soothsayer, taxpayer.
Escaper, notepaper, newspaper, sandpaper, skyscraper, wallpaper.
Creator, curator, debater, dictator, equator, frustrater, narrator, spectator, translator.
Disfavour/disfavor (U.S.), engraver, lifesaver, timesaver.
Abseiler, blackmailer, exhaler, inhaler, loudhailer, regaler, retailer.
Arranger, endanger, exchanger, moneychanger, shortchanger.
[4] **Abdicator**, agitator, alligator, aviator, animator, calculator, captivator, celebrator, commentator, decorator, demonstrator, educator, elevator, escalator, figure-skater, generator, gladiator, hesitater, illustrator, imitator, indicator, innovator, instigator, liberator, mediator, moderator, motivator, operator, orchestrater, percolator, perpetrator, radiator, simulator, speculator, terminator, violator.
[5] **Accelerator**, collaborator, impersonator, incinerator, interrogator, investigator, negotiator, refrigerator, resuscitator, ventilator.

2.2.11 "--ailer" (as in "jailer")
[2] frailer, hailer, jailer, mailer, nailer, paler, sailor, staler, trailer, tailor, wailer, whaler.
[3] abseiler, blackmailer, exhaler, inhaler, loudhailer, regaler, retailer, wholesaler.

SURPRISING RHYMING:
[2] **Greyer/grayer (U.S.)**, layer, mayor, payer, player, prayer, slayer, stayer, strayer.
Fainter, painter, quainter.
Caper, gaper, paper, scraper, shaper, taper, vapour/vapor (U.S.).
Cater, crater, data, dater, greater, hater, later, skater, straighter, traitor, waiter.
Braver, favour/favor (U.S.), flavour/flavor (U.S.), raver, saver, savour/savor (U.S.), shaver.
Disclaimer, exclaimer, framer, gamer, proclaimer, shamer, tamer.
Changer, danger, manger, ranger, stranger.
Chaser, facer, pacer, placer, racer, spacer, tracer.
Blazer, gazer, grazer, laser, phraser, praiser, raiser, razor, tazer.
[3] **Betrayer**, delayer, portrayer, purveyor, record player, soothsayer, taxpayer.
Aider, crusader, degrader, dissuader, evader, first-aider, invader, masquerader, parader, persuader, ram-raider, rollerblader, serenader, wader.
Escaper, notepaper, newspaper, sandpaper, skyscraper, wallpaper.
Creator, curator, debater, dictator, equator, frustrater, narrator, spectator, translator.
Disfavour/disfavor (U.S.), engraver, enslaver, lifesaver, semiquaver, timesaver.
Abseiler, blackmailer, exhaler, inhaler, loudhailer, regaler, retailer.
Arranger, endanger, exchanger, moneychanger, shortchanger.
Embracer, encaser, eraser, horse-racer, misplacer, replacer, retracer, steeplechaser.
[4] **Abdicator**, agitator, alligator, aviator, animator, calculator, captivator, celebrator, commentator, decorator, demonstrator, educator, elevator, escalator, figure-skater, generator, gladiator, hesitater, illustrator, imitator, indicator, innovator, instigator, liberator, mediator, moderator, motivator, operator, orchestrater, percolator, perpetrator, radiator, simulator, speculator, terminator, violator.
[5] **Accelerator**, collaborator, impersonator, incinerator, interrogator, investigator, negotiator, refrigerator, resuscitator, ventilator.

2.2.12 "--aimer" (as in "gamer")
[2] aimer, claimer, disclaimer, exclaimer, framer, gamer, proclaimer, shamer, tamer.

SURPRISING RHYMING:
[2] **Changer**, danger, manger, ranger, stranger.
Braver, favour/favor (U.S.), flavour/flavor (U.S.), raver, saver, savour/savor (U.S.), shaver.
Caper, gaper, paper, scraper, shaper, taper, vapour/vapor (U.S.).
Greyer/grayer (U.S.), layer, mayor, payer, player, prayer, slayer, stayer, strayer.
Cater, crater, data, dater, greater, hater, later, skater, straighter, traitor, waiter.
Frailer, jailer, paler, sailor, staler, trailer, tailor, wailer, whaler.
[3] **Arranger**, endanger, exchanger, moneychanger.
Aider, crusader, degrader, dissuader, evader, first-aider, invader, masquerader, parader, persuader, ram-raider, rollerblader, serenader, wader
Abseiler, blackmailer, exhaler, inhaler, loudhailer, regaler, retailer.
Disfavour/disfavor (U.S.), engraver, enslaver, lifesaver, timesaver.
Escaper, notepaper, newspaper, sandpaper, skyscraper, wallpaper.
Betrayer, delayer, displayer, portrayer, purveyor, record player, soothsayer, taxpayer.
Creator, curator, debater, dictator, equator, frustrater, narrator, spectator, translator.
[4] **Agitator**, alligator, aviator, animator, calculator, captivator, celebrator, commentator, decorator, demonstrator, educator, elevator, escalator, figure-skater, generator, gladiator, hesitater, illustrator, imitator, indicator, innovator, instigator, liberator, mediator, moderator, motivator, operator, orchestrater, percolator, perpetrator, radiator, simulator, speculator, terminator, violator.
[5] **Accelerator**, collaborator, impersonator, incinerator, interrogator, investigator, negotiator, refrigerator, resuscitator, ventilator.

2.2.13 "--ainger" (as in "danger")
[2] changer, danger, manger, ranger, stranger.
[3] arranger, endanger, endangered, exchanger, moneychanger, shortchanger.

SURPRISING RHYMING:
[2] **Fainter**, painter, quainter.
Greyer/grayer (U.S.), layer, mayor, payer, player, prayer, slayer, stayer, strayer.
Frailer, jailer, paler, sailor, staler, trailer, tailor, wailer, whaler.
Chamber, disclaimer, exclaimer, framer, gamer, proclaimer, shamer, tamer.
Chaser, facer, mesa, pacer, placer, racer, spacer, tracer.
Blazer, gazer, grazer, laser, phraser, praiser, raiser, razor, tazer.
[3] **Aider**, blockader, crusader, degrader, dissuader, evader, fader, first-aider, grader, invader, masquerader, parader, persuader, raider, ram-raider, rollerblader, serenader, trader, upgrader, wader.
Container, remainder, remainer, retainer.
Betrayer, delayer, displayer, portrayer, purveyor, record player, soothsayer, taxpayer.
Abseiler, blackmailer, exhaler, inhaler, loudhailer, regaler, retailer.
Embracer, eraser, horse-racer, misplacer, replacer, retracer.
Appraiser, eraser, fundraiser, impresa, stargazer, trail-blazer.

2.2.14 "--amper" (as in "pamper")
[2] camper, clamper, damper, hamper, pamper, scamper, stamper, tamper, tramper.

SURPRISING RHYMING:
[2] **Amber**, camber, clamber, mamba, samba, timbre.
Answer, cancer, chancer, dancer, glancer, lancer, prancer.
Anger, blander, candour/candor (U.S.), dander, gander, grander, panda, pander, slander.
Ambler, brambler, gambler, rambler, scrambler, shambler.
Banter, canter, chanter, granter, grantor, mantra, panter, planter, ranter, scanter, Santa.
Banner, hosanna, manna, manner, manor, nana/nanna, planner, scanner, spanner.
Anchor, banker, blanker, canker, Casablanca, clanker, flanker, franker, hanker, pranker, rancour/rancor (U.S.), ranker, spanker, tanker, thanker, up-anchor, yanker.
After, crafter, dafter, drafter, grafter, laughter, rafter.
Clamour/clamor (U.S.), crammer, glamour/glamor (U.S.), grammar, hammer, jammer, mamma, rammer, slammer, spammer, stammer.
Catcher, capture, matcher, patcher, rapture, scratcher, snatcher, stature, thatcher.
[3] **Advancer**, enhancer, entrancer, romancer.
Backhander, bystander, commander, demander, expander, left-hander, meander, memoranda, outlander, philander, propaganda, right-hander, understander, veranda.
Bandanna, caravanner, savannah.
Enamour/enamor (U.S.), programmer, sledgehammer, windjammer.
Back-scratcher, body-snatcher, cradle-snatcher, dispatcher, dogcatcher, flycatcher, oyster-catcher.

2.2.15 "--amber" (as in "clamber")
[2] amber, camber, clamber, mamba, samba, timbre.

SURPRISING RHYMING:
[2] **Camper**, clamper, damper, hamper, pamper, scamper, stamper, tamper, tramper.
Answer, cancer, chancer, dancer, glancer, lancer, prancer.
Ambler, brambler, gambler, rambler, scrambler, shambler.
Angler, antler, chandler, dangler, handler, sampler, strangler, trampler, wrangler.
Anger, blander, candour/candor (U.S.), dander, gander, grander, pander, slander.
Clamour/clamor (U.S.), crammer, gamma, glamour/glamor (U.S.), grammar, hammer, jammer, mamma, rammer, shammer, slammer, spammer, stammer.
Anchor, banker, blanker, canker, Casablanca, clanker, flanker, franker, hanker, pranker, rancour/rancor (U.S.), ranker, spanker, tanker, thanker, up-anchor, yanker.
After, crafter, dafter, drafter, grafter, laughter, rafter.
Banner, hosanna, manna, manner, manor, nana/nanna, planner, scanner, spanner.

Banter, canter, chanter, granter, grantor, mantra, panter, planter, ranter, scanter, Santa.
Clapper, dapper, flapper, grappa, lapper, napper, rapper, scrapper, slapper, snapper, strapper, tapper, trapper, wrapper, yapper.
[3] **Backhander**, bystander, commander, demander, expander, left-hander, meander, memoranda, outlander, philander, propaganda, right-hander, understander, veranda.
Advancer, enhancer, entrancer, romancer.
Bandanna, caravanner, enamour/enamor (U.S.), programmer, savannah, sledgehammer.
Decanter, enchanter, supplanter, transplanter.
Backslapper, entrapper, hand-clapper, handicapper, kidnapper, knee-capper, recapper, whippersnapper, wiretapper.

2.2.16 "--ambler" (as in "gambler")
[2] ambler, brambler, gambler, rambler, scrambler, shambler.

SURPRISING RHYMING:
[2] **Angler**, antler, chandler, dangler, handler, sampler, strangler, trampler, wrangler.
Amber, camber, clamber, mamba, samba, timbre.
Anger, blander, candour/candor (U.S.), dander, gander, grander, pander, slander.
Camper, clamper, damper, hamper, pamper, scamper, stamper, tamper, tramper.
Answer, cancer, chancer, dancer, glancer, lancer, prancer.
[3] **Backhander**, bystander, commander, demander, expander, left-hander, meander, memoranda, outlander, philander, propaganda, right-hander, understander, veranda.
Bandanna, caravanner, enamour/enamor (U.S.), programmer, savannah, sledgehammer.
Advancer, enhancer, entrancer, romancer.

2.2.17 "--ammer" (as in "hammer")
[2] clamour/clamor (U.S.), crammer, gamma, glamour/glamor (U.S.), grammar, hammer, jammer, mamma, rammer, shammer, slammer, spammer, stammer.
[3] Enamour/enamor (U.S.), programmer, sledgehammer, windjammer.

SURPRISING RHYMING:
[2] **Clamoured/clamored** (U.S.), enamoured/enamored (U.S.), hammered, stammered.
Banner, hosanna, manna, manner, manor, nana/nanna, planner, scanner, spanner.
Amber, camber, clamber, mamba, samba, timbre.
Ambler, brambler, gambler, rambler, scrambler, shambler.
Angler, antler, chandler, dangler, handler, sampler, strangler, trampler, wrangler.
Bagger, blagger, bragger, carpetbagger, dagger, dragger, flagger, gagger, lagger, nagger, snagger, stagger, swagger, zigzagger.
Adder, bladder, gladder, sadder, ladder, madder, step-ladder.
Batter, chatter, clatter, fatter, flatter, hatter, latter, matter, natter, patter, platter, scatter, shatter, smatter, spatter, splatter, yatter.
Anger, blander, candour/candor (U.S.), dander, gander, grander, pander, slander.
[3] **Bandanna**, caravanner, savannah.
Backhander, bystander, commander, demander, expander, left-hander, meander, memoranda, outlander, philander, propaganda, right-hander, understander, veranda.

2.2.18 "--anner" (as in "banner")
[2] banner, canner, fanner, hosanna, manna, manner, manor, nana/nanna, panner, planner, scanner, spanner, tanner.
[3] bandanna, caravanner, savannah.

SURPRISING RHYMING:
[2] **Clamour/clamor** (U.S.), crammer, gamma, glamour/glamor (U.S.), grammar, hammer, jammer, mamma, rammer, shammer, slammer, spammer, stammer.
Adder, bladder, gladder, sadder, ladder, madder, step-ladder.
After, crafter, dafter, drafter, grafter, laughter, rafter.
Anger, blander, candour/candor (U.S.), dander, gander, grander, pander, slander.
Batter, chatter, clatter, fatter, flatter, latter, matter, natter, patter, platter, ratter, scatter, shatter, smatter, spatter, splatter, yatter.

217

Camper, clamper, damper, hamper, pamper, scamper, stamper, tamper, tramper.
Banter, canter, chanter, granter, grantor, mantra, panter, planter, ranter, scanter, Santa.
Amber, camber, clamber, mamba, samba, timbre.
Clapper, dapper, flapper, napper, rapper, scrapper, slapper, snapper, trapper, wrapper.
Answer, cancer, chancer, dancer, glancer, lancer, prancer.
Bagger, blagger, bragger, carpetbagger, dagger, dragger, flagger, gagger, nagger, snagger, stagger, swagger, zigzagger.
[3] **Enamour/enamor** (U.S.), programmer, sledgehammer, windjammer.
Backhander, bystander, commander, demander, expander, left-hander, meander, memoranda, outlander, philander, propaganda, right-hander, understander, veranda.
Backslapper, entrapper, hand-clapper, handicapper, kidnapper, knee-capper, recapper, whippersnapper, wiretapper.
Attacker, backpacker, bushwhacker, firecracker, hijacker, linebacker, lipsmacker, maraca, nutcracker, safecracker, skyjacker, wisecracker.

2.2.19 "--ancer" (as in "dancer")
[2] answer, cancer, chancer, dancer, glancer, lancer, prancer, sir.
[3] advancer, enhancer, entrancer, romancer.

SURPRISING RHYMING:
[2] **Gangster**, gangsta, prankster, salsa, transfer.
Blaster, caster, faster, master, passer, pasta, pastor, plaster, relaxer, vaster, waxer.
Basher, brasher, casher, clasher, crasher, dasher, flasher, gasher, gate-crasher, lasher, masher, rasher, slasher, smasher, splasher, stasher, thrasher.
After, crafter, dafter, drafter, grafter, laughter, rafter.
Catcher, capture, matcher, patcher, rapture, scratcher, snatcher, stature, thatcher.
Banner, hosanna, manna, manner, manor, nana/nanna, planner, scanner, spanner.
Camper, clamper, damper, hamper, pamper, scamper, stamper, tamper, tramper.
Anger, blander, candour/candor (U.S.), dander, gander, grander, pander, slander.
Anchor, banker, blanker, canker, Casablanca, clanker, flanker, franker, hanker, pranker, rancour/rancor (U.S.), ranker, spanker, tanker, thanker, up-anchor, yanker.
Banter, canter, chanter, granter, grantor, mantra, panter, planter, ranter, scanter, Santa.
Amber, camber, clamber, mamba, samba, timbre.
Clamour/clamor (U.S.), crammer, gamma, glamour/glamor (U.S.), grammar, hammer, jammer, mamma, rammer, shammer, slammer, spammer, stammer.
[3] **Bandmaster**, broadcaster, choirmaster, disaster, forecaster, flabbergaster, grandmaster, headmaster, newscaster, paymaster, postmaster, quartermaster, quizmaster, ringmaster, schoolmaster, spymaster, steadfaster, taskmaster.
Enamour/enamor (U.S.), programmer, sledgehammer, windjammer.
Backhander, bystander, commander, demander, expander, left-hander, meander, memoranda, outlander, philander, propaganda, right-hander, understander, veranda.

2.2.20 "--ander" (as in "grander")
[2] bander, blander, brander, candour/candor (U.S.), dander, gander, grander, lander, panda, pander, sander, slander, stander.
[3] backhander, bystander, commander, coriander, demander, disbander, expander, inlander, jacaranda, left-hander, meander, memoranda, oleander, outlander, philander, propaganda, remander, right-hander, understander, veranda.

SURPRISING RHYMING:
[2] **Banter**, canter, chanter, granter, mantra, panter, planter, ranter, scanter, Santa.
Answer, cancer, chancer, dancer, glancer, lancer, prancer.
Ambler, brambler, gambler, rambler, scrambler, shambler.
Angler, antler, dangler, handler, sampler, strangler, wrangler.
Anger, amber, camber, clamber, mamba, samba, timbre.
Camper, clamper, hamper, pamper, scamper, stamper, tamper.
Anchor, banker, blanker, Casablanca, flanker, franker, hanker, rancour/rancor (U.S.), spanker, tanker, thanker, up-anchor, yanker.
Banner, hosanna, manna, manner, manor, nana/nanna, planner, scanner, spanner.
After, crafter, dafter, drafter, grafter, laughter, rafter.

218

[3] **Decanter**, enchanter, supplanter, transplanter.
Advancer, enhancer, entrancer, romancer.
Enamour/enamor (U.S.), programmer, sledgehammer, windjammer.

2.2.21 "--anker" (as in "banker")
[2] anchor, banker, blanker, canker, Casablanca, clanker, flanker, franker, hanker, pranker, rancour/rancor (U.S.), ranker, spanker, tanker, thanker, up-anchor, yanker.

SURPRISING RHYMING:
[2] **Banter**, canter, chanter, granter, mantra, panter, planter, ranter, scanter, Santa.
Actor, factor, gangster, gangsta, prankster, salsa, tractor, transfer.
Camper, clamper, damper, hamper, pamper, scamper, stamper, tamper, tramper.
Anger, blander, candour/candor (U.S.), dander, gander, grander, pander, slander.
Answer, cancer, chancer, dancer, glancer, lancer, prancer.
Amber, camber, clamber, mamba, samba, timbre.
Angler, antler, chandler, dangler, handler, sampler, strangler, trampler, wrangler.
[3] **Backhander**, bystander, commander, demander, expander, left-hander, meander, memoranda, outlander, philander, propaganda, right-hander, understander, veranda.
Ambler, brambler, gambler, rambler, scrambler, shambler.
Decanter, enchanter, supplanter, transplanter.
Advancer, enhancer, entrancer, romancer.

2.2.22 "--anter" (as in "banter")
[2] banter, canter, chanter, granter, grantor, panter, planter, ranter, scanter, Santa.
[3] decanter, enchanter, supplanter, transplanter.

SURPRISING RHYMING:
[2] **Actor**, factor, gangster, gangsta, prankster, salsa, tractor, transfer.
Anchor, banker, blanker, canker, Casablanca, clanker, flanker, franker, hanker, pranker, rancour/rancor (U.S.), ranker, spanker, tanker, thanker, up-anchor, yanker.
Camper, damper, hamper, pamper, scamper, stamper, tamper.
Anger, blander, brander, candour/candor (U.S.), dander, gander, grander, lander, panda, pander, sander, slander, stander.
Answer, cancer, chancer, dancer, glancer, lancer, prancer.
Amber, camber, clamber, mamba, samba, timbre.
Angler, antler, chandler, dangler, handler, sampler, strangler, trampler, wrangler.
[3] **Backhander**, blander, candour/candor (U.S.), dander, gander, grander, panda, pander, slander.
Ambler, brambler, gambler, rambler, scrambler, shambler.
Advancer, enhancer, entrancer, romancer.

2.2.23 "--apper" (as in "rapper")
[2] clapper, dapper, flapper, grappa, lapper, mapper, napper, rapper, sapper, scrapper, slapper, snapper, strapper, tapper, trapper, wrapper, yapper.
[3] backslapper, entrapper, hand-clapper, handicapper, kidnapper, knee-capper, recapper, whippersnapper, wiretapper.

SURPRISING RHYMING:
[2] **Batter**, chatter, clatter, fatter, flatter, hatter, latter, matter, natter, patter, scatter, shatter, smatter, spatter, splatter.
After, crafter, dafter, drafter, grafter, laughter, rafter.
Blaster, caster, castor, faster, master, pasta, pastor, plaster, vaster.
Backer, blacker, cracker, hacker, knacker, slacker, smacker, snacker, stacker, tracker.
Camper, damper, hamper, pamper, scamper, stamper, tamper.
Catcher, capture, matcher, patcher, rapture, scratcher, snatcher, stature, thatcher.
Bagger, blagger, bragger, carpetbagger, dagger, dragger, flagger, gagger, lagger, nagger, snagger, stagger, swagger, zigzagger.

Basher, brasher, clasher, crasher, dasher, flasher, gate-crasher, masher, rasher, slasher, smasher, splasher, stasher, thrasher.
[3] **Attacker**, backpacker, bushwhacker, firecracker, hijacker, linebacker, lipsmacker, maraca, nutcracker, ransacker, repacker, safecracker, skyjacker, unpacker, wisecracker.
Benefactor, chiropractor, contractor, enactor, exactor, extractor, protractor, reactor, redactor, refractor, retractor.
Antimatter, pitter-patter, regatta.
Back-scratcher, body-snatcher, cradle-snatcher, dispatcher, dogcatcher, flycatcher.

2.2.24 "--arber" (as in "barber")
[2] arbor, barber, harbour/harbor (U.S.).

SURPRISING RHYMING:
[2] **Ardour/ardor** (U.S.), armada, harder, lambada, larder, discarder, enchilada, piña colada, promenader, retarder, safeguarder.
Armour/armor (U.S.), calmer, charmer, drama, farmer, harmer, karma, lama, llama.
Barker, darker, larker, marker, parka, parker, sparker, starker.
Barter, carter, charter, garter, martyr, scarper, sharper, smarter, starter, strata, tartar.
[3] **Americana**, banana, cabana, darner, garner, gymkhana, iguana, mañana, nirvana, piranha, sultana, Victoriana.
Bookmarker, moussaka, nosy-parker, postmarker, disembarker.
Cyclorama, disarmer, embalmer, melodrama, panorama, pyjama, snake-charmer.
Discharger, enlarger, maharaja, turbocharger.
Cantata, non-starter, pro rata, sonata.
[4] **Alma mater**, chipolata, inamorata, magna carta, persona non-grata, serenata.

2.2.25 "--archer" (as in "marcher")
[2] archer, departure, marcher, starcher

SURPRISING RHYMING:
[2] **Catcher**, fracture, hatcher, matcher, patcher, scratcher, snatcher, stature, thatcher.
Barger, charger, larger.
Barker, darker, larker, marker, parka, parker, scarper, sharper, sparker, starker.
Armour/armor (U.S.), calmer, charmer, drama, farmer, harmer, karma, lama, llama.
Arbor, barber, harbour/harbor (U.S.).
Barter, charter, darter, garter, martyr, smarter, starter, strata, tartar.
Answer, cancer, chancer, dancer, glancer, lancer, prancer.
[3] **Harder**, lambada, discarder, enchilada, piña colada, promenader, safeguarder.
Discharger, enlarger, maharaja, turbocharger.
Bookmarker, moussaka, nosy-parker, postmarker, disembarker.
Cyclorama, disarmer, embalmer, melodrama, panorama, pyjama, snake-charmer.
Cantata, non-starter, pro rata, sonata.
Advancer, enhancer, entrancer, romancer.
[4] **Alma mater**, chipolata, magna carta, persona non-grata, serenata.
Back-scratcher, body-snatcher, cradle-snatcher, dispatcher, dogcatcher, flycatcher.

2.2.26 "--arder" (as in "harder")
ardour/ardor (U.S.), armada, harder, lambada, larder, discarder, enchilada, piña colada, promenader, retarder, safeguarder.

SURPRISING RHYMING:
[2] **Archer**, barger, charger, departure, larger, marcher, starcher
Barker, darker, larker, marker, parka, parker, sparker, starker.
Arbor, barber, harbour/harbor (U.S.).
Armour/armor (U.S.), calmer, charmer, drama, farmer, harmer, karma, lama, llama.
Barter, charter, darter, garter, martyr, scarper, sharper, smarter, starter, strata, tartar.
Answer, cancer, chancer, dancer, glancer, lancer, prancer.
Catcher, hatcher, latcher, matcher, patcher, scratcher, snatcher, stature, thatcher.
[3] **Discharger**, enlarger, maharaja, turbocharger.

Bookmarker, moussaka, nosy-parker, postmarker, disembarker.
Cyclorama, disarmer, embalmer, melodrama, panorama, pyjama, snake-charmer.
Americana, banana, cabana, darner, garner, gymkhana, iguana, mañana, nirvana, piranha, sultana, Victoriana.
Cantata, non-starter, pro rata, sonata.
Advancer, enhancer, entrancer, romancer.
[4] **Alma mater**, chipolata, inamorata, magna carta, persona non-grata, serenata.
Back-scratcher, body-snatcher, cradle-snatcher, dispatcher, dogcatcher, flycatcher.

2.2.27 "--arger" (as in "larger")
[2] barger, charger, larger.
[3] discharger, enlarger, maharaja, turbocharger.

SURPRISING RHYMING:
[2] **Archer**, departure, marcher, starcher
Ardor/ardour, armada, barber, harbour/harbor (U.S.), harder, lambada, larder, discarder, enchilada, piña colada, promenader, safeguarder.
Barker, darker, larker, marker, parka, parker, sparker, starker.
Armour/armor (U.S.), calmer, charmer, drama, farmer, harmer, karma, lama, llama.
Barter, charter, darter, garter, martyr, scarper, sharper, smarter, starter, strata, tartar.
Answer, cancer, chancer, dancer, glancer, lancer, prancer.
[3] **Bookmarker**, moussaka, nosy-parker, postmarker, disembarker.
Cyclorama, disarmer, embalmer, melodrama, panorama, pyjama, snake-charmer.
Cantata, non-starter, pro rata, sonata.
Advancer, enhancer, entrancer, romancer.
Americana, banana, cabana, darner, garner, gymkhana, iguana, mañana, nirvana, piranha, sultana, Victoriana.
[4] **Alma mater**, chipolata, magna carta, persona non-grata, serenata.
Back-scratcher, body-snatcher, cradle-snatcher, dispatcher, dogcatcher, flycatcher.

2.2.28 "--arker" (as in "darker")
[2] barker, darker, larker, marker, parka, parker, sparker, starker.
[3] bookmarker, moussaka, nosy-parker, postmarker, remarker, disembarker.

SURPRISING RHYMING:
[2] **Barter**, charter, garter, martyr, scarper, sharper, smarter, starter, strata, tartar.
Ardor/ardour, armada, barber, harbour/harbor (U.S.), harder, lambada, larder, discarder, enchilada, piña colada, promenader, retarder, safeguarder.
Archer, barger, charger, departure, larger, marcher, starcher.
Armour/armor (U.S.), calmer, charmer, drama, farmer, harmer, karma, lama, llama.
Answer, cancer, chancer, dancer, glancer, lancer, prancer.
[3] **Cantata**, non-starter, pro rata, sonata.
Discharger, enlarger, maharaja, turbocharger.
Cyclorama, disarmer, embalmer, melodrama, panorama, pyjama, snake-charmer.
Americana, banana, cabana, darner, garner, gymkhana, iguana, mañana, nirvana, piranha, sultana, Victoriana.
Advancer, enhancer, entrancer, romancer.
[4] **Alma mater**, chipolata, inamorata, magna carta, persona non-grata, serenata.

2.2.29 "--armer" (as in "charmer")
[2] Armour/armor (U.S.), calmer, charmer, drama, farmer, harmer, karma, lama, llama.
[3] disarmer, embalmer, melodrama, panorama, pyjama, snake-charmer.

SURPRISING RHYMING:
[2] **Ardour/ardor (U.S.)**, armada, barber, harbour/harbor (U.S.), harder, lambada, larder, discarder, enchilada, piña colada, promenader, retarder, safeguarder.
Barker, darker, larker, marker, parka, parker, sparker, starker.
Barter, charter, darter, garter, martyr, scarper, sharper, smarter, starter, strata, tartar.
Archer, departure, larger, marcher, starcher.

[3] **Bookmarker**, moussaka, nosy-parker, postmarker, disembarker.
Americana, banana, cabana, cantata, darner, garner, gymkhana, iguana, mañana, nirvana, non-starter, piranha, pro rata, sonata, sultana, Victoriana.
Advancer, enhancer, entrancer, romancer.
Discharger, enlarger, maharaja, turbocharger.
[4] **Alma mater**, chipolata, inamorata, magna carta, persona non-grata, serenata.

2.2.30 "--arner" (as in "banana")
Americana, banana, cabana, darner, garner, gymkhana, iguana, mañana, nirvana, piranha, sultana, Victoriana.

SURPRISING RHYMING:
[2] **Ardour/ardor** (U.S.), armada, barber, harbour/harbor (U.S.), harder, lambada, larder, discarder, enchilada, piña colada, promenader, retarder, safeguarder.
Armour/armor (U.S.), calmer, charmer, drama, farmer, harmer, karma, lama, llama.
Barker, darker, larker, marker, parka, parker, sparker, starker.
Barter, charter, darter, garter, martyr, scarper, sharper, smarter, starter, strata, tartar.
[3] **Bookmarker**, moussaka, nosy-parker, postmarker, disembarker.
Cyclorama, disarmer, embalmer, melodrama, panorama, pyjama, snake-charmer.
Discharger, enlarger, maharaja, turbocharger.
Cantata, non-starter, pro rata, sonata.
[4] **Alma mater**, chipolata, inamorata, magna carta, persona non-grata, serenata.

2.2.31 "--arper" (as in "sharper")
carper, cardsharper, harper, scarper, sharper.

SURPRISING RHYMING:
[2] **Barter**, charter, garter, martyr, smarter, starter, strata, tartar.
Barker, darker, marker, parka, parker, sparker, starker.
Armour/armor (U.S.), calmer, charmer, drama, farmer, harmer, karma, lama, llama.
Ardour/ardor (U.S.), armada, barber, harbour/harbor (U.S.), harder, lambada, larder, discarder, enchilada, piña colada, promenader, retarder, safeguarder.
Barger, charger, larger.
Answer, cancer, chancer, dancer, glancer, lancer, prancer.
Archer, departure, marcher, starcher.
[3] **Bookmarker**, moussaka, nosy-parker, postmarker, disembarker.
Cantata, non-starter, pro rata, sonata.
Cyclorama, disarmer, embalmer, melodrama, panorama, pyjama, snake-charmer.
Americana, banana, cabana, darner, garner, gymkhana, iguana, mañana, nirvana, piranha, Victoriana.
[4] **Alma mater**, chipolata, inamorata, magna carta, persona non-grata, serenata.

2.2.32 "--arter" (as in "smarter")
[2] barter, charter, garter, martyr, smarter, starter, strata, tartar.
[3] cantata, non-starter, pro rata, sonata.
[4] alma mater, chipolata, inamorata, magna carta, persona non-grata, serenata.

SURPRISING RHYMING:
[2] **Barker**, darker, larker, marker, parka, parker, scarper, sharper, sparker, starker.
Ardour/ardor (U.S.), armada, barber, harbour/harbor (U.S.), harder, lambada, larder, discarder, enchilada, piña colada, promenader, retarder, safeguarder.
Armour/armor (U.S.), calmer, charmer, drama, farmer, harmer, karma, lama, llama.
Archer, barger, charger, departure, larger, marcher, starcher.
[3] **Bookmarker**, moussaka, nosy-parker, postmarker, disembarker.
Americana, banana, cabana, darner, garner, gymkhana, iguana, mañana, nirvana, piranha, sultana, Victoriana.
Discharger, enlarger, maharaja, turbocharger.
Cyclorama, disarmer, embalmer, melodrama, panorama, pyjama, snake-charmer.

*

2.2.33 "--aster" (as in "faster")

[2] blaster, caster, castor, faster, master, pasta, pastor, plaster, vaster.
[3] alabaster, bandmaster, broadcaster, canasta, choirmaster, disaster, forecaster, flabbergaster, grandmaster, headmaster, newscaster, paymaster, postmaster, quartermaster, quizmaster, ringmaster, schoolmaster, scoutmaster, spymaster, stationmaster, steadfaster, taskmaster.

SURPRISING RHYMING:
Gangster, gangsta, prankster, salsa, transfer.
Answer, cancer, chancer, dancer, glancer, lancer, prancer.
After, crafter, dafter, drafter, grafter, laughter, rafter.
Banter, canter, chanter, granter, grantor, mantra, panter, planter, ranter, scanter, Santa.
Basher, brasher, clasher, crasher, dasher, flasher, gate-crasher, masher, rasher, slasher, smasher, splasher, stasher, thrasher.
Actor, factor, tractor.
Batter, chatter, clatter, fatter, flatter, latter, matter, natter, patter, platter, ratter, scatter, shatter, smatter, spatter, splatter, yatter.
Anger, blander, candour/candor (U.S.), dander, gander, grander, pander, slander.
Anchor, banker, blanker, canker, Casablanca, flanker, franker, hanker, pranker, rancour/rancor (U.S.), ranker, spanker, tanker, thanker, up-anchor, yanker.
Catcher, capture, matcher, patcher, rapture, scratcher, snatcher, stature, thatcher.
Camper, damper, hamper, pamper, scamper, stamper, tamper.
[3] **Benefactor**, chiropractor, contractor, extractor, protractor, reactor, redactor, retractor.
Back-scratcher, body-snatcher, cradle-snatcher, dispatcher, dogcatcher, flycatcher.
Enamour/enamor (U.S.), programmer, sledgehammer, windjammer.
Attacker, backpacker, bushwhacker, firecracker, hijacker, lipsmacker, nutcracker, ransacker, safecracker, skyjacker, unpacker, wisecracker.
Backhander, bystander, commander, demander, expander, left-hander, meander, memoranda, outlander, philander, propaganda, right-hander, understander, veranda.

2.2.34 "--asher" (as in "smasher")

[2] basher, brasher, casher, clasher, crasher, dasher, flasher, gasher, gate-crasher, lasher, masher, rasher, slasher, smasher, splasher, stasher, thrasher.

SURPRISING RHYMING:
[2] **Batter**, chatter, clatter, fatter, flatter, latter, matter, natter, patter, platter, ratter, scatter, shatter, smatter, spatter, splatter, yatter.
Catcher, capture, matcher, patcher, rapture, scratcher, snatcher, stature, thatcher.
Blaster, caster, castor, faster, master, pasta, pastor, plaster, vaster.
After, crafter, dafter, drafter, grafter, laughter, rafter.
Answer, cancer, chancer, dancer, glancer, lancer, prancer.
[3] **Back-scratcher**, body-snatcher, cradle-snatcher, dispatcher, dogcatcher, flycatcher.
Antimatter, pitter-patter, regatta.
Bandmaster, broadcaster, choirmaster, disaster, forecaster, flabbergaster, grandmaster, headmaster, newscaster, paymaster, postmaster, quartermaster, quizmaster, ringmaster, schoolmaster, scoutmaster, spymaster, stationmaster, taskmaster.

2.2.35 "--atcher" (as in "catcher")

[2] catcher, hatcher, latcher, matcher, patcher, scratcher, snatcher, stature, thatcher.
[3+] baby-snatcher, back-scratcher, body-snatcher, cradle-snatcher, dispatcher, dogcatcher, flycatcher, oyster-catcher.

SURPRISING RHYMING:
[2] **Capture**, enrapture, fracture, manufacture, rapture, recapture.
Basher, brasher, clasher, crasher, dasher, flasher, gate-crasher, masher, rasher, slasher, smasher, splasher, stasher, thrasher.
Answer, cancer, chancer, dancer, glancer, lancer, prancer.
Blaster, caster, faster, master, pasta, pastor, plaster, vaster.
Camper, damper, hamper, pamper, scamper, stamper, tamper.

After, crafter, dafter, drafter, grafter, laughter, rafter.
Anger, blander, candour/candor (U.S.), dander, gander, grander, pander, slander.
Backer, blacker, cracker, hacker, knacker, slacker, smacker, snacker, stacker, tracker.
Anchor, banker, blanker, canker, Casablanca, flanker, franker, hanker, pranker, rancour/rancor (U.S.), ranker, spanker, tanker, thanker, up-anchor, yanker.
Banter, canter, chanter, granter, grantor, mantra, panter, planter, ranter, scanter, Santa.
Actor, factor, tractor.
[3] **Bandmaster**, broadcaster, choirmaster, disaster, forecaster, grandmaster, headmaster, newscaster, paymaster, postmaster, quartermaster, quizmaster, ringmaster, schoolmaster, scoutmaster, spymaster, stationmaster, taskmaster.
Attacker, backpacker, bushwhacker, firecracker, hijacker, lipsmacker, nutcracker, ransacker, safecracker, skyjacker, unpacker, wisecracker.
Benefactor, chiropractor, contractor, extractor, protractor, reactor, redactor, retractor.

2.2.36 "--atter" (as in "shatter")
[2] batter, chatter, clatter, fatter, flatter, hatter, latter, matter, natter, patter, platter, ratter, scatter, shatter, smatter, spatter, splatter, yatter.
[3] antimatter, pitter-patter, regatta.

SURPRISING RHYMING:
[2] **Battered**, clattered, flattered, mattered, nattered, pattern, scattered, shattered, spattered, splattered.
Backer, blacker, cracker, hacker, knacker, slacker, smacker, snacker, stacker, tracker.
Clapper, dapper, flapper, napper, rapper, scrapper, slapper, snapper, trapper, wrapper.
Bagger, blagger, bragger, carpetbagger, dagger, dragger, flagger, gagger, lagger, nagger, snagger, stagger, swagger, zigzagger.
Banner, hosanna, manna, manner, manor, nana/nanna, planner, scanner, spanner.
Basher, brasher, clasher, crasher, dasher, flasher, gate-crasher, masher, rasher, slasher, smasher, splasher, stasher, thrasher.
Adder, bladder, gladder, sadder, ladder, madder, step-ladder.
Clamour/clamor (U.S.), crammer, gamma, glamour/glamor (U.S.), grammar, hammer, jammer, mamma, rammer, shammer, slammer, spammer, stammer.
[3] **Attacker**, backpacker, bushwhacker, firecracker, hijacker, lipsmacker, nutcracker, safecracker, skyjacker, wisecracker.
Backslapper, hand-clapper, kidnapper, knee-capper, whippersnapper, wiretapper.
Enamour/enamor (U.S.), programmer, sledgehammer, windjammer.

2.2.37 "--atterer" (as in "scatterer")
[3] batterer, chatterer, clatterer, flatterer, natterer, scatterer, shatterer, splatterer.

SURPRISING RHYMING:
[3] **Camera**, capturer, Nazareth, plasterer, staggerer, stammerer, swaggerer. philanderer.

2.2.38 "--ayer" (as in "player")
[2] greyer/grayer (U.S.), layer, mayor, payer, player, prayer, slayer, stayer, strayer.
[3] betrayer, bill-payer, bricklayer, conveyor, delayer, displayer, gainsayer, portrayer, purveyor, record player, soothsayer, surveyor, taxpayer.

SURPRISING RHYMING:
[2] **Fainter**, painter, quainter.
Cater, crater, data, dater, greater, hater, later, skater, straighter, traitor, waiter.
Braver, favour/favor (U.S.), flavour/flavor (U.S.), raver, saver, savour/savor (U.S.), shaver.
Jailer, mailer, paler, sailor, staler, trailer, tailor, scaler, wailer.
Aimer, disclaimer, exclaimer, gamer, proclaimer, shamer, tamer.
Changer, danger, manger, ranger, stranger.
Acer, bracer, chaser, facer, pacer, placer, racer, spacer, tracer.
Blazer, gazer, grazer, hazer, laser, praiser, raiser, razor, tazer.
[3] **Creator**, curator, debater, dictator, equator, frustrater, narrator, spectator, translator.
Disfavour/disfavor (U.S.), engraver, enslaver, lifesaver, timesaver.

Aider, crusader, degrader, dissuader, evader, first-aider, invader, masquerader, parader, persuader, ram-raider, rollerblader, serenader, wader.
Abseiler, blackmailer, exhaler, inhaler, loudhailer, regaler, retailer, wholesaler.
Arranger, endanger, exchanger, moneychanger, shortchanger.
Embracer, eraser, horse-racer, misplacer, replacer, retrace.
Appraiser, eraser, fundraiser, impresa, stargazer, trail-blazer.
[4] **Agitator**, alligator, aviator, animator, calculator, captivator, celebrator, commentator, decorator, demonstrator, educator, elevator, escalator, figure-skater, generator, gladiator, hesitater, illustrator, imitator, indicator, innovator, instigator, liberator, mediator, moderator, motivator, operator, orchestrater, percolator, perpetrator, radiator, simulator, speculator, terminator, violator.
[5] **Accelerator**, collaborator, impersonator, incinerator, interrogator, investigator, negotiator, refrigerator, resuscitator, ventilator.

2.2.39 "--ayker (as in "taker")
[2] acre, baker, breaker, faker, maker, Quaker, raker, shaker, staker, taker, waker.
[3] backbreaker, boneshaker, bookmaker, caretaker, clockmaker, dressmaker, filmmaker, forsaker, haymaker, heartbreaker, homemaker, housebreaker, icebreaker, Jamaica, kingmaker, lawbreaker, lawmaker, matchmaker, mischief-maker, muckraker, pacemaker, painstaker, partaker, peacemaker, playmaker, rainmaker, safebreaker, sailmaker, saltshaker, shoemaker, strikebreaker, tie-breaker, windbreaker, wiseacre, watchmaker.
[4] bellyacher, holidaymaker, merrymaker, moneymaker, overtaker,
troublemaker. undertaker.

SURPRISING RHYMING:
[2] **Fainter**, painter, quainter.
Cater, crater, data, dater, greater, hater, later, skater, straighter, traitor, waiter.
Braver, favour/favor (U.S.), flavour/flavor (U.S.), raver, saver, savour/savor (U.S.), shaver.
Aider, blockader, crusader, degrader, dissuader, evader, first-aider, invader, masquerader, parader, persuader, ram-raider, rollerblader, serenader, wader.
Frailer, jailer, paler, sailor, staler, trailer, tailor, wailer, whaler.
Disclaimer, exclaimer, framer, gamer, proclaimer, shamer, tamer.
Changer, danger, manger, ranger, stranger.
Chaser, facer, lacer, mesa, pacer, placer, racer, spacer, tracer.
Blazer, gazer, grazer, laser, phraser, praiser, raiser, razor, tazer.
[3] **Creator**, curator, debater, dictator, equator, frustrater, narrator, spectator, translator.
Disfavour/disfavor (U.S.), engraver, enslaver, lifesaver, timesaver.
Abseiler, blackmailer, exhaler, inhaler, loudhailer, regaler, retailer.
Arranger, endanger, exchanger, moneychanger, shortchanger.
Embracer, eraser, horse-racer, misplacer, replacer, retracer, steeplechaser.
Appraiser, eraser, fundraiser, impresa, stargazer, trail-blazer.
[4] **Agitator**, alligator, aviator, animator, calculator, celebrator, commentator, confiscator, contemplator, alligator, aviator, animator, calculator, captivator, celebrator, commentator, decorator, demonstrator, educator, elevator, escalator, figure-skater, generator, gladiator, hesitater, illustrator, imitator, indicator, innovator, instigator, liberator, mediator, moderator, motivator, operator, orchestrater, percolator, perpetrator, radiator, simulator, speculator, terminator, violator.
[5] **Accelerator**, collaborator, impersonator, incinerator, interrogator, investigator, negotiator, refrigerator, resuscitator, ventilator.

2.2.40 "--ayper" (as in "paper")
[2] caper, draper, gaper, paper, scraper, shaper, taper, vapour/vapor (U.S.).
[3] escaper, flypaper, notepaper, newspaper, sandpaper, skyscraper, wallpaper.

SURPRISING RHYMING:
[2] **Cater**, crater, data, dater, greater, hater, later, skater, straighter, traitor, waiter.
Acre, baker, breaker, faker, maker, nature, shaker, taker, waker.
Fainter, painter, quainter.
Greyer/grayer (U.S.), layer, mayor, payer, player, prayer, slayer, stayer, strayer.

Aider, blockader, crusader, degrader, dissuader, evader, first-aider, invader, masquerader, parader, persuader, ram-raider, rollerblader, serenader, wader.
[3] **Creator**, curator, debater, dictator, equator, frustrater, narrator, spectator, translator.
Backbreaker, boneshaker, bookmaker, caretaker, clockmaker, dressmaker, filmmaker, heartbreaker, homemaker, housebreaker, icebreaker, Jamaica, kingmaker, lawbreaker, lawmaker, matchmaker, mischief-maker, muckraker, pacemaker, painstaker, partaker, peacemaker, playmaker, rainmaker, safebreaker, saltshaker, tie-breaker, windbreaker.
Betrayer, delayer, displayer, portrayer, purveyor, record player, soothsayer, taxpayer.
Disclaimer, exclaimer, framer, gamer, proclaimer, shamer, tamer.
[4] **Agitator**, alligator, aviator, animator, calculator, captivator, celebrator, commentator, decorator, demonstrator, educator, elevator, escalator, figure-skater, generator, gladiator, hesitater, illustrator, imitator, indicator, innovator, instigator, liberator, mediator, moderator, motivator, operator, orchestrater, percolator, perpetrator, radiator, simulator, speculator, terminator, violator.
Bellyacher, holidaymaker, merrymaker, moneymaker, overtaker, troublemaker, undertaker.
[5] **Accelerator**, collaborator, impersonator, incinerator, interrogator, investigator, negotiator, refrigerator, resuscitator, ventilator.

2.2.41 "--ayter" (as in "later")

[2] cater, crater, data, dater, freighter, grater, greater, hater, later, skater, slater, straighter, traitor, waiter.
[3] collator, creator, curator, debater, dictator, dumbwaiter, equator, frustrater, gyrator, locator, narrator, negator, peseta, rotator, spectator, translator, vibrator.
[4] abdicator, aggregator, agitator, alligator, aviator, allocator, animator, calculator, captivator, celebrator, commentator, confiscator, contemplator, cultivator, decorator, delegator, demonstrator, detonator, educator, elevator, escalator, estimator, excavator, figure-skater, formulator, generator, gladiator, hesitater, illustrator, imitator, incubator, indicator, infiltrator, innovator, instigator, insulator, isolator, legislator, liberator, liquidator, litigator, lubricator, mediator, moderator, motivator, navigator, operator, orchestrater, percolator, perpetrator, radiator, recreator, regulator, separator, simulator, speculator, terminator, validator, ventilator, violator.
[5] accelerator, adjudicator, collaborator, coordinator, exterminator, impersonator, incinerator, interrogator, investigator, negotiator, refrigerator, resuscitator.

SURPRISING RHYMING:
[2] **Caper**, paper, scraper, shaper, taper, vapour/vapor (U.S.).
Acre, baker, breaker, faker, maker, nature, shaker, taker, waker.
Fainter, painter, quainter.
Aider, blockader, crusader, degrader, dissuader, evader, first-aider, invader, masquerader, parader, persuader, ram-raider, rollerblader, serenader, wader.
Frailer, jailer, paler, sailor, staler, trailer, tailor, wailer, whaler.
Disclaimer, exclaimer, framer, gamer, proclaimer, shamer, tamer.
Changer, danger, manger, ranger, stranger.
Acer, bracer, chaser, facer, pacer, placer, racer, spacer, tracer.
Blazer, gazer, grazer, laser, phraser, praiser, raiser, razor, tazer.
[3] **Escaper**, notepaper, newspaper, sandpaper, skyscraper, wallpaper.
Backbreaker, boneshaker, bookmaker, caretaker, clockmaker, dressmaker, filmmaker, heartbreaker, homemaker, housebreaker, icebreaker, Jamaica, kingmaker, lawbreaker, lawmaker, matchmaker, mischief-maker, muckraker, pacemaker, painstaker, partaker, peacemaker, playmaker, rainmaker, safebreaker, saltshaker, tie-breaker, windbreaker.
Abseiler, blackmailer, exhaler, inhaler, loudhailer, regaler, retailer, wholesaler.
Arranger, endanger, exchanger, moneychanger, shortchanger.
Embracer, eraser, horse-racer, misplacer, replacer, steeplechaser.
Appraiser, eraser, fundraiser, impresa, stargazer, trail-blazer.
[4] **Bellyacher**, holidaymaker, merrymaker, moneymaker, troublemaker, undertaker.

2.2.42 "--ayver" (as in "saver")

[2] braver, caver, craver, favour/favor (U.S.), flavour/flavor (U.S.), graver, paver, quaver, raver, saver, savour/savor (U.S.), shaver, slaver, waiver, waver.

[3] depraver, disfavour/disfavor (U.S.), engraver, enslaver, lifesaver, semiquaver, timesaver.

SURPRISING RHYMING:
[2] **Greyer/grayer (U.S.)**, layer, mayor, payer, player, prayer, slayer, stayer, strayer.
Acre, baker, breaker, faker, maker, Quaker, shaker, taker, waker.
Caper, draper, paper, scraper, shaper, taper, vapour/vapor (U.S.).
Cater, crater, data, dater, greater, hater, later, skater, straighter, traitor, waiter.
Frailer, jailer, paler, sailor, staler, trailer, tailor, wailer, whaler.
Disclaimer, exclaimer, framer, gamer, proclaimer, shamer, tamer.
Changer, danger, manger, ranger, stranger.
Acer, bracer, chaser, facer, pacer, placer, racer, spacer, tracer.
Blazer, gazer, grazer, laser, phraser, praiser, raiser, razor, tazer.
[3] **Betrayer**, delayer, portrayer, purveyor, record player, soothsayer, taxpayer.
Backbreaker, boneshaker, bookmaker, caretaker, clockmaker, dressmaker, boneshaker, bookmaker, caretaker, clockmaker, dressmaker, filmmaker, heartbreaker, homemaker, housebreaker, icebreaker, Jamaica, kingmaker, lawbreaker, lawmaker, matchmaker, mischief-maker, muckraker, pacemaker, painstaker, partaker, peacemaker, playmaker, rainmaker, safebreaker, saltshaker, tie-breaker, windbreaker.
Escaper, notepaper, newspaper, sandpaper, skyscraper, wallpaper.
Creator, curator, debater, dictator, equator, frustrater, narrator, spectator, translator.
Aider, blockader, crusader, degrader, dissuader, evader, first-aider, invader, masquerader, parader, persuader, ram-raider, rollerblader, serenader, wader.
Abseiler, blackmailer, exhaler, inhaler, loudhailer, regaler, retailer.
Arranger, endanger, exchanger, moneychanger, shortchanger.
Embracer, encaser, eraser, horse-racer, misplacer, replacer, retracer, steeplechaser.
Appraiser, eraser, fundraiser, impresa, stargazer, trail-blazer.
[4] **Agitator**, alligator, aviator, animator, calculator, captivator, celebrator, commentator, decorator, demonstrator, educator, elevator, escalator, figure-skater, generator, gladiator, hesitater, illustrator, imitator, indicator, innovator, instigator, liberator, mediator, moderator, motivator, operator, orchestrater, percolator, perpetrator, radiator, simulator, speculator, terminator, violator.
[5] **Accelerator**, collaborator, impersonator, incinerator, interrogator, investigator, negotiator, refrigerator, resuscitator, ventilator.

2.2.43 "--edder" (as in "shredder")
[2] bedder, cheddar, deader, header, homesteader, redder, shedder, shredder, spreader, threader, treader.

SURPRISING RHYMING:
[2] **Clever**, ever, never, sever.
Better, debtor, fetter, fretter, getter, letter, setter, sweater, wetter.
Feather, heather, leather, nether, tether, together, untether, weather, whether.
Cellar, fella, queller, seller, smeller, speller, stellar, teller, yeller.
Dresser, guesser, lesser, presser, yessir.
Leisure, measure, pleasure, treasure.
[3] **Endeavour/endeavor** (U.S.), forever, however, never-never, whatever, whatsoever, whenever, wherever, whichever, whoever, whomever.
Bonesetter, carburettor/carburetor (U.S.), forgetter, go-getter, jet-setter, love-letter, newsletter, operetta, pacesetter, red-letter, typesetter, unfetter, upsetter, vendetta.
Bestseller, cave dweller, dispeller, exceller, expeller, foreteller, novella, paella, propeller, repeller, umbrella.
Displeasure, made-to-measure.
Aggressor, caresser, confessor, contessa, hairdresser, oppressor, possessor, predecessor, processor, professor, possessor, microprocessor, successor, transgressor.

2.2.44 "--eecher" (as in "teacher")
bleacher, breacher, creature, feature, headteacher, leecher, preacher, reacher, schoolteacher, screecher, teacher.

SURPRISING RHYMING:
[2] **Beater**, bleater, cheater, cheetah, eater, fleeter, greeter, heater, litre/liter (U.S.), meter, metre, neater, pleater, seater, skeeter, sweeter, teeter, treater, tweeter.
Bleeper, cheaper, creeper, deeper, leaper, peeper, reaper, sleeper, steeper, weeper.
Beaker, bleaker, eureka, meeker, leaker, loudspeaker, peeker, seeker, shrieker, sleeker, sneaker, speaker, streaker, squeaker, tikka, tweaker, weaker, wreaker.
Freezer, geezer, geyser, pleaser, seizer, sneezer, squeezer, teaser, tweezer, visa.
Beaver, cleaver, diva, fever, griever, leaver, lever, viva, weaver.
Eager, intriguer, meagre/meager (U.S.).
Dealer, feeler, healer, kneeler, spieler, stealer, squealer, wheeler.
Bleeder, breeder, cedar, feeder, heeder, leader, pleader, reader, speeder, weeder.
Beamer, creamer, dreamer, prima, reamer, schemer, screamer, steamer, streamer.
Cleaner, greener, keener, leaner, meaner, screener, serener.
[3] **Achiever**, believer, deceiver, naïver, perceiver, receiver, reliever, repriever, retriever.
Enfant terrible, repealer, revealer, tequila, wheeler-dealer.
Bandleader, cheerleader, lip-reader, ringleader, succeeder.
Appeaser, blasphemer, crowd pleaser, daydreamer, Mona Lisa, redeemer, stripteaser.
Arena, betweener, cantina, convener, demeanour/demeanor (U.S.), hyena, marina, obscener, serener, subpoena, tsarina, uncleaner.
Anteater, beefeater, brow-beater, deleter, discreeter, dolce vita, margarita, mistreater, repeater, señorita, two-seater, windcheater.
Barkeeper, bee-keeper, book-keeper, doorkeeper, gamekeeper, gatekeeper, goalkeeper, housekeeper, innkeeper, peacekeeper, shopkeeper, storekeeper, timekeeper, zookeeper.
[4] **Disbeliever**, make-believer, unbeliever, underachiever.
Ballerina, concertina, in-betweener, intervener, misdemeanour/misdemeanor (U.S.).

2.2.45 "--eeder" (as in "leader")
[2] bleeder, breeder, cedar, feeder, heeder, leader, pleader, reader, speeder, weeder.
[3] bandleader, cheerleader, conceder, lip-reader, misleader, ringleader, succeeder.

SURPRISING RHYMING:
[2] **Beaver**, cleaver, diva, fever, griever, leaver, lever, viva, weaver.
Cleaner, greener, keener, leaner, meaner, screener, serener, weaner.
Dealer, feeler, healer, kneeler, peeler, reeler, spieler, stealer, squealer, wheeler.
Beamer, creamer, dreamer, prima, reamer, schemer, screamer, steamer, streamer.
Eager, intriguer, meagre/meager (U.S.).
Bleeper, cheaper, creeper, deeper, leaper, peeper, reaper, sleeper, steeper, weeper.
Beta, cheater, eater, heater, litre/liter (U.S.), meter/metre, neater, sweeter, tweeter.
Freezer, geezer, geyser, pleaser, seizer, sneezer, squeezer, teaser, tweezer, visa.
Beaker, bleaker, eureka, meeker, leaker, loudspeaker, peeker, seeker, shrieker, sleeker, sneaker, speaker, streaker, squeaker, tikka, tweaker, weaker, wreaker.
[3] **Achiever**, believer, deceiver, naïver, perceiver, receiver, reliever, repriever, retriever.
Arena, betweener, blasphemer, cantina, daydreamer, demeanour/demeanor (U.S.), hyena, marina, obscener, redeemer, serener, subpoena, tsarina, uncleaner.
Appealer, concealer, enfant terrible, tequila, wheeler-dealer.
Barkeeper, bee-keeper, book-keeper, doorkeeper, gamekeeper, gatekeeper, goalkeeper, housekeeper, innkeeper, peacekeeper, shopkeeper, storekeeper, timekeeper, zookeeper.
Anteater, beefeater, brow-beater, deleter, discreeter, dolce vita, eggbeater, maltreater, margarita, mistreater, repeater, retreater, señorita, two-seater, windcheater.
Appeaser, crowd pleaser, Mona Lisa, stripteaser.
[4] **Disbeliever**, make-believer, unbeliever, underachiever.
Ballerina, concertina, in-betweener, misdemeanour/misdemeanor (U.S.), signorina.

2.2.46 "--eeger" (as in "eager")
[2] eager, intriguer, meagre/meager (U.S.).

SURPRISING RHYMING:
[2] **Beaver**, cleaver, diva, fever, griever, heaver, leaver, lever, viva, weaver.
Bleeder, breeder, cedar, feeder, heeder, leader, pleader, reader, speeder.
Dealer, feeler, healer, kneeler, peeler, reeler, sealer, spieler, stealer, squealer, wheeler.

228

Beta, bleater, cheater, cheetah, eater, fleeter, greeter, heater, litre/liter (U.S.), meter, metre, neater, pleater, seater, skeeter, sweeter, teeter, treater, tweeter.
Bleeper, cheaper, creeper, deeper, keeper, reaper, sleeper, steeper, sweeper, weeper.
Beaker, bleaker, eureka, meeker, leaker, loudspeaker, peeker, seeker, shrieker, sleeker, sneaker, speaker, streaker, squeaker, tikka, tweaker, weaker, wreaker.
[3] Achiever, believer, deceiver, naïver, perceiver, receiver, retriever.
Blasphemer, daydreamer, redeemer.
Bandleader, cheerleader, conceder, lip-reader, misleader, ringleader, succeeder.
Appealer, concealer, enfant terrible, repealer, revealer, tequila, wheeler-dealer.
Brow-beater, dolce vita, margarita, mistreater, repeater, señorita, two-seater.
Barkeeper, bee-keeper, book-keeper, doorkeeper, gamekeeper, gatekeeper, goalkeeper, housekeeper, innkeeper, peacekeeper, shopkeeper, storekeeper, timekeeper, zookeeper.

2.2.47 "--eeker" (as in "seeker")
[2] beaker, bleaker, eureka, meeker, leaker, loudspeaker, peeker, seeker, shrieker, sleeker, sneaker, speaker, streaker, squeaker, tikka, tweaker, weaker, wreaker.

SURPRISING RHYMING:
[2] **Eager**, intriguer, meagre/meager (U.S.).
Beeper, bleeper, cheaper, creeper, deeper, keeper, leaper, peeper, reaper, sleeper, steeper, sweeper, weeper.
Beater, cheater, cheetah, eater, fleeter, greeter, heater, litre/liter (U.S.), meter/metre, neater, seater, sweeter, treater, tweeter.
Beaver, cleaver, diva, fever, griever, leaver, lever, viva, weaver.
Dealer, feeler, healer, kneeler, peeler, reeler, sealer, spieler, stealer, squealer, wheeler.
Beamer, creamer, dreamer, prima, reamer, schemer, screamer, steamer, streamer.
Cleaner, greener, keener, leaner, meaner, screener, serener.
Bleeder, breeder, cedar, feeder, heeder, leader, pleader, reader, speeder, weeder.
[3] Barkeeper, bee-keeper, book-keeper, doorkeeper, gamekeeper, gatekeeper, goalkeeper, housekeeper, innkeeper, peacekeeper, storekeeper, timekeeper, zookeeper.
Anteater, beefeater, brow-beater, deleter, discreeter, dolce vita, eggbeater, maltreater, margarita, mistreater, repeater, retreater, , señorita, two-seater, windcheater.
Achiever, believer, deceiver, naïver, perceiver, receiver, reliever, repriever, retriever.
Appealer, concealer, enfant terrible, revealer, tequila, wheeler-dealer.
Arena, betweener, blasphemer, cantina, daydreamer, demeanour/demeanor (U.S.), hyena, marina, obscener, redeemer, serener, subpoena, tsarina, uncleaner.
Bandleader, cheerleader, lip-reader, misleader; ringleader, succeeder.
[4] Ballerina, concertina, in-betweener, intervener, misdemeanour/misdemeanor (U.S.), semolina, signorina.

2.2.48 "--eeler" (as in "healer")
[2] dealer, feeler, healer, heeler, kneeler, peeler, reeler, sealer, spieler, stealer, squealer, wheeler.
[3] appealer, concealer, enfant terrible, repealer, revealer, tequila, wheeler-dealer.

SURPRISING RHYMING:
[2] **Caesar**, easer, freezer, geezer, geyser, pleaser, seizer, sneezer, squeezer, teaser, tweezer, visa, wheezer.
Eager, intriguer, meagre/meager (U.S.).
Bleeder, breeder, cedar, feeder, leader, pleader, reader, speeder.
Cleaner, greener, keener, leaner, meaner, screener, serener.
Beamer, dreamer, prima, schemer, screamer, steamer, streamer.
Beaver, cleaver, diva, fever, griever, leaver, lever, viva, weaver.
Beater, beta, cheater, cheetah, eater, fleeter, greeter, heater, litre/liter (U.S.), meter/metre, neater, seater, sweeter, treater, tweeter.
Beeper, bleeper, cheaper, creeper, deeper, keeper, leaper, peeper, reaper, sleeper, steeper, sweeper, weeper.
Beaker, bleaker, eureka, meeker, leaker, loudspeaker, peeker, seeker, shrieker, sleeker, sneaker, speaker, streaker, squeaker, tikka, tweaker, weaker.
[3] Appeaser, crowd pleaser, Mona Lisa, stripteaser.

Bandleader, cheerleader, lip-reader, misleader, ringleader, succeeder.
Arena, betweener, blasphemer, cantina, daydreamer, demeanour/demeanor (U.S.), hyena, marina, obscener, redeemer, serener, subpoena, tsarina, uncleaner.
Achiever, believer, deceiver, naïver, receiver, reliever, retriever.
Anteater, brow-beater, deleter, discreeter, dolce vita, eggbeater, margarita, mistreater, retreater, señorita, two-seater, windcheater.
Barkeeper, bee-keeper, book-keeper, doorkeeper, gamekeeper, gatekeeper, goalkeeper, housekeeper, innkeeper, peacekeeper,
shopkeeper, storekeeper, timekeeper, zookeeper.
[4] **Ballerin**a, concertina, in-betweener, misdemeanour/misdemeanor.
Disbeliever, make-believer, unbeliever, underachiever.

2.2.49 "--eemer" (as in "dreamer")
[2] beamer, creamer, dreamer, prima, reamer, schemer, screamer, steamer, streamer.
[3] blasphemer, daydreamer, redeemer.

SURPRISING RHYMING:
[2] **Cleaner**, greener, keener, leaner, meaner, screener, serener.
Beaver, cleaver, diva, fever, griever, leaver, lever, viva, weaver.
Bleeder, breeder, cedar, feeder, leader, pleader, reader, speeder.
Eager, intriguer, meagre/meager (U.S.).
Dealer, feeler, healer, kneeler, peeler, reeler, sealer, spieler, stealer, squealer, wheeler.
Beeper, bleeper, cheaper, creeper, deeper, keeper, leaper, peeper, reaper, sleeper, steeper, sweeper, weeper.
Caesar, easer, freezer, geezer, geyser, pleaser, seizer, sneezer, squeezer, teaser, tweezer, visa, wheezer.
Beater, beta, bleater, cheater, cheetah, eater, fleeter, greeter, heater, litre/liter (U.S.), meter, metre, neater, pleater, seater, skeeter, sweeter, teeter, treater, tweeter.
Beaker, bleaker, eureka, meeker, leaker, loudspeaker, peeker, seeker, shrieker, sleeker, sneaker, speaker, streaker, squeaker, tikka, tweaker, weaker, wreaker.
[3] **Arena**, betweener, cantina, demeanour/demeanor (U.S.), hyena, marina, serener.
Achiever, believer, deceiver, naïver, receiver, repriever, retriever.
Bandleader, cheerleader, lip-reader, misleader, ringleader, succeeder.
Enfant terrible, repealer, revealer, tequila, wheeler-dealer.
Barkeeper, bee-keeper, book-keeper, doorkeeper, gamekeeper, gatekeeper, goalkeeper, housekeeper, innkeeper, peacekeeper, shopkeeper, storekeeper, timekeeper, zookeeper.
Anteater, beefeater, brow-beater, deleter, discreeter, dolce vita, eggbeater, maltreater, margarita, mistreater, repeater, retreater, señorita, two-seater, windcheater.
Appeaser, crowd pleaser, Mona Lisa, stripteaser.
[4] **Ballerina**, concertina, in-betweener, intervener, misdemeanour/misdemeanor (U.S.).

2.2.50 "--eener" (as in "greener")
[2] cleaner, gleaner, greener, keener, leaner, meaner, screener, serener, weaner.
[3] arena, betweener, cantina, convener, demeanour/demeanor (U.S.), hyena, marina, obscener, serener, subpoena, tsarina, uncleaner.
[4] ballerina, concertina, in-betweener, intervener, misdemeanour/misdemeanor (U.S.), semolina, signorina.

SURPRISING RHYMING:
[2] **Beamer**, dreamer, prima, schemer, screamer, steamer, streamer.
Bleeder, breeder, cedar, feeder, heeder, leader, pleader, reader, seeder, speeder.
Beaver, cleaver, diva, fever, griever, leaver, lever, viva, weaver.
Eager, intriguer, meagre/meager (U.S.).
Dealer, feeler, healer, kneeler, peeler, reeler, sealer, spieler, stealer, squealer, wheeler.
Caesar, easer, freezer, geezer, geyser, pleaser, seizer, sneezer, squeezer, teaser, tweezer, visa, wheezer.
Beater, beta, bleater, cheater, cheetah, eater, fleeter, greeter, heater, litre/liter (U.S.), metre/meter, neater, pleater, seater, skeeter, sweeter, teeter, treater, tweeter.
Beeper, bleeper, cheaper, creeper, deeper, keeper, leaper, peeper, reaper, sleeper, steeper, sweeper, weeper.

[3] **Blasphemer**, daydreamer, redeemer.
Achiever, believer, deceiver, naïver, perceiver, receiver, reiver, reliever, retriever.
Bandleader, cheerleader, lip-reader, misleader, ringleader.
Appeaser, crowd pleaser, Mona Lisa, stripteaser.
Brow-beater, dolce vita, margarita, mistreater, repeater, retreater, señorita, two-seater.
Barkeeper, bee-keeper, book-keeper, doorkeeper, gamekeeper, gatekeeper, goalkeeper, housekeeper, innkeeper, peacekeeper, shopkeeper, storekeeper, timekeeper, zookeeper.

2.2.51 "--eeper" (as in "keeper")

[2] beeper, bleeper, cheaper, creeper, deeper, keeper, leaper, peeper, reaper, sleeper, steeper, sweeper, weeper.
[3] barkeeper, bee-keeper, book-keeper, doorkeeper, gamekeeper, gatekeeper, goalkeeper, housekeeper, innkeeper, peacekeeper, shopkeeper, storekeeper, timekeeper, zookeeper.

SURPRISING RHYMING:
[2] **Beater**, beta, bleater, cheater, cheetah, eater, greeter, heater, litre/liter (U.S.), meter, metre, neater, pleater, seater, skeeter, sweeter, teeter, treater, tweeter.
Beaver, cleaver, diva, fever, griever, leaver, lever, viva, weaver.
Caesar, easer, freezer, geezer, geyser, pleaser, seizer, sneezer, squeezer, teaser, tweezer, visa, wheezer.
Beaker, bleaker, eureka, meeker, leaker, loudspeaker, peeker, seeker, shrieker, sleeker, sneaker, speaker, streaker, squeaker, tikka, tweaker, weaker, wreaker.
Eager, intriguer, meagre/meager (U.S.).
Dealer, feeler, healer, kneeler, peeler, reeler, sealer, spieler, stealer, squealer, wheeler.
Bleeder, breeder, cedar, feeder, heeder, leader, pleader, reader, speeder, weeder.
Beamer, creamer, dreamer, prima, reamer, schemer, screamer, steamer, streamer.
Cleaner, gleaner, greener, keener, leaner, meaner, screener, serener, weaner, wiener.
[3] **Achiever**, believer, deceiver, naïver, perceiver, receiver, reliever, repriever, retriever.
Anteater, beefeater, brow-beater, deleter, discreeter, dolce vita, eggbeater, maltreater, margarita, mistreater, repeater, retreater, señorita, two-seater, windcheater.
Appeaser, crowd pleaser, Mona Lisa, stripteaser.
Enfant terrible, repealer, revealer, tequila, wheeler-dealer.
Bandleader, cheerleader, conceder, lip-reader, misleader, ringleader, stampeder, succeeder.
Arena, betweener, blasphemer, cantina, daydreamer, demeanour/demeanor (U.S.), hyena, marina, obscener, redeemer, serener, subpoena, tsarina, uncleaner.
[4] **Ballerina**, concertina, in-betweener, intervener, misdemeanour/misdemeanor (U.S.).
Disbeliever, make-believer, unbeliever, underachiever.

2.2.52 "--eeter" (as in "sweeter")

[2] beater, beta, bleater, cheater, cheetah, eater, fleeter, greeter, heater, litre/liter (U.S.), meter, metre, neater, pleater, seater, skeeter, sweeter, teeter, treater, tweeter.
[3] anteater, beefeater, brow-beater, deleter, discreeter, dolce vita, eggbeater, Lolita, maltreater, margarita, mistreater, repeater, retreater, señorita, two-seater, windcheater.

SURPRISING RHYMING:
[2] **Beeper**, bleeper, cheaper, creeper, deeper, keeper, leaper, peeper, reaper, sleeper, steeper, sweeper, weeper.
Beaver, cleaver, diva, fever, griever, leaver, lever, viva, weaver.
Caesar, easer, freezer, geezer, geyser, pleaser, seizer, sneezer, squeezer, teaser, tweezer, visa, wheezer.
Beaker, bleaker, eureka, meeker, leaker, loudspeaker, peeker, seeker, shrieker, sleeker, sneaker, speaker, streaker, squeaker, tikka, tweaker, weaker, wreaker.
Eager, intriguer, meagre/meager (U.S.).
Dealer, feeler, healer, kneeler, peeler, reeler, sealer, spieler, stealer, squealer, wheeler.
Bleeder, breeder, cedar, feeder, heeder, leader, pleader, reader, speeder, weeder.
Beamer, dreamer, prima, schemer, screamer, steamer, streamer.
Cleaner, greener, keener, leaner, meaner, screener, serener.

[3] Barkeeper, bee-keeper, book-keeper, doorkeeper, gamekeeper, gatekeeper, goalkeeper, housekeeper, innkeeper, peacekeeper, storekeeper, timekeeper, zookeeper.
Achiever, believer, deceiver, receiver, reliever, repriever, retriever.
Appeaser, crowd pleaser, Mona Lisa, stripteaser.
Appealer, concealer, enfant terrible, revealer, tequila, wheeler-dealer.
Bandleader, cheerleader, lip-reader, ringleader, succeeder.
Arena, betweener, blasphemer, cantina, daydreamer, demeanour/demeanor (U.S.), hyena, marina, obscener, redeemer, serener, subpoena, tsarina, uncleaner.
[4] Disbeliever, make-believer, unbeliever, underachiever.
Ballerina, concertina, in-betweener, intervener, misdemeanour/misdemeanor (U.S.), semolina, signorina.

2.2.53 "--eever" (as in "leaver")

[2] beaver, cleaver, diva, fever, griever, heaver, leaver, lever, viva, weaver.
[3] achiever, aggriever, believer, deceiver, naïver, perceiver, receiver, reiver, reliever, repriever, retriever.
[4] cantilever, disbeliever, interweaver, make-believer, unbeliever, underachiever.

SURPRISING RHYMING:
[2] **Bleeder**, breeder, cedar, feeder, heeder, leader, pleader, reader, seeder, speeder.
Dealer, feeler, healer, kneeler, peeler, reeler, sealer, spieler, stealer, squealer, wheeler.
Beamer, dreamer, prima, schemer, screamer, steamer, streamer.
Cleaner, greener, keener, leaner, meaner, screener, serener.
Caesar, easer, either, freezer, geezer, geyser, neither, pleaser, seizer, sneezer, squeezer, teaser, tweezer, visa, wheezer.
Beater, beta, bleater, cheater, cheetah, eater, fleeter, greeter, heater, litre/liter (U.S.), meter, metre, neater, pleater, seater, skeeter, sweeter, teeter, treater, tweeter.
Beeper, bleeper, cheaper, creeper, deeper, keeper, leaper, peeper, reaper, sleeper, steeper, sweeper, weeper.
Eager, intriguer, meagre/meager (U.S.).
Beaker, bleaker, eureka, meeker, leaker, loudspeaker, peeker, seeker, shrieker, sleeker, sneaker, speaker, streaker, squeaker, tikka, tweaker, weaker, wreaker.
[3] **Bandleader**, cheerleader, conceder, lip-reader, misleader, ringleader, succeeder.
Appealer, concealer, enfant terrible, revealer, tequila, wheeler-dealer.
Arena, betweener, blasphemer, cantina, daydreamer, demeanour/demeanor (U.S.), hyena, marina, obscener, redeemer, serener, subpoena, tsarina, uncleaner.
Appeaser, crowd pleaser, Mona Lisa, stripteaser.
Anteater, beefeater, brow-beater, deleter, discreeter, dolce vita, eggbeater, maltreater, margarita, mistreater, repeater, retreater, señorita, two-seater, windcheater.
Barkeeper, bee-keeper, book-keeper, doorkeeper, gamekeeper, gatekeeper, goalkeeper, housekeeper, innkeeper, peacekeeper, shopkeeper, storekeeper, timekeeper, zookeeper.
[4] **Ballerina**, concertina, in-betweener, intervener, misdemeanour/misdemeanor (U.S.).

2.2.54 "--eezer" (as in "teaser")

[2] Caesar, easer, freezer, geezer, geyser, pleaser, seizer, sneezer, squeezer, teaser, tweezer, visa, wheezer.
[3] appeaser, crowd pleaser, Mona Lisa, stripteaser.

SURPRISING RHYMING:
[2] **Creature**, feature, preacher, reacher, schoolteacher, screecher, teacher.
Eager, intriguer, meagre/meager (U.S.).
Beaver, cleaver, diva, fever, griever, leaver, lever, viva, weaver.
Dealer, feeler, healer, kneeler, sealer, spieler, stealer, squealer.
Bleeder, breeder, cedar, feeder, heeder, leader, pleader, reader, speeder, weeder.
Beamer, dreamer, prima, schemer, screamer, steamer, streamer.
Cleaner, greener, keener, leaner, meaner, screener, serener.
Beater, beta, bleater, cheater, cheetah, eater, fleeter, greeter, heater, litre/liter (U.S.), meter, metre, neater, pleater, seater, skeeter, sweeter, teeter, treater, tweeter.
Beeper, bleeper, cheaper, creeper, deeper, keeper, leaper, peeper, reaper, sleeper, steeper, sweeper, weeper.

Beaker, bleaker, eureka, meeker, leaker, loudspeaker, peeker, seeker, shrieker, sleeker, sneaker, speaker, streaker, squeaker, tikka, tweaker, weaker, wreaker.
[3] Achiever, believer, deceiver, naïver, perceiver, receiver, reliever, repriever, retriever.
Appealer, concealer, enfant terrible, revealer, tequila, wheeler-dealer.
Bandleader, cheerleader, conceder, lip-reader, misleader, ringleader.
Arena, betweener, blasphemer, cantina, daydreamer, demeanour/demeanor (U.S.), hyena, marina, obscener, redeemer, serener, subpoena, tsarina, uncleaner.
Anteater, beefeater, brow-beater, deleter, discreeter, dolce vita, eggbeater, maltreater, margarita, mistreater, repeater, retreater, señorita, two-seater, windcheater.
Barkeeper, bee-keeper, book-keeper, doorkeeper, gamekeeper, gatekeeper, goalkeeper, housekeeper, innkeeper, peacekeeper, shopkeeper, storekeeper, timekeeper, zookeeper.
[4] Disbeliever, make-believer, unbeliever, underachiever.
Ballerina, concertina, in-betweener, intervener, misdemeanour/misdemeanor (U.S.), semolina, signorina.

2.2.55 "--easure" (as in "treasure")
[2] leisure, measure, pleasure, treasure.
[3] displeasure, made-to-measure.

SURPRISING RHYMING:
[2] **Clever**, ever, never, sever.
Feather, heather, leather, nether, tether, together, weather, whether.
Cellar, dweller, fella, feller, queller, seller, smeller, speller, stellar, teller, yeller.
Cheddar, deader, header, homesteader, redder, shredder, spreader, threader, treader.
Dresser, guesser, lesser, presser, yessir.
[3] Endeavour/endeavor (U.S.), forever, however, never-never, whatever, whatsoever, whenever, wherever, whichever, whoever, whomever.
A capella, Cinderella, fortune-teller, mozzarella, storyteller.
Bestseller, cave dweller, exceller, foreteller, novella, paella, propeller, repeller, umbrella.
Aggressor, assessor, caresser, confessor, contessa, digresser, hairdresser, oppressor, possessor, predecessor, processor, professor, possessor, successor, transgressor.

2.2.56 "--eller" (as in "cellar")
[2] cellar, dweller, fella, feller, queller, seller, smeller, speller, stellar, teller, yeller.
[3] bestseller, cave dweller, dispeller, exceller, expeller, foreteller, novella, paella, propeller, repeller, umbrella.
[4] a capella, Cinderella, fortune-teller, mozzarella, storyteller.

SURPRISING RHYMING:
[2] **Clever**, ever, never, sever.
Feather, heather, leather, nether, tether, together, weather, whether.
Leisure, measure, pleasure, treasure.
Better, debtor, fetter, fretter, getter, letter, setter, sweater, wetter.
[3] Endeavour/endeavor, forever, however, never-never, whatever, whatsoever, whenever, wherever, whichever, whoever, whomever.
Aggressor, assessor, caresser, confessor, contessa, digresser, hairdresser, oppressor, possessor, predecessor, processor, professor, possessor, successor, transgressor.

2.2.57 "--elthier" (as in "wealthier")
[3] healthier, stealthier, wealthier.

SURPRISING RHYMING:
[2] **Caesar**, easer, freezer, geezer, geyser, pleaser, seizer, sneezer, squeezer, teaser, tweezer, visa, wheezer.
Beamer, creamer, dreamer, prima, reamer, schemer, screamer, steamer, streamer.
[3] Breathier, earthier, filthier, frothier, lengthier, stealthier, swarthier, toothier, worthier.
Arena, betweener, cantina, convener, demeanour/demeanor (U.S.), hyena, marina, obscener, serener, subpoena, tsarina, uncleaner.
Eager, intriguer, meagre/meager (U.S.).

2.2.58 "--ember" (as in "remember")
[2] ember, member.
[3] December, dismember, remember, September, November.

SURPRISING RHYMING:
[2] **Blender**, ender, fender, gender, lender, mender, render, sender, slender, spender, splendour/splendor (U.S.), tender, vendor.
Enter, centre/center (U.S.), renter.
Censor, denser, fencer, sensor, tenser, condenser, dispenser.
Altogether, feather, heather, leather, together, weather, whether.
Fester, jester, nester, pester, quester, tester, vesta, wester, zester.
Better, debtor, fetter, fretter, getter, letter, setter, sweater, wetter.
[3] **Agenda**, amender, apprehender, ascender, attender, bartender, contender, defender, descender, extender, hacienda, moneylender, offender, pretender, recommender, surrender, suspender, transcender, transgender, weekender.
Dissenter, epicentre/epicenter (U.S.), frequenter, inventor, lamenter, magenta, presenter, preventer, re-enter, repenter, tormentor.
Ancestor, arrester, digester, fiesta, investor, molester, polyester, protester, semester, siesta, sou'wester, suggester, trimester.
Endeavour/endeavor, forever, however, never-never, whatever, whatsoever, whenever, wherever, whichever, whoever, whomever.
Bonesetter, carburettor/carburetor (U.S.), forgetter, go-getter, jet-setter, love-letter, newsletter, operetta, pacesetter, red-letter, typesetter, unfetter, upsetter, vendetta.

2.2.59 "--ender" (as in "tender")
[2] bender, blender, ender, fender, gender, lender, mender, render, sender, slender, spender, splendour/splendor (U.S.), tender, vender, vendor.
[3] agenda, amender, apprehender, ascender, attender, bartender, contender, defender, descender, extender, hacienda, moneylender, offender, pretender, recommender, surrender, suspender, transcender, transgender, weekender.

SURPRISING RHYMING:
[2] **Centre/center** (U.S.), ember, enter, member, renter.
Clever, ever, never, sever.
Censor, denser, fencer, sensor, tenser, condenser, dispenser.
Altogether, feather, leather, tether, together, weather, whether.
Fester, jester, nester, pester, quester, tester, vesta, wester, zester.
Better, debtor, fetter, fretter, getter, letter, setter, sweater, wetter.
[3] **December**, dismember, remember, September, November.
Endeavour/endeavor, forever, however, never-never, whatever, whatsoever, whenever, wherever, whichever, whoever, whomever.
Dissenter, epicentre/epicenter (U.S.), eventer, fermenter, frequenter, inventor, presenter, preventer, re-enter, repenter, tormentor.
Ancestor, arrester, fiesta, investor, molester, polyester, protester, semester, sequester, siesta, sou'wester, suggester, trimester.
Bonesetter, carburettor/carburetor (U.S.), forgetter, go-getter, jet-setter, love-letter, newsletter, operetta, pacesetter, red-letter, typesetter, unfetter, upsetter, vendetta.

2.2.60 "--enser" (as in "censor")
censor, denser, fencer, Mensa, sensor, tenser, condenser, dispenser.

SURPRISING RHYMING:
[2] **Centre/center** (U.S.), ember, enter, member, renter.
Fester, jester, nester, pester, rester, tester, wester, zester.
Blender, ender, fender, gender, lender, mender, render, sender, slender, spender, splendour/splendor (U.S.), tender, vendor.
[3] **Cementer**, dissenter, epicentre/epicenter (U.S.), eventer, fermenter, frequenter, inventor, lamenter, magenta, presenter, preventer, re-enter, repenter, tormentor.

December, dismember, remember, September, November.
Aggressor, assessor, caresser, confessor, contessa, digresser, hairdresser, oppressor, possessor, predecessor, processor, professor, possessor, successor, transgressor.
Ancestor, arrester, digester, fiesta, investor, molester, polyester, protester, semester, siesta, sou'wester, suggester, trimester.

2.2.61 "--enter" (as in "enter")
[2] enter, centre/center (U.S.), renter.
[3] cementer, dissenter, epicentre/epicenter (U.S.), eventer, fermenter, frequenter, inventor, lamenter, magenta, presenter, preventer, re-enter, repenter, tormentor.

SURPRISING RHYMING:
[2] **Ember**, member, temper.
Blender, ender, fender, gender, lender, mender, render, sender, slender, spender, splendour/splendor (U.S.), tender, vendor.
Censor, denser, fencer, sensor, tenser, condenser, dispenser.
Fester, jester, nester, pester, rester, tester, vesta, wester, zester.
[3] **December**, dismember, remember, September, November.
Ancestor, arrester, contester, digester, fiesta, investor, molester, polyester, protester, semester, siesta, sou'wester, trimester.

2.2.62 "--esser" (as in "lesser")
[2] dresser, guesser, lesser, presser, yessir.
[3] addresser, aggressor, assessor, caresser, compressor, confessor, contessa, depressor, digresser, hairdresser, oppressor, possessor, predecessor, processor, professor, microprocessor, successor, suppresser, transgressor.

SURPRISING RHYMING:
[2] **Censor**, denser, fencer, Mensa, sensor, condenser, dispenser.
Fester, jester, nester, pester, quester, rester, tester, vesta.
Leisure, measure, pleasure, treasure.
[3] **Ancestor**, arrester, contester, digester, fiesta, investor, molester, polyester, protester, semester, siesta, sou'wester, trimester.
Displeasure, made-to-measure.
Bestseller, cave dweller, dispeller, exceller, expeller, foreteller, novella, paella, propeller, repeller, umbrella.
[4] **A capella**, Cinderella, fortune-teller, mozzarella, storyteller.

2.2.63 "--ester" (as in "protester")
[2] fester, jester, nester, pester, quester, rester, tester, vesta, wester, zester.
[3] ancestor, arrester, Celesta, contester, digester, fiesta, investor, molester, polyester, protester, semester, sequester, siesta, sou'wester, suggester, trimester.

SURPRISING RHYMING:
[2] **Censor**, denser, fencer, sensor, tenser, condenser, dispenser.
Enter, centre/center (U.S.), renter.
Dresser, guesser, lesser, presser, yessir.
Better, debtor, fetter, fretter, getter, letter, setter, sweater, wetter.
Leisure, measure, pleasure, treasure.
[3] **Dissenter**, epicentre/epicenter (U.S.), frequenter, inventor, lamenter, magenta, presenter, preventer, repenter, tormentor.
Bonesetter, carburettor/carburetor (U.S.), forgetter, go-getter, jet-setter, love-letter, newsletter, operetta, pacesetter, red-letter, typesetter, unfetter, upsetter, vendetta.

2.2.64 "--etter" (as in "better")
[2] better, debtor, fetter, fretter, getter, letter, setter, sweater, wetter.
[3] bonesetter, carburettor/carburetor (U.S.), forgetter, go-getter, jet-setter, love-letter, newsletter, operetta, pacesetter, red-letter, typesetter, unfetter, upsetter, vendetta.

SURPRISING RHYMING:
[2] **Feather**, heather, leather, nether, tether, together, untether, weather, whether.
Clever, ever, never, sever.
Leisure, measure, pleasure, treasure.
Cheddar, header, redder, shredder, spreader, threader, treader.
Cellar, dweller, fella, seller, smeller, speller, teller, yeller.
[3] **Endeavour/endeavor** (U.S.), forever, forget her, however, never-never, whatever, whatsoever, whenever, wherever, whichever, whoever, whomever.
Bestseller, cave dweller, exceller, foreteller, novella, paella, propeller, repeller, umbrella.

2.2.65 "--ether" (as in "weather")
altogether, feather, heather, leather, tether, together, untether, weather, whether.

SURPRISING RHYMING:
[2] **Clever**, ever, never, sever.
Leisure, measure, pleasure, treasure.
Cheddar, deader, header, homesteader, redder, shredder, spreader, threader, treader.
Cellar, dweller, fella, feller, seller, smeller, speller, teller, yeller.
[3] **Endeavour/endeavor** (U.S.), forever, forget her, however, never-never, whatever, whatsoever, whenever, wherever, whichever, whoever, whomever.
Bestseller, cave dweller, dispeller, exceller, expeller, foreteller, novella, paella, propeller, repeller, umbrella.

2.2.66 "--ever" (as in "never")
[2] clever, ever, never, sever.
[3] endeavour/endeavor (U.S.), forever, however, never-never, whatever, whatsoever, whenever, wherever, whichever, whoever, whomever.

SURPRISING RHYMING:
[2] **Feather**, heather, leather, tether, together, weather, whether.
Leisure, measure, pleasure, treasure.
Better, debtor, fetter, fretter, getter, letter, setter, sweater, wetter.
Cellar, dweller, error, fella, feller, seller, sierra, smeller, speller, teller, terror, yeller.
[3] **Bestseller**, cave dweller, dispeller, displeasure, exceller, expeller, foreteller, made-to-measure, novella, paella, propeller, repeller, umbrella.
Bonesetter, carburettor/carburetor (U.S.), forgetter, go-getter, jet-setter, love-letter, newsletter, operetta, pacesetter, red-letter, typesetter, unfetter, upsetter, vendetta.
Aggressor, assessor, caresser, confessor, contessa, digresser, hairdresser, oppressor, possessor, predecessor, processor, professor, possessor, successor, transgressor.
A capella, Cinderella, fortune-teller, mozzarella, storyteller.

2.2.67 "--ibbler" (as in "nibbler")
[2] dribbler, nibbler, quibbler, scribbler.

SURPRISING RHYMING:
[2] **Giggler**, jiggler, niggler, wiggler, wriggler.
Chiller, driller, filler, griller, killer, miller, pillar, spiller, thriller, villa.
Bigger, digger, figure, rigour/rigor (U.S.), snigger, swigger, trigger, vigour/vigor (U.S.).
Limber, marimba, timber.
Crimper, limper, shrimper, simper, whimper.
[3] **Builder**, bodybuilder, boatbuilder, bewilder, housebuilder.
Caterpillar, flotilla, fulfiller, gorilla, guerilla, man-killer, painkiller, spine-chiller, vanilla.
Configure, disfigure, gold-digger, gravedigger, outrigger, vinegar.

2.2.68 "--iber" (as in "briber")
briber, cyber, fibre/fiber (U.S.), imbiber, inscriber, prescriber, subscriber, transcriber.

SURPRISING RHYMING:
[2] **Diver**, driver, fiver, jiver, skiver, striver, thriver.

Cider, eider, glider, guider, hider, rider, slider, spider, strider, wider.
Diaper, hyper, piper, riper, sniper, striper, swiper, viper, wiper.
China, diner, finer, liner, miner, minor, mynah, piner, shiner, whiner.
[3] Conniver, pearl diver, piledriver, saliva, screwdriver, skydiver, slave driver, survivor.
Backslider, collider, confider, decider, insider, joyrider, nightrider, outrider, outsider, provider, roughrider.
Bagpiper, sandpiper, sideswiper.
Airliner, designer, diviner, eyeliner, hardliner, headliner, moonshiner, recliner, streamliner.

2.2.69 "--icer" (as in "nicer")
dicer, enticer, de-icer, nicer, pricer, slicer, splicer.

SURPRISING RHYMING:
[2] Biter, blighter, brighter, fighter, lighter, slighter, spiter, tighter, triter, whiter, writer.
Kaiser, miser, riser, sizer, visor, wiser.
Cipher, decipher, encipher, knifer, lifer, knife her.
[3] Adviser, chastiser, despiser, deviser, disguiser, incisor, reviser, surmiser, surpriser.
[4] Advertiser, appetizer, atomizer, breathalyzer, compromiser, criticizer, deodorizer, economizer, energizer, equalizer, exerciser, fertilizer, idolizer, immobilizer, improviser, itemizer, jeopardizer, liquidizer, maximiser, memorizer, merchandiser, mesmerizer, minimizer, mobilizer, modernizer, moisturizer, moralizer, neutralizer, organizer, patronizer, philosophizer, plagiarizer, recognizer, sermonizer, socializer, specializer, stabilizer, subsidizer, summarizer, supervisor, sympathizer, synthesizer, terrorizer, tranquillizer, tantalizer, victimizer, womanizer.

2.2.70 "--icker" (as in "kicker")
[2] bicker, clicker, dicker, flicker, kicker, knicker, licker, liquor, nicker, picker, pricker, quicker, sicker, slicker, snicker, sticker, thicker, ticker, tricker, vicar, whicker, wicker.
[3] electronica, erotica, exotica, frolicker, harmonica, lip-syncer, replica, mimicker, moniker, picnicker, trafficker.

SURPRISING RHYMING:
[2] Bitter, critter, fitter, flitter, fritter, glitter, gritter, hitter, jitter, knitter, litter, quitter, sitter, skitter, slitter, spitter, splitter, twitter.
Bigger, figure, rigour/rigor (U.S.), snigger, trigger, vigour/vigor (U.S.).
Bidder, consider, differ, kidder.
Chipper, clipper, dipper, flipper, gripper, hipper, kipper, nipper, quipper, ripper, shipper, sipper, skipper, slipper, stripper, tipper, tripper, whipper, zipper.
Chiller, driller, filler, griller, killer, pillar, spiller, swiller, thriller, villa.
Dinner, grinner, inner, sinner(s), skinner, spinner, thinner, winner(s).
Elixir, fixer, mixer, picture, sixer.
Giver, liver, river, shiver, sliver, quiver.
[3] Auditor, committer, creditor, cricketer, editor, embitter, emitter, housesitter, janitor, Jupiter, monitor, outfitter, permitter, pinch-hitter, submitter, transmitter, visitor.
Configure, disfigure, gold-digger, gravedigger, outrigger, vinegar.
Day-tripper, equipper, juniper, worshiper.
Beginner(s), Berliner, breadwinner, examiner, foreigner, mariner, phenomena, retina, prizewinner, stamina.
Aquiver, deliver, downriver, forgiver, upriver.
[4] Baby-sitter, barometer, competitor, counterfeiter, diameter, exhibitor, interpreter, mileometer/milometer (U.S.), parameter, perimeter, solicitor, speedometer, thermometer.

2.2.71 "--ider" (as in "spider")
[2] chider, cider, eider, glider, guider, hider, rider, slider, spider, strider, wider.
[3] backslider, collider, confider, decider, divider, insider, joyrider, nightrider, outrider, outsider, provider, roughrider.

SURPRISING RHYMING:
[2] China, diner, finer, liner, miner, minor, mynah, piner, shiner, signer, whiner.

237

Biter, blighter, brighter, fighter, lighter, mitre/miter (U.S.), slighter, spiter, tiger, tighter, triter, whiter, writer.
Briber, cyber, fibre/fiber (U.S.), imbiber, inscriber, prescriber, subscriber, transcriber.
[3] Airliner, designer, diviner, eyeliner, hardliner, headliner, moonshiner, recliner, streamliner.
All-nighter, backbiter, bullfighter, copywriter, delighter, exciter, fistfighter, ghostwriter, gunfighter, inciter, igniter, lamplighter, midnighter, moonlighter, overnighter, politer, prizefighter, reciter, rewriter, screenwriter, scriptwriter, signwriter, songwriter, typewriter.
Beguiler, compiler, defiler, hair-styler, profiler, reviler, stockpiler.
Childminder, pathfinder, reminder, rewinder, sidewinder, spellbinder, viewfinder.

2.2.72 "--ier" (as in "liar")
[2] briar, buyer, crier, defier, denier, dire, drier, dryer, dyer, flier/flyer, friar, fryer, higher, liar, Maya, plier, plyer, prier, prior, shyer, sprier, spryer, trier, via.
[3] applier, denier, hairdryer, homebuyer, messiah, papaya, pariah, replier, supplier.
[4] amplifier, beautifier, clarifier, classifier, crucifier, disqualifier, fortifier, glorifier, gratifier, humidifier, identifier, intensifier, jambalaya, justifier, magnifier, mollifier, multiplier, occupier, pacifier, personifier, prettifier, prophesier, purifier, qualifier, rectifier, sanctifier, scarifier, signifier, terrifier, testifier, tumble-dryer, unifier, verifier, vilifier.

SURPRISING RHYMING:
[1] **Choir,** fire, hire, ire, mire, pyre, shire, sire, spire, squire, tire, tyre/tire (U.S.), wire.
[2] **Acquire,** admire, aspire, attire, backfire, barbwire, bonfire, buyer, campfire, ceasefire, conspire, crossfire, desire, empire, enquire, entire, esquire, expire, gunfire, haywire, hellfire, higher, inspire, misfire, perspire, quagmire, sapphire, satire, spitfire, surefire, transpire, tripwire, umpire, vampire, wildfire.
China, diner, finer, liner, miner, minor, mynah, piner, shiner, whiner.
Diver, driver, fiver, jiver, skiver, striver, thriver.
[3] **Airliner,** designer, eyeliner, hardliner, headliner, moonshiner, recliner, streamliner.
Conniver, contriver, piledriver, saliva, screwdriver, skydiver, slave driver, survivor.

2.2.73 "--ieter" (as in "quieter")
[3] dieter, proprietor, quieter, rioter.

SURPRISING RHYMING:
[3] **All-nighter,** backbiter, bullfighter, copywriter, delighter, exciter, fistfighter, ghostwriter, gunfighter, inciter, igniter, lamplighter, midnighter, moonlighter, overnighter, politer, prizefighter, reciter, rewriter, screenwriter, scriptwriter, signwriter, songwriter, typewriter.
Backfire, barbwire, bonfire, bushfire, campfire, ceasefire, crossfire, gunfire, haywire, hellfire, misfire, surefire, tripwire, vampire, wildfire.
Backslider, collider, confider, decider, divider, insider, joyrider, nightrider, outrider, outsider, provider, roughrider.

2.2.74 "--iffer (as in "differ")
conifer, differ, Lucifer, sniffer, stiffer.

SURPRISING RHYMING:
[2] **Giver,** liver, river, shiver, sliver, quiver.
Dinner, grinner, inner, sinner(s), skinner, spinner, thinner, winner(s).
Dimmer, glimmer, primmer, shimmer, simmer, skimmer, slimmer, strimmer, swimmer, trimmer, zimmer.
Drifter, grifter, lifter, shifter, sifter, snifter, swifter.
[3] **Aquiver,** deliver, downriver, forgiver, upriver.
Beginner(s), breadwinner, examiner, foreigner, phenomena, prizewinner, stamina.

2.2.75 "--ifter" (as in "drifter")
[2] drifter, grifter, lifter, shifter, sifter, snifter, swifter.
[3] shoplifter, uplifter, weightlifter.

SURPRISING RHYMING:
[2] **Inter**, into, midwinter, printer, splinter, sprinter, squinter, tinter, winter.
Blister, crisper, mister, sister, trickster, twister, vista, whisper.
Conifer, differ, giver, liver, Lucifer, quiver, river, shiver, sliver, sniffer, sniffler, stiffer.
Filter, jilter, kilter, quilter, tilter.
Bitter, critter, fitter, flitter, fritter, glitter, gritter, hitter, jitter, knitter, litter, pitta, quitter, sitter, slitter, spitter, splitter, titter, twitter.
[3] **Constrictor**, contradictor, depicter, evictor, predictor, victor.
Builder, bodybuilder, boatbuilder, bewilder, housebuilder, shipbuilder.
Aquiver, deliver, downriver, forgiver, upriver.

2.2.76 "--iyger" (as in "tiger")
[2] Geiger, tiger.

SURPRISING RHYMING:
[2] **Briber**, cyber, cypher, fibre/fiber (U.S.).
Cider, eider, glider, guider, hider, rider, slider, spider, strider, wider.
China, diner, finer, liner, miner, minor, mynah, piner, shiner, whiner.
Biter, blighter, brighter, fighter, lighter, mitre/miter (U.S.), slighter, tighter, whiter, writer.
Climber, mimer, primer, rhymer, timer.
Buyer, crier, drier, dryer, dyer, fire, flyer, friar, fryer, higher, liar, prior, shyer, tire, tyre/tire (U.S.), trier, via, wire.
Diaper, hyper, piper, riper, sniper, striper, swiper, viper, wiper.
Biker, hiker, like her, spiker, striker.
[3] **Imbiber**, inscriber, prescriber, subscriber, transcriber.
Backslider, collider, confider, decider, divider, insider, joyrider, nightrider, outrider, outsider, provider, roughrider.
All-nighter, backbiter, bullfighter, copywriter, delighter, exciter, fistfighter, ghostwriter, gunfighter, inciter, igniter, lamplighter, midnighter, moonlighter, overnighter, politer, prizefighter, reciter, rewriter, screenwriter, scriptwriter, signwriter, songwriter, typewriter.
Conniver, contriver, piledriver, saliva, screwdriver, skydiver, slave driver, survivor.

2.2.77 "--igger" (as in "bigger")
[2] bigger, digger, figure, jigger, ligger, rigger, rigour/rigor (U.S.), snigger, swigger, trigger, vigour/vigor (U.S.).
[3] configure, disfigure, gold-digger, gravedigger, outrigger, square-rigger, vinegar.

SURPRISING RHYMING:
[2] **Bitter**, critter, fitter, flitter, fritter, glitter, gritter, hitter, jitter, knitter, litter, pitta, quitter, sitter, skitter, spitter, splitter, titter, twitter.
Dimmer, glimmer, mirror, primmer, shimmer, simmer, skimmer, slimmer, swimmer.
Dinner, grinner, inner, sinner(s), skinner, spinner, thinner, winner(s).
Giver, liver, river, shiver, sliver, quiver.
Chiller, driller, filler, griller, killer, pillar, spiller, thriller, tiller, villa.
Chipper, clipper, dipper, flipper, gripper, hipper, kipper, nipper, quipper, ripper, shipper, sipper, skipper, slipper, stripper, tipper, tripper, whipper, zipper.
Bidder, consider, kidder.
Fizzer, hisser, kisser, quizzer, reminiscer, whizzer.
Giggler, jiggler, niggler, wiggler, wriggler.
[3] **Committer**, embitter, emitter, housesitter, outfitter, remitter, submitter, transmitter.
Beginner(s), breadwinner, examiner, foreigner, mariner, milliner, phenomena, prizewinner, retina, stamina.
Caterpillar, chinchilla, distiller, flotilla, fulfiller, gorilla, guerilla, manilla, man-killer, painkiller, spine-chiller, vanilla, weedkiller.
Bell-ringer, gunslinger, humdinger, left-winger, mud-slinger.
Aquiver, deliver, downriver, forgiver, upriver.

2.2.78 "--iggler" (as in "giggler")
[2] giggler, jiggler, niggler, wiggler, wriggler.

239

SURPRISING RHYMING:
[2] **Crippler**, dribbler, nibbler, quibbler, scribbler, stickler, tippler.
Diddler, fiddler, middler, riddler, tiddler.
Chiller, driller, filler, griller, killer, pillar, spiller, thriller, tiller, villa.

2.2.79 "--iler" (as in "smiler")
[2] filer, smiler, styler, tiler, viler.
[3] beguiler, compiler, defiler, hair-styler, profiler, reviler, stockpiler.

SURPRISING RHYMING:
[2] **China**, diner, finer, liner, miner, minor, mynah, piner, shiner, signer, whiner.
Climber, mimer, primer, rhymer, timer.
Diver, driver, fiver, jiver, skiver, striver, thriver.
Cider, glider, guider, hider, rider, slider, spider, strider, tiger, wider.
Buyer, choir, crier, dire, drier, dryer, dyer, fire, flyer, friar, fryer, higher, hire, inspire, ire, liar, lyre, Maya, mire, plier, plyer, prier, prior, pyre, shire, shyer, sire, spire, sprier, spryer, squire, tire, tyre/tire (U.S.), trier, via, wire.
[3] **Airliner**, designer, diviner, hardliner, headliner, moonshiner, recliner, streamliner.
Old-timer, part-timer, sublimer, two-timer.
Piledriver, saliva, screwdriver, skydiver, slave driver, survivor.
Denier, hairdryer, homebuyer, messiah, papaya, pariah, replier.
[4] **Amplifier**, beautifier, clarifier, disqualifier, glorifier, gratifier, humidifier, identifier, intensifier, jambalaya, justifier, liquefier, magnifier, modifier, mollifier, multiplier, occupier, pacifier, personifier, prettifier, prophesier, purifier, qualifier, rectifier, sanctifier, signifier, terrifier, testifier, tumble-dryer, unifier, verifier, vilifier.

2.2.80 "--iller" (as in "thriller")
[2] chiller, driller, filler, griller, killer, miller, pillar, spiller, swiller, thriller, tiller, villa.
[3] caterpillar, chinchilla, distiller, flotilla, fulfiller, gorilla, guerilla, manilla, man-killer, painkiller, spine-chiller, vanilla, weedkiller.

SURPRISING RHYMING:
[2] **Similar**, dissimilar.
Bigger, digger, figure, rigour/rigor (U.S.), snigger, swigger, trigger, vigour/vigor (U.S.).
Dimmer, glimmer, primmer, shimmer, simmer, skimmer, slimmer, swimmer, trimmer.
Dinner, grinner, inner, sinner(s), skinner, spinner, thinner, winner(s).
Bitter, critter, fitter, flitter, fritter, glitter, gritter, hitter, jitter, knitter, litter, pitta, quitter, sitter, skitter, slitter, spitter, splitter, titter, twitter.
Giver, liver, river, shiver, sliver, quiver.
[3] **Beginner(s)**, Berliner, breadwinner, examiner, foreigner, mariner, phenomena, retina, prizewinner, stamina.
Auditor, committer, creditor, cricketer, editor, embitter, emitter, housesitter, janitor, Jupiter, monitor, outfitter, permitter, pinch-hitter, submitter, transmitter, visitor.

2.2.81 "--illder" (as in "builder")
[3] builder, bodybuilder, boatbuilder, bewilder, housebuilder, rebuilder, shipbuilder.

SURPRISING RHYMING:
[2] **Bewildered**, filter, kilter, pilfer, quilter, tilter.
Drifter, grifter, lifter, shifter, sifter, snifter, swifter.
Midwinter, printer, splinter, sprinter, squinter, tinter, winter.
Limber, marimba, timber.
Dimmer, glimmer, primmer, shimmer, simmer, skimmer, slimmer, swimmer, trimmer.

2.2.82 "--imer" (as in "climber")
[2] climber, mimer, primer, rhymer, timer.
[3] old-timer, part-timer, sublimer, two-timer.

SURPRISING RHYMING:
[2] China, diner, finer, liner, minor, mynah, piner, shiner, whiner.
Binder, blinder, finder, grinder, kinda, kinder, minder, winder.
Buyer, choir, crier, dire, drier, dryer, dyer, fire, flyer, friar, fryer, higher, hire, inspire, ire, liar, lyre, Maya, mire, plier, plyer, prier, prior, pyre, shire, shyer, sire, spire, sprier, spryer, squire, tire, tyre/tire (U.S.), trier, via, wire.
[3] Airliner, designer, diviner, hardliner, headliner, moonshiner, recliner, streamliner.
Childminder, pathfinder, reminder, rewinder, sidewinder, spellbinder, viewfinder.
[4] Amplifier, beautifier, clarifier, classifier, crucifier, disqualifier, fortifier, glorifier, gratifier, humidifier, identifier, intensifier, jambalaya, justifier, liquefier, magnifier, modifier, mollifier, multiplier, occupier, pacifier, personifier, prettifier, prophesier, purifier, qualifier, quantifier, rectifier, scarifier, signifier, specifier, terrifier, testifier, tumble-dryer.

2.2.83 "--imber" (as in "timber")
[2] limber, marimba, timber.

SURPRISING RHYMING:
[2] Builder, filter, kilter, pilfer, quilter, tilter.
Drifter, grifter, lifter, shifter, sifter, snifter, swifter.
Midwinter, printer, splinter, sprinter, squinter, tinter, winter.
Crimper, limper, shrimper, simper, whimper.
Dimmer, glimmer, primmer, shimmer, simmer, skimmer, slimmer, strimmer, swimmer, trimmer, zimmer.
Dinner, grinner, inner, sinner(s), skinner, spinner, thinner, winner(s).
Bringer, clinger, flinger, pinger, ringer, singer, slinger, springer, stinger, stringer, swinger, winger, wringer, zinger.
[3] Bewilder, bewildered, bodybuilder, boatbuilder, housebuilder, rebuilder, shipbuilder.
Beginner(s), Berliner, breadwinner, examiner, foreigner, mariner, phenomena, retina, prizewinner, stamina.
Bell-ringer, gunslinger, humdinger, left-winger, mud-slinger.

2.2.84 "--immer" (as in "swimmer")
[2] dimmer, glimmer, primmer, shimmer, simmer, skimmer, slimmer, strimmer, swimmer, trimmer, zimmer.

SURPRISING RHYMING:
[2] Limber, marimba, timber.
Crimper, limper, shrimper, simper, whimper.
Dinner, grinner, inner, sinner(s), skinner, spinner, thinner, winner(s).
Bringer, clinger, flinger, pinger, ringer, singer, slinger, springer, stinger, stringer, swinger, winger, wringer, zinger.
Midwinter, printer, splinter, sprinter, squinter, tinter, winter.
Conifer, differ, giver, liver, Lucifer, quiver, river, shiver, sliver, sniffer, sniffler, stiffer.
Bigger, digger, figure, rigour/rigor (U.S.), snigger, swigger, trigger, vigour/vigor (U.S.).
[3] Cinema, charisma, eczema, enema, maxima, minima, ultima.
Beginner(s), Berliner, breadwinner, examiner, foreigner, mariner, phenomena, retina, prizewinner, stamina.
Bell-ringer, gunslinger, humdinger, left-winger, mud-slinger.

2.2.85 "--imper" (as in "whimper")
[2] crimper, limper, shrimper, simper, whimper.

SURPRISING RHYMING:
[2] Limber, marimba, timber.
Midwinter, printer, splinter, sprinter, squinter, tinter, winter.
Blinker, drinker, Inca, inker, jinker, linker, pinker, shrinker, sinker, stinker, thinker, tinker, winker, freethinker, headshrinker.
Dimmer, glimmer, shimmer, simmer, skimmer, slimmer, swimmer, trimmer, zimmer.
Dinner, grinner, inner, sinner(s), skinner, spinner, thinner, winner(s).

Bringer, clinger, flinger, pinger, ringer, singer, slinger, springer, stinger, stringer, swinger, winger, wringer, zinger.
Conifer, differ, giver, liver, Lucifer, quiver, river, shiver, sliver, sniffer, sniffler, stiffer.
Bigger, digger, figure, rigour/rigor (U.S.), snigger, swigger, trigger, vigour/vigor (U.S.).
[3] **Cinema**, charisma, eczema, enema, maxima, minima, ultima.
Beginner(s), Berliner, breadwinner, examiner, foreigner, mariner, phenomena, retina, prizewinner, stamina.
Bell-ringer, gunslinger, humdinger, left-winger, mud-slinger.
Configure, disfigure, gold-digger, gravedigger, outrigger, vinegar.

2.2.86 "--inder" (as in "kinder")
[2] binder, blinder, finder, grinder, kinda, kinder, minder, winder.
[3] bookbinder, childminder, pathfinder, rangefinder, reminder, rewinder, ringbinder, sidewinder, spellbinder, viewfinder.

SURPRISING RHYMING:
[2] **China**, diner, finer, liner, miner, minor, mynah, piner, shiner, signer, whiner.
Climber, mimer, primer, rhymer, timer.
Cider, eider, glider, guider, hider, rider, slider, spider, strider, wider.
Biter, blighter, brighter, fighter, lighter, mitre/miter (U.S.), slighter, tighter, whiter, writer.
Briber, cyber, fibre/fiber (U.S.).
Buyer, choir, crier, dire, drier, dryer, fire, flyer, friar, higher, hire, ire, liar, lyre, Maya, mire, prior, pyre, shire, shyer, sire, spire, squire, tire, tyre/tire (U.S.), trier, via, wire.
[3] **Airliner**, designer, diviner, hardliner, headliner, moonshiner, recliner, streamliner.
Old-timer, part-timer, sublimer, two-timer.
Backslider, collider, confider, decider, divider, insider, joyrider, nightrider, outrider, outsider, provider, roughrider.
All-nighter, backbiter, bullfighter, copywriter, delighter, exciter, fistfighter, ghostwriter, gunfighter, inciter, igniter, lamplighter, midnighter, moonlighter, overnighter, politer, prizefighter, reciter, rewriter, screenwriter, scriptwriter, signwriter, songwriter, typewriter.
Imbiber, inscriber, prescriber, subscriber, transcriber.
Applier, denier, hairdryer, homebuyer, messiah, papaya, pariah, replier, supplier.

2.2.87 "--iner" (as in "finer")
[2] china, diner, finer, liner, miner, minor, mynah, piner, shiner, signer, whiner.
[3] airliner, angina, assigner, combiner, consigner, cosigner, decliner, definer, designer, diviner, eyeliner, freightliner, hardliner, headliner, incliner, maligner, moonshiner, recliner, refiner, streamliner.

SURPRISING RHYMING:
[2] **Climber**, mimer, primer, rhymer, timer.
Cider, eider, glider, guider, hider, rider, slider, spider, strider, wider.
Binder, blinder, finder, grinder, kinda, kinder, minder, winder.
Diver, driver, fiver, jiver, skiver, striver, thriver.
Briber, cyber, fibre/fiber (U.S.), imbiber, inscriber, prescriber, subscriber, transcriber.
Buyer, choir, crier, dire, drier, dryer, dyer, fire, flyer, friar, fryer, higher, hire, inspire, ire, liar, lyre, Maya, mire, plier, plyer, prior, pyre, shire, shyer, sire, spire, sprier, squire, tire, tyre/tire (U.S.), trier, via, wire.
[3] **Old-timer**, part-timer, sublimer, two-timer.
Backslider, collider, confider, decider, divider, insider, joyrider, nightrider, outrider, outsider, provider, roughrider.
Childminder, pathfinder, reminder, rewinder, sidewinder, spellbinder, viewfinder.
Conniver, contriver, piledriver, saliva, screwdriver, skydiver, slave driver, survivor.
Applier, denier, hairdryer, homebuyer, messiah, papaya, pariah, replier, supplier.
Beguiler, compiler, defiler, hair-styler, profiler, reviler.
Acquire, admire, aspire, attire, backfire, barbwire, bonfire, buyer, campfire, ceasefire, conspire, crossfire, desire, empire, enquire, entire, esquire, expire, gunfire, haywire, hellfire, higher, inspire, misfire, perspire, quagmire, sapphire, satire, spitfire, surefire, transpire, tripwire, umpire, vampire, wildfire.

2.2.88 "--inger" (as in "singer")
[2] bringer, clinger, flinger, linger, pinger, ringer, singer, slinger, springer, stinger, stringer, swinger, winger, wringer, zinger.
[3] bell-ringer, gunslinger, humdinger, left-winger, mud-slinger.

SURPRISING RHYMING:
[2] **Dinner**, grinner, inner, sinner, skinner, spinner, thinner, winner.
Bigger, digger, figure, rigour/rigor (U.S.), snigger, swigger, trigger, vigour/vigor (U.S.).
Dimmer, glimmer, primmer, shimmer, simmer, skimmer, slimmer, strimmer, swimmer, trimmer, zimmer.
Blinker, drinker, Inca, inker, jinker, linker, pinker, shrinker, sinker, stinker, thinker, tinker, winker, freethinker, headshrinker.
Midwinter, printer, splinter, sprinter, squinter, tinter, winter.
[3] **Beginner(s)**, Berliner, breadwinner, examiner, foreigner, mariner, milliner, phenomena, prizewinner, retina, stamina.

2.2.89 "--inister" (as in "sinister")
[3] administer, minister, sinister.

SURPRISING RHYMING:
[2] **Blister**, crisper, mister, sister, trickster, twister, vista, whisper.
[3] **Administer**, banister, barista, barrister, canister, chorister, enlister, forester, harvester, register, resister, resistor, sinister, sob-sister, stepsister, transistor, visitor.
Brandisher, burnisher, finisher, flourisher, furnisher, kingfisher, languisher, militia, nourisher, perisher, polisher, publisher, punisher, ravisher, vanquisher, well-wisher.
[4] **Expenditure**, furniture, literature, miniature, signature, temperature.

2.2.90 "--inker" (as in "thinker")
blinker, drinker, Inca, inker, jinker, linker, pinker, shrinker, sinker, stinker, thinker, tinker, winker, freethinker, headshrinker.

SURPRISING RHYMING:
[2] **Bicker**, flicker, kicker, knicker, licker, liquor, picker, quicker, sicker, slicker, snicker, sticker, thicker, ticker, tricker, vicar, wicker.
Limber, marimba, timber.
Crimper, limper, shrimper, simper, whimper.
Midwinter, printer, splinter, sprinter, squinter, tinter, winter.
Conifer, differ, giver, liver, Lucifer, quiver, river, shiver, sliver, sniffer, sniffler, stiffer.
Drifter, grifter, lifter, shifter, sifter, snifter, swifter.
Fixture, mixture, scripture, tincture.

2.2.91 "--inner" (as in "dinner")
[2] dinner, grinner, inner, sinner(s), skinner, spinner, thinner, winner(s).
[3] beginner(s), Berliner, breadwinner, examiner, foreigner, mariner, milliner, phenomena, prizewinner, retina, stamina, submariner.

SURPRISING RHYMING:
[2] **Dimmer**, glimmer, shimmer, simmer, skimmer, slimmer, swimmer, trimmer, zimmer.
Bringer, clinger, flinger, ringer, singer, slinger, springer, stinger, stringer, swinger, winger, wringer, zinger.
Conifer, differ, giver, liver, Lucifer, quiver, river, shiver, sliver, sniffer, sniffler, stiffer.
Limber, marimba, timber.
Crimper, limper, shrimper, simper, whimper.
Midwinter, printer, splinter, sprinter, squinter, tinter, winter.
Bigger, digger, figure, rigour/rigor (U.S.), snigger, swigger, trigger, vigour/vigor (U.S.).
Bitter, critter, fitter, flitter, fritter, glitter, gritter, hitter, jitter, knitter, litter, pitta, quitter, sitter, skitter, slitter, spitter, splitter, titter, twitter.
[3] **Cinema**, charisma, eczema, maxima, minima, polymer, ultima.

Bell-ringer, gunslinger, humdinger, left-winger, mud-slinger.
Configure, disfigure, gold-digger, gravedigger, outrigger, vinegar.
Caterpillar, chinchilla, distiller, flotilla, fulfiller, gorilla, guerilla, manilla, man-killer, painkiller, spine-chiller, vanilla, weedkiller.

2.2.92 "--inter" (as in "winter")
midwinter, printer, splinter, sprinter, squinter, tinter, winter.

SURPRISING RHYMING:
[2] Limber, marimba, timber.
Crimper, limper, shrimper, simper, whimper.
Builder, filter, kilter, pilfer, quilter, tilter.
Drifter, grifter, lifter, shifter, sifter, snifter, swifter.
Elixir, fixer, mixer, sixer.
Fixture, minster, mixture, scripture, spinster, tincture.
Clincher, flincher, lyncher, pincher, wincher.
Blister, crisper, mister, resistor, sister, transistor, trickster, twister, vista, whisper.
Blinker, drinker, Inca, inker, jinker, linker, pinker, shrinker, sinker, stinker, thinker, tinker, winker, freethinker, headshrinker.
Dimmer, glimmer, primmer, shimmer, simmer, skimmer, slimmer, strimmer, swimmer, trimmer, zimmer.
Midwinter, printer, splinter, sprinter, squinter, tinter, winter.
Dinner, grinner, inner, sinner(s), skinner, spinner, thinner, winner(s).
Bringer, clinger, ringer, singer, springer, stinger, stringer, swinger, winger, zinger.
[3] Bewilder(ed), bodybuilder, boatbuilder, housebuilder, shipbuilder.
Constrictor, contradictor, depicter, evictor, inflicter, predictor, victor.
Bell-ringer, gunslinger, humdinger, left-winger, mud-slinger.

2.2.93 "--iper" (as in "wiper")
[2] diaper, griper, hyper, piper, riper, sniper, striper, swiper, viper, wiper.
[3] bagpiper, sandpiper, sideswiper.

SURPRISING RHYMING:
[2] Biter, blighter, brighter, fighter, lighter, mitre/miter (U.S.), slighter, spiter, tighter, whiter, writer.
Briber, fibre/fiber (U.S.), inscriber, prescriber, subscriber, transcriber.
Cider, eider, glider, guider, hider, rider, slider, spider, strider, wider.
China, diner, finer, liner, miner, minor, mynah, piner, shiner, whiner.
Climber, mimer, primer, rhymer, timer.
[3] All-nighter, backbiter, bullfighter, copywriter, delighter, exciter, fistfighter, ghostwriter, gunfighter, inciter, igniter, lamplighter, midnighter, moonlighter, overnighter, politer, prizefighter, reciter, rewriter, screenwriter, scriptwriter, signwriter, songwriter, typewriter.
Old-timer, part-timer, sublimer, two-timer.
Backslider, collider, confider, decider, divider, insider, joyrider, nightrider, outrider, outsider, provider, roughrider.
Airliner, designer, diviner, eyeliner, hardliner, headliner, moonshiner, recliner, streamliner.

2.2.94 "--ipper" (as in "slipper")
[2] chipper, clipper, dipper, flipper, gripper, hipper, kipper, nipper, quipper, ripper, shipper, sipper, skipper, slipper, stripper, tipper, tripper, whipper, zipper.
[3] day-tripper, equipper, juniper, worshiper.

SURPRISING RHYMING:
[2] Bitter, critter, fitter, flitter, fritter, glitter, gritter, hitter, jitter, knitter, litter, quitter, sitter, skitter, slitter, spitter, splitter, titter, twitter.
Conifer, differ, giver, liver, Lucifer, quiver, river, shiver, sliver, sniffer, sniffler, stiffer.
Crimper, limper, shrimper, simper, whimper.
Fizzer, hisser, kisser, kiss her, quizzer, reminiscer, whizzer.

Bicker, clicker, dicker, flicker, kicker, knicker, licker, liquor, nicker, picker, pricker, quicker, sicker, slicker, snicker, sticker, thicker, ticker, tricker, vicar, whicker, wicker.
Bigger, digger, figure, jigger, ligger, rigger, rigour/rigor (U.S.), snigger, swigger, trigger, vigour/vigor (U.S.).
Dimmer, glimmer, primmer, shimmer, simmer, skimmer, slimmer, swimmer, trimmer.
[3] **Caterpillar,** chinchilla, distiller, flotilla, fulfiller, gorilla, guerilla, manilla, man-killer, painkiller, spine-chiller, vanilla, weedkiller.
[4] **Baby-sitter,** barometer, competitor, counterfeiter, diameter, exhibitor, interpreter, mileometer/milometer (U.S.), parameter, perimeter, solicitor, speedometer, thermometer.

2.2.95 "--iter" (as in "writer")
[2] biter, blighter, brighter, fighter, lighter, mitre/miter (U.S.), slighter, spiter, tighter, triter, whiter, writer.
[3] all-nighter, backbiter, bullfighter, copywriter, delighter, exciter, expediter, extraditer, fistfighter, ghostwriter, gunfighter, inciter, igniter,
indicter, inviter, lamplighter, midnighter, moonlighter, overnighter, politer, prizefighter, reciter, rewriter, screenwriter, scriptwriter, signwriter, songwriter, spotlighter, typewriter, underwriter, uniter.

SURPRISING RHYMING:
[2] **Cider,** glider, guider, hider, rider, slider, spider, strider, wider.
Diaper, hyper, piper, riper, sniper, striper, swiper, viper, wiper.
Briber, cyber, fibre/fiber (U.S.), imbiber, inscriber, prescriber, subscriber, transcriber.
Dicer, enticer, de-icer, nicer, pricer, slicer, splicer.
Diver, driver, fiver, jiver, skiver, striver, thriver.
[3] **Backslider,** collider, confider, decider, divider, insider, joyrider, nightrider, outrider, outsider, provider, roughrider.
Bagpiper, sandpiper, sideswiper.
Piledriver, saliva, screwdriver, skydiver, slave driver, survivor.
Dieter, proprietor, quieter, rioter.

2.2.96 "--iver" (as in "driver")
[2] diver, driver, fiver, jiver, skiver, striver, thriver.
[3] conniver, contriver, pearl diver, piledriver, reviver, saliva, screwdriver, skydiver, slave driver, survivor.

SURPRISING RHYMING:
[2] **Briber,** cyber, fibre/fiber (U.S.), imbiber, inscriber, prescriber, subscriber, transcriber.
Cider, eider, glider, guider, hider, rider, slider, spider, strider, wider.
China, diner, finer, liner, miner, minor, mynah, piner, shiner, whiner.
Biter, blighter, brighter, fighter, lighter, slighter, spiter, tighter, triter, whiter, writer.
Diaper, hyper, piper, riper, sniper, striper, swiper, viper, wiper.
Dicer, enticer, de-icer, nicer, pricer, slicer, splicer.
[3] **Backslider,** collider, confider, decider, divider, insider, joyrider, nightrider, outrider, outsider, provider, roughrider.
Bagpiper, sandpiper, sideswiper.
All-nighter, backbiter, bullfighter, copywriter, delighter, exciter, fistfighter, ghostwriter, gunfighter, inciter, igniter, lamplighter, midnighter, moonlighter, overnighter, politer, prizefighter, reciter, rewriter, screenwriter, scriptwriter, signwriter, songwriter, typewriter.
Airliner, designer, diviner, eyeliner, hardliner, headliner, moonshiner, recliner, streamliner.

2.2.97 "--isser" (as in "kisser")
[2] fizzer, hisser, kisser, quizzer, reminiscer, whizzer.

SURPRISING RHYMING:
[2] **Blister,** crisper, mister, sister, trickster, twister, vista, whisper.
Conifer, differ, giver, liver, Lucifer, quiver, river, shiver, sliver, sniffer, sniffler, stiffer.
Fisher, fissure, wisher, well-wisher.

Bitter, critter, fitter, flitter, fritter, glitter, gritter, hitter, jitter, knitter, litter, pitta, quitter, sitter, skitter, slitter, spitter, splitter, titter, twitter.
[3] **Barista**, enlister, resister, resistor, sob-sister, stepsister, transistor.
Aquiver, deliver, downriver, forgiver, upriver.

2.2.98 "--isher" (as in "wisher")
fisher, fissure, wisher, well-wisher.
[3] brandisher, Britisher, burnisher, finisher, flourisher, furbisher, furnisher, kingfisher, languisher, militia, nourisher, perisher, polisher, publisher, punisher, ravisher, skirmisher, vanquisher, varnisher, well-wisher.
[4] abolisher, demolisher, embellisher, establisher, extinguisher, replenisher.

SURPRISING RHYMING:
[2] **Ditcher**, hitcher, mixture, picture, pitcher, richer, snitcher, stitcher, stricture, switcher, twitcher.
Fizzer, hisser, kisser, kiss her, quizzer, reminiscer, whizzer.
Blister, crisper, mister, sister, trickster, twister, vista, whisper.
Dimmer, glimmer, shimmer, simmer, skimmer, slimmer, swimmer, trimmer, zimmer.
Conifer, differ, giver, liver, Lucifer, quiver, river, shiver, sliver, sniffer, sniffler, stiffer.
Midwinter, printer, splinter, sprinter, squinter, tinter, winter.
[3] **Administer**, assister, banister, barista, barrister, canister, chorister, forester, harvester, minister, register, resister, resistor, sinister, sob-sister, stepsister, transistor.
Aquiver, deliver, downriver, forgiver, upriver.
Electronica, erotica, exotica, frolicker, harmonica, lip-syncer, replica, mimicker, moniker.

2.2.99 "--ister" (as in "sister")
[2] blister, crisper, glister, lister, mister, sister, trickster, tryster, twister, vista, whisper.
[3] administer, assister, banister, barista, barrister, canister, chorister, enlister, forester, harvester, minister, register, resister, resistor, sinister, sob-sister, stepsister, transistor.

SURPRISING RHYMING:
[2] **Hitcher**, picture, pitcher, richer, snitcher, stitcher, stricture, switcher, twitcher, victor.
Elixir, fixer, mixer, sixer.
Fixture, hipster, minster, mixture, scripture, spinster, tincture.
Clincher, flincher, lyncher, pincher, wincher.
Fizzer, hisser, kisser, kiss her, quizzer, reminiscer, whizzer.
Fisher, fissure, wisher, well-wisher.
Drifter, grifter, lifter, shifter, sifter, snifter, swifter.
Blinker, drinker, freethinker, pinker, shrinker, sinker, stinker, thinker, tinker, winker.
[3] **Constrictor**, contradictor, depicter, evictor, inflicter, predictor, .
Creditor, editor, embitter, housesitter, janitor, Jupiter, monitor, transmitter, visitor.

2.2.100 "--iskier" (as in "riskier")
[3] friskier, riskier.

SURPRISING RHYMING:
[3] **Busier**, crispier, dizzier, fizzier, frizzier.
Electronica, erotica, exotica, frolicker, harmonica, lip-syncer, replica, mimicker, moniker, picnicker, trafficker.
Administer, assister, banister, barista, barrister, canister, chorister, enlister, forester, harvester, minister, register, resister, resistor, sinister, sob-sister, stepsister, transistor.

2.2.101 "--itcher" (as in "richer")
[2] ditcher, hitcher, picture, pitcher, richer, snitcher, stitcher, stricture, switcher, twitcher.

SURPRISING RHYMING:
[2] **Elixir**, fisher, fissure, fixer, fixture, mixer, mixture, scripture, sixer, tincture, wisher.
Clincher, flincher, lyncher, pincher, wincher.
Blister, crisper, mister, sister, trickster, twister, vista, whisper.

[3] Assister, banister, barista, barrister, canister, chorister, enlister, forester, harvester, minister, register, resister, resistor, sinister, sob-sister, stepsister, transistor.
Brandisher, burnisher, finisher, flourisher, furbisher, furnisher, kingfisher, languisher, militia, nourisher, perisher, polisher, publisher, punisher, ravisher, skirmisher, vanquisher, varnisher, well-wisher.
[4] Expenditure, investiture, forfeiture, furniture, literature, miniature, portraiture, signature, temperature.
Abolisher, demolisher, embellisher, establisher, extinguisher.

2.2.102 "--itter (as in "bitter")
[2] bitter, critter, fitter, flitter, fritter, glitter, gritter, hitter, jitter, knitter, litter, pitta, quitter, sitter, skitter, slitter, spitter, splitter, titter, twitter.
[3] auditor, committer, creditor, cricketer, editor, embitter, emitter, housesitter, janitor, Jupiter, monitor, outfitter, permitter, pinch-hitter, remitter, submitter, transmitter, visitor.
[4] baby-sitter, barometer, competitor, counterfeiter, diameter, exhibitor, interpreter, mileometer/milometer (U.S.), parameter, perimeter, solicitor, speedometer, thermometer.

SURPRISING RHYMING:
[2] Bicker, clicker, dicker, flicker, kicker, knicker, licker, liquor, nicker, picker, pricker, quicker, sicker, slicker, snicker, sticker, thicker, ticker, tricker, vicar, whicker, wicker.
Bigger, digger, figure, rigour/rigor (U.S.), snigger, swigger, trigger, vigour/vigor (U.S.).
Bidder, consider, kidder.
Chipper, clipper, dipper, flipper, gripper, hipper, kipper, nipper, quipper, ripper, shipper, sipper, skipper, slipper, stripper, tipper, tripper, whipper, zipper.
Chiller, driller, filler, griller, killer, pillar, spiller, thriller, tiller, villa.
Dinner, grinner, inner, sinner(s), skinner, spinner, thinner, winner(s).
[3] Configure, disfigure, gold-digger, gravedigger, outrigger, vinegar.
Day-tripper, equipper, juniper, worshiper.
Caterpillar, chinchilla, distiller, flotilla, fulfiller, gorilla, guerilla, manilla, man-killer, painkiller, spine-chiller, vanilla, weedkiller.
Beginner(s), breadwinner, examiner, foreigner, phenomena, prizewinner, stamina.
Administer, assister, banister, barista, barrister, canister, chorister, enlister, forester, harvester, minister, register, resister, resistor, sinister, sob-sister, stepsister, transistor.

2.2.103 "--ivver" (as in "river")
[2] giver, liver, river, shiver, sliver, quiver.
[3] aquiver, deliver, downriver, forgiver, upriver.

SURPRISING RHYMING:
[2] Conifer, differ, Lucifer, sniffer, stiffer.
Limber, marimba, timber.
Bitter, critter, fitter, flitter, fritter, glitter, gritter, hitter, jitter, knitter, litter, pitta, quitter, sitter, skitter, slitter, spitter, splitter, titter, twitter.
Bigger, digger, figure, rigour/rigor (U.S.), snigger, swigger, trigger, vigour/vigor (U.S.).
Bidder, consider, differ, kidder.
Chiller, driller, filler, griller, killer, pillar, spiller, thriller, tiller, villa.
Dinner, grinner, inner, sinner(s), skinner, spinner, thinner, winner(s).
Midwinter, printer, splinter, sprinter, squinter, tinter, winter.
[3] Configure, disfigure, gold-digger, gravedigger, outrigger, vinegar.
Day-tripper, equipper, juniper, worshiper.
Beginner(s), breadwinner, examiner, foreigner, phenomena, prizewinner, stamina.

2.2.104 "--ixer" (as in "mixer")
[2] elixir, fixer, mixer, sixer, spritzer.

SURPRISING RHYMING:
[2] Hitcher, picture, pitcher, richer, snitcher, stitcher, stricture, switcher, twitcher.
Blister, crisper, mister, sister, trickster, twister, vista, whisper.
Fizzer, hisser, kisser, kiss her, quizzer, reminiscer, whizzer.

Fisher, fissure, wisher.
Fixture, mixture, scripture.

2.2.105 "--izer" (as in "wiser")
[2] Kaiser, miser, riser, sizer, visor, wiser.
[3] Adviser, chastiser, despiser, deviser, disguiser, reviser, surmiser, surpriser.
[4] advertiser, appetizer, atomizer, breathalyzer, centralizer, civilizer, colonizer, compromiser, criticizer, deodorizer, economizer, energizer, enterpriser, equalizer, exerciser, fertilizer, idolizer, immobilizer, improviser, itemizer, jeopardizer, legalizer, liberalizer, liquidizer, maximiser, memorizer, merchandiser, mesmerizer, minimizer, mobilizer, modernizer, moisturizer, moralizer, neutralizer, organizer, patronizer, philosophizer, plagiarizer, pulverizer, rationalizer, recognizer, sermonizer, socializer, specializer, stabilizer, standardizer, sterilizer, subsidizer, summarizer, supervisor, sympathizer, synthesizer,, tenderizer, terrorizer, tranquillizer, utilizer, tantalizer, vaporizer, verbalizer, victimizer, womanizer.

SURPRISING RHYMING:
[2] **Dicer**, enticer, de-icer, nicer, pricer, slicer, splicer.
China, diner, finer, liner, miner, minor, mynah, piner, shiner, whiner.
Diver, driver, fiver, jiver, skiver, striver, thriver.
Briber, cyber, fibre/fiber (U.S.).
Cider, eider, glider, guider, hider, rider, slider, spider, strider, wider.
Buyer, choir, crier, dire, drier, dryer, dyer, fire, flyer, friar, fryer, higher, hire, ire, liar, lyre, Maya, mire, plier, plyer, prior, pyre, shire, shyer, sire, spire, spryer, squire, tire, tyre/tire (U.S.), trier, via, wire.
[3] **Airliner**, designer, diviner, hardliner, headliner, moonshiner, recliner, streamliner.
Piledriver, saliva, screwdriver, skydiver, slave driver, survivor.
Imbiber, inscriber, prescriber, subscriber, transcriber.
Backslider, collider, confider, decider, divider, insider, joyrider, nightrider, outrider, outsider, provider, roughrider.
Applier, denier, hairdryer, homebuyer, messiah, papaya, pariah.
All-nighter, backbiter, bullfighter, copywriter, delighter, exciter, fistfighter, ghostwriter, gunfighter, inciter, igniter, lamplighter, midnighter, moonlighter, overnighter, politer, prizefighter, reciter, rewriter, screenwriter, scriptwriter, signwriter, songwriter, typewriter.

2.2.106 "--izzier" (as in "dizzier")
[3] busier, dizzier, fizzier, frizzier.

SURPRISING RHYMING:
[3] **Crispier**, envier, friskier, nippier, riskier, trivia.
Administer, linear, minister, sinister, skinnier
Bristlier, chillier, drizzlier, frillier, grizzlier, hillier, sillier.

2.2.107 "--oater" (as in "voter")
[2] boater, doter, floater, gloater, iota, motor, promoter, quota, rota, rotor, voter.

SURPRISING RHYMING:
[2] **Broker**, choker, coca, croaker, joker, ochre, poker, smoker, soaker, stoker, stroker.
Chauffer, closer, dozer, poser, gofer, gopher, loafer, sofa.
Jojoba, October, sober.
Coda, coder, goader, loader, odour/odor (U.S.), ogre, soda, toga, yoga.
Clover, drover, nova, over, rover, soldier.
Coma, donor, comber, groaner, homer, loner, moaner, owner, phoner, roamer, toner.
[3] **Evoker**, non-smoker, pawnbroker, provoker, Rioja, stockbroker.
Bulldozer, composer, disclosure, exposer, forecloser, imposer, opposer, proposer.
Changeover, crossover, flyover, handover, hangover, left-over, makeover, once-over, pullover, pushover, sleepover, stopover, takeover, turnover, walkover, wrapover.
Corroder, decoder, encoder, exploder, freeloader, pagoda, railroader, unloader, vocoder.
Aloha, churchgoer, glassblower, lawnmower, playgoer, racegoer.

Bipolar, cajoler, Coca-Cola, consoler, controller, Ebola, extoller, granola, Moviola, payola, patroller, Pianola, rock 'n' roller, scroller, steamroller, tombola, troller, viola.
Aroma, beachcomber, diploma, misnomer, Oklahoma.
Atoner, condoner, corona, disowner, homeowner, landowner, persona, postponer.
[4] Carioca, mediocre, tapioca.

2.2.108 "--obber" (as in "robber")
[2] clobber, cobber, jobber, mobber, robber, slobber, sobber.

SURPRISING RHYMING:
[2] **Cobbler**, gobbler, hobbler, quabbler, wobbler.
Dodder, fodder, nodder, odder, plodder, prodder.
Bopper, chopper, copper, cropper, dropper, hopper, mopper, poppa, popper, proper, shopper, stopper, swapper, topper, whopper.
Blotter, dotter, gotta, hotter, jotter, knotter, otter, plotter, potter, ricotta, rotter, spotter, squatter, totter, trotter, water, yachter.
Blogger, dogger, flogger, hogger, jogger, logger, slogger.
Collar, corolla, dollar, holler, scholar, squalor, white-collar.
Blocker, chocker, docker, knocker, locker, mocker, rocker, shocker, soccer.
Coffer, cougher, offer, proffer, quaffer, scoffer.
Dormer, former, korma, stormer, swarmer, trauma, warmer.
Absconder, anaconda, blonder, fonder, ponder, responder, squander, wander, yonder.
[3] Eavesdropper, globetrotter, grasshopper, improper, teenybopper, terracotta.

2.2.109 "--obbler" (as in "cobbler")
[2] cobbler, gobbler, hobbler, quabbler, wobbler.

SURPRISING RHYMING:
[2] **Clobber**, cobber, jobber, mobber, robber, slobber, sobber.
Blogger, flogger, hogger, jogger, logger, slogger.
Coffer, cougher, offer, proffer, quaffer, scoffer.
Collar, corolla, dollar, holler, scholar, squalor, white-collar.
Bopper, chopper, copper, cropper, dropper, hopper, mopper, poppa, popper, proper, shopper, stopper, swapper, topper, whopper.
Blotter, gotta, hotter, jotter, knotter, otter, plotter, potter, ricotta, rotter, spotter, squatter, totter, trotter, water, yachter.
Blocker, chocker, docker, knocker, locker, mocha, mocker, rocker, shocker, soccer.
Absconder, anaconda, blonder, fonder, ponder, responder, squander, wander, yonder.
[3] Eavesdropper, globetrotter, grasshopper, improper, teenybopper, terracotta.

2.2.110 "--ocer" (as in "grocer")
anorexia nervosa, closer, grocer, greengrocer, mimosa.

SURPRISING RHYMING:
[2] **Forcer**, saucer, endorser, enforcer, reinforcer.
Chauffer, clover, coaxer, gofer, gopher, hoaxer, loafer, nova, over, rover, sofa.
Coda, coder, goader, loader, odour/odor (U.S.), ogre, sober, soda, toga, yoga.
Bolder, boulder, colder, folder, holder, moulder/molder (U.S.), older, scolder, shoulder, smoulder/smolder (U.S.), solder.
Bowler, cola, molar, polar, roller, solar, stroller.
Coma, donor, comber, groaner, homer, loner, moaner, owner, phoner, roamer, toner.
[3] Changeover, crossover, flyover, handover, hangover, left-over, makeover, moreover, once-over, popover, pullover, pushover, sleepover, slipover, stopover, takeover, turnover, walkover, wrapover.
Bulldozer, composer, disclosure, exposer, forecloser, imposer, opposer, proposer.
Decoder, encoder, freeloader, jojoba, October, pagoda, railroader, reloader, unloader.
Beholder, cold shoulder, enfolder, freeholder, householder, keyholder, leaseholder, remoulder/remolder (U.S.), shareholder, smallholder, stakeholder, stockholder, withholder.

Bipolar, cajoler, Coca-Cola, consoler, controller, Ebola, extoller, granola, Moviola, payola, patroller, Pianola, rock 'n' roller, scroller, steamroller, tombola, troller, viola.
Atoner, condoner, homeowner, landowner, persona, postponer.

2.2.111 "--ocker" (as in "rocker")
[2] blocker, chocker, docker, knocker, locker, mocha, mocker, rocker, shocker, soccer.

SURPRISING RHYMING:
[2] **Blotter**, dotter, gotta, hotter, jotter, knotter, otter, plotter, potter, ricotta, rotter, spotter, squatter, totter, trotter, water, yachter.
Clobber, cobber, jobber, mobber, robber, slobber, sobber.
Bopper, chopper, copper, cropper, dropper, flopper, hopper, mopper, poppa, popper, proper, shopper, stopper, swapper, topper, whopper.
Dodder, fodder, nodder, odder, plodder, prodder.
Blogger, flogger, hogger, jogger, logger, slogger.
Boxer, crosser, dosser, embosser, flosser, glosser, sponsor, tosser.
Collar, corolla, dollar, holler, scholar, squalor, white-collar.
Coffer, cougher, offer, proffer, quaffer, scoffer.
[3] **Eavesdropper**, globetrotter, grasshopper, improper, teenybopper, terracotta.

2.2.112 "--odder" (as in "fodder")
[2] dodder, fodder, nodder, odder, plodder, prodder.

SURPRISING RHYMING:
[2] **Blogger**, flogger, hogger, jogger, logger, slogger.
Blotter, dotter, gotta, hotter, jotter, knotter, otter, plotter, potter, ricotta, rotter, spotter, squatter, totter, trotter, water, yachter.
Bopper, chopper, copper, cropper, dropper, flopper, hopper, Poppa, popper, proper, shopper, stopper, swapper, topper, whopper.
Clobber, cobber, jobber, mobber, robber, slobber, sobber.
Blocker, chocker, docker, knocker, locker, mocha, mocker, rocker, shocker, soccer.
Absconder, anaconda, blonder, fonder, ponder, responder, squander, wander, yonder.
Collar, corolla, dollar, holler, scholar, squalor, white-collar.
Coffer, cougher, offer, proffer, quaffer, scoffer.
[3] **Eavesdropper**, globetrotter, grasshopper, improper, teenybopper, terracotta.

2.2.113 "--oder" (as in "loader")
[2] coda, coder, goader, loader, odour/odor (U.S.), soda.
[3] corroder, decoder, encoder, exploder, freeloader, pagoda, railroader, unloader.

SURPRISING RHYMING:
[2] **Bolder**, boulder, colder, folder, holder, moulder/molder (U.S.), older, scolder, shoulder, smoulder/smolder (U.S.), solder.
Donor, groaner, loaner, loner, moaner, owner, phoner, toner.
Bowler, cola, molar, polar, roller, solar, stroller.
Clover, drover, jojoba, nova, October, ogre, over, rover, sober, soldier, toga, yoga.
[3] **Beholder**, cardholder, cold shoulder, enfolder, freeholder, householder, leaseholder, remoulder/remolder (U.S.), shareholder, smallholder, stakeholder, stockholder, withholder.
Atoner, condoner, homeowner, landowner, persona, postponer.
Bipolar, cajoler, Coca-Cola, consoler, controller, Ebola, extoller, granola, Moviola, payola, patroller, Pianola, rock 'n' roller, scroller, steamroller, tombola, troller, viola.
Changeover, crossover, flyover, handover, hangover, left-over, makeover, moreover, once-over, popover, pullover, pushover, sleepover, slipover, stopover, takeover, turnover, walkover, wrapover.
[4] **Bossa nova**, Casanova, supernova, up-and-over.

2.2.114 "--offer" (as in "offer")
[2] coffer, cougher, offer, proffer, quaffer, scoffer.

SURPRISING RHYMING:
[2] **Bopper**, chopper, copper, cropper, dropper, flopper, hopper, poppa, popper, proper, shopper, stopper, swapper, topper, whopper.
Blotter, gotta, hotter, jotter, knotter, otter, plotter, potter, ricotta, rotter, spotter, squatter, totter, trotter, water, yachter.
Clobber, cobber, jobber, mobber, robber, slobber, sobber.
Dodder, fodder, nodder, odder, plodder, prodder.
Blogger, flogger, hogger, jogger, logger, slogger.
Collar, corolla, dollar, holler, scholar, squalor, white-collar.
Daughter, mortar, porter, quarter, shorter, slaughter, snorter, sorter, water.
Altar, alter, assaulter, defaulter, falter, halter, vaulter, salter.
Author, chauffer, gofer, golfer, gopher, loafer, sofa, softer.
Crosser, dosser, embosser, flosser, glosser, tosser.
Dormer, former, korma, stormer, swarmer, trauma, warmer.
Blonder, fonder, ponder, responder, squander, transponder, wander, yonder.
Blocker, chocker, docker, knocker, locker, mocha, mocker, rocker, shocker, soccer.
[3] **Eavesdropper**, globetrotter, grasshopper, improper, teenybopper, terracotta.

2.2.115 "--ogger" as in "blogger"
[2] blogger, flogger, hogger, jogger, logger, slogger.

SURPRISING RHYMING:
[2] **Bopper**, chopper, copper, cropper, dropper, flopper, hopper, poppa, popper, proper, shopper, stopper, swapper, topper, whopper.
Blotter, gotta, hotter, jotter, knotter, otter, plotter, potter, ricotta, rotter, spotter, squatter, totter, trotter, water.
Clobber, cobber, jobber, mobber, robber, slobber, sobber.
Dodder, fodder, nodder, odder, plodder, prodder.
Collar, corolla, dollar, holler, scholar, squalor, white-collar.
Blocker, chocker, docker, knocker, locker, mocha, mocker, rocker, shocker, soccer, .
Absconder, anaconda, blonder, fonder, ponder, responder, squander, transponder, wander, yonder.
Daughter, porter, quarter, shorter, slaughter, snorter, sorter, water.
Altar, alter, assaulter, defaulter, falter, halter, vaulter, salter.
[3] **Eavesdropper**, globetrotter, grasshopper, improper, teenybopper, terracotta.
Barnstormer, bedwarmer, conformer, informer, performer, reformer, transformer.
Backwater, breakwater, exporter, extorter, firewater, freshwater, granddaughter, importer, manslaughter, reporter, saltwater, supporter, transporter, underwater.

2.2.116 "--ohwer" (as in "slower")
[2] blower, boa, echoer, glower, goer, grower, knower, lower, mower, o'er, rower, sewer, shower, slower, sower, thrower, tower.
[3] aloha, borrower, churchgoer, follower, foregoer, glassblower, lawnmower, playgoer, racegoer, shadower, swallower, widower.
[4] concertgoer, theatregoer/theatergoer (U.S.), winegrower.

SURPRISING RHYMING:
[2] **Coda**, coder, goader, loader, odour/odor, soda, sober.
Chauffer, clover, drover, gofer, gopher, loafer, nova, over, rover, sofa, soldier.
Coma, comber, donor, groaner, homer, loner, moaner, owner, phoner, roamer, toner.
Closer, dozer, poser.
[3] **Bipolar**, cajoler, Coca-Cola, consoler, controller, Ebola, extoller, granola, Moviola, payola, patroller, Pianola, rock 'n' roller, scroller, steamroller, tombola, viola.
Aroma, beachcomber, diploma, misnomer, Oklahoma.
Atoner, condoner, homeowner, landowner, persona, postponer.
Changeover, crossover, flyover, handover, hangover, layover, left-over, makeover, once-over, pullover, pushover, sleepover, stopover, takeover, turnover, walkover.
Bulldozer, composer, disclosure, exposer, forecloser, imposer, opposer, proposer.
Bossa nova, Casanova, jojoba, October, supernova, up-and-over.

2.2.117 "--oiler" (as in "boiler")
[2] boiler, broiler, foiler, oiler, potboiler, soiler, spoiler, toiler.

SURPRISING RHYMING:
[2] **Lawyer**, sawyer, soya, voyeur.
Anointer, appointer, cloister, exploiter, joiner, loiter, oyster, pointer, reconnoiter.
[3] **Annoyer**, deployer, destroyer, employer, enjoyer, paranoia.

2.2.118 "--oker" (as in "joker")
[2] broker, choker, coca, croaker, joker, ochre, poker, smoker, soaker, stoker, stroker.
[3] evoker, invoker, non-smoker, pawnbroker, provoker, revoker, Rioja, stockbroker.
[4] carioca, mediocre, tapioca.

SURPRISING RHYMING:
[2] **Coper**, eloper, groper, hoper, interloper, moper, no-hoper, scoper.
Boater, doter, emoter, floater, gloater, iota, motor, promoter, quota, rota, rotor, voter.
Coma, comber, donor, groaner, homer, loner, moaner, owner, phoner, roamer, toner.
Bolder, boulder, colder, folder, holder, moulder/molder (U.S.), older, scolder, shoulder, smoulder/smolder (U.S.), solder.
Coda, coder, closer, dozer, goader, loader, odour/odor, ogre, poser, soda, toga, yoga.
Chauffer, clover, drover, gofer, gopher, loafer, nova, over, rover, sofa, soldier.
Bowler, cola, molar, polar, roller, solar, stroller.
Donor, groaner, loaner, loner, moaner, owner, phoner, toner.
[3] **Changeover**, crossover, flyover, handover, hangover, left-over, makeover, moreover, once-over, popover, pullover, pushover, sleepover, slipover, stopover, takeover, turnover, walkover, wrapover.
Bulldozer, composer, disclosure, exposure, imposer, opposer.
Decoder, encoder, exploder, freeloader, jojoba, October, pagoda, railroader, unloader.
Beholder, cold shoulder, enfolder, freeholder, householder, keyholder, leaseholder, remoulder/remolder (U.S.), shareholder, smallholder, stakeholder, stockholder, withholder.
Bipolar, cajoler, Coca-Cola, consoler, controller, Ebola, extoller, granola, Moviola, payola, patroller, Pianola, rock 'n' roller, scroller, steamroller, tombola, troller, viola.
Atoner, condoner, homeowner, landowner, persona, postponer.

2.2.119 "--olar" (as in "polar")
[2] bowler, cola, molar, polar, roller, solar, stroller.
[3] bipolar, cajoler, Coca-Cola, comptroller, consoler, controller, Ebola, extoller, Moviola, payola, patroller, Pianola, rock 'n' roller, scroller, steamroller, tombola, troller, viola.

SURPRISING RHYMING:
[2] **Chauffer**, clover, closer, dozer, gopher, loafer, nova, over, poser, rover, sofa.
Coda, coder, goader, loader, odour/odor, soda.
Coma, comber, donor, groaner, homer, loner, moaner, owner, phoner, roamer, toner.
Blower, boa, echoer, glower, goer, grower, knower, lower, mower, o'er, rower, sewer, shower, slower, sower, thrower, tower.
Aura, borer, flora, pourer, roarer, scorer, snorer, soarer, storer.
Coper, eloper, groper, hoper, interloper, moper, no-hoper, scoper.
[3] **Changeover**, crossover, flyover, handover, hangover, left-over, makeover, moreover, once-over, popover, pullover, pushover, sleepover, slipover, stopover, takeover, turnover, walkover, wrapover.
Corroder, decoder, encoder, exploder, freeloader, pagoda, railroader, unloader.
Atoner, condoner, homeowner, landowner, persona, postponer.
Aroma, beachcomber, diploma, misnomer, Oklahoma.
Aloha, borrower, churchgoer, follower, foregoer, lawnmower, playgoer, racegoer, shadower, swallower, widower.
Bulldozer, composer, disclosure, exposure, opposer, proposer.
[4] **Bossa nova**, Casanova, supernova, up-and-over.

*

2.2.120 "--older" (as in "colder")
[2] bolder, boulder, colder, folder, holder, moulder/molder (U.S.), older, scolder, shoulder, smoulder/smolder (U.S.), solder, told her.
[3] beholder, cardholder, cold shoulder, enfolder, freeholder, householder, keyholder, leaseholder, remoulder/remolder (U.S.), shareholder, smallholder, stakeholder, stockholder, withholder.

SURPRISING RHYMING:
[2] **Chauffer**, clover, drover, gofer, gopher, loafer, nova, over, rover, sofa, soldier.
Coper, eloper, groper, hoper, interloper, moper, no-hoper, scoper.
Cobra, coda, coder, goader, loader, odour/odor (U.S.), sober, soda.
Bowler, cola, molar, polar, roller, solar, stroller.
[3] **Changeover**, crossover, flyover, handover, hangover, left-over, makeover, once-over, pullover, pushover, sleepover, stopover, takeover, turnover, walkover, wrapover.
Bipolar, cajoler, Coca-Cola, consoler, controller, Ebola, extoller, granola, Moviola, payola, patroller, Pianola, rock 'n' roller, scroller, steamroller, tombola, troller, viola.
Decoder, encoder, exploder, freeloader, pagoda, railroader, skateboarder, snowboarder.
[4] **Bossa nova**, Casanova, supernova, up-and-over.

2.2.121 "--ollar" (as in "collar")
[2] collar, corolla, dollar, holler, scholar, squalor, white-collar.

SURPRISING RHYMING:
[2] **Altar**, alter, assaulter, defaulter, falter, halter, vaulter, salter.
Clobber, cobber, jobber, mobber, robber, slobber, sobber.
Dodder, fodder, nodder, odder, plodder, prodder.
Blogger, flogger, hogger, jogger, logger, slogger.
Blotter, dotter, gotta, hotter, jotter, knotter, otter, plotter, potter, ricotta, rotter, spotter, squatter, totter, trotter, water, yachter.
Bopper, chopper, copper, cropper, dropper, flopper, hopper, poppa, popper, proper, shopper, stopper, swapper, topper, whopper.
Blocker, knocker, locker, mocha, mocker, rocker, shocker, soccer.
Blonder, fonder, ponder, responder, squander, transponder, wander, yonder.
Daughter, mortar, porter, quarter, shorter, slaughter, water.
[3] **Eavesdropper**, globetrotter, grasshopper, improper, teenybopper, terracotta.
Barnstormer, bedwarmer, conformer, informer, performer, reformer, transformer.

2.2.122 "--olter" (as in "falter")
altar, alter, bolter, assaulter, defaulter, falter, halter, salter, vaulter.

SURPRISING RHYMING:
[2] **Altered**, faltered, unaltered.
Blonder, fonder, ponder, responder, squander, transponder, wander, yonder.
Brawler, caller, crawler, faller, hauler, mauler, trawler.
Blotter, doctor, dotter, gotta, hotter, jotter, knotter, otter, plotter, potter, ricotta, rotter, spotter, squatter, totter, trotter, water, yachter.
Corker, gawker, hawker, polka, stalker, talker, walker.
Aura, borer, flora, horror, pourer, roarer, scorer, snorer, storer.
Bopper, chopper, copper, cropper, dropper, flopper, hopper, poppa, popper, proper, shopper, stopper, swapper, topper, whopper.
Coffer, cougher, offer, proffer, quaffer, scoffer.
[3] **Deerstalker**, jaywalker, nightwalker, sleepwalker, streetwalker.

2.2.123 "--omer" (as in "aroma")
[2] coma, comber, homer, roamer.
[3] aroma, beachcomber, diploma, misnomer, Oklahoma.

SURPRISING RHYMING:
[2] **Donor**, groaner, jojoba, loner, moaner, October, owner, phoner, sober, stoner.

Coda, coder, closer, dozer, goader, loader, odour/odor, ogre, poser, soda, toga, yoga.
Coper, eloper, groper, hoper, interloper, moper, no-hoper, scoper.
Chauffer, clover, drover, gofer, gopher, loafer, nova, over, rover, sofa, soldier.
Blower, boa, echoer, glower, goer, grower, knower, lower, mower, o'er, rower, sewer, shower, slower, sower, thrower, tower.
Bowler, cola, molar, polar, roller, solar, stroller.
[3] Atoner, condoner, corona, disowner, homeowner, landowner, persona, postponer.
Corroder, decoder, encoder, exploder, freeloader, pagoda, railroader, unloader.
Bipolar, cajoler, Coca-Cola, consoler, Moviola, payola, patroller, Pianola, rock 'n' roller, scroller, steamroller, tombola, troller, viola.
Changeover, crossover, flyover, handover, hangover, left-over, makeover, moreover, once-over, popover, pullover, pushover, sleepover, slipover, stopover, takeover, turnover, walkover, wrapover.
Bulldozer, composer, disclosure, exposure, opposer, proposer.
[4] Bossa nova, Casanova, supernova, up-and-over.

2.2.124 "--onder" (as in "wander")
absconder, anaconda, blonder, first-responder, fonder, ponder, responder, squander, transponder, wander, yonder.

SURPRISING RHYMING:
[2] Pondered, squandered, wandered.
Longer, stronger, want her, wonga.
Flaunter, haunter, saunter, taunter.
Boxer, crosser, dosser, embosser, flosser, glosser, sponsor, tosser.
Blotter, dotter, gotta, hotter, jotter, knotter, otter, plotter, potter, ricotta, rotter, spotter, squatter, totter, trotter, water, yachter.
Bopper, chopper, copper, cropper, dropper, flopper, hopper, poppa, popper, proper, shopper, stopper, swapper, topper, whopper.
Dodder, fodder, nodder, odder, plodder, prodder.
Clobber, cobber, jobber, mobber, robber, slobber, sobber.
Blogger, flogger, hogger, jogger, logger, slogger.
Dormer, former, korma, stormer, swarmer, trauma, warmer.
[3] Eavesdropper, globetrotter, grasshopper, improper, teenybopper, terracotta.
Barnstormer, bedwarmer, conformer, informer, performer, reformer, transformer.

2.2.125 "--ooker" (as in "cooker")
[2] booker, cooker, hookah, hooker, looker, good-looker, onlooker.

SURPRISING RHYMING:
[2] Chukka/chukker (U.S.), ducker, mucker, plucker, pucker, succour/succor (U.S.), sucker, trucker, tucker, yucca.
Butter, clutter, cutter, flutter, gutter, mutter, nutter, putter, scutter, shutter, splutter, sputter, stutter, utter.
Judder, rudder, shudder, udder, Buddha, do-gooder.
Hugger, mugger, plugger, rugger, slugger, snugger, sugar.
Bummer, drummer, dumber, glummer, hummer, number, plumber, strummer, summer.
Upper, scupper, supper.
[3] Abductor, conductor, constructor, instructor, obstructer.
Latecomer, midsummer, newcomer, welcomer.

2.2.126 "--opper" (as in "bopper")
[2] bopper, chopper, copper, cropper, dropper, flopper, hopper, mopper, poppa, popper, proper, shopper, stopper, swapper, topper, whopper.
[3] clodhopper, eavesdropper, gobstopper, grasshopper, improper, teenybopper.

SURPRISING RHYMING:
[2] Blotter, dotter, gotta, hotter, jotter, knotter, otter, plotter, potter, ricotta, rotter, spotter, squatter, totter, trotter, water.

Clobber, cobber, jobber, mobber, robber, slobber, sobber.
Blocker, knocker, locker, mocha, mocker, rocker, shocker, soccer.
Dodder, fodder, nodder, odder, plodder, prodder.
Blogger, flogger, hogger, jogger, logger, slogger.
Blonder, fonder, ponder, responder, squander, transponder, wander, yonder.
Boxer, crosser, dosser, embosser, flosser, glosser, sponsor, tosser.
Collar, corolla, dollar, holler, scholar, squalor, white-collar.
Coffer, cougher, offer, proffer, quaffer, scoffer.
Dormer, former, korma, stormer, swarmer, trauma, warmer.
[3] **Barnstormer**, bedwarmer, conformer, globetrotter, informer, performer, reformer, terracotta, transformer.

2.2.127 "--oper" (as in "no-hoper")
[2] coper, doper, eloper, groper, hoper, interloper, moper, no-hoper, scoper.

SURPRISING RHYMING:
[2] **Broker**, choker, coca, croaker, joker, ochre, poker, smoker, soaker, stoker, stroker.
Chauffer, clover, drover, gofer, gopher, loafer, nova, over, rover, sober, sofa, soldier.
Bolder, boulder, colder, folder, holder, moulder/molder (U.S.), older, scolder, shoulder, smoulder/smolder (U.S.), solder.
Coda, coder, closer, dozer, goader, loader, odour/odor, ogre, poser, soda, toga, yoga.
Bowler, cola, molar, polar, roller, solar, stroller.
Donor, loaner, loner, moaner, owner, phoner, stoner, toner.
Closer, dozer, poser.
[3] **Evoker**, invoker, non-smoker, pawnbroker, provoker, stockbroker.
Changeover, crossover, flyover, handover, hangover, left-over, makeover, once-over, pullover, pushover, sleepover, stopover, takeover, turnover, walkover, wrapover.
Bulldozer, composer, disclosure, exposer, forecloser, imposer, opposer, proposer.
Corroder, decoder, encoder, exploder, freeloader, pagoda, railroader, unloader.
Beholder, cardholder, cold shoulder, enfolder, freeholder, householder, keyholder, leaseholder, remoulder/remolder (U.S.), smallholder, stakeholder, stockholder, withholder.
Bipolar, cajoler, Coca-Cola, consoler, controller, Ebola, extoller, granola, Moviola, payola, patroller, Pianola, rock 'n' roller, scroller, steamroller, tombola, troller, viola.
Atoner, condoner, homeowner, landowner, persona, postponer.

2.2.128 "--ora" (as in "aura")
[2] aura, borer, corer, flora, pourer, roarer, scorer, snorer, soarer, storer.
[3] abhorrer, adorer, angora, aurora, explorer, fedora, goalscorer, ignorer, Pandora, restorer, señora, signora.

SURPRISING RHYMING:
[2] **Daughter**, mortar, porter, quarter, shorter, slaughter, snorter, sorter, water.
Corner, former, fauna, forewarner, mourner, sauna, scorner, trauma, warmer, warner.
Boarder, border, hoarder, order, warder.
Coda, coder, goader, jojoba, loader, October, odour/odor, sober, soda.
Donor, loaner, loner, moaner, owner, phoner, stoner, toner.
Chauffer, clover, drover, gofer, gopher, loafer, nova, over, rover, sofa, soldier.
[3] **Backwater,** breakwater, exporter, extorter, firewater, freshwater, granddaughter, importer, manslaughter, reporter, saltwater, transporter, underwater.
Awarder, defrauder, disorder, marauder, recorder.
Aroma, beachcomber, diploma, misnomer, Oklahoma.
Barnstormer, bedwarmer, conformer, informer, performer, reformer, transformer.

2.2.129 "--order" (as in "border")
[2] boarder, border, hoarder, order, warder.
[3] awarder, defrauder, disorder, marauder, recorder.

SURPRISING RHYMING:
[2] **Daughter**, mortar, porter, quarter, shorter, slaughter, water.

Corner, former, fauna, forewarner, mourner, sauna, scorner, trauma, warmer, warner.
Aura, borer, flora, pourer, roarer, scorer, snorer, soarer, storer.
Brawler, caller, crawler, faller, mauler, smaller, staller, taller, trawler.
Augur, author, chauffer, gofer, gopher, loafer, sofa.
Corker, gawker, hawker, stalker, talker, walker.
Courser, forcer, saucer, endorser, enforcer, reinforcer.
[3] **Backwater**, breakwater, exporter, extorter, firewater, freshwater, granddaughter, importer, manslaughter, reporter, saltwater, supporter, transporter, underwater.
Adorer, angora, aurora, explorer, fedora, goalscorer, ignorer, restorer, señora, signora.
Barnstormer, bedwarmer, conformer, informer, performer, reformer, transformer.
Deerstalker, jaywalker, nightwalker, sleepwalker, streetwalker.

2.2.130 "--orker" (as in "walker")
[2] balker, corker, gawker, hawker, stalker, talker, walker.
[3] deerstalker, jaywalker, nightwalker, sleepwalker, streetwalker.

SURPRISING RHYMING:
[2] **Daughter**, mortar, porter, quarter, shorter, slaughter, water.
Corner, former, fauna, forewarner, mourner, sauna, scorner, trauma, warmer, warner.
Courser, forcer, saucer, endorser, enforcer, reinforcer.
Boarder, border, hoarder, order, warder.
[3] **Backwater**, breakwater, exporter, extorter, firewater, freshwater, granddaughter, importer, manslaughter, reporter, saltwater, supporter, transporter, underwater.
Barnstormer, bedwarmer, conformer, informer, performer, reformer, transformer.
Awarder, defrauder, disorder, marauder, recorder.

2.2.131 "--orler" (as in "trawler")
[2] brawler, caller, crawler, faller, hauler, mauler, smaller, staller, taller, trawler.
[3] footballer, forestaller, installer, stonewaller.

SURPRISING RHYMING:
[2] **Bowler**, cola, coma, comber, homer, molar, polar, roamer, roller, solar, stroller.
Daughter, mortar, porter, quarter, shorter, slaughter, sorter, water.
Bolder, boulder, colder, folder, holder, moulder/molder (U.S.), older, scolder, shoulder, smoulder/smolder (U.S.), solder.
Altar, alter, assaulter, defaulter, falter, halter, vaulter, salter.
[3] **Bipolar**, cajoler, Coca-Cola, consoler, controller, Ebola, Moviola, payola, patroller, rock 'n' roller, scroller, steamroller, tombola, viola.
Aroma, beachcomber, diploma, misnomer, Oklahoma.
Backwater, breakwater, exporter, extorter, firewater, freshwater, granddaughter, importer, manslaughter, reporter, saltwater, supporter, transporter, underwater.
Beholder, cardholder, cold shoulder, freeholder, householder, keyholder, remoulder/remolder (U.S.), shareholder, stakeholder.

2.2.132 "--ormer" (as in "warmer")
[2] dormer, former, korma, stormer, swarmer, trauma, warmer.
[3] barnstormer, bedwarmer, conformer, informer, performer, reformer, transformer.

SURPRISING RHYMING:
[2] **Aura**, borer, flora, pourer, roarer, scorer, snorer, soarer, storer.
Coma, comber, donor, homer, loner, moaner, owner, phoner, roamer, stoner, toner.
Boarder, border, hoarder, order, warder.
Daughter, longer, mortar, porter, quarter, shorter, slaughter, sorter, stronger, water.
Brawler, caller, crawler, faller, mauler, smaller, staller, taller, trawler.
Courser, forcer, saucer, endorser, enforcer, reinforcer.
[3] **Atoner**, condoner, homeowner, landowner, persona, postponer.
Aroma, beachcomber, diploma, misnomer, Oklahoma.
Awarder, defrauder, disorder, marauder, recorder.
Backwater, breakwater, exporter, extorter, firewater, freshwater, granddaughter,

importer, manslaughter, reporter, saltwater, supporter, transporter, underwater.
Adorer, aurora, explorer, goalscorer, ignorer, Pandora, restorer, señora, signora.

2.2.133 "--orner" (as in "corner")
[2] corner, fauna, forewarner, mourner, sauna, scorner, warner.

SURPRISING RHYMING:
[2] **Coma**, comber, donor, homer, loner, moaner, owner, phoner, roamer, toner
Aura, borer, flora, former, pourer, roarer, scorer, snorer, storer, trauma, warmer.
Boarder, border, hoarder, October, order, sober, warder.
Daughter, mortar, porter, quarter, shorter, slaughter, sorter, water.
Brawler, caller, crawler, faller, footballer, hauler, mauler, trawler.
[3] **Aroma**, beachcomber, diploma, misnomer, Oklahoma.
Adorer, aurora, explorer, goalscorer, ignorer, Pandora, restorer, señora, signora.
Decoder, encoder, exploder, freeloader, pagoda, railroader.
Backwater, breakwater, exporter, extorter, firewater, freshwater, granddaughter, importer, manslaughter, reporter, saltwater, supporter, transporter, underwater.
Atoner, condoner, homeowner, landowner, persona, postponer.

2.2.134 "--orter" (as in "daughter")
[2] daughter, mortar, porter, quarter, shorter, slaughter, snorter, sorter, water.
[3] backwater, breakwater, deporter, exhorter, exporter, extorter, firewater, freshwater, goddaughter, granddaughter, importer, manslaughter, reporter, saltwater, stepdaughter, supporter, three-quarter, transporter, underwater.

SURPRISING RHYMING:
[2] **Boarder**, border, hoarder, order, warder.
Aura, borer, flora, pourer, roarer, scorer, snorer, soarer, storer.
Corner, former, fauna, forewarner, mourner, sauna, scorner, trauma, warmer, warner.
Brawler, caller, crawler, faller, mauler, smaller, staller, taller, trawler.
Augur, author, chauffer, gofer, gopher, loafer, sofa.
Corker, gawker, hawker, stalker, talker, walker.
[3] **Awarder**, defrauder, disorder, marauder, recorder.
Adorer, aurora, explorer, goalscorer, ignorer, Pandora, restorer, señora, signora.
Aroma, beachcomber, diploma, misnomer, Oklahoma.
Deerstalker, jaywalker, nightwalker, sleepwalker, streetwalker.

2.2.135 "--osser" (as in "embosser")
[2] crosser, dosser, embosser, flosser, glosser, josser, tosser.

SURPRISING RHYMING:
[2] **Blocker**, boxer, docker, knocker, locker, mocker, rocker, shocker, soccer, sponsor.
Bopper, chopper, copper, cropper, dropper, flopper, hopper, poppa, popper, proper, shopper, stopper, swapper, topper, whopper.
Blotter, gotta, hotter, jotter, knotter, otter, plotter, potter, ricotta, rotter, spotter, squatter, totter, trotter, water, yachter.
Clobber, cobber, jobber, mobber, robber, slobber, sobber.
Blogger, flogger, fodder, hogger, jogger, logger, odder, plodder, prodder, slogger.
Collar, corolla, dollar, holler, scholar, squalor, white-collar.
Coffer, cougher, offer, proffer, quaffer, scoffer.
Blonder, fonder, ponder, responder, squander, transponder, wander, yonder.

2.2.136 "--otter" (as in "hotter")
[2] blotter, dotter, gotta, hotter, jotter, knotter, otter, plotter, potter, ricotta, rotter, spotter, squatter, totter, trotter, water, yachter.
[3] globetrotter, terracotta, train-spotter.

SURPRISING RHYMING:
[2] **Bopper**, chopper, copper, cropper, dropper, flopper, hopper, popper, proper,

shopper, stopper, swapper, topper, whopper.
Clobber, cobber, jobber, mobber, robber, slobber, sobber.
Blocker, chocker, docker, knocker, locker, mocha, mocker, rocker, shocker, soccer.
Blogger, flogger, hogger, jogger, logger, slogger.
Cobbler, gobbler, hobbler, quabbler, wobbler.
Dodder, fodder, nodder, odder, plodder, prodder.
Boxer, crosser, dosser, embosser, flosser, glosser, sponsor, tosser.
Blonder, fonder, ponder, responder, squander, transponder, wander, yonder.
Collar, corolla, dollar, holler, scholar, squalor, white-collar.
Coffer, cougher, offer, proffer, quaffer, scoffer.
[3] **Eavesdropper**, globetrotter, grasshopper, improper, teenybopper, terracotta.

2.2.137 "--ounder" (as in "rounder")
[2] bounder, compounder, expounder, flounder, founder, grounder, impounder, pounder, rounder, sounder.

SURPRISING RHYMING:
[2] **Chowder**, gunpowder, louder, powder, prouder.
Doubter, outer, pouter, router (U.S.), scouter, shouter, spouter, sprouter, stouter, touter.
Counter, encounter, mounter.
Browner, downer, frowner, sundowner, downtowner, uptowner.
Lounger, scrounger, sunlounger.
Browser, bouncer, dowser, rabble-rouser, rouser, trouser, wowser.

2.2.138 "--outer" (as in "shouter")
[2] doubter, outer, pouter, router (U.S.), scouter, shouter, spouter, stouter, touter.

SURPRISING RHYMING:
[2] **Counter**, encounter, mounter.
Cower, devour, dower, flour, flower, glower, hour, our, plougher/plower (U.S.), power, rush-hour, scour, shower, sour, tower.
Chowder, gunpowder, louder, powder, prouder.
Browser, carouser, dowser, rabble-rouser, rouser, trouser, wowser.
Bounder, flounder, founder, grounder, pounder, rounder, sounder.
Browner, downer, frowner, sundowner, downtowner, uptowner.
Lounger, scrounger, sunlounger.

2.2.139 "--over" (as in "rover")
[2] clover, drover, nova, over, rover.
[3] all over, blow over, bowl over, changeover, chew over, crossover, fall over, flyover, get over, handover, hangover, layover, left-over, makeover, moreover, once-over, popover, pullover, pushover, sleepover, slipover, spillover, stopover, takeover, turnover, walkover, watch over, wrapover.
[4] bossa nova, Casanova, supernova, up-and-over.

SURPRISING RHYMING:
[2] **Bolder**, boulder, colder, folder, holder, moulder/molder (U.S.), older, scolder, shoulder, smoulder/smolder (U.S.), solder, soldier.
Coda, coder, goader, loader, odour/odor, sober, soda.
Coma, comber, donor, homer, loner, moaner, owner, phoner, roamer, toner.
Blower, boa, echoer, glower, goer, grower, knower, lower, mower, o'er, rower, shower, slower, sower, thrower, tower.
Coper, eloper, groper, hoper, interloper, moper, no-hoper, scoper.
Chauffer, gofer, gopher, loafer, sofa.
[3] **Beholder**, cold shoulder, freeholder, householder, jojoba, keyholder, October, remoulder/remolder (U.S.), shareholder, stakeholder, stockholder.
Bulldozer, composer, disclosure, exposer, foreclosure, imposer, opposer, proposer.
Corroder, decoder, encoder, exploder, freeloader, pagoda, railroader, unloader.
Atoner, condoner, homeowner, landowner, persona, postponer.

Aroma, beachcomber, diploma, misnomer, Oklahoma.
Aloha, borrower, churchgoer, follower, foregoer, glassblower, lawnmower, playgoer, racegoer, shadower, swallower, widower.
Bipolar, cajoler, Coca-Cola, comptroller, consoler, controller, Ebola, extoller, Moviola, payola, patroller, Pianola, rock 'n' roller, scroller, steamroller, tombola, troller, viola.

2.2.140 "--owner" (as in "loner")
[2] donor, groaner, loaner, loner, moaner, owner, phoner, toner.
[3] atoner, condoner, corona, disowner, homeowner, landowner, persona, postponer.

SURPRISING RHYMING:
[2] **Coma**, comber, homer, roamer.
Coda, coder, goader, loader, odour/odor, sober, soda.
Bowler, cola, molar, polar, roller, solar, stroller.
Chauffer, clover, drover, gofer, gopher, loafer, nova, over, rover, sofa, soldier.
Bolder, boulder, colder, folder, holder, moulder/molder (U.S.), older, scolder, shoulder, smoulder/smolder (U.S.), solder.
[3] **Aroma**, beachcomber, diploma, misnomer, Oklahoma.
Corroder, decoder, encoder, exploder, freeloader, pagoda, railroader, unloader.
Bipolar, cajoler, Coca-Cola, comptroller, consoler, controller, Ebola, extoller, Moviola, payola, patroller, Pianola, rock 'n' roller, scroller, steamroller, tombola, troller, viola.
Changeover, crossover, flyover, handover, hangover, layover, left-over, makeover, moreover, once-over, popover, pullover, pushover, sleepover, slipover, stopover, takeover, turnover, walkover, wrapover.
Beholder, cardholder, cold shoulder, enfolder, freeholder, householder, keyholder, leaseholder, October, remoulder/remolder (U.S.), shareholder, smallholder, stakeholder, stockholder, withholder.
[4] **Bossa nova**, Casanova, supernova, up-and-over.

2.2.141 "--oyer" (as in "destroyer")
[2] lawyer, sawyer, soya, voyeur.
[3] annoyer, destroyer, employer, enjoyer, paranoia.

SURPRISING RHYMING:
[2] **Boiler**, broiler, foiler, oiler, potboiler, soiler, spoiler, toiler.
Anointer, appointer, exploiter, jointer, loiter, pointer, reconnoiter.

2.2.142 "--owder" (as in "powder")
[2] chowder, gunpowder, louder, powder, prouder.

SURPRISING RHYMING:
[2] **Cower**, devour, flour, flower, glower, hour, our, plougher/plower (U.S.), power, rush-hour, scour, shower, sour, tower.
Doubter, outer, pouter, router (U.S.), scouter, shouter, spouter, sprouter, stouter, touter.
Counter, encounter, mounter.
Bounder, compounder, expounder, flounder, founder, grounder, impounder, pounder, rounder, sounder.
Browner, downer, sundowner, towner, downtowner, uptowner.
Browser, carouser, dowser, frowner, rabble-rouser, trouser, wowser.
Fowler, fouler, growler, howler, prowler, scowler.
[3] **Brainpower**, cauliflower, deflower, empower, firepower, horsepower, man-hour, manpower, mayflower, overpower, passion flower, sunflower, sweet-and-sour, wallflower, watchtower, willpower.

2.2.143 "--owser" (as in "browser")
[2] browser, carouser, dowser, frowner, rabble-rouser, rouser, trouser, wowser.

SURPRISING RHYMING:
[2] **Chowder**, gunpowder, louder, powder, prouder.

259

Doubter, outer, pouter, router (U.S.), scouter, shouter, spouter, sprouter, stouter, touter.
Counter, encounter, mounter.
Bounder, compounder, expounder, flounder, founder, pounder, rounder, sounder.
Bower, cower, devour, flour, flower, glower, hour, our, plougher/plower (U.S.), power, rush-hour, scour, shower, sour, tower.
[3] **Brainpower**, cauliflower, deflower, empower, firepower, horsepower, man-hour, manpower, mayflower, overpower, passion flower, sunflower, sweet-and-sour, wallflower, watchtower, willpower.

2.2.144 "--ower" (as in "flower")

[2] bower, cower, devour, flour, flower, glower, hour, our, plougher/plower (U.S.), power, rush-hour, scour, shower, sour, tower.
[3] brainpower, deflower, empower, endower, firepower, horsepower, man-hour, manpower, overpower, passion flower, sunflower, sweet-and-sour, wallflower, watchtower, willpower.

SURPRISING RHYMING:
[2] **Chowder**, gunpowder, louder, powder, prouder.
Browser, carouser, dowser, frowner, rabble-rouser, trouser, wowser.
Doubter, outer, pouter, router (U.S.), scouter, shouter, spouter, sprouter, stouter, touter.
Counter, encounter, mounter.
Bounder, compounder, expounder, flounder, founder, pounder, rounder, sounder.
Browner, downer, sundowner, towner, downtowner, uptowner.
Fowler, fouler, growler, howler, prowler, scowler.

2.2.145 "--owler" (as in "prowler")

[2] fowler, fouler, growler, howler, prowler, scowler.

SURPRISING RHYMING:
[2] **Bower,** cower, devour, flour, flower, glower, hour, our, plougher/plower (U.S.), power, rush-hour, scour, shower, sour, tower.
Chowder, gunpowder, louder, powder, prouder.
Browser, carouser, dowser, frowner, rabble-rouser, trouser, wowser.
Doubter, outer, pouter, router (U.S.), scouter, shouter, spouter, sprouter, stouter, touter.
Bounder, compounder, counter, encounter, expounder, flounder, founder, grounder, impounder, lounger, mounter, pounder, rounder, scrounger, sounder, sunlounger.
Browner, downer, sundowner, towner, downtowner, uptowner.
[3] **Brainpower**, cauliflower, empower, firepower, horsepower, man-hour, manpower, overpower, passion flower, sunflower, sweet-and-sour, wallflower, watchtower, willpower.

2.2.146 "--oxer" (as in "boxer")

[2] boxer, sponsor.

SURPRISING RHYMING:
[2] **Crosser**, dosser, embosser, flosser, glosser, tosser.
Blocker, knocker, locker, mocha, mocker, rocker, shocker, soccer.
Bopper, chopper, copper, cropper, dropper, flopper, hopper, popper, proper, shopper, stopper, swapper, topper, whopper.
Blotter, gotta, hotter, jotter, knotter, otter, plotter, potter, ricotta, rotter, spotter, squatter, totter, trotter, water, yachter.
Clobber, cobber, jobber, mobber, robber, slobber, sobber.
Blogger, flogger, hogger, jogger, logger, slogger.
Collar, corolla, dollar, holler, scholar, squalor, white-collar.
Coffer, cougher, offer, proffer, quaffer, scoffer.
[3] **Eavesdropper**, globetrotter, grasshopper, improper, teenybopper, terracotta.

2.2.147 "--ozer" (as in "composer")

[2] closer, dozer, poser.
[3] bulldozer, composer, disclosure, exposer, foreclosher, imposer, opposer, proposer.

260

SURPRISING RHYMING:
[2] **Coda**, coder, goader, jojoba, loader, October, odour/odor (U.S.), sober, soda.
Chauffer, clover, drover, gofer, gopher, loafer, nova, over, rover, sofa, soldier.
Broker, coca, croaker, joker, ochre, poker, smoker, soaker, stroker.
Coma, comber, donor, homer, loner, moaner, owner, phoner, roamer, toner.
Boater, doter, emoter, floater, gloater, iota, motor, promoter, quota, rota, rotor, voter.
[3] **Changeover**, crossover, flyover, handover, hangover, layover, left-over, makeover, moreover, once-over, popover, pullover, pushover, sleepover, slipover, spillover, stopover, takeover, turnover, walkover, wrapover.
Corroder, decoder, encoder, exploder, freeloader, pagoda, railroader, unloader.
Aloha, churchgoer, foregoer, lawnmower, playgoer, racegoer.
Evoker, invoker, non-smoker, pawnbroker, provoker, stockbroker.
Bipolar, cajoler, Coca-Cola, comptroller, consoler, controller, Ebola, extoller, Moviola, payola, patroller, Pianola, rock 'n' roller, scroller, steamroller, tombola, troller, viola.
Aroma, beachcomber, diploma, misnomer, Oklahoma.
Atoner, condoner, homeowner, landowner, persona, postponer.
[4] **Carioca**, mediocre, tapioca.

2.2.148 "--ooder" (as in "intruder")
barracuda, brooder, colluder, cruder, deluder, excluder, intruder, ruder, shrewder, Tudor.

SURPRISING RHYMING:
[2] **Boomer**, bloomer, groomer, humour/humor (U.S.), puma, rumour/rumor (U.S.), roomer, zoomer.
Crooner, lunar, pruner, schooner, sooner, swooner, tuna, tuner.
Boozer, bruiser, chooser, cruiser, looser, loser, smoother, snoozer, soother, user.
Hooter, looter, neuter, pewter, rooter, scooter, shooter, suitor, tutor.
Curer, insurer, juror, poorer, procurer, purer.
[3] **Mea culpa**, paratrooper, party-pooper, peasouper, pooper-scooper, super-duper.
Approver, disapprover, hoover, improver, manoeuvre/maneuver (U.S.), mover, outmanoeuvre/outmaneuver (U.S.), remover.
Commuter, computer, disputer, freebooter, peashooter, persecutor, polluter, prosecutor, recruiter, refuter, saluter, sharpshooter, six-shooter, troubleshooter, uprooter.
Abuser, accuser, medusa, misuser, peruser, producer, refuser, seducer, yakuza.

2.2.149 "--ooer" (as in "fewer")
[2] bluer, brewer, chewer, cure, doer, dour, fewer, newer, poor, screwer, sewer, skewer, spewer, viewer, you're, who're, wooer.
[3] arguer, evil-doer, interviewer, issuer, pursuer, renewer, rescuer, tattooer, wrongdoer.

SURPRISING RHYMING:
[2] **Cooler**, crueler, drooler, dueller, fooler, jeweller/jeweler (U.S.), moolah, pooler, ruler.
Boomer, bloomer, groomer, humour/humor (U.S.), puma, roomer, rumour/rumor (U.S.), zoomer.
Crooner, lunar, pruner, schooner, sooner, swooner, tuna, tuner.
Blooper, duper, future, grouper, hooper, looper, scooper, snooper, stupor, super, swooper, trooper, trouper.
Curer, insurer, juror, poorer, procurer, purer.
Boozer, bruiser, chooser, cruiser, looser, loser, smoother, snoozer, soother, user.
Allure, amour, assure, brochure, cocksure, contour, coiffure, couture, demure, detour, endure, ensure, impure, insure, liqueur, lure, manure, mature, moor, obscure, procure, pure, secure, sure, tour, unsure, velour.
[3] **Abuser**, accuser, diffuser, infuser, medusa, misuser, peruser, producer, refuser, seducer, yakuza.
Mea culpa, paratrooper, party-pooper, peasouper, pooper-scooper, super-duper.
Approver, disapprover, Hoover, improver, manoeuvre/maneuver (U.S.), mover, outmanoeuvre/outmaneuver (U.S.), remover.
Caricature, immature, insecure, manicure, overture, paramour, pedicure, plat du jour, premature, reassure.

2.2.150 "--ooler" (as in "cooler")
[2] cooler, crueler, drooler, dueller, fooler, jeweller/jeweler (U.S.), moolah, pooler, ruler.

SURPRISING RHYMING:
[2] **Bluer,** brewer, chewer, cure, doer, dour, fewer, newer, poor, sewer, skewer, spewer, viewer, you're, who're, wooer.
Boomer, bloomer, groomer, humour/humor (U.S.), puma, roomer, rumour/rumor (U.S.), zoomer.
Crooner, lunar, pruner, schooner, sooner, swooner, tuna, tuner.
Blooper, duper, future, looper, scooper, snooper, stupor, super, swooper, trooper.
Curer, insurer, juror, poorer, procurer, purer.
Boozer, bruiser, chooser, cruiser, looser, loser, smoother, snoozer, soother, user.
[3] **Baby-boomer,** consumer, perfumer, satsuma.
Ballooner, harpooner, honeymooner, lampooner.
Abuser, accuser, medusa, misuser, peruser, producer, refuser, seducer, yakuza.
Arguer, evil-doer, interviewer, issuer, pursuer, renewer, rescuer, tattooer, wrongdoer.
Mea culpa, paratrooper, party-pooper, peasouper, pooper-scooper, super-duper.
Approver, disapprover, Hoover, improver, manoeuvre/maneuver (U.S.), mover, outmanoeuvre/outmaneuver (U.S.), remover.

2.2.151 "--oomer" (as in "boomer")
[2] boomer, bloomer, groomer, humour/humor (U.S.), puma, rumour/rumor (U.S.), roomer, zoomer.
[3] baby-boomer, consumer, perfumer, satsuma.

SURPRISING RHYMING:
[2] **Crooner**, lunar, pruner, schooner, sooner, swooner, tuna, tuner.
Cooler, crueler, drooler, dueller, fooler, jeweller/jeweler (U.S.), moolah, pooler, ruler.
Bluer, brewer, chewer, cure, doer, dour, fewer, newer, poor, screwer, sewer, skewer, spewer, viewer, you're, who're, wooer.
Curer, insurer, juror, poorer, procurer, purer.
[3] **Ballooner**, harpooner, honeymooner, lampooner.
Barracuda, brooder, colluder, cruder, deluder, intruder, ruder, shrewder, Tudor.

2.2.152 "--ooner" (as in "sooner")
[2] crooner, lunar, pruner, schooner, sooner, spooner, swooner, tuna, tuner.
[3] ballooner, harpooner, honeymooner, lampooner.

SURPRISING RHYMING:
[2] **Boomer**, bloomer, groomer, humour/humor (U.S.), puma, rumour/rumor (U.S.), roomer, zoomer.
Cooler, crueler, drooler, dueller, fooler, jeweller/jeweler (U.S.), moolah, pooler, ruler.
Bluer, brewer, chewer, cure, doer, dour, fewer, newer, poor, screwer, sewer, skewer, spewer, viewer, you're, who're, wooer.
Curer, insurer, juror, poorer, procurer, purer.
Blooper, duper, future, looper, scooper, snooper, stupor, super, swooper, trooper.
Hooter, looter, neuter, pewter, rooter, scooter, shooter, suitor, tutor.
Boozer, bruiser, chooser, cruiser, juicer, looser, loser, smoother, snoozer, soother, user.
[3] **Baby-boomer**, consumer, perfumer, satsuma.
Approver, disapprover, hoover, improver, manoeuvre/maneuver (U.S.), mover, outmanoeuvre/outmaneuver (U.S.), remover.
Barracuda, brooder, colluder, cruder, deluder, intruder, ruder, shrewder, Tudor.
Abuser, accuser, medusa, producer, refuser, seducer, yakuza.
Commuter, computer, disputer, freebooter, persecutor, polluter, prosecutor, recruiter, refuter, saluter, sharpshooter, troubleshooter, uprooter.

2.2.153 "--ooper" (as in "super")
[2] blooper, cooper, duper, grouper, hooper, looper, scooper, snooper, stupor, super, swooper, trooper, trouper.

[3] mea culpa, paratrooper, party-pooper, peasouper, pooper-scooper, super-duper.

SURPRISING RHYMING:
[2] **Hooter**, looter, neuter, pewter, scooter, shooter, suitor, tutor.
Boomer, bloomer, groomer, humour/humor (U.S.), roomer, rumour/rumor (U.S.), zoomer.
Crooner, lunar, pruner, schooner, sooner, swooner, tuna, tuner.
Cooler, crueler, drooler, dueller, fooler, jeweller/jeweler (U.S.), moolah, pooler, ruler.
Boozer, bruiser, chooser, juicer, looser, loser, smoother, snoozer, soother, user.
[3] **Commuter**, computer, disputer, persecutor, polluter, prosecutor, recruiter, saluter, sharpshooter, troubleshooter, uprooter.
Baby-boomer, ballooner, consumer, honeymooner, lampooner, perfumer, satsuma.
Barracuda, brooder, colluder, cruder, deluder, intruder, ruder, shrewder, Tudor.
Approver, disapprover, hoover, improver, manoeuvre/maneuver (U.S.), mover, outmanoeuvre/outmaneuver (U.S.), remover.

2.2.154 "--oorer" (as in "poorer")
curer, insurer, juror, poorer, procurer, purer.

SURPRISING RHYMING:
[2] **Boomer,** bloomer, groomer, humour/humor (U.S.), puma, rumour/rumor (U.S.), roomer, zoomer.
Crooner, lunar, pruner, schooner, sooner, swooner, tuna, tuner.
Bluer, brewer, chewer, cure, doer, dour, fewer, newer, poor, screwer, sewer, skewer, spewer, viewer, you're, who're, wooer.
Boozer, bruiser, chooser, cruiser, looser, loser, smoother, snoozer, soother, user.
[3] **Baby-boomer**, ballooner, consumer, honeymooner, lampooner, perfumer, satsuma.
Arguer, evil-doer, interviewer, pursuer, rescuer, tattooer, wrongdoer.
Abuser, accuser, medusa, producer, refuser, seducer, yakuza.
Barracuda, brooder, colluder, cruder, intruder, ruder, shrewder, Tudor.
Approver, disapprover, hoover, improver, manoeuvre/maneuver (U.S.), mover, outmanoeuvre/outmaneuver (U.S.), remover.

2.2.155 "--ooter" (as in "computer")
[2] hooter, looter, neuter, pewter, rooter, scooter, shooter, suitor, tooter, tutor.
[3] commuter, computer, disputer, freebooter, persecutor, polluter, prosecutor, recruiter, refuter, saluter, sharpshooter, six-shooter, transmuter, troubleshooter, uprooter.

SURPRISING RHYMING:
[2] **Blooper,** duper, future, looper, scooper, snooper, stupor, super, swooper, trooper.
Boomer, bloomer, groomer, humour/humor (U.S.), roomer, rumour/rumor (U.S.), zoomer.
Crooner, lunar, pruner, schooner, sooner, swooner, tuna, tuner.
Booster, boozer, bruiser, chooser, cruiser, looser, loser, rooster, smoother, snoozer, soother, user.
[3] **Mea culpa**, paratrooper, party-pooper, peasouper, pooper-scooper, super-duper.
Barracuda, brooder, colluder, cruder, deluder, intruder, ruder, shrewder, Tudor.
Baby-boomer, ballooner, consumer, honeymooner, lampooner, perfumer, satsuma.
Approver, disapprover, hoover, improver, manoeuvre/maneuver (U.S.), mover, outmanoeuvre/outmaneuver (U.S.), remover.
Abuser, accuser, medusa, misuser, peruser, producer, refuser, seducer, yakuza.

2.2.156 "--oover" (as in "remover")
approver, disapprover, groover, hoover, improver, manoeuvre/maneuver (U.S.), mover, outmanoeuvre/outmaneuver (U.S.), remover.

SURPRISING RHYMING:
[2] **Boozer**, bruiser, chooser, cruiser, looser, loser, smoother, snoozer, soother, user.
Cooler, crueler, drooler, dueller, fooler, jeweller/jeweler (U.S.), moolah, pooler, ruler.
Boomer, bloomer, groomer, humour/humor (U.S.), roomer, rumour/rumor (U.S.), zoomer.
Crooner, lunar, pruner, schooner, sooner, swooner, tuna, tuner.

Bluer, brewer, chewer, cure, doer, dour, fewer, newer, poor, sewer, skewer, spewer, viewer, you're, who're, wooer.
Curer, insurer, juror, poorer, procurer, purer.
Blooper, duper, future, looper, scooper, snooper, stupor, super, swooper, trooper.
[3] Abuser, accuser, medusa, misuser, peruser, producer, refuser, seducer, yakuza.
Baby-boomer, ballooner, consumer, honeymooner, lampooner, perfumer, satsuma.
Barracuda, brooder, cruder, intruder, ruder, shrewder, Tudor.
Mea culpa, paratrooper, party-pooper, pooper-scooper, super-duper.

2.2.157 "--oozer" (as in "loser")

[2] boozer, bruiser, chooser, cruiser, juicer, looser, loser, snoozer, user.
[3] abuser, accuser, medusa, misuser, peruser, producer, refuser, seducer, yakuza.

SURPRISING RHYMING:
[2] Bluer, brewer, chewer, cure, doer, dour, fewer, newer, poor, screwer, sewer, skewer, spewer, viewer, you're, who're, wooer.
Cooler, crueler, drooler, dueller, fooler, jeweller/jeweler (U.S.), moolah, pooler, ruler.
Cuba, scuba, tuba, Uber, YouTuber.
Boomer, bloomer, groomer, humour/humor (U.S.), roomer, rumour/rumor (U.S.), zoomer.
Crooner, lunar, pruner, schooner, sooner, swooner, tuna, tuner.
Curer, insurer, juror, poorer, procurer, purer.
Hooter, looter, neuter, pewter, rooter, scooter, shooter, suitor, tutor.
[3] Evil-doer, interviewer, pursuer, rescuer, tattooer, wrongdoer.
Approver, groover, hoover, improver, mover, remover, manoeuvre/maneuver (U.S.), outmanoeuvre/outmaneuver(U.S.).
Baby-boomer, ballooner, consumer, honeymooner, lampooner, perfumer, satsuma.
Barracuda, brooder, cruder, intruder, ruder, shrewder, Tudor.
Commuter, computer, peashooter, persecutor, polluter, prosecutor, recruiter, saluter, sharpshooter, six-shooter, troubleshooter, uprooter.

2.2.158 "--uffer" (as in "suffer")

[2] bluffer, buffer, duffer, huffer, puffer, rougher, scuffer, snuffer, suffer.

SURPRISING RHYMING:
[2] Brother, mother, other, smother, t'other.
Cuppa, scupper, supper, upper.
Judder, rudder, shudder, udder, Buddha, do-gooder.
Hugger, lugger, mugger, plugger, rugger, slugger, snugger, sugar, tugger.
Bummer, drummer, dumber, glummer, gunner, hummer, number, plumber, runner, scunner, stunner, strummer, summer.
Butter, clutter, cutter, flutter, gutter, mutter, nutter, putter, scutter, shutter, splutter, sputter, stutter, utter.
Chukka/chukker (U.S.), ducker, mucker, plucker, pucker, succour/succor (U.S.), sucker, trucker, tucker, yucca.
[3] Another, grandmother, stepmother, godmother, housemother, stepbrother, further.
First-footer, rebutter, six-footer, shot-putter, woodcutter.

2.2.159 "--ugger" (as in "sugar")

[2] hugger, lugger, mugger, plugger, rugger, slugger, snugger, sugar, tugger.

SURPRISING RHYMING:
[2] Brother, mother, other, smother, t'other.
Butter, clutter, cutter, flutter, gutter, mutter, nutter, putter, scutter, shutter, splutter, sputter, stutter, utter.
Cuppa, scupper, supper, upper.
Chukka/chukker (U.S.), ducker, mucker, plucker, pucker, succour/succor (U.S.), sucker, trucker, tucker, yucca.
Bummer, drummer, dumber, glummer, gunner, hummer, number, plumber, runner, scunner, stunner, strummer, summer.

Judder, rudder, shudder, udder, Buddha, do-gooder.
Bluffer, buffer, duffer, huffer, puffer, rougher, scuffer, snuffer, suffer.
Juggler, pergola, smuggler, snuggler, struggler.
[3] First-footer, rebutter, six-footer, shot-putter, woodcutter.
Another, grandmother, stepmother, godmother, stepbrother, further.

2.2.160 "--uggler" (as in "juggler")
[2] juggler, pergola, smuggler, snuggler, struggler.

SURPRISING RHYMING:
[2] **Hugger**, lugger, mugger, plugger, rugger, slugger, snugger, sugar, tugger.
Bubbler, bumbler, crumbler, fumbler, grumbler, humbler, mumbler, tumbler.
Bundler, butler, bungler, bustler, coupler, cutler, doubler, guzzler, hustler, muffler, muzzler, puzzler, rustler, swashbuckler.
Colour/color (U.S.), duller, discolour/discolor (U.S.), fuller, puller, sculler, Technicolor, watercolour/watercolor (U.S.).
Bummer, drummer, dumber, glummer, hummer, number, plumber, strummer, summer.
Butter, clutter, cuppa, cutter, flutter, gutter, mutter, nutter, putter, scupper, scutter, shutter, splutter, sputter, stutter, supper, upper, utter.

2.2.161 "--ukker" (as in "trucker")
[2] chukka/chukker (U.S.), ducker, mucker, plucker, pucker, succour/succor (U.S.), sucker, trucker, tucker, yucca.

SURPRISING RHYMING:
[2] **Booker**, cooker, hookah, hooker, looker, good-looker, onlooker.
Cuppa, scupper, supper, upper.
Butter, busker, clutter, cutter, flutter, gutter, mutter, nutter, putter, scutter, shutter, splutter, sputter, stutter, utter.
Hugger, lugger, mugger, plugger, rugger, slugger, snugger, sugar, tugger.
Judder, rudder, shudder, udder, Buddha, do-gooder.
Bluffer, buffer, duffer, huffer, puffer, rougher, scuffer, snuffer, suffer.
Bummer, bunker, drummer, dumber, glummer, gunner, hummer, number, plumber, runner, scunner, stunner, strummer, summer.

2.2.162 "--uller" (as in "duller")
[2] colour/color (U.S.), duller, discolour/discolor (U.S.), fuller, puller, sculler, Technicolor, watercolour/watercolor (U.S.).

SURPRISING RHYMING:
[2] **Brother**, mother, other, smother, t'other.
Bummer, drummer, dumber, glummer, gunner, hummer, number, plumber, runner, scunner, stunner, strummer, summer.
Judder, rudder, shudder, udder, Buddha, do-gooder.
Hugger, lugger, mugger, plugger, rugger, slugger, snugger, sugar, tugger.
Cuppa, scupper, supper, upper.
Chukka/chukker (U.S.), plucker, pucker, succour/succor (U.S.), sucker, trucker, tucker.
Bluffer, buffer, duffer, huffer, puffer, rougher, scuffer, snuffer, suffer.
[3] **Another**, grandmother, stepmother, godmother, stepbrother.

2.2.163 "--ummer" (as in "summer")
[2] bummer, drummer, dumber, glummer, gummer, hummer, number, plumber, strummer, summer.
[3] latecomer, midsummer, newcomer, welcomer.

SURPRISING RHYMING:
[2] **Gunner**, hunger, runner, scunner, stunner, younger.
Brother, cover, glover, hover, lover, mother, other, shover, smother, t'other.
Bluffer, buffer, duffer, huffer, puffer, rougher, scuffer, snuffer, suffer.

Cumber, lumbar, lumber, number, rumba, slumber, umber.
Bumbler, fumbler, grumbler, humbler, mumbler, stumbler, tumbler.
Bumper, dumper, jumper, lumper, plumper, stumper, thumper.
Hugger, lugger, mugger, plugger, rugger, slugger, snugger, sugar, tugger.
Cuppa, scupper, supper, upper.
Butter, clutter, cutter, flutter, gutter, mutter, nutter, putter, scutter, shutter, splutter, sputter, stutter, utter.
[3] **Forerunner**, front-runner, gunrunner, guv'nor, roadrunner.
Another, further. grandmother, stepmother, godmother, stepbrother.
Discover, hardcover, recover, rediscover, uncover, undercover.

2.2.164 "--umber" (as in "number")
[2] cumber, lumbar, lumber, number, rumba, slumber, umber.
[3] cucumber, encumber, outnumber.

SURPRISING RHYMING:
[2] **Bumbler**, crumbler, fumbler, grumbler, humbler, mumbler, rumbler, stumbler, tumbler.
Blunder, plunder, sunder, thunder, under, wonder.
Bumper, dumper, jumper, lumper, plumper, stumper, thumper.
Gunner, hunger, runner, scunner, stunner, younger.
[3] **Latecomer**, midsummer, newcomer, welcomer.
Asunder, rotunda, up-and-under.

2.2.165 "--umbler" (as in "tumbler")
[2] bumbler, crumbler, fumbler, grumbler, humbler, mumbler, rumbler, stumbler, tumbler.

SURPRISING RHYMING:
[2] **Cumber**, lumbar, lumber, number, rumba, slumber, umber.
Bundler, bungler, muffler, juggler, puzzler, swashbuckler.
Blunder, plunder, sunder, thunder, under, wonder.
Gambler, rambler, scrambler.
Bumper, dumper, jumper, plumper, pumper, stumper, thumper.
Bummer, drummer, dumber, glummer, number, strummer, summer.
[3] **Cucumber**, encumber, outnumber.
Gazumper, latecomer, midsummer, newcomer, showjumper.

2.2.166 "--umper" (as in "jumper")
[2] bumper, dumper, jumper, plumper, pumper, stumper, thumper.
[3] gazumper, showjumper.

SURPRISING RHYMING:
[2] **Blunder**, plunder, sunder, thunder, under, wonder.
Cumber, lumbar, lumber, number, rumba, slumber, umber.
Bummer, drummer, dumber, glummer, plumber, strummer, summer.
Gunner, hunger, runner, scunner, stunner, younger.
Blunder, plunder, sunder, thunder, under, wonder.
Brother, mother, other, smother, t'other.
Bunker, dunker, drunker, flunker, hunker.
Chunter, grunter, hunter, junta, pothunter, punter, shunter.
Bumbler, fumbler, grumbler, humbler, mumbler, stumbler, tumbler.
[3] **Asunder**, boy-wonder, rotunda, up-and-under.
Cucumber, encumber, outnumber.

2.2.167 "--unner" (as in "runner")
[2] gunner, punner, runner, scunner, stunner.
[3] forerunner, front-runner, gunrunner, guv'nor, roadrunner.

SURPRISING RHYMING:
[2] **Drummer**, dumber, glummer, number, strummer, summer.

Brother, cover, further, glover, lover, mother, other, shover, smother, t'other.
Bluffer, buffer, duffer, huffer, puffer, rougher, scuffer, snuffer, suffer.
Blunder, chunder, hunger, plunder, sunder, thunder, under, wonder, younger.
Cumber, lumbar, lumber, number, rumba, slumber, umber.
Bumbler, fumbler, grumbler, humbler, mumbler, stumbler, tumbler.
Bumper, dumper, jumper, plumper, stumper, thumper.
Hugger, lugger, mugger, plugger, rugger, slugger, snugger, sugar, tugger.
Butter, clutter, flutter, gutter, mutter, nutter, shutter, splutter, sputter, stutter, utter.
[3] **Latecomer**, midsummer, newcomer, welcomer.
Another, grandmother, stepmother, godmother, stepbrother.
Discover, hardcover, recover, rediscover, uncover, undercover.
Asunder, rotunda, up-and-under.

2.2.168 "--under" (as in "under")
[2] blunder, chunder, plunder, sunder, thunder, under, wonder.
[3] asunder, rotunda, up-and-under.

SURPRISING RHYMING:
[2] **Gunner**, hunger, runner, scunner, stunner, younger.
Drummer, dumber, glummer, number, plumber, strummer, summer.
Brother, cover, further, glover, lover, mother, other, shover, smother, t'other.
Cumber, lumbar, lumber, number, rumba, slumber, umber.
Bumbler, fumbler, grumbler, humbler, mumbler, stumbler, tumbler.
Bumper, dumper, jumper, plumper, pumper, stumper, thumper.
Hugger, lugger, mugger, plugger, rugger, slugger, snugger, sugar, tugger.
Butter, clutter, flutter, gutter, mutter, nutter, shutter, splutter, sputter, stutter, utter.
[3] **Forerunner**, front-runner, gunrunner, guv'nor, roadrunner.
Latecomer, midsummer, newcomer, welcomer.
Another, grandmother, stepmother, godmother, stepbrother.
Discover, hardcover, recover, rediscover, uncover, undercover.

2.2.169 "--unger" (as in "younger")
[2] hunger, younger.
[3] fishmonger, ironmonger, scandalmonger, scaremonger, warmonger.

SURPRISING RHYMING:
[2] **Blunder**, plunder, sunder, thunder, under, wonder.
Bumper, dumper, jumper, plumper, pumper, stumper, thumper.
Bundler, bungler, muffler, juggler, puzzler, swashbuckler.
Cumber, lumbar, lumber, number, rumba, slumber, umber.
Conjure, expunger, lunger, plunger, sponger.
Chunter, grunter, hunter, junta, pothunter, punter, shunter.
Bunker, dunker, drunker, flunker, hunker.
Gunner, hunger, punner, runner, scunner, stunner, younger.
[3] **Cucumber**, encumber, outnumber.
Gazumper, showjumper.
Asunder, rotunda, up-and-under.

2.2.170 "--unter" (as in "hunter")
[2] chunter, grunter, hunter, junta, pothunter, punter, shunter.

SURPRISING RHYMING:
[2] **Blunder**, chunder, plunder, sunder, thunder, under, wonder.
Bumper, dumper, jumper, plumper, pumper, stumper, thumper.
Cumber, lumbar, lumber, number, rumba, slumber, umber.
Conjure, expunger, lunger, plunger, sponger.
Cruncher, luncher, puncher.
Bunker, dunker, drunker, flunker, hunker.
Gunner, hunger, runner, scunner, stunner, younger.

[3] **Asunder**, rotunda, up-and-under.
Cucumber, encumber, gazumper, outnumber, showjumper.

2.2.171 "--upper" (as in "supper")
[2] cuppa, scupper, supper, upper.

SURPRISING RHYMING:
[2] **Butter**, clutter, flutter, gutter, mutter, nutter, shutter, splutter, sputter, stutter, utter.
Chukka/chukker (U.S.), ducker, mucker, plucker, pucker, succour/succor (U.S.), sucker, trucker, tucker, yucca.
Hugger, mugger, plugger, rugger, slugger, snugger, sugar, tugger.
Bluffer, buffer, duffer, huffer, puffer, rougher, scuffer, snuffer, suffer.
Drummer, dumber, glummer, number, plumber, strummer, summer.
Gunner, punner, runner, scunner, stunner.
Brother, further, mother, other, smother, t'other.
[3] **First-footer**, rebutter, six-footer, shot-putter, woodcutter.
Another, grandmother, stepmother, godmother, stepbrother.

2.2.172 "--urcher" (as in "searcher")
[2] lurcher, nurture, percher, researcher, searcher.

SURPRISING RHYMING:
[2] **Merger**, perjure, purger, scourger, urger, verger.
Fervour/fervor (U.S), observer, server, swerver, surfer, time-server.
Affirmer, firmer, murmur, squirmer, terra firma.
Bursar, curser, cursor, purser, rehearser, reverser, vice versa.
Burger, burglar, curler, twirler, whirler.
Girder, herder, murder, purdah.
Burner, earner, learner, spurner, sterner, taverna, turner, yearner.
Gurkha, circa, lurker, shirker, jerker, smirker, tearjerker, worker.

2.2.173 "--urder" (as in "murder")
[2] girder, herder, murder, purdah.

SURPRISING RHYMING:
[2] **Burner**, earner, learner, spurner, sterner, taverna, turner, yearner.
Merger, perjure, purger, scourger, urger, verger.
Fervour/fervor (U.S), observer, server, swerver, surfer, time-server.
Affirmer, firmer, murmur, squirmer, terra firma.
Burger, burglar, curler, twirler, whirler.
Gurkha, circa, lurker, shirker, jerker, smirker, tearjerker, worker.
Lurcher, nurture, percher, researcher, searcher.

2.2.174 "--urger" (as in "merger")
[2] merger, perjure, purger, scourger, urger, verger.

SURPRISING RHYMING:
[2] **Fervour/fervor** (U.S), observer, server, surfer, time-server.
Lurcher, nurture, percher, researcher, searcher.
Burger, burglar, curler, twirler, whirler.
Girder, herder, murder, purdah.
Burner, earner, learner, spurner, sterner, taverna, turner, yearner.
Gurkha, circa, lurker, shirker, jerker, smirker, tearjerker, worker.
Affirmer, firmer, murmur, squirmer, terra firma.
Bursar, curser, cursor, purser, rehearser, reverser, vice versa.

2.2.175 "--urker" (as in "worker")
[2] Gurkha, circa, lurker, shirker, jerker, smirker, tearjerker, worker.

SURPRISING RHYMING:
[2] **Burger**, burglar, curler, twirler, whirler.
Girder, herder, murder, purdah.
Burner, earner, learner, spurner, sterner, taverna, turner, yearner.
Affirmer, firmer, murmur, squirmer, terra firma.
Fervour/fervor (U.S), observer, server, swerver, surfer, time-server.
Bursar, curser, cursor, purser, rehearser, reverser, vice versa.
Merger, perjure, purger, scourger, urger, verger.
Lurcher, nurture, percher, researcher, searcher.

2.2.176 "--urmer" (as in "firmer")
[2] affirmer, firmer, murmur, squirmer, terra firma.

SURPRISING RHYMING:
[2] **Burner**, earner, learner, spurner, sterner, taverna, yearner.
Girder, herder, murder, purdah.
Burger, burglar, curler, twirler, whirler.
Gurkha, circa, lurker, shirker, jerker, smirker, tearjerker, worker.
Merger, perjure, purger, scourger, urger, verger.
Fervour/fervor (U.S), observer, server, swerver, surfer, time-server.
Bursar, curser, cursor, purser, rehearser, reverser, vice versa.
Lurcher, nurture, percher, researcher, searcher.

2.2.177 "--urner" (as in "earner")
[2] burner, churner, earner, learner, spurner, sterner, taverna, turner, yearner.
[3+] afterburner, discerner, easterner, northerner, returner, southerner, westerner.

SURPRISING RHYMING:
[2] **Fervour/fervor** (U.S), further, observer, server, surfer, time-server.
Affirmer, firmer, murmur, squirmer, terra firma.
Burger, burglar, curler, twirler, whirler.
Bursar, curser, cursor, purser, rehearser, reverser, vice versa.
Gurkha, circa, lurker, shirker, jerker, smirker, tearjerker, worker.
Merger, perjure, purger, scourger, urger, verger.
Girder, herder, murder, purdah.
[3] **Another**, grandmother, stepmother, godmother, stepbrother.

2.2.178 "--urser" (as in "vice versa")
[2] bursar, curser, cursor, purser, rehearser, reverser, vice versa.

SURPRISING RHYMING:
[2] **Fervour/fervor** (U.S), observer, server, surfer, time-server.
Gurkha, circa, lurker, shirker, jerker, smirker, tearjerker, worker.
Burger, burglar, curler, twirler, whirler.
Merger, perjure, purger, scourger, urger, verger.
Affirmer, firmer, murmur, squirmer, terra firma.
Girder, herder, murder, purdah.
Lurcher, nurture, percher, researcher, searcher.
Burner, discerner, earner, learner, spurner, sterner, taverna.

2.2.179 "--urver" (as in "observer")
[2] fervour/fervor (U.S), observer, server, swerver, surfer, time-server.

SURPRISING RHYMING:
[2] **Burger**, burglar, curler, twirler, whirler.
Girder, herder, murder, purdah.
Burner, earner, learner, spurner, sterner, taverna, turner, yearner.
Affirmer, firmer, murmur, squirmer, terra firma.
Bursar, curser, cursor, purser, rehearser, reverser, vice versa.

Merger, perjure, purger, scourger, urger, verger.
Lurcher, nurture, percher, researcher, searcher.
Gurkha, circa, lurker, shirker, jerker, smirker, tearjerker, worker.

2.2.180 "--utter" (as in "butter")

[2] butter, clutter, cutter, flutter, gutter, mutter, nutter, putter, scutter, shutter, splutter, sputter, stutter, utter.
[3] first-footer, rebutter, six-footer, shot-putter, woodcutter.

SURPRISING RHYMING:
[2] **Cuppa**, scupper, supper, upper.
Chukka/chukker (U.S.), ducker, mucker, plucker, pucker, succour/succor (U.S.), sucker, trucker, tucker, yucca.
Booker, cooker, hookah, hooker, looker, good-looker, onlooker.
Bluffer, buffer, duffer, huffer, puffer, rougher, scuffer, snuffer, suffer.
Judder, rudder, shudder, udder, Buddha, do-gooder.
Hugger, mugger, plugger, rugger, slugger, snugger, sugar, tugger.
Bummer, drummer, dumber, glummer, gunner, hummer, number, plumber, runner, scunner, stunner, strummer, summer.
Brother, mother, other, smother, t'other.
[3] **Another**, grandmother, stepmother, godmother, housemother, stepbrother, further.

2.2.181 "--usher" (as in "usher")

[2] blusher, brusher, crusher, flusher, gusher, pusher, plusher, Russia, rusher, usher.

SURPRISING RHYMING:
[2] **Buzzer**, guzzler, hustler, muffler, muzzler, puzzler, rustler.
Bluster, buster, busker, cluster, duster, fluster, lustre/luster (U.S.), muster, thruster.
Brother, cover, further, glover, lover, mother, other, shover, smother, t'other.
Butter, clutter, flutter, gutter, mutter, nutter, shutter, splutter, sputter, stutter, utter.
Bluffer, buffer, duffer, huffer, puffer, rougher, scuffer, snuffer, suffer.
[3] **Another**, grandmother, stepmother, godmother, stepbrother.
Discover, hardcover, recover, rediscover, uncover, undercover.
Adjuster, blockbuster, filibuster, knuckle-duster, lacklustre/lackluster.

2.2.182 "--uster" (as in "buster")

[2] bluster, buster, cluster, duster, fluster, lustre/luster (U.S.), muster, thruster.
[3] adjuster, blockbuster, filibuster, knuckle-duster, lacklustre/lackluster (U.S.).

SURPRISING RHYMING:
[2] **Buzzer**, guzzler, hustler, muffler, muzzler, puzzler, rustler.
Butter, clutter, flutter, gutter, mutter, nutter, shutter, splutter, sputter, stutter, utter.
Blusher, brusher, crusher, gusher, pusher, plusher, rusher, usher.
Chunter, grunter, hunter, junta, pothunter, punter, shunter.
Busker, dumpster, funster, huckster, youngster.
Custard, flustered, mustard.
[3] **Discover**, hardcover, recover, rediscover, uncover, undercover.
Abductor, conductor, constructor, inductor, instructor, obstructer.

2.2.183 "--uvver" (as in "lover")

[2] cover, glover, hover, lover, shover.
[3] discover, hardcover, recover, rediscover, uncover, undercover.

SURPRISING RHYMING:
[2] **Brother**, further, mother, other, smother, t'other.
Bluffer, buffer, duffer, huffer, puffer, rougher, scuffer, snuffer, suffer.
Judder, rudder, shudder, udder, Buddha, do-gooder.
Colour/color (U.S.), duller, discolour/discolor (U.S.), fuller, puller, sculler, Technicolor, watercolour/watercolor (U.S.).

Hugger, mugger, plugger, rugger, slugger, snugger, sugar, tugger.
Drummer, dumber, glummer, number, plumber, strummer, summer.
Gunner, punner, runner, scunner, stunner.
[3] Another, grandmother, stepmother, godmother, stepbrother.
Latecomer, midsummer, newcomer, welcomer.

2.2.184 "--uther" (as in "mother")
[2] brother, mother, other, smother, t'other.
[3] another, grandmother, stepmother, godmother, housemother, stepbrother, further.

SURPRISING RHYMING:
[2] **Cover**, glover, hover, lover, shover.
Bluffer, buffer, duffer, huffer, puffer, rougher, scuffer, snuffer, suffer.
Judder, rudder, shudder, udder, Buddha, do-gooder.
Colour/color (U.S.), duller, discolour/discolor (U.S.), fuller, puller, watercolour/watercolor.
Butter, clutter, flutter, gutter, mutter, nutter, shutter, splutter, sputter, stutter, utter.
Gunner, punner, runner, scunner, stunner.
Blusher, brusher, buzzer, crusher, gusher, pusher, plusher, usher.
[3] Discover, hardcover, recover, rediscover, uncover, undercover.
Latecomer, midsummer, newcomer, welcomer.

2.3 "eer"

2.3.1 "--eer" (as in "cheer")
[1] beer, blear, cheer, clear, dear, deer, ear, fear, gear, hear, here, jeer, leer, mere, near, peer, pier, queer, rear, seer, sear, shear, sheer, smear, sneer, spear, sphere, steer, tear, tears, tier, veer, weir, we're, year.
[2] adhere, appear, arrears, austere, besmear, brassiere, career, cashier, cashmere, cohere, endear, footgear, frontier, headgear, premier, midyear, mishear, nadir, reindeer, revere, severe, Shakespeare, sincere, unclear, veneer.
[3] atmosphere, auctioneer, balladeer, bandolier, bombardier, brigadier, buccaneer, cavalier, chandelier, commandeer, disappear, domineer, engineer, financier, gazetteer, ginger beer, gondolier, grenadier, hemisphere, idea, insincere, interfere, mountaineer, musketeer, overhear, persevere, pioneer, privateer, profiteer, puppeteer, racketeer, reappear, rocketeer, souvenir, stratosphere, volunteer, yesteryear.

SURPRISING RHYMING:
[1] **Beard**, cheered, cleared, feared, geared, jeered, leered, neared, peered, reared, sneered, steered, teared, tiered, veered, weird.
[2] **Adhered**, appeared, careered, cashiered, endeared, lop-eared, revered, veneered.
[3] **Commandeered**, disappeared, domineered, engineered, interfered, mountaineered, persevered, pioneered, privateered, profiteered, reappeared, volunteered.

2.3.2 "--eered" (as in "steered")
[1] beard, cheered, cleared, feared, geared, jeered, leered, neared, peered, reared, seared, sheared, sheered, smeared, sneered, steered, teared, tiered, veered, weird.
[2] adhered, appeared, careered, cashiered, endeared, lop-eared, revered, veneered.
[3] commandeered, disappeared, domineered, engineered, interfered, mountaineered, persevered, pioneered, privateered, profiteered, reappeared, volunteered.

SURPRISING RHYMING:
[1] **Beer**, cheer, clear, dear, deer, ear, fear, gear, hear, here, jeer, leer, mere, near, peer, pier, queer, rear, sheer, smear, sneer, spear, steer, tear, tier, veer, year.
[2] **Adhere**, appear, arrears, austere, besmear, brassiere, career, cashier, cashmere, cohere, endear, footgear, frontier, headgear, premier, midyear, mishear, nadir, reindeer, revere, severe, Shakespeare, sincere, unclear, veneer.
[3] **Atmosphere**, auctioneer, balladeer, bandolier, bombardier, brigadier, buccaneer, cavalier, chandelier, commandeer, disappear, domineer, engineer, financier, gazetteer, ginger beer, gondolier, grenadier, hemisphere, idea, insincere, interfere, mountaineer,

musketeer, overhear, persevere, pioneer, privateer, profiteer, puppeteer, racketeer, reappear, rocketeer, souvenir, stratosphere, volunteer, yesteryear.

2.3.3 "--eerence" (as in "appearance")
[3] appearance, adherence, clearance, coherence, disappearance, incoherence, interference, non-appearance, perseverance, reappearance.

SURPRISING RHYMING:
[3+] **Allegiance**, antecedence, competence, circumstance, convenience, credence, endurance, high-maintenance, impedance, inconvenience, maintenance, malfeasance, obedience, patience, precedence, reassurance, sequence, tea-dance.

2.3.4 "--eerest" (as in "dearest")
[2] clearest, dearest, merest, nearest, queerest, severest, sheerest, sincerest.

SURPRISING RHYMING:
[1] **Best**, blessed, breast, chest, crest, dressed, guest, guessed, jest, messed, nest, pest, quest, stressed, test, vest, west, zest.
[2] **Abreast**, addressed, arrest, attest, Beau Geste, behest, bequest, caressed, contest, depressed, detest, digest, digressed, distressed, divest, expressed, inquest, invest, molest, oppressed, possessed, progressed, recessed, refreshed, repressed, request, suggest, suppressed, transgressed, undressed, unless, unrest.
Cheerless, earless, fearless, gearless, idealess, peerless, tearless.
Cleanest, comfiest, greenest, keenest, leanest, meanest.
Cheapest, deepest, dreamless, fleetest, neatest, seamless, steepest, sweetest.
Decent, needn't, adherent, coherent.
[3] **Defeatist**, elitist, extremist, idealist, lyricist, optimist, realist, strategist, surrealist.
Dispossessed, effervesced, interest, manifest, readdressed, reassessed, self-possessed.

2.3.5 "--eerful" (as in "cheerful")
[2] cheerful, earful, fearful, tearful.

SURPRISING RHYMING:
[2] **People**, steeple, townspeople.
Deceitful, gleeful, heedful, lethal, needful.
Beetle, evil, medieval, primeval, retrieval, upheaval, weevil.
Eagle, feeble, legal, needle, regal, illegal, seagull, wheedle.
Easel, diesel, merciful, peaceful, teasel, weasel.
Equal, sequel, treacle, unequal, unspeakable.
[3] **Cereal**, serial, imperial, material, ethereal.
Amenable, feasible, genial, meaningful, menial, deceitful.
Enfeeble, peaceable, readable, redeemable, unreadable.
Reachable, teachable, impeachable, unteachable.
[4] **Agreeable**, foreseeable, disagreeable, unforeseeable.
Achievable, believable, retrievable, conceivable, unbelievable, inconceivable.
Reasonable, seasonable, unreasonable.

2.3.6 "--eerfully" (as in "tearfully")
[3] cheerfully, fearfully, tearfully.

SURPRISING RHYMING:
[1] **Fee**, gee, he, key, knee, me, sea, see, tee, tea, the, twee, we, wee, whee, zee.
Brie, flea, flee, free, glee, lee, spree, three, tree.
[2] **Carefree**, clearly, dearly, degree, freebie, Frisbee, merely, nearly, queerly, yearly.
Creepy, sleepy, sweetpea, teepee, weepy.
Creamy, dreamy, gleamy, seamy, screamy, steamy.
Beady, greedy, needy, seedy, speedy, sweetie, treaty, weedy.
Beefy, coffee, leafy, toffee.
Beanie, genie, greeny, meanie, queenie, teeny, tweeny, weeny.

Cheeky, marquee, reeky, sleeky, sneaky, squeaky, streaky, whiskey/whisky, Yankee.
Bleakly, meekly, sleekly, weakly, weekly.
Cleanly , seemly, queenly, seemly, steely, wheelie.
Easy, breezy, fleecy, foresee, look-see, queasy, sightsee, specie.
[3] Ancestry, archery, artistry, bakery, battery, bigotry, binary, blackberry, blubbery, blueberry, blustery, brasserie, bravery, brewery, bribery, burglary, calorie, carpentry, carvery, cavalry, celery, century, chemistry, chicory, chivalry, Christmas tree, colliery, contrary, devilry, diary, dietary, disagree, dithery, doddery, drudgery, dungaree, duty-free, eatery, enquiry, estuary, expiry, factory, fakery, feathery, filigree, finery, fishery, flattery, fluttery, forestry, forgery, gallery, geometry, gimmickry, glittery, greenery, grocery, history, imagery, injury, inquiry, ivory, jamboree, jewellery/jewelry (U.S.), jittery, leathery, lingerie, lottery, luxury, memory, mercury, misery, momentary, monastery, mystery, nursery, obituary, obligatory, pageantry, pedigree, perjury, pillory, pleasantry, poetry, pottery, primary, priory, quivery, referee, revelry, reverie, rivalry, robbery, rockery, rosary, rubbery, salary, sanctuary, savagery, savory, scenery, sensory, shimmery, shivery, silvery, slavery, slippery, sorcery, sugary, surgery, tapestry, thundery, treachery, trickery, victory, wintery, wizardry.
Austerely, cavalierly, insincerely, severely, sincerely.
[4] Accessory, adultery, artillery, cautionary, cemetery, compulsory, confectionery, conciliatory, constabulary, contemporary, customary, debauchery, delivery, dictionary, directory, discovery, distillery, elementary, embroidery, explanatory, exploratory, hunky-dory, idolatry, imaginary, incendiary, infirmary, inflammatory, judiciary, laboratory, legendary, literary, machinery, mandatory, mercenary, military, missionary, necessary, ordinary, patisserie, perfumery, preliminary, psychiatry, publicity, reactionary, recovery, secretary, secondary, simplicity, skullduggery, solitary, stationary, stationery, temporary, territory, tomfoolery, upholstery, visionary, vocabulary.

2.3.7 "--eery" (as in "weary")

[2] beery, bleary, carefree, cheery, dearie, degree, dreary, eerie, eyrie/aerie (U.S.), leery, query, teary, theory, smeary, weary.

SURPRISING RHYMING:
[1] Fee, gee, he, key, knee, me, sea, see, tee, tea, the, twee, we, wee, whee, zee.
Brie, flea, flee, free, glee, lee, spree, three, tree.
[2] Carefree, clearly, dearly, degree, freebie, Frisbee, merely, nearly, queerly, yearly.
Creepy, sleepy, sweetpea, teepee, weepy.
Creamy, dreamy, gleamy, seamy, screamy, steamy.
Beady, freely, greedy, needy, reedy, seedy, speedy, sweetie, treaty, tweedy, weedy.
Beefy, coffee, leafy, toffee.
Cleanly, seemly, queenly, seemly, steely, wheelie.
Easy, breezy, fleecy, foresee, look-see, queasy, sightsee, specie.
Cheeky, marquee, reeky, sleeky, sneaky, squeaky, streaky, whiskey/whisky, Yankee.
Bleakly, meekly, sleekly, weakly, weekly.
[3] Ancestry, archery, artistry, bakery, battery, bigotry, binary, blackberry, blubbery, blueberry, blustery, brasserie, bravery, brewery, bribery, burglary, calorie, carpentry, carvery, cavalry, celery, century, chemistry, chicory, chivalry, Christmas tree, colliery, contrary, devilry, diary, dietary, disagree, dithery, doddery, drudgery, dungaree, duty-free, eatery, enquiry, estuary, expiry, factory, fakery, feathery, filigree, finery, fishery, flattery, fluttery, forestry, forgery, gallery, geometry, gimmickry, glittery, greenery, grocery, history, imagery, injury, inquiry, ivory, jamboree, jewellery/jewelry (U.S.), jittery, leathery, lingerie, lottery, luxury, memory, mercury, misery, momentary, monastery, mystery, nursery, obituary, obligatory, pageantry, pedigree, perjury, pillory, pleasantry, poetry, pottery, primary, priory, quivery, referee, revelry, reverie, rivalry, robbery, rockery, rosary, rubbery, salary, sanctuary, savagery, savory, scenery, sensory, shimmery, shivery, silvery, slavery, slippery, sorcery, sugary, surgery, tapestry, thundery, treachery, trickery, victory, wintery, wizardry.
Austerely, cavalierly, insincerely, severely, sincerely.
[4] Accessory, adultery, artillery, cautionary, cemetery, compulsory, confectionery, conciliatory, constabulary, contemporary, customary, debauchery, delivery, dictionary, directory, discovery, elementary, embroidery, explanatory, exploratory, hunky-dory,

idolatry, imaginary, incendiary, infirmary, inflammatory, judiciary, laboratory, legendary, literary, machinery, mandatory, mercenary, military, missionary, necessary, ordinary, patisserie, perfumery, preliminary, psychiatry, publicity, reactionary, recovery, secretary, secondary, simplicity, skullduggery, solitary, stationary, stationery, temporary, territory, tomfoolery, upholstery, visionary, vocabulary.

2.3.8 "--earring" (as in "fearing")
[2] cheering, clearing, earring, fearing, gearing, hearing, jeering, leering, nearing, peering, rearing, searing, shearing, sneering, spearing, steering, tearing, veering.
[3] adhering, appearing, besmearing, disappearing, endearing, God-fearing, veneering.
[4] auctioneering, electioneering, engineering, mountaineering, orienteering, volunteering.

SURPRISING RHYMING:
[2] **Cleaning**, greening, leaning, meaning, screening, weaning.
Breathing, grieving, leaving, seething, teething, thieving, weaving.
Being, fleeing, freeing, seeing, skiing, teeing, treeing.
Ceiling, dealing, feeling, fielding, healing, kneeling, pealing, peeling, reeling, sealing, shielding, stealing, squealing, wheeling, wielding, yielding.
Bleeding, breeding, feeding, heeding, leading, needing, pleading, reading, speeding.
Beaming, dreaming, scheming, screaming, steaming, streaming.
Beating, bleating, cheating, eating, fleeting, greeting, heating, meeting, pleating, seating, sheeting, treating, tweeting.
Creaking, freaking, leaking, peaking, peeking, reeking, seeking, shrieking, sneaking, speaking, streaking, squeaking, tweaking.
Ceasing, creasing, feasting, fleecing, greasing, leasing, piecing.
Beeping, bleeping, cheeping, creeping, heaping, keeping, leaping, peeping, reaping, seeping, sleeping, sweeping, weeping.
Breezing, easing, freezing, pleasing, seizing, sneezing, squeezing, teasing, wheezing.
[3] **Appealing**, revealing, self-sealing, wheeler-dealing.
Convening, demeaning, dry-cleaning, overweening, spring-cleaning, well-meaning.
Conceding, exceeding, impeding, misleading, misreading, preceding, proceeding, receding, re-reading, re-seeding, seceding, stampeding, succeeding, unheeding.
Browbeating, competing, completing, concreting, deceiving, defeating, deleting, depleting, heart beating, maltreating, mistreating, repeating, reseating, retreating.
Appeasing, decreasing, increasing, policing, releasing, subleasing.
Achieving, believing, conceiving, debriefing, deceiving, displeasing, perceiving, receiving, relieving, reprieving, reprising, retrieving.

2.3.9 "--earless" (as in "fearless")
[2] cheerless, earless, fearless, gearless, idealess, peerless, tearless.

SURPRISING RHYMING:
[1] **Best**, blessed, breast, chest, crest, dressed, guest, guessed, jest, messed, nest, pest, quest, stressed, test, vest, west, zest.
[2] **Clearest**, dearest, merest, nearest, queerest, severest, sincerest.
Cleanest, greenest, keenest, leanest, meanest.
Cheapest, deepest, steepest.
Abreast, addressed, arrest, attest, Beau Geste, behest, bequest, caressed, celeste, compressed, contest, depressed, detest, digest, digressed, distressed, divest, expressed, footrest, headrest, ingest, inquest, invest, molest, oppressed, possessed, progressed, recessed, refreshed, repressed, request, suggest, suppressed, transgressed, undressed, unless, unrest.

2.3.10 "--eerly" (as in "nearly")
[2] clearly, dearly, merely, nearly, queerly, yearly.
[3] austerely, cavalierly, insincerely, severely, sincerely.

SURPRISING RHYMING:
[2] **Foresee**, greasy, look-see, maxi, mercy, sightsee, specie, tipsy.

Bleary, carefree, cheery, dearie, debris, dreary, eerie, esprit, hairy, hungry, leery, prairie, quarry, query, storey, story, sultry, teary, theory, smeary, weary.
Freebie, greedy, maybe, needy, ruby, seedy, speedy, would-be, zombie.
Ably, beastly, cleanly, early, earthly, freely, friendly, likely, lowly, medley, mostly, muesli, newly, nightly, oily, paisley, really, seemly, steely, truly, weakly, weekly, yearly.
Creepy, hippie, sleepy, teepee, weepy.
Beamy, creamy, dreamy, gimme, gleamy, seamy.
Achy, beaky, car key, cheeky, cliquey, creaky, freaky, karaoke, leaky, psyche, reeky, risky, sleeky, sneaky, squeaky, streaky.
Acne, any, beanie, genie, greeny, meanie, queenie, teeny, tweeny.
Gritty, guilty, meaty, misty, pity, pretty, sweetie, tasty, treaty.
[3] Ancestry, archery, artistry, bakery, battery, bigotry, binary, blackberry, blubbery, blueberry, blustery, brasserie, bravery, brewery, bribery, burglary, calorie, carpentry, carvery, cavalry, celery, century, chemistry, chicory, chivalry, Christmas tree, colliery, contrary, devilry, diary, dietary, disagree, dithery, doddery, drudgery, dungaree, duty-free, eatery, enquiry, estuary, expiry, factory, fakery, feathery, filigree, finery, fishery, flattery, fluttery, forestry, forgery, gallery, geometry, gimmickry, glittery, greenery, grocery, history, imagery, injury, inquiry, ivory, jamboree, jewellery/jewelry (U.S.), jittery, leathery, lingerie, lottery, luxury, memory, mercury, misery, momentary, monastery, mystery, nursery, obituary, obligatory, pageantry, pedigree, perjury, pillory, pleasantry, poetry, pottery, primary, priory, quivery, referee, revelry, reverie, rivalry, robbery, rockery, rosary, rubbery, salary, sanctuary, savagery, savory, scenery, sensory, shimmery, shivery, silvery, slavery, slippery, sorcery, sugary, surgery, tapestry, thundery, treachery, trickery, victory, wintery, wizardry.
Courtesy, currency, decency, heresy, leniency, odyssey, oversee, prophecy, secrecy.
Cheerily, drearily, eerily, merrily, warily, wearily.
Comedy, remedy, gravity, recipe, sanity.
Alchemy, blasphemy, enemy, infamy, sesame.
Actually, broccoli, brotherly, easterly, equally, fatherly, leisurely.
Certainty, charity, clarity, deputy, dignity, graffiti, gravity, guarantee, honesty, liberty, piety, poverty, quality, sanctity, unity, vanity.
Anchovy, c'est la vie, eau-de-vie, vis-à-vis.

2.4 "eh"

2.4.1 "--easure" (as in "treasure")
leisure, measure, pleasure, pressure, treasure, displeasure, made-to-measure.

SURPRISING RHYMING:
[2] Measured, pleasured, pressured, treasured.
Dresser, fresher, guesser, lesser, presser, yessir.
Feather, heather, leather, nether, tether, together, weather, whether.
Clever, ever, lever, never, sever.
Better, debtor, fetter, fretter, getter, letter, setter, sweater, wetter.
Cellar, dweller, fella, feller, seller, speller, stellar, teller, yeller.
Etcher, fetcher, gesture, lecher, lecture, sketcher, stretcher, venture.
[3] Endeavour/endeavor (U.S.), forever, forget her, however, never-never, whatever, whatsoever, whenever, wherever, whichever, whoever, whomever.
Bestseller, cave dweller, dispeller, exceller, expeller, foreteller, novella, paella, propeller, repeller, umbrella.
Bonesetter, carburettor/carburetor (U.S.), forgetter, go-getter, jet-setter, love-letter, newsletter, operetta, pacesetter, red-letter, typesetter, unfetter, upsetter, vendetta.
Aggressor, assessor, caresser, confessor, contessa, digresser, hairdresser, oppressor, possessor, predecessor, processor, professor, possessor, successor, transgressor.
Adventure, ancestor, arrester, condenser, contester, digester, dispenser, fiesta, investor, molester, polyester, protester, semester, sequester, siesta, sou'wester, trimester.

2.4.2 "--ebble" (as in "pebble")
[2] pebble, rebel, treble.

SURPRISING RHYMING:
[2] **Freckle**, Jekyll, heckle, speckle, shekel.
Bevel, devil, level, medal, meddle, pedal, peddle, revel.
Fettle, kettle, metal, mettle, nettle, petal, re-settle, settle, unsettle.
Dental, gentle, kennel, mental, parental, rental.
Embezzle, nestle, special, trestle, vessel, wrestle.
[3] **Assemble**, dissemble, resemble, tremble.
Bedevil, daredevil, eye-level, high-level, low-level., split-level.
[4] **Accidental**, continental, departmental, detrimental, elemental, environmental, experimental, fundamental, incremental, instrumental, judgmental, monumental, Oriental, sentimental, transcendental.

2.4.3 "--eck" (as in "neck")
[1] check, cheque, deck, fleck, heck, neck, peck, sec, spec, speck, tech, trek, wreck.
[2] breakneck, crew-neck, crosscheck, Dalek, exec, foredeck, henpeck, high tech, raincheck, redneck, rollneck, roughneck, shipwreck, soundcheck, spot-check, sundeck, swan-neck, V-neck.
[3] bodycheck, bottleneck, countercheck, discotheque, leatherneck, rubberneck, quarterdeck, turtleneck.

SURPRISING RHYMING:
[1] **Checked**, decked, flecked, necked, pecked, sect, specked, trekked, wrecked.
Bet, debt, fret, get, jet, let, met, net, pet, set, stet, sweat, threat, vet, wet, whet, yet.
Pep, prep, rep, schlep, step, steppe, yep.
Crept, kept, leapt, prepped, slept, stepped, swept, wept.
Best, blessed, blest, breast, chest, crest, dressed, guest, guessed, jest, lest, messed, nest, pest, quest, rest, stressed, test, vest, west, wrest, zest.
[2] **Abject**, affect, aspect, bisect, bull-necked, collect, connect, correct, defect, deflect, deject, detect, dialect, direct, dissect, effect, eject, elect, erect, expect, henpecked, infect, inflect, inject, insect, inspect, neglect, object, perfect, prefect, project, prospect, protect, reflect, reject, respect, select, subject, suspect, unchecked.
Affects, aspects, bisects, collects, connects, corrects, defects, deflects, detects, dialects, directs, effects, ejects, elects, erects, expects, infects, injects, insects, inspects, neglects, objects, projects, prospects, protects, reflects, rejects, respects, sects, selects, subjects, suspects.
Asset, baguette, banquet, beget, beset, brochette, brunette/brunet (U.S.), cadet, cassette, coquette, cornet, corvette, croquette, dragnet, duet, filmset, fishnet, forget, gazette, handset, headset, in debt, inlet, inset, kismet, mindset, nymphet, octet, offset, onset, outset, pre-set, quartet, quintet, regret, reset, rosette, roulette, sextet, sunset, toilette, upset, vignette.
Doorstep, footstep, instep, misstep, one-step, quickstep, sidestep.
Accept, adept, concept, except, inept, intercept, overslept, over-stepped, precept, rainswept, side-stepped, unswept, windswept.
Burlesque, desk, grotesque, newsdesk, picturesque, statuesque.
Abreast, addressed, arrest, attest, Beau Geste, behest, bequest, caressed, compressed, contest, depressed, detest, digest, digressed, distressed, expressed, inquest, invest, molest, oppressed, possessed, progressed, recessed, refreshed, repressed, request, suggest, suppressed, transgressed, undressed, unless, unrest.
[3] **Aftereffect**, architect, circumspect, dialect, disaffect, disinfect, disconnect, disrespect, incorrect, indirect, intellect, interconnect, interject, intersect, introspect, misdirect, recollect, re-elect, resurrect, retrospect, self-respect.
Alphabet, castanet, cigarette, clarinet, epithet, etiquette, heavy-set, internet, launderette, leatherette, maisonette, marionette, minuet, outlet, pirouette, silhouette, statuette, suffragette, usherette.

2.4.4 "--ecking" (as in "wrecking")
[2] checking, decking, flecking, necking, pecking, specking, trekking, wrecking.
[3] crosschecking, henpecking, sound-checking, spot-checking.
[4] bottlenecking, counterchecking, rubbernecking.

SURPRISING RHYMING:
[2] Betting, fretting, getting, jetting, letting, netting, petting, setting, sweating, vetting, wetting, whetting.
Begging, bootlegging, egging, legging, pegging.
Blessing, dressing, guessing, messing, pressing, stressing, yessing.
Pepping, prepping, schlepping, stepping.
Cresting, guesting, jesting, nesting, questing, resting, testing, vesting, wresting.
Bedding, breading, dreading, heading, shedding, shredding, sledding, spreading, threading, treading, wedding.
[3] Affecting, bisecting, collecting, connecting, correcting, defecting, deflecting, detecting, directing, dissecting, ejecting, electing, erecting, expecting, infecting, injecting, inspecting, neglecting, objecting, perfecting, projecting, prospecting, protecting, reflecting, rejecting, respecting, selecting, subjecting, suspecting.
Arresting, attesting, contesting, detesting, digesting, divesting, infesting, ingesting, interesting, investing, manifesting, molesting, protesting, requesting, suggesting.
Abetting, banqueting, begetting, duetting, forgetting, pirouetting, regretting, resetting, silhouetting, upsetting.
[4] Disinfecting, disconnecting, disrespecting, interjecting, intersecting, misdirecting, recollecting, re-electing, resurrecting, self-respecting.

2.4.5 "--ecks" (as in "checks")
[1] checks, cheques, decks, flex, flecks, hex, necks, pecs, pecks, secs, sex, specs, specks, treks, vex, wrecks.
[2] annex, apex, complex, convex, crosscheck, Daleks, duplex, execs, index, perplex, rednecks, reflex, shipwrecks, soundchecks, spot-checks, vortex.

SURPRISING RHYMING:
[1] Next, sexed, sext, text, vexed.
Checked, decked, flecked, pecked, sect, specked, trekked, wrecked.
Bets, debts, frets, gets, jets, lets, nets, pets, sets, sweats, threats, vets, wets, whets.
Etch(ed), fetch(ed), ketch, lech, retch(ed), sketch(ed), stretch(ed), wretch.
Best, blessed, blest, breast, chest, crest, dressed, guest, guessed, jest, lest, messed, nest, pest, quest, rest, stressed, test, vest, west, wrest, zest.
[2] Annexed, context, indexed, oversexed, perplexed, pretext, subtext, teletext.
Burlesque, desk, grotesque, newsdesk, picturesque, statuesque.
Affects, aspects, bisects, collects, connects, corrects, defects, deflects, detects, dialects, directs, dissects, effects, ejects, elects, erects, expects, infects, injects, insects, inspects, neglects, objects, perfects, projects, prospects, protects, reflects, rejects, respects, sects, selects, subjects, suspects.
Assets, baguettes, banquets, begets, besets, brochettes, brunettes/brunets (U.S.), cadets, cassettes, coquettes, cornets, corvettes, croquettes, duets, filmsets, fishnets, forgets, gazettes, hairnets, handsets, headsets, inlets, nymphets, offsets, quartets, regrets, resets, rosettes, sunsets, toilettes, upsets, vignettes.
Abreast, addressed, armrest, arrest, attest, Beau Geste, behest, bequest, caressed, compressed, confessed, contest, conquest, depressed, detest, digest, digressed, distressed, divest, expressed, impressed, incest, infest, inquest, invest, Midwest, molest, northwest, oppressed, possessed, progressed, protest, recessed, repressed, request, southwest, suggest, suppressed, transgressed, undressed, unrest, well-dressed.
[3] Aftereffects, architects, dialects, disconnects, disrespects, intellects, interconnects, interjects, intersects, introspects, misdirects, recollects, reconnects, re-elects, resurrects.
Castanets, cigarettes, clarinets, epithets, marionettes, outlets, pirouettes, silhouettes, statuettes, suffragettes, usherettes.
Chimneybreast, dispossessed, effervesced, interest, overdressed, reassessed, repossessed, second-best, self-addressed, self-confessed, self-possessed, unimpressed.

2.4.6 "--ect" (as in "checked")
[1] checked, decked, flecked, necked, pecked, sect, specked, trekked, wrecked.
[2] abject, affect, aspect, bisect, bull-necked, collect, connect, correct, defect, deflect, deject, detect, dialect, direct, dissect, effect, eject, elect, erect, expect, henpecked,

infect, inflect, inject, insect, inspect, neglect, object, perfect, prefect, project, prospect, protect, reflect, reject, respect, select, subject, suspect, unchecked.
[3] aftereffect, architect, circumspect, dialect, disaffect, disinfect, disconnect, disrespect, incorrect, indirect, intellect, interconnect, interject, intersect, introspect, misdirect, recollect, re-elect, resurrect, retrospect, self-respect.

SURPRISING RHYMING:
[1] **Check**, cheque, deck, fleck, heck, neck, peck, sec, spec, speck, tech, trek, wreck.
Checks, decks, flecks, necks, pecks, sects, specks, treks, wrecks.
Crept, door-stepped, kept, leapt, prepped, repped, schlepped, sidestepped, slept, stepped, swept, wept.
Next, sexed, sext, text, vexed.
Best, blessed, blest, breast, chest, crest, dressed, guest, guessed, jest, lest, messed, nest, pest, quest, rest, stressed, test, vest, west, wrest, zest.
Bet, debt, fret, get, jet, let, met, net, pet, set, stet, sweat, threat, vet, wet, whet, yet.
[2] **Annexed**, context, indexed, oversexed, perplexed, pretext, subtext, teletext.
Burlesque, desk, grotesque, newsdesk, picturesque, statuesque.
Abject, affect, aspect, bisect, bull-necked, collect, connect, correct, defect, deflect, deject, detect, dialect, direct, dissect, effect, eject, elect, erect, expect, henpecked, infect, inflect, inject, insect, inspect, neglect, object, perfect, prefect, project, prospect, protect, reflect, reject, respect, select, subject, suspect, unchecked.
Abreast, addressed, armrest, arrest, attest, Beau Geste, behest, bequest, caressed, compressed, confessed, contest, conquest, depressed, detest, digest, digressed, distressed, divest, expressed, impressed, incest, infest, inquest, invest, Midwest, molest, northwest, oppressed, possessed, progressed, protest, recessed, repressed, request, southwest, suggest, suppressed, transgressed, undressed, unrest, well-dressed.

2.4.7 "--ects" (as in "reflects")
[2] affects, aspects, bisects, collects, connects, corrects, defects, deflects, detects, dialects, directs, dissects, effects, ejects, elects, erects, expects, infects, injects, insects, inspects, neglects, objects, perfects, projects, prospects, protects, reflects, rejects, respects, sects, selects, subjects, suspects.
[3] aftereffects, architects, dialects, disconnects, disrespects, intellects, interconnects, interjects, intersects, introspects, misdirects, recollects, reconnects, re-elects, resurrects.

SURPRISING RHYMING:
[1] **Checks**, cheques, decks, flex, flecks, hex, necks, pecs, pecks, secs, sex, specs, specks, treks, vex, wrecks.
Checked, decked, necked, pecked, sect, specked, trekked, wrecked.
Next, sexed, sext, text, vexed.
Etched, fetched, retched, sketched, stretched.
Best, blessed, breast, chest, crest, dressed, guest, guessed, jest, lest, messed, nest, pest, quest, rest, stressed, test, vest, west, zest.
Bets, debts, frets, gets, jets, lets, nets, pets, sets, sweats, threats, vets, wets, whets.
[2] **Annex**, apex, complex, Daleks, duplex, execs, index, perplex, rednecks, reflex, shipwrecks, soundchecks, spot-checks, vortex.
Annexed, context, indexed, oversexed, perplexed, pretext, subtext, teletext.
Burlesque, desk, grotesque, newsdesk, picturesque, statuesque.
Abreast, addressed, armrest, arrest, attest, Beau Geste, behest, bequest, caressed, compressed, contest, conquest, depressed, detest, digest, digressed, distressed, divest, expressed, impressed, incest, infest, ingest, inquest, invest, Midwest, molest, northwest, oppressed, possessed, progressed, protest, recessed, repressed, request, road-test, southwest, suggest, suppressed, transgressed, undressed, unrest, well-dressed.
Assets, baguettes, banquets, begets, brunettes/brunets (U.S.), cadets, cassettes, cornets, corvettes, dragnets, duets, filmsets, fishnets, forgets, handsets, headsets, inlets, nymphets, offsets, quartets, regrets, resets, rosettes, sunsets, upsets, vignettes.
[3] **Castanets**, cigarettes, clarinets, epithets, marionettes, outlets, pirouettes, silhouettes, statuettes, suffragettes, usherettes.
Chimneybreast, dispossessed, effervesced, interest, manifest, overdressed, reassessed, repossessed, second-best, self-confessed, self-possessed, unaddressed, unimpressed.

2.4.8 "--eckless" (as in "necklace")
[2] feckless, necklace, reckless.

SURPRISING RHYMING:
[1] **Best**, bless, chess, cress, dress, guess, less, mess, press, rest, stress, tress, yes.
[2] **Abbess**, abscess, access, address, assess, breathless, caress, careless, compress, confess, congress, depress, digress, distress, duchess, duress, egress, excess, express, finesse, headdress, helpless, impress, largesse, legless, nightdress, obsess, oppress, outguess, possess, process, profess, princess, progress, prowess, recess, redress, regress, repress, restless, success, suppress, transgress, undress, unless.
Accessed, addressed, assessed, blessed, caressed, confessed, depressed, digressed, distressed, impressed, obsessed, oppressed, outguessed, possessed, processed, professed, progressed, regressed, repressed, suppressed, transgressed, undressed.
Affects, aspects, bisects, breakfast, collects, connects, corrects, defects, deflects, detects, dialects, directs, dissects, effects, ejects, elects, erects, expects, infects, injects, insects, inspects, neglects, objects, perfects, projects, prospects, protects, reflects, rejects, respects, sects, selects, subjects, suspects.
Against, commenced, condensed, dispensed, incensed, licensed, ring-fenced, sensed, sentenced, sequenced, silenced.
Endless, famous, fellas, friendless, jealous, lettuce, Lexus, menace, nameless, precious, relentless, senseless, zealous.
Chalice, coppice, gratis, haggis, hospice, hubris, jaundice, justice, malice, Memphis, novice, office, palace, Paris, preface, purchase, service, solstice, surface.
[3] **Acquiesce**, baroness, battledress, coalesce, convalesce, dispossess, effervesce, manageress, minidress, murderess, nevertheless, nonetheless, overstress, phosphoresce, poetess, reassess, repossess, SOS, stewardess, tenderness.

2.4.9 "--ection" (as in "affection")
[3] affection, collection, complexion, confection, connection, correction, defection, deflection, dejection, detection, direction, dissection, ejection, election, erection, infection, inflection, injection, inspection, objection, perfection, projection, protection, reflection, rejection, section, selection.
[4] imperfection, insurrection, interjection, intersection, introspection, misdirection, predilection, recollection, re-election, resurrection, retrospection.

SURPRISING RHYMING:
[1] **Done**, fun, gun, hon', none, nun, one, pun, spun, run, sun, son, ton, stun, won.
[2] **Freshen**, mention, pension, session, tension.
Etching, fetching, fencing, retching, sensing, sketching, stretching, tensing.
Alleging, dredging, edging, hedging, pledging, sledging, wedging.
Begun, grandson, homespun, outdone, outrun, well-done.
[3] **Exemption**, pre-emption, redemption.
Abstention, attention, contention, convention, detention, dimension, extension, intention, invention, prevention, retention, suspension.
Conception, deception, exception, inception, objection, perception, reception.
Congestion, digestion, indigestion, ingestion, question, suggestion.
Aviation, citation, creation, donation, duration, elation, fixation, location, mutation, nation, notation, ovation, relation, rotation, station, taxation, vacation, vexation, vocation.
Aggression, concession, confession, depression, discretion, expression, impression, jam session, obsession, oppression, possession, procession, profession, progression, recession, regression, repression, succession, transgression.
Commencing, condensing, dispensing, incensing, licensing, ring-fencing, sentencing, sequencing, silencing.
[4] **Apprehension**, comprehension, condescension, contravention, hypertension, intervention, misapprehension.
Contraception, indiscretion, interception, misconception, repossession, self-expression.

2.4.10 "--ected" (as in "affected")
[3] affected, collected, connected, corrected, defected, deflected, dejected, detected,

directed, dissected, effected, ejected, elected, erected, expected, infected, inflected, injected, inspected, neglected, objected, perfected, projected, protected, reflected, rejected, respected, selected, subjected, suspected.
[4] interjected, misdirected, recollected, re-elected, resurrected.

SURPRISING RHYMING:
[2] **Betted**, fretted, headed, jetted, method, netted, petted, regretted, sweated, tepid, vetted, whetted, wretched.
Credit, edit, medic, readied, steadied.
Dented, rented, scented, tempted, vented.
Bended, blended, ended, friended, mended, tended, vended.
Belted, melted, pelted, smelted.
Bested, crested, jested, nested, rested, tested, vested.
Hectic, sceptic/skeptic (U.S.), pathetic.
Alleges, dredges, edges, hedges, ledges, pledges, sledges, wedges.
[3] **Collective**, connective, corrective, defective, detective, directive, effective, infective, objective, perceptive, perspective, prospective, protective, reflective, respective, retrospective, selective, subjective.
Accepted, arrested, attested, congested, contested, detested, digested, divested, infested, interested, invested, molested, protested, requested, suggested, unrested.
Abetted, banqueted, duetted, indebted, intrepid, pirouetted, regretted, silhouetted.
Augmented, cemented, commented, consented, contented, demented, dissented, fermented, fragmented, frequented, indented, invented, lamented, presented, prevented, relented, repented, resented, segmented, tormented, unrented, unscented.
Aesthetic/esthetic (U.S.), athletic, authentic, balletic, cosmetic, domestic, eclectic, electric, frenetic, genetic, kinetic, magnetic, majestic, pathetic, phonetic, poetic, prophetic, synthetic.
Addicted, afflicted, conflicted, constricted, convicted, depicted, evicted, inflicted, predicted, restricted.
Amended, appended, ascended, attended, befriended, commended, contended, defended, depended, descended, extended, intended, offended, pretended, rear-ended, suspended, transcended, upended.
[4] **Circumvented**, complemented, complimented, discontented, disoriented, experimented, implemented, misrepresented, oriented, represented, supplemented.
Alphabetic, apathetic, apologetic, anaesthetic/anesthetic (U.S.), apathetic, diabetic, energetic, sympathetic, telekinetic, theoretic.
Apprehended, comprehended, condescended, recommended.

2.4.11 "--ector" (as in "collector")
[2] hector, nectar, rector, sector, spectre/specter (U.S.), vector.
[3] collector, connector, corrector, defector, deflector, detector, director, ejector, elector, erector, inspector, objector, projector, prospector, protector, reflector, selector.

SURPRISING RHYMING:
[2] **Checker**, chequer, heckler, pecker, trekker, wrecker.
Etcher, fetcher, lecher, lecture, sketcher, stretcher.
Better, debtor, fetter, fretter, getter, letter, setter, sweater, wetter.
Fester, jester, nester, pester, quester, shelter, swelter, tester, vesta.
Blender, ember, ender, fender, gender, lender, member, mender, render, renter, sender, slender, spender, splendour/splendor (U.S.), temper, tempter, tender, vendor.
Leisure, measure, pleasure, pressure, treasure.
Feather, heather, leather, nether, tether, together, weather, whether.
Censor, centre/center (U.S.), denser, enter, fencer, Mensa, renter, sensor, tenser.
[3] **Bonesetter**, carburettor/carburetor (U.S.), forgetter, go-getter, jet-setter, love-letter, newsletter, operetta, pacesetter, red-letter, typesetter, unfetter, upsetter, vendetta.
Dissenter, epicentre/epicenter (U.S.), eventer, fermenter, frequenter, inventor, lamenter, magenta, presenter, preventer, re-enter, repenter, tormentor.
Ancestor, arrester, condenser, contester, dispenser, fiesta, investor, molester, polyester, protester, semester, sequester, siesta, sou'wester, trimester.
Double-decker, exchequer, woodpecker.

Endeavour/endeavor (U.S.), forever, however, never-never, whatever, whatsoever, whenever, wherever, whichever, whoever, whomever.
Aggressor, assessor, caresser, confessor, contessa, digresser, hairdresser, oppressor, possessor, predecessor, processor, professor, possessor, successor, transgressor.
December, dismember, remember, September, November.
Agenda, apprehender, attender, bartender, contender, defender, extender, hacienda, moneylender, offender, pretender, surrender, suspender, transgender, weekender.

2.4.12 "--ecting" (as in "affecting")

[3] affecting, bisecting, collecting, connecting, correcting, defecting, deflecting, detecting, directing, dissecting, effecting, ejecting, electing, erecting, expecting, infecting, injecting, inspecting, neglecting, objecting, perfecting, projecting, prospecting, protecting, reflecting, rejecting, respecting, selecting, subjecting, suspecting.
[4] disinfecting, disconnecting, disrespecting, interjecting, intersecting, misdirecting, recollecting, re-electing, resurrecting, self-respecting.

SURPRISING RHYMING:
[2] **Checking**, decking, flecking, necking, pecking, specking, trekking, wrecking.
Betting, fretting, heading, jetting, netting, petting, regretting, sweating, vetting, whetting.
Belting, denting, melting, pelting, renting, scenting, tempting, venting.
Bending, blending, ending, friending, mending, tending, vending.
Alleging, dredging, edging, hedging, pledging, sledging, wedging.
Cresting, guesting, jesting, nesting, questing, resting, testing, vesting, wresting.
Etching, fetching, retching, sketching, stretching.
[3] **Banqueting**, duetting, pirouetting, regretting, silhouetting.
Accepting, attempting, augmenting, cementing, commenting, consenting, dissenting, fermenting, fragmenting, frequenting, indenting, inventing, lamenting, presenting, preventing, relenting, repenting, resenting, segmenting, tormenting.
Amending, ascending, attending, befriending, commending, contending, defending, depending, descending, extending, intending, offending, pretending, suspending, transcending, upending.
Crosschecking, henpecking, sound-checking, spot-checking.
Arresting, attesting, contesting, detesting, digesting, divesting, infesting, ingesting, interesting, investing, manifesting, molesting, protesting, requesting, suggesting.
[4] **Circumventing**, complementing, complimenting, disorienting, experimenting, implementing, misrepresenting, orienting, representing, re-presenting, supplementing.
Apprehending, comprehending, condescending, recommending.

2.4.13 "--ective" (as in "reflective")

[3] collective, connective, corrective, defective, detective, directive, effective, elective, infective, invective, objective, perceptive, perspective, prospective, protective, reflective, respective, retrospective, selective, subjective.
[4] ineffective, introspective, irrespective, retrospective.

SURPRISING RHYMING:
[3] **Affected**, collected, connected, corrected, defected, deflected, dejected, detected, directed, dissected, effected, ejected, elected, erected, expected, infected, inflected, injected, inspected, neglected, objected, perfected, projected, protected, reflected, rejected, respected, selected, subjected, suspected.
Deceptive, defensive, expensive, extensive, incentive, intensive, offensive, pensive.
Aggressive, excessive, expressive, impressive, obsessive, oppressive, possessive, progressive, repressive, successive.
Accepted, arrested, attested, congested, contested, detested, digested, divested, infested, arrested, attested, congested, contested, detested, digested, divested, infested, interested, invested, molested, protested, requested, suggested, unrested.
Abetted, banqueted, duetted, indebted, intrepid, pirouetted, regretted, silhouetted.
Augmented, cemented, commented, consented, contented, demented, dissented, fermented, fragmented, frequented, indented, invented, lamented, presented, prevented, relented, repented, resented, segmented, tormented, unscented.

Amended, attended, befriended, commended, defended, depended, descended, extended, intended, offended, pretended, rear-ended, suspended, transcended, upended.
[4] Apprehensive, comprehensive, inexpensive.
Interjected, misdirected, recollected, re-elected, resurrected.
Circumvented, complemented, complimented, discontented, disoriented, experimented, implemented, misrepresented, oriented, represented, re-presented, supplemented.
Apprehended, comprehended, condescended, recommended.

2.4.14 "--ed" (as in "bed")
[1] bed, bled, bread, bred, cred, dead, dread, fed, fled, head, lead, led, Med, read, red, said, shed, shred, sled, sped, spread, stead, thread, tread, wed, zed.
[2] ahead, airbed, airhead, beachhead, bedhead, bedspread, bedstead, behead, bighead, blackhead, blockhead, bloodshed, bobsled, bonehead, breastfed, bridgehead, bulkhead, bullhead, co-ed, cowshed, crossbred, deadhead, deathbed, dickhead, drip-fed, drop dead, drumhead, egghead, embed, faded, farmstead, fathead, flatbed, forehead, highbred, homebred, homestead, hotbed, hothead, inbred, instead, lowbred, masthead, meathead, misled, misread, moped, outspread, pinhead, pothead, pre-med, purebred, railhead, redhead, retread, rested, re-wed, seabed, shortbread, sickbed, skinhead, sleepyhead, sofa-bed, sorehead, spearhead, spoon-fed, sunbed, sweetbread, thickhead, truebred, unfed, unread, unsaid, unwed, warhead, waterbed, watershed, well-fed, well-read, widespread, wingspread, woodshed.
[3] arrowhead, copperhead, dunderhead, figurehead, flowerbed, gingerbread, go-ahead, infrared, knucklehead, letterhead, loggerhead, newlywed, overfed, overhead, overspread, poppy head, riverbed, sleepyhead, thoroughbred, underfed, watershed.

SURPRISING RHYMING:
[1] Bet, debt, fret, get, jet, let, met, net, pet, set, sweat, threat, vet, wet, whet, yet.
Beg, begged, dreg, egg, egged, keg, leg, legged, peg, pegged.
Check, cheque, deck, fleck, heck, neck, peck, sec, spec, speck, tech, trek, wreck.
Pep, prep, rep, schlep, step, steppe, yep.
Bend, blend, den, end, fend, friend, glen, hen, lend, men, mend, pen, penned, send, spend, stemmed, ten, tend, then, trend, wend, when, wren, yen, Zen.
Dwelled, felled, gelled, held, jelled, knelled, meld, quelled, shelled, smelled, spelled, swelled, weld, yelled.
Aired, bared, blared, cared, chaired, dared, erred, faired, flared, glared, haired, laird, paired, pared, shared, snared, spared, squared, stared, there'd, where'd.
Assaulted, bolted, exalted, halted, malted, revolted, salted, vaulted.
[2] Asset, baguette, banquet, beget, beset, brunette/brunet (U.S.), cadet, cassette, coquette, cornet, corvette, dragnet, duet, filmset, fishnet, forget, gazette, handset, headset, in debt, inlet, inset, kismet, mindset, nymphet, octet, offset, onset, outset, quartet, quintet, regret, reset, rosette, roulette, sextet, sunset, toilette, upset, vignette.
Bootleg, clothes peg, dogleg, nutmeg, peg-leg, unpeg.
Breakneck, crew-neck, crosscheck, Dalek, exec, henpeck, high tech, raincheck, redneck, rollneck, roughneck, shipwreck, soundcheck, spot-check, sundeck, V-neck.
Doorstep, footstep, instep, misstep, one-step, quickstep, sidestep.
Amend, ascend, attend, befriend, best friend, bookend, boyfriend, commend, contend, defend, depend, descend, extend, girlfriend, godsend, intend, offend, old friend, overspend, penfriend, portend, pretend, suspend, tail end, transcend, upend, weekend.
Apprehend, comprehend, condemned, condescend, recommend.
Compelled, dispelled, excelled, expelled, impelled, misspelled, propelled, rebelled, repelled, self-propelled, upheld, unparalleled, withheld.
Alleged, dredged, edged, fully-fledged, hedged, ledged, pledged, sledged, wedged.
Compared, declared, despaired, ensnared, impaired, prepared, repaired, shorthaired.
Bended, blended, dented, ended, friended, mended, rented, scented, tended, vented.
Admen, again, amen, bagmen, Big Ben, bitten, broken, burden, cavemen, chosen, conmen, firemen, frontmen, frozen, glisten, he-men, hidden, hitmen, horsemen, jazzmen, lawmen, listen, mailmen, milkmen, newsmen, ocean, oilmen, open, playpen, ragmen, risen, shaken, showmen, snowmen, spoken, strongmen, stuntmen, taken, taxmen, wingmen, woven.

[3] Affected, collected, connected, corrected, defected, deflected, dejected, detected, directed, dissected, effected, ejected, elected, erected, expected, infected, inflected, injected, inspected, neglected, objected, perfected, projected, protected, reflected, rejected, respected, selected, subjected, suspected.
Amended, ascended, attended, befriended, commended, contended, defended, depended, descended, extended, intended, offended, pretended, rear-ended, suspended, transcended, upended.
Augmented, cemented, commented, consented, contented, demented, dissented, fermented, fragmented, frequented, invented, lamented, presented, prevented, relented, repented, resented, segmented, tormented, unscented.
Alphabet, castanet, cigarette, clarinet, epithet, etiquette, internet, launderette, maisonette, marionette, minuet, outlet, pirouette, silhouette, statuette, suffragette.

2.4.15 "--edge" (as in "ledge")
allege, dredge, edge, fledge, hedge, ledge, pledge, sledge, veg, wedge.

SURPRISING RHYMING:
[1] Alleged, dredged, edged, fully-fledged, hedged, ledged, pledged, sledged, wedged.
Beds, heads, sheds, shreds, sleds, spreads, threads, treads, weds.
Etch(ed), fetch(ed), ketch, lech, retch(ed), sketch(ed), stretch(ed), wretch.
Bench, clench, drench, quench, stench, trench, wench, wrench.
Dense, fence, hence, pence, sense, tense, thence, whence.
Best, blessed, breast, chest, crest, dressed, guest, guessed, jest, lest, messed, nest, pest, quest, rest, stressed, test, vest, west.
[2] Airbeds, airheads, beachheads, bedheads, bedspreads, bedsteads, beheads, blackheads, blockheads, boneheads, bridgeheads, bulkheads, cowsheds, deadheads, dickheads, eggheads, fatheads, foreheads, homesteads, hotbeds, hotheads, mopeds, pinheads, potheads, redheads, skinheads, sofa-beds, spearheads, sunbeds, warheads.
Backbench, entrench, frontbench, unclench, workbench.
Against, commenced, condensed, dispensed, experienced, fenced, incensed, inconvenienced, inexperienced, influenced, licensed, recommenced, recompensed, referenced, sensed, sentenced, sequenced, silenced.

2.4.16 "--edged" (as in "pledged")
alleged, dredged, edged, fully-fledged, hedged, ledged, pledged, sledged, wedged.

SURPRISING RHYMING:
[1] Allege, dredge, edge, fledge, hedge, ledge, pledge, sledge, veg, wedge.
Dense, fence, hence, pence, sense, tense, thence, whence.
Etched, fetched, retched, sketched, stretched.
Benched, clenched, drenched, entrenched, quenched, wrenched.
Belt, Celt, dealt, dwelt, felt, heartfelt, knelt, melt, pelt, smelt, spelt, svelte, welt.
[2] Amend, ascend, attend, befriend, best friend, bookend, boyfriend, commend, contend, defend, depend, descend, extend, girlfriend, godsend, intend, offend, old friend, overspend, penfriend, pretend, suspend, tail end, transcend, upend, weekend.
Absence, commence, condense, conscience, credence, defence/defense (U.S.), dispense, essence, expense, immense, incense, intense, licence/license (U.S.), nonsense, offence/offense (U.S.), patience, presence, pretence/pretense (U.S.), prudence, ring-fence, science, sentence, sequence, silence, sixpence, suspense.
Against, commenced, condensed, dispensed, fenced, incensed, licensed, sensed, sentenced, sequenced, silenced.
Attempt, contempt, dreamt, exempt, tempt, pre-empt, unkempt.

2.4.17 "--edded" (as in "threaded")
[2] bedded, breaded, dreaded, headed, leaded, shredded, sledded, threaded, treaded, wedded.
[3] bareheaded, beheaded, bigheaded, bullheaded, cool headed, embedded, flat-headed, hardheaded, hotheaded, imbedded,
lightheaded, pigheaded, redheaded, retreaded, spearheaded,

SURPRISING RHYMING:
[2] **Betted**, fetid, fretted, headed, jetted, method, netted, petted, regretted, sweated, tepid, vetted, whetted.
Credit, edit, medic, readied, steadied.
Dented, rented, scented, vented.
Bended, blended, ended, friended, mended, tended, vended.
Belted, melted, pelted, smelted.
Bested, crested, jested, nested, rested, tested, vested.
[3] **Abetted**, banqueted, duetted, indebted, intrepid, pirouetted, regretted, silhouetted.
Accredit, discredit, paramedic.
Augmented, cemented, commented, consented, contented, demented, dissented, fermented, fragmented, frequented, indented, invented, lamented, presented, prevented, relented, repented, resented, segmented, tormented, unrented, unscented.
Amended, appended, ascended, attended, befriended, commended, contended, defended, depended, descended, extended, intended, offended, pretended, rear-ended, suspended, transcended, upended.
Affected, collected, connected, corrected, defected, deflected, dejected, detected, directed, dissected, effected, ejected, elected, erected, expected, infected, inflected, injected, inspected, neglected, objected, perfected, projected, protected, reflected, rejected, respected, selected, subjected, suspected.
Arrested, attested, congested, contested, detested, digested, divested, infested, ingested, invested, molested, protested, requested, road-tested, suggested, unrested.
[4] **Circumvented**, complemented, complimented, discontented, disoriented, experimented, implemented, misrepresented, oriented, regimented, represented, re-presented, supplemented.
Apprehended, comprehended, condescended, recommended.
Double-breasted, interested, manifested.

2.4.18 "--edder" (as in "shredder")
cheddar, deader, header, homesteader, redder, shedder, shredder, spreader, threader.

SURPRISING RHYMING:
[2] **Clever**, ever, never, sever.
Better, debtor, fetter, fretter, getter, letter, setter, sweater, wetter.
Feather, heather, leather, nether, tether, together, untether, weather, whether.
Cellar, dweller, fella, feller, seller, smeller, speller, stellar, teller, yeller.
Dresser, guesser, lesser, presser, yessir.
Leisure, measure, pleasure, treasure.
[3] **Endeavour/endeavor** (U.S.), forever, however, never-never, whatever, whatsoever, whenever, wherever, whichever, whoever, whomever.
Bonesetter, carburettor/carburetor (U.S.), forgetter, go-getter, jet-setter, love-letter, newsletter, operetta, pacesetter, red-letter, typesetter, unfetter, upsetter, vendetta.
Bestseller, cave dweller, exceller, expeller, novella, paella, propeller, repeller, umbrella.
Displeasure, made-to-measure.
Aggressor, assessor, caresser, confessor, contessa, digresser, hairdresser, oppressor, possessor, predecessor, processor, professor, possessor, successor, transgressor.

2.4.19 "--edding" (as in "wedding")
[2] bedding, breading, dreading, heading, shedding, shredding, sledding, spreading, threading, treading, wedding.
[3] embedding, homesteading, letterheading, retreading, spearheading.

SURPRISING RHYMING:
[2] **Begging**, bootlegging, egging, legging, pegging.
Betting, fretting, getting, jetting, letting, petting, setting, sweating, vetting, wetting.
Blessing, dressing, guessing, messing, pressing, stressing, yessing.
Checking, decking, flecking, pecking, specking, trekking, wrecking.
Bending, blending, ending, fending, lending, mending, pending, sending, spending, tending, trending, vending, wending.
Pepping, prepping, schlepping, stepping.

[3] Banqueting, duetting, forgetting, pirouetting, regretting, silhouetting, upsetting.
Accessing, addressing, assessing, caressing, confessing, depressing, digressing, distressing, expressing, impressing, obsessing, oppressing, possessing, processing, professing, progressing, regressing, suppressing, transgressing, undressing.
Crosschecking, henpecking, rubbernecking, sound-checking, spot-checking.
Amending, ascending, attending, befriending, commending, contending, defending, depending, descending, extending, impending, intending, misspending, offending, overspending, pretending, suspending, transcending, unbending, upending.
[4] Acquiescing, convalescing, dispossessing, effervescing, reassessing, repossessing.
Apprehending, comprehending, condescending, recommending.

2.4.20 "--eddly" (as in "medley")
[2] deadly, medley.

SURPRISING RHYMING:
[2] **Envy**, friendly, gently, healthy, pebbly, stealthy, wealthy.
Belly, deli, edgy, jelly, smelly, tele, telly, veggie.
Bevvy, Chevy, heavy, levee, top-heavy.
Berry, bury, chérie, cherry, ferry, imaginary, merry, sherry, very.
[3] **Readily**, steadily, unreadily, unsteadily.
Already, heady, ready, steady, steady-eddy, teddy,
Brevity, confetti, jetty, levity, libretti, longevity, petty, spaghetti, sweaty.

2.4.21 "--eddline" (as in "headline")
[2] breadline, deadline, headline, redline.

SURPRISING RHYMING:
[1] **Brine**, cryin', fine, line, mine, nine, pine, shine, shrine, sign, spine, stein, swine, tine, twine, vine, whine, wine.
Chime, climb, clime, crime, dime, grime, I'm, lime, mime, prime, rhyme, rime, slime, sublime, thyme, time.
Bind, blind, find, fined, grind, hind, kind, lined, mind, mined, pined, rind, signed, whined, wined.
[2] **Airline**, align, alpine, assign, bassline, benign, bovine, canine, carbine, combine, confine, consign, decline, define, design, divine, enshrine, entwine, feline, gang-sign, goldmine, hairline, helpline, hemline, incline, lifeline, malign, moonshine, outshine, recline, refine, resign, skyline, sunshine, turbine, waistline.
Bedtime, daytime, hard time(s), lifetime, maritime, meantime, nighttime, noontime, overtime, pantomime, pastime, playtime, sometime(s), springtime, sublime, summertime.
Aligned, behind, combined, consigned, cosigned, declined, defined, designed, divined, entwined, free mind, inclined, maligned, mankind, reclined, refined, remind, resigned, rewind, snow-blind, strong mind, unkind, unlined, untwined, unwind, weak mind.
[3] **Alkaline**, auld lang syne, borderline, calamine, concubine, countersign, denying, intertwine, porcupine, realign, storyline, undefine(d), underline, undermine, valentine.
Colour blind/color blind (U.S.), intertwined, mastermind, redesigned, undefined, underlined, womankind.

2.4.22 "--eddlock" (as in "deadlock")
[2] deadlock, dreadlock, headlock, wedlock.

SURPRISING RHYMING:
[1] **Bloc**, block, chock, clock, crock, doc, dock, flock, hock, jock, knock, lock, mock, rock, schlock, shock, smock, sock, stock, wok.
Blot, cot, dot, got, hot, jot, knot, lot, not, plot, pot, rot, shot, slot, spot, squat, swat, swot, tot, trot, watt, what, yacht.
Bop, chop, cop, crop, drop, flop, hop, mop, pop, prop, shop, slop, stop, swap, top.
Box, cox, fox, ox, pox, socks, stocks.
Cough, doff, off, standoff, trough.
Clog, cog, dog, fog, frog, grog, hog, jog, log, slog, smog.

[2] Ad hoc, amok, armlock, Bangkok, baroque, bedrock, deadlock, defrock, epoch, gridlock, Hitchcock, laughing stock, o'clock, padlock, roadblock, shamrock, shell shock, shylock, sunblock, tick-tock, unlock, Van Gogh, warlock, wedlock, windsock, Woodstock.
Abbot, cannot, earshot, forgot, gunshot, red-hot, robot, snapshot, upshot, whatnot.
Desktop, dewdrop, eavesdrop, flip-flop, lollipop, nonstop, pawnshop, raindrop, soda pop, teardrop, tip-top, whistle-stop, workshop.
Bandbox, brainbox, detox, dreadlocks, gearbox, hatbox, icebox, jukebox, mailbox, matchbox, outfox, paintbox, pillbox, shoebox, soapbox, squeezebox, strongbox, toolbox.
Backlog, bulldog, bullfrog, hedgehog, watchdog.
[3] Aftershock, belle époque, chock-a-block, interlock, laughing stock, stumbling block.
Apricot, coffeepot, coffee-shop, counterplot, flowerpot, juggernaut, overshot, patriot.
Chatterbox, chickenpox, equinox, Goldilocks, letter box, orthodox, paradox, smallpox.
Catalogue, dialogue, monologue, prairie dog, synagogue, underdog.

2.4.23 "--edges" (as in "pledges")
[2] alleges, dredges, edges, fledges, hedges, ledges, pledges, sledges, wedges.

SURPRISING RHYMING:
[2] Etches, fetches, ketches, retches, sketches, stretches, wretches.
Benches, clenches, drenches, fences, quenches, senses trenches, wenches, wrenches.
Ages, cages, gauges, pages, rages, sages, stages, wages.
Bridges, fridges, midges, ridges.
Blesses, dresses, guesses, presses, stresses, tresses, yeses.
Engines, legends, lenses, precious, veggies, wages.
[3] Abridges, cabbages, dosages, hostages, languages, leakages, messages, packages, sausages, shortage, voyages.
Absences, commences, condenses, consciences, defences/defenses (U.S.), essences, expenses, licences/licenses (U.S.), offences/offenses (U.S.), pretences/pretenses (U.S.), sentences, sequences.
Addresses, assesses, caresses, confesses, digresses, distresses, excesses, expresses, finesses, impresses, obsesses, oppresses, possesses, princesses, processes, professes, progresses, recesses, regresses, represses, successes, suppresses, undresses.
Collective, corrective, defective, detective, directive, effective, infective, objective, perceptive, perspective, prospective, protective, reflective, respective, retrospective, selective, subjective.

2.4.24 "--edging" (as in "hedging")
[2] alleging, dredging, edging, fledging, hedging, pledging, sledging, wedging.

SURPRISING RHYMING:
[2] Etching, fetching, retching, sketching, stretching.
Benching, clenching, drenching, fencing, quenching, sensing, tensing, wrenching.
Ageing, caging, gauging, paging, raging, staging, waging.
Blessing, dressing, freshen, guessing, messing, pressing, session, stressing, yessing.
Bridging, engine, legend.
[3] Commencing, condensing, dispensing, incensing, licensing, ring-fencing, sentencing, sequencing, silencing.
Accessing, addressing, assessing, caressing, confessing, depressing, digressing, distressing, expressing, impressing, obsessing, oppressing, possessing, processing, progressing, refreshing, regressing, repressing, suppressing, transgressing, undressing.
Abridging, engaging, enraging, messaging, packaging, rampaging.
Annexing, indexing, perplexing, sexting, texting.
Affecting, collecting, connecting, correcting, defecting, deflecting, detecting, directing, dissecting, effecting, ejecting, electing, erecting, expecting, infecting, injecting, inspecting, neglecting, objecting, perfecting, projecting, prospecting, protecting, reflecting, rejecting, respecting, selecting, subjecting, suspecting.
Arresting, contesting, detesting, digesting, divesting, infesting, interesting, investing, manifesting, molesting, protesting, requesting, road-testing, suggesting.

*

2.4.25 "--edible" (as in "edible")
[3] credible, edible, incredible, inedible, spreadable.

SURPRISING RHYMING:
[3] **Chemical**, ethical, festival, medical, pedestal, sensual, sentinel, skeletal, sceptical/skeptical (U.S.), spectacle, tentacle.
Flexible, legible, preferable, sensible, terrible, vegetable.
Bendable, blendable, endable, lendable, mendable, sendable, spendable, unbendable.
Bearable, comparable, repairable, shareable, tearable, unbearable, untearable, wearable.
[4] **Accessible**, commendable, defendable, defensible, dependable, digestible, expendable, impeccable, inflexible, ostensible, recommendable, respectable, suggestible.
Available, eligible, illegible, ineligible, indelible, insatiable, intelligible, negligible, sensational, unassailable, unavailable, unwearable.
[5] **Apprehensible**, comprehensible, inaccessible, indefensible, indispensable, irrepressible, irresistible, reprehensible, unacceptable, unconventional, unforgettable, unintentional, unprofessional.

2.4.26 "--edicate" (as in "dedicate")
[3] dedicate, medicate, predicate.

SURPRISING RHYMING:
[3+] **Authenticate**, communicate, complicate, confiscate, duplicate, educate, extricate, fabricate, implicate, indicate, replicate, syndicate, vindicate.
Candidate, consolidate, intimidate, sedate, validate, aggregate, congregate, delegate, interrogate, investigate, litigate, relegate, segregate.
Annihilate, calculate, circulate, congratulate, emulate, escalate, formulate, isolate, regulate, relate, simulate, speculate, stimulate, stipulate, titillate, ventilate, violate.
Animate, decimate, estimate, guesstimate, intimate, legitimate, underestimate.
Alienate, alternate, contaminate, detonate, discriminate, dominate, eliminate, emanate, exterminate, fascinate, hallucinate, hibernate, illuminate, impersonate, incriminate, originate, pollinate, rejuvenate, resonate, terminate, vaccinate.
Anticipate, dissipate, emancipate, participate.
Accelerate, accommodate, alienate, alleviate, anticipate, associate, authenticate, certificate, collaborate, communicate, concentrate, congratulate, contaminate, cooperate, corroborate, deteriorate, elaborate, eradicate, evaporate, exaggerate, exasperate, exonerate, hallucinate, humiliate, impersonate, infuriate, intimidate, invigorate, investigate, negotiate, participate, recuperate, refrigerate, reverberate.
Agitate, gravitate, hesitate, imitate, irritate, levitate, meditate, necessitate, resuscitate.
Activate, aggravate, captivate, cultivate, elevate, excavate, innovate, motivate, reactivate, renovate, salivate.
Compensate, overweight, paperweight.

2.4.27 "--eddily" (as in "readily")
[3] readily, steadily, unreadily, unsteadily.

SURPRISING RHYMING:
[3] **Breathlessly**, endlessly, helplessly, recklessly, relentlessly, restlessly.
Credibly, desperately, easily, flexibly, heavenly, heavily, merrily, messily, pleasantly, preferably, presently, prettily, secondly, sensibly, sketchily, splendidly, terribly.
Beggingly, caressingly, compellingly, depressingly, despairingly, distressingly, tellingly.
Carefully, dreadfully, fretfully, generally, helpfully, mentally, regretfully, respectfully, revelry, separately, successfully.
Jealousy, jealously, preciously, rebelliously, zealously.
Chemistry, devilry, every, feathery, leathery, pedigree, remedy.
Brevity, clarity, confetti, density, deputy, entity, equity, levity, libretti, penalty, seventy, spaghetti, specialty, velvety.
Clemency, ecstasy, embassy, legacy, pregnancy, tenancy, tendency.
Destiny, ebony, empathy, enemy, felony, melody, sesame, recipe, telepathy, therapy.
[4] **Especially**, essentially, eventually, exceptionally, potentially, professionally, specially.

Acceptably, accessibly, allegedly, contentedly, expectantly, impeccably, incessantly, incredibly, indelibly, intrepidly, irreverently, lamentably, ostensibly, perceptibly, primarily, progressively, regrettably, respectably, tremendously, unpleasantly, unsuccessfully.
Complexity, extremity, fidelity, heredity, indemnity, identity, integrity, intensity, longevity, necessity, nonentity, serenity, solemnity.
Ascendancy, dependency, discrepancy, expectancy, supremacy.
[5] Accidentally, confidentially, consequentially, conscientiously, disrespectfully, fundamentally, incidentally, influentially, instrumentally, monumentally, reverentially, sentimentally, temperamentally, transcendentally, unconventionally, unintentionally.
Independently, high fidelity, infidelity, necessarily, ordinarily, temporarily, unacceptably.

2.4.28 "--eff" (as in "chef")
[1] chef, clef, deaf, ref.
[2] tone-deaf, UNICEF.

SURPRISING RHYMING:
[1] Breath, death, eightieth, fiftieth, fortieth, ninetieth, seventieth, sixtieth, thirtieth, twentieth.
Bereft, cleft, clef, deft, elf, heft, left, self, shelf, theft.
Pep, prep, rep, schlep, step, steppe, yep.
Bet, debt, fret, get, jet, let, met, net, pet, set, stet, sweat, threat, vet, wet, whet, yet.
Bless, dress, guess, mess, press, stress, tress, yes.
[2] Bookshelf, herself, himself, itself, mantelshelf, myself, oneself, yourself.
Address, assess, caress, confess, digress, distress, excess, express, finesse, impress, obsess, oppress, possess, princess, process, profess, progress, recess, redress, regress, success, suppress, transgress, undress.
Doorstep, footstep, instep, misstep, one-step, quickstep, sidestep.
Asset, baguette, banquet, beget, beset, brunette/brunet (U.S.), cadet, cassette, coquette, cornet, corvette, dragnet, duet, filmset, fishnet, forget, gazette, hairnet, handset, headset, indebt, inlet, inset, kismet, mindset, nymphet, octet, offset, onset, outset, pre-set, quartet, quintet, regret, reset, rosette, roulette, sextet, sublet, sunset, thickset, toilette, typeset, upset, vignette.
[3] Alphabet, cigarette, clarinet, epithet, etiquette, heavy-set, internet, intranet, launderette, maisonette, minuet, outlet, pirouette, silhouette, statuette, suffragette.

2.4.29 "--efference" (as in "preference")
[3] deference, preference, reference.

SURPRISING RHYMING:
[2] Absence, commence, condense, conscience, credence, defence/defense (U.S.), dispense, essence, expense, immense, incense, intense, licence/license (U.S.), nonsense, offence/offense (U.S.), patience, presence, pretence/pretense (U.S.), prudence, ring-fence, science, sentence, sequence, silence, suspense, vengeance.
Against, commenced, condensed, dispensed, incensed, licensed, ring-fenced, sensed, sentenced, sequenced, silenced.
[3] Beverage, leverage.
Abstinence, affluence, ambience, audience, coherence, commonsense, competence, condolence, conference, confidence, consequence, dependence, eloquence, emergence, eminence, evidence, excellence, existence, fraudulence, impatience, impudence, impotence, indolence, influence, innocence, insistence, insolence, insurgence, leniency, negligence, occurrence, opulence, penitence, permanence, persistence, prescience, prevalence, prominence, providence, radiance, recommence, recompense, recurrence, residence, resurgence, reticence, reverence, self-defence/self-defense (U.S.), severance, subsistence, succulence, temperance, transcendence, transience, turbulence, violence.
Influenced, recommenced, recompensed, referenced.
Adventurous, effortless, Everest, generous, lecherous, treacherous, venturous.
[4] Acquiescence, adolescence, ambivalence, belligerence, benevolence, coincidence, convenience, correspondence, deliverance, disobedience, ebullience, effervescence, experience, inconvenience, independence, indifference, inexperience, intelligence,

interference, iridescence, irreverence, magnificence, malevolence, obedience, reminiscence, resilience, self-confidence, translucence.
Experienced, inconvenienced, inexperienced.

2.4.30 "--egg" (as in "beg")
[1] beg, dreg, egg, keg, leg, peg.
[2] bootleg, clothes peg, dogleg, nutmeg, peg-leg, unpeg.

SURPRISING RHYMING:
[1] **Bed**, bled, bread, bred, cred, dead, dread, fed, fled, head, lead, led, Med, read, red, said, shed, shred, sled, sped, spread, stead, thread, tread, wed, zed.
Bet, debt, fret, get, jet, let, met, net, pet, set, stet, sweat, threat, vet, wet, whet, yet.
Check, cheque, deck, fleck, heck, neck, peck, sec, spec, speck, tech, trek, wreck.
Pep, prep, rep, schlep, step, steppe, yep.
[2] **Ahead**, airhead, bighead, blockhead, bloodshed, bobsled, bonehead, co-ed, deadhead, deathbed, dickhead, drop dead, forehead, highbred, homebred, homestead, hotbed, hothead, instead, misled, pinhead, pothead, purebred, redhead, sickbed, skinhead, sleepyhead, sofa-bed, sorehead, spearhead, spoon-fed, sunbed, thickhead, unsaid, warhead, waterbed, watershed, well-fed, well-read, widespread.
Asset, baguette, banquet, brunette/brunet (U.S.), cadet, cassette, coquette, cornet, corvette, dragnet, duet, filmset, fishnet, forget, gazette, handset, headset, in debt, inlet, inset, kismet, mindset, nymphet, octet, offset, onset, outset, quartet, quintet, regret, reset, rosette, roulette, sextet, sunset, upset, vignette.
Breakneck, crew-neck, crosscheck, Dalek, high tech, raincheck, redneck, rollneck, roughneck, shipwreck, soundcheck, spot-check, sundeck, swan-neck, V-neck.
Doorstep, footstep, instep, misstep, one-step, quickstep, sidestep.

2.4.31 "--egging" (as in "begging")
[2] begging, bootlegging, egging, legging, pegging.

SURPRISING RHYMING:
[2] **Bedding**, dreading, heading, shedding, shredding, sledding, spreading, threading, treading, wedding.
Betting, fretting, getting, jetting, letting, netting, petting, setting, sweating, vetting, wetting, whetting.
Blessing, dressing, guessing, messing, pressing, stressing, yessing.
Checking, decking, flecking, pecking, specking, trekking, wrecking.
Bending, blending, ending, fending, lending, mending, pending, sending, spending, tending, trending, vending, wending.
Dwelling, felling, gelling, jelling, knelling, quelling, selling, shelling, smelling, spelling, swelling, telling, yelling.
[3] **Embedding**, homesteading, letterheading, spearheading.
Abetting, banqueting, duetting, forgetting, pirouetting, regretting, resetting, upsetting.
Accessing, addressing, assessing, caressing, confessing, depressing, digressing, distressing, expressing, impressing, obsessing, oppressing, possessing, professing, progressing, regressing, suppressing, transgressing, undressing.
Crosschecking, henpecking, rubbernecking, sound-checking, spot-checking.
Amending, ascending, attending, befriending, commending, contending, defending, depending, descending, extending, impending, intending, offending, overspending, pretending, suspending, transcending, unbending, upending.
Compelling, dispelling, excelling, expelling, foretelling, fortune-telling, misspelling, outselling, propelling, rebelling, repelling, re-telling.
Affecting, bisecting, collecting, connecting, correcting, defecting, deflecting, detecting, directing, dissecting, effecting, ejecting, electing, erecting, expecting, infecting, injecting, inspecting, neglecting, objecting, perfecting, projecting, prospecting, protecting, reflecting, rejecting, respecting, selecting, subjecting, suspecting.
[4] **Acquiescing**, convalescing, dispossessing, effervescing, reassessing, repossessing.
Apprehending, comprehending, condescending, recommending.
Disinfecting, disconnecting, disrespecting, recollecting, resurrecting, self-respecting.

2.4.32 "--ell" (as in "tell")
[1] bell, belle, cell, dell, dwell, el, fell, gel, hell, jell, knell, quell, sell, shell, smell, spell, swell, tell, well, yell.
[2] befell, bluebell, bombshell, cartel, Chanel, compel, cowbell, dispel, doorbell, dumbbell, eggshell, excel, expel, farewell, foretell, gazelle, groundswell, handbell, hotel, impel, inkwell, lapel, misspell, motel, noel, nutshell, outsell, propel, rebel, repel, resell, seashell, stairwell, unwell.
[3] bagatelle, caramel, caravel, carousel, citadel, clientele, cockleshell, decibel, infidel, Jezebel, muscatel, ne're-do-well, oversell, parallel, personnel, pimpernel, show-and-tell, undersell, wishing well.
[4] au naturel, crime passionnel, mademoiselle, maître d'hôtel.

SURPRISING RHYMING:
[1] **Dwelled**, felled, gelled/jelled, held, quelled, shelled, smelled, spelled, swelled, yelled.
Delve, elf, health, self, shelf, shelve, stealth, twelfth, twelve, wealth.
[2] **Beheld**, compelled, dispelled, excelled, expelled, impelled, propelled, rebelled, repelled, upheld, unparalleled, withheld.
Bookshelf, herself, himself, itself, myself, oneself, yourself.

2.4.33 "--eld" (as in "held")
[1] dwelled, felled, gelled, held, jelled, knelled, meld, quelled, shelled, smelled, spelled, swelled, weld, yelled.
[2] beheld, compelled, dispelled, excelled, expelled, impelled, misspelled, propelled, rebelled, repelled, self-propelled, upheld, unparalleled, withheld.

SURPRISING RHYMING:
[1] **Bell**, belle, belt, cell, dealt, dell, dwell, dwelt, fell, felt, gel, hell, jell, knell, knelt, melt, pelt, quell, sell, shell, smell, spell, spelt, swell, tell, well, yell.
Elm, helm, overwhelm, realm, underwhelm, whelm.
Delve, elf, health, self, shelf, shelve, stealth, twelfth, twelve, wealth.
[2] **Befell**, bluebell, bombshell, cartel, Chanel, compel, dispel, doorbell, dumbbell, eggshell, excel, expel, farewell, foretell, gazelle, groundswell, hotel, impel, inkwell, lapel, misspell, motel, noel, nutshell, propel, rebel, repel, resell, seashell, unwell.
Heartfelt, seat belt, lifebelt, sunbelt.
[3] **Bagatelle**, caramel, carousel, citadel, clientele, cockleshell, decibel, infidel, Jezebel, ne're-do-well, oversell, parallel, personnel, pimpernel, show-and-tell, wishing well.
[4] **Au naturel**, crime passionnel, mademoiselle, maître d'hôtel.

2.4.34 "--elf" (as in "self")
[1] elf, self, shelf.
[2] bookshelf, herself, himself, itself, mantelshelf, myself, oneself, yourself.

SURPRISING RHYMING:
[1] **Delve**, shelve, twelve.
Breath, chef, clef, deaf, death, else, health, stealth, twelfth, wealth.
Bell, belle, cell, dell, dwell, el, fell, gel, hell, jell, knell, quell, sell, shell, smell, spell, swell, tell, well, yell.
Belt, Celt, dealt, dwelt, felt, heartfelt, help, knelt, melt, pelt, spelt, svelte.
[2] **Befell**, bluebell, bombshell, cartel, Chanel, compel, dispel, doorbell, dumbbell, eggshell, excel, expel, farewell, foretell, gazelle, groundswell, hotel, impel, inkwell, lapel, misspell, motel, noel, nutshell, propel, rebel, repel, resell, seashell, unwell.
[3] **Bagatelle**, caramel, carousel, citadel, clientele, cockleshell, decibel, infidel, Jezebel, ne're-do-well, oversell, parallel, personnel, pimpernel, show-and-tell, wishing well.

2.4.35 "--elm" (as in "realm")
elm, helm, overwhelm, realm, underwhelm, whelm.

SURPRISING RHYMING:
[1] **Crème**, 'em, gem, hem, phlegm, REM, stem, them.

Den, fen, glen, hen, men, pen, ten, then, when, wren, yen, Zen.
Bend, blend, end, fend, friend, lend, mend, penned, send, spend, tend, trend, vend.
[2] Ahem, condemn, crème de la crème, item, mayhem, modem, pro tem, requiem.
Attempt, contempt, dreamt, exempt, tempt, pre-empt, unkempt.
Again, amen, bagmen, Big Ben, bullpen, bushmen, cavemen, cayenne, conmen, crème-de-la- crème, firemen, frontmen, he-men, hitmen, horsemen, jazzmen, lawmen, linkmen, mailmen, milkmen, newsmen, Norsemen, oilmen, pigpen, playpen, ragmen, showmen, snowmen, strongmen, stuntmen, swagmen, taken, taxmen, wingmen.

2.4.36 "--elp" (as in "help")
[1] help, kelp, whelp, yelp.

SURPRISING RHYMING:
[1] Belt, Celt, dealt, dwelt, felt, knelt, melt, pelt, smelt, spelt, svelte, welt.
Bell, belle, cell, dell, dwell, el, fell, gel, hell, jell, knell, quell, sell, shell, smell, spell, swell, tell, well, yell.
Elf, health, self, shelf, shelve, stealth, twelfth, twelve, wealth.
Pep, prep, rep, schlep, step, steppe, yep.
Crept, kept, leapt, prepped, slept, stepped, swept, wept.
[2] Heartfelt, seat belt, lifebelt, sunbelt.
Bookshelf, herself, himself, itself, myself, oneself, yourself.
Accept, adept, concept, except, inept, intercept, overslept, over-stepped, rainswept, side-stepped, unswept, windswept.

2.4.37 "--elt" (as in "belt")
[1] belt, Celt, dealt, dwelt, felt, knelt, melt, pelt, smelt, spelt, svelte, welt.
[2] fan-belt, heartfelt, seat belt, lifebelt, sunbelt.

SURPRISING RHYMING:
[1] Help, kelp, whelp, yelp.
Health, stealth, twelfth, wealth.
Crept, kept, leapt, prepped, slept, stepped, swept, wept.
Checked, decked, flecked, pecked, sect, specked, trekked, wrecked.
Bent, cent, dent, gent, leant, lent, meant, rent, scent, sent, spent, tent, vent, went.
[2] Attempt, contempt, dreamt, exempt, tempt, pre-empt, unkempt.
Accept, adept, concept, except, inept, intercept, overslept, over-stepped, rainswept, side-stepped, unswept, windswept.
Affect, aspect, collect, connect, correct, defect, deflect, detect, dialect, direct, dissect, effect, eject, elect, erect, expect, henpecked, infect, inject, insect, inspect, neglect, object, perfect, project, prospect, protect, reflect, reject, respect, select, subject, suspect, unchecked.
Absent, accent, advent, ascent, assent, augment, cement, comment, consent, content, decent, descent, dissent, event, extent, fragment, frequent, hellbent, intent, invent, lament, moment, percent, portent, present, prevent, relent, repent, resent, torment.
[3] Accident, argument, circumvent, complement, compliment, condiment, confident, diligent, discontent, disorient, document, eminent, evident, excellent, experiment, fraudulent, government, imminent, implement, incident, insolent, instrument, malcontent, management, misrepresent, misspent, monument, negligent, opulent, orient, ornament, overspent, parliament, permanent, punishment, regiment, represent, sacrament, subsequent, succulent, supplement, tenement, testament, tournament, turbulent.

2.4.38 "--elth" (as in "health")
commonwealth, health, stealth, twelfth, wealth.

SURPRISING RHYMING:
[1] Elf, self, shelf.
Belt, Celt, dealt, dwelt, felt, knelt, melt, pelt, spelt, svelte, welt.
Breadth, breath, death, depth, length, strength, wavelength.
Dwelled, felled, gelled/jelled, held, quelled, shelled, smelled, spelled, swelled, yelled.

Bereft, cleft, deft, heft, left, theft.
[2] Bookshelf, herself, himself, itself, myself, oneself, yourself.
Compelled, dispelled, excelled, expelled, impelled, misspelled, propelled, rebelled, repelled, upheld, unparalleled, withheld.
Heartfelt, seat belt, lifebelt, sunbelt.

2.4.39 "--elve" (as in "shelve")
[1] delve, shelve, twelve.

SURPRISING RHYMING:
[1] Delves, elves, selves, shelves.
Elf, health, self, shelf, stealth, twelfth, wealth.
Dwelled, felled, gelled/jelled, held, quelled, shelled, smelled, spelled, swelled, yelled.
Bell, belle, cell, dell, dwell, el, fell, gel, hell, jell, knell, quell, sell, shell, smell, spell, swell, tell, well, yell.
[2] Ourselves, themselves, yourselves.
Bookshelf, herself, himself, itself, myself, oneself, yourself.
Compelled, dispelled, excelled, expelled, impelled, misspelled, propelled, rebelled, repelled, upheld, unparalleled, withheld.

2.4.40 "--elves" (as in "shelves")
[1] delves, elves, selves, shelves.
[2] ourselves, themselves, yourselves.

SURPRISING RHYMING:
[1] Delve, elf, self, shelf, shelve, twelve.
Bells, belles, cells~ dwells, fells, gels, jells, knells, quells, sells, shells, smells, spells, swells, tells, wells, yells.
[2] Bookshelf, herself, himself, itself, myself, oneself, yourself.
Compelled, dispelled, excelled, expelled, impelled, misspelled, propelled, rebelled, repelled, upheld, unparalleled, withheld.
Heartfelt, seat belt, lifebelt, sunbelt.

2.4.41 "--eller" (as in "cellar")
[2] cellar, dweller, fella, feller, seller, smeller, speller, stellar, teller, yeller.
[3] bestseller, cave dweller, dispeller, exceller, expeller, foreteller, impeller, novella, paella, propeller, repeller, reseller, umbrella.
[4] a cappella, Cinderella, fortune-teller, interstellar, mozzarella.

SURPRISING RHYMING:
[2] Clever, ever, never, sever.
Error, feather, heather, leather, nether, terror, tether, together, weather, whether.
Leisure, measure, pleasure, treasure.
Cheddar, deader, header, homesteader, redder, shedder, shredder, spreader, threader.
Better, debtor, fetter, fretter, getter, letter, setter, sweater, wetter.
Fester, jester, nester, pester, quester, shelter, swelter, tester, vesta.
Centre/center (U.S.), enter, renter.
Dresser, guesser, lesser, presser, yessir.
Nectar, rector, sector, spectre/specter (U.S.), vector.
[3] Endeavour/endeavor (U.S.), displeasure, forever, however, made-to-measure, never-never, whatever, whatsoever, whenever, wherever, whichever, whoever.
Bonesetter, carburettor/carburetor (U.S.), forgetter, go-getter, jet-setter, love-letter, newsletter, operetta, pacesetter, red-letter, typesetter, unfetter, upsetter, vendetta.
Aggressor, assessor, caresser, confessor, contessa, digresser, hairdresser, oppressor, possessor, predecessor, processor, professor, possessor, successor, transgressor.
Dissenter, epicentre/epicenter (U.S.), inventor, lamenter, presenter, repenter, tormentor.
Collector, connector, corrector, defector, deflector, detector, director, ejector, elector, erector, inspector, objector, projector, prospector, protector, reflector, selector.

*

2.4.42 "--elling" (as in "telling")
[2] dwelling, felling, gelling, jelling, knelling, quelling, selling, shelling, smelling, spelling, swelling, telling, yelling.
[3] compelling, dispelling, excelling, expelling, foretelling, fortune-telling, misspelling, outselling, overselling, propelling, rebelling, repelling, re-telling.

SURPRISING RHYMING:
[2] Begging, bootlegging, egging, legging, pegging.
Bedding, breading, dreading, heading, shedding, shredding, sledding, spreading, threading, treading, wedding.
Blessing, dressing, guessing, messing, pressing, stressing, yessing.
Belting, melting, pelting, smelting.
Betting, fretting, getting, jetting, letting, petting, setting, sweating, vetting, wetting.
Checking, decking, flecking, pecking, specking, trekking, wrecking.
Bending, blending, ending, fending, lending, mending, pending, sending, spending, tending, trending, vending, wending.
Airing, bearing, blaring, caring, daring, faring, flaring, glaring, pairing, raring, scaring, sharing, snaring, sparing, staring, swearing, tearing, wearing.
Bee sting, key-ring, nose-ring, offspring, plaything, real thing, sexting, shelving, shoestring, spring, string, sun king, texting, upswing.
[3] Embedding, homesteading, letterheading, spearheading.
Abetting, banqueting, duetting, forgetting, pirouetting, regretting, resetting, upsetting.
Accessing, addressing, assessing, caressing, confessing, depressing, digressing, distressing, expressing, impressing, obsessing, oppressing, possessing, processing, professing, progressing, regressing, repressing, suppressing, transgressing, undressing.
Crosschecking, henpecking, sound-checking, spot-checking.
Amending, ascending, attending, befriending, commending, contending, defending, depending, descending, extending, impending, intending, misspending, offending, overspending, pretending, rebellion, suspending, transcending, unbending, upending.
Declaring, despairing, hardwearing, impairing, repairing, seafaring, time-sharing.
Anything, boxing ring, colouring/coloring (U.S.), everything, nuzzling, wedding ring.

2.4.43 "--ello" (as in "hello")
[2] bellow, bordello, cello, fellow, hello, Jell-O, mellow, Othello, yellow.

SURPRISING RHYMING:
[1] Beau, blow, bow, bro, crow, doe, dough, flow, glow, go, grow, hoe, know, low, mow, no, oh, owe, pro, roe, row, sew, slow, snow, so, so-so, sow, throw, toe, tow.
Bold, bowled, coaled, cold, doled, foaled, fold, gold, hold, holed, mould/mold (U.S.), old, polled, rolled, scold, soled, sold, told, tolled.
Bowl, coal, console, control, dole, droll, foal, goal, hole, mole, pole, poll, role, roll, scroll, sole, soul, stole, stroll, toll, troll, shoal, whole.
Bode, code, crowed, goad, load, mode, mowed, ode, owed, road, rode, rowed, sewed, slowed, sowed, stowed, toad, toed, towed.
Blown, bone, cone~ drone, groan, grown, known, loan, lone, moan, own, phone, prone, scone, sewn, shone, shown, sown, stone, throne, thrown, tone, zone.
Bows, chose, close, clothes, doze, foes, froze, glows, goes, knows, nose, owes, pros, prose, rose, rows, sews, snows, sows, those, toes, tows.
Cope, dope, grope, hope, mope, nope, pope, rope, slope, soap.
Boat, coat, float, gloat, goat, moat, note, oat, quote, throat, tote, vote, wrote.
[2] Ago, aglow, also, below, bestow, bureau, crossbow, dunno, escrow, follow, forgo, go-go, hedgerow, hobo, ice-floe, Jell-O, logo, longbow, meadow, moonglow, narrow, no-go, oboe, outgrow, photo, pillow, plateau, pogo, rainbow, scarecrow, shadow, slowmo, Soho, sorrow, tallyho, tiptoe, wallow, window, yellow, yo-ho.
Behold, blindfold, cajoled, controlled, enfold, foothold, foretold, freehold, household, paroled, remould/remold (U.S.), remoulds/remolds (U.S.), re-sold, resoled, retold, stronghold, threshold, twofold, threefold, unfold, uphold, unsold, withhold.
Cajole, charcoal, control, creole, enroll, flagpole, hell-hole, loophole, manhole, maypole, payroll, parole, pinhole, porthole, tadpole.
Abode, bestowed, corrode, elbowed, erode, explode, overload, railroad, reload, unload.

Alone, atone, backbone, cell phone, cologne, condone, dethrone, disown, full-grown, half-grown, hormone, iPhone, jawbone, intone, limestone, ozone, postpone, sandstone, syndrome, tombstone, unknown, unsewn, unsown, well-known, wishbone.
Arose, bulldoze, compose, depose, disclose, enclose, expose, foreclose, impose, oppose, primrose, propose, rainbows, repose, suppose, tiptoes, transpose, wild rose.
Afloat, cutthroat, demote, denote, devote, emote, footnote, houseboat, keynote, lifeboat, promote, remote, re-wrote, sailboat, scapegoat, showboat, topcoat, turncoat.
[3] **Buffalo**, bungalow, cameo, cheerio, counterblow, dynamo, embryo, Eskimo, folio, gigolo, indigo, long ago, overflow, radio, rodeo, Romeo, Scorpio, studio, tomorrow, touch and go, tremolo, undergo, vertigo, video.
Manifold, oversold, pigeonholed, self-controlled, uncontrolled.
Buttonhole, casserole, pigeonhole, rock and roll, self-control, Superbowl.
Anklebone, baritone, chaperone, cornerstone, knucklebone, megaphone, microphone, monotone, overgrown, overthrown, overtone, saxophone, telephone, xylophone.
Decompose, dominoes, indispose, overdose, predispose.
Envelope, horoscope, isotope, kaleidoscope, microscope, periscope, telescope.
Anecdote, antidote, ferryboat, mountain goat, nanny goat, overcoat, petticoat, riverboat.

2.4.44 "--elted" (as in "melted")
[2] belted, melted, pelted, smelted.

SURPRISING RHYMING:
[2] **Blended**, ended, friended, mended, tended, vended, wended.
Dented, rented, scented, vented.
Bested, crested, jested, nested, rested, tested, vested.
Ahead, airhead, bighead, blockhead, bloodshed, bobsled, bonehead, co-ed, deadhead, deathbed, dickhead, drop dead, forehead, highbred, homebred, homestead, hotbed, hothead, instead, misled, pinhead, pothead, purebred, redhead, sickbed, skinhead, sleepyhead, sofa-bed, sorehead, spearhead, spoon-fed, sunbed, thickhead, unsaid, warhead, waterbed, watershed, well-fed, well-read, widespread.
Bedded, breaded, dreaded, headed, leaded, shredded, threaded, treaded, wedded.
Betted, fretted, jetted, netted, sweated, vetted, whetted.
Alleges, edges, fledges, hedges, ledges, pledges, sledges, wedges.
[3] **Arrowhead**, copperhead, dunderhead, figurehead, flowerbed, fountainhead, gingerbread, go-ahead, infrared, knucklehead, letterhead, loggerhead, newlywed, overfed, overhead, riverbed, sleepyhead, thoroughbred, underfed, watershed.
Attempted, augmented, cemented, consented, contented, demented, dissented, fragmented, frequented, invented, lamented, presented, prevented, relented, repented, resented, segmented, tormented, unscented.
Arrested, attested, congested, contested, detested, digested, divested, infested, ingested, invested, molested, protested, requested, road-tested, suggested, unrested.
Bareheaded, beheaded, bigheaded, bullheaded, cool headed, embedded, flat-headed, hardheaded, hotheaded, lightheaded, pigheaded, redheaded, spearheaded.
Affected, collected, connected, corrected, defected, deflected, dejected, detected, directed, dissected, ejected, elected, erected, expected, infected, injected, inspected, neglected, objected, perfected, projected, protected, reflected, rejected, respected, selected, subjected, suspected.
Amended, ascended, attended, befriended, commended, contended, defended, depended, descended, extended, intended, offended, pretended, rear-ended, suspended, transcended, upended.
Abetted, banqueted, duetted, indebted, pirouetted, regretted, silhouetted, unfretted.
[4] **Interjected**, interested, misdirected, recollected, resurrected, unexpected.
Apprehended, comprehended, condescended, recommended.
Complemented, complimented, discontented, disoriented, experimented, implemented, misrepresented, oriented, regimented, represented, re-presented, supplemented.

2.4.45 "--elting" (as in "melting")
[2] belting, melting, pelting, smelting.

SURPRISING RHYMING:
[2] Betting, fretting, getting, jetting, letting, petting, setting, sweating, vetting, wetting.
Bending, blending, ending, fending, lending, mending, pending, sending, spending, tending, trending, vending, wending.
Denting, renting, scenting, tempting, venting.
Cresting, guesting, jesting, nesting, questing, resting, testing, vesting, wresting.
Bedding, dreading, heading, shredding, spreading, threading, treading, wedding.
Alleging, edging, fledging, hedging, pledging, sledging, wedging.
[3] Affecting, collecting, connecting, correcting, defecting, deflecting, detecting, directing, dissecting, ejecting, electing, erecting, expecting, infecting, injecting, inspecting, neglecting, objecting, perfecting, projecting, prospecting, protecting, reflecting, rejecting, respecting, selecting, subjecting, suspecting.
Accepting, attempting, augmenting, cementing, commenting, consenting, dissenting, fermenting, fragmenting, frequenting, indenting, inventing, lamenting, presenting, preventing, relenting, repenting, resenting, segmenting, tormenting.
Abetting, banqueting, duetting, forgetting, pirouetting, regretting, resetting, upsetting.
Amending, ascending, attending, befriending, commending, contending, defending, depending, descending, extending, impending, intending, misspending, offending, overspending, pretending, suspending, transcending, unbending, upending.
Arresting, contesting, detesting, digesting, divesting, infesting, ingesting, interesting, investing, manifesting, molesting, protesting, requesting, road-testing, suggesting.
Embedding, homesteading, letterheading, retreading, spearheading.
[4] Disinfecting, disconnecting, disrespecting, interesting, interjecting, intersecting, misdirecting, recollecting, resurrecting, self-respecting.
Complementing, complimenting, disorienting, experimenting, implementing, misrepresenting, orienting, regimenting, representing, re-presenting, supplementing.
Apprehending, comprehending, condescending, recommending.

2.4.46 "--eltering" (as in "sheltering")
[3] sheltering, sweltering.

SURPRISING RHYMING:
[3] Bettering, censoring, centering, entering, feathering, festering, lecturing, lettering, measuring, mentoring, peppering, pestering, questioning, rendering, severing, tempering, tendering, tethering, texturing, venturing, weathering.
[4] Endeavouring/endeavoring (U.S.), remembering, surrendering.

2.4.47 "--elthier" (as in "wealthier")
[3] healthier, stealthier, wealthier.

SURPRISING RHYMING:
[3] Breathier, earthier, filthier, frothier, lengthier, mouthier, pithier, stealthier, swarthier, toothier, worthier.
Arena, betweener, cantina, convener, demeanour/demeanor (U.S.), hyena, marina, obscener, serener, subpoena, tsarina.
Eager, intriguer, meagre/meager (U.S.).

2.4.48 "--ellously" (as in "jealously")
[3] jealously, zealously.

SURPRISING RHYMING:
[3] Callously, jealousy, preciously, rebelliously.
Aimlessly, breathlessly, endlessly, helplessly, hopelessly, recklessly, restlessly.
Clemency, ecstasy, embassy, legacy, pregnancy, tenancy, tendency.
Destiny, ebony, empathy, enemy, felony, melody, sesame, recipe, telepathy, therapy.
Brevity, clarity, confetti, density, deputy, entity, equity, intensity, levity, libretti, penalty, seventy, spaghetti, specialty, velvety.
Carefully, dreadfully, fretfully, generally, helpfully, mentally, regretfully, respectfully, revelry, separately, successfully.

Credibly, desperately, easily, flexibly, heavenly, heavily, merrily, messily, pleasantly, preferably, presently, prettily, queasily, secondly, sensibly, sketchily, splendidly, terribly.
Readily, steadily, unreadily, unsteadily.
[4] Infectiously, tremendously, unsuccessfully.
Ascendancy, dependency, discrepancy, expectancy, relentlessly, supremacy.
Centrally, especially, essentially, eventually, exceptionally, potentially, professionally, sequentially, specially.
Aggressively, excessively, expressively, impressively, obsessively, oppressively, possessively, progressively.
Acceptably, accessibly, allegedly, contentedly, expectantly, impeccably, incessantly, incredibly, indelibly, intrepidly, irreverently, lamentably, ostensibly, perceptibly, primarily, progressively, regrettably, respectably, unpleasantly.
Amenity, complexity, fidelity, heredity, indemnity, identity, integrity.
[5] Accidentally, confidentially, consequentially, conscientiously, disrespectfully, fundamentally, incidentally, influentially, instrumentally, monumentally, reverentially, sentimentally, temperamentally, transcendentally, unconventionally, unintentionally.
Independently, infidelity, necessarily, ordinarily, reprehensibly, temporarily, unacceptably.

2.4.49 "--ember" (as in "remember")
[2] ember, member.
[3] December, dismember, remember, September, November.

SURPRISING RHYMING:
[2] **Blender**, centre/center (U.S.), ender, enter, fender, gender, lender, mender, render, sender, slender, spender, splendour/splendor (U.S.), tender, vendor.
Censor, denser, fencer, sensor, tenser, condenser, dispenser.
Altogether, feather, heather, leather, tether, together, untether, weather, whether.
Fester, jester, nester, pester, quester, tester, vesta, wester, zester.
Better, debtor, fetter, fretter, getter, letter, setter, sweater, wetter.
[3] **Agenda**, apprehender, attender, bartender, contender, defender, hacienda, moneylender, offender, pretender, surrender, suspender, transgender, weekender.
Dissenter, epicentre/epicenter (U.S.), frequenter, inventor, lamenter, magenta, presenter, preventer, re-enter, repenter, tormentor.
Ancestor, arrester, celesta, contester, digester, fiesta, investor, molester, polyester, protester, semester, sequester, siesta, sou'wester, suggester, trimester.
Endeavour/endeavor (U.S.), forever, however, never-never, whatever, whatsoever, whenever, wherever, whichever, whoever.
Bonesetter, carburettor/carburetor (U.S.), forgetter, go-getter, jet-setter, love-letter, newsletter, operetta, pacesetter, red-letter, typesetter, unfetter, upsetter, vendetta.

2.4.50 "--em" (as in "them")
[1] crème, 'em, gem, hem, phlegm, REM (rem), stem, them.
[2] ahem, condemn, crème de la crème, item, mayhem, modem, pro tem, requiem.
SURPRISING RHYMING:
[1] **Den**, glen, hen, men, pen, ten, then, when, wren, yen, Zen.
Bend, blend, end, fend, friend, lend, mend, penned, send, spend, tend, trend, wend.
Elm, helm, overwhelm, realm, underwhelm, whelm.
[2] **Admen**, again, amen, bagmen, Big Ben, bitten, broken, burden, cavemen, chosen, conmen, firemen, frozen, glisten, he-men, hidden, hitmen, horsemen, jazzmen, lawmen, listen, mailmen, milkmen, newsmen, ocean, oilmen, open, playpen, ragmen, risen, shaken, showmen, snowmen, spoken, strongmen, stuntmen, taken, taxmen, woven.
Amend, ascend, attend, befriend, best friend, bookend, boyfriend, commend, contend, defend, depend, descend, extend, girlfriend, godsend, intend, offend, old friend, overspend, penfriend, portend, pretend, suspend, tail end, transcend, upend, weekend.
Attempt, contempt, dreamt, exempt, tempt, pre-empt, unkempt.
[3] **Cameramen**, citizen, forsaken, fountain pen, gentlemen, lion's den, middlemen, mistaken, newspapermen, oxygen, poison-pen, repairmen, weathermen, wide-open.
Apprehend, comprehend, condescend, recommend, reverend.

*

2.4.51 "--empt" (as in "tempt")
attempt, contempt, dreamt, exempt, kempt, tempt, pre-empt, unkempt.

SURPRISING RHYMING:
[1] **Bent**, cent, dent, gent, leant, lent, meant, rent, scent, sent, spent, tent, vent, went.
Crept, kept, leapt, prepped, slept, stepped, swept, wept.
Belt, dealt, dwelt, felt, heartfelt, knelt, melt, pelt, spelt, svelte, welt.
Den, fen, glen, hen, men, pen, ten, then, when, wren, yen, Zen.
Bend, blend, end, fend, friend, lend, mend, penned, send, spend, tend, trend, wend.
Crème, 'em, gem, hem, phlegm, REM, stem, them.
[2] **Absent**, accent, advent, ascent, assent, augment, cement, comment, consent, content, decent, descent, dissent, event, extent, fragment, frequent, hellbent, intent, invent, lament, moment, percent, present, prevent, relent, repent, resent, torment.
Affect, aspect, collect, connect, correct, defect, deflect, detect, dialect, direct, dissect, effect, eject, elect, erect, expect, henpecked, infect, inject, insect, inspect, neglect, object, perfect, project, prospect, protect, reflect, reject, respect, select, subject, suspect, unchecked.
Accept, adept, concept, except, inept, intercept, overslept, over-stepped, precept, rainswept, side-stepped, unswept, windswept.
Asset, baguette, banquet, brunette/brunet (U.S.), cadet, cassette, coquette, cornet, corvette, dragnet, duet, filmset, fishnet, forget, gazette, handset, headset, in debt, inlet, inset, kismet, mindset, nymphet, octet, offset, onset, outset, quartet, quintet, regret, reset, rosette, roulette, sextet, sunset, upset, vignette.
Admen, again, amen, bagmen, Big Ben, bitten, broken, burden, cavemen, chosen, conmen, firemen, frontmen, frozen, glisten, he-men, hidden, hitmen, horsemen, jazzmen, lawmen, listen, mailmen, milkmen, newsmen, ocean, oilmen, open, playpen, ragmen, risen, shaken, showmen, snowmen, spoken, strongmen, stuntmen, taken, taxmen, wingmen, woven.
Amend, ascend, attend, befriend, best friend, bookend, boyfriend, commend, contend, defend, depend, descend, extend, girlfriend, godsend, intend, offend, old friend, overspend, penfriend, portend, pretend, suspend, tail end, transcend, upend, weekend.
Condemn, crème de la crème, item, mayhem, modem, requiem.
[3] **Accident**, argument, circumvent, complement, compliment, condiment, confident, diligent, discontent, disorient, document, eminent, evident, excellent, experiment, fraudulent, government, imminent, implement, incident, insolent, instrument, malcontent, management, misrepresent, misspent, monument, negligent, opulent, orient, ornament, overspent, parliament, permanent, punishment, regiment, represent, sacrament, subsequent, succulent, supplement, tenement, testament, tournament, turbulent.
Apprehend, comprehend, condescend, dividend, recommend, reprehend, reverend.

2.4.52 "--en" (as in "when")
[1] den, fen, gen, glen, hen, men, pen, ten, then, when, wren, yen, Zen.
[2] admen, again, amen, bagmen, Big Ben, bitten, broken, bullpen, burden, bushmen, cavemen, cayenne, chosen, conmen, firemen, frontmen, frozen, glisten, he-men, hidden, hitmen, horsemen, jazzmen, lawmen, linkmen, listen, mailmen, milkmen, newsmen, Norsemen, ocean, oilmen, open, pigpen, playpen, ragmen, risen, shaken, showmen, snowmen, spoken, strongmen, stuntmen, taken, taxmen, wingmen, woven.
[3] arisen, cameramen, citizen, denizen, Englishmen, forsaken, fountain pen, gentlemen, lion's den, middlemen, mistaken, newspapermen, nitrogen, older men, oxygen, poison-pen, repairmen, specimen, weathermen, wide-open.

SURPRISING RHYMING:
[1] **Crème**, 'em, gem, hem, phlegm, REM (rem), stem, them.
Bend, blend, end, fend, friend, lend, mend, penned, send, spend, tend, trend, wend.
Bent, cent, dent, gent, leant, lent, meant, rent, scent, sent, spent, tent, vent, went.
Elm, helm, overwhelm, realm, underwhelm, whelm.
[2] **A.M.** (ay-em), condemn, item, mayhem, modem, pro tem, requiem, rhythm.
Amend, ascend, attend, befriend, best friend, bookend, boyfriend, commend, contend, defend, depend, descend, extend, girlfriend, godsend, intend, offend, old friend, overspend, penfriend, portend, pretend, suspend, tail end, transcend, upend, weekend.

Lotion, motion, notion, ocean, potion.
Attempt, contempt, dreamt, exempt, tempt, pre-empt, unkempt.
Absent, accent, advent, ascent, assent, augment, cement, comment, consent, content, decent, descent, dissent, event, extent, fragment, frequent, hellbent, intent, invent, lament, moment, percent, portent, present, prevent, relent, repent, resent, torment.
Captain, certain, curtain, fountain, mountain, uncertain.
Awesome, gruesome, lonesome, overcome, quarrelsome, threesome, troublesome, twosome, wholesome.
[3] **Apprehend**, comprehend, condescend, dividend, recommend, reprehend, reverend.

NOTE:
You can also create a two-syllable 'surprising rhyme' for an "--en" word by adding -ing to the end of a one-syllable word (such as "hope") and pronouncing it with a silent 'g' (e.g. hopin'). Similarly, a three-syllable rhyme can be created by adding -ing to a two-syllable word (such as "heartbreak") and pronouncing it with a silent 'g' (e.g. heartbreakin').

2.4.53 "--end" (as in "send")
[1] bend, blend, end, fend, friend, lend, mend, penned, rend, send, spend, tend, trend, vend, wend.
[2] amend, append, ascend, attend, befriend, best friend, bookend, boyfriend, commend, contend, defend, depend, descend, expend, extend, girlfriend, godsend, impend, intend, misspend, offend, old friend, overspend, penfriend, portend, pretend, stipend, suspend, tail end, transcend, U-bend, unbend, upend, weekend.
[3] apprehend, comprehend, condescend, dividend, recommend, reprehend, reverend.

SURPRISING RHYMING:
[1] **Den**, glen, hen, men, pen, ten, then, when, wren, yen, Zen.
Crème, 'em, gem, hem, phlegm, REM, stem, stemmed, them.
Bent, cent, dent, gent, leant, lent, meant, rent, scent, sent, spent, tent, vent, went.
Felled, gelled/jelled, held, knelled, quelled, shelled, smelled, spelled, swelled, yelled.
[2] **Admen**, again, amen, bagmen, Big Ben, bitten, broken, burden, cavemen, chosen, conmen, firemen, frontmen, frozen, glisten, he-men, hidden, hitmen, horsemen, jazzmen, lawmen, listen, mailmen, milkmen, newsmen, ocean, oilmen, open, playpen, ragmen, risen, shaken, showmen, snowmen, spoken, strongmen, stuntmen, taken, woven.
A.M. (ay-em), condemn(ed), crème de la crème, item, mayhem, modem, requiem, rhythm.
Attempt, contempt, dreamt, exempt, tempt, pre-empt, unkempt.
Absent, accent, advent, ascent, assent, augment, cement, comment, consent, content, decent, descent, dissent, event, extent, fragment, frequent, hellbent, intent, invent, lament, moment, percent, portent, present, prevent, relent, repent, resent, torment.
Compelled, dispelled, excelled, expelled, impelled, misspelled, propelled, rebelled, repelled, upheld, withheld.
Captain, certain, curtain, fountain, mountain, uncertain.
[3] **Cameramen**, citizen, Englishmen, forsaken, fountain pen, gentlemen, lion's den, middlemen, mistaken, newspapermen, oxygen, poison-pen, repairmen, specimen, weathermen, wide-open.
Accident, argument, circumvent, complement, compliment, condiment, confident, diligent, discontent, disorient, document, eminent, evident, excellent, experiment, fraudulent, government, imminent, implement, incident, insolent, instrument, malcontent, management, misrepresent, misspent, monument, negligent, opulent, orient, ornament, overspent, parliament, permanent, punishment, regiment, represent, sacrament, subsequent, succulent, supplement, tenement, testament, tournament, turbulent.

2.4.54 "--ench" (as in "clench")
[1] bench, clench, drench, French, quench, stench, trench, wench, wrench.
[2] backbench, entrench, frontbench, unclench, workbench.

SURPRISING RHYMING:
[1] **Dense**, fence, hence, pence, sense, tense, thence, whence.
Etch, fetch, ketch, lech, retch, sketch, stretch, wretch.
Bent, cent, dent, gent, leant, lent, meant, rent, scent, sent, spent, tent, vent, went.

Allege, dredge, edge, hedge, ledge, pledge, sledge, veg, wedge.
[2] Absence, commence, condense, conscience, credence, defence/defense (U.S.), dispense, essence, expense, immense, incense, intense, licence/license (U.S.), nonsense, offence/offense (U.S.), patience, presence, pretence/pretense (U.S.), prudence, ring-fence, science, sentence, sequence, silence, sixpence, suspense.
Against, commenced, condensed, dispensed, fenced, incensed, licensed, sensed, sentenced, sequenced, silenced.
[3] Abstinence, affluence, ambience, audience, coherence, commonsense, competence, condolence, conference, confidence, consequence, dependence, eloquence, emergence, eminence, evidence, excellence, existence, fraudulence, impatience, impudence, impotence, indolence, influence, innocence, insistence, insolence, insurgence, lenience, negligence, occurrence, opulence, penitence, permanence, persistence, prescience, prevalence, prominence, providence, radiance, recommence, recompense, recurrence, residence, resurgence, reticence, reverence, self-defence/self-defense (U.S.), severance, subsistence, succulence, temperance, transcendence, transience, turbulence, violence.
Influenced, recommenced, recompensed, referenced.

2.4.55 "--ence" (as in "fence")
[1] dense, fence, hence, pence, sense, tense, thence, whence.
[2] absence, commence, condense, conscience, credence, defence/defense (U.S.), dispense, essence, expense, immense, incense, intense, licence/license (U.S.), nonsense, offence/offense (U.S.), patience, presence, pretence/pretense (U.S.), prudence, ring-fence, science, sentence, sequence, silence, suspense, vengeance.
[3] abstinence, affluence, ambience, audience, coherence, commonsense, competence, condolence, conference, confidence, consequence, dependence, eloquence, emergence, eminence, evidence, excellence, existence, fraudulence, impatience, impudence, impotence, indolence, influence, innocence, insistence, insolence, insurgence, lenience, negligence, occurrence, opulence, penitence, permanence, persistence, prescience, prevalence, prominence, providence, radiance, recommence, recompense, recurrence, residence, resurgence, reticence, reverence, self-defence/self-defense (U.S.), severance, subsistence, succulence, temperance, transcendence, transience, turbulence, violence.
[4] acquiescence, adolescence, ambivalence, belligerence, benevolence, coincidence, convenience, correspondence, disobedience, ebullience, effervescence, expedience, experience, inconvenience, independence, indifference, inexperience, intelligence, interference, iridescence, irreverence, magnificence, malevolence, obedience, reminiscence, resilience, self-confidence, translucence.

SURPRISING RHYMING:
[1] Fenced, sensed, tensed.
Bench, clench, drench, French, quench, stench, trench, wrench.
Benched, clenched, drenched, quenched, trenched, wrenched.
Best, blessed, blest, breast, chest, crest, dressed, guest, guessed, jest, lest, messed, nest, pest, quest, rest, stressed, test, vest, west.
Bent, cent, dent, gent, leant, lent, meant, rent, scent, sent, spent, tent, vent, went.
Belts, Celts, helps, melts, pelts, whelps, yelps.
Footsteps, reps, schleps, steps, steppes.
[2] Against, commenced, condensed, dispensed, incensed, licensed, ring-fenced, sensed, sentenced, sequenced, silenced.
Backbench, entrench, frontbench, unclench, workbench.
Abreast, addressed, armrest, arrest, Beau Geste, behest, bequest, caressed, confessed, contest, conquest, depressed, detest, digest, digressed, distressed, divest, expressed, impressed, infest, inquest, invest, Midwest, molest, northwest, oppressed, possessed, progressed, protest, recessed, repressed, request, road-test, southwest, suggest, suppressed, transgressed, undressed, unrest, well-dressed.
Absent, accent, advent, ascent, assent, augment, cement, comment, consent, content, decent, descent, dissent, event, extent, fragment, frequent, hellbent, intent, invent, lament, moment, percent, portent, present, prevent, relent, repent, resent, torment.
[3] Influenced, recommenced, recompensed, referenced.
Chimneybreast, dispossessed, effervesced, interest, manifest, overdressed, second-best, self-addressed, self-confessed, self-possessed, unexpressed, unimpressed.

Accident, argument, circumvent, complement, compliment, condiment, confident, diligent, discontent, disorient, document, eminent, evident, excellent, experiment, fraudulent, government, imminent, implement, incident, insolent, instrument, malcontent, management, misrepresent, misspent, monument, negligent, opulent, orient, ornament, overspent, parliament, permanent, punishment, regiment, represent, sacrament, subsequent, succulent, supplement, tenement, testament, tournament, turbulent.

2.4.56 "--enced" (as in "commenced")
[2] against, commenced, condensed, dispensed, incensed, licensed, ring-fenced, sensed, sentenced, sequenced, silenced.
[3] influenced, recommenced, recompensed, referenced.
[4+] experienced, inconvenienced, inexperienced.

SURPRISING RHYMING:
[1] **Dense**, fence(d), hence, pence, sense(d), tense(d), thence, whence.
Benched, clenched, drenched, quenched, trenched, wrenched.
Bench, clench, drench, quench, stench, trench, wench, wrench.
Bent, cent, dent, gent, leant, lent, meant, rent, scent, sent, spent, tent, vent, went.
[2] **Absence**, commence, condense, conscience, credence, defence/defense (U.S.), dispense, essence, expense, immense, incense, intense, licence/license (U.S.), nonsense, offence/offense (U.S.), patience, presence, pretence/pretense (U.S.), prudence, ring-fence, science, sentence, sequence, silence, suspense, vengeance.
Absent, accent, advent, ascent, assent, augment, cement, comment, consent, content, decent, descent, dissent, event, extent, fragment, frequent, hellbent, intent, invent, lament, moment, percent, portent, present, prevent, relent, repent, resent, torment.
Abreast, addressed, armrest, arrest, Beau Geste, behest, bequest, caressed, confessed, contest, conquest, depressed, detest, digest, digressed, distressed, divest, expressed, impressed, infest, inquest, invest, Midwest, molest, northwest, oppressed, possessed, progressed, protest, recessed, repressed, request, road-test, southwest, suggest, suppressed, transgressed, undressed, unrest, well-dressed.
[3] **Abstinence**, affluence, ambience, audience, coherence, commonsense, competence, condolence, conference, confidence, consequence, dependence, eloquence, emergence, eminence, evidence, excellence, existence, fraudulence, impatience, impudence, impotence, indolence, influence, innocence, insistence, insolence, insurgence, lenience, negligence, occurrence, opulence, penitence, permanence, persistence, prescience, prevalence, prominence, providence, radiance, recommence, recompense, recurrence, residence, resurgence, reticence, reverence, self-defence/self-defense (U.S.), severance, subsistence, succulence, temperance, transcendence, transience, turbulence, violence.
Chimneybreast, dispossessed, effervesced, interest, manifest, overdressed, reassessed, second-best, self-addressed, self-confessed, self-possessed, unexpressed, unimpressed.
Accident, argument, circumvent, complement, compliment, condiment, confident, diligent, discontent, disorient, document, eminent, evident, excellent, experiment, fraudulent, government, imminent, implement, incident, insolent, instrument, malcontent, management, misrepresent, misspent, monument, negligent, opulent, orient, ornament, overspent, parliament, permanent, punishment, regiment, represent, sacrament, subsequent, succulent, supplement, tenement, testament, tournament, turbulent.
[4] **Coincidence**, convenience, disobedience, expedience, experience, inconvenience, inexperience, obedience, resilience.

2.4.57 "--ent" (as in "went")
[1] bent, cent, dent, gent, leant, lent, meant, rent, scent, sent, spent, tent, vent, went.
[2] absent, accent, advent, ascent, assent, augment, cement, comment, consent, content, decent, descent, dissent, event, extent, ferment, fragment, frequent, hellbent, indent, intent, invent, lament, moment, percent, portent, present, prevent, relent, repent, resent, segment, torment, unbent, unsent, unspent, well-spent.
[3] accident, ailment, argument, banishment, circumvent, complement, compliment, condiment, confident, diligent, discontent, disorient, document, eminent, evident,

excellent, excrement, experiment, fraudulent, government, imminent, implement, incident, insolent, instrument, malcontent, management, misrepresent, misspent, monument, negligent, opulent, orient, ornament, overspent, parliament, permanent, provident, punishment, ravishment, regiment, represent, rudiment, sacrament, subsequent, succulent, supplement, tenement, testament, tournament, turbulent, underwent.

SURPRISING RHYMING:
[1] Dreamt, kempt, tempt.
Crème, 'em, gem, hem, phlegm, REM, stem, them.
Bend, blend, end, fend, friend, lend, mend, penned, send, spend, tend, trend, wend.
Den, gen, glen, hen, men, pen, ten, then, when, wren, yen, Zen.
Dense, fence, hence, pence, sense, tense, thence, whence.
[2] Attempt, contempt, exempt, pre-empt, unkempt.
Amend, ascend, attend, befriend, best friend, bookend, boyfriend, commend, contend, defend, depend, descend, extend, girlfriend, godsend, intend, offend, old friend, overspend, penfriend, portend, pretend, suspend, tail end, transcend, upend, weekend.
Admen, again, amen, bagmen, Big Ben, bitten, broken, burden, cavemen, chosen, conmen, firemen, frozen, glisten, he-men, hidden, hitmen, horsemen, jazzmen, lawmen, listen, mailmen, milkmen, newsmen, ocean, oilmen, open, playpen, ragmen, risen, shaken, showmen, snowmen, spoken, strongmen, stuntmen, taken, taxmen, woven.
Condemn, crème de la crème, item, mayhem, modem, requiem.
Absence, commence, condense, conscience, credence, defence/defense (U.S.), dispense, essence, expense, immense, incense, intense, licence/license (U.S.), nonsense, offence/offense (U.S.), patience, presence, pretence/pretense (U.S.), prudence, ring-fence, science, sentence, sequence, silence, suspense, vengeance.
[3] Apprehend, comprehend, condescend, dividend, recommend, reprehend, reverend.
Arisen, cameramen, citizen, forsaken, gentlemen, lion's den, middlemen, mistaken, newspapermen, oxygen, poison-pen, repairmen, specimen, weathermen, wide-open.

2.4.58 "--ended" (as in "ended")

[2] bended, blended, ended, friended, mended, tended, vended, wended.
[3] amended, appended, ascended, attended, befriended, commended, contended, defended, depended, descended, extended, intended, offended, pretended, rear-ended, suspended, transcended, upended, unblended.
[4] apprehended, comprehended, condescended, recommended.

SURPRISING RHYMING:
[2] Dented, rented, scented, vented.
Bedded, dreaded, headed, leaded, shredded, sledded, threaded, treaded, wedded.
Betted, fretted, headed, jetted, method, netted, petted, regretted, sweated, tepid, vetted, whetted.
Belted, melted, pelted, smelted.
Bending, blending, ending, fending, lending, mending, pending, sending, spending, tending, trending, vending, wending.
Bested, crested, fences, jested, nested, rested, senses, tenses, tested, vested.
[3] Augmented, cemented, consented, contented, demented, dissented, fragmented, frequented, invented, lamented, presented, prevented, relented, repented, resented, segmented, tormented, unscented.
Affected, collected, connected, corrected, deflected, dejected, detected, directed, dissected, ejected, elected, erected, expected, infected, injected, inspected, neglected, objected, perfected, projected, protected, reflected, rejected, respected, selected, subjected, suspected.
Bareheaded, beheaded, bigheaded, cool headed, embedded, hardheaded, hotheaded, lightheaded, pigheaded, redheaded, spearheaded, thickheaded, unwedded.
Abetted, banqueted, duetted, indebted, intrepid, pirouetted, regretted, silhouetted.
Amending, ascending, attending, befriending, commending, contending, defending, depending, descending, extending, impending, intending, misspending, offending, overspending, pretending, suspending, transcending, unbending, upending.
Attendant, defendant, dependent, descendant, pendant, superintendent, transcendent.

301

Arrested, congested, contested, detested, digested, divested, infested, invested, molested, protested, requested, road-tested, suggested.
[4] **Interjected**, interested, misdirected, recollected, re-elected, resurrected.
Apprehending, comprehending, condescending, recommending.

2.4.59 "--endent" (as in "dependent")
[3] ascendant, attendant, defendant, dependent, descendant, pendant, transcendent.

SURPRISING RHYMING:
[1] **Bent**, cent, dent, gent, leant, lent, meant, rent, scent, sent, spent, tent, vent, went.
[2] **Absent**, accent, advent, ascent, assent, augment, cement, comment, consent, content, decent, descent, dissent, event, extent, fragment, frequent, hellbent, intent, invent, lament, moment, percent, present, prevent, relent, repent, resent, torment.
Bended, blended, ended, friended, mended, tended, vended.
Ardent, apparent, couldn't, dormant, needn't, didn't, remnant, sergeant, wouldn't.
[3] **Accident**, argument, circumvent, complement, compliment, condiment, confident, diligent, discontent, disorient, document, eminent, evident, excellent, experiment, fraudulent, government, imminent, implement, incident, insolent, instrument, malcontent, management, misrepresent, misspent, monument, negligent, opulent, orient, ornament, overspent, parliament, permanent, punishment, regiment, represent, sacrament, subsequent, succulent, supplement, tenement, testament, tournament, turbulent.
Amended, ascended, attended, befriended, commended, defended, depended, descended, extended, intended, offended, pretended, rear-ended, suspended, upended.
Crescent, depressant, fluorescent, incessant, quiescent.
Arrested, congested, contested, detested, digested, divested, infested, invested, molested, protested, requested, road-tested, suggested, untested.
Arrogant, confidant, covenant, debutante, dominant, elegant, elephant, hesitant, ignorant, immigrant, important, informant, irritant, jubilant, militant, nonchalant, radiant, relevant, stimulant, sycophant, tolerant, triumphant, vigilant.
[4] **Apprehended**, comprehended, condescended, recommended.
Acquiescent, effervescent, iridescent, incandescent, adolescent, obsolescent, convalescent, antidepressant.

2.4.60 "--ender" (as in "tender")
[2] bender, blender, ender, fender, gender, lender, mender, render, sender, slender, spender, splendour/splendor (U.S.), tender, vender, vendor.
[3] agenda, amender, apprehender, ascender, attender, bartender, contender, defender, descender, extender, hacienda, moneylender, offender, pretender, recommender, surrender, suspender, transgender, weekender.

SURPRISING RHYMING:
[2] **Ember**, member, temper.
Clever, ever, feather, heather, leather, never, sever, tether, together, weather, whether.
Censor, denser, fencer, sensor, tenser, condenser, dispenser.
Enter, centre/center (U.S.), renter.
Fester, jester, nester, pester, quester, tester, vesta, zester.
Better, debtor, fetter, fretter, getter, letter, setter, sweater, wetter.
[3] **December**, dismember, remember, September, November.
Altogether, endeavour/endeavor (U.S.), forever, however, never-never, whatever, whatsoever, whenever, wherever, whichever, whoever, whomever.
Dissenter, epicentre/epicenter (U.S.), eventer, fermenter, frequenter, inventor, lamenter, magenta, presenter, preventer, re-enter, repenter, tormentor.
Ancestor, fiesta, investor, molester, polyester, protester, semester, siesta, sou'wester.
Bonesetter, carburettor/carburetor (U.S.), forgetter, go-getter, jet-setter, love-letter, newsletter, operetta, pacesetter, red-letter, typesetter, unfetter, upsetter, vendetta.

2.4.61 "--ending" (as in "sending")
[2] bending, blending, ending, fending, lending, mending, pending, sending, spending, tending, trending, vending, wending.

[3] amending, ascending, attending, befriending, commending, contending, defending, depending, descending, extending, impending, intending, misspending, offending, pretending, suspending, transcending, unbending, upending.
[4] apprehending, comprehending, condescending, never-ending, recommending.

SURPRISING RHYMING:
[2] **Denting**, renting, scenting, temping, tempting, tenpin, venting.
Gelding, helping, melting, welding.
Cresting, fencing, guesting, jesting, nesting, questing, resting, sensing, tensing, testing.
Dwelling, felling, gelling/jelling, quelling, smelling, spelling, swelling, telling, yelling.
Dreading, heading, shedding, shredding, spreading, threading, treading, wedding.
Begging, bootlegging, egging, legging, pegging.
Betting, fretting, getting, jetting, letting, petting, setting, sweating, vetting, wetting.
[3] **Deadening**, deafening, fledgling, freshening, leveling/levelling, reckoning, second-string, settling, strengthening, threatening, trembling, welcoming,
Abetting, banqueting, begetting, duetting, forgetting, pirouetting, regretting, upsetting.
Attempting, exempting, stemming, tempting, pre-empting.
Augmenting, cementing, consenting, dissenting, fragmenting, frequenting, inventing, lamenting, presenting, preventing, relenting, repenting, resenting, tormenting.
Compelling, condemning, dispelling, excelling, expelling, foretelling, fortune-telling, rebelling, repelling.
Commencing, condensing, dispensing, incensing, licensing, ring-fencing, sequencing.
Embedding, homesteading, letterheading, spearheading.
Affecting, collecting, connecting, correcting, deflecting, detecting, directing, dissecting, ejecting, erecting, expecting, infecting, injecting, inspecting, neglecting, objecting, perfecting, projecting, prospecting, protecting, reflecting, rejecting, respecting, selecting, subjecting, suspecting.
Arresting, contesting, detesting, digesting, divesting, infesting, interesting, investing, manifesting, molesting, protesting, requesting, road-testing, suggesting.
[4] **Complimenting**, complementing, documenting, experimenting, implementing, misrepresenting, orienting, overwhelming, representing, supplementing.
Disinfecting, disconnecting, disrespecting, interjecting, intersecting, misdirecting, recollecting, re-electing, resurrecting, self-respecting.

2.4.62 "--enser" (as in "censor")

[2] censor, denser, fencer, Mensa, sensor, tenser.
[3] condenser, dispenser.

SURPRISING RHYMING:
[2] **Centre/center** (U.S.), ember, enter, member, renter, temper.
Jester, nester, pester, quester, tester, vesta, wester, zester.
Dresser, guesser, lesser, presser, yessir.
Feather, heather, leather, tether, together, weather, whether.
Leisure, measure, pleasure, treasure.
Blender, ender, fender, gender, lender, mender, render, sender, slender, spender, splendour/splendor (U.S.), tender, vendor.
Better, debtor, fetter, fretter, getter, letter, setter, sweater, wetter.
Nectar, rector, sector, spectre/specter (U.S.), vector.
[3] **Dissenter**, epicentre/epicenter (U.S.), inventor, lamenter, presenter, preventer, repenter, tempter, tormentor.
Ancestor, fiesta, investor, molester, polyester, protester, semester, siesta, sou'wester.
Aggressor, caresser, confessor, depressor, digresser, hairdresser, oppressor, possessor, predecessor, processor, professor, successor, suppresser, transgressor.
Agenda, apprehender, ascender, attender, bartender, contender, defender, hacienda, moneylender, offender, pretender, surrender, suspender, transgender, weekender.
Carburettor/carburetor (U.S.), dead letter, go-getter, jet-setter, love-letter, newsletter, operetta, pacesetter, red-letter, upsetter, vendetta.
Collector, connector, corrector, defector, deflector, detector, director, elector, inspector, objector, projector, protector, reflector, selector.
December, dismember, remember, September, November.

2.4.63 "--ential" (as in "essential")
[3] credential, essential, potential, prudential, sequential, torrential.
[4] confidential, consequential, deferential, differential, evidential, existential, experiential, exponential, influential, preferential, presidential, quintessential, residential.

SURPRISING RHYMING:
[2] **Pencil**, stencil, utensil.
Mention, pension, tension.
Bluebell, bombshell, cartel, Chanel, compel, dispel, doorbell, dumbbell, eggshell, excel, expel, farewell, foretell, gazelle, groundswell, hotel, impel, inkwell, lapel, misspell, motel, noel, nutshell, propel, rebel, repel, resell, seashell, unwell.
Central, dental, gentle, kennel, mental, parental, rental.
Embezzle, nestle, special, trestle, vessel, wrestle.
[3] **Attention**, contention, convention, detention, dimension, extension, intention, invention, prevention, retention, suspension.
Bagatelle, caramel, carousel, citadel, clientele, decibel, infidel, Jezebel, ne're-do-well, oversell, parallel, personnel, pimpernel, show-and-tell, undersell, wishing well.
[4] **Accidental**, continental, detrimental, elemental, environmental, experimental, fundamental, instrumental, judgmental, monumental, Oriental, sentimental, transcendental.

2.4.64 "--ention" (as in "mention")
[2] mention, pension, tension.
[3] ascension, attention, contention, convention, detention, dimension, extension, intention, invention, pretension, prevention, retention, suspension.
[4] apprehension, comprehension, condescension, contravention, hypertension, intervention, misapprehension.

SURPRISING RHYMING:
[2] **Freshen**, session, discretion.
Etching, fetching, retching, sketching, stretching.
Alleging, edging, fledging, hedging, pledging, sledging, wedging.
[3] **Abstention**, attention, contention, convention, detention, dimension, exemption, extension, intention, invention, prevention, redemption, retention, suspension.
Conception, deception, exception, objection, perception, reception.
Congestion, digestion, indigestion, ingestion, question, suggestion.
Aggression, concession, confession, depression, discretion, expression, impression, jam session, obsession, oppression, possession, procession, profession, progression, recession, regression, repression, succession, transgression.
Affection, collection, complexion, confection, connection, correction, dejection, detection, direction, dissection, ejection, election, infection, injection, objection, perfection, projection, protection, reflection, rejection, section, selection.
Commencing, condensing, dispensing, incensing, licensing, ring-fencing, sentencing, sequencing, silencing.
[4] **Contraception**, interception, misconception.
Indiscretion, repossession, self-expression.
Imperfection, insurrection, interjection, intersection, introspection, recollection, resurrection, retrospection.

2.4.65 "--encing" (as in "commencing")
[2] fencing, sensing, tensing.
[3] commencing, condensing, dispensing, incensing, licensing, ring-fencing, sentencing, sequencing, silencing.
[4+] experiencing, inconveniencing, influencing, recommencing, recompensing, referencing.

SURPRISING RHYMING:
[2] **Blessing**, dressing, guessing, messing, pressing, stressing, yessing.
Etching, fetching, retching, sketching, stretching.
Alleging, edging, fledging, hedging, pledging, sledging, wedging.

Mention, pension, tension.
Guesting, jesting, nesting, questing, resting, testing, vesting.
Bending, blending, ending, fending, lending, mending, pending, sending, spending, tending, trending, vending, wending.
Denting, renting, scenting, tempting, venting.
[3] Accessing, addressing, assessing, caressing, confessing, convincing, depressing, distressing, expressing, impressing, obsessing, oppressing, possessing, processing, professing, progressing, regressing, repressing, suppressing, transgressing, undressing.
Arresting, contesting, detesting, digesting, divesting, infesting, interesting, investing, molesting, protesting, requesting, road-testing, suggesting.
Amending, ascending, attending, befriending, commending, contending, defending, depending, descending, extending, impending, intending, offending, overspending, pretending, suspending, transcending, unbending, upending.
Attempting, augmenting, consenting, dissenting, fragmenting, frequenting, inventing, lamenting, presenting, preventing, relenting, repenting, resenting, tormenting.
Attention, contention, convention, detention, dimension, extension, intention, invention, prevention, retention, suspension.
[4] Apprehending, comprehending, condescending, never-ending, recommending.
Acquiescing, convalescing, effervescing, reassessing, repossessing.
Complementing, complimenting, experimenting, implementing, misrepresenting, orienting, representing, supplementing, unrelenting.

2.4.66 "--ensive" (as in "expensive")
apprehensive, comprehensive, defensive, expensive, extensive, inexpensive, intensive, offensive, pensive.

SURPRISING RHYMING:
[2] Fences, lenses, senses, tenses, Texas.
Fencing, sensing, tensing.
Pencil, stencil, utensil.
Dented, rented, scented, splendid, vented.
Freshen, lesson, mention, pension, session, tension.
[3] Aggressive, excessive, expressive, impressive, obsessive, oppressive, possessive, progressive, repressive, successive.
Collective, connective, corrective, defective, detective, directive, effective, infective, objective, perceptive, perspective, prospective, protective, reflective, respective, retrospective, selective, subjective.
Commences, condenses, defences/defenses (U.S.), dispenses, expenses, incenses, licences/licenses (U.S.), offences/offenses (U.S.), pretences/pretenses (U.S.).
Commencing, condensing, dispensing, incensing, licensing, ring-fencing, sentencing, sequencing, silencing.
Abstention, attention, contention, convention, detention, dimension, extension, intention, invention, prevention, retention, suspension.
Consented, contented, demented, dissented, fragmented, frequented, invented, lamented, presented, prevented, relented, repented, resented, tormented.

2.4.67 "--ented" (as in "scented")
[2] dented, rented, scented, vented.
[3] augmented, cemented, consented, contented, demented, dissented, fermented, fragmented, frequented, invented, lamented, presented, prevented, relented, repented, resented, segmented, tormented, unscented.
[4] circumvented, complemented, complimented, discontented, disoriented, experimented, implemented, misrepresented, oriented, regimented, represented, supplemented.

SURPRISING RHYMING:
[2] Bended, blended, ended, friended, mended, tended, vended.
Bedded, dreaded, headed, leaded, shredded, sledded, threaded, treaded, wedded.
Belted, melted, pelted, smelted.
Bested, crested, jested, nested, rested, tested, vested.

[3] Amended, attended, befriended, commended, defended, depended, descended, extended, intended, offended, pretended, rear-ended, suspended, transcended.
Attempted, exempted, tempted, pre-empted.
Bareheaded, beheaded, bigheaded, cool headed, embedded, hardheaded, hotheaded, lightheaded, pigheaded, redheaded, spearheaded, thickheaded, unwedded.
Affected, collected, connected, corrected, dejected, detected, directed, dissected, ejected, elected, erected, expected, infected, injected, inspected, neglected, objected, perfected, projected, protected, reflected, rejected, respected, selected, suspected.
Arrested, congested, contested, detested, digested, divested, infested, invested, molested, protested, requested, road-tested, suggested, untested.
Deceptive, defensive, expensive, extensive, incentive, intensive, offensive, pensive.
[4] Apprehended, comprehended, condescended, recommended.
Interjected, interested, misdirected, recollected, re-elected, resurrected.
Apprehensive, comprehensive, inexpensive.

2.4.68 "--enter" (as in "enter")
[2] centre/center (U.S.), enter, renter.
[3] cementer, dissenter, epicentre/epicenter (U.S.), eventer, fermenter, frequenter, inventor, lamenter, magenta, presenter, preventer, re-enter, repenter, tormentor.

SURPRISING RHYMING:
[2] Ember, ender, fender, gender, lender, member, mender, render, sender, slender, spender, splendour/splendor (U.S.), temper, tender, vendor.
Censor, denser, fencer, sensor, tenser, condenser, dispenser.
Fester, jester, nester, pester, quester, tester, vesta, zester.
[3] Agenda, apprehender, attender, bartender, contender, defender, hacienda, moneylender, offender, pretender, surrender, suspender, transgender, weekender.
December, dismember, remember, September, November.
Ancestor, fiesta, investor, molester, polyester, protester, semester, sequester, siesta.

2.4.69 "--endable" (as in "mendable")
bendable, blendable, commendable, defendable, dependable, expendable, extendable, lendable, mendable, recommendable, sendable, spendable, unbendable.

SURPRISING RHYMING:
[3] Credible, edible, flexible, incredible, legible, preferable, sensible, terrible.
Chemical, ethical, festival, medical, pedestal, sensual, sentinel, skeletal, sceptical/skeptical (U.S.), spectacle, tentacle, vegetable.
Kissable, miserable, missable, possible, syllable, visible.
[4] Accessible, acceptable, adorable, avoidable, compatible, confessional, corruptible, defensible, delectable, deplorable, desirable, detectable, dispensable, forgettable, impeccable, improbable, infallible, inflexible, insatiable, lamentable, ostensible, presentable, preventable, regrettable, remarkable, respectable, responsible, satiable, unflappable, unmissable, unstoppable, untouchable.
Available, contemptible, eligible, illegible, ineligible, indelible, intelligible, negligible, susceptible, unassailable, unavailable.
Accidental, confidential, conventional, disrespectful, exceptional, fundamental, hypothetical, incidental, influential, instrumental, intentional, monumental, professional, sentimental, temperamental, three-dimensional, unconventional, unintentional.
[5] Comprehensible, inaccessible, indefensible, indispensable, irrepressible, irresistible, reprehensible, unacceptable, unconventional, unforgettable, unintentional, unprofessional.

2.4.70 "--enderest" (as in "tenderest")
[3] slenderest, tenderest.

SURPRISING RHYMING:
[1] Best, blessed, breast, chest, crest, dressed, guest, guessed, jest, lest, messed, nest, pest, quest, rest, stressed, test, vest, west.
[2] Abreast, addressed, armrest, arrest, Beau Geste, behest, bequest, caressed,

confessed, contest, conquest, depressed, detest, digest, digressed, distressed, divest, expressed, impressed, infest, inquest, invest, Midwest, molest, northwest, oppressed, possessed, progressed, protest, recessed, repressed, request, road-test, southwest, suggest, suppressed, transgressed, undressed, unrest, well-dressed.
[3] **Dispossessed**, effervesced, interest, overdressed, reassessed, second-best, self-addressed, self-confessed, self-possessed, unexpressed, unimpressed.

2.4.71 "--entering" (as in "entering")
[3] centering, entering, mentoring, re-entering.

SURPRISING RHYMING:
[3] **Bartendering**, bettering, censoring, festering, feathering, lecturing, lettering, measuring, menacing, offering, peppering, pestering, questioning, rendering, severing, sheltering, splintering, sweltering, tempering, tendering, tethering, texturing, venturing, weathering, whispering, wondering.
Anything, boxing ring, chicken wing, colouring/coloring (U.S.), everything, nuzzling, pencil-in, splattering, stenciling, wedding ring.
[4] **Endeavouring/endeavoring** (U.S.), remembering, surrendering.

2.4.72 "--ep" (as in "step")
[1] pep, prep, rep, schlep, step, steppe, yep.
[2] doorstep, footstep, goosestep, instep, misstep, one-step, quickstep, sidestep.

SURPRISING RHYMING:
[1] **Crept**, kept, leapt, prepped, slept, stepped, swept, wept.
Bed, bled, bread, bred, cred, dead, dread, fed, fled, head, lead, led, Med, read, red, said, shed, shred, sled, sped, spread, stead, thread, tread, wed, zed.
Bet, debt, fret, get, jet, let, met, net, pet, set, stet, sweat, threat, vet, wet, whet, yet. Check, cheque, deck, fleck, heck, neck, peck, sec, spec, speck, tec, tech, trek, wreck.
[2] **Accept**, adept, concept, except, inept, intercept, overslept, over-stepped, precept, rainswept, side-stepped, unswept, windswept.
Ahead, airhead, bighead, blockhead, bloodshed, bobsled, bonehead, co-ed, deadhead, deathbed, dickhead, drop dead, forehead, highbred, homebred, homestead, hotbed, hothead, instead, misled, pinhead, pothead, purebred, redhead, sickbed, skinhead, sleepyhead, sofa-bed, sorehead, spearhead, spoon-fed, sunbed, thickhead, unsaid, warhead, waterbed, watershed, well-fed, well-read, widespread.
Asset, baguette, banquet, brunette/brunet (U.S.), cadet, cassette, coquette, cornet, corvette, dragnet, duet, filmset, fishnet, forget, gazette, handset, headset, in debt, inlet, inset, kismet, mindset, nymphet, octet, offset, onset, outset, quartet, quintet, regret, reset, rosette, roulette, sextet, sunset, upset, vignette.
Breakneck, crew-neck, crosscheck, exec, foredeck, henpeck, high tech, raincheck, redneck, rollneck, roughneck, shipwreck, soundcheck, spot-check, sundeck, V-neck.

2.4.73 "--ept" (as in "slept")
[1] crept, kept, leapt, prepped, slept, stepped, swept, wept.
[2] accept, adept, concept, except, inept, intercept, overslept, over-stepped, precept, rainswept, side-stepped, unswept, windswept.

SURPRISING RHYMING:
[1] **Checked**, decked, flecked, necked, pecked, sect, specked, trekked, wrecked.
Check, cheque, deck, fleck, heck, neck, peck, sec, spec, speck, tech, trek, wreck.
Pep, prep, rep, schlep, step, steppe, yep.
Next, sexed, sext, text, vexed.
Best, blessed, breast, chest, crest, dressed, guest, guessed, jest, lest, messed, nest, pest, quest, rest, stressed, test, vest, west, zest.
Bet, debt, fret, get, jet, let, met, net, pet, set, stet, sweat, threat, vet, wet, whet, yet.
[2] **Affect**, aspect, collect, connect, correct, defect, deflect, detect, dialect, direct, dissect, effect, eject, elect, erect, expect, henpecked, infect, inject, insect, inspect,

neglect, object, perfect, project, prospect, protect, reflect, reject, respect, select, subject, suspect, unchecked.
Doorstep, footstep, instep, misstep, one-step, quickstep, sidestep.
Annexed, context, oversexed, perplexed, pretext, subtext, teletext.
Burlesque, desk, grotesque, newsdesk, picturesque, statuesque.
Abreast, addressed, armrest, arrest, Beau Geste, behest, bequest, caressed, confessed, contest, conquest, depressed, detest, digest, digressed, distressed, divest, expressed, impressed, infest, inquest, invest, Midwest, molest, northwest, oppressed, possessed, progressed, protest, recessed, repressed, request, road-test, southwest, suggest, suppressed, transgressed, undressed, unrest, well-dressed.
Asset, baguette, banquet, brunette/brunet (U.S.), cadet, cassette, coquette, cornet, corvette, dragnet, duet, filmset, fishnet, forget, gazette, handset, headset, in debt, inlet, inset, kismet, mindset, nymphet, octet, offset, onset, outset, quartet, quintet, regret, reset, rosette, roulette, sextet, sunset, upset, vignette.
[3] **Aftereffect**, architect, circumspect, dialect, disaffect, disinfect, disconnect, disrespect, incorrect, indirect, intellect, misdirect, recollect, resurrect, retrospect, self-respect.
Alphabet, cigarette, clarinet, epithet, etiquette, heavy-set, internet, launderette, maisonette, marionette, minuet, outlet, pirouette, silhouette, statuette, suffragette.

2.4.74 "--eption" (as in "deception")
[3] conception, deception, exception, inception, interception, misconception, objection, perception, reception.

SURPRISING RHYMING:
[2] **Freshen**, lesson, mention, pension, session, tension, weapon.
Etching, fetching, retching, sketching, stretching.
[3] **Affection**, collection, complexion, confection, connection, correction, deflection, dejection, detection, direction, ejection, election, infection, inflection, injection, inspection, objection, perfection, projection, protection, reflection, rejection, section, selection.
Attention, contention, convention, detention, dimension, extension, exemption, intention, invention, pretension, prevention, redemption, retention, suspension.
Aggression, concession, confession, depression, digression, direction, discretion, expression, impression, jam session, obsession, oppression, possession, procession, profession, progression, recession, regression, repression, succession.
Congestion, digestion, indigestion, question, suggestion.
[4] **Imperfection**, indiscretion, insurrection, interjection, intersection, introspection, misdirection, predilection, recollection, resurrection, retrospection, self-expression.
Apprehension, comprehension, condescension, contravention, hypertension, intervention.

2.4.75 "--erry" (as in "very")
[2] berry, bury, chérie, cherry, ferry, merry, sherry, very.
[3] blackberry, blueberry, cranberry, gooseberry, raspberry, strawberry.

SURPRISING RHYMING:
[2] **Berries**, buries, buried, cherries, ferries.
Breathy, envy, friendly, gently, healthy, pebbly, stealthy, wealthy.
Belly, deli, edgy, jelly, smelly, tele, telly, veggie.
Any, bevvy, Chevy, heavy, levee, many, penny, top-heavy.
Airy, angry, belfry, dairy, debris, entry, esprit, every, fairy, flowery, gentry, hairy, hurry, prairie, rarely, scary, sentry, squarely, squarely, treachery, vary, vestry, wary, weary.
Barely, fairly, rarely, squarely, unfairly.
Dressy, emcee, lessee, messy, sexy.
Hefty, jetty, lefty, petit, petty, settee, sweaty.
[3] **Blackberries**, blue berries, cranberries, gooseberries, raspberries, strawberries.
Already, heady, ready, steady, teddy, unready, unsteady.
Confetti, jetty, libretti, petty, spaghetti, sweaty.
Ancestry, archery, artistry, bakery, battery, bigotry, binary, blackberry, blubbery, blueberry, blustery, brasserie, bravery, brewery, bribery, burglary, calorie, carpentry, carvery, cavalry, celery, century, chemistry, chicory, chivalry, Christmas tree, colliery, contrary, devilry, diary, dietary, disagree, dithery, doddery, drudgery, dungaree, duty-

free, eatery, enquiry, estuary, expiry, factory, fakery, feathery, filigree, finery, fishery, flattery, fluttery, forestry, forgery, gallery, geometry, gimmickry, glittery, greenery, grocery, history, imagery, injury, inquiry, ivory, jamboree, jewellery/jewelry (U.S.), jittery, leathery, lingerie, lottery, luxury, memory, mercury, misery, momentary, monastery, mystery, nursery, obituary, obligatory, pageantry, pedigree, perjury, pillory, pleasantry, poetry, pottery, primary, priory, quivery, referee, revelry, reverie, rivalry, robbery, rockery, rosary, rubbery, salary, sanctuary, savagery, savory, scenery, sensory, shimmery, shivery, silvery, slavery, slippery, sorcery, sugary, surgery, tapestry, thundery, treachery, trickery, victory, wintery, wizardry.
[4] Accessory, adultery, artillery, cautionary, cemetery, compulsory, confectionery, conciliatory, constabulary, contemporary, customary, debauchery, delivery, dictionary, directory, discovery, distillery, elementary, embroidery, explanatory, exploratory, hunky-dory, idolatry, imaginary, incendiary, infirmary, inflammatory, judiciary, laboratory, legendary, literary, machinery, mandatory, mercenary, military, missionary, necessary, ordinary, patisserie, perfumery, preliminary, psychiatry, publicity, reactionary, recovery, secretary, secondary, simplicity, skullduggery, solitary, stationary, stationery, temporary, territory, tomfoolery, upholstery, visionary, vocabulary.
[5] Anniversary, beneficiary, camaraderie, complementary, complimentary, contradictory, directory, documentary, elementary, evolutionary, intermediary, mocumentary, revolutionary, rudimentary, supplementary.

2.4.76 "--erries" (as in "berries")
[2] berries, buries, cherries, ferries.
[3] blackberries, blue berries, cranberries, gooseberries, raspberries, strawberries.

SURPRISING RHYMING:
[2] Berry, breathy, bury, chérie, cherry, ferry, merry, sherry, very.
Aries, dairies, debris, dresses, emcees, entries, fairies, hurries, sentries, varies.
Bevvies, envies, friendlies, heavies, jellies, levees, pennies, selfies.
[3] Blackberry, blueberry, cranberry, gooseberry, raspberry, strawberry.
Bakeries, batteries, boundaries, breweries, burglaries, calories, canaries, centuries, diaries, disagrees, dungarees, eateries, enquiries, estuaries, factories, fisheries, friaries, histories, industries, injuries, inquiries, jamborees, libraries, luxuries, memories, monasteries, mortuaries, mysteries, notaries, nurseries, obituaries, pleasantries, referees, revelries, reveries, rivalries, robberies, rockeries, salaries, summaries, surgeries, symmetries, tandooris, tapestries, victories.
[4] Accessories, adversaries, allegories, categories, dictionaries, luminaries, mercenaries, missionaries, preliminaries, secretaries, subsidiaries, territories.

2.4.77 "--ess" (as in "dress")
[1] bless, chess, cress, dress, guess, less, mess, press, stress, tress, yes.
[2] abscess, access, address, assess, caress, compress, confess, congress, depress, digress, distress, duress, excess, express, finesse, headdress, impress, largesse, nightdress, obsess, oppress, outguess, possess, process, profess, princess, progress, recess, redress, regress, repress, success, suppress, transgress, undress, unless.
[3] acquiesce, baroness, battledress, coalesce, convalesce, dispossess, effervesce, manageress, minidress, murderess, nevertheless, nonetheless, overstress, poetess, reassess, repossess, shepherdess, SOS, stewardess, tenderness.

SURPRISING RHYMING:
[1] Bets, debts, frets, gets, jets, lets, pets, sets, sweats, threats, vets, wets, whets.
Best, blessed, blest, breast, chest, crest, dressed, guest, guessed, jest, messed, nest, pest, quest, rest, stressed, test, vest, west, zest.
Breath, death.
[2] Assets, baguettes, banquets, begets, brunettes/brunets (U.S.), cadets, cassettes, cornets, corvettes, dragnets, duets, filmsets, fishnets, forgets, handsets, headsets, inlets, nymphets, offsets, quartets, regrets, resets, rosettes, sunsets, upsets, vignettes.
Abreast, addressed, armrest, arrest, Beau Geste, behest, bequest, caressed, confessed, contest, conquest, depressed, detest, digest, digressed, distressed, divest,

expressed, impressed, infest, inquest, invest, Midwest, molest, northwest, oppressed, possessed, progressed, protest, recessed, repressed, request, road-test, southwest, suggest, suppressed, transgressed, undressed, unrest, well-dressed.
Arabesque, burlesque, desk, grotesque, newsdesk, picturesque, statuesque.
[3] **Castanets**, cigarettes, clarinets, epithets, outlets, silhouettes, statuettes, suffragettes. **Chimneybreast**, dispossessed, effervesced, interest, manifest, overdressed, reassessed, second-best, self-addressed, self-confessed, self-possessed, unexpressed, unimpressed.
Eightieth, fiftieth, fortieth, ninetieth, seventieth, sixtieth, thirtieth, twentieth.

2.4.78 "--esk" (as in "desk")

arabesque, burlesque, desk, grotesque, newsdesk, picturesque, statuesque.

SURPRISING RHYMING:
[1] **Check**, cheque, deck, fleck, heck, neck, peck, sec, spec, speck, tech, trek, wreck.
Crept, kept, leapt, prepped, slept, stepped, swept, wept.
Best, blessed, blest, breast, chest, crest, dressed, guest, guessed, jest, lest, messed, nest, pest, quest, rest, stressed, test, vest, west.
[2] **Abreast**, addressed, armrest, arrest, Beau Geste, behest, bequest, caressed, confessed, contest, conquest, depressed, detest, digest, digressed, distressed, divest, expressed, impressed, infest, inquest, invest, Midwest, molest, northwest, oppressed, possessed, progressed, protest, recessed, repressed, request, road-test, southwest, suggest, suppressed, transgressed, undressed, unrest, well-dressed.
Affect, aspect, collect, connect, correct, defect, deflect, detect, dialect, direct, dissect, effect, eject, elect, erect, expect, henpecked, infect, inject, insect, inspect, neglect, object, perfect, project, prospect, protect, reflect, reject, respect, select, subject, suspect, unchecked.
Accept, adept, concept, except, inept, intercept, overslept, over-stepped, precept, rainswept, side-stepped, unswept, windswept.
Asset, baguette, banquet, brunette/brunet (U.S.), cadet, cassette, coquette, cornet, corvette, dragnet, duet, filmset, fishnet, forget, gazette, handset, headset, in debt, inlet, inset, kismet, mindset, nymphet, octet, offset, onset, outset, quartet, quintet, regret, reset, rosette, roulette, sextet, sunset, upset, vignette.
Breakneck, crew-neck, crosscheck, foredeck, henpeck, high tech, raincheck, redneck, rollneck, roughneck, shipwreck, soundcheck, spot-check, sundeck, swan-neck, V-neck.
[3] **Bodycheck**, bottleneck, discotheque, leatherneck, rubberneck, turtleneck.
Aftereffect, architect, circumspect, dialect, disaffect, disinfect, disconnect, disrespect, incorrect, indirect, intellect, introspect, recollect, resurrect, retrospect, self-respect.
Alphabet, castanet, cigarette, clarinet, epithet, etiquette, internet, launderette, maisonette, marionette, minuet, outlet, pirouette, silhouette, statuette, suffragette.

2.4.79 "--est" (as in "best")

[1] best, blessed, blest, breast, chest, crest, dressed, guest, guessed, jest, lest, messed, nest, pest, quest, rest, stressed, test, vest, west, wrest, zest.
[2] abreast, addressed, armrest, arrest, attest, Beau Geste, behest, bequest, caressed, compressed, confessed, contest, conquest, depressed, detest, digest, digressed, distressed, divest, expressed, footrest, headrest, impressed, incest, infest, ingest, inquest, invest, Midwest, molest, northwest, oppressed, possessed, progressed, protest, recessed, repressed, request, road-test, southwest, suggest, suppressed, transgressed, undressed, unrest, unstressed, well-dressed.
[3] chimneybreast, dispossessed, effervesced, interest, manifest, overdressed, readdressed, reassessed, repossessed, second-best, self-addressed, self-confessed, self-possessed, unaddressed, unexpressed, unimpressed.

SURPRISING RHYMING:
[1] **Crept**, kept, leapt, prepped, slept, stepped, swept, wept.
Next, sexed, sext, text, vexed.
Checks, decks, flecks, necks, pecks, sects, specks, treks, wrecks.
Bet, debt, fret, get, jet, let, met, net, pet, set, stet, sweat, threat, vet, wet, whet, yet.
Bless, chess, cress, dress, guess, less, mess, press, stress, yes.
Pep, prep, rep, schlep, step, steppe, yep.

[2] Aspects, collects, connects, corrects, deflects, detects, directs, dissects, effects, ejects, erects, expects, infects, injects, insects, inspects, neglects, objects, perfects, projects, prospects, protects, reflects, rejects, respects, selects, subjects, suspects.
Against, commenced, condensed, dispensed, incensed, licensed, ring-fenced, sensed, sentenced, sequenced, silenced.
Doorstep, footstep, instep, misstep, one-step, quickstep, sidestep.
Burlesque, desk, grotesque, newsdesk, picturesque, statuesque.
Accept, adept, concept, except, inept, intercept, overslept, over-stepped, precept, rainswept, side-stepped, unswept, windswept.
Annexed, context, oversexed, perplexed, pretext, subtext, teletext.
Asset, baguette, banquet, brunette/brunet (U.S.), cadet, cassette, coquette, cornet, corvette, dragnet, duet, filmset, fishnet, forget, gazette, handset, headset, in debt, inlet, inset, kismet, mindset, nymphet, octet, offset, onset, outset, quartet, quintet, regret, reset, rosette, roulette, sextet, sunset, upset, vignette.
Access, address, assess, caress, compress, confess, congress, depress, digress, distress, duress, excess, express, finesse, headdress, impress, largesse, nightdress, obsess, oppress, possess, process, profess, princess, progress, recess, redress, regress, repress, success, suppress, transgress, undress, unless.
[3] Aftereffects, architects, dialects, disconnects, disrespects, intellects, intersects, recollects, reconnects, resurrects.
Influenced, recommenced, recompensed, referenced.
Acquiesce, baroness, battledress, coalesce, convalesce, dispossess, effervesce, manageress, minidress, murderess, nevertheless, nonetheless, overstress, poetess, reassess, repossess, shepherdess, SOS, stewardess, tenderness.

2.4.80 "--estion" (as in "question")
[3] congestion, digestion, indigestion, ingestion, question, suggestion.

SURPRISING RHYMING:
[2] Freshen, lessen, lesson, mention, pension, session, tension.
Blessing, dressing, guessing, messing, pressing, stressing, yessing.
Etching, fetching, retching, sketching, stretching.
Alleging, edging, fledging, hedging, pledging, sledging, wedging.
Guesting, jesting, nesting, questing, resting, testing, vesting.
[3] Attention, contention, convention, detention, dimension, extension, intention, invention, pretension, prevention, retention, suspension.
Affection, collection, complexion, confection, connection, correction, dejection, detection, direction, ejection, election, infection, injection, inspection, objection, perfection, projection, protection, reflection, rejection, section, selection.
Conception, deception, exception, inception, interception, misconception, objection, perception, reception.
Aggression, concession, confession, depression, discretion, expression, impression, jam session, obsession, oppression, possession, procession, profession, progression, recession, regression, repression, succession, transgression.
Accessing, addressing, assessing, caressing, confessing, depressing, digressing, distressing, expressing, impressing, obsessing, oppressing, possessing, processing, professing, progressing, regressing, repressing, suppressing, transgressing, undressing.
Arresting, contesting, detesting, digesting, divesting, infesting, interesting, investing, manifesting, molesting, protesting, requesting, road-testing, suggesting.
[4] Apprehension, comprehension, condescension, contravention, hypertension, intervention, misapprehension.
Imperfection, indiscretion, insurrection, interjection, intersection, introspection, misdirection, recollection, resurrection, retrospection, self-expression.
Acquiescing, convalescing, dispossessing, effervescing, reassessing, repossessing.

2.4.81 "--escent" (as in "crescent")
[3] crescent, depressant, excrescent, fluorescent, incessant, quiescent.
[4] acquiescent, effervescent, iridescent, incandescent, adolescent, obsolescent, convalescent, antidepressant.

SURPRISING RHYMING:
[1] **Bent**, cent, dent, gent, leant, lent, meant, rent, scent, sent, spent, tent, vent, went.
Dreamt, kempt, tempt.
[2] **Freshen**, lesson, mention, pension, second, session, tension, weapon.
Absent, accent, advent, ascent, assent, augment, cement, comment, consent, content, decent, descent, dissent, event, extent, fragment, frequent, hellbent, intent, invent, lament, moment, percent, portent, present, prevent, relent, repent, resent, torment.
Errant, parent, apparent, inherent, transparent.
Attempt, contempt, exempt, pre-empt, unkempt.
Ardent, apparent, garment, peasant, pheasant, pleasant, remnant, sergeant.
Blessing, dressing, guessing, messing, pressing, stressing, yessing.
Absence, cadence, commence, condense, conscience, defence/defense (U.S.), dispense, essence, expense, immense, incense, intense, licence/license (U.S.), nonsense, offence/offense (U.S.), patience, presence, pretence/pretense (U.S.), prudence, ring-fence, science, sentence, sequence, silence, sixpence, suspense.
[3] **Accident**, argument, circumvent, complement, compliment, condiment, confident, diligent, discontent, disorient, document, eminent, evident, excellent, experiment, fraudulent, government, imminent, implement, incident, insolent, instrument, malcontent, management, misrepresent, misspent, monument, negligent, opulent, orient, ornament, overspent, parliament, permanent, punishment, regiment, represent, sacrament, subsequent, succulent, supplement, tenement, testament, tournament, turbulent.
Attendant, defendant, dependent, descendant, pendant, superintendent, transcendent.
Accessing, addressing, assessing, caressing, confessing, depressing, digressing, distressing, expressing, impressing, obsessing, oppressing, possessing, processing, professing, progressing, regressing, suppressing, transgressing, undressing.
[4] **Acquiescence**, adolescence, adolescents, effervescence, reminiscent.

2.4.82 "--esser" (as in "lesser")
[2] dresser, guesser, lesser, presser, yessir.
[3] aggressor, assessor, caresser, confessor, contessa, digresser, hairdresser, oppressor, possessor, predecessor, processor, professor, microprocessor, successor, suppresser, transgressor.

SURPRISING RHYMING:
[2] **Censor**, denser, fencer, sensor, tenser, condenser, dispenser.
Fester, jester, nester, pester, quester, tester, vesta, wester, zester.
Leisure, measure, pleasure, treasure.
[3] **Ancestor**, fiesta, investor, molester, polyester, protester, semester, siesta, trimester.
Displeasure, made-to-measure.
Bestseller, cave dweller, dispeller, exceller, expeller, foreteller, novella, paella, propeller, repeller, umbrella.
[4] **A Capella**, Cinderella, fortune-teller, mozzarella, storyteller.

2.4.83 "--esses" (as in "caresses")
[2] blesses, dresses, guesses, messes, presses, stresses, tresses, yeses.
[3] addresses, assesses, caresses, compresses, confesses, digresses, distresses, egresses, excesses, expresses, finesses, impresses, obsesses, oppresses, possesses, princesses, processes, professes, progresses, recesses, redresses, regresses, represses, successes, suppresses, transgresses, undresses.
[4] acquiesces, baronesses, coalesces, convalesces, dispossesses, effervesces, reassesses, repossesses, stewardesses.

SURPRISING RHYMING:
[2] **Fences**, lenses, senses, tenses, Texas.
Freshens, lessons, mentions, pensions, sessions, tensions.
Alleges, edges, fledges, hedges, ledges, pledges, sledges, wedges.
Blessing(s), dressing, guessing, messing, pressing, stressing.
Bested, crested, jested, nested, rested, tested, vested.
Aces, bases, cases, faces, laces, places, races, traces, vases.

[3] Aggressive, excessive, expressive, impressive, obsessive, oppressive, possessive, progressive, repressive, successive.
Apprehensive, comprehensive, defensive, expensive, intensive, offensive, pensive.
Attentive, collective, connective, corrective, defective, detective, directive, effective, incentive, infective, invective, inventive, objective, perceptive, perspective, preventive, prospective, protective, reflective, retrospective, selective, subjective.
Arrested, congested, contested, detested, digested, infested, ingested, invested, molested, protested, requested, suggested.
Backspaces, birthplaces, bookcases, bootlaces, briefcases, debases, defaces, disgraces, displaces, effaces, embraces, encases, erases, fireplaces, misplaces, nutcases, outpaces, replaces, retraces, shoelaces, showcases, staircases, suitcases, typefaces, unlaces, wheelbases, workplaces, workspaces.
[4] Angel faces, databases, hiding places, interfaces, interlaces, nutcases, packing cases, pillowcases, resting places.

2.4.84 "--ession" (as in "confession")
[2] freshen, session.
[3] aggression, concession, confession, depression, digression, discretion, expression, impression, jam session, obsession, oppression, possession, procession, profession, progression, recession, regression, repression, succession, transgression.
[4] indiscretion, repossession, self-expression.

SURPRISING RHYMING:
[2] **Lesson**, mention, pension, tension, weapon.
Blessing *(silent 'g')*, dressing, guessing, messing, pressing, stressing, yessing.
Etching *(silent 'g')*, fetching, retching, sketching, stretching.
Alleging *(silent 'g')*, edging, fledging, hedging, pledging, sledging, wedging.
Deafen, eleven, heaven, seven.
Bridging, engine, legend.
Fencing, sensing, tensing.
[3] **Attention**, contention, convention, detention, dimension, extension, intention, invention, pretension, prevention, retention, suspension.
Congestion, digestion, indigestion, ingestion, question, suggestion.
Affection, collection, complexion, connection, correction, defection, deflection, dejection, detection, direction, dissection, ejection, election, erection, infection, injection, inspection, objection, perfection, projection, protection, reflection, rejection, section, selection.
Conception, deception, exception, inception, interception, misconception, objection, perception, reception.
Accessing *(silent 'g')*, addressing, assessing, caressing, confessing, depressing, digressing, distressing, expressing, impressing, obsessing, oppressing, possessing, processing, professing, progressing, regressing, suppressing, transgressing, undressing.
Commencing *(silent 'g')*, condensing, dispensing, incensing, licensing, ring-fencing, sentencing, sequencing, silencing.
[4] **Apprehension**, comprehension, condescension, contravention, hypertension, intervention, misapprehension.
Imperfection, insurrection, interjection, intersection, introspection, misdirection, recollection, resurrection, retrospection.
Acquiescing *(silent 'g')*, convalescing, effervescing, reassessing, repossessing.

2.4.85 "--essing" (as in "caressing")
[2] blessing, dressing, guessing, messing, pressing, stressing, yessing.
[3] accessing, addressing, assessing, caressing, confessing, depressing, digressing, distressing, expressing, impressing, obsessing, oppressing, possessing, processing, professing, progressing, regressing, repressing, suppressing, transgressing, undressing.
[4] acquiescing, convalescing, dispossessing, effervescing, reassessing, repossessing.

SURPRISING RHYMING:
[2] **Betting**, fretting, getting, jetting, letting, netting, petting, setting, sweating, vetting, wetting, whetting.

Cresting, guesting, jesting, nesting, questing, resting, testing..
Etching, fetching, retching, sketching, stretching.
Fencing, sensing, tensing.
Bedding, dreading, heading, shedding, shredding, spreading, treading, wedding.
Checking, decking, flecking, pecking, specking, trekking, wrecking.
Dwelling, felling, gelling/jelling, quelling, selling, shelling, smelling, spelling, swelling, telling, yelling.
[3] **Abetting**, banqueting, begetting, duetting, forgetting, pirouetting, regretting, upsetting.
Arresting, detesting, digesting, divesting, infesting, interesting, investing, molesting, protesting, requesting, suggesting.
Commencing, condensing, dispensing, incensing, licensing, ring-fencing, sentencing, sequencing, silencing.
Embedding, homesteading, letterheading, retreading, spearheading.
Annexing, indexing, perplexing, sexting, texting.
Affecting, collecting, connecting, correcting, deflecting, detecting, directing, dissecting, ejecting, electing, erecting, expecting, infecting, injecting, inspecting, neglecting, objecting, perfecting, projecting, prospecting, protecting, reflecting, rejecting, respecting, selecting, subjecting, suspecting.
Compelling, excelling, foretelling, fortune-telling, misspelling, rebelling, repelling.

2.4.86 "--essive" (as in "impressive")
[3] aggressive, excessive, expressive, impressive, obsessive, oppressive, possessive, progressive, recessive, repressive, successive, suppressive.

SURPRISING RHYMING:
[2] **Blesses**, dresses, guesses, message, messes, presses, stresses, tresses, yeses.
Blessing, dressing, guessing, messing, pressing, session, stressing.
Deafen, eleven, heaven, seven.
Endless, fellas, jealous, Lexus, menace, precious, relentless, senseless, zealous.
[3] **Collective**, corrective, defective, detective, effective, objective, perceptive, perspective, prospective, protective, reflective, respective, selective, subjective.
Deceptive, defensive, expensive, festive, incentive, intensive, offensive, pensive.
Accessing, addressing, assessing, caressing, confessing, depressing, digressing, distressing, expressing, impressing, obsessing, oppressing, possessing, processing, professing, progressing, regressing, repressing, suppressing, transgressing, undressing.
Addresses, caresses, confesses, digresses, distresses, excesses, expresses, impresses, obsesses, oppresses, possesses, princesses, processes, professes, progresses, recesses, redresses, regresses, successes, transgresses, undresses.

2.4.87 "--ested" (as in "rested")
[2] bested, crested, jested, nested, rested, tested, vested.
[3] arrested, attested, congested, contested, detested, digested, divested, infested, ingested, invested, molested, protested, requested, road-tested, suggested, unrested.
[4] double-breasted, interested, manifested.

SURPRISING RHYMING:
[2] **Dented**, rented, scented, vented.
Betted, fretted, jetted, netted, sweated, vetted, whetted.
Bended, blended, ended, mended, tended, vended, wended.
Bedded, dreaded, headed, leaded, shredded, sledded, threaded, treaded, wedded.
Ahead, airhead, bighead, blockhead, bloodshed, bobsled, bonehead, co-ed, deadhead, deathbed, dickhead, drop dead, forehead, highbred, homebred, homestead, hotbed, hothead, instead, misled, pinhead, pothead, purebred, redhead, sickbed, skinhead, sleepyhead, sofa-bed, sorehead, spearhead, spoon-fed, sunbed, thickhead, unsaid, warhead, waterbed, watershed, well-fed, well-read, widespread.
Asset, baguette, banquet, beget, beset, brunette/brunet (U.S.), cadet, cassette, coquette, cornet, corvette, dragnet, duet, filmset, fishnet, forget, gazette, handset, headset, in debt, inlet, kismet, mindset, nymphet, octet, offset, onset, outset, quartet, quintet, regret, rosette, roulette, sextet, sunset, upset, vignette.

[3] Augmented, cemented, consented, contented, demented, dissented, fragmented, frequented, invented, lamented, presented, prevented, relented, repented, resented, segmented, tormented, unscented.
Abetted, duetted, indebted, pirouetted, regretted, silhouetted.
Amended, ascended, attended, befriended, commended, defended, depended, descended, extended, intended, offended, pretended, rear-ended, suspended, upended.
Bareheaded, beheaded, bigheaded, cool headed, embedded, hardheaded, hotheaded, lightheaded, pigheaded, redheaded, spearheaded, thickheaded, unwedded.
Arrowhead, copperhead, dunderhead, figurehead, flowerbed, fountainhead, gingerbread, go-ahead, infrared, knucklehead, letterhead, loggerhead, newlywed, overfed, overhead, poppy head, riverbed, sleepyhead, thoroughbred, underfed, watershed.
Affected, collected, connected, corrected, deflected, dejected, detected, directed, dissected, ejected, erected, expected, infected, injected, inspected, neglected, objected, perfected, projected, protected, reflected, rejected, respected, selected, suspected.
Alphabet, castanet, cigarette, clarinet, epithet, etiquette, internet, launderette, maisonette, marionette, minuet, outlet, pirouette, silhouette, statuette, suffragette.
[4] Complemented, complimented, discontented, disoriented, experimented, implemented, recollected, represented, resurrected, supplemented.
Apprehended, comprehended, condescended, recommended.

2.4.88 "--ester" (as in "protester")
[2] fester, jester, nester, pester, quester, tester, vesta, zester.
[3] ancestor, arrester, celesta, contester, digester, fiesta, investor, molester, polyester, protester, semester, sequester, siesta, sou'wester, suggester, trimester.

SURPRISING RHYMING:
[2] Censor, centre/center (U.S.), denser, enter, fencer, sensor, tenser, dispenser.
Dresser, guesser, lesser, presser, yessir.
Better, debtor, fetter, fretter, getter, letter, setter, sweater, wetter.
Leisure, measure, pleasure, treasure.
[3] Dissenter, epicentre/epicenter (U.S.), inventor, lamenter, magenta, presenter, preventer, re-enter, repenter, tormentor.
Bonesetter, carburettor/carburetor (U.S.), forgetter, go-getter, jet-setter, love-letter, newsletter, operetta, pacesetter, red-letter, typesetter, unfetter, upsetter, vendetta.

2.4.89 "--esting" (as in "resting")
[2] cresting, guesting, jesting, nesting, questing, resting, testing, vesting.
[3] arresting, contesting, detesting, digesting, divesting, infesting, ingesting, interesting, investing, manifesting, molesting, protesting, requesting, road-testing, suggesting.

SURPRISING RHYMING:
[2] Crept in, leapt in, slept in, stepped in, swept in.
Blessing, dressing, guessing, messing, pressing, stressing, yessing.
Bee sting, Beijing, key-ring, nose-ring, offspring, plaything, real thing, sexting, shoestring, sun king, texting, upswing, vexing.
Checking, decking, pecking, trekking, wrecking.
Betting, fretting, getting, jetting, letting, petting, setting, sweating, vetting, wetting.
Bending, blending, ending, fending, lending, mending, pending, sending, spending, tending, trending, vending, wending.
Pepping, prepping, schlepping, stepping.
Dreading, heading, shedding, shredding, spreading, threading, treading, wedding.
Etching, fetching, retching, sketching, stretching.
[3] Accessing, addressing, assessing, caressing, confessing, depressing, digressing, distressing, expressing, impressing, obsessing, oppressing, possessing, processing, professing, progressing, regressing, suppressing, transgressing, undressing.
Abetting, banqueting, begetting, duetting, forgetting, regretting, silhouetting, upsetting.
Commencing, condensing, dispensing, incensing, licensing, perplexing, ring-fencing, sentencing, sequencing, silencing.

Amending, ascending, attending, befriending, commending, defending, depending, descending, extending, impending, intending, misspending, offending, overspending, pretending, suspending, transcending, unbending, upending.
Affecting, collecting, connecting, correcting, deflecting, detecting, directing, dissecting, ejecting, erecting, expecting, infecting, injecting, inspecting, neglecting, objecting, perfecting, projecting, protecting, reflecting, rejecting, respecting, selecting, suspecting.
[4] **Acquiescing**, convalescing, dispossessing, effervescing, reassessing, repossessing.
Bottlenecking, counterchecking, rubbernecking.
Apprehending, comprehending, condescending, recommending.

2.4.90 "--esents" (as in "presents")
adolescents, depressants, peasants, pheasants, presence, presents.

SURPRISING RHYMING:
[2] **Crescent**, peasant, pheasant, pleasant, present.
Against, commenced, condensed, dispensed, fenced, incensed, inconvenienced, influenced, licensed, recommenced, sensed, sentenced, sequenced, silenced.
Absence, cadence, commence, condense, conscience, defence/defense (U.S.), dispense, essence, expense, immense, incense, intense, licence/license (U.S.), nonsense, offence/offense (U.S.), patience, pretence/pretense (U.S.), prudence, remnants, ring-fence, science, segments, sentence, sequence, silence, sixth sense, suspense.
[3] **Attendants**, defendants, dependents, descendants, pendants, superintendents.
Audience, elegance, preference, reference, difference, inference.
Deliverance, irreverence, presidents, residence, residents, reverence, severance.
Experienced, inexperienced, influenced, recommended, recompensed, referenced.
Abstinence, affluence, ambience, audience, commonsense, competence, confidence, consequence, dependence, eloquence, emergence, eminence, evidence, excellence, impudence, impotence, indolence, influence, innocence, insistence, insolence, insurgence, negligence, opulence, penitence, permanence, persistence, prescience, prominence, providence, radiance, recommence, resurgence, reticence, reverence, self-defence/self-defense (U.S.), severance, subsistence, succulence, temperance, turbulence, violence.
[4] **Acquiescence**, adolescence, belligerence, benevolence, coincidence, convenience, correspondence, effervescence, independence, irreverence, magnificence, quintessence.

2.4.91 "--esidents" (as in "presidents")
[3] presidents, residence, residents.

SURPRISING RHYMING:
[2] **Absence**, cadence, commence, condense, conscience, defence/defense (U.S.), dispense, essence, expense, immense, incense, intense, licence/license (U.S.), nonsense, offence/offense, patience, presence, pretence/pretense (U.S.), prudence, science, sentence, sequence, silence, sixpence, suspense.
Against, commenced, condensed, dispensed, incensed, licensed, ring-fenced, sensed, sentenced, sequenced, silenced.
[3] **Accidents**, arguments, compliments, complements, documents, experiments, governments, implements, incidents, instruments, malcontents, misrepresents, monuments, ornaments, represents, sacraments, supplements, tenements, tournaments.
Abstinence, affluence, ambience, audience, coherence, commonsense, competence, condolence, conference, confidence, consequence, dependence, eloquence, emergence, eminence, evidence, excellence, existence, fraudulence, impatience, impudence, impotence, indolence, influence, innocence, insistence, insolence, insurgence, lenience, negligence, occurrence, opulence, penitence, permanence, persistence, prescience, prevalence, prominence, providence, radiance, recommence, recompense, recurrence, residence, resurgence, reticence, reverence, self-defence/self-defense (U.S.), severance, subsistence, succulence, temperance, transcendence, transience, turbulence, violence.
Influenced, recommenced, recompensed, referenced.
[4] **Acquiescence**, adolescence, ambivalence, belligerence, coincidence, convenience,

correspondence, disobedience, effervescence, experienced, inconvenience, independence, inexperience, intelligence, interference, irreverence, magnificence, malevolence, obedience, reminiscence, resilience, self-confidence.

2.4.92 "--et" (as in "bet")
[1] ate, bet, debt, fret, get, jet, let, met, net, pet, set, stet, sweat, threat, vet, wet, whet, yet.
[2] asset, baguette, banquet, beget, beset, bonnet, brochette, brunette/brunet (U.S.), cadet, cassette, closet, coquette, comet, cornet, corvette, croquette, dragnet, duet, faucet, filmset, fishnet, forget, gazette, hairnet, handset, headset, indebt, inlet, inset, jacket, kismet, locket, mindset, nymphet, octet, offset, onset, outset, pocket, pre-set, prophet, quartet, quintet, regret, reset, rocket, rosette, roulette, sextet, socket, sublet, subset, sunset, thickset, toilette, typeset, upset, vignette, wallet.
[3] alphabet, castanet, cigarette, clarinet, epithet, etiquette, heavy-set, internet, intranet, launderette, leatherette, maisonette, marionette, minuet, novelette, outlet, pirouette, silhouette, statuette, suffragette, usherette.

SURPRISING RHYMING:
[1] **Pep**, prep, rep, schlep, step, steppe, yep.
Crept, kept, leapt, prepped, slept, stepped, swept, wept.
Check, cheque, deck, fleck, heck, neck, peck, sec, spec, speck, tech, trek, wreck.
Checked, decked, flecked, pecked, sect, specked, trekked, wrecked.
Best, blessed, blest, breast, chest, crest, dressed, guest, guessed, jest, lest, messed, nest, pest, quest, rest, stressed, test, vest, west.
Chef, clef, deaf, ref.
[2] **Accept**, adept, concept, except, inept, intercept, overslept, over-stepped, rainswept, side-stepped, unswept, windswept.
Doorstep, footstep, instep, misstep, one-step, quickstep, sidestep.
Breakneck, crew-neck, crosscheck, Dalek, exec, henpeck, high tech, raincheck, redneck, rollneck, roughneck, shipwreck, soundcheck, spot-check, sundeck, V-neck.
Affect, aspect, collect, connect, correct, defect, deflect, detect, dialect, direct, dissect, effect, eject, elect, erect, expect, henpecked, infect, inject, insect, inspect, neglect, object, perfect, project, prospect, protect, reflect, reject, respect, select, subject, suspect, unchecked.
Abreast, addressed, armrest, arrest, Beau Geste, behest, bequest, caressed, confessed, contest, conquest, depressed, detest, digest, digressed, distressed, divest, expressed, impressed, infest, inquest, invest, Midwest, molest, northwest, oppressed, possessed, progressed, protest, recessed, repressed, request, road-test, southwest, suggest, suppressed, transgressed, undressed, unrest, well-dressed.
[3] **Aftereffect**, architect, circumspect, dialect, disaffect, disinfect, disconnect, disrespect, incorrect, indirect, intellect, recollect, resurrect, retrospect, self-respect.
Dispossessed, effervesced, interest, manifest, overdressed, reassessed, repossessed, second-best, self-confessed, self-possessed, unaddressed, unexpressed, unimpressed.

2.4.93 "--eth" (as in "breath")
[1] breath, death, eightieth, fiftieth, fortieth, ninetieth, seventieth, sixtieth, thirtieth, twentieth.

SURPRISING RHYMING:
[1] **Bereft**, cleft, deft, elf, heft, left, self, shelf, theft.
Breadth, breath, death, depth, length, strength, wavelength.
Bless, dress, guess, mess, press, stress, tress, yes.
Health, stealth, twelfth, wealth.
[2] **Tone-deaf**, UNICEF.
Address, assess, caress, compress, confess, digress, distress, egress, excess, express, finesse, impress, obsess, oppress, possess, princess, process, profess, progress, recess, redress, regress, repress, success, suppress, transgress, undress.
Bookshelf, herself, himself, itself, myself, oneself, yourself.

*

2.4.94 "--etching" (as in "fetching")
[2] etching, fetching, retching, sketching, stretching.

SURPRISING RHYMING:
[2] **Benching**, clenching, drenching, fencing, quenching, sensing, tensing, wrenching.
Alleging, edging, fledging, hedging, pledging, sledging, wedging.
Blessing, dressing, freshen, guessing, messing, pressing, stressing, session, yessing.
Cresting, guesting, jesting, nesting, questing, resting, testing.
[3] **Commencing**, condensing, dispensing, incensing, sentencing, sequencing, silencing.
Aggression, concession, confession, depression, discretion, expression, impression, jam session, obsession, oppression, possession, procession, profession, progression, recession, regression, repression, succession, transgression.
Accessing, addressing, assessing, caressing, confessing, depressing, digressing, distressing, expressing, impressing, obsessing, oppressing, possessing, professing, progressing, regressing, repressing, suppressing, transgressing, undressing.
Annexing, indexing, perplexing, sexting, texting.
Affecting, collecting, connecting, correcting, deflecting, detecting, directing, dissecting, ejecting, electing, erecting, expecting, infecting, injecting, inspecting, neglecting, objecting, perfecting, projecting, prospecting, protecting, reflecting, rejecting, respecting, selecting, subjecting, suspecting.
Arresting, contesting, detesting, digesting, divesting, infesting, ingesting, interesting, investing, manifesting, molesting, protesting, requesting, road-testing, suggesting.
[4] **Indiscretion**, repossession, self-expression.
Acquiescing, convalescing, dispossessing, effervescing, reassessing, repossessing.
Disinfecting, disconnecting, disrespecting, interjecting, intersecting, misdirecting, recollecting, re-electing, resurrecting, self-respecting.

2.4.95 "--etch" (as in "sketch")
[1] etch, fetch, ketch, lech, retch, sketch, stretch, wretch.

SURPRISING RHYMING:
[1] **Etched**, fetched, next, retched, sexed, sext, sketched, stretched, text, vexed.
Allege, edge, fledge, hedge, ledge, pledge, sledge, veg, wedge.
Checks, cheques, decks, flex, flecks, hex, necks, pecs, pecks, secs, sex, specs, specks, treks, vex, wrecks.
Best, blessed, blest, breast, chest, crest, dressed, guest, guessed, jest, lest, messed, nest, pest, quest, rest, stressed, test, vest, west.
[2] **Annexed**, context, oversexed, perplexed, pretext, subtext.
Annex, apex, complex, duplex, execs, perplex, rednecks, reflex, shipwrecks, soundchecks, spot-checks, vortex.
Affects, aspects, collects, connects, corrects, defects, deflects, detects, dialects, directs, dissects, effects, ejects, elects, erects, expects, infects, injects, insects, inspects, neglects, objects, perfects, projects, prospects, protects, reflects, rejects, respects, sects, selects, subjects, suspects.
Burlesque, desk, grotesque, newsdesk, picturesque, statuesque.
Abreast, addressed, armrest, arrest, Beau Geste, behest, bequest, caressed, confessed, contest, conquest, depressed, detest, digest, digressed, distressed, divest, expressed, impressed, infest, inquest, invest, Midwest, molest, northwest, oppressed, possessed, progressed, protest, recessed, repressed, request, road-test, southwest, suggest, suppressed, transgressed, undressed, unrest, well-dressed.
[3] **Aftereffects**, architects, dialects, disconnects, disrespects, recollects, resurrects.
Dispossessed, effervesced, interest, manifest, overdressed, reassessed, second-best, self-addressed, self-confessed, self-possessed, unaddressed, unexpressed, unimpressed.

2.4.96 "--etched" (as in "stretched")
[1] etched, fetched, retched, sketched, stretched.

SURPRISING RHYMING:
[1] **Etch**, fetch, ketch, lech, retch, sketch, stretch, wretch.

Best, blessed, breast, chest, crest, dressed, guest, guessed, jest, lest, messed, nest, pest, quest, rest, stressed, test, vest, west.
Benched, clenched, drenched, entrenched, quenched, wrenched.
Alleged, dredged, edged, fledged, fully-fledged, hedged, ledged, pledged, wedged.
Checked, decked, flecked, pecked, sect, specked, trekked, wrecked.
[2] **Abreast**, addressed, armrest, arrest, Beau Geste, behest, bequest, caressed, confessed, contest, conquest, depressed, detest, digest, digressed, distressed, divest, expressed, impressed, infest, inquest, invest, Midwest, molest, northwest, oppressed, possessed, progressed, protest, recessed, repressed, request, road-test, southwest, suggest, suppressed, transgressed, undressed, unrest, well-dressed.
Affect, aspect, collect, connect, correct, deflect, detect, dialect, direct, effect, eject, elect, erect, expect, henpecked, infect, inject, insect, inspect, neglect, object, perfect, project, prospect, protect, reflect, reject, respect, select, subject, suspect.
Burlesque, desk, grotesque, newsdesk, picturesque, statuesque.
[3] **Aftereffect**, architect, circumspect, dialect, disinfect, disconnect, disrespect, incorrect, indirect, intellect, introspect, recollect, resurrect, retrospect, self-respect.

2.4.97 "--etted" (as in "regretted")
[2] betted, fretted, jetted, netted, sweated, vetted, whetted.
[3] abetted, banqueted, duetted, indebted, pirouetted, regretted, silhouetted, unfretted.

SURPRISING RHYMING:
[2] **Bested**, chested, crested, guested, jested, nested, rested, tested, vested.
Bedded, dreaded, headed, leaded, shredded, sledded, threaded, treaded, wedded.
Dented, rented, scented, vented.
Bended, blended, ended, mended, tended, vended, wended.
[3] **Accepted**, arrested, congested, contested, detested, digested, divested, infested, interested, invested, molested, protested, requested, road-tested, suggested, untested.
Affected, collected, connected, corrected, deflected, dejected, detected, directed, dissected, ejected, elected, erected, expected, infected, injected, inspected, neglected, objected, perfected, protected, reflected, rejected, respected, selected, suspected.
Bareheaded, beheaded, bigheaded, cool headed, embedded, hardheaded, hotheaded, lightheaded, pigheaded, redheaded, spearheaded, thickheaded, unwedded.
Amended, attended, befriended, commended, defended, depended, descended, extended, intended, offended, pretended, rear-ended, suspended, transcended, upended.
Augmented, cemented, consented, contented, demented, dissented, fragmented, frequented, invented, lamented, presented, prevented, relented, repented, resented, segmented, tormented, unscented.
[4] **Double-breasted**, intercepted, interested, manifested.
Disaffected, disinfected, disconnected, disrespected, recollected, resurrected.
Complemented, complimented, discontented, experimented, oriented, represented.

2.4.98 "--etter" (as in "better")
[2] better, debtor, fetter, fretter, getter, letter, setter, sweater, wetter.
[3] bonesetter, carburettor/carburetor (U.S.), dead letter, forgetter, go-getter, jet-setter, love-letter, newsletter, operetta, pacesetter, red-letter, typesetter, upsetter, vendetta.

SURPRISING RHYMING:
[2] **Feather**, heather, leather, nether, tether, together, untether, weather, whether.
Clever, ever, leisure, measure, never, pleasure, sever, treasure.
Cheddar, deader, header, homesteader, redder, shedder, shredder, spreader, threader.
Cellar, fella, feller, seller, smeller, speller, stellar, teller, yeller.
[3] **Endeavour/endeavor** (U.S.), forever, forget her, however, never-never, whatever, whatsoever, whenever, wherever, whichever, whoever, whomever.
Bestseller, cave dweller, exceller, foreteller, novella, paella, propeller, repeller, umbrella.

2.4.99 "--ether" (as in "weather")
altogether, feather, heather, leather, nether, tether, together, untether, weather, whether.

319

SURPRISING RHYMING:
[2] **Clever**, ever, never, sever.
Leisure, measure, pleasure, treasure.
Cheddar, deader, header, homesteader, redder, shedder, shredder, spreader, threader.
Better, debtor, fetter, fretter, getter, letter, setter, sweater, wetter.
Cellar, fella, feller, seller, smeller, speller, stellar, teller, yeller.
[3] **Endeavour/endeavor** (U.S.), forever, forget her, however, never-never, whatever, whatsoever, whenever, wherever, whichever, whoever, whomever.
Bestseller, cave dweller, exceller, foreteller, novella, paella, propeller, repeller, umbrella.
Displeasure, made-to-measure.
Bonesetter, carburettor/carburetor (U.S.), forgetter, go-getter, jet-setter, love-letter, newsletter, operetta, pacesetter, red-letter, typesetter, unfetter, upsetter, vendetta.

2.4.100 "--ethered" (as in "weathered")
[2] feathered, leathered, tethered, weathered.

SURPRISING RHYMING:
[2] **Feather**, heather, leather, tether, weather, whether.
Measure, measured, pleasure, pleasured, pressure, pressured, treasure, treasured.
Bettered, checkered, effort, endeavoured/endeavored (U.S.), fettered, leopard, record, severed, shepherd, stretchered, unfettered.
Censored, centred/centered (U.S.), entered, festered, pestered, preferred, rendered, sheltered, tendered, ventured.
[3] **Re-enter(ed)**, remember(ed), surrender(ed), together.

2.4.101 "--etty" (as in "petty")
confetti, jetty, libretti, petty, spaghetti, sweaty.

SURPRISING RHYMING:
[2] **Any**, envy, friendly, gently, healthy, many, penny, pebbly, stealthy, wealthy.
Belly, deli, edgy, jelly, smelly, tele, telly, veggie.
Bevvy, Chevy, heavy, levee, top-heavy.
Berry, bury, chérie, cherry, ferry, imaginary, merry, sherry, very.
Empty, plenty, twenty.
Dressy, emcee, jealousy, lessee, messy, sexy.
Betting, fretting, getting, jetting, letting, petting, setting, sweating, vetting, wetting.
[3] **Already**, heady, ready, steady, steady-eddy, teddy, unready, unsteady.
Abetting, banqueting, begetting, duetting, forgetting, pirouetting, regretting, resetting, silhouetting, upsetting.

2.4.102 "--ettic" (as in "poetic")
[3] aesthetic/esthetic (U.S.), athletic, balletic, cosmetic, frenetic, genetic, kinetic, magnetic, pathetic, phonetic, poetic, synthetic.
[4] alphabetic, apathetic, apologetic, anaesthetic/anesthetic (U.S.), apathetic, diabetic, diuretic, energetic, sympathetic, telekinetic, theoretic.

SURPRISING RHYMING:
[2] **Credit**, edit, epic, ethic, medic, metric, relic.
Hectic, septic, sceptic/skeptic (U.S.), pathetic.
Betted, fretted, jetted, netted, sweated, vetted, whetted.
Arsenic, homesick, lipstick, lovesick, picnic, pinprick, rock chick, seasick, toothpick.
[3] **Accredit**, discredit, paramedic.
Angelic, authentic, eccentric, eclectic, electric, epidemic, generic, majestic, paramedic.
Affected, collected, connected, corrected, deflected, dejected, detected, directed, dissected, ejected, elected, erected, expected, infected, injected, inspected, neglected, objected, perfected, projected, protected, reflected, rejected, respected, selected, subjected, suspected.
Abetted, banqueted, duetted, indebted, pirouetted, regretted, silhouetted, unfretted.
Candlestick, candlewick, heretic, limerick, maverick, politic, rhetoric, walking-stick.

2.4.103 "--etting" (as in "getting")
[2] betting, fretting, getting, jetting, letting, netting, petting, setting, sweating, vetting, wetting, whetting.
[3] abetting, banqueting, begetting, duetting, forgetting, pirouetting, regretting, resetting, silhouetting, upsetting.

SURPRISING RHYMING:
[2] **Crept in**, get in, kept in, leapt in, slept in, stepped in, swept in.
Checking, decking, pecking, trekking, wrecking.
Pepping, prepping, schlepping, stepping.
Blessing, dressing, guessing, messing, pressing, stressing, yessing.
Besting, cresting, guesting, jesting, nesting, questing, resting, testing, wresting.
Belting, melting, pelting, smelting.
Bee sting, Beijing, key-ring, nose-ring, offspring, plaything, real thing, sexting, shoestring, sun king, texting, upswing, vexing.
Begging, bootlegging, ebbing, egging, legging, pegging, webbing.
Dreading, heading, shedding, shredding, spreading, threading, treading, wedding.
Denting, renting, scenting, tempting, venting.
Dwelling, felling, gelling/jelling, quelling, selling, shelling, smelling, spelling, swelling, telling, yelling.
Etching, fetching, retching, sketching, stretching.
[3] **Affecting**, collecting, connecting, correcting, deflecting, detecting, directing, dissecting, effecting, ejecting, erecting, expecting, infecting, injecting, inspecting, neglecting, objecting, perfecting, projecting, prospecting, protecting, reflecting, rejecting, respecting, selecting, suspecting.
Crosschecking, henpecking, sound-checking, spot-checking.
Arresting, detesting, digesting, divesting, infesting, interesting, investing, molesting, protesting, requesting, road-testing, suggesting.
Amending, ascending, attending, befriending, commending, defending, depending, descending, extending, impending, intending, offending, overspending, pretending, suspending, transcending, unbending, upending.
Accepting, attempting, augmenting, consenting, dissenting, fragmenting, frequenting, inventing, lamenting, presenting, preventing, relenting, repenting, resenting, tormenting.
Compelling, dispelling, excelling, expelling, foretelling, fortune-telling, misspelling, overselling, propelling, rebelling, repelling, re-telling.
Accessing, addressing, assessing, caressing, confessing, depressing, digressing, distressing, expressing, impressing, obsessing, oppressing, possessing, processing, professing, progressing, regressing, suppressing, transgressing, undressing.

2.4.104 "--ettal" (as in "metal")
[2] fettle, kettle, metal, mettle, nettle, petal, re-settle, settle, unsettle.

SURPRISING RHYMING:
[2] **Freckle**, Jekyll, heckle, speckle, shekel.
Bevel, devil, level, peril, revel.
Medal, meddle, pebble, pedal, peddle, rebel, treble.
Central, dental, gentle, kennel, mental, parental, rental, temple.
Embezzle, nestle, special, trestle, vessel, wrestle.
Pencil, several, stencil, utensil.
[3] **Bedevil**, daredevil, dishevel, eye-level, high-level, low-level., split-level.
[4] **Accidental**, continental, detrimental, elemental, environmental, experimental, fundamental, instrumental, judgmental, monumental, Oriental, sentimental, transcendental.

2.4.105 "--ethery" (as in "feathery")
[3] feathery, heathery, leathery.

SURPRISING RHYMING:
[3] **Ancestry**, archery, artistry, bakery, battery, bigotry, binary, blackberry, blubbery, blueberry, blustery, brasserie, bravery, brewery, bribery, burglary, calorie, carpentry,

carvery, cavalry, celery, century, chemistry, chicory, chivalry, Christmas tree, colliery, contrary, devilry, diary, dietary, disagree, dithery, doddery, drudgery, dungaree, duty-free, eatery, enquiry, estuary, expiry, factory, fakery, feathery, filigree, finery, fishery, flattery, fluttery, forestry, forgery, gallery, geometry, gimmickry, glittery, greenery, grocery, history, imagery, injury, inquiry, ivory, jamboree, jewellery/jewelry (U.S.), jittery, leathery, lingerie, lottery, luxury, memory, mercury, misery, momentary, monastery, mystery, nursery, obituary, obligatory, pageantry, pedigree, perjury, pillory, pleasantry, poetry, pottery, primary, priory, quivery, referee, revelry, reverie, rivalry, robbery, rockery, rosary, rubbery, salary, sanctuary, savagery, savory, scenery, sensory, shimmery, shivery, silvery, slavery, slippery, sorcery, sugary, surgery, tapestry, thundery, treachery, trickery, victory, wintery, wizardry.
Readily, steadily, unreadily, unsteadily.
[4] Accessory, adultery, artillery, cautionary, cemetery, compulsory, confectionery, conciliatory, constabulary, contemporary, customary, debauchery, delivery, dictionary, directory, discovery, distillery, elementary, embroidery, explanatory, exploratory, hunky-dory, idolatry, imaginary, incendiary, infirmary, inflammatory, judiciary, laboratory, legendary, literary, machinery, mandatory, mercenary, military, missionary, necessary, ordinary, patisserie, perfumery, preliminary, psychiatry, publicity, reactionary, recovery, secretary, secondary, simplicity, skullduggery, solitary, stationary, stationery, temporary, territory, tomfoolery, upholstery, visionary, vocabulary.
[5] Anniversary, beneficiary, camaraderie, complementary, complimentary, contradictory, documentary, evolutionary, intermediary, revolutionary, rudimentary, supplementary.

2.4.106 "--ever" (as in "never")
[2] clever, ever, never, sever.
[3] endeavour/endeavor (U.S.), forever, however, never-never, whatever, whatsoever, whenever, wherever, whichever, whoever, whomever.

SURPRISING RHYMING:
[2] **Error**, feather, heather, leather, tether, terror, together, untether, weather, whether.
Leisure, measure, pleasure, treasure.
Better, debtor, fetter, fretter, getter, letter, setter, sweater, wetter.
Cellar, fella, feller, seller, smeller, speller, stellar, teller, yeller.
[3] **Displeasure**, made-to-measure.
Bestseller, cave dweller, exceller, foreteller, fortune-teller, novella, propeller, umbrella.
Bonesetter, carburettor/carburetor (U.S.), forgetter, go-getter, jet-setter, love-letter, newsletter, operetta, pacesetter, red-letter, typesetter, unfetter, upsetter, vendetta.
Aggressor, caresser, confessor, hairdresser, oppressor, possessor, predecessor, processor, professor, possessor, microprocessor, successor, suppresser, transgressor.

2.4.107 "--everence" (as in "reverence")
[3] deliverance, irreverence, reverence, severance.

SURPRISING RHYMING:
[2] **Against**, commenced, condensed, experienced, fenced, incensed, inconvenienced, inexperienced, influenced, licensed, recommenced, recompensed, sensed, sentenced, sequenced, silenced.
[3] **Abstinence**, affluence, ambience, audience, coherence, commonsense, competence, condolence, conference, confidence, consequence, dependence, eloquence, emergence, eminence, evidence, excellence, existence, fraudulence, impatience, impudence, impotence, indolence, influence, innocence, insistence, insolence, insurgence, lenience, negligence, occurrence, opulence, penitence, permanence, persistence, prescience, prevalence, prominence, providence, radiance, recommence, recompense, recurrence, residence, resurgence, reticence, reverence, self-defence/self-defense (U.S.), severance, subsistence, succulence, temperance, transcendence, transience, turbulence, violence.

2.4.108 "--evity" (as in "levity")
[3] brevity, levity, longevity.

SURPRISING RHYMING:
[3] **Amnesty**, casualty, certainty, chastity, confetti, density, deputy, devotee, dignity, dynasty, entity, faculty, fidgety, graffiti, gravity, guarantee, honesty, karate, liberty, majesty, modesty, nudity, oddity, penalty, piety, poverty, property, puberty, purity, quality, repartee, rickety, sanctity, sanctuary, sanity, scarcity, seventy, sovereignty, spaghetti, specialty, trinity, unity, uppity, vanity, velvety, warranty.
Allergy, effigy, elegy, energy, lethargy, prodigy, refugee, strategy, synergy, trilogy.
Bodily, family, fleur-de-lis, heavenly, homily, icily, jubilee, melancholy, miserly, readily.
Mimicry, ministry, misery, priory, reverie.
Gossipy, recipe, slap-happy, syrupy/syrupy, therapy, unhappy.
Burgundy, chickadee, COD, comedy, custody, dogsbody, embody, fool-hardy, jeopardy, melody, nobody, parody, Ph.D., raggedy, remedy, rhapsody, somebody, tragedy.
[4] **Absurdity**, affinity, amenity, anxiety, barbarity, calamity, cognoscenti, community, conformity, credulity, difficulty, dilettante, enormity, equality, eternity, fatality, fidelity, fifty-fifty, fraternity, frivolity, glitterati, heredity, hilarity, humanity, humidity, immunity, impunity, indemnity, infinity, intercity, literati, maternity, modernity, morality, nitty-gritty, obscenity, profanity, reality, senility, serenity, sobriety, solemnity, virility, stupidity, timidity, totality, twenty-twenty, variety, vicinity, vigilante, virginity, vulgarity.
Ability, facility, fertility, fragility, futility, hostility, humility, mobility, nobility, stability, tranquillity/tranquility (U.S.), utility, virility.
[5] **Ambiguity**, anonymity, continuity, familiarity, femininity, impropriety, ingenuity, irregularity, masculinity, notoriety, opportunity, peculiarity, popularity, positivity, regularity, serendipity, similarity, solidarity, spontaneity, uniformity.
Edibility, liability, responsibility, usability, versatility, viability, volatility.

2.4.109 "--ext" (as in "next")
[1] next, sexed, sext, text, vexed.
[2] annexed, context, indexed, oversexed, perplexed, pretext, subtext, teletext.

SURPRISING RHYMING:
[1] **Best**, blessed, blest, breast, chest, crest, dressed, guest, guessed, jest, lest, messed, nest, pest, quest, rest, stressed, test, vest, west, wrest, zest.
Etch(ed), fetch(ed), ketch, lech, retch(ed), sketch(ed), stretch(ed), wretch.
Peps, preps, rep, schlep, step, steppes.
Checks, decks, flecks, necks, pecks, sects, specks, treks, wrecks.
Checked, decked, flecked, pecked, sect, specked, trekked, wrecked.
Benched, clenched, drenched, entrenched, quenched, wrenched.
[2] **Affects**, aspects, collects, connects, corrects, deflects, detects, dialects, directs, dissects, effects, ejects, elects, erects, expects, infects, injects, insects, inspects, neglects, objects, perfects, projects, protects, reflects, rejects, respects, suspects.
Abreast, addressed, armrest, arrest, Beau Geste, behest, bequest, caressed, confessed, contest, conquest, depressed, detest, digest, digressed, distressed, divest, expressed, impressed, infest, inquest, invest, Midwest, molest, northwest, oppressed, possessed, progressed, protest, recessed, repressed, request, road-test, southwest, suggest, suppressed, transgressed, undressed, unrest, well-dressed.
Doorsteps, footsteps, missteps, quicksteps, sidesteps.
Against, commenced, condensed, dispensed, experienced, fenced, incensed, inconvenienced, inexperienced, influenced, licensed, recommenced, referenced, sensed, sentenced, sequenced, silenced.
Burlesque, desk, grotesque, newsdesk, picturesque, statuesque.
[3] **Dispossessed**, effervesced, interest, manifest, overdressed, readdressed, reassessed, repossessed, second-best, self-addressed, self-confessed, self-possessed, unaddressed, unexpressed, unimpressed.

* * *

PART 3

'I'

3.1 "i" sounds (as in *"it"*)..........................Index on Page 326
3.2 "īy" sounds (as in *"eye"*)........................Index on Page 330

3.1 "i" (as in "it")

3.1.1 "--ib" (as in "rib") ... 333
3.1.2 "--ibbit" (as in "exhibit") ... 333
3.1.3 "--ibble" (as in "nibble") ... 333
3.1.4 "--ibbled" (as in "nibbled") ... 334
3.1.5 "--ibbler" (as in "nibbler") ... 334
3.1.6 "--ibbling" (as in "nibbling") ... 334
3.1.7 "--ibute" (as in "tribute") ... 334
3.1.8 "--ick" (as in "kick") ... 335
3.1.9 "--icked" (as in "kicked") ... 335
3.1.10 "--icken" (as in "chicken") ... 336
3.1.11 "--icker" (as in "quicker") ... 336
3.1.12 "--ickest" (as in "quickest") ... 336
3.1.13 "--icket" (as in "ticket") ... 337
3.1.14 "--icky" (as in "tricky") ... 337
3.1.15 "--icking" (as in "kicking") ... 337
3.1.16 "--ickle" (as in "tickle") ... 338
3.1.17 "--ickly" (as in "quickly") ... 338
3.1.18 "--ickness" (as in "sickness") ... 338
3.1.19 "--icted" (as in "addicted") ... 338
3.1.20 "--icting" (as in "predicting") ... 339
3.1.21 "--ictive" (as in "addictive") ... 339
3.1.22 "--ickup" (as in "pickup") ... 339
3.1.23 "--ickening" (as in "sickening") ... 339
3.1.24 "--id" (as in "forbid") ... 340
3.1.25 "--idden" (as in "hidden") ... 340
3.1.26 "--idding" (as in "kidding") ... 341
3.1.27 "--iddel" (as in "fiddle") ... 341
3.1.28 "--iddler" (as in "fiddler") ... 341
3.1.29 "--iddling" (as in "fiddling") ... 342
3.1.30 "--idge" (as in "bridge") ... 342
3.1.31 "--idget" (as in "fidget") ... 342
3.1.32 "--idgid" (as in "rigid") ... 343
3.1.33 "--idgen" (as in "religion") ... 343
3.1.34 "--if" (as in "cliff") ... 343
3.1.35 "--ift" (as in "lift") ... 344
3.1.36 "--iffer" (as in "differ") ... 344
3.1.37 "--iffic" (as in "terrific") ... 345
3.1.38 "--ifted" (as in "gifted") ... 345
3.1.39 "--ifter" (as in "drifter") ... 345
3.1.40 "--ifty" (as in "thrifty") ... 345
3.1.41 "--ifting" (as in "drifting") ... 346
3.1.42 "--ig" (as in "big") ... 346
3.1.43 "--igger" (as in "bigger") ... 347
3.1.44 "--igging" (as in "digging") ... 347
3.1.45 "--iggle" (as in "giggle") ... 347
3.1.46 "--iggler" (as in "giggler") ... 348

3.1.47 "--iggly" (as in "wiggly") ... 348
3.1.48 "--iggling" (as in "giggling") ... 348
3.1.49 "--igment" (as in "figment") ... 348
3.1.50 "--ignant" (as in "indignant") ... 349
3.1.51 "--iggot" (as in "bigot") ... 349
3.1.52 "--igure" (as in "figure") ... 349
3.1.53 "--ignify" (as in "dignify") ... 349
3.1.54 "--igidly" (as in "rigidly") ... 350
3.1.55 "--ikshun" (as in "friction") ... 350
3.1.56 "--ill" (as in "still") ... 350
3.1.57 "--illed" (as in "thrilled") ... 351
3.1.58 "--ilk" (as in "milk") ... 351
3.1.59 "--ilt" (as in "guilt") ... 351
3.1.60 "--illa" (as in "vanilla") ... 351
3.1.61 "--illder" (as in "builder") ... 352
3.1.62 "--iller" (as in "thriller") ... 352
3.1.63 "--illy" (as in "silly") ... 352
3.1.64 "--illing" (as in "willing") ... 353
3.1.65 "--ilky" (as in "silky") ... 353
3.1.66 "--illow" (as in "pillow") ... 353
3.1.67 "--ilted" (as in "jilted") ... 354
3.1.68 "--ilting" (as in "tilting") ... 354
3.1.69 "--illyun" (as in "million") ... 354
3.1.70 "--ilitee" (as in "ability") ... 355
3.1.71 "--illable" (as in "syllable") ... 355
3.1.72 "--illfully" (as in "skillfully") ... 355
3.1.73 "--illiest" (as in "silliest") ... 355
3.1.74 "--ilkiest" (as in "silkiest") ... 356
3.1.75 "--illowy" (as in "willowy") ... 356
3.1.76 "--imm" (as in "him") ... 356
3.1.77 "--immed" (as in "slimmed") ... 357
3.1.78 "--imp" (as in "limp") ... 357
3.1.79 "--imps" (as in "glimpse") ... 357
3.1.80 "--imbal" (as in "symbol") ... 358
3.1.81 "--imber" (as in "timber") ... 358
3.1.82 "--immer" (as in "swimmer") ... 358
3.1.83 "--immy" (as in "gimme") ... 358
3.1.84 "--immick" (as in "gimmick") ... 359
3.1.85 "--imming" (as in "swimming") ... 359
3.1.86 "--imper" (as in "whimper") ... 359
3.1.87 "--imping" (as in "limping") ... 360
3.1.88 "--imple" (as in "simple") ... 360
3.1.89 "--imsy" (as in "flimsy") ... 360
3.1.90 "--in" (as in "skin") ... 360
3.1.91 "--inch" (as in "pinch") ... 361
3.1.92 "--inched" (as in "pinched") ... 361
3.1.93 "--inned" (as in "grinned") ... 361

3.1.94 "--ing" (as in "sing") 362
3.1.95 "--inge" (as in "hinge") 362
3.1.96 "--ink" (as in "pink") 362
3.1.97 "--inx" (as in "drinks") 363
3.1.98 "--inked" (as in "blinked") 363
3.1.99 "--ince" (as in "prince") 363
3.1.100 "--int" (as in "hint") 364
3.1.101 "--inching" (as in "flinching") 364
3.1.102 "--indle" (as in "kindle") 364
3.1.103 "--indling" (as in "dwindling") 364
3.1.104 "--inner" (as in "dinner") 365
3.1.105 "--inger" (as in "singer") 365
3.1.106 "--inging" (as in "swinging") 365
3.1.107 "--ingle" (as in "tingle") 366
3.1.108 "--ingless" (as in "wingless") 366
3.1.109 "--ingling" (as in "tingling") 366
3.1.110 "--indicate" (as in "indicate") 366
3.1.111 "--inical" (as in "cynical") 367
3.1.112 "--inister" (as in "sinister") 367
3.1.113 "--inkable" (as in "drinkable") 367
3.1.114 "--inny" (as in "skinny") 367
3.1.115 "--inning" (as in "spinning") 368
3.1.116 "--injes" (as in "cringes") 368
3.1.117 "--injing" (as in "hinging") 368
3.1.118 "--inker" (as in "thinker") 369
3.1.119 "--inking" (as in "blinking") 369
3.1.120 "--inkle" (as in "sprinkle") 370
3.1.121 "--inkling" (as in "sprinkling") 370
3.1.122 "--inctive" (as in "instinctive") 370
3.1.123 "--inctly" (as in "distinctly") 370
3.1.124 "--incing" (as in "wincing") 371
3.1.125 "--inted" (as in "sprinted") 371
3.1.126 "--inter" (as in "winter") 371
3.1.127 "--inting" (as in "sprinting") 372
3.1.128 "--ip" (as in "ship") 372
3.1.129 "--ips" (as in "lips") 372
3.1.130 "--ippie" (as in "hippie") 373
3.1.131 "--ipped" (as in "ripped") 373
3.1.132 "--ipper" (as in "slipper") 374
3.1.133 "--ipping" (as in "slipping") 374
3.1.134 "--ipple" (as in "ripple") 374
3.1.135 "--ipshun" (as in "description") 375
3.1.136 "--iracle" (as in "miracle") 375
3.1.137 "--iss" (as in "kiss") 375
3.1.138 "--ish" (as in "wish") 375
3.1.139 "--isk" (as in "risk") 376
3.1.140 "--ist" (as in "list") 376

3.1.141 "--issiv" (as in "permissive") 377
3.1.142 "--issen" (as in "listen") 377
3.1.143 "--issel" (as in "whistle") 377
3.1.144 "--ishul" (as in "official") 378
3.1.145 "--ishun" (as in "mission") 378
3.1.146 "--ishent" (as in "efficient") 379
3.1.147 "--isher" (as in "wisher") 379
3.1.148 "--ishing" (as in "wishing") 379
3.1.149 "--ishus" (as in "vicious") 380
3.1.150 "--issing" (as in "kissing") 380
3.1.151 "--issit" (as in "illicit") 381
3.1.152 "--isky" (as in "risky") 381
3.1.153 "--istence" (as in "resistance") 381
3.1.154 "--istent" (as in "persistent") 381
3.1.155 "--isted" (as in "twisted") 382
3.1.156 "--ister" (as in "sister") 382
3.1.157 "--istic" (as in "stylistic") 382
3.1.158 "--istics" (as in "statistics") 383
3.1.159 "--isting (as in "twisting") 383
3.1.160 "--ision" (as in "vision") 383
3.1.161 "--iskier" (as in "riskier") 384
3.1.162 "--iskiest" (as in "riskiest") 384
3.1.163 "--istory" (as in "mystery") 384
3.1.164 "--it" (as in "admit") 384
3.1.165 "--itch" (as in "rich") 385
3.1.166 "--itched" (as in "hitched") 385
3.1.167 "--ith" (as in "myth") 386
3.1.168 "--itcher" (as in "richer") 386
3.1.169 "--itches" (as in "riches") 386
3.1.170 "--itching" (as in "switching") 387
3.1.171 "--itted (as in "outwitted") 387
3.1.172 "--itter (as in "bitter") 387
3.1.173 "--ittee" (as in "pretty") 388
3.1.174 "--aritee" (as in "charity") 388
3.1.175 "--itting" (as in "sitting") 389
3.1.176 "--ittle" (as in "little") 389
3.1.177 "--itten" (as in "kitten") 390
3.1.178 "--itness" (as in "witness") 390
3.1.179 "--ittiest" (as in "prettiest") 390
3.1.180 "--ittingly" (as in "wittingly") 390
3.1.181 "--iv" (as in "give") 391
3.1.182 "--iven" (as in "driven") 391
3.1.183 "--ivver" (as in "river") 392
3.1.184 "--ivered" (as in "delivered") 392
3.1.185 "--ivid" (as in "vivid") 392
3.1.186 "--iving" (as in "living") 392
3.1.187 "--ivel" (as in "swivel") 393

3.1.188 "--iveling" (as in "sniveling") 393
3.1.189 "--ivery" (as in "shivery") 393
3.1.190 "--ivering" (as in "shivering") 394
3.1.191 "--ix" (as in "fix") 394
3.1.192 "--ixer" (as in "mixer") 395
3.1.193 "--ixing" (as in "fixing") 395
3.1.194 "--ixture" (as in "mixture") 395
3.1.195 "--ixable" (as in "fixable") 396
3.1.196 "--iz" (as in "his") 396
3.1.197 "--izum" (as in "prism") 396
3.1.198 "--izard" (as in "lizard") 397
3.1.199 "--izzy" (as in "dizzy") 397
3.1.200 "--izzing" (as in "fizzing") 397
3.1.201 "--izzle" (as in "sizzle") 397
3.1.202 "--izzen" (as in "prison") 398
3.1.203 "--izzier" (as in "dizzier") 398
3.1.204 "--izziest" (as in "dizziest") 398
3.1.205 "--izzical" (as in "quizzical") 399
3.1.206 "--izzily" (as in "dizzily") 399

3.2 "iy" (as in "eye")

3.2.1 "--eye" (as in "eye") 399
3.2.2 "--eyeing" (as in "crying") 401
3.2.3 "--bye" (as in "goodbye") 402
3.2.4 "--fie" (as in "satisfy") 402
3.2.5 "--lie" (as in "reply") 402
3.2.6 "--pie" (as in "spy") 403
3.2.7 "--rye" (as in "dry") 403
3.2.8 "--ial" (as in "dial") 404
3.2.9 "--iance" (as in "defiance") 404
3.2.10 "--iant" (as in "defiant") 404
3.2.11 "--iable" (as in "liable") 404
3.2.12 "--ibe" (as in "tribe") 405
3.2.13 "--ibed" (as in "described") 406
3.2.14 "--iber" (as in "cyber") 406
3.2.15 "--ibing" (as in "describing") 407
3.2.16 "--ice" (as in "nice") 407
3.2.17 "--icer" (as in "nicer") 408
3.2.18 "--ices" (as in "prices") 408
3.2.19 "--icing" (as in "dicing") 408
3.2.20 "--iceless" (as in "priceless") 408
3.2.21 "--icycle" (as in "bicycle") 409
3.2.22 "--ide" (as in "lied") 409
3.2.23 "--ided" (as in "decided") 410
3.2.24 "--ider" (as in "spider") 410
3.2.25 "--iding" (as in "hiding") 410
3.2.26 "--ier" (as in "liar") 411

3.2.27 "--iest" (as in "highest") 411
3.2.28 "--iet" (as in "diet") 411
3.2.29 "--ieter" (as in "quieter") 412
3.2.30 "--ieting" (as in "rioting") 412
3.2.31 "--ife" (as in "life") 412
3.2.32 "--ifen" (as in "hyphen") 413
3.2.33 "--ifel" (as in "stifle") 413
3.2.34 "--ike" (as in "like") 414
3.2.35 "--iking" (as in "liking") 414
3.2.36 "--ile" (as in "smile") 415
3.2.37 "--iled" (as in "child") 415
3.2.38 "--ildly" (as in "wildly") 416
3.2.39 "--iler" (as in "smiler") 416
3.2.40 "--iling" (as in "smiling") 416
3.2.41 "--ime" (as in "time") 416
3.2.42 "--imed" (as in "climbed") 417
3.2.43 "--imer" (as in "climber") 418
3.2.44 "--iming" (as in "timing") 418
3.2.45 "--imeless" (as in "timeless") 418
3.2.46 "--ine" (as in "mine") 418
3.2.47 "--ined" (as in "kind") 419
3.2.48 "--inded" (as in "blinded") 420
3.2.49 "--inder" (as in "kinder") 420
3.2.50 "--inding" (as in "finding") 420
3.2.51 "--iner" (as in "finer") 421
3.2.52 "--iness" (as in "shyness") 421
3.2.53 "--ining" (as in "shining") 422
3.2.54 "--inement" (as in "refinement") 422
3.2.55 "--ipe" (as in "pipe") 422
3.2.56 "--iped" (as in "wiped") 423
3.2.57 "--iper" (as in "wiper") 423
3.2.58 "--iping" (as in "typing") 423
3.2.59 "--ire" (as in "fire") 424
3.2.60 "--ired" (as in "tired") 424
3.2.61 "--iring" (as in "inspiring") 424
3.2.62 "--ising" (as in "rising") 425
3.2.63 "--ite" (as in "might") 426
3.2.64 "--ited" (as in "delighted") 426
3.2.65 "--iten" (as in "brighten") 426
3.2.66 "--iter" (as in "writer") 427
3.2.67 "--itest" (as in "brightest") 427
3.2.68 "--iteful" (as in "spiteful") 427
3.2.69 "--iting" (as in "fighting") 428
3.2.70 "--itel" (as in "vital") 428
3.2.71 "--itely" (as in "brightly") 428
3.2.72 "--itement" (as in "excitement") 428
3.2.73 "--iteness" (as in "brightness") 429

3.2.74 "--itening" (as in "lightning") 429
3.2.75 "--itefully" (as in "spitefully") 429
3.2.76 "--ive" (as in "drive") 429
3.2.77 "--ival" (as in "survival") 430
3.2.78 "--iver" (as in "driver") 430
3.2.79 "--iving" (as in "driving") 430
3.2.80 "--ize" (as in "prize") 431
3.2.81 "--ized" (as in "disguised") 431

* * *

3.1 "i" (as in "it")

3.1.1 "--ib" (as in "rib")
adlib, bib, crib, dib, fib, glib, lib, nib, rib(s), sparerib, squib.

SURPRISING RHYMING:
[1] Bid, did, grid, id, kid, lid, quid, skid, slid, squid.
Give, live, sieve, spiv.
Big, dig, fig, gig, jig, pig, prig, rig, swig, twig, wig.
Been, bin, chin, fin, gin, grin, in, inn, kin, pin, shin, sin, skin, spin, thin, twin, win.
Bit, fit, grit, hit, it, kit, knit, lit, pit, quit, skit, slit, spit, split, wit.
Biz, fizz, his, is, quiz, whiz.
Blip, chip, clip, dip, drip, flip, grip, hip, kip, lip, nip, pip, quip, rip, ship, sip, skip, slip, snip, strip, tip, trip, whip, yip, zip.
[2] Amid, eyelid, forbid, outbid, rapid, undid.
Begin, bearskin, chagrin, dolphin, has-been, hatpin, herein, kingpin, Kremlin, Latin, Mickey Finn, muffin, napkin, paraffin, penguin, pippin, pushpin, robin, satin, sheepskin, therein, urchin, wherein, within.
Active, captive, festive, forgive, massive, misgive, missive, motive, native, octave, olive, outlive, passive, pensive, relive.
Acquit, admit, armpit, cockpit, commit, emit, habit, misfit, moonlit, omit, outfit, outwit, remit, spirit, submit, sunlit, tidbit, transmit, unfit.
Airship, catnip, courtship, equip, flagship, friendship, hardship, horsewhip, kinship, outstrip, steamship, township, warship, worship.
[3] Invalid, pyramid, overbid, overdid, underbid.
Antonym, cherubim, homonym, interim, pseudonym, synonym.
Aspirin, bulletin, crystalline, discipline, feminine, genuine, glycerin, harlequin, heroin, heroine, insulin, intestine, javelin, mandolin, mannequin, margarine, masculine, moccasin, mortal sin, origin, saccharin, tarpaulin, thick and thin, violin, vitamin, zeppelin.
Abrasive, abusive, adhesive, aggressive, combative, compulsive, conclusive, conducive, corrosive, decisive, defensive, depressive, divisive, effusive, elusive, emotive, evasive, excessive, exclusive, expansive, expensive, expletive, explosive, expressive, impassive, impressive, impulsive, incisive, inclusive, intensive, intrusive, narrative, negative, obsessive, offensive, oppressive, percussive, permissive, persuasive, possessive, progressive, reclusive, repulsive, responsive, sedative, submissive, subversive, talkative.
Counterfeit, definite, exquisite, favourite/favorite (U.S.), hypocrite, infinite, opposite.

3.1.2 "--ibbit" (as in "exhibit")
[3] exhibit, inhibit, prohibit.

SURPRISING RHYMING:
[1] Bit, fit, grit, hit, it, kit, knit, lit, pit, quit, skit, slit, spit, split, wit.
[2] Acquit, admit, armpit, cockpit, commit, emit, habit, misfit, moonlit, omit, outfit, outwit, remit, spirit, submit, sunlit, tidbit, transmit, unfit.
Digit, fidget, legit, midget, widget.
Cricket, picket, snippet, stick it, thicket, ticket, wicket.
Dinted, glinted, hinted, minted, printed, sprinted, squinted, tinted.
Drifted, gifted, lifted, livid, rifted, shifted, sifted, vivid.
[3] Counterfeit, definite, exquisite, favourite/favorite (U.S.), hypocrite, infinite, opposite.
Ballistic, elicit, explicit, illicit, implicit, linguistic, logistic, solicit, statistic.
Acquitted, admitted, committed, dimwitted, emitted, fitted, half-witted, knitted, omitted, outwitted, permitted, quick-witted, spirited, submitted, transmitted, unfitted.
Imprinted, misprinted, reprinted.

3.1.3 "--ibble" (as in "nibble")
[2] dribble, nibble, quibble, scribble, sibyl.

SURPRISING RHYMING:
[2] Dribbled, nibbled, quibbled, scribbled.

Dribbles, nibbles, quibbles, scribbles.
Diddle, fiddle, griddle, idyll, middle, paradiddle, riddle, twiddle.
Giggle, jiggle, niggle, squiggle, wiggle, wriggle.
Civil, drivel, shrivel, skiffle, sniffle, snivel, swivel.
Bristle, chisel, drizzle, fizzle, missile, sizzle, swizzle, thistle, whistle.
Cripple, nipple, ripple, stipple, tipple, triple.
Belittle, brittle, committal, hospital, it'll, little, skittle, spittle, whittle.
Cymbal, nimble, symbol, thimble, timbale.
Fickle, nickel, pickle, prickle, tickle, trickle.

3.1.4 "--ibbled" (as in "nibbled")
[2] dribbled, nibbled, quibbled, ribald, scribbled.

SURPRISING RHYMING:
[2] **Dribble**, nibble, quibble, scribble, sibyl.
Dribbles, nibbles, quibbles, scribbles.
Diddled, fiddled, middle, riddled, twiddled.
Giggled, jiggled, niggled, squiggled, wiggled, wriggled.
Civil, drivel, shrivel, skiffle, sniffle, snivel, swivel.
Chiseled, drizzled, fizzled, frizzled, sizzled, swizzled, whistled.
Crippled, rippled, stippled, tippled, tripled.
Belittled, brittle, committal, hospital, it'll, little, skittle, spittle, whittled.
Fickle, nickel, pickled, prickled, tickled, trickled.

3.1.5 "--ibbler" (as in "nibbler)
[2] dribbler, nibbler, quibbler, scribbler.

SURPRISING RHYMING:
[2] **Giggler**, niggler, wiggler, wriggler.
Diddler, fiddler, riddler, twiddler.
Chiller, driller, filler, griller, killer, pillar, spiller, thriller, tiller, villa.
Bigger, digger, figure, jigger, ligger, rigger, rigour/rigor (U.S.), snigger, trigger, vigour/vigor (U.S.).
Limber, marimba, timber.
Crimper, limper, shrimper, simper, whimper.
[3] **Builder**, bodybuilder, boatbuilder, bewilder(ed), housebuilder, rebuilder, shipbuilder.
Caterpillar, flotilla, fulfiller, gorilla, guerilla, man-killer, painkiller, spine-chiller, vanilla.
Configure, disfigure, gold-digger, gravedigger, vinegar.

3.1.6 "--ibbling" (as in "nibbling")
[2] dribbling, nibbling, quibbling, scribbling, sibling.

SURPRISING RHYMING:
[2] **Diddling**, fiddling, middling, piddling, riddling, twiddling.
Giggling, jiggling, niggling, squiggling, wiggling, wriggling.
Driveling, shriveling, sniffling, sniveling, swiveling.
Chiseling, drizzling, fizzling, sizzling, whistling.
Crippling, rippling, stippling, tippling, tripling.
Building, bodybuilding, boatbuilding, bewildering, housebuilding, rebuilding, shipbuilding.

3.1.7 "--ibute" (as in "tribute")
attribute, contribute, distribute, tribute.

SURPRISING RHYMING:
[1] **Boot**, brute, chute, cute, flute, fruit, hoot, loot, mute, root, route, scoot, shoot, suit.
Bloop, coop, coupe, droop, dupe, group, loop, scoop, sloop, snoop, soup, stoop, swoop, troop, troupe.
Booed, brewed, brood, chewed, crude, feud, food, glued, lewd, mood, nude, prude, rude, screwed, shrewd, stewed, viewed.

[2] **Acute**, astute, commute, dilute, dispute, lawsuit, minute, pollute, pursuit, salute.
Accrued, allude, conclude, elude, etude, exclude, include, intrude, issued, preclude, prelude, previewed, protrude, pursued, renewed, reviewed, seclude, shampooed, tabooed, unscrewed.
[3] **Absolute**, constitute, convolute, destitute, dissolute, execute - institute, parachute, persecute, resolute, substitute.
Continued, discontinued, reissued, reviewed.
Fortitude, gratitude, latitude, magnitude, multitude, solitude.

3.1.8 "--ick" (as in "kick")
[1] brick, chick, click, crick, dick, flick, hick, kick, lick, nick, pick, prick, quick, sic, sick, slick, stick, thick, tic, tick, trick, wick.
[2] arsenic, broomstick, chopstick, drumstick, heartsick, homesick, lipstick, lovesick, seasick, toothpick.
[3] candlestick, heretic, limerick, lunatic, maverick, politic, rhetoric, walking-stick.

SURPRISING RHYMING:
[1] **Bricked**, clicked, flicked, kicked, licked, picked, pricked, strict, ticked, tricked.
Bit, fit, grit, hit, it, kit, knit, lit, pit, quit, skit, slit, spit, split, wit.
Blink, brink, chink, clink, drink, hoodwink, ice-rink, ink, kink, link, mink, pink, rink, shrink, sink, slink, stink, sync, think, wink, zinc.
Asterisk, bisque, brisk, disc/disk (U.S.), frisk, risk, obelisk, whisk.
Blip, chip, clip, dip, drip, flip, grip, hip, kip, lip(s), nip, pip, quip, rip, ship, sip, skip, slip, snip, strip, tip, trip, whip, yip, zip.
Dissed, fist, gist, grist, hissed, kissed, list, midst, missed, mist, pissed, tryst, twist, whist, wrist.
[2] **Addict**, conflict, constrict, contradict, convict, depict, evict, predict, restrict.
Acquit, admit, armpit, cockpit, commit, emit, habit, misfit, moonlit, omit, outfit, outwit, remit, spirit, submit, sunlit, tidbit, transmit, unfit.
Airship, catnip, courtship, equip, flagship, friendship, hardship, horsewhip, kinship, outstrip, steamship, township, warship, worship.
Assist, consist, dismissed, enlist, exist, insist, persist, resist, subsist.
[3] **Counterfeit**, definite, exquisite, favourite/favorite (U.S.), hypocrite, infinite, opposite.
Battleship, fellowship, horsemanship, leadership, membership, partnership, penmanship, scholarship, sportsmanship, workmanship.
Activist, anarchist, atheist, analyst, botanist, catalyst, columnist, communist, egotist, Eucharist, exorcist, fatalist, hobbyist, humourist/humorist (U.S.), hypnotist, journalist, lobbyist, moralist, motorist, novelist, optimist, organist, pacifist, pessimist, pre-exist, publicist, socialist, soloist, specialist, strategist, terrorist.

3.1.9 "--icked" (as in "kicked")
[1] bricked, clicked, flicked, kicked, licked, picked, pricked, strict, ticked, tricked.
[2] addict, conflict, constrict, contradict, convict, depict, evict, predict, restrict.

SURPRISING RHYMING:
[1] **Brick**, chick, click, crick, dick, flick, hick, kick, lick, nick, pick, prick, quick, sic, sick, slick, stick, thick, tic, tick, trick, wick.
Blinked, inked, linked, winked.
Drift, gift, lift, miffed, rift, shift, shrift, sniffed, swift, thrift, whiffed.
Chipped, clipped, crypt, dipped, dripped, flipped, gripped, nipped, pipped, quipped, ripped, script, shipped, sipped, skipped, slipped, snipped, stripped, tipped, tripped, whipped, zipped.
Dissed, fist, gist, grist, hissed, kissed, list, midst, missed, mist, pissed, tryst, twist, whist, wrist.
Bitched, ditched, hitched, itched, pitched, snitched, stitched, switched, twitched.
[2] **Arsenic**, broomstick, chopstick, drumstick, heartsick, homesick, lipstick, lovesick, seasick, toothpick.
Adrift, airlift, facelift, gearshift, makeshift, nightshift, snowdrift, spendthrift, uplift.
Assist, consist, dismissed, enlist, exist, insist, persist, resist, subsist.
Encrypt, equipped, horsewhipped, outstripped, postscript, transcript, worshipped.

Bewitched, enriched, snitched, re-stitched, switched, twitched.
[3] Candlestick, heretic, limerick, lunatic, maverick, politic, rhetoric, walking-stick.
Manuscript, superscript, unzipped.

3.1.10 "--icken" (as in "chicken")
[2] chicken, quicken, sicken, stricken, thicken.

SURPRISING RHYMING:
[2] Didn't, forbidden, hidden, ridden.
Clicking, flicking, kicking, licking, picking, pricking, ticking, tricking.
Blinking, clinking, drinking, hoodwinking, inking, inkling, linking, shrinking, sinking, slinking, sprinkling, stinking, syncing, thinking, twinkling, winking.
Chipping, clipping, dipping, dripping, flipping, gripping, nipping, quipping, ripping, shipping, sipping, skipping, slipping, snipping, stripping, tipping, tripping, unzipping, whipping, zipping.
Bitten, kitten, mitten, smitten, written.
Christen, emission, fission, intermission, magician, mission, musician, titian.
Fitting, gritting, hitting, knitting, quitting, sitting, spitting, splitting.
Digging, jigging, rigging, swigging.
Grinning, pinning, sinning, skinning, spinning, thinning, winning.
Bidding, forbidding, kidding, outbidding, ridding, skidding.
Bitching, ditching, hitching, itching, pitching, snitching, stitching, switching, twitching.
[3] Flea-bitten, frostbitten, rewritten, unwritten.
Acquitting, admitting, emitting, omitting, permitting, remitting, side-splitting, transmitting, unremitting, unwitting.

3.1.11 "--icker" (as in "quicker")
[2] bicker, clicker, dicker, flicker, kicker, knicker, licker, liquor, nicker, picker, quicker, sicker, slicker, snicker, sticker, thicker, ticker, vicar, whicker, wicker.
[3] electronica, erotica, exotica, frolicker, harmonica, lip-syncer, replica, mimicker, moniker, picnicker, trafficker.

SURPRISING RHYMING:
[2] Bitter, critter, fitter, flitter, fritter, glitter, gritter, hitter, jitter, knitter, litter, pitta, quitter, sitter, skitter, slitter, splitter, titter, twitter.
Bigger, digger, figure, jigger, ligger, rigger, rigour/rigor (U.S.), snigger, trigger, vigour/vigor (U.S.).
Bidder, consider, differ, kidder.
Chipper, clipper, dipper, flipper, hipper, kipper, nipper, ripper, shipper, sipper, skipper, slipper, stripper, tipper, tripper, zipper.
Blinker, drinker, Inca, inker, linker, pinker, shrinker, sinker, stinker, thinker, tinker, winker, freethinker, headshrinker.
Chiller, driller, filler, killer, miller, pillar, spiller, thriller, tiller, villa.
Dinner, grinner, inner, sinner(s), skinner, spinner, thinner, winner(s).
Elixir, fixer, mixer, picture, sixer.
Giver, liver, river, shiver, sliver, quiver.
[3] Creditor, editor, embitter, housesitter, janitor, Jupiter, monitor, transmitter, visitor.
Configure, disfigure, gold-digger, gravedigger, vinegar.
Caliper, day-tripper, equipper, juniper, worshiper.
Beginner(s), Berliner, breadwinner, examiner, foreigner, mariner, milliner, phenomena, prizewinner, retina, stamina, submariner.
Aquiver, deliver, downriver, forgiver, upriver.
[4] Baby-sitter, barometer, competitor, counterfeiter, depositor, diameter, exhibitor, interpreter, mileometer/milometer (U.S.), parameter, perimeter, solicitor, speedometer, thermometer.

3.1.12 "--ickest" (as in "quickest")
[2] quickest, sickest, thickest.

SURPRISING RHYMING:
[2] **Biggest**, fittest, hippest, richest, simplest, thinnest, witnessed.
Crickets, pickets, thickets, tickets, wickets.
[3] **Busiest**, chilliest, dizziest, fizziest, frizziest, hilliest, silliest.
Friskiest, milkiest, riskiest, silkiest, skinniest.
Grittiest, prettiest, wittiest.

3.1.13 "--icket" (as in "ticket")
[2] cricket, picket, stick it, thicket, ticket, wicket.

SURPRISING RHYMING:
[2] **Bigot**, biscuit, dig it, milk it, snippet, wicked.
Emit, limit, minute, misfit, remit, tidbit.
Digit, fidget, legit, midget, widget.
[3] **Elicit**, explicit, illicit, implicit, solicit, re-visit.
Acquitted, admitted, committed, dimwitted, fitted, half-witted, knitted, omitted, outwitted, permitted, quick-witted, spirited, transmitted.
Exhibit, inhibit, prohibit, speed limit.

3.1.14 "--icky" (as in "tricky")
[2] dickey, hickey, picky, quickie, sickie, slicky, sticky, tricky, wiki.

SURPRISING RHYMING:
[2] **Bitty**, city, ditty, gritty, guilty, kitty, pity, pretty, sixty, witty.
Chippy, clippie, crispy, dippy, drippy, hippie, lippy, nippy, snippy, trippy, whippy, yippee, zippy.
Milky, prickly, quickly, sickly, silky, slickly, tickly, thickly.
Dixie, frisky, risky, whiskey, whisky.
Cine, gimme, guinea, lemme, mini, skinny, spinney, tinny, whinny.
Busy, dizzy, fizzy, frizzy, missy, silly, tizzy.
Diddy, giddy, kiddie, midi.
[3] **Ability**, agility, anxiety, equality, gravity, hostility, humanity, humility, humidity, notoriety, nudity, oddity, quality, responsibility, sanity, self-pity, sobriety, society, stupidity, vanity, variety.

3.1.15 "--icking" (as in "kicking")
[2] clicking, flicking, kicking, licking, nicking, picking, pricking, ticking, tricking.

SURPRISING RHYMING:
[2] **Chicken**, quicken, sicken, stricken, thicken.
Blinking, drinking, hoodwinking, inkling, linking, shrinking, sinking, slinking, sprinkling, stinking, syncing, thinking, twinkling, winking.
Bitten, kitten, mitten, smitten, written.
Bidding, forbidding, kidding, outbidding, ridding, skidding.
Digging, jigging, rigging, swigging.
Glinting, hinting, minting, printing, sprinting, squinting, tinting.
Chipping, clipping, dipping, dripping, flipping, gripping, nipping, ripping, shipping, sipping, skipping, slipping, snipping, stripping, tipping, tripping, unzipping, whipping, .
Fitting, hitting, knitting, quitting, sitting, slitting, spitting, splitting.
Drifting, gifting, lifting, rifting, shifting, sifting, sixteen.
Beginning, grinning, inning, pinning, sinning, skinning, spinning, thinning, winning.
Bringing, clinging, flinging, pinging, ringing, singing, slinging, springing, stinging, stringing, swinging, winging, wringing.
Giving, living, forgiving, misgiving, outliving, thanksgiving, unforgiving.
Bitching, ditching, hitching, itching, snitching, stitching, switching, twitching, witching.
Dissing, hissing, kissing, missing.
[3] **Equipping**, frostbitten, horsewhipping, outstripping, rewritten, unwritten, unzipping.
Acquitting, admitting, omitting, permitting, side-splitting, transmitting, unwitting.
Conflicting, convicting, depicting, evicting, inflicting, predicting, restricting.

337

3.1.16 "--ickle" (as in "tickle")
[2] fickle, nickel, pickle, prickle, tickle, trickle.
[3] chronicle, classical, cyclical, follicle, icicle, popsicle, radical, tricycle, tropical.
[4+] tyrannical, lackadaisical, mathematical, philosophical.

SURPRISING RHYMING:
[2] **Pickled**, prickled, tickled, trickled.
Belittle, brittle, committal, hospital, it'll, little, skittle, spittle, whittle.
Cripple, nipple, ripple, stipple, tipple, triple.
Dribble, nibble, quibble, scribble, sibyl.
Chicken, quicken, sicken, stricken, thicken.
Diddle, fiddle, griddle, idyll, middle, paradiddle, riddle, twiddle.
Giggle, jiggle, niggle, squiggle, wiggle, wriggle.
Civil, drivel, shrivel, skiffle, sniffle, snivel, swivel.
Bristle, chisel, drizzle, fizzle, missile, sizzle, swizzle, thistle, whistle.
[3] **Acquittal**, belittle, committal, hospital.

3.1.17 "--ickly" (as in "quickly")
[2] prickly, quickly, sickly, slickly, tickly, thickly.

SURPRISING RHYMING:
[2] **Dickey**, hickey, picky, quickie, sickie, slicky, sticky, tricky, wiki.
Dixie, frisky, richly, risky, whiskey, whisky.
Guilty, milky, minty, misty, nasty, nicety, nifty, shifty, silky, simply, sixty, swiftie, thrifty.
Crinkly, sprinkly, tinkly, wrinkly.
Giggly, hygge, niggly, squiggly, tingly, wiggly, wriggly.
[3] **Ability**, agility, anxiety, equality, gravity, hostility, humanity, humility, humidity, notoriety, nudity, oddity, quality, responsibility, sanity, self-pity, sobriety, society, stupidity, vanity, variety.
Distinctly, physically, quizzically, succinctly.

3.1.18 "--ickness" (as in "sickness")
[2] quickness, sickness, slickness, thickness.

SURPRISING RHYMING:
[2] **Business**, citrus, illness, fitness, witness.
Quickest, sickest, thickest.
Biggest, fittest, hippest, richest, richness, simplest, witnessed.
Crickets, pickets, thickets, tickets, wickets.
[3] **Ambitious**, auspicious, Christmas, delicious, fictitious, forgiveness, inauspicious, malicious, nutritious, suspicious, vicious.
Busiest, chilliest, dizziest, dizziness, fizziest, frizziest, hilliest, silliest.
Friskiest, grittiest, milkiest, prettiest, riskiest, silkiest, skinniest, wittiest.

3.1.19 "--icted" (as in "addicted")
[3] addicted, afflicted, conflicted, convicted, depicted, evicted, predicted, restricted.

SURPRISING RHYMING:
[2] **Drifted**, frigid, gifted, lifted, rigid, rifted, scripted, shifted, sifted.
Bigot, biscuit, dig it, snippet, wicked.
Emit, limit, minute, misfit, remit, tidbit.
Digit, fidget, legit, midget, widget.
Jilted, kilted, lilted, quilted, silted, stilted, tilted, wilted.
Listed, liquid, misted, twisted.
Cricket, picket, stick it, thicket, ticket, wicket.
Dinted, glinted, hinted, minted, printed, sprinted, squinted, tinted.
Bitten, kitten, mitten, smitten, victim, written.
[3] **Acquitted**, admitted, committed, dimwitted, emitted, fitted, half-witted, knitted, omitted, outwitted, permitted, quick-witted, spirited, submitted, transmitted, unfitted.

Artistic, ballistic, linguistic, logistic, realistic, sadistic, simplistic, statistic, stylistic.
Addictive, constrictive, predictive, restrictive, vindictive.
Assisted, blacklisted, consisted, enlisted, existed, insisted, persisted, predicted, resisted, tight-fisted, two-fisted, unlisted.
Elicit, explicit, illicit, implicit, solicit, re-visit.
Exhibit, inhibit, prohibit, speed limit.
Conscripted, encrypted, expected, infected, unscripted.

3.1.20 "--icting" (as in "predicting")
[3] addicting, conflicting, convicting, depicting, evicting, inflicting, predicting, restricting.

SURPRISING RHYMING:
[2] **Fitting,** hitting, knitting, quitting, sitting, slitting, spitting, splitting.
Blinking, drinking, hoodwinking, inking, inkling, linking, shrinking, sinking, sprinkling, stinking, syncing, thinking, twinkling, winking.
Clicking, flicking, kicking, licking, picking, pricking, ticking, tricking.
Drifting, gifting, lifting, rifting, shifting, sifting, sixteen.
Glinting, hinting, minting, printing, sprinting, squinting, tinting.
Glistening, listening, listing, misting, twisting.
[3] **Addicted,** afflicted, conflicted, convicted, depicted, evicted, predicted, restricted.
Addictive, constrictive, predictive, restrictive, vindictive.
Drifting, gifting, lifting, rifting, shifting, sifting, sixteen.
Emitting, exhibiting, inhibiting, limiting, prohibiting, remitting.
Assisting, blacklisting, consisting, enlisting, existing, insisting, persisting, resisting, subsisting, untwisting.
Acquitting, admitting, emitting, omitting, permitting, remitting, side-splitting, transmitting, unremitting, unwitting.

3.1.21 "--ictive" (as in "addictive")
[3] addictive, constrictive, predictive, restrictive, vindictive.

SURPRISING RHYMING:
[2] **Active,** captive, festive, forgive, massive, misgive, missive, motive, native, octave, olive, outlive, passive, pensive, relive.
Drifted, frigid, gifted, lifted, liquid, listed, misted, rigid, scripted, shifted, sifted, twisted.
[3] **Addicted,** afflicted, conflicted, convicted, depicted, evicted, predicted, restricted.
Dismissive, emissive, missive, permissive, submissive.
Distinctive, instinctive, protective.
Artistic, ballistic, linguistic, logistic, realistic, sadistic, simplistic, statistic, stylistic.
Assisted, blacklisted, close-fisted, consisted, enlisted, existed, insisted, persisted, predicted, resisted, subsisted, tight-fisted, two-fisted, unlisted, untwisted.
Abrasive, abusive, adhesive, aggressive, compulsive, conclusive, conducive, corrosive, decisive, defensive, divisive, elusive, emotive, evasive, excessive, exclusive, expensive, expletive, explosive, expressive, impassive, impressive, impulsive, incisive, inclusive, intensive, intrusive, narrative, negative, obsessive, offensive, oppressive, percussive, permissive, persuasive, possessive, progressive, reclusive, repulsive, responsive, sedative, submissive, subversive, talkative.

3.1.22 "--ickup" (as in "pickup")
[2] hiccup, pickup, stick-up.

SURPRISING RHYMING:
[2] **Gossip,** syrup.
Build-up, chin up, dig up, give up, ketchup, lift, link-up, mix-up, pin-up, rip up, sit up, slipup, split up, stirrup, trip up, zip-up.
Bigot, frigate, minute.

3.1.23 "--ickening" (as in "sickening")
[3] quickening, sickening, thickening.

SURPRISING RHYMING:
[3] **Cricketing,** picketing, ticketing.
Pickling, prickling, tickling, trickling.
Crinkling, inkling, sprinkling, tinkling, twinkling, winkling, wrinkling.
Exhibiting, inhibiting, prohibiting.
Glistening, listening, listing, misting, twisting.
Crippling, rippling, stippling, tippling, tripling.
Dribbling, nibbling, quibbling, scribbling, sibling.
Jingling, mingling, tingling.
Dwindling, kindling, spindling, swindling
Chiseling, drizzling, fizzling, frizzling, sizzling, whistling.
Driveling, shriveling, sniffling, sniveling, swiveling.
Delivering, quivering, shivering.

3.1.24 "--id" (as in "forbid")
[1] bid, did, grid, id, kid, lid, quid, skid, slid, squid.
[2] amid, eyelid, forbid, outbid, rapid, undid.
[3] excited, invalid, pyramid, overbid, overdid, underbid.

SURPRISING RHYMING:
[1] **Adlib,** bib, crib, dib, fib, glib, lib, nib, rib(s), sparerib, squib.
Bit, fit, grit, hit, it, kit, knit, lit, pit, quit, skit, slit, spit, split, wit.
Drift, gift, lift, miffed, shift, sniffed, swift, thrift, whiffed.
Big, dig, fig, gig, jig, pig, prig, rig, swig, twig, wig.
Brick, chick, click, crick, dick, flick, hick, kick, lick, nick, pick, prick, quick, sic, sick, slick, stick, thick, tic, tick, trick, wick.
Blip, chip, clip, dip, drip, flip, grip, hip, kip, lip, nip, pip, quip, rip, ship, sip, skip, slip, snip, strip, tip, trip, whip, yip, zip.
Built, gilt, guilt, jilt, kilt, lilt, quilt, silt, spilt, stilt, tilt, wilt.
[2] **Acquit,** admit, armpit, commit, emit, habit, misfit, moonlit, omit, outfit, outwit, spirit, submit, sunlit, tidbit, transmit, unfit.
Gearshift, makeshift, snowdrift, spendthrift, uplift.
Arsenic, broomstick, chopstick, drumstick, heartsick, homesick, lipstick, lovesick, seasick.
Airship, catnip, courtship, equip, flagship, friendship, hardship, horsewhip, kinship, outstrip, steamship, township, warship, worship.
Assist, consist, dismissed, enlist, insist, persist, resist, subsist.
Addict, afflict, constrict, convict, evict, predict, restrict.
[3] **Counterfeit,** definite, exquisite, favourite/favorite (U.S.), hypocrite, infinite, opposite.
Elicit, explicit, illicit, implicit, solicit.
Battleship, fellowship, horsemanship, leadership, membership, partnership, scholarship, sportsmanship, workmanship.
Activist, anarchist, atheist, analyst, botanist, catalyst, columnist, communist, egotist, exorcist, fatalist, hobbyist, humourist/humorist (U.S.), hypnotist, journalist, lobbyist, moralist, motorist, novelist, optimist, organist, pacifist, pessimist, pre-exist, publicist, socialist, soloist, specialist, strategist, terrorist.

3.1.25 "--idden" (as in "hidden")
forbidden, hidden, ridden.

SURPRISING RHYMING:
[2] **Bidding,** didn't, kidding, ridding, skidding.
Bitten, kitten, mitten, smitten, written.
Digging, jigging, ligging, rigging, swigging.
Bringing, clinging, flinging, pinging, ringing, singing, slinging, springing, stinging, stringing, swinging, winging, wringing.
Fitting, hitting, knitting, quitting, sitting, slitting, spitting, splitting.
Christen, criticism, isn't, listen, rhythm - vision.
Chicken, quicken, sicken, stricken, thicken.
Emission, fission, intermission, magician, mission, musician, titian.
Arisen, glisten, imprison, prison, risen.

Pigeon, religion, smidgen, stool-pigeon.
[3] **Flea-bitten**, frostbitten, rewritten, unwritten.
Acquitting, admitting, omitting, permitting, side-splitting, transmitting, unwitting.
Efficient, proficient, sufficient.

3.1.26 "--idding" (as in "kidding")
bidding, forbidding, kidding, outbidding, ridding, skidding.

SURPRISING RHYMING:
[2] **Didn't**, forbidden, hidden, ridden.
Bitten, kitten, mitten, smitten, written.
Fitting, hitting, knitting, quitting, sitting, slitting, spitting, splitting.
Digging, jigging, rigging, swigging.
Drifting, gifting, lifting, rifting, shifting, sifting, sixteen.
Bringing, clinging, flinging, pinging, ringing, singing, slinging, springing, stinging, stringing, swinging, winging, wringing.
Chipping, clipping, dipping, dripping, flipping, gripping, nipping, ripping, shipping, sipping, skipping, slipping, stripping, tipping, tripping, unzipping, whipping, zipping.
Chicken, quicken, sicken, stricken, thicken.
Clicking, flicking, kicking, licking, picking, pricking, ticking, tricking.
Brimming, dimming, skimming, slimming, swimming, trimming.
Grinning, pinning, sinning, skinning, spinning, thinning, winning.
Billing, chilling, drilling, filling, grilling, killing, shilling, spilling, stilling, swilling, thrilling, tilling, willing.
Giving, driven, given, forgiving, living, misgiving, outliving, thanksgiving, unforgiving.
Dissing, hissing, kissing, missing.
Emission, fission, intermission, magician, mission, musician, titian.
Arisen, glisten, imprison, prison, risen.
Pigeon, religion, smidgen, stool-pigeon.
[3] **Flea-bitten**, frostbitten, rewritten, unwritten.
Acquitting, admitting, omitting, permitting, side-splitting, transmitting, unwitting.

3.1.27 "--iddel" (as in "fiddle")
[2] diddle, fiddle, griddle, idyll, middle, paradiddle, riddle, twiddle.

SURPRISING RHYMING:
[2] **Driven**, given, forbidden, hidden, ridden.
Bidding, didn't, kidding, ridding, skidding.
Dwindle, kindle, spindle, swindle.
Dribble, nibble, quibble, scribble, sibyl.
Dribbled, nibbled, quibbled, ribald, scribbled.
Cripple, nipple, ripple, stipple, tipple, triple.
Belittle, brittle, committal, hospital, it'll, little, skittle, spittle, whittle.
Giggle, jiggle, squiggle, wiggle, wriggle.
Civil, drivel, shrivel, skiffle, sniffle, snivel, swivel.
Fickle, nickel, pickle, prickle, tickle, trickle.
Crinkle, sprinkle, tinkle, twinkle, winkle, wrinkle.
Jingle, mingle, single, tingle.
Giving, living, forgiving, misgiving, outliving, thanksgiving, unforgiving.
Bristle, chisel, drizzle, fizzle, frizzle, gristle, missile, sizzle, swizzle, thistle, whistle.

3.1.28 "--iddler" (as in "fiddler")
[2] diddler, fiddler, riddler, tiddler.

SURPRISING RHYMING:
[2] **Crippler**, dribbler, nibbler, quibbler, scribbler, simpler, sprinkler, stickler, tippler.
Chiller, driller, filler, killer, miller, pillar, spiller, thriller, tiller, villa.
Giggler, niggler, wiggler, wriggler.
Bigger, digger, figure, rigour/rigor (U.S.), snigger, trigger, vigour/vigor (U.S.).

Crimper, limper, shrimper, simper, whimper.
Drifter, grifter, lifter, shifter, sifter, snifter, swifter.
Dinner, grinner, inner, sinner(s), skinner, spinner, thinner, winner.
Bringer, clinger, finger, flinger, linger, ringer, singer, slinger, springer, stinger, stringer, swinger, winger, wringer, zinger.
Bitter, critter, fitter, flitter, fritter, glitter, gritter, hitter, jitter, knitter, litter, pitta, quitter, sitter, skitter, slitter, splitter, titter, twitter.
Blister, crisper, mister, sister, trickster, twister, vista, whisper.
[3] **Builder**, bodybuilder, boatbuilder, bewilder, housebuilder.
Caterpillar, chinchilla, distiller, flotilla, fulfiller, gorilla, guerilla, manila, man-killer, painkiller, spine-chiller, vanilla, weed killer.
Configure, disfigure, gold-digger, gravedigger, vinegar.

3.1.29 "--iddling" (as in "fiddling")
[2] diddling, fiddling, middling, piddling, riddling, twiddling.

SURPRISING RHYMING:
[2] **Dribbling**, nibbling, quibbling, scribbling, sibling.
Giggling, jiggling, niggling, squiggling, wiggling, wriggling.
Driveling, shriveling, sniffling, sniveling, swiveling.
Chiseling, drizzling, fizzling, sizzling, whistling.
Crippling, rippling, stippling, tippling, tripling.
Drifting, gifting, lifting, rifting, shifting, sifting, sixteen.
Bringing, clinging, flinging, pinging, ringing, singing, slinging, springing, stinging, stringing, swinging, winging, wringing.
[3] **Building**, bodybuilding, boatbuilding, bewildering, housebuilding.
Figuring, sniggering, triggering.

3.1.30 "--idge" (as in "bridge")
[1] bridge, midge, ridge.
[2] abridge, bondage, cabbage, carnage, cribbage, dosage, hostage, language, leakage, message, package, postage, sausage, shortage, storage, usage, voyage.
[3] anchorage, appendage, average, beverage, brokerage, cartilage, foliage, heritage, leverage, patronage, pilgrimage.

SURPRISING RHYMING:
[1] **Bitch**, ditch, glitch, hitch, itch, kitsch, niche, pitch, rich, snitch, stitch, switch, twitch, which, witch.
Cinch, clinch, finch, flinch, Grinch, inch, lynch, pinch, winch.
Binge, cringe, fringe, hinge, singe, tinge, twinge.
Dish, fish, squish, swish, wish.
[2] **Bewitch**, enrich, sales pitch, unhitch.
Infringe, syringe, unhinge.
Anguish, blueish, brownish, feverish, flourish, goldfish, greenish, jellyfish, nourish, reddish, selfish, shellfish, starfish, yellowish.

3.1.31 "--idget" (as in "fidget")
[2] digit, fidget, legit, midget, widget.

SURPRISING RHYMING:
[2] **Acquit**, admit, armpit, biscuit, cockpit, commit, habit, limit, minute, misfit, moonlit, omit, outwit, spirit, sunlit, tidbit, unfit.
Commit, edit, emit, outfit, permit, rabbit, submit, transmit, visit.
Exhibit, inhibit, prohibit.
Drifted, frigid, gifted, lifted, rigid, rifted, shifted, sifted.
Ninja, pigeon, religion, smidgen, stool-pigeon.
[3] **Artistic**, ballistic, linguistic, logistic, realistic, sadistic, simplistic, statistic, stylistic.
Elicit, explicit, illicit, implicit, solicit.

Acquitted, admitted, committed, dimwitted, fitted, knitted, omitted, outwitted, permitted, quick-witted, spirited, submitted, transmitted.

3.1.32 "--idgid" (as in "rigid")
[2] frigid, rigid.

SURPRISING RHYMING:
[2] **Digit**, fidget, legit, midget, widget.
Drifted, frigid, gifted, lifted, rigid, rifted, scripted, shifted, sifted.
Dinted, glinted, hinted, minted, printed, sprinted, squinted, tinted.
Listed, liquid, livid, misted, timid, twisted, vivid, wicked.
Biscuit, limit, minute, misfit, sunlit, tidbit, transmit, unfit.
Bridges, fridge, midges, ridges.
Binges, cringes, fringes, hinges, singes, tinges, twinges.
Bitches, breeches, britches, ditches, hitches, itches, niches, pitches, riches, snitches, stitches, switches, twitches, witches, which is.
Jilted, kilted, lilted, quilted, silted, stilted, tilted, wilted.
[3] **Acquitted**, admitted, committed, dimwitted, fitted, half-witted, knitted, omitted, outwitted, permitted, quick-witted, spirited, submitted.
Assisted, blacklisted, consisted, enlisted, existed, insisted, persisted, predicted, resisted, tight-fisted, two-fisted, unlisted, untwisted.
Addicted, afflicted, conflicted, convicted, depicted, evicted, predicted, restricted.
Elicit, explicit, illicit, implicit, solicit.

3.1.33 "--idgen" (as in "religion")
pigeon, religion, smidgen, stool-pigeon.

SURPRISING RHYMING:
[2] **Bitching**, ditching, hitching, itching, snitching, stitching, switching, twitching, witching.
Diction, fiction, friction.
Bitten, didn't, forbidden, glisten, hidden, isn't, listen, rhythm.
Emission, fission, intermission, magician, mission, musician, titian, vision.
Billion, million, civilian, pavilion, trillion, vermillion.
Cinching, clinching, flinching, inching, lynching, pinching.
Dishing, fishing, phishing, squishing, swishing, wishing.
Dissing, hissing, kissing, missing.
Arisen, driven, given, glisten, imprison, prison, risen.
Digit, fidget, legit, midget, widget.
[3] **Abridging**, averaging, bridging, leveraging, messaging, packaging, voyaging.
Addiction, affliction, constriction, conviction, depiction, eviction, prediction, restriction.
Description, inscription, prescription, subscription, transcription.
Addition, admission, ambition, attrition, audition, condition, contrition, edition, emission, fruition, ignition, magician, musician, nutrition, omission, optician, partition, petition, permission, physician, position, remission, rendition, submission, suspicion, tactician, technician, tradition, transition, transmission, tuition, volition.
Efficient, proficient, sufficient.
Collision, decision, derision, division, envision, incision, precision, provision, revision.

3.1.34 "--if" (as in "cliff")
[1] if, cliff, miff, riff, skiff, sniff, stiff, tiff, whiff.
[3] handkerchief, neckerchief.

SURPRISING RHYMING:
[1] **Drift**, gift, lift, miffed, shift, sniffed, swift, thrift, whiffed.
Myth, pith, smith, with.
Built, gilt, guilt, jilt, kilt, lilt, quilt, silt, spilt, stilt, tilt, wilt.
Blip, chip, clip, dip, drip, flip, grip, hip, kip, lip, nip, pip, quip, rip, ship, sip, skip, slip, snip, strip, tip, trip, whip, yip, zip.
Bliss, diss, hiss, kiss, miss, sis, this.

Dissed, fist, gist, hissed, kissed, list, midst, missed, mist, pissed, tryst, twist, wrist.
[2] Gearshift, makeshift, snowdrift, spendthrift, uplift.
Forthwith, goldsmith, gunsmith, herewith, locksmith, wordsmith.
Airship, catnip, courtship, equip, flagship, friendship, hardship, horsewhip, kinship, outstrip, steamship, township, warship, worship.
Amiss, bodice, chalice, coppice, dismiss, gratis, haggis, hospice, hubris, jaundice, justice, malice, Memphis, novice, office, palace, Paris, preface, purchase, remiss, service, solstice, surface.
Assist, consist, dismissed, enlist, exist, insist, persist, resist.
[3] Activist, anarchist, atheist, analyst, botanist, catalyst, columnist, communist, egotist, exorcist, fatalist, hobbyist, humourist/humorist (U.S.), hypnotist, journalist, lobbyist, moralist, motorist, novelist, optimist, organist, pacifist, pessimist, pre-exist, publicist, socialist, soloist, specialist, strategist, terrorist.
Accomplice, cowardice, edifice, emphasis, genesis, kinesis, liquorice/licorice (U.S.), nemesis, prejudice, reminisce, synthesis.

3.1.35 "--ift" (as in "lift")
[1] drift, gift, lift, miffed, rift, shift, shrift, sniffed, swift, thrift, whiffed.
[2] adrift, airlift, facelift, gearshift, makeshift, nightshift, snowdrift, spendthrift, uplift.

SURPRISING RHYMING:
[1] If, cliff, miff, riff, skiff, sniff, stiff, tiff, whiff.
Myth, pith, smith, with.
Give, live, sieve, spiv.
Dissed, fist, gist, hissed, kissed, list, midst, missed, mist, pissed, tryst, twist.
Dished, fished, squished, swished, wished.
[2] Forthwith, goldsmith, gunsmith, herewith, locksmith, wordsmith.
Active, captive, festive, forgive, massive, misgive, missive, motive, native, octave, olive, outlive, passive, pensive, relive.
Assist, consist, dismissed, enlist, exist, insist, persist, resist, subsist.
[3] Abrasive, abusive, adhesive, aggressive, compulsive, conclusive, conducive, corrosive, decisive, defensive, divisive, elusive, emotive, evasive, excessive, exclusive, expensive, expletive, explosive, expressive, impassive, impressive, impulsive, incisive, inclusive, intensive, intrusive, narrative, negative, obsessive, offensive, oppressive, percussive, permissive, persuasive, possessive, progressive, reclusive, repulsive, responsive, sedative, submissive, subversive, talkative.
Activist, anarchist, atheist, analyst, botanist, catalyst, coexist, columnist, communist, egotist, exorcist, fatalist, hobbyist, humourist/humorist (U.S.), hypnotist, journalist, lobbyist, moralist, motorist, novelist, optimist, organist, pacifist, pessimist, pre-exist, publicist, socialist, soloist, specialist, strategist, terrorist.

3.1.36 "--iffer" (as in "differ")
conifer, differ, Lucifer, sniffer, stiffer.

SURPRISING RHYMING:
[2] Giver, liver, river, shiver, sliver, quiver.
Dither, hither, slither, whither, wither, zither.
Dinner, grinner, inner, sinner, skinner, spinner, thinner, winner.
Dimmer, glimmer, primmer, shimmer, simmer, skimmer, slimmer, swimmer, trimmer.
Bidder, consider, kidder.
Bigger, digger, figure, rigour/rigor (U.S.), snigger, trigger, vigour/vigor (U.S.).
Drifter, grifter, lifter, shifter, sifter, snifter, swifter.
Fisher, fissure, fizzer, hisser, kisser, quizzer, reminiscer, scissor, whizzer, wisher.
Chipper, clipper, dipper, flipper, hipper, kipper, nipper, ripper, shipper, sipper, skipper, slipper, stripper, tipper, tripper, zipper.
Bicker, flicker, kicker, knicker, licker, liquor, picker, quicker, sicker, slicker, snicker, sticker, thicker, ticker, tricker, vicar, whicker, wicker.
Bitter, critter, fitter, flitter, fritter, glitter, gritter, hitter, jitter, knitter, litter, pitta, quitter, sitter, skitter, slitter, splitter, titter, twitter.
Blister, crisper, mister, sister, trickster, twister, vista, whisper.

[3] **Aquiver**, deliver, downriver, forgiver, upriver.
Beginner, Berliner, breadwinner, examiner, foreigner, mariner, milliner, phenomena, prizewinner, retina, stamina, submariner.

3.1.37 "--iffic" (as in "terrific")
[3] horrific, pacific, prolific, specific, terrific.
[4] colorific, hieroglyphic, non-specific, scientific.

SURPRISING RHYMING:
[2] **Civic**, clinic, critic, cynic, filmic, gimmick, lipstick, lyric, matchstick, mimic, mystic, mythic, traffic.
Cricket, picket, snippet, stick it, thicket, ticket, wicket.
Affix, crucifix, intermix, matchsticks, prefix, suffix.
[3] **Eccentric**, exhibit, inhibit, prohibit.
Elicit, explicit, illicit, implicit, solicit.
Artistic, ballistic, linguistic, logistic, realistic, sadistic, simplistic, statistic, stylistic.
Dismissive, emissive, missive, permissive, submissive.

3.1.38 "--ifted" (as in "gifted")
[2] drifted, gifted, lifted, rifted, shifted, sifted.

SURPRISING RHYMING:
[2] **Dinted**, glinted, hinted, minted, printed, sprinted, squinted, tinted.
Listed, liquid, misted, twisted.
[3] **Acquitted**, admitted, committed, dimwitted, emitted, fitted, half-witted, knitted, omitted, outwitted, permitted, quick-witted, spirited, submitted, transmitted, unfitted.
Assisted, blacklisted, consisted, enlisted, existed, insisted, persisted, predicted, resisted, subsisted, tight-fisted, two-fisted, unlisted.
Imprinted, misprinted, reprinted.

3.1.39 "--ifter" (as in "drifter")
drifter, grifter, lifter, shifter, shoplifter, sifter, snifter, swifter, weightlifter.

SURPRISING RHYMING:
[2] **Midwinter**, printer, splinter, sprinter, squinter, winter.
Blister, crisper, mister, sister, trickster, twister, vista, whisper.
Conifer, differ, Lucifer, sniffer, sniffler, stiffer.
Giver, liver, quiver, river, shiver, sliver.
Filter, jilter, kilter, quilter, tilter.
Bitter, critter, fitter, flitter, fritter, glitter, gritter, hitter, jitter, knitter, litter, pitta, quitter, sitter, skitter, slitter, splitter, titter, twitter.
Ditcher, hitcher, picture, pitcher, richer, snitcher, stitcher, stricture, switcher, twitcher.
Elixir, scissor, fizzer, hisser, kisser, quizzer, reminiscer, whizzer.
[3] **Contradictor**, depicter, descriptor, evictor, predictor, victor.
Builder, bodybuilder, boatbuilder, bewilder, housebuilder, shipbuilder.
Aquiver, deliver, downriver, forgiver, upriver.

3.1.40 "--ifty" (as in "thrifty")
[2] fifty, nifty, shifty, thrifty.

SURPRISING RHYMING:
[2] **Drifting**, gifting, lifting, rifting, shifting, sifting, sixteen.
Bitty, chitty, city, ditty, gritty, kitty, pity, pretty, witty.
Guilty, milky, silky, distinctly, succinctly.
Prickly, quickly, slickly, tickly, thickly.
Dickey, hickey, picky, quickie, slicky, sticky, tricky.
Frisky, history, mystery, risky, whiskey, whisky.
Giggly, hygge, niggly, squiggly, tingly, wiggly, wriggly.
Guinea, ninny, pinny, skinny, tinny, whinny.

Busy, dizzy, fizzy, flimsy, frizzy, kiss me, tizzy, whimsy.
Chili, chilly, filly, frilly, hilly, hillbilly, icily, lily, silly, willy-nilly, rockabilly.
[3] Gravity, nudity, oddity, quality, sanity, self-pity, vanity.
Delivery, livery, quivery, shivery.
[4] Ability, agility, anxiety, equality, facility, fertility, fragility, futility, hostility, humanity, humidity, humility, mobility, nitty-gritty, nobility, sobriety, society, stability, stupidity, tranquillity/tranquility (U.S.), utility, variety, virility.
[5] Edibility, liability, notoriety, responsibility, usability, versatility, viability, volatility.

3.1.41 "--ifting" (as in "drifting")
[2] drifting, gifting, lifting, rifting, shifting, sifting.

SURPRISING RHYMING:
[2] **Jilting**, lilting, quilting, silting, stilting, tilting, wilting.
Glinting, hinting, minting, printing, sprinting, squinting, tinting.
Listing, misting, twisting.
Fitting, hitting, knitting, quitting, sitting, slitting, spitting, splitting.
Bidding, forbidding, kidding, outbidding, ridding, skidding.
Diddling, fiddling, middling, piddling, riddling, twiddling.
Affixing, fixing, mixing, nixing.
Crimping, limping, pimping, primping, skimping.
Blinking, drinking, hoodwinking, inking, inkling, linking, shrinking, sinking, sprinkling, stinking, syncing, thinking, twinkling, winking.
Clicking, flicking, kicking, licking, picking, pricking, ticking, tricking.
Giggling, jiggling, wiggling, wriggling.
Bringing, clinging, flinging, pinging, ringing, singing, slinging, springing, stinging, stringing, swinging, winging, wringing.
Dishing, fishing, phishing, squishing, swishing, wishing.
Dissing, hissing, kissing, missing.
Grinning, pinning, sinning, skinning, spinning, thinning, winning.
Billing, chilling, drilling, filling, grilling, killing, shilling, spilling, stilling, thrilling, willing.
[3] Giving, living, forgiving, misgiving, thanksgiving, unforgiving.
Assisting, blacklisting, consisting, enlisting, existing, insisting, persisting, resisting.
Conflicting, constricting, convicting, depicting, evicting, inflicting, predicting, restricting.
Acquitting, admitting, omitting, permitting, side-splitting, transmitting, unwitting.
Distilling, fulfilling, instilling, unwilling.

3.1.42 "--ig" (as in "big")
[1] big, dig, fig, gig, jig, pig, prig, rig, swig, twig, wig.

SURPRISING RHYMING:
[1] **Adlib**, bib, crib, dib, fib, glib, lib, nib, rib(s), sparerib, squib.
Bid, did, grid, id, kid, lid, quid, skid, slid, squid.
Give, live, sieve, spiv.
Been, bin, chin, din, gin, grin, in, inn, kin, pin, shin, sin, skin, spin, thin, twin, win.
Bit, fit, grit, hit, it, kit, knit, lit, pit, quit, skit, slit, spit, split, wit.
Drift, gift, lift, miffed, shift, sniffed, swift, thrift, whiffed.
Brick, chick, click, crick, dick, flick, hick, kick, lick, nick, pick, prick, quick, sic, sick, slick, stick, thick, tic, tick, trick, wick.
Blip, chip, clip, dip, drip, flip, grip, hip, kip, lip, nip, pip, quip, rip, ship, sip, skip, slip, snip, strip, tip, trip, whip, yip, zip.
Biz, fizz, his, is, quiz, whiz.
[2] **Amid**, eyelid, forbid, outbid, rapid, undid.
Active, captive, festive, forgive, massive, misgive, missive, motive, native, octave, olive, outlive, passive, pensive, relive.
Acquit, admit, armpit, cockpit, commit, emit, habit, misfit, moonlit, omit, outfit, outwit, remit, spirit, submit, sunlit, tidbit, transmit, unfit.
Gearshift, makeshift, snowdrift, spendthrift, uplift.
Airship, catnip, courtship, equip, flagship, friendship, hardship, horsewhip, kinship, outstrip, steamship, township, warship, worship.

3.1.43 "--igger" (as in "bigger")
[2] bigger, digger, figure, jigger, ligger, rigger, rigour/rigor (U.S.), snigger, trigger, vigour/vigor (U.S.).
[3] configure, disfigure, gold-digger, gravedigger, outrigger, square-rigger, vinegar.

SURPRISING RHYMING:
[2] **Bitter**, critter, fitter, flitter, fritter, glitter, gritter, hitter, jitter, knitter, litter, pitta, quitter, sitter, skitter, slitter, splitter, titter, twitter.
Dimmer, glimmer, primmer, shimmer, simmer, skimmer, slimmer, swimmer, trimmer.
Beginner, dinner, grinner, inner, sinner(s), spinner, thinner, winner.
Giver, liver, mirror, river, shiver, sliver, quiver.
Bringer, clinger, finger, flinger, linger, ringer, singer, slinger, springer, stinger, stringer, swinger, winger, wringer, zinger.
Chiller, filler, griller, killer, miller, pillar, spiller, thriller, tiller, villa.
Chipper, clipper, dipper, flipper, gripper, hipper, kipper, nipper, ripper, shipper, sipper, skipper, slipper, stripper, tipper, tripper, whipper, zipper.
Bidder, consider, kidder.
Scissor, fizzer, hisser, kisser, quizzer, reminiscer, whizzer.
Giggler, niggler, wiggler, wriggler.
Crippler, dribbler, nibbler, quibbler, scribbler, simpler, sprinkler, stickler, tippler.
Bicker, flicker, kicker, knicker, licker, liquor, nicker, picker, quicker, sicker, slicker, snicker, sticker, thicker, ticker, vicar, whicker, wicker.
[3] **Administer,** assister, banister, barista, barrister, canister, chorister, enlister, forester, harvester, minister, register, resister, resistor, sinister, sob-sister, stepsister, transistor.
Committer, embitter, outfitter, pinch-hitter, rail-splitter, remitter, submitter, transmitter.
Beginner(s), Berliner, breadwinner, examiner, foreigner, mariner, milliner, phenomena, prizewinner, retina, stamina, submariner.
Caterpillar, distiller, flotilla, fulfiller, gorilla, guerilla, painkiller, spine-chiller, vanilla.
Bell-ringer, gunslinger, humdinger, left-winger, mud-slinger.
Aquiver, deliver, downriver, forgiver, upriver.

3.1.44 "--igging" (as in "digging")
[2] digging, jigging, rigging, swigging.

SURPRISING RHYMING:
[2] **Giggling**, jiggling, niggling, squiggling, wiggling, wriggling.
Bidding, didn't, kidding, ridding, skidding.
Bringing, clinging, flinging, pinging, ringing, singing, slinging, springing, stinging, stringing, swinging, winging, wringing.
Brimming, dimming, skimming, slimming, swimming, trimming.
Grinning, pinning, sinning, skinning, spinning, thinning, winning.
Giving, driven, given, forgiving, living, misgiving, outliving, thanksgiving, unforgiving.
Billing, chilling, drilling, filling, grilling, killing, shilling, spilling, stilling, thrilling, willing.
Fitting, hitting, knitting, quitting, sitting, slitting, spitting, splitting.
Drifting, gifting, lifting, rifting, shifting, sifting, sixteen.
Glinting, hinting, minting, printing, sprinting, squinting, tinting.
Clicking, flicking, kicking, licking, picking, pricking, ticking, tricking.
Blinking, drinking, hoodwinking, inking, inkling, linking, shrinking, sinking, sprinkling, stinking, syncing, thinking, twinkling, winking.
Dwindling, kindling, spindling, swindling.
Dishing, fishing, phishing, squishing, swishing, wishing.
Dissing, hissing, kissing, missing.
[3] **Acquitting**, admitting, emitting, omitting, permitting, remitting, side-splitting, transmitting, unremitting, unwitting.
Distilling, fulfilling, instilling, unwilling.

3.1.45 "--iggle" (as in "giggle")
[2] giggle, jiggle, squiggle, wiggle, wriggle.

SURPRISING RHYMING:
[2] **Giggled**, jiggled, niggled, squiggled, wiggled, wriggled.
Dribble, nibble, quibble, scribble, sibyl.
Brittle, it'll, little, skittle, spittle, whittle.
Diddle, fiddle, griddle, idyll, middle, paradiddle, riddle, twiddle.
Civil, drivel, shrivel, skiffle, sniffle, snivel, swivel.
Cripple, nipple, ripple, stipple, tipple, triple.
Fickle, nickel, pickle, prickle, tickle, trickle.
Crinkle, sprinkle, tinkle, twinkle, winkle, wrinkle.
Bristle, chisel, drizzle, fizzle, missile, sizzle, swizzle, thistle, whistle.
Jingle, mingle, single, tingle.
Dimple, pimple, simple, wimple.
[3] **Acquittal**, belittle, committal, hospital.

3.1.46 "--iggler" (as in "giggler")
[2] giggler, niggler, wiggler, wriggler.

SURPRISING RHYMING:
[2] **Dribbler**, nibbler, quibbler, scribbler, simpler, sprinkler, stickler, tippler.
Diddler, fiddler, griddler, riddler, tiddler, twiddler.
Chiller, filler, griller, killer, miller, pillar, spiller, thriller, tiller, villa.
Dribbler, nibbler, quibbler, scribbler.
Chiseler, fizzler, frizzler, sizzler, swizzler, whistler.
Jingler, mingler, singular, tingler.

3.1.47 "--iggly" (as in "wiggly")
[2] giggly, niggly, squiggly, tingly, wiggly, wriggly.

SURPRISING RHYMING:
[2] **Chili**, chilly, filly, frilly, hilly, hillbilly, icily, lily, silly, willy-nilly, rockabilly.
Fifty, nifty, shifty, thrifty.
Prickly, quickly, slickly, tickly, thickly.
Cine, flimsy, gimme, lemme, mini, ninny, shinny, skinny, tinny, whimsy, whinny.
[3] **Frigidly**, rigidly, vividly.
Fittingly, unwillingly, willingly.
Busily, dizzily, misery.
Graffiti, liberty, rickety, snippety, trinity.
Chivalry, disagree, dithery, imagery, jittery, livery, pillory, quivery, shimmery, shivery, silvery, wizardry.
[4] **Ability**, agility, civility, dignity, fidgety, facility, fertility, fragility, futility, hostility, humility, mobility, nobility, stability, tranquillity/tranquility (U.S.), utility, virility.
Agility, fragility, hostility, infinity, stability.

3.1.48 "--iggling" (as in "giggling")
[2] giggling, jiggling, niggling, wiggling, wriggling.

SURPRISING RHYMING:
[2] **Dribbling**, nibbling, quibbling, scribbling, sibling.
Belittling, skittling, whittling.
Diddling, fiddling, griddling, middling, riddling, twiddling.
Driveling, shriveling, sniffling, sniveling, swiveling.
Crippling, rippling, stippling, tippling, tripling.
Pickling, prickling, tickling, trickling.
Crinkling, inkling, sprinkling, tinkling, twinkling, winkling, wrinkling.
Chiseling, drizzling, fizzling, frizzling, sizzling, whistling.
Jingling, mingling, singling, tingling.

3.1.49 "--igment" (as in "figment")
[2] figment, pigment.

SURPRISING RHYMING:
[2] Different, dinted, glinted, hinted, minted, minute, mitten, printed, splinted, sprinted, squinted, tinted.
Fitment, instant, shipment.
Listen, missing, mission.
[3] Enigma, indignant, malignant, stigma.
Assistant, commitment, consistent, distant, delinquent, equipment, existent, insistent, persistent, resilient, resistant.
Efficient, proficient, sufficient.

3.1.50 "--ignant" (as in "indignant")
[2] indignant, malignant.

SURPRISING RHYMING:
[2] Enigma, figment, pigment, stigma.
Different, dinted, glinted, hinted, minted, minute, mitten, printed, splinted, sprinted, squinted, tinted.
Fitment, instant, shipment.
[3] Assistant, commitment, consistent, distant, delinquent, equipment, existent, insistent, persistent, resilient, resistant.
Efficient, proficient, sufficient.

3.1.51 "--iggot" (as in "bigot")
[2] bigot, frigate.

SURPRISING RHYMING:
[2] Emit, limit, minute, misfit, remit, tidbit.
Digit, fidget, legit, midget, widget.
Cricket, picket, snippet, stick it, thicket, ticket, wicket.
Dinted, glinted, hinted, printed, splinted, sprinted, squinted, tinted.
Drifted, gifted, lifted, rifted, shifted, sifted.
[3] Counterfeit, definite, exquisite, favourite/favorite (U.S.), hypocrite, infinite, opposite.
Elicit, exhibit, explicit, illicit, implicit, inhibit, prohibit, solicit.
Addicted, afflicted, conflicted, convicted, depicted, evicted, predicted, restricted.
Acquitted, admitted, committed, dimwitted, emitted, fitted, knitted, omitted, outwitted, permitted, quick-witted, spirited, transmitted.

3.1.52 "--igure" (as in "figure")
configure, disfigure, figure, transfigure.

SURPRISING RHYMING:
[2] Configured, disfigured, figured, transfigured.
Bigger, jigger, ligger, rigour/rigor (U.S.), snigger, trigger, vigour/vigor.
Giver, liver, river, shiver, silver, sliver, quiver.
Bidder, consider, differ, kidder.
Bicker, flicker, kicker, knicker, licker, liquor, nicker, picker, quicker, sicker, slicker, snicker, sticker, thicker, ticker, vicar, whicker, wicker.
Dinner, grinner, inner, sinner, skinner, spinner, thinner, winner.
Bitter, critter, fitter, flitter, fritter, glitter, hitter, jitter, knitter, litter, quitter, sitter, twitter.
[3] Aquiver, deliver, downriver, forgiver, upriver.
Electronica, erotica, exotica, frolicker, harmonica, lip-syncer, replica, mimicker, moniker, picnicker, trafficker.
Gold-digger, gravedigger, outrigger, square-rigger, vinegar.

3.1.53 "--ignify" (as in "dignify")
[3] dignify, signify.

349

SURPRISING RHYMING:
[1] **Aye**, buy, by, cry, die, dry, dye, eye, fly, fry, guy, hi, high, I, lie, my, pi, pie, ply, pry, rye, sci-fi, shy, sigh, sky, sly, spry, spy, tie, try, vie, why, wry.
[2] **Ally**, apply, awry, belie, blow-dry, bowtie, bye-bye, comply, decry, defy, deny, drip-dry, drive-by, espy, flyby, gadfly, goodbye, good-buy, hereby, hi-fi, humble pie, imply, I-spy, July, low-fi, magpie, mince pie, nearby, occupy, outcry, rely, reply, retry, samurai, sci-fi, spin-dry, stir-fry, supply, tumble-dry, untie, whereby.
[3] **Alibi**, amplify, beautify, butterfly, by and by, certify, clarify, dignify, dragonfly, falsify, firefly, fortify, glorify, horrify, justify, lullaby, magnify, multiply, mummify, mystify, notify, nullify, pacify, passer-by, petrify, purify, qualify, rectify, rockabye, sanctify, satisfy, signify, simplify, specify, speechify, stimuli, stupefy, terrify, testify, underlie, unify, verify.
[4] **Disqualify**, diversify, electrify, exemplify, humidify, identify, indemnify, intensify, objectify, solidify, personify.

3.1.54 "--igidly" (as in "rigidly")
[3] frigidly, rigidly.

SURPRISING RHYMING:
[3] **Fittingly**, unwillingly, unwittingly, vividly, willingly, wittingly.
Busily, dizzily, misery.
Chivalry, disagree, dithery, imagery, jittery, livery, pillory, quivery, shimmery, shivery, silvery, wizardry.
Allergy, effigy, energy, eulogy, lethargy, prodigy, refugee, strategy, synergy, trilogy.
Bodily, family, fleur-de-lis, heavenly, homily, icily, jubilee, melancholy, miserly, readily.
Mimicry, ministry, misery, priory, reverie.
Gossipy, recipe, slap-happy, syrupy/syrupy, therapy, unhappy.
Distinctly, physically, quizzically, succinctly.
Critically, cynically, rhythmically, specifically, typically, wickedly.
[4] **Ability**, absurdity, affinity, agility, anxiety, calamity, community, conformity, convincingly, credulity, difficulty, dilettante, divinity, enormity, equality, eternity, fatality, fertility, fidelity, fragility, fraternity, frivolity, futility, glitterati, hostility, humanity, humidity, humility, immunity, impunity, infinity, maternity, mobility, modernity, morality, obscenity, profanity, publicity, reality, senility, serenity, sobriety, stability, stupidity, tranquillity, variety, vicinity, virginity, virility.

3.1.55 "--ikshun" (as in "friction")
[2] diction, fiction, friction.
[3] addiction, affliction, conviction, depiction, eviction, nonfiction, prediction, restriction.

SURPRISING RHYMING:
[2] **Fixing**, mixing, nixing.
Fixture, hipster, minster, mixture, picture, scripture, spinster, tincture, tipster, trickster.
Efficient, proficient, sufficient.
Bitching, ditching, hitching, itching, kitchen, pitching, snitching, stitching, switching, twitching, vixen, witching.
Emission, fission, intermission, magician, mission, musician, titian.
Arisen, glisten, imprison, listen, prison, risen.
Cinching, clinching, flinching, inching, lynching, pinching, winching.
[3] **Addition**, admission, ambition, attrition, audition, condition, contrition, edition, emission, fruition, ignition, magician, musician, nutrition, omission, optician, partition, petition, permission, physician, position, remission, rendition, submission, suspicion, tactician, technician, tradition, transition, transmission, tuition, volition.
Description, distinction, inscription, prescription, restriction, subscription, transcription.
[4] **Opposition**, contradiction, intuition, politician, premonition, prohibition, superstition.

3.1.56 "--ill" (as in "still")
[1] bill, chill, dill, drill, fill, frill, gill, grill, hill, ill, kill, mill, nil, pill, quill, shrill, sill, skill, spill, still, swill, thrill, till, trill, twill, will.

[2] anthill, bluegill, distill, downhill, fulfill, goodwill, ill-will, instill, molehill, peril, playbill, quadrille, refill, sawmill, standstill, treadmill, until, uphill, wind chill, windmill.
[3] chlorophyll, espadrille, hotel bill, daffodil, dollar bill, overkill, Pleasantville, sleeping pill, volatile, whippoorwill, window-sill.

SURPRISING RHYMING:
[1] Billed, build, chilled, drilled, filled, frilled, gild, grilled, guild, killed, milled, skilled, spilled, swilled, thrilled, tilled, willed.
Built, gilt, guilt, jilt, kilt, lilt, quilt, silt, spilt, stilt, tilt, wilt.
Been, bin, chin, din, gin, grin, in, inn, kin, pin, shin, sin, skin, spin, thin, twin, win.
[2] Distilled, fulfilled, instilled, rebuild, refilled, strong-willed, unchilled, unfilled, unskilled, weak-willed.
Begin, bearskin, chagrin, dolphin, has-been, hatpin, herein, kingpin, kremlin, Latin, Mickey Finn, muffin, napkin, paraffin, penguin, pippin, pushpin, robin, satin, sheepskin, therein, urchin, wherein, within.

3.1.57 "--illed" (as in "thrilled")
[1] billed, build, chilled, drilled, filled, frilled, gild, grilled, guild, killed, milled, skilled, spilled, swilled, thrilled, tilled, willed.
[2] fulfilled, instilled, rebuild, refilled, strong-willed, unchilled, unskilled, weak-willed.

SURPRISING RHYMING:
[1] Bill, chill, dill, drill, fill, frill, gill, grill, hill, ill, kill, mill, nil, pill, quill, shrill, sill, skill, spill, still, swill, thrill, till, trill, twill, will.
Built, gilt, guilt, jilt, kilt, lilt, quilt, silt, spilt, stilt, tilt, wilt.
[2] Anthill, bluegill, distill, downhill, fulfill, goodwill, ill-will, instill, molehill, playbill, quadrille, refill, sawmill, standstill, treadmill, until, uphill, wind chill, windmill.
Begin, bearskin, chagrin, dolphin, has-been, hatpin, herein, kingpin, kremlin, Latin, Mickey Finn, muffin, napkin, paraffin, penguin, pippin, pushpin, robin, satin, sheepskin, therein, urchin, wherein, within.
[3] Daffodil, dollar bill, overkill, sleeping pill, volatile, window-sill.

3.1.58 "--ilk" (as in "milk")
[1] bilk, ilk, milk, silk.

SURPRISING RHYMING:
[1] Built, gilt, guilt, jilt, kilt, lilt, quilt, silt, spilt, stilt, tilt, wilt.

3.1.59 "--ilt" (as in "guilt")
[1] built, gilt, guilt, jilt, kilt, lilt, quilt, silt, spilt, stilt, tilt, wilt.

SURPRISING RHYMING:
[1] Billed, build, chilled, drilled, filled, frilled, gild, grilled, guild, killed, milled, skilled, spilled, swilled, tilled, willed.
Bilk, ilk, milk, silk.
Brimmed, dimmed, rimmed, skimmed, slimmed, trimmed.
[2] Fulfilled, instilled, rebuild, refilled, strong-willed, unchilled, unfilled, unskilled, weak-willed.

3.1.60 "--illa" (as in "vanilla")
cedilla, flotilla, Godzilla, gorilla, guerilla, vanilla, villa.

SURPRISING RHYMING:
[2] Chiller, filler, gorilla, killer, pillar, spiller, stiller, thriller, tiller, villa.
Dinner, grinner, inner, sinner, skinner, spinner, thinner, winner.
[3] Beginner, Berliner, breadwinner, examiner, foreigner, mariner, milliner, phenomena, prizewinner, retina, stamina, submariner.
A Capella, Cinderella, salmonella.
Enigma, indignant, stigma.

3.1.61 "--ildder" (as in "builder")
[3] builder, bodybuilder, boatbuilder, bewilder, housebuilder, rebuilder, shipbuilder.

SURPRISING RHYMING:
[2] **Bewilder(ed)**, filter, kilter, pilfer, quilter, tilter.
Cinder, hinder, limber, marimba, timber, tinder.
Giver, liver, river, shiver, silver, sliver, quiver.
Bidder, consider, differ, kidder.
Bigger, digger, rigour/rigor (U.S.), snigger, trigger, vigour/vigor (U.S.).
Drifter, grifter, lifter, shifter, sifter, snifter, swifter.
Bringer, finger, flinger, linger, ringer, singer, slinger, springer, stinger, stringer, swinger, winger, wringer, zinger.
Midwinter, printer, splinter, sprinter, squinter, winter.
Crimper, limper, shrimper, simper, whimper.
Dimmer, glimmer, primmer, shimmer, simmer, skimmer, slimmer, swimmer, trimmer.
Dinner, grinner, inner, sinner, skinner, spinner, thinner, winner.
Bitter, critter, fitter, flitter, fritter, glitter, gritter, hitter, jitter, knitter, litter, pitta, quitter, sitter, skitter, slitter, splitter, titter, twitter.
Chiller, filler, gorilla, killer, pillar, spiller, stiller, thriller, tiller, villa.
[3] **Configure**, disfigure, figure, transfigure.
Aquiver, deliver, downriver, forgiver, upriver.
Gold-digger, gravedigger, outrigger, square-rigger, vinegar.

3.1.62 "--iller" (as in "thriller")
[2] chiller, driller, filler, griller, killer, miller, pillar, spiller, stiller, thriller, tiller, villa.
[3] caterpillar, chinchilla, distiller, flotilla, fulfiller, Godzilla, gorilla, guerilla, man-killer, painkiller, spine-chiller, vanilla, weedkiller.

SURPRISING RHYMING:
[2] **Similar**, dissimilar.
Bigger, digger, figure, jigger, ligger, rigger, rigour/rigor (U.S.), snigger, trigger, vigour/vigor (U.S.).
Dimmer, glimmer, primmer, shimmer, simmer, skimmer, slimmer, swimmer, trimmer.
Dinner, grinner, inner, sinner, skinner, spinner, thinner, winner.
Bitter, critter, fitter, flitter, fritter, glitter, gritter, hitter, jitter, knitter, litter, pitta, quitter, sitter, splitter, titter, twitter, winter.
Bidder, consider, kidder.
Giver, liver, river, shiver, silver, sliver, quiver.
Differ, drifter, grifter, lifter, shifter, snifter, sniffer, stiffer, swifter.
Scissor, fizzer, hisser, kisser, quizzer, reminiscer, whizzer.
Bringer, clinger, finger, flinger, linger, ringer, singer, slinger, springer, stinger, stringer, swinger, winger, wringer, zinger.
Chipper, clipper, dipper, flipper, hipper, kipper, nipper, ripper, shipper, sipper, skipper, slipper, stripper, tipper, tripper, zipper.
[3] **Beginner(s)**, Berliner, breadwinner, examiner, foreigner, mariner, milliner, phenomena, prizewinner, retina, stamina, submariner.
Builder, bodybuilder, boatbuilder, bewilder, housebuilder, shipbuilder.
Aquiver, deliver, downriver, forgiver, upriver.

3.1.63 "--illy" (as in "silly")
[2] chili, chilly, filly, frilly, hilly, hillbilly, icily, lily, silly, willy-nilly, rockabilly.

SURPRISING RHYMING:
[2] **Billing**, chilling, drilling, filling, grilling, killing, shilling, spilling, stilling, swilling, thrilling, tilling, willing.
Cine, gimme, mini, ninny, shinny, skinny, spinney, tinny, whinny.
Diddy, giddy, kiddie, midi.
Busy, dizzy, fizzy, flimsy, frizzy, kiss me, tizzy, whimsy.
Chippy, clippie, crispy, dippy, drippy, hippie, lippy, nippy, trippy, whippy, yippee, zippy.

352

Guilty, minty, misty, nifty, shifty, sixty, swiftie, thrifty.
Bitty, chitty, city, ditty, gritty, kitty, pity, pretty, witty.
Fifty, fifty-fifty, iffy, jiffy, miffy, nifty, pithy, shifty, sniffy, spiffy, thrifty.
Dixie, glitzy, kissy, missy, prissy, ritzy, sissy.
Brickie, hickey, icky, kinky, mickey, milky, picky, pinkie, pinky, quickie, sickie, silky, sticky, tricky, whiskey/whisky.
[3] **Fulfilling**, instilling, unwilling.

3.1.64 "--illing" (as in "willing")
[2] billing, chilling, drilling, filling, grilling, killing, shilling, spilling, stilling, swilling, thrilling, tilling, willing.
[3] distilling, fulfilling, instilling, unwilling.

SURPRISING RHYMING:
[2] **Bringing**, clinging, flinging, giving, living, pinging, ringing, singing, springing, stinging, stringing, swinging, winging, wringing.
Brimming, dimming, skimming, slimming, swimming, trimming.
Bidding, forbidding, kidding, outbidding, ridding, skidding.
Digging, jigging, rigging, swigging.
Grinning, pinning, sinning, spinning, thinning, winning.
Begin, herein, kingpin, satin, sheepskin, therein, urchin, within.
Dissing, hissing, kissing, missing.
Chipping, clipping, dipping, dripping, flipping, gripping, nipping, ripping, shipping, sipping, skipping, slipping, snipping, stripping, tipping, tripping, unzipping, whipping.
Fitting, hitting, knitting, quitting, sitting, slitting, spitting, splitting.
[3] **Beginning**, forgiving, misgiving, outliving, thanksgiving, unforgiving.
Bee-sting, blurring, bluffing, changeling, coiling, earring, evening, fledgling, hamstring, mainspring, nose-ring, nothing, offspring, plaything, purring, shoestring, slurring, something, stirring, wielding.
Acquitting, admitting, omitting, permitting, side-splitting, transmitting, unwitting.

3.1.65 "--ilky" (as in "silky")
[2] milky, silky.

SURPRISING RHYMING:
[2] **Guilty**, minty, misty, nifty, shifty, simply, sixty, swiftie, thrifty.
Prickly, quickly, sickly, slickly, tickly, thickly.
Frisky, history, mystery, risky, whiskey, whisky.
Fifty, fifty-fifty, filthy, guilty, iffy, jiffy, miffy, minty, misty, nifty, pithy, shifty, simply, sixty, sniffy, spiffy, stiffy, smithy, swiftie, thrifty, whiffy.
Inky, crinkly, kinky, dinky, slinky, pinkie, wrinkly.
Hickey, icky, kinky, mickey, picky, pinkie, quickie, sickie, slinky, sticky, tricky, wiki.
Giggly, hygge, niggly, squiggly, tingly, wiggly, wriggly.
Chili, chilly, filly, frilly, hilly, hillbilly, icily, lily, silly, rockabilly.
Bitty, chitty, city, ditty, gritty, guilty, kitty, pity, pretty, witty.
Chippy, clippie, crispy, dippy, drippy, hippie, lippy, nippy, trippy, whippy, yippee, zippy.
Busy, dizzy, fizzy, flimsy, frizzy, kiss me, tizzy, whimsy.
Cine, chimney, mini, pinny, skinny, spinney, tinny, whinny, windy.

3.1.66 "--illow" (as in "pillow")
armadillo, billow, cigarillo, peccadillo, pillow, willow.

SURPRISING RHYMING:
[1] **Beau**, bo, bow, doe, dough, go, no, know, oh, owe, sew, snow, so, so-so, sow, toe, tow.
Blow, flow, glow, low, sloe, slow, snow.
Bro, crow, grow, pro, roe, row, throw.
[2] **Aglow**, ago, also, below, bestow, dunno, fellow, follow, hello, ice-floe, Jell-O, moonglow, overflow, swallow, wallow, yellow.

Crossbow, hobo, longbow, oboe, rainbow, window.
Ago, go, forgo, go-go, logo, no-go, outgo, pogo, tiptoe.
Soho, tallyho, westward ho!, yo-ho.
Bureau, hedgerow, narrow, outgrow, scarecrow, sorrow, tomorrow.
[3] Buffalo, bungalow, counterblow, gigolo, overflow, tremolo.
Cameo, cheerio, folio, radio, rodeo, Romeo, Scorpio, studio, video.
Indigo, long ago, touch and go, undergo, vertigo.
Dynamo, Eskimo, mow, slowmo.

3.1.67 "--ilted" (as in "jilted")
[2] jilted, kilted, lilted, quilted, silted, stilted, tilted, wilted.

SURPRISING RHYMING:
[2] **Jilting**, lilting, quilting, silting, stilting, tilting, wilting.
Listed, misted, twisted.
Dinted, glinted, hinted, printed, splinted, sprinted, squinted, tinted.
Drifted, gifted, lifted, rifted, shifted, sifted.
Digit, fidget, frigid, legit, midget, rigid, widget.
[3] **Assisted**, blacklisted, close-fisted, consisted, enlisted, existed, insisted, persisted, predicted, resisted, subsisted, tight-fisted, two-fisted, unlisted, untwisted.
Acquitted, admitted, committed, dimwitted, fitted, half-witted, knitted, omitted, outwitted, permitted, quick-witted, spirited, transmitted.

3.1.68 "--ilting" (as in "tilting")
[2] jilting, lilting, quilting, silting, stilting, tilting, wilting.

SURPRISING RHYMING:
[2] **Jilted**, kilted, lilted, quilted, silted, stilted, tilted, wilted.
Listing, misting, twisting.
Glinting, hinting, minting, printing, sprinting, squinting, tinting.
Fitting, hitting, knitting, quitting, sitting, slitting, spitting, splitting.
Drifting, gifting, lifting, rifting, shifting, sifting.
Blinking, drinking, hoodwinking, inking, inkling, linking, shrinking, sinking, sprinkling, stinking, syncing, thinking, twinkling, winking.
Dwindling, kindling, spindling, swindling.
Bidding, forbidding, kidding, outbidding, ridding, skidding.
Diddling, fiddling, middling, piddling, riddling, twiddling.
Affixing, fixing, mixing, nixing.
Crimping, limping, pimping, primping, skimping.
[3] **Assisting**, blacklisting, consisting, enlisting, existing, insisting, persisting, resisting, subsisting, untwisting.
Acquitting, admitting, emitting, omitting, permitting, remitting, side-splitting, transmitting, unremitting, unwitting.

3.1.69 "--illyun" (as in "million")
billion, million, civilian, pavilion, trillion, vermillion.

SURPRISING RHYMING:
[2] **Bitten**, forbidden, hidden, isn't, listen, rhythm, ribbon, vision.
Emission, efficient, fission, intermission, magician, mission, musician, sufficient, titian.
Dishing, fishing, phishing, squishing, swishing, wishing.
Dissing, hissing, kissing, missing.
Arisen, glisten, imprison, listen, prison, risen.
Pigeon, religion, smidgen.
[3] **Addition**, admission, ambition, attrition, audition, condition, contrition, edition, emission, fruition, ignition, magician, musician, nutrition, omission, optician, partition, petition, permission, physician, position, remission, rendition, submission, suspicion, tactician, technician, tradition, transition, transmission, tuition, volition.
Collision, decision, derision, division, envision, incision, precision, revision, vision.

3.1.70 "--ilitee" (as in "ability")
[4] ability, agility, civility, facility, fertility, fragility, futility, hostility, humility, mobility, nobility, stability, tranquillity/tranquility (U.S.), utility, virility.
[5] edibility, liability, responsibility, usability, versatility, viability, volatility.

SURPRISING RHYMING:
[2] **Bitty**, chitty, city, ditty, gritty, kitty, pity, pretty, witty.
[3] **Burgundy**, COD, comedy, custody, dogsbody, embody, fool-hardy, jeopardy, melody, nobody, parody, Ph.D., raggedy, remedy, rhapsody, somebody, tragedy.
Amnesty, casualty, certainty, chastity, confetti, density, deputy, devotee, dignity, dynasty, entity, faculty, fidgety, graffiti, gravity, guarantee, honesty, karate, liberty, majesty, modesty, nudity, oddity, penalty, piety, poverty, property, puberty, purity, quality, repartee, rickety, sanctity, sanctuary, sanity, scarcity, seventy, sovereignty, spaghetti, specialty, trinity, unity, uppity, vanity, velvety, warranty.
Allergy, effigy, elegy, energy, eulogy, lethargy, prodigy, refugee, synergy, trilogy.
Bodily, family, fleur-de-lis, heavenly, homily, icily, jubilee, melancholy, miserly, readily.
Mimicry, ministry, misery, priory, reverie.
Gossip, recipe, slap-happy, syrupy/syrupy, therapy, unhappy.
[4] **Ability**, agility, anxiety, equality, facility, fertility, fragility, futility, hostility, humanity, humidity, humility, mobility, nitty-gritty, nobility, sobriety, society, stability, stupidity, tranquillity/tranquility (U.S.), utility, variety, virility.
[5] **Ambiguity**, anonymity, continuity, familiarity, femininity, impropriety, ingenuity, irregularity, masculinity, notoriety, opportunity, peculiarity, popularity, regularity, serendipity, similarity, solidarity, spontaneity, uniformity.

3.1.71 "--illable" (as in "syllable")
[3] fillable, killable, refillable, syllable, thrillable, tillable, willable.

SURPRISING RHYMING:
[3] **Kissable**, miserable, missable, possible, syllable, visible.
Feasible, fixable, flexible, forcible, mixable, plausible, taxable.
Fallible, gullible, legible, miserable, saleable, scalable.
Additional, conditional, criminal, digital, fictional, minimal, original, pivotal, principal, principle, subliminal.
[4] **Admissible**, charitable, deliverable, despicable, discernible, dismissible, divisible, exhaustible, forgivable, formidable, inadmissible, indivisible, inexhaustible, invincible, invisible, irresistible, noticeable, permissible, resistible, serviceable, unforgivable.
Applicable, equivocal, explicable, political, predictable, reciprocal, unpredictable.
Disposable, exhaustible, implausible, impossible, inflexible, observable, traditional.
Available, eligible, illegible, intelligible, negligible, unassailable, unavailable.

3.1.72 "--illfully" (as in "skillfully")
[3] skillfully, willfully.

SURPRISING RHYMING:
[3] **Busily**, dizzily, physically, quizzically, succinctly.
Critically, cynically, gimmickry, rhythmically, typically, wickedly.
[4] **Artistically**, linguistically, realistically, sadistically, specifically, statistically, stylistically.
Ability, agility, anxiety, calamity, community, convincingly, difficulty, enormity, equality, eternity, fatality, fidelity, fragility, fraternity, frivolity, futility, hostility, humanity, humility, immediately, immunity, impunity, infinity, modernity, morality, obscenity, profanity, publicity, reality, senility, serenity, sobriety, solemnity, stability, stupidity, timidity, totality, tranquillity/tranquility, variety, vicinity, virginity, virility.

3.1.73 "--illiest" (as in "silliest")
[3] chilliest, hilliest, silliest.

SURPRISING RHYMING:
[3] **Guiltiest**, nastiest, shiftiest, thriftiest.

Accomplice, cowardice, emphasis, genesis, kinesis, liquorice/licorice (U.S.), nemesis, orifice, prejudice, reminisce, synthesis.
Milkiest, friskiest, riskiest, silkiest, stickiest, trickiest.
Grittiest, prettiest, wittiest.
Busiest, dizziest, fizziest, frizziest.
Hideous, oblivious, silliness, skinniest.
Fatalist, hobbyist, humourist/humorist (U.S.), hypnotist, journalist, lobbyist, moralist, motorist, novelist, optimist, organist, pacifist, pessimist, publicist, socialist, soloist, specialist.
Ambivalence, belligerence, brilliance, deliverance, difference, diligence, dissonance, inheritance, insolence, innocence, magnificence, reminiscence, penitence, reticence.
Activist, anarchist, atheist, analyst, catalyst, columnist, communist, egotist, Eucharist, exorcist, fatalist, hobbyist, humourist/humorist (U.S.), hypnotist, journalist, lobbyist, moralist, motorist, novelist, optimist, organist, pacifist, pessimist, pre-exist, publicist, socialist, soloist, specialist, strategist, terrorist.

3.1.74 "--ilkiest" (as in "silkiest")
[3] milkiest, silkiest.

SURPRISING RHYMING:
[3] **Grittiest**, prettiest, wittiest.
Friskiest, prickliest, riskiest, sickliest, stickiest, trickiest.
Filthiest, guiltiest, shiftiest, thriftiest, wealthiest.
Chilliest, hilliest, silliest.
Busiest, dizziest, fizziest, friskiest, frizziest, riskiest.
Activist, anarchist, atheist, analyst, catalyst, egotist, exorcist, fatalist, hobbyist, humourist/humorist (U.S.), hypnotist, journalist, lobbyist, motorist, novelist, optimist, pacifist, pessimist, pre-exist, publicist, socialist, soloist, specialist, strategist, terrorist.

3.1.75 "--illowy" (as in "willowy")
[3] billowy, pillowy, willowy.

SURPRISING RHYMING:
[3] **Bodily**, family, fleur-de-lis, heavenly, homily, icily, jubilee, miserly, readily.
Gossipy, recipe, syrupy/syrupy, therapy.
Comedy, jeopardy, melody, nobody, remedy, rhapsody, somebody, subsidy, tragedy.
Amnesty, brevity, casualty, certainty, charity, chastity, clarity, density, dignity, dynasty, enmity, entity, fidgety, graffiti, gravity, guarantee, honesty, liberty, majesty, modesty, nudity, oddity, parity, penalty, piety, poverty, property, purity, quality, sanctity, sanity, specialty, trinity, unity, uppity, vanity, velvety.
Effigy, elegy, energy, eulogy, lethargy, prodigy, refugee, strategy, synergy, trilogy.
Mimicry, ministry, misery, priory, reverie.
Chivalry, disagree, dithery, history, imagery, injury, history, mystery, quivery, shimmery, shivery, silvery, slippery, slithery, symmetry, tapestry, trickery, victory, wintery.
[4] **Ability**, agility, civility, facility, fertility, fragility, futility, hostility, humility, mobility, nobility, stability, tranquillity/tranquility (U.S.), virility.

3.1.76 "--im" (as in "him")
[1] brim, dim, grim, gym, him, hymn, limb, rim, skim, slim, swim, trim, vim, whim.
[3] antonym, cherubim, homonym, interim, pseudonym, synonym, victim.

SURPRISING RHYMING:
[1] **Brimmed**, dimmed, rimmed, skimmed, slimmed, trimmed.
Been, bin, chin, din, gin, grin, in, inn, kin, pin, shin, sin, skin, spin, thin, twin, win.
Didn't, dint, flint, glint, hint, lint, mint, print, skint, splint, sprint, stint, squint, tint.
Bling, bring, cling, ding, fling, king, Ming, ping, ring, sing, sling, spring, sting, string, swing, thing, wing, zing.
Grinned, pinned, sinned, thinned, tinned, twinned, winged, wind.
[2] **Begin**, bearskin, chagrin, dolphin, has-been, kingpin, kremlin, Latin, Mickey Finn,

muffin, napkin, paraffin, penguin, robin, satin, sheepskin, therein, urchin, within.
Blueprint, footprint, hoof print, imprint, misprint, newsprint, paw print, peppermint, reprint, skinflint, spearmint.
Bee-sting, blurring, bluffing, changeling, coiling, earring, evening, fledgling, mainspring, nose-ring, nothing, offspring, plaything, purring, shoestring, Sing-Sing, slurring, something, stirring, wielding.
Rescind, thick-skinned, thin-skinned, trade wind, unpinned, whirlwind.
[3] **Aspirin**, bulletin, crystalline, discipline, feminine, genuine, glycerin, harlequin, heroin, heroine, imagine, insulin, intestine, javelin, mandolin, mannequin, margarine, masculine, moccasin, mortal sin, origin, saccharin, tarpaulin, violin, vitamin, zeppelin.
Angering, answering, anything, arguing, auctioning, boxing-ring, copying, colouring/coloring (U.S.), conferring, coveting, deafening, deferring, deterring, echoing, everything, fastening, fattening, featuring, financing, foraging, fracturing, happening, hastening, hollering, incurring, inferring, issuing, lecturing, limiting, lobbying, maddening, menacing, moistening, motoring, murdering, occurring, opening, picturing, pillaging, preferring, promising, publishing, purchasing, questioning, rationing, ravishing, recurring, rivaling, sickening, softening, strengthening, swallowing, suffering, sweetening, thickening, threatening, toughening, trafficking, transferring, varying, volleying, weathering, whirring, widening, witnessing, worshiping.

3.1.77 "--immed" (as in "slimmed")
[1] brimmed, dimmed, rimmed, skimmed, slimmed, trimmed.

SURPRISING RHYMING:
[1] **Brim,** dim, grim, gym, him, hymn, limb, rim, skim, slim, swim, trim, vim, whim.
Grinned, pinned, sinned, thinned, tinned, twinned, winged, wind.
Didn't, dint, flint, glint, hint, lint, mint, print, skint, splint, sprint, stint, squint, tint.
[2] **Rescind**, thick-skinned, thin-skinned, trade wind, whirlwind.
Blueprint, footprint, hoof print, imprint, misprint, newsprint, paw print, peppermint, reprint, skinflint, spearmint.
[3] **Antonym**, cherubim, homonym, interim, pseudonym, synonym.

3.1.78 "--imp" (as in "limp")
[1] blimp, chimp, crimp, gimp, imp, limp, pimp, primp, shrimp, skimp, scrimp, wimp.

SURPRISING RHYMING:
[1] **Blimps**, crimps, glimpse, imps, limps, pimps, shrimps, skimps.
Brim, dim, grim, gym, him, hymn, limb, rim, skim, slim, swim, trim, vim, whim.
Didn't, dint, flint, glint, hint, lint, mint, print, skint, splint, sprint, stint, squint, tint.
Blink, brink, chink, clink, drink, hoodwink, ice-rink, ink, kink, link, mink, pink, rink, shrink, sink, slink, stink, sync, think, wink, zinc.
Brimmed, dimmed, rimmed, skimmed, slimmed, trimmed.
[2] **Blueprint,** footprint, hoof print, imprint, misprint, newsprint, paw print, peppermint, reprint, skinflint, spearmint.
[3] **Antonym**, cherubim, homonym, interim, pseudonym, synonym.

3.1.79 "--imps" (as in "glimpse")
[1] blimps, crimps, glimpse, imps, limps, pimps, primps, shrimps, skimps, wimps.

SURPRISING RHYMING:
[1] **Blimp**, chimp, crimp, gimp, imp, limp, pimp, primp, shrimp, skimp, scrimp, wimp.
Brims, dims, hymns, limbs, rims, skims, slims, swims, trims, whims.
Chintz, hints, mints, prints, splints, sprints, stints, squints, tints.
Blinks, drinks, hoodwinks, ice-rinks, inks, jinx, kinks, links, lynx, minks, minx, rinks, shrinks, sinks, sphinx, stinks, thinks, winks.
Convince, evince, mince, prince, rinse, since, wince.
Cinch, clinch, finch, flinch, Grinch, inch, lynch, pinch, winch.
Binge, cringe, fringe, hinge, singe, tinge, twinge.
[2] **Blueprints,** footprints, imprints, misprints, peppermints, reprints, skinflints.

3.1.80 "--imbal" (as in "symbol")
[2] cymbal, nimble, symbol, thimble, timbale.

SURPRISING RHYMING:
[2] **Dwindle**, hymnal, kindle, sinful, spindle, swindle.
Dimple, pimple, simple, wimple.
Jingle, mingle, shingle, signal, single, tingle.
Crinkle, skillful, sprinkle, tinkle, twinkle, willful, winkle, wrinkle.
Bristle, crystal, gristle, missal, missile, pistol, thistle, whistle.
Civil, drivel, shrivel, skiffle, sniffle, snivel, swivel.
Dribble, nibble, quibble, scribble, sibyl.
Fiddle, griddle, idyll, middle, paradiddle, riddle, twiddle.
Cripple, nipple, ripple, stipple, tipple, triple.
Giggle, jiggle, squiggle, wiggle, wriggle.
[3] **Fillable**, killable, syllable, thrillable, tillable.
Clinical, cynical, lyrical, miracle, pinnacle, satirical.

3.1.81 "--imber" (as in "timber")
[2] limber, marimba, timber.

SURPRISING RHYMING:
[2] **Builder**, filter, kilter, pilfer, quilter, tilter.
Drifter, grifter, lifter, shifter, sifter, snifter, swifter.
Midwinter, printer, splinter, sprinter, squinter, winter.
Crimper, limper, shrimper, simper, whimper.
Dimmer, glimmer, primmer, shimmer, simmer, skimmer, slimmer, swimmer, trimmer.
Dinner, grinner, inner, sinner(s), skinner, spinner, thinner, winner(s).
Bringer, finger, flinger, ringer, singer, slinger, springer, stinger, stringer, swinger, winger, wringer, zinger.
[3] **Bewilder(ed)**, bodybuilder, boatbuilder, housebuilder, shipbuilder.
Beginner(s), Berliner, breadwinner, examiner, foreigner, mariner, milliner, phenomena, prizewinner, retina, stamina, submariner.
Bell-ringer, gunslinger, humdinger, left-winger, mud-slinger.

3.1.82 "--immer" (as in "swimmer")
[2] dimmer, glimmer, primmer, shimmer, simmer, skimmer, slimmer, strimmer, swimmer, trimmer, zimmer.

SURPRISING RHYMING:
[2] **Limber**, marimba, timber.
Crimper, limper, shrimper, simper, whimper.
Dinner, grinner, inner, sinner(s), skinner, spinner, thinner, winner(s).
Bringer, finger, flinger, ringer, singer, slinger, springer, stinger, stringer, swinger, winger, wringer, zinger.
Midwinter, printer, splinter, sprinter, squinter, winter.
Conifer, differ, Lucifer, sniffer, stiffer.
Bigger, figure, ligger, rigour/rigor (U.S.), snigger, trigger, vigour/vigor (U.S.).
[3] **Cinema**, charisma, enema, maxima, minima, polymer, ultima.
Beginner, Berliner, breadwinner, examiner, foreigner, mariner, milliner, phenomena, prizewinner, retina, stamina, submariner.
Bell-ringer, gunslinger, humdinger, left-winger, mud-slinger.
Configure, disfigure, gold-digger, gravedigger, vinegar.

3.1.83 "--immy" (as in "gimme")
[2] gimme, jimmy, shimmy.

SURPRISING RHYMING:
[2] **Cine**, chimney, guinea, mini, ninny, pinny, shinny, skinny, spinney, tinny, whinny.
Diddy, giddy, kiddie, midi.

Bitty, chitty, city, ditty, gritty, kitty, pity, pretty, witty.
Busy, dizzy, fizzy, frizzy, tizzy.
Chippy, clippie, crispy, dippy, drippy, grippy, hippie, lippy, nippy, snippy, trippy, whippy, yippie, zippy.
Chili, chilly, filly, frilly, hilly, hillbilly, lily, silly, willy-nilly, rockabilly.
Fifty, fifty-fifty, iffy, jiffy, miffy, nifty, pithy, shifty, sniffy, thrifty.
Dixie, glitzy, kissy, missy, prissy, ritzy, sissy.

3.1.84 "--immick" (as in "gimmick")
[2] filmic, gimmick, mimic, rhythmic.

SURPRISING RHYMING:
[2] **Civic,** clinic, critic, cynic, lipstick, lyric, matchstick, mimicked, mystic, mythic, traffic.
Exhibit, inhibit, prohibit, speed limit.
Cricket, kick it, picket, snippet, stick it, thicket, ticket, wicket.
Image, limit, minute, misfit, spirit, sunlit, tidbit, transmit, unfit, visit.
Biscuit, digit, fidget, legit, midget, pivot, widget.
Liquid, livid, misted, timid, twisted, vivid, wicked.
[3] **Acidic**, horrific, idyllic, pacific, prolific, specific, terrific, epidemic.
Artistic, ballistic, explicit, illicit, implicit, realistic, sadistic, simplistic, solicit, stylistic.
[4] **Colorific**, hieroglyphic, non-specific, scientific

3.1.85 "--imming" (as in "swimming")
[2] brimming, dimming, skimming, slimming, swimming, trimming.

SURPRISING RHYMING:
Beginning, grinning, inning, pinning, sinning, skinning, spinning, thinning, winning.
Bringing, clinging, flinging, pinging, ringing, singing, slinging, springing, stinging, stringing, swinging, winging, wringing.
Giving, living, forgiving, misgiving, thanksgiving, unforgiving.
Fizzing, frizzing, quizzing, whizzing.
Billing, chilling, drilling, filling, fulfilling, grilling, killing, shilling, spilling, stilling, swilling, thrilling, tilling, unwilling, willing.
Glinting, hinting, minting, printing, sprinting, squinting, tinting.
Digging, jigging, ligging, rigging, swigging.
Chipping, clipping, dipping, dripping, flipping, gripping, nipping, ripping, sipping, skipping, slipping, snipping, stripping, tipping, tripping, unzipping, whipping, zipping.
Fitting, hitting, knitting, quitting, sitting, slitting, spitting, splitting.
Drifting, gifting, lifting, rifting, shifting, sifting, sixteen.
Glistening, listening, listing, misting, twisting.

3.1.86 "--imper" (as in "whimper")
[2] crimper, limper, shrimper, simper, whimper.

SURPRISING RHYMING:
[2] **Limber**, marimba, timber.
Midwinter, printer, splinter, sprinter, squinter, winter.
Blinker, drinker, Inca, shrinker, sinker, stinker, thinker, tinker, winker, freethinker.
Dimmer, glimmer, shimmer, simmer, skimmer, slimmer, swimmer, trimmer, zimmer.
Dinner, grinner, inner, sinner(s), skinner, spinner, thinner, winner(s).
Bringer, clinger, finger, flinger, ringer, singer, slinger, springer, stinger, stringer, swinger, winger, wringer, zinger.
Blister, crisper, differ, mister, sister, sniffer, stiffer, trickster, twister, vista, whisper.
Bigger, figure, rigour/rigor (U.S.), snigger, trigger, vigour/vigor (U.S.).
[3] **Bewilder(ed)**, bodybuilder, boatbuilder, housebuilder, shipbuilder.
Beginner(s), Berliner, breadwinner, charisma, cinema, examiner, foreigner, mariner, milliner, phenomena, prizewinner, retina, stamina, submariner.
Bell-ringer, gunslinger, humdinger, left-winger, mud-slinger.
Configure, disfigure, gold-digger, gravedigger, vinegar.

3.1.87 "--imping" (as in "limping")
[2] crimping, limping, pimping, primping, shrimping, skimping.

SURPRISING RHYMING:
[2] **Glinting**, hinting, minting, printing, sprinting, squinting, tinting.
Blinking, drinking, hoodwinking, inkling, linking, shrinking, sinking, sprinkling, stinking, syncing, thinking, twinkling, winking.
Jilting, lilting, quilting, silting, stilting, tilting, wilting.
Brimming, dimming, skimming, slimming, swimming, trimming.
Glistening, listening, listing, misting, twisting.
Beginning, grinning, pinning, sinning, spinning, thinning, winning.
Bringing, clinging, flinging, pinging, ringing, singing, slinging, springing, stinging, stringing, swinging, winging, wringing.
Dwindling, jingling, kindling, mingling, spindling, swindling, tingling.
Billing, chilling, filling, grilling, killing, spilling, thrilling, willing.
Giving, driven, forgiving, living, misgiving, thanksgiving, unforgiving.
Cinching, clinching, flinching, inching, lynching, pinching.
[3] **Convincing**, evincing, mincing, wincing.
Conflicting, convicting, depicting, evicting, inflicting, predicting, restricting.

3.1.88 "--imple" (as in "simple")
[2] dimple, pimple, simple, wimple.

SURPRISING RHYMING:
[2] **Crinkle**, skillful, sprinkle, tinkle, twinkle, willful, winkle, wrinkle.
Cymbal, nimble, symbol, thimble, timbale.
Dwindle, hymnal, kindle, rekindle, sinful, spindle, swindle.
Jingle, mingle, shingle, signal, single, tingle.
Brittle, cripple, it'll, little, nipple, ripple, skittle, tipple, triple, whittle.
Fiddle, griddle, idyll, middle, paradiddle, riddle, twiddle.
Dribble, nibble, quibble, scribble, sibyl.
Giggle, jiggle, squiggle, wiggle, wriggle.
Bristle, chisel, crystal, drizzle, fizzle, frizzle, gristle, missal, missile, official, pistol, sizzle, swizzle, thistle, whistle.
Civil, drivel, shrivel, skiffle, sniffle, snivel, swivel.
Fickle, nickel, pickle, prickle, tickle, trickle.

3.1.89 "--imsy" (as in "flimsy")
[2] flimsy, whimsy.

SURPRISING RHYMING:
[2] **Busy**, chintzy, dizzy, fizzy, frizzy, tizzy.
Busily, dizzily, drizzly, grisly, grizzly.
Dixie, glitzy, kissy, missy, prissy, ritzy, sissy.
Chimney, Disney, gimme, mini, skinny, spinney, tinny, whinny.
Chili, chilly, filly, frilly, hilly, lily, silly, willy-nilly.
Guilty, milky, minty, misty, prickly, quickly, nifty, shifty, sickly, silky, simply, sixty, slickly, thrifty, thickly.
Frisky, frisbee, history, mystery, risky, whiskey, whisky.
[3] **Delivery**, history, livery, mystery, quivery, shivery.
[4] **Ability**, agility, civility, facility, fertility, fragility, futility, hostility, humility, mobility, nobility, stability, tranquillity/tranquility (U.S.), virility.

3.1.90 "--in" (as in "skin")
[1] been, bin, chin, din, fin, gin, grin, in, inn, kin, pin, shin, sin, skin, spin, thin, tin, twin, win.
[2] begin, bearskin, believe in, chagrin, dolphin, has-been, hatpin, herein, kingpin, kremlin, Latin, livin', Mickey Finn, muffin, napkin, paraffin, penguin, pippin, pushpin, robin, satin, sheepskin, therein, urchin, virgin, wherein, within.

360

[3] aspirin, bulletin, crystalline, discipline, feminine, genuine, glycerin, harlequin, heroin, heroine, imagine, insulin, intestine, javelin, mandolin, mannequin, margarine, masculine, moccasin, mortal sin, origin, saccharin, tarpaulin, thick and thin, violin, vitamin, zeppelin.

SURPRISING RHYMING:
[1] **Brim**, dim, grim, gym, him, hymn, limb, rim, skim, slim, swim, trim, vim, whim.
Grinned, pinned, ringed, sinned, skinned, thinned, tinned, twinned, winged, wind.
Bling, bring, cling, ding, fling, king, Ming, ping, ring, sing, sling, spring, sting, string, swing, thing, wing, zing.
[2] **Rescind**, thick-skinned, thin-skinned, trade wind, whirlwind.
Bee-sting, blurring, bluffing, changeling, earring, evening, fledgling, hamstring, mainspring, nose-ring, nothing, offspring, plaything, purring, shoestring, Sing Sing, slurring, something, stirring, wielding.
Bacon, certain, fakin', shaken, taken, waken.
[3] **Angering**, answering, anything, arguing, copying, colouring/coloring (U.S.), coveting, deafening, deterring, echoing, everything, fastening, fattening, featuring, foraging, fracturing, happening, hastening, hollering, issuing, lecturing, limiting, maddening, menacing, moistening, motoring, murdering, occurring, opening, picturing, preferring, promising, publishing, purchasing, questioning, ravishing, recurring, rivaling, sickening, softening, strengthening, swallowing, suffering, sweetening, thickening, threatening, toughening, trafficking, varying, weathering, whirring, widening, witnessing, worshiping.

3.1.91 "--inch" (as in "pinch")
[1] cinch, clinch, finch, flinch, Grinch, inch, lynch, pinch, winch.

SURPRISING RHYMING:
[1] **Cinched**, clinched, flinched, inched, lynched, pinched, winched.
Bitch, bridge, ditch, glitch, hitch, itch, kitsch, niche, pitch, rich, ridge, snitch, stitch, switch, twitch, which, witch.
Bitched, ditched, hitched, itched, pitched, snitched, stitched, switched, twitched.
Binge, cringe, fringe, hinge, singe, tinge, twinge.
Chintz, hints, mints, prints, splints, sprints, stints, squints, tints.
Blinks, drinks, hoodwinks, ice-rinks, inks, jinx, kinks, links, lynx, minks, minx, rinks, shrinks, sinks, sphinx, stinks, thinks, winks.
Convince, evince, mince, prince, rinse, since, wince.
Blimps, glimpse, imps, limps, pimps, shrimps, skimps, wimps.
Dish, fish, squish, swish, wish.
[2] **Bewitch**, enrich, sales pitch, unhitch.
Bewitched, enriched, unhitched, snitched, re-stitched, switched, twitched, unstitched.
Infringe, syringe, unhinge.
Abridge, bondage, cabbage, carnage, hostage, language, message, package, postage, sausage, shortage, storage, usage, voyage.

3.1.92 "--inched" (as in "pinched")
[1] cinched, clinched, flinched, inched, lynched, pinched, winched.

SURPRISING RHYMING:
[1] **Cinch**, clinch, finch, flinch, Grinch, inch, lynch, pinch, winch.
Chintz, hints, mints, prints, splints, sprints, stints, squints, tints.
Convinced, evinced, minced, rinsed, winced.
[2] **Bewitched**, enriched, snitched, switched, twitched, unstitched.

3.1.93 "--inned" (as in "grinned")
[1] grinned, pinned, ringed, sinned, skinned, thinned, tinned, twinned, winged, wind.
[2] rescind, thick-skinned, thin-skinned, trade wind, unpinned, whirlwind.

SURPRISING RHYMING:
[1] **Been**, bin, chin, din, gin, grin, in, inn, pin, shin, sin, skin, spin, thin, tin, twin, win.
Brimmed, dimmed, rimmed, skimmed, slimmed, trimmed.

Bling, bring, cling, ding, fling, king, Ming, ping, ring, sing, sling, spring, sting, string, swing, thing, wing, zing.
Didn't, dint, flint, glint, hint, lint, mint, print, skint, splint, sprint, stint, squint, tint.
[2] Begin, believe in, chagrin, dolphin, has-been, kingpin, kremlin, Latin, livin', Mickey Finn, muffin, napkin, penguin, pippin, robin, satin, sheepskin, urchin, virgin, within.
Blueprint, footprint, imprint, misprint, newsprint, peppermint, reprint, skinflint, spearmint.
[3] Aspirin, discipline, feminine, genuine, harlequin, heroin, heroine, imagine, insulin, interim, javelin, mandolin, mannequin, margarine, masculine, moccasin, mortal sin, origin, pseudonym, saccharin, violin, vitamin, zeppelin.

3.1.94 "--ing" (as in "sing")
[1] bling, bring, cling, ding, fling, king, Ming, ping, ring, sing, sling, spring, sting, string, swing, thing, wing, wring, zing.
[2] bee-sting, blurring, bluffing, changeling, coiling, earring, evening, fledgling, mainspring, nose-ring, nothing, offspring, plaything, purring, shoestring, Sing Sing, slurring, something, stirring, wielding.
[3] angering, answering, anything, arguing, auctioning, balloting, boxing-ring, copying, colouring/coloring (U.S.), conferring, coveting, deafening, deferring, deterring, echoing, everything, fastening, fattening, featuring, financing, foraging, fracturing, happening, hastening, hollering, incurring, inferring, issuing, lecturing, limiting, lobbying, maddening, menacing, moistening, motoring, murdering, occurring, opening, picturing, pillaging, preferring, promising, publishing, purchasing, questioning, rationing, ravishing, recurring, rivaling, sickening, softening, strengthening, swallowing, suffering, sweetening, thickening, threatening, toughening, trafficking, transferring, varying, volleying, weathering, whirring, widening, witnessing, worshiping.

SURPRISING RHYMING:
[1] **Been**, bin, chin, din, gin, grin, in, inn, pin, shin, sin, skin, spin, thin, tin, twin, win.
Brim, dim, grim, gym, him, hymn, limb, rim, skim, slim, swim, trim, vim, whim.
Brimmed, dimmed, rimmed, skimmed, slimmed, trimmed.
Grinned, pinned, ringed, sinned, skinned, thinned, tinned, twinned, winged, wind.
[2] **Begin**, believe in, chagrin, dolphin, has-been, kingpin, kremlin, Latin, livin', Mickey Finn, muffin, napkin, penguin, pippin, robin, satin, sheepskin, urchin, virgin, within.
Rescind, thick-skinned, thin-skinned, trade wind, unpinned, whirlwind.
Fixing, mixing, nixing.
[3] **Aspirin**, discipline, feminine, genuine, harlequin, heroin, heroine, imagine, insulin, interim, javelin, mandolin, mannequin, margarine, masculine, moccasin, mortal sin, origin, pseudonym, saccharin, violin, vitamin, zeppelin.

3.1.95 "--inge" (as in "hinge")
[1] binge, cringe, dinge, fringe, hinge, singe, tinge, twinge.
[2] infringe, syringe, unhinge.

SURPRISING RHYMING:
[1] **Bridge**, fridge, midge, ridge, smidge.
Convince, evince, mince, prince, rinse, since, wince.
Cinch, clinch, finch, flinch, Grinch, inch, lynch, pinch, winch.
Been, bin, chin, din, gin, grin, in, inn, pin, shin, sin, skin, spin, thin, tin, twin, win.
Grinned, pinned, sinned, thinned, tinned, twinned, winged, wind.
Brimmed, dimmed, rimmed, skimmed, slimmed, trimmed.
[2] **Rescind**, thick-skinned, thin-skinned, trade wind, whirlwind.
Begin, chagrin, dolphin, has-been, kingpin, kremlin, Latin, livin', napkin, penguin, robin, satin, sheepskin, urchin, virgin, within.
[3] **Discipline**, feminine, genuine, heroin, heroine, imagine, mandolin, mannequin, margarine, masculine, moccasin, mortal sin, origin, saccharin, violin, vitamin, zeppelin.

3.1.96 "--ink" (as in "pink")
[1] blink, brink, chink, clink, drink, fink, hoodwink, ice-rink, Inc., ink, kink, link, mink, pink, rink, shrink, sink, slink, stink, sync, think, unlink, wink, zinc.

SURPRISING RHYMING:
[1] **Blinked**, inked, linked, winked.
Blinks, drinks, hoodwinks, ice-rinks, inks, jinx, kinks, links, lynx, minks, minx, rinks, shrinks, sinks, sphinx, stinks, thinks, winks.
Bricked, clicked, flicked, kicked, licked, picked, pricked, strict, ticked, tricked.
Built, gilt, guilt, jilt, kilt, lilt, myth, quilt, spilt, stilt, tilt, wilt, with.
Didn't, dint, flint, glint, hint, lint, mint, print, skint, splint, sprint, stint, squint, tint.
Cinch, clinch, finch, flinch, Grinch, inch, lynch, pinch, winch.
Been, bin, chin, din, gin, grin, in, inn, pin, shin, sin, skin, spin, thin, tin, twin, win.
[2] **Distinct**, extinct, indistinct, instinct, precinct, succinct.
Addict, conflict, contradict, convict, depict, evict, predict, restrict.
Blueprint, footprint, imprint, misprint, newsprint, peppermint, reprint, skinflint, spearmint.
Bee-sting, blurring, bluffing, changeling, earring, evening, nothing, offspring, plaything, purring, shoestring, slurring, something, stirring.
Begin, chagrin, dolphin, has-been, kingpin, kremlin, Latin, livin', Mickey Finn, muffin, napkin, paraffin, penguin, pippin, robin, satin, sheepskin, urchin, virgin, within.
[3] **Discipline**, feminine, genuine, heroin, heroine, imagine, mandolin, mannequin, margarine, masculine, moccasin, mortal sin, origin, saccharin, violin, vitamin, zeppelin.

3.1.97 "--inx" (as in "drinks")
[1] blinks, drinks, finks, hoodwinks, ice-rinks, inks, jinx, kinks, links, lynx, minks, minx, rinks, shrinks, sinks, slinks, sphinx, stinks, thinks, unlinks, winks.

SURPRISING RHYMING:
[1] **Blink**, brink, chink, clink, drink, hoodwink, ice-rink, ink, kink, link, mink, pink, rink, shrink, sink, stink, sync, think, wink, zinc.
Blinked, inked, linked, winked.
Convince, evince, mince, prince, rinse, since, wince.
Blimps, glimpse, imps, limps, pimps, shrimps, skimps, wimps.
Bricks, chicks, fix, flicks, hicks, kicks, licks, mix, nix, picks, pix, pricks, six, slicks, sticks, tics, ticks, tricks, wicks.
Bricked, clicked, flicked, kicked, licked, picked, pricked, strict, ticked, tricked.
Cinch, clinch, finch, flinch, Grinch, inch, lynch, pinch, winch.
Chintz, hints, mints, prints, splints, sprints, stints, squints, tints.
[2] **Affix,** crucifix, intermix, matchsticks, prefix, suffix.
Bewitched, enriched, unhitched, snitched, switched, twitched.
Blueprints, footprints, imprints, misprints, paw prints, peppermints, reprints, skinflints.

3.1.98 "--inked" (as in "blinked")
[1] blinked, clinked, inked, linked, slinked, winked, hoodwinked.

SURPRISING RHYMING:
[1] **Blink**, brink, chink, clink, drink, fink, hoodwink, ice-rink, Inc., ink, kink, link, mink, pink, rink, shrink, sink, slink, stink, sync, think, unlink, wink, zinc.
Blinks, drinks, hoodwinks, ice-rinks, inks, jinx, kinks, links, lynx, minks, minx, rinks, shrinks, sinks, sphinx, stinks, thinks, winks.
Didn't, dint, flint, glint, hint, lint, mint, print, skint, splint, sprint, stint, squint, tint.
Blimp, chimp, crimp, imp, limp, pimp, shrimp, skimp, scrimp, wimp.
Cinched, clinched, flinched, inched, lynched, pinched, winched.
[2] **Distinct**, extinct, indistinct, instinct, precinct, succinct.
Convinced, evinced, minced, rinsed, winced.
Blueprint, footprint, imprint, misprint, newsprint, peppermint, reprint, skinflint, spearmint.

3.1.99 "--ince" (as in "prince")
convince, evince, mince, prince, rinse, since, wince.

SURPRISING RHYMING:
[1] **Blimps**, glimpse, imps, limps, pimps, shrimps, skimps, wimps.
Chintz, hints, mints, prints, splints, sprints, stints, squints, tints.

Blinks, drinks, finks, hoodwinks, ice-rinks, inks, jinx, kinks, links, lynx, minks, minx, rinks, shrinks, sinks, sphinx, stinks, thinks, winks.
Cinch, clinch, finch, flinch, Grinch, inch, lynch, pinch, winch.
[2] **Blueprints**, footprints, imprints, misprints, peppermints, skinflints.

3.1.100 "--int" (as in "hint")

[1] didn't, dint, flint, glint, hint, lint, mint, print, skint, splint, sprint, stint, squint, tint.
[2] blueprint, footprint, hoof print, imprint, misprint, newsprint, paw print, peppermint, reprint, skinflint, spearmint.

SURPRISING RHYMING:
[1] **Been**, bin, chin, din, gin, grin, in, inn, pin, shin, sin, skin, spin, thin, tin, twin, win.
Brim, dim, grim, gym, him, hymn, limb, rim, skim, slim, swim, trim, vim, whim.
Brimmed, dimmed, rimmed, skimmed, slimmed, trimmed.
Blimp, chimp, crimp, imp, limp, pimp, shrimp, skimp, scrimp, wimp.
Grinned, pinned, sinned, thinned, tinned, twinned, winged, wind.
Blinked, clinked, inked, linked, slinked, winked, hoodwinked.
[2] **Rescind**, thick-skinned, thin-skinned, trade wind, unpinned, whirlwind.
[3] **Discipline**, feminine, genuine, harlequin, heroin, heroine, imagine, interim, insulin, javelin, mandolin, mannequin, margarine, masculine, moccasin, mortal sin, origin, pseudonym, saccharin, violin, vitamin, zeppelin.

3.1.101 "--inching" (as in "flinching")

[2] cinching, clinching, flinching, inching, lynching, pinching.

SURPRISING RHYMING:
[2] **Bitching**, ditching, hitching, itching, snitching, stitching, switching, twitching, witching.
Binging, cringing, hinging, infringing, singeing, twinging, unhinging.
Dishing, fishing, phishing, squishing, swishing, wishing.
Diction, fiction, kitchen, friction.
Glinting, hinting, minting, printing, sprinting, squinting, tinting.
Fizzing, frizzing, quizzing, whizzing.
Listing, misting, twisting.
Drifting, gifting, lifting, rifting, shifting, sifting.
Jilting, lilting, quilting, silting, stilting, tilting, wilting.
Inkling, sprinkling, twinkling.
[3] **Convincing**, evincing, glimpsing, mincing, wincing.
Assisting, blacklisting, consisting, enlisting, existing, insisting, persisting, resisting.

3.1.102 "--indle" (as in "kindle")

[2] dwindle, kindle, spindle, swindle.

SURPRISING RHYMING:
[2] **Cymbal,** nimble, symbol, thimble, timbale.
Dimple, pimple, simple, wimple.
Jingle, mingle, shingle, signal, single, tingle.
Crinkle, skillful, sprinkle, tinkle, twinkle, willful, winkle, wrinkle.
Dribble, nibble, quibble, scribble, sibyl.
Fiddle, griddle, idyll, middle, paradiddle, riddle, twiddle.
Cripple, nipple, ripple, stipple, tipple, triple.
Giggle, jiggle, squiggle, wiggle, wriggle.
[3] **Initial**, judicial, official, prejudicial, unofficial.
Clinical, cynical, lyrical, miracle, pinnacle, satirical.

3.1.103 "--indling" (as in "dwindling")

[2] dwindling, kindling, spindling, swindling.

SURPRISING RHYMING:
[2] **Jingling**, mingling, signaling, singling, tingling.

Crinkling, inkling, sprinkling, tinkling, twinkling, winkling, wrinkling.
Dribbling, nibbling, quibbling, scribbling, sibling.
Diddling, fiddling, griddling, middling, piddling, riddling, twiddling.
Crippling, rippling, stippling, tippling, tripling.
Giggling, jiggling, niggling, squiggling, wiggling, wriggling.
Driveling, shriveling, sniffling, sniveling, swiveling.
Chiseling, drizzling, fizzling, sizzling, whistling.
Building, bodybuilding, bewildering, housebuilding, rebuilding.

3.1.104 "--inner" (as in "dinner")
[2] dinner, grinner, inner, sinner(s), skinner, spinner, thinner, winner(s).
[3] beginner(s), Berliner, breadwinner, examiner, foreigner, mariner, milliner, phenomena, prizewinner, retina, stamina, submariner.

SURPRISING RHYMING:
[2] **Dimmer**, glimmer, primmer, shimmer, simmer, skimmer, slimmer, strimmer, swimmer, trimmer, zimmer.
Bringer, clinger, finger, flinger, linger, ringer, singer, slinger, springer, stinger, stringer, swinger, winger, wringer, zinger.
Giver, liver, river, shiver, sliver, quiver.
Limber, marimba, timber.
Crimper, limper, shrimper, simper, whimper.
Midwinter, printer, splinter, sprinter, squinter, winter.
Conifer, differ, Lucifer, sniffer, stiffer.
Bigger, figure, ligger, rigour/rigor (U.S.), snigger, trigger, vigour/vigor.
Bidder, consider, kidder.
Bitter, critter, fitter, flitter, fritter, glitter, gritter, hitter, jitter, knitter, litter, pitta, quitter, sitter, splitter, titter, twitter.
[3] **Cinema**, charisma, enema, maxima, minima, polymer, ultima.
Bell-ringer, gunslinger, humdinger, left-winger, mud-slinger.
Configure, disfigure, gold-digger, gravedigger, vinegar.
Caterpillar, flotilla, fulfiller, gorilla, guerilla, man-killer, painkiller, spine-chiller, vanilla.

3.1.105 "--inger" (as in "singer")
[2] bringer, clinger, finger, flinger, linger, ringer, singer, slinger, springer, stinger, stringer, swinger, winger, wringer, zinger.
[3] bell-ringer, gunslinger, humdinger, left-winger, mud-slinger, right-winger.

SURPRISING RHYMING:
[2] **Dinner**, grinner, inner, sinner, skinner, spinner, thinner, winner.
Bigger, figure, ligger, rigour/rigor (U.S.), snigger, trigger, vigour/vigor.
Dimmer, glimmer, mirror, shimmer, simmer, skimmer, slimmer, swimmer, trimmer.
Midwinter, printer, splinter, sprinter, squinter, winter.
Cinder, hinder, injure, tinder.
Chiller, filler, gorilla, killer, pillar, spiller, stiller, thriller, tiller, villa.
Chipper, clipper, dipper, flipper, hipper, kipper, nipper, ripper, shipper, sipper, skipper, slipper, stripper, tipper, tripper, zipper.
Blinker, drinker, pinker, shrinker, sinker, stinker, thinker, tinker, winker, freethinker.
[3] **Beginner(s)**, Berliner, breadwinner, examiner, foreigner, mariner, milliner, phenomena, prizewinner, retina, stamina, submariner.

3.1.106 "--inging" (as in "swinging")
[2] bringing, clinging, flinging, pinging, ringing, singing, slinging, springing, stinging, stringing, swinging, winging, wringing.

SURPRISING RHYMING:
[2] **Beginning**, grinning, inning, pinning, sinning, skinning, spinning, thinning, winning.
Brimming, dimming, skimming, slimming, swimming, trimming.
Grinning, pinning, sinning, skinning, spinning, thinning, winning.

Giving, driven, given, forgiving, living, misgiving, outliving, thanksgiving, unforgiving.
Bidding, didn't, forbidding, forbidden, hidden, kidding, ridding, ridden, skidding.
Fitting, hitting, knitting, quitting, sitting, slitting, spitting, splitting.
Drifting, gifting, lifting, rifting, shifting, sifting, sixteen.
Chilling, drilling, filling, grilling, killing, shilling, spilling, stilling, swilling, thrilling, willing.
Digging, jigging, rigging, swigging.
Glinting, hinting, minting, printing, sprinting, squinting, tinting.
Arisen, glisten, imprison, listen, prison, risen.
Chipping, clipping, dipping, dripping, flipping, gripping, nipping, ripping, shipping, sipping, skipping, slipping, snipping, stripping, tipping, tripping, unzipping, zipping.
Fizzing, frizzing, quizzing, whizzing.
[3] **Acquitting**, admitting, omitting, permitting, side-splitting, transmitting, unwitting.

3.1.107 "--ingle" (as in "tingle")
[2] jingle, mingle, single, tingle.

SURPRISING RHYMING:
[2] **Dimple**, pimple, simple, wimple.
Dwindle, hymnal, kindle, sinful, spindle, swindle.
Crinkle, skillful, sprinkle, tinkle, twinkle, willful, winkle, wrinkle.
Bristle, crystal, gristle, missal, missile, pistol, thistle, whistle.
Civil, drivel, shrivel, skiffle, sniffle, snivel, swivel.
Dribble, nibble, quibble, scribble, sibyl.
Fiddle, griddle, idyll, middle, paradiddle, riddle, twiddle.
Cripple, nipple, ripple, stipple, tipple, triple.
Giggle, jiggle, squiggle, wiggle, wriggle.

3.1.108 "--ingless" (as in "wingless")
[2] ringless, stingless, stringless, wingless.

SURPRISING RHYMING:
[2] **Binges**, cringes, fringes, hinges, singes, tinges, twinges.
Business, citrus, illness, fitness, witness, willingness.
Quickest, sickest, thickest.
Biggest, fittest, hippest, richest, simplest, thinnest, witnessed.
[3] **Ambitious**, auspicious, Christmas, delicious, fictitious, inauspicious, judicious, malicious, nutritious, suspicious, vicious.

3.1.109 "--ingling" (as in "tingling")
[2] jingling, mingling, tingling.

SURPRISING RHYMING:
[2] **Dwindling**, kindling, spindling, swindling.
Dribbling, nibbling, quibbling, scribbling, sibling.
Diddling, fiddling, griddling, middling, piddling, riddling, twiddling.
Crippling, rippling, stippling, tippling, tripling.
Giggling, jiggling, niggling, squiggling, wiggling, wriggling.
Crinkling, inkling, sprinkling, tinkling, twinkling, winkling, wrinkling.
Driveling, shriveling, sniffling, sniveling, swiveling.
Chiseling, drizzling, fizzling, sizzling, whistling.

3.1.110 "--indicate" (as in "indicate")
[3] indicate, syndicate, vindicate.

SURPRISING RHYMING:
[3] **Abdicate**, activate, aggravate, alienate, allocate, alternate, animate, automate, calculate, candidate, captivate, celebrate, circulate, complicate, consecrate, concentrate, confiscate, congregate, consummate, contemplate, cultivate, decorate, dedicate, demonstrate, desolate, devastate, deviate, discriminate, dominate, duplicate, educate,

elevate, eliminate, emigrate, emulate, escalate, estimate, fascinate, fluctuate, generate, graduate, heavyweight, hesitate, hibernate, illuminate, illustrate, imitate, implicate, infiltrate, innovate, instigate, interstate, intimate, intricate, irritate, isolate, liberate, litigate, mediate, meditate, moderate, motivate, navigate, operate, orchestrate, overstate, overweight, paperweight, penetrate, percolate, permeate, perpetuate, pollinate, procreate, punctuate, radiate, relocate, renovate, segregate, separate, simulate, situate, stimulate, stipulate, suffocate, syncopate, terminate, tête-à-tête, tolerate, violate.
[4] **Accelerate**, accommodate, alienate, alleviate, anticipate, associate, collaborate, communicate, concentrate, congratulate, contaminate, cooperate, corroborate, deteriorate, elaborate, exaggerate, exonerate, hallucinate, humiliate, impersonate, infuriate, initiate, infatuate, intimidate, investigate, necessitate, negotiate, orientate, participate, recuperate, refrigerate, reverberate.

3.1.111 "--inical" (as in "cynical")
[3] clinical, cynical, pinnacle.

SURPRISING RHYMING:
[3] **Biblical**, critical, lyrical, miracle, mystical, mythical, physical, pitiful, quizzical, rhythmical, satirical, typical, visible, whimsical.
Additional, conditional, criminal, digital, fictional, minimal, original, pivotal, principal, principle, subliminal, thrillable.
[4] **Applicable**, despicable, equivocal, explicable, extricable, logistical, medicinal, political, predictable, reciprocal, satirical, uncritical, unequivocal, untypical, unpredictable.
Admissible, forgivable, formidable, impossible, invincible, invisible, irresistible, noticeable, permissible, resistible, serviceable, traditional, unforgivable.

3.1.112 "--inister" (as in "sinister")
[3] administer, minister, sinister.

SURPRISING RHYMING:
[2] **Blister**, crisper, mister, sister, trickster, twister, vista, whisper.
[3] **Banister**, barista, barrister, canister, chorister, register, sob-sister, stepsister, transistor, visitor.
Brandisher, extinguisher, finisher, flourisher, furnisher, kingfisher, languisher, militia, nourisher, perisher, polisher, publisher, punisher, ravisher, villager, well-wisher.
Cylinder, insular, listener, prisoner, senator, similar, swindler.
[4] **Expenditure**, furniture, literature, miniature, perimeter, signature, temperature.

3.1.113 "--inkable" (as in "drinkable")
drinkable, shrinkable, sinkable, thinkable, unsinkable, unthinkable.

SURPRISING RHYMING:
[3] **Biblical**, clinical, critical, cynical, lyrical, miracle, mystical, mythical, physical, pinnacle, pitiful, quizzical, rhythmical, satirical, typical, whimsical.
Feasible, fixable, flexible, forcible, mixable, plausible, taxable.
Fillable, miserable, refillable, syllable, thrillable, tillable, visible.
[4] **Applicable**, despicable, equivocal, explicable, extricable, political, predictable, reciprocal, unpredictable.
Admissible, charitable, forgivable, formidable, inadmissible, indivisible, invincible, invisible, irresistible, noticeable, permissible, resistible, unforgivable.
Disposable, exhaustible, implausible, impossible, inflexible, provisional, traditional.
Additional, conditional, criminal, digital, fictional, minimal, original, pivotal, principal, principle, subliminal.

3.1.114 "--inny" (as in "skinny")
[2] cine, chimney, guinea, mini, ninny, pinny, skinny, spinney, tinny, whinny.

SURPRISING RHYMING:
[2] **Gimme**, jimmy, shimmy.

Beginning, grinning, inning, pinning, sinning, skinning, spinning, thinning, winning.
Diddy, giddy, kiddie, midi., windy
Busy, dizzy, fizzy, flimsy, frizzy, kiss me, tizzy, whimsy.
Chili, chilly, filly, frilly, hilly, hillbilly, icily, lily, silly, rockabilly.
Chippy, clippie, crispy, dippy, drippy, hippie, lippy, nippy, trippy, whippy, yippee, zippy.
Bitty, chitty, city, ditty, gritty, kitty, pity, pretty, witty.
Hickey, icky, kinky, mickey, milky, picky, pinkie, pinky, quickie, sickie, silky, slinky, sticky, tricky, whiskey/whisky.
[4] Ability, agility, civility, facility, fertility, fragility, futility, hostility, humility, mobility, nobility, stability, tranquillity/tranquility (U.S.), virility.

3.1.115 "--inning" (as in "spinning")
[2] beginning, grinning, inning, pinning, sinning, skinning, spinning, thinning, winning.

SURPRISING RHYMING:
[2] **Brimming**, dimming, skimming, slimming, swimming, trimming.
Bringing, clinging, flinging, pinging, ringing, singing, slinging, springing, stinging, stringing, swinging, winging, wringing.
Giving, living, forgiving, misgiving, outliving, thanksgiving, unforgiving.
Bidding, forbidding, kidding, outbidding, ridding, skidding.
Forbidden, hidden, ridden.
Digging, jigging, rigging, swigging.
Chilling, drilling, filling, grilling, killing, shilling, spilling, stilling, swilling, thrilling, willing.
Fitting, hitting, knitting, quitting, sitting, slitting, spitting, splitting.
Bitten, didn't, kitten, mitten, smitten, written.
Chipping, clipping, dipping, dripping, flipping, gripping, nipping, ripping, shipping, sipping, skipping, slipping, snipping, stripping, tipping, tripping, unzipping, zipping.
Glinting, hinting, minting, printing, sprinting, squinting, tinting.
Fizzing, frizzing, quizzing, whizzing.
Dissing, hissing, kissing, missing.
Dishing, fishing, phishing, squishing, swishing, wishing.
Clicking, flicking, kicking, licking, picking, pricking, ticking, tricking.
Chicken, quicken, sicken, stricken, thicken.
[3] **Distilling**, fulfilling, instilling, unwilling.
Acquitting, admitting, omitting, permitting, side-splitting, transmitting, unwitting.

3.1.116 "--injes" (as in "cringes")
[2] binges, cringes, fringes, hinges, infringes, singes, tinges, twinges, unhinges.

SURPRISING RHYMING:
[2] **Clinches**, finches, flinches, inches, lynches, pinches, winches.
Dishes, fishes, squishes, swishes, wishes.
Bridges, fridges, midges, ridges.
Bitches, breeches, britches, ditches, hitches, itches, niches, pitches, riches, snitches, stitches, switches, twitches, witches.
Convinces, evinces, minces, princes, rinses, winces.
Business, citrus, illness, fitness, witness.
Quickness, sickness, slickness, thickness.

3.1.117 "--injing" (as in "hinging")
[2] binging, cringing, fringing, hinging, infringing, singeing, tingeing, twinging, unhinging.

SURPRISING RHYMING:
[2] **Convincing**, evincing, mincing, wincing.
Cinching, clinching, flinching, inching, lynching, pinching, winching.
Bitching, ditching, hitching, itching, snitching, stitching, switching, twitching, witching.
Bridging, pigeon, religion, smidgen, stool-pigeon.
Dishing, fishing, phishing, squishing, swishing, wishing.
Fizzing, frizzing, quizzing, whizzing.

Bee-sting, blurring, bluffing, changeling, earring, evening, fledgling, nose-ring, nothing, offspring, plaything, purring, questioning, shoestring, Sing Sing, slurring, something, stirring, wielding.
Efficient, proficient, sufficient.
Bringing, clinging, flinging, pinging, ringing, singing, slinging, springing, stinging, stringing, swinging, winging, wringing.
Dwindling, kindling, spindling, swindling.
Brimming, dimming, skimming, slimming, swimming, trimming.
Drifting, gifting, lifting, rifting, shifting, sifting.
Giving, driven, forgiving, living, misgiving, thanksgiving, unforgiving.
[3] Abridging, averaging, leveraging, messaging, packaging, voyaging.

3.1.118 "--inker" (as in "thinker")
[2] blinker, drinker, Inca, inker, linker, pinker, shrinker, sinker, stinker, thinker, tinker, winker, freethinker, headshrinker.

SURPRISING RHYMING:
[2] **Bicker**, flicker, kicker, knicker, licker, liquor, picker, quicker, sicker, slicker, snicker, sticker, thicker, ticker, vicar, whicker, wicker.
Limber, marimba, timber.
Dimmer, glimmer, mirror, shimmer, simmer, skimmer, slimmer, swimmer, trimmer.
Crimper, limper, shrimper, simper, whimper.
Cinder, hinder, injure, tinder.
Dinner, grinner, inner, sinner, skinner, spinner, thinner, winner.
Inter, midwinter, printer, splinter, sprinter, squinter, winter.
Bringer, clinger, finger, flinger, linger, ringer, singer, slinger, springer, stinger, stringer, swinger, winger, wringer, zinger.
Bigger, digger, figure, rigour/rigor (U.S.), snigger, trigger, vigour/vigor.
Crippler, dribbler, nibbler, quibbler, scribbler, simpler, sprinkler, stickler, tippler.
Conifer, differ, Lucifer, sniffer, stiffer.
Drifter, grifter, lifter, shifter, sifter, snifter, swifter.
Fixture, mixture, scripture, tincture.

3.1.119 "--inking" (as in "blinking")
[2] blinking, clinking, drinking, hoodwinking, inking, linking, shrinking, sinking, slinking, stinking, syncing, thinking, winking.

SURPRISING RHYMING:
[2] **Inkling**, sprinkling, twinkling, winkling.
Clicking, flicking, kicking, licking, picking, pricking, ticking, tricking.
Affixing, fixing, mixing, nixing.
Glinting, hinting, minting, printing, sprinting, squinting, tinting.
Jilting, lilting, quilting, silting, stilting, tilting, wilting.
Listing, misting, twisting.
Fitting, hitting, knitting, quitting, sitting, slitting, spitting, splitting.
Crimping, limping, pimping, primping, shrimping, skimping.
Brimming, dimming, skimming, slimming, swimming, trimming.
Bitching, ditching, hitching, itching, snitching, stitching, switching, twitching, witching.
Cinching, clinching, flinching, inching, lynching, pinching.
Dissing, hissing, kissing, missing.
Bidding, forbidding, kidding, outbidding, ridding, skidding.
Bringing, clinging, flinging, jingling, mingling, pinging, ringing, singing, slinging, springing, stinging, stringing, swinging, tingling, winging, wringing.
Beginning, grinning, pinning, sinning, spinning, thinning, winning.
[3] Quickening, sickening, thickening.
Conflicting, constricting, convicting, depicting, evicting, inflicting, predicting, restricting.
Assisting, blacklisting, consisting, enlisting, existing, insisting, persisting, resisting, subsisting, untwisting.
Acquitting, admitting, omitting, permitting, side-splitting, transmitting, unwitting.

3.1.120 "--inkle" (as in "sprinkle")
[2] crinkle, sprinkle, tinkle, twinkle, winkle, wrinkle.

SURPRISING RHYMING:
[2] **Crinkled**, sprinkled, tinkled, twinkled, winkled, wrinkled.
Jingle, mingle, shingle, signal, single, tingle.
Fickle, nickel, pickle, prickle, tickle, trickle.
Dwindle, hymnal, kindle, rekindle, sinful, spindle, swindle.
Cymbal, nimble, symbol, thimble, timbale.
Dimple, pimple, simple, wimple.
Bristle, chisel, drizzle, fizzle, frizzle, missile, sizzle, swizzle, thistle, tinsel, whistle.
Diddle, fiddle, griddle, idyll, middle, riddle, twiddle.
Cripple, nipple, ripple, stipple, tipple, triple.
[3] **Clinical**, cynical, lyrical, miracle, physical, pinnacle, quizzical, satirical.

3.1.121 "--inkling" (as in "sprinkling")
[2] crinkling, inkling, sprinkling, tinkling, twinkling, winkling, wrinkling.

SURPRISING RHYMING:
[2] **Crinkle**, sprinkle, tinkle, twinkle, winkle, wrinkle.
Blinking, drinking, hoodwinking, inking, inkling, linking, shrinking, sinking, sprinkling, stinking, syncing, thinking, twinkling, winking.
Jingling, mingling, singling, tingling.
Pickling, prickling, tickling, trickling.
Glistening, listening, listing, misting, twisting.
Glinting, hinting, minting, printing, sprinting, squinting, tinting.
Giggling, jiggling, niggling, wiggling, wriggling.
Affixing, fixing, mixing, nixing.
Crippling, rippling, stippling, tippling, tripling.
Dribbling, nibbling, quibbling, scribbling, sibling.
Jilting, lilting, quilting, silting, stilting, tilting, wilting.
Dwindling, kindling, spindling, swindling.
Diddling, fiddling, griddling, middling, riddling, twiddling.
Driveling, shriveling, sniffling, sniveling, swiveling.
Chiseling, drizzling, fizzling, frizzling, sizzling, whistling.
[3] **Conflicting**, convicting, depicting, inflicting, predicting, restricting.

3.1.122 "--inctive" (as in "instinctive")
[3] distinctive, instinctive.

SURPRISING RHYMING:
[2] **Drifted**, frigid, gifted, lifted, liquid, listed, misted, rigid, scripted, shifted, twisted.
[3] **Constrictive**, descriptive, predictive, restrictive, vindictive.
Addicted, afflicted, conflicted, convicted, evicted, predicted, restricted.
Artistic, ballistic, linguistic, realistic, sadistic, simplistic, stylistic.
Dismissive, emissive, missive, permissive, submissive.
Abrasive, abusive, adhesive, aggressive, compulsive, conclusive, conducive, corrosive, decisive, defensive, divisive, elusive, emotive, evasive, excessive, exclusive, expensive, expletive, explosive, expressive, impassive, impressive, impulsive, incisive, inclusive, intensive, intrusive, narrative, negative, obsessive, offensive, oppressive, percussive, permissive, persuasive, possessive, repulsive, responsive, sedative, submissive, talkative.
Assisted, blacklisted, consisted, enlisted, existed, insisted, persisted, resisted, tight-fisted, two-fisted, unlisted, untwisted.

3.1.123 "--inctly" (as in "distinctly")
[3] distinctly, succinctly.

SURPRISING RHYMING:
[2] **Prickly**, quickly, sickly, slickly, swiftly, tickly, thickly.

Crinkly, sprinkly, strictly, tinkly, wrinkly.
Brickie, briskly, hickey, icky, kinky, mickey, milky, picky, pinkie, pinky, quickie, sickie, silky, slinky, sticky, tricky, whiskey/whisky.
[4] Artistically, linguistically, realistically, sadistically, stylistically.

3.1.124 "--incing" (as in "wincing")
convincing, evincing, mincing, wincing.

SURPRISING RHYMING:
[2] Binging, cringing, hinging, infringing, singeing, twinging.
Affixing, fixing, mixing, nixing.
Dishing, fishing, phishing, squishing, swishing, wishing.
Dissing, hissing, kissing, listing, missing, misting, twisting.
Blinking, clinking, drinking, hoodwinking, linking, shrinking, sinking, slinking, stinking, syncing, thinking, winking.
Inkling, sprinkling, twinkling.
Cinching, clinching, flinching, inching, lynching, pinching.
Glinting, hinting, minting, printing, sprinting, squinting, tinting.
Drifting, gifting, lifting, rifting, shifting, sifting.
Bringing, clinging, flinging, pinging, ringing, singing, slinging, springing, stinging, stringing, swinging, winging, wringing.
Crimping, limping, pimping, primping, shrimping, skimping.
[3] Assisting, blacklisting, consisting, enlisting, existing, insisting, persisting, resisting, subsisting, untwisting.

3.1.125 "--inted" (as in "sprinted")
[2] dinted, glinted, hinted, minted, printed, splinted, sprinted, squinted, tinted.
[3] imprinted, misprinted, reprinted.

SURPRISING RHYMING:
[2] Drifted, gifted, lifted, listed, misted, rifted, shifted, sifted, twisted.
Jilted, kilted, lilted, quilted, silted, stilted, tilted, wilted.
Big head, bridgehead, figurehead, inbred, instead, invented, kindred, misled, misread, rescinded, skinhead, spearhead, winded.
[3] Addicted, afflicted, conflicted, constricted, convicted, depicted, dickhead, evicted, predicted, restricted.
Assisted, blacklisted, consisted, enlisted, existed, insisted, persisted, predicted, resisted, tight-fisted, two-fisted, unlisted, untwisted.
Acquitted, admitted, committed, dimwitted, fitted, half-witted, knitted, outwitted, permitted, quick-witted, spirited, transmitted.

3.1.126 "--inter" (as in "winter")
[2] midwinter, printer, splinter, sprinter, squinter, winter.

SURPRISING RHYMING:
[2] Crimper, limper, shrimper, simper, whimper.
Limber, marimba, timber.
Cinder, hinder, injure, tinder.
Builder, filter, kilter, pilfer, quilter, tilter.
Drifter, grifter, lifter, shifter, sifter, snifter, swifter, victor.
Elixir, fixer, fixture, minster, mixer, mixture, scripture, spinster, tipster, trickster.
Clincher, flincher, pincher, wincher.
Blister, crisper, mister, sister, trickster, twister, vista, whisper.
Blinker, drinker, pinker, shrinker, sinker, stinker, thinker, tinker, winker, freethinker.
Dimmer, glimmer, primmer, shimmer, simmer, skimmer, slimmer, swimmer, trimmer.
Dinner, grinner, inner, sinner(s), skinner, spinner, thinner, winner(s).
Bringer, clinger, finger, flinger, ringer, singer, slinger, springer, stinger, stringer, swinger, winger, wringer, zinger.
[3] Bewilder(ed), bodybuilder, boatbuilder, housebuilder, rebuilder.

3.1.127 "--inting" (as in "sprinting")
[2] glinting, hinting, minting, printing, sprinting, squinting, tinting.

SURPRISING RHYMING:
[2] **Crimping**, limping, pimping, primping, shrimping, skimping.
Dinted, glinted, hinted, minted, printed, sprinted, squinted, tinted.
Drifting, gifting, lifting, rifting, shifting, sifting, sixteen.
Blinking, clinking, drinking, hoodwinking, inking, linking, shrinking, sinking, slinking, stinking, syncing, thinking, winking.
Clicking, flicking, kicking, licking, picking, pricking, ticking, tricking.
Chipping, clipping, dipping, dripping, flipping, gripping, nipping, ripping, shipping, sipping, skipping, slipping, snipping, stripping, tipping, tripping, unzipping, whipping.
Bringing, clinging, flinging, pinging, ringing, singing, slinging, springing, stinging, stringing, swinging, winging, wringing.
Brimming, dimming, skimming, slimming, swimming, trimming.
Fitting, hitting, knitting, quitting, sitting, slitting, spitting, splitting.
Bidding, forbidding, forbidden, hidden, kidding, ridding, skidding.
Beginning, grinning, pinning, sinning, spinning, thinning, winning.
Giving, living, forgiving, misgiving, outliving, thanksgiving, unforgiving.
[3] **Acquitting**, admitting, omitting, permitting, side-splitting, transmitting, unwitting.

3.1.128 "--ip" (as in "ship")
[1] blip, chip, clip, dip, drip, flip, grip, hip, kip, lip, nip, pip, quip, rip, ship, sip, skip, slip, snip, strip, tip, trip, whip, yip, zip.
[2] airship, catnip, courtship, equip, flagship, friendship, hardship, horsewhip, kinship, outstrip, steamship, township, warship, worship.
[3] battleship, fellowship, horsemanship, leadership, membership, partnership, penmanship, scholarship, sportsmanship, workmanship.

SURPRISING RHYMING:
[1] **Chipped**, clipped, crypt, dipped, dripped, flipped, gripped, nipped, pipped, quipped, ripped, script, shipped, sipped, skipped, slipped, snipped, stripped, tipped, tripped, whipped, zipped.
Blips, chips, clips, dips, drips, flips, grips, hips, kips, lips, nips, pips, quips, rips, scripts, ships, sips, skips, slips, snips, strips, tips, trips, whips, zips.
Bit, fit, grit, hit, it, kit, knit, lit, pit, quit, skit, slit, spit, split, wit.
Brick, chick, click, crick, dick, flick, hick, kick, lick, nick, pick, prick, quick, sic, sick, slick, stick, thick, tic, tick, trick, wick.
[2] **Conscript**, equipped, horsewhipped, outstripped, postscript, transcript, worshipped.
Eclipse, ellipse, equips, friendships, hardships, outstrips, steamships, townships, warships, worships.
Acquit, admit, armpit, cockpit, commit, emit, habit, misfit, moonlit, omit, outfit, outwit, remit, spirit, submit, sunlit, tidbit, transmit, unfit.
Broomstick, chopstick, drumstick, heartsick, homesick, lipstick, lovesick, seasick.
[3] **Apocalypse**, fish and chips, midships, manuscript, unzipped.
Counterfeit, definite, exquisite, favourite/favorite (U.S.), hypocrite, infinite, opposite.
Candlestick, heretic, limerick, lunatic, maverick, politic, rhetoric, walking-stick.
Exhibit, inhibit, prohibit.

3.1.129 "--ips" (as in "lips")
[1] blips, chips, clips, dips, drips, flips, grips, hips, kips, lips, nips, pips, quips, rips, scripts, ships, sips, skips, slips, snips, strips, tips, trips, whips, zips.
[2] eclipse, ellipse, equips, friendships, hardships, outstrips, steamships, townships, unzips, warships, worships.
[3] amidships, apocalypse, fish and chips, midships.

SURPRISING RHYMING:
[1] **Blip**, chip, clip, dip, drip, flip, grip, hip, kip, lip, nip, pip, quip, rip, ship, sip, skip, slip, snip, strip, tip, trip, whip, yip, zip.

Chipped, clipped, crypt, dipped, dripped, flipped, gripped, nipped, pipped, quipped, ripped, script, shipped, sipped, skipped, slipped, snipped, stripped, tipped, tripped, whipped, zipped.
Bits, blitz, fits, grits, hits, its/it's, kits, knits, pits, quits, skits, slits, spits, splits, wits.
Bricks, chicks, fix, flicks, hicks, kicks, licks, mix, nix, picks, pix, pricks, six, slicks, sticks, tics, ticks, tricks, wicks.
[2] Airship, courtship, equip, flagship, friendship, hardship, kinship, outstrip, steamship, township, warship, worship.
Conscript, equipped, horsewhipped, outstripped, postscript, transcript, worshipped.
Acquits, admits, commits, habits, misfits, outfits, outwits, spirits, submits, tidbits.
Affix, crucifix, intermix, matchsticks, prefix, suffix.
[3] Battleship, fellowship, horsemanship, leadership, membership, partnership, penmanship, scholarship, sportsmanship, workmanship.
Manuscript, superscript, unzipped.
Favourites/favorites (U.S.), hypocrites, opposites, requisites.
Candlesticks, heretics, limericks, lunatics, mavericks, politics, rhetoric, walking-sticks.

3.1.130 "--ippie" (as in "hippie")
[2] chippy, clippie, crispy, dippy, drippy, hippie, lippy, nippy, snippy, trippy, whippy, yippee, zippy.

SURPRISING RHYMING:
[2] Bitty, chitty, city, ditty, gritty, kitty, pity, pretty, sixty, witty.
Diddy, giddy, kiddie, midi.
Busy, dizzy, fizzy, frizzy, tizzy.
Dixie, glitzy, kissy, missy, prissy, ritzy, sissy.
Hickey, icky, kinky, mickey, milky, picky, pinkie, pinky, quickie, sickie, silky, slinky, sticky, tricky, whiskey/whisky.
Chili, chilly, filly, frilly, hilly, hillbilly, icily, lily, silly, rockabilly.
Fifty, fifty-fifty, iffy, jiffy, miffy, nifty, pithy, shifty, sniffy, spiffy, thrifty.
Guilty, minty, misty, nasty, nicety, nifty, shifty, sixty, swiftie, thrifty.
Cine, chimney, gimme, lemme, mini, ninny, skinny, tinny, whinny.
[3] Ability, agility, anxiety, equality, facility, fertility, fragility, futility, hostility, humanity, humidity, humility, mobility, nitty-gritty, nobility, sobriety, society, stability, stupidity, tranquillity/tranquility (U.S.), utility, variety, virility.

3.1.131 "--ipped" (as in "ripped")
[1] chipped, clipped, crypt, dipped, dripped, flipped, gripped, nipped, pipped, quipped, ripped, script, shipped, sipped, skipped, slipped, snipped, stripped, tipped, tripped, whipped, zipped.
[2] conscript, encrypt, equipped, horsewhipped, outstripped, postscript, subscript, transcript, unzipped, worshipped.
[3] ill-equipped, manuscript, nondescript, superscript, unequipped.

SURPRISING RHYMING:
[1] Blip, chip, clip, dip, drip, flip, grip, hip, kip, lip, nip, pip, quip, rip, ship, sip, skip, slip, snip, strip, tip, trip, whip, yip, zip.
Bit, fit, grit, hit, it, kit, knit, lit, pit, quit, skit, slit, spit, split, wit.
Drift, gift, lift, miffed, rift, shift, shrift, sniffed, swift, thrift, whiffed.
Bricked, clicked, flicked, kicked, licked, picked, pricked, strict, ticked, tricked.
Built, gilt, guilt, jilt, kilt, lilt, quilt, silt, spilt, stilt, tilt, wilt.
Blinked, clinked, inked, linked, slinked, winked, hoodwinked.
[2] Airship, equip, flagship, friendship, hardship, kinship, outstrip, steamship, worship.
Acquit, admit, armpit, cockpit, commit, emit, habit, misfit, moonlit, omit, outfit, outwit, remit, spirit, submit, sunlit, tidbit, transmit, unfit.
Adrift, airlift, facelift, gearshift, makeshift, nightshift, snowdrift, spendthrift, uplift.
Addict, afflict, conflict, contradict, convict, depict, predict, restrict.
[3] Counterfeit, definite, exquisite, favourite/favorite (U.S.), hypocrite, infinite, opposite, pre-requisite, requisite.

3.1.132 "--ipper" (as in "slipper")
[2] chipper, clipper, dipper, flipper, gripper, hipper, kipper, nipper, quipper, ripper, shipper, sipper, skipper, slipper, stripper, tipper, tripper, whipper, zipper.
[3] caliper, day-tripper, equipper, juniper, worshiper.

SURPRISING RHYMING:
[2] **Bitter**, critter, fitter, flitter, fritter, glitter, gritter, hitter, jitter, kidder, knitter, litter, pitta, quitter, sitter, skitter, slitter, splitter, titter, twitter.
Dinner, grinner, inner, sinner, skinner, spinner, thinner, winner(s).
Chiller, filler, killer, miller, pillar, spiller, stiller, thriller, tiller, villa.
Differ, Lucifer, river, sniffer, stiffer.
Crimper, limper, shrimper, simper, whimper.
Scissor, fizzer, hisser, kisser, quizzer, reminiscer, whizzer.
Bicker, flicker, kicker, knicker, licker, liquor, picker, quicker, sicker, slicker, snicker, sticker, thicker, ticker, vicar, whicker, wicker.
Bigger, figure, rigour/rigor (U.S.), snigger, trigger, vigour/vigor (U.S.).
Dimmer, glimmer, primmer, shimmer, simmer, skimmer, slimmer, swimmer, trimmer.
[3] **Caterpillar**, consider, distiller, flotilla, fulfiller, gorilla, guerilla, man-killer, painkiller, spine-chiller, vanilla, weedkiller.
Beginner, breadwinner, deliver, downriver, examiner, forgiver, foreigner, mariner, milliner, phenomena, prizewinner, retina, stamina, upriver.
[4] **Baby-sitter**, barometer, competitor, counterfeiter, depositor, diameter, exhibitor, interpreter, parameter, perimeter, solicitor, speedometer, thermometer.

3.1.133 "--ipping" (as in "slipping")
[2] chipping, clipping, dipping, dripping, flipping, gripping, nipping, quipping, ripping, shipping, sipping, skipping, slipping, snipping, stripping, tipping, tripping, whipping.
[3] equipping, horsewhipping, outstripping, unzipping.

SURPRISING RHYMING:
[2] **Crimping**, limping, pimping, primping, skimping.
Fitting, hitting, knitting, quitting, sitting, slitting, spitting, splitting.
Drifting, gifting, lifting, rifting, shifting, sifting, sixteen, sniffing.
Glinting, hinting, minting, printing, sprinting, squinting, tinting.
Clicking, flicking, kicking, licking, picking, pricking, ticking, tricking.
Bidding, forbidding, kidding, outbidding, ridding, skidding.
Brimming, dimming, skimming, slimming, swimming, trimming.
Grinning, pinning, sinning, spinning, thinning, winning.
Chilling, drilling, filling, grilling, killing, shilling, spilling, stilling, swilling, thrilling, willing.
Giving, driven, forgiving, living, misgiving, thanksgiving, unforgiving.
Digging, jigging, rigging, swigging.
Bringing, clinging, flinging, pinging, ringing, singing, slinging, springing, stinging, stringing, swinging, winging, wringing.
Fizzing, frizzing, hissing, kissing, quizzing, reminiscing, whizzing.
[3] **Acquitting**, admitting, omitting, permitting, side-splitting, transmitting, unwitting.
Assisting, consisting, existing, insisting, persisting, resisting.

3.1.134 "--ipple" (as in "ripple")
[2] cripple, nipple, ripple, stipple, tipple, triple.

SURPRISING RHYMING:
[2] **Dimple**, nimble, pimple, simple, symbol, thimble, wimple.
Dribble, nibble, quibble, scribble, sibyl.
Bristle, chisel, drizzle, fizzle, missile, sizzle, swizzle, thistle, whistle.
Diddle, fiddle, griddle, idyll, middle, piddle, riddle, twiddle.
Belittle, brittle, committal, hospital, it'll, little, skittle, spittle, whittle.
Fickle, nickel, pickle, prickle, tickle, trickle.
Giggle, jiggle, niggle, squiggle, wiggle, wriggle.
Civil, drivel, shrivel, skiffle, sniffle, snivel, swivel.

374

3.1.135 "--ipshun" (as in "description")
[3] description, inscription, prescription, subscription, transcription.

SURPRISING RHYMING:
[2] **Bitching**, ditching, hitching, itching, snitching, stitching, switching, twitching, witching.
Diction, fiction, kitchen, friction.
Emission, fission, intermission, magician, mission, musician, titian.
Cinching, clinching, flinching, inching, lynching, pinching.
Dishing, fishing, phishing, squishing, swishing, wishing.
Christen, criticism, glisten, isn't, listen, rhythm, vision.
Pigeon, religion, smidgen, stool-pigeon.
[3] **Averaging**, bridging, leveraging, messaging, packaging, voyaging.
Addiction, affliction, conviction, eviction, prediction, restriction.
Addition, admission, ambition, audition, condition, contrition, edition, fruition, ignition, magician, musician, nutrition, omission, optician, permission, physician, position, remission, rendition, submission, suspicion, tradition, transition, transmission, tuition.
Efficient, proficient, sufficient.
Collision, decision, derision, division, envision, incision, precision, provision, revision.
[4] **Composition**, contradiction, crucifixion, definition, dereliction, intuition, jurisdiction, politician, prohibition, recognition, superstition.

3.1.136 "--iracle" (as in "miracle")
[3] lyrical, miracle.

SURPRISING RHYMING:
[3] **Biblical,** clinical, criminal, critical, cynical, difficult, digital, fictional, minimal, mystical, mythical, physical, pinnacle, pitiful, principal, principle, quizzical, rhythmical, satirical, typical, visible, whimsical.
[4] **Applicable,** despicable, explicable, extricable, hypocritical, hysterical, political, predictable, reciprocal, unpredictable.
Additional, conditional, invisible, original, subliminal.

3.1.137 "--iss" (as in "kiss")
[1] bliss, diss, hiss, kiss, miss, piss, sis, 'tis, this.
[2] abyss, amiss, bodice, chalice, coppice, dismiss, gratis, haggis, hospice, hubris, jaundice, justice, malice, Memphis, novice, office, palace, Paris, preface, purchase, remiss, service, solstice, surface.
[3] accomplice, cowardice, edifice, emphasis, genesis, kinesis, liquorice/licorice (U.S.), nemesis, orifice, prejudice, reminisce, synthesis.

SURPRISING RHYMING:
[1] **Dissed**, fist, gist, grist, hissed, kissed, list, midst, missed, mist, pissed, tryst, twist, whist, wrist.
Biz, fizz, his, is, quiz, whiz.
Bits, blitz, fits, grits, hits, its/it's, kits, knits, pits, quits, skits, slits, spits, splits, wits.
If, cliff, miff, myth, riff, skiff, sniff, stiff, tiff, whiff, with.
Dished, fished, squished, swished, wished.
Anguish, dish, fish, flourish, nourish, squish, swish, wish.
[2] **Assist**, consist, dismissed, enlist, exist, insist, persist, resist.
Acquits, admits, armpits, cockpits, commits, emits, habits, misfits, omits, outfits, outwits, remits, spirits, submits, tidbits, transmits.
Chalice, gratis, haggis, malice, palace, solstice, surface.
[3] **Activist,** anarchist, atheist, catalyst, columnist, communist, egotist, exorcist, fatalist, humourist/humorist (U.S.), hypnotist, journalist, lobbyist, motorist, novelist, optimist, organist, pacifist, pessimist, publicist, socialist, soloist, specialist, strategist, terrorist.

3.1.138 "--ish" (as in "wish")
[1] dish, fish, ish, squish, swish, wish.
[2] anguish, blackfish, bluefish, blueish, brownish, catfish, crayfish, crawfish, devilfish,

dogfish, feverish, flourish, goldfish, greenish, jellyfish, kingfish, nourish, reddish, selfish, shellfish, starfish, swordfish, yellowish.

SURPRISING RHYMING:
[1] Dished, fished, squished, swished, wished.
Bliss, diss, hiss, kiss, miss, myth, piss, sis, 'tis, this, with.
Bitch, ditch, glitch, hitch, itch, kitsch, niche, pitch, rich, snitch, stitch, switch, twitch, which, witch.
Convince, evince, mince, prince, rinse, since, wince.
Dissed, fist, gist, hissed, kissed, list, midst, missed, mist, pissed, tryst, twist, wrist.
[2] Abyss, amiss, bodice, chalice, coppice, dismiss, gratis, haggis, hospice, hubris, jaundice, justice, malice, Memphis, novice, office, palace, Paris, preface, purchase, remiss, service, solstice, surface.
Bewitch, enrich, sales pitch, unhitch.
Bewitched, enriched, snitched, switched, twitched, unstitched.
[3] Accomplice, cowardice, edifice, emphasis, genesis, kinesis, liquorice/licorice (U.S.), nemesis, orifice, prejudice, reminisce.

3.1.139 "--isk" (as in "risk")
asterisk, bisque, brisk, disc/disk (U.S.), frisk, risk, obelisk, whisk.

SURPRISING RHYMING:
[1] Bliss, diss, hiss, kiss, miss, piss, sis, 'tis, this.
Blink, brink, chink, clink, drink, fink, hoodwink, ice-rink, ink, kink, link, mink, pink, rink, shrink, sink, stink, sync, think, wink, zinc.
Brick(s), chick(s), click(s), crick(s), dick, fix, flick(s), hick(s), kick(s), lick(s), mix, nick, nix, pick(s), pix, prick(s), quick, sic, sick, six, slick(s), stick(s), thick, tic(s), tick(s), trick(s), wick(s).
Dissed, fist, gist, hissed, kissed, list, midst, missed, mist, pissed, tryst, twist, wrist.
Drift, gift, lift, miffed, rift, shift, shrift, sniffed, swift, thrift, whiffed.
Biz, fizz, his, is, quiz, whiz.
[2] Affix, crucifix, intermix, matchsticks, prefix, suffix.
Abyss, amiss, bodice, chalice, dismiss, gratis, haggis, hospice, hubris, jaundice, justice, malice, Memphis, novice, office, palace, Paris, preface, purchase, remiss, service, solstice, surface.
Broomstick, chopstick, drumstick, heartsick, homesick, lipstick, lovesick, seasick.
Assist, consist, dismissed, enlist, exist, insist, persist, resist.
Adrift, airlift, facelift, gearshift, makeshift, nightshift, snowdrift, spendthrift, uplift.
[3] Accomplice, cowardice, edifice, emphasis, genesis, kinesis, liquorice/licorice (U.S.), nemesis, orifice, prejudice, reminisce.
Candlestick, heretic, limerick, lunatic, maverick, politic, rhetoric, walking-stick.
Activist, anarchist, atheist, botanist, catalyst, columnist, communist, egotist, exorcist, fatalist, humourist/humorist (U.S.), hypnotist, journalist, moralist, motorist, novelist, optimist, organist, pacifist, pessimist, publicist, socialist, soloist, specialist, terrorist.

3.1.140 "--ist" (as in "list")
[1] cyst, dissed, fist, gist, grist, hissed, kissed, list, midst, missed, mist, pissed, tryst, twist, wrist.
[2] assist, consist, dismissed, enlist, exist, insist, persist, resist, subsist, untwist.
[3] activist, anarchist, atheist, analyst, botanist, catalyst, columnist, communist, egotist, Eucharist, exorcist, fatalist, hobbyist, humourist/humorist (U.S.), hypnotist, journalist, lobbyist, moralist, motorist, novelist, optimist, organist, pacifist, pessimist, pre-exist, publicist, socialist, soloist, specialist, strategist, terrorist.

SURPRISING RHYMING:
[1] Drift, gift, lift, miffed, rift, shift, sift, sniffed, swift, thrift, whiffed.
Bricked, clicked, flicked, kicked, licked, picked, pricked, strict, ticked, tricked.
Dished, fished, squished, swished, wished.
Bliss, diss, hiss, kiss, miss, piss, sis, 'tis, this.

Blips, chips, clips, dips, drips, flips, grips, hips, kips, lips, nips, pips, quips, rips, scripts, ships, sips, skips, slips, snips, strips, tips, trips, whips, zips.
Dish, fish, ish, squish, swish, wish.
Brisk, disc/disk (U.S.), frisk, risk, obelisk, whisk.
[2] **Eclipse**, ellipse, equips, friendships, hardships, outstrips, steamships, townships, unzips, warships, worships.
Adrift, facelift, makeshift, nightshift, snowdrift, spendthrift, uplift.
Addict, conflict, contradict, convict, depict, evict, predict, restrict.
Abyss, amiss, bodice, chalice, coppice, dismiss, gratis, haggis, hospice, hubris, jaundice, justice, malice, Memphis, novice, office, palace, Paris, preface, purchase, remiss, service, solstice, surface.
Anguish, feverish, flourish, goldfish, nourish, selfish, shellfish.
[3] **Accomplice**, cowardice, edifice, emphasis, genesis, kinesis, liquorice/licorice (U.S.), nemesis, orifice, prejudice, reminisce.
Amidships, apocalypse, fish and chips, midships.

3.1.141 "--issiv" (as in "permissive")
dismissive, emissive, missive, permissive, submissive.

SURPRISING RHYMING:
[1] **Give**, live, sieve, spiv.
If, cliff, miff, myth, riff, skiff, sniff, stiff, tiff, whiff, with
[2] **Active**, captive, festive, forgive, massive, misgive, motive, native, octave, olive, outlive, passive, pensive, relive.
Adrift, facelift, makeshift, nightshift, snowdrift, spendthrift, uplift.
[3] **Abrasive**, abusive, adhesive, aggressive, compulsive, conclusive, conducive, corrosive, decisive, defensive, depressive, divisive, elusive, emotive, evasive, excessive, exclusive, expensive, expletive, explosive, expressive, impassive, impressive, impulsive, incisive, inclusive, intensive, intrusive, narrative, negative, obsessive, offensive, oppressive, percussive, persuasive, possessive, repulsive, responsive, sedative.

3.1.142 "--issen" (as in "listen")
[2] christen, glisten, listen.

SURPRISING RHYMING:
[2] **Bristle**, gristle, missal, missile, thistle, whistle.
Emission, fission, intermission, magician, mission, musician, vision.
Arisen, forgiven, glistened, imprison, listened, prison, risen.
Dishing, fishing, phishing, squishing, swishing, wishing.
Diction, fiction, kitchen, friction.
Dissing, hissing, kissing, missing.
Forbidden, hidden, ridden.
Bitten, kitten, mitten, smitten, written.
Driven, given, pigeon, religion, smidgen, stool-pigeon.
Chicken, quicken, sicken, stricken, thicken.
[3] **Addition**, admission, ambition, audition, condition, edition, emission, fruition, ignition, magician, musician, nutrition, omission, optician, petition, permission, physician, position, remission, submission, suspicion, tradition, transition, transmission, tuition.
Description, inscription, prescription, subscription, suspicion, transcription.
Efficient, proficient, sufficient.
Initial, judicial, official, prejudicial, unofficial.

3.1.143 "--issel" (as in "whistle")
[2] bristle, gristle, missile, thistle, whistle.

SURPRISING RHYMING:
[2] **Chisel**, drizzle, fizzle, frizzle, sizzle, swizzle.
Belittle, brittle, committal, hospital, it'll, little, skittle, spittle, whittle.
Dimple, pimple, simple, wimple.

Cripple, nipple, ripple, stipple, tipple, triple.
Dribble, nibble, quibble, scribble, sibyl.
Diddle, fiddle, griddle, idyll, middle, paradiddle, riddle, twiddle.
Giggle, jiggle, niggle, squiggle, wiggle, wriggle.
Jingle, mingle, shingle, signal, single, tingle.
Civil, drivel, shrivel, skiffle, sniffle, snivel, swivel.
Dwindle, kindle, spindle, swindle.
Cymbal, nimble, symbol, thimble, timbale.
Fickle, nickel, pickle, prickle, tickle, trickle.
Crinkle, skillful, sprinkle, tinkle, twinkle, willful, winkle, wrinkle.
[3] **Initial**, judicial, official, prejudicial, unofficial.

3.1.144 "--ishul" (as in "official")
[3] initial, judicial, official, prejudicial, unofficial.

SURPRISING RHYMING:
[2] **Bristle**, chisel, crystal, drizzle, fizzle, frizzle, gristle, grizzle, missal, missile, pistol, sizzle, swizzle, thistle, whistle, wishful.
Emission, fission, intermission, magician, mission, musician, titian.
Civil, drivel, shrivel, skiffle, sniffle, snivel, swivel.
Belittle, brittle, committal, hospital, it'll, little, ritual, skittle, whittle.
Giggle, jiggle, niggle, squiggle, wiggle, wriggle.
Dribble, nibble, quibble, scribble, sibyl.
Fiddle, griddle, idyll, middle, paradiddle, riddle, twiddle.
Cripple, nipple, ripple, stipple, tipple, triple.
Diddle, fiddle, griddle, idyll, middle, paradiddle, riddle, twiddle.
Fickle, nickel, pickle, prickle, tickle, trickle.
Cymbal, nimble, symbol, thimble, timbale.
Jingle, mingle, shingle, signal, single, tingle.
[3] **Addition**, admission, ambition, attrition, audition, condition, contrition, edition, emission, fruition, ignition, magician, musician, nutrition, omission, optician, partition, petition, permission, physician, position, remission, rendition, submission, suspicion, tactician, technician, tradition, transition, transmission, tuition, volition.

3.1.145 "--ishun" (as in "mission")
[2] fission, magician, mission, musician, titian.
[3] addition, admission, ambition, attrition, audition, cognition, commission, condition, contrition, edition, emission, fruition, ignition, magician, munition, musician, nutrition, omission, optician, partition, patrician, petition, permission, physician, position, remission, rendition, submission, suspicion, tactician, technician, tradition, transition, transmission, tuition, volition.
[4] abolition, acquisition, ammunition, apparition, coalition, competition, composition, definition, demolition, deposition, dietician, disposition, electrician, exhibition, expedition, exposition, extradition, imposition, inhibition, intuition, inquisition, malnutrition, opposition, politician, precognition, precondition, premonition, preposition, prohibition, proposition, recognition, repetition, reposition, requisition, statistician, superstition.

SURPRISING RHYMING:
[2] **Dishing**, fishing, phishing, squishing, swishing, wishing.
Dissing, hissing, kissing, missing.
Arisen, christen, criticism, glisten, imprison, isn't, listen, prison, rhythm, risen, vision.
Fizzing, frizzing, quizzing, whizzing.
Pigeon, religion, smidgen, stool-pigeon.
Diction, fiction, friction.
Billion, million, civilian, pavilion, trillion, vermillion.
Bitching, ditching, hitching, itching, pitching, snitching, stitching, switching, twitching.
Cinching, clinching, flinching, inching, lynching, pinching.
Binging, cringing, hinging, infringing, singeing, twinging, unhinging.
Convincing, evincing, mincing, wincing.
Driven, forbidden, given, hidden, ridden.

Chicken, quicken, sicken, stricken, thicken.
Bitten, kitten, mitten, smitten, written.
[3] Collision, decision, derision, division, envision, incision, precision, provision.
Efficient, proficient, sufficient.
Addiction, affliction, conviction, eviction, prediction, restriction.
Description, inscription, prescription, subscription, transcription.

3.1.146 "--ishent" (as in "efficient")
[3] efficient, proficient, sufficient.

SURPRISING RHYMING:
[2] **Emission**, magician, mission, musician, titian.
Arisen, glisten, imprison, isn't, listen, prison, rhythm, risen, vision.
Diction, fiction, kitchen, friction.
Dishing, fishing, phishing, squishing, swishing, wishing.
Bristle, gristle, missal, missile, thistle, whistle.
Figment, indignant, malignant, pigment.
[3] Assistant, consistent, distant, existent, insistent, persistent, reminiscent, resistant.
Initial, judicial, official, prejudicial, unofficial.
Addition, admission, ambition, audition, condition, edition, emission, fruition, ignition, magician, musician, nutrition, omission, optician, petition, permission, physician, position, remission, rendition, submission, suspicion, tradition, transition, transmission, tuition.
Collision, decision, derision, division, envision, incision, precision, provision, revision.
[4] Abolition, acquisition, ammunition, apparition, competition, composition, definition, demolition, dietician, electrician, exhibition, expedition, imposition, inhibition, intuition, inquisition, malnutrition, opposition, politician, premonition, prohibition, proposition, recognition, repetition, reposition, requisition, superstition.

3.1.147 "--isher" (as in "wisher")
[2] fisher, fissure, wisher.
[3+] brandisher, embellisher, extinguisher, finisher, flourisher, furbisher, furnisher, kingfisher, languisher, militia, nourisher, perisher, polisher, publisher, punisher, ravisher, vanquisher, well-wisher.

SURPRISING RHYMING:
[2] **Hitcher**, picture, pitcher, richer, stitcher, switcher, twitcher.
Scissor, fizzer, hisser, kisser, quizzer, reminiscer, whizzer.
Dimmer, glimmer, primmer, shimmer, simmer, skimmer, slimmer, swimmer, trimmer.
Dinner, grinner, inner, sinner, skinner, spinner, thinner, winner.
Differ, giver, liver, river, shiver, sliver, sniffer, stiffer, quiver.
Bigger, digger, figure, rigour/rigor (U.S.), snigger, trigger, vigour/vigor (U.S.).
Bicker, flicker, kicker, knicker, licker, liquor, nicker, picker, quicker, sicker, slicker, snicker, sticker, thicker, ticker, vicar, whicker, wicker.
Fixture, hipster, minster, mixture, scripture, spinster, tipster, trickster.
Blister, crisper, mister, sister, trickster, twister, vista, whisper.
Midwinter, printer, splinter, sprinter, squinter, winter.
[3] Banister, barista, barrister, canister, chorister, forester, minister, resistor, sinister, sob-sister, stepsister, transistor.
Aquiver, deliver, downriver, forgiver, upriver.
Beginner, breadwinner, examiner, foreigner, mariner, phenomena, prizewinner, stamina.
Electronica, erotica, exotica, frolicker, harmonica, lip-syncer, replica, mimicker, moniker, picnicker, trafficker.

3.1.148 "--ishing" (as in "wishing")
[2] dishing, fishing, phishing, squishing, swishing, wishing.

SURPRISING RHYMING:
[2] **Emission**, fission, intermission, magician, mission, musician.
Dissing, hissing, kissing, missing.

Fizzing, frizzing, quizzing, whizzing.
Cinching, clinching, flinching, inching, lynching, pinching.
Bewitching, bitching, ditching, hitching, itching, pitching, snitching, stitching, switching, twitching, witching.
Listing, misting, twisting.
Drifting, gifting, lifting, rifting, shifting, sifting.
Affixing, fixing, mixing, nixing.
[3] Convincing, evincing, mincing, wincing.
Efficient, proficient, sufficient.
Addition, admission, ambition, audition, condition, edition, emission, fruition, ignition, magician, musician, nutrition, omission, optician, petition, permission, physician, position, remission, rendition, submission, suspicion, tradition, transition, transmission, tuition.
Assisting, consisting, existing, insisting, persisting, resisting.

3.1.149 "--ishus" (as in "vicious")
ambitious, auspicious, delicious, fictitious, inauspicious, judicious, malicious, nutritious, suspicious, vicious.

SURPRISING RHYMING:
[2] Dishes, fishes, squishes, swishes, wishes.
Bridges, fridges, midges, ridges.
Bitches, breeches, britches, ditches, hitches, itches, niches, pitches, riches, snitches, stitches, switches, twitches, witches, which is.
Hisses, kisses, misses, Mrs., this is.
Business, citrus, illness, fitness, witness.
Quickest, sickest, thickest.
Elixirs, fixers, mixers, pictures.
Cinches, clinches, finches, fitness, flinches, inches, lynches, pinches, winches, witness.
Convinces, evinces, glimpses, minces, princes, rinses, winces.

3.1.150 "--issing" (as in "kissing")
[2] dissing, hissing, kissing, missing.

SURPRISING RHYMING:
[2] Dishing, fishing, phishing, squishing, swishing, wishing.
Fission, intermission, magician, mission, musician, titian.
Fizzing, frizzing, quizzing, whizzing.
Christen, criticism, glisten, isn't, listen, rhythm, vision.
Fitting, hitting, knitting, quitting, sitting, slitting, spitting, splitting.
Bitten, kitten, mitten, smitten, written.
Chipping, clipping, dipping, dripping, flipping, gripping, nipping, ripping, shipping, sipping, skipping, slipping, snipping, stripping, tipping, tripping, unzipping, zipping.
Bidding, forbidding, kidding, outbidding, ridding, skidding.
Grinning, pinning, sinning, skinning, spinning, thinning, winning.
Bringing, clinging, flinging, pinging, ringing, singing, slinging, springing, stinging, stringing, swinging, winging, wringing.
Billing, chilling, filling, killing, spilling, swilling, thrilling, tilling, willing.
Giving, driven, forgiving, living, misgiving, thanksgiving, unforgiving.
Listing, misting, twisting.
Affixing, diction, fiction, fixing, friction, kitchen, mixing, nixing.
Bitching, ditching, hitching, itching, pitching, snitching, stitching, switching, twitching.
Chiseling, drizzling, fizzling, sizzling, whistling.
Drifting, gifting, lifting, rifting, shifting, sifting, sixteen, sniffing.
Clicking, flicking, kicking, licking, picking, pricking, ticking, tricking.
[3] Convincing, evincing, glimpsing, mincing, wincing.
Efficient, proficient, sufficient.
Assisting, consisting, existing, insisting, persisting, resisting.
Addiction, affliction, conviction, depiction, eviction, infliction, prediction, restriction.

*

3.1.151 "--issit" (as in "illicit")
[3] elicit, explicit, illicit, implicit, solicit.

SURPRISING RHYMING:
[2] **Biscuit**, limit, minute, misfit, outfit, outwit, permit, snippet, spirit, sunlit, tidbit, transmit, unfit, visit, vivid.
Hisses, kisses, misses, Mrs., this is, vicious.
Digit, fidget, legit, midget, pivot, widget.
Civic, clinic, critic, cynic, gimmick, lyric, matchstick, mimic, mimicked, mystic, mythic, physics, rhythmic, traffic.
Listed, misted, twisted.
Cricket, picket, snippet, stick it, thicket, ticket, wicked, wicket.
Glisten, dissing, hissing, kissing, listen, missing, prison.
[3] **Exhibit,** inhibit, prohibit, speed limit.
Artistic, ballistic, linguistic, realistic, sadistic, simplistic, stylistic.
Horrific, pacific, prolific, specific, terrific.
Acquitted, admitted, committed, dimwitted, fitted, half-witted, knitted, omitted, outwitted, permitted, quick-witted, submitted, transmitted.
Assisted, blacklisted, consisted, existed, insisted, persisted, predicted, resisted, tight-fisted, two-fisted, unlisted, untwisted.
Dismissive, permissive, submissive.

[3.1.152 "--isky" (as in "risky")
[2] frisky, risky, whiskey, whisky.

SURPRISING RHYMING:
[2] **Briskly**, hickey, icky, kinky, mickey, milky, picky, pinkie, pinky, quickie, sickie, silky, slinky, sticky, tricky, whiskey/whisky, wiki.
Guilty, milky, minty, misty, silky, simply, sixty, swiftie, thrifty, distinctly, succinctly.
Fifty, nifty, shifty, thrifty.
Prickly, quickly, slickly, tickly, thickly.
Busy, Dixie, dizzy, fizzy, flimsy, frisbee, frizzy, history, kiss me, mystery, tizzy, whimsy.
Chippy, crispy, drippy, hippie, lippy, nippy, trippy, yippee, zippy.
[3] **Gravity,** nudity, oddity, quality, sanity, self-pity, vanity.
[4] **Ability,** agility, anxiety, civility, equality, facility, fertility, fragility, futility, hostility, humanity, humidity, humility, mobility, nitty-gritty, nobility, sobriety, society, stability, stupidity, tranquillity/tranquility (U.S.), utility, variety, virility.
[5] **Liability,** responsibility, usability, versatility, viability, volatility.

3.1.153 "--istence" (as in "resistance")
[3] assistance, distance, existence, insistence, persistence, resistance, subsistence.

SURPRISING RHYMING:
[2] **Listen(ed)**, listless, mistress, riddance, twisted, twisting, vicious.
[3] **Assistant**, commitment, consistent, distant, delinquent, existent, equipment, insistent, persistent, reminiscent, resilient, resistant.
Admittance, competence, hesitance, importance, remittance, reminiscence, significance.
Allegiance, ambivalence, belligerence, brilliance, deliverance, deviance, difference, diligence, indolence, inheritance, insolence, innocence, magnificence, reminiscence, penitence, reticence.
[4] **Inconsistent**, nonexistent, reminiscent.

3.1.154 "--istent" (as in "persistent")
[3] assistant, consistent, distant, existent, inconsistent, insistent, nonexistent, persistent, resistant.

SURPRISING RHYMING:
[2] **Figment**, fitment, instant, pigment, shipment, system.
[3] **Assistance**, distance, existence, insistence, instance, persistence, resistance.

Brilliant, different, indignant, malignant.
Commitment, delinquent, equipment, resilient.
Deficient, efficient, magician, proficient, sufficient.

3.1.155 "--isted" (as in "twisted")
[2] listed, misted, twisted.
[3] assisted, blacklisted, close-fisted, consisted, enlisted, existed, insisted, persisted, predicted, resisted, subsisted, tight-fisted, two-fisted, unlisted, untwisted.

SURPRISING RHYMING:
[2] **Biscuit,** limit, minute, misfit, outfit, outwit, permit, spirit, sunlit, transmit, unfit, visit.
Drifted, frigid, gifted, lifted, liquid, rigid, scripted, shifted, sifted, vivid.
Jilted, kilted, lilted, quilted, silted, stilted, tilted, wicked, wilted.
Glisten, listen, prison.
Dinted, glinted, hinted, minted, printed, splinted, sprinted, squinted, tinted, whiz kid.
Civic, clinic, critic, cynic, lipstick, lyric, matchstick, mimic, mystic, mythic, traffic.
[3] **Acquitted,** admitted, committed, dimwitted, fitted, knitted, omitted, outwitted, permitted, quick-witted, spirited, submitted.
Dismissive, emissive, missive, permissive, submissive.
Addicted, afflicted, conflicted, convicted, depicted, evicted, predicted, restricted.

3.1.156 "--ister" (as in "sister")
[2] blister, crisper, glister, lister, mister, sister, twister, vista, whisper.
[3] administer, assister, banister, barista, barrister, canister, chorister, enlister, forester, harvester, minister, register, resister, resistor, sinister, sob-sister, stepsister, transistor.

SURPRISING RHYMING:
[2] **Drifter,** grifter, lifter, shifter, sifter, snifter, swifter.
Listed, misted, twisted.
Hitcher, picture, pitcher, richer, snitcher, stricture, switcher, twitcher.
Elixir, fixer, mixer, sixer, spritzer.
Fixture, hipster, minster, mixture, scripture, spinster, tipster, trickster.
Clincher, flincher, pincher, wincher.
Fisher, fissure, scissor, fizzer, hisser, kisser, quizzer, reminiscer, whizzer, wisher.
Giver, liver, mirror, river, shiver, sliver, quiver.
Bicker, flicker, kicker, knicker, licker, liquor, picker, quicker, sicker, slicker, snicker, sticker, thicker, ticker, vicar, victor, whicker, wicker.
Bigger, figure, rigour/rigor (U.S.), snigger, trigger, vigour/vigor (U.S.).
Baby-sitter, bitter, critter, fitter, flitter, fritter, glitter, hitter, jitter, knitter, litter, pitta, quitter, sitter, splitter, titter, twitter.
Blinker, drinker, pinker, sinker, stinker, thinker, tinker, winker, freethinker, headshrinker.
[3] **Creditor,** editor, embitter, housesitter, janitor, Jupiter, monitor, transmitter, visitor.
Assisted, blacklisted, consisted, existed, insisted, persisted, predicted, resisted, tight-fisted, two-fisted, unlisted, untwisted.

3.1.157 "--istic" (as in "stylistic")
[3] artistic, ballistic, holistic, linguistic, realistic, sadistic, simplistic, statistic, stylistic.
[4] altruistic, chauvinistic, euphemistic, fatalistic, futuristic, hedonistic, jingoistic, journalistic, naturalistic, optimistic, pessimistic, realistic, unrealistic, voyeuristic.
[5] anachronistic, antagonistic, characteristic, idealistic, materialistic, opportunistic, ritualistic, surrealistic, uncharacteristic.

SURPRISING RHYMING:
[2] **Civic,** clinic, critic, cynic, gimmick, lyric, matchstick, mimic, mimicked, mystic, mythic, physics, rhythmic, traffic.
Broomstick, chopstick, drumstick, heartsick, homesick, lipstick, lovesick, seasick.
Addict, conflict, contradict, convict, depict, evict, predict, restrict.
Cricket, picket, stick it, thicket, ticket, wicket.
[3] **Horrific,** pacific, prolific, specific, terrific.

Candlestick, heretic, limerick, lunatic, maverick, politic, rhetoric, walking-stick.
Ballistics, linguistics, logistics, statistics.
Elicit, explicit, illicit, implicit, solicit.
Exhibit, inhibit, prohibit.
Addicted, afflicted, conflicted, convicted, evicted, predicted, restricted.
[4] **Colorific**, hieroglyphic, non-specific, scientific.

3.1.158 "--istics" (as in "statistics")
[3] ballistics, linguistics, logistics, statistics.

SURPRISING RHYMING:
[2] **Clinics**, critics, cynics, gimmicks, lyrics, matchsticks, mimics, mystics, physics.
Broomsticks, chopsticks, drumsticks, lipsticks, toothpicks.
Addicts, conflicts, contradicts, convicts, evicts, predicts, restricts.
Crickets, pickets, thickets, tickets, wickets.
Biscuits, limits, minutes, misfits, outfits, outwits, permits, spirits, transmits, visits.
Listed, misted, twisted.
[3] **Candlesticks**, heretics, limericks, lunatics, mavericks, politics.
Exhibits, inhibits, prohibits, specifics.
Assisted, blacklisted, consisted, existed, insisted, persisted, predicted, resisted, tight-fisted, two-fisted, unlisted, untwisted.
[4] **Analytics**, hieroglyphics.

3.1.159 "--isting (as in "twisting")
[2] listing, misting, twisting.
[3] assisting, blacklisting, consisting, enlisting, existing, insisting, persisting, resisting, subsisting, untwisting.

SURPRISING RHYMING:
[2] **Listed**, misted, twisted.
Dissing, fizzing, hissing, kissing, missing, quizzing, whizzing.
Dishing, fishing, phishing, squishing, swishing, wishing.
Affixing, fixing, mixing, nixing.
Frisking, risking, whisking.
Convincing, evincing, mincing, wincing.
Cinching, clinching, flinching, inching, lynching, pinching, winching.
Bitching, ditching, hitching, itching, pitching, snitching, stitching, switching, twitching.
Drifting, gifting, lifting, rifting, shifting, sifting, sixteen.
Chiseling, drizzling, fizzling, sizzling, whistling.
Bringing, clinging, flinging, pinging, ringing, singing, slinging, springing, stinging, stringing, swinging, winging, wringing.
Fitting, hitting, knitting, quitting, sitting, slitting, spitting, splitting.
Chipping, clipping, dipping, dripping, flipping, gripping, nipping, ripping, shipping, sipping, skipping, slipping, snipping, stripping, tipping, tripping, unzipping, whipping.
[3] **Acquitting**, admitting, emitting, omitting, permitting, remitting, side-splitting, transmitting, unremitting, unwitting.
Giving, forgiving, living, misgiving, thanksgiving, unforgiving.

3.1.160 "--ision" (as in "vision")
collision, decision, derision, division, envision, incision, precision, provision, vision.

SURPRISING RHYMING:
[2] **Emission**, fission, intermission, magician, mission, musician, prism, schism.
Dishing, fishing, phishing, squishing, swishing, wishing.
Arisen, driven, forgiven, given, glisten, imprison, prison, risen.
Bitten, forbidden, didn't, glisten, hidden, isn't, listen, rhythm, vision.
Diction, fiction, kitchen, friction.
Pigeon, religion, smidgen, stool-pigeon.
Didn't, giving, living, ribbon, stiffen, villain, written.

[3] Addition, admission, ambition, audition, condition, edition, emission, fruition, ignition, magician, musician, nutrition, omission, optician, petition, permission, physician, position, remission, rendition, submission, suspicion, tradition, transition, tuition.
Efficient, proficient, sufficient.
[4] Abolition, acquisition, ammunition, apparition, competition, composition, definition, demolition, dietician, electrician, exhibition, expedition, imposition, inhibition, intuition, inquisition, malnutrition, opposition, politician, premonition, prohibition, proposition, recognition, repetition, reposition, requisition, superstition.

3.1.161 "--iskier" (as in "riskier")
[3] friskier, riskier.

SURPRISING RHYMING:
[3] **Busier**, crispier, dizzier, fizzier, frizzier.
Kinkier, milkier, niftier, shiftier, silkier, slinkier, thriftier, trickier.
Electronica, erotica, exotica, harmonica, lip-syncer, replica, trafficker.
Administer, banister, barista, barrister, canister, chorister, forester, minister, register, resistor, sinister, sob-sister, stepsister, transistor.
Chillier, drizzlier, frillier, grizzlier, hillier, sillier.

3.1.162 "--iskiest" (as in "riskiest")
[3] friskiest, riskiest.

SURPRISING RHYMING:
[3] **Grittiest,** prettiest, wittiest.
Busiest, crispiest, dizziest, fizziest, frizziest.
Kinkiest, milkiest, shiftiest, silkiest, skinniest, slinkiest, stickiest, thriftiest, trickiest.
Chilliest, drizzliest, frilliest, grizzliest, hilliest, silliest.

3.1.163 "--istory" (as in "mystery")
[3] history, mystery.

SURPRISING RHYMING:
[3] **Bitterly**, blistery, glittery, jittery, sisterly, whispery.
Ancestry, archery, artistry, bakery, battery, bigotry, binary, blackberry, blubbery, blueberry, blustery, brasserie, bravery, brewery, bribery, burglary, calorie, carpentry, carvery, cavalry, celery, century, chemistry, chicory, chivalry, Christmas tree, colliery, contrary, devilry, diary, dietary, disagree, dithery, doddery, drudgery, dungaree, duty-free, eatery, enquiry, estuary, expiry, factory, fakery, feathery, filigree, finery, fishery, flattery, fluttery, forestry, forgery, gallery, geometry, gimmickry, glittery, greenery, grocery, history, imagery, injury, inquiry, ivory, jamboree, jewellery/jewelry (U.S.), jittery, leathery, lingerie, lottery, luxury, memory, mercury, misery, momentary, monastery, mystery, nursery, obituary, obligatory, pageantry, pedigree, perjury, pillory, pleasantry, poetry, pottery, primary, priory, quivery, referee, revelry, reverie, rivalry, robbery, rockery, rosary, rubbery, salary, sanctuary, savagery, savory, scenery, sensory, shimmery, shivery, silvery, slavery, slippery, sorcery, sugary, surgery, tapestry, thundery, treachery, trickery, victory, wintery, wizardry.
[4] Accessory, adultery, artillery, cautionary, cemetery, compulsory, confectionery, conciliatory, constabulary, contemporary, customary, debauchery, delivery, dictionary, directory, discovery, distillery, elementary, embroidery, explanatory, exploratory, hunky-dory, idolatry, imaginary, incendiary, infirmary, inflammatory, judiciary, laboratory, legendary, literary, machinery, mandatory, mercenary, military, missionary, necessary, ordinary, patisserie, perfumery, preliminary, psychiatry, publicity, reactionary, recovery, secretary, secondary, simplicity, skullduggery, solitary, stationary, stationery, temporary, territory, tomfoolery, upholstery, visionary, vocabulary.

3.1.164 "--it" (as in "admit")
[1] bit, fit, grit, hit, it, kit, knit, lit, pit, quit, skit, slit, spit, split, wit.
[2] acquit, admit, armpit, cockpit, commit, emit, habit, misfit, moonlit, omit, outfit,

outwit, remit, spirit, submit, sunlit, tidbit, transmit, unfit.
[3] counterfeit, definite, exquisite, favourite/favorite (U.S.), hypocrite, infinite, opposite.

SURPRISING RHYMING:
[1] **Bib**, crib, dib, fib, glib, lib, nib, rib(s), sparerib, squib.
Bid, did, grid, id, kid, lid, quid, skid, slid, squid.
Drift, gift, lift, miffed, shift, sniffed, swift, thrift, whiffed.
Big, dig, fig, gig, jig, pig, prig, rig, swig, twig, wig.
Brick, chick, click, crick, dick, flick, hick, kick, lick, nick, pick, prick, quick, sic, sick, slick, stick, thick, tic, tick, trick, wick.
Blip, chip, clip, dip, drip, flip, grip, hip, kip, lip, nip, pip, quip, rip, ship, sip, skip, slip, snip, strip, tip, trip, whip, yip, zip.
Dissed, fist, gist, hissed, kissed, list, midst, missed, mist, pissed, tryst, twist, wrist.
Built, gilt, guilt, jilt, kilt, lilt, quilt, silt, spilt, stilt, tilt, wilt.
[2] **Adlib**, amid, eyelid, forbid, outbid, rapid, undid.
Gearshift, makeshift, snowdrift, spendthrift, uplift.
Broomstick, chopstick, drumstick, heartsick, homesick, lipstick, lovesick, seasick.
Airship, catnip, courtship, equip, flagship, friendship, hardship, horsewhip, kinship, outstrip, steamship, township, warship, worship.
Assist, consist, dismissed, enlist, exist, insist, persist, resist.
Addict, afflict, constrict, convict, evict, predict, restrict.
[3] **Elicit**, explicit, illicit, implicit, solicit.
Excited, invalid, pyramid, overbid, overdid, underbid.
Candlestick, heretic, limerick, lunatic, maverick, politic, rhetoric, walking-stick.
Battleship, fellowship, horsemanship, leadership, membership, partnership, penmanship, scholarship, sportsmanship, workmanship.

3.1.165 "--itch" (as in "rich")
[1] bitch, ditch, glitch, hitch, itch, kitsch, niche, pitch, rich, snitch, stitch, switch, twitch, which, witch.
[2] bewitch, enrich, sales pitch, unhitch.

SURPRISING RHYMING:
[1] **Bitched**, ditched, hitched, itched, pitched, snitched, stitched, switched, twitched.
Bricks, chicks, fix, flicks, hicks, kicks, licks, mix, nix, picks, pix, pricks, six, slicks, sticks, tics, ticks, tricks, wicks.
Bridge, fridge, midge, ridge, smidge.
Cinch, clinch, finch, flinch, Grinch, inch, lynch, pinch, winch.
Dish, fish, squish, swish, wish.
Blimps, glimpse, imps, limps, pimps, shrimps, skimps, wimps.
Convince, evince, mince, prince, rinse, since, wince.
[2] **Bewitched**, enriched, snitched, switched, twitched, unstitched.
Affix, crucifix, intermix, matchsticks, prefix, suffix.
Bondage, cabbage, carnage, dosage, hostage, language, message, package, postage, sausage, shortage, storage, usage, voyage.
Anguish, blueish, brownish, catfish, crayfish, crawfish, devilfish, dogfish, feverish, flourish, goldfish, greenish, jellyfish, kingfish, nourish, reddish, selfish, shellfish, starfish, swordfish, yellowish.

3.1.166 "--itched" (as in "hitched")
[1] bitched, ditched, hitched, itched, pitched, snitched, stitched, switched, twitched.
[2] bewitched, enriched, unhitched, snitched, re-stitched, switched, twitched, unstitched.

SURPRISING RHYMING:
[1] **Bitch**, ditch, glitch, hitch, itch, kitsch, niche, pitch, rich, snitch, stitch, switch, twitch, which, witch.
Bricks, chicks, fix, flicks, hicks, kicks, licks, mix, nix, picks, pix, pricks, six, slicks, sticks, tics, ticks, tricks, wicks.
Bridge, fridge, midge, ridge, smidge.
Cinch, clinch, finch, flinch, Grinch, inch, lynch, pinch, winch.

Dish, fish, squish, swish, wish.
Blimps, glimpse, imps, limps, pimps, shrimps, skimps, wimps.
Convince, evince, mince, prince, rinse, since, wince.
[2] **Affix**, bewitch, enrich, intermix, matchsticks, prefix, suffix, unhitch.
Bondage, cabbage, carnage, dosage, hostage, language, message, package, postage, sausage, shortage, storage, usage, voyage.
Anguish, blueish, brownish, feverish, flourish, goldfish, greenish, jellyfish, nourish, reddish, selfish, shellfish, starfish, yellowish.

3.1.167 "--ith" (as in "myth")
[1] myth, pith, smith, with.
[2] forthwith, goldsmith, gunsmith, herewith, locksmith, therewith, wordsmith.
[3] coppersmith, metalsmith, silversmith.

SURPRISING RHYMING:
[1] **If,** cliff, miff, riff, skiff, sniff, stiff, tiff, whiff.
Drift, gift, lift, miffed, rift, shift, shrift, sniffed, swift, thrift, whiffed.
Give, live, sieve, spiv.
Bliss, diss, hiss, kiss, miss, piss, sis, 'tis, this.
[2] **Active**, captive, festive, forgive, massive, misgive, missive, motive, native, octave, olive, outlive, passive, pensive, relive.
Adrift, airlift, facelift, gearshift, makeshift, nightshift, snowdrift, spendthrift, uplift.
Abyss, amiss, bodice, chalice, coppice, dismiss, gratis, haggis, hospice, hubris, jaundice, justice, malice, Memphis, novice, office, palace, Paris, remiss, service, solstice, surface.
[3] **Abrasive**, abusive, adhesive, aggressive, compulsive, conclusive, conducive, corrosive, decisive, defensive, depressive, divisive, elusive, emotive, evasive, excessive, exclusive, expensive, expletive, explosive, expressive, impassive, impressive, impulsive, incisive, inclusive, intensive, intrusive, narrative, negative, obsessive, offensive, oppressive, percussive, permissive, persuasive, possessive, repulsive, responsive, sedative, submissive, subversive, talkative.
Accomplice, cowardice, edifice, emphasis, genesis, kinesis, liquorice/licorice (U.S.), nemesis, orifice, prejudice, reminisce.

3.1.168 "--itcher" (as in "richer")
[2] ditcher, hitcher, picture, pitcher, richer, snitcher, stitcher, stricture, switcher, twitcher.

SURPRISING RHYMING:
[2] **Clincher**, flincher, pincher, wincher.
Drifter, grifter, lifter, shifter, shoplifter, sifter, swifter, weightlifter.
Blister, crisper, lister, mister, sister, trickster, twister, vista, whisper, wisher.
Elixir, fisher, fissure, fixer, mixer, sixer, spritzer.
Fixture, hipster, minster, mixture, scripture, spinster, tipster, trickster.
Scissor, fizzer, hisser, kisser, quizzer, reminiscer, whizzer.
[3] **Contradictor**, depicter, evictor, inflictor, predictor, victor.
Administer, banister, barista, barrister, canister, chorister, forester, minister, register, resistor, sinister, sob-sister, stepsister, transistor.
Brandisher, finisher, flourisher, furnisher, kingfisher, militia, nourisher, perisher, polisher, publisher, punisher, vanquisher, well-wisher.
[4] **Expenditure**, furniture, literature, miniature, portraiture, signature, temperature.

3.1.169 "--itches" (as in "riches")
[2] bitches, breeches, britches, ditches, hitches, itches, niches, pitches, riches, snitches, stitches, switches, twitches, witches.

SURPRISING RHYMING:
[2] **Dishes**, fishes, squishes, swishes, wishes.
Bridges, fridges, midges, ridges.
Binges, cringes, fringes, hinges, singes, tinges, twinges.

Convinces, evinces, glimpses, minces, princes, rinses, winces.
Cinches, clinches, inches, lynches, pinches, witness.
Hisses, kisses, misses, Mrs., princess, this is.
Elixirs, fixers, mixers, pictures.
[3] **Infringes**, syringe, unhinges.
Ambitious, auspicious, delicious, fictitious, inauspicious, judicious, malicious, nutritious, suspicious, vicious.

3.1.170 "--itching" (as in "switching")
[2] bitching, ditching, hitching, itching, pitching, snitching, stitching, switching, twitching, witching.

SURPRISING RHYMING:
[2] **Cinching**, clinching, flinching, inching, lynching, pinching.
Affixing, fixing, listing, misting, mixing, nixing, twisting.
Dishing, fishing, phishing, squishing, swishing, wishing.
Diction, fiction, kitchen, friction.
Emission, fission, intermission, magician, mission, musician, titian.
Binging, cringing, hinging, infringing, singeing, twinging, unhinging.
Dissing, hissing, kissing, missing.
[3] **Averaging**, bridging, leveraging, messaging, packaging, voyaging.
Conflicting, convicting, depicting, inflicting, predicting, restricting.
Addiction, affliction, conviction, depiction, prediction, restriction.
Description, inscription, prescription, subscription, transcription.
Assisting, consisting, existing, insisting, persisting, resisting.
Convincing, evincing, mincing, wincing.
Addition, admission, ambition, audition, condition, edition, emission, fruition, ignition, magician, musician, nutrition, omission, optician, petition, permission, physician, position, remission, rendition, submission, suspicion, tradition, transition, transmission, tuition.
Efficient, proficient, sufficient.

3.1.171 "--itted (as in "outwitted")
acquitted, admitted, committed, dimwitted, emitted, fitted, half-witted, knitted, omitted, outwitted, permitted, quick-witted, spirited, submitted, transmitted, unfitted.

SURPRISING RHYMING:
[2] **Drifted**, frigid, gifted, lifted, rigid, pitied, scripted, shifted, sifted.
Listed, liquid, livid, misted, timid, twisted, vivid, wicked.
Jilted, kilted, lilted, quilted, silted, stilted, tilted, wilted.
Dinted, glinted, hinted, minted, printed, sprinted, squinted, tinted.
Cricket, picket, snippet, stick it, thicket, ticket, wicket.
Fitting, hitting, knitting, quitting, sitting, slitting, spitting, splitting.
Bitten, kitten, mitten, smitten, written.
[3] **Addicted**, afflicted, conflicted, constricted, convicted, depicted, distinctive, evicted, instinctive, predicted, restricted.
Elicit, explicit, illicit, implicit, solicit.
Flea-bitten, frostbitten, rewritten, unwritten.
Assisted, blacklisted, consisted, existed, insisted, persisted, predicted, resisted, tight-fisted, two-fisted, unlisted, untwisted.

3.1.172 "--itter (as in "bitter")
[2] bitter, critter, fitter, flitter, fritter, glitter, gritter, hitter, jitter, knitter, litter, pitta, quitter, sitter, splitter, titter, twitter.
[3] auditor, committer, creditor, cricketer, editor, embitter, emitter, housesitter, janitor, Jupiter, monitor, outfitter, pinch-hitter, rail-splitter, remitter, submitter, transmitter, visitor.
[4] baby-sitter, barometer, competitor, counterfeiter, depositor, diameter, exhibitor, interpreter, mileometer/milometer (U.S.), parameter, perimeter, solicitor, speedometer, thermometer.

SURPRISING RHYMING:
[2] **Bicker**, flicker, kicker, knicker, licker, liquor, picker, quicker, sicker, slicker, snicker, sticker, thicker, ticker, vicar, whicker, wicker.
Bigger, digger, figure, jigger, ligger, rigger, rigour/rigor (U.S.), snigger, trigger, vigour/vigor (U.S.).
Bidder, consider, kidder.
Chipper, clipper, dipper, flipper, hipper, kipper, nipper, ripper, shipper, sipper, skipper, slipper, stripper, tipper, tripper, zipper.
Chiller, filler, griller, killer, miller, pillar, spiller, thriller, tiller, villa.
Dinner, grinner, inner, sinner, skinner, spinner, thinner, winner.
[3] **Day-tripper**, disfigure, gold-digger, gravedigger, vinegar.
Caterpillar, flotilla, gorilla, guerilla, man-killer, painkiller, spine-chiller, vanilla, weedkiller.
Beginner, breadwinner, foreigner, phenomena, prizewinner, retina, stamina, submariner.
Administer, banister, barista, barrister, canister, chorister, forester, minister, register, resistor, sinister, sob-sister, stepsister, transistor.
Character, limiter, perimeter, scimitar, trumpeter.

3.1.173 "--ittee" (as in "pretty")
[2] bitty, chitty, city, ditty, gritty, kitty, pity, pretty, witty.
[3] ability, agility, anxiety, committee, equality, gravity, hostility, humanity, humility, nitty-gritty, humidity, notoriety, nudity, oddity, quality, responsibility, sanity, self-pity, sobriety, society, stupidity, vanity, variety.

SURPRISING RHYMING:
[2] **Diddy**, giddy, kiddie, midi.
Busy, dizzy, fizzy, frizzy, tizzy.
Dixie, glitzy, kissy, missy, prissy, ritzy, sissy.
Chippy, crispy, dippy, drippy, hippie, lippy, nippy, snippy, trippy, whippy, yippie, zippy.
Hickey, icky, kinky, mickey, milky, picky, pinkie, pinky, quickie, sickie, silky, slinky, sticky, tricky, whiskey/whisky.
Filly, frilly, hilly, hillbilly, silly, willy, rockabilly.
Fifty, iffy, jiffy, miffy, nifty, pithy, shifty, sniffy, spiffy, smithy, thrifty.
Guilty, minty, misty, nasty, nicety, nifty, shifty, sixty, swiftie, thrifty.
Cine, gimme, lemme, mini, ninny, shimmy, shinny, skinny, spinney, tinny, whinny.
Burly, curly, early, hurly-burly, pearly, surly, swirly, twirly, whirly.

3.1.174 "--aritee" (as in "charity")
[3] charity, clarity, parity.
[4] barbarity, hilarity, polarity, vulgarity.
[5+] familiarity, irregularity, peculiarity, popularity, regularity, similarity, solidarity.

SURPRISING RHYMING:
[3] **Amnesty**, casualty, certainty, chastity, confetti, density, deputy, devotee, dignity, dynasty, entity, faculty, fidgety, graffiti, gravity, guarantee, honesty, karate, liberty, majesty, modesty, nudity, oddity, penalty, piety, poverty, property, puberty, purity, quality, repartee, rickety, sanctity, sanctuary, sanity, scarcity, seventy, sovereignty, spaghetti, specialty, trinity, unity, uppity, vanity, velvety, warranty.
Bodily, family, fleur-de-lis, heavenly, homily, icily, jubilee, melancholy, miserly, readily.
Comedy, custody, jeopardy, melody, nobody, parody, perfidy, raggedy, remedy, rhapsody, somebody, subsidy, tragedy.
Agony, balcony, company, destiny, harmony, Houdini, irony, mutiny, symphony, tiffany, timpani, tyranny, villainy.
Ancestry, archery, artistry, bakery, battery, bigotry, binary, blackberry, blubbery, blueberry, blustery, brasserie, bravery, brewery, bribery, burglary, calorie, carpentry, carvery, cavalry, celery, century, chemistry, chicory, chivalry, Christmas tree, colliery, contrary, devilry, diary, dietary, disagree, dithery, doddery, drudgery, dungaree, duty-free, eatery, enquiry, estuary, expiry, factory, fakery, feathery, filigree, finery, fishery, flattery, fluttery, forestry, forgery, gallery, geometry, gimmickry, glittery, greenery, grocery, history, imagery, injury, inquiry, ivory, jamboree, jewellery/jewelry (U.S.), jittery,

leathery, lingerie, lottery, luxury, memory, mercury, misery, momentary, monastery, mystery, nursery, obituary, obligatory, pageantry, pedigree, perjury, pillory, pleasantry, poetry, pottery, primary, priory, quivery, referee, revelry, reverie, rivalry, robbery, rockery, rosary, rubbery, salary, sanctuary, savagery, savory, scenery, sensory, shimmery, shivery, silvery, slavery, slippery, sorcery, sugary, surgery, tapestry, thundery, treachery, trickery, victory, wintery, wizardry.
[4] Ability, agility, anxiety, equality, facility, fertility, fragility, futility, hostility, humanity, humidity, humility, mobility, nitty-gritty, nobility, sobriety, society, stability, stupidity, tranquillity/tranquility (U.S.), utility, variety, virility.
[5] Ambiguity, anonymity, continuity, familiarity, femininity, impropriety, ingenuity, irregularity, masculinity, notoriety, opportunity, peculiarity, popularity, regularity, serendipity, similarity, solidarity, spontaneity, uniformity.
Edibility, liability, responsibility, usability, versatility, viability, volatility.

3.1.175 "--itting" (as in "sitting")
[2] fitting, gritting, hitting, knitting, quitting, sitting, slitting, spitting, splitting.
[3] acquitting, admitting, emitting, omitting, permitting, remitting, side-splitting, transmitting, unremitting, unwitting.

SURPRISING RHYMING:
[2] Bitten, kitten, mitten, smitten, written.
Listing, misting, twisting.
Chipping, clipping, dipping, dripping, flipping, gripping, nipping, ripping, shipping, sipping, skipping, slipping, snipping, stripping, tipping, tripping, unzipping, whipping.
Chicken, clicking, flicking, kicking, licking, picking, pricking, stricken, ticking, tricking.
Blinking, clinking, drinking, hoodwinking, inking, linking, shrinking, sinking, slinking, stinking, syncing, thinking, winking.
Glinting, hinting, minting, printing, sprinting, squinting, tinting.
Jilting, lilting, quilting, silting, stilting, tilting, wilting.
Crimping, limping, pimping, primping, shrimping, skimping.
Digging, jigging, rigging, swigging.
Bidding, forbidding, kidding, outbidding, ridding, skidding.
Drifting, gifting, lifting, rifting, shifting, sifting, sixteen.
Bringing, clinging, flinging, pinging, ringing, singing, slinging, springing, stinging, stringing, swinging, winging, wringing.
Chilling, filling, killing, spilling, swilling, thrilling, tilling, willing.
Grinning, pinning, sinning, skinning, spinning, thinning, winning.
Affixing, fixing, mixing, nixing.
[3] Addicting, conflicting, convicting, depicting, evicting, inflicting, predicting, restricting.
Assisting, blacklisting, consisting, enlisting, existing, insisting, persisting, resisting.

3.1.176 "--ittle" (as in "little")
belittle, brittle, committal, hospital, it'll, little, skittle, spittle, whittle.

SURPRISING RHYMING:
[2] Bitten, didn't, kitten, mitten, smitten, written.
Fickle, nickel, pickle, prickle, ripple, tickle, tipple, trickle, triple.
Dribble, nibble, quibble, scribble, sibyl.
Crinkle, skillful, sprinkle, tinkle, twinkle, willful, winkle, wrinkle.
Bristle, chisel, drizzle, fizzle, frizzle, gristle, missal, missile, sizzle, swizzle, thistle, whistle.
Diddle, fiddle, griddle, idyll, middle, piddle, riddle, twiddle.
Giggle, jiggle, niggle, squiggle, wiggle, wriggle.
Jingle, mingle, shingle, signal, single, tingle.
Civil, drivel, shrivel, skiffle, sniffle, snivel, swivel, vigil.
Dimple, pimple, simple, wimple.
Dwindle, hymnal, kindle, rekindle, sinful, spindle, swindle.
[3] Initial, judicial, official, prejudicial, unofficial.

*

3.1.177 "--itten" (as in "kitten")
[2] bitten, kitten, mitten, smitten, written.
[3] flea-bitten, frostbitten, rewritten, unwritten.

SURPRISING RHYMING:
[2] **Fitting**, hitting, knitting, quitting, sitting, slitting, spitting, splitting.
Chicken, quicken, sicken, stricken, thicken.
Clicking, flicking, kicking, licking, picking, pricking, ticking, tricking.
Chipping, clipping, dipping, dripping, flipping, gripping, nipping, ripping, shipping, sipping, skipping, slipping, snipping, stripping, tipping, tripping, unzipping, whipping.
Digging, jigging, rigging, swigging.
Didn't, forbidden, glisten, hidden, isn't, listen, ribbon, ridden, risen.
Bidding, forbidding, kidding, outbidding, ridding, skidding.
Grinning, pinning, sinning, skinning, spinning, thinning, winning.
Dissing, hissing, kissing, missing.
Giving, driven, given, living, stiffen.
Belittle, brittle, committal, hospital, it'll, little, skittle, spittle, whittle.
[3] **Acquitting**, admitting, committing, emitting, omitting, permitting, remitting, side-splitting, transmitting, unremitting, unwitting.
Acquitted, admitted, committed, dimwitted, emitted, fitted, knitted, omitted, outwitted, permitted, quick-witted, submitted, transmitted.
Efficient, proficient, sufficient.
Forgiving, lawgiving, misgiving, outliving, thanksgiving, unforgiving.

3.1.178 "--itness" (as in "witness")
[2] fitness, witness.

SURPRISING RHYMING:
[2] **Business**, Christmas, illness, sickness, slickness, stiffness, stillness, sweetness, swiftness, thickness.
Biggest, fittest, hippest, richest, simplest, thinnest, witnessed.
Quickest, sickest, thickest.
Assist, consist, dismissed, enlist, exist, hit list, insist, persist, resist, subsist, untwist.
Grimace, listless, mistress, riddance, systems, vicious.
[3] **Activist**, anarchist, atheist, catalyst, columnist, communist, egotist, exorcist, fatalist, hobbyist, humourist/humorist (U.S.), hypnotist, journalist, moralist, motorist, novelist, optimist, organist, pacifist, pessimist, publicist, socialist, soloist, specialist, terrorist.
Ambitious, auspicious, delicious, fictitious, forgiveness, inauspicious, judicious, malicious, nutritious, religious, suspicious.

3.1.179 "--ittiest" (as in "prettiest")
[3] grittiest, prettiest, wittiest.

SURPRISING RHYMING:
[3] **Friskiest**, milkiest, prickliest, riskiest, sickliest, silkiest, stickiest, trickiest.
Filthiest, guiltiest, shiftiest, thriftiest, wealthiest.
Chilliest, hilliest, silliest.
Busiest, dizziest, fizziest, friskiest, frizziest, riskiest.
Activist, anarchist, atheist, catalyst, columnist, communist, egotist, exorcist, fatalist, humourist/humorist (U.S.), hypnotist, journalist, moralist, motorist, novelist, optimist, organist, pacifist, pessimist, publicist, socialist, soloist, specialist, terrorist.

3.1.180 "--ittingly" (as in "wittingly")
fittingly, unwittingly, wittingly.

SURPRISING RHYMING:
[3] **Critically**, cynically, explicitly, rhythmically, specifically, typically.
Consistently, distantly, insistently, instantly, persistently, resiliently.
Mimicry, ministry, misery, priory, reverie.

Distinctly, physically, quizzically, succinctly.
Fidgety, frigidly, rigidly, timidly, twistedly, vividly, wickedly.
Gossipy, recipe, slap-happy, syrupy/syrupy, therapy, unhappy.
Efficiently, proficiently, sufficiently.
Bruisingly, chillingly, grippingly, thrillingly, unwillingly, willingly.
Bitterly, chivalry, disagree, dithery, imagery, jittery, livery, pillory, quivery, shimmery, shivery, silvery, wizardry.
Bodily, family, fleur-de-lis, heavenly, homily, icily, jubilee, melancholy, miserly, readily.
Gossipy, recipe, slap-happy, syrupy/syrupy, therapy, unhappy.
[4] Ability, agility, anxiety, differently, equality, gravity, hostility, humanity, humility, humidity, nudity, oddity, quality, responsibility, sanity, self-pity, sobriety, society, stupidity, vanity, variety.
Artistically, distinctively, instinctively, linguistically, physically, quizzically, realistically, sadistically, statistically, stylistically.
Ambitiously, auspiciously, deliciously, fictitiously, inauspiciously, judiciously, maliciously, nutritiously, suspiciously, viciously.

3.1.181 "--iv" (as in "give")
[1] give, live, sieve, spiv.
[2] active, captive, festive, forgive, massive, misgive, missive, motive, native, octave, olive, outlive, passive, pensive, relive.
[3] abrasive, abusive, adhesive, aggressive, combative, compulsive, conclusive, conducive, convulsive, corrosive, decisive, defensive, depressive, divisive, effusive, elusive, emotive, evasive, excessive, exclusive, expansive, expensive, expletive, explosive, expressive, extensive, impassive, impressive, impulsive, incisive, inclusive, intensive, intrusive, narrative, negative, obsessive, offensive, oppressive, percussive, permissive, persuasive, pervasive, possessive, progressive, reclusive, repulsive, responsive, sedative, submissive, subversive, successive, talkative.
[4] apprehensive, comprehensive.

SURPRISING RHYMING:
[1] Myth, pith, smith, with.
If, cliff, miff, riff, skiff, sniff, stiff, tiff, whiff.
Drift, gift, lift, miffed, rift, shift, shrift, sniffed, swift, thrift, whiffed.
Bid, did, grid, id, kid, lid, lived, quid, skid, slid, squid.
[2] Amid, eyelid, forbid, outbid, rapid, undid.
Adrift, facelift, makeshift, nightshift, snowdrift, spendthrift, uplift.
[3] Excited, invalid, pyramid, overbid, overdid, underbid.

3.1.182 "--iven" (as in "driven")
[2] driven, given.

SURPRISING RHYMING:
[2] Forbidden, giving, hidden, living, ridden, stiffen.
Arisen, glisten, imprison, listen, prison, risen.
Bitten, kitten, mitten, smitten, written.
Didn't, forbidden, glisten, hidden, isn't, listen, ribbon, ridden, risen.
Chicken, quicken, sicken, stricken, thicken.
Pigeon, religion, smidgen, stool-pigeon.
Emission, fission, intermission, magician, mission, musician, titian, vision.
Beginning, grinning, pinning, sinning, spinning, thinning, winning.
Brimming, dimming, skimming, slimming, swimming, trimming.
Dishing, dissing, fishing, hissing, kissing, missing, phishing, swishing, wishing.
[3] Forgiving, misgiving, outliving, thanksgiving, unforgiving.
Collision, decision, derision, division, envision, incision, precision, provision, revision.
Efficient, proficient, sufficient.
Addition, admission, ambition, audition, condition, edition, emission, fruition, ignition, magician, musician, nutrition, omission, optician, petition, permission, physician, position, remission, rendition, submission, suspicion, tradition, transition, transmission, tuition.

3.1.183 "--ivver" (as in "river")
[2] giver, liver, river, shiver, sliver, quiver.
[3] aquiver, deliver, downriver, forgiver, upriver.

SURPRISING RHYMING:
[2] **Dimmer**, glimmer, primmer, shimmer, simmer, skimmer, slimmer, swimmer, trimmer.
Bitter, critter, fitter, flitter, fritter, glitter, gritter, hitter, jitter, knitter, litter, pitta, quitter, sitter, skitter, slitter, splitter, titter, twitter.
Chipper, clipper, dipper, flipper, hipper, kipper, nipper, ripper, shipper, sipper, skipper, slipper, stripper, tipper, tripper, zipper.
Bigger, digger, figure, rigour/rigor (U.S.), snigger, trigger, vigour/vigor (U.S.).
Bicker, flicker, kicker, knicker, licker, liquor, picker, quicker, sicker, slicker, snicker, sticker, thicker, ticker, vicar, whicker, wicker.
Bidder, consider, kidder.
Chiller, filler, griller, killer, miller, pillar, spiller, thriller, tiller, villa.
Dinner, grinner, inner, sinner, skinner, spinner, thinner, winner.
Midwinter, printer, splinter, sprinter, squinter, winter.
Blister, crisper, mister, sister, trickster, twister, vista, whisper.
Fisher, fissure, miss her, wisher.
Differ, dither, hither, slither, sniffer, stiffer, thither, whither, wither, with her, zither.
Scissor, fizzer, hisser, kisser, quizzer, reminiscer, whizzer.
[3] **Day-tripper**, disfigure, gold-digger, gravedigger, vinegar.
Beginner, Berliner, breadwinner, examiner, foreigner, mariner, milliner, phenomena, prizewinner, retina, stamina, submariner.

3.1.184 "--ivered" (as in "delivered")
delivered, quivered, shivered, slivered.

SURPRISING RHYMING:
[2] **Giver**, liver, river, shiver, sliver, quiver.
Glimmered, shimmered, simmered.
Blistered, flittered, frittered, glittered, littered, twittered, whispered.
Differed, dithered, figured, slithered, sniggered, triggered, withered.
Bickered, blinkered, flickered, stickered.
Blizzard, lizard, wizard.
[3] **Aquiver**, deliver, downriver, forgiver, upriver.
Bewildered, configured, considered, disfigured, lounge lizard.

3.1.185 "--ivid" (as in "vivid")
[2] chivvied, livid, vivid.

SURPRISING RHYMING:
[1] **Bid**, did, grid, id, kid, lid, quid, skid, slid, squid.
Bib, crib, dib, fib, glib, lib, nib, rib, squib.
[2] **Adlib**, amid, eyelid, forbid, Frigid, outbid, rapid, rigid, undid.
Dinted, glinted, hinted, minted, printed, sprinted, squinted, tinted.
Drifted, gifted, lifted, rifted, shifted, sifted.
Jilted, kilted, lilted, quilted, silted, stilted, tilted, wilted.
Listed, misted, twisted.
Digit, fidget, frigid, legit, midget, rigid, widget.
[3] **Acquitted**, admitted, committed, dimwitted, emitted, fitted, knitted, omitted, outwitted, permitted, quick-witted, spirited, submitted.
Exhibit, inhibit, prohibit.

3.1.186 "--iving" (as in "living")
giving, living, forgiving, lawgiving, misgiving, outliving, thanksgiving, unforgiving.

SURPRISING RHYMING:
[2] **Driven**, given, forbidden, hidden, livid, ridden.

Bringing, clinging, flinging, pinging, ringing, singing, slinging, springing, stinging, stringing, swinging, winging, wringing.
Brimming, dimming, skimming, slimming, swimming, trimming.
Beginning, grinning, pinning, sinning, spinning, thinning, winning.
Bidding, forbidding, kidding, outbidding, ridding, skidding.
Fitting, hitting, knitting, quitting, sitting, slitting, spitting, splitting.
Drifting, gifting, lifting, rifting, shifting, sifting.
Billing, chilling, filling, killing, spilling, swilling, thrilling, willing.
Dissing, fizzing, hissing, kissing, missing, quizzing, whizzing.
Dishing, fishing, phishing, squishing, swishing, wishing.
Dwindling, kindling, spindling, swindling.
Building, bodybuilding, bewildering, housebuilding, rebuilding.
[3] **Acquitting**, admitting, emitting, omitting, permitting, remitting, side-splitting, transmitting, unremitting, unwitting.

3.1.187 "--ivel" (as in "swivel")
[2] civil, drivel, shrivel, skiffle, sniffle, snivel, swivel.

SURPRISING RHYMING:
[2] **Dribble**, nibble, quibble, scribble, sibyl.
Diddle, fiddle, griddle, idyll, middle, paradiddle, riddle, twiddle.
Dwindle, hymnal, kindle, rekindle, sinful, spindle, swindle.
Giggle, jiggle, niggle, squiggle, wiggle, wriggle.
Fickle, nickel, pickle, prickle, tickle, trickle.
Crinkle, skillful, sprinkle, tinkle, twinkle, willful, winkle, wrinkle.
Initial, judicial, official, prejudicial, unofficial.
Cripple, nipple, ripple, stipple, tipple, triple.
Bristle, chisel, dismissal, drizzle, fizzle, missile, sizzle, swizzle, thistle, whistle.
Belittle, brittle, committal, hospital, it'll, little, skittle, spittle, whittle.
Dimple, pimple, simple, wimple.
Jingle, mingle, shingle, signal, single, tingle.
[3+] **Artificial**, beneficial, initial, judicial, official, superficial, unofficial.

3.1.188 "--iveling" (as in "sniveling")
[3] driveling, shriveling, sniveling, swiveling.

SURPRISING RHYMING:
[2] **Dribbling**, nibbling, quibbling, scribbling, sibling.
Diddling, fiddling, middling, piddling, riddling, twiddling.
Giggling, jiggling, niggling, squiggling, wiggling, wriggling.
Belittling, bristling, chiseling, drizzling, fizzling, sizzling, whistling.
Crippling, rippling, stippling, tippling, tripling.
Dwindling, kindling, rekindling, spindling, swindling
Crinkling, inkling, sprinkling, tinkling, twinkling, winkling, wrinkling.
Pickling, prickling, tickling, trickling.
Jingling, mingling, singling, tingling.

3.1.189 "--ivery" (as in "shivery")
[3] delivery, livery, quivery, shivery.

SURPRISING RHYMING:
[3] **Bitterly**, blistery, glittery, jittery, sisterly, whispery.
Ancestry, archery, artistry, bakery, battery, bigotry, binary, blackberry, blubbery, blueberry, blustery, brasserie, bravery, brewery, bribery, burglary, calorie, carpentry, carvery, cavalry, celery, century, chemistry, chicory, chivalry, Christmas tree, colliery, contrary, devilry, diary, dietary, disagree, dithery, doddery, drudgery, dungaree, duty-free, eatery, enquiry, estuary, expiry, factory, fakery, feathery, filigree, finery, fishery, flattery, fluttery, forestry, forgery, gallery, geometry, gimmickry, glittery, greenery, grocery, history, imagery, injury, inquiry, ivory, jamboree, jewellery/jewelry (U.S.), jittery,

393

leathery, lingerie, lottery, luxury, memory, mercury, misery, momentary, monastery, mystery, nursery, obituary, obligatory, pageantry, pedigree, perjury, pillory, pleasantry, poetry, pottery, primary, priory, quivery, referee, revelry, reverie, rivalry, robbery, rockery, rosary, rubbery, salary, sanctuary, savagery, savory, scenery, sensory, shimmery, shivery, silvery, slavery, slippery, sorcery, sugary, surgery, tapestry, thundery, treachery, trickery, victory, wintery, wizardry.
Ability, agility, anxiety, equality, gravity, hostility, humanity, humility, nitty-gritty, humidity, notoriety, nudity, oddity, quality, responsibility, sanity, self-pity, sobriety, society, stupidity, vanity, variety.
Critically, cynically, explicitly, gimmickry, rhythmically, specifically, typically, wickedly.
Amnesty, casualty, certainty, chastity, confetti, density, deputy, devotee, dignity, dynasty, entity, faculty, fidgety, graffiti, gravity, guarantee, honesty, karate, liberty, majesty, modesty, nudity, oddity, penalty, piety, poverty, property, puberty, purity, quality, repartee, rickety, sanctity, sanctuary, sanity, scarcity, seventy, sovereignty, spaghetti, specialty, trinity, unity, uppity, vanity, velvety, warranty.
Allergy, effigy, elegy, energy, eulogy, lethargy, prodigy, refugee, synergy, trilogy.
[4] Accessory, adultery, artillery, cautionary, cemetery, compulsory, confectionery, conciliatory, constabulary, contemporary, customary, debauchery, delivery, dictionary, directory, discovery, distillery, elementary, embroidery, explanatory, exploratory, hunky-dory, idolatry, imaginary, incendiary, infirmary, inflammatory, judiciary, laboratory, legendary, literary, machinery, mandatory, mercenary, military, missionary, necessary, ordinary, patisserie, perfumery, preliminary, psychiatry, publicity, reactionary, recovery, secretary, secondary, simplicity, skullduggery, solitary, stationary, stationery, temporary, territory, tomfoolery, upholstery, visionary, vocabulary.
Artistically, distinctively, instinctively, linguistically, logistically, officially, physically, quizzically, realistically, sadistically, statistically, stylistically.

3.1.190 "--ivering" (as in "shivering")
[3] delivering, quivering, shivering.

SURPRISING RHYMING:
[3] **Differing**, dithering, shriveling, sniveling, swiveling, withering.
Figuring, sniggering, triggering.
Dribbling, nibbling, quibbling, scribbling, sibling.
Glistening, listening, listing, misting, twisting.
Bickering, flickering, quickening, sickening, thickening, tinkering.
Glimmering, shimmering, simmering, whimpering.
Blistering, bristling, drizzling, fizzling, sizzling, whispering, whistling.
Fingering, lingering, limbering, splintering, timbering.
Bewildering, considering, hindering, injuring, picturing
Filtering, flittering, frittering, glittering, littering, tittering, twittering.

3.1.191 "--ix" (as in "fix")
[1] bricks, chicks, fix, flicks, hicks, kicks, licks, mix, nix, picks, pix, pricks, six, slicks, sticks, tics, ticks, tricks, wicks.
[2] affix, crucifix, intermix, matchsticks, prefix, suffix.

SURPRISING RHYMING:
[1] **Dissed**, fist, gist, hissed, kissed, list, midst, missed, mist, pissed, tryst, twist, wrist.
Bits, blitz, fits, grits, hits, its, it's, kits, knits, pits, quits, skits, slits, spits, splits, wits.
Blinks, drinks, hoodwinks, ice-rinks, inks, jinx, kinks, links, lynx, minks, minx, rinks, shrinks, sinks, sphinx, stinks, thinks, winks.
Asterisk, bisque, brisk, disc/disk (U.S.), frisk, risk, obelisk, whisk.
Blips, chips, clips, dips, drips, flips, grips, hips, kips, lips, nips, pips, quips, rips, scripts, ships, sips, skips, slips, snips, strips, tips, trips, whips, zips.
Bliss, diss, hiss, kiss, miss, sis, this.
[2] **Assist**, consist, dismissed, enlist, exist, insist, persist, resist.
Amiss, bodice, chalice, dismiss, gratis, haggis, hospice, hubris, jaundice, justice, malice, Memphis, novice, office, palace, Paris, purchase, service, solstice, surface.

Acquits, admits, armpits, cockpits, commits, emits, habits, misfits, omits, outfits, outwits, remits, spirit, submits, tidbits, transmits.
Broomsticks, chopsticks, drumsticks, lipsticks, toothpicks.
Eclipse, ellipse, equips, fish and chips, friendships, hardships, outstrips, steamships, townships, warships, worships.
Addicts, afflicts, constricts, convicts, evicts, predicts, restricts.

3.1.192 "--ixer" (as in "mixer")
[2] elixir, fixer, mixer, sixer, spritzer.

SURPRISING RHYMING:
[2] **Fixture,** hipster, minster, mixture, picture, scripture, spinster, tipster, trickster.
Hitcher, picture, pitcher, richer, stitcher, stricture, switcher, twitcher.
Blister, crisper, mister, sister, trickster, twister, vista, whisper.
Scissor, fisher, fissure, fizzer, hisser, kisser, quizzer, reminiscer, whizzer, wisher.
Drifter, grifter, lifter, shoplifter, snifter, swifter, victor, weightlifter.
Bicker, flicker, kicker, knicker, licker, liquor, picker, quicker, sicker, slicker, snicker, sticker, thicker, ticker, vicar, whicker, wicker.
[3] **Brandisher**, finisher, flourisher, furnisher, kingfisher, militia, nourisher, polisher, publisher, punisher, vanquisher, well-wisher.

3.1.193 "--ixing" (as in "fixing")
affixing, fixing, mixing, nixing.

SURPRISING RHYMING:
[2] **Dishing**, dissing, fishing, hissing, kissing, missing, phishing, swishing, wishing.
Bitching, ditching, hitching, itching, pitching, snitching, stitching, switching, twitching.
Convincing, evincing, glimpsing, mincing, wincing.
Binging, cringing, fringing, hinging, infringing, singeing, twinging.
Diction, fiction, friction.
Drifting, gifting, lifting, rifting, shifting, sifting, sixteen.
Conflicting, convicting, depicting, inflicting, predicting, restricting.
Jilting, lilting, quilting, listing, misting, silting, stilting, tilting, twisting, wilting.
Fitting, hitting, knitting, quitting, sitting, slitting, spitting, splitting.
Cinching, clinching, flinching, inching, lynching, pinching.
Fixture, hipster, minster, mixture, picture, scripture, spinster, tincture, tipster, trickster.
Blinking, drinking, hoodwinking, inking, inkling, linking, shrinking, sinking, sprinkling, stinking, syncing, thinking, twinkling, winking.
Glinting, hinting, minting, printing, sprinting, squinting, tinting.
Bringing, clinging, flinging, pinging, ringing, singing, slinging, springing, stinging, stringing, swinging, winging, wringing.
Fizzing, frizzing, quizzing, whizzing.
[3] **Addiction**, affliction, conviction, depiction, eviction, nonfiction, prediction, restriction.
Assisting, consisting, enlisting, existing, insisting, persisting, resisting.
Acquitting, admitting, omitting, permitting, side-splitting, transmitting, unwitting.

3.1.194 "--ixture" (as in "mixture")
[2] fixture, mixture.

SURPRISING RHYMING:
[2] **Elixir,** fixer, mixer, sixer, spritzer.
Blister, crisper, lister, mister, sister, trickster, twister, vista, whisper.
Fisher, fissure, miss her, wisher.
Ditcher, hitcher, injure, picture, pitcher, richer, scripture, snitcher, stitcher, stricture, switcher, twitcher.
Bicker, flicker, kicker, knicker, licker, liquor, picker, quicker, sicker, slicker, snicker, sticker, thicker, ticker, vicar, whicker, wicker.
[3] **Administer**, banister, barista, barrister, canister, chorister, forester, minister, resistor, sinister, sob-sister, stepsister, transistor.

Furnisher, nourisher, polisher, publisher, punisher, vanquisher, well-wisher.
[4] Expenditure, furniture, literature, miniature, signature, temperature.
Abolisher, demolisher, embellisher, establisher, extinguisher.

3.1.195 "--ixable" (as in "fixable")
[3] fixable, mixable.

SURPRISING RHYMING:
[3] Kissable, miserable, missable, possible, syllable, visible.
Feasible, flexible, forcible, plausible, taxable.
Biblical, critical, cynical, lyrical, miracle, mystical, physical, pinnacle, quizzical, typical.
Drinkable, shrinkable, sinkable, thinkable, unsinkable, unthinkable.
Additional, conditional, criminal, digital, fictional, minimal, original, pivotal, principal, principle, subliminal.
[4] Admissible, dismissible, exhaustible, forgivable, formidable, inadmissible, indivisible, invincible, invisible, irresistible, noticeable, permissible, resistible, unforgivable.
Despicable, explicable, extricable, political, predictable, reciprocal, unpredictable.
Disposable, exhaustible, implausible, impossible, inflexible, provisional, traditional.

3.1.196 "--iz" (as in "his")
[1] biz, fizz, frizz, gee-whiz, his, is, Ms (mizz), quiz, tizz, viz, whiz.

SURPRISING RHYMING:
[1] Bliss, diss, hiss, kiss, miss, piss, sis, 'tis, this.
Dissed, fist, gist, hissed, kissed, list, midst, missed, mist, pissed, tryst, twist, wrist.
Bits, blitz, fits, grits, hits, its, it's, kits, knits, pits, quits, skits, slits, spits, splits, wits.
If, cliff, miff, myth, pith, riff, skiff, sniff, stiff, tiff, whiff, with.
Anguish, dish, fish, flourish, nourish, squish, swish, wish.
Give, live, sieve, spiv.
[2] Abyss, amiss, bodice, chalice, dismiss, gratis, haggis, hospice, hubris, jaundice, justice, malice, novice, office, palace, purchase, service, solstice, surface.
Assist, consist, dismissed, enlist, exist, insist, persist, resist.
Active, captive, festive, forgive, massive, misgive, missive, motive, native, octave, olive, outlive, passive, pensive, relive.
[3] Accomplice, cowardice, edifice, emphasis, genesis, kinesis, liquorice/licorice (U.S.), nemesis, orifice, prejudice, reminisce.
Abrasive, abusive, adhesive, aggressive, compulsive, conclusive, conducive, corrosive, decisive, defensive, depressive, divisive, elusive, emotive, evasive, excessive, exclusive, expensive, expletive, explosive, expressive, impassive, impressive, impulsive, incisive, inclusive, intensive, intrusive, narrative, negative, obsessive, offensive, oppressive, percussive, permissive, persuasive, possessive, repulsive, responsive, sedative, submissive, subversive, talkative.

3.1.197 "--izum" (as in "prism")
[2] -ism, prism, racism, schism, tourism.
[4] atheism, cataclysm, chauvinism, communism, criticism, cynicism, dogmatism, egotism, euphemism, extremism, feminism, heroism, hypnotism, journalism, magnetism, mannerism, modernism, mysticism, nepotism, optimism, pacifism, pessimism, plagiarism, rheumatism, Satanism, scepticism/skepticism (U.S.), socialism, symbolism.

SURPRISING RHYMING:
[1] Bum, chum, come, crumb, drum, dumb, gum, hum. glum, mum, numb, plum, plumb, rum, scrum, scum, slum, some, strum, sum, swum, thumb, tum, yum.
[2] Bitten, didn't, glisten, hidden, isn't, listen, rhythm, vision.
Emission, fission, intermission, magician, mission, musician, titian, vision.
Dishing, fishing, phishing, squishing, swishing, wishing.
Arisen, dissing, glisten, hissing, imprison, kissing, missing, prison, risen.
Chilling, drilling, filling, grilling, killing, shilling, spilling, stilling, swilling, thrilling, willing.
[3] Addition, admission, ambition, audition, condition, edition, emission, fruition,

ignition, magician, musician, nutrition, omission, optician, petition, permission, physician, position, remission, rendition, submission, suspicion, tradition, transition, tuition.
Efficient, proficient, sufficient.
Collision, decision, derision, division, envision, incision, precision, provision, revision.

3.1.198 "--izard" (as in "lizard")
[2] blizzard, gizzard, lizard, wizard.

SURPRISING RHYMING:
[2] **Delivered**, mirrored, quivered, shivered, slivered.
Differed, dithered, figured, slithered, sniggered, triggered, withered.
Glimmered, shimmered, simmered.
Blistered, flittered, frittered, glittered, littered, tittered, skippered, twittered, whispered.
Bickered, blinkered, flickered, stickered.
[3] **Bewildered**, configured, considered, disfigured.

3.1.199 "--izzy" (as in "dizzy")
[2] busy, dizzy, fizzy, frizzy, tizzy.

SURPRISING RHYMING:
[2] **Drizzly**, flimsy, frisbee, grisly, grizzly, whimsy.
Dishy, fishy, squishy, swishy, wishy.
Chili, chilly, filly, frilly, hilly, hillbilly, icily, lily, silly, rockabilly.
Dixie, glitzy, hissy, kissy, missy, prissy, ritzy, sissy.
Diddy, giddy, kiddie, midi.
Hickey, icky, kinky, mickey, milky, picky, pinkie, pinky, quickie, sickie, silky, slinky, sticky, tricky, whiskey/whisky.
Iffy, chivvy, fifty, jiffy, miffy, pithy, privy, sniffy, spiffy, squiffy, stiffy.
Bitty, chitty, city, ditty, fifty, gritty, kitty, pity, pretty, sixty, witty.
Chippy, clippie, crispy, dippy, drippy, hippie, lippy, nippy, snippy, trippy, whippy, yippee, zippy.
Cine, chimney, gimme, lemme, mini, ninny, skinny, tinny, whinny.

3.1.200 "--izzing" (as in "fizzing")
[2] fizzing, frizzing, quizzing, whizzing.

SURPRISING RHYMING:
[2] **Dissing**, hissing, kissing, missing, sizzling.
Dishing, fishing, phishing, squishing, swishing, wishing.
Emission, fission, intermission, magician, mission, musician, titian, vision.
Arisen, glisten, imprison, prison, risen.
Chilling, filling, killing, spilling, swilling, thrilling, willing.
Bidding, forbidding, kidding, outbidding, ridding, skidding.
Bitten, forbidden, didn't, glisten, hidden, isn't, listen, rhythm.
Brimming, dimming, skimming, slimming, swimming, trimming.
Grinning, pinning, sinning, skinning, spinning, thinning, winning.
[3] **Addition**, admission, ambition, audition, condition, edition, emission, fruition, ignition, magician, musician, nutrition, omission, optician, petition, permission, physician, position, remission, rendition, submission, suspicion, tradition, transition, tuition.
Efficient, proficient, sufficient.
Collision, decision, derision, division, envision, incision, precision, provision, revision.
Distilling, fulfilling, instilling, unwilling.

3.1.201 "--izzle" (as in "sizzle")
[2] bristle, chisel, drizzle, fizzle, frizzle, gristle, missile, sizzle, swizzle, thistle, whistle.

SURPRISING RHYMING:
[2] **Bristled**, chiseled, drizzled, fizzled, grizzled, sizzled, whistled.
Civil, drivel, shrivel, skiffle, sniffle, snivel, swivel.

Belittle, brittle, committal, crystal, hospital, it'll, little, skittle, spittle, visual, whittle.
Diddle, fiddle, griddle, idyll, middle, paradiddle, riddle, twiddle.
Dribble, nibble, quibble, scribble, sibyl.
Giggle, jiggle, niggle, squiggle, wiggle, wriggle.
Cripple, nipple, ripple, stipple, tipple, triple.
Fickle, nickel, pickle, prickle, tickle, trickle.
[3+] Artificial, beneficial, dismissal, initial, judicial, official, superficial, unofficial.

3.1.202 "--izzen" (as in "prison")
[2] arisen, glisten, imprison, listen, prison, risen.

SURPRISING RHYMING:
[2] **Emission,** fission, intermission, magician, mission, musician.
Dissing, hissing, kissing, missing.
Bitten, christen, didn't, forbidden, hidden, isn't, listen, rhythm, vision, wisdom.
Driven, given, giving, forgiven, forgiving, living, misgiving, outliving, stiffen, thanksgiving.
Didn't, ribbon, stiffen, villain, women, written.
Diction, fiction, kitchen, friction.
Pigeon, religion, smidgen, stool-pigeon.
Chicken, quicken, sicken, stricken, thicken.
Ism, prism, racism, schism, tourism.
[3] **Addition,** admission, ambition, audition, condition, edition, emission, fruition, ignition, magician, musician, nutrition, omission, optician, petition, permission, physician, position, remission, rendition, submission, suspicion, tradition, transition, tuition.
Efficient, proficient, sufficient.
Collision, decision, derision, division, envision, incision, precision, provision, revision, supervision, vision.
[4] **Abolition,** acquisition, ammunition, apparition, competition, composition, definition, demolition, dietician, electrician, exhibition, expedition, inhibition, intuition, inquisition, malnutrition, opposition, politician, premonition, prohibition, proposition, recognition, repetition, reposition, requisition, superstition.
Atheism, cataclysm, chauvinism, communism, criticism, cynicism, dogmatism, egotism, euphemism, extremism, feminism, heroism, hypnotism, journalism, magnetism, mannerism, modernism, mysticism, nepotism, optimism, pacifism, pessimism, plagiarism, rheumatism, Satanism, scepticism/skepticism (U.S.), socialism, symbolism.

3.1.203 "--izzier" (as in "dizzier")
[3] busier, dizzier, fizzier, frizzier.

SURPRISING RHYMING:
[3] **Crispier,** friskier, riskier, trivia.
Chillier, drizzlier, frillier, grizzlier, hillier, sillier.
Kinkier, milkier, niftier, shiftier, silkier, stickier, thriftier, trickier.
Electronica, erotica, exotica, frolicker, harmonica, lip-syncer, replica, mimicker, moniker, picnicker, trafficker.
Barista, barrister, minister, resistor, sinister, sob-sister, stepsister, transistor.
Billionaire, connoisseur, debonair, disrepair, in the air, love affair, millionaire, questionnaire, solitaire.

3.1.204 "--izziest" (as in "dizziest")
[3] busiest, dizziest, fizziest, frizziest.

SURPRISING RHYMING:
[3] **Chilliest,** hilliest, silliest.
Filthiest, guiltiest, shiftiest, thriftiest, wealthiest.
Grittiest, prettiest, wittiest.
Milkiest, friskiest, riskiest, silkiest, stickiest, trickiest.
Ambitious, auspicious, delicious, fictitious, hideous, inauspicious, judicious, malicious, nutritious, oblivious, silliness, suspicious, vicious.

3.1.205 "--izzical" (as in "quizzical")
[3] physical, quizzical.

SURPRISING RHYMING:
[3] **Biblical,** comical, critical, cynical, lyrical, miracle, mystical, mythical, pinnacle, typical.
Additional, conditional, criminal, digital, fictional, minimal, original, pivotal, principal, principle, subliminal.
Kissable, fixable, miserable, missable, possible, syllable, visible.
[4] **Admissible,** charitable, deliverable, discernible, dismissible, divisible, exhaustible, forgivable, formidable, inadmissible, invincible, invisible, irresistible, noticeable, permissible, resistible, unforgivable.
Applicable, despicable, equivocal, explicable, extricable, inexplicable, political, predictable, reciprocal, unpredictable.

3.1.206 "--izzily" (as in "dizzily")
[3] busily, dizzily.

SURPRISING RHYMING:
[2] **Drizzly,** flimsy, frisbee, grisly, grizzly, whimsy.
Giggly, hygge, niggly, squiggly, tingly, wiggly, wriggly.
Prickly, quickly, slickly, tickly, thickly.
[3] **Frigidly,** rigidly, skillfully, vividly, willfully.
Liberty, rickety, snippety, trinity.
Chivalry, disagree, history, imagery, infantry, injury, mystery, pillory, shimmery, shivery, silvery, slippery, tapestry, trickery, victory, wintery.
Allergy, effigy, elegy, energy, eulogy, lethargy, liturgy, ology, prodigy, refugee, strategy, synergy, trilogy.
Bodily, family, fleur-de-lis, heavenly, homily, icily, jubilee, melancholy, miserly, readily.
Gossipy, recipe, syrupy/syrupy, therapy, unhappy.
[4] **Ability,** admittedly, agility, civility, dignity, fidgety, facility, fertility, fragility, futility, hostility, humility, mobility, nobility, stability, tranquillity/tranquility (U.S.), utility, virility.

3.2 "iy" (as in "eye")

3.2.1 "--eye" (as in "eye")
[1] aye, buy, by, cry, die, dry, dye, eye, fly, fry, guy, hi, high, I, lie, my, pi, pie, ply, pry, rye, sci-fi, shy, sigh, sky, sly, spry, spy, tie, try, vie, why, wry.
[2] ally, apply, awry, belie, blow-dry, bowtie, bye-bye, comply, decry, defy, deny, drip-dry, drive-by, espy, fish fry, flyby, gadfly, goodbye, good-buy, hereby, hi-fi, horsefly, housefly, humble pie, imply, I-spy, July, low-fi, magpie, mince pie, nearby, occupy, outcry, rabbi, rely, reply, retry, samurai, sci-fi, spin-dry, stir-fry, supply, thereby, tumble-dry, untie, whereby.
[3] alibi, alkali, amplify, beautify, butterfly, by and by, certify, clarify, classify, codify, crucify, dignify, dragonfly, dulcify, edify, falsify, firefly, fortify, gentrify, glorify, gratify, horrify, jollify, justify, ladyfy, liquefy, lullaby, magnify, modify, mollify, mortify, multiply, mummify, mystify, notify, nullify, pacify, passer-by, petrify, preachify, prettify, purify, qualify, quantify, ramify, rarefy, ratify, reapply, rectify, rockabye, sanctify, satisfy, signify, simplify, specify, speechify, stimuli, stupefy, terrify, testify, underlie, unify, verify.
[4] disqualify, diversify, electrify, exemplify, humidify, identify, indemnify, intensify, objectify, solidify, personify.

SURPRISING RHYMING:
[1] **I've,** chive, dive, drive, five, hive, jive, live, strive, thrive.
Aisle, dial, file, guile, I'll, isle, mile(s), pile, smile(s), style, tile, trial, vial, vile, while.
Child, filed, mild, piled, smiled, styled, wild.
Chime, climb, clime, crime, dime, grime, I'm, lime, mime, prime, rhyme, rime, slime, sublime, thyme, time.
Chimed, climbed, mimed, primed, rhymed, timed.

Bind, blind, find, fined, grind, kind, lined, mind, mined, pined, signed, whined, wined.
Bide, bride, chide, cried, died, dried, dyed, eyed, glide, guide, hide, I'd, lied, pied, pried, pride, ride, sighed, side, slide, snide, spied, stride, tide, tied, tried, wide.
Bribe, jibe, scribe, tribe, vibe.
Bite, blight, bright, cite, fight, flight, fright, height, kite, knight, light, mite, might, night, plight, quite, right, rite, sight, site, slight, smite, spite, sprite, tight, trite, white, write.
Gripe, hype, pipe, ripe, snipe, stripe, swipe, tripe, type, wipe.
Griped, hyped, piped, sniped, striped, swiped, typed, wiped.
Bike, dyke/dike, hike, like, mike/mic, psych, spike, strike, trike, tyke.
Dice, ice, lice, mice, nice, price, rice, slice, spice, splice, thrice, twice, vice.
Cries, dies, eyes, guise, lies, prize, rise, size, skies, tries, wise.
[2] Alive, arrive, contrive, deprive, nose-dive, overdrive, revive, survive, swan-dive.
Abide, allied, applied, aside, astride, backside, backslide, bedside, beside, broadside, black-eyed, blue-eyed, brown-eyed, cock-eyed, collide, confide, cross-eyed, decide, denied, deride, divide, downside, fireside, green-eyed, hawk-eyed, high tide, hillside, inside, lakeside, landslide, low tide, misguide, nearside, offside, outside, pop-eyed, preside, provide, red-eyed, reside, riptide, seaside, stateside, subside, tie-dyed, tongue-tied, topside, untied, untried, upside, wayside, well-tried, wide-eyed, worldwide, Yuletide.
Airline, align, alpine, assign, benign, bovine, canine, carbine, carmine, combine, confine, consign, cosign, deadline, decline, define, design, divine, enshrine, entwine, feline, gang-sign, goldmine, hairline, headline, hemline, incline, lifeline, malign, moonshine, outshine, recline, refine, resign, skyline, sunshine, turbine, waistline.
Good life, highlife, housewife, jackknife, lowlife, midlife, midwife, nightlife, paperknife, penknife, pocketknife, shelf-life, still-life, wildlife.
Bedtime, daytime, every time, lifetime, maritime, meantime, nighttime, noontime, overtime, pantomime, pastime, playtime, sometime, sublime, springtime, summertime.
Ascribe, describe, imbibe, inscribe, prescribe, subscribe, transcribe.
Ascribed, described, imbibed, inscribed, prescribed, subscribed, transcribed.
Alike, catlike, childlike, dislike, dreamlike, ghostlike, godlike, hitchhike, lifelike, psyche, pushbike, spring-like, star-like, suchlike, turnpike, unlike, warlike, witchlike, wolf-like.
Awhile, beguile, compile, defile, exile, futile, hostile, meanwhile, profile, reptile, revile, senile, turnstile, worthwhile.
Beguiled, compiled, defiled, exiled, godchild, grandchild, reconciled, reviled, self-styled.
Denial, misdial, mistrial, retrial, self-denial, sundial.
Aligned, behind, combined, consigned, cosigned, declined, defined, designed, divined, entwined, free mind, inclined, maligned, mankind, reclined, refined, remind, resigned, rewind, snow-blind, strong mind, unkind, unlined, untwined, unwind, weak mind.
Advice, choc-ice, concise, de-ice, device, entice, half-price, precise, sacrifice, suffice.
Advise, arise, baptize, blue eyes, brown eyes, capsize, chastise, clockwise, comprise, crosswise, demise, despise, devise, disguise, energize, eulogize, excise, first prize, green eyes, likewise, moonrise, oxidize, revise, sunrise, surmise, surprise, unwise.
Advised, apprised, baptized, capsized, chastised, comprised, despised, devised, disguised, prized, revised, surmised, surprised.
Airtight, all night, alright, birthright, bullfight, daylight, delight, despite, downright, eyesight, excite, expedite, extradite, fistfight, flashlight, floodlight, footlight, foresight, fortnight, goodnight, green light, hindsight, ignite, incite, indict, insight, invite, lamplight, midnight, moonlight, outright, playwright, polite, recite, red light, searchlight, skylight, spotlight, starlight, stoplight, sunlight, termite, tonight, twilight, unite, upright.
Bagpipe, blowpipe, overripe, pitch-pipe, retype, sideswipe, stereotype, windpipe.
[3] Alongside, amplified, beautified, bona fide, certified, classified, coincide, countryside, dignified, dissatisfied, dry-eyed, eagle-eyed, evil-eyed, falsified, glorified, goggle-eyed, gratified, homicide, justified, magnified, mortified, mountainside, multiplied, mystified, nationwide, notified, nullified, occupied, oceanside, override, qualified, pacified, pie-eyed, petrified, preoccupied, qualified, riverside, sanctified, satisfied, specified, stupefied, suicide, terrified, testified, undignified, unqualified, waterside.
Businesslike, ladylike, lookalike, soundalike, sportsmanlike, statesmanlike, workmanlike.
Crocodile, infantile, juvenile, mercantile, reconcile, versatile, volatile.
Colour blind/color blind (U.S.), intertwined, mastermind, one of a kind, underlined.
Edelweiss, merchandise, paradise, sacrifice.

Advertise, agonize, burglarize, civilize, compromise, criticize, demoralize, dramatize, emphasize, enterprise, fertilize, finalize, fossilize, harmonize, hypnotize, idolize, immunize, jeopardize, magnetize, memorize, mesmerize, modernize, otherwise, publicize, realize, recognize, satirize, scrutinize, sensitize, socialize, specialize, stabilize, symbolize, sympathize, tantalize, terrorize, victimize.
Advertised, agonized, burglarized, civilized, compromised, criticized, dramatized, emphasized, energized, fertilized, finalized, fossilized, harmonized, hypnotized, idolized, immunized, jeopardized, magnetized, memorized, mesmerized, modernized, moralized, publicized, realized, recognized, satirized, sensitized, socialized, specialized, stabilized, sterilized, symbolized, sympathized, tantalized, terrorized, victimized.
Appetite, candlelight, copyright, copywrite, day and night, dynamite, Fahrenheit, impolite, overnight, oversight, reunite, second sight.
[4] Disqualified, diversified, electrified, exemplified, humidified, identified, indemnified, intensified, solidified, personified.

3.2.2 "--eying" (as in "crying")
[2] buying, crying, drying, dyeing, dying, eyeing, flying, frying, lying, plying, prying, sighing, spying, trying, tying, vying.
[3] allying, applying, belying, complying, decrying, defying, denying, implying, relying, replying, supplying, untying.
[4] amplifying, beautifying, certifying, clarifying, classifying, codifying, crucifying, dignifying, edifying, falsifying, fortifying, glorifying, gratifying, horrifying, justifying, liquefying, magnifying, modifying, mollifying, mortifying, multiplying, mummifying, mystifying, notifying, nullifying, occupying, pacifying, petrifying, purifying, qualifying, quantifying, ratifying, reapplying, rectifying, sanctifying, satisfying, signifying, simplifying, specifying, terrifying, testifying, underlying, unifying, verifying.
[5] disqualifying, diversifying, electrifying, identifying, indemnifying, intensifying, solidifying, personifying.

SURPRISING RHYMING:
[2] Client, defiant, giant, lion, pliant, reliant, silent, triumph, tyrant.
Diving, driving, high-fiving, jiving, skiving, striving, thriving.
Dialing, filing, piling, smiling, styling, tiling, trialing.
Chiming, climbing, miming, priming, rhyming, timing.
Binding, blinding, finding, grinding, minding, winding.
Biding, gliding, guiding, hiding, riding, siding, sliding, striding, tiding.
Bribing, jibing, scribing.
Biting, blighting, citing, fighting, knighting, lighting, righting, sighting, siting, writing.
Griping, hyping, piping, sniping, swiping, typing, wiping.
Biking, hiking, liking, psyching, spiking, striking.
Dicing, icing, pricing, prizing, sizing, slicing, spicing, splicing.
Horizon, Mayan, python, ripen.
[3] Arriving, conniving, contriving, depriving, deriving, reviving, skydiving, surviving.
Abiding, backsliding, coinciding, colliding, confiding, deciding, deriding, dividing, overriding, presiding, providing, residing, subsiding.
Aligning, combining, confining, declining, defining, designing, entwining, flatlining, headlining, inclining, outshining, reclining, refining, resigning, streamlining, toplining.
Describing, imbibing, inscribing, prescribing, subscribing.
Beguiling, compiling, defiling, profiling, reconciling, reviling.
Advising, arising, capsizing, chastising, comprising, de-icing, despising, devising, disguising, downsizing, energizing, enticing, revising, rising, surprising, uprising.
Bullfighting, delighting, exciting, expediting, extraditing, igniting, inciting, indicting, inviting~ moonlighting, reciting, spotlighting, uniting.
[4] Advertising, agonizing, burglarizing, civilizing, compromising, criticizing, demoralizing, dramatizing, emphasizing, enterprising, finalizing, harmonizing, hypnotizing, idolizing, immunizing, jeopardizing, legalizing, magnetizing, memorizing, mesmerizing, modernizing, moralizing, publicizing, realizing, recognizing, sacrificing, satirizing, socializing, specializing, stabilizing, symbolizing, sympathizing, tantalizing, terrorizing, unsurprising, victimizing.

*

3.2.3 "--bye" (as in "goodbye")
[1] by, bye, buy.
[2] bye-bye, flyby, goodbye, good-buy, hereby, nearby, rabbi, thereby, whereby.
[3] alibi, by and by, drive-by, lullaby, passer-by, passers-by, rockabye.

SURPRISING RHYMING:
[1] **Die**, fly, lie, ply, sly.
Eye, I, guy, high, Pi, pie, shy, sigh, sky, spy, why.
Cry, dry, fry, pry, rye, spry, try, wry.
Bite, blight, bright, cite, fight, flight, fright, height, kite, knight, light, mite, might, night, plight, quite, right, rite, sight, site, slight, smite, spite, sprite, tight, trite, white, write.
Bind, blind, find, fined, grind, kind, lined, mind, mined, pined, signed, whined, wined.
Chime, climb, clime, crime, dime, grime, I'm, lime, mime, prime, rhyme, rime, slime, sublime, thyme, time.
Bide, bride, chide, cried, died, dried, dyed, eyed, glide, guide, hide, I'd, lied, pied, pried, pride, ride, sighed, side, slide, snide, spied, stride, tide, tied, tried, wide.
[2] **Defy**, hi-fi, low-fi, sci-fi, untie.
Ally, apply, bowtie, comply, deny, horsefly, housefly, imply, July, rely, reply, supply.
Awry, decry, fish fry, outcry.
Alive, arrive, beehive, contrive, deprive, nose-dive, overdrive, revive, survive.
[3] **Alibi**, amplify, beautify, butterfly, by and by, certify, clarify, dignify, dragonfly, falsify, firefly, fortify, glorify, horrify, justify, lullaby, magnify, multiply, mummify, mystify, notify, nullify, pacify, passer-by, petrify, purify, qualify, reapply, rectify, rockabye, sanctify, satisfy, signify, simplify, specify, speechify, stimuli, stupefy, terrify, testify.
Apple pie, humble pie, magpie, mince pie, occupy, potpie.

3.2.4 "--fie" (as in "satisfy")
[2] defy, hi-fi, low-fi, sci-fi.
[3] amplify, beautify, certify, clarify, classify, codify, crucify, dignify, dulcify, edify, falsify, fortify, gentrify, glorify, gratify, horrify, jollify, justify, ladyfy, liquefy, magnify, modify, mollify, mortify, mummify, mystify, notify, nullify, pacify, petrify, preachify, prettify, purify, qualify, ~quantify, ramify, rarefy, ratify, rectify, sanctify, satisfy, signify, simplify, specify, speechify, stupefy, terrify, testify, unify, verify.
[4] disqualify, diversify, electrify, exemplify, humidify, identify, indemnify, intensify, objectify, solidify, personify.

SURPRISING RHYMING:
[1] **By**, bye, buy, high, why.
Die, fly, lie, ply, sly.
Eye, I, guy, high, Pi, pie, shy, sigh, sky, spy, why.
Cry, dry, fry, pry, rye, spry, try, wry.
Bite, blight, bright, cite, fight, flight, fright, height, kite, knight, light, mite, might, night, plight, quite, right, rite, sight, site, slight, smite, spite, sprite, tight, trite, white, write.
Bind, blind, find, fined, grind, kind, lined, mind, mined, pined, signed, whined, wined.
Chime, climb, crime, dime, grime, I'm, mime, prime, rhyme, slime, sublime, thyme, time.
Bide, bride, chide, cried, died, dried, dyed, eyed, glide, guide, hide, I'd, lied, pied, pried, pride, ride, sighed, side, slide, snide, spied, stride, tide, tied, tried, wide.
[2] **Bye-bye**, bowtie, flyby, goodbye, hereby, nearby, thereby.
Ally, apply, comply, deny, housefly, imply, July, rely, reply, supply.
Alive, arrive, beehive, contrive, deprive, nose-dive, overdrive, revive, survive.
Awry, blow-dry, decry, drip-dry, outcry, retry, samurai, spin-dry, stir-fry, tumble-dry.
Alibi, by and by, drive-by, lullaby, passer-by, passers-by, rockabye.
Alkali, butterfly, dragonfly, firefly, multiply, reapply, stimuli, underlie.
Apple pie, espy, humble pie, I-spy, magpie, mince pie, occupy.

3.2.5 "--lie" (as in "reply")
[1] die, fly, lie, ply, sly.
[2] ally, apply, belie, comply, gadfly, horsefly, housefly, imply, July, rely, reply, supply.
[3] alkali, butterfly, dragonfly, firefly, multiply, reapply, stimuli, underlie.

SURPRISING RHYMING:
[1] By, bye, buy, high, why.
Eye, I, guy, high, Pi, pie, shy, sigh, sky, spy, why.
Cry, dry, fry, pry, rye, spry, try, wry.
Bind, blind, find, fined, grind, kind, lined, mind, mined, pined, signed, whined, wined.
Bite, blight, bright, cite, fight, flight, fright, height, kite, knight, light, mite, might, night, plight, quite, right, rite, sight, site, slight, smite, spite, sprite, tight, trite, white, write.
Chime, climb, crime, dime, grime, I'm, mime, prime, rhyme, slime, sublime, thyme, time.
Bide, bride, chide, cried, died, dried, dyed, eyed, glide, guide, hide, I'd, lied, pied, pried, pride, ride, sighed, side, slide, snide, spied, stride, tide, tied, tried, wide.
[2] Bye-bye, bowtie, flyby, goodbye, hereby, nearby, thereby.
Defy, hi-fi, low-fi, sci-fi, untie.
Awry, blow-dry, deny, drip-dry, outcry, retry, samurai, spin-dry, stir-fry, tumble-dry.
Alive, arrive, deprive, nose-dive, overdrive, revive, survive.
[3] Alibi, by and by, drive-by, lullaby, passer(s)-by, rockabye.
Amplify, beautify, certify, clarify, classify, dignify, falsify, fortify, glorify, gratify, horrify, justify, magnify, modify, mortify, mummify, mystify, notify, nullify, pacify, petrify, purify, qualify, rectify, sanctify, satisfy, simplify, specify, stupefy, terrify, testify, verify.
Apple pie, espy, humble pie, I-spy, magpie, mince pie, occupy.
[4] Disqualify, diversify, identify, indemnify, intensify, objectify, solidify, personify.

3.2.6 "--pie" (as in "spy")
apple pie, humble pie, I-spy, magpie, mince pie, occupy, pi, pie, ply, potpie, spy.

SURPRISING RHYMING:
[1] By, bye, buy, eye, guy, high, I, why.
Die, fly, lie, ply, sly.
Cry, dry, fry, pry, rye, spry, try, wry.
Eye, I, guy, high, Pi, pie, shy, sigh, sky, spy, why.
Bind, blind, find, fined, grind, kind, lined, mind, mined, pined, signed, whined, wined.
Bite, blight, bright, cite, fight, flight, fright, height, kite, knight, light, mite, might, night, plight, quite, right, rite, sight, site, slight, smite, spite, sprite, tight, trite, white, write.
Chime, climb, crime, dime, grime, I'm, mime, prime, rhyme, slime, sublime, thyme, time.
Bide, bride, chide, cried, died, dried, dyed, eyed, glide, guide, hide, I'd, lied, pied, pried, pride, ride, sighed, side, slide, snide, spied, stride, tide, tied, tried, wide.
[2] Bye-bye, bowtie, flyby, goodbye, hereby, nearby, thereby.
Defy, hi-fi, low-fi, sci-fi, untie.
Awry, blow-dry, drip-dry, outcry, retry, samurai, spin-dry, stir-fry, tumble-dry.
Ally, apply, comply, deny, housefly, imply, July, rely, reply, supply.
Alive, arrive, deprive, nose-dive, overdrive, revive, survive.
[3] Alibi, by and by, drive-by, lullaby, passer(s)-by, rockabye.
Amplify, beautify, certify, clarify, classify, dignify, falsify, fortify, glorify, gratify, horrify, justify, magnify, modify, mortify, mummify, mystify, notify, nullify, pacify, petrify, purify, qualify, rectify, sanctify, satisfy, simplify, specify, stupefy, terrify, testify, verify.
Alkali, butterfly, dragonfly, firefly, multiply, reapply, stimuli, underlie.
[4] Disqualify, diversify, identify, indemnify, intensify, objectify, solidify, personify.

3.2.7 "--rye" (as in "dry")
[1] cry, dry, fry, pry, rye, spry, try, wry.
[2] awry, blow-dry, drip-dry, fish fry, outcry, retry, samurai, spin-dry, stir-fry, tumble-dry.

SURPRISING RHYMING:
[1] By, bye, buy, high, why.
Die, fly, lie, ply, sly.
Eye, I, guy, high, Pi, pie, shy, sigh, sky, spy, why.
Bite, blight, bright, cite, fight, flight, fright, height, kite, knight, light, mite, might, night, plight, quite, right, rite, sight, site, slight, smite, spite, sprite, tight, trite, white, write.
Bind, blind, find, fined, grind, kind, lined, mind, mined, pined, signed, whined, wined.
Chime, climb, crime, dime, grime, I'm, mime, prime, rhyme, slime, sublime, thyme, time.

Bide, bride, chide, cried, died, dried, dyed, eyed, glide, guide, hide, I'd, lied, pied, pried, pride, ride, sighed, side, slide, snide, spied, stride, tide, tied, tried, wide.
[2] **Bye-bye**, bowtie, flyby, goodbye, good-buy, hereby, nearby, thereby, whereby.
Defy, hi-fi, low-fi, sci-fi, untie.
Ally, apply, comply, deny, housefly, imply, July, rely, reply, supply.
Alive, arrive, deprive, nose-dive, overdrive, revive, survive.
[3] **Alibi**, by and by, drive-by, lullaby, passer(s)-by, rockabye.
Amplify, beautify, certify, clarify, classify, dignify, falsify, fortify, glorify, gratify, horrify, justify, magnify, modify, mortify, mummify, mystify, notify, nullify, pacify, petrify, purify, qualify, rectify, sanctify, satisfy, simplify, specify, stupefy, terrify, testify, verify.
Alkali, butterfly, dragonfly, firefly, multiply, reapply, stimuli, underlie.
Apple pie, humble pie, I-spy, magpie, mince pie, occupy.
[4] **Disqualify**, diversify, identify, indemnify, intensify, objectify, solidify, personify.

3.2.8 "--ial" (as in "dial")
[2] dial, trial, vial.
[3] denial, misdial, mistrial, retrial, self-denial, sundial.

SURPRISING RHYMING:
[1] **Child**, filed, mild, piled, smiled, styled, wild.
Aisle, file, guile, I'll, isle, mile(s), pile, smile(s), style, tile, vile, while, wile.
I've, chive, dive, drive, five, hive, jive, live, strive, thrive.
Die, eye, fly, I, guy, high, lie, Pi, pie, shy, sigh, sky, sly, spy, why.
Cry, dry, fry, pry, rye, spry, try, wry.
Chime, climb, crime, dime, grime, I'm, mime, prime, rhyme, slime, sublime, thyme, time.
[2] **Beguiled**, exiled, godchild, grandchild, reconciled, reviled, self-styled.
Awhile, beguile, compile, defile, exile, futile, hostile, meanwhile, profile, reptile, revile, senile, turnstile, worthwhile.
Alive, arrive, deprive, nose-dive, overdrive, revive, survive.
[3] **Crocodile**, infantile, juvenile, reconcile, versatile, volatile.

3.2.9 "--iance" (as in "defiance")
[3] alliance, appliance, compliance, dalliance, defiance, reliance, science.

SURPRISING RHYMING:
[2] **Clients**, giants, lions, triumphs.
Client, compliant, defiant, giant, pliant, reliant.
Bias, highest, pious, shyest.
Guidance, licence/license (U.S.), silence, sirens, violence.
[3] **Annoyance**, connivance, contrivance, impatience, subsidence.

3.2.10 "--iant" (as in "defiant")
[2] client, compliant, defiant, giant, pliant, reliant.

SURPRISING RHYMING:
[2] **Buying**, crying, drying, dyeing, dying, eyeing, flying, frying, lying, plying, prying, sighing, spying, trying, tying, vying.
Licensed, silent, silenced, siren, violent.
Brighten, client, climate, crying, diamond, diet, hydrant, island, quiet, riot, triumph, tyrant, vibrant.
[3] **Alliance**, appliance, compliance, defiance, reliance, science.
Applying, complying, decrying, defying, denying, implying, relying, replying, satisfying, supplying, terrifying, unifying, untying.

3.2.11 "--iable" (as in "liable")
[3] liable, pliable, reliable, viable.
[4] deniable, reliable.
[5] certifiable, classifiable, identifiable, justifiable, notifiable, undeniable, unreliable, verifiable.

SURPRISING RHYMING:
[2] **Bible**, libel, tribal, liable, libel.
Bridal, bridle, idle, idol, sidle, tidal.
Rival, spiral, title, trial, viral, vital.
Delightful, eyeful, frightful, mindful, rifle, rightful, spiteful, stifle, trifle.
[3] **Bicycle**, icicle, tricycle.
[4] **Advisable**, desirable, devisable, excitable, inadvisable, likeable, recognizable, sizable, unrecognizable.

3.2.12 "--ibe" (as in "tribe")
[1] bribe, jibe, scribe, tribe, vibe.
[2] ascribe, describe, imbibe, inscribe, prescribe, proscribe, subscribe, transcribe.

SURPRISING RHYMING:
[1] **Bribed**, jibed.
Bide, bride, chide, cried, died, dried, dyed, eyed, glide, guide, hide, I'd, lied, pied, pried, pride, ride, sighed, side, slide, snide, spied, stride, tide, tied, tried, wide.
Knife, life, rife, strife, wife.
Bite, blight, bright, cite, fight, flight, fright, height, kite, knight, light, mite, might, night, plight, quite, right, rite, sight, site, slight, smite, spite, sprite, tight, trite, white, write.
Gripe, hype, pipe, ripe, snipe, stripe, swipe, tripe, type, wipe.
Brine, cryin', fine, line, mine, nine, pine, shine, shrine, sign, spine, swine, vine, wine.
Chime, climb, crime, dime, grime, I'm, mime, prime, rhyme, slime, sublime, thyme, time.
By, bye, buy.
Die, fly, lie, ply, sly.
Pi, pie, ply, spy.
Cry, dry, fry, pry, rye, spry, try, wry.
[2] **Described**, inscribed, prescribed, subscribed, transcribed.
Abide, allied, applied, aside, astride, backside, backslide, bedside, beside, broadside, black-eyed, blue-eyed, brown-eyed, cock-eyed, collide, confide, cross-eyed, decide, denied, deride, divide, downside, fireside, green-eyed, hawk-eyed, high tide, hillside, inside, lakeside, landslide, low tide, misguide, nearside, offside, outside, pop-eyed, preside, provide, red-eyed, reside, riptide, seaside, stateside, subside, tie-dyed, tongue-tied, topside, untied, untried, upside, wayside, well-tried, wide-eyed, worldwide, Yuletide.
Bagpipe, blowpipe, overripe, pitch-pipe, retype, sideswipe, stereotype, windpipe.
Airline, align, alpine, benign, canine, combine, confine, deadline, decline, define, design, divine, enshrine, entwine, feline, gang-sign, goldmine, hairline, headline, incline, lifeline, malign, moonshine, outshine, recline, refine, resign, skyline, sunshine, waistline.
Bedtime, daytime, every time, lifetime, maritime, meantime, nighttime, noontime, overtime, pantomime, pastime, playtime, sometime, sublime, springtime, summertime.
Fishwife, highlife, housewife, jackknife, lowlife, midlife, midwife, nightlife, paperknife, penknife, pocketknife, shelf-life, still-life, wildlife.
Bye-bye, flyby, goodbye, hereby, nearby, rabbi, thereby, whereby.
Defy, hi-fi, low-fi, sci-fi, untie.
Ally, apply, belie, comply, gadfly, horsefly, housefly, imply, July, rely, reply, supply.
Awry, blow-dry, decry, drip-dry, outcry, retry, samurai, spin-dry, stir-fry, tumble-dry.
I-spy, magpie, mince pie.
[3] **Alongside**, amplified, beautified, bona fide, certified, classified, coincide, countryside, dignified, dissatisfied, dry-eyed, eagle-eyed, evil-eyed, falsified, glorified, goggle-eyed, gratified, homicide, justified, magnified, mortified, mountainside, multiplied, mystified, nationwide, notified, nullified, occupied, oceanside, override, qualified, pacified, pie-eyed, petrified, preoccupied, qualified, riverside, sanctified, satisfied, specified, stupefied, suicide, terrified, testified, undignified, unqualified, waterside.
Afterlife, bowie knife, pocketknife.
Alibi, apple pie, by and by, drive-by, humble pie, lullaby, occupy, passer(s)-by, rockabye.
Amplify, beautify, certify, clarify, classify, dignify, falsify, fortify, glorify, gratify, horrify, justify, magnify, modify, mortify, mummify, mystify, notify, nullify, pacify, petrify, purify, qualify, rectify, sanctify, satisfy, simplify, specify, stupefy, terrify, testify, verify.
Butterfly, dragonfly, firefly, multiply, reapply, stimuli, underlie.
[4] **Disqualify**, electrify, identify, indemnify, intensify, objectify, solidify, personify.

3.2.13 "--ibed" (as in "described")
[1] bribed, jibed.
[2] described, imbibed, inscribed, prescribed, proscribed, subscribed, transcribed.

SURPRISING RHYMING:
[1] **Bribe**, jibe, scribe, tribe, vibe.
Bite, blight, bright, cite, fight, flight, fright, height, kite, knight, light, mite, might, night, plight, quite, right, rite, sight, site, slight, smite, spite, sprite, tight, trite, white, write.
Bide, bride, chide, cried, died, dried, dyed, eyed, glide, guide, hide, I'd, lied, pied, pried, pride, ride, sighed, side, slide, snide, spied, stride, tide, tied, tried, wide.
Gripe, hype, pipe, ripe, snipe, stripe, swipe, tripe, type, wipe.
Brine, cryin', fine, line, mine, nine, pine, shine, shrine, sign, spine, stein, swine, tine, twine, vine, whine, wine.
Chime, climb, clime, crime, dime, grime, I'm, lime, mime, prime, rhyme, rime, slime, sublime, thyme, time.
By, bye, buy.
Die, fly, lie, ply, sly.
Pi, pie, ply, spy.
Cry, dry, fry, pry, rye, spry, try, wry.
[2] **Describe**, diatribe, inscribe, prescribe, subscribe, transcribe.
Abide, allied, applied, aside, astride, backside, backslide, bedside, beside, broadside, black-eyed, blue-eyed, brown-eyed, cock-eyed, collide, confide, cross-eyed, decide, denied, deride, divide, downside, fireside, green-eyed, hawk-eyed, high tide, hillside, inside, lakeside, landslide, low tide, misguide, nearside, offside, outside, pop-eyed, preside, provide, red-eyed, reside, riptide, seaside, stateside, subside, tie-dyed, tongue-tied, topside, untied, untried, upside, wayside, well-tried, wide-eyed, worldwide, Yuletide.
Bagpipe, blowpipe, overripe, pitch-pipe, retype, sideswipe, stereotype, under-ripe.
Bedtime, daytime, every time, lifetime, maritime, meantime, nighttime, noontime, overtime, pantomime, pastime, playtime, sometime, sublime, springtime, summertime.
Bye-bye, flyby, goodbye, hereby, nearby, rabbi, thereby, whereby.
Defy, hi-fi, low-fi, sci-fi, untie.
Ally, apply, belie, comply, housefly, imply, July, rely, reply, supply.
Awry, blow-dry, decry, drip-dry, outcry, retry, samurai, spin-dry, stir-fry, tumble-dry.
[3] **Alongside**, amplified, beautified, bona fide, certified, classified, coincide, countryside, dignified, dissatisfied, dry-eyed, eagle-eyed, evil-eyed, falsified, glorified, goggle-eyed, gratified, homicide, justified, magnified, mortified, mountainside, multiplied, mystified, nationwide, notified, nullified, occupied, oceanside, override, pacified, pie-eyed, petrified, preoccupied, qualified, riverside, sanctified, satisfied, specified, stupefied, suicide, terrified, testified, undignified, unqualified, waterside.

3.2.14 "--iber" (as in "cyber")
[2] briber, cyber, fibre/fiber (U.S.), imbiber, inscriber, prescriber, subscriber, transcriber.

SURPRISING RHYMING:
[2] **Cipher**, decipher, encipher, knifer, lifer.
Biter, blighter, brighter, fighter, lighter, slighter, tiger, tighter, triter, whiter, writer.
Diver, driver, fiver, jiver, skiver, striver, thriver.
Chider, cider, eider, glider, guider, hider, rider, slider, spider, strider, wider.
Diaper, hyper, piper, riper, sniper, striper, swiper, viper, wiper.
China, diner, finer, liner, miner, minor, piner, shiner, signer, whiner.
Climber, mimer, primer, rhymer, timer.
Buyer, choir, crier, dire, drier, dryer, dyer, fire, flyer, friar, fryer, higher, hire, inspire, ire, liar, mire, plier, plyer, prier, prior, pyre, shire, shyer, sire, spire, sprier, spryer, squire, tire, tyre/tire (U.S.), trier, via, wire.
Kaiser, miser, riser, sizer, visor, wiser.
[3] **All-nighter**, backbiter, bullfighter, copywriter, delighter, exciter, fistfighter, ghostwriter, gunfighter, inciter, igniter, lamplighter, midnighter, moonlighter, overnighter, politer, prizefighter, reciter, rewriter, screenwriter, scriptwriter, signwriter, songwriter, typewriter.
Conniver, contriver, pearl diver, piledriver, saliva, screwdriver, skydiver, survivor.

Backslider, collider, confider, decider, divider, insider, hang-glider, joyrider, nightrider, outrider, outsider, provider, roughrider.
Bagpiper, sandpiper, sideswiper.
Airliner, angina, decliner, definer, designer, diviner, eyeliner, hardliner, headliner, maligner, moonshiner, recliner, streamliner.
Old-timer, part-timer, two-timer.

3.2.15 "--ibing" (as in "describing")
[3] bribing, describing, imbibing, inscribing, prescribing, proscribing, subscribing, transcribing.

SURPRISING RHYMING:
[2] **Diving,** driving, high-fiving, jiving, skiving, striving, thriving.
Chiming, climbing, miming, priming, rhyming, timing.
Biting, citing, fighting, lighting, sighting, slighting, spiting, writing.
Biding, chiding, gliding, guiding, hiding, riding, siding, sliding, striding, tiding.
Griping, hyping, piping, retyping, sideswiping, sniping, striping, swiping, wiping.
Dining, lining, mining, shining, signing, whining, wining.
Buying, crying, drying, dyeing, dying, eyeing, flying, frying, lying, plying, prying, sighing, spying, trying, tying, vying.
[3] **Bullfighting,** delighting, exciting, handwriting, inciting, indicting, inviting, reciting, requiting, rewriting, spotlighting, uniting.
Abiding, backsliding, colliding, confiding, dividing, misguiding, presiding, providing, residing, subsiding.
Aligning, assigning, combining, confining, consigning, declining, defining, designing, divining, entwining, flatlining, headlining, inclining, outshining, reclining, refining, resigning, streamlining, toplining.
Applying, complying, decrying, defying, denying, implying, relying, replying, satisfying, supplying, terrifying, unifying, untying.
Arriving, conniving, contriving, depriving, deriving, reviving, skydiving, surviving.

3.2.16 "--ice" (as in "nice")
[1] dice, ice, lice, mice, nice, price, rice, slice, spice, splice, thrice, twice, vice.
[2] advice, allspice, choc-ice, concise, de-ice, device, entice, half-price, precise, sacrifice, suffice.
[3] edelweiss, merchandise, paradise, sacrifice.

SURPRISING RHYMING:
[1] **Bite(s),** blight, bright, cite, fight(s), flight(s), fright, height(s), kite(s), knight(s), light(s), might, night(s), plight, quite, right(s), rite(s), sight(s), site(s), slight, spite, sprite, tight(s), trite, white, write(s).
Cries, dies, eyes, guise, lies, prize, rise, size, skies, tries, wise.
Knife, life, rife, strife, wife.
[2] **Airtight,** all night, alright, birthright, bullfight, daylight, delight, despite, downright, eyesight, excite, expedite, extradite, fistfight, flashlight, floodlight, footlight, foresight, fortnight, goodnight, green light, hindsight, ignite, incite, indict, insight, invite, lamplight, midnight, moonlight, outright, playwright, polite, recite, red light, searchlight, skylight, spotlight, starlight, stoplight, sunlight, termite, tonight, twilight, unite, upright.
Advise, arise, baptize, blue eyes, brown eyes, capsize, chastise, clockwise, comprise, crosswise, demise, despise, devise, disguise, energize, eulogize, excise, first prize, green eyes, likewise, moonrise, revise, sunrise, surmise, surprise, unwise, wide eyes.
Good life, highlife, housewife, jackknife, lowlife, midlife, midwife, nightlife, paperknife, penknife, pocketknife, shelf-life, still-life, wildlife.
[3] Afterlife, appetite, candlelight, copyright, day and night, dynamite, Fahrenheit, impolite, overnight, oversight, overwrite, parasite, reunite, satellite, second sight.
Agonize, burglarize, civilize, compromise, criticize, demoralize, dramatize, emphasize, enterprise, finalize, harmonize, hypnotize, idolize, jeopardize, magnetize, memorize, mesmerize, modernize, otherwise, publicize, realize, recognize, scrutinize, sensitize, socialize, specialize, stabilize, symbolize, sympathize, tantalize, terrorize, victimize.

3.2.17 "--icer" (as in "nicer")
dicer, enticer, de-icer, nicer, slicer, splicer.

SURPRISING RHYMING:
[2] **Biter**, brighter, fighter, lighter, slighter, tighter, triter, whiter, writer.
Kaiser, miser, riser, sizer, visor, wiser.
Cipher, decipher, encipher, knifer, lifer.
Cider, eider, glider, guider, hider, rider, slider, spider, strider, wider.
[3] **Adviser**, chastiser, despiser, deviser, disguiser, surpriser.
Backslider, confider, decider, insider, joyrider, nightrider, outrider, outsider, provider.
[4] **Advertiser,** appetizer, breathalyzer, compromiser, criticizer, equalizer, exerciser, improviser, jeopardizer, memorizer, mesmerizer, mobilizer, modernizer, moisturizer, moralizer, organizer, philosophizer, recognizer, socializer, stabilizer, supervisor, sympathizer, synthesizer, terrorizer, tranquillizer, tantalizer, victimizer, womanizer.

3.2.18 "--ices" (as in "prices")
[2] crisis, dices, ices, prices, slices, spices, splices, vices.
[3] de-ices, devices, entices, suffices.

SURPRISING RHYMING:
[2] **Crises**, guises, high seas, prizes, rises, sizes.
Finest, highness, kindest, lightless, lightness, Midas, minus, nicest, sightless, sinus, tightness, virus, widest, wildest, wisest.
[3] **Arises**, arthritis, baptizes, bronchitis, capsizes, chastises, comprises, despises, devises, disguises, revises, sunrises, surprises.
[4] **Advertises**, agonizes, compromises, criticizes, dramatizes, emphasizes, energizes, enterprises, finalizes, harmonizes, hypnotizes, idolizes, immunizes, jeopardizes, magnetizes, memorizes, mesmerizes, modernizes, publicizes, realizes, recognizes, satirizes, scrutinizes, specializes, symbolizes, sympathizes, tantalizes, terrorizes.

3.2.19 "--icing" (as in "dicing")
de-icing, dicing, enticing, icing, pricing, sacrificing, slicing, splicing.

SURPRISING RHYMING:
[2] **Bison**, prizing, rising, sizing.
Biting, blighting, citing, fighting, lighting, righting, sighting, slighting, spiting, writing.
Diving, driving, high-fiving, jiving, skiving, striving, thriving.
Buying, crying, drying, dyeing, dying, eyeing, flying, frying, lying, plying, prying, sighing, spying, trying, tying, vying.
Biding, chiding, gliding, guiding, hiding, riding, siding, sliding, striding, tiding.
Filing, piling, riling, smiling, styling, tiling, wiling.
[3] **Advising**, arising, capsizing, chastising, comprising, de-icing, despising, devising, disguising, downsizing, energizing, enticing, revising, rising, surprising, uprising.
Delighting, exciting, handwriting, inciting, inviting, reciting, rewriting, spotlighting, uniting.
Arriving, conniving, contriving, depriving, deriving, reviving, skydiving, surviving.
Defying, denying, implying, relying, replying, satisfying, supplying, terrifying, unifying.
Abiding, backsliding, colliding, confiding, dividing, presiding, providing, residing.
Beguiling, compiling, defiling, exiling, profiling, reconciling, restyling, reviling, unsmiling.
[4] **Agonizing**, burglarizing, civilizing, compromising, criticizing, demoralizing, dramatizing, emphasizing, enterprising, finalizing, harmonizing, hypnotizing, idolizing, jeopardizing, legalizing, magnetizing, memorizing, mesmerizing, modernizing, publicizing, realizing, recognizing, sacrificing, socializing, specializing, symbolizing, sympathizing, tantalizing, terrorizing, unsurprising, victimizing.

3.2.20 "--iceless" (as in "priceless")
[2] iceless, priceless, spiceless, viceless.

SURPRISING RHYMING:
[2] **Crisis**, finest, highness, kindest, Midas, minus, nicest, shyness, sightless, sinus,

slyness, stylus, virus, widest, wildest, wisest.
Brightness, lifeless, lightness, rightness, righteous, slightness, tightness, tireless, triteness, whiteness, wireless.
Brightest, lightest, slightest, tightest, tritest, whitest.
Bias, biased, pious.
Blindness, childless, kindness, mindless, spineless, wildness.
Driest, highest, shyest, slyest, spryest.

3.2.21 "--icycle" (as in "bicycle")
[3] bicycle, icicle, popsicle, tricycle.

SURPRISING RHYMING:
[3] **Entitle**, mistitle, recital, requital, retitle, subtitle, title, vital.
Delightful, disciple, insightful, recycle, reprisal.
Archival, arrival, revival, survival.
[4] **Deniable**, identifiable, justifiable, pliable, reliable, unreliable, undeniable,
Advisable, desirable, excitable, inadvisable, likeable, recognizable, sizable, unrecognizable.

3.2.22 "--ide" (as in "lied")
[1] bide, bride, chide, cried, died, dried, dyed, eyed, glide, guide, hide, I'd, lied, pied, pried, pride, ride, sighed, side, slide, snide, spied, stride, tide, tied, tried, wide.
[2] abide, allied, applied, aside, astride, backside, backslide, bedside, beside, bromide, broadside, black-eyed, blue-eyed, brown-eyed, child bride, cock-eyed, collide, confide, cowhide, cross-eyed, decide, denied, deride, divide, downside, fireside, frontside, green-eyed, hawk-eyed, high tide, hillside, inside, lakeside, landslide, low tide, misguide, nearside, offside, outside, pop-eyed, preside, provide, rawhide, red-eyed, reside, riptide, seaside, stateside, subside, tie-dyed, tongue-tied, topside, untied, untried, upside, wayside, well-tried, wide-eyed, worldwide, Yuletide.

SURPRISING RHYMING:
[1] **Die**, eye, fly, guy, high, I, I've, lie, pie, ply, shy, sigh, sky, sly, spy, why.
Cry, dry, fry, pry, rye, spry, try, wry.
Bite, blight, bright, cite, fight, flight, fright, height, kite, knight, light, mite, might, night, plight, quite, right, rite, sight, site, slight, smite, spite, sprite, tight, trite, white, write.
Bind, blind, find, fined, grind, kind, lined, mind, mined, pined, signed, whined, wined.
Cries, dies, eyes, guise, lies, prize, rise, size, skies, tries, wise.
Bribe, bribed, jibe, scribe, tribe, vibe.
[2] **Advised**, baptized, capsized, chastised, comprised, despised, devised, disguised, prized, revised, surmised, surprised.
Advise, arise, baptize, blue eyes, brown eyes, capsize, chastise, clockwise, comprise, crosswise, demise, despise, devise, disguise, energize, first prize, green eyes, likewise, moonrise, revise, sunrise, surmise, surprise, unwise, wide eyes.
Alive, arrive, deprive, nose-dive, overdrive, revive, survive.
Defy, hi-fi, low-fi, sci-fi, untie.
Ally, apply, bye-bye, comply, deny, flyby, goodbye, hereby, imply, July, nearby, rely, reply, supply, thereby, whereby..
Awry, blow-dry, decry, drip-dry, outcry, retry, samurai, spin-dry, stir-fry, tumble-dry.
[3] **Advertised**, agonized, burglarized, civilized, compromised, criticized, dramatized, emphasized, energized, fertilized, finalized, fossilized, harmonized, hypnotized, idolized, immunized, jeopardized, magnetized, memorized, mesmerized, modernized, moralized, publicized, realized, recognized, satirized, sensitized, socialized, specialized, stabilized, symbolized, sympathized, tantalized, terrorized, victimized.
Alibi, by and by, drive-by, lullaby, passer-by, passers-by, rockabye.
Amplify, beautify, certify, clarify, classify, dignify, falsify, fortify, glorify, gratify, horrify, justify, magnify, modify, mortify, mummify, mystify, notify, nullify, pacify, petrify, purify, qualify, rectify, sanctify, satisfy, simplify, specify, stupefy, terrify, testify, verify.
Apple pie, humble pie, magpie, mince pie, occupy, potpie.
Alkali, butterfly, dragonfly, firefly, multiply, reapply, stimuli, underlie.

3.2.23 "--ided" (as in "decided")
[2] bided, chided, glided, guided, prided, sided, tided.
[3] abided, collided, confided, decided, derided, divided, lopsided, misguided, one-sided, presided, provided, two-sided, undecided.

SURPRISING RHYMING:
[2] **Blighted**, knighted, lighted, righted, sighted, slighted, spited.
Blinded, eyelid, hybrid, minded, winded.
[3] **Free-minded**, high-minded, like-minded, reminded, snow-blinded, strong-minded, weak-minded.
Clear-sighted, decided, delighted, excited, farsighted, ignited, incited, indicted, invited, nearsighted, recited, shortsighted, spotlighted, united, unrequited.

3.2.24 "--ider" (as in "spider")
[2] chider, cider, eider, glider, guider, hider, rider, slider, spider, strider, wider.
[3] backslider, collider, confider, decider, divider, insider, joyrider, nightrider, outrider, outsider, provider, roughrider.

SURPRISING RHYMING:
[2] **Binder**, blinder, finder, grinder, kinda, kinder, minder, winder.
China, diner, finer, liner, miner, minor, piner, shiner, signer, smiler, tiger, viler, whiner.
Biter, blighter, brighter, fighter, lighter, slighter, tighter, triter, whiter, writer.
Briber, cyber, fibre/fiber (U.S.), inscriber, prescriber, subscriber.
[3] **Bookbinder**, childminder, pathfinder, rangefinder, reminder, rewinder, ringbinder, sidewinder, spellbinder, viewfinder.
Beguiler, compiler, defiler, hair-styler, profiler, reviler, stockpiler.
Airliner, decliner, definer, designer, diviner, eyeliner, hardliner, headliner, maligner, moonshiner, recliner, refiner, streamliner.
All-nighter, backbiter, bullfighter, copywriter, delighter, exciter, fist fighter, ghostwriter, gunfighter, inciter, igniter, lamplighter, midnighter, moonlighter, overnighter, politer, prizefighter, reciter, rewriter, screenwriter, scriptwriter, signwriter, songwriter, typewriter.

3.2.25 "--iding" (as in "hiding")
[2] biding, chiding, gliding, guiding, hiding, riding, siding, sliding, striding, tiding.
[3] abiding, backsliding, colliding, confiding, dividing, misguiding, presiding, providing, residing, subsiding.

SURPRISING RHYMING:
[2] **Bribing**, describing, inscribing, prescribing, subscribing.
Diving, driving, high-fiving, jiving, skiving, striving, thriving.
Biking, disliking, hiking, hitchhiking, liking, spiking, striking, Viking.
De-icing, dicing, icing, pricing, slicing, splicing.
Buying, crying, drying, dyeing, dying, eyeing, flying, frying, lying, plying, prying, sighing, spying, trying, tying, vying.
Chiming, climbing, miming, priming, rhyming, timing.
Binding, blinding, finding, grinding, minding, winding.
Filing, piling, riling, smiling, styling, tiling.
Dining, fining, lining, mining, pining, shining, signing, whining.
Biting, citing, fighting, lighting, righting, sighting, spiting, writing.
Griping, hyping, piping, retyping, sniping, striping, swiping, wiping.
Firing, hiring, squiring, tiring, wiring.
[3] **Arriving**, conniving, contriving, depriving, deriving, reviving, skydiving, surviving.
Advising, arising, baptizing, capsizing, chastising, comprising, de-icing, despising, disguising, downsizing, energizing, enticing, revising, rising, surmising, surprising.
Applying, complying, decrying, defying, denying, implying, relying, replying, satisfying, supplying, terrifying, unifying, untying.
Acquiring, admiring, aspiring, attiring, backfiring, conspiring, desiring, expiring, inquiring, inspiring, misfiring, perspiring, rehiring, retiring, re-wiring, transpiring.
Childminding, pathfinding, reminding, rewinding, sidewinding, spellbinding.

Beguiling, compiling, hair-styling, profiling, stockpiling.
Aligning, combining, confining, declining, defining, designing, flatlining, headlining, outshining, reclining, refining, resigning, streamlining, toplining.
Backbiting, bullfighting, copywriting, delighting, exciting, ghostwriting, gunfighting, inciting, igniting, inviting, lamplighting, midnighting, moonlighting, reciting, rewriting, screenwriting, scriptwriting, signwriting, songwriting, typewriting.

3.2.26 "--ier" (as in "liar")
[2] briar, buyer, crier, denier, dire, drier, dryer, dyer, flier/flyer, friar, fryer, higher, liar, Maya, plier, plyer, prier, prior, shyer, sprier, spryer, trier, via.
[3] applier, denier, hairdryer, homebuyer, messiah, papaya, pariah, replier, supplier.
[4] amplifier, beautifier, clarifier, classifier, crucifier, disqualifier, fortifier, glorifier, gratifier, humidifier, identifier, intensifier, jambalaya, justifier, liquefier, magnifier, modifier, mollifier, multiplier, occupier, pacifier, prophesier, purifier, qualifier, quantifier, rectifier, sanctifier, signifier, specifier, testifier, tumble-dryer, unifier, verifier, vilifier.

SURPRISING RHYMING:
[1] **Choir**, dire, fire, higher, hire, mire, pyre, sire, spire, tire, tyre/tire (U.S), wire.
[2] **Acquire**, admire, aspire, attire, backfire, barbwire, bonfire, bushfire, buyer, campfire, ceasefire, choir, conspire, crossfire, desire, empire, enquire, entire, esquire, expire, gunfire, haywire, hellfire, inspire, misfire, perspire, quagmire, sapphire, satire, spitfire, surefire, transpire, tripwire, umpire, vampire, wildfire.
China, diner, finer, liner, miner, minor, piner, shiner, signer, whiner.
Diver, driver, fiver, jiver, skiver, striver, thriver.
[3] **Airliner**, decliner, definer, designer, diviner, eyeliner, hardliner, headliner, maligner, moonshiner, recliner, refiner, streamliner.
Conniver, contriver, pile-driver, saliva, screwdriver, skydiver, survivor.
Beguiler, compiler, defiler, hair-styler, profiler, reviler, stockpiler.

3.2.27 "--iest" (as in "highest")
[2] driest, highest, shyest, slyest, spryest.

SURPRISING RHYMING:
[2] **Brightest**, lightest, slightest, tightest, tritest, whitest.
Bias, biased, pious.
Crisis, finest, highness, kindest, lightless, lightness, Midas, minus, nicest, sightless, sinus, tightness, virus, widest, wildest, wisest.
[3] **Arthritis**, bronchitis, ignited, invited, reliant, united.

3.2.28 "--iet" (as in "diet")
[2] diet, disquiet, quiet, riot.

SURPRISING RHYMING:
[1] **Fired**, hired, mired, sired, squired, tired, wired.
[2] **Client**, defiant, giant, lion, pliant, reliant, silent, triumph, tyrant.
Blighted, knighted, lighted, righted, sighted, slighted, spited.
Bias, biased, driest, finest, highest, pious, shyest, slyest, spryest.
Climate, pilot, pirate, private.
Acquired, admired, aspired, backfired, barbwired, conspired, desired, expired, inquired, inspired, misfired, perspired, required, retired, rewired, transpired, undesired, uninspired.
Blinded, free-minded, like-minded, minded, reminded, strong-minded, weak-minded.
Airtight, all night, alright, birthright, bullfight, daylight, delight, despite, downright, eyesight, excite, expedite, extradite, fistfight, flashlight, floodlight, footlight, foresight, fortnight, goodnight, green light, hindsight, ignite, incite, indict, insight, invite, lamplight, midnight, moonlight, outright, playwright, polite, recite, red light, searchlight, skylight, spotlight, starlight, stoplight, sunlight, termite, tonight, twilight, unite, upright.
[3] **Appetite,** candlelight, copyright, day and night, dynamite, Fahrenheit, impolite, overnight, oversight, overwrite, parasite, reunite, satellite, second sight, stalagmite, traffic light, underwrite.

3.2.29 "--ieter" (as in "quieter")
[3] dieter, proprietor, quieter, rioter.

SURPRISING RHYMING:
[3] **All-nighter**, backbiter, bullfighter, copywriter, delighter, exciter, fistfighter, ghostwriter, gunfighter, inciter, igniter, lamplighter, midnighter, moonlighter, overnighter, politer, prizefighter, reciter, rewriter, screenwriter, scriptwriter, signwriter, songwriter, typewriter.
Backfire, barbwire, bonfire, campfire, ceasefire, crossfire, gunfire, haywire, hellfire, misfire, spitfire, surefire, tripwire, vampire, wildfire.
Backslider, collider, confider, decider, divider, insider, joyrider, nightrider, outrider, outsider, provider, roughrider.

3.2.30 "--ieting" (as in "rioting")
[3] dieting, quieting, rioting.

SURPRISING RHYMING:
[2] **Biting**, citing, fighting, lighting, righting, sighting, spiting, writing.
Brightening, frightening, heightening, lightning, tightening, whitening.
Griping, hyping, piping, retyping, sideswiping, sniping, striping, swiping, wiping.
[3] **Bribing**, describing, inscribing, prescribing, subscribing.
Backbiting, bullfighting, copywriting, delighting, exciting, ghostwriting, gunfighting, inciting, igniting, inviting, moonlighting, reciting, rewriting, screenwriting, scriptwriting, signwriting, songwriting, typewriting.
Abiding, backsliding, colliding, confiding, dividing, misguiding, presiding, providing.
Aligning, combining, confining, declining, defining, designing, divining, entwining, flatlining, headlining, outshining, reclining, refining, resigning, streamlining, toplining.
Applying, complying, decrying, defying, denying, implying, relying, replying, satisfying, supplying, terrifying, unifying, untying.
Acquiring, admiring, aspiring, backfiring, conspiring, desiring, expiring, inquiring, inspiring, misfiring, perspiring, retiring, transpiring.
Advising, arising, capsizing, chastising, comprising, de-icing, despising, devising, disguising, downsizing, enticing, revising, rising, surprising, uprising.

3.2.31 "--ife" (as in "life")
[1] knife, life, rife, strife, wife.
[2] fishwife, good life, highlife, housewife, jackknife, lowlife, midlife, midwife, nightlife, paperknife, penknife, pocketknife, shelf-life, still-life, wildlife.
[3] afterlife, bowie knife, pocketknife.

SURPRISING RHYMING:
[1] **I've**, chive, dive, drive, five, hive, jive, live, strive, thrive.
Dice, ice, mice, nice, price, rice, slice, spice, thrice, twice, vice.
Die, fly, lie(s), ply, sly.
Eye, I, guy, high, Pi, pie, shy, sigh, sky, spy, why.
Bide, bride, chide, cried, died, dried, dyed, eyed, glide, guide, hide, I'd, lied, pied, pried, pride, ride, sighed, side, slide, snide, spied, stride, tide, tied, tried, wide.
Chime, climb, crime, dime, grime, I'm, mime, prime, rhyme, rime, slime, sublime, time.
Cryin', fine, line, mine, nine, pine, shine, shrine, sign, spine, swine, twine, vine, wine.
Cry, dry, fry, pry, rye, spry, try, wry.
Bite, blight, bright, cite, fight, flight, fright, height, kite, knight, light, mite, might, night, plight, quite, right, rite, sight, site, slight, smite, spite, sprite, tight, trite, white, write.
Bike, hike, like, mike/mic, psych, pike, spike, strike, trike, tyke.
Bind, blind, find, fined, grind, kind, lined, mind, mined, pined, signed, whined, wined.
[2] **Alive**, arrive, deprive, nose-dive, overdrive, revive, survive.
Advice, concise, device, entice, paradise, precise, sacrifice, suffice.
Ally, apply, comply, defy, deny, hi-fi, imply, July, low-fi, rely, reply, sci-fi, supply, untie.
Abide, allied, applied, aside, astride, backside, backslide, bedside, beside, broadside, black-eyed, blue-eyed, brown-eyed, cock-eyed, collide, confide, cross-eyed, decide, denied, deride, divide, downside, fireside, green-eyed, hawk-eyed, high tide, hillside,

412

inside, lakeside, landslide, low tide, misguide, nearside, offside, outside, pop-eyed, preside, provide, red-eyed, reside, riptide, seaside, stateside, subside, tie-dyed, tongue-tied, topside, untied, untried, upside, wayside, well-tried, wide-eyed, worldwide, Yuletide.
Bedtime, daytime, every time, lifetime, maritime, meantime, nighttime, noontime, overtime, pantomime, pastime, playtime, sometime, sublime, springtime, summertime.
Aligned, behind, combined, consigned, cosigned, declined, defined, designed, divined, entwined, free mind, inclined, maligned, mankind, reclined, refined, remind, resigned, rewind, snow-blind, strong mind, unkind, unlined, untwined, unwind, weak mind.
Airline, alpine, benign, canine, combine, confine, deadline, decline, define, design, divine, enshrine, entwine, gang-sign, goldmine, headline, incline, lifeline, malign, moonshine, outshine, recline, refine, resign, skyline, sunshine, turbine, waistline.
Airtight, all night, alright, birthright, bullfight, daylight, delight, despite, downright, eyesight, excite, expedite, extradite, fistfight, flashlight, floodlight, footlight, foresight, fortnight, goodnight, green light, hindsight, ignite, incite, indict, insight, invite, lamplight, midnight, moonlight, outright, playwright, polite, recite, red light, searchlight, skylight, spotlight, starlight, stoplight, sunlight, termite, tonight, twilight, unite, upright.
Apple pie, espy, humble pie, I-spy, magpie, mince pie, occupy.
Alike, catlike, childlike, dislike, dreamlike, ghostlike, godlike, hitchhike, lifelike, pushbike, spring-like, sponge-like, star-like, suchlike, sun-like, turnpike, unlike, warlike, witchlike.
[3] Alkali, butterfly, dragonfly, firefly, multiply, stimuli, underlie.
Amplify, beautify, certify, clarify, classify, dignify, falsify, fortify, glorify, gratify, horrify, justify, magnify, modify, mortify, mummify, mystify, notify, nullify, pacify, petrify, purify, qualify, rectify, sanctify, satisfy, simplify, specify, stupefy, terrify, testify, verify.
Awry, blow-dry, drip-dry, outcry, retry, samurai, stir-fry, tumble-dry.
Alongside, amplified, beautified, bona fide, certified, classified, coincide, countryside, dignified, dissatisfied, dry-eyed, eagle-eyed, evil-eyed, falsified, glorified, goggle-eyed, gratified, homicide, justified, magnified, mortified, mountainside, multiplied, mystified, nationwide, notified, nullified, occupied, oceanside, override, qualified, pacified, pie-eyed, petrified, preoccupied, qualified, riverside, sanctified, satisfied, specified, stupefied, suicide, terrified, testified, undignified, unqualified, waterside.
Appetite, candlelight, copyright, day and night, dynamite, Fahrenheit, impolite, overnight, oversight, parasite, reunite, satellite, second sight.
Auld lang syne, concubine, countersign, denying, intertwine, porcupine, realign, storyline, underline, undermine, valentine.

3.2.32 "--ifen" (as in "hyphen")
[2] hyphen, siphon.

SURPRISING RHYMING:
[2] Brighten, enlighten, frighten, heighten, lighten, liken, lion, siren, tighten, titan, whiten, widen.
Crying, diamond, diet, giant, island, pliant, quiet, reliant, riot, triumph, tyrant, vibrant.
Diving, driving, high-fiving, jiving, skiving, striving, thriving.
Buying, crying, drying, dyeing, dying, eyeing, flying, frying, lying, plying, prying, sighing, spying, trying, tying, vying.
Chiming, climbing, miming, priming, rhyming, timing.
Binding, blinding, finding, grinding, minding, winding.
Filing, piling, riling, smiling, styling, tiling.
Dining, fining, lining, mining, pining, shining, signing, whining.
Biting, fighting, lighting, righting, sighting, slighting, spiting, writing.
Biking, disliking, hiking, hitchhiking, liking, spiking, striking, Viking.
Dicing, horizon, icing, pricing, python, ripen, slicing, splicing.

3.2.33 "--ifel" (as in "stifle")
[2] eyeful, rifle, stifle, trifle.

SURPRISING RHYMING:
[2] Frightful, rightful, spiteful.
Hyphen, siphon.
Dial, phial, rival, spiral, title, trial, viral, vital.

Bible, libel, tribal, liable, libel.
Bridal, bridle, idle, idol, sidle, tidal.
Cycle, final, primal, spinal.
[3] Entitle, mistitle, recital, requital, retitle, subtitle, title, vital.
Denial, misdial, mistrial, retrial, self-denial, sundial.
Certifiable, deniable, identifiable, justifiable, notifiable, pliable, reliable, unreliable, undeniable, verifiable, viable.
Archival, arrival, revival, survival.
Archetypal, delightful, disciple, insightful, recycle, reprisal.
Desirable, excitable, inadvisable, likeable, recognizable, sizable, unrecognizable.
Homicidal, quarterfinal, semifinal, suicidal, unbridle, urinal.

3.2.34 "--ike" (as in "like")
[1] bike, dyke/dike, hike, like, mike/mic, psych, pike, spike, strike, trike, tyke.
[2] alike, catlike, childlike, crablike, dislike, dreamlike, ghostlike, godlike, hitchhike, homelike, Klondike, lifelike, psyche, pushbike, rose-like, spring-like, sponge-like, star-like, suchlike, sun-like, turnpike, unlike, warlike, witchlike, wolf-like.
[3] businesslike, ladylike, lookalike, motorbike, soundalike, sportsmanlike, statesmanlike, workmanlike.

SURPRISING RHYMING:
[1] Biked, disliked, hiked, hitchhiked, liked, psyched, spiked.
Bite, blight, bright, cite, fight, flight, fright, height, kite, knight, light, mite, might, night, plight, quite, right, rite, sight, site, slight, smite, spite, sprite, tight, trite, white, write.
Gripe, hype, pipe, ripe, snipe, stripe, swipe, tripe, type, wipe.
Die, eye, fly, I, guy, high, lie, Pi, pie, shy, sigh, sky, sly, spy, why.
Cry, dry, fry, pry, rye, spry, try, wry.
Bide, bride, chide, cried, died, dried, dyed, eyed, glide, guide, hide, I'd, lied, pied, pried, pride, ride, sighed, side, slide, snide, spied, stride, tide, tied, tried, wide.
Bribe, jibe, scribe, tribe, vibe.
Bind, blind, find, fined, grind, kind, lined, mind, mined, pined, signed, whined, wined.
[2] Bagpipe, blowpipe, overripe, pitch-pipe, retype, sideswipe, stereotype, under-ripe.
Airtight, all night, alright, birthright, bullfight, daylight, delight, despite, downright, eyesight, excite, expedite, extradite, fistfight, flashlight, floodlight, footlight, foresight, fortnight, goodnight, green light, hindsight, ignite, incite, indict, insight, invite, lamplight, midnight, moonlight, outright, playwright, polite, recite, red light, searchlight, skylight, spotlight, starlight, stoplight, sunlight, termite, tonight, twilight, unite, upright.
Defy, hi-fi, low-fi, sci-fi.
Ascribe, describe, diatribe, inscribe, prescribe, subscribe, transcribe.
[3] Appetite, black and white, candlelight, copyright, day and night, dynamite, impolite, overnight, oversight, overwrite, parasite, reunite, satellite, second sight, underwrite.

3.2.35 "--iking" (as in "liking")
biking, disliking, hiking, hitchhiking, liking, spiking, striking, Viking.

SURPRISING RHYMING:
[2] Biting, citing, fighting, lighting, righting, sighting, spiting, writing.
Griping, hyping, piping, retyping, sniping, striping, swiping, wiping.
Biding, chiding, gliding, guiding, hiding, riding, siding, sliding, striding, tiding.
Binding, blinding, finding, grinding, minding, winding.
Diving, driving, high-fiving, jiving, skiving, striving, thriving.
Buying, crying, drying, dyeing, dying, eyeing, flying, frying, lying, plying, prying, sighing, spying, trying, tying, vying.
Chiming, climbing, miming, priming, rhyming, timing.
Filing, piling, riling, smiling, styling, tiling.
Dining, fining, lining, mining, pining, shining, signing, whining.
Firing, hiring, squiring, tiring, wiring.
[3] Abiding, backsliding, colliding, confiding, dividing, misguiding, presiding, providing.
Backbiting, delighting, exciting, ghostwriting, gunfighting, inciting, igniting, inviting, moonlighting, reciting, rewriting, scriptwriting, songwriting, typewriting, uniting.

Arriving, conniving, contriving, depriving, deriving, reviving, skydiving, surviving.
Advising, arising, baptizing, capsizing, chastising, comprising, de-icing, despising, devising, disguising, downsizing, energizing, enticing, rising, surprising, uprising.
Applying, complying, decrying, defying, denying, implying, relying, replying, satisfying, supplying, terrifying, unifying, untying.
Aligning, combining, confining, declining, defining, designing, entwining, flatlining, headlining, inclining, outshining, reclining, refining, resigning, streamlining, toplining.

3.2.36 "--ile" (as in "smile")
[1] aisle, bile, file, guile, I'll, isle, mile(s), pile, smile(s), style, tile, vile, while, wile.
[2] awhile, beguile, compile, defile, exile, futile, hostile, meanwhile, profile, reptile, revile, senile, turnstile, worthwhile.
[3] crocodile, infantile, juvenile, mercantile, reconcile, versatile, volatile.

SURPRISING RHYMING:
[1] **Child**, filed, mild, piled, smiled, styled, wild.
I've, chive, dive, drive, five, hive, jive, live, strive, thrive.
Bide, bride, chide, cried, died, dried, dyed, eyed, glide, guide, hide, I'd, lied, pied, pried, pride, ride, sighed, side, slide, snide, spied, stride, tide, tied, tried, wide.
Bite, blight, bright, cite, fight, flight, fright, height, kite, knight, light, mite, might, night, plight, quite, right, rite, sight, site, slight, smite, spite, sprite, tight, trite, white, write.
Dial, trial, vial.
Die, eye, fly, I, guy, high, lie, Pi, pie, shy, sigh, sky, sly, spy, why.
Cry, dry, fry, pry, rye, spry, try, wry.
Chime, climb, crime, dime, grime, I'm, mime, prime, rhyme, rime, slime, sublime, time.
[2] **Beguiled**, defiled, exiled, godchild, grandchild, reconciled, reviled, self-styled.
Denial, misdial, mistrial, retrial, self-denial, sundial.
Alive, arrive, contrive, deprive, nose-dive, overdrive, revive, survive.
Ally, apply, belie, comply, imply, July, rely, reply, supply.
[3] **Butterfly**, dragonfly, firefly, multiply, reapply, stimuli, underlie.
Amplify, beautify, certify, clarify, classify, dignify, falsify, fortify, glorify, gratify, horrify, justify, magnify, modify, mortify, mummify, mystify, notify, nullify, pacify, petrify, purify, qualify, rectify, sanctify, satisfy, simplify, specify, stupefy, terrify, testify, verify.

3.2.37 "--iled" (as in "child")
[1] child, filed, mild, piled, smiled, styled, wild.
[2] beguiled, compiled, defiled, domiciled, exiled, godchild, grandchild, reconciled, reviled, self-styled.

SURPRISING RHYMING:
[1] **Aisle**, file, guile, I'll, isle, mile(s), pile, smile(s), style, vile, while.
I've, chive, dive, drive, five, hive, jive, live, strive, thrive.
Bide, bride, chide, cried, died, dried, dyed, eyed, glide, guide, hide, I'd, lied, pied, pried, pride, ride, sighed, side, slide, snide, spied, stride, tide, tied, tried, wide.
Bite, blight, bright, cite, fight, flight, fright, height, kite, knight, light, mite, might, night, plight, quite, right, rite, sight, site, slight, smite, spite, sprite, tight, trite, white, write.
Dial, trial, vial.
Die, eye, fly, I, guy, high, lie, Pi, pie, shy, sigh, sky, sly, spy, why.
Cry, dry, fry, pry, rye, spry, try, wry.
Chime, climb, crime, dime, grime, I'm, mime, prime, rhyme, rime, slime, sublime, time.
[2] **Awhile**, beguile, compile, defile, exile, futile, hostile, meanwhile, profile, reptile, revile, senile, turnstile, worthwhile.
Denial, misdial, mistrial, retrial, self-denial, sundial.
Alive, arrive, contrive, deprive, nose-dive, overdrive, revive, survive.
Ally, apply, belie, comply, imply, July, rely, reply, supply.
[3] **Crocodile**, infantile, juvenile, reconcile, versatile, volatile.
Alkali, butterfly, dragonfly, firefly, multiply, reapply, stimuli, underlie.
Amplify, beautify, certify, clarify, dignify, falsify, fortify, glorify, gratify, horrify, justify, magnify, modify, mortify, mummify, mystify, notify, nullify, pacify, petrify, purify, qualify, rectify, sanctify, satisfy, simplify, specify, stupefy, terrify, testify, verify.

3.2.38 "--ildly" (as in "wildly")
[2] mildly, wildly.

SURPRISING RHYMING:
[2] **Brightly**, lightly, likely, nightly, politely, quietly, rightly, slightly, sprightly, tightly, tritely, unlikely, unsightly.
Drily, highly, idly, shyly, slyly, smiley, wily, wryly.
Finely, benignly, lively, malignly, sublimely, timely.
Blindly, Friday, kindly, unkindly, widely.
Concisely, nicely, precisely, wisely.

3.2.39 "--iler" (as in "smiler")
[2] filer, smiler, styler, tiler, viler.
[3] beguiler, compiler, defiler, profiler, reviler, stockpiler.

SURPRISING RHYMING:
[2] **China**, diner, finer, liner, miner, minor, piner, signer, whiner.
Climber, mimer, primer, rhymer, timer.
Diver, driver, fiver, jiver, skiver, striver.
Chider, cider, eider, glider, guider, hider, rider, slider, spider, strider, tiger, wider.
Buyer, choir, crier, dire, drier, dryer, dyer, fire, flyer, friar, fryer, higher, hire, inspire, ire, liar, mire, prior, pyre, shyer, sire, spire, squire, tire, tyre/tire (U.S.), trier, via, wire.
[3] **Airliner**, designer, eyeliner, hardliner, headliner, moonshiner, recliner, streamliner.
Old-timer, part-timer, two-timer.
Conniver, contriver, piledriver, saliva, screwdriver, skydiver, survivor.
Applier, hairdryer, homebuyer, messiah, pariah, replier, supplier.
[4] **Amplifier**, clarifier, disqualifier, glorifier, gratifier, humidifier, identifier, intensifier, jambalaya, justifier, magnifier, occupier, pacifier, prophesier, testifier, verifier.

3.2.40 "--iling" (as in "smiling")
[2] filing, piling, riling, smiling, styling, tiling, wiling.
[3] beguiling, compiling, defiling, exiling, profiling, reconciling, reviling, unsmiling.

SURPRISING RHYMING:
[2] **Dialing**, trialing.
Diving, driving, high-fiving, jiving, skiving, striving, thriving.
Chiming, climbing, miming, priming, rhyming, timing.
Biting, citing, fighting, lighting, righting, sighting, spiting, writing.
Biding, chiding, gliding, guiding, hiding, riding, siding, sliding, striding, tiding.
Griping, hyping, piping, retyping, sniping, striping, swiping, wiping.
Dining, lining, mining, shining, signing, whining, wining.
Buying, crying, drying, dyeing, dying, eyeing, flying, frying, lying, plying, prying, sighing, spying, trying, tying, vying.
[3] **Abiding**, backsliding, colliding, confiding, dividing, presiding, providing, residing.
Combining, confining, declining, defining, designing, entwining, headlining, inclining, outshining, reclining, refining, streamlining.
Applying, complying, decrying, defying, denying, implying, relying, replying, satisfying, supplying, terrifying, unifying, untying.
Arriving, conniving, contriving, depriving, deriving, reviving, skydiving, surviving.
[4] **Amplifying**, beautifying, clarifying, dignifying, falsifying, glorifying, gratifying, horrifying, justifying, magnifying, mortifying, multiplying, mummifying, mystifying, notifying, occupying, pacifying, petrifying, purifying, qualifying, rectifying, sanctifying, satisfying, signifying, simplifying, terrifying, testifying, underlying, verifying.
[5] **Disqualifying**, diversifying, electrifying, identifying, intensifying, personifying.

3.2.41 "--ime" (as in "time")
[1] chime, climb, clime, crime, dime, grime, I'm, lime, mime, prime, rhyme, rime, slime, thyme, time.

[2] aftertime, bedtime, daytime, every time, hard time(s), lifetime, maritime, meantime, nighttime, noontime, overtime, pantomime, pastime, playtime, sometime(s), springtime, sublime, summertime.

SURPRISING RHYMING:
[1] **Chimed**, climbed, mimed, primed, rhymed, timed.
Buy, by, cry, die, dry, dye, eye, fly, fry, guy, hi, high, I, lie, my, pi, pie, ply, pry, rye, sci-fi, shy, sigh, sky, sly, spry, spy, tie, try, vie, why, wry.
Brine, cryin', fine, line, mine, nine, pine, shine, shrine, sign, spine, stein, swine, tine, twine, vine, whine, wine.
Bind, blind, find, fined, grind, kind, lined, mind, mined, pined, signed, whined, wined.
Bide, bride, chide, cried, died, dried, dyed, eyed, glide, guide, hide, I'd, lied, pied, pried, pride, ride, sighed, side, slide, snide, spied, stride, tide, tied, tried, wide.
Knife, life, rife, strife, wife.
[2] **Apply**, awry, belie, blow-dry, bowtie, bye-bye, comply, decry, defy, deny, drip-dry, drive-by, espy, flyby, goodbye, hi-fi, humble pie, imply, I-spy, July, low-fi, magpie, mince pie, nearby, occupy, outcry, rely, reply, samurai, sci-fi, stir-fry, supply, untie.
Airline, align, alpine, benign, canine, combine, confine, deadline, decline, define, design, divine, enshrine, entwine, feline, gang-sign, goldmine, headline, incline, lifeline, malign, moonshine, outshine, recline, refine, resign, skyline, sunshine, turbine, waistline.
Aligned, behind, combined, declined, defined, designed, entwined, free mind, inclined, maligned, mankind, reclined, refined, remind, resigned, rewind, snow-blind, unkind, untwined, unwind, weak mind.
Abide, allied, applied, aside, astride, backside, backslide, bedside, beside, broadside, black-eyed, blue-eyed, brown-eyed, cock-eyed, collide, confide, cross-eyed, decide, denied, deride, divide, downside, fireside, green-eyed, hawk-eyed, high tide, hillside, inside, lakeside, landslide, low tide, misguide, nearside, offside, outside, pop-eyed, preside, provide, red-eyed, reside, riptide, seaside, stateside, subside, tie-dyed, tongue-tied, topside, untied, untried, upside, wayside, well-tried, wide-eyed, worldwide, Yuletide.
[3] **Alibi**, by and by, drive-by, lullaby, passer(s)-by, rockabye.
Amplify, beautify, certify, clarify, classify, dignify, falsify, fortify, glorify, gratify, horrify, justify, magnify, modify, mortify, mummify, mystify, notify, nullify, pacify, petrify, purify, qualify, rectify, sanctify, satisfy, simplify, specify, stupefy, terrify, testify, verify.
Auld lang syne, concubine, countersign, denying, intertwine, porcupine, realign, storyline, underline, undermine, valentine.
[4] Disqualify, diversify, electrify, exemplify, humidify, identify, indemnify, intensify, objectify, solidify, personify.

3.2.42 "--imed" (as in "climbed")
[1] chimed, climbed, mimed, primed, rhymed, timed.

SURPRISING RHYMING:
[1] **Chime**, climb, clime, crime, dime, grime, I'm, lime, mime, prime, rhyme, rime, slime, sublime, thyme, time.
Cryin', fine, line, mine, nine, pine, shine, shrine, sign, spine, swine, twine, vine, whine, wine.
Bind, blind, find, fined, grind, kind, lined, mind, mined, pined, signed, whined, wined.
Bide, bride, chide, cried, died, dried, dyed, eyed, glide, guide, hide, I'd, lied, pied, pried, pride, ride, sighed, side, slide, snide, spied, stride, tide, tied, tried, wide.
[2] **Bedtime**, daytime, every time, lifetime, maritime, meantime, nighttime, noontime, overtime, pantomime, pastime, playtime, sometime, sublime, springtime, summertime.
Airline, align, alpine, benign, canine, combine, confine, deadline, decline, define, design, divine, enshrine, entwine, feline, gang-sign, goldmine, headline, incline, lifeline, malign, moonshine, outshine, recline, refine, resign, skyline, sunshine, turbine, waistline.
Aligned, behind, combined, declined, defined, designed, entwined, free mind, inclined, maligned, mankind, reclined, refined, remind, resigned, rewind, unkind, unwind.
Abide, allied, applied, aside, astride, backside, backslide, bedside, beside, broadside, black-eyed, blue-eyed, brown-eyed, cock-eyed, collide, confide, cross-eyed, decide, denied, deride, divide, downside, fireside, green-eyed, hawk-eyed, high tide, hillside,

inside, lakeside, landslide, low tide, misguide, nearside, offside, outside, pop-eyed, preside, provide, red-eyed, reside, riptide, seaside, stateside, subside, tie-dyed, tongue-tied, topside, untied, untried, upside, wayside, well-tried, wide-eyed, worldwide, Yuletide.
[3] **Amplify**, beautify, certify, clarify, classify, crucify, dignify, falsify, fortify, glorify, gratify, horrify, justify, magnify, modify, mystify, notify, nullify, pacify, petrify, purify, qualify, rectify, sanctify, satisfy, simplify, specify, stupefy, terrify, testify, unify, verify.
[3] **Auld lang syne**, concubine, denying, intertwine, porcupine, realign, storyline, underline, undermine, valentine.

3.2.43 "--imer" (as in "climber")
[2] climber, mimer, primer, rhymer, timer.
[3] old-timer, part-timer, two-timer.

SURPRISING RHYMING:
[2] **China**, diner, finer, liner, miner, minor, piner, signer, whiner.
Binder, blinder, finder, grinder, kinda, kinder, minder, winder.
Diver, driver, fiver, jiver, skiver, striver, thriver.
Briber, cyber, fibre/fiber (U.S.), inscriber, prescriber, subscriber.
Buyer, choir, crier, dire, drier, dryer, dyer, fire, flyer, friar, fryer, higher, hire, inspire, ire, liar, Maya, mire, prior, pyre, sire, spire, tire, tyre/tire (U.S.), trier, via, wire.
Chider, cider, eider, glider, guider, hider, rider, slider, spider, strider, tiger, wider.
[3] **Airliner**, decliner, definer, designer, diviner, eyeliner, hardliner, headliner, moonshiner, recliner, refiner, streamliner, topliner.
Childminder, pathfinder, rangefinder, reminder, sidewinder, spellbinder, viewfinder.
Backslider, collider, confider, decider, divider, insider, joyrider, nightrider, outrider, outsider, provider, roughrider.
Conniver, contriver, piledriver, reviver, saliva, screwdriver, skydiver, survivor.

3.2.44 "--iming" (as in "timing")
[2] chiming, climbing, miming, priming, rhyming, timing.

SURPRISING RHYMING:
[2] **Dining**, fining, lining, mining, pining, shining, signing, whining.
Binding, blinding, finding, grinding, minding, winding.
Diving, driving, high-fiving, jiving, skiving, striving, thriving.
Buying, crying, drying, dying, flying, frying, plying, shying, trying.
Chiding, gliding, guiding, hiding, riding, sliding, striding.
[3] **Bribing**, imbibing, inscribing, prescribing, subscribing, transcribing.
Aligning, combining, confining, declining, defining, designing, divining, entwining, flatlining, headlining, inclining, reclining, refining, resigning, streamlining, toplining.
Bookbinding, childminding, reminding, spellbinding.
Backsliding, colliding, confiding, deciding, dividing, joyriding, providing.
Conniving, contriving, reviving, skydiving, slave driving, surviving.

3.2.45 "--imeless" (as in "timeless")
[2] chimeless, dimeless, rhymeless, timeless.

SURPRISING RHYMING:
[2] **Blindness**, childless, kindness, mindless, spineless, wildness.
Driest, highest, shyest, slyest, spryest.
Crisis, dryness, finest, highness, kindest, lightless, lightness, Midas, minus, nicest, shyness, sightless, sinus, slyness, stylus, tightness, virus, widest, wildest, wisest.
Brightest, lightest, slightest, tightest, tritest, whitest.
Bias, biased, lifeless, pious, priceless, righteous, tireless, viceless, wireless.
Guidance, licence/license (U.S.), silence, sirens, violence.

3.2.46 "--ine" (as in "mine")
[1] brine, cryin', fine, line(s), mine, nine, pine, shine, shrine, sign, spine, stein, swine, tine, twine, vine, whine, wine.

[2] airline, align, alpine, assign, bassline, benign, bovine, breadline, canine, carbine, carmine, combine, confine, consign, cosign, deadline, decline, define, design, divine, enshrine, entwine, feline, gang-sign, goldmine, hairline, headline, hemline, incline, lifeline, lupine, malign, moonshine, outshine, quinine, recline, refine, resign, skyline, sunshine, turbine, waistline.
[3] alkaline, auld lang syne, borderline, calamine, concubine, countersign, crystalline, denying, intertwine, porcupine, realign, storyline, turpentine, undefine(d), underline, undermine, valentine.

SURPRISING RHYMING:
[1] Chime, climb, clime, crime, dime, grime, I'm, lime, mime, prime, rhyme, rime, slime, sublime, thyme, time.
Bind, blind, find, fined, grind, kind, lined, mind, mined, pined, signed, whined, wined.
Bide, bride, chide, cried, died, dried, dyed, eyed, glide, guide, hide, I'd, lied, pied, pried, pride, ride, sighed, side, slide, snide, spied, stride, tide, tied, tried, wide.
Bite, blight, bright, cite, fight, flight, fright, height, kite, knight, light, mite, might, night, plight, quite, right, rite, sight, site, slight, smite, spite, sprite, tight, trite, white, write.
[2] Bedtime, daytime, hard time(s), lifetime, maritime, meantime, nighttime, noontime, overtime, pantomime, pastime, playtime, sometime(s), springtime, sublime, summertime.
Aligned, behind, combined, declined, defined, designed, entwined, free mind, inclined, maligned, mankind, reclined, refined, remind, resigned, rewind, unkind, unwind.
Abide, allied, applied, aside, astride, backside, backslide, bedside, beside, broadside, black-eyed, blue-eyed, brown-eyed, cock-eyed, collide, confide, cross-eyed, decide, denied, deride, divide, downside, fireside, green-eyed, hawk-eyed, high tide, hillside, inside, lakeside, landslide, low tide, misguide, nearside, offside, outside, pop-eyed, preside, provide, red-eyed, reside, riptide, seaside, stateside, subside, tie-dyed, tongue-tied, topside, untied, untried, upside, wayside, well-tried, wide-eyed, worldwide, Yuletide.
Airtight, all night, alright, birthright, bullfight, daylight, delight, despite, downright, eyesight, excite, expedite, extradite, fistfight, flashlight, floodlight, footlight, foresight, fortnight, goodnight, green light, hindsight, ignite, incite, indict, insight, invite, lamplight, midnight, moonlight, outright, playwright, polite, recite, red light, searchlight, skylight, spotlight, starlight, stoplight, sunlight, termite, tonight, twilight, unite, upright.
[3] Appetite, candlelight, copyright, day and night, dynamite, Fahrenheit, impolite, overnight, oversight, reunite, satellite.
Colour blind/color blind (U.S.), intertwined, mastermind, redesigned, undefined, underlined, womankind.

3.2.47 "--ined" (as in "kind")

[1] bind, blind, find, fined, grind, kind, lined, mind, mined, pined, signed, whined.
[2] aligned, behind, combined, consigned, cosigned, declined, defined, designed, divined, entwined, free mind, inclined, maligned, mankind, reclined, refined, remind, resigned, rewind, snow-blind, strong mind, unkind, unlined, untwined, unwind.
[3] colour blind/color blind (U.S.), countersigned, intertwined, mastermind, one of a kind, redesigned, undefined, underlined, unsigned, womankind.

SURPRISING RHYMING:
[1] Brine, cryin', fine, line(s), mine, nine, pine, shine, shrine, sign, spine, stein, swine, tine, twine, vine, whine, wine.
Chime, climb, crime, dime, grime, I'm, mime, prime, rhyme, rime, slime, sublime, time.
Bide, bride, chide, cried, died, dried, dyed, eyed, glide, guide, hide, I'd, lied, pied, pried, pride, ride, sighed, side, slide, snide, spied, stride, tide, tied, tried, wide.
Bite, blight, bright, cite, fight, flight, fright, height, kite, knight, light, mite, might, night, plight, quite, right, rite, sight, site, slight, smite, spite, sprite, tight, trite, white, write.
Knife, life, rife, strife, wife.
By, bye, buy, cry, die, dry, eye, fly, fry, goodbye, guy, high, I, lie, pi, pie, ply, pry, rye, shy, sigh, sky, sly, spy, spry, try, wry, why.
Child, filed, mild, piled, smiled, styled, wild.
Cries, dies, eyes, guise, lies, prize, rise, size, skies, thighs, tries, wise.
[2] Airline, align, alpine, benign, canine, combine, confine, deadline, decline, define,

design, divine, enshrine, entwine, feline, gang-sign, goldmine, headline, incline, lifeline, malign, moonshine, outshine, recline, refine, resign, skyline, sunshine, waistline.
Bedtime, daytime, hard time(s), lifetime, maritime, meantime, nighttime, noontime, overtime, pantomime, pastime, playtime, sometime(s), springtime, sublime, summertime.
Abide, allied, applied, aside, astride, backside, backslide, bedside, beside, broadside, black-eyed, blue-eyed, brown-eyed, cock-eyed, collide, confide, cross-eyed, decide, denied, deride, divide, downside, fireside, green-eyed, hawk-eyed, high tide, hillside, inside, lakeside, landslide, low tide, misguide, nearside, offside, outside, pop-eyed, preside, provide, red-eyed, reside, riptide, seaside, stateside, subside, tie-dyed, tongue-tied, topside, untied, untried, upside, wayside, well-tried, wide-eyed, worldwide, Yuletide.
Airtight, all night, alright, birthright, bullfight, daylight, delight, despite, downright, eyesight, excite, expedite, extradite, fistfight, flashlight, floodlight, footlight, foresight, fortnight, goodnight, green light, hindsight, ignite, incite, indict, insight, invite, lamplight, midnight, moonlight, outright, playwright, polite, recite, red light, searchlight, skylight, spotlight, starlight, stoplight, sunlight, termite, tonight, twilight, unite, upright.
Afterlife, highlife, housewife, jackknife, lowlife, midlife, midwife, nightlife, paperknife, penknife, pocketknife, shelf-life, still-life, wildlife.
Beguiled, compiled, exiled, godchild, grandchild, reconciled, reviled.
[3] **Auld lang syne**, borderline, concubine, countersign, crystalline, denying, intertwine, porcupine, realign, storyline, turpentine, undefine(d), underline, undermine, valentine.
Appetite, black and white, candlelight, copyright, copywrite, dynamite, impolite, neophyte, overnight, oversight, overwrite, parasite, reunite, satellite, second sight.

3.2.48 "--inded" (as in "blinded")
blinded, free-minded, like-minded, minded, reminded, re-winded, snow-blinded, strong-minded, weak-minded.

SURPRISING RHYMING:
[2] **Blighted**, cited, knighted, lighted, righted, sighted, spited.
Bided, chided, eyelid, hybrid, glided, guided, prided, sided, tided.
[3] **Abided**, collided, confided, decided, derided, divided, lopsided, misguided, one-sided, presided, provided, two-sided, undecided.
Decided, delighted, excited, farsighted, ignited, incited, invited, nearsighted, recited, shortsighted, spotlighted, united, unrequited.

3.2.49 "--inder" (as in "kinder")
[2] binder, blinder, finder, grinder, kinda, kinder, minder, winder.
[3] bookbinder, childminder, pathfinder, rangefinder, reminder, re-winder, ringbinder, sidewinder, spellbinder, viewfinder.

SURPRISING RHYMING:
[2] **China**, diner, finer, liner, miner, minor, shiner, signer, whiner.
Climber, mimer, primer, rhymer, timer.
Cyber, cider, eider, fibre/fiber (U.S.), glider, guider, hider, rider, slider, spider, wider.
Biter, brighter, fighter, lighter, slighter, tiger, tighter, triter, whiter, writer.
Buyer, choir, crier, dire, drier, dryer, fire, flyer, friar, fryer, higher, hire, ire, liar, Maya, mire, prior, pyre, shyer, sire, spire, squire, tire, tyre/tire (U.S.), trier, via, wire.
[3] **Airliner**, decliner, definer, designer, diviner, eyeliner, hardliner, headliner, maligner, moonshiner, recliner, refiner, streamliner.
Old-timer, part-timer, two-timer.
Backslider, collider, confider, decider, divider, insider, joyrider, nightrider, outrider, outsider, provider, roughrider.
All-nighter, backbiter, bullfighter, copywriter, delighter, exciter, ghostwriter, gunfighter, inciter, igniter, lamplighter, midnighter, moonlighter, overnighter, politer, prizefighter, reciter, rewriter, screenwriter, scriptwriter, signwriter, songwriter, typewriter.
Applier, hairdryer, homebuyer, messiah, pariah, replier, supplier.

3.2.50 "--inding" (as in "finding")
[2] binding, blinding, finding, grinding, minding, winding.

[3] childminding, pathfinding, reminding, rewinding, sidewinding, spellbinding, unwinding.

SURPRISING RHYMING:
[2] **Diving**, driving, high-fiving, jiving, skiving, striving, thriving.
Chiming, climbing, miming, priming, rhyming, timing.
Biting, fighting, lighting, righting, sighting, slighting, spiting, writing.
Biding, chiding, gliding, guiding, hiding, riding, siding, sliding, striding, tiding.
Griping, hyping, piping, retyping, sniping, striping, swiping, wiping.
Dining, lining, mining, shining, signing, whining, wining.
Buying, crying, drying, dyeing, dying, eyeing, flying, frying, lying, plying, prying, sighing, spying, trying, tying, vying.
Biking, hiking, liking, psyching, spiking, striking.
[3] **Aligning**, combining, confining, declining, defining, designing, divining, entwining, flatlining, headlining, inclining, reclining, refining, resigning, streamlining, toplining.
Arriving, conniving, contriving, depriving, deriving, reviving, skydiving, surviving.
Advising, arising, baptizing, capsizing, chastising, comprising, de-icing, despising, devising, disguising, downsizing, energizing, enticing, resizing, revising, rising, surmising, surprising, uprising.
Applying, complying, decrying, defying, denying, implying, relying, replying, satisfying, supplying, terrifying, unifying, untying.
Acquiring, admiring, aspiring, backfiring, conspiring, desiring, expiring, inquiring, inspiring, misfiring, perspiring, retiring, transpiring.
Beguiling, compiling, defiling, hair-styling, profiling, stockpiling.
Backbiting, bullfighting, copywriting, delighting, exciting, ghostwriting, gunfighting, inciting, igniting, inviting, moonlighting, reciting, rewriting, screenwriting, scriptwriting, signwriting, songwriting, typewriting, uniting.

3.2.51 "--iner" (as in "finer")
[2] china, diner, finer, liner, miner, minor, mynah, piner, shiner, signer, whiner.
[3] airliner, assigner, combiner, decliner, definer, designer, diviner, eyeliner, freightliner, hardliner, headliner, incliner, maligner, moonshiner, recliner, refiner, streamliner.

SURPRISING RHYMING:
[2] **Climber**, mimer, primer, rhymer, timer.
Chider, cider, glider, guider, hider, rider, slider, spider, wider.
Binder, blinder, finder, grinder, kinda, kinder, minder, winder.
Diver, driver, fiver, jiver, skiver, striver.
Briber, cyber, fibre/fiber (U.S.), inscriber, prescriber, subscriber.
Buyer, choir, crier, dire, drier, dryer, dyer, fire, flyer, friar, fryer, higher, hire, inspire, ire, liar, mire, prior, pyre, shyer, sire, spire, tire, tyre/tire (U.S.), trier, via, wire.
[3] **Old-timer**, part-timer, two-timer.
Backslider, collider, confider, decider, divider, insider, joyrider, nightrider, outrider, outsider, provider, roughrider.
Childminder, pathfinder, rangefinder, reminder, sidewinder, spellbinder, viewfinder.
Conniver, contriver, pearl diver, piledriver, saliva, screwdriver, skydiver, survivor.
Applier, hairdryer, homebuyer, messiah, pariah, replier, supplier.
Beguiler, compiler, defiler, hair-styler, profiler, reviler.
Conniver, piledriver, saliva, screwdriver, skydiver, survivor.
Acquire, admire, aspire, attire, backfire, barbwire, bonfire, campfire, ceasefire, conspire, crossfire, empire, enquire, entire, esquire, expire, gunfire, haywire, hellfire, inspire, perspire, quagmire, sapphire, satire, spitfire, surefire, tripwire, umpire, vampire, wildfire.

3.2.52 "--iness" (as in "shyness")
[2] dryness, highness, shyness, slyness, spryness.

SURPRISING RHYMING:
[2] **Blindness**, childless, kindness, mindless, spineless, timeless.
Driest, highest, shyest, slyest, spryest.
Crisis, finest, kindest, lightless, lightness, Midas, minus, nicest, sinus, slyness, stylus, tightness, virus, widest, wildest, wisest.

Brightness, lightness, rightness, tightness, triteness, whiteness.
Brightest, lightest, slightest, tightest, tritest, whitest.
Bias, biased, pious.
Iceless, lifeless, priceless, righteous, tireless, viceless, wireless.
Guidance, licence/license (U.S.), silence, sirens, violence.

3.2.53 "--ining" (as in "shining")
[2] dining, lining, mining, shining, signing, whining, wining.
[3] aligning, assigning, combining, confining, consigning, cosigning, declining, defining, designing, divining, entwining, flatlining, headlining, inclining, outshining, reclining, refining, resigning, streamlining, toplining.

SURPRISING RHYMING:
[2] Chiming, climbing, miming, priming, rhyming, timing.
Binding, blinding, finding, grinding, minding, winding.
Diving, driving, high-fiving, jiving, skiving, striving, thriving.
Buying, crying, drying, dyeing, dying, eyeing, flying, frying, lying, plying, prying, sighing, spying, trying, tying, vying.
Chiding, gliding, guiding, hiding, riding, sliding, striding.
Filing, piling, riling, smiling, styling, tiling.
Biting, citing, fighting, lighting, righting, sighting, spiting, writing.
[3] Bribing, describing, imbibing, inscribing, prescribing, subscribing.
Childminding, reminding, rewinding, spellbinding.
Backsliding, colliding, confiding, deciding, dividing, joyriding, providing.
Arriving, conniving, contriving, depriving, deriving, reviving, skydiving, surviving.
Applying, complying, decrying, defying, denying, implying, relying, replying, satisfying, supplying, terrifying, unifying, untying.
Advising, arising, capsizing, chastising, comprising, de-icing, despising, devising, disguising, downsizing, energizing, enticing, revising, rising, surprising, uprising.
Acquiring, admiring, aspiring, backfiring, conspiring, desiring, expiring, inquiring, inspiring, misfiring, perspiring, retiring, transpiring.
Beguiling, compiling, defiling, hair-styling, profiling, stockpiling.
Backbiting, copywriting, delighting, exciting, ghostwriting, gunfighting, inciting, igniting, inviting, midnighting, moonlighting, reciting, scriptwriting, songwriting, typewriting, uniting.

3.2.54 "--inement" (as in "refinement")
[3] alignment, assignment, confinement, consignment, enshrinement, refinement, realignment, reassignment.

SURPRISING RHYMING:
[2] Diamond, fireman, frightened, heightened, highland, island, lineman, silent, tightened, widened.
[3] Chastisement, compliant, excitement, horizon, incitement, reliant, retirement.

3.2.55 "--ipe" (as in "pipe")
[1] gripe, hype, pipe, ripe, snipe, stripe, swipe, tripe, type, wipe.
[2] bagpipe, blowpipe, overripe, pitch-pipe, retype, sideswipe, stereotype, under-ripe.

SURPRISING RHYMING:
[1] Griped, hyped, piped, sniped, striped, swiped, typed, wiped.
Bite, blight, bright, cite, fight, flight, fright, height, kite, knight, light, mite, might, night, plight, quite, right, rite, sight, site, slight, smite, spite, sprite, tight, trite, white, write.
Bike, dyke/dike, hike, like, mike/mic, psych, spike, strike, trike, tyke.
Bribe, jibe, scribe, tribe, vibe.
Bide, bride, chide, cried, died, dried, dyed, eyed, glide, guide, hide, I'd, lied, pied, pried, pride, ride, sighed, side, slide, snide, spied, stride, tide, tied, tried, wide.
Knife, life, rife, strife, wife.
By, bye, buy, cry, die, dry, eye, fly, fry, goodbye, guy, high, I, lie, pi, pie, ply, pry, rye, shy, sigh, sky, sly, spy, spry, try, wry, why.

[2] Airtight, all night, alright, birthright, bullfight, daylight, delight, despite, downright, eyesight, excite, expedite, extradite, fistfight, flashlight, floodlight, footlight, foresight, fortnight, goodnight, green light, hindsight, ignite, incite, indict, insight, invite, lamplight, midnight, moonlight, outright, playwright, polite, recite, red light, searchlight, skylight, spotlight, starlight, stoplight, sunlight, termite, tonight, twilight, unite, upright.
Alike, catlike, childlike, dislike, dreamlike, ghostlike, godlike, hitchhike, lifelike, pushbike, spring-like, sponge-like, star-like, suchlike, sun-like, turnpike, unlike, warlike, witchlike.
Describe, diatribe, imbibe, inscribe, prescribe, subscribe, transcribe.
Abide, applied, aside, astride, backside, backslide, bedside, beside, broadside, black-eyed, blue-eyed, brown-eyed, cock-eyed, collide, confide, cross-eyed, decide, denied, deride, divide, downside, fireside, green-eyed, hawk-eyed, high tide, hillside, inside, lakeside, landslide, low tide, misguide, nearside, offside, outside, pop-eyed, preside, provide, red-eyed, reside, riptide, seaside, stateside, subside, tie-dyed, tongue-tied, topside, untied, untried, upside, wayside, well-tried, wide-eyed, worldwide, Yuletide.
Afterlife, good life, highlife, housewife, jackknife, lowlife, midlife, midwife, nightlife, penknife, pocketknife, shelf-life, still-life, wildlife.
[3] Businesslike, ladylike, lookalike, motorbike, soundalike, sportsmanlike.

3.2.56 "--iped" (as in "wiped")

[1] griped, hyped, piped, retyped, sideswiped, sniped, striped, swiped, typed, wiped.

SURPRISING RHYMING:
[1] Gripe, hype, pipe, ripe, snipe, stripe, swipe, tripe, type, wipe.
Bite, blight, bright, cite, fight, flight, fright, height, kite, knight, light, mite, might, night, plight, quite, right, rite, sight, site, slight, smite, spite, sprite, tight, trite, white, write.
Bike(d), hike(d), like(d), mike/mic, psych(ed), spike(d), strike, trike.
[2] Bagpipe, blowpipe, overripe, pitch-pipe, retype, sideswipe, stereotype, under-ripe.
Airtight, all night, alright, birthright, bullfight, daylight, delight, despite, downright, eyesight, excite, expedite, extradite, fistfight, flashlight, floodlight, footlight, foresight, fortnight, goodnight, green light, hindsight, ignite, incite, indict, insight, invite, lamplight, midnight, moonlight, outright, playwright, polite, recite, red light, searchlight, skylight, spotlight, starlight, stoplight, sunlight, termite, tonight, twilight, unite, upright.
Alike, catlike, childlike, dislike(d), dreamlike, ghostlike, godlike, hitchhike(d), lifelike, psyched, pushbike, spring-like, sponge-like, star-like, suchlike, turnpike, unlike(d).

3.2.57 "--iper" (as in "wiper")

[2] diaper, griper, hyper, piper, riper, sniper, striper, swiper, viper, wiper.
[3] bagpiper, sandpiper, sideswiper.

SURPRISING RHYMING:
[2] Biter, brighter, fighter, lighter, mitre/miter (U.S.), slighter, tighter, triter, whiter, writer.
Briber, fibre/fiber (U.S.), inscriber, prescriber, subscriber, transcriber.
Cider, cipher, glider, guider, hider, lifer, rider, slider, spider, wider.
China, diner, finer, liner, miner, minor, piner, shiner, signer, whiner.
Climber, mimer, primer, rhymer, timer.
[3] All-nighter, backbiter, bullfighter, copywriter, delighter, exciter, fistfighter, ghostwriter, gunfighter, inciter, igniter, lamplighter, midnighter, moonlighter, overnighter, politer, prizefighter, reciter, rewriter, screenwriter, scriptwriter, songwriter, typewriter.
Backslider, collider, confider, decider, divider, insider, joyrider, nightrider, outrider, outsider, provider, roughrider.
Airliner, decliner, definer, designer, eyeliner, hardliner, headliner, incliner, maligner, moonshiner, recliner, refiner, streamliner.

3.2.58 "--iping" (as in "typing")

griping, hyping, piping, retyping, sideswiping, sniping, striping, swiping, wiping.

SURPRISING RHYMING:
[2] Biting, citing, fighting, lighting, righting, sighting, spiting, writing.
Biding, chiding, gliding, guiding, hiding, riding, siding, sliding, striding, tiding.

Bribing, describing, imbibing, inscribing, prescribing, subscribing.
Chiming, climbing, miming, priming, rhyming, timing.
Dining, lining, mining, shining, signing, whining, wining.
Diving, driving, high-fiving, jiving, skiving, striving, thriving.
Buying, crying, drying, dyeing, dying, eyeing, flying, frying, lying, plying, prying, sighing, spying, trying, tying, vying.
[3] **Delighting**, exciting, handwriting, inciting, inviting, reciting, spotlighting, uniting.
Abiding, backsliding, colliding, confiding, dividing, misguiding, presiding, providing.
Aligning, assigning, combining, confining, declining, defining, designing, divining, entwining, flatlining, headlining, outshining, reclining, resigning, streamlining, toplining.
Applying, complying, decrying, defying, denying, implying, relying, replying, satisfying, supplying, terrifying, unifying, untying.
Arriving, conniving, contriving, depriving, deriving, reviving, skydiving, surviving.

3.2.59 "--ire" (as in "fire")
[1] choir, dire, fire, hire, ire, mire, pyre, shire, sire, spire, tire, tyre/tire (U.S), wire.
[2] acquire, admire, aspire, attire, backfire, barbwire, bonfire, bushfire, buyer, campfire, ceasefire, conspire, crossfire, desire, empire, enquire, entire, esquire, expire, gunfire, haywire, hellfire, higher, inquire, inspire, misfire, perspire, quagmire, require, retire, rewire, sapphire, satire, spitfire, surefire, transpire, tripwire, umpire, vampire, wildfire.

SURPRISING RHYMING:
[1] **Fired**, hired, mired, sired, squired, tired, wired.
[2] **Acquired**, admired, aspired, backfired, barbwired, conspired, desired, expired, inquired, inspired, misfired, overtired, perspired, required, retired, rewired, transpired, undesired, uninspired, unwired.
Briar, buyer, crier, denier, dire, drier, dryer, dyer, flier/flyer, friar, higher, liar, Maya, plier, plyer, prier, prior, shyer, trier, via.
[3] **Applier**, denier, hairdryer, homebuyer, messiah, papaya, pariah, replier, supplier.
[4] **Amplifier**, beautifier, clarifier, disqualifier, glorifier, humidifier, identifier, intensifier, jambalaya, justifier, magnifier, multiplier, occupier, pacifier, prophesier, purifier, qualifier, rectifier, signifier, specifier, terrifier, testifier, tumble-dryer, unifier, verifier, vilifier.

3.2.60 "--ired" (as in "tired")
[1] fired, hired, mired, sired, squired, tired, wired.
[2] acquired, admired, aspired, attired, backfired, barbwired, conspired, desired, expired, inquired, inspired, misfired, overtired, perspired, rehired, required, retired, rewired, transpired, undesired, uninspired, unwired.

SURPRISING RHYMING:
[1] **Choir**, dire, fire, hire, ire, mire, pyre, shire, sire, spire, tire, tyre/tire (U.S), wire.
[2] **Acquire**, admire, aspire, backfire, barbwire, bonfire, buyer, campfire, ceasefire, conspire, crossfire, desire, empire, enquire, entire, esquire, expire, gunfire, haywire, hellfire, higher, inquire, inspire, misfire, perspire, quagmire, require, retire, rewire, sapphire, satire, spitfire, surefire, transpire, tripwire, umpire, vampire, wildfire.
Buyer, crier, defier, denier, dire, drier, dryer, flier/flyer, higher, liar, prior, trier, via.
[3] **Applier**, denier, hairdryer, homebuyer, messiah, papaya, pariah, replier, supplier.
[4] **Amplifier**, beautifier, clarifier, disqualifier, glorifier, humidifier, identifier, intensifier, jambalaya, justifier, magnifier, multiplier, occupier, pacifier, prophesier, purifier, qualifier, rectifier, signifier, specifier, terrifier, testifier, tumble-dryer, unifier, verifier, vilifier.

3.2.61 "--iring" (as in "inspiring")
[2] firing, hiring, squiring, tiring, wiring.
[3] acquiring, admiring, aspiring, attiring, backfiring, conspiring, desiring, expiring, inquiring, inspiring, misfiring, perspiring, rehiring, retiring, re-wiring, transpiring, uninspiring, untiring.

SURPRISING RHYMING:
[2] **Diving**, driving, high-fiving, jiving, rising, skiving, striving, thriving.

Biking, disliking, hiking, hitchhiking, liking, spiking, striking, Viking.
Biting, citing, fighting, lighting, righting, sighting, spiting, writing.
Griping, hyping, piping, retyping, sideswiping, sniping, striping, swiping, wiping.
Dining, fining, lining, mining, pining, shining, siren, signing, whining.
Buying, crying, drying, dyeing, dying, eyeing, flying, frying, lying, plying, prying, sighing, spying, trying, tying, vying.
Chiming, climbing, miming, priming, rhyming, timing.
Binding, blinding, finding, grinding, minding, winding.
Filing, piling, riling, smiling, styling, tiling.
[3] Advising, arising, baptizing, capsizing, chastising, comprising, de-icing, despising, devising, disguising, downsizing, energizing, enticing, revising, surprising, uprising.
Arriving, conniving, contriving, depriving, deriving, reviving, skydiving, surviving.
Bribing, describing, imbibing, inscribing, prescribing, subscribing.
Aligning, combining, confining, declining, defining, designing, entwining, flatlining, headlining, inclining, outshining, reclining, refining, resigning, streamlining, toplining.
Delighting, exciting, ghostwriting, gunfighting, inciting, igniting, inviting, midnighting, moonlighting, reciting, screenwriting, songwriting, spotlighting, typewriting, uniting.
Applying, complying, decrying, defying, denying, implying, relying, replying, satisfying, supplying, terrifying, unifying, untying.
[4] Agonizing, burglarizing, civilizing, compromising, criticizing, demoralizing, dramatizing, emphasizing, enterprising, finalizing, harmonizing, hypnotizing, idolizing, immunizing, jeopardizing, legalizing, magnetizing, memorizing, mesmerizing, modernizing, moralizing, publicizing, realizing, recognizing, sacrificing, satirizing, socializing, specializing, symbolizing, sympathizing, tantalizing, terrorizing, unsurprising, victimizing.

3.2.62 "--ising" (as in "rising")

[3] advising, apprising, arising, baptizing, capsizing, chastising, comprising, de-icing, despising, devising, disguising, downsizing, enticing, excising, resizing, revising, rising, surmising, surprising, uprising, upsizing.
[4] advertising, agonizing, analyzing, authorizing, burglarizing, categorizing, centralizing, civilizing, colonizing, compromising, criticizing, demoralizing, dramatizing, emphasizing, energizing, enterprising, eulogizing, fertilizing, finalizing, fraternizing, harmonizing, hypnotizing, idolizing, immunizing, jeopardizing, legalizing, magnetizing, memorizing, mesmerizing, modernizing, moralizing, neutralizing, publicizing, realizing, recognizing, sacrificing, satirizing, scrutinizing, sensitizing, socializing, specializing, stabilizing, standardizing, sterilizing, subsidizing, symbolizing, sympathizing, tantalizing, tenderizing, terrorizing, theorizing, unsurprising, utilizing, vaporizing, verbalizing, victimizing.

SURPRISING RHYMING:
[2] De-icing, dicing, enticing, horizon, icing, pricing, sacrificing, slicing, splicing.
Diving, driving, high-fiving, jiving, skiving, striving, thriving.
Bribing, describing, imbibing, inscribing, prescribing, subscribing.
Biding, gliding, guiding, hiding, riding, siding, sliding, striding, tiding.
Chiming, climbing, miming, priming, rhyming, timing.
Filing, piling, riling, smiling, styling, tiling, wiling.
Dining, lining, mining, shining, signing, whining, wining.
Biting, citing, fighting, lighting, righting, sighting, spiting, writing.
Griping, hyping, piping, retyping, sniping, striping, swiping, wiping.
Buying, crying, drying, dyeing, dying, eyeing, flying, frying, lying, plying, prying, sighing, spying, trying, tying, vying.
Binding, blinding, finding, grinding, minding, winding.
Brightening, enlightening, frightening, heightening, lightning, tightening, whitening.
Firing, hiring, squiring, tiring, wiring.
Biking, disliking, hiking, hitchhiking, liking, spiking, striking, Viking.
[3] Arriving, conniving, contriving, depriving, deriving, reviving, skydiving, surviving.
Abiding, backsliding, colliding, confiding, dividing, presiding, providing, residing.
Beguiling, compiling, profiling, reconciling, restyling, unsmiling.
Combining, declining, defining, designing, entwining, flatlining, headlining, outshining, reclining, refining, resigning, streamlining, toplining.
Delighting, exciting, handwriting, inciting, inviting, reciting, rewriting, spotlighting, uniting.

Applying, complying, decrying, defying, denying, implying, relying, replying, satisfying, supplying, terrifying, unifying, untying.
Acquiring, admiring, aspiring, backfiring, conspiring, desiring, inquiring, inspiring, perspiring, retiring, uninspiring, untiring.

3.2.63 "--ite" (as in "might")
[1] bite, blight, bright, cite, fight, flight, fright, height, kite, knight, light, might, night, plight, quite, right, rite, sight, site, slight, smite, spite, sprite, tight, trite, white, write.
[2] airtight, all night, alright, birthright, bobwhite, bullfight, cartwright, cockfight, daylight, delight, despite, downright, eyesight, excite, expedite, extradite, fistfight, flashlight, floodlight, footlight, foresight, fortnight, goodnight, graphite, green light, hindsight, ignite, incite, indict, insight, invite, lamplight, midnight, moonlight, outright, playwright, polite, recite, red light, requite, searchlight, skylight, spotlight, starlight, stoplight, sunlight, termite, tonight, twilight, unite, upright.
[3] appetite, black and white, candlelight, copyright, copywrite, day and night, dynamite, Fahrenheit, impolite, neophyte, overnight, oversight, overwrite, parasite, reunite, satellite, second sight, stalagmite, traffic light, underwrite.

SURPRISING RHYMING:
[1] Bike(d), hike(d), like(d), mike/mic, psych(d), spike(d), strike.
Dice, ice, mice, nice, price, rice, slice, spice, splice, twice, vice.
Knife, life, rife, strife, wife.
Bribe, jibe, scribe, tribe, vibe.
Gripe(d), hype(d), pipe(d), ripe, snipe(d), stripe(d), swipe(d), tripe, type(d), wipe(d).
Bide, bride, chide, cried, died, dried, dyed, eyed, glide, guide, hide, I'd, lied, pied, pried, pride, ride, sighed, side, slide, snide, spied, stride, tide, tied, tried, wide.
I've, chive, dive, drive, five, hive, jive, live, strive, thrive.
Cry, dry, fry, pry, rye, sky, spry, try, wry.
[2] Advice, choc-ice, concise, device, entice, half-price, precise, sacrifice, suffice.
Good life, highlife, housewife, jackknife, lowlife, midlife, midwife, nightlife, paperknife, penknife, pocketknife, shelf-life, still-life, wildlife.
Describe, imbibe, inscribe, prescribe, subscribe, transcribe.
Bagpipe, blowpipe, overripe, pitch-pipe, retype, sideswipe, stereotype, under-ripe.
Alike, catlike, childlike, dislike(d), dreamlike, ghostlike, godlike, hitchhike(d), lifelike, psyched, pushbike, spring-like, sponge-like, suchlike, turnpike, unlike, warlike, witchlike.
Alive, arrive, contrive, deprive, nose-dive, overdrive, revive, survive.
Abide, allied, applied, aside, astride, backside, backslide, bedside, beside, broadside, black-eyed, blue-eyed, brown-eyed, cock-eyed, collide, confide, cross-eyed, decide, denied, deride, divide, downside, fireside, green-eyed, hawk-eyed, high tide, hillside, inside, lakeside, landslide, low tide, misguide, nearside, offside, outside, pop-eyed, preside, provide, red-eyed, reside, riptide, seaside, stateside, subside, tie-dyed, tongue-tied, topside, untied, untried, upside, wayside, well-tried, wide-eyed, worldwide, Yuletide.
[3] Cold as ice, edelweiss, merchandise, paradise, sacrifice.

3.2.64 "--ited" (as in "delighted")
[2] blighted, cited, knighted, lighted, righted, sighted, sited, slighted, spited.
[3] clear-sighted, delighted, excited, farsighted, ignited, incited, indicted, invited, nearsighted, recited, requited, shortsighted, spotlighted, united, unrequited, unsighted.

SURPRISING RHYMING:
[2] Bided, chided, fight it, glided, guided, prided, private, sided.
Blinded, eyelid, hybrid, minded, winded.
[3] Abided, collided, confided, decided, derided, divided, lopsided, misguided, one-sided, presided, provided, two-sided, undecided.
Free-minded, high-minded, like-minded, reminded, snow-blinded, strong-minded, weak-minded.

3.2.65 "--iten" (as in "brighten")
brighten, enlighten, frighten, heighten, lighten, retighten, tighten, titan, whiten.

SURPRISING RHYMING:
[2] **Brightened**, enlightened, fireman, frightened, heightened, highland, island, lineman, lightened, silent, tightened, widen, widened, whitened.
Biting, citing, fighting, lighting, righting, sighting, spiting, writing.
Horizon, hyphen, liken, lion, siren, python, ripen, siphon.
Diving, driving, high-fiving, jiving, skiving, striving, thriving.
Chiming, climbing, item, miming, priming, rhyming, timing.
Binding, blinding, finding, grinding, minding, winding.
Filing, piling, riling, smiling, styling, tiling.
Dining, fining, lining, mining, pining, shining, signing, whining.
Biking, disliking, hiking, hitchhiking, liking, spiking, striking, Viking.
Dicing, icing, pricing, slicing, splicing.
[3] **Delighting**, exciting, handwriting, inciting, indicting, inviting, reciting, requiting, rewriting, spotlighting, uniting.

3.2.66 "--iter" (as in "writer")
[2] biter, brighter, fighter, lighter, mitre/miter (U.S.), slighter, tighter, triter, whiter, writer.
[3] all-nighter, backbiter, bullfighter, copywriter, delighter, exciter, expediter, fistfighter, ghostwriter, gunfighter, inciter, igniter, indicter, inviter, lamplighter, midnighter, moonlighter, overnighter, politer, prizefighter, reciter, rewriter, screenwriter, scriptwriter, signwriter, songwriter, typewriter, underwriter.

SURPRISING RHYMING:
[2] **Biker,** hiker, like her, spiker, striker, tiger.
Chider, cider, glider, guider, hider, rider, slider, spider, wider.
Diaper, hyper, piper, riper, sniper, striper, swiper, viper, wiper.
Briber, cyber, fibre/fiber (U.S.), inscriber, prescriber, subscriber.
Dicer, enticer, de-icer, nicer, slicer, splicer.
Diver, driver, fiver, jiver, skiver, striver, thriver.
China, diner, finer, liner, miner, minor, piner, shiner, signer, whiner.
Binder, blinder, finder, grinder, kinda, kinder, minder, winder.
[3] **Backslider**, collider, confider, decider, divider, insider, joyrider, nightrider, outrider, outsider, provider, roughrider, screwdriver, skydiver, survivor.
Dieter, proprietor, quieter, rioter.
Airliner, decliner, definer, designer, eyeliner, hardliner, headliner, maligner, moonshiner, recliner, refiner, streamliner.
Childminder, pathfinder, rangefinder, reminder, re-winder, ringbinder, sidewinder, spellbinder, viewfinder.

3.2.67 "--itest" (as in "brightest")
[2] brightest, lightest, slightest, tightest, tritest, whitest.

SURPRISING RHYMING:
[2] **Clients**, finest, giants, highness, kindest, lightness, lions, Midas, minus, nicest, sinus, tightness, virus, widest, wildest, wisest.
Bias, biased, driest, finest, highest, pious, shyest, slyest, spryest.
Guidance, licence/license (U.S.), silence, sirens, violence.
Chimeless, dimeless, rhymeless, timeless.
Blindness, childless, kindness, mindless, spineless, wildness.
Lifeless, priceless, righteous, tireless, viceless, wireless.

3.2.68 "--iteful" (as in "spiteful")
delightful, frightful, rightful, spiteful.

SURPRISING RHYMING:
[2] **Rival**, spiral, title, trial, viral, vital.
Bible, libel, tribal, liable, libel.
Bridal, bridle, idle, idol, sidle, tidal.

Cycle, final, primal, spinal.
Eyeful, mindful, rifle, stifle, trifle.
[3] Entitle, entitled, recital, requital, retitle, subtitle, title, vital.
Arrival, delightful, disciple, insightful, recycle, reprisal, revival, survival.

3.2.69 "--iting" (as in "fighting")
[2] biting, citing, fighting, lighting, righting, sighting, siting, slighting, spiting, writing.
[3] bullfighting, cockfighting, delighting, exciting, fistfighting, handwriting, igniting, inciting, indicting, inviting, moonlighting, reciting, requiting, rewriting, spotlighting, uniting.
[4] copyrighting, copywriting, dynamiting, expediting, extraditing, reuniting, underwriting.

SURPRISING RHYMING:
[2] Frightening, heightening, lightning, tightening, whitening.
Brighten, enlighten, frighten, heighten, lighten, tighten, titan, whiten.
Biking, disliking, hiking, hitchhiking, liking, spiking, striking, Viking.
De-icing, dicing, icing, pricing, slicing, splicing.
Griping, hyping, piping, retyping, sniping, striping, swiping, wiping.
Biding, gliding, guiding, hiding, riding, siding, sliding, striding, tiding.
Diving, driving, high-fiving, jiving, skiving, striving, thriving.
[3] Bribing, describing, imbibing, inscribing, prescribing, subscribing.
Advising, arising, baptizing, capsizing, chastising, comprising, de-icing, despising, devising, disguising, downsizing, energizing, enticing, resizing, revising, rising, sacrificing, surprising, uprising.
Ascribing, describing, imbibing, inscribing, prescribing, subscribing.
Arriving, conniving, contriving, depriving, reviving, skydiving, surviving.
Abiding, backsliding, colliding, confiding, dividing, presiding, providing, residing.

3.2.70 "--itel" (as in "vital")
entitle, mistitle, recital, requital, retitle, subtitle, title, vital.

SURPRISING RHYMING:
[2] Frightful, rifle, rightful, spiteful, stifle, trifle.
Dial, phial, rival, spiral, title, titled, trial, viral, vital.
Bible, bridal, bridle, idle, idol, libel, sidle, tidal, tribal, liable, libel.
Cycle, final, hyphen, primal, recycle, life cycle, siphon, spinal, vinyl.
[3] Arrival, denial, misdial, mistrial, retrial, revival, self-denial, sundial, survival.
Deniable, identifiable, justifiable, reliable, unreliable, undeniable, verifiable, viable.
Archetypal, delightful, disciple, insightful, recycle, reprisal.
Advisable, desirable, excitable, inadvisable, likeable, (un)recognizable, sizable.
Doctrinal, homicidal, quarterfinal, semifinal, suicidal, unbridle, urinal.

3.2.71 "--itely" (as in "brightly")
brightly, contritely, fortnightly, lightly, nightly, politely, rightly, slightly, sprightly/spritely, tightly, tritely, unsightly.

SURPRISING RHYMING:
Likely, mildly, quietly, unlikely, wildly.
Concisely, nicely, precisely, wisely.
Drily, highly, idly, shyly, slyly, smiley, wily, wryly.
Blindly, defiantly, finely, Friday, kindly, lively, sublimely, timely, unkindly, widely.

3.2.72 "--itement" (as in "excitement")
[3] excitement, incitement, indictment.

SURPRISING RHYMING:
[2] Diet, giant, hydrant, island, quiet, riot, triumph, tyrant, vibrant.
Diamond, frightened, heightened, highland, island, lineman, silent, tightened, widened.
[3] Alignment, assignment, confinement, refinement, realignment, reassignment.
Compliant, defiant, horizon, reliant, requirement, retirement.

3.2.73 "--iteness" (as in "brightness")
[2] brightness, lightness, politeness, rightness, slightness, tightness, whiteness.

SURPRISING RHYMING:
[2] **Brightest**, lightest, slightest, tightest, tritest, whitest.
Digress, dryness, highness, likeness, shyness, slyness, spryness.
Blindness, childless, kindness, mindless, spineless, timeless, wildness.
Bias, biased, driest, highest, pious, shyest, slyest, spryest.
Crisis, finest, kindest, lightness, Midas, minus, nicest, sightless, slyness, stylus, virus, widest, wildest, wisest.
Chimeless, dimeless, rhymeless, timeless.
Iceless, lifeless, priceless, righteous, tireless, viceless, wireless.

3.2.74 "--itening" (as in "lightning")
[2] brightening, enlightening, frightening, heightening, lightning, tightening, whitening.

SURPRISING RHYMING:
[2] **Biting**, citing, fighting, lighting, righting, sighting, spiting, writing.
Griping, hyping, piping, sniping, striping, swiping, wiping.
Biking, disliking, hiking, hitchhiking, liking, spiking, striking, Viking.
Biding, gliding, guiding, hiding, riding, siding, sliding, striding, tiding.
Binding, blinding, finding, grinding, minding, winding.
Chiming, climbing, miming, priming, rhyming, timing.
Dining, fining, lining, mining, pining, shining, signing, whining.
[3] **Backbiting**, bullfighting, delighting, exciting, ghostwriting, gunfighting, highlighting, inciting, igniting, inviting, lamplighting, midnighting, moonlighting, reciting, rewriting, screenwriting, scriptwriting, signwriting, songwriting, spotlighting, typewriting, uniting.
Aligning, assigning, combining, confining, declining, defining, designing, entwining, flatlining, headlining, inclining, outshining, reclining, refining, resigning, toplining.
Abiding, backsliding, colliding, confiding, dividing, presiding, providing, residing.
Arriving, conniving, contriving, depriving, deriving, reviving, skydiving, surviving.

3.2.75 "--itefully" (as in "spitefully")
[3] delightfully, frightfully, rightfully, spitefully.

SURPRISING RHYMING:
[2] **Brightly**, lightly, likely, nightly, rightly, slightly, sprightly, tightly.
[3] **Contritely**, politely, quietly, unlikely, unsightly.
Rivalry, silently, vibrantly, violently.
Mightily, righteously, privacy, privately, sobriety, tirelessly, vibrancy.
Finally, irony, mindfully.
[4] **Decidedly**, delightedly, excitedly.

3.2.76 "--ive" (as in "drive")
[1] I've, chive, dive, drive, five, hive, jive, live, strive, thrive.
[2] alive, arrive, beehive, contrive, deprive, nose-dive, overdrive, revive, survive.

SURPRISING RHYMING:
[1] **Bite**, blight, bright, cite, fight, flight, fright, height, kite, knight, light, might, night, plight, quite, right, rite, sight, site, slight, smite, spite, sprite, tight, trite, white, write.
Bide, bride, chide, cried, died, dried, dyed, eyed, glide, guide, hide, I'd, lied, pied, pried, pride, ride, sighed, side, slide, snide, spied, stride, tide, tied, tried, wide.
Cries, dies, eyes, guise, lies, prize, rise, size, skies, tries, wise.
By, bye, buy, cry, die, dry, eye, fly, fry, goodbye, guy, high, I, lie, pi, pie, ply, pry, rye, shy, sigh, sky, sly, spy, spry, try, wry, why.
[2] **Airtight**, all night, alright, birthright, bullfight, daylight, delight, despite, downright, eyesight, excite, expedite, extradite, fistfight, flashlight, floodlight, footlight, foresight, fortnight, goodnight, green light, hindsight, ignite, incite, indict, insight, invite, lamplight,

midnight, moonlight, outright, playwright, polite, recite, red light, searchlight, skylight, spotlight, starlight, stoplight, sunlight, termite, tonight, twilight, unite, upright.
Abide, allied, applied, aside, astride, backside, backslide, bedside, beside, broadside, black-eyed, blue-eyed, brown-eyed, cock-eyed, collide, confide, cross-eyed, decide, denied, deride, divide, downside, fireside, green-eyed, hawk-eyed, high tide, hillside, inside, lakeside, landslide, low tide, misguide, nearside, offside, outside, pop-eyed, preside, provide, red-eyed, reside, riptide, seaside, stateside, subside, tie-dyed, tongue-tied, topside, untied, untried, upside, wayside, well-tried, wide-eyed, worldwide, Yuletide.
Advise, arise, blue eyes, brown eyes, chastise, clockwise, comprise, demise, despise, devise, disguise, energize, green eyes, likewise, moonrise, sunrise, surprise, unwise.
[3] **Alibi,** by and by, drive-by, lullaby, passer(s)-by, rockabye.
Appetite, candlelight, copyright, day and night, dynamite, Fahrenheit, impolite, neophyte, overnight, oversight, overwrite, parasite, reunite, satellite, second sight, underwrite.
Advertise, agonize, burglarize, civilize, compromise, criticize, demoralize, dramatize, emphasize, enterprise, fertilize, finalize, fossilize, harmonize, hypnotize, idolize, immunize, jeopardize, magnetize, memorize, mesmerize, modernize, otherwise, publicize, realize, recognize, satirize, scrutinize, sensitize, socialize, specialize, stabilize, symbolize, sympathize, tantalize, terrorize, victimize.

3.2.77 "--ival" (as in "survival")
archival, arrival, revival, rival, survival.

SURPRISING RHYMING:
[2] **Spiral**, title, trial, viral, vital.
Bible, libel, tribal, liable, libel.
Bridal, bridle, idle, idol, sidle, tidal.
Cycle, final, primal, spinal, vinyl.
Delightful, eyeful, frightful, mindful, rifle, rightful, spiteful, stifle, trifle.
[3] **Entitle**, entitled, recital, recycle, requital, retitle, subtitle.
Denial, misdial, mistrial, retrial, self-denial, sundial.
Archetypal, disciple, insightful, reprisal.

3.2.78 "--iver" (as in "driver")
[2] diver, driver, fiver, jiver, skiver, striver, thriver.
[3] conniver, contriver, piledriver, reviver, saliva, screwdriver, skydiver, survivor.

SURPRISING RHYMING:
[2] **Briber**, cyber, fibre/fiber (U.S.), inscriber, prescriber, subscriber.
Chider, cider, glider, guider, hider, rider, slider, spider, wider.
China, diner, finer, liner, miner, minor, piner, shiner, signer, whiner.
Biter, brighter, fighter, lighter, mitre/miter (U.S.), slighter, tighter, triter, whiter, writer.
Diaper, hyper, piper, riper, sniper, striper, swiper, viper, wiper.
Dicer, enticer, de-icer, nicer, slicer, splicer.
[3] **Backslider**, bagpiper, collider, confider, decider, divider, insider, hang-glider, joyrider, nightrider, outrider, outsider, provider, roughrider, sandpiper, sideswiper.
All-nighter, backbiter, bullfighter, copywriter, delighter, exciter, fistfighter, ghostwriter, gunfighter, inciter, igniter, lamplighter, midnighter, moonlighter, overnighter, politer, prizefighter, reciter, rewriter, screenwriter, scriptwriter, signwriter, songwriter, typewriter.
Airliner, designer, eyeliner, hardliner, headliner, moonshiner, recliner, refiner.

3.2.79 "--iving" (as in "driving")
[2] diving, driving, high-fiving, jiving, skiving, striving, thriving.
[3] arriving, conniving, contriving, depriving, deriving, reviving, skydiving, surviving.

SURPRISING RHYMING:
[2] **Bribing**, imbibing, inscribing, prescribing, subscribing, transcribing.
Chiding, gliding, guiding, hiding, riding, sliding, striding.
Dining, lining, mining, pining, shining, signing, whining.
Biting, blighting, citing, fighting, lighting, sighting, writing.

Griping, hyping, piping, sniping, striping, swiping, wiping.
Dicing, enticing, de-icing, slicing, splicing.
[3] **Backsliding**, colliding, confiding, deciding, dividing, hang-gliding, joyriding, providing.
Backbiting, bullfighting, copywriting, delighting, exciting, ghostwriting, gunfighting, inciting, igniting, inviting, midnighting, moonlighting, prizefighting, reciting, rewriting, screenwriting, scriptwriting, signwriting, songwriting, typewriting, uniting.
Combining, declining, defining, designing, headlining, inclining, reclining, refining.

3.2.80 "--ize" (as in "prize")

[1] cries, dies, eyes, guise, lies, prize, rise, size, skies, thighs, tries, wise.
[2] advise, apprise, arise, baptize, blue eyes, brown eyes, capsize, chastise, clockwise, comprise, crosswise, demise, despise, devise, disguise, energize, eulogize, excise, first prize, green eyes, likewise, moonrise, revise, sunrise, surmise, surprise, unwise.
[3] advertise, agonize, analyze, authorize, burglarize, categorize, centralize, civilize, colonize, compromise, criticize, demoralize, dramatize, emphasize, enterprise, feminize, fertilize, finalize, fossilize, fraternize, harmonize, hypnotize, idolize, immunize, jeopardize, legalize, magnetize, mechanize, memorize, mesmerize, modernize, moralize, neutralize, otherwise, pasteurize, publicize, realize, recognize, satirize, scrutinize, sensitize, socialize, specialize, stabilize, standardize, sterilize, subsidize, symbolize, sympathize, tantalize, tenderize, terrorize, theorize, utilize, verbalize, victimize.

SURPRISING RHYMING:
[1] **Bide**, bride, chide, cried, died, dried, dyed, eyed, glide, guide, hide, I'd, lied, pied, pried, pride, ride, sighed, side, slide, snide, spied, stride, tide, tied, tried, wide.
Dice, ice, mice, nice, price, rice, slice, spice, splice, twice, vice.
I've, chive, dive, drive, five, hive, jive, live, strive, thrive.
By, bye, buy, cry, die, dry, eye, fly, fry, goodbye, guy, high, I, lie, pi, pie, ply, pry, rye, shy, sigh, sky, sly, spy, spry, try, wry, why.
Knife, life, rife, strife, wife.
[2] **Advice**, choc-ice, concise, de-ice, device, entice, half-price, precise, sacrifice.
Abide, allied, applied, aside, astride, backside, backslide, bedside, beside, broadside, black-eyed, blue-eyed, brown-eyed, cock-eyed, collide, confide, cross-eyed, decide, denied, deride, divide, downside, fireside, green-eyed, hawk-eyed, high tide, hillside, inside, lakeside, landslide, low tide, misguide, nearside, offside, outside, pop-eyed, preside, provide, red-eyed, reside, riptide, seaside, stateside, subside, tie-dyed, tongue-tied, topside, untied, untried, upside, wayside, well-tried, wide-eyed, worldwide, Yuletide.
Alive, arrive, beehive, contrive, deprive, nose-dive, overdrive, revive, survive.
Afterlife, good life, highlife, housewife, jackknife, lowlife, midlife, midwife, nightlife, paperknife, penknife, pocketknife, shelf-life, still-life, wildlife.
[3] **Alibis**, cold as ice, lullabies, merchandise, paradise, sacrifice.

3.2.81 "--ized" (as in "disguised")

[2] advised, apprised, baptized, capsized, chastised, comprised, demised, despised, devised, disguised, excised, prized, revised, surmised, surprised.
[3] advertised, agonized, analyzed, authorized, burglarized, categorized, centralized, civilized, colonized, compromised, criticized, dramatized, emphasized, energized, eulogized, feminized, fertilized, finalized, fossilized, fraternized, harmonized, hypnotized, idolized, immunized, jeopardized, legalized, magnetized, mechanized, memorized, mesmerized, modernized, moralized, neutralized, oxidized, pasteurized, publicized, ~ realized, recognized, satirized, scrutinized, sensitized, socialized, specialized, stabilized, standardize, sterilized, subsidized, symbolized, sympathized, tantalized, tenderized, terrorized, theorized, utilized, verbalized, victimized.

SURPRISING RHYMING:
[1] **Bide**, bride, chide, cried, died, dried, dyed, eyed, glide, guide, hide, I'd, lied, pied, pried, pride, ride, sighed, side, slide, snide, spied, stride, tide, tied, tried, wide.
Diced, heist, iced, priced, sliced, spiced, spliced.
I've, chive, dive, drive, five, hive, jive, live, strive, thrive.
By, bye, buy, cry, die, dry, eye, fly, fry, goodbye, guy, high, I, lie, pi, pie, ply, pry, rye, shy, sigh, sky, sly, spy, spry, try, wry, why.

Knife, life, rife, strife, wife.
[2] **Advice**, choc-ice, concise, de-ice, device, entice, half-price, precise, sacrifice.
Abide, allied, applied, aside, astride, backside, backslide, bedside, beside, broadside, black-eyed, blue-eyed, brown-eyed, cock-eyed, collide, confide, cross-eyed, decide, denied, deride, divide, downside, fireside, green-eyed, hawk-eyed, high tide, hillside, inside, lakeside, landslide, low tide, misguide, nearside, offside, outside, pop-eyed, preside, provide, red-eyed, reside, riptide, seaside, stateside, subside, tie-dyed, tongue-tied, topside, untied, untried, upside, wayside, well-tried, wide-eyed, worldwide, Yuletide.
Alive, arrive, contrive, deprive, nose-dive, overdrive, revive, survive.
Afterlife, good life, highlife, housewife, jackknife, lowlife, midlife, midwife, nightlife, penknife, pocketknife, shelf-life, still-life, wildlife.
[3] **Alibis**, cold as ice, lullabies, merchandise, paradise, poltergeist, sacrifice underpriced.

* * *

432

PART 4

'O'

4.1 "oe" sounds (as in "toe")................................Index on Page 434
4.2 "o̲" sounds (as in "hot")..................................Index on Page 436
4.3 "or" sounds (as in "for").................................Index on Page 437
4.4 "oy" sounds (as in "toy")................................Index on Page 438
4.5 "ow" sounds (as in "how").............................Index on Page 439
4.6 "oo" sounds (as in "boo")...............................Index on Page 439

4.1 "oe" (as in "toe")

4.1.1 "--oe" (as in "blow") 443
4.1.2 "--bo" (as in "bow") 445
4.1.3 "--doe" (as in "doe") 445
4.1.4 "--go" (as in "indigo") 446
4.1.5 "--ho" (as in "show") 447
4.1.6 "--lo" (as in "hello") 447
4.1.7 "--mo" (as in "dynamo") 448
4.1.8 "--no" (as in "know") 448
4.1.9 "--ro" (as in "grow") 449
4.1.10 "--so" (as in "also") 450
4.1.11 "--tow" (as in "toe") 450
4.1.12 "--oach" (as in "coach") 451
4.1.13 "--oached" (as in "poached") 451
4.1.14 "--oaf" (as in "loaf") 452
4.1.15 "--oast" (as in "toast") 452
4.1.16 "--oaches" (as in "coaches") 453
4.1.17 "--oaching" (as in "coaching") 453
4.1.18 "--oax" (as in "hoax") 453
4.1.19 "--oaxing" (as in "coaxing") 453
4.1.20 "--oasted" (as in "boasted") 454
4.1.21 "--oasting" (as in "hosting") 454
4.1.22 "--ocal" (as in "local") 454
4.1.23 "--oco" (as in "loco") 455
4.1.24 "--ocer" (as in "grocer") 455
4.1.25 "--ocious" (as in "ferocious") 455
4.1.26 "--ode" (as in "road") 456
4.1.27 "--oda" (as in "soda") 457
4.1.28 "--oded" (as in "loaded") 457
4.1.29 "--oding" (as in "loading") 457
4.1.30 "--ogue" (as in "rogue") 458
4.1.31 "--oke" (as in "joke") 458
4.1.32 "--oked" (as in "joked") 459
4.1.33 "--oken" (as in "spoken") 459
4.1.34 "--oker" (as in "joker") 459
4.1.35 "--oking" (as in "joking") 460
4.1.36 "--ole" (as in "hole") 460
4.1.37 "--old" (as in "told") 461
4.1.38 "--olded" (as in "folded") 462
4.1.39 "--olden" (as in "golden") 462
4.1.40 "--older" (as in "colder") 463
4.1.41 "--oldest" (as in "boldest") 463
4.1.42 "--olding" (as in "holding") 463
4.1.43 "--olar" (as in "polar") 464
4.1.44 "--oly" (as in "holy") 464
4.1.45 "--olling" (as in "rolling") 465

4.1.46 "--olo" (as in "solo") 465
4.1.47 "--olt" (as in "bolt") 466
4.1.48 "--olted" (as in "bolted") 466
4.1.49 "--olting" (as in "revolting") 466
4.1.50 "--oma" (as in "aroma") 467
4.1.51 "--oming" (as in "roaming") 467
4.1.52 "--ome" (as in "home") 467
4.1.53 "--omeless" (as in "homeless") 468
4.1.54 "--omen" (as in "omen") 468
4.1.55 "--oned" (as in "phoned") 469
4.1.56 "--onent" (as in "opponent") 469
4.1.57 "--oner" (as in "loner") 470
4.1.58 "--ony" (as in "pony") 470
4.1.59 "--oning" (as in "phoning") 471
4.1.60 "--oneless" (as in "toneless") 471
4.1.61 "--only" (as in "lonely") 471
4.1.62 "--onement" (as in "atonement") 471
4.1.63 "--ope" (as in "hope") 472
4.1.64 "--oped" (as in "hoped") 472
4.1.65 "--oping" (as in "hoping") 473
4.1.66 "--opeless" (as in "hopeless") 473
4.1.67 "--ose" (as in "close") 473
4.1.68 "--osis" (as in "hypnosis") 474
4.1.69 "--osive" (as in "explosive") 474
4.1.70 "--ostal" (as in "postal") 474
4.1.71 "--ote" (as in "boat") 474
4.1.72 "--oth" (as in "both") 475
4.1.73 "--otion" (as in "emotion") 475
4.1.74 "--oted" (as in "devoted") 476
4.1.75 "--oting" (as in "floating") 476
4.1.76 "--ove" (as in "drove") 477
4.1.77 "--oves" (as in "loaves") 477
4.1.78 "--over" (as in "rover") 478
4.1.79 "--own" (as in "phone") 478
4.1.80 "--ower" (as in "slower") 479
4.1.81 "--owest" (as in "slowest") 479
4.1.82 "--owing" (as in "glowing") 479
4.1.83 "--oze" (as in "doze") 480
4.1.84 "--ozed" (as in "dozed") 480
4.1.85 "--ozing" (as in "dozing") 481
4.1.86 "--ozen" (as in "frozen") 481
4.1.87 "--ozer" (as in "composer") 482
4.1.88 "--ozes" (as in "roses") 482
4.1.89 "--ozure" (as in "closure") 482
4.1.90 "--ozion" (as in "explosion") 483

* * *

4.2. "o" (as in "hot")

4.2.1 "--ob" (as in "sob") 483
4.2.2 "--obber" (as in "robber") 484
4.2.3 "--obbing" (as in "robbing") 484
4.2.4 "--obby" (as in "hobby") 484
4.2.5 "--obble" (as in "wobble") 484
4.2.6 "--obbler" (as in "cobbler") 485
4.2.7 "--obbling" (as in "hobbling") 485
4.2.8 "--ock" (as in "rock") 485
4.2.9 "--ocker" (as in "locker") 486
4.2.10 "--ocked" (as in "rocked") 486
4.2.11 "--ocking" as in "rocking") 487
4.2.12 "--ocket" (as in "locket") 487
4.2.13 "--ockey" (as in "jockey") 487
4.2.14 "--odd" (as in "odd") 487
4.2.15 "--odded" (as in "nodded") 488
4.2.16 "--odder" (as in "fodder") 488
4.2.17 "--oddle" (as in "model") 489
4.2.18 "--ody as in "body") 489
4.2.19 "--odic" (as in "melodic") 489
4.2.20 "--off" (as in "cough") 489
4.2.21 "--offer" (as in "offer") 490
4.2.22 "--oft" (as in "soft") 490
4.2.23 "--offen" (as in "soften") 490
4.2.24 "--ogg" (as in "dog") 490
4.2.25 "--oggy" (as in "foggy") 491
4.2.26 "--ogger" (as in "blogger") 491
4.2.27 "--ogging" (as in "jogging") 491
4.2.28 "--ogged" (as in "jogged") 492
4.2.29 "--oggle" as in "goggle") 492
4.2.30 "--olve" (as in "evolve") 492
4.2.31 "--olved" (as in "resolved") 492
4.2.32 "--olving" (as in "solving") 493
4.2.33 "--olt" (as in "fault") 493
4.2.34 "--olting" (as in "revolting") 493
4.2.35 "--olted" (as in "halted") 494
4.2.36 "--olter" (as in "falter") 494
4.2.37 "--ollar" as in "collar") 494
4.2.38 "--ollege" as in "college") 494
4.2.39 "--olly" (as in "holly") 495
4.2.40 "--omm" (as in "bomb") 495
4.2.41 "--omp" (as in "pomp") 495
4.2.42 "--on" (as in "gone") 496
4.2.43 "--ond" (as in "bond") 496
4.2.44 "--onding" (as in "responding") 496
4.2.45 "--onting" (as in "haunting") 497
4.2.46 "--onder" (as in "ponder") 497

4.2.47 "--onded" (as in "responded") 497
4.2.48 "--ong" (as in "song") 498
4.2.49 "--onged" (as in "wronged") 498
4.2.50 "--onging" (as in "longing") 498
4.2.51 "--onic" (as in "tonic") 499
4.2.52 "--op" (as in "drop") 499
4.2.53 "--opped" (as in "dropped") 499
4.2.54 "--opping" (as in "dropping") 500
4.2.55 "--oppy" (as in "poppy") 500
4.2.56 "--opper" (as in "proper") 500
4.2.57 "--oral" (as in "moral") 501
4.2.58 "--ost" (as in "lost") 501
4.2.59 "--osh" (as in "wash") 501
4.2.60 "--oshed" (as in "washed") 501
4.2.61 "--oshing" (as in "washing") 502
4.2.62 "--oss" (as in "boss") 502
4.2.63 "--ossing" (as in "crossing") 502
4.2.64 "--ossy" (as in "bossy") 503
4.2.65 "--ot" (as in "what") 503
4.2.66 "--otty" (as in "dotty") 504
4.2.67 "--otter" (as in "hotter") 504
4.2.68 "--otting" (as in "spotting") 504
4.2.69 "--otted" (as in "spotted") 504
4.2.70 "--otless" (as in "spotless") 505
4.2.71 "--otten" (as in "forgotten") 505
4.2.72 "--otto" (as in "motto") 505
4.2.73 "--otch" (as in "watch") 505
4.2.74 "--otched" (as in "watched") 506
4.2.75 "--otching" (as in "watching") 506
4.2.76 "--oth" (as in "cloth") 506
4.2.77 "--ox" (as in "box") 507
4.2.78 "--oz" (as in "because") 507

4.3 "or" (as in "for")

4.3.1 "--or" (as in "for") 508
4.3.2 "--oarer" (as in "aura") 509
4.3.3 "--oral" (as in "choral") 509
4.3.4 "--orch" (as in "porch") 509
4.3.5 "--orchard" (as in "orchard") 510
4.3.6 "--orching" (as in "scorching") 510
4.3.7 "--ord" (as in "sword") 510
4.3.8 "--order" (as in "border") 511
4.3.9 "--orded" (as in "awarded") 511
4.3.10 "--ordered" (as in "ordered") 511
4.3.11 "--ording" (as in "recording") 512
4.3.12 "--orful" (as in "awful") 512
4.3.13 "--oring" (as in "roaring") 512
4.3.14 "--orick" (as in "historic") 513

4.3.15 "--ork" (as in "walk") ... 513
4.3.16 "--orker" (as in "walker") ... 513
4.3.17 "--orless" (as in "flawless") ... 513
4.3.18 "--orl" (as in "fall") ... 513
4.3.19 "--orling" (as in "falling") ... 514
4.3.20 "--orled" (as in "called") ... 514
4.3.21 "--orlest" (as in "tallest") ... 515
4.3.22 "--olding" (as in "balding") ... 515
4.3.23 "--orm" (as in "warm") ... 515
4.3.24 "--ormed" (as in "formed") ... 516
4.3.25 "--ormal" (as in "normal") ... 516
4.3.26 "--ormat" (as in "format") ... 516
4.3.27 "--ormer" (as in "former") ... 517
4.3.28 "--orming" (as in "swarming") ... 517
4.3.29 "--orn" (as in "torn") ... 517
4.3.30 "--orner" (as in "corner") ... 518
4.3.31 "--orning" (as in "morning") ... 518
4.3.32 "--orned" (as in "warned") ... 519
4.3.33 "--ornful" (as in "scornful") ... 519
4.3.34 "--orny" (as in "corny") ... 519
4.3.35 "--ornt" (as in "haunt") ... 519
4.3.36 "--ornting" (as in "haunting") ... 519
4.3.37 "--ornted" (as in "haunted") ... 520
4.3.38 "--ors" (as in "doors") ... 520
4.3.39 "--orse" (as in "remorse") ... 520
4.3.40 "--orsing" (as in "forcing") ... 521
4.3.41 "--orsely" (as in "coarsely") ... 521
4.3.42 "--ort" (as in "short") ... 521
4.3.43 "--ortal" (as in "mortal") ... 522
4.3.44 "--orty" (as in "naughty") ... 522
4.3.45 "--orted" (as in "sorted") ... 522
4.3.46 "--orter" (as in "quarter") ... 522
4.3.47 "--ortly" (as in "shortly") ... 522
4.3.48 "--orting" (as in "sporting") ... 523
4.3.49 "--oawing" (as in "drawing") ... 523
4.3.50 "--ory" (as in "glory") ... 523
4.3.51 "--orz" (as in "jaws") ... 524

4.4. "oy" (as in "toy")

4.4.1 "--oy" (as in "boy") ... 524
4.4.2 "--oyz" (as in "noise") ... 524
4.4.3 "--oid" (as in "avoid") ... 525
4.4.4 "--oil" (as in "boil") ... 525
4.4.5 "--oiler" (as in "boiler") ... 525
4.4.6 "--oiling" (as in "spoiling") ... 525
4.4.7 "--oiled" (as in "spoiled") ... 525
4.4.8 "--oin" (as in "coin") ... 526
4.4.9 "--oint" (as in "point") ... 526

4.4.10 "--ointed" (as in "pointed") 526
4.4.11 "--ointing" (as in "pointing") 526
4.4.12 "--oice" (as in "choice") 526
4.4.13 "--oist" (as in "moist") 527
4.4.14 "--oyal" (as in "loyal") 527
4.4.15 "--oyant" (as in "buoyant") 527
4.4.16 "--oyer" (as in "destroyer") 527
4.4.17 "--oying" (as in "annoying") 527

4.5 "ow" (as in "how")

4.5.1 "--ow" (as in "how") 528
4.5.2 "--ouch" (as in "couch") 528
4.5.3 "--oud" (as in "cloud") 529
4.5.4 "--owded" (as in "crowded") 529
4.5.5 "--owder" (as in "powder") 529
4.5.6 "--owdy" (as in "cloudy") 530
4.5.7 "--owl" (as in "howl") 530
4.5.8 "--oun" (as in "down") 530
4.5.9 "--ound" (as in "found") 531
4.5.10 "--ounded" (as in "grounded") 531
4.5.11 "--ounding" (as in "astounding") 532
4.5.12 "--ounds" (as in "pounds") 532
4.5.13 "--ounce" (as in "bounce") 532
4.5.14 "--ouncing" (as in "pouncing") 533
4.5.15 "--ouncement" (as in "announcement") 533
4.5.16 "--ount" (as in "count") 533
4.5.17 "--ounty" (as in "bounty") 534
4.5.18 "--ountain" (as in "mountain") 534
4.5.19 "--ounting" (as in "counting") 534
4.5.20 "--our" (as in "hour") 534
4.5.21 "--ours" (as in "flowers") 534
4.5.22 "--owering" (as in "towering") 535
4.5.23 "--ouse" (as in "house") 535
4.5.24 "--ouser" (as in "browser") 536
4.5.25 "--out" (as in "doubt") 536
4.5.26 "--outed" (as in "shouted") 536
4.5.27 "--outer" (as in "shouter") 536
4.5.28 "--outing" (as in "shouting") 537
4.5.29 "--outh" (as in "mouth") 537
4.5.30 "--owel" (as in "towel") 538
4.5.31 "--owwing" (as in "vowing") 538

4.6 "oo" (as in "boo")

4.6.1 "--oo" (as in "ooh") 538
4.6.2 "--ooing" (as in "doing") 539
4.6.3 "--boo" (as in "taboo") 540
4.6.4 "--doo" (as in "voodoo") 541

4.6.5 "--loo" (as in "clue") 542
4.6.6 "--noo" (as in "canoe") 543
4.6.7 "--roo" (as in "grew") 544
4.6.8 "--too" (as in "tattoo") 545
4.6.9 "--ook" (as in "book") 546
4.6.10 "--ooking" (as in "looking") 547
4.6.11 "--ooker" (as in "cooker") 547
4.6.12 "--oob" (as in "tube") 547
4.6.13 "--oober" (as in "YouTuber") 548
4.6.14 "--ood" (as in "food") 548
4.6.15 "--oods" (as in "moods") 549
4.6.16 "--oodest" (as in "rudest") 550
4.6.17 "--oodly" (as in "shrewdly") 550
4.6.18 "--ooel" (as in "cruel") 550
4.6.19 "--ooer" (as in "fewer") 550
4.6.20 "--ooey" (as in "chewy") 551
4.6.21 "--ooest" (as in "truest") 551
4.6.22 "--oof" (as in "proof") 551
4.6.23 "--oogle" (as in "google") 552
4.6.24 "--oohk" (as in "spook") 552
4.6.25 "--ool" (as in "fool") 552
4.6.26 "--ooler" (as in "cooler") 553
4.6.27 "--ooly" (as in "truly") 553
4.6.28 "--ooling" (as in "cooling") 553
4.6.29 "--oom" (as in "room") 554
4.6.30 "--ooman" (as in "human") 554
4.6.31 "--oomer" (as in "rumour/rumor") 555
4.6.32 "--oomered" (as in "rumoured/rumored") 555
4.6.33 "--oon" (as in "moon") 555
4.6.34 "--ooned" (as in "marooned") 556
4.6.35 "--ooner" (as in "sooner") 556
4.6.36 "--oonful" (as in "spoonful") 557
4.6.37 "--ooning" (as in "swooning") 557
4.6.38 "--oonist" (as in "cartoonist") 557
4.6.39 "--oop" (as in "swoop") 557
4.6.40 "--ooped" (as in "swooped") 558
4.6.41 "--ooping" (as in "swooping") 558
4.6.42 "--ooper" (as in "super") 559
4.6.43 "--oor" (as in "poor") 559
4.6.44 "--oored" (as in "moored") 559
4.6.45 "--oorer" (as in "poorer") 560
4.6.46 "--oorest" (as in "poorest") 560
4.6.47 "--ooral" (as in "rural") 560
4.6.48 "--ooring" (as in "during") 560
4.6.49 "--oorly" (as in "poorly") 561
4.6.50 "--oose" (as in "loose") 561
4.6.51 "--ooshun" (as in "illusion") 562
4.6.52 "--oosive" (as in "elusive") 562

440

4.6.53 "--oot" (as in "shoot") 562
4.6.54 "--ooter" (as in "shooter") 563
4.6.55 "--ooth" (as in "truth") 563
4.6.56 "--ooted" (as in "rooted") 564
4.6.57 "--ooty" (as in "beauty") 564
4.6.58 "--ooting" (as in "shooting") 564
4.6.59 "--oove" (as in "groove") 565
4.6.60 "--ooved" (as in "moved") 565
4.6.61 "--oover" (as in "mover") 566
4.6.62 "--oovie" (as in "movie") 566
4.6.63 "--ooze" (as in "choose") 566
4.6.64 "--oozed" (as in "used") 567
4.6.65 "--oozer" (as in "loser") 568
4.6.66 "--oozes" (as in "chooses") 568
4.6.67 "--oozing" (as in "choosing") 568

* * *

4.1 "oe" (as in "toe")

4.1.1 "--oe" (as in "blow")
[1] beau, blow, bow, bro, crow, doe, doh, dough, floe, flow, foe, glow, go, grow, hoe, know, low, mo., mow, no, oh, owe, pro, row, sew, show, slow, snow, so, stow, though, throw, toe, tow, whoa, woe, yo.
[2] aglow, ago, aggro, airflow, also, alto, although, ammo, arrow, auto, banjo, barrow, beano, below, bellow, bestow, billow, bimbo, bingo, biro, bistro, blotto, bolo, bongo, Bordeaux, borrow, bozo, bravo, bronco, bureau, burrow, capo, cargo, cashflow, cello, chateau, chat show, cheapo, chino, coco, cocoa, combo, condo, credo, crossbow, Day-Glo, deathblow, demo, depot, dingo, dipso, disco, ditto, dodo, Dumbo, dunno, duo, echo, ego, elbow, escrow, euro, fallow, farrow, fellow, follow, forgo, furlough, furrow, gaucho, ghetto, giro/gyro, gizmo, go-go, go-slow, gringo, grotto, gumbo, gung-ho, gusto, halo, heave-ho, hedgerow, heigh-ho, hello, hero, hippo, hobo, hollow, honcho, impro, info, intro, jello, jingo, judo, kilo, K.O., jumbo, kendo, largo, lido, lilo, limbo, limo, lingo, lino, loco, logo, longbow, lotto, Ludo, macho, macro, maestro, mallow, mambo, mango, marrow, meadow, mellow, memo, metro, mezzo, micro, mojo, mono, motto, muso, nacho, narrow, no-go, no-show, oboe, outgo, outgrow, panto, peepshow, photo, pillow, pinko, pinto, plateau, poco, polo, poncho, pongo, presto, promo, pronto, pseudo, psycho, rainbow, Rambo, repo, repro, retro, rhino, Rio, roadshow, rondeau, rondo, salvo, say-so, scarecrow, schizo, shadow, shallow, sideshow, silo, sicko, slow-mo, Soho, solo, so-so, sorrow, sparrow, speedo, sumo, swallow, taco, tango, tarot, techno, tempo, thicko, tiptoe, torso, trio, turbo, typo, uno, Velcro, veto, vino, whacko, wallow, widow, weirdo, willow, window, wino, yellow, yo-yo, zero.
[3] afterglow, a-gogo, akimbo, alfresco, amigo, arroyo, art deco, art nouveau, audio, bambino, billy-o, bolero, bordello, bravado, buffalo, bungalow, burrito, calico, calypso, cameo, casino, castrato, cheerio, commando, concerto, cornetto, crescendo, curio, de facto, domino, dynamo, electro, embargo, embryo, Eskimo, espresso, eyeshadow, falsetto, fandango, fiasco, flamenco, flamingo, folio, foreshadow, gazebo, gelato, gigolo, glissando, indigo, inferno, kimono, Latino, libido, machismo, marshmallow, memento, mistletoe, mosquito, overflow, overthrow, patio, pedalo, pharaoh, physio, piano, piccolo, Pierrot, placebo, potato, proviso, quid pro quo, radio, ratio, rodeo, Romeo, Scorpio, semipro, sombrero, so-and-so, soprano, staccato, status quo, stereo, stiletto, studio, subzero, supremo, tally-ho, tic-tac-toe, to and fro, tobacco, tomato, tomorrow, tornado, torpedo, tremolo, tuxedo, UFO, undergo, undertow, up-tempo, vertigo, vibrato, video, volcano, yo-ho-ho, wheelbarrow.
[4] aficionado, adagio, alter ego, Americano, arpeggio, avocado, cappuccino, cigarillo, desperado, Eldorado, impresario, incognito, incommunicado, innuendo, Lothario, mafioso, magnifico, manifesto, mumbo-jumbo, oratorio, overshadow, palomino, paparazzo, politico, portfolio, scenario, simpatico, superhero, virtuoso.

SURPRISING RHYMING:
[1] **Bode**, code, crowed, flowed, goad, load, mode, mowed, node, ode, owed, road, rode, rowed, sewed, showed, slowed, sowed, stowed, strode, toad, toed, towed, woad.
Both, growth, loath, oath, sloth.
Clove, cove, dove, drove, grove, mauve, rove, stove, strove, wove.
Bowl, coal, dole, droll, foal, goal, hole, knoll, mole, pole, poll, role, roll, scroll, shoal, sole, soul, stole, stroll, toll, troll, whole.
Bold, bowled, coaled, cold, doled, foaled, fold, gold, hold, holed, mould/mold (U.S.), old, polled, rolled, scold, soled, sold, told, tolled.
Chrome, comb, dome, foam, gnome, home, roam, Rome, tome.
Blown, bone, clone, cone, drone, flown, groan, grown, hone, known, loan, lone, moan, mown, own, phone, prone, scone, sewn, shown, sown, stone, throne, thrown, tone, zone.
Cloned, coned, droned, groaned, honed, loaned, loaned, moaned, owned, phoned, stoned, toned, zoned.

Blows, bows, chose, close, clothes, crows, doze, flows, foes, froze, glows, goes, grows, hose, knows, lows, mows, nose, owes, pose, pros, prose, rose, rows, sews, shows, slows, snows, sows, stows, those, throes, throws, toes, tows, woes.
Close(d), doze(d), hose(d), nose(d), pose(d).
Coped, doped, groped, hoped, moped, roped, scoped, soaped.
Bolt, colt, halt, jolt, moult/molt (U.S.), salt, vault, volt.
Boast, coast, ghost, grossed, host, most, post, roast, toast.
Brogue, rogue, vogue.
Bloke, broke, choke, cloak, coke, croak, folk, joke, oak, poke, smoke, soak, spoke, stoke, stroke, woke, yolk.
Broached, coached, poached.
Loaf, oaf, sugarloaf.
Cope, dope, grope, hope, lope, mope, nope, pope, rope, scope, slope, soap.
Boat, coat, dote, float, gloat, goat, moat, note, oat, quote, throat, tote, vote, wrote.
[2] **Alone**, atone, backbone, bemoan, birthstone, bloodstone, brownstone, cellphone, cheekbone, cologne, condone, cyclone, disown, earphone, end zone, full-blown, full-grown, gemstone, gravestone, half-grown, headphone, headstone, high-flown, home-grown, hormone, jawbone, kerbstone/curbstone (U.S.), keystone, limestone, lodestone, milestone, millstone, moonstone, outgrown, ozone, payphone, postpone, rhinestone, ringtone, sandstone, tombstone, touchstone, trombone, unknown, windblown, wishbone.
Abode, barcode, bestowed, corrode, decode, download, elbowed, episode, erode, explode, forebode, freeload, hallowed, highroad, implode, inroad, offload, overflowed, overload, payload, postcode, railroad, reload, unload, upload, workload, zip code.
Atoll, bankroll, bargepole, beanpole, bolthole, cajole, charcoal, console, control, Creole, dustbowl, enrol/enroll (U.S.), fishbowl, flagpole, hellhole, keyhole, loophole, payroll, parole, patrol, peephole, pinhole, plughole, pothole, punchbowl.
Behold, blindfold, cajoled, controlled, cuckold, foothold, foretold, household, millionfold, outsold, paroled, remould(s)/remold(s) (U.S.), re-sold, retold, scaffold, stronghold, tenfold, threshold, toehold, twofold, threefold, unfold, uphold, unsold, untold, withhold.
Genome, in-home, re-home, syndrome, toothcomb.
Atoned, bemoaned, condoned, disowned, intoned, postponed.
Approached, encroached, reproached.
Almost, bedpost, eloped, endmost, engrossed, foremost, gatepost, goalpost, lamppost, outpost, seacoast, signpost, tightrope, topmost, towrope, utmost.
Arose, bulldoze, compose, depose, disclose, dispose, enclose, expose, foreclose, forgoes, gallows, glucose, impose, oppose, outgrows, pillows, plainclothes, primrose, propose, rainbows, suppose, tiptoes, transpose, undergoes, wild rose.
Engross, lactose, morose, verbose, viscose.
Bulldozed, composed, deposed, disclosed, disposed, enclosed, exposed, imposed, opposed, proposed, supposed, transposed.
Assault, default, exalt, pole-vault, revolt, somersault, unbolt.
Awoke, backstroke, baroque, bespoke, breaststroke, cowpoke, egg yolk, evoke, heatstroke, invoke, keystroke, kinfolk, menfolk, provoke, revoke, slowpoke, sunstroke, townsfolk, uncloak, woodsmoke.
Alcove, behove/behoove (U.S.), interwove, mangrove.
Afloat, banknote, cutthroat, denote, devote, dovecote, dreamboat, emote, footnote, houseboat, keynote, lifeboat, misquote, promote, raincoat, remote, rowboat, sailboat, scapegoat, showboat, speedboat, steamboat, topcoat, tugboat, turncoat, waistcoat.
[3] **Buttonhole**, casserole, cubbyhole, hidey-hole, pigeonhole, rigmarole, rock and roll, self-control, waterhole.
Innermost, northernmost, southernmost, uppermost, whipping-post.
Centrefold/centerfold (U.S.), manifold, marigold, oversold, pigeonholed, self-controlled, stranglehold, uncontrolled, undersold.
Aerodrome, backcomb, catacomb, honeycomb, monochrome, motorhome, pocket comb, pressure dome, Styrofoam, velodrome.
Chaperoned, cobblestoned, telephoned.
Anklebone, answerphone, baritone, chaperone, cobblestone, cornerstone, fully-grown, gramophone, herringbone, megaphone, methadone, microphone, monotone, overblown, overgrown, overthrown, overtone, pheromone, saxophone, semitone, silicone, stepping stone, telephone, undertone, xylophone.

Adios, comatose, decompose, diagnose, dominoes, grandiose, indispose, overdose, overexpose, presuppose, superimpose.
Diagnosed, indisposed, overdosed, overexposed, predisposed, superimposed.
Antelope, Cinemascope, envelope, horoscope, kaleidoscope, microscope, periscope, skipping-rope, stethoscope, telescope.
Anecdote, antidote, ferryboat, motorboat, mountain goat, overcoat, petticoat, powerboat, riverboat, sugarcoat, table d'hôte, undercoat.

4.1.2 "--bo" (as in "bow")
[1] beau, bo, bow.
[2] bimbo, combo, crossbow, Dumbo, elbow, gumbo, hobo, jumbo, limbo, longbow, mambo, oboe, Rambo, rainbow, turbo.
[3] akimbo, gazebo, mumbo-jumbo, placebo.

SURPRISING RHYMING:
[1] **Blow**, bro, crow, doe, doh, dough, flow, foe, glow, go, grow, hoe, know, K.O., low, mow, no, owe, pro, row, sew, show, slow, snow, so, stow, though, throw, toe, tow, woe.
[2] **Aglow**, ago, aggro, also, alto, although, ammo, arrow, auto, banjo, barrow, below, bestow, billow, bingo, biro, bistro, blotto, bolo, bongo, Bordeaux, borrow, bozo, bravo, bronco, bureau, burrow, cargo, cashflow, cello, chateau, cheapo, chino, coco, cocoa, condo, credo, Day-Glo, deathblow, demo, depot, dingo, dipso, disco, ditto, dodo, dunno, duo, echo, ego, escrow, euro, fellow, follow, forgo, furlough, furrow, gaucho, gelato, ghetto, giro/gyro, gizmo, go-go, go-slow, gringo, grotto, gung-ho, gusto, halo, heave-ho, hedgerow, heigh-ho, hello, hero, hippo, hollow, honcho, info, intro, jello, jingo, judo, kilo, K.O., lido, limo, lingo, loco, logo, lotto, macho, macro, maestro, mango, meadow, mellow, memo, metro, mezzo, micro, mojo, mono, motto, muso, nacho, narrow, no-show, outgo, outgrow, panto, peepshow, photo, pillow, pinto, plateau, poco, polo, poncho, pongo, presto, promo, pronto, pseudo, psycho, repo, repro, retro, rhino, Rio, roadshow, rondeau, rondo, salvo, say-so, scarecrow, schizo, shadow, shallow, sideshow, slow-mo, Soho, solo, so-so, sorrow, sparrow, speedo, stiletto, sumo, swallow, taco, tango, tarot, techno, tempo, tiptoe, torso, trio, typo, Velcro, veto, vino, wallow, widow, weirdo, willow, window, wino, yellow, yo-yo, zero.
[3] **Afterglow**, a-gogo, alfresco, amigo, arroyo, art deco, art nouveau, audio, bambino, billy-o, bolero, bordello, bravado, buffalo, bungalow, burrito, calypso, cameo, casino, cheerio, commando, concerto, cornetto, crescendo, curio, de facto, domino, dynamo, electro, espresso, eyeshadow, falsetto, fandango, fiasco, flamenco, flamingo, foreshadow, gigolo, indigo, inferno, kimono, Latino, libido, machismo, marshmallow, memento, mistletoe, mosquito, overflow, overthrow, patio, pharaoh, physio, piano, piccolo, Pierrot, potato, proviso, quid pro quo, radio, ratio, rodeo, Romeo, sombrero, so-and-so, soprano, staccato, status quo, stereo, studio, subzero, supremo, tally-ho, tic-tac-toe, to and fro, tobacco, tomato, tomorrow, tornado, torpedo, tremolo, tuxedo, UFO, undergo, undertow, up-tempo, vertigo, vibrato, video, volcano, yo-ho-ho, wheelbarrow.
[4] **Aficionado**, adagio, alter ego, cappuccino, desperado, incognito, innuendo, mafioso, oratorio, overshadow, paparazzo, politico, scenario, simpatico, superhero, virtuoso.

4.1.3 "--doe" (as in "doe")
[1] doe, doh, dough.
[2] Bordeaux, condo, credo, dodo, judo, kendo, lido, Ludo, meadow, pseudo, rondeau, rondo, shadow, speedo, widow, weirdo, window.
[3] bravado, commando, crescendo, eyeshadow, foreshadow, glissando, libido, tornado, torpedo, tuxedo.
[4] aficionado, avocado, desperado, Eldorado, incommunicado, innuendo, overshadow.

SURPRISING RHYMING:
[1] **Beau**, blow, bow, bro, crow, flow, foe, glow, go, grow, hoe, know, low, mow, no, oh, owe, pro, row, sew, show, slow, snow, so, stow, though, throw, toe, tow, woe.
[2] **Aglow**, ago, aggro, also, alto, although, ammo, arrow, auto, banjo, barrow, below, bestow, billow, bingo, biro, bistro, blotto, bolo, bongo, borrow, bozo, bravo, bronco,

bureau, burrow, cargo, cello, chateau, cheapo, chino, coco, cocoa, condo, credo, Day-Glo, deathblow, demo, depot, dingo, disco, ditto, dodo, dunno, duo, echo, ego, euro, fellow, follow, forgo, furlough, furrow, gaucho, gelato, ghetto, giro/gyro, gizmo, go-go, go-slow, gringo, grotto, gung-ho, gusto, halo, heave-ho, hedgerow, heigh-ho, hello, hero, hippo, hollow, honcho, info, intro, jello, jingo, judo, kilo, K.O., lido, limo, lingo, loco, logo, lotto, macho, maestro, mango, meadow, mellow, memo, metro, mezzo, micro, mojo, mono, motto, muso, nacho, narrow, no-show, outgo, outgrow, panto, peepshow, photo, pillow, pinto, plateau, poco, polo, poncho, pongo, presto, promo, pronto, pseudo, psycho, repo, repro, retro, rhino, Rio, roadshow, rondo, salvo, say-so, scarecrow, schizo, shadow, shallow, sideshow, slow-mo, Soho, solo, so-so, sorrow, sparrow, speedo, stiletto, swallow, taco, tango, tarot, techno, tempo, tiptoe, torso, trio, Velcro, veto, vino, wallow, widow, weirdo, willow, window, wino, yellow, yo-yo, zero.
[3] Afterglow, a-gogo, akimbo, alfresco, amigo, arroyo, art deco, art nouveau, audio, bambino, billy-o, bolero, bordello, bravado, buffalo, bungalow, burrito, calypso, cameo, casino, cheerio, commando, concerto, cornetto, crescendo, curio, de facto, domino, dynamo, electro, espresso, eyeshadow, falsetto, fandango, fiasco, flamenco, flamingo, foreshadow, gigolo, indigo, inferno, kimono, Latino, libido, machismo, marshmallow, memento, mistletoe, overflow, overthrow, patio, physio, piano, piccolo, Pierrot, potato, proviso, quid pro quo, radio, ratio, rodeo, Romeo, sombrero, so-and-so, soprano, staccato, status quo, stereo, studio, subzero, supremo, tally-ho, tic-tac-toe, to and fro, tobacco, tomato, tomorrow, tornado, torpedo, tuxedo, UFO, undergo, undertow, up-tempo, vertigo, vibrato, video, volcano.
[4] Adagio, alter ego, cappuccino, desperado, Eldorado, incognito, innuendo, mafioso, overshadow, paparazzo, politico, portfolio, scenario, simpatico, superhero, virtuoso.

4.1.4 "--go" (as in "indigo")
[2] ago, bingo, bongo, cargo, dingo, ego, forgo, go, go-go, gringo, jingo, largo, lingo, logo, mango, no-go, outgo, pogo, pongo, tango.
[3] a-gogo, alter ego, amigo, embargo, fandango, flamingo, indigo, long ago, touch and go, undergo, vertigo.

SURPRISING RHYMING:
[2] **Aglow**, ago, aggro, also, alto, although, ammo, arrow, auto, banjo, barrow, below, bestow, billow, bingo, biro, bistro, blotto, bolo, bongo, borrow, bozo, bravo, bronco, bureau, burrow, cargo, cello, chateau, cheapo, chino, coco, cocoa, condo, credo, Day-Glo, deathblow, demo, depot, dingo, disco, ditto, dodo, dunno, duo, echo, ego, euro, fellow, follow, forgo, furlough, furrow, gaucho, gelato, ghetto, giro/gyro, gizmo, go-go, go-slow, gringo, grotto, gung-ho, gusto, halo, heave-ho, hedgerow, heigh-ho, hello, hero, hippo, hollow, honcho, info, intro, jello, jingo, judo, kilo, K.O., lido, limo, lingo, loco, logo, lotto, macho, maestro, mango, meadow, mellow, memo, metro, mezzo, micro, mojo, mono, motto, muso, nacho, narrow, no-show, outgo, outgrow, panto, peepshow, photo, pillow, pinto, plateau, poco, polo, poncho, pongo, presto, promo, pronto, pseudo, psycho, repo, repro, retro, rhino, Rio, roadshow, rondo, salvo, say-so, scarecrow, schizo, shadow, shallow, sideshow, slow-mo, Soho, solo, so-so, sorrow, sparrow, speedo, stiletto, swallow, tango, tarot, techno, tempo, tiptoe, torso, trio, typo, Velcro, veto, vino, wallow, widow, weirdo, willow, window, wino, yellow, yo-yo, zero.
[3] Afterglow, a-gogo, alfresco, amigo, arroyo, art deco, art nouveau, audio, bambino, billy-o, bolero, bordello, bravado, buffalo, bungalow, burrito, calypso, cameo, casino, cheerio, commando, concerto, cornetto, crescendo, curio, de facto, domino, dynamo, electro, espresso, eyeshadow, falsetto, fandango, fiasco, flamenco, flamingo, foreshadow, gigolo, indigo, inferno, kimono, Latino, libido, machismo, marshmallow, memento, mistletoe, overflow, overthrow, patio, physio, piano, piccolo, Pierrot, potato, proviso, quid pro quo, radio, ratio, rodeo, Romeo, sombrero, so-and-so, soprano, staccato, status quo, stereo, studio, subzero, supremo, tally-ho, tic-tac-toe, to and fro, tobacco, tomato, tomorrow, tornado, torpedo, tuxedo, UFO, undergo, undertow, up-tempo, vertigo, vibrato, video, volcano.
[4] Adagio, alter ego, cappuccino, desperado, Eldorado, incognito, innuendo, mafioso, overshadow, paparazzo, politico, portfolio, scenario, simpatico, superhero, virtuoso.

*

4.1.5 "--ho" (as in "show")
[1] hoe, show.
[2] chat show, echo, gaucho, gung-ho, heave-ho, heigh-ho, honcho, ho-ho, macho, nacho, no-show, peepshow, poncho, psycho, roadshow, sideshow, Soho, tallyho, westward ho!, yo-ho-ho.

SURPRISING RHYMING:
[1] **Beau**, blow, bow, bro, crow, doe, doh, dough, floe, flow, foe, glow, go, grow, know, low, mo., mow, no, oh, owe, pro, row, sew, slow, snow, so, stow, though, throw, toe, tow, whoa, woe, yo.
[2] **Aglow**, ago, aggro, also, alto, although, ammo, arrow, auto, banjo, barrow, below, bestow, billow, bingo, biro, bistro, blotto, bolo, bongo, borrow, bozo, bravo, bronco, bureau, burrow, cargo, cello, chateau, cheapo, chino, coco, cocoa, condo, credo, Day-Glo, deathblow, demo, depot, dingo, disco, ditto, dodo, dunno, duo, echo, ego, euro, fellow, follow, forgo, furlough, furrow, gaucho, gelato, ghetto, giro/gyro, gizmo, go-go, go-slow, gringo, grotto, gung-ho, gusto, halo, heave-ho, hedgerow, heigh-ho, hello, hero, hippo, hollow, honcho, info, intro, jello, jingo, judo, kilo, K.O., lido, limo, lingo, loco, logo, lotto, macho, maestro, mango, meadow, mellow, memo, metro, mezzo, micro, mojo, mono, motto, muso, nacho, narrow, no-show, outgo, outgrow, panto, peepshow, photo, pillow, pinto, plateau, poco, polo, poncho, pongo, presto, promo, pronto, pseudo, psycho, repo, repro, retro, rhino, Rio, roadshow, rondo, salvo, say-so, scarecrow, schizo, shadow, shallow, sideshow, slow-mo, Soho, solo, so-so, sorrow, sparrow, speedo, stiletto, swallow, tango, tarot, techno, tempo, tiptoe, torso, trio, typo, Velcro, veto, vino, wallow, widow, weirdo, willow, window, wino, yellow, yo-yo, zero.
[3] **Afterglow**, a-gogo, akimbo, alfresco, amigo, arroyo, art deco, art nouveau, audio, bambino, billy-o, bolero, bordello, bravado, buffalo, bungalow, burrito, calypso, cameo, casino, cheerio, commando, concerto, cornetto, crescendo, curio, de facto, domino, dynamo, electro, espresso, eyeshadow, falsetto, fandango, fiasco, flamenco, flamingo, foreshadow, gigolo, indigo, inferno, kimono, Latino, libido, machismo, marshmallow, memento, mistletoe, overflow, overthrow, patio, physio, piano, piccolo, Pierrot, potato, proviso, quid pro quo, radio, ratio, rodeo, Romeo, sombrero, so-and-so, soprano, staccato, status quo, stereo, studio, subzero, supremo, tally-ho, tic-tac-toe, to and fro, tobacco, tomato, tomorrow, tornado, torpedo, tuxedo, UFO, undergo, undertow, up-tempo, vertigo, vibrato, video, volcano.
[4] **Adagio**, alter ego, cappuccino, desperado, Eldorado, incognito, innuendo, mafioso, overshadow, paparazzo, politico, portfolio, scenario, simpatico, superhero, virtuoso.

4.1.6 "--lo" (as in "hello")
[1] blow, flow, glow, lo, low, sloe, slow.
[2] aglow, airflow, bellow, below, billow, bolo, cashflow, cello, Day-Glo, deathblow, fallow, farrow, fellow, follow, furlough, Jell-O, go-slow, halo, hello, hollow, ice-floe, kilo, lilo, mallow, mellow, moonglow, outflow, pillow, polo, shallow, silo, solo, swallow, wallow, willow, yellow.
[3] afterglow, bordello, buffalo, bungalow, cigarillo, counterblow, gigolo, marshmallow, overflow, pedalo, piccolo, tremolo.

SURPRISING RHYMING:
[1] **Beau**, bow, bro, crow, doe, doh, dough, foe, go, grow, hoe, know, mow, no, oh, owe, pro, row, sew, show, snow, so, stow, though, throw, toe, tow, whoa, woe, yo.
[2] Aglow, ago, aggro, also, alto, although, ammo, arrow, auto, banjo, barrow, below, bestow, billow, bingo, biro, bistro, blotto, bolo, bongo, borrow, bozo, bravo, bronco, bureau, burrow, cargo, cello, chateau, cheapo, chino, coco, cocoa, condo, credo, Day-Glo, deathblow, demo, depot, dingo, disco, ditto, dodo, dunno, duo, echo, ego, euro, fellow, follow, forgo, furlough, furrow, gaucho, gelato, ghetto, giro/gyro, gizmo, go-go, go-slow, gringo, grotto, gung-ho, gusto, halo, heave-ho, hedgerow, heigh-ho, hello, hero, hippo, hollow, honcho, info, intro, jello, jingo, judo, kilo, K.O., lido, limo, lingo, loco, logo, lotto, macho, maestro, mango, meadow, mellow, memo, metro, mezzo, micro, mojo, mono, motto, muso, nacho, narrow, no-show, outgo, outgrow, panto, peepshow, photo, pillow, plateau, poco, polo, poncho, pongo, presto, promo, pronto,

447

pseudo, psycho, repo, repro, retro, rhino, Rio, roadshow, salvo, say-so, scarecrow, schizo, shadow, shallow, sideshow, slow-mo, solo, so-so, sorrow, speedo, stiletto, sumo, swallow, taco, tango, tarot, techno, tempo, tiptoe, torso, trio, typo, Velcro, veto, vino, wallow, widow, weirdo, willow, window, wino, yellow, yo-yo, zero.
[3] **Afterglow**, a-gogo, akimbo, alfresco, amigo, arroyo, art deco, art nouveau, audio, bambino, billy-o, bolero, bordello, bravado, buffalo, bungalow, calypso, cameo, casino, cheerio, commando, concerto, cornetto, crescendo, curio, de facto, domino, dynamo, electro, espresso, eyeshadow, falsetto, fandango, fiasco, flamenco, flamingo, foreshadow, gigolo, indigo, inferno, kimono, Latino, libido, machismo, marshmallow, memento, mistletoe, overflow, overthrow, patio, physio, piano, piccolo, Pierrot, potato, proviso, quid pro quo, radio, ratio, rodeo, Romeo, sombrero, so-and-so, soprano, staccato, status quo, stereo, studio, subzero, supremo, tally-ho, tic-tac-toe, to and fro, tobacco, tomato, tomorrow, tornado, torpedo, tuxedo, UFO, undergo, undertow, up-tempo, vertigo, vibrato, video, volcano.
[4] **Adagio**, alter ego, cappuccino, desperado, Eldorado, incognito, innuendo, mafioso, overshadow, paparazzo, politico, portfolio, scenario, simpatico, superhero, virtuoso.

4.1.7 "--mo" (as in "dynamo")
[2] ammo, demo, gizmo, limo, memo, mow, promo, slow-mo, sumo.
[3] dynamo, Eskimo, machismo, supremo.

SURPRISING RHYMING:
[1] **Beau**, blow, bow, bro, crow, doe, doh, dough, floe, flow, foe, glow, go, grow, hoe, know, low, no, oh, owe, pro, row, sew, show, slow, snow, so, stow, though, throw, toe, tow, whoa, woe, yo.
[2] **Aglow**, ago, aggro, also, alto, although, ammo, arrow, auto, banjo, barrow, below, bestow, billow, bingo, biro, bistro, blotto, bolo, bongo, borrow, bozo, bravo, bronco, bureau, burrow, cargo, cello, chateau, cheapo, chino, coco, cocoa, condo, credo, Day-Glo, deathblow, demo, depot, dingo, disco, ditto, dodo, dunno, duo, echo, ego, euro, fellow, follow, forgo, furlough, furrow, gaucho, gelato, ghetto, giro/gyro, gizmo, go-go, go-slow, gringo, grotto, gung-ho, gusto, halo, heave-ho, hedgerow, heigh-ho, hello, hero, hippo, hollow, honcho, info, intro, jello, jingo, judo, kilo, K.O., lido, limo, lingo, loco, logo, lotto, macho, maestro, mango, meadow, mellow, memo, metro, mezzo, micro, mojo, mono, motto, muso, nacho, narrow, no-show, outgo, outgrow, panto, peepshow, photo, pillow, plateau, poco, polo, poncho, pongo, presto, promo, pronto, pseudo, psycho, repo, repro, retro, rhino, Rio, roadshow, salvo, say-so, scarecrow, schizo, shadow, shallow, sideshow, slow-mo, solo, so-so, sorrow, speedo, stiletto, sumo, swallow, taco, tango, tarot, techno, tempo, tiptoe, torso, trio, typo, Velcro, veto, vino, wallow, widow, weirdo, willow, window, wino, yellow, yo-yo, zero.
[3] **Afterglow**, a-gogo, akimbo, alfresco, amigo, arroyo, art deco, art nouveau, audio, bambino, billy-o, bolero, bordello, bravado, buffalo, bungalow, calypso, cameo, casino, cheerio, commando, concerto, cornetto, crescendo, curio, de facto, domino, dynamo, electro, espresso, eyeshadow, falsetto, fandango, fiasco, flamenco, flamingo, foreshadow, gigolo, indigo, inferno, kimono, Latino, libido, machismo, marshmallow, memento, mistletoe, overflow, overthrow, patio, physio, piano, piccolo, Pierrot, potato, proviso, quid pro quo, radio, ratio, rodeo, Romeo, sombrero, so-and-so, soprano, staccato, status quo, stereo, studio, subzero, supremo, tally-ho, tic-tac-toe, to and fro, tobacco, tomato, tomorrow, tornado, torpedo, tuxedo, UFO, undergo, undertow, up-tempo, vertigo, vibrato, video, volcano, wheelbarrow.
[4] **Adagio**, alter ego, cappuccino, desperado, Eldorado, incognito, innuendo, mafioso, overshadow, paparazzo, politico, portfolio, scenario, simpatico, superhero, virtuoso.

4.1.8 "--no" (as in "know")
[1] know, no, snow.
[2] beano, chino, dunno, lino, mono, rhino, techno, uno, vino, winnow, wino.
[3] bambino, casino, domino, inferno, kimono, Latino, piano, soprano, tornado, volcano.
[4] Americano, cappuccino, palomino.

SURPRISING RHYMING:
[1] Beau, blow, bow, bro, crow, doe, doh, dough, floe, flow, foe, glow, go, grow, hoe, low, mo., mow, oh, owe, pro, row, sew, show, slow, so, stow, though, throw, toe, tow, whoa, woe, yo.
[2] Aglow, ago, aggro, also, alto, although, ammo, arrow, auto, banjo, barrow, below, bestow, billow, bingo, biro, bistro, blotto, bolo, bongo, borrow, bozo, bravo, bronco, bureau, burrow, cargo, cello, chateau, cheapo, chino, coco, cocoa, condo, credo, Day-Glo, deathblow, demo, depot, dingo, disco, ditto, dodo, dunno, duo, echo, ego, euro, fellow, follow, forgo, furlough, furrow, gaucho, gelato, ghetto, giro/gyro, gizmo, go-go, go-slow, gringo, grotto, gung-ho, gusto, halo, heave-ho, hedgerow, heigh-ho, hello, hero, hippo, hollow, honcho, info, intro, jello, jingo, judo, kilo, K.O., lido, limo, lingo, loco, logo, lotto, macho, maestro, mango, meadow, mellow, memo, metro, mezzo, micro, mojo, mono, motto, muso, nacho, narrow, no-show, outgo, outgrow, panto, peepshow, photo, pillow, plateau, poco, polo, poncho, pongo, presto, promo, pronto, pseudo, psycho, repo, repro, retro, rhino, Rio, roadshow, salvo, say-so, scarecrow, schizo, shadow, shallow, sideshow, slow-mo, solo, so-so, sorrow, speedo, stiletto, sumo, swallow, taco, tango, tarot, techno, tempo, tiptoe, torso, trio, typo, Velcro, veto, vino, wallow, widow, weirdo, willow, window, wino, yellow, yo-yo, zero.
[3] Afterglow, a-gogo, akimbo, alfresco, amigo, arroyo, art deco, art nouveau, audio, bambino, billy-o, bolero, bordello, bravado, buffalo, bungalow, calypso, cameo, casino, cheerio, commando, concerto, cornetto, crescendo, curio, de facto, domino, dynamo, electro, espresso, eyeshadow, falsetto, fandango, fiasco, flamenco, flamingo, foreshadow, gigolo, indigo, inferno, kimono, Latino, libido, machismo, marshmallow, memento, mistletoe, overflow, overthrow, patio, physio, piano, piccolo, Pierrot, potato, proviso, quid pro quo, radio, ratio, rodeo, Romeo, sombrero, so-and-so, soprano, staccato, status quo, stereo, studio, subzero, supremo, tally-ho, tic-tac-toe, to and fro, tobacco, tomato, tomorrow, tornado, torpedo, tuxedo, UFO, undergo, undertow, up-tempo, vertigo, vibrato, video, volcano, wheelbarrow.
[4] Adagio, alter ego, cappuccino, desperado, Eldorado, incognito, innuendo, mafioso, overshadow, paparazzo, politico, portfolio, scenario, simpatico, superhero, virtuoso.

4.1.9 "--ro" (as in "grow")
[1] bro, crow, fro, grow, pro, row, throw.
[2] aggro, arrow, barrow, biro, bistro, borrow, bureau, burrow, escrow, euro, farrow, furrow, giro, gyro, hedgerow, hero, impro, intro, macro, maestro, marrow, metro, micro, morrow, narrow, outgrow, repro, retro, scarecrow, sorrow, sparrow, tarot, Velcro, zero.
[3] bolero, electro, overthrow, pharaoh, Pierrot, semipro, sombrero, subzero, superhero, to and fro, tomorrow, wheelbarrow.

SURPRISING RHYMING:
[1] Beau, blow, bow, doe, doh, dough, flow, foe, glow, go, hoe, know, low, mow, no, oh, owe, sew, show, slow, snow, so, stow, though, toe, tow, whoa, woe, yo.
[2] Aglow, ago, aggro, also, alto, although, ammo, arrow, auto, banjo, barrow, below, bestow, billow, bingo, biro, bistro, blotto, bolo, bongo, borrow, bozo, bravo, bronco, bureau, burrow, cargo, cello, chateau, cheapo, chino, coco, cocoa, condo, credo, Day-Glo, deathblow, demo, depot, dingo, disco, ditto, dodo, dunno, duo, echo, ego, euro, fellow, follow, forgo, furlough, furrow, gaucho, gelato, ghetto, giro/gyro, gizmo, go-go, go-slow, gringo, grotto, gung-ho, gusto, halo, heave-ho, hedgerow, heigh-ho, hello, hero, hippo, hollow, honcho, info, intro, jello, jingo, judo, kilo, K.O., lido, limo, lingo, loco, logo, lotto, macho, maestro, mango, meadow, mellow, memo, metro, mezzo, micro, mojo, mono, motto, muso, nacho, narrow, no-show, outgo, outgrow, panto, peepshow, photo, pillow, plateau, poco, polo, poncho, pongo, presto, promo, pronto, pseudo, psycho, repo, repro, retro, rhino, Rio, roadshow, salvo, say-so, scarecrow, schizo, shadow, shallow, sideshow, slow-mo, solo, so-so, sorrow, speedo, stiletto, sumo, swallow, taco, tango, tarot, techno, tempo, tiptoe, torso, trio, typo, Velcro, veto, vino, wallow, widow, weirdo, willow, window, wino, yellow, yo-yo, zero.
[3] Afterglow, a-gogo, akimbo, alfresco, amigo, arroyo, art deco, art nouveau, audio, bambino, billy-o, bolero, bordello, bravado, buffalo, bungalow, calypso, cameo, casino, cheerio, commando, concerto, cornetto, crescendo, curio, de facto, domino, dynamo, electro, espresso, eyeshadow, falsetto, fandango, fiasco, flamenco, flamingo,

foreshadow, gigolo, indigo, inferno, kimono, Latino, libido, machismo, marshmallow, memento, mistletoe, overflow, overthrow, patio, physio, piano, potato, proviso, quid pro quo, radio, rodeo, Romeo, sombrero, so-and-so, soprano, staccato, status quo, stereo, studio, supremo, tally-ho, tic-tac-toe, to and fro, tobacco, tomato, tomorrow, tornado, torpedo, tuxedo, UFO, undergo, undertow, up-tempo, vertigo, vibrato, video, volcano.
[4] Adagio, alter ego, cappuccino, desperado, Eldorado, incognito, innuendo, Lothario, overshadow, paparazzo, superhero, virtuoso.

4.1.10 "--so" (as in "also")
[1] sew, so, sow.
[2] also, bozo, dipso, mezzo, muso, say-so, schizo, so-so, torso.
[3] calypso, espresso, proviso, so-and-so.
[4] mafioso, paparazzo, virtuoso.

SURPRISING RHYMING:
[1] Beau, blow, bow, bro, crow, doe, doh, dough, floe, flow, foe, glow, go, grow, hoe, know, low, mo., mow, no, oh, owe, pro, row, show, slow, snow, stow, though, throw, toe, tow, whoa, woe, yo.
[2] Aglow, ago, aggro, also, alto, although, ammo, arrow, auto, banjo, barrow, below, bestow, billow, bingo, biro, bistro, blotto, bolo, bongo, borrow, bozo, bravo, bronco, bureau, burrow, cargo, cello, chateau, cheapo, chino, coco, cocoa, condo, credo, Day-Glo, deathblow, demo, depot, dingo, disco, ditto, dodo, dunno, duo, echo, ego, euro, fellow, follow, forgo, furlough, furrow, gaucho, gelato, ghetto, giro/gyro, gizmo, go-go, go-slow, gringo, grotto, gung-ho, gusto, halo, heave-ho, hedgerow, heigh-ho, hello, hero, hippo, hollow, honcho, info, intro, jello, jingo, judo, kilo, K.O., lido, limo, lingo, loco, logo, lotto, macho, maestro, mango, meadow, mellow, memo, metro, mezzo, micro, mojo, mono, motto, muso, nacho, narrow, no-show, outgo, outgrow, panto, peepshow, photo, pillow, plateau, poco, polo, poncho, pongo, presto, promo, pronto, pseudo, psycho, repo, repro, retro, rhino, Rio, roadshow, salvo, say-so, scarecrow, schizo, shadow, shallow, sideshow, slow-mo, solo, so-so, sorrow, speedo, stiletto, sumo, swallow, taco, tango, tarot, techno, tempo, tiptoe, torso, trio, typo, Velcro, veto, vino, wallow, widow, weirdo, willow, window, wino, yellow, yo-yo, zero.
[3] Afterglow, a-gogo, akimbo, alfresco, amigo, arroyo, art deco, art nouveau, audio, bambino, billy-o, bolero, bordello, bravado, buffalo, bungalow, calypso, cameo, casino, cheerio, commando, concerto, cornetto, crescendo, curio, de facto, domino, dynamo, electro, espresso, eyeshadow, falsetto, fandango, fiasco, flamenco, flamingo, foreshadow, gigolo, indigo, inferno, kimono, Latino, libido, machismo, marshmallow, memento, mistletoe, overflow, overthrow, patio, physio, piano, piccolo, Pierrot, potato, proviso, quid pro quo, radio, ratio, rodeo, Romeo, sombrero, so-and-so, soprano, staccato, status quo, stereo, studio, subzero, supremo, tally-ho, tic-tac-toe, to and fro, tobacco, tomato, tomorrow, tornado, torpedo, tuxedo, UFO, undergo, undertow, up-tempo, vertigo, vibrato, video, volcano, wheelbarrow.
[4] Adagio, alter ego, cappuccino, desperado, Eldorado, incognito, innuendo, mafioso, overshadow, paparazzo, politico, portfolio, scenario, simpatico, superhero, virtuoso.

4.1.11 "--tow" (as in "toe")
[1] stow, toe, tow.
[2] alto, auto, bestow, blotto, chateau, ditto, gelato, ghetto, grotto, gusto, lotto, motto, panto, photo, pinto, plateau, presto, pronto, tiptoe, veto.
[3] burrito, castrato, concerto, cornetto, de facto, falsetto, memento, mistletoe, mosquito, potato, staccato, stiletto, tic-tac-toe, tomato, undertow, vibrato.
[4] incognito, manifesto.

SURPRISING RHYMING:
[1] Beau, blow, bow, bro, crow, doe, doh, dough, floe, flow, foe, glow, go, grow, hoe, know, low, mo., mow, no, oh, owe, pro, row, sew, show, slow, snow, so, though, throw, whoa, woe, yo.
[2] Aglow, ago, aggro, also, alto, although, ammo, arrow, auto, banjo, barrow, below, bestow, billow, bingo, biro, bistro, blotto, bolo, bongo, borrow, bozo, bravo, bronco,

bureau, burrow, cargo, cello, chateau, cheapo, chino, coco, cocoa, condo, credo, Day-Glo, deathblow, demo, depot, dingo, disco, ditto, dodo, dunno, duo, echo, ego, euro, fellow, follow, forgo, furlough, furrow, gaucho, gelato, ghetto, giro/gyro, gizmo, go-go, go-slow, gringo, grotto, gung-ho, gusto, halo, heave-ho, hedgerow, heigh-ho, hello, hero, hippo, hollow, honcho, info, intro, jello, jingo, judo, kilo, K.O., lido, limo, lingo, loco, logo, lotto, macho, maestro, mango, meadow, mellow, memo, metro, mezzo, micro, mojo, mono, motto, muso, nacho, narrow, no-show, outgo, outgrow, panto, peepshow, photo, pillow, plateau, poco, polo, poncho, pongo, presto, promo, pronto, pseudo, psycho, repo, repro, retro, rhino, Rio, roadshow, salvo, say-so, scarecrow, schizo, shadow, shallow, sideshow, slow-mo, solo, so-so, sorrow, speedo, stiletto, sumo, swallow, taco, tango, tarot, techno, tempo, tiptoe, torso, trio, typo, Velcro, veto, vino, wallow, widow, weirdo, willow, window, wino, yellow, yo-yo, zero.
[3] Afterglow, a-gogo, akimbo, alfresco, amigo, arroyo, art deco, art nouveau, audio, bambino, billy-o, bolero, bordello, bravado, buffalo, bungalow, calypso, cameo, casino, cheerio, commando, concerto, cornetto, crescendo, curio, de facto, domino, dynamo, electro, espresso, eyeshadow, falsetto, fandango, fiasco, flamenco, flamingo, foreshadow, gigolo, indigo, inferno, kimono, Latino, libido, machismo, marshmallow, memento, mistletoe, overflow, overthrow, patio, physio, piano, piccolo, Pierrot, potato, proviso, quid pro quo, radio, ratio, rodeo, Romeo, sombrero, so-and-so, soprano, staccato, status quo, stereo, studio, subzero, supremo, tally-ho, tic-tac-toe, to and fro, tobacco, tomato, tomorrow, tornado, torpedo, tuxedo, UFO, undergo, undertow, up-tempo, vertigo, vibrato, video, volcano, wheelbarrow.
[4] Adagio, alter ego, cappuccino, desperado, Eldorado, incognito, innuendo, mafioso, overshadow, paparazzo, politico, portfolio, scenario, simpatico, superhero, virtuoso.

4.1.12 "--oach" (as in "coach")
[1] broach, brooch, coach, loach, poach, roach.
[2] approach, cockroach, encroach, reproach, slowcoach, stagecoach.

SURPRISING RHYMING:
[1] Broached, coached, coaxed, hoaxed, poached
Bloke(s), broke, choke(s), cloak(s), coax, coke(s), croak(s), folk(s), hoax, joke(s), oak(s), poke(s), smoke(s), soak(s), spoke, stoke(s), stroke(s), woke, yolk.
Choked, cloaked, croaked, joked, poked, smoked, soaked, stoked, stroked.
Boast, close, coast, dose, ghost, gross(ed), host, most, post, roast, toast.
Cope(d), dope(d), grope(d), hope(d), mope(d), nope, rope(d), scope(d), slope(d), soap.
[2] Approached, encroached, reproached.
Awoke, backstroke, baroque, bespoke, breaststroke, cowpoke, egg yolk, evoke, heatstroke, invoke, keystroke, kinfolk, menfolk, provoke, revoke, slowpoke, sunstroke, townsfolk, woodsmoke.
Evoked, invoked, provoked, revoked, uncloaked.
Almost, bedpost, engrossed, foremost, gatepost, goalpost, lamppost, outmost, outpost, seacoast, signpost, topmost, utmost.
Elope(d), tightrope, towrope.
[3] Okey-doke, gentlefolk, masterstroke, stony-broke/stone-broke (U.S.), womenfolk.
Diagnosed, innermost, outermost, uppermost, whipping-post.
Antelope, Cinemascope, envelope, horoscope, kaleidoscope, microscope, periscope, skipping-rope, stethoscope, telescope.

4.1.13 "--oached" (as in "poached")
[1] broached, coached, poached.
[2] approached, encroached, reproached.

SURPRISING RHYMING:
[1] Broach, brooch, coach, coax, hoax, loach, poach, roach.
Choked, cloaked, croaked, joked, poked, smoked, soaked, stoked, stroked.
Boast, close, coast, coaxed, dose, ghost, hoaxed, host, most, post, roast, toast.
Close, dose, gross.
Coped, doped, groped, eloped, hoped, loped, moped, roped, scoped, sloped, soaped.
Boat, coat, dote, float, gloat, goat, moat, note, oat, quote, throat, tote, vote, wrote.

[2] **Approach**, encroach, reproach, slowcoach, stagecoach.
Evoked, invoked, provoked, revoked, uncloaked.
Almost, bedpost, engrossed, foremost, gatepost, goalpost, lamppost, outmost, outpost, seacoast, signpost, topmost, utmost.
Afloat, banknote, cutthroat, demote, denote, devote, dreamboat, emote, houseboat, keynote, lifeboat, misquote, promote, raincoat, remote, re-wrote, rowboat, sailboat, scapegoat, showboat, speedboat, steamboat, tailcoat, topcoat, tugboat, waistcoat.
[3] **Diagnosed**, innermost, outermost, uppermost, whipping-post.
Anecdote, antidote, ferryboat, motorboat, mountain goat, overcoat, petticoat, powerboat, riverboat, sugarcoat, table d'hôte, undercoat.

4.1.14 "--oaf" (as in "loaf")
[1] loaf, oaf, sugarloaf.

SURPRISING RHYMING:
[1] **Both**, growth, loath, oath, sloth.
Clove, cove, dove, drove, grove, mauve, stove, strove, trove, wove.
Bode, code, crowed, flowed, goad, load, lode, mode, mowed, node, ode, owed, road, rode, rowed, sewed, showed, slowed, sowed, stowed, strode, toad, toed, towed.
Cope, dope, grope, hope, mope, pope, rope, scope, slope, soap.
Blows, bows, chose, close, clothes, crows, dose, doze, flows, foes, froze, glows, goes, gross, grows, hose, knows, lows, mows, nose, owes, pose, pros, prose, rose, rows, sews, shows, slows, snows, sows, those, throes, throws, toes, tows, woes.
[2] **Alcove**, behove/behoove (U.S.), interwove, mangrove.
Abode, barcode, bestowed, corrode, decode, download, elbowed, encode, episode, erode, explode, forebode, freeload, hallowed, highroad, inroad, offload, overflowed, overload, payload, postcode, railroad, reload, unload, upload, workload, zip code.
Elope, tightrope, towrope.
Engross, lactose, morose, verbose, viscose.
Arose, compose, disclose, dispose, enclose, expose, forgoes, gallows, impose, oppose, outgrows, pillows, plainclothes, primrose, propose, rainbows, repose, suppose, tiptoes, undergoes, wild rose.
[3] **Antelope**, Cinemascope, envelope, horoscope, kaleidoscope, microscope, periscope, skipping-rope, stethoscope, telescope.
Adios, comatose, diagnose, dominoes, grandiose, indispose, overdose, overexpose, presuppose, superimpose.

4.1.15 "--oast" (as in "toast")
[1] boast, coast, ghost, grossed, host, most, post, roast, toast.
[2] almost, bedpost, endmost, engrossed, foremost, Freepost, gatepost, goalpost, guidepost, lamppost, milepost, outmost, outpost, seacoast, signpost, topmost, utmost.
[3] diagnosed, innermost, outermost, uppermost, whipping-post.

SURPRISING RHYMING:
[1] **Close**, cloves, coves, dose, droves, gross, loaves, stoves.
Closed, dozed, hosed, nosed, posed.
Coax(ed), hoax(ed).
Blows, bows, chose, close, clothes, crows, doze, flows, foes, froze, glows, goes, grows, hose, knows, lows, mows, nose, owes, pose, pros, prose, rose, rows, sews, shows, slows, snows, sows, stows, those, throes, throws, toes, tows, woes.
Choked, cloaked, croaked, joked, poked, smoked, soaked, stoked, stroked.
[2] **Engross**, lactose, morose, verbose, viscose.
Bulldozed, composed, deposed, disclosed, disposed, enclosed, exposed, imposed, opposed, proposed, supposed, transposed.
Arose, compose, disclose, dispose, enclose, expose, forgoes, gallows, impose, oppose, outgrows, pillows, plainclothes, primrose, propose, rainbows, repose, suppose, tiptoes, undergoes, wild rose.
[3] **Adios**, comatose(d), diagnose(d), dominoes, grandiose, indispose(d), innermost, outermost, overdose(d), overexpose(d), predispose(d), superimpose(d), uppermost.

4.1.16 "--oaches" (as in "coaches")
[2] coaches, broaches, brooches, poaches, roaches.
[3] approaches, cockroaches, encroaches, reproaches, slowcoaches, stagecoaches.
SURPRISING RHYMING:
[2] **Closes**, doses, dozes, hoses, noses, poses, roses.
Coaxes, hoaxes, torches.
Emotions, lotions, motions, notions, oceans, potions.
Boasters, coasters, poachers, posters, toasters.
Cronies, moanies, phonies, ponies.
[3] **Bulldozes**, composes, diagnoses, discloses, exposes, forecloses, imposes, opposes, overdoses, proposes.
Atrocious, ferocious, precocious.

4.1.17 "--oaching" (as in "coaching")
[2] broaching, coaching, poaching.
[3] approaching, encroaching, reproaching.

SURPRISING RHYMING:
[2] **Choking**, cloaking, croaking, evoking, joking, poking, smoking, soaking, stroking.
Boasting, coasting, coaxing, hoaxing, hosting, posting, roasting, toasting.
Closing, dozing, hosing, nosing, posing.
Coping, doping, eloping, groping, hoping, moping, roping, sloping.
Boating, coating, doting, floating, gloating, noting, quoting, voting.
Cloning, groaning, honing, loaning, moaning, owning, phoning, stoning, toning, zoning.
Blowing, bowing, crowing, flowing, glowing, going, growing, knowing, loathing, mowing, owing, rowing, sewing, showing, slowing, snowing, sowing, throwing, toeing, towing.
[3] **Bulldozing**, composing, deposing, disclosing, disposing, enclosing, exposing, imposing, opposing, proposing, supposing.
Evoking, invoking, provoking, revoking, stockbroking.
Consoling, controlling, extolling, paroling, patrolling, potholing.
Atoning, condoning, disowning, postponing.
[4] **Diagnosing**, overdosing, presupposing, superimposing.

4.1.18 "--oax" (as in "hoax")
[1] blokes, chokes, cloaks, coax, cokes, croaks, folks, hoax, jokes, oaks, pokes, smokes, soaks, stokes, strokes, yolks.
[2] egg yolks, evokes, invokes, keystrokes, provokes, revokes.

SURPRISING RHYMING:
[1] **Broach**, brooch, coach, loach, poach, roach.
Boast, coast, ghost, host, post, roast, signpost, toast.
Boats, coats, dotes, floats, gloats, goats, moats, notes, oats, quotes, throats, votes.
Close, doze, hose, nose, pose.
Cope(s), dope(s), grope(s), hope(s), mope(s), nope, rope(s), scope, slope(s), soap.
[2] **Approach**, encroach, reproach, slowcoach, stagecoach.
Banknotes, denotes, devotes, dreamboats, lifeboats, raincoats, rowboats, sailboats, scapegoats, showboats, speedboats, waistcoats.
[3] **Anecdotes**, antidotes, ferryboats, motorboats, mountain goats, overcoats, petticoats, powerboats, riverboats.
Antelope, Cinemascope, envelope(s), horoscope(s), kaleidoscope, microscope, periscope, skipping-rope(s), stethoscope, telescope.

4.1.19 "--oaxing" (as in "coaxing")
[2] coaxing, hoaxing.

SURPRISING RHYMING:
[2] **Boasting**, coasting, hosting, posting, roasting, toasting.
Broaching, coaching, poaching.
Choking, cloaking, croaking, evoking, joking, poking, smoking, soaking, stroking.

Boating, coating, doting, floating, gloating, noting, quoting, voting.
Closing, dozing, hosing, nosing, posing.
Coping, doping, eloping, groping, hoping, moping, roping, sloping.
Coding, goading, loading.
Lotion, motion, notion, ocean, potion.
[3] **Evoking**, invoking, provoking, revoking, stockbroking.
Approaching, encroaching, reproaching.
Bulldozing, composing, deposing, disclosing, disposing, enclosing, exposing, imposing, opposing, proposing, supposing.
Demoting, denoting, devoting, emoting, misquoting, promoting.
Corroding, decoding, encoding, eroding, exploding, foreboding, freeloading, overloading, railroading, reloading, unloading.
Commotion, devotion, emotion, locomotion, promotion, slow-motion.
[4] **Diagnosing**, overdosing, presupposing, superimposing.

4.1.20 "--oasted" (as in "boasted")

[2] boasted, coasted, ghosted, hosted, posted, roasted, signposted, toasted.

SURPRISING RHYMING:
[2] **Boated**, coated, doted, floated, gloated, noted, quoted, voted.
Folded, moulded/molded (U.S.), scolded.
Bolted, halted, jolted, moulted/molted (U.S.), salted, vaulted.
Boded, coded, goaded, loaded.
[3] **Demoted**, denoted, devoted, misquoted, outvoted, promoted.
Blindfolded, cuckolded, remoulded/remolded (U.S.), unfolded.
Assaulted, defaulted, exalted, revolted, somersaulted, unbolted.
Corrosive, erosive, explosive.
Corroded, decoded, encoded, eroded, exploded, imploded, overloaded, outmoded, railroaded, reloaded, unloaded.

4.1.21 "--oasting" (as in "hosting")

[2] boasting, coasting, hosting, posting, roasting, toasting.

SURPRISING RHYMING:
[2] **Closing**, coaxing, dozing, hoaxing, hosing, nosing, posing.
Boating, coating, doting, floating, gloating, noting, quoting, voting.
Choking, cloaking, croaking, evoking, joking, poking, smoking, soaking, stroking.
Folding, holding, moulding/molding (U.S.), scolding
Cloning, groaning, honing, loaning, moaning, owning, phoning, stoning, toning, zoning.
Bowling, polling, rolling, scrolling, strolling, tolling, trolling.
Blowing, bowing, crowing, flowing, glowing, going, growing, knowing, loathing, mowing, owing, rowing, sewing, showing, slowing, snowing, sowing, throwing, toeing, towing.
Coding, goading, loading.
Coping, doping, eloping, groping, hoping, moping, roping, sloping.
[3] **Demoting**, denoting, devoting, emoting, misquoting, promoting.
Evoking, invoking, provoking, revoking, stockbroking.
Bulldozing, composing, disclosing, disposing, enclosing, exposing, foreclosing, imposing, opposing, proposing, supposing, transposing.
Remoulding/remolding (U.S.), shareholding, stockholding, unfolding, withholding.
Consoling, controlling, extolling, paroling, patrolling, potholing.
Churchgoing, easy-going, following, foregoing, harrowing, ongoing, outgoing, overflowing, seagoing, stowing, tiptoeing, unknowing.
Corroding, decoding, encoding, eroding, exploding, foreboding, freeloading, imploding, overloading, railroading, reloading, unloading.
[4] **Diagnosing**, overdosing, presupposing, superimposing.

4.1.22 "--ocal" (as in "local")

[2] bi-focal, focal, local, vocal, yokel.

SURPRISING RHYMING:
[2] **Broken**, oaken, spoken, token, woken.
Coastal, postal, social, total, woeful - yodel, zonal.
Global, hopeful, ignoble, mobile, noble, ogle, oval.
[3] **Awoken**, heartbroken, outspoken, plain-spoken, re-open, soft-spoken, unbroken, unspoken, well-spoken.
Anecdotal, disposal, proposal, subtotal.

4.1.23 "--oco" (as in "loco")
[2] coco, cocoa, loco, poco.

SURPRISING RHYMING:
[2] **Ago**, aggro, also, alto, although, ammo, arrow, auto, banjo, barrow, below, bestow, billow, bingo, biro, bistro, blotto, bolo, bongo, borrow, bozo, bravo, bronco, bureau, burrow, cargo, cello, chateau, cheapo, chino, coco, cocoa, condo, credo, Day-Glo, deathblow, demo, depot, dingo, disco, ditto, dodo, dunno, duo, echo, ego, euro, fellow, follow, forgo, furlough, furrow, gaucho, gelato, ghetto, giro/gyro, gizmo, go-go, go-slow, gringo, grotto, gung-ho, gusto, halo, heave-ho, hedgerow, heigh-ho, hello, hero, hippo, hollow, honcho, info, intro, jello, jingo, judo, kilo, K.O., lido, limo, lingo, loco, logo, lotto, macho, maestro, mango, meadow, mellow, memo, metro, mezzo, micro, mojo, mono, motto, muso, nacho, narrow, no-show, outgo, outgrow, panto, peepshow, photo, pillow, plateau, poco, polo, poncho, pongo, presto, promo, pronto, pseudo, psycho, repo, repro, retro, rhino, Rio, roadshow, salvo, say-so, scarecrow, schizo, shadow, shallow, sideshow, slow-mo, solo, so-so, sorrow, speedo, stiletto, sumo, swallow, taco, tango, tarot, techno, tempo, tiptoe, torso, trio, typo, Velcro, veto, vino, wallow, widow, weirdo, willow, window, wino, yellow, yo-yo, zero.

4.1.24 "--ocer" (as in "grocer")
anorexia nervosa, closer, greengrocer, grocer, mimosa, Via Dolorosa.

SURPRISING RHYMING:
[2] **Boaster**, coaster, poacher, poster, toaster.
Chauffeur, clover, dozer, drover, nova, over, poser, rover.
Coder, goader, loader, odour/odor (U.S.).
Donor, groaner, loaner, loner, moaner, owner, toner.
Aura, broker, choker, coaxer, coca, hoaxer, joker, poker, smoker.
Boater, doter, floater, gloater, motor, quota, rota, rotor, voter.
Coper, doper, eloper, groper, hoper, moper, no-hoper, ogre, sober.
Bolder, boulder, colder, folder, holder, moulder/molder (U.S.), older, scolder, shoulder, smoulder/smolder (U.S.), solder, told her.
Blower, boa, goer, grower, lower, mower, rower, sewer, shower, slower, thrower.
Bowler, cola, molar, polar, roller, solar, stroller.
[3] **Composure**, closure, disclosure, enclosure, exposure.
Bulldozer, composer, discloser, exposer, imposer, proposer.
All over, blow over, bowl over, changeover, chew over, crossover, fall over, fly-over, get over, handover, hangover, leftover, makeover, moreover, once-over, pullover, pushover, sleepover, slipover, stopover, takeover, turnover, walkover, watch over.
Decoder, encoder, exploder, freeloader, railroader, unloader.
Beholder, cardholder, cold shoulder, freeholder, householder, keyholder, leaseholder, shareholder, stakeholder, stockholder.
Bipolar, cajoler, consoler, controller, payola, rock 'n' roller, steamroller, tombola, viola.
Aroma, beachcomber, diploma, glaucoma, misnomer.
Atoner, condoner, homeowner, landowner, persona.
Borrower, churchgoer, concertgoer, follower, lawnmower, racegoer, swallower, theatregoer/theatergoer (U.S.), widower, winegrower.

4.1.25 "--ocious" (as in "ferocious")
[3] atrocious, ferocious, precocious.

SURPRISING RHYMING:
[2] **Coaches**, broaches, brooches, grocers, poaches, roaches.
Bogus, bonus, focus(ed), notice(d), onus, opus, wholeness.
Boldness, coldness, hostess, locust, poets, smokeless.
Hopeless, homeless, ropeless, soapless, soulless.
Closes, dozes, hoses, noses, poses, roses.
Boldest, closest, coldest, lowest, oldest, omelets, poets, slowest.
Boasters, coasters, poachers, poster, toasters.
Brokers, chokers, jokers, provokers, smokers.
Codas, coders, goaders, loaders, odours/odors (U.S.).
[3] **Hypnosis**, neurosis, osmosis, prognosis, psychosis.
Approaches, encroaches, reproaches, slowcoaches, stagecoaches.
Bulldozes, composes, discloses, exposes, exposures, imposes, opposes, proposes.
Decoders, encoders, freeloaders, railroaders.
[4] **Diagnosis**, halitosis, metamorphosis, overdoses, symbiosis.

4.1.26 "--ode" (as in "road")
[1] bode, code, crowed, flowed, goad, load, lode, mode, mowed, node, ode, owed, road, rode, rowed, sewed, showed, slowed, sowed, stowed, strode, toad, toed, towed.
[2] abode, anode, barcode, bestowed, boatload, carload, cathode, commode, corrode, decode, download, elbowed, encode, episode, erode, explode, forebode, freeload, hallowed, highroad, implode, inroad, offload, overflowed, overload, payload, postcode, railroad, reload, truckload, unload, upload, workload, zip code.

SURPRISING RHYMING:
[1] **Bold**, bowled, coaled, cold, doled, foaled, fold, gold, hold, holed, mould/mold (U.S.), old, poled, polled, rolled, scold, soled, sold, told, tolled.
Closed, dozed, hosed, nosed, posed.
Blow, bro, crow, doe, doh, dough, flow, glow, grow, know, lo, low, no, pro, row, slow, snow, stow, throw, toe, tow.
Clove, cove, dove, drove, grove, mauve, stove, strove, trove, wove.
Brogue, rogue, vogue.
Boat, coat, dote, float, gloat, goat, moat, note, quote, rote, throat, tote, vote, wrote.
Cloned, coned, droned, groaned, honed, loaned, loaned, moaned, owned, phoned, stoned, toned, zoned.
[2] **Behold**, blindfold, cajoled, controlled, cuckold, foothold, foretold, household, millionfold, outsold, paroled, remould(s)/remold(s) (U.S.), retold, scaffold, stronghold, tenfold, threshold, toehold, twofold, threefold, unfold, uphold, unsold, untold, withhold.
Bulldozed, composed, deposed, disclosed, disposed, enclosed, exposed, imposed, opposed, proposed, supposed, transposed.
Afloat, banknote, cutthroat, demote, devote, dovecote, dreamboat, emote, houseboat, keynote, lifeboat, misquote, promote, raincoat, remote, re-wrote, rowboat, sailboat, scapegoat, showboat, speedboat, steamboat, tugboat, turncoat, waistcoat.
Atoned, condoned, dethroned, disowned, postponed.
Ago, bingo, bongo, cargo, dingo, ego, forgo, go, lingo, mango, no-go, pogo, tango.
Bimbo, combo, crossbow, elbow, hobo, jumbo, limbo, mambo, oboe, rainbow.
Bordeaux, condo, credo, dodo, judo, kendo, meadow, pseudo, rondeau, rondo, shadow, speedo, widow, weirdo, window.
Aglow, below, cashflow, cello, deathblow, fellow, follow, furlough, go-slow, halo, hello, hollow, mellow, moonglow, pillow, polo, shallow, solo, swallow, wallow, willow, yellow.
Arrow, barrow, bistro, borrow, bureau, burrow, euro, farrow, furrow, hedgerow, hero, intro, macro, maestro, marrow, metro, micro, narrow, outgrow, repro, retro, scarecrow, sorrow, tarot, Velcro, zero.
Alto, auto, bestow, blotto, chateau, ditto, ghetto, grotto, gusto, lotto, motto, photo, pinto, plateau, presto, pronto, tiptoe, veto.
[3] **Centrefold/centerfold** (U.S.), manifold, marigold, oversold, pigeonholed, self-controlled, stranglehold, uncontrolled, undersold.
Diagnosed, indisposed, interposed, juxtaposed, overdosed, overexposed, predisposed, presupposed, recomposed, superimposed.

Anecdote, antidote, ferryboat, motorboat, mountain goat, overcoat, petticoat, powerboat, riverboat, sugarcoat, table d'hôte, undercoat.
Bravado, commando, crescendo, libido, tornado, torpedo, tuxedo.
Bambino, casino, domino, inferno, kimono, Latino, piano, soprano, tornado, volcano.

4.1.27 "--oda" (as in "soda")
[2] coda, coder, goader, loader, odour/odor (U.S.), soda.
[3] corroder, decoder, encoder, exploder, freeloader, pagoda, railroader, unloader.

SURPRISING RHYMING:
[2] **Donor**, groaner, loaner, loner, moaner, owner, toner.
Bolder, boulder, colder, folder, holder, moulder/molder (U.S.), older, scolder, shoulder, smoulder/smolder (U.S.), solder, told her.
Broker, choker, coaxer, coca, evoker, hoaxer, joker, poker, smoker.
Bowler, clover, cola, molar, over, polar, roller, rover, solar, stroller.
Blower, boa, chauffer, glower, goer, grower, knower, lower, mower, rower, sewer, shower, slower, sower, thrower, tower.
Closer, dozer, grocer, poser.
[3] **Aroma**, beachcomber, diploma, glaucoma, misnomer.
Atoner, condoner, homeowner, landowner, persona, postponer.
All over, blow over, bowl over, changeover, chew over, crossover, fall over, fly-over, get over, handover, hangover, leftover, makeover, moreover, once-over, pullover, pushover, sleepover, slipover, stopover, takeover, turnover, walkover, watch over.
Beholder, cardholder, cold shoulder, freeholder, householder, leaseholder, shareholder, smallholder, stakeholder, stockholder.
Bipolar, cajoler, Coca-Cola, comptroller, consoler, controller, extoller, granola, patroller, payola, rock 'n' roller, steamroller, tombola, viola.
Bulldozer, composer, discloser, exposer, imposer, proposer.
[4] **Bossa nova**, Casanova, supernova, up-and-over.

4.1.28 "--oded" (as in "loaded")
[2] boded, coded, goaded, loaded.
[3] corroded, decoded, encoded, eroded, exploded, imploded, overloaded, outmoded, railroaded, reloaded, unloaded.

SURPRISING RHYMING:
[2] **Boated**, coated, doted, floated, gloated, noted, quoted, voted.
Folded, moulded/molded (U.S.), scolded.
Bolted, halted, jolted, moulted/molted (U.S.), salted, vaulted.
Boasted, ghosted, hosted, posted, roasted, signposted, toasted.
Beholden, bolden, embolden, golden, olden.
[3] **Demoted**, denoted, devoted, misquoted, outvoted, promoted.
Blindfolded, cuckolded, remoulded/remolded (U.S.), unfolded.

4.1.29 "--oding" (as in "loading")
[2] coding, goading, loading.
[3] corroding, decoding, encoding, eroding, exploding, foreboding, freeloading, imploding, overloading, railroading, reloading, unloading.

SURPRISING RHYMING:
[2] **Closing**, dozing, hosing, nosing, posing.
Combing, foaming, gloaming, homing, roaming.
Folding, holding, moulding/molding (U.S.), scolding.
Cloning, groaning, honing, loaning, moaning, owning, phoning, stoning, toning, zoning.
Boating, coating, doting, floating, gloating, noting, quoting, voting.
Blowing, crowing, flowing, glowing, going, growing, knowing, mowing, owing, rowing, sewing, showing, slowing, snowing, sowing, throwing, toeing, towing.
Bowling, polling, rolling, scrolling, strolling, tolling, trolling.
Choking, cloaking, croaking, evoking, joking, poking, smoking, soaking, stroking.

Coping, doping, eloping, groping, hoping, moping, roping, sloping.
[3] **Bulldozing**, composing, deposing, disclosing, disposing, enclosing, exposing, imposing, opposing, proposing, supposing.
Enfolding, shareholding, stockholding, unfolding, withholding.
Consoling, controlling, extolling, paroling, patrolling, potholing.
Atoning, condoning, disowning, postponing.
Demoting, denoting, devoting, emoting, misquoting, promoting.
Churchgoing, easy-going, foregoing, ongoing, outgoing, overflowing, seagoing, stowing, tiptoeing, unknowing.
[4] **Diagnosing**, overdosing, presupposing, superimposing.

4.1.30 "--ogue" (as in "rogue")
[1] brogue, rogue, vogue.

SURPRISING RHYMING:
[1] **Clove**, cove, dove, drove, grove, mauve, stove, strove, wove.
Bloke, broke, choke, cloak, coke, croak, folk, joke, oak, poke, smoke, soak, spoke, stoke, stroke, woke, yolk.
Bode, code, flowed, goad, load, mode, mowed, ode, owed, road, rode, rowed, sewed, showed, slowed, sowed, stowed, strode, towed.
Bold, bowled, cold, doled, fold, gold, hold, holed, mould/mold (U.S.), old, poled, polled, rolled, scold, soled, sold, told, tolled.
Blown, bone, clone, cone, drone, flown, groan, grown, hone, known, loan, lone, moan, mown, own, phone, prone, scone, sewn, shone, shown, sown, stone, throne, thrown, tone, zone.
Cope, dope, grope, hope, mope, oath, pope, rope, scope, slope, soap.
Coped, groped, eloped, hoped, moped, roped, sloped, soaped.
Boat, coat, dote, float, gloat, goat, moat, note, oat, quote, throat, tote, vote, wrote.
[2] **Awoke**, backstroke, bespoke, breaststroke, cowpoke, evoke, heatstroke, invoke, keystroke, kinfolk, menfolk, provoke, revoke, slowpoke, sunstroke, townsfolk, uncloak.
Abode, barcode, bestowed, corrode, decode, download, elbowed, encode, episode, erode, explode, forebode, freeload, hallowed, highroad, implode, inroad, offload, overflowed, overload, postcode, railroad, reload, unload, upload, workload, zip code.
Behold, blindfold, cajoled, controlled, cuckold, foothold, foretold, household, millionfold, outsold, paroled, remould(s)/remold(s) (U.S.), re-sold, retold, scaffold, stronghold, tenfold, threshold, toehold, twofold, threefold, unfold, uphold, unsold, untold, withhold.
Afloat, banknote, cutthroat, demote, denote, devote, dreamboat, emote, houseboat, keynote, lifeboat, misquote, promote, raincoat, remote, re-wrote, rowboat, sailboat, scapegoat, showboat, speedboat, steamboat, tugboat, turncoat, waistcoat.
[3] **Okey-doke**, masterstroke, stony-broke/stone-broke.
Centrefold/centerfold (U.S.), manifold, marigold, oversold, pigeonholed, self-controlled, stranglehold, uncontrolled, undersold.
Antelope, Cinemascope, envelope, horoscope, kaleidoscope, microscope, periscope, skipping-rope, stethoscope, telescope.
Anecdote, antidote, ferryboat, motorboat, mountain goat, overcoat, petticoat, powerboat, riverboat, sugarcoat, table d'hôte, undercoat.

4.1.31 "--oke" (as in "joke")
[1] bloke, broke, choke, cloak, coke, croak, folk, joke, oak, poke, smoke, soak, spoke, stoke, stroke, woke, yolk.
[2] awoke, backstroke, baroque, bespoke, breaststroke, egg yolk, evoke, heatstroke, invoke, keystroke, kinfolk, menfolk, provoke, revoke, slowpoke, sunstroke, townsfolk, uncloak, woodsmoke.
[3] artichoke, okey-doke, gentlefolk, masterstroke, stony-broke/stone-broke (U.S.).

SURPRISING RHYMING:
[1] **Choked**, cloaked, croaked, joked, poked, smoked, soaked, stoked, stroked.
Boat, coat, dote, float, gloat, goat, moat, note, oat, quote, throat, tote, vote, wrote.
Brogue, rogue, vogue.
Cope, dope, grope, hope, mope, pope, rope, scope, slope, soap.

Boast, coast, ghost, grossed, host, most, post, roast, toast.
[2] Evoked, invoked, provoked, revoked, uncloaked.
Afloat, banknote, cutthroat, demote, denote, devote, dreamboat, emote, houseboat, keynote, lifeboat, misquote, promote, raincoat, remote, rowboat, sailboat, scapegoat, showboat, speedboat, steamboat, tugboat, turncoat, waistcoat.
Elope, tightrope, towrope.
Almost, bedpost, engrossed, foremost, gatepost, goalpost, lamppost, milepost, outmost, outpost, seacoast, signpost, topmost, utmost.
[3] Anecdote, antidote, ferryboat, motorboat, overcoat, petticoat, powerboat, riverboat.
Envelope, horoscope, kaleidoscope, microscope, skipping-rope, telescope.

4.1.32 "--oked" (as in "joked")
[1] choked, cloaked, croaked, joked, poked, smoked, soaked, stoked, stroked.
[2] convoked, evoked, invoked, provoked, revoked, uncloaked.

SURPRISING RHYMING:
[1] **Bloke**, broke, choke, cloak, coke, croak, folk, joke, oak, poke, smoke, soak, spoke, stoke, stroke, woke, yolk.
Boat, coat, dote, float, gloat, goat, moat, note, oat, quote, throat, tote, vote, wrote.
Brogue, rogue, vogue.
Coped, doped, groped, hoped, moped, roped, sloped, soaped.
Boast, coast, ghost, grossed, host, most, post, roast, toast.
[2] Awoke, backstroke, baroque, breaststroke, evoke, heatstroke, invoke, keystroke, menfolk, provoke, revoke, slowpoke, sunstroke
Afloat, banknote, cutthroat, demote, denote, devote, dreamboat, elope(d), emote, houseboat, keynote, lifeboat, misquote, promote, raincoat, remote, re-wrote, rowboat, sailboat, scapegoat, showboat, speedboat, steamboat, tugboat, turncoat, waistcoat.
Almost, bedpost, engrossed, foremost, gatepost, goalpost, lamppost, milepost, outmost, outpost, seacoast, signpost, topmost, utmost.
[3] Artichoke, okey-doke, masterstroke, stony-broke/stone-broke (U.S.).
Anecdote, antidote, ferryboat, motorboat, overcoat, petticoat, powerboat, riverboat.
Envelope, horoscope, kaleidoscope, microscope, periscope, skipping-rope, telescope.
Diagnosed, innermost, uppermost, whipping-post.

4.1.33 "--oken" (as in "spoken")
[2] broken, oaken, spoken, token, woken.
[3] awoken, heartbroken, outspoken, plain-spoken, re-open, soft-spoken, unbroken, unspoken, well-spoken.

SURPRISING RHYMING:
[2] **Beholden**, bolden, embolden, golden, olden.
Chosen, frozen, lederhosen, unfrozen.
Copin' [silent "g"], dopin', elopin', gropin', hopin', mopin'.
Chokin', croakin', evokin', jokin', pokin', smokin', soakin', strokin'.
Boastin', coastin', hostin', postin', roastin', toastin'.
Closin', dozin', hosin', nosin', posin'.
Glowin', goin', growin', knowin', mowin', owin', rowin', sewin', showin', slowin', snowin', sowin', throwin', towin'.
Boltin' [silent "g"], haltin', joltin', saltin'.
Boatin' [silent "g"], coatin', dotin', floatin', gloatin', notin', quotin', votin'.
[3] **Component**, exponent, opponent, proponent.
Bulldozin' [silent "g"], composin', disclosin', disposin', enclosin', exposin', imposin', opposin', proposin', supposin'.
Churchgoin' [silent "g"], easy-goin', followin', ongoin', outgoin', overflowin', seagoin', tiptoein', unknowin'.

4.1.34 "--oker" (as in "joker")
[2] broker, choker, coca, evoker, joker, ochre, poker, soaker, smoker, stroker.
[3] carioca, invoker, mediocre, nonsmoker, pawnbroker, provoker, Rioja, stockbroker.

SURPRISING RHYMING:
[2] **Boater**, doter, floater, gloater, motor, quota, rota, rotor, voter.
Coper, doper, eloper, groper, hoper, moper, no-hoper, ogre, sober.
Boaster, coaster, poacher, poster, toaster.
Bolder, boulder, colder, folder, holder, moulder/molder (U.S.), older, scolder, shoulder, smoulder/smolder (U.S.), solder, told her.
Donor, groaner, loaner, loner, moaner, owner, toner.
Closer, dozer, grocer, poser.
Chauffeur, clover, drover, nova, over, rover.
Coder, goader, loader, loafer, odour/odor (U.S.).
Bowler, cola, molar, polar, roller, solar, stroller.
[3] **Bulldozer**, composer, exposer, imposer, mimosa, proposer.
Atoner, condoner, homeowner, landowner, persona.
All over, blow over, bowl over, changeover, chew over, crossover, fall over, fly-over, get over, handover, hangover, leftover, makeover, moreover, once-over, pullover, pushover, sleepover, slipover, stopover, takeover, turnover, walkover, watch over.
Decoder, encoder, exploder, freeloader, railroader, unloader.
Beholder, cardholder, cold shoulder, freeholder, householder, leaseholder, shareholder, smallholder, stakeholder, stockholder.
Bipolar, cajoler, Coca-Cola, consoler, controller, patroller, payola, pianola, rock 'n' roller, steamroller, tombola, viola.
[4] **Bossa nova**, Casanova, supernova, up-and-over.

4.1.35 "--oking" (as in "joking")
[2] choking, cloaking, croaking, evoking, joking, poking, smoking, soaking, stroking.
[3] evoking, invoking, provoking, revoking, stockbroking.

SURPRISING RHYMING:
[2] **Boating**, doting, floating, gloating, loading, noting, quoting, voting.
Coping, eloping, groping, hoping, moping, roping, sloping, soaping.
Boasting, coaxing, hoaxing, hosting, posting, roasting, toasting.
Cloning, groaning, honing, loaning, moaning, owning, phoning, stoning, toning, zoning.
Bowling, polling, rolling, scrolling, strolling, tolling, trolling.
Closing, dozing, hosing, nosing, posing.
Folding, holding, moulding/molding (U.S.), scolding.
Broken, oaken, spoken, token, woken.
[3] **Demoting**, denoting, devoting, emoting, misquoting, promoting.
Consoling, controlling, extolling, paroling, patrolling, potholing.
Atoning, condoning, disowning, postponing.
Churchgoing, easy-going, following, foregoing, harrowing, ongoing, outgoing, overflowing, seagoing, stowing, tiptoeing, unknowing.
Corroding, decoding, encoding, eroding, exploding, foreboding, freeloading, imploding, overloading, railroading, reloading, unloading.
Bulldozing, composing, deposing, disclosing, disposing, enclosing, exposing, imposing, opposing, proposing, supposing.
Enfolding, remoulding/remolding (U.S.), unfolding, withholding.
Awoken, heartbroken, outspoken, plain-spoken, soft-spoken, unbroken, well-spoken.
[4] **Diagnosing**, overdosing, presupposing, superimposing.

4.1.36 "--ole" (as in "hole")
[1] bowl, coal, dole, droll, foal, goal, hole, knoll, mole, pole, poll, role, roll, scroll, shoal, sole, soul, stole, stroll, toll, troll, vole, whole.
[2] atoll, bankroll, bargepole, beanpole, bedroll, bolthole, cajole, charcoal, console, control, Creole, dustbowl, enrol/enroll (U.S.), extol, fishbowl, flagpole, hellhole, insole, keyhole, loophole, manhole, maypole, payroll, parole, patrol, peephole, pinhole, plughole, porthole, pothole, punchbowl, tadpole.
[3] buttonhole, casserole, cubbyhole, hidey-hole, pigeonhole, rigmarole, rock and roll, self-control, waterhole.

460

SURPRISING RHYMING:
[1] **Bold**, bowled, cold, doled, fold, gold, hold, holed, mould/mold, old, poled, polled, rolled, scold, soled, sold, told, tolled.
Both, growth, loath, oath, sloth.
Blow, flow, glow, lo, low, sew, slow, so, sow.
Cope, dope, grope, hope, mope, pope, rope, scope, slope, soap.
Clove, cove, dove, drove, grove, mauve, stove, strove, trove, wove.
Bolt, colt, halt, jolt, moult/molt (U.S.), salt, vault, volt.
[2] **Behold**, blindfold, cajoled, controlled, cuckold, foothold, foretold, household, millionfold, outsold, paroled, remould(s)/remold(s) (U.S.), retold, scaffold, stronghold, tenfold, threshold, toehold, twofold, threefold, unfold, uphold, unsold, untold, withhold.
Aglow, airflow, bellow, below, billow, bolo, cashflow, cello, deathblow, fellow, follow, furlough, Jell-O, go-slow, halo, hello, hollow, kilo, mallow, mellow, moonglow, pillow, polo, shallow, solo, swallow, wallow, willow, yellow.
Alcove, behove/behoove (U.S.), interwove, mangrove.
Assault, deadbolt, default, exalt, revolt, somersault, unbolt.
Chat show, echo, gaucho, gung-ho, heave-ho, honcho, macho, no-show, peepshow, poncho, psycho, roadshow, sideshow, tallyho.
Also, bozo, dipso, mezzo, muso, say-so, schizo, so-so, torso.
[3] **Centrefold/centerfold** (U.S.), manifold, marigold, oversold, pigeonholed, self-controlled, stranglehold, uncontrolled, undersold.
Afterglow, bordello, buffalo, bungalow, cigarillo, counterblow, gigolo, marshmallow, overflow, piccolo, tremolo.
Calypso, espresso, mafioso, paparazzo, proviso, so-and-so.

4.1.37 "--old" (as in "told")
[1] bold, bowled, cold, doled, fold, gold, hold, holed, mould/mold (U.S.), old, poled, polled, rolled, scold, soled, sold, told, tolled.
[2] behold, billfold, blindfold, cajoled, controlled, cuckold, enfold, enrolled, foothold, foretold, fourfold, freehold, gatefold, handhold, household, leasehold, millionfold, outsold, paroled, remould/remold (U.S.), remoulds/remolds (U.S.), retold, scaffold, stronghold, tenfold, threshold, toehold, twofold, threefold, unfold, uphold, unsold, untold, withhold.
[3] centrefold/centerfold (U.S.), manifold, marigold, oversold, pigeonholed, self-controlled, stranglehold, uncontrolled, undersold.

SURPRISING RHYMING:
[1] **Bowl**, coal, dole, droll, foal, goal, hole, knoll, mole, pole, poll, role, roll, scroll, shoal, sole, soul, stole, stroll, toll, troll, vole, whole.
Bode, code, crowed, flowed, goad, load, lode, mode, mowed, node, ode, owed, road, rode, rowed, sewed, showed, slowed, sowed, stowed, strode, toad, toed, towed.
Closed, dozed, hosed, nosed, posed.
Beau, blow, bow, bro, crow, doe, doh, dough, flow, foe, glow, go, grow, hoe, know, low, mo., mow, no, oh, owe, pro, row, sew, show, slow, snow, so, stow, though, throw, toe, tow, woe, yo.
Brogue, rogue, vogue.
Boat, coat, dote, float, gloat, goat, moat, note, oat, quote, throat, tote, vote, wrote.
Blows, bows, chose, close, clothes, crows, doze, flows, foes, froze, glows, goes, grows, hose, knows, lows, mows, nose, owes, pose, pros, prose, rose, rows, sews, shows, slows, snows, sows, stows, those, throes, throws, toes, tows, woes.
[2] **Atoll**, bankroll, bargepole, beanpole, bolthole, cajole, console, control, Creole, dustbowl, enrol/enroll (U.S.), fishbowl, flagpole, hellhole, keyhole, loophole, manhole, maypole, payroll, parole, patrol, peephole, pinhole, plughole, pothole, punchbowl.
Abode, barcode, bestowed, corrode, decode, download, elbowed, encode, episode, erode, explode, forebode, freeload, hallowed, highroad, implode, inroad, offload, overflowed, overload, postcode, railroad, reload, unload, upload, workload, zip code.
Bulldozed, composed, deposed, disclosed, disposed, enclosed, exposed, imposed, opposed, proposed, supposed, transposed.
Afloat, banknote, cutthroat, demote, denote, devote, dreamboat, emote, houseboat, keynote, lifeboat, misquote, promote, raincoat, remote, rowboat, sailboat, scapegoat, showboat, speedboat, steamboat, tugboat, turncoat, waistcoat.

Bordeaux, condo, credo, dodo, judo, kendo, lido, Ludo, meadow, pseudo, rondeau, rondo, shadow, speedo, widow, weirdo, window.
Ago, bingo, bongo, cargo, dingo, ego, forgo, go, go-go, gringo, jingo, largo, lingo, logo, mango, no-go, outgo, pogo, pongo, tango.
Beano, chino, dunno, mono, rhino, techno, vino, winnow, wino.
Aggro, arrow, barrow, biro, bistro, borrow, bureau, burrow, escrow, euro, furrow, hedgerow, hero, intro, macro, maestro, metro, micro, narrow, outgrow, repro, retro, scarecrow, sorrow, tarot, Velcro, zero.
Arose, bulldoze, compose, depose, disclose, dispose, enclose, expose, forgoes, gallows, impose, oppose, outgrows, pillows, plainclothes, primrose, propose, rainbows, repose, suppose, tiptoes, transpose, undergoes, wild rose.
[3] **Buttonhole**, casserole, cubbyhole, hidey-hole, pigeonhole, rigmarole, rock and roll, self-control, waterhole.
Bravado, commando, crescendo, eyeshadow, libido, tornado, torpedo, tuxedo.
Anecdote, antidote, ferryboat, motorboat, mountain goat, overcoat, petticoat, powerboat, riverboat, sugarcoat, table d'hôte, undercoat.
Alter ego, amigo, embargo, fandango, flamingo, indigo, long ago, touch and go, undergo, vertigo.
Bambino, casino, domino, inferno, kimono, Latino, piano, soprano, tornado, volcano.
Bolero, electro, overthrow, pharaoh.
Cellulose, diagnose, dominoes, indispose, juxtapose, overdose, overexpose, predispose, presuppose, recompose, superimpose.
[4] **Aficionado**, desperado, Eldorado, incommunicado, overshadow.

4.1.38 "--olded" (as in "folded")

[2] folded, moulded/molded (U.S.), scolded.
[3] blindfolded, cuckolded, remoulded/remolded (U.S.), unfolded.

SURPRISING RHYMING:
[2] **Folding**, holding, moulding/molding (U.S.), scolding.
Boded, coded, goaded, loaded.
Boated, coated, doted, floated, gloated, noted, quoted, voted.
Bolted, halted, jolted, moulted/molted (U.S.), salted, vaulted.
Boasted, ghosted, hosted, posted, roasted, signposted, toasted.
Beholden, bolden, embolden, golden, olden.
[3] **Beholding**, enfolding, remoulding/remolding (U.S.), shareholding, stockholding, unfolding, withholding.
Corroded, decoded, encoded, eroded, exploded, imploded, overloaded, outmoded, railroaded, reloaded, unloaded.
Demoted, denoted, devoted, misquoted, promoted.
Assaulted, defaulted, exalted, revolted, somersaulted, unbolted.

4.1.39 "--olden" (as in "golden")

beholden, bolden, embolden, golden, olden.

SURPRISING RHYMING:
[2] **Bolder**, boulder, colder, folder, holder, moulder/molder (U.S.), older, scolder, shoulder, smoulder/smolder (U.S.), solder, told her.
Broken, oaken, open, slogan, spoken, stolen, token, woken, woven.
Chosen, frozen, lederhosen, molten, unfrozen.
Omen, Roman, showman, snowman, snowmen, yeoman.
Cloning, groaning, honing, loaning, moaning, owning, phoning, stoning, toning, zoning.
Lotion, motion, notion, ocean, potion.
Folding, holding, moulding/molding (U.S.), scolding.
Bowling, polling, rolling, scrolling, strolling, tolling, trolling.
[3] **Beholder**, cardholder, cold shoulder, freeholder, householder, keyholder, leaseholder, shareholder, stakeholder, stockholder.
Awoken, heartbroken, outspoken, plain-spoken, re-open, soft-spoken, unbroken, unspoken, well-spoken.
Corrosion, erosion, explosion, implosion.

Commotion, devotion, emotion, locomotion, promotion, slow-motion.
Consoling, controlling, patrolling, shareholding, stockholding, unfolding, withholding.
Blindfolded, cuckolded, remoulded/remolded (U.S.), unfolded.
Atonement, component, exponent, opponent, postponement.

4.1.40 "--older" (as in "colder")
[2] bolder, boulder, colder, folder, holder, hold her, moulder/molder (U.S.), older, scolder, shoulder, smoulder/smolder (U.S.), solder.
[3] beholder, cardholder, cold shoulder, freeholder, householder, keyholder, leaseholder, shareholder, smallholder, stakeholder, stockholder.

SURPRISING RHYMING:
[2] **Bowler**, cola, molar, polar, roller, solar, stroller.
Coder, goader, loader, odour/odor (U.S.).
Donor, groaner, loaner, loner, moaner, owner, toner.
Coma, comber, homer, roamer.
Blower, boa, glower, goer, grower, knower, lower, mower, rower, sewer, shower, slower, sower, thrower, tower.
Broker, choker, coca, evoker, joker, ochre, poker, soaker, smoker.
Chauffeur, clover, drover, nova, over, rover.
Boaster, coaster, poacher, poster, toaster.
Coper, doper, eloper, groper, hoper, moper, no-hoper, ogre, sober.
[3] **Bipolar**, cajoler, Coca-Cola, consoler, controller, Moviola, patroller, payola, rock 'n' roller, steamroller, tombola, viola.
Decoder, encoder, exploder, freeloader, railroader, unloader.
Atoner, condoner, homeowner, landowner, persona.
Borrower, churchgoer, concertgoer, follower, foregoer, lawnmower, racegoer, theatregoer/theatergoer (U.S.), widower, winegrower.
Bulldozer, closer, composer, dozer, exposer, imposer, opposer, poser, proposer.
Composure, closure, disclosure, enclosure, exposure, foreclosure.
All over, blow over, bowl over, changeover, chew over, crossover, fall over, fly-over, get over, handover, hangover, leftover, makeover, moreover, once-over, pullover, pushover, sleepover, slipover, stopover, takeover, turnover, walkover, watch over.
[4] **Bossa nova**, Casanova, supernova, up-and-over.

4.1.41 "--oldest" (as in "boldest")
[2] boldest, coldest, oldest.

SURPRISING RHYMING:
[2] **Closest**, hostess, locust, lowest, moment, poets, slowest.
Bogus, bonus, focus(ed), notice(d), onus, opus, wholeness.
Boneless, homeless, phoneless, throneless, toneless, zoneless.
Hopeless, ropeless, soapless, soulless.
Folded, moulded/molded (U.S.), scolded.
[3] **Hypnosis**, neurosis, osmosis, prognosis, psychosis, unnoticed.
Blindfolded, cuckolded, remoulded/remolded (U.S.), unfolded.
[4] **Diagnosis**, halitosis, metamorphosis, symbiosis.

4.1.42 "--olding" (as in "holding")
[2] folding, holding, moulding/molding (U.S.), scolding.
[3] beholding, enfolding, remoulding/remolding (U.S.), shareholding, stockholding, unfolding, withholding.

SURPRISING RHYMING:
[2] **Boding**, coding, goading, loading.
Beholden, bolden, embolden, golden, olden.
Combing, foaming, gloaming, homing, roaming.
Blowing, bowing, clothing, crowing, flowing, glowing, going, growing, knowing, mowing, owing, rowing, sewing, showing, slowing, snowing, sowing, throwing, toeing, towing.

Cloning, groaning, honing, loaning, moaning, owning, phoning, stoning, toning, zoning.
Choking, cloaking, croaking, evoking, joking, poking, smoking, soaking, stroking.
Bowling, holing, polling, rolling, scrolling, strolling, tolling, trolling.
Boasting, coasting, hosting, posting, roasting, toasting.
Boating, coating, doting, floating, gloating, noting, quoting, voting.
Bolting, halting, jolting, moulting/molting (U.S.), salting.
Coping, eloping, groping, hoping, moping, roping, sloping, soaping.
Closing, dozing, hosing, nosing, posing.
[3] **Corroding**, decoding, encoding, eroding, exploding, foreboding, freeloading, imploding, overloading, railroading, reloading, unloading.
Atoning, condoning, disowning, postponing.
Churchgoing, easy-going, following, foregoing, harrowing, ongoing, outgoing, overflowing, seagoing, stowing, tiptoeing, unknowing.
Evoking, invoking, provoking, revoking, stockbroking.
Consoling, controlling, extolling, paroling, patrolling.
Demoting, denoting, devoting, emoting, misquoting, promoting.
Assaulting, defaulting, exalting, revolting, somersaulting, unbolting.
Bulldozing, composing, deposing, disclosing, disposing, enclosing, exposing, imposing, opposing, proposing, supposing, transposing.

4.1.43 "--olar" (as in "polar")

[2] bowler, cola, molar, polar, roller, solar, stroller.
[3] bipolar, cajoler, Coca-Cola, comptroller, consoler, controller, extoller, granola, Moviola, patroller, payola, pianola, potholer, rock 'n' roller, steamroller, tombola, viola.

SURPRISING RHYMING:
[2] **Donor**, groaner, loaner, loner, moaner, owner, toner.
Chauffeur, clover, drover, nova, over, rover.
Coder, goader, loader, odour/odor (U.S.).
Blower, boa, glower, goer, grower, knower, lower, mower, rower, sewer, shower, slower, sower, thrower, tower.
Bolder, boulder, colder, folder, holder, moulder/molder (U.S.), older, scolder, shoulder, smoulder/smolder (U.S.), solder, told her.
Broker, choker, coca, evoker, joker, ochre, poker, soaker, smoker.
Boater, doter, floater, gloater, motor, quota, rota, rotor, voter.
Coper, doper, eloper, groper, hoper, moper, no-hoper, ogre, sober.
[3] **Atoner**, condoner, homeowner, landowner, persona.
All over, blow over, bowl over, changeover, chew over, crossover, fall over, fly-over, get over, handover, hangover, leftover, makeover, moreover, once-over, pullover, pushover, sleepover, slipover, stopover, takeover, turnover, walkover, watch over.
Bulldozer, closer, composer, dozer, exposer, imposer, opposer, poser, proposer.
Decoder, encoder, exploder, freeloader, October, railroader.
Borrower, churchgoer, concertgoer, follower, lawnmower, racegoer, swallower, theatregoer/theatergoer (U.S.), widower, winegrower.
Beholder, cardholder, cold shoulder, freeholder, householder, leaseholder, shareholder, smallholder, stakeholder, stockholder.
Carioca, mediocre, nonsmoker, pawnbroker, provoker, stockbroker.
Anorexia nervosa, closer, greengrocer, grocer, mimosa.
[4] **Bossa nova**, Casanova, supernova, up-and-over.

4.1.44 "--oly" (as in "holy")

[2] goalie, holy, lowly, ravioli, roly-poly, slowly, solely, wholly.

SURPRISING RHYMING:
[2] **Bony**, lonely, moany, only, phoney/phony (U.S.), pony, stony.
Cosy/cozy (U.S.), dozy, mosey, nosy, posy, rosy.
Bogey, boldly, closely, coyote, dopey, homely, homie, low-key, mouldy/moldy (U.S.), oldie, roadie, smoky, snowy, soapy, trophy.
[3] **Agony**, balcony, baloney, barony, colony, cottony, cushiony, ebony, felony, gluttony, harmony, irony, lemony, symphony.

[4] **Acrimony**, alimony, cacophony, cannelloni, ceremony, macaroni, matrimony, minestrone, monotony, pepperoni, rigatoni, testimony.

4.1.45 "--olling" (as in "rolling")
[2] bowling, polling, rolling, scrolling, strolling, tolling, trolling.
[3] consoling, controlling, extolling, paroling, patrolling, potholing.

SURPRISING RHYMING:
[2] **Blowing**, bowing, crowing, flowing, glowing, going, growing, knowing, mowing, owing, roving, rowing, sewing, showing, slowing, snowing, sowing, throwing, towing.
Combing, foaming, gloaming, homing, roaming.
Folding, holding, moulding/molding (U.S.), scolding.
Cloning, groaning, honing, loaning, moaning, owning, phoning, stoning, toning, zoning.
Coding, goading, loading, loafing.
Chosen, closing, dozing, frozen, nosing, omen, posing, snowman, stolen, woven.
Coping, doping, eloping, groping, hoping, moping, roping, sloping.
Boating, coating, doting, floating, gloating, noting, quoting, voting.
Broken, oaken, open, slogan, spoken, stolen, token, woken, woven.
[3] **Churchgoing**, easy-going, following, harrowing, ongoing, outgoing, overflowing, seagoing, stowing, tiptoeing, unknowing.
Atoning, condoning, disowning, postponing.
Beholding, enfolding, shareholding, stockholding, unfolding, withholding.
Corroding, decoding, encoding, eroding, exploding, foreboding, freeloading, imploding, overloading, railroading, reloading, unloading.
Bulldozing, composing, deposing, disclosing, disposing, enclosing, exposing, imposing, opposing, proposing, supposing, transposing.
Demoting, denoting, devoting, emoting, misquoting, promoting.
Awoken, heartbroken, outspoken, plain-spoken, re-open, soft-spoken, unbroken, unspoken, well-spoken.
[4] **Diagnosing**, overdosing, presupposing, superimposing.

4.1.46 "--olo" (as in "solo")
bolo, follow, gigolo, hollow, piccolo, polo, solo, swallow, tremolo, wallow.

SURPRISING RHYMING:
[2] **Aglow**, ago, aggro, also, alto, although, ammo, arrow, auto,
banjo, barrow, below, bestow, billow, bingo, biro, bistro, blotto, bolo, bongo, borrow, bozo, bravo, bronco, bureau, burrow, cargo, cello, chateau, cheapo, chino, coco, cocoa, condo, credo, Day-Glo, deathblow, demo, depot, dingo, disco, ditto, dodo, dunno, duo, echo, ego, euro, fellow, follow, forgo, furlough, furrow, gaucho, gelato, ghetto, giro/gyro, gizmo, go-go, go-slow, gringo, grotto, gung-ho, gusto, halo, heave-ho, hedgerow, heigh-ho, hello, hero, hippo, hollow, honcho, info, intro, jello, jingo, judo, kilo, K.O., lido, limo, lingo, loco, logo, lotto, macho, maestro, mango, meadow, mellow, memo, metro, mezzo, micro, mojo, mono, motto, muso, nacho, narrow, no-show, outgo, outgrow, panto, peepshow, photo, pillow, plateau, poco, polo, poncho, pongo, presto, promo, pronto, pseudo, psycho, repo, repro, retro, rhino, Rio, roadshow, salvo, say-so, scarecrow, schizo, shadow, shallow, sideshow, slow-mo, solo, so-so, sorrow, speedo, stiletto, sumo, swallow, tango, tarot, techno, tempo, tiptoe, torso, trio, typo, Velcro, veto, vino, wallow, widow, willow, window, wino, yellow, yo-yo, zero.
[3] **Afterglow**, a-gogo, akimbo, alfresco, amigo, art deco, art nouveau, audio, bambino, billy-o, bolero, bordello, bravado, buffalo, bungalow, calypso, cameo, casino, cheerio, commando, concerto, cornetto, crescendo, curio, de facto, domino, dynamo, electro, espresso, eyeshadow, falsetto, fandango, fiasco, flamenco, flamingo, foreshadow, gigolo, indigo, inferno, kimono, Latino, libido, machismo, marshmallow, memento, mistletoe, overflow, overthrow, patio, physio, piano, piccolo, Pierrot, potato, proviso, quid pro quo, radio, ratio, rodeo, Romeo, sombrero, so-and-so, soprano, staccato, status quo, stereo, studio, subzero, supremo, tally-ho, tic-tac-toe, to and fro, tobacco, tomato, tomorrow, tornado, torpedo, tuxedo, UFO, undergo, undertow, up-tempo, vertigo, vibrato, video, volcano, wheelbarrow.

4.1.47 "--olt" (as in "bolt")
[1] bolt, colt, halt, jolt, moult/molt (U.S.), salt, vault, volt.
[2] assault, default, exalt, pole-vault, revolt, somersault, unbolt.

SURPRISING RHYMING:
[1] **Bloat**, boat, coat, don't, dote, float, gloat, goat, moat, mote, note, oat, quote, rote, throat, tote, vote, won't, wrote.
Boast, coast, ghost, grossed, host, most, post, roast, toast.
Choked, cloaked, croaked, joked, poked, smoked, soaked, stoked, stroked.
Coped, doped, groped, eloped, hoped, moped, roped, sloped.
Broached, coached, poached.
[2] **Afloat**, banknote, cutthroat, demote, denote, devote, dreamboat, emote, houseboat, keynote, lifeboat, misquote, promote, raincoat, remote, rowboat, sailboat, scapegoat, showboat, speedboat, steamboat, tugboat, turncoat, waistcoat.
Evoked, invoked, provoked, revoked, uncloaked.
Almost, bedpost, endmost, engrossed, foremost, gatepost, goalpost, lamppost, outpost, seacoast, signpost, topmost, utmost.
Approached, encroached, reproached.
[3] **Anecdote**, antidote, ferryboat, motorboat, overcoat, petticoat, powerboat, riverboat, sugarcoat, table d'hôte, undercoat.

4.1.48 "--olted" (as in "bolted")
[2] bolted, halted, jolted, moulted/molted (U.S.), salted, vaulted.
[3] assaulted, defaulted, exalted, pole-vaulted, revolted, somersaulted, unbolted.

SURPRISING RHYMING:
[2] **Boated**, coated, doted, floated, gloated, noted, quoted, voted.
Boasted, coasted, ghosted, hosted, posted, roasted, toasted.
Folded, moulded/molded (U.S.), scolded.
Boded, coded, goaded, loaded.
Boasted, coasted, ghosted, hosted, posted, roasted, toasted.
Bolden, embolden, golden, olden.
[3] **Demoted**, denoted, devoted, emoted, misquoted, promoted.
Blindfolded, cuckolded, remoulded/remolded (U.S.), unfolded.
Corroded, decoded, encoded, eroded, exploded, overloaded, outmoded, railroaded, reloaded, unloaded.

4.1.49 "--olting" (as in "revolting")
[2] bolting, halting, jolting, moulting/molting (U.S.), salting.
[3] assaulting, defaulting, exalting, pole-vaulting, revolting, somersaulting, unbolting.

SURPRISING RHYMING:
[2] **Bolted**, halted, jolted, moulted/molted (U.S.), salted, vaulted.
Boating, coating, doting, floating, gloating, noting, quoting, voting.
Choking, cloaking, croaking, evoking, joking, poking, smoking, soaking, stroking.
Boasting, coasting, hosting, posting, roasting, toasting.
Coping, eloping, groping, hoping, moping, roping, sloping, soaping.
Broaching, coaching, poaching.
Coding, folding, goading, going, holding, loading, scolding.
Closing, dozing, hosing, nosing, posing.
[3] **Assaulted**, defaulted, exalted, revolted, somersaulted, unbolted.
Evoking, invoking, provoking, revoking, stockbroking.
Demoting, denoting, devoting, emoting, misquoting, promoting.
Approaching, encroaching, reproaching.
Corroding, decoding, encoding, eroding, exploding, foreboding, freeloading, imploding, overloading, railroading, reloading, unloading.
Beholding, enfolding, shareholding, stockholding, unfolding, withholding.
Bulldozing, composing, deposing, disclosing, disposing, enclosing, exposing, imposing, opposing, proposing, supposing, transposing.

4.1.50 "--oma" (as in "aroma")
[2] coma, comber, homer, roamer.
[3] aroma, beachcomber, diploma, glaucoma, misnomer.

SURPRISING RHYMING:
[2] **Donor**, groaner, loaner, loner, moaner, owner, toner.
Bolder, boulder, colder, folder, holder, moulder/molder (U.S.), older, scolder, shoulder, smoulder/smolder (U.S.), solder, told her.
Chauffeur, clover, drover, nova, over, rover.
Coda, coder, decoder, encoder, exploder, freeloader, goader, loader, loafer, odour/odor (U.S.), pagoda, soda, sofa, toga.
Coper, doper, eloper, groper, hoper, moper, no-hoper, ogre, sober.
Bowler, cola, molar, polar, roller, solar, stroller.
Boater, doter, floater, gloater, motor, quota, rota, rotor, voter.
Broker, choker, coca, joker, ochre, poker, soaker, smoker, stroker.
Blower, boa, glower, goer, grower, knower, lower, mower, rower, sewer, shower, slower, sower, thrower, tower.
[3] **Atoner**, condoner, homeowner, landowner, persona.
Beholder, cardholder, cold shoulder, freeholder, householder, leaseholder, shareholder, smallholder, stakeholder, stockholder.
Carioca, mediocre, nonsmoker, pawnbroker, provoker, stockbroker.
All over, blow over, bowl over, changeover, chew over, crossover, fall over, fly-over, get over, handover, hangover, leftover, makeover, moreover, once-over, pullover, pushover, sleepover, slipover, stopover, takeover, turnover, walkover, watch over.
Bipolar, cajoler, Coca-Cola, consoler, controller, Moviola, patroller, payola, pianola, potholer, rock 'n' roller, steamroller, tombola, viola.
[4] **Bossa nova**, Casanova, supernova, up-and-over.

4.1.51 "--oming" (as in "roaming")
[2] backcombing, combing, foaming, gloaming, homing, roaming.

SURPRISING RHYMING:
[2] **Cloning**, groaning, honing, loaning, moaning, owning, phoning, toning, zoning.
Omen, Roman, showman, snowman, yeoman.
Folding, holding, moulding/molding (U.S.), scolding.
Bowling, polling, rolling, scrolling, strolling, tolling, trolling.
Coding, goading, loading.
Coping, doping, eloping, groping, hoping, moping, roping, sloping.
Closing, dozing, hosing, nosing, posing.
Blowing, bowing, crowing, flowing, glowing, going, growing, knowing, mowing, owing, rowing, sewing, showing, slowing, snowing, sowing, throwing, toeing, towing.
Choking, cloaking, croaking, evoking, joking, poking, smoking, soaking, stroking.
Boating, coating, doting, floating, gloating, noting, quoting, voting.
Beholden, bolden, embolden, golden, olden.
[3] **Atoning**, condoning, disowning, postponing.
Enfolding, remoulding/remolding (U.S.), unfolding, withholding.
Consoling, controlling, extolling, paroling, patrolling.
Corroding, decoding, encoding, eroding, exploding, foreboding, freeloading, imploding, overloading, railroading, reloading, unloading.
Bulldozing, composing, deposing, disclosing, disposing, enclosing, exposing, imposing, opposing, proposing, supposing, transposing.
Churchgoing, easy-going, following, foregoing, harrowing, ongoing, outgoing, overflowing, seagoing, stowing, tiptoeing, unknowing.
Evoking, invoking, provoking, revoking, stockbroking.
Demoting, denoting, devoting, emoting, misquoting, promoting.

4.1.52 "--ome" (as in "home")
[1] chrome, comb, dome, foam, gnome, home, roam, Rome, tome.
[2] genome, in-home, re-home, syndrome, toothcomb.

[3] aerodrome, backcomb, catacomb, chromosome, honeycomb, monochrome, motorhome, pressure dome, Styrofoam, velodrome.

SURPRISING RHYMING:
[1] **Blown**, bone, clone, cone, drone, flown, groan, grown, hone, known, loan, lone, moan, mown, own, phone, prone, scone, sewn, shone, shown, sown, stone, throne, thrown, tone, zone.
Combed, domed, foamed, homed, re-homed, roamed.
Cloned, coned, droned, groaned, honed, loaned, loaned, moaned, owned, phoned, stoned, toned, zoned.
Beau, blow, bow, bro, crow, doe, doh, dough, flow, foe, glow, go, grow, hoe, know, low, mo., mow, no, oh, owe, pro, row, sew, show, slow, snow, so, stow, though, throw, toe, tow, woe, yo.
Both, growth, loath, oath, sloth.
Bold, bowled, cold, doled, fold, gold, hold, holed, mould/mold (U.S.), old, poled, polled, rolled, scold, soled, sold, told, tolled.
[2] **Alone**, atone, backbone, bemoan, birthstone, bloodstone, brownstone, cellphone, cheekbone, cologne, condone, cyclone, disown, earphone, end zone, full-blown, full-grown, gemstone, gravestone, half-grown, headphone, headstone, high-flown, home-grown, hormone, jawbone, kerbstone/curbstone (U.S.), keystone, lodestone, milestone, millstone, moonstone, outgrown, ozone, payphone, postpone, rhinestone, ringtone, sandstone, tombstone, touchstone, trombone, unknown, windblown, wishbone.
Atoned, bemoaned, condoned, disowned, enthroned, postponed.
Beano, chino, dunno, mono, rhino, techno, vino, winnow, wino.
Behold, blindfold, cajoled, controlled, cuckold, foothold, foretold, household, millionfold, outsold, paroled, remould(s)/remold(s) (U.S.), re-sold, retold, scaffold, stronghold, tenfold, threshold, toehold, twofold, threefold, unfold, uphold, unsold, untold, withhold.
[3] **Anklebone**, answerphone, baritone, chaperone, cobblestone, cornerstone, fully-grown, gramophone, herringbone, megaphone, methadone, microphone, monotone, overblown, overgrown, overthrown, overtone, pheromone, saxophone, semitone, silicone, stepping stone, telephone, undertone, xylophone.
Chaperoned, cobblestoned, telephoned.
Dynamo, Eskimo, machismo, supremo.
Bambino, casino, domino, inferno, kimono, piano, soprano, volcano.
Centrefold/centerfold (U.S.), manifold, marigold, oversold, pigeonholed, self-controlled, stranglehold, uncontrolled, undersold.

4.1.53 "--omeless" (as in "homeless")
[2] combless, foamless, homeless.

SURPRISING RHYMING:
[2] **Boneless**, phoneless, stoneless, throneless, toneless, zoneless.
Hopeless, ropeless, soapless, soulless.
Bogus, bonus, focus(ed), notice(d), onus, opus, wholeness.
Boldest, closest, coldest, oldest, omelets, poets.
Boldness, hostess, locust, lowest, poets, slowest, smokeless.
[3] **Hypnosis**, neurosis, osmosis, prognosis, psychosis, unnoticed.
Atrocious, ferocious, precocious.
Aromas, beachcombers, diplomas.
[4] **Diagnosis**, halitosis, metamorphosis, symbiosis.

4.1.54 "--omen" (as in "omen")
[2] omen, Roman, showman, showmen, snowman, snowmen, yeoman, yeomen.

SURPRISING RHYMING:
[2] **Broken**, open, poem, slogan, spoken, stolen, token, woken.
Beholden, bolden, embolden, golden, olden, swollen.
Combing, foaming, gloaming, homing, roaming.
Chosen, frozen, lederhosen, unfrozen, woven.
Lotion, motion, notion, ocean, potion.

[3] **Awoken**, heartbroken, outspoken, plain-spoken, re-open, soft-spoken, unbroken, unspoken, well-spoken.
Component, exponent, moment, opponent, proponent.
Commotion, devotion, emotion, locomotion, promotion, slow-motion.

4.1.55 "--oned" (as in "phoned")
[1] cloned, coned, droned, groaned, honed, loaned, loaned, moaned, owned, phoned, stoned, toned, zoned.
[2] atoned, bemoaned, condoned, dethroned, disowned, enthroned, intoned, postponed.
[3] chaperoned, cobblestoned, telephoned.

SURPRISING RHYMING:
[1] **Blown**, bone, clone, cone, drone, flown, groan, grown, hone, known, loan, lone, moan, mown, own, phone, prone, scone, sewn, shone, shown, sown, stone, throne, thrown, tone, zone.
Combed, domed, foamed, homed, roamed.
Beau, blow, bow, bro, crow, doe, dough, floe, flow, foe, glow, go, grow, hoe, know, low, mo., mow, no, oh, owe, pro, row, sew, show, slow, snow, so, stow, though, throw, toe, tow, whoa, woe.
[2] **Alone**, atone, backbone, bemoan, birthstone, bloodstone, brownstone, cellphone, cheekbone, cologne, condone, cyclone, disown, earphone, end zone, full-blown, full-grown, gemstone, gravestone, half-grown, headphone, headstone, high-flown, home-grown, hormone, jawbone, kerbstone/curbstone (U.S.), keystone, lodestone, milestone, millstone, moonstone, outgrown, ozone, payphone, postpone, rhinestone, ringtone, sandstone, tombstone, touchstone, trombone, unknown, windblown, wishbone.
Beano, chino, dunno, mono, rhino, techno, vino, wino.
Bordeaux, condo, credo, dodo, judo, kendo, lido, Ludo, meadow, pseudo, rondeau, rondo, shadow, speedo, widow, weirdo, window.
Ago, bingo, bongo, cargo, dingo, ego, forgo, go, go-go, gringo, jingo, largo, lingo, logo, mango, no-go, outgo, pogo, pongo, tango.
Chat show, echo, gung-ho, heave-ho, heigh-ho, honcho, macho, no-show, peepshow, poncho, psycho, roadshow, sideshow, tallyho.
Aglow, below, cashflow, cello, Day-Glo, deathblow, fellow, follow, furlough, Jell-O, go-slow, halo, hello, hollow, kilo, mellow, moonglow, pillow, polo, shallow, solo, swallow, wallow, willow, yellow.
[3] **Anklebone**, answerphone, baritone, chaperone, cobblestone, cornerstone, fully-grown, gramophone, herringbone, megaphone, methadone, microphone, monotone, overblown, overgrown, overthrown, overtone, pheromone, saxophone, semitone, silicone, stepping stone, telephone, undertone, xylophone.
Casino, domino, inferno, kimono, piano, soprano, tornado, volcano.
Amigo, embargo, fandango, flamingo, indigo, long ago, touch and go, undergo, vertigo.
Afterglow, bordello, buffalo, bungalow, cigarillo, counterblow, gigolo, marshmallow, overflow, piccolo, tremolo.

4.1.56 "--onent" (as in "opponent")
[3] component, exponent, opponent, proponent.

SURPRISING RHYMING:
[1] **Bent**, cent, dent, gent, leant, lent, meant, rent, scent, sent, spent, tent, vent, went.
[2] **Omen**, Roman, showman, snowman, yeoman.
Attempt, contempt, exempt, moment, potent, pre-empt, unkempt.
Cloning, groaning, honing, loaning, moaning, owning, phoning, stoning, toning, zoning.
Broken, open, poem, slogan, spoken, stolen, token, woken, woven.
Beholden, bolden, embolden, golden, olden, swollen.
Combing, foaming, gloaming, homing, roaming.
Chosen, frozen, lederhosen, unfrozen.
Lotion, motion, notion, ocean, potion.
Boldest, closest, coldest, oldest, poet.
[3] **Atonement**, enrollment, enthronement, postponement.
Atoning, condoning, disowning, postponing.

469

Awoken, heartbroken, outspoken, plain-spoken, re-open, soft-spoken, unbroken, unspoken, well-spoken.

4.1.57 "--oner" (as in "loner")

[2] donor, groaner, loaner, loner, moaner, owner, toner.
[3] atoner, condoner, homeowner, landowner, persona, postponer.

SURPRISING RHYMING:
[2] **Coma**, comber, homer, roamer.
Bowler, cola, molar, polar, roller, solar, stroller.
Coda, coder, decoder, encoder, exploder, freeloader, goader, loader, loafer, odour/odor (U.S.), pagoda, soda, sofa, toga.
Blower, boa, glower, goer, grower, knower, lower, mower, rower, sewer, shower, slower, sower, thrower, tower.
Chauffeur, clover, drover, nova, over, rover.
Bolder, boulder, colder, folder, holder, moulder/molder (U.S.), older, scolder, shoulder, smoulder/smolder (U.S.), solder, told her.
Aura, broker, choker, coca, evoker, joker, poker, soaker, smoker.
Coper, doper, eloper, groper, hoper, moper, no-hoper, ogre, sober.
Boater, doter, floater, gloater, motor, quota, rota, rotor, voter.
[3] **Aroma**, beachcomber, diploma, glaucoma, misnomer.
Bipolar, cajoler, Coca-Cola, consoler, controller, Moviola, patroller, payola, pianola, potholer, rock 'n' roller, steamroller, tombola, viola.
Churchgoer, concertgoer, follower, foregoer, lawnmower, racegoer, swallower, theatregoer/theatergoer (U.S.), widower, winegrower.
All over, blow over, bowl over, changeover, chew over, crossover, fall over, fly-over, get over, handover, hangover, leftover, makeover, moreover, once-over, pullover, pushover, sleepover, slipover, stopover, takeover, turnover, walkover, watch over.
Beholder, cardholder, cold shoulder, freeholder, householder, leaseholder, shareholder, smallholder, stakeholder, stockholder.
Carioca, mediocre, nonsmoker, pawnbroker, provoker, stockbroker.
Bulldozer, closer, composer, dozer, exposer, opposer, poser.
[4] **Bossa nova**, Casanova, supernova, up-and-over.

4.1.58 "--ony" (as in "pony")

[2] bony, crony, moany, phoney/phony (U.S.), pony, stony.
[3] agony, balcony, baloney, barony, colony, cottony, cushiony, ebony, felony, gluttony, harmony, irony, lemony, symphony.
[4] acrimony, alimony, cacophony, cannelloni, ceremony, macaroni, matrimony, minestrone, monotony, pepperoni, rigatoni, testimony.

SURPRISING RHYMING:
[2] **Lonely**, lowly, mostly, only.
Bogey, boldly, closely, dopey, homely, homie, jokey, low-key, mouldy/moldy (U.S.), oldie, roadie, smoky, snowy, soapy, trophy.
Cosy/cozy (U.S.), dozy, mosey, nosy, posy, rosy.
Goalie, holy, lowly, ravioli, roly-poly, slowly, solely, wholly.
Blowy, bluey, chewy, dewy, gluey, gooey, hooey, phooey, screwy.
Bonny, brawny, cockney, corny, horny, money, scrawny, thorny.
Brolly, collie, dolly, folly, golly, holly, jolly, lolly, trolley, volley, wally.
Croaky, folkie, folky, hokey, jokey, karaoke, pokey, smoky.
Gaudy, mouldy/moldy (U.S.), oldie, roadie.
Coffee, comfy, toffee, TV, trophy.
Glory, gory, lorry, poultry, scot-free, sorry, storey, story, tawdry.
Body, copy, crawly, foamy, ghostly, glossy, poppy, ropy, stormy.
[3] **Bigotry**, calorie, chicory, chivalry, Christmas tree, cursory, disagree, doddery, enquiry, factory, furore, hickory, history, ivory, jamboree, memory, misery, obligatory, olive tree, poetry, potpourri, referee, savory, sensory, signatory, third degree, victory.
COD, comedy, custody, dogsbody, embody, melody, monarchy, nobody, parody, rhapsody, somebody.

Anatomy, astronomy, blossomy, bonhomie, economy, epitome, nominee, timpani.
Eulogy, ology, prodigy, trilogy.
ABC, absentee, bourgeoisie, bumblebee, Cherokee, devotee, divorcee, escapee, guarantee, Hawaii, honeybee, invitee, licensee, oversee, reality, spelling bee, undersea, VIP, wannabe, water ski.

4.1.59 "--oning" (as in "phoning")
[2] cloning, groaning, honing, loaning, moaning, owning, phoning, toning, zoning.
[3] atoning, condoning, disowning, postponing.

SURPRISING RHYMING:
[2] **Combing**, foaming, gloaming, homing, roaming.
Folding, holding, moulding/molding (U.S.), scolding.
Bowling, polling, rolling, scrolling, strolling, tolling, trolling.
Coping, doping, eloping, groping, hoping, moping, roping, sloping.
Closing, dozing, hosing, nosing, posing.
Blowing, bowing, crowing, flowing, glowing, going, growing, knowing, mowing, owing, rowing, sewing, showing, slowing, snowing, sowing, throwing, toeing, towing.
Choking, cloaking, croaking, evoking, joking, poking, smoking, soaking, stroking.
Boating, coating, doting, floating, gloating, noting, quoting, voting.
[3] **Enfolding**, remoulding/remolding (U.S.), unfolding, withholding.
Consoling, controlling, extolling, paroling, patrolling.
Corroding, decoding, encoding, eroding, exploding, foreboding, freeloading, imploding, overloading, railroading, reloading, unloading.
Bulldozing, composing, deposing, disclosing, disposing, enclosing, exposing, imposing, opposing, proposing, supposing, transposing.
Churchgoing, easy-going, following, foregoing, harrowing, ongoing, outgoing, overflowing, seagoing, stowing, tiptoeing, unknowing.
Evoking, invoking, provoking, revoking, stockbroking.
Demoting, denoting, devoting, emoting, misquoting, promoting.
Component, exponent, moment, opponent, proponent.

4.1.60 "--oneless" (as in "toneless")
[2] boneless, phoneless, stoneless, throneless, toneless, zoneless.

SURPRISING RHYMING:
[2] **Hopeless**, homeless, ropeless, soapless, soulless.
Bogus, bonus, focus(ed), notice(d), onus, opus, wholeness.
Boldest, closest, coldest, oldest, omelets, poets.
Boldness, coldness, hostess, locust, lowest, moment, poets, slowest, smokeless.
[3] **Hypnosis**, neurosis, osmosis, prognosis, psychosis, unnoticed.
Atrocious, ferocious, precocious.
Aromas, beachcombers, diplomas.
[4] **Diagnosis**, halitosis, metamorphosis, symbiosis.

4.1.61 "--only" (as in "lonely")
[2] lonely, only.

SURPRISING RHYMING:
[2] **Bony**, homely, homie, moany, phoney/phony (U.S.), pony, stony.
Bogey, boldly, closely, coldly, coyote, dopey, foamy, jokey, low-key, mouldy/moldy (U.S.), oldie, roadie, smoky, snowy, soapy, trophy.
Cosy/cozy (U.S.), dozy, mosey, nosy, posy, rosy, showy, snowy.
Goalie, holy, lowly, ravioli, roly-poly, slowly, solely, wholly.
Glory, gory, lorry, poultry, scot-free, sorry, storey, story, tawdry.
[3] **Agony**, balcony, colony, cushiony, ebony, felony, harmony, irony, symphony.

4.1.62 "--onement" (as in "atonement")
[3] atonement, enthronement, intonement, postponement.

SURPRISING RHYMING:
[2] **Chosen**, frozen, omen, showman, snowman, stolen, woven.
Beholden, bolden, embolden, golden, olden.
Broken, oaken, spoken, token, woken.
Groaning, honing, loaning, moaning, owning, phoning, rolling, stoning, toning, zoning.
Combing, foaming, gloaming, homing, roaming.
Lotion, motion, notion, ocean, potion.
[3] **Atoning**, condoning, disowning, postponing.
Component, enrollment, exponent, opponent, proponent.
Awoken, heartbroken, outspoken, plain-spoken, re-open, soft-spoken, unbroken, unspoken, well-spoken.
Commotion, devotion, emotion, locomotion, promotion, slow-motion.

4.1.63 "--ope" (as in "hope")
[1] cope, dope, grope, hope, lope, mope, nope, pope, rope, scope, slope, soap.
[2] elope, tightrope, towrope.
[3] antelope, cantaloupe, Cinemascope, envelope, gyroscope, horoscope, interlope, kaleidoscope, microscope, periscope, skipping-rope, stethoscope, telescope.

SURPRISING RHYMING:
[1] **Coped**, groped, eloped, hoped, moped, roped, sloped, soaped.
Boat, coat, dote, float, gloat, goat, note, quote, throat, vote, wrote.
Bloke, broke, choke, cloak, coke, croak, folk, joke, oak, poke, smoke, soak, spoke, stoke, stroke, woke, yolk.
Boast, coast, ghost, grossed, host, most, post, roast, toast.
Beau, blow, bow, bro, crow, doe, doh, dough, flow, foe, glow, go, grow, hoe, know, low, mo., mow, no, oh, owe, pro, row, sew, show, slow, snow, so, stow, though, throw, toe, tow, woe, yo.
Bode, code, crowed, flowed, goad, load, lode, mode, mowed, node, ode, owed, road, rode, rowed, sewed, showed, slowed, sowed, stowed, strode, toad, toed, towed.
Both, growth, loath, oath, sloth.
[2] **Afloat**, banknote, cutthroat, demote, denote, devote, dreamboat, emote, houseboat, keynote, lifeboat, misquote, promote, raincoat, remote, rowboat, sailboat, scapegoat, showboat, speedboat, steamboat, tugboat, turncoat, waistcoat.
Almost, bedpost, endmost, engrossed, foremost, gatepost, goalpost, lamppost, outpost, seacoast, signpost, topmost, utmost.
Abode, barcode, bestowed, corrode, decode, download, elbowed, encode, episode, erode, explode, forebode, freeload, hallowed, highroad, implode, inroad, offload, overflowed, overload, payload, postcode, railroad, reload, unload, upload, workload, zip code.
Awoke, backstroke, baroque, breaststroke, evoke, heatstroke, keystroke, menfolk, provoke, slowpoke, sunstroke, woodsmoke.
[3] **Anecdote**, antidote, ferryboat, motorboat, overcoat, petticoat, powerboat, riverboat, sugarcoat, table d'hôte, undercoat.
Okey-doke, masterstroke, stony-broke/stone-broke (U.S.).

4.1.64 "--oped" (as in "hoped")
coped, doped, groped, eloped, hoped, loped, moped, roped, scoped, sloped, soaped.

SURPRISING RHYMING:
[1] **Cope**, grope, hope, mope, pope, rope, scope, slope, soap.
Boat, coat, dote, float, gloat, goat, note, quote, throat, vote, wrote.
Choked, cloaked, croaked, joked, poked, smoked, soaked, stroked.
Boast, coast, ghost, grossed, host, most, post, roast, toast.
Beau, blow, bow, bro, crow, doe, doh, dough, flow, foe, glow, go, grow, know, low, mow, no, owe, pro, row, sew, show, slow, snow, so, though, throw, toe, tow, woe.
Bode, code, crowed, flowed, goad, load, lode, mode, mowed, node, ode, owed, road, rode, rowed, sewed, showed, slowed, sowed, stowed, strode, toad, toed, towed.
[2] **Elope**, tightrope, towrope.

Afloat, banknote, cutthroat, demote, denote, devote, dreamboat, emote, houseboat, keynote, lifeboat, misquote, promote, raincoat, remote, rowboat, sailboat, scapegoat, showboat, speedboat, steamboat, tugboat, turncoat, waistcoat.
Awoke, evoked, invoked, provoked, revoked, uncloaked.
Almost, bedpost, engrossed, foremost, gatepost, goalpost, lamppost, milepost, outpost, seacoast, signpost, topmost, utmost.
Abode, barcode, bestowed, corrode, decode, download, elbowed, encode, episode, erode, explode, forebode, freeload, hallowed, highroad, implode, inroad, offload, overflowed, overload, postcode, railroad, reload, unload, upload, workload, zip code.
[3] **Envelope**, horoscope, kaleidoscope, microscope, skipping-rope, telescope.
Anecdote, antidote, ferryboat, motorboat, mountain goat, overcoat, petticoat, powerboat, riverboat, sugarcoat, table d'hôte, undercoat.
Okey-doke, masterstroke, stony-broke/stone-broke (U.S.).

4.1.65 "--oping" (as in "hoping")
[2] coping, doping, eloping, groping, hoping, moping, roping, scoping, sloping, soaping.

SURPRISING RHYMING:
[2] **Boating**, doting, floating, gloating, noting, quoting, voting.
Choking, cloaking, croaking, evoking, joking, poking, smoking, soaking, stroking.
Broken, oaken, spoken, token, woken.
Chosen, closing, dozing, frozen, nosing, posing, unfrozen.
Boasting, coasting, hosting, posting, roasting, toasting.
Combing, foaming, gloaming, homing, roaming.
Cloning, groaning, honing, loaning, moaning, owning, phoning, stoning, toning, zoning.
Coding, goading, loading, omen, Roman, showman, snowman, yeoman.
[3] **Demoting**, denoting, devoting, emoting, misquoting, promoting.
Evoking, invoking, provoking, revoking, stockbroking.
Awoken, heartbroken, outspoken, plain-spoken, soft-spoken, unspoken, well-spoken.
Atoning, condoning, disowning, postponing.
Corroding, decoding, encoding, eroding, exploding, foreboding, freeloading, imploding, overloading, railroading, reloading, unloading.
Bulldozing, composing, deposing, disclosing, disposing, enclosing, exposing, imposing, opposing, proposing, supposing, transposing.
Consoling, controlling, extolling, paroling, patrolling, potholing.

4.1.66 "--opeless" (as in "hopeless")
[2] hopeless, ropeless, soapless.

SURPRISING RHYMING:
[2] **Homeless**, phoneless, lowest, slowest, soulless, toneless.
Boldness, coldness, hostess, locust, lowest, moment, poets, slowest, smokeless.
Boldest, closest, coldest, oldest, poets.
Bogus, bonus, focus, focused, notice, noticed, onus, opus, shown us, slowness.
[3] **Hypnosis**, neurosis, osmosis, prognosis, psychosis, unnoticed.
Atrocious, ferocious, precocious.

4.1.67 "--ose" (as in "close")
[1] close, dose, gross.
[2] engross, lactose, morose, verbose, viscose.
[3] adios, bellicose, cellulose, comatose, diagnose, grandiose, overdose, varicose.

SURPRISING RHYMING:
[1] **Boast**, coast, ghost, grossed, host, most, post, roast, toast.
Both, growth, loath, oath, sloth.
Blows, bows, chose, close, clothes, crows, doze, flows, foes, froze, glows, goes, grows, hose, knows, lows, mows, nose, owes, pose, pros, prose, rose, rows, sews, shows, slows, snows, sows, stows, those, throes, throws, toes, tows, woes.
Cloves, coves, droves, groves, loaves, stoves.

473

Blokes, chokes, cloaks, coax, cokes, croaks, folks, hoax, jokes, oaks, pokes, smokes, soaks, stokes, strokes, yolks.
Broach, brooch, coach, loach, poach, roach.
[2] Almost, bedpost, endmost, engrossed, foremost, gatepost, goalpost, lamppost, outpost, seacoast, signpost, topmost, utmost.
Arose, bellows, bulldoze, compose, depose, disclose, dispose, enclose, expose, forgoes, gallows, impose, oppose, outgrows, pillows, plainclothes, primrose, propose, rainbows, repose, suppose, tiptoes, transpose, undergoes, wild rose.
Approach, cockroach, encroach, reproach, slowcoach, stagecoach.
[3] Diagnose(d), dominoes, innermost, outermost, overdose, uppermost, whipping-post..

4.1.68 "--osis" (as in "hypnosis")
[3] hypnosis, neurosis, osmosis, prognosis, psychosis.
[4] diagnosis, halitosis, metamorphosis, symbiosis.

SURPRISING RHYMING:
[2] Coaches, broaches, brooches, poaches, roaches.
Bogus, bonus, focus(ed), notice(d), onus, opus, wholeness.
Boldness, coldness, hostess, locust, poets, smokeless.
Hopeless, ropeless, soapless, soulless.
Closes, dozes, doses, hoses, noses, poses, roses.
Boldest, closest, coldest, lowest, oldest, omelets, poets, slowest.
Boasters, coasters, poachers, poster, toasters.
[3] Atrocious, ferocious, precocious.
Approaches, encroaches, reproaches, slowcoaches, stagecoaches.
Bulldozers, composers, disclosures, exposures, posers, proposers.
Composes, discloses, exposes, imposes, opposes, proposes.
Corrosive, erosive, explosive.

4.1.69 "--osive" (as in "explosive")
[3] corrosive, erosive, explosive.

SURPRISING RHYMING:
[2] Closes, dosage, doses, dozes, hoses, noses, poses, roses.
Notice, noticed, showbiz, unnoticed.
Boasted, ghosted, hosted, posted, roasted, signposted, toasted.
Boded, coded, goaded, loaded.
Folded, moulded/molded (U.S.), scolded.
Boated, doted, floated, gloated, moated, noted, quoted, voted.
Bolted, halted, jolted, moulted/molted (U.S.), salted, vaulted.
[3] Hypnosis, neurosis, osmosis, prognosis, psychosis.
Diagnoses, engrosses, overdoses.
Blindfolded, cuckolded, remoulded/remolded (U.S.), unfolded.
Demoted, denoted, devoted, misquoted, promoted.
Assaulted, defaulted, exalted, revolted, somersaulted, unbolted.
[4] Automotive, emotive, locomotive, motive.

4.1.70 "--ostal" (as in "postal")
[2] coastal, postal.

SURPRISING RHYMING:
[2] Bi-focal, focal, local, vocal, yokel.
Global, hold-all, hopeful, ignoble, know-all, mobile, mogul, noble, ogle, oval, social, total, yodel, zonal.
Boastful, hopeful, soulful, woeful.
[3] Anecdotal, antisocial, disposal, proposal, remorseful, resourceful, sorrowful.

4.1.71 "--ote" (as in "boat")
[1] boat, coat, dote, float, gloat, goat, moat, note, oat, quote, throat, tote, vote, wrote.

[2] afloat, banknote, cutthroat, demote, denote, devote, dovecote, dreamboat, emote, footnote, gunboat, houseboat, keynote, lifeboat, misquote, promote, raincoat, redcoat, remote, re-wrote, rowboat, sailboat, scapegoat, showboat, speedboat, steamboat, tailcoat, topcoat, tugboat, turncoat, waistcoat.
[3] anecdote, antidote, creosote, ferryboat, motorboat, mountain goat, nanny goat, overcoat, petticoat, powerboat, riverboat, sugarcoat, table d'hôte, undercoat.

SURPRISING RHYMING:
[1] Bloke, broke, choke, cloak, coke, croak, folk, joke, oak, poke, smoke, soak, spoke, stoke, stroke, woke, yolk.
Choked, cloaked, croaked, joked, poked, smoked, soaked, stoked, stroked.
Cope, dope, grope, hope, mope, pope, rope, scope, slope, soap.
Coped, groped, eloped, hoped, moped, roped, sloped, soaped.
Boast, coast, ghost, grossed, host, most, post, roast, toast.
Bode, code, crowed, flowed, goad, load, mode, mowed, ode, owed, road, rode, rogue, rowed, sewed, showed, slowed, sowed, stowed, strode, toad, toed, towed, vogue.
Bold, bowled, cold, doled, fold, gold, hold, holed, mould/mold (U.S.), old, poled, polled, rolled, scold, soled, sold, told, tolled.
Beau, blow, bow, bro, crow, doe, doh, dough, flow, foe, glow, go, grow, hoe, know, low, mo., mow, no, oh, owe, pro, row, sew, show, slow, snow, so, stow, though, throw, toe, tow, woe, yo.
[2] Awoke, backstroke, baroque, bespoke, breaststroke, elope, evoke, heatstroke, keystroke, provoke, revoke, sunstroke, tightrope, towrope, woodsmoke.
Almost, bedpost, endmost, engrossed, foremost, gatepost, goalpost, lamppost, outpost, seacoast, signpost, topmost, utmost.
Abode, barcode, bestowed, corrode, decode, download, elbowed, encode, episode, erode, explode, forebode, freeload, hallowed, highroad, implode, inroad, offload, overflowed, overload, postcode, railroad, reload, unload, upload, workload, zip code.
Behold, blindfold, cajoled, controlled, cuckold, foothold, foretold, household, millionfold, outsold, paroled, remould(s)/remold(s) (U.S.), re-sold, retold, scaffold, stronghold, tenfold, threshold, toehold, twofold, threefold, unfold, uphold, unsold, untold, withhold.
[3] Okey-doke, masterstroke, stony-broke/stone-broke.
Envelope, horoscope, kaleidoscope, microscope, periscope, skipping-rope, telescope.
Centrefold/centerfold (U.S.), manifold, marigold, oversold, pigeonholed, self-controlled, stranglehold, uncontrolled, undersold.

4.1.72 "--oth" (as in "both")
[1] both, growth, loath, oath, sloth.

SURPRISING RHYMING:
[1] Close, dose, gross, loaf, oaf, sugarloaf.
Cloves, coves, droves, groves, loaves, stoves.
Bold, bowled, cold, doled, fold, gold, hold, holed, mould/mold (U.S.), old, poled, polled, rolled, scold, soled, sold, told, tolled.
Clove, cove, dove, drove, grove, mauve, stove, strove, trove, wove.
Beau, blow, bow, bro, crow, doe, doh, dough, flow, foe, glow, go, grow, hoe, know, low, mo., mow, no, oh, owe, pro, row, sew, show, slow, snow, so, stow, though, throw, toe, tow, woe, yo.
[2] Behold, blindfold, cajoled, controlled, cuckold, foothold, foretold, household, millionfold, outsold, paroled, remould(s)/remold(s) (U.S.), retold, scaffold, stronghold, tenfold, threshold, toehold, twofold, threefold, unfold, uphold, unsold, untold, withhold.
[3] Adios, bellicose, comatose, diagnose, grandiose, overdose.
Centrefold/centerfold (U.S.), self-controlled, stranglehold, uncontrolled, undersold.

4.1.73 "--otion" (as in "emotion")
[2] lotion, motion, notion, ocean, potion.
[3] commotion, demotion, devotion, emotion, locomotion, promotion, slow-motion.

SURPRISING RHYMING:
[2] Chosen, closing, dozing, frozen, omen, posing, showman, snowman, stolen, woven.

Broaching, coaching, poaching.
Boasting, coasting, hosting, posting, roasting, toasting.
Combing, foaming, gloaming, homing, roaming.
Cloning, groaning, honing, loaning, moaning, owning, phoning, stoning, toning, zoning.
Broken, open, slogan, spoken, stolen, swollen, token, woken.
Choking, croaking, evoking, joking, poking, smoking, stroking.
Coping, eloping, groping, hoping, moping, roping, sloping, soaping.
Boating, coating, doting, floating, gloating, noting, quoting, voting.
Coding, goading, loading.
Folding, holding, moulding/molding (U.S.), scolding.
Bowling, polling, rolling, scrolling, strolling, tolling, trolling.
[3] **Corrosion**, erosion, explosion, implosion.
Approaching, encroaching, reproaching.
Bulldozing, composing, deposing, disclosing, disposing, enclosing, exposing, imposing, opposing, proposing, supposing, transposing.
Atoning, condoning, disowning, postponing.
Demoting, denoting, devoting, emoting, misquoting, promoting.
Evoking, invoking, provoking, revoking, stockbroking.
Corroding, decoding, encoding, eroding, exploding, foreboding, freeloading, imploding, overloading, railroading, reloading, unloading.
Enfolding, remoulding/remolding (U.S.), unfolding, withholding.
Consoling, controlling, extolling, paroling, patrolling, potholing.
[4] **Diagnosing**, overdosing, presupposing, superimposing.

4.1.74 "--oted" (as in "devoted")
[2] bloated, boated, coated, doted, floated, gloated, moated, noted, quoted, voted.
[3] demoted, denoted, devoted, misquoted, promoted.

SURPRISING RHYMING:
[2] **Boded**, coded, folded, goaded, loaded, moulded/molded, scolded.
Bolted, halted, jolted, moulted/molted (U.S.), salted, vaulted.
Boasted, coasted, ghosted, hosted, noticed, posted, roasted, signposted, toasted.
Beholden, bolden, embolden, golden, olden.
Closes, dozes, hoses, noses, poses, roses.
Boatin' [*silent 'g'*], coatin', dotin', floatin', gloatin', notin', quotin', votin'.
[3] **Corroded**, decoded, encoded, eroded, exploded, imploded, overloaded, outmoded, railroaded, reloaded, unloaded.
Blindfolded, cuckolded, remoulded/remolded (U.S.), unfolded.
Assaulted, defaulted, exalted, revolted, somersaulted, unbolted.
[4] **Automotive**, emotive, locomotive, overloaded, unexploded.

4.1.75 "--oting" (as in "floating")
[2] bloating, boating, coating, doting, floating, gloating, noting, quoting, voting.
[3] demoting, denoting, devoting, emoting, misquoting, promoting.

SURPRISING RHYMING:
[2] **Coping**, eloping, groping, hoping, moping, roping, sloping.
Boasting, coasting, hosting, posting, roasting, toasting.
Choking, croaking, evoking, joking, poking, smoking, stroking.
Broken, oaken, spoken, token, woken.
Coding, goading, loading.
Folding, holding, moulding/molding (U.S.), scolding.
Combing, foaming, gloaming, homing, roaming.
Cloning, groaning, honing, loaning, moaning, owning, phoning, stoning, toning, zoning.
Chosen, closing, dozing, frozen, nosing, posing, stolen, woven.
Broaching, coaching, poaching.
Bowling, polling, rolling, scrolling, strolling, tolling, trolling.
Blowing, bowing, crowing, flowing, glowing, going, growing, knowing, mowing, owing, rowing, sewing, showing, slowing, snowing, sowing, throwing, toeing, towing.
[3] **Evoking**, invoking, provoking, revoking, stockbroking.

Awoken, heartbroken, outspoken, soft-spoken, unbroken, unspoken, well-spoken.
Atoning, condoning, disowning, postponing.
Assaulting, defaulting, exalting, revolting, somersaulting, unbolting.
Corroding, decoding, encoding, eroding, exploding, foreboding, freeloading, imploding, overloading, railroading, reloading, unloading.
Bulldozing, composing, deposing, disclosing, disposing, enclosing, exposing, imposing, opposing, proposing, supposing, transposing.
Approaching, encroaching, reproaching.
Consoling, controlling, extolling, paroling, patrolling.
Churchgoing, easy-going, following, foregoing, harrowing, ongoing, outgoing, overflowing, seagoing, stowing, tiptoeing, unknowing.
[4] **Diagnosing**, overdosing, presupposing, superimposing.

4.1.76 "--ove" (as in "drove")
[1] clove, cove, dove, drove, grove, mauve, stove, strove, wove.
[2] alcove, behove/behoove (U.S.), interwove, mangrove.

SURPRISING RHYMING:
[1] **Both**, growth, loaf, oaf, oath, sloth, sugarloaf.
Close, cloves, coves, dose, droves, gross, groves, loaves, stoves.
Brogue, rogue, vogue.
Bowl, coal, dole, droll, foal, goal, hole, knoll, mole, pole, poll, role, roll, scroll, shoal, sole, soul, stole, stroll, toll, troll, vole, whole.
Beau, blow, bow, bro, crow, doe, doh, dough, flow, foe, glow, go, grow, hoe, know, low, mo., mow, no, oh, owe, pro, row, sew, show, slow, snow, so, stow, though, throw, toe, tow, woe, yo.
Blows, bows, chose, close, clothes, crows, doze, flows, foes, froze, glows, goes, grows, hose, knows, lows, mows, nose, owes, pose, pros, prose, rose, rows, sews, shows, slows, snows, sows, stows, those, throes, throws, toes, tows, woes.
[2] **Bankroll**, bargepole, beanpole, cajole, charcoal, console, control, Creole, dustbowl, enrol/enroll (U.S.), fishbowl, flagpole, hellhole, insole, keyhole, loophole, manhole, maypole, payroll, parole, patrol, peephole, pinhole, plughole, pothole, punchbowl.
Engross, lactose, morose, verbose, viscose.
Arose, bellows, bulldoze, compose, depose, disclose, dispose, enclose, expose, forgoes, gallows, glucose, impose, oppose, outgrows, pillows, plainclothes, primrose, propose, rainbows, repose, suppose, tiptoes, transpose, undergoes, wild rose.
[3] **Buttonhole**, casserole, cubbyhole, hidey-hole, pigeonhole, rigmarole, rock and roll, self-control, waterhole.
Adios, diagnose, dominoes, grandiose, overdose, overexpose, superimpose.

4.1.77 "--oves" (as in "loaves")
[1] cloves, coves, droves, groves, loaves, stoves.

SURPRISING RHYMING:
[1] **Clove**, cove, dove, drove, grove, mauve, stove, strove, wove.
Blows, bows, chose, close, clothes, crows, doze, flows, foes, froze, glows, goes, grows, hose, knows, lows, mows, nose, owes, pose, pros, prose, rose, rows, sews, shows, slows, snows, sows, stows, those, throes, throws, toes, tows, woes.
Boast, coast, ghost, grossed, host, most, post, roast, toast.
Bones, clones, cones, drones, groans, hones, loans, moans, owns, phones, scones, stones, thrones, tones, zones.
Combs, domes, foams, gnomes, homes, roams, tomes.
[2] **Alcove**, behove/behoove (U.S.), interwove, mangrove.
Arose, bellows, bulldoze, compose, depose, disclose, dispose, enclose, expose, foreclose, forgoes, gallows, glucose, impose, oppose, outgrows, pillows, plainclothes, primrose, propose, rainbows, repose, suppose, tiptoes, transpose, undergoes, wild rose.
Almost, bedpost, endmost, engrossed, foremost, gatepost, goalpost, lamppost, outpost, seacoast, signpost, topmost, utmost.
[3] **Diagnose**, dominoes, overdose, presuppose, superimpose.

4.1.78 "--over" (as in "rover")
[2] clover, drover, nova, over, rover.
[3] all over, blow over, bowl over, changeover, chew over, crossover, fall over, fly-over, get over, handover, hangover, leftover, makeover, moreover, once-over, pullover, pushover, sleepover, slipover, stopover, takeover, turnover, walkover, watch over.
[4] bossa nova, Casanova, supernova, up-and-over.

SURPRISING RHYMING:
[2] **Coda**, coder, coaxer, goader, hoaxer, loader, loafer, odour/odor (U.S.), soda.
Coma, comber, homer, roamer.
Aura, donor, groaner, loaner, loner, moaner, owner, toner.
Bolder, boulder, colder, folder, holder, older, scolder, shoulder, smoulder/smolder (U.S.).
Bowler, cola, molar, polar, roller, solar, stroller.
Blower, boa, glower, goer, grower, knower, lower, mower, o'er, rower, sewer, shower, slower, sower, thrower, tower.
Boater, doter, floater, gloater, motor, quota, rota, rotor, voter.
Broker, choker, coca, evoker, joker, ochre, poker, soaker, smoker.
[3] **Decoder**, encoder, freeloader, pagoda, railroader, unloader.
Beholder, cardholder, cold shoulder, freeholder, householder, shareholder, stakeholder.
Aroma, beachcomber, diploma, glaucoma, misnomer.
Atoner, condoner, homeowner, landowner, persona.
Bipolar, cajoler, Coca-Cola, consoler, controller, Moviola, patroller, payola, pianola, rock 'n' roller, steamroller, tombola, viola.
Bulldozer, composer, discloser, exposer, opposer, poser, proposer.
Composure, closure, disclosure, enclosure, exposure, foreclosure.
Aloha, borrower, churchgoer, concertgoer, follower, lawnmower, racegoer, theatregoer/theatergoer (U.S.), widower, winegrower.
Anorexia nervosa, closer, greengrocer, grocer, mimosa.

4.1.79 "--own" (as in "phone")
[1] blown, bone, clone, cone, drone, flown, groan, grown, hone, known, loan, lone, moan, mown, own, phone, prone, scone, sewn, shone, shown, sown, stone, throne, thrown, tone, zone.
[2] alone, atone, backbone, bemoan, birthstone, bloodstone, brownstone, cellphone, cheekbone, cologne, condone, cyclone, dethrone, disown, earphone, end zone, enthrone, flagstone, Freephone, full-blown, full-grown, gallstone, gemstone, gravestone, half-grown, headphone, headstone, high-flown, home-grown, hormone, intone, jawbone, kerbstone/curbstone (U.S.), keystone, limestone, lodestone, milestone, millstone, moonstone, outgrown, ozone, payphone, pinecone, postpone, rhinestone, ringtone, sandstone, shinbone, tombstone, touchstone, trombone, unknown, unsewn, unsown, whalebone, windblown, wishbone.
[3] anklebone, answerphone, baritone, chaperone, cobblestone, cornerstone, Dictaphone, fully-grown, gramophone, herringbone, knucklebone, marrowbone, megaphone, methadone, microphone, monotone, overblown, overgrown, overthrown, overtone, pheromone, saxophone, semitone, silicone, stepping stone, telephone, unbeknown, undertone, xylophone.

SURPRISING RHYMING:
[1] **Cloned**, coned, droned, groaned, honed, loaned, loaned, moaned, owned, phoned, stoned, toned, zoned.
Chrome, comb, dome, foam, gnome, home, roam, Rome, tome.
Beau, blow, bow, bro, crow, doe, doh, dough, floe, flow, foe, glow, go, grow, hoe, know, low, mo., mow, no, oh, owe, pro, row, sew, show, slow, snow, so, stow, though, throw, toe, tow, woe, yo.
[2] **Atoned**, bemoaned, condoned, disowned, enthroned, postponed.
Genome, in-home, re-home, syndrome, toothcomb.
Beano, chino, dunno, mono, rhino, techno, vino, winnow, wino.
Bordeaux, condo, credo, dodo, judo, kendo, lido, Ludo, meadow, pseudo, rondeau, rondo, shadow, speedo, widow, weirdo, window.

Ago, bingo, bongo, cargo, dingo, ego, forgo, go, go-go, gringo, jingo, largo, lingo, logo, mango, no-go, outgo, pogo, pongo, tango.
Chat show, echo, gung-ho, heave-ho, heigh-ho, honcho, macho, no-show, peepshow, poncho, psycho, roadshow, sideshow, tallyho.
Aglow, below, billow, bolo, cashflow, cello, deathblow, fellow, follow, furlough, Jell-O, go-slow, halo, hello, hollow, mellow, moonglow, pillow, polo, shallow, solo, swallow, wallow, willow, yellow.
[3] **Chaperoned**, cobblestoned, telephoned.
Casino, inferno, kimono, Latino, piano, soprano, tornado, volcano.
Amigo, embargo, fandango, flamingo, indigo, long ago, touch and go, undergo, vertigo.
Afterglow, bordello, buffalo, bungalow, cigarillo, counterblow, gigolo, marshmallow, overflow, piccolo, tremolo.

4.1.80 "--ower" (as in "slower")

[2] blower, boa, glower, goer, grower, knower, lower, mower, o'er, rower, sewer, shower, slower, sower, thrower, tower.
[3] aloha, borrower, burrower, churchgoer, concertgoer, echoer, follower, foregoer, glass-blower, harrower, lawnmower, playgoer, racegoer, shadower, swallower, theatregoer/theatergoer (U.S.), widower, winegrower.

SURPRISING RHYMING:
{2} **Bowler**, cola, molar, polar, roller, solar, stroller.
Broker, choker, coca, evoker, joker, ochre, poker, smoker.
Closer, dozer, grocer, poser.
Chauffeur, clover, drover, nova, over, rover.
Bolder, boulder, colder, folder, holder, older, scolder, shoulder, smoulder/smolder (U.S.).
Coma, comber, homer, roamer.
Coder, goader, loader, odour/odor (U.S.).
Donor, groaner, loaner, loner, moaner, owner, toner.
[3] **Bipolar**, cajoler, Coca-Cola, consoler, controller, Moviola, patroller, payola, pianola, rock 'n' roller, steamroller, tombola, viola.
Mediocre, nonsmoker, pawnbroker, provoker, stockbroker, tapioca.
All over, blow over, bowl over, changeover, chew over, crossover, fall over, fly-over, get over, handover, hangover, leftover, makeover, moreover, once-over, pullover, pushover, sleepover, slipover, stopover, takeover, turnover, walkover, watch over.
Beholder, cardholder, cold shoulder, freeholder, householder, shareholder, stakeholder.
Aroma, beachcomber, diploma, glaucoma, misnomer.
Decoder, encoder, exploder, freeloader, railroader, unloader.
Bulldozer, composer, discloser, exposer, imposer, proposer.
[4] **Bossa nova**, Casanova, supernova, up-and-over.

4.1.81 "--owest" (as in "slowest")

[2] lowest, slowest.

SURPRISING RHYMING:
[2] **Boldest**, closest, coldest, oldest, poets.
Bogus, bonus, focus(ed), notice(d), onus, opus, wholeness.
Homeless, hopeless, ropeless, soapless.
[3] **Diagnosis**, hypnosis, neurosis, osmosis, prognosis, psychosis, unnoticed.

4.1.82 "--owing" (as in "glowing")

[2] blowing, bowing, crowing, flowing, glowing, going, growing, knowing, mowing, owing, rowing, sewing, showing, slowing, snowing, sowing, throwing, toeing, towing.
[3] churchgoing, easy-going, following, foregoing, harrowing, ongoing, outgoing, overflowing, seagoing, stowing, tiptoeing, unknowing.

SURPRISING RHYMING:
[2] **Folding**, holding, moulding/molding (U.S.), scolding.
Bowling, polling, rolling, scrolling, strolling, tolling, trolling.

Combing, foaming, gloaming, homing, roaming.
Cloning, groaning, honing, loaning, moaning, owning, phoning, stoning, toning, zoning.
Coping, doping, eloping, groping, hoping, moping, roping, sloping.
Boating, coating, doting, floating, gloating, noting, quoting, voting.
Chosen, closing, dozing, frozen, nosing, omen, posing, stolen.
Choking, croaking, joking, poking, smoking, soaking, stroking.
Beholden, bolden, embolden, golden, olden.
[3] **Enfolding**, remoulding/remolding (U.S.), unfolding, withholding.
Corroding, decoding, encoding, eroding, exploding, foreboding, freeloading, imploding, overloading, railroading, reloading, unloading.
Consoling, controlling, extolling, paroling, patrolling, potholing.
Atoning, condoning, disowning, postponing.
Demoting, denoting, devoting, emoting, misquoting, promoting.
Bulldozing, composing, deposing, disclosing, disposing, enclosing, exposing, imposing, opposing, proposing, supposing, transposing.
[4] **Diagnosing**, overdosing, presupposing, superimposing.

4.1.83 "--oze" (as in "doze")

[1] blows, bows, chose, close, clothes, crows, doze, flows, foes, froze, glows, goes, grows, hose, knows, lows, mows, nose, owes, pose, pros, prose, rose, rows, sews, shows, slows, snows, sows, stows, those, throes, throws, toes, tows, woes.
[2] arose, bellows, bulldoze, compose, depose, disclose, dispose, enclose, expose, foreclose, forgoes, gallows, glucose, impose, oppose, outgrows, pillows, plainclothes, primrose, propose, rainbows, repose, suppose, tiptoes, transpose, undergoes, wild rose.
[3] cellulose, decompose, diagnose, dominoes, indispose, interpose, juxtapose, overdose, overexpose, predispose, presuppose, recompose, superimpose.

SURPRISING RHYMING:
[1] **Closed**, dozed, hosed, nosed, posed.
Cloves, coves, dose, droves, groves, loaves, stoves.
Bowls, coals, foals, goals, holes, moles, poles, polls, roles, rolls, scrolls, shoals, soles, souls, strolls, tolls, trolls, voles.
Boast, coast, ghost, grossed, host, most, post, roast, toast.
Blokes, chokes, cloaks, coax, cokes, croaks, folks, hoax, jokes, oaks, pokes, smokes, soaks, stokes, strokes, yolks.
Bones, clones, cones, drones, groans, hones, loans, moans, owns, phones, scones, stones, thrones, tones, zones.
Beau, blow, bow, bro, crow, doe, doh, dough, flow, foe, glow, go, grow, hoe, know, low, mo., mow, no, oh, owe, pro, row, sew, show, slow, snow, so, stow, though, throw, toe, tow, woe, yo.
Both, growth, loath, oath, sloth.
Bold, bowled, cold, doled, fold, gold, hold, holed, mould/mold (U.S.), old, poled, polled, rolled, scold, soled, sold, told, tolled.
[2] **Bulldozed**, composed, deposed, disclosed, disposed, enclosed, exposed, imposed, opposed, proposed, supposed, transposed.
Engross, lactose, morose, verbose, viscose.
Almost, bedpost, endmost, engrossed, foremost, gatepost, goalpost, lamppost, outpost, seacoast, signpost, topmost, utmost.
Behold, blindfold, cajoled, controlled, cuckold, foothold, foretold, household, millionfold, outsold, paroled, remould(s)/remold(s) (U.S.), re-sold, retold, scaffold, stronghold, tenfold, threshold, toehold, twofold, threefold, unfold, uphold, unsold, untold, withhold.
[3] **Diagnosed**, indisposed, overdosed, overexposed, predisposed, presupposed, superimposed.
Adios, comatose, decompose, diagnose, dominoes, grandiose, indispose, overdose, overexpose, presuppose, superimpose.
Centrefold/centerfold (U.S.), manifold, marigold, oversold, pigeonholed, self-controlled, stranglehold, uncontrolled, undersold.

4.1.84 "--ozed" (as in "dozed")

[1] closed, dozed, hosed, nosed, posed.

480

[2] bulldozed, composed, deposed, disclosed, disposed, enclosed, exposed, imposed, opposed, proposed, supposed, transposed.
[3] diagnosed, indisposed, interposed, juxtaposed, overdosed, overexposed, predisposed, presupposed, recomposed, superimposed.

SURPRISING RHYMING:
[1] **Blows**, bows, chose, close, clothes, crows, doze, flows, foes, froze, glows, goes, grows, hose, knows, lows, mows, nose, owes, pose, pros, prose, rose, rows, sews, shows, slows, snows, sows, stows, those, throes, toes, tows, woes.
Cloves, coves, droves, groves, loaves, stoves.
Bowls, coals, foals, goals, holes, moles, poles, polls, roles, rolls, scrolls, shoals, soles, souls, strolls, tolls, trolls, voles.
Boast, coast, ghost, grossed, host, most, post, roast, toast.
Bones, clones, cones, drones, groans, hones, loans, moans, owns, phones, scones, stones, thrones, tones, zones.
[2] **Arose**, bellows, bulldoze, compose, depose, disclose, dispose, enclose, expose, foreclose, forgoes, gallows, glucose, impose, oppose, outgrows, pillows, plainclothes, primrose, propose, rainbows, repose, suppose, tiptoes, transpose, undergoes, wild rose.
Engrossed, lactose, morose, verbose, viscose.
Almost, bedpost, endmost, engrossed, foremost, gatepost, goalpost, lamppost, outpost, seacoast, signpost, topmost, utmost.
[3] **Adios**, comatose, decompose, diagnose, dominoes, grandiose, indispose, overdose, overexpose, presuppose, superimpose.

4.1.85 "--ozing" (as in "dozing")
[2] closing, dozing, hosing, nosing, posing.
[3] bulldozing, composing, deposing, disclosing, disposing, enclosing, exposing, imposing, opposing, proposing, supposing, transposing.
[4] diagnosing, interposing, juxtaposing, overdosing, overexposing, predisposing, presupposing, recomposing, superimposing.

SURPRISING RHYMING:
[2] **Bowling**, polling, rolling, scrolling, strolling, tolling, trolling.
Boasting, coasting, coaxing, hoaxing, hosting, posting, roasting, toasting.
Cloning, groaning, honing, loaning, moaning, owning, phoning, stoning, toning, zoning.
Blowing, bowing, crowing, flowing, glowing, going, growing, knowing, loathing, mowing, owing, rowing, sewing, showing, slowing, snowing, sowing, throwing, toeing, towing.
Choking, croaking, joking, poking, smoking, soaking, stroking.
Coping, eloping, groping, hoping, moping, roping, sloping, soaping.
Boating, coating, doting, floating, gloating, noting, quoting, voting.
[3] **Consoling**, controlling, extolling, paroling, patrolling, potholing.
Atoning, condoning, disowning, postponing.
Churchgoing, easy-going, following, foregoing, harrowing, ongoing, outgoing, overflowing, seagoing, stowing, tiptoeing, unknowing.
Corroding, decoding, encoding, eroding, exploding, foreboding, freeloading, imploding, overloading, railroading, reloading, unloading.
Evoking, invoking, provoking, revoking, stockbroking.
Demoting, denoting, devoting, emoting, misquoting, promoting.

4.1.86 "--ozen" (as in "frozen")
chosen, frozen, lederhosen, unfrozen.

SURPRISING RHYMING:
[2] **Lotion**, motion, notion, ocean, potion.
Closing, dozing, hosing, nosing, posing.
Beholden, bolden, embolden, golden, olden.
Omen, Roman, showman, snowman, yeoman.
Broken, open, spoken, stolen, swollen, token, woken, woven.
Coping, doping, eloping, groping, hoping, moping, roping, soaping.
Cloning, groaning, honing, loaning, moaning, owning, phoning.

Bowling, polling, rolling, scrolling, strolling, tolling, trolling.
[3] **Commotion**, devotion, emotion, locomotion, slow-motion.
Corrosion, erosion, explosion, implosion.
Awoken, heartbroken, outspoken, plain-spoken, soft-spoken, unbroken, unspoken.
Bulldozing, composing, deposing, disclosing, disposing, enclosing, exposing, imposing, opposing, proposing, supposing, transposing.
Consoling, controlling, extolling, paroling, patrolling.

4.1.87 "--ozer" (as in "composer")
bulldozer, closer, composer, discloser, dozer, exposer, forecloser, imposer, mimosa, opposer, poser, proposer.

SURPRISING RHYMING:
[2] **Coder**, goader, loader, odour/odor (U.S.).
Bolder, boulder, colder, folder, holder, older, scolder, shoulder, smoulder/smolder (U.S.).
Blower, boa, glower, goer, grower, knower, lower, mower, o'er, rower, sewer, shower, slower, sower, thrower, tower.
Coper, doper, eloper, groper, hoper, moper, no-hoper, ogre, sober.
Broker, choker, coca, evoker, joker, ochre, poker, soaker, smoker.
Donor, groaner, loaner, loner, moaner, owner, toner.
Chauffeur, clover, drover, gopher, loafer, nova, over, rover.
Bowler, cola, molar, polar, roller, solar, stroller.
[3] **Composure**, closure, disclosure, enclosure, exposure, grocer.
Decoder, encoder, exploder, freeloader, railroader, unloader.
Beholder, cardholder, cold shoulder, freeholder, householder, shareholder, stakeholder.
Borrower, churchgoer, concertgoer, follower, lawnmower, racegoer, swallower, theatregoer/theatergoer (U.S.), widower, winegrower.
Mediocre, nonsmoker, pawnbroker, provoker, stockbroker, tapioca.
Atoner, condoner, homeowner, landowner, persona, postponer.
All over, blow over, bowl over, changeover, chew over, crossover, fall over, fly-over, get over, handover, hangover, leftover, makeover, moreover, once-over, pullover, pushover, sleepover, slipover, stopover, takeover, turnover, walkover, watch over.
Bipolar, cajoler, Coca-Cola, consoler, controller, Moviola, patroller, payola, pianola, potholer, rock 'n' roller, steamroller, tombola, viola.
[4] **Bossa nova**, Casanova, supernova, up-and-over.

4.1.88 "--ozes" (as in "roses")
[2] closes, dozes, hoses, noses, poses, roses.
[3] bulldozes, composes, discloses, exposes, forecloses, imposes, opposes, proposes.

SURPRISING RHYMING:
[2] **Coaches**, coaxes, brooches, hoaxes, poaches, roaches.
Boldness, hostess, lowest, moment, poets, slowest, smokeless.
Boldest, closest, coldest, homeless, hopeless, oldest, poets.
Bogus, bonus, focus(ed), notice(d), onus, opus, showbiz, wholeness.
[3] **Hypnosis**, neurosis, osmosis, prognosis, psychosis.
Approaches, encroaches, explosives, slowcoaches, stagecoaches.
Atrocious, ferocious, precocious.
[4] **Diagnosis**, halitosis, metamorphosis, symbiosis.

4.1.89 "--ozure" (as in "closure")
[3] composure, closure, disclosure, enclosure, exposure, foreclosure.

SURPRISING RHYMING:
[2] **Chauffeur**, closer, clover, drover, grocer, nova, over, poser, rover.
Coda, coder, goader, loader, odour/odor (U.S.), soda.
Bolder, boulder, colder, folder, holder, older, scolder, shoulder, smoulder/smolder (U.S.), solder, soldier, told her.
Boaster, coaster, coaxer, hoaxer, poacher, poster, toaster.

Blower, boa, glower, goer, grower, knower, lower, mower, o'er, rower, sewer, shower, slower, sower, thrower, tower.
Bowler, cola, molar, polar, roller, solar, stroller.
Donor, groaner, loaner, loner, moaner, owner, toner.
[3] Bulldozer, composer, disposer, exposer, proposer.
Beholder, cardholder, cold shoulder, freeholder, householder, shareholder, stakeholder.
All over, blow over, bowl over, changeover, chew over, crossover, fall over, fly-over, get over, handover, hangover, leftover, makeover, moreover, once-over, pullover, pushover, sleepover, slipover, stopover, takeover, turnover, walkover, watch over.
Borrower, churchgoer, concertgoer, follower, lawnmower, racegoer, swallower, theatregoer/theatergoer (U.S.), widower, winegrower.
Decoder, encoder, exploder, freeloader, pagoda, railroader, unloader.
Bipolar, cajoler, Coca-Cola, consoler, controller, Moviola, patroller, payola, pianola, rock 'n' roller, steamroller, tombola, viola.
Atoner, condoner, homeowner, landowner, persona, postponer.

4.1.90 "--ozion" (as in "explosion")
[3] corrosion, erosion, explosion, implosion.

SURPRISING RHYMING:
[2] Lotion, motion, notion, ocean, potion.
Chosen, closing, dozing, frozen, nosing, omen, posing, stolen.
Beholden, bolden, embolden, golden, olden.
Broaching, coaching, poaching.
Boasting, coasting, coaxing, hoaxing, hosting, posting, roasting, toasting.
Omen, Roman, showman, snowman, yeoman.
Cloning, groaning, honing, loaning, moaning, owning, phoning.
Folding, holding, moulding/molding (U.S.), scolding.
Bowling, polling, rolling, scrolling, strolling, tolling, trolling.
Coping, doping, eloping, groping, hoping, moping, roping, sloping.
Broken, oaken, spoken, token, woken.
Boating, coating, doting, floating, gloating, noting, quoting, voting.
[3] Commotion, demotion, devotion, emotion, locomotion, promotion, slow-motion.
Bulldozing, composing, deposing, disclosing, disposing, enclosing, exposing, imposing, opposing, proposing, supposing, transposing.
Approaching, encroaching, reproaching.
Atoning, condoning, disowning, postponing.
Awoken, heartbroken, outspoken, plain-spoken, re-open, soft-spoken, unbroken, unspoken, well-spoken.
Consoling, controlling, extolling, paroling, patrolling.
Demoting, denoting, devoting, emoting, misquoting, promoting.
[4] Diagnosing, overdosing, presupposing, superimposing.

4.2. "o" (as in "hot")

4.2.1 "--ob" (as in "sob")
[1] blob, bob, cob, daub, fob, gob, hob, job, knob, lob, mob, rob, slob, snob, sob, swab, throb, yob.
[2] doorknob, heartthrob, hobnob, thingamabob.

SURPRISING RHYMING:
[1] Lobbed, mobbed, robbed, sobbed, swabbed, throbbed.
Bop, chop, clop, cop, crop, drop, flop, fop, hop, lop, mop, op, plop, pop, prop, shop, slop, sop, stop, strop, swap, top.
Blog, bog, clog, cog, dog, flog, fog, frog, grog, hog, jog, log, nog, prog, slog, smog, snog, sprog, tog.
Bod, clod, cod, god, mod, nod, odd, plod, pod, prod, quad, rod, shod, sod, squad, trod, wad.

[2] **Atop**, backdrop, bebop, bellhop, bookshop, bus-stop, car-hop, coin-op, co-op, cough drop, desktop, dewdrop, doorstop, eavesdrop, face-swap, flat-top, flip-flop, full stop, hardtop, hilltop, hip-hop, laptop, namedrop, nonstop, pawnshop, raindrop, rooftop, screwtop, sweatshop, sweetshop, teardrop, tea-shop, tip-top, toyshop, treetop.
Backlog, bulldog, bullfrog, groundhog, hangdog, hedgehog, hotdog, lapdog, leapfrog, prologue/prolog (U.S.), roadhog, seadog, watchdog.
Hotrod, iPod, tripod, ramrod, roughshod, slipshod, tightwad.
[3] **Barbershop**, coffeeshop, lollipop, soda pop, spinning-top, whistle-stop, window-shop.
Analogue/analog (U.S.), catalogue/catalog (U.S.), dialogue, travelogue, underdog.

4.2.2 "--obber" (as in "robber")
[2] clobber, cobber, jobber, robber, sobber.

SURPRISING RHYMING:
[2] **Bopper**, chopper, copper, cropper, dropper, hopper, poppa, popper, proper, shopper, stopper, swapper, topper, whopper.
Coffer, cougher, hover, offer, proffer, scoffer.
Blotter, gotta, globetrotter, hotter, jotter, otter, plotter, potter, rotter, spotter, squatter, terracotta, totter, trotter, water, yachter.
Author, bother, boxer, daughter, foster, roster, slaughter, softer.
Augur, blogger, flogger, jogger, lager, logger, slogger, snogger.
Dodder, fodder, odder, plodder, prodder.
Caller, collar, dollar, holler, horror, scholar, squalor.
[3] **Eavesdropper**, gobstopper, grasshopper, improper, teenybopper.

4.2.3 "--obbing" (as in "robbing")
[2] bobbing, jobbing, lobbing, mobbing, robbing, sobbing, throbbing.

SURPRISING RHYMING:
[2] **Bopping**, chopping, dropping, flopping, hopping, lopping, mopping, popping, propping, shopping, stopping, swapping, topping, whopping.
Blogging, bogging, clogging, flogging, hogging, jogging, logging, slogging, snogging.
Blotting, clotting, dotting, globetrotting, jotting, knotting, plotting, rotting, slotting, spotting, squatting, train-spotting, trotting, yachting.
Nodding, plodding, prodding, wadding.
Blocking, clocking, crocking, docking, flocking, knocking, locking, mocking, rocking, shocking, stocking.
Bossing, crossing, double-crossing, flossing, glossing, tossing.
Coffin, coughing, often, scoffing, soften.
[3] **Eavesdropping**, namedropping, window-shopping.

4.2.4 "--obby" (as in "hobby")
[2] bobby, hobby, lobby, slobby, snobby.

SURPRISING RHYMING:
[2] **Bawdy**, body, gaudy, shoddy, squaddie, toddy, wadi.
Boggy, doggy, foggy, groggy, smoggy, soggy.
Coffee, faulty, lofty, softie, toffee.
Choppy, copy, floppy, jalopy, poppy, sloppy, soppy, stroppy.
Dotty, foxy, grotty, hottie, naughty, potty, snotty, spotty.
Brolly, collie, dolly, finale, folly, golly, holly, jolly, lolly, trolley, volley.
Cocky, disc jockey/disk jockey (U.S.), hockey, rocky, schlocky, stocky.
Bossy, flossy, glossy, posse, saucy.
[3] **Anybody**, busybody, dogsbody, everybody, nobody, somebody.

4.2.5 "--obble" (as in "wobble")
[2] bauble, bobble, cobble, gobble, hobble, knobble, nobble, squabble, warble, wobble.

484

SURPRISING RHYMING:
[2] **Coddle**, dawdle, doddle, modal, model, molly-coddle, noddle, remodel, swaddle, toddle, twaddle, waddle, yodel.
Boggle, boondoggle, goggle, joggle, ogle, toggle, woggle.
Aristotle, bottle, horizontal, hostel, mottle, throttle.
Awful, brothel, grovel, hovel, lawful, novel, offal, waffle.
Amoral, choral, coral, floral, immoral, laurel, moral, oral, quarrel.
Apostle, colossal, fossil, gospel, jostle, morsel, nozzle, schnozzle, shovel, topple.

4.2.6 "--obbler" (as in "cobbler")
[2] cobbler, gobbler, hobbler, nobbler, squabbler, wobbler.

SURPRISING RHYMING:
[2] **Clobber**, cobber, jobber, robber, sobber.
Coddler, modeller/modeler (U.S.), toddler, waddler.
Altar, alter, assaulter, defaulter, exalter, falter, halter, salter, vaulter.
Groveller/groveler (U.S.), quarreller/quarreler (U.S.), shoveller.
Bomber, comma, momma, trauma.
Absconder, anaconda, blonder, fonder, ponder, responder, squander, wander, yonder.
Bopper, chopper, copper, cropper, dropper, hopper, poppa, popper, poplar, proper, shopper, stopper, swapper, topper, whopper.
Blotter, gotta, globetrotter, hotter, jotter, otter, plotter, potter, rotter, spotter, squatter, terracotta, totter, trotter, water, yachter.
Brawler, collar, dollar, holler, horror, scholar, squalor.
Dodder, fodder, odder, plodder, prodder.
Blogger, flogger, hogger, jogger, lager, logger, slogger, snogger.
Blocker, boxer, docker, doctor, knocker, locker, mocker, rocker, shocker, soccer.
[3] **Eavesdropper**, gobstopper, grasshopper, improper, teenybopper.

4.2.7 "--obbling" (as in "hobbling")
[2] bobbling, cobbling, gobbling, goblin, hobbling, nobbling, squabbling, wobbling.

SURPRISING RHYMING:
[2] **Coddling**, modelling/modeling (U.S.), swaddling, toddling, waddling, yodelling/yodeling (U.S.).
Fondling, grovelling/groveling (U.S.), quarrelling/quarreling (U.S.).
Belonging, bonging, gonging, longing, thronging, wronging.
Daunting, flaunting, haunting, jaunting, taunting, wanting.
Faulting, halting, malting, salting, vaulting.
All in, balding, folding, holding, moulding/molding (U.S.), scolding.
Boggling, bottling, jostling, throttling, toppling.
[3] **Dissolving**, evolving, involving, resolving, revolving, solving.
Assaulting, exalting, pole-vaulting, revolting, somersaulting.
Absconding, bonding, corresponding, responding.

4.2.8 "--ock" (as in "rock")
[1] bloc, block, choc, chock, clock, crock, doc, dock, flock, frock, hock, jock, knock, loch, lock, mock, pock, rock, schlock, shock, smock, sock, Spock, stock, wok.
[2] ad hoc, airlock, amok, armlock, Bangkok, baroque, bedrock, bed sock, breeze block, deadlock, defrock, epoch, forelock, gridlock, hemlock, Hitchcock, laughing stock, livestock, o'clock, padlock, peacock, restock, roadblock, shamrock, shell shock, sunblock, tick-tock, unfrock, unlock, Van Gogh, warlock, wedlock, windsock, Woodstock.
[3] aftershock, chock-a-block, interlock, laughing stock, overstock, poppycock, shuttlecock, stopcock, stumbling block.

SURPRISING RHYMING:
[1] **Blocked**, clocked, cocked, crocked, docked, flocked, hocked, knocked, locked, mocked, pocked, rocked, shocked, socked, stocked.
Blocks, box, chocs, clocks, cox, docks, fox, frocks, ox, pox, knocks, locks, mocks,

485

rocks, shocks, smocks, socks, stocks, woks.
Bop, chop, clop, cop, crop, drop, flop, fop, hop, lop, mop, op, plop, pop, prop, shop, slop, sop, stop, strop, swap, top.
Blot, clot, cot, dot, got, hot, jot, knot, lot, not, plot, pot, rot, Scot, shot, slot, snot, spot, squat, swat, swot, tot, trot, watt, what, yacht.
[2] **Deadlocked**, gridlocked, padlocked, shell shocked, unlocked.
Bandbox, brainbox, breadbox, detox, dreadlocks, gearbox, hatbox, horsebox, icebox, jukebox, mailbox, matchbox, outfox, padlocks, peacocks, paintbox, pillbox, sandbox, shadowbox, shoebox, snuffbox, soapbox, soundbox, squeezebox, strongbox, toolbox.
Atop, backdrop, bebop, bellhop, bookshop, bus-stop, car-hop, coin-op, co-op, cough drop, desktop, dewdrop, doorstop, eavesdrop, face-swap, flat-top, flip-flop, full stop, hardtop, hilltop, hip-hop, laptop, namedrop, nonstop, pawnshop, raindrop, rooftop, screwtop, sweatshop, sweetshop, teardrop, tea-shop, tip-top, toyshop, treetop.
Adopt, bopped, chopped, cropped, dropped, flopped, hopped, mopped, opt, popped, propped, shopped, stopped, swapped, topped.
Blackspot, bloodshot, boycott, cannot, crackpot, despot, earshot, forgot, fusspot, gunshot, hotpot, hotshot, hotspot, jackpot, mailshot, mascot, moonshot, mugshot, nightspot, potshot, robot, sexpot, snapshot, somewhat, sunspot, teapot, upshot.
[3] **Chatterbox**, equinox, Goldilocks, letter box, orthodox, paradox.
Barbershop, coffeeshop, lollipop, soda pop, spinning-top, whistle-stop, window-shop.
Apricot, Camelot, carrycot, chimneypot, coffeepot, diddly-squat, flowerpot, forget-me-not, kilowatt, Lancelot, overshot, polka dot.

4.2.9 "--ocker" (as in "locker")
[2] blocker, doctor, knocker, locker, mocker, rocker, shocker, soccer.

SURPRISING RHYMING:
[2] **Bopper**, chopper, copper, cropper, dropper, hopper, poppa, popper, proper, prosper, shopper, stopper, swapper, topper, whopper.
Blotter, bother, boxer, daughter, gotta, globetrotter, hotter, jotter, plotter, potter, rotter, slaughter, softer, spotter, squatter, totter, water.
Blogger, flogger, hogger, jogger, lager, logger, slogger, snogger.
Clobber, cobber, jobber, robber, sober.
Collar, dollar, holler, horror, scholar, squalor.
[3] **Eavesdropper**, gobstopper, grasshopper, improper, teenybopper.

4.2.10 "--ocked" (as in "rocked")
[1] blocked, clocked, crocked, docked, flocked, hocked, knocked, locked, mocked, pocked, rocked, shocked, socked, stocked.
[2] deadlocked, defrocked, gridlocked, interlocked, overstocked, padlocked, restocked, shell shocked, unfrocked, unlocked.

SURPRISING RHYMING:
[1] **Bloc**, block, choc, chock, clock, crock, doc, dock, flock, frock, hock, jock, knock, loch, lock, mock, pock, rock, schlock, shock, smock, sock, Spock, stock, wok.
Adopt, bopped, chopped, cropped, dropped, flopped, hopped, mopped, opt, popped, propped, shopped, stopped, swapped, topped.
Blot, clot, cot, dot, got, hot, jot, knot, lot, not, plot, pot, rot, Scot, shot, slot, snot, spot, squat, swat, swot, tot, trot, watt, what, yacht.
Blocks, box, chocs, clocks, cox, docks, fox, frocks, ox, pox, knocks, locks, mocks, rocks, shocks, smocks, socks, stocks, woks.
[2] **Ad hoc**, airlock, amok, armlock, Bangkok, baroque, bedrock, deadlock, defrock, epoch, gridlock, Hitchcock, laughing stock, o'clock, padlock, roadblock, shamrock, shell shock, sunblock, tick-tock, unlock, Van Gogh, warlock, wedlock, windsock, Woodstock.
Blackspot, bloodshot, boycott, cannot, crackpot, despot, earshot, forgot, fusspot, gunshot, hotpot, hotshot, hotspot, jackpot, mailshot, mascot, moonshot, mugshot, nightspot, potshot, robot, sexpot, snapshot, somewhat, sunspot, teapot, upshot.
Eavesdropped, flat-topped, flip-flopped, hard-topped, namedropped.

Bandbox, brainbox, breadbox, detox, dreadlocks, gearbox, hatbox, horsebox, icebox, jukebox, mailbox, matchbox, outfox, padlocks, peacocks, paintbox, pillbox, sandbox, shadowbox, shoebox, snuffbox, soapbox, soundbox, squeezebox, strongbox, toolbox.
[3] **Aftershock**, chock-a-block, interlock, laughing stock, overstock, poppycock, shuttlecock, stopcock, stumbling block.
Barbershop, coffeeshop, lollipop, soda pop, spinning-top, whistle-stop, window-shop.
Apricot, Camelot, carrycot, chimneypot, coffeepot, diddly-squat, flowerpot, forget-me-not, kilowatt, Lancelot, overshot, polka dot.
Chatterbox, equinox, Goldilocks, letter box, orthodox, paradox.

4.2.11 "--ocking" as in "rocking"
[2] blocking, clocking, crocking, docking, flocking, knocking, locking, mocking, rocking, shocking, stocking.
[3] defrocking, interlocking, overstocking, padlocking, restocking, unblocking, undocking, unfrocking, unlocking.

SURPRISING RHYMING:
[2] **Bopping**, chopping, cropping, dropping, flopping, hopping, mopping, popping, shopping, stopping, swapping, topping, whopping.
Blotting, clotting, dotting, hotting, jotting, knotting, plotting, rotting, rotten, slotting, spotting, squatting, swatting, trotting, yachting.
Hawking, sleepwalking, squawking, stalking, talking, walking.
Docket, knock it, locket, pocket, rocket, socket, sock it, sprocket.
Blogging, clogging, flogging, hogging, jogging, slogging, snogging.
Bobbing, jobbing, lobbing, mobbing, robbing, sobbing, throbbing.
Coffin, coughing, often, soften.
[3] **Boxing**, detoxing, foxing, outfoxing, shadowboxing.
Clip-clopping, eavesdropping, namedropping, window-shopping.

4.2.12 "--ocket" (as in "locket")
[2] docket, knock it, locket, pocket, rocket, socket, sock it, sprocket.
[3] air pocket, hip pocket, pickpocket, skyrocket.

SURPRISING RHYMING:
[2] **Bonnet**, brochette, chocolate, closet, coquette, comet, cornet, corvette, croquette, faucet, offset, profit, prophet, rosette, wallet.
Blocker, docker, knocker, locker, mocker, rocker, shocker, soccer.
Allotted, blotted, boycotted, clotted, dotted, jotted, knotted, plotted, slotted, spotted, squatted, swatted, trotted.
Chronic, phonic, sonic, tonic, topic, tropic.
[3] **Bionic**, demonic, electronic, iconic, ironic, laconic, platonic, supersonic, symphonic.

4.2.13 "--ockey" (as in "jockey")
[2] cocky, hockey, jockey, rocky, schlocky, stocky.

SURPRISING RHYMING:
[2] **Choppy**, copy, floppy, jalopy, poppy, sloppy, soppy, stroppy.
Dotty, grotty, hottie, naughty, potty, snotty, spotty.
Bobby, hobby, lobby, slobby, snobby.
Boggy, doggy, foggy, groggy, smoggy, soggy.
Bawdy, body, gaudy, shoddy, squaddie, toddy, wadi.
Bossy, flossy, glossy, posse, saucy.
Brolly, collie, dolly, folly, golly, holly, jolly, lolly, poly, trolley, volley.
[3] **Anybody**, busybody, dogsbody, everybody, nobody, somebody.

4.2.14 "--odd" (as in "odd")
[1] bod, clod, cod, god, hod, mod, nod, odd, plod, pod, prod, quad, rod, shod, sod, squad, trod, wad.
[2] demigod, hotrod, iPod, tripod, ramrod, roughshod, slipshod.

SURPRISING RHYMING:
[1] **Awed**, board, bored, chord, fjord, floored, ford, hoard, horde, lord, oared, pored, poured, roared, scored, snored, soared, stored, sword, toward, ward.
Blob, cob, fob, gob, hob, job, knob, lob, mob, rob, slob, snob, sob, swab, throb, yob.
Blog, bog, clog, cog, dog, flog, fog, frog, grog, hog, jog, log, nog, prog, slog, smog, snog, sprog, tog.
Blot, clot, cot, dot, got, hot, jot, knot, lot, not, plot, pot, rot, Scot, shot, slot, snot, spot, squat, swat, swot, tot, trot, watt, what, yacht.
Bop, chop, clop, cop, crop, drop, flop, fop, hop, lop, mop, op, plop, pop, prop, shop, slop, sop, stop, strop, swap, top.
[2] **Doorknob**, heartthrob, hobnob, thingamabob.
Abhorred, aboard, accord, adored, afford, award, billboard, blackboard, cardboard, chessboard, clipboard, dartboard, dashboard, deplored, explored, floorboard, headboard, ignored, keyboard, landlord, onboard, record, restored, reward, scoreboard, sideboard, skateboard, snowboard, springboard, surfboard, switchboard.
Backlog, bulldog, bullfrog, groundhog, hangdog, hedgehog, hotdog, lapdog, leapfrog, prologue/prolog (U.S.), roadhog, seadog, watchdog.
Blackspot, bloodshot, boycott, cannot, crackpot, despot, earshot, forgot, fusspot, gunshot, hotpot, hotshot, hotspot, jackpot, mailshot, mascot, moonshot, mugshot, nightspot, potshot, robot, sexpot, snapshot, somewhat, sunspot, teapot, upshot.
Atop, backdrop, bebop, bellhop, bookshop, bus-stop, car-hop, coin-op, co-op, cough drop, desktop, dewdrop, doorstop, eavesdrop, face-swap, flat-top, flip-flop, full stop, hardtop, hilltop, hip-hop, laptop, namedrop, nonstop, pawnshop, raindrop, rooftop, screwtop, sweatshop, sweetshop, teardrop, tea-shop, tip-top, toyshop, treetop.
[3] **Harpsichord**, notice board, overawed, overboard.
Analogue/analog (U.S.), catalogue/catalog (U.S.), dialogue, underdog.
Apricot, Camelot, carrycot, chimneypot, coffeepot, diddly-squat, flowerpot, forget-me-not, kilowatt, Lancelot, polka dot.
Barbershop, coffeeshop, lollipop, soda pop, spinning-top, whistle-stop, window-shop.

4.2.15 "--odded" (as in "nodded")
[2] nodded, plodded, prodded, sodded, wadded.

SURPRISING RHYMING:
[2] **Florid**, horrid, solid, torrid.
Boarded, dogged, forded, hoarded, sordid, warded.
Allotted, blotted, boycotted, clotted, dotted, jotted, knotted, plotted, slotted, spotted, squatted, swatted, trotted.
Assaulted, bolted, exalted, halted, malted, revolted, salted, vaulted.
Daunted, flaunted, haunted, taunted, unwanted, wanted.
Folded, moulded/molded (U.S.), scolded.
Bonnet, chocolate, closet, comet, faucet, profit, prophet, wallet.
Docket, knock it, locket, pocket, rocket, socket, sock it, sonnet.
[3] **Accorded**, afforded, awarded, recorded, rewarded.
Absconded, bonded, corresponded, responded, unbonded.

4.2.16 "--odder" (as in "fodder")
[2] dodder, fodder, nodder, odder, plodder, prodder.

SURPRISING RHYMING:
[2] **Clobber**, cobber, jobber, robber, sobber.
Blogger, flogger, hogger, jogger, lager, logger, slogger, snogger.
Bopper, chopper, copper, cropper, dropper, hopper, poppa, popper, proper, shopper, stopper, swapper, topper, whopper.
Boarder, border, disorder, former, hoarder, order, recorder, warder.
Blotter, bother, gotta, globetrotter, hotter, jotter, plotter, potter, rotter, squatter, totter.
Bomber, comma, goner, momma, trauma.
Blocker, boxer, doctor, knocker, locker, rocker, shocker, soccer.
[3] **Eavesdropper**, gobstopper, grasshopper, improper, teenybopper.

4.2.17 "--oddle" (as in "model")

[2] Coddle, dawdle, doddle, modal, model, molly-coddle, noddle, remodel, swaddle, toddle, twaddle, waddle, yodel.

SURPRISING RHYMING:
[2] **Bauble**, bobble, cobble, gobble, hobble, squabble, wobble.
Boggle, boondoggle, goggle, joggle, ogle, toggle, woggle.
Aristotle, bottle, horizontal, hostel, mottle, throttle.
Apostle, colossal, fossil, gospel, jostle, morsel, nozzle, topple.
Awful, brothel, grovel, hovel, lawful, novel, offal, waffle.
Amoral, choral, coral, floral, immoral, laurel, moral, oral, quarrel.

4.2.18 "--ody as in "body")

[2] bawdy, body, gaudy, shoddy, squaddie, toddy, wadi.
[3] anybody, busybody, dogsbody, embody, homebody, everybody, nobody, somebody.

SURPRISING RHYMING:
[2] **Bobby**, hobby, lobby, slobby, snobby.
Boggy, cloggy, doggy, foggy, groggy, smoggy, soggy.
Coffee, faulty, lofty, softie, toffee.
Choppy, copy, floppy, jalopy, poppy, sloppy, soppy, stroppy.
Dotty, foxy, grotty, haughty, hottie, lordy, naughty, potty, spotty.
Brolly, dolly, finale, folly, golly, holly, jolly, lolly, poly, trolley, volley.
Disc/disk jockey (U.S.), hockey, jockey, rocky, schlocky, stocky.
Bossy, flossy, glossy, posse, saucy.

4.2.19 "--odic" (as in "melodic")

episodic, melodic, methodic, periodic, spasmodic.

SURPRISING RHYMING:
[2] **Atomic**, comic, chopstick, con trick, cosmic, frolic, homesick, logic, lovesick, topic, tropic, toxic, vomit.
Closet, knock it, locket, pocket, profit, rocket, socket, sonnet, wallet.
Chronic, conic, phonic, sonic, tonic, topic, tropic.
Bawdy, body, gaudy, shoddy, squaddie, toddy, wadi.
[3] **Bionic**, demonic, iconic, ironic, laconic, platonic, symphonic.
Aerobic, agnostic, chaotic, erotic, euphoric, exotic, historic, hypnotic, meteoric, neurotic, psychotic, robotic, symbolic.
Anybody, busybody, dogsbody, everybody, nobody, somebody.
[4] **Electronic**, embryonic, philharmonic, quadraphonic, stereophonic, supersonic.
Alcoholic, astronomic, catastrophic, claustrophobic, economic, gastronomic, idiotic, melancholic, microscopic, patriotic.

4.2.20 "--off" (as in "cough")

[2] cough, doff, off, quaff, scoff, trough, bakeoff.

SURPRISING RHYMING:
[1] **Aloft**, coughed, croft, cross, loft, morph, oft, soft, waft, wharf.
Broth, cloth, froth, Goth, moth, troth, wrath.
Boss, 'cos, cross, dross, floss, gloss, joss, loss, moss, sauce, toss.
Cosh, dosh, gosh, josh, nosh, posh, quash, slosh, squash, wash.
Blot, clot, cot, dot, got, hot, jot, knot, lot, not, plot, pot, rot, Scot, shot, slot, snot, spot, squat, swat, swot, tot, trot, watt, what, yacht.
[2] **Behemoth**, dishcloth, facecloth, J-cloth, loincloth, tablecloth.
Across, chaos, cosmos, crisscross, emboss, Eros, kudos, pathos.
Blackspot, bloodshot, boycott, cannot, crackpot, despot, earshot, forgot, fusspot, gunshot, hotpot, hotshot, hotspot, jackpot, mailshot, mascot, moonshot, mugshot, nightspot, potshot, robot, sexpot, snapshot, somewhat, sunspot, teapot, upshot.

*

4.2.21 "--offer" (as in "offer")
[2] coffer, cougher, offer, proffer, quaffer, scoffer.

SURPRISING RHYMING:
[2] **Author**, blotter, bother, boxer, daughter, foster, gotta, hotter, jotter, often, plotter, roster, rotter, slaughter, softer, soften, spotter, squatter, water.
Absconder, fonder, ponder, responder, squander, wander, yonder.
Bopper, chopper, copper, cropper, dropper, hopper, poppa, popper, proper, prosper, shopper, stopper, swapper, topper, whopper.
Blocker, doctor, knocker, locker, mocker, rocker, shocker, soccer.
Dodder, fodder, odder, plodder, prodder.
Blogger, flogger, hogger, jogger, lager, logger, slogger, snogger.
Clobber, cobber, jobber, robber, sobber.
Collar, dollar, holler, horror, scholar, squalor.
Altar, alter, assaulter, defaulter, exalter, falter, halter, salter, vaulter.
[3] **Eavesdropper**, gobstopper, grasshopper, improper, teenybopper.

4.2.22 "--oft" (as in "soft")
[1] aloft, coughed, croft, loft, oft, soft, waft.

SURPRISING RHYMING:
[1] **Bossed**, cost, crossed, flossed, frost, glossed, lost, tossed.
Boss, 'cos, cross, dross, floss, gloss, loss, moss, sauce, toss.
Lobbed, mobbed, robbed, sobbed, swabbed, throbbed.
Coshed, joshed, quashed, sloshed, squashed, washed.
Blogged, clogged, dogged, flogged, jogged, logged, slogged.
Blot, clot, cot, dot, got, hot, jot, knot, lot, not, plot, pot, rot, Scot, shot, slot, snot, spot, squat, swat, swot, tot, trot, watt, what, yacht.
Blocked, clocked, crocked, docked, flocked, hocked, knocked, locked, mocked, pocked, rocked, shocked, socked.
Adopt, bopped, chopped, cropped, dropped, flopped, hopped, mopped, opt, popped, propped, shopped, stopped, swapped, topped.
[2] **Accost**, compost, defrost, exhaust, double-crossed, low-cost, riposte, star-crossed.

4.2.23 "--offen" (as in "soften")
[2] boffin, coffin, coughing, often, soften.

SURPRISING RHYMING:
[2] **Broaden**, caution, fallen, foreign, gotten, orphan, rotten, softened.
Bobbin' *(silent 'g')*, jobbin', lobbin', mobbin', robbin', sobbin', throbbin'.
Noddin' *(silent 'g')*, ploddin', proddin'.
Bloggin' *(silent 'g')*, floggin', hoggin', joggin', loggin', sloggin', snoggin'.
Boppin' *(silent 'g')*, choppin', droppin', floppin', hoppin', moppin', poppin', proppin', shoppin', stoppin', swappin', toppin', whoppin'.
Blottin' *(silent 'g')*, clottin', dottin', globetrottin', jottin', knottin', plottin', slottin', spottin', squattin', train-spottin', trottin', yachtin'.
Bossin' *(silent 'g')*, crossin', double-crossin', flossin', glossin', tossin'.
Blockin' *(silent 'g')*, clockin', dockin', flockin', knockin', lockin', mockin', rockin', shockin'.
Awesome, blossom, lonesome, ownsome, wholesome.
Bottom, column, common, cotton, ho-hum, solemn.
[3] **Begotten**, forgotten, ill-gotten, unforgotten.

4.2.24 "--ogg" (as in "dog")
[1] blog, bog, clog, cog, dog, flog, fog, frog, grog, hog, jog, log, nog, prog, slog, smog, snog, sprog, tog.
[2] agog, backlog, bulldog, bullfrog, firedog, groundhog, gundog, hangdog, hedgehog, hotdog, lapdog, leapfrog, prologue/prolog (U.S.), roadhog, seadog, sheepdog, watchdog.
[3] analogue/analog (U.S.), catalogue/catalog (U.S.), demagogue, dialogue, epilogue/epilog (U.S.), synagogue, travelogue, underdog.

SURPRISING RHYMING:
[1] **Blogged**, clogged, dogged, flogged, jogged, logged, slogged.
Blob, cob, fob, gob, hob, job, knob, lob, mob, rob, slob, snob, sob, swab, throb, yob.
Bod, cod, god, mod, nod, odd, plod, prod, quad, rod, shod, sod, squad, trod, wad.
Bop, chop, clop, cop, crop, drop, flop, fop, hop, lop, mop, op, plop, pop, prop, shop, slop, sop, stop, strop, swap, top.
Block, choc, clock, crock, dock, flock, frock, hock, jock, knock, loch, lock, mock, pock, rock, schlock, shock, smock, sock, wok.
Chalk, cork, fork, hawk, squawk, stalk, stork, talk, walk.
[2] **Doorknob**, heartthrob, hobnob, thingamabob.
Hotrod, iPod, tripod, ramrod, roughshod, slipshod, tightwad.
Atop, backdrop, bebop, bellhop, bookshop, bus-stop, car-hop, coin-op, co-op, cough drop, desktop, dewdrop, doorstop, eavesdrop, face-swap, flat-top, flip-flop, full stop, hardtop, hilltop, hip-hop, laptop, namedrop, nonstop, pawnshop, raindrop, rooftop, screwtop, sweatshop, sweetshop, teardrop, tea-shop, tip-top, toyshop, treetop.
[3] **Barbershop**, coffeeshop, lollipop, soda pop, spinning-top, whistle-stop, window-shop.

4.2.25 "--oggy" (as in "foggy")
[2] boggy, doggy, foggy, groggy, smoggy, soggy.

SURPRISING RHYMING:
[2] **Bobby**, hobby, lobby, slobby, snobby.
Coffee, faulty, lofty, softie, toffee.
Bawdy, body, gaudy, shoddy, squaddie, toddy, wadi.
Choppy, copy, floppy, jalopy, poppy, sloppy, soppy, stroppy.
Dotty, grotty, hottie, naughty, potty, snotty, spotty.
Disc jockey/disk jockey (U.S.), hockey, jockey, rocky, stocky, talkie.
Brolly, collie, dolly, folly, golly, holly, jolly, lolly, poly, trolley, volley.
Bossy, flossy, glossy, posse, saucy.
[3] **Anybody**, busybody, dogsbody, everybody, nobody, somebody.

4.2.26 "--ogger" (as in "blogger")
[2] augur, blogger, flogger, hogger, jogger, logger, slogger, snogger.

SURPRISING RHYMING:
[2] **Clobber**, cobber, jobber, robber, sobber.
Dodder, fodder, odder, plodder, prodder.
Bomber, comma, momma, trauma.
Coffer, cougher, hover, offer, proffer, scoffer.
Blotter, bother, boxer, daughter, gotta, globetrotter, hotter, jotter, plotter, potter, rotter, slaughter, softer, spotter, squatter, totter, water.
Bopper, chopper, copper, cropper, dropper, hopper, poppa, popper, proper, prosper, shopper, stopper, swapper, topper, whopper.
Blocker, doctor, knocker, locker, mocker, rocker, shocker, soccer.
Collar, dollar, holler, horror, scholar, squalor.
[3] **Eavesdropper**, gobstopper, grasshopper, improper, teenybopper.

4.2.27 "--ogging" (as in "jogging")
[2] blogging, bogging, clogging, flogging, hogging, jogging, logging, slogging, snogging.

SURPRISING RHYMING:
[2] **Bobbing**, jobbing, lobbing, mobbing, robbing, sobbing, throbbing.
Nodding, plodding, prodding, wadding.
Bopping, chopping, dropping, flopping, hopping, mopping, popping, propping, shopping, stopping, swapping, topping, whopping.
Blotting, clotting, dotting, globetrotting, jotting, knotting, plotting, rotting, slotting, spotting, squatting, train-spotting, trotting, yachting.
Bossing, crossing, double-crossing, flossing, glossing, tossing.
Coffin, coughing, often, scoffing, soften.

Blocking, clocking, crocking, docking, flocking, knocking, locking, mocking, rocking, shocking, stocking.
[3] Eavesdropping, namedropping, window-shopping.

4.2.28 "--ogged" (as in "jogged")
[1] blogged, clogged, dogged, flogged, jogged, logged, slogged.

SURPRISING RHYMING:
[1] Blog, bog, clog, cog, dog, flog, fog, frog, grog, hog, jog, log, nog, prog, slog, smog, snog, sprog, tog.
Lobbed, mobbed, robbed, sobbed, swabbed, throbbed.
Bod, cod, god, mod, nod, odd, plod, prod, quad, rod, shod, sod, squad, trod, wad.
Adopt, bopped, chopped, cropped, dropped, flopped, hopped, mopped, opt, popped, propped, shopped, stopped, swapped, topped.
Bossed, cost, crossed, flossed, frost, glossed, lost, tossed.
Blot, clot, cot, dot, got, hot, jot, knot, lot, not, plot, pot, rot, Scot, shot, slot, snot, spot, squat, swat, swot, tot, trot, watt, what, yacht.
[2] Backlog, bulldog, bullfrog, groundhog, hangdog, hedgehog, hotdog, lapdog, leapfrog, prologue/prolog (U.S.), roadhog, seadog, watchdog.
Hotrod, iPod, tripod, ramrod, roughshod, slipshod, tightwad.
[3] Analogue/analog (U.S.), catalogue/catalog, dialogue, underdog.

4.2.29 "--oggle" as in "goggle")
[2] boggle, boondoggle, goggle, joggle, ogle, toggle, woggle.

SURPRISING RHYMING:
[2] Awful, brothel, grovel, hovel, lawful, novel, offal, waffle.
Bauble, bobble, cobble, gobble, hobble, nobble, squabble, wobble.
Coddle, dawdle, doddle, model, toddle, twaddle, waddle, yodel.
Aristotle, bottle, horizontal, hostel, mottle, throttle.
Apostle, colossal, fossil, gospel, jostle, morsel, nozzle, shovel.
Aural, choral, coral, floral, immoral, laurel, moral, oral, quarrel.
Chortle, formal, mortal, normal, portal, snorkel.
[3] Abnormal, informal, immortal, paranormal.

4.2.30 "--olve" (as in "evolve")
absolve, devolve, dissolve, evolve, involve, resolve, revolve, solve.

SURPRISING RHYMING:
[1] Bald, bawled, brawled, called, crawled, drawled, hauled, mauled, scrawled, shawled, sprawled, stalled, trawled, walled.
[2] Dissolved, evolved, involved, resolved, revolved, solved.
Behold, blindfold, cajoled, controlled, cuckold, foothold, foretold, household, millionfold, outsold, paroled, remould(s)/remold(s) (U.S.), re-sold, retold, scaffold, stronghold, tenfold, threshold, toehold, twofold, threefold, unfold, uphold, unsold, untold, withhold.
Atoll, bankroll, bargepole, beanpole, bolthole, cajole, charcoal, console, control, Creole, dustbowl, enrol/enroll (U.S.), fishbowl, flagpole, hellhole, keyhole, loophole, payroll, parole, patrol, peephole, pinhole, plughole, pothole, punchbowl.
Appalled, blackballed, enthralled, eyeballed, installed, mothballed, overhauled, recalled, snowballed, so-called, sprawled, stonewalled.
[3] Centrefold/centerfold (U.S.), pigeonholed, self-controlled, stranglehold, uncontrolled.

4.2.31 "--olved" (as in "resolved")
absolved, dissolved, evolved, involved, resolved, revolved, solved.

SURPRISING RHYMING:
[1] Bald, bawled, brawled, called, crawled, drawled, hauled, mauled, rolled, scrawled, shawled, sprawled, stalled, tolled, trawled, walled.
[2] Absolve, dissolve, evolve, involve, resolve, revolve, solve.

Behold, blindfold, cajoled, controlled, cuckold, foothold, foretold, household, millionfold, outsold, paroled, remould(s)/remold(s) (U.S.), re-sold, retold, scaffold, stronghold, tenfold, threshold, toehold, twofold, threefold, unfold, uphold, unsold, untold, withhold.
Appalled, blackballed, enthralled, eyeballed, installed, mothballed, overhauled, recalled, snowballed, so-called, sprawled, stonewalled.
Abscond, beyond, correspond, respond, second, vagabond.
Atoll, bankroll, bargepole, beanpole, bolthole, cajole, charcoal, console, control, Creole, dustbowl, enrol/enroll (U.S.), fishbowl, flagpole, hellhole, keyhole, loophole, payroll, parole, patrol, peephole, pinhole, plughole, pothole, punchbowl.
[3] **Centrefold/centerfold** (U.S.), pigeonholed, self-controlled, stranglehold, uncontrolled.

4.2.32 "--olving" (as in "solving")
[3] absolving, devolving, dissolving, evolving, involving, resolving, revolving, solving.

SURPRISING RHYMING:
[2] **Bawling**, brawling, calling, crawling, drawling, hauling, installing, mauling, scrawling, sprawling, stalling, trawling.
Balding, folding, holding, moulding/molding (U.S.), scolding.
Bobbing, jobbing, lobbing, mobbing, robbing, sobbing, throbbing.
Bobbling, cobbling, gobbling, hobbling, squabbling, wobbling.
Blogging, flogging, hogging, jogging, logging, slogging, snogging.
[3] **Blindfolding**, cajoling, handholding, remoulding/remolding (U.S.), unfolding, upholding, withholding.
Appalling, bankrolling, befalling, cajoling, consoling, controlling, enthralling, freefalling, installing, mothballing, name calling, patrolling, recalling, snowballing, stonewalling.

4.2.33 "--olt" (as in "fault")
[1] bolt, colt, dolt, fault, halt, jolt, malt, moult, salt, vault, volt.
[2] assault, default, exalt, revolt, somersault, thunderbolt, unbolt.

SURPRISING RHYMING:
[1] **Flaunt**, gaunt, haunt, jaunt, taunt, want.
Bought, brought, caught, fought, fraught, naught, ought, sought, taught, thought.
Bald, bawled, brawled, called, crawled, drawled, hauled, mauled, scrawled, shawled, sprawled, stalled, trawled, walled.
Aloft, coughed, croft, cross, loft, oft, soft, waft.
Blot, clot, cot, dot, got, hot, jot, knot, lot, not, plot, pot, rot, Scot, shot, slot, snot, spot, squat, swat, swot, tot, trot, watt, what, yacht.
[2] **Atoll**, bankroll, bargepole, beanpole, bolthole, cajole, charcoal, console, control, enrol/enroll (U.S.), fishbowl, flagpole, hellhole, keyhole, loophole, payroll, parole, patrol, pinhole, punchbowl.
Appalled, blackballed, enthralled, eyeballed, installed, mothballed, overhauled, recalled, snowballed, so-called, sprawled, stonewalled.
Absolved, dissolved, evolved, involved, resolved, revolved, solved.

4.2.34 "--olting" (as in "revolting")
[2] faulting, halting, malting, salting, vaulting.
[3] assaulting, exalting, pole-vaulting, revolting, somersaulting.

SURPRISING RHYMING:
[2] **Bonding**, daunting, flaunting, haunting, taunting, wanting, waltzing.
Balding, folding, holding, moulding/molding (U.S.), scolding.
Bobbling, cobbling, hobbling, nobbling, squabbling, wobbling.
Blogging, flogging, hogging, jogging, logging, slogging, snogging.
[3] **Blindfolding**, cajoling, handholding, remoulding/remolding (U.S.), unfolding, upholding, withholding.
Absolving, evolving, involving, resolving, revolving, solving.
Appalling, bankrolling, befalling, cajoling, consoling, controlling, enrolling, enthralling, extolling, freefalling, installing, mothballing, patrolling, recalling, snowballing.

4.2.35 "--olted" (as in "halted")
assaulted, bolted, exalted, halted, malted, revolted, salted, vaulted.

SURPRISING RHYMING:
[1] **Allotted**, blotted, boycotted, clotted, dotted, jotted, knotted, plotted, slotted, spotted, squatted, swatted, trotted.
Daunted, flaunted, haunted, taunted, unwanted, wanted.
Folded, moulded/molded (U.S.), scolded.
Blockhead, bobsled, bonehead, co-ed, crossbred, drop dead, forehead, homebred, homestead, hotbed, hothead, moped, shortbread, sofa-bed, sorehead, watershed.
Nodded, plodded, prodded, sodded, wadded.
[3] **Absconded**, bonded, corresponded, responded, unbonded.
Blindfolded, remoulded/remolded (U.S.), unfolded.

4.2.36 "--olter" (as in "falter")
altar, alter, assaulter, defaulter, exalter, falter, halter, salter, vaulter.

SURPRISING RHYMING:
[2] **Altered**, faltered, unaltered.
Author, blotter, bother, boxer, daughter, foster, gotta, globetrotter, golfer, hotter, imposter, jotter, plotter, roster, shorter, slaughter, softer, spotter, squatter, totter, water.
Bopper, chopper, copper, cropper, dropper, hopper, poppa, popper, proper, shopper, stopper, swapper, topper, whopper.
Clobber, cobber, jobber, robber, sobber.
Augur, blogger, flogger, hogger, jogger, logger, slogger, snogger.
Collar, dollar, holler, scholar, squalor.
Blocker, doctor, knocker, locker, mocker, rocker, shocker, soccer.
Absconder, fonder, ponder, responder, squander, wander, yonder.
[3] **Eavesdropper**, grasshopper, improper, revolver, teenybopper.

4.2.37 "--ollar" (as in "collar")
[2] collar, dollar, holler, scholar, squalor.

SURPRISING RHYMING:
[2] **Bawler**, blue-collar, brawler, caller, crawler, dog collar, drawler, faller, hauler, mauler, scrawler, smaller, solar, taller, trawler, troller.
Coffer, cougher, offer, proffer, quaffer, scoffer.
Clobber, cobber, jobber, robber, sobber.
Dodder, fodder, nodder, odder, plodder, prodder.
Blogger, flogger, hogger, jogger, lager, logger, slogger, snogger.
Bopper, chopper, copper, cropper, dropper, hopper, poppa, popper, proper, shopper, stopper, swapper, topper, whopper.
Blotter, gotta, globetrotter, hotter, jotter, plotter, potter, rotter, spotter, squatter, terracotta, totter, water.
[3] **Eavesdropper**, gobstopper, grasshopper, improper, teenybopper.

4.2.38 "--ollege" (as in "college")
acknowledge, college, knowledge.

SURPRISING RHYMING:
[1] **Allege**, dredge, edge, hedge, ledge, pledge, sledge, veg, wedge.
[2] **Blockage**, bondage, cottage, forage, hostage, incense, mileage, mortgage, porridge, sausage, silence, snobbish, solace, storage, voyage.
Airheads, beachheads, bedheads, bedspreads, bedsteads, beheads, blackheads, blockheads, boneheads, bridgeheads, bulkheads, cowsheds, deadheads, dickheads, eggheads, fatheads, foreheads, homesteads, hotbeds, hotheads, mopeds, pinheads, potheads, redheads, skinheads, sofa-beds, spearheads, sunbeds, warheads.
[3] **Abolish**, astonish, demolish.

*

4.2.39 "--olly" (as in "holly")
[2] brolly, collie, dolly, finale, folly, golly, holly, jolly, lolly, poly, trolley, volley, wally.

SURPRISING RHYMING:
[2] **Bobby**, hobby, lobby, mommy, slobby, snobby.
Coffee, faulty, lofty, softie, toffee.
Bawdy, body, gaudy, godly, oddly, shoddy, squaddie, toddy, wadi.
Boggy, doggy, foggy, groggy, smoggy, soggy.
Choppy, copy, floppy, jalopy, poppy, sloppy, soppy, stroppy.
Dotty, foxy, grotty, hottie, naughty, potty, snotty, spotty.
Glory, gory, hoary, lorry, quarry, sorry, starry, storey, story.
Disc/disk jockey (U.S.), hockey, jockey, rocky, schlocky, stocky.
Bossy, flossy, glossy, posse, saucy.
[3] **Anybody**, busybody, dogsbody, everybody, nobody, somebody.

4.2.40 "--omm" (as in "bomb")
[1] bomb, from, mom, prom, rom, Somme.
[2] aplomb, dot.com, peeping tom, photobomb, rom-com, sitcom.

SURPRISING RHYMING:
[1] **Con**, don, gone, none, on, one, scone, shone, swan, yon.
Blond/blonde, bond, dawned, conned, fond, pawned, pond, spawned, wand, yawned.
Bong, gong, long, prong, song, strong, thong, throng, tong, wrong.
Bomp, chomp, clomp, comp, pomp, romp, stomp, swamp.
Arm, balm, calm, charm, farm, harm, ma'am, palm, psalm, qualm.
[2] **Anon**, baton, begone, bygone, chiffon, coupon, doggone, eon, fatten, flatten, foregone, icon, krypton, log-on, moron, neon, neutron, nylon, pattern, salon, Saturn, someone, thereon, upon.
Abscond, beyond, correspond, respond, second, vagabond.
Along, among, belong, birdsong, bouffant, chaise longue, croissant, ding-dong, furlong, headlong, headstrong, lifelong, mahjong, oblong, penchant, ping-pong, prolong, singalong, singsong, swansong.
Alarm, becalm, disarm, firearm, forearm, rearm, schoolmarm.
[3] **Amazon**, anyone, echelon, electron, everyone, hexagon, leprechaun, liaison, one-on-one, pentagon, silicon, undergone.

4.2.41 "--omp" (as in "pomp")
[1] bomp, chomp, clomp, comp, pomp, romp, stomp, swamp.

SURPRISING RHYMING:
[1] **Bomb**, from, mom, prom, prompt, rom, Somme.
Fault, halt, malt, salt, vault.
Flaunt, haunt, jaunt, taunt, want.
Blond/blonde, bond, dawned, conned, fond, pawned, pond, spawned, wand, yawned.
Con, don, gone, none, on, one, scone, shone, swan, yon.
Bop, chop, clop, cop, crop, drop, flop, fop, hop, lop, mop, op, plop, pop, prop, shop, slop, sop, stop, strop, swap, top.
[2] **Aplomb**, dot.com, peeping tom, photobomb, rom-com, sitcom.
Assault, exalt, pole-vault, revolt, somersault.
Abscond, beyond, correspond, respond, second, vagabond.
Anon, baton, begone, bygone, chiffon, coupon, doggone, eon, icon, krypton, log-on, moron, neon, neutron, nylon, pattern, salon, Saturn, someone.
Atop, backdrop, bebop, bellhop, bookshop, bus-stop, car-hop, coin-op, co-op, cough drop, desktop, dewdrop, doorstop, eavesdrop, face-swap, flat-top, flip-flop, full stop, hardtop, hilltop, hip-hop, laptop, namedrop, nonstop, pawnshop, raindrop, rooftop, screwtop, sweatshop, sweetshop, teardrop, tea-shop, tip-top, toyshop, treetop.
[3] **Amazon**, anyone, echelon, electron, everyone, hexagon, leprechaun, liaison, one-on-one, pentagon, silicon, undergone.
Barbershop, coffeeshop, lollipop, soda pop, spinning-top, whistle-stop, window-shop.

4.2.42 "--on" (as in "gone")
[1] con, don, gone, none, on, one, scone, shone, swan, yon.
[2] anon, baton, batten, begone, bonbon, bygone, chiffon, coupon, crouton, doggone, eon, fatten, flatten, foregone, hereon, icon, krypton, log-on, Manhattan, moron, neon, neuron, neutron, nylon, pattern, pecan, salon, Saturn, someone, thereon, upon.
[3] Amazon, anyone, echelon, electron, everyone, hexagon, leprechaun, liaison, octagon, one-on-one, pentagon, silicon, thereupon, undergone, whereupon.

SURPRISING RHYMING:
[1] **Bomb**, from, mom, prom, rom, Somme.
Born, brawn, corn, dawn(ed), drawn, fawn(ed), horn, lawn, mourn, pawn, scorn, shorn, sworn, thorn, torn, warn, worn, yawn(ed).
Flaunt, gaunt, haunt, jaunt.
Blond/blonde, bond, dawned, donned, fond, pond, spawned, wand.
Bong, gong, long, prong, song, strong, thong, throng, tong, wrong.
Bun, begun, done, fun, gun, nun, pun, run, shun, son, spun, stun, ton, won.
[2] **Aplomb**, dot.com, peeping tom, photobomb, rom-com, sitcom.
Adorn, forlorn, forewarn, morn, redrawn, withdrawn.
Abscond, beyond, correspond, respond, second, vagabond.
Along, among, belong, birdsong, bouffant, chaise longue, croissant, ding-dong, furlong, headlong, headstrong, lifelong, mahjong, oblong, penchant, ping-pong, prolong, singalong, singsong, swansong.
Awesome, become, breadcrumb, eardrum, gruesome, humdrum, kingdom, lonesome, outcome, succumb, twosome, wholesome.
[3] **Atrium**, bothersome, bubblegum, chromium, cumbersome, helium, idiom, martyrdom, medium, meddlesome, opium, overcome, petroleum, platinum, premium, quarrelsome, requiem, solarium, stadium, sugarplum, troublesome.
[4] **Auditorium**, consortium, crematorium, delirium, emporium, equilibrium, gymnasium, millennium, pandemonium, uranium.

4.2.43 "--ond" (as in "bond")
[1] blond/blonde, bond, dawned, conned, donned, fond, pawned, pond, spawned, wand, yawned.
[2] abscond, beyond, correspond, despond, respond, second, vagabond.

SURPRISING RHYMING:
[1] **Con**, don, gone, none, on, one, scone, shone, swan, yon.
Bomb, from, mom, prom, rom, Somme.
Born, brawn, corn, dawn, drawn, fawn, horn, lawn, mourn, pawn, prawn, scorn, shorn, spawn, sworn, thorn, torn, warn, worn, yawn.
Flaunt, gaunt, haunt, jaunt.
Bong, gong, long, prong, song, strong, thong, throng, tong, wrong.
Bun, begun, done, fun, gun, nun, pun, run, shun, son, spun, stun, ton, won.
[2] **Anon**, baton, begone, bygone, chiffon, coupon, doggone, eon, fatten, flatten, foregone, icon, krypton, log-on, moron, neon, neutron, nylon, pattern, salon, Saturn, someone, thereon, upon.
Aplomb, dot.com, peeping tom, photobomb, rom-com, sitcom.
Adorn, forlorn, forewarn, morn, redrawn, withdrawn.
Along, among, belong, birdsong, bouffant, chaise longue, croissant, ding-dong, furlong, headlong, headstrong, lifelong, mahjong, oblong, penchant, ping-pong, prolong, singalong, singsong, swansong.
[3] **Amazon**, anyone, echelon, electron, everyone, hexagon, leprechaun, liaison, one-on-one, pentagon, silicon, undergone.

4.2.44 "--onding" (as in "responding")
[3] absconding, bonding, corresponding, responding.

SURPRISING RHYMING:
[2] **Belonging**, bonging, gonging, longing, thronging, wronging.

496

Daunting, flaunting, haunting, jaunting, nothing, taunting, wanting.
Blogging, flogging, hogging, jogging, logging, slogging, snogging.
Blotting, dotting, globetrotting, jotting, knotting, plotting, potting, rotting, slotting, spotting, squatting, train-spotting, trotting, yachting.
Bossing, crossing, flossing, glossing, rejoicing, tossing, voicing.
Blocking, clocking, flocking, knocking, locking, mocking, rocking, shocking, stocking.
Bopping, chopping, dropping, flopping, hopping, lopping, mopping, popping, propping, shopping, stopping, swapping, topping, whopping.
Bobbling, cobbling, hobbling, nobbling, squabbling, wobbling.
[3] **Assaulting**, exalting, revolting, revolving, somersaulting.
Dissolving, evolving, involving, resolving, revolving, solving.
Eavesdropping, namedropping, window-shopping.

4.2.45 "--onting" (as in "haunting")
[2] daunting, flaunting, haunting, jaunting, taunting, wanting.

SURPRISING RHYMING:
[2] **Belonging**, bonging, gonging, longing, thronging, wronging.
All in, balding, folding, holding, moulding/molding (U.S.), scolding.
Adorning, awning, dawning, fawning, forewarning, mid-morning, morning, mourning, scorning, sworn-in, warming, warning, yawning.
Faulting, halting, malting, salting, vaulting.
Blogging, flogging, hogging, jogging, logging, slogging, snogging.
Bobbling, cobbling, gobbling, hobbling, nobbling, squabbling, wobbling.
Bossing, crossing, double-crossing, flossing, glossing, tossing.
Boring, flooring, pouring, roaring, soaring, scoring, snoring, storing.
[3] **Blindfolding**, cajoling, handholding, remoulding/remolding (U.S.), unfolding, upholding, withholding.
Assaulting, exalting, revolting, revolving, somersaulting.
Absconding, bonding, corresponding, responding.
According, affording, awarding, boarding, recording, rewarding.

4.2.46 "--onder" (as in "ponder")
[2] absconder, blonder, fonder, ponder, responder, squander, wander, yonder.

SURPRISING RHYMING:
[2] **Conga**, longer, sombre/somber (U.S.), stronger.
Pondered, squandered, wandered.
Altar, alter, assaulter, defaulter, exalter, falter, halter, salter, vaulter.
Flaunter, haunter, saunter, taunter.
Broader, dodder, fodder, marauder, odder, plodder, prodder.
Clobber, cobber, jobber, robber, sobber.
Blotter, bother, dotter, gotta, hotter, jotter, otter, plotter, potter, rotter, spotter, squatter, terracotta, totter, trotter, water.
[3] **Absolver**, evolver, resolver, revolver, solver.

4.2.47 "--onded" (as in "responded")
absconded, bonded, corresponded, responded, unbonded.

SURPRISING RHYMING:
[2] **Daunted**, flaunted, haunted, taunted, unwanted, wanted.
Folded, moulded/molded (U.S.), scolded.
Nodded, plodded, prodded, sodded, wadded.
Assaulted, bolted, exalted, halted, malted, revolted, salted, vaulted.
Congaed/conga'd, pondered, squandered, wandered.
Allotted, blotted, boycotted, clotted, dotted, jotted, knotted, plotted, slotted, spotted, squatted, swatted, trotted.
[3] **Blindfolded**, remoulded/remolded (U.S.), unfolded.

*

4.2.48 "--ong" (as in "song")
[1] bong, dong, gong, long, pong, prong, song, strong, thong, throng, tong, wrong.
[2] along, among, belong, birdsong, bouffant, chaise longue, croissant, ding-dong, furlong, headlong, headstrong, lifelong, mahjong, oblong, overlong, penchant, ping-pong, prolong, sarong, singalong, singsong, swansong.

SURPRISING RHYMING:
[1] **Belonged**, gonged, longed, ponged, prolonged, pronged, thronged, wronged.
Con, don, gone, none, on, one, scone, shone, swan, yon.
Blond/blonde, bond, dawned, donned, fond, pond, spawned, wand.
Bomb, from, mom, prom, rom, Somme.
Born, brawn, corn, dawn, dawned, drawn, fawn, fawned, horn, lawn, mourn, pawn, prawn, scorn, scorned, shorn, spawn, sworn, thorn, torn, warn, worn, yawn, yawned.
Flaunt, gaunt, haunt, jaunt.
[2] **Anon**, baton, begone, bygone, chiffon, coupon, doggone, eon, fatten, flatten, foregone, icon, krypton, log-on, moron, neon, neutron, nylon, pattern, salon, Saturn, someone, thereon, upon.
Abscond, beyond, correspond, respond, second, vagabond.
Aplomb, dot.com, peeping tom, photobomb, rom-com, sitcom.
Adorn, forlorn, forewarn, morn, redrawn, withdrawn.
[3] **Amazon**, anyone, echelon, electron, everyone, hexagon, leprechaun, liaison, one-on-one, pentagon, silicon, undergone.

4.2.49 "--onged" (as in "wronged")
belonged, bonged, gonged, longed, ponged, prolonged, pronged, thronged, wronged.

SURPRISING RHYMING:
[1] **Bong**, gong, long, prong, song, strong, thong, throng, wrong.
Blond/blonde, bond, bombed, conned, dawned, donned, fond, lawned, mourned, pawned, pond, scorned, wand, warned, yawned.
Con, don, gone, none, on, one, scone, shone, swan, yon.
[2] **Along**, among, belong, birdsong, bouffant, ding-dong, headlong, headstrong, lifelong, mahjong, oblong, penchant, prolong, singalong, singsong, swansong.
Anon, baton, begone, bygone, chiffon, coupon, doggone, eon, fatten, flatten, foregone, icon, krypton, log-on, moron, neon, neutron, nylon, salon, Saturn, someone, upon.
Abscond, adorned, beyond, forewarned, respond, vagabond.
Aplomb, dot.com, peeping tom, photobomb, rom-com, sitcom.
[3] **Amazon**, anyone, echelon, electron, everyone, hexagon, leprechaun, liaison, one-on-one, pentagon, silicon, undergone.

4.2.50 "--onging" (as in "longing")
[2] belonging, bonging, gonging, longing, thronging, wronging.

SURPRISING RHYMING:
[1] **Daunting**, flaunting, haunting, jaunting, taunting, wanting.
Adorning, awning, dawning, fawning, forming, morning, mourning, pawning, scorning, spawning, storming, warming, warning, yawning.
Bawling, brawling, calling, crawling, drawling, falling, hauling, installing, mauling, scrawling, sprawling, stalling, trawling.
Boring, flooring, pouring, roaring, soaring, scoring, snoring, storing.
Bobbing, jobbing, lobbing, mobbing, robbing, sobbing, throbbing.
Bossing, crossing, double-crossing, flossing, glossing, tossing.
Blogging, flogging, hogging, jogging, logging, slogging, snogging.
Bopping, chopping, dropping, flopping, hopping, lopping, mopping, popping, propping, shopping, stopping, swapping, topping, whopping.
Bobbling, cobbling, hobbling, nobbling, squabbling, wobbling.
[3] **Absconding**, bonding, corresponding, responding, seconding.
Eavesdropping, namedropping, window-shopping.

*

4.2.51 "--onic" (as in "tonic")
[2] chronic, conic, phonic, sonic, tonic.
[3] bionic, bubonic, Byronic, carbonic, demonic, harmonic, iconic, ironic, laconic, moronic, platonic, sardonic, symphonic.
[4] catatonic, electronic, embryonic, harmonic, histrionic, mnemonic, philharmonic, polyphonic, quadraphonic, stereophonic, supersonic.

SURPRISING RHYMING:
[2] **Atomic**, comic, chopstick, con trick, cosmic, frolic, homesick, logic, lovesick, topic, tropic, toxic, vomit.
Closet, docket, got it, knock it, locket, pocket, profit, rocket, socket, sock it, sonnet, sprocket, wallet.
[3] **Aerobic**, agnostic, chaotic, episodic, erotic, euphoric, exotic, historic, hypnotic, melodic, methodic, metaphoric, meteoric, myopic, neurotic, periodic, psychotic, robotic, spasmodic, symbolic.
[4] **Alcoholic**, astronomic, catastrophic, claustrophobic, economic, ergonomic, gastronomic, homophobic, idiotic, microscopic, patriotic.

4.2.52 "--op" (as in "drop")
[1] bop, chop, clop, cop, crop, drop, flop, fop, hop, lop, mop, op, plop, pop, prop, shop, slop, sop, stop, strop, swap, top.
[2] atop, backdrop, bebop, bellhop, bookshop, bus-stop, car-hop, clip-clop, coin-op, co-op, cough drop, desktop, dewdrop, doorstop, eavesdrop, face-swap, flat-top, flip-flop, full stop, gumdrop, hardtop, hedgehop, hilltop, hip-hop, laptop, namedrop, nonstop, outcrop, pawnshop, raindrop, rooftop, screwtop, snowdrop, sweatshop, sweetshop, teardrop, tea-shop, tip-top, toyshop, treetop, workshop.
[3] barbershop, coffeeshop, bellyflop, lollipop, malaprop, soda pop, spinning-top, tabletop, turboprop, whistle-stop, window-shop.

SURPRISING RHYMING:
[1] **Blob**, fob, gob, hob, job, knob, lob, mob, rob, slob, snob, sob, swab, throb, yob.
Blot, clot, cot, dot, got, hot, jot, knot, lot, not, plot, pot, rot, Scot, shot, slot, snot, spot, squat, swat, swot, tot, trot, watt, what, yacht.
Bod, cod, god, mod, nod, odd, plod, pod, prod, quad, rod, shod, squad, trod, wad.
Block, choc, clock, crock, doc, dock, flock, frock, hock, jock, knock, loch, lock, mock, pock, rock, schlock, shock, smock, sock, wok.
Blog, bog, clog, cog, dog, flog, fog, frog, grog, hog, jog, log, nog, prog, slog, smog, snog, sprog, tog.
Broth, cloth, froth, Goth, moth, troth, wrath.
[2] **Doorknob**, heartthrob, hobnob, thingamabob.
Blackspot, bloodshot, boycott, cannot, crackpot, despot, earshot, forgot, fusspot, gunshot, hotpot, hotshot, hotspot, jackpot, mailshot, mascot, moonshot, mugshot, nightspot, potshot, robot, sexpot, snapshot, somewhat, sunspot, teapot, upshot.
Demigod, hotrod, iPod, tripod, ramrod, roughshod, slipshod.
Ad hoc, amok, armlock, Bangkok, baroque, bedrock, deadlock, defrock, epoch, gridlock, Hitchcock, laughing stock, o'clock, padlock, roadblock, shamrock, shell shock, shylock, sunblock, tick-tock, unlock, Van Gogh, warlock, wedlock, windsock, Woodstock.
Backlog, bulldog, bullfrog, groundhog, hangdog, hedgehog, hotdog, lapdog, leapfrog, prologue/prolog (U.S.), roadhog, seadog, watchdog.
[3] **Apricot**, Camelot, carrycot, chimneypot, coffeepot, diddly-squat, flowerpot, forget-me-not, kilowatt, Lancelot, overshot, polka dot.
Aftershock, chock-a-block, laughing stock, poppycock, shuttlecock, stumbling block.

4.2.53 "--opped" (as in "dropped")
[1] adopt, bopped, chopped, cropped, dropped, flopped, hopped, lopped, mopped, opt, plopped, popped, propped, shopped, slopped, stopped, stropped, swapped, topped.

SURPRISING RHYMING:
[1] **Bop**, chop, cop, crop, drop, flop, hop, lop, mop, pop, prop, shop, stop, swap, top.

Blocked, docked, flocked, hocked, knocked, locked, mocked, rocked, shocked, socked.
Block, choc, clock, crock, doc, dock, flock, frock, hock, jock, knock, loch, lock, mock, pock, rock, schlock, shock, smock, sock, wok.
Blot, clot, cot, dot, got, hot, jot, knot, lot, not, plot, pot, rot, Scot, shot, slot, snot, spot, squat, swat, swot, tot, trot, watt, what, yacht.
Lobbed, mobbed, robbed, sobbed, swabbed, throbbed.
Blogged, flogged, jogged, logged, slogged, snogged, togged.
[2] **Atop**, backdrop, bebop, bellhop, bookshop, bus-stop, car-hop, coin-op, co-op, cough drop, desktop, dewdrop, doorstop, eavesdrop, face-swap, flat-top, flip-flop, full stop, hardtop, hilltop, hip-hop, laptop, namedrop, nonstop, pawnshop, raindrop, rooftop, screwtop, sweatshop, sweetshop, teardrop, tea-shop, tip-top, toyshop, treetop.
Blackspot, bloodshot, boycott, cannot, crackpot, despot, earshot, forgot, fusspot, gunshot, hotpot, hotshot, hotspot, jackpot, mailshot, mascot, moonshot, mugshot, nightspot, potshot, robot, sexpot, snapshot, somewhat, sunspot, teapot, upshot.
Ad hoc, amok, armlock, Bangkok, baroque, bedrock, deadlock, defrock, epoch, gridlock, Hitchcock, laughing stock, o'clock, padlock, roadblock, shamrock, shell shock, shylock, sunblock, tick-tock, unlock, Van Gogh, warlock, wedlock, windsock, Woodstock.
[3] **Barbershop**, coffeeshop, lollipop, soda pop, spinning-top, whistle-stop, window-shop.
Apricot, Camelot, carrycot, chimneypot, coffeepot, diddly-squat, flowerpot, forget-me-not, kilowatt, Lancelot, overshot, polka dot.
Aftershock, chock-a-block, laughing stock, poppycock, shuttlecock, stumbling block.

4.2.54 "--opping" (as in "dropping")
[2] bopping, chopping, dropping, flopping, hopping, mopping, popping, propping, shopping, stopping, swapping, topping, whopping.
[3] eavesdropping, namedropping, window-shopping.

SURPRISING RHYMING:
[2] **Blotting**, clotting, dotting, jotting, knotting, opting, plotting, potting, rotting, slotting, spotting, squatting, trotting, yachting.
Bobbing, jobbing, lobbing, mobbing, robbing, sobbing, throbbing.
Blocking, clocking, docking, flocking, hocking, knocking, locking, mocking, rocking, shocking, stocking, talking, walking.
Blogging, flogging, hogging, jogging, logging, slogging, snogging.
Nodding, plodding, prodding, wadding.
Boffin, coffin, coughing, often, soften.
Bossing, crossing, double-crossing, flossing, glossing, tossing.

4.2.55 "--oppy" (as in "poppy")
[2] choppy, copy, floppy, jalopy, poppy, sloppy, soppy, stroppy.

SURPRISING RHYMING:
[2] **Bobby**, gobby, hobby, lobby, slobby, snobby.
Dotty, grotty, hottie, naughty, potty, snotty, spotty, totty.
Bawdy, body, gaudy, shoddy, squaddie, toddy, wadi.
Cocky, hockey, jockey, rocky, schlocky, stocky.
Boggy, doggy, foggy, groggy, smoggy, soggy.
Bossy, flossy, glossy, posse, saucy.
Brolly, collie, dolly, folly, golly, holly, jolly, lolly, poly, trolley, volley.
[3] **Anybody**, busybody, dogsbody, everybody, nobody, somebody.

4.2.56 "--opper" (as in "proper")
[2] bopper, chopper, copper, cropper, dropper, hopper, poppa, popper, proper, shopper, stopper, swapper, topper, whopper.
[3] eavesdropper, gobstopper, grasshopper, improper, sharecropper, teenybopper.

SURPRISING RHYMING:
[2] **Blotter**, bother, boxer, daughter, gotta, globetrotter, hotter, jotter, plotter, potter, rotter, slaughter, softer, spotter, squatter, totter, water.

Blocker, boxer, doctor, knocker, locker, rocker, shocker, soccer.
Dodder, fodder, odder, plodder, prodder.
Augur, blogger, flogger, hogger, jogger, logger, slogger, snogger.
Clobber, cobber, jobber, robber, sobber.
Collar, dollar, holler, horror, scholar, squalor.

4.2.57 "--oral" (as in "moral")
amoral, choral, coral, floral, immoral, laurel, moral, oral, quarrel.

SURPRISING RHYMING:
[2] **Awful**, brothel, grovel, hovel, lawful, novel, offal, waffle.
Chortle, formal, mortal, normal, portal, snorkel.
Coddle, dawdle, doddle, model, molly-coddle, noddle, remodel, swaddle, toddle, twaddle, waddle, yodel.
Bauble, bobble, cobble, gobble, hobble, nobble, squabble, wobble.
Boggle, boondoggle, goggle, joggle, ogle, toggle, woggle.
Aristotle, bottle, horizontal, hostel, mottle, throttle.
Apostle, colossal, fossil, gospel, jostle, morsel, nozzle, schnozzle.
[3] **Abnormal**, informal, immortal, paranormal.

4.2.58 "--ost" (as in "lost")
[1] bossed, cost, crossed, flossed, frost, glossed, lost, tossed.
[2] accost, compost, defrost, exhaust, double-crossed, embossed, low-cost, riposte, star-crossed.

SURPRISING RHYMING:
[1] **Boss**, 'cos, cross, dross, floss, gloss, loss, moss, sauce, toss.
Aloft, bakeoff, coughed, croft, cross, loft, oft, soft, waft.
Adopt, bopped, chopped, cropped, dropped, flopped, hopped, mopped, opt, popped, propped, shopped, stopped, swapped, topped.
Coshed, joshed, quashed, sloshed, squashed, unwashed, washed.
Blot, clot, cot, dot, got, hot, jot, knot, lot, not, plot, pot, rot, Scot, shot, slot, snot, spot, squat, swat, swot, tot, trot, watt, what, yacht.
[2] **Across**, chaos, cosmos, crisscross, Eros, ethos, kudos, pathos.
Blackspot, bloodshot, boycott, cannot, crackpot, despot, earshot, forgot, fusspot, gunshot, hotpot, hotshot, hotspot, jackpot, mailshot, mascot, moonshot, mugshot, nightspot, potshot, robot, sexpot, snapshot, somewhat, sunspot, teapot, upshot.
[3] **Albatross**, candyfloss, double-cross, rally-cross.
Apricot, Camelot, carrycot, chimneypot, coffeepot, diddly-squat, flowerpot, forget-me-not, kilowatt, Lancelot, overshot, polka dot.

4.2.59 "--osh" (as in "wash")
[1] cosh, dosh, gosh, josh, nosh, posh, quash, slosh, squash, wash.
[2] awash, car wash, eyewash, hogwash, mouthwash, whitewash.

SURPRISING RHYMING:
[1] **Coshed**, joshed, quashed, sloshed, squashed, washed.
Blotch, botch(ed), crotch, notch(ed), scotch(ed), Scotch, splotch, swatch, watch(ed).
Boss, 'cos, cross, dross, floss, gloss, joss, loss, moss, sauce, toss.
Bossed, cost, crossed, flossed, glossed, lost, sauced, tossed.
[2] **Across**, chaos, cosmos, crisscross, Eros, ethos, kudos, pathos.
Butterscotch, hopscotch, hotchpotch, skywatch, stopwatch, topnotch, wristwatch.
[3] **Albatross**, candyfloss, double-cross, rally-cross.

4.2.60 "--oshed" (as in "washed")
coshed, joshed, quashed, sloshed, squashed, washed, whitewashed.

SURPRISING RHYMING:
[1] **Cosh**, gosh, josh, nosh, posh, quash, slosh, squash, wash.

Blotch, botch(ed), crotch, notch(ed), scotch(ed), Scotch, splotch, swatch, watch(ed).
Boss, 'cos, cross, dross, floss, gloss, joss, loss, moss, sauce, toss.
Bossed, cost, crossed, flossed, glossed, lost, sauced, tossed.
Aloft, coughed, croft, loft, oft, soft, waft.
[2] Awash, car wash, eyewash, hogwash, mouthwash, whitewash.
Across, chaos, cosmos, crisscross, Eros, ethos, kudos, pathos.
Butterscotch, hopscotch, hotchpotch, skywatch, stopwatch, topnotch, wristwatch.
[3] Albatross, candyfloss, double-cross, rally-cross.

4.2.61 "--oshing" (as in "washing")
brainwashing, coshing, dishwashing, joshing, quashing, sloshing, squashing, washing.

SURPRISING RHYMING:
[2] Blotching, botching, notching, scotching, watching.
Bossing, crossing, dossing, flossing, frosting, glossing, tossing.
Boxing, detoxing, foxing, outfoxing, shadowboxing.
Dodging, lodging, dislodging.
Auction, caution, concoction, launching, precaution, option, scorching, torching.
Blotting, coughing, dotting, globetrotting, jotting, knotting, plotting, rotting, slotting, spotting, squatting, train-spotting, trotting, yachting.
Bopping, chopping, dropping, flopping, hopping, lopping, mopping, popping, propping, shopping, stopping, swapping, topping, whopping.
Blocking, clocking, crocking, docking, flocking, knocking, locking, mocking, rocking, shocking, stocking, walking.
[3] Crisscrossing, defrosting, double-crossing, skywatching.
Eavesdropping, namedropping, window-shopping.

4.2.62 "--oss" (as in "boss")
[1] boss, 'cos, cross, doss, dross, floss, gloss, joss, loss, moss, sauce, toss.
[2] across, chaos, cosmos, crisscross, emboss, Eros, ethos, kudos, lacrosse, pathos.
[3] albatross, candyfloss, double-cross, rally-cross.

SURPRISING RHYMING:
[1] Bossed, cost, crossed, flossed, frost, glossed, lost, tossed.
'Coz, cause, clause, claws, draws, drawers, flaws, gauze, gnaws, jaws, laws, pause, paws, squaws, straws, was, yours.
Cosh, dosh, gosh, josh, nosh, posh, quash, slosh, squash, wash.
Blots, dots, hots, knots, lots, plots, pots, rots, Scots, shots, slots, spots, squats, swats, trots, watts, yachts.
Blocks, box, chocs, clocks, cox, docks, fox, frocks, ox, pox, knocks, locks, mocks, rocks, shocks, smocks, socks, stocks, woks.
Chops, cops, crops, drops, flops, hops, mops, pops, props, shops, slops, stops, tops.
[2] Accost, defrost, exhaust, embossed, low-cost, riposte, star-crossed.
Applause, because, indoors, outdoors, Santa Claus.
Awash, car wash, eyewash, hogwash, mouthwash, whitewash.
Apricots, chimneypots, coffeepots, flowerpots, forget-me-nots, polka dots.
Bandbox, brainbox, breadbox, detox, dreadlocks, gearbox, hatbox, horsebox, icebox, jukebox, mailbox, matchbox, outfox, padlocks, peacocks, paintbox, pillbox, sandbox, shadowbox, shoebox, snuffbox, soapbox, soundbox, squeezebox, strongbox, toolbox.
Bookshops, desktops, doorstops, eavesdrops, flip-flops, hilltops, laptops, lollipops, raindrops, rooftops, teardrops, toyshops, treetops.
[3] Chatterbox, double-crossed, equinox, Goldilocks, letter box, orthodox, paradox.

4.2.63 "--ossing" (as in "crossing")
bossing, crossing, double-crossing, flossing, glossing, tossing.

SURPRISING RHYMING:
[2] Boxing, causing, detoxing, forcing, foxing, outfoxing, pausing, shadowboxing.
Bossy, flossy, glossy, posse, saucy.

502

Coffin, coughing, often, scoffing, soften.
Accosting, costing, defrosting, frosting, exhausting.
Blotting, dotting, globetrotting, jotting, knotting, plotting, potting, rotting, slotting, spotting, squatting, train-spotting, trotting, yachting.
Bopping, chopping, dropping, flopping, hopping, mopping, popping, propping, shopping, stopping, swapping, topping, whopping.
Brainwashing, joshing, quashing, sloshing, squashing, washing.
Blocking, clocking, crocking, docking, flocking, knocking, locking, mocking, rocking, shocking, stocking.
Blogging, flogging, hogging, jogging, logging, slogging, snogging.
[3] **Eavesdropping**, namedropping, window-shopping.

4.2.64 "--ossy" (as in "bossy")
[2] bossy, flossy, glossy, posse, saucy.

SURPRISING RHYMING:
[2] **Coffee**, faulty, frosty, frothy, lofty, softie, toffee.
Brolly, dolly, finale, folly, golly, holly, jolly, lolly, poly, trolley, volley.
Bobby, hobby, lobby, slobby, snobby.
Dotty, foxy, grotty, hottie, naughty, potty, snotty, spotty.
Choppy, copy, floppy, jalopy, poppy, sloppy, soppy, stroppy.
Bawdy, body, gaudy, shoddy, squaddie, toddy, wadi.
Boggy, doggy, foggy, groggy, smoggy, soggy.
[3] **Anybody**, busybody, dogsbody, everybody, nobody, somebody.

4.2.65 "--ot" (as in "what")
[1] blot, clot, cot, dot, got, hot, jot, knot, lot, not, plot, pot, rot, shot, slot, snot, spot, squat, swat, swot, tot, trot, watt, what, yacht.
[2] abbot, allot, begot, blackspot, bloodshot, boycott, buckshot, cannot, crackpot, despot, dovecote, earshot, forgot, foxtrot, fusspot, gunshot, hotpot, hotshot, hotspot, jackpot, mailshot, mascot, moonshot, mugshot, nightspot, potshot, robot, sexpot, slingshot, slipknot, snapshot, somewhat, stewpot, subplot, sunspot, teapot, upshot.
[3] apricot, Camelot, carrycot, chimneypot, coffeepot, counterplot, diddly-squat, flowerpot, forget-me-not, kilowatt, Lancelot, megawatt, overshot, polka dot.

SURPRISING RHYMING:
[1] **Block,** choc, clock, crock, doc, dock, flock, frock, hock, jock, knock, loch, lock, mock, pock, rock, schlock, shock, smock, sock, wok.
Bop, chop, clop, cop, crop, drop, flop, fop, hop, lop, mop, op, plop, pop, prop, shop, slop, sop, stop, strop, swap, top.
Blocked, clocked, crocked, docked, flocked, hocked, knocked, locked, mocked, pocked, rocked, shocked, socked, stocked.
Adopt, bopped, chopped, cropped, dropped, flopped, hopped, mopped, opt, popped, propped, shopped, stopped, swapped, topped.
Bossed, cost, crossed, flossed, frost, glossed, lost, tossed.
Bod, cod, god, mod, nod, odd, plod, pod, prod, quad, rod, shod, squad, trod, wad.
[2] **Deadlocked**, gridlocked, padlocked, shell shocked, unlocked.
Ad hoc, amok, armlock, Bangkok, baroque, bedrock, deadlock, defrock, epoch, gridlock, Hitchcock, laughing stock, o'clock, padlock, roadblock, shamrock, shell shock, shylock, sunblock, tick-tock, unlock, Van Gogh, warlock, wedlock, windsock, Woodstock.
Atop, backdrop, bebop, bellhop, bookshop, bus-stop, car-hop, coin-op, co-op, cough drop, desktop, dewdrop, doorstop, eavesdrop, face-swap, flat-top, flip-flop, full stop, hardtop, hilltop, hip-hop, laptop, namedrop, nonstop, pawnshop, raindrop, rooftop, screwtop, sweatshop, sweetshop, teardrop, tea-shop, tip-top, toyshop, treetop.
Clear-cut, doughnut, haircut, peanut, rebut, somewhat, uncut, walnut.
[3] **Aftershock**, chock-a-block, interlock, laughing stock, poppycock, shuttlecock, stopcock, stumbling block.
Barbershop, coffeeshop, lollipop, soda pop, spinning-top, whistle-stop, window-shop.

*

4.2.66 "--otty" (as in "dotty")
[2] dotty, grotty, haughty, hottie, naughty, potty, snotty, spotty.

SURPRISING RHYMING:
[2] **Cocky**, hockey, jockey, rocky, schlocky, stocky.
Choppy, copy, floppy, jalopy, poppy, sloppy, soppy, stroppy.
Coffee, faulty, lofty, softie, toffee.
Bobby, gobby, hobby, lobby, slobby, snobby.
Boggy, doggy, foggy, groggy, smoggy, soggy.
Bawdy, body, forty, gaudy, shoddy, sporty, squaddie, toddy, wadi.
Bossy, flossy, frosty, glossy, posse, saucy.
Brolly, collie, dolly, folly, golly, holly, jolly, lolly, poly, trolley, volley.
[3] **Anybody**, busybody, dogsbody, everybody, nobody, somebody.

4.2.67 "--otter" (as in "hotter")
[2] blotter, dotter, gotta, globetrotter, hotter, jotter, knotter, otter, plotter, potter, rotter, spotter, squatter, terracotta, totter, trotter.

SURPRISING RHYMING:
[2] **Blocker**, doctor, knocker, locker, rocker, shocker, soccer.
Bopper, chopper, copper, cropper, dropper, hopper, poppa, popper, proper, prosper, shopper, stopper, swapper, topper, whopper.
Dodder, fodder, odder, plodder, prodder.
Blogger, flogger, hogger, jogger, lager, logger, slogger, snogger.
Clobber, cobber, jobber, robber, sobber.
Coffer, cougher, offer, proffer, scoffer.
Collar, dollar, holler, horror, scholar, squalor.
Author, bother, boxer, daughter, foster, roster, slaughter, softer.
[3] **Eavesdropper**, gobstopper, grasshopper, improper, teenybopper.

4.2.68 "--otting" (as in "spotting")
[2] blotting, clotting, dotting, globetrotting, jotting, knotting, plotting, rotting, slotting, spotting, squatting, train-spotting, trotting, yachting.

SURPRISING RHYMING:
[2] **Bopping**, chopping, clopping, dropping, flopping, hopping, lopping, mopping, opting, popping, propping, shopping, stopping, swapping, topping, whopping.
Blocking, docking, flocking, knocking, locking, mocking, rocking, shocking, stocking.
Nodding, plodding, prodding, wadding.
Bobbing, fobbing, lobbing, mobbing, robbing, sobbing, throbbing.
Blogging, flogging, hogging, jogging, logging, slogging, snogging.
Bossing, crossing, double-crossing, flossing, glossing, tossing.
Boffin, coffin, coughing, often, soften.
[3] **Eavesdropping**, namedropping, window-shopping.
Defrocking, interlocking, padlocking, unblocking, unlocking.

4.2.69 "--otted" (as in "spotted")
[2] allotted, blotted, boycotted, clotted, dotted, jotted, knotted, plotted, potted, rotted, slotted, spotted, squatted, swatted, totted, trotted, yachted.

SURPRISING RHYMING:
[2] **Nodded**, plodded, prodded, sodded, wadded.
Dogged, horrid, solid, torrid.
Assaulted, bolted, exalted, halted, revolted, salted, vaulted, wanted.
Closet, docket, goddess, got it, knock it, locket, pocket, profit, rocket, socket, sock it, sonnet, sprocket, wallet.
Daunted, flaunted, haunted, taunted, unwanted, wanted.
Chronic, conic, phonic, sonic, tonic, topic, tropic.
Melodic, methodic, periodic, spasmodic.

504

[3] **Air pocket**, hip pocket, pickpocket, skyrocket.
Absconded, bonded, corresponded, responded, unbonded.
Accosted, costed, defrosted, exhausted, faucet, frosted.
Bionic, demonic, iconic, ironic, laconic, platonic, symphonic.
[4] **Electronic**, embryonic, philharmonic, quadraphonic, stereophonic, supersonic.

4.2.70 "--otless" (as in "spotless")
[2] plotless, spotless.

SURPRISING RHYMING:
[1] **Bless**, chess, dress, guess, less, mess, press, stress, yes.
[2] **Compress**, confess, congress, obsess, oppress, outguess, possess, process, profess, thoughtless.
Cautious, chorus, conscious, faultless, flawless, fortress, goddess, godless, heartless, hottest, jobless, lawless, nauseous, noxious, obnoxious, pompous, promise, smallest, softness, solace, topless.

4.2.71 "--otten" (as in "forgotten")
[2] cotton, gotten, rotten.
[3] begotten, forgotten, ill-gotten, unforgotten.

SURPRISING RHYMING:
[2] **Autumn**, bottom, column, common, orphan, solemn.
Blotting, clotting, dotting, jotting, knotting, plotting, potting, rotting, rotten, slotting, spotting, squatting, swatting, trotting, yachting.
Bopping, chopping, dropping, flopping, hopping, mopping, opting, popping, propping, shopping, stopping, swapping, topping, whopping.
Bobbing, jobbing, lobbing, mobbing, robbing, sobbing, throbbing.
Blogging, flogging, hogging, jogging, logging, slogging, snogging.
Broaden, caution, fallen, foreign.
Blossom, coffin, coffin, coughing, often, soften.
[3] **Eavesdropping**, namedropping, window-shopping.

4.2.72 "--otto" (as in "motto")
[2] blotto, grotto, lotto, motto, risotto.

SURPRISING RHYMING:
[1] **Apollo**, bolo, follow, hollow, pronto, wallow, wallow.
Auto, bestow, chateau, gateau, photo, plateau, shadow, taco, tiptoe.
Atoll, bankroll, bargepole, beanpole, bolthole, cajole, charcoal, console, control, Creole, dustbowl, enrol/enroll (U.S.), fishbowl, flagpole, hellhole, keyhole, loophole, payroll, parole, patrol, pinhole, plughole, pothole, punchbowl.
Appalled, blackballed, enthralled, eyeballed, installed, mothballed, overhauled, recalled, snowballed, so-called, sprawled, stonewalled.
[3] **Falsetto**, Picasso, soprano, staccato, stiletto, tomato.
[4] **Avocado**, bravado, desperado, Eldorado.

4.2.73 "--otch" (as in "watch")
[1] blotch, botch, crotch, notch, scotch, splotch, swatch, watch.
[2] butterscotch, hopscotch, hotchpotch, skywatch, stopwatch, topnotch, wristwatch.

SURPRISING RHYMING:
[1] **Blot**, clot, cot, dot(s), got, hot, jot, knot(s), lot(s), not, plot(s), pot(s), rot, Scot(s), shot(s), slot, snot, spot, squat, swat, swot, tot, trot(s), watt(s), what, yacht(s).
Cosh, dosh, gosh, josh, nosh, posh, quash, slosh, squash, wash.
Dodge, lodge, splodge, stodge, dislodge.
Broth, cloth, froth, Goth, moth, troth, wrath.
Gods, Mods, nods, odds, plods, pods, prods, rods, squads, wads.
[2] **Awash**, car wash, eyewash, hogwash, mouthwash, whitewash.

Blackspot(s), bloodshot, boycott, cannot, crackpot(s), earshot, forgot, foxtrot, fusspot, gunshot(s), hotpot, hotshot(s), hotspot(s), jackpot, mailshot(s), mascot(s), moonshot(s), mugshot(s), nightspot(s), potshot(s), robot(s), sexpot, slingshot, slipknot, snapshot(s), somewhat, sunspot(s), teapot(s), upshot.
[3] Apricot(s), Camelot, chimneypot(s), coffeepot(s), diddly-squat, flowerpot(s), forget-me-not(s), Lancelot, overshot, polka dot(s).

4.2.74 "--otched" (as in "watched")
[1] blotched, botched, notched, scotched, watched.

SURPRISING RHYMING:
[1] Blotch, botch, crotch, notch, scotch, splotch, swatch, watch.
Blot, clot, cot, dot, got, hot, jot, knot, lot, not, plot, pot, rot, Scot, shot, slot, snot, spot, squat, swat, swot, tot, trot, watt, what, yacht.
Coshed, joshed, quashed, sloshed, squashed, washed, whitewashed.
Bossed, cost, crossed, flossed, frost, glossed, lost, tossed.
Aloft, coughed, croft, cross, loft, oft, soft, waft.
Adopt, bopped, chopped, cropped, dropped, flopped, hopped, lopped, mopped, opt, plopped, popped, propped, shopped, slopped, stopped, stropped, swapped, topped.
Blocked, clocked, crocked, docked, flocked, hocked, knocked, locked, mocked, pocked, rocked, shocked, socked, stocked.
Bought, brought, caught, fought, fraught, naught, ought, sought, taught, thought, wrought.
[2] Butterscotch, hopscotch, hotchpotch, skywatch, stopwatch, topnotch, wristwatch.

4.2.75 "--otching" (as in "watching")
[2] blotching, botching, notching, scotching, watching.

SURPRISING RHYMING:
[2] Joshing, squashing, washing, brainwashing.
Boxing, detoxing, foxing, outfoxing, shadowboxing.
Bossing, crossing, double-crossing, flossing, glossing, tossing.
Dodging, lodging, splodging, dislodging.
Blotting, dotting, globetrotting, jotting, knotting, plotting, potting, rotting, slotting, spotting, squatting, train-spotting, trotting, yachting.
Blocking, clocking, crocking, docking, flocking, knocking, locking, mocking, rocking, shocking, stocking, walking.
Coffin, coughing, often, soften.
Bopping, chopping, dropping, flopping, hopping, mopping, popping, propping, shopping, stopping, swapping, topping, whopping.
Daunting, flaunting, haunting, jaunting, taunting, wanting.
Auction, concoction, launching, scorching, torching.
[3] Eavesdropping, namedropping, window-shopping.
Assaulting, exalting, pole-vaulting, revolting, somersaulting.

4.2.76 "--oth" (as in "cloth")
[1] broth, cloth, froth, Goth, moth, troth, wrath.
[2] backcloth, behemoth, betroth, broadcloth, dishcloth, facecloth, J-cloth, loincloth, oilcloth, tablecloth.

SURPRISING RHYMING:
[1] Aloft, bakeoff, cough, croft, loft, off, oft, soft, toff, waft.
Forth, fourth, henceforth, north.
Bop, chop, clop, cop, crop, drop, flop, fop, hop, lop, mop, op, plop, pop, prop, shop, slop, sop, stop, strop, swap, top.
Boss, 'cos, cross, dross, floss, gloss, joss, loss, moss, sauce, toss.
Cause, clause, claws, draws, drawers, flaws, gauze, gnaws, jaws, laws, Oz, pause, paws, squaws, straws, was, yours.
Blot, clot, cot, dot, got, hot, jot, knot, lot, not, plot, pot, rot, Scot, shot, slot, snot,

spot, squat, swat, swot, tot, trot, watt, what, yacht.
[2] **Atop**, backdrop, bebop, bellhop, bookshop, bus-stop, car-hop, coin-op, co-op, cough drop, desktop, dewdrop, doorstop, eavesdrop, face-swap, flat-top, flip-flop, full stop, hardtop, hilltop, hip-hop, laptop, namedrop, nonstop, pawnshop, raindrop, rooftop, screwtop, sweatshop, sweetshop, teardrop, tea-shop, tip-top, toyshop, treetop.
Across, chaos, cosmos, crisscross, Eros, ethos, kudos, pathos.
Applause, because, indoors, outdoors, Santa Claus.
Blackspot, bloodshot, boycott, cannot, crackpot, despot, earshot, forgot, fusspot, gunshot, hotpot, hotshot, hotspot, jackpot, mailshot, mascot, moonshot, mugshot, nightspot, potshot, robot, sexpot, slipknot, snapshot, somewhat, sunspot, teapot, upshot, whatnot.
[3] **Barbershop**, coffeeshop, lollipop, soda pop, spinning-top, whistle-stop, window-shop.
Albatross, candyfloss, double-cross, rally-cross.
Apricot, Camelot, coffeepot, diddly-squat, flowerpot, forget-me-not, kilowatt, polka dot.

4.2.77 "--ox" (as in "box")

[1] blocks, box, chocs, clocks, cox, docks, fox, frocks, ox, pox, knocks, locks, mocks, rocks, shocks, smocks, socks, stocks, woks.
[2] bandbox, brainbox, breadbox, detox, dreadlocks, gearbox, hatbox, horsebox, icebox, jukebox, mailbox, matchbox, outfox, padlocks, peacocks, paintbox, pillbox, sandbox, shadowbox, shoebox, smallpox, snuffbox, soapbox, soundbox, squeezebox, strongbox, toolbox, workbox.
[3] chatterbox, equinox, Goldilocks, letter box, orthodox, paradox.

SURPRISING RHYMING:
[1] **Block**, choc, clock, crock, doc, dock, flock, frock, hock, knock, loch, lock, mock, pock, rock, schlock, shock, smock, sock, wok.
Blotch, botch, crotch, notch, scotch, Scotch, splotch, swatch, watch.
Corks, dorks, forks, hawks, squawks, stalks, storks, talks, walks.
Chops, cops, crops, drops, flops, hops, mops, pops, props, shops, slops, stops, tops.
Blots, dots, knots, lots, plots, pots, rots, Scots, shots, slots, spots, squats, swats, trots, watts, yachts.
Jobs, knobs, mobs, robs, slobs, snobs, sobs, swabs, throbs, yobs.
Gods, nods, odds, plods, pods, rods, sods.
Blogs, clogs, cogs, dogs, flogs, frogs, hogs, jogs, logs, snogs, togs.
Bossed, cost, crossed, flossed, frost, glossed, lost, tossed.
Boss, 'cos, cross, dross, floss, gloss, joss, loss, moss, sauce, toss.
Cosh, dosh, gosh, josh, nosh, posh, quash, slosh, squash, wash.
[2] **Ad hoc**, amok, armlock, Bangkok, baroque, bedrock, deadlock, epoch, gridlock, Hitchcock, laughing stock, o'clock, padlock, roadblock, shamrock, shell shock, sunblock, tick-tock, unlock, Van Gogh, warlock, wedlock, windsock, Woodstock.
Deathwatch, hopscotch, hotchpotch, skywatch, stopwatch, topnotch, wristwatch.
Accost, defrost, exhaust, double-crossed, riposte, star-crossed.
Bookshops, desktops, doorstops, eavesdrops, flip-flops, hilltops, laptops, lollipops, raindrops, rooftops, teardrops, toyshops, treetops.
Blackspots, boycotts, crackpots, fusspots, gunshots, hotshots, hotspots, jackpots, mascots, nightspots, robots, snapshots.
Bulldogs, bullfrogs, hedgehogs, hotdogs, lapdogs, roadhogs, sandhogs, seadogs, sheepdogs, unclogs, underdogs, watchdogs.
Across, chaos, cosmos, crisscross, Eros, ethos, kudos, pathos.
Awash, car wash, eyewash, hogwash, mouthwash, whitewash.
[3] **Aftershock**, chock-a-block, laughing stock, poppycock, shuttlecock, stumbling block.
Chimneypots, coffeepots, flowerpots, forget-me-nots, polka dots.
Albatross, candyfloss, double-cross, rally-cross.

4.2.78 "--oz" (as in "because")

[1] 'coz, cause, clause, claws, draws, drawers, flaws, gauze, gnaws, jaws, laws, Oz, pause, paws, squaws, straws, was, yours.
[2] applause, because, indoors, outdoors, Santa Claus.

SURPRISING RHYMING:
[1] **Coarse**, course, force, hoarse, horse, Morse.
Bores, doors, floors, force, oars, pores, pours, roars, scores, snores, shores, soars, sores, stores, wars.
Boss, 'cos, cross, dross, floss, gloss, joss, loss, moss, sauce, toss.
Bossed, cost, crossed, flossed, frost, glossed, lost, tossed.
Blocks, box, chocs, clocks, cox, docks, fox, frocks, ox, pox, knocks, locks, mocks, rocks, shocks, smocks, socks, stocks, woks.
Chops, cops, crops, drops, flops, hops, mops, pops, props, shops, slops, stops, tops.
Dots, hots, knots, lots, plots, pots, rots, Scots, shots, slots, spots, squats, swats, trots, watts, yachts.
[2] **Divorce**, endorse, enforce, recourse, reinforce, remorse.
Across, chaos, cosmos, crisscross, Eros, ethos, kudos, pathos.
Adores, deplores, downpours, drugstores, explores, eyesores, ignores, indoors, outdoors, outpours, restores.
Awash, car wash, eyewash, hogwash, mouthwash, whitewash.
Bandbox, brainbox, breadbox, detox, dreadlocks, gearbox, hatbox, horsebox, icebox, jukebox, mailbox, matchbox, outfox, padlocks, peacocks, paintbox, pillbox, sandbox, shadowbox, shoebox, snuffbox, soapbox, soundbox, squeezebox, strongbox, toolbox.
Bookshops, desktops, doorstops, eavesdrops, flip-flops, hilltops, laptops, lollipops, raindrops, rooftops, teardrops, toyshops, treetops.
Accost, defrost, exhaust, double-crossed, riposte, star-crossed.
Chimneypots, coffeepots, flowerpots, forget-me-nots, polka dots.
[3] **Carnivores**, commodores, dinosaurs, matadors, meteors, stevedores, sycamores, troubadours, underscores.
Chatterbox, equinox, Goldilocks, letter box, orthodox, paradox.
Albatross, candyfloss, double-cross, rally-cross.

4.3 "or" (as in "for")

4.3.1 "--or" (as in "for")

[1] awe, boar, bore, chore, claw, core, corps, door, draw, drawer, flaw, floor, for, fore, four, gnaw, gore, jaw, law, lore, more, nor, oar, o'er, or, ore, paw, pore, pour, raw, roar, saw, score, snore, shore, soar, sore, store, squaw, straw, swore, thaw, tore, war, whore, wore, yore, your, you're.
[2] abhor, adore, amore, ashore, before, bylaw, centaur, coleslaw, condor, décor, deplore, downpour, drugstore, encore, explore, eyesore, folklore, footsore, foresaw, furor, galore, guffaw, hacksaw, hardcore, heehaw, ignore, implore, indoor, jackdaw, jigsaw, mentor, offshore, outdoor, outlaw, outpour, postwar, prewar, rapport, restore, rickshaw, rigour/rigor (U.S.), seashore, seesaw, señor, sensor, signor, therefore, trapdoor, uproar, vendor, wherefore, withdraw.
[3] anymore, carnivore, commodore, corridor, dinosaur, evermore, forevermore, furthermore, humidor, Labrador, man-o'-war, matador, megastore, meteor, nevermore, overawe, petit fours, picador, pinafore, semaphore, sophomore, stevedore, superstore, sycamore, toreador, troubadour, tug of war, two-by-four, underscore.

SURPRISING RHYMING:
[1] **Bores**, chores, claws, doors, draws, drawers, flaws, floors, force, jaws, laws, oars, paws, pores, pours, roars, scores, snores, shores, soars, sores, stores, wars, yours.
Awed, board, bored, broad, chord, fjord, flawed, floored, ford, fraud, hoard, horde, lord, laud, oared, pored, poured, roared, scored, snored, soared, stored, sword, ward.
Dorm, form, norm, storm, swarm, warm.
Are, ah, bar, bra, blah, car, char, czar, dah, far, ha, hah, jar, la, ma, mar, noir, pa, par, scar, spa, spar, star, tar, tsar, yah.
Bought, brought, caught, court, fort, fought, fraught, naught/nought, ought, port, short, snort, sort, sought, sport, taught, taut, thought, thwart.
Born, borne, brawn, corn, dawn, drawn, fawn, horn, lawn, morn, mourn, pawn, porn, prawn, sawn, scorn, shorn, spawn, sworn, thorn, torn, warn, worn, yawn.
[2] **Adores**, deplores, downpours, drugstores, encores, explores, eyesores, rickshaws,

508

ignores, indoors, in-laws, jigsaws, mentors, outdoors, outlaws, outpours, restores.
Abhorred, aboard, accord, adored, afford, award, billboard, blackboard, cardboard, chessboard, clipboard, dartboard, dashboard, deplored, explored, floorboard, headboard, ignored, keyboard, landlord, onboard, record, restored, reward, scoreboard, sideboard, skateboard, snowboard, springboard, surfboard, switchboard.
Barnstorm, brainstorm, conform, firestorm, inform, lukewarm, misinform, perform, platform, rainstorm, reform, sandstorm, snowstorm, transform, uniform.
Abort, airport, assort, carport, cavort, cohort, consort, contort, deport, distort, distraught, escort, export, forecourt, forethought, import, onslaught, outfought, passport, purport, report, resort, retort, seaport, self-taught, spoilsport, support, transport.
Acorn, adorn, airborne, careworn, firstborn, foghorn, forewarn, forlorn, greenhorn, lovelorn, mid-morn, newborn, outworn, popcorn, reborn, sweetcorn, time-worn, unborn, unicorn, war-torn, withdrawn.
[3] **Carnivores**, commodores, corridors, dinosaurs, matadors, meteors, stevedores, sycamores, troubadours, underscores.
Chequerboard/checkerboard (U.S.), clapperboard, diving board, harpsichord, notice board, overawed, overboard, smorgasbord, storyboard, unexplored, untoward.
Chloroform, outperform, thunderstorm, underperform.
Aforethought, afterthought, astronaut, cosmonaut, juggernaut.

4.3.2 "--oarer" (as in "aura")
[2] aura, borer, scorer, flora, roarer, snorer, pourer.
[3] adorer, angora, explorer, fedora, goalscorer, ignorer, aurora, restorer, signora.

SURPRISING RHYMING:
[2] **Boarder**, border, broader, hoarder, order, warder.
Daughter, snorter, porter, quarter, shorter, slaughter, sorter, water.
Corner, fauna, mourner, sauna, scorner, warner, yawner.
Dormer, former, korma, stormer, trauma, warmer.
Corker, gawker, hawker, squawker, stalker, talker, walker.
Flaunter, haunter, saunter, taunter.
[3] **Court order**, defrauder, disorder, mail order, marauder, recorder.
Backwater, breakwater, freshwater, granddaughter, importer, manslaughter, reporter, supporter, transporter, underwater.
Barnstormer, conformer, informer, performer, reformer, transformer.
Back talker, deerstalker, jaywalker, New Yorker, nightwalker, skywalker, sleepwalker, smooth-talker, streetwalker, sweet-talker.

4.3.3 "--oral" (as in "choral")
[2] aural, choral, coral, floral, immoral, laurel, moral, oral, quarrel.

SURPRISING RHYMING:
[1] **All**, ball, bawl, brawl, call, crawl, doll, drawl, fall, gall, hall, haul, loll, maul, mall, moll, pall, scrawl, shawl, small, sprawl, squall, stall, tall, trawl, wall.
[2] **Awful**, formal, lawful, mournful, normal, lawful, scornful.
Baseball, befall, birdcall, blackball, catcall, catchall, dance hall, downfall, enthral/enthrall (U.S.), eyeball, fireball, firewall, football, goofball, handball, hardball, highball, install, jackal, landfall, meatball, mothball, nightfall, oddball, paintball, pinball, pitfall, rainfall, recall, rollcall, shorthaul, snowball, snowfall, stonewall, windfall.
[3] **Alcohol**, all in all, basketball, cannonball, free-for-all, know-it-all, overall, overhaul, protocol, volleyball, waterfall, wherewithal.
Abnormal, informal, paranormal.

4.3.4 "--orch" (as in "porch")
debauch, blow-torch, porch, scorch, torch.

SURPRISING RHYMING:
[1] **Courts**, ports, shorts, snorts, sorts, sports, thoughts, thwarts.
Coarse, course, force, gorse, hoarse, horse, Morse, sauce, source.

Boards, broads, chords, hoards, hordes, swords, wards.
Bought, brought, caught, court, fought, fraught, ought, port, short, snort, sort, sought, sport, taught, taut, thought, thwart.
[2] **Airports**, cavorts, cohorts, consorts, contorts, distorts, escorts, exports, imports, passports, reports, resorts, supports, transports.
Divorce, endorse/indorse (U.S.), enforce, reinforce, remorse.
Affords, applauds, awards, billboards, blackboards, dashboards, floorboards, keyboards, landlords, records, rewards, towards.
Abort, airport, assort, carport, cavort, cohort, contort, distort, distraught, escort, forecourt, forethought, import, onslaught, outfought, passport, report, resort, self-taught, spoilsport, support, transport.
[3] **Afterthought(s)**, astronaut(s), cosmonaut(s), juggernaut(s).

4.3.5 "--orchard" (as in "orchard")
[2] orchard, tortured.

SURPRISING RHYMING:
[2] **Courted**, snorted, sorted, sported, thwarted.
Boarded, hoarded, lauded, morbid, orchid, orbit, sordid.
Daunted, flaunted, haunted, taunted, wanted.
Awkward, forward, homeward, onward, shoreward, straightforward.
Bordered, cornered, ordered, sauntered, slaughtered, watered.
[3] **Aborted**, assorted, cavorted, contorted, distorted, escorted, exported, imported, reported, resorted, supported, transported.
Afforded, applauded, awarded, defrauded, recorded, rewarded.

4.3.6 "--orching" (as in "scorching")
debauching, scorching, torching.

SURPRISING RHYMING:
[2] **Causing**, coursing, forcing, pausing, saucing, sourcing.
Courting, snorting, sorting, sporting, thwarting.
Daunting, flaunting, haunting, jaunting, taunting, vaunting, wanting.
Awning, dawning, fawning, morning, mourning, pawning, scorning, spawning, sworn-in, warning, yawning.
[3] **Divorcing**, endorsing/indorsing (U.S.), enforcing, reinforcing.
Aborting, cavorting, contorting, distorting, escorting, extorting, reporting, resorting, supporting, transporting.
According, affording, applauding, awarding, boarding, defrauding, hoarding, lauding, marauding, recording, rewarding.
Adoring, deploring, downpouring, exploring, ignoring, imploring, mentoring, outpouring, restoring, underscoring.

4.3.7 "--ord" (as in "sword")
[1] awed, board, bored, broad, chord, fjord, flawed, floored, ford, fraud, hoard, horde, lord, laud, oared, pored, poured, roared, scored, snored, soared, stored, sword, ward.
[2] abhorred, aboard, abroad, accord, adored, afford, applaud, award, billboard, blackboard, cardboard, chessboard, chipboard, clapboard, clipboard, concord, dartboard, dashboard, defraud, deplored, discord, explored, floorboard, four-doored, headboard, ignored, implored, inboard, keyboard, landlord, maraud, milord, onboard, outboard, record, restored, reward, ripcord, scoreboard, seaboard, sideboard, skateboard, snowboard, springboard, surfboard, switchboard, toward, two-doored, warlord.
[3] chequerboard/checkerboard (U.S.), clapperboard, diving board, harpsichord, notice board, overawed, overboard, overlord, sandwich board, shuffleboard, smorgasbord, storyboard, unexplored, untoward.

SURPRISING RHYMING:
[1] **Awe**, bore, chore, claw, core, corps, door, draw, drawer, flaw, floor, for, fore, four, gnaw, jaw, law, more, nor, oar, or, paw, pour, raw, roar, saw, score, snore, shore,

510

soar, sore, store, straw, swore, thaw, tore, war, whore, wore, yore, your, you're.
Bought, brought, caught, court, fought, fraught, ought, port, short, snort, sort, sought, sport, taught, taut, thought, thwart.
Formed, stormed, swarmed, warmed.
Daunt, flaunt, font, gaunt, haunt, jaunt, taunt, vaunt, want.
Born, borne, brawn, corn, dawn, drawn, fawn, horn, lawn, morn, mourn, pawn, porn, prawn, sawn, scorn, shorn, spawn, sworn, thorn, torn, warn, worn, yawn.
[2] **Adore**, amore, ashore, before, condor, décor, deplore, downpour, drugstore, encore, explore, eyesore, folklore, footsore, foresaw, furor, galore, guffaw, hardcore, ignore, implore, indoor, jigsaw, mentor, offshore, outdoor, outlaw, outpour, postwar, prewar, rapport, restore, rickshaw, seashore, seesaw, señor, sensor, signor, therefore, trapdoor, uproar, vendor, wherefore, withdraw.
Airport, cavort, contort, distort, distraught, escort, export, forecourt, forethought, import, onslaught, outfought, passport, report, resort, self-taught, spoilsport, support, transport.
Barnstormed, brainstormed, conformed, informed, misinformed, performed, reformed, transformed, uniformed.
Acorn, adorn, airborne, careworn, firstborn, foghorn, forewarn, forlorn, greenhorn, lovelorn, mid-morn, newborn, outworn, popcorn, reborn, sweetcorn, time-worn, unborn, unicorn, war-torn, withdrawn.
[3] **Anymore**, corridor, dinosaur, evermore, forevermore, man-o'-war, matador, megastore, meteor, overawe, picador, pinafore, semaphore, sophomore, superstore, sycamore, toreador, troubadour, tug of war.
Aforethought, afterthought, astronaut, cosmonaut, juggernaut.

4.3.8 "--order" (as in "border")
[2] boarder, border, broader, hoarder, order, warder.
[3] court order, defrauder, disorder, mail order, marauder, recorder.

SURPRISING RHYMING:
[2] **Corner**, fauna, mourner, sauna, scorner, warner, yawner.
Aura, borer, scorer, flora, snorer, pourer.
Dormer, former, korma, stormer, trauma, warmer.
Corker, gawker, hawker, squawker, stalker, talker, walker.
Daughter, snorter, porter, quarter, shorter, slaughter, sorter, water.
[3] **Barnstormer**, bedwarmer, conformer, informer, performer, reformer, transformer.
Back talker, deerstalker, jaywalker, New Yorker, nightwalker, skywalker, sleepwalker, smooth-talker, streetwalker, sweet-talker.
Backwater, breakwater, exporter, freshwater, granddaughter, importer, manslaughter, reporter, supporter, transporter, underwater.
[3] **Explorer**, fedora, goalscorer, ignorer, aurora, restorer, signora.

4.3.9 "--orded" (as in "awarded")
[2] boarded, hoarded, lauded, morbid, orchid, orbit, sordid.
[3] afforded, applauded, awarded, defrauded, recorded, rewarded.

SURPRISING RHYMING:
[2] **Daunted**, flaunted, haunted, taunted, wanted.
Courted, orbit, snorted, sorted, sported, thwarted, torrid.
[3] **Aborted**, assorted, cavorted, contorted, distorted, escorted, exported, imported, reported, resorted, supported, transported.

4.3.10 "--ordered" (as in "ordered")
[2] bordered, ordered.

SURPRISING RHYMING:
[2] **Cornered**, sauntered, quartered, slaughtered, watered.
Boarded, hoarded, lauded, morbid, orchid, orbit, sordid.
Awkward, forward, northward, orchard, straightforward, tortured.
Altered, collared, hollered, faltered., offered.

[3] **Afforded**, applauded, awarded, defrauded, recorded, rewarded.

4.3.11 "--ording" (as in "recording")
according, affording, applauding, awarding, boarding, defrauding, hoarding, lauding, marauding, recording, rewarding.

SURPRISING RHYMING:
[2] **Boring**, pouring, roaring, scoring, snoring, soaring, warring.
Courting, snorting, sorting, sporting, thwarting.
Forming, storming, swarming, warming.
Daunting, flaunting, haunting, taunting, wanting.
Awning, dawning, fawning, morning, mourning, pawning, scorning, spawning, sworn-in, warning, yawning.
Bawling, brawling, calling, crawling, drawling, falling, hauling, mauling, scrawling, sprawling, squalling, stalling, trawling.
[3] **Adoring**, deploring, downpouring, exploring, ignoring, imploring, mentoring, outpouring, restoring, underscoring, withdrawing.
Aborting, cavorting, contorting, distorting, escorting, extorting, reporting, resorting, supporting, transporting.
Barnstorming, brainstorming, conforming, housewarming, informing, misinforming, performing, reforming, transforming.
Appalling, bankrolling, blackballing, cajoling, consoling, controlling, enthralling, freefalling, mothballing, name calling, patrolling, recalling, snowballing, stonewalling.

4.3.12 "--orful" (as in "awful")
[2] awful, lawful, unlawful.

SURPRISING RHYMING:
[2] **Aural**, choral, coral, floral, formal, immoral, laurel, moral, mournful, normal, novel, oral, quarrel, scornful, thoughtful.
Dawdle, doddle, fondle, modal, model, molly-coddle, noddle, remodel, role model, rondel, swaddle, toddle, twaddle, yodel, waddle.
Bauble, bobble, cobble, gobble, hobble, nobble, squabble, wobble.
Colossal, fossil, gospel, hostile, jostle, morsel.
[3] **Abnormal**, informal, immortal, paranormal.

4.3.13 "--oring" (as in "roaring")
[2] boring, flooring, poring, pouring, roaring, scoring, snoring, soaring, storing, warring.
[3] adoring, deploring, downpouring, exploring, ignoring, imploring, mentoring, outpouring, restoring, underscoring.

SURPRISING RHYMING:
[2] **Glory**, gory, hoary, sorry, storey, story.
Boarding, forming, hoarding, lauding, storming, swarming, warming.
Bawling, brawling, calling, crawling, drawling, falling, hauling, mauling, scrawling, sprawling, squalling, stalling, trawling.
Clawing, drawing, gnawing, jawing, pawing, sawing, thawing.
Courting, shorting, snorting, sorting, sporting, thwarting.
Dawning, fawning, morning, mourning, pawning, scorning, sworn-in, warning, yawning.
Causing, coursing, forcing, saucing, sourcing.
[3] **According**, affording, applauding, awarding, defrauding, marauding, recording, rewarding, skateboarding, snowboarding.
Barnstorming, brainstorming, conforming, housewarming, informing, misinforming, performing, reforming, transforming.
Appalling, bankrolling, befalling, blackballing, cajoling, consoling, controlling, enthralling, freefalling, mothballing, name calling, patrolling, recalling, snowballing, stonewalling.
Cavorting, distorting, escorting, extorting, reporting, resorting, supporting, transporting.

*

4.3.14 "--orick" (as in "historic")
[3] caloric, euphoric, historic, meteoric.

SURPRISING RHYMING:
[1] **Brick**, chick, click, crick, dick, flick, hick, kick, lick, nick, pick, prick, quick, sic, sick, slick, stick, thick, tic, tick, trick, wick.
Clicked, flicked, kicked, licked, picked, pricked, strict, ticked, tricked.
[2] **Arsenic**, broomstick, chopstick, con trick, drumstick, heartsick, homesick, joss stick, lipstick, lovesick, seasick, toothpick, yardstick.
Addict, conflict, contradict, convict, depict, evict, predict, restrict.
[3] **Candlestick**, candlewick, double quick, heretic, limerick, lunatic, maverick, politic, rhetoric, walking-stick.

4.3.15 "--ork" (as in "walk")
[1] chalk, cork, dork, fork, gawk, hawk, pork, squawk, stalk, stork, talk, torque, walk.
[2] back talk, beanstalk, boardwalk, cakewalk, catwalk, crosstalk, crosswalk, jaywalk, mohawk, newshawk, nighthawk, pep talk, pitchfork, shoptalk, sidewalk, skywalk, sleepwalk, small talk, smooth-talk, spacewalk, sweet-talk, tomahawk, uncork.

SURPRISING RHYMING:
[1] **Chalked**, forked, hawked, squawked, stalked, talked, walked.
Bought, brought, caught, court, fort, fought, fraught, nought, ought, port, short, snort, sort, sought, sport, taught, taut, thought, thwart.
[2] **Jaywalked**, sleepwalked, uncorked.
Airport, assort, cavort, distort, distraught, escort, export, forecourt, forethought, import, onslaught, outfought, passport, report, resort, self-taught, spoilsport, support, transport.
Ad-hoc, bedrock, deadlock, gridlock, o'clock, padlock, peacock, roadblock, shellshock, unlock, wall clock, warlock, Woodstock.
[3] **Afterthought**, astronaut, cosmonaut, juggernaut.

4.3.16 "--orker" (as in "walker")
[2] corker, gawker, hawker, squawker, stalker, talker, walker.
[3] back talker, deerstalker, jaywalker, New Yorker, nightwalker, skywalker, sleepwalker, smooth-talker, streetwalker, sweet-talker.

SURPRISING RHYMING:
[2] **Daughter**, oughta, porter, quarter, shorter, slaughter, water.
Blocker, docker, knocker, loch, locker, mocker, rocker, shocker.
Boarder, border, broader, hoarder, order, warder.
Corner, fauna, former, mourner, sauna, scorner, stormer, trauma, warmer, warner.
Flaunter, haunter, saunter, taunter.
Longer, sombre/somber (U.S.), stronger.
[3] **Backwater**, breakwater, freshwater, granddaughter, importer, manslaughter, reporter, supporter, transporter, underwater.
Court order, defrauder, disorder, mail order, marauder, recorder.
Barnstormer, bedwarmer, informer, performer, reformer, transformer.

4.3.17 "--orless" (as in "flawless")
[2] coreless, flawless, jawless, lawless, scoreless, shoreless.

SURPRISING RHYMING:
[2] **Smallest**, tallest.
Courses, forces, horses, sauces, sources.
[3] **Divorces**, enforces, racehorses, reinforces, resources, seahorses.

4.3.18 "--orl" (as in "fall")
[1] all, ball, bawl, brawl, call, crawl, doll, drawl, fall, gall, hall, haul, loll, maul, mall, moll, pall, scrawl, shawl, small, sprawl, squall, stall, tall, trawl, wall.
[2] appal/appall (U.S.), baseball, befall, birdcall, blackball, bookstall, catcall, catchall,

dance hall, downfall, enthral/enthrall (U.S.), eyeball, fireball, firewall, football, goofball, handball, hardball, highball, install, jackal, landfall, meatball, miscall, mothball, nightfall, oddball, paintball, pinball, pitfall, punchbowl, rainfall, recall, rollcall, sea wall, shorthaul, snowball, snowfall, stonewall, windfall.
[3] alcohol, all in all, basketball, cannonball, free-for-all, know-it-all, overall, overhaul, protocol, volleyball, waterfall, wherewithal.

SURPRISING RHYMING:
[1] **Bald**, balled, bawled, brawled, called, crawled, drawled, hauled, lolled, mauled, scald, scrawled, sprawled, stalled, trawled, walled.
Bolt, colt, dolt, fault, halt, jolt, malt, moult, salt, vault, volt.
Awe, bore, chore, claw, core, door, draw, drawer, flaw, floor, for, fore, four, gnaw, gore, jaw, law, more, nor, oar, or, paw, pour, raw, roar, saw, score, snore, shore, soar, sore, store, straw, swore, thaw, tore, war, whore, wore, yore, your, you're.
[2] **Appalled**, enthralled, eyeballed, installed, mothballed, overhauled, recalled, snowballed, so-called, sprawled, stonewalled.
Assault, cobalt, default, exalt, revolt, somersault, thunderbolt, unbolt.
Atoll, bankroll, bargepole, beanpole, befall, bolthole, cajole, control, enrol/enroll (U.S.), fishbowl, flagpole, freefall, hellhole, keyhole, loophole, payroll, parole, patrol, peephole.
Adore, amore, ashore, before, décor, deplore, downpour, drugstore, encore, explore, eyesore, folklore, footsore, foresaw, furor, galore, hardcore, ignore, implore, indoor, jigsaw, mentor, offshore, outdoor, outlaw, outpour, postwar, prewar, rapport, restore, rickshaw, seashore, seesaw, señor, sensor, therefore, trapdoor, uproar, withdraw.

4.3.19 "--orling" (as in "falling")
[2] balling, bawling, brawling, calling, crawling, drawling, falling, hauling, mauling, scrawling, sprawling, squalling, stalling, trawling.
[3] appalling, bankrolling, befalling, blackballing, cajoling, consoling, controlling, enrolling, enthralling, freefalling, installing, mothballing, name calling, patrolling, recalling, snowballing, stonewalling.

SURPRISING RHYMING:
[2] **All in**, balding, folding, holding, moulding/molding (U.S.), scolding.
Causing, coursing, forcing, pausing, saucing, sourcing.
Clawing, drawing, gnawing, jawing, pawing, sawing, thawing.
Dawning, fawning, morning, mourning, pawning, spawning, sworn-in, warning, yawning.
Boring, clawing, drawing, gnawing, pawing, pouring, roaring, sawing, scoring, shoring, snoring, soaring, storing, thawing, warring.
Adorning, awning, dawning, fawning, forewarning, mid-morning, morning, mourning, scorning, spawning, sworn-in, warning, yawning.
Daunting, flaunting, haunting, jaunting, nothing, taunting, wanting.
Bossing, crossing, flossing, glossing, rejoicing, tossing, voicing
[3] **Blindfolding**, cajoling, handholding, unfolding, upholding, withholding.
Assaulting, exalting, revolting, revolving, somersaulting.
Adoring, deploring, exploring, ignoring, outpouring, restoring.

4.3.20 "--orled" (as in "called")
[1] bald, balled, bawled, brawled, called, crawled, drawled, hauled, lolled, mauled, scald, scrawled, sprawled, stalled, trawled, walled.
[2] appalled, blackballed, enthralled, eyeballed, installed, mothballed, overhauled, recalled, snowballed, so-called, sprawled, stonewalled.

SURPRISING RHYMING:
[1] **All**, ball, bawl, brawl, call, crawl, doll, drawl, fall, hall, haul, maul, mall, moll, pall, scrawl, shawl, small, sprawl, squall, stall, tall, trawl, wall.
Formed, stormed, swarmed, warmed.
Dawned, fawned, horned, lawned, mourned, pawned, scorned, warned, yawned.
Awed, board, bored, broad, chord, fjord, flawed, floored, ford, fraud, gored, hoard, horde, lord, poured, roared, scored, snored, soared, stored, sword, ward.

[2] **Appal/appall** (U.S.), baseball, befall, birdcall, blackball, catcall, catchall, downfall, enthral/enthrall (U.S.), eyeball, fireball, firewall, football, goofball, handball, hardball, highball, install, jackal, landfall, meatball, mothball, nightfall, oddball, paintball, pinball, pitfall, rainfall, recall, rollcall, shorthaul, snowball, snowfall, stonewall, windfall.
Barnstormed, brainstormed, conformed, informed, misinformed, performed, reformed, transformed, uniformed.
Aboard, abroad, accord, adored, afford, applaud, award, billboard, blackboard, cardboard, chessboard, clipboard, concord, dartboard, dashboard, defraud, deplored, discord, explored, floorboard, headboard, ignored, keyboard, landlord, maraud, onboard, outboard, record, restored, reward, ripcord, scoreboard, sideboard, skateboard, snowboard, springboard, surfboard, switchboard, toward.
[3] **Alcohol**, all in all, basketball, cannonball, free-for-all, know-it-all, overall, overhaul, protocol, volleyball, waterfall, wherewithal.

4.3.21 "--orlest" (as in "tallest")
[2] smallest, tallest.

SURPRISING RHYMING:
[2] **Baldest**, flawless, lawless, scoreless, shoreless, shortest, warmest.
Abreast, addressed, armrest, arrest, behest, bequest, caressed, confessed, contest, conquest, depressed, detest, digest, digressed, distressed, expressed, headrest, impressed, infest, inquest, invest, oppressed, possessed, progressed, protest, repressed, request, suggest, suppressed, transgressed, undressed, unrest, well-dressed.

4.3.22 "--olding" (as in "balding")
[2] balding, scalding.

SURPRISING RHYMING:
[1] **Halting**, salting, vaulting.
Daunting, flaunting, haunting, jaunting, nothing, taunting, wanting.
All in, folding, holding, moulding/molding (U.S.), scolding.
Dawning, fawning, morning, mourning, pawning, scorning, sworn-in, warning, yawning.
Forming, storming, swarming, warming.
Bawling, brawling, calling, crawling, drawling, falling, hauling, mauling, scrawling, sprawling, squalling, stalling, trawling.
Boring, flooring, pouring, roaring, scoring, snoring, soaring, warring.
[3] **Appalling**, bankrolling, befalling, blackballing, cajoling, consoling, controlling, enthralling, freefalling, mothballing, name calling, patrolling, recalling, stonewalling.
According, affording, applauding, awarding, boarding, defrauding, hoarding, lauding, marauding, recording, rewarding.
Assaulting, exalting, revolting, revolving, somersaulting.
Barnstorming, brainstorming, conforming, housewarming, informing, misinforming, performing, reforming, transforming.

4.3.23 "--orm" (as in "warm")
[1] dorm, form, norm, storm, swarm, warm.
[2] barnstorm, brainstorm, conform, deform, firestorm, inform, lukewarm, misinform, perform, platform, rainstorm, reform, sandstorm, snowstorm, transform, uniform.
[3] chloroform, outperform, thunderstorm, underperform.

SURPRISING RHYMING:
[1] **Formed**, stormed, swarmed, warmed.
Born, borne, brawn, corn, dawn, drawn, fawn, horn, lawn, morn, mourn, pawn, porn, prawn, sawn, scorn, shorn, spawn, sworn, thorn, torn, warn, worn, yawn.
Dawned, fawned, horned, mourned, pawned, scorned, thorned, warned, yawned.
Awe, bore, chore, claw, core, corps, door, draw, drawer, flaw, floor, for, fore, four, gnaw, jaw, law, more, nor, oar, or, paw, pour, raw, roar, saw, score, snore, shore, soar, sore, store, straw, swore, thaw, tore, war, whore, wore, yore, your, you're.
[2] **Barnstormed**, brainstormed, informed, performed, reformed, transformed, uniformed.

515

Acorn, adorn(ed), airborne, careworn, firstborn, foghorn, forewarn(ed), forlorn, greenhorn, lovelorn, mid-morn, newborn, outworn, popcorn, reborn, sweetcorn, time-worn, unborn, unicorn, war-torn, withdrawn.
Adore, amore, ashore, before, décor, deplore, downpour, drugstore, encore, explore, eyesore, folklore, footsore, foresaw, furor, galore, hardcore, ignore, implore, indoor, jigsaw, mentor, offshore, outdoor, outlaw, outpour, postwar, prewar, rapport, restore, rickshaw, seashore, seesaw, señor, sensor, therefore, trapdoor, uproar, withdraw.
[3] **Anymore**, corridor, dinosaur, evermore, forevermore, man-o'-war, matador, megastore, meteor, overawe, pinafore, semaphore, sophomore, superstore, sycamore, toreador, troubadour, tug of war, underscore.

4.3.24 "--ormed" (as in "formed")
[1] formed, stormed, swarmed, warmed.
[2] barnstormed, brainstormed, conformed, deformed, informed, misinformed, performed, reformed, transformed, uniformed.

SURPRISING RHYMING:
[1] **Dorm**, form, norm, storm, swarm, warm.
Dawned, fawned, horned, mourned, pawned, scorned, thorned, warned, yawned.
Born, borne, brawn, corn, dawn, drawn, fawn, horn, lawn, morn, mourn, pawn, porn, prawn, sawn, scorn, shorn, spawn, sworn, thorn, torn, warn, worn, yawn.
Bald, balled, bawled, brawled, called, crawled, drawled, hauled, lolled, mauled, scald, scrawled, sprawled, stalled, trawled, walled.
Daunt, flaunt, font, gaunt, haunt, jaunt, taunt, vaunt, want.
[2] **Barnstorm**, brainstorm, conform, firestorm, inform, lukewarm, misinform, perform, platform, rainstorm, reform, sandstorm, snowstorm, transform, uniform.
Adorned, forewarned.
Acorn, adorn, airborne, careworn, firstborn, foghorn, forewarn, forlorn, greenhorn, lovelorn, mid-morn, newborn, outworn, popcorn, reborn, sweetcorn, time-worn, unborn, unicorn, war-torn, withdrawn.
Appalled, blackballed, enthralled, eyeballed, installed, mothballed, overhauled, recalled, snowballed, so-called, sprawled, stonewalled.
[3] **Chloroform**, outperform, thunderstorm, underperform.

4.3.25 "--ormal" (as in "normal")
abnormal, formal, informal, normal, paranormal.

SURPRISING RHYMING:
[2] **Aural**, choral, coral, floral, immoral, moral, oral, quarrel, warble.
Awful, armful, artful, boastful, forceful, harmful, hopeful, hurtful, joyful, lawful, mournful, scornful, soulful, thoughtful, woeful, wrongful.
[3] **Forceful**, forgetful, remorseful, resourceful, sorrowful, unlawful.

4.3.26 "--ormat" (as in "format")
[2] doormat, format.

SURPRISING RHYMING:
[1] **At**, bat, brat, cat, chat, drat, fat, flat, frat, gnat, hat, mat, matte, pat, prat, rat, sat, scat, slat, spat, splat, sprat, stat, tat, that, vat.
Act, fact, pact, tact, tract.
Ad, add, bad, cad, clad, dad, fad, glad, grad, had, lad, mad, pad, plaid, sad, tad.
App, cap, chap, clap, crap, flap, gap, knap, lap, map, nap, pap, rap, sap, scrap, slap, snap, strap, tap, trap, wrap, yap.
Back, black, clack, crack, fact, flak, hack, jack, knack, lack, mac, pack, plaque, quack, rack, sack, shack, slack, smack, snack, stack, tack, track, yak, whack
Blast, cast, caste, fast, last, mast, massed, past, passed, vast.
[2] **Backchat**, bobcat, brickbat, chitchat, combat, fat cat, hard hat, hellcat, high-hat, howzat, sun hat, that's that, tomcat, top hat, wildcat.
Abstract, attract, compact, contact, contract, detract, distract, enact, exact, extract,

hunchbacked, impact, intact, play act, protract, ransacked, react, redact, retract, sidetracked, subtract, unpacked.
Aghast, amassed, at last, breakfast, broadcast, contrast, downcast, forecast, gymnast, harassed, hold fast, fly-past, miscast, outcast, outlast, outclassed, steadfast, surpassed.
Backslap, flat-cap, icecap, kneecap, mishap, nightcap, recap.
Entrap, madcap, mantrap, roadmap, stopgap, uncap.
[3] **Acrobat**, aristocrat, autocrat, baseball bat, bureaucrat, copycat, cricket bat, democrat, diplomat, habitat, kitty cat, lariat, laundromat, pussycat, scaredy-cat, technocrat, that's that, thermostat, tit-for-tat.

4.3.27 "--ormer" (as in "former")
[2] dormer, former, korma, stormer, trauma, warmer.
[3] barnstormer, bedwarmer, conformer, informer, performer, reformer, transformer.

SURPRISING RHYMING:
[2] **Corner**, fauna, mourner, sauna, scorner, warner, yawner.
Boarder, border, broader, hoarder, order, warder.
Daughter, mortar, porter, quarter, shorter, slaughter, sorter, water.
Corker, gawker, hawker, squawker, stalker, talker, walker.
Flaunter, haunter, saunter, taunter.
[3] **Court order**, defrauder, disorder, mail order, marauder, recorder.
Back talker, deerstalker, jaywalker, New Yorker, nightwalker, skywalker, sleepwalker, smooth-talker, streetwalker, sweet-talker.
Backwater, breakwater, freshwater, granddaughter, importer, manslaughter, reporter, supporter, transporter, underwater.

4.3.28 "--orming" (as in "swarming")
[2] forming, storming, swarming, warming.
[3] barnstorming, brainstorming, conforming, housewarming, informing, misinforming, performing, reforming, transforming.

SURPRISING RHYMING:
[2] **Awning**, dawning, fawning, morning, mourning, pawning, scorning, spawning, sworn-in, warning, yawning.
Boring, flooring, pawing, pouring, roaring, scoring, snoring, soaring, thawing, warring.
Bawling, brawling, calling, crawling, drawling, falling, hauling, mauling, scrawling, sprawling, squalling, stalling, trawling.
Courting, shorting, snorting, sorting, sporting, thwarting.
Daunting, flaunting, haunting, taunting, vaunting, wanting.
[3] **Adoring**, deploring, downpouring, exploring, ignoring, imploring, mentoring, outpouring, restoring, underscoring, withdrawing.
According, affording, applauding, awarding, defrauding, marauding, recording, rewarding, skateboarding, snowboarding.
Appalling, bankrolling, blackballing, cajoling, consoling, controlling, enthralling, freefalling, installing, mothballing, name calling, patrolling, recalling, stonewalling.
Aborting, cavorting, contorting, distorting, escorting, extorting, reporting, resorting, supporting, transporting.

4.3.29 "--orn" (as in "torn")
[1] born, borne, brawn, corn, dawn, drawn, fawn, horn, lawn, morn, mourn, pawn, porn, prawn, sawn, scorn, shorn, spawn, sworn, thorn, torn, warn, worn, yawn.
[2] acorn, adorn, airborne, careworn, firstborn, foghorn, forewarn, forlorn, greenhorn, longhorn, lovelorn, mid-morn, newborn, outworn, popcorn, reborn, shoehorn, shopworn, sweetcorn, time-worn, tinhorn, unborn, unicorn, war-torn, withdrawn.
[3] leprechaun, overdrawn, peppercorn, weatherworn.

SURPRISING RHYMING:
[1] **Dawned**, fawned, mourned, pawned, scorned, spawned, thorned, warned, yawned.
Dorm, form(ed), norm, storm(ed), swarm(ed), warm(ed).

Daunt, flaunt, font, gaunt, haunt, jaunt, taunt, vaunt, want.
Fore, four, gnaw, jaw, law, more, nor, oar, o'er, or, ore, paw, pore, pour, raw, roar, saw, score, snore, shore, soar, sore, store, squaw, straw, swore, thaw, tore, war, whore, wore, yore, your, you're.
[2] Adorned, forewarned.
Barnstorm, brainstorm, conform, firestorm, inform, lukewarm, misinform, perform, platform, rainstorm, reform, sandstorm, snowstorm, transform, uniform.
Barnstormed, brainstormed, conformed, informed, misinformed, performed, reformed, transformed, uniformed.
Adore, amore, ashore, before, décor, deplore, downpour, drugstore, encore, explore, eyesore, folklore, footsore, foresaw, furor, galore, hardcore, ignore, implore, indoor, jigsaw, mentor, offshore, outdoor, outlaw, outpour, postwar, prewar, rapport, restore, rickshaw, seashore, seesaw, señor, sensor, therefore, trapdoor, uproar, withdraw.
[3] Chloroform, outperform, thunderstorm, underperform.
Anymore, corridor, dinosaur, evermore, forevermore, man-o'-war, matador, megastore, meteor, overawe, pinafore, semaphore, sophomore, superstore, sycamore, toreador, troubadour, tug of war.

4.3.30 "--orner" (as in "corner")
[2] corner, fauna, mourner, sauna, scorner, warner, yawner.

SURPRISING RHYMING:
[2] Dormer, former, korma, stormer, trauma, warmer.
Boarder, border, broader, hoarder, order, warder.
Corker, gawker, hawker, squawker, stalker, talker, walker.
Flaunter, haunter, saunter, taunter.
Daughter, snorter, porter, quarter, shorter, slaughter, sorter, water.
[3] Barnstormer, conformer, informer, performer, reformer.
Court order, defrauder, disorder, mail order, marauder, recorder.
Back talker, deerstalker, jaywalker, New Yorker, nightwalker, skywalker, sleepwalker, smooth-talker, streetwalker, sweet-talker.
Backwater, breakwater, freshwater, granddaughter, importer, manslaughter, reporter, supporter, transporter, underwater.

4.3.31 "--orning" (as in "morning")
[2] awning, dawning, fawning, morning, mourning, pawning, scorning, spawning, sworn-in, warning, yawning.
[3] adorning, forewarning, mid-morning.

SURPRISING RHYMING:
[2] Forming, storming, swarming, warming.
Daunting, flaunting, haunting, taunting, vaunting, wanting.
Boarding, hoarding, lauding.
Bawling, brawling, calling, crawling, drawling, falling, hauling, mauling, scrawling, sprawling, squalling, stalling, trawling.
Boring, flooring, gnawing, pawing, pouring, roaring, sawing, scoring, snoring, shoring, soaring, storing, thawing, warring.
Courting, shorting, snorting, sorting, sporting, thwarting.
[3] Barnstorming, brainstorming, conforming, informing, misinforming, performing, reforming, transforming.
Adoring, deploring, downpouring, exploring, ignoring, imploring, mentoring, outpouring, restoring, underscoring, withdrawing.
According, affording, applauding, awarding, defrauding, marauding, recording, rewarding, skateboarding, snowboarding.
Appalling, bankrolling, befalling, blackballing, cajoling, consoling, controlling, enthralling, freefalling, installing, mothballing, name calling, patrolling, recalling, stonewalling.
Aborting, cavorting, contorting, distorting, escorting, extorting, reporting, resorting, supporting, transporting.

*

4.3.32 "--orned" (as in "warned")
[1] dawned, fawned, horned, lawned, mourned, pawned, scorned, spawned, thorned, warned, yawned.
[2] adorned, forewarned.

SURPRISING RHYMING:
[1] **Formed**, stormed, swarmed, warmed.
Born, borne, brawn, dawn, drawn, horn, lawn, morn, mourn, pawn, porn, sawn, scorn, shorn, sworn, thorn, torn, warn, worn, yawn.
Daunt, flaunt, font, gaunt, haunt, jaunt, taunt, vaunt, want.
Bald, bawled, brawled, called, crawled, drawled, hauled, mauled, scald, scrawled, sprawled, stalled, trawled, walled.
[2] **Barnstormed**, brainstormed, conformed, deformed, informed, misinformed, performed, reformed, transformed, uniformed.
Adorn, careworn, firstborn, foghorn, forewarn, forlorn, greenhorn, lovelorn, mid-morn, newborn, outworn, popcorn, reborn, time-worn, unborn, unicorn, war-torn, withdrawn.
Appalled, blackballed, enthralled, eyeballed, installed, mothballed, overhauled, recalled, snowballed, so-called, sprawled, stonewalled.

4.3.33 "--ornful" (as in "scornful")
[2] mournful, scornful.

SURPRISING RHYMING:
[2] **Awful**, lawful, thoughtful, unlawful.
Aural, choral, floral, formal, immoral, moral, normal, oral, quarrel.
Bauble, bobble, cobble, gobble, hobble, nobble, squabble, wobble.
Colossal, forceful, fossil, gospel, hostile, jostle, morsel.
[3] **Abnormal**, informal, immortal, paranormal, remorseful, resourceful.

4.3.34 "--orny" (as in "corny")
[2] brawny, corny, horny, scrawny, tawny, thorny.

SURPRISING RHYMING:
[2] **Glory**, gory, hoary, sorry, stormy, storey, story.
Forty, haughty, naughty, pianoforte, shorty, UB40, sporty, warty.
Chalky, corky, croaky, dorky, gawky, hokey, jokey, karaoke, pokey, scot-free, smoky, talkie, tawdry, walkie.
Bawdy, broadly, courtly, gaudy, lordy, portly, shortly.

4.3.35 "--ornt" (as in "haunt")
[1] daunt, flaunt, font, gaunt, haunt, jaunt, taunt, vaunt, want.

SURPRISING RHYMING:
[1] **Bought**, brought, caught, court, fort, fought, fraught, naught/nought, ought, port, quart, short, snort, sort, sought, sport, taught, taut, thought, thwart, tort, wart.
Formed, stormed, swarmed, warmed.
Dawned, fawned, horned, mourned, pawned, scorned, thorned, warned, yawned.
[2] **Airport**, cavort, distort, distraught, escort, export, forecourt, forethought, import, onslaught, outfought, passport, report, resort, self-taught, spoilsport, support, transport.
Acorn, adorn, airborne, careworn, firstborn, foghorn, forewarn, forlorn, greenhorn, lovelorn, mid-morn, newborn, outworn, popcorn, reborn, sweetcorn, time-worn, unborn, unicorn, war-torn, withdrawn.
Barnstormed, brainstormed, conformed, informed, misinformed, performed, reformed, transformed, uniformed.
[3] **Croissant**, debutante, confidant, detente, non-chalant, restaurant.
Aforethought, afterthought, astronaut, cosmonaut, juggernaut.

4.3.36 "--ornting" (as in "haunting")
[2] daunting, flaunting, haunting, jaunting, taunting, wanting.

SURPRISING RHYMING:
[2] **Courting**, snorting, sorting, sporting, thwarting.
Forming, storming, swarming, warming.
Awning, dawning, fawning, morning, mourning, pawning, scorning, spawning, sworn-in, warning, yawning.
[3] **Aborting**, cavorting, contorting, distorting, escorting, extorting, reporting, resorting, supporting, transporting.
Barnstorming, brainstorming, conforming, housewarming, informing, misinforming, performing, reforming, transforming.
According, adorning, affording, applauding, awarding, boarding, defrauding, forewarning, hoarding, lauding, marauding, mid-morning, recording, rewarding.

4.3.37 "--ornted" (as in "haunted")
[2] daunted, flaunted, haunted, taunted, wanted.

SURPRISING RHYMING:
[2] **Courted**, snorted, sorted, sported, thwarted.
Boarded, hoarded, lauded, morbid, orchid, orbit, sordid.
Bolted, bonded, frosted, halted, malted, salted, vaulted.
[3] **Aborted**, assorted, cavorted, contorted, distorted, escorted, exported, imported, reported, resorted, supported, transported.
Afforded, applauded, awarded, blindfolded, defrauded, recorded, rewarded, unfolded.
Assaulted, exalted, exhausted, revolted.

4.3.38 "--ors" (as in "doors")
[1] bores, chores, claws, doors, draws, drawers, flaws, floors, force, jaws, laws, oars, paws, pores, pours, roars, scores, snores, shores, soars, sores, stores, wars, yours.
[2] adores, deplores, downpours, drugstores, encores, explores, eyesores, rickshaws, ignores, indoors, in-laws, jigsaws, mentors, outdoors, outlaws, outpours, restores.
[3] carnivores, commodores, corridors, dinosaurs, matadors, meteors, stevedores, sycamores, troubadours, underscores.

SURPRISING RHYMING:
[1] **Awe**, bore, chore, claw, core, corps, door, draw, drawer, flaw, floor, for, fore, four, gnaw, jaw, law, more, nor, oar, or, paw, pour, raw, roar, saw, score, snore, shore, soar, sore, store, straw, swore, thaw, tore, war, whore, wore, yore, your, you're.
Awes, cause, clause, claws, draws, drawers, flaws, gauze, gnaws, jaws, laws, pause, paws, squaws, straws, was, yours.
Coarse, course, force, gorse, hoarse, horse, Morse, sauce, source.
[2] **Adore**, amore, ashore, before, décor, deplore, downpour, drugstore, encore, explore, eyesore, folklore, footsore, foresaw, furor, galore, hardcore, ignore, implore, indoor, jigsaw, mentor, offshore, outdoor, outlaw, outpour, postwar, prewar, rapport, restore, seashore, seesaw, señor, sensor, therefore, trapdoor, uproar, withdraw.
Applause, because, indoors, in-laws, outdoors, Santa Claus.
Divorce, endorse/indorse (U.S.), enforce, reinforce, remorse.
[3] **Anymore**, corridor, dinosaur, evermore, forevermore, man-o'-war, matador, megastore, meteor, overawe, pinafore, semaphore, sophomore, superstore, sycamore, toreador, troubadour, tug of war, underscore.

4.3.39 "--orse" (as in "remorse")
[1] coarse, course, force, hoarse, horse, Morse, sauce, source.
[2] discourse, divorce, endorse/indorse (U.S.), enforce, intercourse, racecourse, racehorse, recourse, reinforce, remorse, resource, seahorse, workforce.

SURPRISING RHYMING:
[1] **Cause**, caused, clause, claws, draws, drawers, flaws, forced, gauze, gnaws, jaws, laws, pause(d), paws, sauced, sourced, squaws, straws, was, yours.
Dawns, fawns, horns, lawns, mourns, pawns, prawns, scorns, thorns, warns, yawns.
Dorms, forms, norms, storms, swarms, warms.

[2] Applause, because, indoors, in-laws, outdoors, Santa Claus.
Adores, deplores, downpours, drugstores, encores, explores, eyesores, ignores, in-laws, jigsaws, outdoors, outlaws, restores.
Divorced, endorsed/indorsed (U.S.), enforce, reinforced.
Acorns, adorns, forewarns, newborns, unicorns.
Conforms, informs, performs, platforms, reforms, sandstorms, snowstorms, thunderstorms, transforms, uniforms.
[3] Corridors, dinosaurs, matadors, meteors, troubadours.

4.3.40 "--orsing" (as in "forcing")
[2] coursing, forcing, saucing, sourcing.
[3] divorcing, endorsing/indorsing (U.S.), enforcing, reinforcing, resourcing.

SURPRISING RHYMING:
[2] Causing, pausing.
Bawling, brawling, calling, crawling, drawling, falling, hauling, mauling, scrawling, sprawling, squalling, stalling, trawling.
Boring, pouring, roaring, scoring, snoring, soaring, storing, warring.
Debauching, scorching, torching.
Awning, dawning, fawning, morning, mourning, pawning, scorning, spawning, sworn-in, warning, yawning.
Forming, storming, swarming, warming.
Courting, snorting, sorting, sporting, thwarting.
Daunting, flaunting, haunting, jaunting, taunting, vaunting, wanting.
[3] Appalling, bankrolling, blackballing, cajoling, consoling, controlling, enthralling, freefalling, installing, mothballing, name calling, patrolling, recalling, stonewalling.
Adoring, deploring, exploring, ignoring, outpouring, restoring.
Adorning, forewarning, mid-morning.
Barnstorming, brainstorming, conforming, housewarming, informing, misinforming, performing, reforming, transforming.
Aborting, cavorting, contorting, distorting, escorting, extorting, reporting, resorting, supporting, transporting.

4.3.41 "--orsely" (as in "coarsely")
[2] coarsely, hoarsely.

SURPRISING RHYMING:
[2] Forty, haughty, naughty, pianoforte, shorty, UB40, sporty, warty.
Boldly, closely, dopey, homely, homie, low-key, mouldy/moldy (U.S.), oldie, roadie, smoky, snowy, soapy, trophy.
Brolly, collie, dolly, folly, golly, holly, jolly, lolly, trolley, volley.

4.3.42 "--ort" (as in "short")
[1] bought, brought, caught, court, fort, fought, fraught, naught/nought, ought, port, quart, short, snort, sort, sought, sport, taught, taut, thought, thwart, tort, wart.
[2] abort, airport, assort, carport, cavort, cohort, consort, contort, deport, distort, distraught, escort, exhort, export, forecourt, forethought, import, onslaught, outfought, passport, purport, report, resort, retort, self-taught, spoilsport, support, transport.
[3] aforethought, afterthought, astronaut, cosmonaut, juggernaut.

SURPRISING RHYMING:
[1] Awed, board, bored, broad, chord, flawed, floored, fraud, hoard, horde, lord, poured, roared, scored, snored, soared, sword, ward.
Chalk, cork, dork, fork, gawk, hawk, pork, squawk, stalk, stork, talk, torque, walk.
[2] Aboard, abroad, accord, adored, afford, applaud, award, billboard, blackboard, cardboard, chessboard, clipboard, concord, dartboard, dashboard, defraud, deplored, discord, explored, floorboard, headboard, ignored, keyboard, landlord, maraud, onboard, outboard, record, restored, reward, ripcord, scoreboard, sideboard, skateboard, snowboard, springboard, surfboard, switchboard, toward.

Back talk, boardwalk, cakewalk, catwalk, crosstalk, crosswalk, jaywalk, newshawk, nighthawk, pep talk, pitchfork, shoptalk, sidewalk, skywalk, sleepwalk, small talk, smooth-talk, spacewalk, sweet-talk.
[3] **Chequerboard/checkerboard** (U.S.), clapperboard, diving board, harpsichord, open-doored, overawed, overboard, smorgasbord, storyboard, unexplored, untoward.

4.3.43 "--ortal" (as in "mortal")
[2] chortle, immortal, mortal, portal.

SURPRISING RHYMING:
[2] **Aural**, choral, floral, immoral, laurel, moral, oral, quarrel, warble.
Awful, armful, artful, boastful, forceful, harmful, hopeful, hurtful, joyful, lawful, mournful, scornful, soulful, thoughtful, woeful, wrongful.
[3] **Abnormal**, formal, informal, normal, paranormal.

4.3.44 "--orty" (as in "naughty")
[2] forty, haughty, naughty, pianoforte, shorty, UB40, sporty, warty.

SURPRISING RHYMING:
[2] **Bawdy**, broadly, courtly, gaudy, lordy, portly, saucy, shortly.
Brawny, corny, horny, scrawny, tawny, thorny.
Glory, gory, hoary, sorry, storey, story, faulty.
Boating, doting, floating, gloating, noting, quoting, voting.
Chalky, croaky, dorky, folky, gawky, hokey, jokey, karaoke, pokey, scot-free, smoky, talkie, tawdry, walkie.
[3] **Furore**, hunky-dory, multi-storey.

4.3.45 "--orted" (as in "sorted")
[2] courted, snorted, sorted, sported, thwarted.
[3] aborted, assorted, cavorted, contorted, deported, distorted, escorted, exported, extorted, imported, purported, reported, resorted, retorted, supported, transported.

SURPRISING RHYMING:
[2] **Boarded**, hoarded, lauded, morbid, orchid, orbit, sordid.
Daunted, flaunted, haunted, taunted, wanted.
[3] **Afforded**, applauded, awarded, defrauded, marauded, recorded, rewarded.

4.3.46 "--orter" (as in "quarter")
[2] daughter, mortar, oughta, snorter, porter, quarter, shorter, slaughter, sorter, water.
[3] backwater, breakwater, deporter, exporter, extorter, freshwater, granddaughter, importer, manslaughter, reporter, supporter, transporter, underwater.

SURPRISING RHYMING:
[2] **Boarder**, border, broader, hoarder, order, warder.
Corker, gawker, hawker, squawker, stalker, talker, walker.
Corner, fauna, former, mourner, sauna, scorner, stormer, trauma, warmer, warner.
Flaunter, haunter, saunter, taunter.
Longer, sombre/somber (U.S.), stronger.
[3] **Court order**, defrauder, disorder, mail order, marauder, recorder.
Back talker, deerstalker, jaywalker, New Yorker, nightwalker, skywalker, sleepwalker, smooth-talker, streetwalker, sweet-talker.
Barnstormer, conformer, informer, performer, reformer, transformer.

4.3.47 "--ortly" (as in "shortly")
[2] courtly, portly, shortly.

SURPRISING RHYMING:
[2] **Forty**, haughty, naughty, pianoforte, shorty, shorty, sporty.
Bawdy, broadly, courtly, gaudy, lordy, portly, saucy, shortly.

Brawny, corny, horny, scrawny, stormy, tawny, thorny.
Coarsely, hoarsely, saucy.
Crawly, glory, gory, hoary, sorry, storey, story, faulty.
Chalky, croaky, dorky, folky, gawky, hokey, jokey, karaoke, pokey, scot-free, smoky, talkie, tawdry, walkie.
Dolly, folly, golly, holly, jolly, lolly, trolley, volley.

4.3.48 "--orting" (as in "sporting")
[2] courting, snorting, sorting, sporting, thwarting.
[3] aborting, cavorting, consorting, contorting, deporting, distorting, escorting, exhorting, extorting, purporting, reporting, resorting, retorting, supporting, transporting.

SURPRISING RHYMING:
[2] **Daunting**, flaunting, haunting, jaunting, taunting, wanting.
Awning, dawning, morning, mourning, pawning, warning, yawning.
Forming, storming, swarming, warming.
Boring, pouring, roaring, scoring, snoring, soaring, storing, warring.
Coursing, forcing, saucing, sourcing.
[3] **Adorning**, forewarning, mid-morning.
Affording, applauding, awarding, boarding, defrauding, hoarding, lauding, marauding, recording, rewarding.
Barnstorming, brainstorming, conforming, housewarming, informing, misinforming, performing, reforming, transforming.
Adoring, deploring, exploring, ignoring, outpouring, restoring.
Divorcing, endorsing/indorsing (U.S.), enforcing, reinforcing.

4.3.49 "--oawing" (as in "drawing")
[2] clawing, drawing, gnawing, pawing, sawing, seesawing, thawing.

SURPRISING RHYMING:
[2] **Bawling**, brawling, calling, crawling, drawling, falling, hauling, mauling, scrawling, sprawling, squalling, stalling, trawling.
Awning, dawning, morning, mourning, pawning, warning, yawning.
Forming, storming, swarming, warming.
Boring, pouring, roaring, scoring, snoring, soaring, storing, warring.
[3] **Appalling**, bankrolling, befalling, blackballing, cajoling, consoling, controlling, enrolling, enthralling, freefalling, installing, mothballing, name calling, patrolling, recalling, snowballing, stonewalling.
Adoring, deploring, exploring, ignoring, outpouring, restoring.
Barnstorming, brainstorming, conforming, housewarming, informing, misinforming, performing, reforming, transforming.
Affording, applauding, awarding, boarding, defrauding, hoarding, lauding, marauding, recording, rewarding.

4.3.50 "--ory" (as in "glory")
[2] glory, gory, hoary, sorry, storey, story.
[3] furore, hunky-dory, multi-storey.

SURPRISING RHYMING:
[2] **Forty**, haughty, naughty, pianoforte, shorty, sporty, warty.
Brawny, corny, horny, scrawny, shortly, thorny.
Boring, pouring, roaring, scoring, snoring, soaring, storing, warring.
Bony, crony, lonely, moany, only, phoney/phony (U.S.), pony, stony.
Croaky, folky, hokey, jokey, karaoke, pokey, scot-free, smoky.
Coffee, comfy, toffee, trophy.
[3] **Calorie**, cursory, disagree, doddery, factory, hickory, history, ivory, jamboree, memory, misery, poetry, savory, sensory, victory.
Adoring, deploring, exploring, ignoring, outpouring, restoring.
Anatomy, astronomy, bonhomie, economy, epitome, nominee.

Agony, balcony, colony, ebony, felony, harmony, irony, symphony.
[4] **Acrimony**, alimony, cacophony, cannelloni, ceremony, macaroni, matrimony, minestrone, monotony, pepperoni, rigatoni, testimony.

4.3.51 "--orz" (as in "jaws")
[1] awes, cause, clause, claws, draws, drawers, flaws, gauze, gnaws, jaws, laws, pause, paws, saws, squaws, straws, was, yours.
[2] applause, because, indoors, in-laws, outdoors, Santa Claus.

SURPRISING RHYMING:
[1] **Coarse**, course, force, hoarse, horse, Morse, sauce, source.
Bores, chores, doors, floors, force, oars, pores, pours, roars, scores, snores, shores, soars, sores, stores, wars.
Caused, forced, paused, sauced, sourced.
Dawns, fawns, horns, lawns, mourns, pawns, prawns, scorns, thorns, warns, yawns.
Dorms, forms, norms, storms, swarms, warms.
[2] **Divorce(d)**, endorse/indorse (U.S.), enforce(d), racecourse, racehorse, reinforce(d), remorse, resource, seahorse, workforce.
Adores, deplores, downpours, drugstores, encores, explores, eyesores, ignores, jigsaws, outdoors, outlaws, outpours, restores.
Acorns, adorns, forewarns, newborns, unicorns.
Conforms, informs, performs, platforms, reforms, sandstorms, snowstorms, thunderstorms, transforms, uniforms.
[3] **Corridors**, dinosaurs, matadors, meteors, troubadours.

4.4. "oy" (as in "toy")

4.4.1 "--oy" (as in "boy")
[1] boy, buoy, coy, joy, ploy, toy, troy.
[2] ahoy, alloy, annoy, ballboy, bellboy, choirboy, convoy, cowboy, decoy, deploy, destroy, employ, enjoy, hoi polloi, killjoy, pageboy, paperboy, playboy, savoy, schoolboy, tannoy, tomboy, toyboy.
[3] altar boy, attaboy, corduroy, overjoy, saveloy.

SURPRISING RHYMING:
[1] **Boys**, noise, ploys, poise, toys.
Buoyed, toyed, void.
Boil, broil, coil, foil, oil, soil, spoil, toil.
Bitcoin, coin, groin, join, loin, purloin, sirloin.
Choice, invoice, rejoice, voice.
[2] **Annoys**, ballboys, bellboys, choirboys, convoys, cowboys, decoys, destroys, employs, enjoys, killjoys, newsboys, pageboys, paperboys, playboys, schoolboys, tomboys, toyboys, turquoise.
Android, annoyed, avoid, devoid, employed, enjoyed, tabloid.
Embroil, gargoyle, recoil, tinfoil, turmoil, uncoil.
[3] **Alkaloid**, asteroid, celluloid, overjoyed, paranoid, unemployed.

4.4.2 "--oyz" (as in "noise")
[1] boys, noise, ploys, poise, toys.
[2] annoys, ballboys, bellboys, choirboys, convoys, corduroys, cowboys, decoys, deploys, destroys, employs, enjoys, envoys, killjoys, newsboys, pageboys, paperboys, playboys, schoolboys, tomboys, toyboys, turquoise.

SURPRISING RHYMING:
[1] **Boy**, buoy, coy, joy, ploy, toy, troy.
Choice, foist, hoist, invoice(d), joist, moist, rejoice(d), voice(d).
Boils, coils, foils, oils, soils, spoils, toils.
Buoyed, toyed, void.

[2] **Ahoy**, annoy, ballboy, bellboy, choirboy, convoy, cowboy, decoy, deploy, destroy, employ, enjoy, hoi polloi, killjoy, newsboy, pageboy, paperboy, playboy, savoy, schoolboy, tannoy, tomboy, toyboy.
Android, annoyed, avoid, devoid, employed, enjoyed, tabloid.
[3] **Alkaloid**, asteroid, celluloid, overjoyed, paranoid, unemployed.

4.4.3 "--oid" (as in "avoid")
[1] buoyed, toyed, void.
[2] alloyed, android, annoyed, avoid, decoyed, deployed, devoid, employed, enjoyed, tabloid, typhoid.
[3] alkaloid, asteroid, celluloid, overjoyed, paranoid, unemployed.

SURPRISING RHYMING:
[1] **Boy**, buoy, coy, joy, ploy, toy, troy.
Boil, broil, coil, foil, oil, soil, spoil, toil.
[2] **Ahoy**, annoy, ballboy, bellboy, choirboy, convoy, cowboy, decoy, deploy, destroy, employ, enjoy, hoi polloi, killjoy, newsboy, pageboy, paperboy, playboy, schoolboy, tannoy, tomboy, toyboy.
Bitcoin, coin, groin, join, loin, purloin, sirloin.
Embroil, gargoyle, recoil, tinfoil, turmoil, uncoil.
[3] **Altar boy**, attaboy, corduroy, overjoy.

4.4.4 "--oil" (as in "boil")
[1] boil, broil, coil, foil, oil, soil, spoil, toil.
[2] embroil, gargoyle, recoil, tinfoil, turmoil, uncoil.

SURPRISING RHYMING:
[1] **Boiled**, coiled, foiled, oiled, soiled, spoiled, spoilt, toiled, void.
Boy, buoy(ed), coy, joy, ploy, toy(ed), troy.
[2] **Disloyal**, embroiled, loyal, recoiled, royal, uncoiled.
Ahoy, annoy, ballboy, bellboy, choirboy, convoy, cowboy, decoy, deploy, destroy, employ, enjoy, hoi polloi, killjoy, newsboy, pageboy, paperboy, playboy, schoolboy, tannoy, tomboy, toyboy.
Android, annoyed, avoid, devoid, employed, enjoyed, tabloid.
[3] **Altar boy**, attaboy, corduroy, overjoy.
Asteroid, celluloid, overjoyed, paranoid, unemployed.

4.4.5 "--oiler" (as in "boiler")
[2] boiler, broiler, oiler, potboiler, soiler, spoiler, toiler.

SURPRISING RHYMING:
[2] **Coiner**, joiner, loiter, oyster, pointer, roller, solar.
[3] **Annoyer**, destroyer, employer, enjoyer, foyer, lawyer, paranoia.
Avoider, embroider, purloiner.

4.4.6 "--oiling" (as in "spoiling")
[2] boiling, broiling, coiling, embroiling, foiling, oiling, recoiling, soiling, spoiling, toiling.

SURPRISING RHYMING:
[2] **Coining**, enjoying, hoisting, joining, pointing, rejoicing, rolling.
[3] **Annoying**, deploying, destroying, employing, enjoying, toying.
Anointing, avoiding, appointing, disappointing, pinpointing.

4.4.7 "--oiled" (as in "spoiled")
[1] boiled, broiled, coiled, foiled, oiled, soiled, spoiled, toiled.
[2] embroiled, recoiled, uncoiled.

SURPRISING RHYMING:
[1] **Boil**, broil, coil, foil, oil, soil, spoil, toil.

Boy, buoy(ed), coy, joy, ploy, toy(ed), void.
[2] **Embroil**, gargoyle, recoil, tinfoil, turmoil, uncoil.
Android, annoyed, avoid, devoid, employed, enjoyed, tabloid.
Ahoy, annoy, ballboy, bellboy, choirboy, convoy, cowboy, decoy, deploy, destroy, employ, enjoy, hoi polloi, killjoy, newsboy, pageboy, paperboy, playboy, schoolboy, tannoy, tomboy, toyboy.

4.4.8 "--oin" (as in "coin")
adjoin, bitcoin, coin, groin, join, loin, purloin, sirloin.

SURPRISING RHYMING:
[1] **Coined**, joined, joint, point, purloined.
Boy, buoy(ed), coy, joy, ploy, toy(ed), void.
[2] **Appoint**, breakpoint, cashpoint, checkpoint, disappoint, flashpoint, gunpoint, knifepoint, pinpoint, standpoint, strongpoint, viewpoint.
Android, annoyed, avoid, devoid, employed, enjoyed, tabloid.
Ahoy, annoy, ballboy, bellboy, choirboy, convoy, cowboy, decoy, deploy, destroy, employ, enjoy, hoi polloi, killjoy, newsboy, pageboy, paperboy, playboy, schoolboy, tannoy, tomboy, toyboy.

4.4.9 "--oint" (as in "point")
anoint, appoint, breakpoint, cashpoint, checkpoint, counterpoint, disappoint, disjoint, flashpoint, gunpoint, joint, knifepoint, pinpoint, point, point-to-point, standpoint, strongpoint, viewpoint.

SURPRISING RHYMING:
[1] **Bitcoin**, coin(ed), groin, join(ed), loin, purloin(ed), sirloin.
Boy, buoy(ed), coy, joy, ploy, toy(ed), void.
[2] **Android**, annoyed, avoid, devoid, employed, enjoyed, tabloid.
Ahoy, annoy, ballboy, bellboy, choirboy, convoy, cowboy, decoy, deploy, destroy, employ, enjoy, hoi polloi, killjoy, newsboy, pageboy, paperboy, playboy, schoolboy, tannoy, tomboy, toyboy.
Adroit, Detroit, exploit, rejoiced, spoilt, voiced.

4.4.10 "--ointed" (as in "pointed")
[2] jointed, pointed.
[3] anointed, appointed, disappointed, disjointed, pinpointed.

SURPRISING RHYMING:
[2] **Buoyant**, ointment, poignant.
[3] **Avoided**, appointment, clairvoyant, disappointment, enjoyment, exploited, flamboyant.
Assaulted, exalted, revolted, salted.
Augmented, cemented, consented, contented, demented, dissented, fragmented, frequented, invented, lamented, presented, prevented, relented, repented, resented, segmented, tormented.
[4] **Complemented**, complimented, discontented, disoriented, experimented, implemented, represented, supplemented.

4.4.11 "--ointing" (as in "pointing")
[2] jointing, pointing.
[3] anointing, appointing, disappointing, disjointing, pinpointing.

SURPRISING RHYMING:
[2] **Boiling**, coiling, foiling, oiling, recoiling, soiling, spoiling, toiling.
Enjoying, foisting, hoisting, rejoicing, voicing.
[3] **Annoying**, avoiding, destroying, employing, enjoying, toying.

4.4.12 "--oice" (as in "choice")
choice, invoice, rejoice, Rolls Royce, voice.

526

SURPRISING RHYMING:
[1] Foist, hoist, invoiced, joist, moist, rejoiced, spoilt, voiced.
Boys, noise, ploys, poise, toys.
Boils, coils, foils, oils, soils, spoils, toils.
[2] Annoys, choirboys, cowboys, decoys, destroys, enjoys, killjoys, pageboys, paperboys, playboys, schoolboys, tomboys, toyboys.
Anoint, appoint, breakpoint, cashpoint, checkpoint, disappoint, flashpoint, gunpoint, knifepoint, pinpoint, standpoint, viewpoint.

4.4.13 "--oist" (as in "moist")
[1] foist, hoist, invoiced, joist, moist, rejoiced, voiced.

SURPRISING RHYMING:
[1] Boys, choice, noise, poise, rejoice, toys, Rolls Royce, voice.
Boils, coils, foils, oils, soils, spoils, toils.
Boiled, coiled, foiled, oiled, point, soiled, spoiled, toiled.
[2] Annoys, choirboys, cowboys, decoys, destroys, enjoys, killjoys, pageboys, paperboys, playboys, schoolboys, tomboys, toyboys.
Anoint, appoint, breakpoint, cashpoint, checkpoint, disappoint, flashpoint, gunpoint, knifepoint, pinpoint, standpoint, strongpoint, viewpoint.

4.4.14 "--oyal" (as in "loyal")
disloyal, loyal, royal.

SURPRISING RHYMING:
[1] Boil, broil, coil, foil, oil, soil, spoil, toil.
[2] Embroil, gargoyle, recoil, tinfoil, turmoil, uncoil.
Boiled, broiled, coiled, foiled, oiled, soiled, spoiled, toiled.
Embroiled, recoiled, uncoiled.

4.4.15 "--oyant" (as in "buoyant")
buoyant, clairvoyant, flamboyant.

SURPRISING RHYMING:
[2] Disloyal, Goya, joyful, joyous, loyal, royal, voyage
Compliant, defiant, giant, pliant, reliant.
[3] Annoyance, clairvoyance, flamboyance.
Appointment, disappointment, enjoyment, ointment, poignant.
Avoided, appointed, exploited, disappointed, pointed.
Annoyer, destroyer, employer, lawyer, paranoia.

4.4.16 "--oyer" (as in "destroyer")
[3] annoyer, destroyer, employer, enjoyer, foyer, lawyer, paranoia.

SURPRISING RHYMING:
Disloyal, Goya, loyal, royal,
Boiler, broiler, coiler, foiler, oiler, recoiler, soiler, spoiler, toiler.
Avoider, embroider, joiner, loiter, oyster, pointer, purloiner.

4.4.17 "--oying" (as in "annoying")
annoying, deploying, destroying, employing, enjoying, toying.

SURPRISING RHYMING:
[2] Boiling, coiling, foiling, oiling, recoiling, soiling, spoiling, toiling.
Coining, joining, purloining.
Blowing, bowing, crowing, flowing, glowing, going, growing, hoeing, knowing, loathing, mowing, owing, rowing, sewing, showing, slowing, snowing, throwing, toeing, towing.
[3] Avoiding, appointing, disappointing, disjointing, pinpointing.

* * *

4.5 "ow" (as in "how")

4.5.1 "--ow" (as in "how")
[1] bough, bow, brow, chow, ciao, cow, dhow, how, now, ow, plough/plow (U.S.), pow, row, sow, thou, vow, wow.
[2] allow, avow, bow-wow, endow, eyebrow, highbrow, know-how, kowtow, lowbrow, meow, nohow, powwow, somehow.
[3] anyhow, disallow, disavow, middlebrow.

SURPRISING RHYMING:
[1] **Bowed**, cloud, crowd, loud, ploughed/plowed (U.S.), proud, rowed, vowed, wowed.
Bout, clout, doubt, drought, flout, lout, mouth, out, pout, rout, route (U.S.), scout, shout, snout, south, spout, sprout, stout, tout, trout.
Brown, clown, crown, down, drown, frown, gown, noun, town.
Bound, browned, clowned, crowned, downed, drowned, found, frowned, ground, hound, mound, pound, round, sound, wound.
Foul, fowl, growl, howl, jowl, owl, prowl, scowl, yowl.
Blouse, browse, douse/dowse (U.S.), house, mouse, scouse, spouse.
[2] **Allowed**, aloud, avowed, endowed, meowed, unbowed.
About, blackout, blowout, breakout, buyout, checkout, clear-out, cookout, copout, cut-out, devout, dropout, dugout, fallout, handout, hangout, hideout, knockout, layout, litter-lout, lock-out, lookout, payout, printout, pull-out, scout, sell-out, shoot-out, shutout, spin-out, standout, stakeout, takeout, throughout, timeout, tryout, turnout, walkout, washout, way-out, white-out, wipeout, without, workout.
Breakdown, clampdown, climbdown, comedown, countdown, crackdown, downtown, hoedown, hometown, letdown, lowdown, markdown, meltdown, midtown, nightgown, put-down, renown, rubdown, rundown, shakedown, showdown, shutdown, sit-down, slowdown, splashdown, sundown, takedown, touchdown, uptown.
Abound, aground, around, astound, background, bloodhound, confound, dumbfound, earthbound, eastbound, fairground, fogbound, foreground, foxhound, greyhound, hellhound, hidebound, housebound, icebound, inbound, newshound, northbound, outbound, playground, profound, rebound, renowned, showground, snowbound, southbound, spellbound, stormbound, surround, unwound, westbound, whip-round.
Alehouse, birdhouse, boathouse, clubhouse, courthouse, doghouse, dollhouse, farmhouse, glasshouse, greenhouse, guesthouse, hothouse, jailhouse, lighthouse, madhouse, penthouse, playhouse, teahouse, townhouse, treehouse, warehouse.
Bad-mouth, bigmouth, goalmouth, loudmouth.
[3] **Overcrowd**, thundercloud, well-endowed.
Down-and-out, hereabout, in-and-out, knockabout, layabout, out-and-out, roundabout, runabout, thereabout, turnabout, walk-about.
Chinatown, eiderdown, hand-me-down, upside-down.
Blabbermouth, motormouth, mouth-to-mouth.

4.5.2 "--ouch" (as in "couch")
[1] couch, crouch, grouch, ouch, pouch, slouch, vouch.

SURPRISING RHYMING:
[1] **Couched**, crouched, pouched, slouched, vouched.
Blouse, browse, douse, dowse, house, mouse, scouse, spouse.
Bounce, flounce, ounce, pounce, trounce.
Bout, clout, doubt, drought, flout, lout, out, pout, route (U.S.), scout, shout, snout, spout, sprout, stout, tout.
Bough, bow, brow, chow, ciao, cow, how, now, plough/plow (U.S.), row, vow, wow.
[2] **Alehouse**, birdhouse, boathouse, clubhouse, courthouse, doghouse, dollhouse, farmhouse, glasshouse, greenhouse, guesthouse, henhouse, hothouse, jailhouse, lighthouse, madhouse, penthouse, playhouse, townhouse, treehouse, warehouse.
Announce, denounce, mispronounce, pronounce, renounce.
About, blackout, blowout, breakout, checkout, clear-out, cookout, copout, cut-out, devout, dropout, dugout, fallout, handout, hangout, hideout, knockout, layout,

litter-lout, lock-out, lookout, payout, printout, pull-out, scout, sell-out, shoot-out, shutout, spin-out, standout, stakeout, takeout, throughout, timeout, tryout, turnout, walkout, washout, way-out, white-out, wipeout, without, workout.
Allow, endow, eyebrow, highbrow, know-how, lowbrow, somehow.
[3] **Down-and-out**, in-and-out, knockabout, layabout, out-and-out, roundabout, runabout, thereabout, turnabout, walk-about.

4.5.3 "--oud" (as in "cloud")
[1] bowed, cloud, crowd, loud, ploughed/plowed (U.S.), proud, shroud, vowed, wowed.
[2] allowed, aloud, avowed, endowed, meowed, unbowed, unploughed/unplowed (U.S.).
[3] overcrowd, thundercloud, unavowed, well-endowed.

SURPRISING RHYMING:
[1] **Brown**, clown, crown, down, drown, frown, gown, noun, town.
Bout, clout, doubt, drought, flout, lout, out, pout, route (U.S.), scout, shout, snout, spout, sprout, stout, tout.
Bound(s), clowned, crowned, downed, drowned, found, frowned, ground(s), hound(s), mound(s), pound(s), round(s), sound(s), wound.
Fouled, growled, howled, prowled, scowled.
[2] **Breakdown**, clampdown, climbdown, comedown, countdown, crackdown, downtown, hoedown, hometown, letdown, lowdown, markdown, meltdown, midtown, nightgown, put-down, renown, rubdown, rundown, shakedown, showdown, shutdown, sit-down, slowdown, splashdown, sundown, takedown, touchdown, uptown.
Aground, around, astound(s), background, bloodhound, confound(s), dumbfound, earthbound, eastbound, fairground, fogbound, foreground, foxhound, greyhound(s), hellhound(s), hidebound, housebound, icebound, inbound, newshound, northbound, outbound, playground, profound, rebound, renowned, showground, snowbound, southbound, spellbound, stormbound, surround, unwound, westbound, whip-round.
Astounds, bloodhounds, compounds, confounds, dumbfounds, expounds, greyhounds, hellhounds, impounds, surrounds.
About, blackout, blowout, breakout, buyout, checkout, clear-out, cookout, copout, cut-out, devout, dropout, dugout, fallout, handout, hangout, hideout, knockout, layout, litter-lout, lock-out, lookout, payout, printout, pull-out, scout, sell-out, shoot-out, shutout, spin-out, standout, stakeout, takeout, throughout, timeout, tryout, turnout, walkout, washout, way-out, white-out, wipeout, without, workout.
Account, amount, discount, dismount, headcount, recount, surmount.
[3] **Chinatown**, eiderdown, hand-me-down, upside-down.
Battleground, merry-go-round, runaround, turnaround, underground.
Down-and-out, in-and-out, knockabout, layabout, out-and-out, roundabout, runabout, thereabout, turnabout, walk-about.

4.5.4 "--owded" (as in "crowded")
clouded, crowded, enshrouded, overcrowded, shrouded.

SURPRISING RHYMING:
[2] **Bounded**, counted, grounded, hounded, mounted, pounded, rounded, sounded.
Clouted, doubted, flouted, outed, pouted, routed (U.S.), scouted, shouted, spouted, sprouted, touted.
[3] **Astounded**, confounded, dumbfounded, expounded, impounded, rebounded, surrounded, unfounded.
Accounted, amounted, discounted, dismounted, surmounted.

4.5.5 "--owder" (as in "powder")
chowder, gunpowder, louder, powder, prouder.

SURPRISING RHYMING:
[2] **Doubter**, down-and-outer, flouter, outer, pouter, shouter, touter.
Browner, crowner, counter, downer, drowner, frowner.
Bounder, founder, flounder, grounder, pounder, rounder, sounder.

Browser, dowser, mouser, rouser, trouser, wowser.
Cower, flower, glower, hour, our, power, shower, sour, tower.
Fouler, growler, howler, prowler, scowler.
[3] **Downtowner**, midtowner, out-of-towner, sundowner, uptowner.
Compounder, confounder, dumbfounder, expounder, rebounder.

4.5.6 "--owdy" (as in "cloudy")
[2] cloudy, dowdy, howdy, rowdy.

SURPRISING RHYMING:
[2] **Bouncy**, boundary, bounty, brownie, cowardly, devoutly, drowsy, hourly, loudly, lousy, Mountie, mousey, mouthy, proudly, profoundly, roundly, soundly, sourly, stoutly, townie.

4.5.7 "--owl" (as in "howl")
[1] cowl, foul, fowl, growl, howl, jowl, owl, prowl, scowl, yowl.

SURPRISING RHYMING:
[1] **Bowel**, dowel, towel, trowel, vowel.
Bough, bow, brow, chow, ciao, cow, how, now, plough/plow (U.S.), row, vow, wow.
Bowed, cloud, crowd, loud, ploughed/plowed (U.S.), proud, shroud, vowed, wowed.
Brown, clown, crown, down, drown, frown, gown, noun, town.
Bound, clowned, crowned, downed, drowned, found, frowned, ground, hound, mound, pound, round, sound, wound.
[2] **Allow**, endow, eyebrow, highbrow, know-how, lowbrow, somehow.
Allowed, aloud, avowed, endowed, unbowed, unploughed/unplowed.
Breakdown, clampdown, climbdown, comedown, countdown, crackdown, downtown, hoedown, hometown, letdown, lowdown, markdown, meltdown, midtown, nightgown, put-down, renown, rubdown, rundown, shakedown, showdown, shutdown, sit-down, slowdown, splashdown, sundown, takedown, touchdown, uptown.
Abound, aground, around, astound, background, bloodhound, confound, dumbfound, earthbound, eastbound, fairground, fogbound, foreground, foxhound, greyhound, hellhound, hidebound, housebound, icebound, inbound, newshound, northbound, outbound, playground, profound, rebound, renowned, showground, snowbound, southbound, spellbound, stormbound, surround, unwound, westbound, whip-round.
[3] **Anyhow**, disallow, disavow, middlebrow.
Overcrowd, thundercloud, unavowed, well-endowed.
Chinatown, eiderdown, hand-me-down, upside-down.
Battleground, merry-go-round, runaround, turnaround, underground.

4.5.8 "--oun" (as in "down")
[1] brown, clown, crown, down, drown, frown, gown, noun, town.
[2] breakdown, clampdown, climbdown, comedown, countdown, crackdown, downtown, hoedown, hometown, letdown, lowdown, markdown, meltdown, midtown, Motown, nightgown, put-down, renown, rubdown, rundown, shakedown, showdown, shutdown, sit-down, slowdown, splashdown, sundown, takedown, touchdown, toytown, uptown.
[3] Chinatown, eiderdown, hand-me-down, upside-down.

SURPRISING RHYMING:
[1] **Bound**, browned, clowned, crowned, downed, drowned, found, frowned, ground, hound, mound, pound, round, sound, wound.
Bough, bow, brow, chow, ciao, cow, dhow, how, now, ow, plough/plow (U.S.), pow, row, sow, thou, vow, wow.
Bowed, cloud, crowd, loud, ploughed/plowed (U.S.), proud, shroud, vowed, wowed.
Bout, clout, count, doubt, drought, flout, fount, lout, mount, out, pout, rout, route (U.S.), scout, shout, snout, spout, sprout.
[2] **Allow**, endow, eyebrow, highbrow, know-how, lowbrow, somehow.
Abound, aground, around, astound, background, bloodhound, confound, dumbfound, earthbound, eastbound, fairground, fogbound, foreground, foxhound, greyhound,

hellhound, hidebound, housebound, icebound, inbound, newshound, northbound, outbound, playground, profound, rebound, renowned, showground, snowbound, southbound, spellbound, stormbound, surround, unwound, westbound, whip-round.
Allowed, aloud, avowed, endowed, unbowed, unploughed/unplowed.
Account, amount, discount, dismount, headcount, recount, surmount.
About, blackout, blowout, breakout, buyout, checkout, clear-out, cookout, copout, cut-out, devout, dropout, dugout, fallout, handout, hangout, hideout, knockout, layout, litter-lout, lock-out, lookout, payout, printout, pull-out, scout, sell-out, shoot-out, shutout, spin-out, standout, stakeout, takeout, throughout, timeout, tryout, turnout, walkout, washout, way-out, white-out, wipeout, without, workout.
[3] **Battleground**, merry-go-round, runaround, turnaround.
Anyhow, disallow, disavow, middlebrow.
Overcrowd, thundercloud, unavowed, well-endowed.
Down-and-out, in-and-out, knockabout, layabout, out-and-out, paramount, roundabout, runabout, tantamount, turnabout, walk-about.

4.5.9 "--ound" (as in "found")

[1] bound, browned, clowned, crowned, downed, drowned, found, frowned, ground, hound, mound, pound, round, sound, wound.
[2] abound, aground, around, astound, background, bloodhound, compound, confound, dumbfound, earthbound, eastbound, expound, fairground, fogbound, foreground, foxhound, greyhound, hellhound, hidebound, housebound, icebound, impound, inbound, newshound, northbound, outbound, playground, profound, rebound, renowned, showground, snowbound, southbound, spellbound, stormbound, surround, unsound, unwound, westbound, whip-round.
[3] battleground, merry-go-round, runaround, turnaround, underground.

SURPRISING RHYMING:
[1] **Brown**, clown, crown, down, drown, frown, gown, noun, town.
Bough, bow, brow, chow, ciao, cow, how, now, plough/plow (U.S.), row, vow, wow.
Bowed, cloud, crowd, loud, ploughed/plowed (U.S.), proud, shroud, vowed, wowed.
Bout, clout, doubt, drought, flout, lout, out, pout, route (U.S.), scout, shout, snout, spout, sprout, stout, tout.
[2] **Breakdown**, clampdown, climbdown, comedown, countdown, crackdown, downtown, hoedown, hometown, letdown, lowdown, markdown, meltdown, midtown, nightgown, put-down, renown, rubdown, rundown, shakedown, showdown, shutdown, sit-down, slowdown, splashdown, sundown, takedown, touchdown, uptown.
Allow, endow, eyebrow, highbrow, know-how, lowbrow, somehow.
Allowed, aloud, avowed, endowed, unbowed, unploughed/unplowed.
Account, amount, discount, dismount, headcount, recount, surmount.
About, blackout, blowout, breakout, buyout, checkout, clear-out, cookout, copout, cut-out, devout, dropout, dugout, fallout, handout, hangout, hideout, knockout, layout, litter-lout, lock-out, lookout, payout, printout, pull-out, scout, sell-out, shoot-out, shutout, spin-out, standout, stakeout, takeout, throughout, timeout, tryout, turnout, walkout, washout, way-out, white-out, wipeout, without, workout.
[3] **Anyhow**, disallow, disavow, middlebrow.
Overcrowd, thundercloud, unavowed, well-endowed.
Down-and-out, in-and-out, knockabout, layabout, out-and-out, paramount, roundabout, runabout, tantamount, turnabout, walk-about.

4.5.10 "--ounded" (as in "grounded")

[2] bounded, founded, grounded, hounded, pounded, rounded, sounded.
[3] astounded, compounded, confounded, dumbfounded, expounded, impounded, rebounded, surrounded, unfounded.

SURPRISING RHYMING:
[2] **Clouded**, counted, crowded, mounted, shrouded.
Clouted, doubted, flouted, fountain, ousted, outed, mountain, pouted, routed (U.S.), scouted, shouted, spouted, sprouted, touted.
[3] **Enshrouded**, overcrowded.

Accounted, amounted, discounted, dismounted, surmounted.

4.5.11 "--ounding" (as in "astounding")
[2] bounding, founding, grounding, hounding, pounding, rounding, sounding.
[3] astounding, compounding, confounding, dumbfounding, expounding, rebounding, resounding, surrounding.

SURPRISING RHYMING:
[2] **Counting**, clouding, crowding, mounting, overcrowding, shrouding.
Clowning, crowning, downing, drowning, frowning.
Clouting, doubting, outing, pouting, routing (U.S.), scouting, shouting.
Bouncing, flouncing, pouncing, trouncing.
Cowering, flowering, glowering, powering, showering, towering.
Bowing, ploughing/plowing (U.S.), rowing, vowing, wowing.
[3] **Accounting**, amounting, discounting, dismounting, surmounting.
Allowing, avowing, disallowing, disavowing, endowing.
Announcing, denouncing, mispronouncing, pronouncing, renouncing.

4.5.12 "--ounds" (as in "pounds")
[1] bounds, grounds, hounds, mounds, pounds, rounds, sounds.
[2] astounds, bloodhounds, compounds, confounds, dumbfounds, expounds, greyhounds, hellhounds, impounds, surrounds.

SURPRISING RHYMING:
[1] **Bound**, clowned, crowned, downed, drowned, found, frowned, ground, hound, mound, pound, round, sound, wound.
Clowns, crowns, downs, drowns, frowns, gowns, nouns, towns.
Bounce, flounce, ounce, pounce, trounce.
Clouds, crowds, shrouds, thunderclouds.
[2] **Abound**, aground, around, astound, background, bloodhound, confound, dumbfound, earthbound, eastbound, fairground, fogbound, foreground, foxhound, greyhound, hellhound, hidebound, housebound, icebound, inbound, newshound, northbound, outbound, playground, profound, rebound, renowned, showground, snowbound, southbound, spellbound, stormbound, surround, unwound, westbound, whip-round.
Breakdowns, climbdowns, comedowns, countdowns, crackdowns, hand-me-downs, letdowns, put-downs, showdowns, slowdowns.
Announce, denounce, mispronounce, pronounce, renounce.
Accounts, amounts, counts, discounts, founts, mounts, recounts.
[3] **Battleground**, merry-go-round, runaround, turnaround, underground.

4.5.13 "--ounce" (as in "bounce")
[1] bounce, flounce, ounce, pounce, trounce.
[2] announce, denounce, mispronounce, pronounce, renounce.

SURPRISING RHYMING:
[1] **Bounds**, grounds, hounds, mounds, pounds, rounds, sounds.
Clowns, crowns, downs, drowns, frowns, gowns, nouns, towns.
Clouds, crowds, shrouds, thunderclouds.
Couch, crouch, grouch, ouch, pouch, slouch, vouch.
Blouse, browse, douse, dowse, house, mouse, scouse, spouse.
Bouts, clouts, doubts, louts, pouts, routes (U.S.), shouts, touts.
[2] **Astounds**, bloodhounds, confounds, hellhounds, surrounds.
Breakdowns, clampdowns, climbdowns, comedowns, countdowns, crackdowns, hand-me-downs, letdowns, put-downs, showdowns.
Accounts, amounts, counts, discounts, founts, mounts, recounts.
Alehouse, birdhouse, boathouse, clubhouse, courthouse, doghouse, dollhouse, farmhouse, glasshouse, greenhouse, guesthouse, henhouse, hothouse, jailhouse, lighthouse, madhouse, penthouse, playhouse, townhouse, treehouse, warehouse.

Blackouts, blowouts, breakouts, checkouts, clear-outs, cut-outs, dropouts, handouts, hangouts, hideouts, knockouts, layouts, lookouts, payouts, shoot-outs, stakeouts, takeouts, timeouts, tryouts, walkouts.
[3] **Down-and-outs**, ins-and-outs, layabouts, roundabouts, thereabouts.

4.5.14 "--ouncing" (as in "pouncing")
[2] bouncing, flouncing, pouncing, trouncing.
[3] announcing, denouncing, mispronouncing, pronouncing, renouncing.

SURPRISING RHYMING:
[2] **Browsing**, crouching, dowsing, housing, slouching, vouching.
Bounding, grounding, hounding, pounding, rounding, sounding.
Clouding, crowding, enshrouding, overcrowding, shrouding.
Browning, clowning, crowning, downing, drowning, frowning.
Clouting, counting, doubting, fountain, mountain, mounting, outing, pouting, routing (U.S.), scouting, shouting, spouting.
[3] **Astounding**, confounding, rebounding, resounding, surrounding.
Accounting, amounting, discounting, dismounting, surmounting.

4.5.15 "--ouncement" (as in "announcement")
[3] announcement, denouncement, pronouncement, renouncement.

SURPRISING RHYMING:
[2] **Bouncing**, flouncing, pouncing, trouncing.
Browsing, dowsing, gouging, grousing, housing.
Browning, clowning, crowning, downing, drowning, frowning.
Bounding, counting, founding, fountain, grounding, hounding, mountain, mounting, pounding, rounding, sounding.
[3] **Announcing**, denouncing, pronouncing, renouncing.
Accountant, amounting, dismounting, recounting, surmounting.

4.5.16 "--ount" (as in "count")
[1] count, fount, mount.
[2] account, amount, discount, dismount, headcount, surmount.
[3] paramount, tantamount.

SURPRISING RHYMING:
[1] **Bout**, clout, doubt, drought, flout, lout, out, pout, route (U.S.), scout, shout, snout, spout, sprout, stout, tout.
Couched, crouched, pouched, slouched, vouched.
Bounced, flounced, pounced, trounced.
Bound, browned, clowned, crowned, downed, drowned, found, frowned, ground, hound, mound, pound, round, sound, wound.
Bowed, cloud, crowd, loud, ploughed/plowed (U.S.), proud, shroud, vowed, wowed.
[2] **About**, blackout, blowout, breakout, buyout, checkout, clear-out, cookout, copout, cut-out, devout, dropout, dugout, fallout, handout, hangout, hideout, knockout, layout, litter-lout, lock-out, lookout, payout, printout, pull-out, scout, sell-out, shoot-out, shutout, spin-out, standout, stakeout, takeout, throughout, timeout, tryout, turnout, walkout, washout, way-out, white-out, wipeout, without, workout.
Abound, aground, around, astound, background, bloodhound, confound, dumbfound, earthbound, eastbound, fairground, fogbound, foreground, foxhound, greyhound, hellhound, hidebound, housebound, icebound, inbound, newshound, northbound, outbound, playground, profound, rebound, renowned, showground, snowbound, southbound, spellbound, stormbound, surround, unwound, westbound, whip-round.
Announced, denounced, mispronounced, pronounced, renounced.
Allowed, aloud, avowed, endowed, enshroud, meowed, unbowed.
[3] **Down-and-out**, in-and-out, knockabout, layabout, out-and-out, paramount, roundabout, runabout, tantamount, turnabout, walk-about.
Battleground, merry-go-round, runaround, turnaround, underground.

4.5.17 "--ounty" (as in "bounty")
[2] bounty, county, Mountie.

SURPRISING RHYMING:
[2] **Bouncy**, boundary, brownie, cowardly, devoutly, drowsy, hourly, loudly, lousy, mouthy, proudly, profoundly, roundly, soundly, townie.
Cloudy, dowdy, howdy, rowdy.
Coffee, frothy, toffee.

4.5.18 "--ountain" (as in "mountain")
[2] fountain, mountain.

SURPRISING RHYMING:
[2] **Counting**, mounting.
Browning, clowning, crowning, downing, drowning, frowning.
Doubting, outing, pouting, routing (U.S.), scouting, shouting, spouting.
Bounding, grounding, hounding, pounding, rounding, sounding.
Bouncing, flouncing, pouncing, trouncing.
[3] **Accounting**, amounting, discounting, dismounting, surmounting.
Astounding, confounding, dumbfounding, rebounding, resounding, surrounding.
Announcing, denouncing, mispronouncing, pronouncing, renouncing.

4.5.19 "--ounting" (as in "counting")
[2] counting, mounting.
[3] accounting, amounting, discounting, dismounting, surmounting.

SURPRISING RHYMING:
[2] **Fountain**, mountain.
Clouting, doubting, outing, pouting, routing (U.S.), scouting, shouting.
Clouding, crowding, enshrouding, overcrowding, shrouding.
Browning, clowning, crowning, downing, drowning, frowning.
Bounding, grounding, hounding, pounding, rounding, sounding.
Bouncing, browsing, flouncing, pouncing, trouncing.
[3] **Astounding**, confounding, dumbfounding, rebounding, resounding, surrounding.
Announcing, denouncing, mispronouncing, pronouncing, renouncing.

4.5.20 "--our" (as in "hour")
[1] cower, dour, flour, flower, glower, hour, our, plougher/plower (U.S.), power, scour, shower, sour, tower.
[2] brainpower, cornflour, cornflower, devour, empower, firepower, flower-power, horsepower, man-hour, manpower, mayflower, moonflower, rush hour, sunflower, wallflower, watchtower, willpower.
[3] cauliflower, overpower, passion flower, superpower, sweet-and-sour.

SURPRISING RHYMING:
[1] **Cowers**, flowers, glowers, hours, ours, powers, showers, towers.
Doubter, down-and-outer, outer, pouter, router (U.S.), shouter, touter.
Browner, crowner, counter, downer, frowner.
Founder, flounder, grounder, louder, powder, pounder, prouder, rounder, sounder.
Browser, dowser, mouser, rouser, trouser, wowser.
Fouler, growler, howler, prowler, scowler, voyeur.
[2] **Devours**, empowers, man-hours, sunflowers, wallflowers.
[3] **Overpowers**, passion flowers, sunflowers, superpowers.

4.5.21 "--ours" (as in "flowers")
[1] cowers, flowers, glowers, hours, ours, ploughers/plowers (U.S.), powers, scours, showers, towers.
[2] devours, empowers, man-hours, sunflowers, wallflowers.
[3] moonflowers, overpowers, passion flowers, sunflowers, superpowers.

SURPRISING RHYMING:
[1] **Cower**, flower, glower, hour, our, power, shower, sour, tower.
Foulers, growlers, howlers, prowlers, scowlers, voyeurs.
Doubters, down-and-outers, pouters, scouters, shouters, touters.
Bounders, founders, flounders, pounders, rounders.
Browsers, dowsers, rousers, trousers, wowsers.
[2] **Brainpower**, devour, empower, firepower, flower-power, horsepower, man-hour, manpower, mayflower, moonflower, rush hour, sunflower, wallflower, watchtower, willpower.
[3] **Bridal shower**, overpower, passion flower, superpower, sweet-and-sour.

4.5.22 "--owering" (as in "towering")
[2] cowering, flowering, glowering, powering, scouring, showering, souring, towering.

SURPRISING RHYMING:
[1] **Clouding**, crowding, enshrouding, overcrowding, shrouding.
Browning, clowning, crowning, downing, drowning, frowning.
Doubting, outing, pouting, routing (U.S.), scouting, shouting, spouting.
Bouncing, flouncing, pouncing, trouncing.
Bowing, ploughing/plowing (U.S.), rowing, vowing, wowing.
Browsing, dowsing, gouging, housing.
Bounding, grounding, hounding, pounding, rounding, sounding.
[3] **Devouring**, empowering, floundering, powdering.
Astounding, compounding, confounding, dumbfounding, expounding, rebounding, resounding, surrounding.
Accounting, amounting, discounting, dismounting, surmounting.
Allowing, avowing, disallowing, disavowing, endowing.

4.5.23 "--ouse" (as in "house")
[1] blouse, browse, dowse, grouse, house, louse, mouse, nous, scouse, spouse.
[2] alehouse, birdhouse, boathouse, clubhouse, coach house, cookhouse, courthouse, doghouse, dollhouse, dormouse, farmhouse, glasshouse, greenhouse, guardhouse, guesthouse, henhouse, hothouse, in-house, jailhouse, lighthouse, madhouse, outhouse, penthouse, playhouse, poorhouse, steakhouse, storehouse, teahouse, townhouse, treehouse, warehouse, White House.
[3] counting house, powerhouse, summerhouse.

SURPRISING RHYMING:
[1] **Bough**(s), bow(s), brow, chow, ciao, cow(s), how, mouth(s), now, plough(s)/plow(s) (U.S.), pow, row(s), south, thou, vow(s), wow.
Bounce, flounce, ounce, pounce, trounce.
Couch, crouch, grouch, ouch, pouch, slouch, vouch.
Bout(s), clout(s), doubt(s), drought(s), flout(s), lout(s), out, pout(s), route(s) (U.S.), scout(s), shout(s), snout(s), spout(s), stout, tout(s).
[2] **Allow**, avow(s), endow(s), eyebrow(s), highbrow, know-how, kowtow(s), lowbrow, nohow, powwow, somehow.
Announce, denounce, mispronounce, pronounce, renounce.
About, blackout(s), blowout(s), breakout(s), buyout(s), checkout(s), clear-out(s), cookout(s), copout(s), cut-out(s), devout, dropout(s), dugout(s), fallout, handout(s), hangout(s), hideout(s), knockout(s), layout(s), litter-lout(s), lock-out, lookout(s), payout, printout(s), pull-out(s), sell-out, shoot-out(s), shutout, spin-out, standout, stakeout(s), takeout(s), throughout, timeout, tryout(s), turnout, walkout(s), washout, way-out, white-out, wipeout, without, workout(s).
Bad-mouth, bigmouth, goalmouth, loudmouth.
[3] **Anyhow**, disallow(s), disavow(s), middlebrow.
Down-and-out(s), hereabout(s), in-and-out, knockabout, layabout(s), out-and-out, paramount, roundabout(s), runabout, tantamount, thereabout(s), turnabout, walk-about.
Blabbermouth, motormouth, mouth-to-mouth.

*

4.5.24 "--ouser" (as in "browser")
[2] browser, dowser, mouser, rouser, trouser, wowser.
[3] carouser, espouser, rabble-rouser.

SURPRISING RHYMING:
[2] **Bouncer**, flouncer, pouncer, sloucher, trouncer, voucher.
Cower, dour, flower, glower, hour, our, power, shower, sour, tower.
Chowder, gunpowder, louder, powder, prouder.
Browner, crowner, counter, downer, frowner.
Bounder, founder, flounder, grounder, pounder, rounder, sounder.
Doubter, down-and-outer, flouter, pouter, router (U.S.), shouter.
Fouler, growler, howler, prowler, scowler.
[3] **Announcer**, denouncer, renouncer.
Downtowner, midtowner, out-of-towner, sundowner, uptowner.

4.5.25 "--out" (as in "doubt")
[1] bout, clout, doubt, drought, flout, gout, lout, out, pout, rout, route (U.S.), scout, shout, snout, spout, sprout, stout, tout, trout.
[2] about, blackout, blowout, boy scout, breakout, buyout, checkout, clear-out, cookout, copout, cut-out, devout, dropout, dugout, fallout, handout, hangout, hideout, knockout, layout, litter-lout, lock-out, lookout, payout, printout, pull-out, sell-out, shoot-out, shutout, spin-out, standout, stakeout, takeout, throughout, timeout, tryout, turnout, walkout, washout, way-out, white-out, wipeout, without, workout.
[3] down-and-out, hereabout, in-and-out, knockabout, layabout, out-and-out, roundabout, runabout, thereabout, turnabout, walk-about.

SURPRISING RHYMING:
[1] **Count**, fount, mount.
Bough, bow(ed), brow, cow(ed), how, mouth, now, row(ed), south, vow(ed), wow(ed).
Cloud, crowd, loud, ploughed/plowed (U.S.), proud, shroud.
Bound, clowned, crowned, downed, drowned, found, frowned, ground, hound, mound, pound, round, sound, wound.
[2] **Account**, amount, discount, dismount, headcount, surmount.
Allow, endow, eyebrow, highbrow, know-how, lowbrow, somehow.
Allowed, aloud, avowed, endowed, unbowed, unploughed/unplowed.
Bad-mouth, bigmouth, goalmouth, loudmouth.
[3] **Anyhow**, disallow, disavow, middlebrow.
Overcrowd, thundercloud, well-endowed.
Blabbermouth, motormouth, mouth-to-mouth, paramount, tantamount.

4.5.26 "--outed" (as in "shouted")
[2] clouted, doubted, flouted, grouted, outed, pouted, routed (U.S.), scouted, shouted, spouted, sprouted, touted.

SURPRISING RHYMING:
[1] **Counted**, mounted.
Clouded, crowded, enshrouded, shrouded.
Founded, grounded, hounded, pounded, rounded, sounded.
[3] **Accounted**, amounted, discounted, dismounted, overcrowded, surmounted.
Astounded, compounded, confounded, dumbfounded, expounded, impounded, rebounded, surrounded, unfounded.

4.5.27 "--outer" (as in "shouter")
[2] doubter, down-and-outer, flouter, outer, pouter, router (U.S.), scouter, shouter, spouter, stouter, touter.

SURPRISING RHYMING:
[2] **Counter**, downer, frowner, gunpowder, louder, powder, prouder.
Bounder, founder, flounder, pounder, rounder, sounder, voucher.

Browser, dowser, mouser, ouster, rouser, trouser, wowser.
Cower, dour, flower, glower, hour, our, power, shower, sour, tower.
Fouler, growler, howler, prowler, scowler.
[3] Downtowner, midtowner, out-of-towner, sundowner, uptowner.
Compounder, confounder, encounter, expounder, rebounder.
[4] Baking powder, chili powder, take a powder, talcum powder.

4.5.28 "--outing" (as in "shouting")
[2] clouting, doubting, grouting, outing, pouting, routing (U.S.), scouting, shouting, spouting, sprouting

SURPRISING RHYMING:
[2] Counting, fountain, mountain, mounting, mouthing.
Clouding, crowding, enshrouding, overcrowding, shrouding.
Bounding, grounding, hounding, pounding, rounding, sounding.
Browning, clowning, crowning, downing, drowning, frowning.
Bouncing, browsing, flouncing, housing, pouncing, trouncing.
Couching, crouching, pouching, slouching, vouching.
Bowing, ploughing/plowing (U.S.), rowing, vowing, wowing.
[3] Accounting, amounting, discounting, dismounting, surmounting.
Astounding, compounding, confounding, dumbfounding, expounding, rebounding, resounding, surrounding.
Allowing, avowing, disallowing, disavowing, endowing, kowtowing.

4.5.29 "--outh" (as in "mouth")
[1] mouth, south.
[2] bad-mouth, bigmouth, goalmouth, loudmouth.
[3] blabbermouth, motormouth, mouth-to-mouth.

SURPRISING RHYMING:
[1] Bow, brow, cow, how, now, plough/plow (U.S.), row, vow, wow.
Brown, clown, crown, down, drown, frown, gown, noun, town.
Bowed, cloud, crowd, loud, ploughed/plowed (U.S.), proud, shroud, vowed, wowed.
Blouse, browse, house, louse, mouse, nous, scouse, spouse.
Bound, browned, clowned, crowned, downed, drowned, found, frowned, ground, hound, mound, pound, round, sound, wound.
Bout, clout, doubt, drought, flout, lout, out, pout, rout, route (U.S.), scout, shout, snout, spout, sprout, stout, tout, trout.
[2] Allow, endow, eyebrow, highbrow, know-how, lowbrow, somehow.
Breakdown, clampdown, climbdown, comedown, countdown, crackdown, downtown, hoedown, hometown, letdown, lowdown, markdown, meltdown, midtown, nightgown, put-down, renown, rubdown, rundown, shakedown, showdown, shutdown, sit-down, slowdown, splashdown, sundown, takedown, touchdown, uptown.
Alehouse, birdhouse, boathouse, clubhouse, courthouse, doghouse, dollhouse, farmhouse, glasshouse, greenhouse, guesthouse, henhouse, hothouse, jailhouse, lighthouse, madhouse, penthouse, playhouse, townhouse, treehouse, warehouse.
Abound, aground, around, astound, background, bloodhound, confound, dumbfound, earthbound, eastbound, fairground, fogbound, foreground, foxhound, greyhound, hellhound, hidebound, housebound, icebound, inbound, newshound, northbound, outbound, playground, profound, rebound, renowned, showground, snowbound, southbound, spellbound, stormbound, surround, unwound, westbound, whip-round.
Allowed, aloud, avowed, endowed, enshroud, unbowed.
About, blackout, blowout, breakout, buyout, checkout, clear-out, cookout, copout, cut-out, devout, dropout, dugout, fallout, handout, hangout, hideout, knockout, layout, litter-lout, lock-out, lookout, payout, printout, pull-out, sell-out, shoot-out, shutout, standout, stakeout, takeout, throughout, timeout, tryout, turnout, walkout, washout, way-out, white-out, wipeout, without, workout.
[3] Anyhow, disallow, disavow, middlebrow.
Overcrowd, thundercloud, well-endowed.

Down-and-out, in-and-out, knockabout, layabout, out-and-out, paramount, roundabout, runabout, tantamount, turnabout, walk-about.

4.5.30 "--owel" (as in "towel")
avowal, bowel, disavowal, dowel, towel, trowel, vowel.

SURPRISING RHYMING:
[1] **Cowl**, foul, fowl, growl, howl, jowl, owl, prowl, scowl, yowl.
Bough, bow, brow, cow, how, mouth, now, plough/plow (U.S.), row, south, vow, wow.
Cower, flower, glower, hour, our, power, shower, sour, tower.
[2] **Allow**, endow, eyebrow, highbrow, know-how, lowbrow, somehow.
Brainpower, devour, empower, firepower, flower-power, horsepower, man-hour, manpower, moonflower, rush hour, sunflower, wallflower, watchtower, willpower.
[3] **Bridal shower**, overpower, passion flower, superpower, sweet-and-sour.

4.5.31 "--owwing" (as in "vowing")
[2] bowing, ploughing/plowing (U.S.), rowing, vowing, wowing.
[3] allowing, avowing, disallowing, disavowing, endowing, kowtowing.

SURPRISING RHYMING:
[1] **Fouling**, growling, howling, prowling, scowling.
Cowering, flowering, glowering, powering, showering, souring, towering.
Browning, clowning, crowning, downing, drowning, frowning.
Bounding, grounding, hounding, pounding, rounding, sounding.
Clouding, crowding, enshrouding, overcrowding, shrouding.
Bouncing, counting, flouncing, mounting, pouncing, trouncing.
Clouting, doubting, outing, pouting, routing (U.S.), shouting, spouting.
[3] **Astounding**, confounding, dumbfounding, rebounding, resounding, surrounding.

4.6 "oo" (as in "boo")

4.6.1 "--oo" (as in "ooh")
[1] blew, blue, boo, brew, chew, clue, coo, coup, crew, cue, dew, do, drew, due, ewe, few, flew, flu, flue, glue, goo, grew, hue, knew, lieu, loo, mew, new, ooh, pew, phew, queue, screw, shoe, shoo, shrew, Sioux, skew, slew, spew, stew, strew, sue, threw, through, thru, to, too, true, two, view, who, woo, yew, you, zoo.
[2] accrue, adieu, ado, aircrew, anew, argue, askew, bamboo, bayou, bijou, booboo, boohoo, breakthrough, canoe, cashew, construe, corkscrew, cuckoo, curfew, debut, déjà vu, derring-do, diss you, emu, ensue, eschew, fondue, gumshoe, guru, hairdo, hoodoo, horseshoe, igloo, imbue, in lieu, into, in two, issue, juju, kazoo, kung fu, lasso, menu, mildew, miscue, nephew, onto, outdo, outgrew, preview, pursue, rescue, redo, renew, review, revue, sea-view, see-through, set-to, shampoo, sinew, statue, subdue, taboo, tattoo, thumb-screw, tissue, to-do, true-blue, tutu, undo, undue, unscrew, untrue, value, venue, virtue, voodoo, walk-through, withdrew, yahoo.
[3] autocue, avenue, ballyhoo, barbecue, buckaroo, caribou, cockatoo, continue, devalue, didgeridoo, discontinue, hitherto, honeydew, hullabaloo, impromptu, ingénue, interview, I.O.U., kangaroo, misconstrue, overdue, overthrew, overview, peekaboo, rendezvous, residue, superglue, switcheroo, toodle-oo, well-to-do.

SURPRISING RHYMING:
[1] **Bloom**, boom, broom, doom, fume, gloom, groom, loom, plume, room, tomb, vroom, whom, womb, zoom.
Boon, croon, dune, goon, June, loon, moon, noon, prune, rune, soon, spoon, strewn, swoon, tune.
Groove, move, prove, you've.
Booth, couth, sleuth, smooth, sooth, tooth, truth, youth.
Booed, brewed, brood, chewed, cooed, crude, cued, dude, feud, food, glued, lewd, mood, nude, prude, rude, screwed, shoed, shrewd, skewed, spewed, stewed, sued, viewed, who'd, you'd.

538

Boob, cube, lube, tube, YouTube.
Goof, hoof, proof, roof, spoof, woof.
Cool, cruel, drool, fool, ghoul, mule, pool, rule, school, stool, tool, who'll, you'll, yule.
Blues, boos, booze, bruise, chews, choose, clues, crews, cruise, do's, dues, fuse, lose, mews, muse, news, ooze, ruse, schmooze, shoes, shoos, snooze, stews, sues, use, who's, whose, zoos.
Bruised, cruised, fused, mused, oozed, schmoozed, snoozed, used.
[2] **Assume**, backroom, ballroom, bathroom, bedroom, boardroom, bridegroom, classroom, cloakroom, consume, costume, courtroom, darkroom, elbow-room, entomb, exhume, greenroom, headroom, heirloom, leg-room, newsroom, perfume, playroom, presume, resume, schoolroom, sickroom, stockroom, vacuum, volume.
Balloon, buffoon, cartoon, cocoon, commune, festoon, fortune, harpoon, immune, impugn, lagoon, lampoon, maroon, monsoon, platoon, pontoon, saloon, teaspoon, tycoon, typhoon.
Approve, behoove, disapprove, disprove, improve, remove, reprove.
Eyetooth, forsooth, post-truth, uncouth, untruth.
Accrued, allude, argued, boohooed, canoed, collude, conclude, construed, debuted, delude, elude, ensued, exclude, exude, imbued, include, intrude, miscued, preclude, prelude, previewed, protrude, pursued, queued, renewed, rescued, reviewed, seafood, seclude, shampooed, subdued, tabooed, tattooed, valued, wholefood.
Aloof, bulletproof, childproof, fireproof, flameproof, foolproof, living proof, rainproof, shockproof, soundproof, stormproof, sunroof.
Ampoule, capsule, granule, misrule, module, playschool, preschool, schedule, slide-rule, toadstool, tomfool, whirlpool.
Abuse(d), accuse(d), amuse(d), argues, bemuse(d), breakthroughs, canoes, cashews, confuse(d), construes, curfews, debuts, defuse(d), diffuse, ensues, enthuse(d), excuse(d), gurus, hairdos, hoodoos, horseshoes, infuse(d), igloos, issues, menus, miscues, misuse(d), nephews, peruse(d), previews, pursues, refuse(d), rescues, renews, reviews, revues, rhythm-and-blues, shampoos, sinews, statues, subdues, taboos, tattoos, tissues, unscrews, values, venues, virtues.
[3] **Afternoon**, harvest moon, honeymoon, misfortune, opportune.
Altitude, aptitude, attitude, barbecued, continued, fortitude, gratitude, interlude, interviewed, latitude, longitude, magnitude, misconstrued, multitude, platitude, rendezvoused, solitude, superglued.
April fool, overrule, ridicule, Sunday school, supercool, swimming pool.

4.6.2 "--ooing" (as in "doing")
[2] booing, brewing, chewing, cooing, doing, gluing, mewing, queuing, screwing, mooing, ruin, shooing, skewing, spewing, stewing, strewing, suing, viewing, wooing.
[3] accruing, arguing, boohooing, canoeing, construing, debuting, ensuing, imbuing, issuing, lassoing, miscuing, outdoing, previewing, pursuing, redoing, renewing, rescuing, reviewing, shampooing, subduing, tattooing, undoing, unscrewing, valuing.
[4] barbecuing, continuing, devaluing, discontinuing, interviewing, misconstruing, overdoing, overviewing, rendezvousing, supergluing.

SURPRISING RHYMING:
[2] **Grooving**, moving, proving.
Cooling, drooling, fooling, pooling, ruling, schooling, spooling.
Curing, during, luring, mooring, touring.
Goofing, hoofing, roofing, sleuthing, spoofing, smoothing, soothing.
Blooming, booming, brooding, feuding, fuming, grooming, looming.
Crooning, looning, mooning, pruning, spooning, swooning, tuning.
Boozing, bruising, choosing, cruising, fusing, losing, musing, oozing, schmoozing, snoozing, using.
Drooping, duping, grouping, looping, pooping, scooping, snooping, stooping, swooping, trooping, whooping.
Booting, hooting, looting, rooting, scooting, shooting, suiting, tooting.
[3] **Approving**, disapproving, disproving, improving, removing.
Alluring, assuring, enduring, ensuring, insuring, maturing, obscuring, posturing, procuring, reassuring, securing.

Assuming, consuming, perfuming, presuming, resuming, vacuuming.
Ballooning, communing, honeymooning, lampooning, marooning.
Abusing, accusing, amusing, bemusing, confusing, defusing, effusing, enthusing, excusing, infusing, misusing, perusing, refusing.
Commuting, computing, diluting, disputing, polluting, recruiting, saluting, uprooting.

4.6.3 "--boo" (as in "taboo")
boo, bamboo, booboo, boohoo, caribou, marabou, peekaboo, taboo.

SURPRISING RHYMING:
[1] **Blew**, blue, brew, chew, clue, coup, crew, cue, dew, do, drew, due, few, flew, flu, glue, grew, hue, knew, new, pew, queue, screw, shoe, shoo, skew, stew, sue, threw, through, thru, to, too, true, two, view, who, woo, yew, you, zoo.
Boon, croon, dune, goon, June, loon, moon, noon, rune, soon, spoon, swoon, tune.
Bloom, boom, broom, doom, fume, gloom, groom, loom, plume, room, tomb, vroom, whom, womb, zoom.
Booth, groove, move, prove, sleuth, sooth, tooth, truth, youth, you've.
Booed, brewed, brood, chewed, cooed, crude, cued, dude, feud, food, glued, lewd, mood, nude, prude, rude, screwed, shoed, shrewd, skewed, spewed, stewed, sued, viewed, who'd, you'd.
Goof, hoof, proof, roof, spoof, woof.
Cool, cruel, drool, fool, pool, rule, school, stool, tool, who'll, you'll.
[2] **Accrue**, adieu, ado, anew, argue, askew, bayou, bijou, boohoo, breakthrough, canoe, construe, corkscrew, cuckoo, curfew, debut, déjà vu, derring-do, diss you, ensue, gumshoe, guru, hairdo, hoodoo, horseshoe, igloo, in lieu, into, in two, issue, juju, kazoo, kung fu, lasso, menu, mildew, miscue, nephew, onto, outdo, outgrew, preview, pursue, rescue, redo, renew, review, revue, sea-view, see-through, set-to, shampoo, sinew, statue, subdue, tattoo, thumb-screw, tissue, to-do, true-blue, undo, undue, untrue, value, venue, virtue, voodoo, walk-through, withdrew, yahoo.
Balloon, buffoon, cartoon, cocoon, commune, festoon, fortune, harpoon, immune, impugn, lagoon, lampoon, maroon, monsoon, platoon, pontoon, saloon, teaspoon, tycoon, typhoon.
Assume, backroom, ballroom, bathroom, bedroom, boardroom, bridegroom, classroom, cloakroom, consume, costume, courtroom, darkroom, elbow-room, entomb, exhume, greenroom, headroom, heirloom, leg-room, newsroom, perfume, playroom, presume, resume, schoolroom, stockroom, vacuum, volume.
Eyetooth, forsooth, post-truth, uncouth, untruth.
Approve, behoove, disapprove, disprove, improve, remove, reprove.
Accrued, allude, argued, boohooed, canoed, collude, conclude, construed, debuted, delude, elude, ensued, exclude, exude, imbued, include, intrude, miscued, preclude, prelude, previewed, protrude, pursued, queued, renewed, rescued, reviewed, seafood, seclude, shampooed, subdued, tabooed, tattooed, valued, wholefood.
Aloof, bulletproof, childproof, fireproof, flameproof, foolproof, living proof, rainproof, shockproof, soundproof, stormproof, sunroof.
Capsule, granule, misrule, module, playschool, preschool, schedule, slide-rule, toadstool, tomfool, whirlpool.
Brewing, chewing, cooing, doing, gluing, queuing, screwing, ruin, shooing, skewing, stewing, suing, viewing, wooing.
[3] **Avenue**, ballyhoo, barbecue, buckaroo, continue, devalue, discontinue, hitherto, hullabaloo, impromptu, interview, I.O.U., misconstrue, overdue, overthrew, overview, rendezvous, residue, superglue, switcheroo, well-to-do.
Afternoon, harvest moon, honeymoon, misfortune, opportune.
Altitude, aptitude, attitude, barbecued, continued, fortitude, gratitude, interlude, interviewed, latitude, longitude, magnitude, misconstrued, multitude, platitude, rendezvoused, solitude, superglued.
April fool, overrule, ridicule, Sunday school, supercool, swimming pool.
Accruing, arguing, construing, debuting, ensuing, issuing, miscuing, outdoing, previewing, pursuing, redoing, renewing, rescuing, reviewing, shampooing, subduing, tattooing, undoing, valuing.

[4] Barbecuing, continuing, devaluing, discontinuing, interviewing, misconstruing, overdoing, overviewing, rendezvousing, supergluing.

4.6.4 "--doo" (as in "voodoo")
[1] dew, do, due
[2] adieu, ado, hairdo, hoodoo, mildew, outdo, redo, subdue, to-do, undo, voodoo.
[3] derring-do, didgeridoo, well-to-do.

SURPRISING RHYMING:
[1] **Blew**, blue, brew, chew, clue, coup, crew, cue, drew, few, flew, flu, glue, grew, hue, knew, new, pew, queue, screw, shoe, shoo, skew, stew, sue, threw, through, thru, to, too, true, two, view, who, woo, yew, you, zoo.
Booed, brewed, brood, chewed, cooed, crude, cued, dude, feud, food, glued, lewd, mood, nude, prude, rude, screwed, shoed, shrewd, skewed, spewed, stewed, sued, viewed, who'd, you'd.
Cool, cruel, drool, fool, pool, rule, school, stool, tool, who'll, you'll.
Goof, groove, hoof, move, prove, proof, roof, spoof, woof, you've.
Bloom, boom, broom, doom, fume, gloom, groom, loom, plume, room, tomb, vroom, whom, womb, zoom.
Boon, croon, dune, moon, noon, soon, spoon, strewn, swoon, tune.
Boob, cube, lube, tube, YouTube.
Blues, boos, booze, bruise, chews, choose, clues, crews, cruise, do's, dues, fuse, lose, mews, muse, news, ooze, ruse, schmooze, shoes, snooze, stews, sues, use, who's, whose, zoos.
Booth, couth, sleuth, smooth, sooth, tooth, truth, youth.
[2] **Accrue**, anew, argue, askew, bamboo, bayou, bijou, boohoo, breakthrough, canoe, construe, corkscrew, cuckoo, curfew, debut, déjà vu, derring-do, diss you, ensue, fondue, gumshoe, guru, horseshoe, igloo, in lieu, into, in two, issue, juju, kazoo, kung fu, lasso, menu, miscue, nephew, onto, outgrew, preview, pursue, rescue, renew, review, revue, sea-view, see-through, set-to, shampoo, sinew, statue, taboo, tattoo, thumb-screw, tissue, true-blue, undue, untrue, value, venue, virtue, walk-through, withdrew, yahoo.
Accrued, allude, argued, boohooed, canoed, collude, conclude, construed, debuted, delude, elude, ensued, exclude, exude, imbued, include, intrude, miscued, preclude, prelude, previewed, protrude, pursued, queued, renewed, rescued, reviewed, seafood, seclude, shampooed, subdued, tabooed, tattooed, valued, wholefood.
Capsule, granule, misrule, module, playschool, preschool, schedule, tomfool, whirlpool.
Aloof, bulletproof, childproof, fireproof, flameproof, foolproof, living proof, rainproof, shockproof, soundproof, stormproof, sunroof.
Approve, behoove, disapprove, disprove, improve, remove, reprove.
Assume, backroom, ballroom, bathroom, bedroom, boardroom, bridegroom, classroom, cloakroom, consume, costume, courtroom, darkroom, elbow-room, entomb, exhume, greenroom, headroom, heirloom, leg-room, newsroom, perfume, playroom, presume, resume, schoolroom, stockroom, vacuum, volume.
Baboon, Balloon, buffoon, cartoon, cocoon, commune, festoon, fortune, harpoon, immune, impugn, lagoon, lampoon, maroon, monsoon, platoon, pontoon, saloon, teaspoon, tycoon, typhoon.
Abuse, accuse, amuse, argues, bemuse, breakthroughs, canoes, confuse, construes, curfews, debuts, defuse, diffuse, ensues, enthuse, excuse, gurus, hairdos, hoodoos, horseshoes, infuse, igloos, issues, menus, miscues, misuse, nephews, peruse, previews, pursues, refuse, rescues, renews, reviews, revues, rhythm-and-blues, shampoos, sinews, statues, subdues, taboos, tattoos, tissues, values, venues, virtues.
[3] **Avenue**, ballyhoo, barbecue, buckaroo, continue, devalue, discontinue, hitherto, hullabaloo, impromptu, interview, I.O.U., misconstrue, overdue, overthrew, overview, rendezvous, residue, superglue, switcheroo.
Altitude, aptitude, attitude, barbecued, continued, fortitude, gratitude, interlude, interviewed, latitude, longitude, magnitude, misconstrued, multitude, platitude, rendezvoused, solitude, superglued.
April fool, overrule, ridicule, Sunday school, supercool, swimming pool.
Afternoon, harvest moon, honeymoon, misfortune, opportune.

541

4.6.5 "--loo" (as in "clue")
[1] blew, blue, clue, flew, flu, flue, glue, lieu, loo, slew.
[2] curlew, igloo, in lieu, lulu, sky-blue, true-blue, Zulu.
[3] hullabaloo, superglue, toodle-oo.

SURPRISING RHYMING:
[1] **Boo**, brew, chew, coup, crew, cue, dew, do, drew, due, few, goo, grew, hue, knew, new, queue, screw, shoe, shoo, stew, sue, threw, through/thru, too, true, two, view, who, woo, yew, you, zoo.
Cure, lure, moor, poor, pure, sure, tour, your, you're.
Cool, cruel, drool, fool, pool, rule, school, stool, tool, who'll, you'll.
Booth, groove, move, prove, sleuth, sooth, tooth, truth, youth, you've.
Booed, brewed, brood, chewed, cooed, crude, cued, dude, feud, food, glued, lewd, mood, nude, prude, rude, screwed, shoed, shrewd, skewed, spewed, stewed, sued, viewed, who'd, you'd.
Bloom, boom, broom, doom, fume, gloom, groom, loom, plume, room, tomb, vroom, whom, womb, zoom.
Boon, croon, dune, moon, noon, soon, spoon, strewn, swoon, tune.
Blues, boos, booze, bruise, chews, choose, clues, crews, cruise, do's, dues, fuse, lose, mews, muse, news, ooze, ruse, schmooze, shoes, snooze, stews, sues, use, who's, whose, zoos.
Boob, cube, lube, tube, YouTube.
Deuce, juice, loose, moose, mousse, noose, spruce, truce, use.
Beaut, boot, brute, chute, cute, flute, fruit, hoot, jute, loot, lute, moot, mute, newt, root, route, scoot, shoot, snoot, suit, toot.
Coop, coupe, droop, dupe, group, hoop, loop, poop, scoop, sloop, snoop, soup, stoop, swoop, troop, troupe, whoop.
[2] **Accrue**, adieu, ado, anew, argue, askew, bamboo, bayou, bijou, boohoo, breakthrough, canoe, construe, corkscrew, cuckoo, curfew, debut, déjà vu, derring-do, diss you, ensue, fondue, gumshoe, guru, hairdo, hoodoo, horseshoe, in lieu, into, in two, issue, juju, kazoo, kung fu, lasso, menu, mildew, miscue, nephew, onto, outdo, outgrew, preview, pursue, rescue, redo, renew, review, revue, sea-view, see-through, set-to, shampoo, sinew, statue, subdue, taboo, tattoo, thumb-screw, tissue, to-do, true-blue, undo, undue, untrue, value, venue, virtue, voodoo, walk-through, withdrew, yahoo.
Allure, amour, assure, brochure, contour, couture, demure, detour, endure, ensure, impure, insure, liqueur, manure, mature, obscure, secure, unsure.
Barstool, capsule, granule, module, playschool, preschool, schedule, tomfool, whirlpool.
Aloof, bulletproof, childproof, fireproof, flameproof, foolproof, living proof, rainproof, shockproof, soundproof, stormproof, sunroof.
Eyetooth, forsooth, post-truth, uncouth, untruth.
Approve, behoove, disapprove, disprove, improve, remove, reprove.
Accrued, allude, argued, boohooed, canoed, collude, conclude, construed, debuted, delude, elude, ensued, exclude, exude, imbued, include, intrude, miscued, preclude, prelude, previewed, protrude, pursued, queued, renewed, rescued, reviewed, seafood, seclude, shampooed, subdued, tabooed, tattooed, valued, wholefood.
Balloon, buffoon, cartoon, cocoon, commune, festoon, fortune, harpoon, immune, lagoon, lampoon, maroon, monsoon, platoon, saloon, teaspoon, tycoon, typhoon.
Abuse, accuse, amuse, argues, bemuse, breakthroughs, canoes, confuse, construes, curfews, debuts, defuse, ensues, enthuse, hairdos, hoodoos, horseshoes, infuse, igloos, issues, menus, miscues, nephews, peruse, previews, pursues, rescues, renews, reviews, revues, rhythm-and-blues, shampoos, sinews, statues, subdues, taboos, tattoos, tissues, unscrews, values, venues, virtues.
Abuse (noun), caboose, deduce, diffuse, excuse, footloose, induce, misuse, obtuse, produce, profuse, reduce, refuse, seduce, vamoose.
Acute, astute, Canute, commute, compute, dilute, dispute, en route, grapefruit, jackboot, lawsuit, minute, offshoot, pollute, pursuit, recruit, refute, salute, spacesuit, statute, swimsuit, tracksuit, tribute, uproot.
[3] **Avenue**, ballyhoo, barbecue, buckaroo, continue, devalue, discontinue, hitherto, hullabaloo, impromptu, interview, I.O.U., misconstrue, overdue, overthrew, overview, rendezvous, residue, switcheroo, well-to-do.

Aperture, caricature, furniture, immature, insecure, manicure, overture, paramour, premature, reassure, signature, troubadour.
April fool, overrule, ridicule, Sunday school, supercool, swimming pool.
Altitude, aptitude, attitude, barbecued, continued, fortitude, gratitude, interlude, interviewed, latitude, longitude, magnitude, misconstrued, multitude, platitude, rendezvoused, solitude, superglued.
Assume, backroom, ballroom, bathroom, bedroom, boardroom, bridegroom, classroom, cloakroom, consume, costume, courtroom, darkroom, elbow-room, entomb, exhume, greenroom, headroom, heirloom, leg-room, newsroom, perfume, playroom, presume, resume, schoolroom, stockroom, vacuum, volume.
Afternoon, harvest moon, honeymoon, misfortune, opportune.
Calaboose, introduce, reproduce.
Absolute, attribute, constitute, contribute, destitute, disrepute, distribute, electrocute, execute, institute, parachute, persecute, prostitute, resolute, substitute.

4.6.6 "--noo" (as in "canoe")
[1] gnu, knew, new.
[2] anew, canoe, menu, renew, sinew, venue.
[3] avenue, ingénue, revenue.

SURPRISING RHYMING:
[1] **Blew**, blue, brew, chew, clue, coup, crew, cue, dew, do, drew, due, few, flew, flu, glue, grew, hue, pew, queue, screw, shoe, shoo, skew, stew, sue, threw, through, thru, to, too, true, two, view, who, woo, yew, you, zoo.
Booed, brewed, brood, chewed, cooed, crude, cued, dude, feud, food, glued, lewd, mood, nude, prude, rude, screwed, shoed, shrewd, skewed, spewed, stewed, sued, viewed, who'd, you'd.
Boob, cube, lube, tube, YouTube.
Goof, groove, hoof, move, prove, proof, roof, spoof, woof, you've.
Cool, cruel, drool, fool, pool, rule, school, stool, tool, who'll, you'll.
Bloom, boom, broom, doom, fume, gloom, groom, loom, plume, room, tomb, vroom, whom, womb, zoom.
Boon, croon, dune, moon, noon, soon, spoon, strewn, swoon, tune.
Booth, couth, sleuth, sooth, tooth, truth, youth.
Cure, dour, lure, moor, poor, pure, sure, tour, your, you're.
Cruel, dual, duel, fuel, gruel, jewel, refuel, renewal.
Blues, boos, booze, bruise, chews, choose, clues, crews, cruise, do's, dues, fuse, lose, mews, muse, news, ooze, ruse, schmooze, shoes, snooze, stews, sues, use, who's, whose, zoos.
[2] **Accrue**, adieu, ado, argue, askew, bamboo, bayou, bijou, boohoo, breakthrough, construe, corkscrew, cuckoo, curfew, debut, déjà vu, derring-do, diss you, ensue, fondue, gumshoe, guru, hairdo, hoodoo, horseshoe, igloo, in lieu, into, in two, issue, juju, kazoo, kung fu, lasso, mildew, miscue, nephew, onto, outdo, outgrew, preview, pursue, rescue, redo, review, revue, sea-view, see-through, set-to, shampoo, statue, subdue, taboo, tattoo, thumb-screw, tissue, to-do, true-blue, undo, undue, untrue, value, virtue, voodoo, walk-through, withdrew, yahoo.
Accrued, allude, argued, boohooed, canoed, collude, conclude, construed, debuted, delude, elude, ensued, exclude, exude, imbued, include, intrude, miscued, preclude, prelude, previewed, protrude, pursued, queued, renewed, rescued, reviewed, seafood, seclude, shampooed, subdued, tabooed, tattooed, valued, wholefood.
Aloof, bulletproof, childproof, fireproof, flameproof, foolproof, living proof, rainproof, shockproof, soundproof, stormproof, sunroof.
Barstool, capsule, granule, module, playschool, preschool, schedule, tomfool, whirlpool.
Balloon, buffoon, cartoon, cocoon, commune, festoon, fortune, harpoon, immune, impugn, lagoon, lampoon, maroon, monsoon, platoon, pontoon, saloon, teaspoon, tycoon, typhoon.
Assume, backroom, ballroom, bathroom, bedroom, boardroom, bridegroom, classroom, cloakroom, consume, costume, courtroom, darkroom, elbow-room, entomb, exhume, greenroom, headroom, heirloom, leg-room, newsroom, perfume, playroom, presume, resume, schoolroom, stockroom, vacuum, volume.

Eyetooth, forsooth, post-truth, uncouth, untruth.
Approve, behoove, disapprove, disprove, improve, remove, reprove.
Allure, amour, assure, brochure, contour, couture, demure, detour, endure, ensure, insure, liqueur, mature, obscure, secure, unsure.
Abuse, accuse, amuse, argues, bemuse, breakthroughs, canoes, confuse, construes, curfews, debuts, defuse, diffuse, ensues, enthuse, excuse, gurus, hairdos, hoodoos, horseshoes, infuse, igloos, issues, menus, miscues, misuse, nephews, peruse, previews, pursues, refuse, rescues, renews, reviews, revues, rhythm-and-blues, shampoos, sinews, statues, subdues, taboos, tattoos, tissues, values, venues, virtues.
[3] **Autocue**, ballyhoo, barbecue, buckaroo, continue, devalue, discontinue, hitherto, hullabaloo, impromptu, interview, I.O.U., misconstrue, overdue, overthrew, overview, rendezvous, residue, superglue, switcheroo, well-to-do.
Altitude, aptitude, attitude, barbecued, continued, fortitude, gratitude, interlude, interviewed, latitude, longitude, magnitude, misconstrued, multitude, platitude, rendezvoused, solitude, superglued.
April fool, overrule, ridicule, Sunday school, supercool, swimming pool.
Afternoon, harvest moon, honeymoon, misfortune, opportune.
Aperture, caricature, furniture, immature, insecure, manicure, overture, paramour, premature, reassure, signature, troubadour.

4.6.7 "--roo" (as in "grew")

[1] brew, crew, drew, grew, rue, screw, shrew, strew, threw, through, thru, true.
[2] accrue, breakthrough, construe, corkscrew, guru, outgrew, see-through, thumbscrew, unscrew, untrue, walk-through, withdrew.
[3] buckaroo, kangaroo, misconstrue, overthrew, switcheroo.

SURPRISING RHYMING:
[1] **Blew**, blue, chew, clue, coup, cue, dew, do, due, few, flew, flu, glue, grew, hue, knew, new, pew, queue, shoe, shoo, skew, stew, sue, to, too, two, view, who, woo, yew, you, zoo.
Boon, croon, dune, moon, noon, soon, spoon, strewn, swoon, tune.
Cure, dour, lure, moor, poor, pure, sure, tour, your, you're.
Bloom, boom, broom, doom, fume, gloom, groom, loom, plume, room, tomb, vroom, whom, womb, zoom.
Cruel, dual, duel, fuel, gruel, jewel, refuel, renewal.
Cool, drool, fool, pool, rule, school, stool, tool, who'll, you'll, yule.
Booth, couth, sleuth, smooth, sooth, tooth, truth, youth.
Groove, move, prove, you've.
Goof, hoof, proof, roof, spoof, woof.
Booed, brewed, brood, chewed, cooed, crude, cued, dude, feud, food, glued, lewd, mood, nude, prude, rude, screwed, shoed, shrewd, skewed, spewed, stewed, sued, viewed, who'd, you'd.
Boob, cube, lube, tube, YouTube.
Blues, boos, booze, bruise, chews, choose, clues, crews, cruise, do's, dues, fuse, lose, mews, muse, news, ooze, ruse, schmooze, shoes, snooze, stews, sues, use, who's, whose, zoos.
Coop, coupe, droop, dupe, group, hoop, loop, scoop, sloop, snoop, soup, stoop, swoop, troop, troupe, whoop.
[2] **Argue**, askew, bamboo, bayou, bijou, boohoo, canoe, cuckoo, curfew, debut, déjà vu, derring-do, diss you, ensue, fondue, gumshoe, hairdo, hoodoo, horseshoe, igloo, in lieu, into, in two, issue, juju, kazoo, kung fu, lasso, menu, mildew, miscue, nephew, onto, outdo, preview, pursue, rescue, redo, renew, review, revue, sea-view, set-to, shampoo, sinew, statue, subdue, taboo, tattoo, tissue, to-do, true-blue, tutu, undo, undue, value, venue, virtue, voodoo, withdrew, yahoo.
Balloon, buffoon, cartoon, cocoon, commune, festoon, fortune, harpoon, immune, impugn, lagoon, lampoon, maroon, monsoon, platoon, pontoon, saloon, teaspoon, tycoon, typhoon.
Allure, amour, assure, brochure, contour, couture, demure, detour, endure, ensure, impure, insure, liqueur, manure, mature, obscure, secure, unsure.

Assume, backroom, ballroom, bathroom, bedroom, boardroom, bridegroom, classroom, cloakroom, consume, costume, courtroom, darkroom, elbow-room, entomb, exhume, greenroom, headroom, heirloom, leg-room, newsroom, perfume, playroom, presume, resume, schoolroom, stockroom, vacuum, volume.
Eyetooth, forsooth, post-truth, uncouth, untruth.
Approve, behoove, disapprove, disprove, improve, remove, reprove.
Aloof, bulletproof, childproof, fireproof, flameproof, foolproof, living proof, rainproof, shockproof, soundproof, stormproof, sunroof.
Accrued, allude, argued, boohooed, canoed, collude, conclude, construed, debuted, delude, elude, ensued, exclude, exude, imbued, include, intrude, miscued, preclude, prelude, previewed, protrude, pursued, queued, renewed, rescued, reviewed, seafood, seclude, shampooed, subdued, tabooed, tattooed, valued, wholefood.
Barstool, capsule, granule, module, playschool, preschool, schedule, tomfool, whirlpool.
Abuse, accuse, amuse, argues, bemuse, breakthroughs, canoes, confuse, construes, curfews, debuts, defuse, diffuse, ensues, enthuse, excuse, gurus, hairdos, hoodoos, horseshoes, infuse, igloos, issues, menus, miscues, misuse, nephews, peruse, previews, pursues, refuse, rescues, renews, reviews, revues, rhythm-and-blues, shampoos, sinews, statues, subdues, taboos, tattoos, tissues, values, venues, virtues.
Cock-a-hoop, hencoop, hula-hoop, playgroup, recoup, regroup.
[3] Avenue, autocue, ballyhoo, barbecue, continue, devalue, discontinue, hitherto, hullabaloo, impromptu, interview, I.O.U., overdue, overview, rendezvous, residue, superglue, well-to-do.
Afternoon, harvest moon, honeymoon, misfortune, opportune.
Aperture, caricature, furniture, immature, insecure, manicure, overture, paramour, premature, reassure, signature, troubadour.
Altitude, aptitude, attitude, barbecued, continued, fortitude, gratitude, interlude, interviewed, latitude, longitude, magnitude, misconstrued, multitude, platitude, rendezvoused, solitude, superglued.
April fool, overrule, ridicule, Sunday school, supercool, swimming pool.

4.6.8 "--too" (as in "tattoo")
[1] stew, to, too, two
[2] hereto, into, lean-to, onto, set-to, tattoo, tutu, unto, whereto.
[3] cockatoo, hitherto, impromptu.

SURPRISING RHYMING:
[1] **Blew**, blue, brew, chew, clue, coup, crew, cue, dew, do, drew, due, few, flew, flu, glue, grew, hue, knew, new, pew, queue, screw, shoe, shoo, skew, sue, threw, through, thru, true, view, who, woo, yew, you, zoo.
Boon, croon, dune, moon, noon, soon, spoon, strewn, swoon, tune.
Bloom, boom, broom, doom, fume, gloom, groom, loom, plume, room, tomb, vroom, whom, womb, zoom.
Cruel, dual, duel, fuel, gruel, jewel, refuel, renewal.
Cool, drool, fool, pool, rule, school, stool, tool, who'll, you'll, yule.
Booth, couth, sleuth, smooth, sooth, tooth, truth, youth.
Goof, groove, hoof, move, prove, proof, roof, spoof, woof, you've.
Booed, brewed, brood, chewed, cooed, crude, cued, dude, feud, food, glued, lewd, mood, nude, prude, rude, screwed, shoed, shrewd, skewed, spewed, stewed, sued, viewed, who'd, you'd.
Boob, cube, lube, tube, YouTube.
Blues, boos, booze, bruise, chews, choose, clues, crews, cruise, do's, dues, fuse, lose, mews, muse, news, ooze, ruse, schmooze, shoes, snooze, stews, sues, use, who's, whose, zoos.
Coop, coupe, droop, dupe, group, hoop, loop, scoop, sloop, snoop, soup, stoop, swoop, troop, troupe, whoop.
Booth, couth, sleuth, smooth, sooth, tooth, truth, youth.
Boot, brute, cute, flute, fruit, hoot, loot, mute, root, route, scoot, shoot, suit, toot.
[2] **Accrue**, anew, argue, askew, bamboo, bayou, bijou, boohoo, breakthrough, canoe, construe, corkscrew, cuckoo, curfew, debut, déjà vu, derring-do, diss you, ensue, fondue, gumshoe, guru, hairdo, hoodoo, horseshoe, igloo, in lieu, in two, issue, juju,

545

kazoo, kung fu, lasso, menu, mildew, miscue, nephew, outdo, outgrew, preview, pursue, rescue, redo, renew, review, revue, sea-view, see-through, shampoo, sinew, statue, subdue, taboo, thumb-screw, tissue, to-do, true-blue, undo, undue, untrue, value, venue, virtue, voodoo, walk-through, withdrew, yahoo.
Accrued, allude, argued, boohooed, canoed, collude, conclude, construed, debuted, delude, elude, ensued, exclude, exude, imbued, include, intrude, miscued, preclude, prelude, previewed, protrude, pursued, queued, renewed, rescued, reviewed, seafood, seclude, shampooed, subdued, tabooed, tattooed, valued, wholefood.
Balloon, buffoon, cartoon, cocoon, commune, festoon, fortune, harpoon, immune, impugn, lagoon, lampoon, maroon, monsoon, platoon, pontoon, saloon, teaspoon, tycoon, typhoon.
Allure, amour, assure, brochure, contour, couture, demure, detour, endure, ensure, impure, insure, liqueur, manure, mature, obscure, secure, unsure.
Assume, backroom, ballroom, bathroom, bedroom, boardroom, bridegroom, classroom, cloakroom, consume, costume, courtroom, darkroom, elbow-room, entomb, exhume, greenroom, headroom, heirloom, leg-room, newsroom, perfume, playroom, presume, resume, schoolroom, stockroom, vacuum, volume.
Eyetooth, forsooth, post-truth, uncouth, untruth.
Approve, behoove, disapprove, disprove, improve, remove, reprove.
Aloof, bulletproof, childproof, fireproof, flameproof, foolproof, living proof, rainproof, shockproof, soundproof, stormproof, sunroof.
Barstool, capsule, granule, module, playschool, preschool, schedule, tomfool, whirlpool.
Abuse, accuse, amuse, argues, bemuse, breakthroughs, canoes, confuse, construes, curfews, debuts, defuse, diffuse, ensues, enthuse, excuse, gurus, hairdos, hoodoos, horseshoes, infuse, igloos, issues, menus, miscues, misuse, nephews, peruse, previews, pursues, refuse, rescues, renews, reviews, revues, rhythm-and-blues, shampoos, sinews, statues, subdues, taboos, tattoos, tissues, values, venues, virtues.
Cock-a-hoop, hencoop, hula-hoop, playgroup, recoup, regroup.
Acute, astute, Canute, commute, compute, dilute, dispute, en route, grapefruit, jackboot, lawsuit, minute, offshoot, pollute, pursuit, recruit,
refute, salute, spacesuit, statute, swimsuit, tracksuit, tribute, uproot.
[3] Avenue, autocue, ballyhoo, barbecue, buckaroo, continue, devalue, discontinue, hullabaloo, interview, IOU, misconstrue, overdue, overthrew, overview, rendezvous, residue, superglue, switcheroo, well-to-do.
Afternoon, harvest moon, honeymoon, misfortune, opportune.
Aperture, caricature, furniture, immature, insecure, manicure, overture, paramour, premature, reassure, signature, troubadour.
Altitude, aptitude, attitude, barbecued, continued, fortitude, gratitude, interlude, interviewed, latitude, longitude, magnitude, misconstrued, multitude, platitude, rendezvoused, solitude, superglued.
April fool, overrule, ridicule, Sunday school, supercool, swimming pool.
Absolute, attribute, constitute, contribute, destitute, disrepute, dissolute, distribute, electrocute, execute, institute, parachute, persecute, prostitute, resolute, substitute.

4.6.9 "--ook" (as in "book")
[1] book, brook, cook, crook, hook, look, nook, rook, schnook, schtuck, shook, took.
[2] chequebook, cookbook, fishhook, forsook, guidebook, handbook, mistook, notebook, outlook, partook, phrasebook, playbook, scrapbook, sketchbook, songbook, storybook, textbook, workbook.
[3] inglenook, overcook, overlook, overtook, picture book, pocketbook, storybook, tenterhook, undercook, undertook.

SURPRISING RHYMING:
[1] **Booked**, cooked, hooked, looked.
But, butt, cut, foot, gut, hut, mutt, nut, put, rut, shut, soot, what.
Buck, chuck, duck, luck, muck, pluck, puck, ruck, schmuck, struck, stuck, suck, truck, tuck, yuck.
Blood, could, good, hood, should, stood, wood, would.
[2] **Barefoot**, hotfoot, input, kaput, output, pussyfoot, tenderfoot, underfoot, wrong-foot.
Awestruck, dumbstruck, moonstruck, stagestruck, thunderstruck.

Blue-blood, cold-blood, deadwood, driftwood, firewood, knighthood, manhood, misunderstood, redwood, rosewood, understood, withstood.
[3] **Overcooked**, overlooked, undercooked, unhooked.

4.6.10 "--ooking" (as in "looking")
[2] booking, cooking, hooking, looking.
[4] overcooking, overlooking, undercooking, unhooking.

SURPRISING RHYMING:
[2] **Bucking**, chucking, ducking, plucking, sucking, trucking, tucking.
Butting, cutting, footing, jutting, putting, shutting, strutting, tutting.
Cupping, supping, upping, whooping.
Clubbing, dubbing, pubbing, rubbing, scrubbing, stubbing, subbing.
Bugging, hugging, lugging, mugging, plugging, slugging, tugging.
Blooding, budding, flooding, thudding.
Bumming, coming, drumming, dumbing, humming, numbing, plumbing, slumming, strumming, summing, thumbing.
Cunning, funning, gunning, running, stunning, sunning.
Bluffing, buffing, cuffing, fluffing, huffing, loving, puffing, roughing, shoving, stuffing.
[3] **Barefooting**, hotfooting, inputting, pussyfooting, wrong-footing.

4.6.11 "--ooker" (as in "cooker")
[2] booker, cooker, hookah, hooker, looker, onlooker, snooker.

SURPRISING RHYMING:
[2] **Mucker**, plucker, pucker, sucker, trucker.
Butter, clutter, flutter, gutter, mutter, nutter, putter, shutter, splutter, stutter, utter.
Cuppa, scupper, supper, upper.
Hugger, slugger, smugger, snugger, sugar, tugger.
Butcher, future, pusher, toucher, Worcester.
Clubber, rubber, scrubber.
Bluffer, buffer, rougher, tougher, woofer.

4.6.12 "--oob" (as in "tube")
boob, cube, lube, tube, YouTube.

SURPRISING RHYMING:
[1] **Booed**, brewed, brood, chewed, cooed, crude, cued, dude, feud, food, glued, lewd, mood, nude, prude, rude, screwed, shoed, shrewd, skewed, spewed, stewed, sued, viewed, who'd, you'd.
Coop, coupe, droop, dupe, group, hoop, loop, scoop, sloop, snoop, soup, stoop, swoop, troop, troupe, whoop.
Groove(d), move(d), prove(d), you've.
Bruised, cruised, fused, mused, oozed, schmoozed, snoozed, used.
Booth, couth, sleuth, smooth, sooth, tooth, truth, youth.
Blew, blue, brew, chew, clue, coup, crew, cue, dew, do, drew, due, few, flew, flu, glue, grew, hue, knew, new, pew, queue, screw, shoe, shoo, skew, stew, sue, threw, through, thru, to, too, true, two, view, who, woo, yew, you, zoo.
[2] **Approve**, behoove, disapprove, disprove, improve, remove.
Approved, disapproved, disproved, improved, removed, unmoved.
Cock-a-hoop, hencoop, hula-hoop, playgroup, recoup, regroup.
Accrued, allude, argued, boohooed, canoed, collude, conclude, construed, debuted, delude, elude, ensued, exclude, exude, imbued, include, intrude, miscued, preclude, prelude, previewed, protrude, pursued, queued, renewed, rescued, reviewed, seafood, seclude, shampooed, subdued, tabooed, tattooed, valued, wholefood.
Accrue, anew, argue, askew, bamboo, bayou, bijou, boohoo, breakthrough, canoe, construe, corkscrew, cuckoo, curfew, debut, déjà vu, derring-do, diss you, ensue, fondue, gumshoe, guru, hairdo, hoodoo, horseshoe, igloo, in lieu, into, in two, issue, juju, kazoo, kung fu, lasso, menu, mildew, miscue, nephew, onto, outdo, outgrew,

547

preview, pursue, rescue, redo, renew, review, revue, sea-view, see-through, set-to, shampoo, sinew, statue, subdue, taboo, tattoo, thumb-screw, tissue, to-do, true-blue, tutu, undo, undue, untrue, value, venue, virtue, voodoo, walk-through, withdrew, yahoo.
[3] **Altitude**, aptitude, attitude, barbecued, continued, fortitude, gratitude, interviewed, magnitude, misconstrued, multitude, platitude, rendezvoused, solitude, superglued.
Avenue, autocue, ballyhoo, barbecue, buckaroo, continue, devalue, discontinue, hitherto, hullabaloo, impromptu, interview, I.O.U., misconstrue, overdue, overthrew, overview, rendezvous, residue, superglue, switcheroo, well-to-do.

4.6.13 "--oober" (as in "YouTuber")
Cuba, scuba, tuba, Uber, YouTuber.

SURPRISING RHYMING:
[2] **Brooder**, cruder, intruder, lewder, ruder, shrewder.
Groover, mover, prover, smoother, soother.
Boomer, groomer, humour/humor (U.S.), rumour/rumor (U.S.), roomer, zoomer.
Crooner, lunar, pruner, schooner, sooner, swooner, tuna, tuner.
Boozer, bruiser, chooser, cruiser, loser, schmoozer, snoozer, user.
Bluer, brewer, chewer, doer, fewer, newer, poor, sewer, skewer, stewer, truer, viewer, who're, wooer, you're.
Blooper, drooper, duper, grouper, looper, pooper, scooper, snooper, stupor, super, swooper, trooper, trouper, whooper.
[3] **Approver**, improver, manoeuvre/maneuver (U.S.), remover.
Baby-boomer, consumer, costumer, perfumer, satsuma.
Ballooner, harpooner, honeymooner, lampooner.
Abuser, accuser, amuser, excuser, medusa, refuser, yakuza.
Evil-doer, interviewer, pursuer, rescuer, reviewer, wrongdoer.

4.6.14 "--ood" (as in "food")
[1] booed, brewed, brood, chewed, cooed, crewed, crude, cued, dude, feud, food, glued, hued, lewd, mewed, mood, mooed, nude, oohed, prude, rude, screwed, shoed, shooed, shrewd, skewed, spewed, stewed, sued, viewed, who'd, you'd.
[2] accrued, allude, argued, boohooed, canoed, collude, conclude, construed, debuted, delude, elude, ensued, eschewed, exclude, extrude, exude, imbued, include, intrude, lassoed, miscued, preclude, prelude, previewed, protrude, pursued, queued, renewed, rescued, reviewed, seafood, seclude, shampooed, subdued, tabooed, tattooed, unglued, unscrewed, valued, wholefood.
[3] altitude, amplitude, aptitude, attitude, barbecued, continued, fortitude, gratitude, interlude, interviewed, latitude, longitude, magnitude, misconstrued, multitude, platitude, quietude, rectitude, rendezvoused, servitude, solitude, superglued, unvalued.

SURPRISING RHYMING:
[1] **Grooved**, hooved, moved, proved.
Bruised, cruised, fused, mused, oozed, schmoozed, snoozed, used.
Cured, lured, moored, obscured, secured, toured.
Blew, blue, brew, chew, clue, coup, crew, cue, dew, do, drew, due, few, flew, flu, glue, grew, hue, knew, new, pew, queue, screw, shoe, shoo, skew, stew, sue, threw, through, thru, to, too, true, two, view, who, woo, yew, you, zoo.
Boob, cube, lube, tube, YouTube.
Goof, groove, hoof, move, prove, proof, roof, spoof, woof, you've.
Bloom, boom, broom, doom, fume, gloom, groom, loom, plume, room, tomb, vroom, whom, womb, zoom.
Boon, croon, dune, moon, noon, soon, spoon, strewn, swoon, tune.
Cool, cruel, drool, fool, pool, rule, school, stool, tool, who'll, you'll.
Blues, boos, booze, bruise, chews, choose, clues, crews, cruise, do's, dues, fuse, lose, mews, muse, news, ooze, ruse, schmooze, shoes, snooze, stews, sues, use, who's, whose, zoos.
Booth, couth, sleuth, smooth, sooth, tooth, truth, youth.
[2] **Endured**, ensured, insured, manicured, matured, obscured, reassured, secured.
Approved, disapproved, disproved, improved, removed, unmoved.

Abuse(d), accuse(d), amuse(d), argues, bemuse(d), breakthroughs, canoes, confuse(d), construes, curfews, debuts, defuse(d), diffuse, ensues, enthuse(d), excuse(d), gurus, hairdos, hoodoos, horseshoes, infuse(d), igloos, issues, menus, miscues, misuse(d), nephews, peruse(d), previews, pursues, refuse(d), rescues, renews, reviews, revues, rhythm-and-blues, shampoos, sinews, statues, subdues, taboos, tattoos, tissues, unscrews, values, venues, virtues.
Accrue, anew, argue, askew, bamboo, bayou, bijou, boohoo, breakthrough, canoe, construe, corkscrew, cuckoo, curfew, debut, déjà vu, derring-do, diss you, ensue, fondue, gumshoe, guru, hairdo, hoodoo, horseshoe, igloo, in lieu, into, in two, issue, juju, kazoo, kung fu, lasso, menu, mildew, miscue, nephew, onto, outdo, outgrew, preview, pursue, rescue, redo, renew, review, revue, sea-view, see-through, set-to, shampoo, sinew, statue, subdue, taboo, tattoo, thumb-screw, tissue, to-do, true-blue, tutu, undo, undue, untrue, value, venue, virtue, voodoo, walk-through, withdrew, yahoo.
Aloof, bulletproof, childproof, fireproof, flameproof, foolproof, living proof, rainproof, shockproof, soundproof, stormproof, sunroof.
Assume, backroom, ballroom, bathroom, bedroom, boardroom, bridegroom, classroom, cloakroom, consume, costume, courtroom, darkroom, elbow-room, entomb, exhume, greenroom, headroom, heirloom, leg-room, newsroom, perfume, playroom, presume, resume, schoolroom, stockroom, vacuum, volume.
Balloon, buffoon, cartoon, cocoon, commune, festoon, fortune, harpoon, immune, impugn, lagoon, lampoon, maroon, monsoon, platoon, pontoon, saloon, teaspoon, tycoon, typhoon.
Barstool, capsule, granule, module, playschool, preschool, schedule, tomfool, whirlpool.
Approve, behoove, disapprove, disprove, improve, remove, reprove.
[3] Avenue, autocue, ballyhoo, barbecue, buckaroo, continue, devalue, discontinue, hitherto, hullabaloo, impromptu, interview, I.O.U., misconstrue, overdue, overthrew, overview, rendezvous, residue, superglue, switcheroo, well-to-do.
Afternoon, harvest moon, honeymoon, misfortune, opportune.
April fool, overrule, ridicule, Sunday school, supercool, swimming pool.

4.6.15 "--oods" (as in "moods")
[1] broods, dudes, feuds, foods, moods, nudes, prudes.
[2] alludes, colludes, concludes, deludes, excludes, extrudes, exudes, includes, intrudes, precludes, preludes, protrudes, seafoods.
[3] aptitudes, attitudes, interludes, multitudes, platitudes.

SURPRISING RHYMING:
[1] Booed, brewed, brood, chewed, cooed, crude, cued, dude, feud, food, glued, lewd, mood, nude, prude, rude, screwed, shoed, shrewd, skewed, spewed, stewed, sued, viewed, who'd, you'd.
Blew, blue, brew, chew, clue, coup, crew, cue, dew, do, drew, due, few, flew, flu, glue, grew, hue, knew, new, pew, queue, screw, shoe, shoo, skew, stew, sue, threw, through, thru, to, too, true, two, view, who, woo, yew, you, zoo.
Boobs, cubes, tubes.
Booths, grooves, moves, proves, smooths, soothes, truths, youths.
Blues, boos, booze, bruise, chews, choose, clues, crews, cruise, do's, dues, fuse, lose, mews, muse, news, ooze, ruse, schmooze, shoes, snooze, stews, sues, use, who's, whose, zoos.
Blooms, booms, brooms, fumes, grooms, rooms, tombs, zooms.
Dunes, goons, loons, moons, runes, spoons, swoons, tunes.
Drools, fools, ghouls, mules, pools, rules, schools, stools, tools.
Cures, lures, moors, obscures, secures, tours, yours.
[2] Accrued, allude, argued, boohooed, canoed, collude, conclude, construed, debuted, delude, elude, ensued, exclude, exude, imbued, include, intrude, miscued, preclude, prelude, previewed, protrude, pursued, queued, renewed, rescued, reviewed, seafood, seclude, shampooed, subdued, tabooed, tattooed, valued, wholefood.
Approves, disapproves, disproves, improves, removes.
Abuse, accuse, amuse, argues, bemuse, breakthroughs, canoes, confuse, construes, curfews, debuts, defuse, diffuse, ensues, enthuse, excuse, gurus, hairdos, hoodoos,

horseshoes, infuse, igloos, issues, menus, miscues, misuse, nephews, peruse, previews, pursues, refuse, rescues, renews, reviews, revues, rhythm-and-blues, shampoos, sinews, statues, subdues, taboos, tattoos, tissues, values, venues, virtues.
Assumes, backrooms, bathrooms, bedrooms, boardrooms, bridegrooms, classrooms, consumes, costumes, courtrooms, entombs, exhumes, heirlooms, mushrooms, newsrooms, perfumes, presumes, resumes, schoolrooms, vacuums, volumes.
Balloons, buffoons, cartoons, communes, fortunes, lagoons, maroons, monsoons, saloons, teaspoons, tycoons, typhoons.
[3] Altitude, aptitude, attitude(s), barbecued, continued, fortitude, gratitude, interlude, interviewed, latitude, longitude, magnitude, misconstrued, multitude, platitude(s), rendezvoused, solitude, superglued.
Avenues, barbecues, buckaroos, continues, devalues, interviews, IOUs, kangaroos, misconstrues, rendezvous (*pron. "rondayvooz"*).

4.6.16 "--oodest" (as in "rudest")
[2] crudest, lewdest, rudest, shrewdest.

SURPRISING RHYMING:
[2] Bluest, fewest, newest, soonest, truest.
Newness, poorest, purest, surest.
Buddhist, coolest, cutest, loosest, nudist, purest, smoothest, soonest, surest, tourist.
[3] Balloonist, cartoonist, illusionist, lampoonist, opportunist.
Chewiest, cruelest, fruitiest, humourist/humorist (U.S.).

4.6.17 "--oodly" (as in "shrewdly")
[2] crudely, rudely, shrewdly.

SURPRISING RHYMING:
[2] Beauty, booty, cutie, duty, fruity, snooty, tutti-frutti.
Coolie, coolly, duly, newly, truly, unduly, unruly.
Dourly, poorly, purely, surely.
Chewy, gloomy, gluey, gooey, groovy, hooey, phooey, screwy.
Bluesy, boozy, choosey, floozy.
[3] Assuredly, demurely, impurely, maturely, obscurely, securely.

4.6.18 "--ooel" (as in "cruel")
cruel, dual, duel, fuel, gruel, jewel, refuel, renewal.

SURPRISING RHYMING:
[1] Cool, cruel, drool, fool, pool, rule, school, stool, tool, who'll, you'll, yule.
Fooled, pooled, ruled, schooled, spooled.
[2] Barstool, capsule, granule, misrule, module, playschool, preschool, schedule, tomfool, whirlpool.
Cure-all, mural, neural, plural, rural.
Bugle, frugal, google.
[3] April fool, overrule, ridicule, supercool, swimming pool.

4.6.19 "--ooer" (as in "fewer")
[2] bluer, brewer, chewer, doer, fewer, newer, poor, sewer, skewer, stewer, truer, viewer, who're, wooer, you're.
[3] evil-doer, interviewer, pursuer, rescuer, reviewer, wrongdoer.

SURPRISING RHYMING:
[1] Cured, lured, moored, obscured, secured, toured.
[2] Groover, hoover, mover, prover, roofer, smoother, soother.
Cooler, crueler, dueller/dueler (U.S.), fooler, jeweller/jeweler (U.S.), moolah, ruler.
Allure, amour, assure, brochure, contour, couture, demure, detour, endure, ensure, insure, liqueur, mature, obscure, secure, unsure.
Brooder, cruder, intruder, lewder, ruder, shrewder.

550

Assured, contoured, endured, ensured, insured, manicured, matured, obscured, reassured, secured.
Crooner, lunar, pruner, schooner, sooner, swooner, tuna, tuner.
Boomer, groomer, humour/humor (U.S.), rumour/rumor (U.S.), roomer, zoomer.
Blooper, cooper, duper, grouper, looper, pooper, scooper, snooper, stupor, super, swooper, trooper, trouper, whooper.
Boozer, bruiser, chooser, cruiser, loser, schmoozer, snoozer, user.
Cuter, future, hooter, looter, neuter, scooter, shooter, suitor, tutor.
[3] **Approver**, improver, manoeuvre/maneuver (U.S.), remover.
Baby-boomer, consumer, costumer, perfumer, satsuma.
Aperture, caricature, furniture, immature, insecure, manicure, overture, paramour, premature, reassure, signature, troubadour.
Commuter, computer, polluter, prosecutor, recruiter, troubleshooter.

4.6.20 "--ooey" (as in "chewy")
[2] chewy, chop suey, gluey, gooey, hooey, phooey, screwy.

SURPRISING RHYMING:
Broody, gloomy, groovy, loony, moody, movie.
Beauty, booty, cutie, duty, fruity, snooty, tutti-frutti.
Droopy, groupie, kooky, loopy, snoopy, spooky.
Bluesy, boozy, choosy, floozy, snoozy.
Demurely, maturely, poorly, purely, obscurely, securely, surely.

4.6.21 "--ooest" (as in "truest")
[2] bluest, fewest, newest, truest.

SURPRISING RHYMING:
[2] **Coolest**, cruelest, fewest, loosest, newest.
Poorest, purest, smoothest, soonest, surest, tourist.
Crudest, cutest, lewdest, rudest, shrewdest.
[3] **Balloonist**, cartoonist, humourist/humorist (U.S.), illusionist, lampoonist, opportunist, tattooist.

4.6.22 "--oof" (as in "proof")
[1] goof, hoof, proof, roof, spoof, woof.
[2] aloof, bulletproof, childproof, fireproof, flameproof, foolproof, living proof, rainproof, shockproof, soundproof, stormproof, sunroof.

SURPRISING RHYMING:
[1] **Blew**, blue, brew, chew, clue, coup, crew, cue, dew, do, drew, due, few, flew, flu, glue, grew, hue, knew, new, pew, queue, screw, shoe, shoo, skew, stew, sue, threw, through, thru, to, too, true, two, view, who, woo, yew, you, zoo.
Booth, couth, sleuth, smooth, sooth, tooth, truth, youth.
Groove(d), move(d), prove(d), you've.
Boob, cube, lube, tube, YouTube.
[2] **Accrue**, anew, argue, askew, bamboo, bayou, bijou, boohoo, breakthrough, canoe, construe, corkscrew, cuckoo, curfew, debut, déjà vu, derring-do, diss you, ensue, fondue, gumshoe, guru, hairdo, hoodoo, horseshoe, igloo, in lieu, into, in two, issue, juju, kazoo, kung fu, lasso, menu, mildew, miscue, nephew, onto, outdo, outgrew, preview, pursue, rescue, redo, renew, review, revue, sea-view, see-through, set-to, shampoo, sinew, statue, subdue, taboo, tattoo, thumb-screw, tissue, to-do, true-blue, tutu, undo, undue, untrue, value, venue, virtue, voodoo, walk-through, withdrew, yahoo.
Eyetooth, forsooth, post-truth, uncouth, untruth.
Approve, behoove, disapprove, disprove, improve, remove, reprove.
Approved, disapproved, disproved, improved, removed, unmoved.
[3] **Avenue**, autocue, ballyhoo, barbecue, buckaroo, continue, devalue, discontinue, hitherto, hullabaloo, impromptu, interview, I.O.U., misconstrue, overdue, overthrew, overview, rendezvous, residue, superglue, switcheroo, well-to-do.

4.6.23 "--oogle" (as in "google")
[2] bugle, frugal, google.

SURPRISING RHYMING:
[2] **Canoodle**, doodle, feudal, noodle, oodles, poodle, strudel.
Cruel, dual, duel, fuel, gruel, jewel, pupil, refuel, renewal, scruple.
Cure-all, mural, neural, plural, rural.
Spoonful, tuneful.
Brutal, crucial, fruitful, futile, neutral, rueful, truthful, useful, youthful.
[3] **Approval**, bamboozle, disapproval, refusal, removal.

4.6.24 "--oohk" (as in "spook")
duke, fluke, gobbledegook, kook, nuke, puke, rebuke, spook, uke.

SURPRISING RHYMING:
[1] **Nuked**, puked, rebuked, spooked.
Boot, brute, chute, cute, flute, fruit, hoot, jute, loot, lute, moot, mute, newt, root, route, scoot, shoot, snoot, suit, toot.
Coop(ed), coupe, droop(ed), dupe(d), group(ed), hoop(ed), loop(ed), scoop(ed), sloop, snoop(ed), soup, stoop(ed), swoop(ed), troop(ed), troupe, whoop(ed).
Blew, blue, brew, chew, clue, coup, crew, cue, dew, do, drew, due, few, flew, flu, glue, grew, hue, knew, new, pew, queue, screw, shoe, shoo, skew, stew, sue, threw, through, thru, to, too, true, two, view, who, woo, yew, you, zoo.
[2] **Acute**, astute, commute, compute, dilute, dispute, en route, grapefruit, jackboot, lawsuit, minute, offshoot, pollute, pursuit, recruit, refute, salute, spacesuit, statute, swimsuit, tracksuit, tribute, uproot.
Cock-a-hoop, hencoop, hula-hoop, playgroup, recoup, regroup.
Accrue, anew, argue, askew, bamboo, bayou, bijou, boohoo, breakthrough, canoe, construe, corkscrew, cuckoo, curfew, debut, déjà vu, derring-do, diss you, ensue, fondue, gumshoe, guru, hairdo, hoodoo, horseshoe, igloo, in lieu, into, in two, issue, juju, kazoo, kung fu, lasso, menu, mildew, miscue, nephew, onto, outdo, outgrew, preview, pursue, rescue, redo, renew, review, revue, sea-view, see-through, set-to, shampoo, sinew, statue, subdue, taboo, tattoo, thumb-screw, tissue, to-do, true-blue, tutu, undo, undue, untrue, value, venue, virtue, voodoo, walk-through, withdrew, yahoo.
[3] **Absolute**, attribute, constitute, contribute, destitute, disrepute, distribute, electrocute, execute, institute, parachute, persecute, prostitute, resolute, substitute.
Avenue, autocue, ballyhoo, barbecue, buckaroo, continue, devalue, discontinue, hitherto, hullabaloo, impromptu, interview, I.O.U., misconstrue, overdue, overthrew, overview, rendezvous, residue, superglue, switcheroo, well-to-do.

4.6.25 "--ool" (as in "fool")
[1] cool, drool, fool, ghoul, mule, pool, rule, school, stool, tool, who'll, you'll, yule.
[2] ampoule, barstool, befool, capsule, cesspool, footstool, granule, misrule, module, nodule, playschool, preschool, schedule, slide-rule, toadstool, tomfool, whirlpool.
[3] April fool, miniscule, molecule, overrule, ridicule, Sunday school, supercool, swimming pool, vestibule, wading pool.

SURPRISING RHYMING:
[1] **Cruel**, dual, duel, fuel, gruel, jewel, refuel, renewal.
Drools, fools, ghouls, mules, pools, rules, schools, stools, tools.
Fooled, pooled, ruled, schooled, spooled.
Bloom, boom, broom, doom, fume, gloom, groom, loom, plume, room, tomb, vroom, whom, womb, zoom.
Blew, blue, brew, chew, clue, coup, crew, cue, dew, do, drew, due, few, flew, flu, glue, grew, hue, knew, new, pew, queue, screw, shoe, shoo, skew, stew, sue, threw, through, thru, to, too, true, two, view, who, woo, yew, you, zoo.
Boon, croon, dune, moon, noon, soon, spoon, strewn, swoon, tune.
Groove, move, prove, you've.
[2] **Barstools**, capsules, granules, modules, schedules, toadstools.

Assume, backroom, ballroom, bathroom, bedroom, boardroom, bridegroom, classroom, cloakroom, consume, costume, courtroom, darkroom, elbow-room, entomb, exhume, greenroom, headroom, heirloom, leg-room, newsroom, perfume, playroom, presume, resume, schoolroom, stockroom, vacuum, volume.
Accrue, anew, argue, askew, bamboo, bayou, bijou, boohoo, breakthrough, canoe, construe, corkscrew, cuckoo, curfew, debut, déjà vu, derring-do, diss you, ensue, fondue, gumshoe, guru, hairdo, hoodoo, horseshoe, igloo, in lieu, into, in two, issue, juju, kazoo, kung fu, lasso, menu, mildew, miscue, nephew, onto, outdo, outgrew, preview, pursue, rescue, redo, renew, review, revue, sea-view, see-through, set-to, shampoo, sinew, statue, subdue, taboo, tattoo, thumb-screw, tissue, to-do, true-blue, tutu, undo, undue, untrue, value, venue, virtue, voodoo, walk-through, withdrew, yahoo.
Approve, behoove, disapprove, disprove, improve, remove, reprove.
[3] **Avenue**, autocue, ballyhoo, barbecue, buckaroo, continue, devalue, discontinue, hitherto, hullabaloo, impromptu, interview, I.O.U., misconstrue, overdue, overthrew, overview, rendezvous, residue, superglue, switcheroo, well-to-do.
Overruled, ridiculed.

4.6.26 "--ooler" (as in "cooler")
[2] cooler, drooler, dueller/dueler (U.S.), fooler, hula, moolah, ruler.
[3] crueler, jeweller/jeweler (U.S.).

SURPRISING RHYMING:
[2] **Bluer**, brewer, chewer, doer, fewer, newer, poor, sewer, skewer, stewer, truer, viewer, who're, wooer, you're.
Curer, insurer, juror, poorer, purer, tourer.
Brooder, cruder, groover, intruder, lewder, mover, ruder, shrewder.
Crooner, lunar, pruner, schooner, sooner, swooner, tuna, tuner.
Boomer, groomer, humour/humor (U.S.), rumour/rumor (U.S.), roomer, zoomer.
Boozer, bruiser, chooser, cruiser, loser, schmoozer, snoozer, user.
Blooper, pooper, scooper, snooper, stupor, super, swooper, trooper.
[3] **Crueler**, jeweller/jeweler (U.S.).
Evil-doer, interviewer, pursuer, rescuer, reviewer, wrongdoer.
Abuser, accuser, amuser, excuser, misuser, refuser, yakuza.
Baby-boomer, consumer, costumer, perfumer, satsuma.
Approver, improver, manoeuvre/maneuver (U.S.), remover.

4.6.27 "--ooly" (as in "truly")
[2] coolie, coolly, duly, newly, truly, unduly, unruly.

SURPRISING RHYMING:
[2] **Groovy**, movie, poorly, purely, smoothie, surely.
Chewy, gloomy, gluey, gooey, groovy, hooey, phooey, screwy.
Bluesy, boozy, choosey, floozy, juicy, loosely.
Crudely, moody, rudely, shrewdly.
Droopy, groupie, kooky, loopy, snoopy, spooky.
Beauty, booty, cruelty, cutie, duty, fruity, snooty, tutti-frutti.
[3] **Cruelly**, demurely, impurely, maturely, obscurely, securely.

4.6.28 "--ooling" (as in "cooling")
[2] cooling, drooling, fooling, pooling, ruling, schooling, tooling.
[4] April fooling, overruling, ridiculing.

SURPRISING RHYMING:
[2] **Booing**, brewing, chewing, cooing, doing, gluing, mewing, queuing, screwing, ruin, shooing, strewing, suing, viewing, wooing.
Coolie, coolly, duly, newly, truly, unduly, unruly.
Goofing, grooving, moving, proving, sleuthing, smoothing, soothing.
Curing, during, luring, mooring, touring.
Blooming, booming, brooding, feuding, fuming, grooming, looming, rooming, zooming.

Crooning, looning, mooning, pruning, spooning, swooning, tuning.
Boozing, bruising, choosing, cruising, fusing, losing, musing, oozing, schmoozing, snoozing, using.
[3] **Accruing**, arguing, construing, debuting, ensuing, issuing, miscuing, outdoing, previewing, pursuing, renewing, rescuing, reviewing, shampooing, subduing, tattooing, undoing, valuing.
Alluring, assuring, enduring, ensuring, insuring, maturing, obscuring, posturing, procuring, reassuring, securing.
Assuming, consuming, mushrooming, presuming, resuming.
Abusing, accusing, amusing, bemusing, confusing, defusing, effusing, enthusing, excusing, infusing, misusing, perusing, refusing.
[4] **Barbecuing**, interviewing, overdoing, overviewing, rendezvousing.

4.6.29 "--oom" (as in "room")
[1] bloom, boom, broom, doom, flume, fume, gloom, groom, loom, plume, room, tomb, vroom, whom, womb, zoom.
[2] assume, backroom, ballroom, barroom, bathroom, bedroom, boardroom, bridegroom, classroom, cloakroom, consume, costume, courtroom, darkroom, dayroom, deplume, elbow-room, entomb, exhume, greenroom, guardroom, headroom, heirloom, legroom, mushroom, newsroom, perfume, playroom, presume, resume, schoolroom, sickroom, spare room, stateroom, stockroom, storeroom, tea-room, vacuum, volume, workroom.

SURPRISING RHYMING:
[1] **Bloomed**, boomed, doomed, fumed, groomed, loomed, zoomed.
Boon, croon, dune, moon, noon, soon, spoon, strewn, swoon, tune.
Blew, blue, brew, chew, clue, coup, crew, cue, dew, do, drew, due, few, flew, flu, glue, grew, hue, knew, new, pew, queue, screw, shoe, shoo, skew, stew, sue, threw, through, thru, to, too, true, two, view, who, woo, yew, you, zoo.
Cool, cruel, drool, fool, pool, rule, school, stool, tool, who'll, you'll.
Booth, couth, sleuth, smooth, sooth, tooth, truth, youth.
Crooned, mooned, pruned, spooned, swooned, tuned, wound.
[2] **Assumed**, consumed, entombed, perfumed, presumed, resumed, vacuumed.
Balloon, buffoon, cartoon, cocoon, commune, festoon, fortune, harpoon, immune, lagoon, lampoon, maroon, monsoon, platoon, saloon, teaspoon, tycoon, typhoon.
Accrue, anew, argue, askew, bamboo, bayou, bijou, boohoo, breakthrough, canoe, construe, corkscrew, cuckoo, curfew, debut, déjà vu, derring-do, diss you, ensue, fondue, gumshoe, guru, hairdo, hoodoo, horseshoe, igloo, in lieu, into, in two, issue, juju, kazoo, kung fu, lasso, menu, mildew, miscue, nephew, onto, outdo, outgrew, preview, pursue, rescue, redo, renew, review, revue, sea-view, see-through, set-to, shampoo, sinew, statue, subdue, taboo, tattoo, thumb-screw, tissue, to-do, true-blue, tutu, undo, undue, untrue, value, venue, virtue, voodoo, walk-through, withdrew, yahoo.
Barstool, capsule, granule, module, playschool, preschool, schedule, tomfool, whirlpool.
Ballooned, cocooned, communed, festooned, honeymooned, lampooned, marooned.
[3] **Afternoon**, harvest moon, honeymoon, misfortune, opportune.
Avenue, autocue, ballyhoo, barbecue, buckaroo, continue, devalue, discontinue, hitherto, hullabaloo, impromptu, interview, I.O.U., misconstrue, overdue, overthrew, overview, rendezvous, residue, superglue, switcheroo, well-to-do.
April fool, overrule, ridicule, Sunday school, supercool, swimming pool.
Arguin' (with a silent 'g'), boohooin', canoein', ensuin', miscuin', outdoin', overdoin', pursuin', redoin', renewin', rescuin', shampooin', subduin', tattooin', undoin', unscrewin'.

4.6.30 "--ooman" (as in "human")
crewman, human, inhuman, new man, sub-human, superhuman.

SURPRISING RHYMING:
[2] **Blooming**, booming, fuming, looming, rooming, zooming.
Crooning, looning, mooning, pruning, spooning, swooning, tuning.
Grooving, moving, proving.
Cuban, movement, mutant, proven, student, union, woman.
Couldn't, shouldn't, wooden, wouldn't.

Booing, brewing, chewing, cooing, doing, gluing, queuing, ruin, screwing, shooing, stewing, suing, viewing, wooing.
[3] **Assuming**, consuming, perfuming, presuming, resuming.
Collusion, conclusion, confusion, delusion, exclusion, fusion, illusion, inclusion, intrusion, pollution, seclusion, solution, transfusion.
Ballooning, communing, festooning, honeymooning, lampooning.
Accruing, arguing, construing, debuting, ensuing, issuing, miscuing, outdoing, previewing, pursuing, redoing, renewing, rescuing, reviewing, shampooing, subduing, tattooing, undoing, valuing.
[4] **Absolution**, attribution, constitution, destitution, disillusion, electrocution, evolution, execution, persecution, retribution, revolution.

4.6.31 "--oomer" (as in "rumour/rumor")
[2] bloomer, boomer, groomer, humour/humor (U.S.), puma, roomer, rumour/rumor (U.S.), zoomer.
[3] baby-boomer, consumer, costumer, perfumer, satsuma.

SURPRISING RHYMING:
[1] **Crooner**, lunar, pruner, schooner, sooner, swooner, tuna, tuner.
Groover, hoover, improver, mover, prover, smoother, soother.
Brooder, cruder, intruder, lewder, ruder, shrewder.
Boozer, bruiser, chooser, cruiser, loser, schmoozer, snoozer, user.
Cooler, drooler, dueller/dueler (U.S.), fooler, hula, moolah, ruler.
Blooper, duper, pooper, scooper, snooper, stupor, super, trooper.
Bluer, brewer, chewer, doer, fewer, newer, poor, truer, viewer, who're.
Cuter, future, hooter, looter, neuter, scooter, shooter, suitor, tutor.
Curer, insurer, juror, poorer, purer, tourer.
[3] **Ballooner**, harpooner, honeymooner, lampooner.
Approver, improver, manoeuvre/maneuver (U.S.), remover.
Crueler, jeweller/jeweler (U.S.).

4.6.32 "--oomered" (as in "rumoured/rumored")
[2] humoured/humored (U.S.), rumoured/rumored (U.S.).

SURPRISING RHYMING:
[1] **Cured**, lured, moored, toured.
[2] **Assured**, endured, ensured, insured, manicured, matured, obscured, reassured, secured, snookered.

4.6.33 "--oon" (as in "moon")
[1] boon, croon, dune, goon, June, loon, moon, noon, prune, rune, soon, spoon, strewn, swoon, tune.
[2] baboon, balloon, bassoon, bestrewn, buffoon, cartoon, cocoon, commune, doubloon, dragoon, festoon, fortune, harpoon, immune, impugn, lagoon, lampoon, maroon, monsoon, platoon, raccoon, saloon, spittoon, teaspoon, tribune, tycoon, typhoon.
[3] afternoon, harvest moon, honeymoon, misfortune, tablespoon.

SURPRISING RHYMING:
[1] **Crooned**, mooned, pruned, spooned, swooned, tuned, wound.
Bloom(ed), boom(ed), broom, doom(ed), fume(d), gloom, groom(ed), loom(ed), plume, room(ed), tomb, vroom, whom, womb, zoom(ed).
Blew, blue, brew, chew, clue, coup, crew, cue, dew, do, drew, due, few, flew, flu, glue, grew, hue, knew, new, pew, queue, screw, shoe, shoo, skew, stew, sue, threw, through, thru, to, too, true, two, view, who, woo, yew, you, zoo.
Groove, move, prove, you've.
[2] **Ballooned**, cocooned, communed, festooned, harpooned, honeymooned, impugned, lampooned, marooned, ruined.
Assume(d), backroom, ballroom, bathroom, bedroom, boardroom, bridegroom,

classroom, cloakroom, consume(d), costume, courtroom, darkroom, elbow-room, entomb(ed), greenroom, headroom, heirloom, leg-room, mushroom(ed), newsroom, perfume(d), playroom, presume(d), resume(d), schoolroom, vacuum(ed), volume.
Accrue, anew, argue, askew, bamboo, bayou, bijou, boohoo, breakthrough, canoe, construe, corkscrew, cuckoo, curfew, debut, déjà vu, derring-do, diss you, ensue, fondue, gumshoe, guru, hairdo, hoodoo, horseshoe, igloo, in lieu, into, in two, issue, juju, kazoo, kung fu, lasso, menu, mildew, miscue, nephew, onto, outdo, outgrew, preview, pursue, rescue, redo, renew, review, revue, sea-view, see-through, set-to, shampoo, sinew, statue, subdue, taboo, tattoo, thumb-screw, tissue, to-do, true-blue, tutu, undo, undue, untrue, value, venue, virtue, voodoo, walk-through, withdrew, yahoo.
Approve, behoove, disapprove, disprove, improve, remove, reprove.
[3] **Avenue**, autocue, ballyhoo, barbecue, buckaroo, continue, devalue, discontinue, hitherto, hullabaloo, impromptu, interview, I.O.U., misconstrue, overdue, overthrew, overview, rendezvous, residue, superglue, switcheroo, well-to-do.

4.6.34 "--ooned" (as in "marooned")

[1] crooned, mooned, pruned, spooned, swooned, tuned, wound.
[2] ballooned, cocooned, communed, festooned, harpooned, honeymooned, impugned, lampooned, marooned.

SURPRISING RHYMING:
[1] **Bloom(ed)**, boom(ed), broom, doom(ed), fume(ed), gloom, groom(ed), room(ed), tomb, vroom, whom, womb, zoom(ed).
Boon, croon, dune, moon, noon, soon, spoon, strewn, swoon, tune.
Blew, blue, brew, chew, clue, coup, crew, cue, dew, do, drew, due, few, flew, flu, glue, grew, hue, knew, new, pew, queue, screw, shoe, shoo, skew, stew, sue, threw, through, thru, to, too, true, two, view, who, woo, yew, you, zoo.
[2] **Assumed**, consumed, mushroomed, perfumed, presumed, resumed.
Balloon, buffoon, cartoon, cocoon, commune, festoon, fortune, harpoon, immune, lagoon, lampoon, maroon, monsoon, platoon, saloon, teaspoon, tycoon, typhoon.
Assume, backroom, ballroom, bathroom, bedroom, boardroom, bridegroom, classroom, cloakroom, consume, costume, courtroom, darkroom, elbow-room, entomb, exhume, greenroom, headroom, heirloom, leg-room, newsroom, perfume, playroom, presume, resume, schoolroom, stockroom, vacuum, volume.
Accrue, anew, argue, askew, bamboo, bayou, bijou, boohoo, breakthrough, canoe, construe, corkscrew, cuckoo, curfew, debut, déjà vu, derring-do, diss you, ensue, fondue, gumshoe, guru, hairdo, hoodoo, horseshoe, igloo, in lieu, into, in two, issue, juju, kazoo, kung fu, lasso, menu, mildew, miscue, nephew, onto, outdo, outgrew, preview, pursue, rescue, redo, renew, review, revue, sea-view, see-through, set-to, shampoo, sinew, statue, subdue, taboo, tattoo, thumb-screw, tissue, to-do, true-blue, tutu, undo, undue, untrue, value, venue, virtue, voodoo, walk-through, withdrew, yahoo.
[3] **Afternoon**, harvest moon, honeymoon, misfortune, opportune.
Avenue, autocue, ballyhoo, barbecue, buckaroo, continue, devalue, discontinue, hitherto, hullabaloo, impromptu, interview, I.O.U., misconstrue, overdue, overthrew, overview, rendezvous, residue, superglue, switcheroo, well-to-do.

4.6.35 "--ooner" (as in "sooner")

[2] crooner, lunar, pruner, schooner, sooner, swooner, tuna, tuner.
[3] ballooner, harpooner, honeymooner, lampooner.

SURPRISING RHYMING:
[1] **Boomer**, groomer, humour/humor (U.S.), rumour/rumor (U.S.), roomer, zoomer.
Groover, hoover, improver, mover, prover, smoother, soother.
Brooder, cruder, intruder, lewder, ruder, shrewder.
Boozer, bruiser, chooser, cruiser, loser, schmoozer, snoozer, user.
Cooler, dueller/dueler (U.S.), fooler, hula, moolah, pooler, ruler.
Blooper, duper, pooper, scooper, snooper, stupor, super, trooper.
Bluer, brewer, chewer, doer, fewer, newer, poor, truer, viewer, you're.
Cuter, future, hooter, looter, neuter, scooter, shooter, suitor, tutor.
Crueler, insurer, jeweller/jeweler (U.S.), juror, poorer, purer, tourer.

[3] **Baby-boomer**, consumer, costumer, perfumer, satsuma.
Approver, improver, manoeuvre/maneuver (U.S.), remover.
Abuser, accuser, amuser, excuser, medusa, refuser, yakuza.

4.6.36 "--oonful" (as in "spoonful")
[2] spoonful, tuneful.

SURPRISING RHYMING:
[1] **Bull**, cull, dull, full, gull, hull, lull, mull, null, pull, skull, wool.
[2] **Fruitful**, graceful, grateful, hurtful, jugful, mournful, numbskull, roomful, rueful, truthful, useful, youthful.

4.6.37 "--ooning" (as in "swooning")
[2] crooning, looning, mooning, pruning, spooning, swooning, tuning.
[3] ballooning, communing, festooning, honeymooning, lampooning.

SURPRISING RHYMING:
[2] **Blooming**, booming, fuming, grooming, looming, rooming, zooming.
Grooving, moving, proving.
Cooling, drooling, fooling, pooling, ruling, schooling, tooling, Yuling.
Booing, brewing, chewing, cooing, doing, gluing, queuing, screwing, ruin, shooing, skewing, stewing, strewing, suing, viewing, wooing.
Boozing, bruising, choosing, cruising, fusing, losing, musing, oozing, schmoozing, snoozing, using.
Curing, during, luring, mooring, touring.
[3] **Assuming**, consuming, mushrooming, presuming, resuming.
Approving, disapproving, disproving, improving, removing.
Accruing, arguing, construing, debuting, ensuing, issuing, miscuing, outdoing, previewing, pursuing, redoing, renewing, rescuing, reviewing, shampooing, subduing, tattooing, undoing, valuing.
Abusing, accusing, amusing, confusing, defusing, enthusing, excusing, misusing, perusing, refusing.
Alluring, enduring, ensuring, insuring, maturing, obscuring, reassuring, securing.

4.6.38 "--oonist" (as in "cartoonist")
[3] balloonist, bassoonist, cartoonist, lampoonist, opportunist.

SURPRISING RHYMING:
[2] **Bluest**, coolest, cruelest, cutest, fewest, loosest, newest, nudist, poorest, purest, smoothest, soonest, surest, tourist, truest, tuneless.
Crudest, lewdest, rudest, shrewdest.
[3] **Chewiest**, fruitiest, humourist/humorist (U.S.), illusionist, shampooist, tattooist.

4.6.39 "--oop" (as in "swoop")
[1] bloop, coop, coupe, croup, droop, dupe, group, hoop, loop, poop, scoop, sloop, snoop, soup, stoop, swoop, troop, whoop.
[2] cock-a-hoop, hencoop, hula-hoop, playgroup, recoup, regroup.

SURPRISING RHYMING:
[1] **Cooped**, drooped, duped, grouped, hooped, looped, pooped, recouped, scooped, snooped, stooped, swooped, trooped, whooped.
Beaut, boot, brute, chute, cute, flute, fruit, hoot, jute, loot, lute, moot, mute, newt, root, route, scoot, shoot, snoot, suit, toot.
Duke, fluke, gobbledegook, kook, nuke, puke, rebuke, spook, uke.
Boob, cube, lube, tube, YouTube.
Booth, goof, hoof, proof, roof, sleuth, smooth, sooth, spoof, tooth, truth, youth.
Blew, blue, brew, chew, clue, coup, crew, cue, dew, do, drew, due, few, flew, flu, glue, grew, hue, knew, new, pew, queue, screw, shoe, shoo, skew, stew, sue, threw, through, thru, to, too, true, two, view, who, woo, yew, you, zoo.

557

[2] Acute, astute, Canute, commute, compute, dilute, dispute, en route, grapefruit, jackboot, lawsuit, minute, offshoot, pollute, pursuit, recruit, refute, salute, spacesuit, swimsuit, tracksuit, tribute, uproot.
Aloof, bulletproof, childproof, fireproof, flameproof, foolproof, living proof, rainproof, shockproof, soundproof, stormproof, sunroof.
Accrue, anew, argue, askew, bamboo, bayou, bijou, boohoo, breakthrough, canoe, construe, corkscrew, cuckoo, curfew, debut, déjà vu, derring-do, diss you, ensue, fondue, gumshoe, guru, hairdo, hoodoo, horseshoe, igloo, in lieu, into, in two, issue, juju, kazoo, kung fu, lasso, menu, mildew, miscue, nephew, onto, outdo, outgrew, preview, pursue, rescue, redo, renew, review, revue, sea-view, see-through, set-to, shampoo, sinew, statue, subdue, taboo, tattoo, thumb-screw, tissue, to-do, true-blue, tutu, undo, undue, untrue, value, venue, virtue, voodoo, walk-through, withdrew, yahoo.
[3] Absolute, attribute, contribute, destitute, disrepute, distribute, electrocute, execute, parachute, persecute, resolute, substitute.
Avenue, autocue, ballyhoo, barbecue, buckaroo, continue, devalue, discontinue, hitherto, hullabaloo, impromptu, interview, I.O.U., misconstrue, overdue, overthrew, overview, rendezvous, residue, superglue, switcheroo, well-to-do.

4.6.40 "--ooped" (as in "swooped")
cooped, drooped, duped, grouped, hooped, looped, pooped, recouped, scooped, snooped, stooped, swooped, trooped, whooped.

SURPRISING RHYMING:
[1] Coop, coupe, droop, dupe, goop, group, hoop, loop, poop, scoop, sloop, snoop, soup, stoop, swoop, troop, troupe, whoop.
Beaut, boot, brute, chute, cute, flute, fruit, hoot, jute, loot, lute, moot, mute, newt, root, route, scoot, shoot, snoot, suit, toot.
Fluked, cooked, nuked, puked, rebuked, spooked.
Goofed, hoofed, roofed, spoofed, woofed.
Booed, brewed, brood, chewed, cooed, crude, cued, dude, feud, food, glued, lewd, mood, nude, prude, rude, screwed, shoed, shrewd, skewed, spewed, stewed, sued, viewed, who'd, you'd.
[2] Cock-a-hoop, hencoop, hula-hoop, playgroup, recoup, regroup.
Acute, astute, Canute, commute, compute, dilute, dispute, en route, grapefruit, jackboot, lawsuit, minute, offshoot, pollute, pursuit, recruit, refute, salute, spacesuit, statute, swimsuit, tracksuit, tribute, uproot.
Accrued, allude, argued, boohooed, canoed, collude, conclude, construed, debuted, delude, elude, ensued, exclude, exude, imbued, include, intrude, miscued, preclude, prelude, previewed, protrude, pursued, queued, renewed, rescued, reviewed, seafood, seclude, shampooed, subdued, tabooed, tattooed, valued, wholefood.
[3] Absolute, attribute, contribute, destitute, disrepute, distribute, electrocute, execute, parachute, persecute, resolute, substitute.

4.6.41 "--ooping" (as in "swooping")
[2] drooping, duping, grouping, looping, pooping, scooping, snooping, stooping, swooping, trooping, whooping.

SURPRISING RHYMING:
[2] Booting, hooting, looting, rooting, scooting, shooting, tooting.
Nuking, puking, rebuking, spooking.
Blooming, booming, fuming, grooming, looming, rooming, zooming.
Crooning, looning, mooning, pruning, spooning, swooning, tuning.
Goofing, hoofing, roofing, sleuthing, spoofing, smoothing, soothing.
Cooling, drooling, fooling, pooling, ruling, schooling, tooling, Yuling.
Booing, brewing, chewing, cooing, doing, gluing, queuing, screwing, ruin, shooing, skewing, suing, viewing, wooing.
Boozing, bruising, choosing, cruising, fusing, losing, musing, oozing, schmoozing, snoozing, using.
[3] Commuting, computing, diluting, disputing, polluting, uprooting.
Assuming, consuming, perfuming, presuming, resuming, vacuuming.

Ballooning, communing, festooning, honeymooning, lampooning.
Accruing, arguing, construing, debuting, ensuing, issuing, miscuing, outdoing, previewing, pursuing, redoing, renewing, rescuing, reviewing, shampooing, subduing, tattooing, undoing, valuing.
Abusing, accusing, amusing, confusing, enthusing, excusing, refusing.
[4] **Contributing**, electrocuting, executing, persecuting, substituting.
Barbecuing, continuing, devaluing, discontinuing, interviewing, misconstruing, overdoing, overviewing, rendezvousing, supergluing.

4.6.42 "--ooper" (as in "super")

[2] blooper, drooper, duper, grouper, hooper, looper, pooper, scooper, snooper, stupor, super, swooper, trooper, trouper, whooper.
[4] mea culpa, party-pooper, paratrooper, pea-souper, pooper-scooper, super-duper.

SURPRISING RHYMING:
[2] **Cuter**, hooter, looter, neuter, scooter, shooter, suitor, tutor.
Brooder, cruder, intruder, lewder, ruder, shrewder.
Boomer, groomer, humour/humor (U.S.), rumour/rumor (U.S.), roomer, zoomer.
Crooner, lunar, pruner, schooner, sooner, swooner, tuna, tuner.
Curer, insurer, juror, poorer, purer, tourer.
Cooler, crueler, fooler, hula, jeweller/jeweler (U.S.), moolah, ruler.
Groover, hoover, improver, mover, prover, smoother, soother.
Boozer, bruiser, chooser, cruiser, loser, schmoozer, snoozer, user.
Booster, future, rooster.
Bluer, brewer, chewer, doer, fewer, newer, truer, viewer, wooer.
[3] **Commuter**, computer, polluter, prosecutor, troubleshooter.
Baby-boomer, consumer, costumer, perfumer, satsuma.
Ballooner, harpooner, honeymooner, lampooner.
Evil-doer, interviewer, pursuer, rescuer, reviewer, wrongdoer.

4.6.43 "--oor" (as in "poor")

[1] cure, dour, lure, moor, poor, pure, sure, tour, your, you're.
[2] allure, amour, assure, brochure, contour, couture, demure, detour, endure, ensure, gravure, impure, insure, liqueur, manure, mature, obscure, secure, tenure, unsure.
[3] aperture, caricature, curvature, forfeiture, furniture, immature, insecure, manicure, overture, paramour, plat de jour, premature, reassure, signature, tablature, troubadour.

SURPRISING RHYMING:
[1] **Cured**, lured, moored, obscured, secured, toured.
[2] **Endured**, ensured, insured, manicured, matured, obscured, reassured, secured.
Bluer, brewer, chewer, doer, fewer, newer, truer, viewer, wooer.
Crooner, lunar, pruner, schooner, sooner, swooner, tuna, tuner.
Boomer, groomer, humour/humor (U.S.), rumour/rumor (U.S.), roomer, zoomer.
Cooler, drooler, dueller/dueler (U.S.), fooler, hula, moolah, ruler.
Groover, hoover, improver, mover, newer, prover, roofer.
Boozer, bruiser, chooser, cruiser, loser, schmoozer, snoozer, user.
[3] **Evil-doer**, interviewer, pursuer, rescuer, reviewer, wrongdoer.
Baby-boomer, consumer, honeymooner, lampooner.
Abuser, accuser, excuser, medusa, misuser, refuser, yakuza.

4.6.44 "--oored" (as in "moored")

[1] cured, lured, moored, obscured, secured, toured.
[2] assured, contoured, endured, ensured, insured, manicured, matured, obscured, reassured, secured.

SURPRISING RHYMING:
[1] **Cure**, dour, lure, moor, poor, pure, sure, tour, your, you're.

Booed, brewed, brood, chewed, cooed, crude, cued, dude, feud, food, glued, lewd, mood, nude, prude, rude, screwed, shoed, shrewd, skewed, spewed, stewed, sued, viewed, who'd, you'd.
[2] **Allure**, amour, assure, brochure, contour, couture, demure, detour, endure, ensure, impure, insure, liqueur, manure, mature, obscure, secure, unsure.
Bluer, brewer, chewer, doer, fewer, newer, truer, viewer, wooer.
Accrued, allude, argued, boohooed, canoed, collude, conclude, construed, debuted, delude, elude, ensued, exclude, exude, imbued, include, intrude, miscued, preclude, prelude, previewed, protrude, pursued, queued, renewed, rescued, reviewed, seafood, seclude, shampooed, subdued, tabooed, tattooed, valued, wholefood.
[3] **Aperture**, caricature, furniture, immature, insecure, manicure, overture, paramour, premature, reassure, signature, troubadour.
Evil-doer, interviewer, pursuer, rescuer, reviewer, wrongdoer.

4.6.45 "--oorer" (as in "poorer")
[2] curer, insurer, juror, poorer, purer, tourer.

SURPRISING RHYMING:
[2] **Bluer**, brewer, chewer, doer, fewer, newer, truer, viewer, wooer.
Crooner, lunar, pruner, schooner, sooner, swooner, tuna, tuner.
Boomer, groomer, humour/humor (U.S.), rumour/rumor (U.S.), roomer, zoomer.
Cooler, drooler, fooler, groover, hoover, mover, newer, prover, ruler.
Boozer, bruiser, chooser, cruiser, loser, schmoozer, snoozer, user.
[3] **Evil-doer**, interviewer, pursuer, rescuer, reviewer, wrongdoer.
Baby-boomer, consumer, costumer, perfumer, satsuma.
Abuser, accuser, amuser, excuser, medusa, refuser, yakuza.

4.6.46 "--oorest" (as in "poorest")
[2] poorest, purest, surest.

SURPRISING RHYMING:
[2] **Crudest**, lewdest, rudest, shrewdest.
Bluest, coolest, cruelest, cutest, fewest, loosest, newest, nudist, purest, smoothest, soonest, surest, tourist, truest.
[3] **Balloonist**, bassoonist, cartoonist, lampoonist, opportunist.

4.6.47 "--ooral" (as in "rural")
[2] cure-all, mural, neural, plural, rural.

SURPRISING RHYMING:
[2] **Brutal**, crucial, fruitful, futile, neutral, truthful, useful, youthful.
Canoodle, doodle, feudal, noodle, poodle, spoonful, tuneful.
Bugle, frugal, google.
Cruel, dual, duel, fuel, jewel, pupil, refuel, renewal, scruple.
[3] **Approval**, bamboozle, disapproval, refusal, removal.

4.6.48 "--ooring" (as in "during")
[2] curing, during, luring, mooring, touring.
[3] alluring, assuring, enduring, ensuring, insuring, maturing, obscuring, posturing, procuring, reassuring, securing.

SURPRISING RHYMING:
[2] **Grooving**, moving, proving, sleuthing, smoothing, soothing.
Cooling, drooling, fooling, pooling, ruling, schooling, tooling, Yuling.
Blooming, booming, brooding, feuding, fuming, grooming, looming, rooming, zooming.
Crooning, looning, mooning, pruning, spooning, swooning, tuning.
Boozing, bruising, choosing, cruising, losing, musing, oozing, snoozing, using.
Booing, brewing, chewing, cooing, doing, gluing, queuing, screwing, ruin, shooing, skewing, suing, viewing, wooing.

[3] Approving, disapproving, disproving, improving, removing.
Assuming, consuming, mushrooming, presuming, resuming.
Ballooning, communing, festooning, honeymooning, lampooning.
Abusing, accusing, amusing, confusing, enthusing, excusing, refusing.
Commuting, computing, diluting, disputing, polluting, uprooting.
Accruing, arguing, construing, debuting, ensuing, issuing, miscuing, outdoing, previewing, pursuing, redoing, renewing, rescuing, reviewing, shampooing, subduing, tattooing, undoing, valuing.
[4] Barbecuing, interviewing, overdoing, overviewing, rendezvousing.

4.6.49 "--oorly" (as in "poorly")
[2] dourly, poorly, purely, surely.
[3] demurely, impurely, maturely, obscurely, securely.

SURPRISING RHYMING:
[2] **Broody**, gloomy, groovy, loony, moody, movie.
Coolie, coolly, cruelly, duly, newly, truly, unduly, unruly.
Bluesy, boozy, choosy, floozy, loosely, smoothly, snoozy.
Crudely, rudely, shrewdly.
Beauty, booty, cruelty, cutie, duty, fruity, snooty, tutti-frutti.
Droopy, groupie, kooky, loopy, snoopy, spooky.

4.6.50 "--oose" (as in "loose")
[1] deuce, goose, juice, loose, moose, mousse, noose, puce, sluice, spruce, truce, use, Zeus.
[2] abuse, caboose, deduce, diffuse, effuse, excuse, footloose, induce, misuse, mongoose, obtuse, produce, profuse, recluse, reduce, refuse, seduce, vamoose.
[3] calaboose, introduce, reproduce.

SURPRISING RHYMING:
[1] **Blues**, boos, booze, bruise, chews, choose, clues, crews, cruise, do's, dues, fuse, lose, mews, muse, news, ooze, ruse, schmooze, shoes, snooze, stews, sues, use, who's, whose, zoos.
Booth, couth, sleuth, smooth, sooth, tooth, truth, youth.
Booths, grooves, moves, proves, smooths, soothes, truths, youths.
Bruise(d), cruise(d), fuse(d), muse(d), ooze(d), schmooze(d), snooze(d), use(d).
Blew, blue, brew, chew, clue, coup, crew, cue, dew, do, drew, due, few, flew, flu, glue, grew, hue, knew, new, pew, queue, screw, shoe, shoo, skew, stew, sue, threw, through, thru, to, too, true, two, view, who, woo, yew, you, zoo.
Broods, dudes, feuds, foods, moods, nudes, prudes.
Drools, fools, ghouls, mules, pools, rules, schools, stools, tools.
[2] **Abuse**, accuse, amuse, argues, bemuse, breakthroughs, canoes, confuse, construes, curfews, debuts, defuse, diffuse, ensues, enthuse, excuse, gurus, hairdos, hoodoos, horseshoes, infuse, igloos, issues, menus, miscues, misuse, nephews, peruse, previews, pursues, refuse, rescues, renews, reviews, revues, rhythm-and-blues, shampoos, sinews, statues, subdues, taboos, tattoos, tissues, values, venues, virtues.
Accrue, anew, argue, askew, bamboo, bayou, bijou, boohoo, breakthrough, canoe, construe, corkscrew, cuckoo, curfew, debut, déjà vu, derring-do, diss you, ensue, fondue, gumshoe, guru, hairdo, hoodoo, horseshoe, igloo, in lieu, into, in two, issue, juju, kazoo, kung fu, lasso, menu, mildew, miscue, nephew, onto, outdo, outgrew, preview, pursue, rescue, redo, renew, review, revue, sea-view, see-through, set-to, shampoo, sinew, statue, subdue, taboo, tattoo, thumb-screw, tissue, to-do, true-blue, tutu, undo, undue, untrue, value, venue, virtue, voodoo, walk-through, withdrew, yahoo.
Abused, accused, amused, bemused, confused, defused, disused, enthused, excused, infused, misused, perused, refused, transfused.
[3] **Avenues**, barbecues, buckaroos, continues, devalues, interviews, IOUs, misconstrues, rendezvous (plural, *pronounced "rondayvooz"*).
Avenue, autocue, ballyhoo, barbecue, buckaroo, continue, devalue, discontinue, hitherto, hullabaloo, impromptu, interview, I.O.U., misconstrue, overdue, overthrew, overview, rendezvous, residue, superglue, switcheroo, well-to-do.

Aptitudes, attitudes, interludes, multitudes, platitudes.

4.6.51 "--ooshun" (as in "illusion")
[3] allusion, collusion, conclusion, confusion, delusion, dilution, exclusion, fusion, illusion, inclusion, infusion, intrusion, pollution, profusion, seclusion, solution, transfusion.
[4] absolution, attribution, constitution, contribution, counter-revolution, destitution, disillusion, electrocution, evolution, execution, institution, persecution, resolution, retribution, revolution, substitution.

SURPRISING RHYMING:
[2] **Boozing**, bruising, choosing, cruising, losing, musing, oozing, schmoozing, snoozing, using.
Cuban, human, movement, mutant, proven, student, union, woman.
Cooling, drooling, fooling, grooving, moving, pooling, proving, ruling, schooling, spooling, tooling, Yuling.
Curing, during, luring, mooring, touring.
Booing, brewing, chewing, cooing, doing, gluing, queuing, screwing, ruin, shooing, skewing, suing, viewing, wooing.
[3] **Abusing**, accusing, amusing, confusing, excusing, refusing.
Approving, disapproving, disproving, improving, removing.
Accruing, arguing, construing, debuting, ensuing, issuing, miscuing, outdoing, previewing, pursuing, redoing, renewing, rescuing, reviewing, shampooing, subduing, tattooing, undoing, valuing.
Alluring, assuring, enduring, ensuring, insuring, maturing, obscuring, posturing, procuring, reassuring, securing.
[4] **Barbecuing**, interviewing, overdoing, overviewing, rendezvousing.

4.6.52 "--oosive" (as in "elusive")
[3] abusive, conclusive, conducive, effusive, elusive, exclusive, inconclusive, inclusive, intrusive, obtrusive, reclusive.

SURPRISING RHYMING:
[2] **Bruises**, chooses, cruises, floozies, fuses, loses, muses, nooses, oozes, ruses, schmoozes, snoozes, uses.
Cupid, druid, fluid, hooted, looted, lucid, mooted, muted, rooted, scooted, stupid, suited, tooted.
[3] **Abuses**, accuses, amuses, confuses, enthuses, excuses, refuses.
Commuted, computed, diluted, disputed, polluted, reputed, uprooted.
Alluded, colluded, concluded, deluded, eluded, excluded, included, intruded, precluded, protruded, secluded.

4.6.53 "--oot" (as in "shoot")
[1] beaut, boot, brute, chute, cute, flute, fruit, hoot, jute, loot, lute, moot, mute, newt, root, route, scoot, shoot, snoot, suit, toot.
[2] acute, astute, beetroot, breadfruit, Canute, commute, compute, dilute, dispute, en route, grapefruit, jackboot, lawsuit, minute, offshoot, pollute, pursuit, recruit, refute, repute, salute, spacesuit, statute, swimsuit, tracksuit, tribute, uproot.
[3] absolute, attribute, constitute, contribute, convolute, destitute, disrepute, dissolute, electrocute, execute, institute, parachute, persecute, prostitute, resolute, substitute.

SURPRISING RHYMING:
[1] **Coop**, coupe, droop, dupe, group, hoop, loop, scoop, sloop, snoop, soup, stoop, swoop, troop, troupe, whoop.
Cooped, drooped, duped, looped, pooped, recouped, scooped, snooped, stooped, swooped, trooped, whooped.
Duke, fluke, gobbledegook, kook, nuke, puke, rebuke, spook, uke.
Booth, sleuth, smooth, sooth, tooth, truth, youth.
Boob, cube, lube, tube, YouTube.

Booed, brewed, brood, chewed, crude, cued, dude, feud, food, glued, grooved, lewd, mood, moved, nude, proved, prude, rude, screwed, shrewd, skewed, sued, viewed, who'd, you'd.
Blew, blue, brew, chew, clue, coup, crew, cue, dew, do, drew, due, few, flew, flu, glue, grew, hue, knew, new, pew, queue, screw, shoe, shoo, skew, stew, sue, threw, through, thru, to, too, true, two, view, who, woo, yew, you, zoo.
[2] Cock-a-hoop, hencoop, hula-hoop, playgroup, recoup, regroup.
Approved, disapproved, disproved, improved, removed, unmoved.
Aloof, bulletproof, childproof, fireproof, flameproof, foolproof, living proof, rainproof, shockproof, soundproof, stormproof, sunroof.

4.6.54 "--ooter" (as in "shooter")
[2] cuter, hooter, looter, neuter, pewter, rooter, scooter, shooter, suitor, tutor.
[3] commuter, computer, persecutor, polluter, prosecutor, recruiter, sharpshooter, troubleshooter.

SURPRISING RHYMING:
[2] Blooper, duper, pooper, scooper, snooper, stupor, super, trooper.
Booster, future, rooster.
Brooder, cruder, groover, intruder, mover, ruder, shrewder.
Boomer, groomer, humour/humor (U.S.), rumour/rumor (U.S.), roomer, zoomer.
Crooner, lunar, pruner, schooner, sooner, swooner, tuna, tuner.
Cooler, crueler, fooler, jeweller/jeweler (U.S.), ruler, smoother, soother.
Boozer, bruiser, chooser, cruiser, loser, schmoozer, snoozer, user.
[3] Baby-boomer, consumer, costumer, perfumer, satsuma.
Abuser, accuser, amuser, excuser, medusa, refuser, yakuza.
[4] Mea culpa, party-pooper, pooper-scooper, super-duper.

4.6.55 "--ooth" (as in "truth")
[1] booth, couth, sleuth, smooth, sooth, strewth, tooth, truth, youth.
[2] eyetooth, forsooth, post-truth, uncouth, untruth.

SURPRISING RHYMING:
[1] Goof, groove(d), move(d), prove(d), proof, roof, spoof, you've.
Boob, cube, lube, tube, YouTube.
Bloom, boom, broom, doom, fume, gloom, groom, loom, plume, room, tomb, vroom, whom, womb, zoom.
Deuce, goose, juice, loose, noose, sluice, spruce, truce, use, Zeus.
Blew, blue, brew, chew, clue, coup, crew, cue, dew, do, drew, due, few, flew, flu, glue, grew, hue, knew, new, pew, queue, screw, shoe, shoo, skew, stew, sue, threw, through, thru, to, too, true, two, view, who, woo, yew, you, zoo.
[2] Aloof, bulletproof, childproof, fireproof, flameproof, foolproof, living proof, rainproof, shockproof, soundproof, stormproof, sunroof.
Approve(d), behoove(d), disapprove(d), disprove(d), improve(d), remove(d), unmoved.
Blues, boos, booze, bruise, chews, choose, clues, crews, cruise, do's, dues, fuse, lose, mews, muse, news, ooze, ruse, schmooze, shoes, snooze, stews, sues, use, who's, whose, zoos.
Abuse (noun), caboose, deduce, diffuse, excuse, footloose, induce, misuse, obtuse, produce, profuse, reduce, refuse, seduce, vamoose.
Assume, backroom, ballroom, bathroom, bedroom, boardroom, bridegroom, classroom, cloakroom, consume, costume, courtroom, darkroom, elbow-room, entomb, exhume, greenroom, headroom, heirloom, leg-room, newsroom, perfume, playroom, presume, resume, schoolroom, stockroom, vacuum, volume.
Accrue, anew, argue, askew, bamboo, bayou, bijou, boohoo, breakthrough, canoe, construe, corkscrew, curfew, debut, déjà vu, derring-do, diss you, ensue, fondue, gumshoe, guru, hairdo, hoodoo, horseshoe, igloo, in lieu, into, in two, issue, juju, kazoo, kung fu, lasso, menu, mildew, miscue, nephew, onto, outdo, outgrew, preview, pursue, rescue, redo, renew, review, revue, sea-view, see-through, set-to, shampoo, sinew, statue, subdue, taboo, tattoo, thumb-screw, tissue, to-do, true-blue, tutu, undo, undue, untrue, value, venue, virtue, voodoo, walk-through, withdrew, yahoo.

[3] **Avenue**, autocue, ballyhoo, barbecue, buckaroo, continue, devalue, discontinue, hitherto, hullabaloo, impromptu, interview, I.O.U., misconstrue, overdue, overthrew, overview, rendezvous, residue, superglue, switcheroo, well-to-do.
Calaboose, introduce, reproduce.

4.6.56 "--ooted" (as in "rooted")
[2] booted, fluted, fruited, hooted, looted, muted, rooted, scooted, suited, tooted.
[3] commuted, computed, diluted, disputed, polluted, recruited, refuted, reputed, saluted, uprooted
[4] attributed, constituted, contributed, convoluted, distributed, electrocuted, executed, instituted, parachuted, persecuted, substituted.

SURPRISING RHYMING:
[2] **Cupid**, druid, fluid, humid, lucid, putrid, stupid, wounded.
Boosted, roosted.
Booting, fluting, hooting, looting, rooting, scooting, shooting.
[3] **Alluded**, colluded, concluded, deluded, eluded, excluded, included, intruded, precluded, protruded, secluded.
Abusive, conclusive, conducive, effusive, elusive, exclusive, inconclusive, inclusive, intrusive, obtrusive.

4.6.57 "--ooty" (as in "beauty")
[2] beauty, booty, cutie, duty, fruity, snooty, tutti-frutti.

SURPRISING RHYMING:
[2] **Droopy**, groupie, hooky, kooky, loopy, snoopy, spooky.
Broody, gloomy, groovy, loony, moody, movie, smoothie.
Crudely, rudely, shrewdly.
Coolie, coolly, cruelly, duly, newly, truly, unduly, unruly.
Chewy, choosy, goofy, groovy, hooey, juicy, phooey, screwy.
Boogie, boogie-woogie, newbie.
[3] **Ambiguity**, annuity, continuity, gratuity, ingenuity, maturity, obscurity, promiscuity, purity, security, surety.
Absolutely, acutely, astutely, cruelty, crudity, nudity, resolutely.

4.6.58 "--ooting" (as in "shooting")
[2] booting, hooting, looting, rooting, scooting, shooting, tooting.
[3] commuting, computing, diluting, disputing, polluting, recruiting, refuting, saluting, uprooting.
[4] constituting, contributing, convoluting, distributing, electrocuting, executing, instituting, parachuting, persecuting, substituting.

SURPRISING RHYMING:
[2] **Drooping**, duping, grouping, looping, pooping, scooping, snooping, stooping, swooping, trooping, whooping.
Nuking, puking, rebuking, spooking.
Blooming, booming, brooding, fuming, grooming, rooming, zooming.
Crooning, looning, mooning, pruning, spooning, swooning, tuning.
Cooling, drooling, fooling, grooving, moving, proving, ruling, schooling.
Booing, brewing, chewing, doing, gluing, queuing, screwing, ruin, skewing, suing, viewing, wooing.
Boozing, boosting, bruising, choosing, cruising, fusing, losing, musing, oozing, schmoozing, snoozing, using.
[3] **Assuming**, consuming, mushrooming, presuming, resuming.
Ballooning, communing, festooning, honeymooning, lampooning.
Concluding, eluding, excluding, including, intruding, protruding.
Approving, disapproving, disproving, improving, removing.
Accruing, arguing, construing, debuting, ensuing, issuing, miscuing, outdoing, previewing, pursuing, redoing, renewing, rescuing, reviewing, shampooing, subduing, tattooing, undoing, valuing.

Abusing, accusing, amusing, bemusing, confusing, defusing, effusing, enthusing, excusing, infusing, misusing, perusing, refusing.

4.6.59 "--oove" (as in "groove")
[1] groove, move, prove, you've.
[2] approve, behoove, disapprove, disprove, improve, remove.

SURPRISING RHYMING:
[1] **Grooved**, hooved, moved, proved.
Grooves, hooves, moves, proves, roofs, spoofs.
Booth, goof, proof, sleuth, smooth, sooth, spoof, tooth, truth, youth.
Blues, boos, booze, bruise, chews, choose, clues, crews, cruise, do's, dues, fuse, lose, mews, muse, news, ooze, ruse, schmooze, shoes, snooze, stews, sues, use, who's, whose, zoos.
Bruised, cruised, fused, mused, oozed, schmoozed, snoozed, used.
Boob, cube, lube, tube, YouTube.
Boon, croon, dune, moon, noon, soon, spoon, strewn, swoon, tune.
Blew, blue, brew, chew, clue, coup, crew, cue, dew, do, drew, due, few, flew, flu, glue, grew, hue, knew, new, pew, queue, shoe, screw, shoo, skew, stew, sue, threw, through, thru, to, too, true, two, view, who, woo, yew, you, zoo.
[2] **Approved**, disapproved, improved, removed, unmoved.
Approves, disapproves, disproves, improves, removes.
Aloof, bulletproof, childproof, fireproof, flameproof, foolproof, living proof, rainproof, shockproof, soundproof, stormproof, sunroof.
Abuse(d), accuse(d), amuse(d), argues, bemuse(d), breakthroughs, canoes, confuse(d), construes, curfews, debuts, defuse(d), diffuse, ensues, enthuse(d), excuse(d), gurus, hairdos, hoodoos, horseshoes, infuse(d), igloos, issues, menus, miscues, misuse(d), nephews, peruse(d), previews, pursues, refuse(d), rescues, renews, reviews, revues, rhythm-and-blues, shampoos, sinews, statues, subdues, taboos, tattoos, tissues, unscrews, values, venues, virtues.
Balloon, buffoon, cartoon, cocoon, commune, festoon, fortune, harpoon, immune, impugn, lagoon, lampoon, maroon, monsoon, platoon, pontoon, saloon, teaspoon, tycoon, typhoon.
Accrue, anew, argue, askew, bamboo, bayou, bijou, boohoo, breakthrough, canoe, construe, corkscrew, curfew, debut, déjà vu, derring-do, diss you, ensue, fondue, gumshoe, guru, hairdo, hoodoo, horseshoe, igloo, in lieu, into, in two, issue, juju, kazoo, kung fu, lasso, menu, mildew, miscue, nephew, onto, outdo, outgrew, preview, pursue, rescue, redo, renew, review, revue, sea-view, see-through, set-to, shampoo, sinew, statue, subdue, taboo, tattoo, thumb-screw, tissue, to-do, true-blue, tutu, undo, undue, untrue, value, venue, virtue, voodoo, walk-through, withdrew, yahoo.
[3] **Afternoon**, harvest moon, honeymoon, misfortune, opportune.
Avenue, autocue, ballyhoo, barbecue, buckaroo, continue, devalue, discontinue, hitherto, hullabaloo, impromptu, interview, I.O.U., misconstrue, overdue, overthrew, overview, rendezvous, residue, superglue, switcheroo, well-to-do.

4.6.60 "--ooved" (as in "moved")
[1] grooved, hooved, moved, proved.
[2] approved, disapproved, disproved, improved, removed, unmoved.

SURPRISING RHYMING:
[1] **Groove**, move, prove, you've.
Booth, couth, sleuth, smooth, sooth, tooth, truth, youth.
Goofed, hoofed, roofed, spoofed.
Bruised, cruised, fused, mused, oozed, schmoozed, snoozed, used.
Booed, brewed, brood, chewed, cooed, crude, cued, dude, feud, food, glued, lewd, mood, nude, prude, rude, screwed, shoed, shrewd, skewed, spewed, stewed, sued, viewed, who'd, you'd.
Crooned, mooned, pruned, spooned, swooned, tuned, wound.
Bloomed, boomed, doomed, fumed, groomed, roomed, zoomed.

Blew, blue, brew, chew, clue, coup, crew, cue, dew, do, drew, due, few, flew, flu, glue, grew, hue, knew, new, pew, queue, screw, shoe, shoo, skew, stew, sue, threw, through, thru, to, too, true, two, view, who, woo, yew, you, zoo.
[2] **Approve**, behoove, disapprove, disprove, improve, remove.
Accrued, allude, argued, boohooed, canoed, collude, conclude, construed, debuted, delude, elude, ensued, exclude, exude, imbued, include, intrude, miscued, preclude, prelude, previewed, protruded, pursued, queued, renewed, rescued, reviewed, seafood, seclude, shampooed, subdued, tabooed, tattooed, valued, wholefood.
Abused, accused, amused, bemused, confused, defused, disused, enthused, excused, infused, misused, perused, refused, transfused.

4.6.61 "--oover" (as in "mover")
[2] groover, mover, prover.
[3] approver, improver, manoeuvre/maneuver (U.S.), remover.

SURPRISING RHYMING:
[2] **Bluer**, brewer, chewer, doer, fewer, newer, truer, viewer, wooer.
Brooder, cruder, intruder, lewder, ruder, shrewder.
Boomer, groomer, humour/humor (U.S.), rumour/rumor (U.S.), smoother, soother.
Crooner, lunar, pruner, schooner, sooner, swooner, tuna, tuner.
Curer, insurer, juror, poorer, purer, tourer.
Cooler, dueller/dueler (U.S.), fooler, hula, moolah, pooler, ruler.
Boozer, bruiser, chooser, cruiser, loser, schmoozer, snoozer, user.
Blooper, duper, pooper, scooper, snooper, stupor, super, trooper.
Cuter, future, hooter, looter, scooter, shooter, suitor, tutor.
[3] **Evil-doer**, interviewer, pursuer, rescuer, reviewer, wrongdoer.
Baby-boomer, consumer, costumer, perfumer, satsuma.
Mea culpa, party-pooper, paratrooper, pooper-scooper, super-duper.
Abuser, accuser, amuser, excuser, medusa, seducer, yakuza.
Commuter, computer, persecutor, polluter, troubleshooter.

4.6.62 "--oovie" (as in "movie")
[2] groovy, movie.

SURPRISING RHYMING:
[1] **Bluesy**, boozy, choosey, floozy, jacuzzi, juicy, loosely, woozy.
Chewy, gloomy, gooey, goofy, groovy, hooey, phooey, screwy.
Coolie, coolly, duly, newly, toothy, truly, unduly, unruly.
Dourly, poorly, purely, surely.
Broody, gloomy, loony, moody, smoothie.
Beauty, booty, cruelty, cutie, duty, fruity, snooty, tutti-frutti.
Droopy, groupie, kooky, loopy, snoopy, spooky.
[3] **Cruelly**, demurely, impurely, maturely, obscurely, securely.

4.6.63 "--ooze" (as in "choose")
[1] blues, boos, booze, brews, bruise, chews, choose, clues, coos, crews, cruise, do's, dues, flues, fuse, loos, lose, mews, muse, news, ooze, ruse, schmooze, shoes, shoos, snooze, stews, sues, trews, use, who's, whose, zoos.
[2] abuse, accrues, accuse, amuse, argues, bamboos, bemuse, breakthroughs, canoes, cashews, confuse, construes, corkscrews, cuckoos, curfews, curlews, debuts, defuse, diffuse, effuse, ensues, enthuse, excuse, gurus, hairdos, hoodoos, horseshoes, infuse, igloos, imbues, issues, lassos, menus, miscues, misuse, nephews, peruse, previews, pursues, refuse, rescues, renews, reviews, revues, rhythm-and-blues, shampoos, sinews, statues, subdues, taboos, tattoos, tissues, transfuse, values, venues, virtues.

SURPRISING RHYMING:
[1] **Bruised**, cruised, fused, oozed, schmoozed, snoozed, used.
Grooves, hooves, moves, proves, roofs, spoofs.
Booth(s), sleuth, smooth(s), sooth(es), tooth, truth(s), youth(s).

Drools, fools, ghouls, mules, pools, rules, schools, stools, tools.
Deuce, goose, juice, loose, noose, spruce, truce, use, Zeus.
Blooms, brooms, fumes, grooms, looms, rooms, tombs, zooms.
Broods, dudes, feuds, foods, moods, nudes, prudes.
Blew, blue, brew, chew, clue, coup, crew, cue, dew, do, drew, due, few, flew, flu, glue, grew, hue, knew, new, pew, queue, screw, shoe, shoo, skew, stew, sue, threw, through, thru, to, too, true, two, view, who, woo, yew, you, zoo.
[2] Approves, behooves, disapproves, disproves, improves, removes.
Abused, accused, amused, bemused, confused, defused, disused, enthused, excused, infused, misused, perused, refused, transfused.
Abuse (*noun*), caboose, deduce, diffuse, effuse, excuse, footloose, induce, misuse, mongoose, obtuse, produce, profuse, recluse, reduce, refuse, seduce, vamoose.
Assumes, backrooms, bathrooms, bedrooms, boardrooms, bridegrooms, classrooms, consumes, costumes, courtrooms, entombs, heirlooms, mushrooms, newsrooms, perfumes, presumes, resumes, schoolrooms, vacuums, volumes.
Alludes, colludes, concludes, deludes, excludes, exudes, includes, intrudes, precludes, preludes, protrudes, seafoods.
Accrue, anew, argue, askew, bamboo, bayou, bijou, boohoo, breakthrough, canoe, construe, corkscrew, curfew, debut, déjà vu, derring-do, diss you, ensue, fondue, gumshoe, guru, hairdo, hoodoo, horseshoe, igloo, in lieu, into, in two, issue, juju, kazoo, kung fu, lasso, menu, mildew, miscue, nephew, onto, outdo, outgrew, preview, pursue, rescue, redo, renew, review, revue, sea-view, see-through, set-to, shampoo, sinew, statue, subdue, taboo, tattoo, thumb-screw, tissue, to-do, true-blue, tutu, undo, undue, untrue, value, venue, virtue, voodoo, walk-through, withdrew, yahoo.
[3] Calaboose, introduce, reproduce.
Aptitudes, attitudes, interludes, multitudes, platitudes.
Avenue, autocue, ballyhoo, barbecue, buckaroo, continue, devalue, discontinue, hitherto, hullabaloo, impromptu, interview, I.O.U., misconstrue, overdue, overthrew, overview, rendezvous, residue, superglue, switcheroo, well-to-do.

4.6.64 "--oozed" (as in "used")
[1] bruised, cruised, mused, oozed, schmoozed, snoozed, used.
[2] abused, accused, amused, bemused, confused, defused, disused, enthused, excused, infused, misused, perused, refused, transfused.

SURPRISING RHYMING:
[1] Blues, boos, booze, bruise, chews, choose, clues, crews, cruise, do's, dues, fuse, lose, mews, muse, news, ooze, ruse, schmooze, shoes, snooze, stews, sues, use, who's, whose, zoos.
Broods, dudes, feuds, foods, moods, nudes, prudes.
Grooves, hooves, moves, proves, roofs, spoofs.
Grooved, hooved, moved, proved, smoothed.
Booths, smooths, soothes, truths, youths.
Goosed, juiced, loosed, spruced, used.
Blew, blue, brew, chew, clue, coup, crew, cue, dew, do, drew, due, few, flew, flu, glue, grew, hue, knew, new, pew, queue, screw, shoe, shoo, skew, stew, sue, threw, through, thru, to, too, true, two, view, who, woo, yew, you, zoo.
[2] Abuse, accuse, amuse, argues, bemuse, breakthroughs, canoes, confuse, construes, curfews, debuts, defuse, diffuse, ensues, enthuse, excuse, gurus, hairdos, hoodoos, horseshoes, infuse, igloos, issues, menus, miscues, misuse, nephews, peruse, previews, pursues, refuse, rescues, renews, reviews, revues, rhythm-and-blues, shampoos, sinews, statues, subdues, taboos, tattoos, tissues, values, venues, virtues.
Approved, disapproved, disproved, improved, removed, unmoved.
Approves, behooves, disapproves, disproves, improves, removes.
Alludes, colludes, concludes, deludes, excludes, extrudes, exudes, includes, intrudes, precludes, preludes, protrudes, seafoods.
Accrue, anew, argue, askew, bamboo, bayou, bijou, boohoo, breakthrough, canoe, construe, corkscrew, curfew, debut, déjà vu, derring-do, diss you, ensue, fondue,

gumshoe, guru, hairdo, hoodoo, horseshoe, igloo, in lieu, into, in two, issue, juju, kazoo, kung fu, lasso, menu, mildew, miscue, nephew, onto, outdo, outgrew, preview, pursue, rescue, redo, renew, review, revue, sea-view, see-through, set-to, shampoo, sinew, statue, subdue, taboo, tattoo, thumb-screw, tissue, to-do, true-blue, tutu, undo, undue, untrue, value, venue, virtue, voodoo, walk-through, withdrew, yahoo.
[3] Calaboose, introduce, reproduce.
Avenue, autocue, ballyhoo, barbecue, buckaroo, continue, devalue, discontinue, hitherto, hullabaloo, impromptu, interview, I.O.U., misconstrue, overdue, overthrew, overview, rendezvous, residue, superglue, switcheroo, well-to-do.

4.6.65 "--oozer" (as in "loser")
[2] boozer, bruiser, chooser, cruiser, loser, schmoozer, snoozer, user.
[3] abuser, accuser, amuser, excuser, medusa, refuser, yakuza.

SURPRISING RHYMING:
[2] **Groover**, hoover, mover, prover, roofer, smoother, soother.
Curer, insurer, juror, poorer, purer, tourer.
Booster, future, looser, rooster.
Crooner, lunar, pruner, schooner, sooner, swooner, tuna, tuner.
Boomer, groomer, humour/humor (U.S.), rumour/rumor (U.S.), roomer, zoomer.
Brooder, cruder, intruder, lewder, ruder, shrewder.
Cuter, hooter, looter, scooter, shooter, suitor, tutor.
Cooler, dueller/dueler (U.S.), fooler, hula, moolah, pooler, ruler.
Bluer, brewer, chewer, doer, fewer, newer, truer, viewer, wooer.
[3] **Approver**, improver, manoeuvre/maneuver (U.S.), remover.
Abuser, excuser, introducer, producer, refuser, seducer.
Baby-boomer, ballooner, consumer, honeymooner, lampooner.
Commuter, computer, persecutor, polluter, troubleshooter.
Blooper, duper, pooper, scooper, snooper, stupor, super, trooper.
Crueler, jeweller/jeweler (U.S.).
Evil-doer, interviewer, pursuer, rescuer, reviewer, wrongdoer.

4.6.66 "--oozes" (as in "chooses")
[2] bruises, chooses, cruises, floozies, fuses, loses, muses, oozes, ruses, schmoozes, snoozes, uses.
[3] abuses, accuses, amuses, bemuses, confuses, defuses, diffuses, effuses, enthuses, excuses, infuses, misuses, peruses, refuses.

SURPRISING RHYMING:
[2] **Juices**, movies, nooses, spruces, truces.
Bluest, fewest, newest, poorest, purest, soonest, surest, truest.
Crudest, lewdest, rudest, shrewdest.
Boozing, bruising, choosing, cruising, fusing, losing, musing, oozing, schmoozing, snoozing, using.
[3] **Abuses**, deduces, excuses, introduces, produces, reduces, reproduces, seduces.
Abusive, conclusive, conducive, effusive, elusive, exclusive, inconclusive, inclusive, intrusive, obtrusive, reclusive.
Abusing, accusing, amusing, confusing, enthusing, excusing, refusing.

4.6.67 "--oozing" (as in "choosing")
[2] boozing, bruising, choosing, cruising, fusing, losing, musing, oozing, schmoozing, snoozing, using.
[3] abusing, accusing, amusing, bemusing, confusing, defusing, effusing, enthusing, excusing, infusing, misusing, perusing, refusing.

SURPRISING RHYMING:
[2] **Goofing**, grooving, moving, proving, roofing, smoothing, soothing.
Booing, brewing, chewing, cooing, doing, gluing, queuing, screwing, ruin, skewing, suing, viewing, wooing.

Curing, during, luring, mooring, touring.
Cooling, drooling, fooling, pooling, ruling, schooling, tooling.
Blooming, booming, brooding, fuming, grooming, rooming, zooming.
Crooning, looning, mooning, pruning, spooning, swooning, tuning.
[3] **Approving**, disapproving, disproving, improving, removing.
Assuming, consuming, mushrooming, presuming, resuming.
Alluring, assuring, enduring, ensuring, insuring, maturing, obscuring, posturing, procuring, reassuring, securing.
Concluding, eluding, excluding, including, intruding, protruding.
Accruing, arguing, construing, debuting, ensuing, issuing, miscuing, outdoing, previewing, pursuing, redoing, renewing, rescuing, reviewing, shampooing, subduing, tattooing, undoing, valuing.
[4] **April fooling**, overruling, ridiculing.

* * *

PART 5

'U'

5.1 "uh" sounds (as in "up").............................Index on Page 572
5.2 "ur" sounds (as in "her").............................Index on Page 574

5.1 "uh" (as in "up")

5.1.1 "--ub" (as in "club") 577
5.1.2 "--ubby" (as in "clubby") 577
5.1.3 "--ubble" (as in "trouble") 577
5.1.4 "--ubbled" (as in "troubled") 578
5.1.5 "--ubbling" (as in "bubbling") 578
5.1.6 "--ubbed" (as in "rubbed") 578
5.1.7 "--uck" (as in "truck") 579
5.1.8 "--ucked" (as in "bucked") 579
5.1.9 "--uckel" (as in "buckle") 580
5.1.10 "--uct" (as in "obstruct") 580
5.1.11 "--ucker" (as in "trucker") 580
5.1.12 "--ucking" (as in "trucking") 581
5.1.13 "--uction" (as in "seduction") 581
5.1.14 "--ucted" (as in "abducted") 581
5.1.15 "--uctor" (as in "conductor") 581
5.1.16 "--uctive" (as in "seductive") 582
5.1.17 "--ud" (as in "good") 582
5.1.18 "--udded" (as in "wooded") 582
5.1.19 "--udge" (as in "judge") 582
5.1.20 "--udges" (as in "judges") 583
5.1.21 "--udged" (as in "judged") 583
5.1.22 "--udging" (as in "judging") 583
5.1.23 "--idul" (as in "idol") 583
5.1.24 "--oddull" (as in "model") 584
5.1.25 "--uddull" (as in "cuddle") 584
5.1.26 "--iddull" (as in "riddle") 584
5.1.27 "--addull" (as in "saddle") 584
5.1.28 "--uff" (as in "bluff") 585
5.1.29 "--uffer" (as in "suffer") 585
5.1.30 "--uffel" (as in "scuffle") 585
5.1.31 "--ug" (as in "bug") 585
5.1.32 "--ugged" (as in "tugged") 586
5.1.33 "--uggle" (as in "struggle") 586
5.1.34 "--uggler" (as in "juggler") 586
5.1.35 "--angull" (as in "angle") 587
5.1.36 "--oggull" (as in "goggle") 587
5.1.37 "--oogull" (as in "google") 587
5.1.38 "--ingull" (as in "tingle") 587
5.1.39 "--ull" (as in "full") 588
5.1.40 "--ully" (as in "bully") 589
5.1.41 "--ulk" (as in "hulk") 589
5.1.42 "--ult" (as in "insult") 589
5.1.43 "--ulted" (as in "insulted") 590
5.1.44 "--kull" (as in "uncle") 590
5.1.45 "--akull" (as in "crackle") 590
5.1.46 "--inkull" (as in "twinkle") 590
5.1.47 "--ikkull" (as in "tickle") 590

5.1.48 "--ekkull" (as in "freckle") 591
5.1.49 "--um" (as in "thumb") 591
5.1.50 "--ummer" (as in "summer") 592
5.1.51 "--ummy" (as in "dummy") 592
5.1.52 "--umming" (as in "humming") 592
5.1.53 "--ump" (as in "bump") 592
5.1.54 "--umping" (as in "bumping") 593
5.1.55 "--umper" (as in "jumper") 593
5.1.56 "--umpy" (as in "jumpy") 593
5.1.57 "--umber" (as in "number") 594
5.1.58 "--umble" (as in "humble") 594
5.1.59 "--umbler" (as in "tumbler") 594
5.1.60 "--umbling" (as in "fumbling") 594
5.1.61 "--mull" (as in "normal") 595
5.1.62 "--un" (as in "run") 595
5.1.63 "--unned" (as in "stunned") 595
5.1.64 "--unning" (as in "running") 596
5.1.65 "--unch" (as in "lunch") 596
5.1.66 "--unching" (as in "punching") 596
5.1.67 "--unk" (as in "drunk") 596
5.1.68 "--unt" (as in "hunt") 597
5.1.69 "--under" (as in "under") 597
5.1.70 "--unnel" (as in "tunnel") 597
5.1.71 "--ung" (as in "young") 598
5.1.72 "--unger" (as in "younger") 598
5.1.73 "--unny" (as in "funny") 598
5.1.74 "--unky" (as in "funky") 599
5.1.75 "--shun" (as in "passion") 599
5.1.76 "--annull" (as in "channel") 600
5.1.77 "--urnell" (as in "journal") 600
5.1.78 "--onull" (as in "zonal") 600
5.1.79 "--shunnell" (as in "fictional") 601
5.1.80 "--appull" (as in "apple") 601
5.1.81 "--ippull" (as in "ripple") 601
5.1.82 "--uppell" (as in "couple") 601
5.1.83 "--eepull" (as in "people") 602
5.1.84 "--ampull" (as in "sample") 602
5.1.85 "--up" (as in "cup") 602
5.1.86 "--upper" (as in "supper") 603
5.1.87 "--orrul" (as in "quarrel") 603
5.1.88 "--arrull" (as in "barrel") 603
5.1.89 "--oorull" (as in "rural") 603
5.1.90 "--errull" (as in "peril") 604
5.1.91 "--uss" (as in "bus") 604
5.1.92 "--ust" (as in "trust") 605
5.1.93 "--usk" (as in "tusk") 605
5.1.94 "--ush" (as in "push") 606
5.1.95 "--ushed" (as in "pushed") 606

5.1.96 "--ushing" (as in "pushing") 606
5.1.97 "--usher" (as in "usher") 607
5.1.98 "--ustle" (as in "hustle") 607
5.1.99 "--usted" (as in "busted") 607
5.1.100 "--uster" (as in "buster") 607
5.1.101 "--ustard" (as in "custard") 608
5.1.102 "--ustful" (as in "trustful") 608
5.1.103 "--usty" (as in "trusty") 608
5.1.104 "--usting" (as in "trusting") 608
5.1.105 "--ussion" (as in "percussion") 609
5.1.106 "--ut" (as in "foot") 609
5.1.107 "--utter" (as in "butter") 610
5.1.108 "--utton" (as in "button") 610
5.1.109 "--uttel" (as in "shuttle") 610
5.1.110 "--utch" (as in "touch") 611
5.1.111 "--utched" (as in "touched") 611
5.1.112 "--uv" (as in "love") 611
5.1.113 "--uvved" (as in "loved") 611
5.1.114 "--uvver" (as in "lover") 612
5.1.115 "--uvving" (as in "loving") 612
5.1.116 "--uz" (as in "buzz") 612
5.1.117 "--uzzen" (as in "dozen") 612
5.1.118 "--uzzle" (as in "puzzle") 613

5.2 "ur" (as in "her")

5.2.1 "--urr" (as in "fur") 613
5.2.2 "--urch" (as in "church") 614
5.2.3 "--urches" (as in "churches") 614
5.2.4 "--urd" (as in "bird") 614
5.2.5 "--urge" (as in "urge") 614
5.2.6 "--urging" (as in "urging") 615
5.2.7 "--urk" (as in "work") 615
5.2.8 "--urking" (as in "working") 616
5.2.9 "--url" (as in "girl") 616
5.2.10 "--urly" (as in "early") 616
5.2.11 "--urled" (as in "world") 616
5.2.12 "--urm" (as in "germ") 617
5.2.13 "--urmur" (as in "murmur") 617
5.2.14 "--urn" (as in "turn") 617
5.2.15 "--urned" (as in "turned") 617
5.2.16 "--urning" (as in "burning") 618
5.2.17 "--urse" (as in "curse") 618
5.2.18 "--urses" (as in "nurses") 618
5.2.19 "--ursing" (as in "nursing") 619
5.2.20 "--ursion" (as in "excursion") 619
5.2.21 "--urst" (as in "worst") 619
5.2.22 "--urt" (as in "hurt") 619
5.2.23 "--urted" (as in "flirted") 620

5.2.24 "--urting" (as in "hurting") 620
5.2.25 "--urtin" (as in "certain") 620
5.2.26 "--urth" (as in "earth") 620
5.2.27 "--urve" (as in "curve") 621
5.2.28 "--urved" (as in "curved") 621
5.2.29 "--urving" (as in "curving") 622

* * *

5.1 "uh" (as in "up")

5.1.1 "--ub" (as in "club")
[1] blub, bub, chub, club, cub, drub, dub, flub, grub, hub, nub, pub, rub, scrub, shrub, snub, stub, sub, tub.
[2] bathtub, Beelzebub, cherub, hubbub, nightclub, washtub.

SURPRISING RHYMING:
[1] **Blubbed**, clubbed, drubbed, dubbed, rubbed, scrubbed, snubbed, stubbed, subbed.
Bug, chug, drug, dug, glug, hug, jug, lug, mug, plug, rug, shrug, slug, smug, snug, thug, tug.
Blood, bud, could, crud, dud, flood, good, hood, mud, should, spud, stood, stud, thud, wood, would.
Bum, chum, come, crumb, drum, dumb, glum, gum, hum, mum, numb, plum, plumb, rum, scrum, scum, slum, some, strum, sum, swum, thumb, tum, yum.
Bump, chump, clump, dump, frump, grump, hump, jump, lump, plump, pump, rump, slump, stump, thump, trump.
Cup, pup, sup, up, yup.
But, butt, cut, glut, gut, hut, jut, mutt, nut, put, putt, rut, shut, slut, smut, strut, tut.
[2] **Bedbug**, debug, earplug, firebug, hearthrug, humbug, unplug.
Boyhood, childhood, deadwood, driftwood, falsehood, firewood, knighthood, lifeblood, manhood, priesthood, touchwood, withstood.
Album, autumn, awesome, become, boredom, bottom, breadcrumb, bubblegum, column, eardrum, fearsome, forum, freedom, fulsome, gruesome, handsome, hokum, hoodlum, humdrum, income, -ism, kingdom, loathsome, lonesome, magnum, outcome, prism, problem, quantum, ransom, sanctum, schism, seldom, spasm, spectrum, stardom, tantrum, tiresome, twosome, welcome, wholesome, wisdom.
Backup, bishop, break-up, checkup, cleanup, closeup, cock-up, cut-up, dollop, Europe, fry-up, gallop, grown-up, hang-up, hiccup, hold-up, hook-up, ketchup, let-up, lineup, linkup, lock-up, lookup, makeup, markup, nosh-up, pickup, pile-up, pinup, press-up, pull up, punch-up, rave-up, roundup, run-up, scallop, set-up, shake-up, sit-up, slap-up, snarl-up, start-up, stick-up, stirrup, straight-up, stuck up, sun-up, syrup/sirup (U.S.), take-up, teacup, top-up, toss-up, trollop, turn-up, two-up, warmup, wash-up, wind-up, zip-up.
Clean-cut, clear-cut, crewcut, doughnut/donut (U.S.), haircut, half-shut, peanut, shortcut.
[3] **Doodlebug**, jitterbug, ladybug, litterbug.
Adulthood, brotherhood, fatherhood, Hollywood, likelihood, livelihood, misunderstood, motherhood, neighbourhood/neighborhood (U.S.), parenthood, sisterhood, stick-in-the-mud, understood.
Bothersome, bubblegum, burdensome, chromium, conundrum, cumbersome, helium, idiom, maximum, medium, meddlesome, minimum, momentum, museum, opium, optimum, orgasm, overcome, petroleum, phantasm, platinum, podium, premium, quarrelsome, requiem, rhythm, rock-bottom, sadism, sarcasm, stadium, sugarplum, tedium, troublesome, unwelcome, valium.

5.1.2 "--ubby" (as in "clubby")
[2] chubby, clubby, grubby, hubby, nubby, scrubby, stubby, tubby.

SURPRISING RHYMING:
[2] **Bunny**, funny, honey, money, runny, sonny, sunny.
Chummy, crummy, dummy, mummy, plummy, tummy, yummy.
Bully, fully, gully, pulley, woolly.
Bumpy, dumpy, frumpy, grumpy, jumpy, lumpy, rumpy-pumpy.
Chunky, clunky, flunky, funky, hunky, junkie, monkey, punky.

5.1.3 "--ubble" (as in "trouble")
[2] bubble, double, Hubble, rubble, stubble, trouble.

SURPRISING RHYMING:
[2] **Bubbled**, doubled, stubbled, troubled.
Juggle, smuggle, snuggle, struggle.
Cuddle, fuddle, funnel, huddle, muddle, puddle, tunnel.
Bumble, bundle, crumble, fumble, grumble, humble, jumble, mumble, rumble, stumble, trundle, tumble.
Bustle, guzzle, hustle, muscle, muzzle, nuzzle, puzzle, rustle, tussle.
Couple, supple, decouple, uncouple.
Duffel, muffle, ruffle, scuffle, shuffle, snuffle, truffle.
Cuttle, scuttle, shuttle, subtle, rebuttal.
Buckle, chuckle, knuckle, suckle, unbuckle.
[3] **Honeysuckle**, kerfuffle, reshuffle.

5.1.4 "--ubbled" (as in "troubled")
[2] bubbled, doubled, stubbled, troubled.

SURPRISING RHYMING:
[2] **Bubble**, double, Hubble, rubble, stubble, trouble.
Juggled, smuggled, snuggled, struggled.
Befuddled, cuddled, fuddled, funneled, huddled, muddled, tunneled.
Guzzled, muzzled, nuzzled, puzzled.
Bumbled, bundled, crumbled, fumbled, grumbled, humbled, jumbled, mumbled, rumbled, stumbled, trundled, tumbled.
Bustled, hustled, muscled, rustled, tussled.
Coupled, decoupled, uncoupled.
Muffled, ruffled, scuffled, shuffled, snuffled.
Buckled, chuckled, knuckled, scuttled, shuttled, suckled, unbuckled.

5.1.5 "--ubbling" (as in "bubbling")
[2] bubbling, doubling, troubling.

SURPRISING RHYMING:
[2] **Juggling**, smuggling, snuggling, struggling.
Cuddling, coupling, decoupling, fuddling, huddling, muddling.
Bumbling, bundling, crumbling, fumbling, grumbling, humbling, jumbling, mumbling, rumbling, stumbling, trundling, tumbling.
Coming, drumming, dumbing, humming, numbing, slumming, strumming, thumbing.
Cunning, funning, gunning, punning, running, stunning, sunning.
Guzzling, muzzling, nuzzling, puzzling.
Bustling, hustling, muscling, rustling, tussling.
Muffling, ruffling, scuffling, shuffling, snuffling.
Bumping, dumping, jumping, lumping, pumping, slumping, thumping.
Buckling, chuckling, knuckling, suckling, unbuckling.

5.1.6 "--ubbed" (as in "rubbed")
[1] blubbed, clubbed, drubbed, dubbed, grubbed, rubbed, scrubbed, snubbed, stubbed, subbed.

SURPRISING RHYMING:
[1] **Club**, cub, drub, dub, flub, grub, hub, nub, pub, rub, scrub, shrub, snub, stub, sub, tub.
Bugged, chugged, drugged, glugged, hugged, mugged, plugged, rugged, shrugged, slugged, tugged, unplugged.
Gloved, loved, shoved.
Blood, bud, could, crud, dud, flood, good, hood, mud, should, spud, stood, stud, thud, wood, would.
Bluffed, cuffed, duffed, fluffed, huffed, puffed, roughed, scuffed, stuffed, woofed.
Budged, fudged, grudged, judged, nudged, smudged, trudged.

[2] **Bathtub**, Beelzebub, cherub, hubbub, nightclub, washtub.
Adjudged, begrudged, misjudged, prejudged.

5.1.7 "--uck" (as in "truck")
[1] book, brook, buck, chuck, cook, crook, duck, hook, look, luck, muck, pluck, puck, ruck, schmuck, schtuck, shook, shuck, struck, stuck, suck, took, truck, tuck, yuck.
[2] amok, awestruck, chequebook, cookbook, dumbstruck, fishhook, forsook, guidebook, handbook, megabuck, mistook, moonstruck, notebook, outlook, partook, phrasebook, playbook, potluck, scrapbook, sketchbook, songbook, stagestruck, storybook, textbook, thunderstruck, unhook, unstuck, wet look, workbook.
[3] inglenook, overcook, overlook, overtook, picture book, pocketbook, storybook, tenterhook, undercook, undertook.

SURPRISING RHYMING:
[1] **Booked**, bucked, chucked, clucked, cooked, ducked, hooked, looked, mucked, plucked, rucked, sucked, trucked, tucked.
But, butt, cut, glut, gut, hut, jut, mutt, nut, put, putt, rut, shut, slut, smut, strut, tut.
Brusque, busk, bust, bussed, cussed, crust, dusk, dust, fussed, gust, husk, just, lust, musk, must, rust, thrust, trussed, trust, tusk.
Cup, pup, sup, up, yup.
Bulk, hulk, skulk, sulk.
Bunk, chunk, clunk, drunk, dunk, flunk, funk, gunk, hunk, junk, monk, plunk, punk, shrunk, skunk, slunk, stunk, sunk, trunk.
[2] **Clean-cut**, clear-cut, crewcut, crosscut, doughnut/donut (U.S.), haircut, half-shut, peanut, rebut, shortcut, somewhat, uncut.
Abduct, conduct, deduct, construct, instruct, obstruct, product.
Backup, bishop, break-up, checkup, cleanup, closeup, cock-up, cut-up, dollop, Europe, fry-up, gallop, grown-up, hang-up, hiccup, hold-up, hook-up, ketchup, let-up, lineup, linkup, lock-up, lookup, makeup, markup, nosh-up, pickup, pile-up, pinup, press-up, pull up, punch-up, rave-up, roundup, run-up, set-up, shake-up, sit-up, slap-up, snarl-up, start-up, stick-up, stirrup, straight-up, stuck up, sun-up, syrup/sirup (U.S.), take-up, teacup, top-up, toss-up, trollop, turn-up, two-up, wallop, warmup, wash-up, wind-up.
Adjust, august, blood lust, combust, discussed, disgust, distrust, entrust, gold dust, mistrust, robust, stardust, unjust, wanderlust.
[3] **Coconut**, hazelnut, overcooked, overlooked, undercooked, unhooked, undercut.
Aqueduct, misconduct, reconstruct, safe-conduct, viaduct.
Buttercup, develop, giddy-up, pick-me-up, summing-up, washing-up.

5.1.8 "--ucked" (as in "bucked")
[1] booked, bucked, chucked, clucked, cooked, ducked, hooked, looked, mucked, plucked, rucked, sucked, trucked, tucked.
[3] overcooked, overlooked, undercooked, unhooked.

SURPRISING RHYMING:
[1] **Book**, brook, buck, chuck, cook, crook, duck, hook, look, luck, muck, pluck, puck, ruck, schmuck, schtuck, shook, shuck, struck, stuck, suck, took, truck, tuck, yuck.
But, butt, cut, glut, gut, hut, jut, mutt, nut, put, putt, rut, shut, slut, smut, strut, tut.
Cup, pup, sup, up, yup.
Brusque, busk, bust, bussed, cussed, crust, dusk, dust, fussed, gust, husk, just, lust, musk, must, rust, thrust, trussed, trust, tusk.
[2] **Awestruck**, chequebook, cookbook, dumbstruck, fishhook, guidebook, megabuck, mistook, moonstruck, notebook, outlook, partook, playbook, potluck, scrapbook, sketchbook, songbook, stagestruck, storybook, textbook, thunderstruck, unhook, unstuck.
Clean-cut, clear-cut, crewcut, doughnut/donut (U.S.), haircut, half-shut, peanut, shortcut, somewhat, uncut.
Abduct, conduct, deduct, construct, instruct, obstruct, product.
Backup, bishop, break-up, checkup, cleanup, closeup, cock-up, cut-up, Europe, fry-up, gallop, grown-up, hang-up, hiccup, hold-up, hook-up, ketchup, let-up, lineup, linkup, lock-up, lookup, makeup, markup, nosh-up, pickup, pile-up, pinup, press-up, pull up, punch-up, rave-up, roundup, run-up, set-up, shake-up, sit-up, slap-up, snarl-up, start-up,

stick-up, stirrup, straight-up, stuck up, sun-up, syrup/sirup (U.S.), take-up, teacup, top-up, toss-up, trollop, turn-up, two-up, wallop, warmup, wash-up, wind-up.
Adjust, august, blood lust, combust, discussed, disgust, distrust, entrust, gold dust, mistrust, robust, stardust, unjust, wanderlust.
[3] **Overlook**, picture book, pocketbook, storybook, tenterhook.
Aqueduct, misconduct, reconstruct, safe-conduct, viaduct.
Buttercup, develop, giddy-up, pick-me-up, summing-up, washing-up.

5.1.9 "--uckel" (as in "buckle")
buckle, chuckle, honeysuckle, knuckle, suckle, unbuckle.

SURPRISING RHYMING:
[2] **Buckled**, chuckled, suckled, unbuckled.
Couple, decouple, rebuttal, scuttle, shuttle, subtle, supple, uncouple.
Bubble, double, Hubble, rubble, stubble, trouble.
Juggle, smuggle, snuggle, struggle.
Cuddle, fuddle, funnel, huddle, muddle, puddle, tunnel.
Bustle, guzzle, hustle, muscle, muzzle, nuzzle, puzzle, rustle, tussle.
Duffel, muffle, ruffle, scuffle, shuffle, snuffle, truffle.

5.1.10 "--uct" (as in "obstruct")
[2] abduct, conduct, deduct, construct, instruct, obstruct, product.
[3] aqueduct, misconduct, reconstruct, safe-conduct, viaduct.

SURPRISING RHYMING:
[1] **Booked**, bucked, chucked, clucked, cooked, ducked, hooked, looked, mucked, plucked, rucked, sucked, trucked, tucked.
Book, brook, buck, chuck, cluck, cook, crook, duck, hook, look, luck, muck, pluck, puck, ruck, schmuck, shook, shuck, struck, stuck, suck, took, truck, tuck, yuck.
Bust, bussed, cussed, crust, dust, fussed, gust, just, lust, must, rust, thrust, trust.
But, butt, cut, glut, gut, hut, jut, mutt, nut, put, putt, rut, shut, slut, smut, strut, tut.
Blunt, brunt, bunt, front, grunt, hunt, punt, runt, shunt, stunt.
Bunk, chunk, clunk, drunk, dunk, flunk, funk, gunk, hunk, junk, monk, plunk, punk, shrunk, skunk, slunk, stunk, sunk, trunk.
Bugged, chugged, drugged, glugged, hugged, mugged, plugged, rugged, shrugged, slugged, tugged, unplugged.
[2] **Adjust**, august, blood lust, combust, discussed, disgust, distrust, entrust, gold dust, mistrust, robust, stardust, unjust, wanderlust.
Clean-cut, clear-cut, crewcut, doughnut/donut (U.S.), haircut, half-shut, shortcut, uncut.
Amok, awestruck, chequebook, cookbook, dumbstruck, fishhook, guidebook, megabuck, mistook, moonstruck, notebook, outlook, partook, playbook, potluck, scrapbook, sketchbook, songbook, stagestruck, storybook, textbook, thunderstruck, unhook, unstuck.
Affront, confront, couldn't, forefront, headhunt, manhunt, seafront, shouldn't, storefront, upfront, waterfront, witch-hunt, wouldn't.
[3] **Overcooked**, overlooked, undercooked, unhooked.

5.1.11 "--ucker" (as in "trucker")
[2] cooker, hooker, looker, plucker, pucker, sucker, trucker, tucker.

SURPRISING RHYMING:
[2] **Butter**, clutter, cutter, flutter, footer, gutter, mutter, nutter, putter, scutter, shutter, splutter, sputter, strutter, stutter, utter, woodcutter.
Cuppa, scupper, supper, upper.
Hugger, mugger, plugger, shrugger, slugger, snugger, tugger.
Busker, buster, cluster, duster, fluster, lacklustre/lackluster (U.S.), lustre/luster (U.S.), muster, thruster.
Bummer, drummer, dumber, glummer, gunner, hummer, number, plumber, runner, shunner, stunner, strummer, summer.
Bluffer, brother, buffer, duffer, other, rougher, suffer, tougher.

Cover, glover, hover, lover, shover.
[3] **Discover**, helluva, latecomer, midsummer, recover, rediscover, uncover, undercover.

5.1.12 "--ucking" (as in "trucking")
[2] booking, bucking, chucking, clucking, cooking, ducking, hooking, looking, mucking, plucking, sucking, trucking, tucking.

SURPRISING RHYMING:
[2] **Butting**, cutting, footing, jutting, putting, shutting, strutting, tutting.
Busking, busting dusting, gusting, lusting, rusting, thrusting, trusting.
Bunking, clunking, dunking, flunking, junking, skulking, sulking, Sun-King.
Bugging, drugging, hugging, lugging, mugging, plugging, shrugging, slugging, tugging.
Bumping, dumping, jumping, lumping, pumping, slumping, thumping.
Bluffing, cuffing, fluffing, huffing, puffing, roughing, scuffing, stuffing.
[3] **Abducting**, conducting, deducting, instructing, obstructing.
Adjusting, combusting, disgusting, distrusting, entrusting, mistrusting.

5.1.13 "--uction" (as in "seduction")
[2] ruction, suction.
[3] abduction, construction, deduction, destruction, induction, instruction, obstruction, production, reduction, seduction.
[4] introduction, reproduction.

SURPRISING RHYMING:
[2] **Function**, junction, luncheon, touching.
Bunching, crunching, lunching, munching, punching, scrunching.
Budging, fudging, grudging, judging, nudging, smudging, trudging.
Blushing, brushing, crushing, cushion, flushing, gushing, hushing, pushing, rushing.
[3] **Concussion**, discussion, percussion, pincushion.
Assumption, compulsion, expulsion, presumption, repulsion.
Corruption, disruption, eruption, interruption, malfunction, T-junction.
Begrudging, misjudging, prejudging.

5.1.14 "--ucted" (as in "abducted")
[3] abducted, constructed, deducted, inducted, instructed, obstructed.

SURPRISING RHYMING:
[2] **Busted**, dusted, gusted, lusted, rusted, thrusted, trusted.
Blunted, fronted, grunted, hunted, punted, shunted, stunted.
[3] **Adjusted**, disgusted, distrusted, entrusted, mistrusted.
Corrupted, disrupted, erupted, interrupted, uninterrupted.
Catapulted, consulted, exulted, insulted, resulted.
Compulsive, destructive, disruptive, impulsive, productive, repulsive, seductive.
Affronted, confronted, headhunted.

5.1.15 "--uctor" (as in "conductor")
[3] abductor, conductor, instructor, obstructer.

SURPRISING RHYMING:
[2] **Cooker**, hooker, looker, plucker, pucker, sucker, trucker, tucker.
Bunker, debunker, drunker, dunker, flunker, hunger, younger.
Blunter, chunter, grunter, hunter, junta, punter, shunter.
Bluster, buster, cluster, duster, fluster, funster, funkster, lacklustre/lackluster (U.S.), lustre/luster (U.S.), muster, thruster.
Bumper, dumper, jumper, plumper, pumper, stumper, thumper.
[3] **Corrupter**, disrupter, interrupter, sculptor.
Blockbuster, filibuster, gangbuster.
Scandalmonger, scaremonger, warmonger.

5.1.16 "--uctive" (as in "seductive")
[3] constructive, deductive, destructive, instructive, obstructive, productive, seductive.

SURPRISING RHYMING:
[2] **Busted**, dusted, gusted, justice, lusted, rusted, thrusted, trusted.
[3] **Abducted**, constructed, deducted, instructed, obstructed.
Corrupted, disrupted, erupted, interrupted, uninterrupted.
Compulsive, disruptive, impulsive, percussive, repulsive.
Adjusted, disgusted, distrusted, encrusted, entrusted, mistrusted.
Catapulted, consulted, exulted, insulted, resulted.
Abusive, conducive, effusive, elusive, exclusive, intrusive, reclusive.

5.1.17 "--ud" (as in "good")
[1] blood, bud, could, crud, dud, flood, good, hood, mud, should, spud, stood, stud, thud, wood, would.
[2] boyhood, childhood, deadwood, dogwood, driftwood, falsehood, firewood, girlhood, hardwood, knighthood, lifeblood, manhood, priesthood, sainthood, touchwood, withstood.
[3] adulthood, babyhood, brotherhood, fatherhood, Hollywood, likelihood, livelihood, misunderstood, motherhood, nationhood, neighbourhood/neighborhood (U.S.), parenthood, sisterhood, stick-in-the-mud, understood.

SURPRISING RHYMING:
[1] **Blub**, bub, chub, club, cub, drub, dub, flub, grub, hub, nub, pub, rub, scrub, shrub, snub, stub, sub, tub.
Dove, glove(d), guv, love(d), shove(d), above.
Bug, chug, drug, dug, fug, glug, hug, jug, lug, mug, plug, rug, shrug, slug, smug, snug, thug, tug.
Bugged, chugged, drugged, glugged, hugged, mugged, plugged, rugged, shrugged, slugged, tugged, unplugged.
But, butt, cut, glut, gut, hut, jut, mutt, nut, put, putt, rut, shut, slut, smut, strut, tut.
Buzz, 'cuz, does, fuzz, was.
Budge, fudge, grudge, judge, nudge, sludge, smudge, trudge.
[2] **Bathtub**, Beelzebub, cherub, hubbub, nightclub, washtub.
Bedbug, debug, earplug, firebug, hearthrug, humbug, unplug.
Clean-cut, clear-cut, crewcut, crosscut, doughnut/donut (U.S.), haircut, half-shut, peanut, rebut, shortcut, somewhat, uncut, walnut.
Adjudge, begrudge, misjudge, prejudge.
[3] **Tug-of-love**, true love, turtledove, ladylove.
Doodlebug, jitterbug, ladybug, litterbug.

5.1.18 "--udded" (as in "wooded")
[2] blooded, flooded, hooded, studded, thudded, wooded.
[3] blue-blooded, cold-blooded, hot-blooded, red-blooded.

SURPRISING RHYMING:
[2] **Butted**, crooked, footed, gutted, jutted, putted, rugged, studied.
Busted, crusted, dusted, hunted, thrusted, trusted.
[3] **Barefooted**, hotfooted, inputted, pussyfooted, wrong-footed.
Adjusted, disgusted, distrusted, disgusted, distrusted.

5.1.19 "--udge" (as in "judge")
[1] budge, fudge, grudge, judge, nudge, sludge, smudge, trudge.
[2] adjudge, begrudge, misjudge, prejudge.

SURPRISING RHYMING:
[1] **Budged**, fudged, grudged, judged, nudged, smudged, trudged.
Butch, clutch(ed), crutch, hutch, much, putsch, such, touch(ed).
Blush, brush, bush, crush, flush, gush, hush, lush, mush, plush, push, rush, slush.
Brunch, bunch, crunch, honeybunch, hunch, lunch, munch, punch.

Bugged, chugged, drugged, glugged, hugged, mugged, plugged, rugged, shrugged, slugged, tugged, unplugged.
[2] Adjudged, begrudged, misjudged, prejudged.

5.1.20 "--udges" (as in "judges")
[2] budges, fudges, grudges, judges, nudges, smudges, trudges.

SURPRISING RHYMING:
[2] Brunches, bunches, crunches, clutches, crutches, hunches, lunches, munches, punches, scrunches, touches.
Blushes, brushes, buses, bushes, crushes, flushes, gushes, hushes, pushes, rushes.

5.1. 21 "--udged" (as in "judged")
[1] budged, fudged, grudged, judged, nudged, smudged, trudged.
[2] adjudged, begrudged, misjudged, prejudged.

SURPRISING RHYMING:
[1] Budge, fudge, grudge, judge, nudge, sludge, smudge, trudge.
Clutched, touched, untouched.
Blushed, brushed, bushed, crushed, flushed, gushed, hushed, mushed, pushed, rushed, shushed, slushed, swooshed.
Bunched, crunched, hunched, lunched, munched, punched.
Bugged, drugged, hugged, mugged, plugged, shrugged, slugged, tugged, unplugged.
Gloved, loved, shoved.
Blubbed, clubbed, drubbed, dubbed, rubbed, scrubbed, snubbed, stubbed, subbed.
[2] Adjudge, begrudge, misjudge, prejudge.

5.1.22 "--udging" (as in "judging")
[2] budging, fudging, grudging, judging, nudging, smudging, trudging.
[3] begrudging, misjudging, prejudging.

SURPRISING RHYMING:
[2] Clutching, retouching, touching.
Blushing, brushing, crushing, gushing, hushing, pushing, rushing.
Brunching, bunching, crunching, lunching, munching, punching.
Bugging, chugging, drugging, glugging, hugging, mugging, plugging, shrugging, slugging, tugging, unplugging.
Bluffing, buffing, cuffing, fluffing, handcuffing, huffing, puffing, rebuffing, roughing, scuffing, snuffing, stuffing, woofing.
Buzzing, loving, shoving.
Busking, busting, disgusting, dusting, gusting, lusting, rusting, thrusting, trusting.
Bumping, dumping, jumping, lumping, pumping, slumping, thumping.
[3] Abducting, conducting, deducting, instructing, obstructing.
Adjusting, disgusting, distrusting, encrusting, entrusting, mistrusting.

5.1.23 "--idul" (as in "idol")
bridal, bridle, dull, homicidal, idle, idol, sidle, suicidal, tidal, unbridle.

SURPRISING RHYMING:
[2] Bible, libel, tribal, liable, libel
Eyeful, frightful, rifle, rightful, spiteful, stifle, trifle.
Dial, phial, rival, spiral, title, trial, viral, vital.
Cycle, final, primal, spinal.
[3] Entitle, mistitle, recital, requital, retitle, subtitle, title, vital.
Denial, misdial, mistrial, retrial, self-denial, sundial.
Certifiable, deniable, identifiable, justifiable, notifiable, pliable, reliable, unreliable, undeniable, verifiable, viable.
Archival, arrival, revival, survival.
Archetypal, delightful, disciple, insightful, recycle, reprisal.

Advisable, desirable, excitable, likeable, recognizable, sizable.
Doctrinal, quarterfinal, semifinal, urinal.

5.1.24 "--oddull" (as in "model")
[2] coddle, dawdle, doddle, model, molly-coddle, swaddle, toddle, twaddle, waddle, yodel.

SURPRISING RHYMING:
[2] **Bauble**, bobble, fondle, gobble, hobble, squabble, wobble.
Boggle, boondoggle, goggle, joggle, ogle, toggle, woggle.
Aristotle, bottle, horizontal, hostel, mottle, throttle.
Apostle, colossal, fossil, gospel, jostle, morsel, nozzle, shovel.
Awful, brothel, grovel, hovel, lawful, novel, offal, waffle.
Amoral, choral, coral, floral, immoral, laurel, moral, oral, quarrel.

5.1.25 "--uddull" (as in "cuddle")
[2] befuddle, cuddle, fuddle, huddle, muddle, puddle.

SURPRISING RHYMING:
[1] **Bull**, cull, full, gull, hull, lull, mull, null, pull, skull, wool.
[2] **Befuddled**, cuddled, fuddled, huddled, muddled.
Bubble(d), double(d), Hubble, rubble, stubble, trouble(d).
Juggle, smuggle, snuggle, struggle.
Duffel, muffle, ruffle, scuffle, shuffle, snuffle, truffle.
Couple, supple, decouple, uncouple.
Bumble, bundle, bungle, crumble, fumble, grumble, humble, jumble, jungle, mumble, rumble, stumble, trundle, tumble, tunnel.
Bustle, guzzle, hustle, muscle, muzzle, nuzzle, puzzle, rustle, tussle.
Scuttle, shuttle, subtle, rebuttal.
Buckle, chuckle, knuckle, suckle, unbuckle, uncle.
[3] **Honeysuckle**, kerfuffle, reshuffle.

5.1.26 "--iddull" (as in "riddle")
[2] diddle, fiddle, griddle, idyll, middle, paradiddle, riddle, twiddle.

SURPRISING RHYMING:
[2] **Dribble(d),** nibble(d), quibble(d), scribble(d).
Cripple, nipple, ripple, stipple, tipple, triple.
Belittle, brittle, committal, hospital, it'll, little, skittle, spittle, whittle.
Giggle, jiggle, squiggle, wiggle, wriggle.
Civil, drivel, shrivel, skiffle, sniffle, snivel, swivel.
Fickle, nickel, pickle, prickle, tickle, trickle.
Crinkle, sprinkle, tinkle, twinkle, winkle, wrinkle.
Driven, given, forbidden, hidden, ridden.
Bidding, didn't, kidding, ridding, skidding.
Dwindle, jingle, kindle, mingle, single, spindle, swindle, tingle.
Giving, living, forgiving, misgiving, thanksgiving, unforgiving.
Bristle, chisel, drizzle, fizzle, missile, sizzle, swizzle, thistle, whistle.

5.1.27 "--addull" (as in "saddle")
paddle, saddle, skedaddle, straddle, unsaddle.

SURPRISING RHYMING:
[2] **Addled**, paddled, saddled, skedaddled, straddled.
Babble, dabble, rabble, scrabble.
Bedraggle, draggle, gaggle, haggle, straggle, waggle.
Apple, battle, cattle, chapel, chattel, embattle, grapple, prattle, rattle, tattle, tittle-tattle.
Baffle, gavel, gravel, raffle, ravel, snaffle, travel, unravel.
Bedazzle, castle, dazzle, frazzle, hassle, razzle, tassel, vassal.
Cackle, crackle, hackle, jackal, shackle, tackle.

Candle, handle, manhandle, mishandle, sandal, scandal, vandal.
Amble, gamble, preamble, ramble, scramble, shamble, unscramble.
Angle, bangle, dangle, jangle, strangle, tangle, wangle, wrangle.

5.1.28 "--uff" (as in "bluff")
[1] bluff, buff, cuff, duff, fluff, guff, gruff, huff, muff, puff, rough, ruff, scruff, scuff, slough, snuff, stuff, tough, tuff, woof.
[2] cream puff, dandruff, earmuff, enough, foodstuff, green stuff, handcuff, powder puff, rebuff, sho'nuff.

SURPRISING RHYMING:
[1] **Bluffed**, buffed, cuffed, fluffed, gulf, huffed, puffed, roughed, scuffed, stuffed.
Cuffs, muffs, puffs, roughs, scruffs, scuffs.
Above, dove, glove(d), guv, love(d), shove(d).
Buzz, 'cuz, does, fuzz.
Blub, bub, chub, club, cub, drub, dub, flub, grub, hub, nub, pub, rub, scrub, shrub, snub, stub, sub, tub.
Blood, could, dud, flood, good, hood, mud, should, stood, stud, thud, wood, would.
[2] **Boyhood**, childhood, deadwood, driftwood, falsehood, firewood, knighthood, lifeblood, manhood, priesthood, touchwood, withstood.
[3] **Tug-of-love**, turtledove, ladylove, true love.

5.1.29 "--uffer" (as in "suffer")
[2] bluffer, buffer, duffer, puffer, rougher, suffer, tougher, woofer.

SURPRISING RHYMING:
[2] **Cover**, glover, hover, lover, shover.
Brother, further, mother, other, smother, t'other.
Clubber, rubber, scrubber, snubber.
Bummer, drummer, dumber, glummer, gunner, hummer, number, plumber, runner, shunner, stunner, strummer, summer.
Hugger, mugger, plugger, shrugger, slugger, snugger, tugger.
[3] **Discover**, helluva, recover, rediscover, uncover, undercover.
Another, blood brother, grandmother, stepbrother, stepmother.
Latecomer, midsummer, newcomer.

5.1.30 "--uffel" (as in "scuffle")
[2] duffel, muffle, ruffle, scuffle, shuffle, snuffle, truffle.
[3] kerfuffle, reshuffle.

SURPRISING RHYMING:
[2] **Muffled**, ruffled, scuffled, shuffled.
Bubble, double, Hubble, rubble, stubble, trouble.
Cuddle, fuddle, huddle, muddle, puddle, tunnel.
Juggle, smuggle, snuggle, struggle.
Couple, decouple, rebuttal, scuttle, shuttle, subtle, supple, uncouple.
Bustle, guzzle, hustle, muscle, muzzle, nuzzle, puzzle, rustle, tussle.
Buckle, chuckle, honeysuckle, knuckle, suckle, unbuckle.
Bumble, crumble, fumble, grumble, humble, jumble, mumble, rumble, stumble, tumble.

5.1.31 "--ug" (as in "bug")
[1] bug, chug, drug, dug, fug, glug, hug, jug, lug, mug, plug, rug, shrug, slug, smug, snug, thug, tug.
[2] bedbug, debug, earplug, firebug, hearthrug, humbug, unplug.
[3] doodlebug, jitterbug, ladybug, litterbug.

SURPRISING RHYMING:
[1] **Bugged**, chugged, drugged, glugged, hugged, mugged, plugged, rugged, shrugged, slugged, tugged, unplugged.

Club, cub, drub, dub, grub, hub, nub, pub, rub, scrub, shrub, snub, stub, sub, tub.
Above, dove, glove, guv, love, shove.
Blood, could, dud, flood, good, hood, mud, should, stood, stud, thud, wood, would.
But, butt, cut, glut, gut, hut, jut, mutt, nut, put, putt, rut, shut, slut, smut, strut, tut.
Budge, fudge, grudge, judge, nudge, sludge, smudge, trudge.
Bluff, buff, cuff, duff, fluff, guff, gruff, huff, muff, puff, rough, ruff, scruff, scuff, slough, snuff, stuff, tough, tuff, woof.
Buzz, 'cuz, does, fuzz, was.
[2] Bathtub, Beelzebub, cherub, hubbub, nightclub, washtub.
Boyhood, childhood, deadwood, driftwood, falsehood, firewood, knighthood, lifeblood, manhood, priesthood, touchwood, withstood.
Clean-cut, clear-cut, crewcut, doughnut/donut (U.S.), haircut, half-shut, peanut, shortcut, somewhat, uncut, walnut.
Dandruff, earmuff, enough, foodstuff, handcuff, rebuff, sho'nuff.
Backup, bishop, break-up, checkup, cleanup, closeup, cock-up, cut-up, Europe, fry-up, gallop, grown-up, hang-up, hiccup, hold-up, hook-up, ketchup, let-up, lineup, linkup, lock-up, lookup, makeup, markup, nosh-up, pickup, pile-up, pinup, press-up, pull up, punch-up, rave-up, roundup, run-up, set-up, shake-up, sit-up, slap-up, snarl-up, start-up, stick-up, stirrup, straight-up, stuck up, sun-up, syrup/sirup (U.S.), take-up, teacup, top-up, toss-up, trollop, turn-up, two-up, wallop, warmup, wash-up, wind-up.

5.1.32 "--ugged" (as in "tugged")

[1] bugged, chugged, drugged, glugged, hugged, mugged, plugged, rugged, shrugged, slugged, tugged, unplugged.

SURPRISING RHYMING:
[1] Bug, chug, drug, dug, fug, glug, hug, jug, lug, mug, plug, rug, shrug, slug, smug, snug, thug, tug.
Clubbed, dubbed, rubbed, scrubbed, snubbed, stubbed, subbed.
Blood, could, dud, flood, good, hood, mud, should, stood, stud, thud, wood, would.
Gloved, loved, shoved.
Budged, fudged, grudged, judged, nudged, smudged, trudged.
[2] Bedbug, debug, earplug, firebug, hearthrug, humbug, unplug.
Boyhood, childhood, deadwood, driftwood, falsehood, firewood, knighthood, lifeblood, manhood, priesthood, touchwood, withstood.

5.1.33 "--uggle" (as in "struggle")

[2] juggle, smuggle, snuggle, struggle.

SURPRISING RHYMING:
[2] Juggled, smuggled, snuggled, struggled.
Bubble(d), double(d), Hubble, rubble, stubble, trouble(d).
Cuddle, fuddle, funnel, huddle, muddle, puddle, tunnel.
Duffel, muffle, ruffle, scuffle, shuffle, snuffle, truffle.
Bumble, bundle, bungle, crumble, fumble, grumble, humble, jumble, jungle, mumble, rumble, stumble, trundle, tumble.
Bustle, guzzle, hustle, muscle, muzzle, nuzzle, puzzle, rustle, tussle.
Couple, decouple, rebuttal, scuttle, shuttle, subtle, supple, uncouple.
Buckle, chuckle, knuckle, suckle, unbuckle, uncle.
[3] Honeysuckle, kerfuffle, reshuffle.

5.1.34 "--uggler" (as in "juggler")

[2] juggler, smuggler, struggler.

SURPRISING RHYMING:
[2] Bungler, fumbler, grumbler, humbler, mumbler, number, slumber.
Lumber, number, rumba, slumber.
Blunder, hunger, plunder, thunder, under, wonder, younger.
Muffler, ruffler, scuffler, shuffler, snuffler, sufferer.

Cuddler, huddler, muddler.
Bumper, dumper, jumper, plumper, pumper, thumper.
Guzzler, muzzler, nuzzler, puzzler.
Bustler, butler, hustler, rustler.
Coupler, doubler, suppler, uncoupler.
[3] **Scandalmonger**, scaremonger, warmonger.

5.1.35 "--angull" (as in "angle")
[2] angle, bangle, dangle, jangle, strangle, tangle, wangle, wrangle.
[3] bespangle, disentangle, entangle, fandangle, pentangle, quadrangle, rectangle, right-angle, triangle, untangle, wide-angle.

SURPRISING RHYMING:
[1] **Bull**, cull, dull, full, hull, lull, mull, null, pull, skull, wool.
[2] **Candle,** handle, manhandle, mishandle, sandal, scandal, vandal.
Amble, gamble, preamble, ramble, scramble, shamble, unscramble.
Apple, chapel, dapple, grapple.
Dabble, paddle, rabble, saddle, scrabble, skedaddle, straddle.
Bedraggle, draggle, gaggle, haggle, straggle, waggle.
Battle, cattle, chattel, embattle, prattle, rattle, tattle, tittle-tattle.
Baffle, gavel, gravel, raffle, ravel, snaffle, travel, unravel.
Bedazzle, castle, dazzle, frazzle, hassle, razzle, tassel, vassal.
Cackle, crackle, hackle, jackal, shackle, tackle.
Actual, casual, mammal, manual, rascal, sexual, virtual, visual.

5.1.36 "--oggull" (as in "goggle")
[2] boggle, goggle, ogle, toggle, woggle.

SURPRISING RHYMING:
[1] **Bull**, cull, dull, full, hull, lull, mull, null, pull, skull, wool.
[2] **Bauble**, bobble, cobble, gobble, hobble, squabble, wobble.
Coddle, dawdle, doddle, model, molly-coddle, swaddle, toddle, twaddle, waddle, yodel.
Awful, brothel, grovel, hovel, lawful, novel, offal, waffle.
Aristotle, bottle, horizontal, hostel, mottle, throttle.
Apostle, colossal, fossil, gospel, jostle, morsel, nozzle, shovel.
Aural, choral, coral, floral, immoral, laurel, moral, oral, quarrel.
Chortle, formal, mortal, normal, portal, snorkel.
[3] **Abnormal**, informal, immortal, paranormal.

5.1.37 "--oogull" (as in "google")
[2] bugle, frugal, google.

SURPRISING RHYMING:
[1] **Bull**, cull, dull, full, hull, lull, mull, null, pull, skull, wool.
[2] **Canoodle**, doodle, feudal, noodle, oodles, poodle, strudel.
Cruel, dual, duel, fuel, gruel, jewel, pupil, refuel, renewal, scruple.
Cure-all, mural, plural, rural, spoonful, tuneful.
Brutal, crucial, fruitful, futile, neutral, rueful, truthful, useful, youthful.
[3] **Approval**, bamboozle, disapproval, refusal, removal.

5.1.38 "--ingull" (as in "tingle")
[2] jingle, mingle, single, tingle.

SURPRISING RHYMING:
[2] **Dimple**, pimple, simple, wimple.
Dwindle, hymnal, kindle, sinful, spindle, swindle.
Crinkle, skillful, sprinkle, tinkle, twinkle, willful, winkle, wrinkle.
Bristle, crystal, gristle, missal, missile, pistol, thistle, whistle.
Civil, drivel, shrivel, skiffle, sniffle, snivel, swivel.

Dribble, giggle, nibble, quibble, scribble, squiggle, wiggle, wriggle.
Fiddle, griddle, idyll, middle, riddle, twiddle.
Cripple, nipple, ripple, stipple, tipple, triple.

5.1.39 "--ull" (as in "full")

[1] bull, cull, dull, full, gull, hull, lull, mull, null, pull, skull, wool.

[2] annul, armful, artful, awful, bagful, baneful, bashful, blameful, blissful, boastful, brimful, capful, careful, changeful, cheerful, cupful, doubtful, dreadful, earful, equal, eyeful, faithful, fateful, fearful, fitful, forceful, fretful, frightful, fruitful, gainful, glassful, gleeful, graceful, grateful, half-full, handful, harmful, hateful, hatful, heedful, helpful, hopeful, hurtful, joyful, jugful, lapful, lawful, lustful, manful, mindful, mirthful, mournful, mouthful, mugful, needful, numbskull, painful, peaceful, plateful, playful, potful, prayerful, push-pull, restful, rightful, ring-pull, roomful, rueful, schedule, seagull, sequel, shameful, sinful, scornful, skillful, skinful, soulful, spiteful, spoonful, stressful, tactful, tankful, tasteful, tearful, thankful, thoughtful, trustful, truthful, tubful, tuneful, useful, vengeful, wakeful, wasteful, watchful, wilful/willful (U.S.), wishful, wistful, woeful, wrongful, youthful.

[3] beautiful, bellyful, bountiful, colourful/colorful (U.S.), deceitful, delightful, disdainful, disgraceful, disrespectful, distasteful, distrustful, dutiful, eventful, fanciful, forgetful, masterful, meaningful, merciful, neglectful, pitiful, plentiful, pocketful, powerful, purposeful, regardful, regretful, remindful, remorseful, resentful, residual, resourceful, respectful, revengeful, sorrowful, successful, uneventful, unfaithful, ungrateful, unlawful, unmindful, untruthful, wonderful, worshipful.

SURPRISING RHYMING:
[2] Bustle, hustle, muscle, mussel, rustle, tussle.
Juggle, smuggle, snuggle, struggle.
Cackle, chuckle, circle, crackle, crinkle, cull, cycle, debacle, fickle, freckle, heckle, knuckle, nickel, pickle, prickle, shackle, sparkle, sprinkle, suckle, tackle, tickle, tinkle, trickle, twinkle, uncle, wrinkle.
Angle, bangle, boggle, bugle, dangle, frugal, goggle, gull, jangle, jingle, mingle, single, strangle, tangle, tingle, wangle, wrangle.
Bridal, bridle, coddle, cuddle, diddle, doddle, dull, fiddle, fuddle, huddle, idle, idol, middle, model, muddle, paddle, piddle, puddle, riddle, saddle, straddle, tidal, toddle, twaddle, twiddle, waddle.
Camel, dismal, formal, mammal, normal.
Channel, colonel, final, flannel, journal, kernel, kennel, panel, penal.
Apple, chapel, cripple, couple, dapple, grapple, nipple, opal, people, pull, ripple, sample, steeple, stipple, supple, tipple, topple, triple.
Barrel, carol, choral, floral, laurel, moral, mural, oral, rural, quarrel.
[3] Article, bicycle, chemical, chronicle, classical, clinical, comical, critical, cynical, ethical, icicle, logical, lyrical, magical, medical, miracle, musical, mystical, mythical, obstacle, oracle, physical, pinnacle, Popsicle, practical, quizzical, radical, recycle, sceptical, spectacle, stoical, surgical, tactical, tentacle, topical, tropical, typical, pinnacle, ramshackle, vehicle, whimsical.
Triangle, entangle, disentangle, fandangle, rectangle.
Abnormal, abysmal, animal, informal, minimal, optimal, paranormal.
Arsenal, cardinal, criminal, enamel, eternal, infernal, internal, fictional, fraternal, marginal, maternal, national, nocturnal, paternal, personal, rational, seasonal, seminal, sentinel, terminal, virginal.
Disciple, example, multiple, pineapple, principal, principle, unequal.
Admiral, cultural, funeral, immoral, liberal, mineral, natural, several.
[4] Alphabetical, angelical, biographical, diabolical, electrical, fanatical, historical, hypocritical, hysterical, identical, illogical, ironical, methodical, motorcycle, mythological, nonsensical, philosophical, political, psychological, satirical, theatrical.
Additional, conditional, confessional, conventional, conversational, emotional, exceptional, impersonal, inspirational, intentional, international, irrational, medicinal, nutritional, occasional, original, phenomenal, professional, promotional, recreational, sensational, subliminal, three-dimensional, traditional, two-dimensional, unconditional.

5.1.40 "--ully" (as in "bully")
[2] bully, fully, gully, pulley, woolly.
[3] artfully, awfully, banefully, bashfully, blamefully, blissfully, boastfully, carefully, cheerfully, doubtfully, dreadfully, faithfully, fatefully, fearfully, fitfully, forcefully, fretfully, frightfully, gainfully, gleefully, gracefully, gratefully, harmfully, hatefully, helpfully, hopefully, hurtfully, joyfully, lawfully, lustfully, manfully, mindfully, mirthfully, mournfully, painfully, peacefully, playfully, restfully, rightfully, ruefully, shamefully, sinfully, scornfully, skillfully, soulfully, spitefully, tactfully, tastefully, tearfully, thankfully, thoughtfully, trustfully, truthfully, tunefully, usefully, vengefully, wastefully, watchfully, willfully, wishfully, wistfully, woefully, wrongfully, youthfully.
[4] beautifully, colourfully/colorfully (U.S.), deceitfully, delightfully, disdainfully, disgracefully, disrespectfully, distastefully, distrustfully, dutifully, eventfully, fancifully, masterfully, meaningfully, mercifully, neglectfully, pitifully, plentifully, powerfully, purposefully, regretfully, remorsefully, resentfully, resourcefully, respectfully, successfully, unfaithfully, ungratefully, unlawfully, wonderfully.

SURPRISING RHYMING:
[2] **Chubby**, clubby, grubby, hubby, nubby, scrubby, stubby, tubby.
Bunny, funny, honey, money, runny, sonny, sunny.
Chummy, crummy, dummy, mummy, plummy, tummy, yummy.
Bumpy, dumpy, frumpy, grumpy, jumpy, lumpy, rumpy-pumpy.
Bushy, gushy, mushy, pushy, slushy.
Bookie, cookie, ducky, hooky, lucky, mucky, plucky, rookie, yucky.
Bloody, buddy, goody, hoodie, muddy, study, woody.

5.1.41 "--ulk" (as in "hulk")
[1] bulk, hulk, skulk, sulk.

SURPRISING RHYMING:
[1] **Bunk**, chunk, clunk, drunk, dunk, flunk, funk, gunk, hunk, junk, monk, plunk, punk, shrunk, skunk, slunk, stunk, sunk, trunk.
Brusque, busk, dusk, husk, musk, rusk, tusk.
Adult, catapult, consult, cult, difficult, exult, insult, occult, result.
[2] **Amok**, awestruck, chequebook, cookbook, dumbstruck, guidebook, megabuck, mistook, moonstruck, notebook, outlook, partook, playbook, potluck, scrapbook, sketchbook, songbook, stagestruck, storybook, textbook, thunderstruck, unhook, unstuck.
Abduct, conduct, deduct, construct, instruct, obstruct, product.

5.1.42 "--ult" (as in "insult")
adult, catapult, consult, cult, difficult, exult, insult, occult, result.

SURPRISING RHYMING:
[1] **Bust**, cussed, dust, fussed, gust, just, lust, must, rust, thrust, touched, trust.
But, butt, cut, glut, gut, hut, jut, mutt, nut, put, putt, rut, shut, slut, smut, strut, tut.
Blunt, brunt, front, grunt, hunt, punt, runt, shunt, stunt.
Bunk, chunk, clunk, drunk, dunk, flunk, funk, gunk, hunk, junk, monk, plunk, punk, shrunk, skunk, slunk, stunk, sulk, sunk, trunk.
Culled, lulled, mulled, pulled.
[2] **Abduct**, conduct, deduct, construct, instruct, obstruct, product.
Abrupt, corrupt, cupped, disrupt, erupt, interrupt.
Adjust, august, blood lust, combust, discussed, disgust, distrust, entrust, gold dust, mistrust, robust, stardust, unjust, wanderlust.
Clean-cut, clear-cut, crewcut, crosscut, doughnut/donut (U.S.), haircut, half-shut, peanut, rebut, shortcut, somewhat, uncut.
Confront, couldn't, forefront, headhunt, manhunt, seafront, shouldn't, storefront, upfront, waterfront, witch-hunt, wouldn't.

*

5.1.43 "--ulted" (as in "insulted")
[3] catapulted, consulted, exulted, insulted, resulted.

SURPRISING RHYMING:
[2] **Busted**, dusted, gusted, lusted, rusted, thrusted, trusted.
Blunted, fronted, grunted, hunted, punted, shunted, stunted.
[3] **Abducted**, conducted, deducted, instructed, obstructed.
Confronted, disrupted, erupted, headhunted, interrupted.
Adjusted, corrupted, disgusted, distrusted, entrusted, mistrusted.
Compulsive, impulsive, percussive, repulsive.

5.1.44 "--kull" (as in "uncle")
circle, cull, cycle, sparkle, uncle, yokel, monocle, recycle.

SURPRISING RHYMING:
[1] **Bull**, dull, full, gull, hull, lull, mull, null, pull, skull, wool.
[3] **Audible**, constable, hospital, laudable, nominal, obstacle, optional, responsible, possible, probable, prodigal, volatile.
[4] **Impossible**, improbable, irresponsible, phenomenal, responsible.

5.1.45 "--akull" (as in "crackle")
[2] cackle, crackle, debacle, hackle, jackal, shackle, tackle.
[3] obstacle, oracle, pinnacle, spectacle, tentacle, ramshackle.

SURPRISING RHYMING:
[2] **Apple**, chapel, dapple, grapple, pineapple, pull.
Battle, cattle, prattle, rattle, tattle, tittle-tattle.
Haggle, paddle, saddle, skedaddle, straddle, straggle, waggle.
Babble, dabble, rabble, scrabble.
Angle, bangle, dangle, jangle, strangle, tangle, wangle, wrangle.
Barrel, carol, channel, final, flannel, kennel, panel.
[3] **Criminal**, marginal, original, regional, seasonal, seminal, sentinel, terminal, virginal.

5.1.46 "--inkull" (as in "twinkle")
[2] crinkle, sprinkle, tinkle, twinkle, winkle, wrinkle.

SURPRISING RHYMING:
[1] **Bull**, dull, full, hull, lull, mull, null, pull, skull, wool.
[2] **Crinkled**, sprinkled, tinkled, twinkled, winkled, wrinkled.
Dwindle, jingle, kindle, mingle, rekindle, sinful, single, tingle.
Cymbal, dimple, nimble, pimple, simple, symbol, thimble, timbale.
Fickle, nickel, pickle, prickle, tickle, trickle.
Diddle, fiddle, griddle, idyll, middle, riddle, twiddle.
Bristle, chisel, drizzle, fizzle, missile, sizzle, thistle, tinsel, whistle.

5.1.47 "--ikkull" (as in "tickle")
[2] fickle, nickel, pickle, prickle, tickle, trickle.
[3] article, bicycle, chemical, chronicle, classical, clinical, comical, critical, cubicle, cyclical, cynical, ethical, follicle, icicle, logical, lyrical, magical, medical, miracle, musical, mystical, mythical, physical, Popsicle, practical, quizzical, radical, sceptical, stoical, surgical, tactical, topical, tropical, tricycle, typical, vehicle, whimsical.
[4] alphabetical, angelical, diabolical, electrical, fanatical, historical, hypocritical, hysterical, identical, illogical, lackadaisical, mathematical, methodical, motorcycle, mythological, nonsensical, philosophical, political, psychological, satirical, theatrical.

SURPRISING RHYMING:
[2] **Pickled**, prickled, tickled, trickled.
Belittle, brittle, committal, hospital, it'll, little, skittle, spittle, whittle.
Cripple, nipple, ripple, stipple, tipple, triple.

Chicken, quicken, sicken, stricken, thicken.
Dribble, fiddle, idyll, middle, nibble, quibble, riddle, scribble, twiddle.
Giggle, jiggle, niggle, squiggle, wiggle, wriggle.
Civil, drivel, shrivel, skiffle, sniffle, snivel, swivel.
Bristle, chisel, drizzle, fizzle, missile, sizzle, swizzle, thistle, whistle.
[3] **Acquittal**, belittle, committal, hospital.

5.1.48 "--ekkull" (as in "freckle")
[2] freckle, heckle, Jekyll, speckle.

SURPRISING RHYMING:
[2] **Kettle**, metal, mettle, nettle, petal, re-settle, settle, unsettle.
Medal, meddle, pebble, pedal, peddle, rebel, treble.
Devil, embezzle, level, nestle, peril, revel, special, vessel, wrestle.
Central, dental, gentle, kennel, mental, parental, rental, temple.
[3] **Daredevil**, dishevel, eye-level, high-level, low-level., split-level.

5.1.49 "--um" (as in "thumb")
[1] bum, chum, come, crumb, drum, dumb, glum, gum, hum, mum, numb, plum, plumb, rum, scrum, scum, slum, some, strum, sum, swum, thumb, tum, yum.
[2] album, autumn, awesome, become, boredom, bottom, breadcrumb, bubblegum, column, dictum, dumdum, eardrum, fearsome, forum, foursome, freedom, fulsome, gruesome, handsome, ho-hum, hokum, hoodlum, humdrum, income, irksome, -ism, kingdom, lithesome, loathsome, lonesome, magnum, outcome, plectrum, prism, problem, quantum, ransom, sanctum, schism, seldom, spasm, spectrum, stardom, succumb, tantrum, threesome, tiresome, twosome, welcome, wholesome, wisdom, yum-yum.
[3] atrium, bothersome, bubblegum, burdensome, calcium, cadmium, Christendom, chromium, conundrum, cumbersome, decorum, helium, idiom, kettledrum, linoleum, lithium, martyrdom, maximum, medium, meddlesome, minimum, momentum, museum, opium, optimum, orgasm, overcome, petroleum, phantasm, platinum, podium, premium, quarrelsome, requiem, rhythm, rock-bottom, sadism, sarcasm, sodium, solarium, stadium, sugarplum, tedium, tourism, troublesome, Tweedledum, unwelcome, valium.
[4] aquarium, auditorium, capitalism, colosseum, consortium, crematorium, criticism, cynicism, emporium, enthusiasm, equilibrium, gymnasium, harmonium, harum-scarum, heroism, hypnotism, magnetism, mannerism, mausoleum, millennium, officialdom, optimism, pandemonium, patriotism, pessimism, realism, uranium.

SURPRISING RHYMING:
[1] **Bummed**, drummed, hummed, numbed, plumbed, strummed, succumbed, summed, thumbed, welcomed.
Bun, done, fun, gun, none, nun, one, pun, run, shun, son, spun, stun, sun, ton, won.
Fund, gunned, shunned, stunned, sunned.
Bung, clung, dung, flung, hung, lung, rung, slung, sprung, strung, stung, sung, swung, tongue, wrung, young.
Bump, chump, clump, dump, frump, grump, hump, jump, lump, plump, pump, rump, slump, stump, thump, trump.
Blunt, brunt, front, grunt, hunt, punt, runt, shunt, stunt.
[2] **Begun**, godson, grandson, handgun, homespun, outdone, outrun, rerun, shotgun, someone, stepson, undone, well-done.
Atom, anthem, bedlam, blossom, bosom, buxom, emblem, fathom, harem, phantom, slalom, solemn, symptom, system, totem, venom.
Caution(ed), cushion(ed), freshen(ed), mention(ed), motion(ed), outgunned, ration(ed), refund, sanction(ed), station(ed).
Among, aqualung, hamstrung, highly-strung, unsung.
Confront, couldn't, forefront, headhunt, manhunt, seafront, shouldn't, storefront, upfront, waterfront, witch-hunt, wouldn't.
[3] **Anyone**, everyone, honeybun, one-to-one, overdone, overrun.
Audition(ed), petition(ed), position(ed).

5.1.50 "--ummer" (as in "summer")
[2] bummer, drummer, dumber, glummer, hummer, plumber, strummer, summer.
[3] customer, latecomer, midsummer, newcomer, welcomer.

SURPRISING RHYMING:
[2] **Gunner**, runner, shunner, stunner.
Butter, clutter, flutter, mutter, nutter, shutter, splutter, stutter, utter.
Brother, further, mother, other, smother, t'other.
Bumper, dumper, jumper, lumber, number, rumba, slumber.
Cuppa, scupper, supper, upper.
Bluffer, brother, buffer, cover, duffer, gruffer, lover, other, puffer, rougher, shover, suffer, tougher, woofer.
Blubber, clubber, rubber, rudder, shudder, should-a, snubber.
Cooker, hooker, looker, plucker, pucker, sucker, trucker, tucker.
Blunder, hunger, plunder, thunder, under, wonder, younger.
Blunter, chunter, grunter, hunter, junta, punter, shunter.
[3] **Discover**, helluva, recover, rediscover, uncover, undercover.
Another, blood brother, grandmother, stepbrother, stepmother.

5.1.51 "--ummy" (as in "dummy")
[2] chummy, crummy, dummy, mummy, plummy, tummy, yummy.
[3] alchemy, bigamy, blasphemy, blossomy, infamy, sesame.

SURPRISING RHYMING:
[2] **Bunny**, funny, honey, money, runny, sonny, sunny.
Bumpy, dumpy, frumpy, grumpy, jumpy, lumpy, rumpy-pumpy.
Bloody, buddy, goody, hoodie, muddy, study, woody.
Chubby, clubby, grubby, hubby, nubby, scrubby, stubby, tubby.
Bully, fully, gully, pulley, woolly.
Busty, crusty, dusty, gusty, lusty, musty, rusty, trusty.

5.1.52 "--umming" (as in "humming")
[2] chumming, coming, drumming, dumbing, humming, numbing, plumbing, slumming, strumming, thumbing.
[3] becoming, forthcoming, homecoming, incoming, oncoming, shortcoming, unbecoming.

SURPRISING RHYMING:
[2] **Cunning**, funning, gunning, punning, running, stunning, sunning.
Buzzing, loving, shoving.
Bluffing, cuffing, fluffing, huffing, puffing, roughing, stuffing, toughing.
Bumping, dumping, jumping, lumping, pumping, slumping, thumping.
Bumbling, crumbling, fumbling, grumbling, humbling, jumbling, mumbling, rumbling, stumbling, tumbling.
Blooding, budding, flooding, pudding, thudding.
Bugging, chugging, drugging, glugging, hugging, mugging, plugging, shrugging, slugging, tugging, unplugging.
Blushing, brushing, crushing, gushing, hushing, pushing, rushing.
Booking, cooking, ducking, hooking, looking, plucking, sucking, trucking, tucking.

5.1.53 "--ump" (as in "bump")
[1] bump, chump, clump, crump, dump, frump, grump, hump, jump, lump, plump, pump, rump, slump, stump, thump, trump.
[2] gazump, mugwump, showjump, ski-jump.

SURPRISING RHYMING:
[1] **Bumped**, dumped, jumped, pumped, slumped, stumped, thumped.
Bum, chum, come, crumb, drum, dumb, glum, gum, hum, mum, numb, plum, rum, scrum, scum, slum, some, strum, sum, swum, thumb, tum, yum.
Blunt, brunt, bunt, front, grunt, hunt, punt, runt, shunt, stunt.

Bun, done, fun, gun, none, nun, one, pun, run, shun, son, spun, stun, sun, ton, won.
Bunk, chunk, clunk, drunk, dunk, flunk, funk, gunk, hunk, junk, monk, plunk, punk, shrunk, skunk, slunk, stunk, sunk, trunk.
[2] Confront, couldn't, forefront, headhunt, manhunt, seafront, shouldn't, storefront, upfront, waterfront, witch-hunt, wouldn't.
Chipmunk, cyberpunk, debunk, punch-drunk.

5.1.54 "--umping" (as in "bumping")
[2] bumping, dumping, jumping, lumping, pumping, slumping, thumping, trumping.
[3] gazumping, showjumping, ski-jumping.

SURPRISING RHYMING:
[2] Blunting, bunting, fronting, grunting, hunting, punting, shunting, something.
Bumbling, bundling, crumbling, fumbling, grumbling, humbling, jumbling, mumbling, rumbling, stumbling, trundling, tumbling.
Bugging, chugging, drugging, glugging, hugging, lugging, mugging, plugging, shrugging, slugging, tugging.
Butting, cutting, footing, jutting, putting, shutting, strutting, tutting.
Busking, busting dusting, gusting, lusting, rusting, thrusting, trusting.
Bubbling, doubling, rubbing, troubling.
Bumming, coming, drumming, humming, numbing, slumming, strumming, thumbing.
Cunning, funning, gunning, punning, running, stunning, sunning.
Bluffing, cuffing, fluffing, huffing, puffing, roughing, stuffing, toughing.
Buzzing, loving, shoving.
[3] Adjusting, disgusting, distrusting, entrusting, mistrusting.
Becoming, forthcoming, homecoming, incoming, oncoming, shortcoming, unbecoming.

5.1.55 "--umper" (as in "jumper")
[2] bumper, dumper, jumper, plumper, pumper, stumper, thumper.

SURPRISING RHYMING:
[2] Blunter, chunter, grunter, hunter, junta, punter, shunter.
Blunder, plunder, rotunda, sunder, thunder, under, wonder.
Hunger, lumber, number, rumba, slumber, younger.
Bumbler, bungler, fumbler, grumbler, humbler, mumbler, tumbler.
Bunker, debunker, drunker, dunker, flunker, hunger, younger.
Bummer, drummer, dumber, glummer, number, strummer, summer.
Gunner, runner, shunner, stunner.
Bluffer, brother, buffer, gruffer, mother, other, rougher, smother, suffer, tougher.
Bluster, buster, cluster, duster, fluster, funster, funkster, lacklustre/lackluster (U.S.), lustre/luster (U.S.), thruster.
Cover, glover, hover, lover, shover.
Butter, clutter, cuppa, cutter, flutter, gutter, mutter, nutter, putter, shutter, splutter, strutter, stutter, supper, upper, utter.
[3] Scandalmonger, scaremonger, warmonger.
Customer, latecomer, midsummer, newcomer.

5.1.56 "--umpy" (as in "jumpy")
[2] bumpy, clumpy, dumpy, frumpy, grumpy, jumpy, lumpy, rumpy-pumpy, scrumpy.

SURPRISING RHYMING:
[2] Chunky, flunky, funky, hunky, junkie, lucky, monkey, punky.
Busty, clumsy, crusty, dusty, gusty, lusty, musty, rusty, trusty.
Chummy, crummy, dummy, hungry, mummy, tummy, yummy.
Crumbly, grumbly, humbly, dumbly, glumly, numbly.
Bunny, funny, honey, money, runny, sonny, sunny.
Someday, Monday, one day, sundae, Sunday, undies.
Bubbly, buddy, cuddly, comfy, fussy, fuzzy, lovely, roughly, toughly.

5.1.57 "--umber" (as in "number")
cucumber, encumber, lumber, number, outnumber, rumba, slumber.

SURPRISING RHYMING:
[2] **Encumbered**, lumbered, numbered, outnumbered, slumbered.
Blunder, hunger, plunder, thunder, under, wonder, younger.
Bumper, dumper, jumper, plumper, pumper, thumper.
Blunter, chunter, grunter, hunter, junta, punter, shunter.
Another, cover, glover, hover, lover, other.
Bummer, drummer, dumber, glummer, number, strummer, summer.
Gunner, runner, shunner, stunner.
Butter, clutter, flutter, mutter, nutter, shutter, splutter, stutter, utter.
[3] **Customer**, latecomer, midsummer, newcomer.

5.1.58 "--umble" (as in "humble")
bumble, crumble, fumble, grumble, humble, jumble, mumble, rumble, stumble, tumble.

SURPRISING RHYMING:
[2] **Crumbled**, fumbled, grumbled, humbled, jumbled, mumbled, rumbled, stumbled, tumbled.
Bundle, funnel, trundle, tunnel.
Bubble, double, Hubble, rubble, stubble, trouble.
Couple, supple, decouple, uncouple.
Bustle, hustle, muscle, mussel, rustle, tussle.
Juggle, smuggle, snuggle, struggle.
Cuddle, fuddle, huddle, muddle, puddle.
Guzzle, muzzle, nuzzle, puzzle.
Duffel, muffle, ruffle, scuffle, shuffle, snuffle, truffle.
Buckle, chuckle, circle, knuckle, shuttle, subtle, suckle, uncle.

5.1.59 "--umbler" (as in "tumbler")
[2] bumbler, fumbler, grumbler, humbler, mumbler, rumbler, stumbler, tumbler.

SURPRISING RHYMING:
[2] **Bungler**, hunger, lumber, number, rumba, slumber, younger.
Juggler, smuggler, struggler.
Blunder, plunder, rotunda, sunder, thunder, under, wonder.
Muffler, scuffler, shuffler, snuffler, sufferer.
Bumper, dumper, jumper, plumper, pumper, thumper.
Bustler, butler, guzzler, hustler, muzzler, nuzzler, puzzler, rustler.
Bubbler, coupler, doubler, suppler, uncoupler.
Bummer, drummer, dumber, glummer, number, strummer, summer.

5.1.60 "--umbling" (as in "fumbling")
[2] bumbling, crumbling, fumbling, grumbling, humbling, jumbling, mumbling, rumbling, stumbling, tumbling.

SURPRISING RHYMING:
[2] **Bundling**, bungling, juggling, smuggling, snuggling, struggling.
Blundering, hungering, lumbering, numbering, plundering, thundering, underling, slumbering, wondering.
Muffling, ruffling, scuffling, shuffling, snuffling, suffering.
Cuddling, huddling, muddling.
Bumping, dumping, jumping, lumping, pumping, slumping, thumping.
Bustling, guzzling, hustling, muscling, nuzzling, puzzling, rustling.
Bubbling, coupling, doubling, troubling, uncoupling.
Coming, drumming, dumbing, humming, numbing, slumming, strumming, thumbing.
[3] **Becoming**, forthcoming, homecoming, oncoming, shortcoming, unbecoming.

5.1.61 "--mull" (as in "normal")
[2] camel, dismal, formal, mammal, normal.
[3] abnormal, abysmal, animal, informal, minimal, paranormal.

SURPRISING RHYMING:
[1] **Bull**, cull, dull, full, gull, hull, lull, null, pull, skull, wool.
[2] **Aural**, choral, floral, immoral, laurel, moral, oral, quarrel, warble.
Awful, armful, artful, boastful, forceful, harmful, hopeful, hurtful, joyful, lawful, mournful, scornful, soulful, thoughtful, woeful, wrongful.
Apple, chapel, dapple, grapple, paddle, saddle, skedaddle, straddle.
Babble, baffle, dabble, rabble, raffle, scrabble.
Barrel, carol, apparel, gavel, gravel, ravel, travel, unravel.
Basil, bedazzle, dazzle, frazzle, razzle, razzle-dazzle.
Battle, cattle, chattel, embattle, prattle, rattle, tattle, tittle-tattle.
Angle, bangle, dangle, jangle, strangle, tangle, wangle, wrangle.

5.1.62 "--un" (as in "run")
[1] bun, done, dun, fun, gun, hon', none, nun, one, pun, run, shun, son, spun, stun, sun, ton, tonne, won.
[2] begun, godson, grandson, handgun, homespun, outdone, outgun, outrun, rerun, shotgun, someone, stepson, undone, well-done.
[3] anyone, everyone, honeybun, one-to-one, overdone, overrun.

SURPRISING RHYMING:
[1] **Fund**, gunned, shunned, stunned, sunned.
Bum, chum, come, crumb, drum, dumb, glum, gum, hum, mum, numb, plum, plumb, rum, scrum, scum, slum, some, strum, sum, swum, thumb, tum, yum.
Bung, clung, dung, flung, hung, lung, rung, slung, sprung, strung, stung, sung, swung, tongue, wrung, young.
Bump, chump, clump, crump, dump, frump, grump, hump, jump, lump, plump, pump, rump, slump, stump, thump, trump.
Blunt, brunt, bunt, front, grunt, hunt, punt, runt, shunt, stunt.
[2] **Cautioned**, cushioned, freshened, mentioned, moribund, motioned, outgunned, rationed, refund, rotund, sanctioned, stationed.
Album, autumn, awesome, become, boredom, bottom, breadcrumb, bubblegum, column, dumdum, eardrum, fearsome, forum, freedom, gruesome, handsome, ho-hum, hokum, hoodlum, humdrum, income, irksome, kingdom, lithesome, loathsome, lonesome, magnum, outcome, prism, problem, quantum, ransom, sanctum, schism, seldom, spasm, spectrum, stardom, succumb, tantrum, tiresome, twosome, welcome, wholesome, wisdom, yum-yum.
Among, aqualung, hamstrung, highly-strung, unsung.
Confront, couldn't, forefront, headhunt, manhunt, seafront, shopfront, shouldn't, storefront, upfront, waterfront, witch-hunt, wouldn't.
Lotion, motion, notion, ocean, potion.
[3] **Bothersome**, bubblegum, burdensome, chromium, conundrum, cumbersome, helium, idiom, maximum, medium, meddlesome, minimum, momentum, museum, opium, optimum, orgasm, overcome, petroleum, phantasm, platinum, podium, premium, quarrelsome, requiem, rhythm, rock-bottom, sadism, sarcasm, stadium, sugarplum, tedium, troublesome, unwelcome, valium.
[4] **Aquarium**, auditorium, colosseum, crematorium, criticism, cynicism, emporium, enthusiasm, equilibrium, gymnasium, harmonium, heroism, hypnotism, magnetism, millennium, optimism, pandemonium, patriotism, pessimism, realism, uranium.

5.1.63 "--unned" (as in "stunned")
[1] fund, gunned, shunned, stunned, sunned.
[2] cautioned, cushioned, freshened, mentioned, moribund, motioned, outgunned, rationed, refund, rotund, sanctioned, stationed.
[3] auditioned, petitioned, positioned.

SURPRISING RHYMING:
[1] **Bun**, done, dun, fun, gun, hon', none, nun, one, pun, run, shun, son, spun, stun, sun, ton, tonne, won.
Bummed, drummed, dumbed, hummed, numbed, plumbed, strummed, succumbed, summed, thumbed, welcomed.
Bum, chum, come, crumb, drum, dumb, glum, gum, hum, mum, numb, rum, scrum, scum, slum, some, strum, sum, swum, thumb.
[2] **Begun**, godson, grandson, handgun, homespun, outdone, outgun, outrun, shotgun, someone, stepson, undone, well-done.
Album, autumn, awesome, become, boredom, bottom, breadcrumb, bubblegum, column, eardrum, fearsome, forum, freedom, fulsome, gruesome, handsome, hokum, hoodlum, humdrum, income, kingdom, loathsome, lonesome, magnum, outcome, prism, problem, quantum, ransom, sanctum, schism, seldom, spasm, spectrum, stardom, tantrum, tiresome, twosome, welcome, wholesome, wisdom.

5.1.64 "--unning" (as in "running")
[2] cunning, funning, gunning, punning, running, stunning, sunning.

SURPRISING RHYMING:
[2] **Coming**, drumming, dumbing, humming, numbing, slumming, strumming, thumbing.
Crumbling, fumbling, grumbling, humbling, mumbling, rumbling, stumbling, tumbling.
Bluffing, huffing, puffing, roughing, scuffing, stuffing, toughing.
Bugging, chugging, drugging, glugging, hugging, mugging, plugging, shrugging, slugging, tugging, unplugging.
Buzzing, cousin, dozen, loving, nothing, shoving.
Blooding, budding, flooding, pudding, sudden, thudding.
Bumping, dumping, jumping, lumping, pumping, slumping, thumping.
Blushing, brushing, crushing, gushing, hushing, pushing, rushing.
Bubbling, doubling, rubbing, troubling.
[3] **Becoming**, forthcoming, homecoming, oncoming, shortcoming, unbecoming.

5.1.65 "--unch" (as in "lunch")
[1] brunch, bunch, crunch, honeybunch, hunch, lunch, munch, punch, scrunch.

SURPRISING RHYMING:
[1] **Bunched**, crunched, hunched, lunched, munched, punched.
Grunge, lunge, plunge, sponge, expunge.
Budge(d), fudge(d), grudge(d), judge(d), nudge(d), smudge(d), trudge(d).
Bumps, dumps, jumps, lumps, slumps, stumps, thumps, trumps.
Blunt, brunt, bunt, front, grunt, hunt, punt, runt, shunt, stunt.
[2] **Adjudge**, begrudge, misjudge, prejudge.

5.1.66 "--unching" (as in "punching")
[2] bunching, crunching, lunching, munching, punching, scrunching.

SURPRISING RHYMING:
[2] **Dungeon**, grunging, lunging, plunging, sponging, expunging.
Budging, fudging, grudging, judging, nudging, smudging, trudging.
Cushion, clutching, function, junction, luncheon, touching.
Blushing, brushing, crushing, gushing, hushing, pushing, rushing.
Bumping, dumping, jumping, pumping, slumping, thumping.
Blunting, bunting, fronting, grunting, hunting, shunting, something.
Bumbling, bundling, crumbling, fumbling, grumbling, humbling, jumbling, mumbling, rumbling, stumbling, trundling, tumbling.
Busking, busting, dusting, gusting, lusting, thrusting, trusting.
[2] **Begrudging**, bulging, divulging, indulging, misjudging, prejudging.

5.1.67 "--unk" (as in "drunk")
[1] bunk, chunk, clunk, drunk, dunk, flunk, funk, gunk, hunk, junk, monk, plunk, punk,

shrunk, skunk, slunk, stunk, sunk, trunk.
[2] chipmunk, cyberpunk, debunk, punch-drunk.

SURPRISING RHYMING:
[1] **Blunt**, brunt, bunt, front, grunt, hunt, punt, runt, shunt, stunt.
Bump, chump, clump, dump, frump, grump, hump, jump, lump, plump, pump, rump, slump, stump, thump, trump.
[2] **Confront**, couldn't, forefront, headhunt, manhunt, seafront, shouldn't, storefront, upfront, waterfront, witch-hunt, wouldn't.
Abduct, conduct, deduct, instruct, obstruct, product.
Adult, catapult, consult, cult, difficult, exult, insult, occult, result.

5.1.68 "--unt" (as in "hunt")
[1] blunt, brunt, bunt, front, grunt, hunt, punt, runt, shunt, stunt.
[2] affront, confront, couldn't, forefront, headhunt, manhunt, seafront, shouldn't, storefront, upfront, waterfront, witch-hunt, wouldn't.

SURPRISING RHYMING:
[1] **Bunk**, chunk, clunk, drunk, dunk, flunk, funk, gunk, hunk, junk, monk, plunk, punk, shrunk, skunk, slunk, stunk, sunk, trunk.
Bump, chump, clump, crump, dump, frump, grump, hump, jump, lump, plump, pump, rump, slump, stump, thump, trump.
Bust, bussed, clutched, cussed, crust, dust, fussed, gust, just, lust, must, rust, thrust, touched, trussed, trust.
Blushed, brushed, bushed, crushed, flushed, gushed, hushed, mushed, pushed, rushed, shushed, slushed, swooshed.
Bluffed, cuffed, fluffed, huffed, puffed, roughed, scuffed, stuffed.
[2] **Chipmunk**, cyberpunk, debunk, punch-drunk.
Abduct, conduct, deduct, construct, instruct, obstruct, product.
Abrupt, corrupt, cupped, disrupt, erupt, interrupt.
Adult, catapult, consult, cult, difficult, exult, insult, occult, result.
Adjust, august, blood lust, combust, discussed, disgust, distrust, entrust, gold dust, mistrust, robust, stardust, unjust, wanderlust.

5.1.69 "--under" (as in "under")
[2] blunder, plunder, rotunda, sunder, thunder, under, wonder.

SURPRISING RHYMING:
[2] **Blundered**, plundered, thundered, wondered.
Bumper, dumper, jumper, plumper, pumper, stumper, thumper.
Lumber, number, rumba, slumber.
Blunter, chunter, grunter, hunter, junta, punter, shunter.
Bunker, debunker, drunker, dunker, flunker, hunger, younger.
Bummer, drummer, dumber, glummer, gunner, hummer, number, plumber, runner, shunner, strummer, stunner, summer.
Brother, cover, further, lover, mother, other, smother.
[3] **Outnumber**, scandalmonger, scaremonger, warmonger.
Abductor, conductor, instructor, obstructer.
Discover, helluva, recover, rediscover, uncover, undercover.
Another, godmother, grandmother, stepbrother, stepmother.
Latecomer, midsummer, newcomer.

5.1.70 "--unnel" (as in "tunnel")
[2] funnel, gunwale, tunnel.

SURPRISING RHYMING:
[2] **Bumble**, bundle, crumble, fumble, grumble, humble, jumble, mumble, rumble, stumble, trundle, tumble.
Juggle, smuggle, snuggle, struggle.

Cuddle, fuddle, huddle, muddle, puddle.
Bubble, double, Hubble, rubble, stubble, trouble.
Couple, decouple, rebuttal, scuttle, shuttle, subtle, supple, uncouple.
Duffel, muffle, ruffle, scuffle, shuffle, snuffle, truffle.
Buckle, chuckle, knuckle, suckle, unbuckle.
Guzzle, muzzle, nuzzle, puzzle.

5.1.71 "--ung" (as in "young")
[1] bung, clung, dung, flung, hung, lung, rung, slung, sprung, strung, stung, sung, swung, tongue, wrung, young.
[2] among, aqualung, hamstrung, highly-strung, unsung.

SURPRISING RHYMING:
[1] **Bun**, done, dun, fun, gun, hon', none, nun, one, pun, run, shun, son, spun, stun, sun, ton, tonne, won.
Fund, gunned, shunned, stunned, sunned.
Bum, chum, come, crumb, drum, dumb, glum, gum, hum, mum, numb, plum, plumb, rum, scrum, scum, slum, some, strum, sum, swum, thumb, tum, yum.
Bump, chump, clump, crump, dump, frump, grump, hump, jump, lump, plump, pump, rump, slump, stump, thump, trump.
[2] **Begun**, godson, grandson, handgun, homespun, outdone, outgun, outrun, shotgun, someone, stepson, undone, well-done.
Album, autumn, awesome, become, boredom, bottom, breadcrumb, bubblegum, column, eardrum, fearsome, forum, freedom, fulsome, gruesome, handsome, hokum, hoodlum, humdrum, income, kingdom, loathsome, lonesome, magnum, outcome, prism, problem, quantum, ransom, sanctum, schism, seldom, spasm, spectrum, stardom, tantrum, tiresome, twosome, welcome, wholesome, wisdom.
Cautioned, cushioned, freshened, mentioned, moribund, motioned, outgunned, rationed, refund, rotund, sanctioned, stationed.
[3] **Anyone**, everyone, honeybun, one-to-one, overdone, overrun.
Bothersome, bubblegum, burdensome, chromium, conundrum, cumbersome, helium, idiom, maximum, medium, meddlesome, minimum, momentum, museum, opium, optimum, orgasm, overcome, petroleum, phantasm, platinum, podium, premium, quarrelsome, requiem, rhythm, rock-bottom, sadism, sarcasm, stadium, sugarplum, tedium, troublesome, unwelcome, valium.
[4] **Aquarium**, auditorium, colosseum, consortium, crematorium, criticism, cynicism, emporium, enthusiasm, equilibrium, gymnasium, harmonium, hypnotism, magnetism, mannerism, mausoleum, millennium, optimism, pandemonium, pessimism, realism.

5.1.72 "--unger" (as in "younger")
[2] hunger, younger.
[3] scandalmonger, scaremonger, warmonger.

SURPRISING RHYMING:
[2] **Blunder**, plunder, rotunda, sunder, thunder, under, wonder.
Lumber, number, outnumber, rumba, slumber.
Bumper, dumper, jumper, plumper, pumper, thumper.
Bumbler, bungler, fumbler, grumbler, humbler, mumbler, tumbler.
Hugger, juggler, mugger, smuggler, struggler.
Blunter, bunker, drunker, dunker, flunker, grunter, hunter, youngster.
Bummer, drummer, dumber, glummer, gunner, hummer, number, plumber, runner, shunner, stunner, strummer, summer.
[3] **Latecomer**, midsummer, newcomer.

5.1.73 "--unny" (as in "funny")
[2] bunny, funny, honey, money, runny, sonny, sunny.

SURPRISING RHYMING:
[2] **Chummy**, dummy, mummy, plummy, scrummy, tummy, yummy.

Someday, Monday, one day, sundae, Sunday, undies.
Bumpy, dumpy, frumpy, grumpy, jumpy, lumpy, rumpy-pumpy.
Bloody, buddy, goody, hoodie, muddy, study, woody.
Chubby, clubby, grubby, hubby, nubby, scrubby, stubby, tubby.
Chunky, clunky, flunky, funky, hunky, junkie, lucky, monkey, punky.
Bubbly, buddy, cuddly, comfy, fluffy, fussy, fuzzy, gruffly, lovely, roughly, toughly.
Crumbly, grumbly, humbly, dumbly, glumly, numbly.

5.1.74 "--unky" (as in "funky")
[2] chunky, clunky, flunky, funky, hunky, junkie, monkey, punky.

SURPRISING RHYMING:
[2] **Bulky**, hulky, sulky.
Bumpy, dumpy, frumpy, grumpy, jumpy, lumpy, rumpy-pumpy.
Country, gumtree, hungry, sultry, sundry.
Busty, crusty, dusky, dusty, gusty, lusty, musky, rusty, trusty.
Butty, nutty, putty, slutty, smutty.
Chubby, clubby, grubby, hubby, nubby, scrubby, stubby, tubby.
Bloody, buddy, goody, hoodie, muddy, study, woody.
Bunny, funny, honey, money, runny, sonny, sunny.
Bubbly, buddy, cuddly, comfy, fluffy, fussy, fuzzy, lovely, roughly.
Crumbly, grumbly, humbly, dumbly, glumly, numbly.
Someday, Monday, one day, sundae, Sunday, undies.
[3] **Alchemy**, bigamy, blasphemy, blossomy, infamy, sesame.

5.1.75 "--shun" (as in "passion")
[2] **Action**, caption, faction, fraction, traction.
Ashen, fashion, mansion, passion, ration.
Diction, fiction, fission, freshen, friction, mission, session, vision.
Function, junction, luncheon, mention, pension, section, tension.
Lotion, motion, notion, nation, ocean, potion, station.
Auction, caution, portion, sanction, version.
[3] **Abduction**, construction, deduction, destruction, instruction, obstruction, production, reduction, seduction.
Abstention, ascension, attention, confession, contention, convention, detention, dimension, dissention, extension, impression, intention, invention, prevention, obsession, retention, suspension.
Addiction, affliction, conviction, depiction, eviction.
Addition, ambition, audition, edition, petition, tradition, tuition, volition.
Adoption, option, concoction.
Affection, connection, correction, discretion, ejection, election, infection, injection, inspection, objection, perfection, projection, protection, reflection, rejection, selection.
Aspersion, assertion, aversion, conversion, desertion, diversion, excursion, exertion, immersion, insertion.
Assumption, compulsion, presumption, repulsion.
Attraction, contraction, extraction, subtraction, transaction.
Fruition, ignition, magician, musician, optician, physician, suspicion.
Citation, creation, donation, duration, elation, fixation, location, mutation, ovation, persuasion, relation, rotation, taxation, vacation.
Commotion, devotion, emotion, promotion, proportion.
Collection, complexion, confection, convection, defection, deflection, dejection, detection, direction.
Conception, deception, exception, inception, perception, reception.
Corruption, disruption, eruption, malfunction, T-junction.
Completion, deletion, depletion.
Description, inscription, prescription.
Confusion, dilution, illusion, pollution, seclusion, solution.
Distinction, exemption, expansion, extinction, redemption.
Collision, emission, omission, permission, position, remission.
[4] **Apprehension**, comprehension, contravention, intervention, misapprehension.

Constitution, contribution, destitution, electrocution, elocution, evolution, execution, persecution, prosecution, substitution.
Contraception, interception, misconception.
Imperfection, insurrection, interaction, interjection, intersection, introspection, resurrection, retrospection, satisfaction.
Admiration, aviation, explanation, occasion.
Interruption, introduction, locomotion, mathematician, politician.

SURPRISING RHYMING:
[1] **Bun**, done, dun, fun, gun, hon', none, nun, one, pun, run, shun, son, spun, stun, sun, ton, tonne, won.
[2] **Begun**, godson, grandson, handgun, homespun, lesson, outdone, outgun, outrun, shotgun, someone, undone, well-done.
Bitten, hidden, rhythm, criticism, listen.
Bashin' (*silent 'g'*), cashin', clashin', crashin', dashin', flashin', lashin', mashin', slashin', smashin', splashin', thrashin'.
Cushion, concussion, discussion, percussion, pincushion, Russian.
Clutchin' (*silent 'g'*), retouchin', touchin'.
Catchin' (*silent 'g'*), hatchin', matchin', patchin', scratchin', snatchin'.
Blushin' (*silent 'g'*), brushin', crushin', flushin', gushin', hushin', pushin', rushin.
Budgin' (*silent 'g'*), fudgin', grudgin', judgin', nudgin', smudgin', trudgin'.
Fasten, fashioned, haven't, happen, rationed, relaxin'.
Fund, gunned, shunned, stunned, sunned.
[3] **Anyone**, everyone, honeybun, one-to-one, overdone, overrun, underdone.
Earbashin' (*silent 'g'*), gatecrashin', mishmashin', rehashin'.
Attachin' (*silent 'g'*), back-scratchin', detachin', dispatchin', mismatchin'.
Begrudgin' (*silent 'g'*), misjudgin', prejudgin'.
Amassin' (*silent 'g'*), breakfastin', broadcastin', contrastin', everlastin', outlastin'.

5.1.76 "--annull" (as in "channel")
[2] annul, channel, flannel, panel.
[3] cardinal, criminal, marginal, regional, seasonal, seminal, sentinel, terminal, virginal.
[4] original, subliminal.

SURPRISING RHYMING:
[1] **Bull**, cull, dull, full, hull, lull, mull, pull, skull, wool.
[2] **Candle**, handle, manhandle, mishandle, sandal, scandal, vandal.
Amble, camel, gamble, mammal, mantle, ramble, scramble, shamble.
Angle, bangle, dangle, jangle, strangle, tangle, wangle, wrangle.
Ample, example, sample, trample.
Babble, barrel, carol, dabble, rabble, scrabble.
Baffle, gavel, gravel, raffle, ravel, travel, snaffle, unravel.
Bedraggle, gaggle, haggle, straggle, waggle.
Addle, paddle, saddle, skedaddle, straddle, unsaddle.
Apple, chapel, dapple, grapple.
Battle, cattle, chattel, embattle, prattle, rattle, tattle, tittle-tattle.

5.1.77 "--urnell" (as in "journal")
[2] colonel, journal, kernel.
[3] eternal, external, infernal, internal, maternal, nocturnal, paternal.

SURPRISING RHYMING:
[2] **Burgle**, curdle, girdle, gurgle, herbal, hurdle, verbal.
Fertile, hurtle, myrtle, purple, turtle.
Circle, hurtful, mirthful, referral, reversal, thermal, universal.

5.1.78 "--onull" (as in "zonal")
[2] tonal, zonal.
[3] hormonal, personal.

[4] diagonal, impersonal, medicinal, phenomenal.

SURPRISING RHYMING:
[2] **Global**, hopeful, know-all, mobile, mogul, noble, ogle, woeful.
Focal, local, vocal, yokel.
Boastful, coastal, postal, social, soulful, total, woeful, yodel.
[3] **Anecdotal**, disposal, proposal, subtotal.

5.1.79 "--shunnell" (as in "fictional")
[3] fictional, functional, national, optional, rational.
[4] additional, conditional, confessional, conventional, conversational, educational, emotional, exceptional, inspirational, intentional, international, irrational, notional, nutritional, occasional, occupational, professional, promotional, proportional, recreational, sensational, three-dimensional, traditional, two-dimensional, unconditional, unintentional.

SURPRISING RHYMING:
[2] **Cuddle**, fuddle, funnel, huddle, muddle, puddle, tunnel.
Bubble, double, Hubble, rubble, stubble, trouble.
Juggle, smuggle, snuggle, struggle.
Guzzle, muzzle, nuzzle, puzzle.
Duffel, muffle, ruffle, scuffle, shuffle, snuffle, truffle.

5.1.80 "--appull" (as in "apple")
apple, chapel, dapple, grapple, pineapple, pull.

SURPRISING RHYMING:
[2] **Battle**, cattle, chattel, embattle, prattle, rattle, tattle, tittle-tattle.
Dabble, paddle, rabble, saddle, scrabble, skedaddle, straddle.
Baffle, gavel, gravel, raffle, ravel, snaffle, travel, unravel.
Cackle, crackle, hackle, jackal, shackle, tackle.
Bedraggle, draggle, gaggle, haggle, straggle, waggle.
Bedazzle, castle, dazzle, frazzle, hassle, tassel, razzle.
Amble, gamble, preamble, ramble, scramble, shamble, unscramble.
Angle, bangle, dangle, jangle, mangle, spangle, strangle, tangle, wangle, wrangle.

5.1.81 "--ippull" (as in "ripple")
[2] cripple, nipple, ripple, stipple, tipple, triple.
[3] multiple, principal, principle.

SURPRISING RHYMING:
[2] **Belittle**, brittle, committal, hospital, it'll, little, skittle, whittle.
Fickle, nickel, pickle, prickle, tickle, trickle.
Dribble, giggle, jiggle, nibble, niggle, quibble, scribble, squiggle, wiggle, wriggle.
Diddle, fiddle, griddle, idyll, middle, piddle, riddle, twiddle.
Civil, drivel, shrivel, skiffle, sniffle, snivel, swivel.
Bristle, chisel, drizzle, fizzle, missile, sizzle, swizzle, thistle, whistle.
Cymbal, dimple, nimble, pimple, simple, symbol, thimble, timbale.
[3] **Acquittal**, belittle, committal, hospital, noncommittal.

5.1.82 "--uppell" (as in "couple")
couple, decouple, supple, uncouple.

SURPRISING RHYMING:
[2] **Scuttle**, shuttle, subtle, rebuttal.
Buckle, chuckle, honeysuckle, knuckle, suckle, unbuckle.
Bubble, double, Hubble, rubble, stubble, trouble.
Juggle, smuggle, snuggle, struggle.
Cuddle, fuddle, funnel, huddle, muddle, puddle, tunnel.
Bustle, guzzle, hustle, muscle, muzzle, nuzzle, puzzle, rustle, tussle.

Duffel, muffle, ruffle, scuffle, shuffle, snuffle, truffle.
Crumble, crumple, fumble, grumble, humble, jumble, mumble, rumble, stumble, tumble.

5.1.83 "--eepull" (as in "people")
people, steeple, townspeople.

SURPRISING RHYMING:
[2] **Cheerful**, earful, fearful, tearful.
Beetle, evil, weevil, medieval, upheaval, primeval, retrieval.
Eagle, feeble, legal, needle, regal, illegal, seagull, wheedle.
Easel, diesel, peaceful, teasel, weasel.
Equal, sequel, unequal.
Gleeful, heedful, lethal, needful.
[3] **Amenable**, feasible, genial, meaningful, menial, deceitful.
[4] **Agreeable**, foreseeable, disagreeable, unforeseeable.
Achievable, believable, conceivable, unbelievable, irretrievable, inconceivable.

5.1.84 "--ampull" (as in "sample")
ample, example, sample, trample.

SURPRISING RHYMING:
[2] **Amble**, gamble, preamble, ramble, scramble, shamble.
Angle, bangle, dangle, jangle, strangle, tangle, wangle, wrangle.
Candle, handle, manhandle, mishandle, sandal, scandal, vandal.
Dabble, paddle, rabble, saddle, scrabble, skedaddle, straddle.
Apple, chapel, dapple, grapple.
Battle, cattle, chattel, embattle, prattle, rattle, tattle, tittle-tattle.
Bedraggle, draggle, gaggle, haggle, straggle, waggle.
Baffle, gavel, gravel, raffle, ravel, snaffle, travel, unravel.
Bedazzle, castle, dazzle, frazzle, hassle, tassel, razzle.
Cackle, crackle, hackle, jackal, shackle, tackle.
[3] **Disentangle**, entangle, pentangle, quadrangle, rectangle, right-angle, triangle, untangle, wide-angle.

5.1.85 "--up" (as in "cup")
[1] cup, pup, sup, up, yup.
[2] backup, bishop, break-up, checkup, cleanup, closeup, cock-up, cut-up, dollop, Europe, fry-up, gallop, grown-up, hang-up, hiccup, hold-up, hook-up, ketchup, let-up, lineup, linkup, lock-up, lookup, makeup, markup, nosh-up, pickup, pile-up, pinup, press-up, pull up, punch-up, rave-up, roundup, run-up, scallop, set-up, shake-up, sit-up, slap-up, snarl-up, start-up, stick-up, stirrup, straight-up, stuck up, sun-up, syrup/sirup (U.S.), take-up, teacup, top-up, toss-up, trollop, turn-up, two-up, walk up, wallop, warmup, wash-up, wind-up, zip-up.
[3] buttercup, coffee cup, develop, escalope, giddy-up, pick-me-up, summing-up, totting-up, washing-up.

SURPRISING RHYMING:
[1] **But**, butt, cut, gut, hut, jut, nut, put, rut, shut, slut, smut, strut.
Bluff, buff, cuff, duff, fluff, guff, gruff, huff, muff, puff, rough, ruff, scruff, scuff, slough, snuff, stuff, tough, tuff, woof.
Blub, bub, chub, club, cub, drub, dub, flub, grub, hub, nub, pub, rub, scrub, shrub, snub, stub, sub, tub.
Book, buck, cook, crook, duck, hook, look, luck, muck, pluck, puck, ruck, shook, shuck, struck, stuck, suck, took, truck, tuck, yuck.
Bust, cussed, crust, dust, fussed, gust, just, lust, must, rust, thrust, trussed, trust.
[2] **Clean-cut**, clear-cut, crewcut, crosscut, doughnut/donut (U.S.), haircut, half-shut, peanut, rebut, shortcut, somewhat, uncut.
Dandruff, earmuff, enough, foodstuff, green stuff, handcuff, powder puff, rebuff, sho'nuff.
Bathtub, Beelzebub, cherub, hubbub, nightclub, washtub.

Amok, awestruck, chequebook, cookbook, dumbstruck, fishhook, guidebook, megabuck, mistook, moonstruck, notebook, outlook, partook, playbook, potluck, scrapbook, sketchbook, songbook, stagestruck, storybook, textbook, thunderstruck, unhook, unstuck.
Abduct, conduct, deduct, construct, instruct, obstruct, product.
Adjust, august, blood lust, combust, discussed, disgust, distrust, entrust, gold dust, mistrust, robust, stardust, unjust, wanderlust.
[3] **Overlook**, overtook, picture book, pocketbook, storybook, tenterhook, undertook.
Coconut, hazelnut, undercut.

5.1.86 "--upper" (as in "supper")
[2] cuppa, scupper, supper, upper.

SURPRISING RHYMING:
[2] **Butter**, clutter, flutter, gutter, mutter, nutter, putter, scutter, shutter, splutter, sputter, stutter, utter, woodcutter.
Cooker, hooker, looker, mucker, pucker, sucker, trucker, tucker.
Bluster, buster, cluster, duster, fluster, lacklustre/lackluster (U.S.), lustre/luster (U.S.), muster, thruster.
Blubber, clubber, rubber, scrubber.
Bummer, drummer, dumber, glummer, gunner, hummer, number, plumber, runner, shunner, stunner, strummer, summer.
Bluffer, brother, buffer, duffer, gruffer, other, rougher, suffer, tougher.
[3] **Abductor**, conductor, instructor, obstructer.
Latecomer, midsummer, newcomer.
Discover, helluva, recover, rediscover, uncover, undercover.

5.1.87 "--orrul" (as in "quarrel")
[2] aural, choral, coral, floral, laurel, moral, oral, quarrel.
[3] amoral, doctoral, immoral.

SURPRISING RHYMING:
[1] **Bull**, cull, dull, full, hull, lull, mull, null, pull, skull, wool.
[2] **Awful**, grovel, hovel, mournful, novel, scornful, waffle.
Chortle, formal, mortal, normal, portal, snorkel.
Bauble, bobble, cobble, gobble, hobble, squabble, wobble.
Colossal, fossil, gospel, jostle, morsel, nozzle, schnozzle, shovel.
Dawdle, doddle, model, molly-coddle, toddle, twaddle, waddle, yodel.
Aristotle, bottle, boggle, goggle, mottle, ogle, throttle, toggle.
[3] **Alcohol**, all in all, coverall, free-for-all, know-it-all, overall, overhaul, protocol, volleyball, waterfall, withdrawal, wherewithal.

5.1.88 "--arrull" (as in "barrel")
[2] barrel, carol.
[3] apparel, admiral, liberal, literal, mineral.

SURPRISING RHYMING:
[2] **Apple**, chapel, dapple, grapple, pineapple.
Bedraggle, draggle, gaggle, haggle, straggle, waggle.
Channel, final, flannel, panel.
Baffle, cure-all, gavel, gravel, raffle, ravel, snaffle, travel, unravel.
Dabble, paddle, rabble, saddle, scrabble, skedaddle, straddle.
Battle, cattle, chattel, embattle, prattle, rattle, tattle, tittle-tattle.
Cackle, crackle, hackle, jackal, shackle, tackle.
Bedazzle, castle, dazzle, frazzle, hassle, razzle, tassel.
Amble, gamble, preamble, ramble, scramble, shamble, unscramble.
Angle, bangle, dangle, jangle, strangle, tangle, wangle, wrangle.

5.1.89 "--oorull" (as in "rural")
cultural, cure-all, mural, natural, plural, rural, supernatural, unnatural.

SURPRISING RHYMING:
[2] **Brutal**, bugle, crucial, frugal, google, fruitful, futile, neutral, rueful, spoonful, truthful, tuneful, useful, youthful.
Canoodle, doodle, feudal, noodle, oodles, poodle, strudel.
Cruel, dual, duel, fuel, gruel, jewel, pupil, refuel, renewal, scruple.
Colonel, journal, kernel.
[3] **Approval**, bamboozle, disapproval, refusal, removal.

5.1.90 "--errull" (as in "peril")
[2] feral, peril, sterile.
[3] cockerel, federal, funeral, general, mackerel, numeral, several.
[4] collateral, electoral.

SURPRISING RHYMING:
[2] **Fettle**, kettle, metal, mettle, nettle, petal, settle, unsettle.
Medal, meddle, pebble, pedal, peddle, rebel, treble.
Central, dental, gentle, kennel, mental, parental, rental, temple.
Embezzle, nestle, special, trestle, vessel, wrestle.
Pencil, several, stencil, utensil.
Careful, devil, level, prayerful, revel.
Freckle, heckle, Jekyll, speckle.
[3] **Bedevil**, daredevil, eye-level, high-level, low-level., split-level.

5.1.91 "--uss" (as in "bus")
[1] bus, cuss, fuss, plus, puss, suss, thus, truss, us.
[2] anxious, bias, bogus, bonus, cactus, callous, campus, canvas, cautious, census, chorus, circus, citrus, compass, conscious, discuss, famous, focus, fractious, gorgeous, gracious, grievous, hocus, jealous, joyous, luscious, monstrous, nervous, opus, pious, pompous, precious, purpose, raucous, righteous, ruckus, rumpus, scrumptious, spacious, status, sumptuous, surplus, versus, vicious, virus, walrus, wondrous, zealous.
[3] alias, ambitious, amorous, arduous, atrocious, audacious, auspicious, boisterous, chivalrous, colossus, consensus, contagious, contentious, courageous, courteous, curious, dangerous, delicious, devious, disastrous, dubious, envious, fabulous, ferocious, fictitious, flirtatious, frivolous, furious, genius, generous, glamorous, glorious, hazardous, hideous, horrendous, humorous, impetus, infectious, lecherous, ludicrous, malicious, marvellous/marvelous (U.S.), minibus, mischievous, momentous, murderous, nauseous, nucleus, numerous, nutritious, obnoxious, obvious, octopus, odious, ominous, outrageous, perilous, poisonous, precocious, prestigious, pretentious, previous, prosperous, radius, rapturous, ravenous, religious, rigorous, riotous, ruinous, scandalous, scrupulous, sensuous, serious, slanderous, sourpuss, stimulus, strenuous, studious, subconscious, sumptuous, suspicious, tedious, tenacious, thunderous, tortuous, treacherous, tremendous, various, vigorous, villainous, virtuous.
[4] acrimonious, adulterous, advantageous, adventurous, ambiguous, bootylicious, calamitous, conscientious, continuous, delirious, gregarious, harmonious, hilarious, illustrious, impetuous, inconspicuous, ingenious, luxurious, melodious, meticulous, miraculous, monotonous, mysterious, notorious, oblivious, precarious, rebellious, ridiculous, simultaneous, splendiferous, spontaneous, superfluous, superstitious, surreptitious, tempestuous, tumultuous, tyrannosaurus, victorious, vociferous.

SURPRISING RHYMING:
[1] **Bust**, cussed, crust, dust, fussed, gust, just, lust, must, rust, thrust, trussed, trust.
Brusque, busk, dusk, husk, musk, rusk, tusk.
Buzz, 'cuz, does, fuzz, was.
[2] **Adjust**, august, blood lust, combust, discussed, disgust, distrust, entrust, gold dust, mistrust, robust, stardust, unjust, wanderlust.
Fierce, pierce.
Dishes, fishes, squishes, swishes, wishes.
Business, citrus, illness, fitness, forgiveness, weakness, witness.
Captures, departures, fractures, pastures, raptures.

5.1.92 "--ust" (as in "trust")
[1] bust, cussed, crust, dust, fussed, gust, just, lust, must, rust, thrust, trussed, trust.
[2] adjust, august, discussed, disgust, distrust, encrust, entrust, gold dust, mistrust, robust, sawdust, stardust, unjust, wanderlust.

SURPRISING RHYMING:
[1] **Bus**, cuss, fuss, plus, puss, suss, thus, truss, us.
Brusque, busk, dusk, husk, musk, rusk, tusk.
Blushed, brushed, bushed, crushed, flushed, gushed, hushed, mushed, pushed, rushed, shushed, slushed, swooshed, touched.
Bluff(ed), buff(ed), cuff(ed), duff(ed), fluff(ed), guff, gruff, huff(ed), muff, puff(ed), rough, scruff, scuff(ed), snuff, stuff(ed), tough, tuff.
[2] **Anxious**, bias, bogus, bonus, cactus, callous, campus, canvas, cautious, chorus, circus, citrus, compass, conscious, discuss, famous, focus, fractious, gorgeous, gracious, grievous, jealous, joyous, luscious, monstrous, nervous, nonplus, opus, pious, pompous, precious, purpose, raucous, righteous, ruckus, rumpus, scrumptious, spacious, status, sumptuous, surplus, versus, vicious, virus, walrus, wondrous, zealous.
Dandruff, earmuff, enough, handcuff, powder puff, rebuff, sho'nuff.
[3] **Alias**, ambitious, amorous, arduous, atrocious, audacious, auspicious, boisterous, chivalrous, colossus, contagious, contentious, courageous, courteous, curious, dangerous, delicious, devious, disastrous, dubious, envious, fabulous, ferocious, fictitious, flirtatious, frivolous, furious, genius, generous, glamorous, glorious, hazardous, hideous, horrendous, humorous, infectious, ludicrous, malicious, marvellous/marvelous (U.S.), mischievous, momentous, murderous, nauseous, nucleus, numerous, nutritious, obnoxious, obvious, ominous, outrageous, perilous, poisonous, precocious, prestigious, pretentious, previous, prosperous, rapturous, ravenous, religious, rigorous, riotous, ruinous, scandalous, scrupulous, sensuous, serious, slanderous, sourpuss, stimulus, strenuous, studious, subconscious, sumptuous, suspicious, tedious, tenacious, thunderous, tortuous, treacherous, tremendous, various, vigorous, virtuous.
[4] **Acrimonious**, adulterous, adventurous, ambiguous, bootylicious, calamitous, continuous, delirious, hilarious, hocus-pocus, illustrious, impetuous, inconspicuous, ingenious, luxurious, meticulous, miraculous, monotonous, mysterious, notorious, oblivious, precarious, rebellious, ridiculous, simultaneous, splendiferous, spontaneous, superstitious, surreptitious, tempestuous, tyrannosaurus, victorious.

5.1.93 "--usk" (as in "tusk")
[1] brusque, busk, dusk, husk, musk, rusk, tusk.

SURPRISING RHYMING:
[1] **Bus**, cuss, fuss, plus, puss, suss, thus, truss, us.
Bust, bussed, cussed, dust, fussed, gust, just, lust, must, rust, trust.
Bulk, hulk, skulk, sulk.
Book, buck, chuck, cook, crook, duck, hook, look, luck, muck, pluck, schmuck, shook, struck, stuck, suck, took, truck, tuck, yuck.
Blushed, brushed, bushed, crushed, flushed, gushed, hushed, mushed, pushed, rushed, shushed, slushed, swooshed.
Bluffed, cuffed, fluffed, huffed, puffed, roughed, scuffed, stuffed.
Clutched, touched, untouched.
[2] **Abduct**, conduct, deduct, construct, instruct, obstruct, product.
Adjust, august, blood lust, combust, discussed, disgust, distrust, entrust, gold dust, mistrust, robust, stardust, unjust, wanderlust.
Amok, awestruck, chequebook, cookbook, dumbstruck, fishhook, guidebook, megabuck, mistook, moonstruck, notebook, outlook, partook, playbook, potluck, scrapbook, sketchbook, songbook, stagestruck, storybook, textbook, thunderstruck, unhook, unstuck.
Anxious, bogus, bonus, cactus, callous, campus, canvas, cautious, census, chorus, circus, citrus, compass, conscious, discuss, famous, focus, gorgeous, gracious, grievous, hocus, jealous, joyous, luscious, monstrous, nervous, nonplus, opus, pious, pompous, precious, purpose, raucous, righteous, ruckus, rumpus, spacious, status, sumptuous, surplus, versus, vicious, virus, wondrous, zealous.

[3] **Aqueduct**, misconduct, reconstruct, safe-conduct, viaduct.
Alias, ambitious, amorous, arduous, atrocious, audacious, auspicious, boisterous, chivalrous, colossus, contagious, contentious, courageous, courteous, curious, dangerous, delicious, devious, disastrous, dubious, envious, fabulous, ferocious, fictitious, flirtatious, frivolous, furious, genius, generous, glamorous, glorious, hazardous, hideous, humorous, infectious, ludicrous, malicious, marvellous/marvelous (U.S.), mischievous, momentous, murderous, nauseous, nucleus, numerous, nutritious, obnoxious, obvious, ominous, outrageous, perilous, poisonous, precocious, prestigious, pretentious, previous, prosperous, rapturous, ravenous, religious, rigorous, riotous, ruinous, scandalous, scrupulous, sensuous, serious, slanderous, sourpuss, stimulus, strenuous, subconscious, sumptuous, suspicious, tedious, tenacious, thunderous, tortuous, treacherous, tremendous, various, vigorous, virtuous.
[4] **Acrimonious**, adulterous, adventurous, ambiguous, bootylicious, calamitous, continuous, delirious, hilarious, hocus-pocus, illustrious, impetuous, inconspicuous, ingenious, luxurious, meticulous, miraculous, monotonous, mysterious, notorious, oblivious, precarious, rebellious, ridiculous, simultaneous, splendiferous, spontaneous, superstitious, surreptitious, tempestuous, tyrannosaurus, victorious.

5.1.94 "--ush" (as in "push")
[1] blush, brush, bush, crush, flush, gush, hush, lush, mush, plush, push, rush, shush, slush, swoosh, thrush, tush, whoosh.
[2] airbrush, ambush, bell push, hairbrush, hush-hush, mancrush, nailbrush, onrush, paintbrush, rosebush, sagebrush, toothbrush.

SURPRISING RHYMING:
[1] **Blushed**, brushed, bushed, crushed, flushed, gushed, hushed, mushed, pushed, rushed, shushed, slushed, swooshed.
Bust, bussed, cussed, dust, fussed, gust, just, lust, must, rust, trust.
Butch, clutch, crutch, Dutch, hutch, much, putsch, such, touch.
Bluff, buff, cuff, duff, fluff, guff, gruff, huff, muff, puff, rough, ruff, scruff, scuff, snuff, stuff, tough, tuff, woof.
[2] **Adjust**, august, blood lust, combust, discussed, disgust, distrust, entrust, gold dust, mistrust, robust, stardust, unjust, wanderlust.
Airbrushed, ambushed.
Dandruff, earmuff, enough, handcuff, powder puff, rebuff, sho'nuff.

5.1.95 "--ushed" (as in "pushed")
[1] blushed, brushed, bushed, crushed, flushed, gushed, hushed, mushed, pushed, rushed, shushed, slushed, swooshed.
[2] airbrushed, ambushed.

SURPRISING RHYMING:
[1] **Blush**, brush, bush, crush, flush, gush, hush, lush, mush, plush, push, rush, shush, slush, swoosh, thrush, tush, whoosh.
Bust, bussed, cussed, dust, fussed, gust, just, lust, must, rust, trust.
Clutched, touched, untouched.
Budged, fudged, grudged, judged, nudged, smudged, trudged.
[2] **Airbrush**, ambush, hairbrush, hush-hush, mancrush, onrush, paintbrush, toothbrush.
Adjust, august, blood lust, combust, discussed, disgust, distrust, entrust, gold dust, mistrust, robust, stardust, unjust, wanderlust.
Bluffed, cuffed, duffed, fluffed, huffed, puffed, scuffed, stuffed.
Adjudged, begrudged, misjudged, prejudged.

5.1.96 "--ushing" (as in "pushing")
[2] blushing, brushing, crushing, gushing, hushing, pushing, rushing.

SURPRISING RHYMING:
[2] **Cushion(ed)**, concussion, discussion, percussion, pincushion.
Bustling, fussing, hustling, muscling, rustling, tussling.

Clutching, retouching, touching.
Bluffing, cuffing, fluffing, huffing, puffing, stuffing, toughing, woofing.
Busking, busting dusting, gusting, lusting, rusting, thrusting, trusting.
Butting, cutting, footing, jutting, putting, shutting, strutting, tutting.
Budging, fudging, grudging, judging, nudging, smudging, trudging.
Buzzing, cousin, dozen, loving, nothing, shoving.
[3] **Begrudging**, misjudging, prejudging.

5.1.97 "--usher" (as in "usher")
[2] blusher, brusher, crusher, flusher, gusher, plusher, pusher, rusher, Russia, usher.

SURPRISING RHYMING:
[2] **Bluffer**, brother, buffer, mother, other, rougher, suffer, tougher.
Bluster, buster, buzzer, cover, cusser, duster, fluster, fusser, lacklustre/lackluster (U.S.), lustre/luster (U.S.), lover, muster, thruster.
Blustered, clustered, custard, flustered, mustard, mustered.
Bustler, butler, guzzler, hustler, muzzler, nuzzler, puzzler, rustler.
Butter, clutter, flutter, gutter, mutter, shutter, splutter, stutter, utter.
Bummer, drummer, dumber, glummer, gunner, hummer, number, plumber, runner, shunner, stunner, strummer, summer.
[3] **Discover**, helluva, recover, rediscover, uncover, undercover.
Another, big brother, blood brother, godmother, grandmother.
Latecomer, midsummer, newcomer.

5.1.98 "--ustle" (as in "hustle")
[2] bustle, hustle, muscle, mussel, rustle, tussle.

SURPRISING RHYMING:
[2] **Bustled**, hustled, muscled, rustled, tussled.
Guzzle, muzzle, nuzzle, puzzle.
Duffel, muffle, ruffle, scuffle, shuffle, snuffle, truffle.
Bubble, double, Hubble, rubble, stubble, trouble.
Juggle, smuggle, snuggle, struggle.
Cuddle, fuddle, funnel, huddle, muddle, puddle, tunnel.
Bundle, crumble, fumble, grumble, humble, jumble, mumble, rumble, stumble, tumble.
Couple, decouple, rebuttal, scuttle, shuttle, subtle, supple, uncouple.
Buckle, chuckle, knuckle, suckle, unbuckle.
[3] **Honeysuckle**, kerfuffle, reshuffle.

5.1.99 "--usted" (as in "busted")
[2] busted, crusted, dusted, gusted, lusted, rusted, thrusted, trusted.
[3] adjusted, disgusted, distrusted, encrusted, entrusted, mistrusted.

SURPRISING RHYMING:
[2] **Blustered**, clustered, custard, flustered, mustard, mustered.
Busting, disgusting, dusting, justice, lusting, rusting, rustic, trusting.
Blunted, fronted, grunted, hunted, punted, shunted, stunted, tufted.
[3] **Corrupted**, disrupted, erupted, interrupted, uninterrupted.
Abducted, constructed, deducted, inducted, instructed, obstructed.
Catapulted, consulted, exulted, insulted, resulted.
Compulsive, corruptive, disruptive, impulsive, percussive, repulsive.

5.1.100 "--uster" (as in "buster")
[2] bluster, buster, cluster, duster, fluster, lacklustre/lackluster (U.S.), lustre/luster (U.S.), muster, thruster.
[3] blockbuster, filibuster, gangbuster.

SURPRISING RHYMING:
[2] **Blustered**, clustered, custard, flustered, mustard, mustered.

Bustler, busker, butler, huckster, hustler, rustler.
Guzzler, juggler, muzzler, nuzzler, puzzler, smuggler, struggler.
Blusher, brusher, crusher, plusher, pusher, rusher, Russia, usher.
Butter, clutter, flutter, gutter, mutter, shutter, splutter, stutter, utter.
Blunter, chunter, grunter, hunter, junta, punter, shunter.
Bluffer, buffer, duffer, gruffer, puffer, rougher, suffer, tougher.
Bumper, dumper, jumper, plumper, pumper, stumper, thumper.
[3] **Abductor**, conductor, instructor, obstructer.
Corrupter, disrupter, interrupter, sculptor.

5.1.101 "--ustard" (as in "custard")
[2] blustered, clustered, custard, flustered, mustard, mustered.

SURPRISING RHYMING:
[2] **Absurd**, backward, blackbird, bluebird, buzzword, byword, conferred, covered, crossword, drunkard, firebird, forward, homeward, jailbird, keyword, lovebird, misheard, occurred, onward, password, recurred, seabird, snowbird, songbird, unheard, upward.
Bluster, busker, buster, cluster, duster, fluster, lacklustre/lackluster (U.S.), muster.
Busted, crusted, dusted, gusted, lusted, rusted, thrusted, trusted.
Buttered, cluttered, fluttered, muttered, shuttered, spluttered, stuttered, uttered.
[3] **Afterward**, ladybird, mockingbird, overheard, undeterred.
Blockbuster, filibuster, gangbuster, ghostbuster.
Adjusted, disgusted, distrusted, encrusted, entrusted, mistrusted.
Discovered, recovered, rediscovered, uncovered.
Corrupted, disrupted, erupted, interrupted, uninterrupted.

5.1.102 "--ustful" (as in "trustful")
[2] lustful, trustful.

SURPRISING RHYMING:
[2] **Cupful**, hurtful, numbskull, truthful, tuneful, useful, youthful.
Bustle, guzzle, hustle, muscle, muzzle, nuzzle, puzzle, rustle, tussle.
Bumble, crumble, fumble, grumble, humble, jumble, mumble, rumble, stumble, tumble.
Duffel, muffle, ruffle, scuffle, shuffle, snuffle, truffle.
Bubble, double, Hubble, rubble, stubble, trouble.
Cuddle, huddle, juggle, muddle, puddle, smuggle, snuggle, struggle.
Couple, decouple, rebuttal, scuttle, shuttle, subtle, supple, uncouple.

5.1.103 "--usty" (as in "trusty")
[2] busty, crusty, dusty, gusty, lusty, musty, rusty, trusty.

SURPRISING RHYMING:
[2] **Bulky**, bushy, gushy, mushy, pushy, slushy, sulky, touchy.
Bumpy, dumpy, frumpy, grumpy, jumpy, lumpy, rumpy-pumpy.
Bookie, cookie, ducky, hooky, lucky, mucky, plucky, rookie, yucky.
Dusky, flunky, funky, hunky, husky, junkie, monkey, musky, punky.
Bubbly, cuddly, comfy, fluffy, fussy, fuzzy, lovely, roughly, toughly.
Budgie, grungy, gungy, spongy.
Bloody, buddy, goody, hoodie, muddy, study, woody.
Chummy, crummy, gummy, dummy, mummy, plummy, scrummy, tummy, yummy.
Bully, fully, funny, honey, money, runny, sonny, sunny.
Chubby, clubby, grubby, hubby, nubby, scrubby, stubby, tubby.

5.1.104 "--usting" (as in "trusting")
[2] busting, disgusting, dusting, gusting, husting, lusting, rusting, thrusting, trusting.

SURPRISING RHYMING:
[2] **Bustling**, busking, fussing, hustling, muscling, rustling, tussling.
Blushing, brushing, crushing, gushing, hushing, pushing, rushing.

Buzzing, cousin, dozen, loving, nothing, shoving.
Bunching, clutching, crunching, lunching, munching, punching, scrunching, touching.
Budging, fudging, grudging, judging, nudging, smudging, trudging.
Juggling, smuggling, snuggling, struggling.
Cuddling, coupling, huddling, muddling.
Bluffing, cuffing, fluffing, huffing, puffing, roughing, stuffing, toughing.
Muffling, ruffling, scuffling, shuffling, snuffling, suffering.
Bumping, dumping, jumping, lumping, pumping, slumping, thumping.
Bumbling, bundling, crumbling, fumbling, grumbling, humbling, jumbling, mumbling, rumbling, stumbling, trundling, tumbling.
Bunting, fronting, grunting, hunting, punting, shunting, something.
[3] **Abducting**, conducting, deducting, constructing, instructing, obstructing.

5.1.105 "--ussion" (as in "percussion")
cushion, concussion, discussion, percussion, pincushion, Russian.

SURPRISING RHYMING:
[2] **Blushin'** (*silent 'g'*), brushin', cushioned, crushin', gushin', hushin', pushin', rushin', shushin', touchin'.
Bustlin' (*silent 'g'*), fussin', hustlin', musclin', rustlin', tusslin'.
Buzzin' (*silent 'g'*), cousin, dozen, lovin', nothin', shovin'.
Bluffin' (*silent 'g'*), cuffin', fluffin', huffin', puffin', roughin', stuffin', toughen.
Bunchin' (*silent 'g'*), crunchin', lunchin', munchin', punchin', scrunchin'.
Buskin' (*silent 'g'*), bustin' dustin', gustin', lustin', rustin', thrustin', trustin'.
Budgin' (*silent 'g'*), fudgin', grudgin', judgin', nudgin', smudgin', trudgin'.
Bustin' (*silent 'g'*), disgustin', dustin', gustin', lustin', rustin', thrustin', trustin'.
[3] **Begrudgin'** (*silent 'g'*), misjudgin', prejudgin'.
Abduction, construction, deduction, destruction, instruction, obstruction, production, reduction, seduction.
[4] **Introduction**, reproduction.

5.1.106 "--ut" (as in "foot")
[1] but, butt, cut, foot, glut, gut, hut, jut, mutt, nut, put, putt, rut, shut, slut, smut, soot, strut, tut, what.
[2] afoot, barefoot, beechnut, butternut, chestnut, clean-cut, clear-cut, crewcut, crosscut, doughnut/donut (U.S.), haircut, half-shut, hotfoot, input, kaput, output, peanut, pussyfoot, rebut, shortcut, somewhat, tenderfoot, uncut, underfoot, walnut, wrong-foot.
[3] coconut, hazelnut, undercut.

SURPRISING RHYMING:
[1] **Book**, buck, chuck, cook(ed), crook, duck(ed), hook(ed), look(ed), luck, muck, nook, pluck(ed), schmuck, shook, struck, stuck, suck, took, truck, tuck.
Blood, bud, could, flood, good, hood, mud, should, stood, stud, thud, wood, would.
Cup, pup, sup, up, yup.
Bluff, cuff, duff, fluff, guff, gruff, huff, muff, puff, rough, scruff, scuff, snuff, stuff, tough, tuff, woof.
Busk, bust, bussed, cussed, crust, dusk, dust, fussed, gust, just, lust, musk, must, rust, skulk, sulk, thrust, trussed, trust, tusk.
[2] **Amok**, awestruck, chequebook, cookbook, dumbstruck, fishhook, guidebook, megabuck, mistook, moonstruck, notebook, outlook, playbook, potluck, scrapbook, sketchbook, songbook, stagestruck, storybook, textbook, thunderstruck, unhook, unstuck.
Blue-blood, cold-blood, deadwood, driftwood, firewood, knighthood, manhood, misunderstood, redwood, rosewood, understood, withstood.
Backup, bishop, break-up, checkup, cleanup, closeup, cock-up, cut-up, dollop, Europe, fry-up, gallop, grown-up, hang-up, hiccup, hold-up, hook-up, ketchup, let-up, lineup, linkup, lock-up, lookup, makeup, markup, nosh-up, pickup, pile-up, pin-up, press-up, pull up, punch-up, rave-up, roundup, run-up, scallop, set-up, shake-up, sit-up, slap-up, snarl-up, start-up, stick-up, stirrup, straight-up, stuck up, sun-up, syrup/sirup (U.S.), take-up, teacup, top-up, toss-up, trollop, turn-up, two-up, walk up, wallop, warmup, wash-up, wind-up, zip-up.

Dandruff, earmuff, enough, handcuff, powder puff, rebuff, sho'nuff.
Abduct, conduct, deduct, construct, instruct, obstruct, product.
Adjust, august, blood lust, combust, discussed, disgust, distrust, entrust, gold dust, mistrust, robust, stardust, unjust, wanderlust.
[3] Overlook(ed), overtook, picture book, pocketbook, storybook, tenterhook, undercook(ed), undertook.
Aqueduct, misconduct, reconstruct, safe-conduct, viaduct.
Buttercup, giddy-up, pick-me-up, summing-up, totting-up, washing-up.

5.1.107 "--utter" (as in "butter")
[2] butter, clutter, cutter, flutter, footer, gutter, mutter, nutter, putter, scutter, shutter, splutter, sputter, strutter, stutter, utter, woodcutter.

SURPRISING RHYMING:
[2] Cooker, hooker, looker, pucker, sucker, trucker, tucker.
Cuppa, clubber, rubber, scupper, supper, upper.
Hugger, mugger, plugger, shrugger, slugger, snugger, tugger.
Bluffer, buffer, duffer, gruffer, other, puffer, rougher, suffer, tougher.
Brother, buzzer, cover, hover, lover, mother, other, shover.
Bummer, drummer, dumber, glummer, gunner, hummer, number, plumber, runner, shudder, should-a, shunner, stunner, summer.
Bumper, dumper, jumper, plumper, pumper, stumper, thumper.
Bustler, butler, hustler, rustler.
[3] Abductor, conductor, instructor, obstructer.
Discover, helluva, latecomer, midsummer, newcomer, recover, uncover, undercover.

5.1.108 "--utton" (as in "button")
button, glutton, mutton, unbutton, belly-button.

SURPRISING RHYMING:
[2] Buttin' (*silent 'g'*), cuttin', footin', juttin', shuttin', struttin', tuttin'.
Couldn't, shouldn't, sudden, wooden, wouldn't.
Bookin' (*silent 'g'*), buckin', cookin', hookin', lookin', suckin', truckin'.
Begun, godson, grandson, handgun, homespun, outdone, outgun, outrun, rerun, shotgun, someone, stepson, undone, well-done.
Bumpin' (*silent 'g'*), dumpin', jumpin', lumpin', pumpin', slumpin', thumpin'.
Buddin' (*silent 'g'*), floodin', puddin', thuddin', wooden.
Comin' (*silent 'g'*), drummin', hummin', slummin', strummin', summon, thumbin'.
Cunnin' (*silent 'g'*), funnin', gunnin', runnin', stunnin', sunnin'.
Buzzin' (*silent 'g'*), cousin, dozen, lovin', nothin', shovin'.
Buggin' (*silent 'g'*), huggin', muggin', shruggin', sluggin', tuggin', unpluggin'.
Bluffin' (*silent 'g'*), fluffin', huffin', puffin', stuffin', toughen, toughin', woofin'.
Album, autumn, awesome, become, bottom, column, fearsome, fulsome, gruesome, handsome, hoodlum, humdrum, loathsome, prism, problem, quantum, ransom, sanctum, tantrum, welcome, wisdom.

5.1.109 "--uttel" (as in "shuttle")
[2] scuttle, shuttle, subtle, rebuttal.

SURPRISING RHYMING:
[2] Bustle, guzzle, hustle, muscle, nuzzle, puzzle, rustle, tussle.
Buckle, chuckle, knuckle, suckle, unbuckle.
Bubble, double, Hubble, rubble, stubble, trouble.
Juggle, smuggle, snuggle, struggle.
Cuddle, fuddle, huddle, muddle, puddle.
Duffel, muffle, ruffle, scuffle, shuffle, snuffle, truffle.
Couple, supple, decouple, uncouple.
[3] Honeysuckle, kerfuffle, reshuffle.

5.1.110 "--utch" (as in "touch")
[1] butch, clutch, crutch, hutch, much, putsch, such, touch.

SURPRISING RHYMING:
[1] **Clutched**, touched, untouched.
Budge, fudge, grudge, judge, nudge, sludge, smudge, trudge.
Brunch, bunch, crunch, honeybunch, hunch, lunch, munch, punch.
Bust, bussed, cussed, dust, fussed, just, lust, must, rust, trust.
Books, cooks, crooks, hooks, looks, plucks, schmucks, shucks, sucks, trucks, tucks.
Blush, brush, bush, crush, flush, gush, hush, lush, mush, plush, push, rush, shush, slush, swoosh, thrush, tush, whoosh.
Bus, busk, cuss, dusk, fuss, musk, plus, puss, suss, thus, tusk, us.
Bluff, cuff, fluff, guff, gruff, huff, puff, rough, scruff, stuff, tough.
But, butt, cut, glut, gut, hut, jut, nut, put, rut, shut, smut, strut, tut.
[2] **Adjudge**, begrudge, misjudge, prejudge.
Adjust, august, blood lust, combust, discussed, disgust, distrust, entrust, gold dust, mistrust, robust, stardust, unjust, wanderlust.
Dandruff, earmuff, enough, handcuff, powder puff, rebuff, sho'nuff.
Airbrush, ambush, hairbrush, hush-hush, mancrush, nailbrush, paintbrush, toothbrush.
Clean-cut, clear-cut, crewcut, crosscut, doughnut/donut (U.S.), haircut, half-shut, peanut, rebut, shortcut, somewhat, uncut, walnut.

5.1.111 "--utched" (as in "touched")
[1] clutched, touched, untouched.

SURPRISING RHYMING:
[1] **Butch**, clutch(ed), crutch, Dutch, hutch, much, such, touch(ed).
Bust, bussed, cussed, dust, fussed, gust, just, lust, must, rust, trust.
Blushed, brushed, bushed, crushed, flushed, gushed, hushed, mushed, pushed, rushed, shushed, slushed, swooshed.
Budged, fudged, grudged, judged, nudged, smudged, trudged.
Bluffed, cuffed, duffed, fluffed, huffed, puffed, roughed, stuffed.
Bunched, crunched, hunched, lunched, munched, punched.
[2] **Adjust**, august, blood lust, combust, discussed, disgust, distrust, entrust, gold dust, mistrust, robust, stardust, unjust, wanderlust.
Abduct, conduct, deduct, construct, instruct, obstruct, product.
Abrupt, corrupt, cupped, disrupt, erupt, interrupt.
Dandruff, earmuff, enough, handcuff, powder puff, rebuff, sho'nuff.

5.1.112 "--uv" (as in "love")
above, dove, glove, guv, love, shove, true love, tug-of-love, turtledove, ladylove.

SURPRISING RHYMING:
[1] **Gloved**, loved, of, shoved.
Bluff, buff, cuff, duff, fluff, guff, gruff, huff, muff, puff, rough, scruff, scuff, slough, snuff, stuff, tough, tuff, woof.
Blood, bud, could, dud, flood, good, hood, mud, should, spud, stood, stud, thud, wood, would.
[2] **Dandruff**, earmuff, enough, handcuff, rebuff, sho'nuff.

5.1.113 "--uvved" (as in "loved")
[1] gloved, loved, shoved.

SURPRISING RHYMING:
[1] **Above**, dove, glove, guv, love, shove.
Bluffed, cuffed, duffed, fluffed, huffed, puffed, rebuffed, roughed, scuffed, stuffed.
Blood, could, dud, flood, good, hood, mud, should, stood, stud, thud, wood, would.
Bugged, chugged, drugged, hugged, mugged, plugged, shrugged, tugged, unplugged.
Budged, fudged, grudged, judged, nudged, smudged, trudged.

[2] **Boyhood**, childhood, driftwood, falsehood, firewood, knighthood, lifeblood, manhood, priesthood, touchwood, withstood.

5.1.114 "--uvver" (as in "lover")
[2] cover, glover, hover, lover, shover.
[3] discover, helluva, recover, rediscover, uncover, undercover.

SURPRISING RHYMING:
[2] **Brother**, further, mother, other, smother.
Bluffer, brother, buffer, duffer, other, rougher, suffer, tougher.
Bummer, drummer, dumber, glummer, gunner, hummer, number, runner, shunner, stunner, summer.
Hugger, mugger, shudder, should-a, slugger, snugger, tugger.
Butter, clutter, flutter, gutter, mutter, shutter, splutter, stutter, utter.
Blunder, number, plunder, rumba, slumber, thunder, under, wonder.
[3] **Another**, big brother, blood brother, godmother, grandmother, love her, stepmother.
Covered, discovered, recovered, rediscovered, uncovered.
Latecomer, midsummer, newcomer.

5.1.115 "--uvving" (as in "loving")
[2] loving, shoving.

SURPRISING RHYMING:
[2] **Buzzing**, cousin, dozen.
Bluffing, cuffing, fluffing, huffing, nothing, puffing, roughing, stuffing.
Coming, drumming, humming, numbing, slumming, thumbing.
Cunning, funning, gunning, punning, running, stunning, sunning.
Blooding, budding, flooding, pudding, sudden, thudding.
Bugging, drugging, hugging, mugging, shrugging, slugging, tugging.
Blushing, brushing, crushing, gushing, hushing, pushing, rushing, shushing, touching.
Butting, cutting, footing, jutting, putting, shutting, strutting, tutting, trusting.
[3] **Becoming**, forthcoming, homecoming, oncoming, shortcoming, unbecoming.

5.1.116 "--uz" (as in "buzz")
[1] buzz, 'cuz, does, fuzz, was.

SURPRISING RHYMING:
[1] **Doves**, gloves, loves, shoves.
Bus, cuss, fuss, plus, puss, suss, thus, us.
Bust, bussed, cussed, crust, dust, fussed, gust, just, lust, must, rust, thrust, trust.
Blush, brush, bush, crush, flush, gush, hush, lush, mush, plush, push, rush, shush, slush, tush, whoosh.
Budge, fudge, grudge, judge, nudge, sludge, smudge, trudge.
Blood, bud, could, dud, flood, good, hood, mud, should, spud, stood, stud, thud, wood, would.
Becomes, bums, chums, comes, crumbs, drums, gums, hums, mums, numbs, plums, slums, strums, sums, thumbs.
Buns, guns, ones, puns, runs, shuns, sons, stuns, suns, tons.
[2] **Above**, true love.
Adjust, august, blood lust, combust, discussed, disgust, distrust, entrust, gold dust, mistrust, robust, stardust, unjust, wanderlust.

5.1.117 "--uzzen" (as in "dozen")
[2] cousin, dozen.

SURPRISING RHYMING:
[2] **Buzzing**, doesn't, fussing, loving, nothing, shoving.
Blushing, brushing, crushing, gushing, hushing, pushing, rushing.
Bluffing, fluffing, handcuffing, huffing, puffing, stuffing, toughen.

Coming, drumming, dumbing, humming, numbing, summon.
Couldn't, shouldn't, sudden, wooden, wouldn't.
Cunning, funning, gunning, running, stunning, sunning.
Awesome, bosom, fearsome, gruesome, handsome, loathsome, prism, ransom, wisdom.
[3] **Cushion**, concussion, discussion, percussion, pincushion.
Becoming, forthcoming, homecoming, incoming, oncoming, shortcoming, unbecoming.

5.1.118 "--uzzle" (as in "puzzle")
[2] guzzle, muzzle, nuzzle, puzzle.

SURPRISING RHYMING:
[2] **Guzzled**, muzzled, nuzzled, puzzled.
Bustle, hustle, muscle, mussel, rustle, tussle.
Buzzing, cousin, dozen, loving, nothing, shoving.
Duffel, muffle, ruffle, scuffle, shuffle, snuffle, truffle.
Bubble, double, Hubble, rubble, stubble, trouble.
Cuddle, fuddle, huddle, muddle, puddle.
Juggle, smuggle, snuggle, struggle.
Couple, supple, decouple, uncouple.
Scuttle, shuttle, subtle, rebuttal.
Buckle, chuckle, knuckle, suckle, unbuckle.

5.2 "ur" (as in "her")

5.2.1 "--urr" (as in "fur")
[1] blur, burr, cur, er, err, fir, fur, her, myrrh, purr, sir, slur, spur, stir, were, whirr.
[2] chauffer, coiffeur, concur, confer, defer, demur, deter, hipster, incur, infer, inter, liqueur, liquor, lover, masseur, occur, poseur, prefer, recur, refer, transfer, voyeur.
[3] amateur, bon viveur, calendar, caliber, caliper, challenger, copier, connoisseur, cordon-bleu, cri de coeur, de rigueur, entrepreneur, lavender, manager, massacre, messenger, nourisher, orator, passenger, polisher, predator, publisher, punisher, raconteur, saboteur, scavenger, senator, theatre/theater (U.S.), villager, voyager.

SURPRISING RHYMING:
[1] **Bird**, blurred, heard, nerd, slurred, stirred, third, whirred, word.
Burn, churn, earn, fern, learn, spurn, stern, turn, urn, yearn.
Blurt, cert, curt, dirt, flirt, hurt, pert, shirt, skirt, spurt, squirt.
[2] **Bluffer**, buffer, differ, duffer, puffer, rougher, snuffer, suffer.
Coffer, cougher, offer, proffer, scoffer.
Brother, cover, lover, mother, other, shover, smother.
Censor, denser, fencer, Mensa, sensor, tenser, dispenser.
Altogether, feather, leather, tether, together, weather, whether.
Clever, ever, leisure, measure, never, pleasure, sever, treasure.
Better, debtor, fetter, fretter, getter, letter, setter, sweater, wetter.
Absurd, backward, blackbird, bluebird, buzzword, byword, crossword, firebird, forward, homeward, jailbird, keyword, lovebird, misheard, occurred, password, seabird, snowbird, songbird, unheard.
Adjourn, concern, discern, eastern, heartburn, intern, northern, return, Saturn, sideburn, southern, sunburn, upturn, U-turn, western.
Advert, alert, assert, avert, concert, convert, desert, dessert, divert, exert, expert, nightshirt, overt, pervert, sweatshirt, T-shirt, unhurt.
[3] **Another**, grandmother, stepmother, stepbrother, further.
Discover, hardcover, recover, rediscover, uncover, undercover.
Endeavour/endeavor (U.S.), forever, however, whatever, whatsoever, whenever, wherever, whichever, whoever, whomever.
Inventor, presenter, preventer, repenter, tormentor.
Ancestor, arrester, fiesta, protester, semester, siesta, sou'wester.

5.2.2 "--urch" (as in "church")
[1] birch, church, lurch, perch, search, smirch, wordsearch.

SURPRISING RHYMING:
[1] **Dirge**, merge, purge, scourge, splurge, surge, urge, verge.
Curse, hearse, nurse, purse, terse, verse, worse.
Blurs, firs, furs, hers, purrs, sirs, slurs, spurs, stirs, whirrs.
Burst, cursed, first, nursed, pursed, thirst, worst.
Blurts, certs, flirts, hurts, shirts, skirts, spurts, squirts.
Berth, birth, dearth, earth, girth, mirth, worth.
Berk, clerk (U.S.), dirk, irk, jerk, lurk, perk, quirk, shirk, smirk, work.
[2] **Converge**, diverge, emerge, submerge, upsurge.
Adverse, averse, coerce, commerce, converse, disperse, diverse, immerse, perverse, rehearse, reimburse, reverse, universe.
Chauffeurs, confers, defers, deters, hipsters, incurs, infers, liqueurs, liquors, lovers, occurs, poseurs, prefers, recurs, transfers, voyeurs.
Cloudburst, coerced, dispersed, headfirst, immersed, outburst, rehearsed, reversed, starburst, sunburst.
Alerts, averts, converts, diverts, exerts, experts, inserts, nightshirts, perverts, reverts, sweatshirts, T-shirts

5.2.3 "--urches" (as in "churches")
[2] birches, churches, lurches, perches, searches.

SURPRISING RHYMING:
[2] **Curses**, hearses, nurses, purses, verses.
Dirges, merges, purges, scourges, splurges, surges, urges, verges.
[3] **Coerces**, converses, disburses, disperses, immerses, rehearses, reverses, submerses, traverses, universes.
Converges, diverges, emerges, submerges, upsurges.

5.2.4 "--urd" (as in "bird")
[1] bird, blurred, burred, curd, heard, herd, nerd, slurred, stirred, third, whirred, word.
[2] absurd, backward, blackbird, bluebird, buzzword, byword, catchword, conferred, crossword, firebird, foreword, forward, homeward, inferred, jailbird, keyword, lovebird, misheard, occurred, onward, password, recurred, reword, seabird, seaward, snowbird, songbird, swearword, unheard, unstirred, upward, watchword.
[3] afterward, ladybird, mockingbird, overheard, undeterred.

SURPRISING RHYMING:
[1] **Curved**, served, swerved.
Blur, fur, her, purr, sir, slur, spur, stir, were, whirr.
Blurt, cert, curt, dirt, flirt, hurt, pert, shirt, skirt, spurt, squirt.
Burn(ed), earn(ed), fern, learn(ed), spurn(ed), turn(ed), yearn(ed).
[2] **Conserved**, deserved, observed, preserved, reserved, unnerved.
Chauffer, coiffeur, concur, confer, defer, demur, deter, hipster, incur, infer, lover, occur, poseur, prefer, voyeur.
Adjourn(ed), concern(ed), discern, eastern, heartburn, intern, northern, return(ed), sideburn, southern, sunburn, western.
Advert, alert, assert, avert, concert, convert, desert, dessert, divert, exert, expert, nightshirt, overt, pervert, sweatshirt, T-shirt, unhurt.
[3] **Amateur**, bon viveur, calendar, challenger, connoisseur, cordon-bleu, cri de coeur, de rigueur, entrepreneur, lavender, manager, massacre, messenger, passenger, predator, punisher, raconteur, saboteur, scavenger, senator, theatre/theater (U.S.), villager, voyager.

5.2.5 "--urge" (as in "urge")

[1] dirge, merge, purge, scourge, splurge, surge, urge, verge.

[2] converge, diverge, emerge, submerge, upsurge.

SURPRISING RHYMING:
[1] **Birch**, church, lurch, perch, search, wordsearch.
Curse, hearse, nurse, purse, terse, verse, worse.
Curve, nerve, perv, serve, swerve, verve.
Berth, birth, dearth, earth, girth, mirth, worth.
Bird, blurred, heard, herd, slurred, stirred, third, whirred, word.
Blurt, cert, curt, dirt, flirt, hurt, pert, shirt, skirt, spurt, squirt.
[2] **Conserve**, deserve, observe, preserve, reserve, unnerve.
Adverse, averse, coerce, commerce, converse, disperse, diverse, immerse, perverse, rehearse, reverse, universe.
Cloudburst, coerced, dispersed, headfirst, immersed, outburst, rehearsed, reversed, starburst, sunburst.
Alert, assert, avert, concert, convert, divert, exert, expert, insert, nightshirt, overt, pay dirt, pervert, revert, sweatshirt, T-shirt, unhurt.
Absurd, backward, blackbird, bluebird, buzzword, byword, conferred, crossword, firebird, forward, homeward, jailbird, keyword, lovebird, misheard, occurred, onward, password, recurred, seabird, snowbird, songbird, unheard, upward, watchword.

5.2.6 "--urging" (as in "urging")
[2] merging, purging, scourging, splurging, surging, urging, verging.
[3] converging, diverging, emerging, submerging.

SURPRISING RHYMING:
[2] **Bursting**, cursing, curving, nursing, pursing, serving, swerving.
Ka-ching, lurching, perching, searching, surfing, surgeon, urgent.
Curling, hurling, swirling, twirling, whirling.
Burning, churning, earning, learning, spurning, turning, yearning.
Blurring, furring, purring, slurring, spurring, stirring, whirring.
Blurting, flirting, hurting, skirting, spurting, squirting.
Irking, lurking, networking, shirking, smirking, twerking, working.
[3] **Assertion**, aversion, coercion, conversion, desertion, diversion, excursion, exertion, immersion, insertion, perversion, version.
Adjourning, concerning, discerning, returning.
Coercing, conversing, dispersing, immersing, rehearsing, reversing.
Conserving, deserving, observing, preserving, reserving, unnerving.
Conferring, deterring, incurring, inferring, occurring, preferring, recurring, transferring.
Alerting, asserting, converting, deserting, diverting, exerting, inserting, reverting.

5.2.7 "--urk" (as in "work")
[1] clerk (U.S.), dirk, irk, jerk, lurk, perk, quirk, shirk, smirk, work.
[2] artwork, berserk, bookwork, brickwork, clockwork, fieldwork, firework, footwork, framework, groundwork, guesswork, homework, housework. legwork, network, paintwork, patchwork, rework, roadwork, spadework, stonework, waxwork, woodwork.
[3] bodywork, donkeywork, handiwork, overwork, paperwork.

SURPRISING RHYMING:
[1] **Blurt**, cert, curt, dirt, flirt, hurt, pert, shirt, skirt, spurt, squirt.
Burp, chirp, perp, slurp, twerp, usurp.
Burst, cursed, first, nursed, pursed, thirst, worst.
Birth, dearth, earth, girth, mirth, worth.
Blur, fur, her, myrrh, per, purr, sir, slur, spur, stir, were, whirr.
Bird, blurred, heard, herd, nerd, slurred, stirred, third, whirred, word.
Burn, churn, earn, fern, learn, spurn, stern, turn, urn, yearn.
[2] **Advert**, alert, assert, avert, concert, convert, dessert, divert, exert, expert, nightshirt, overt, pervert, sweatshirt, T-shirt, unhurt.
Cloudburst, coerced, dispersed, headfirst, immersed, outburst, rehearsed, reversed, starburst, sunburst.
[3] **Extrovert**, introvert, miniskirt, undershirt, underskirt.

5.2.8 "--urking" (as in "working")
irking, jerking, lurking, networking, overworking, shirking, smirking, twerking, working.

SURPRISING RHYMING:
[2] **Blurting**, flirting, hurting, skirting, spurting, squirting.
Burping, bursting, chirping, cursing, nursing, person, slurping.
Blurring, purring, slurring, spurring, stirring, whirring.
Burning, churning, earning, learning, spurning, turning, yearning.
Curling, hurling, serving, surfing, swerving, swirling, twirling, whirling.
Merging, purging, searching, surging, urging, urgent, verging, virgin.
[3] **Alerting**, averting, deserting, diverting, exerting, inserting.
Coercing, dispersing, immersing, rehearsing, reversing.

5.2.9 "--url" (as in "girl")
[1] curl, earl, furl, girl, hurl, pearl, purl, swirl, twirl, whirl.
[2] ballgirl, call girl, choirgirl, cowgirl, mother-of-pearl, salesgirl, schoolgirl, showgirl, unfurl, weathergirl.

SURPRISING RHYMING:
[1] **Curled**, furled, hurled, swirled, twirled, unfurled, whirled, world.
Curve, nerve, perv, serve, swerve, verve.
[2] **Dreamworld**, underworld.
Conserve, deserve, observe, preserve, reserve, unnerve.

5.2.10 "--urly" (as in "early")
[2] burly, curly, early, girlie, hurly-burly, surly, swirly, twirly, yearly.

SURPRISING RHYMING:
[2] **Blurry**, curvy, earthly, firmly, furry, germ-free, gumtree, hurry, hungry, jury, nervy, sultry, sundry, surrey, teary, theory, worry.
Crumbly, grumbly, humbly, dumbly, glumly, numbly.
Bubbly, bully, dully, duly, fully, gulley, gully, lovely, monthly, newly, poorly, pulley, purply, rumbly, surely, termly, truly, ugly, worldly.
Bumpy, droopy, dumpy, frumpy, grumpy, jumpy, puppy, whoopee.
Curtsy, fussy, gutsy, hussy, look-see, mercy, pussy.
[3] **Allergy**, effigy, emoji, energy, eulogy, lethargy, prodigy, refugee, strategy, synergy.
Brotherly, cowardly, dastardly, directly, easterly, family, fatherly, gingerly, gravelly, leisurely, masterly, motherly, neighbourly/neighborly, northerly, otherworldly, sisterly, southerly, westerly, womanly.
Ancestry, archery, artistry, bakery, battery, bigotry, binary, blackberry, blubbery, blueberry, blustery, brasserie, bravery, brewery, bribery, burglary, calorie, carpentry, carvery, cavalry, celery, century, chemistry, chicory, chivalry, Christmas tree, colliery, contrary, devilry, diary, dietary, disagree, dithery, doddery, drudgery, dungaree, duty-free, eatery, enquiry, estuary, expiry, factory, fakery, feathery, filigree, finery, fishery, flattery, fluttery, forestry, forgery, friary, gallery, geometry, gimmickry, glittery, greenery, grocery, history, imagery, injury, inquiry, ivory, jamboree, jewellery/jewelry, jittery, leathery, lingerie, lottery, luxury, memory, mercury, misery, momentary, monastery, mystery, nursery, obituary, obligatory, pageantry, pedigree, perjury, pillory, pleasantry, poetry, pottery, primary, priory, quivery, referee, revelry, reverie, rivalry, robbery, rockery, rosary, rubbery, salary, sanctuary, savagery, savory, scenery, sensory, shimmery, shivery, silvery, slavery, slippery, sorcery, sugary, surgery, tapestry, thundery, treachery, trickery, victory, wintery, wizardry.

5.2.11 "--urled" (as in "world")
[1] curled, furled, hurled, swirled, twirled, unfurled, whirled, world.
[2] dreamworld, underworld.

SURPRISING RHYMING:
[1] **Curl**, earl, furl, girl, hurl, pearl, purl, swirl, twirl, whirl.
Curve(d), nerve, perv, serve(d), swerve(d), verve.
Burned, churned, earned, learned, spurned, turned, yearned.
Burn, churn, earn, fern, learn, spurn, stern, turn, urn, yearn.
Bird, blurred, heard, nerd, slurred, stirred, third, whirred, word.
[2] **Choirgirl**, cowgirl, mother-of-pearl, salesgirl, schoolgirl, showgirl, unfurl, weathergirl.
Conserved, deserved, observed, preserved, reserved, unnerved.
Conserve, deserve, observe, preserve, reserve, unnerve.
Adjourned, affirmed, concerned, confirmed, returned, sunburned.
Adjourn, concern, discern, eastern, heartburn, intern, northern, return, sideburn, southern, sunburn, upturn, U-turn, western.

5.2.12 "--urm" (as in "germ")
[1] firm, germ, perm, squirm, term, worm.
[2] affirm, confirm, infirm, midterm, long-term, reaffirm, short-term.

SURPRISING RHYMING:
[1] **Permed**, squirmed, termed.
Burn, churn, earn, fern, learn, spurn, stern, turn, urn, yearn.
Burned, churned, earned, learned, spurned, turned, yearned.
[2] **Affirmed**, confirmed, reaffirmed, unconfirmed.
Adjourn(ed), astern, concern(ed), discern(ed), eastern, heartburn, intern, nocturne, northern, return(ed), Saturn, sideburn, southern, sunburn(ed), upturn, U-turn, western.

5.2.13 "--urmur" (as in "murmur")
firmer, murmur, squirmer, terra firma, wormer.

SURPRISING RHYMING:
[2] **Burner**, earner, learner, returner, sterner, taverna, yearner.
Fervour/fervor (U.S), further, observer, server, surfer, time-server.
Burger, burglar, curler, murmured, twirler, whirler.
Curser, cursor, lurker, shirker, tearjerker, vice versa, worker.
Girder, herder, merger, murder, perjure, purdah, purger, verger.
Lurcher, nurture, researcher, searcher.

5.2.14 "--urn" (as in "turn")
[1] burn, churn, earn, fern, learn, spurn, stern, turn, urn, yearn.
[2] adjourn, astern, concern, discern, eastern, heartburn, intern, nocturne, northern, return, Saturn, sideburn, southern, sunburn, taciturn, upturn, U-turn, western.

SURPRISING RHYMING:
[1] **Burned**, churned, earned, learned, spurned, turned, yearned.
Firm, germ, perm, squirm, term, worm.
Curve, nerve, perv, serve, swerve, verve.
[2] **Adjourned**, concerned, returned, sunburned.
Affirm, confirm, infirm, midterm, long-term, short-term.
Affirmed, confirmed, reaffirmed, unconfirmed.
Conserve, deserve, observe, preserve, reserve, unnerve.

5.2.15 "--urned" (as in "turned")
[1] burned, churned, earned, learned, spurned, turned, yearned.
[2] adjourned, concerned, returned, sunburned.

SURPRISING RHYMING:
[1] **Burn**, churn, earn, fern, learn, spurn, stern, turn, urn, yearn.
Firm, germ, perm, squirm, term, worm.
Curled, furled, hurled, swirled, twirled, unfurled, whirled, world.
Bird, blurred, heard, nerd, slurred, stirred, third, whirred, word.

[2] **Adjourn**, astern, concern, discern, eastern, heartburn, intern, northern, return, sideburn, southern, sunburn, U-turn, western.
Affirm(ed), confirm(ed), infirm, reaffirmed, unconfirmed.
Conserved, deserved, observed, preserved, reserved, unnerved.
Absurd, blackbird, bluebird, buzzword, conferred, crossword, firebird, jailbird, keyword, lovebird, misheard, occurred, password, recurred, seabird, snowbird, songbird, unheard, unstirred, upward, watchword.

5.2.16 "--urning" (as in "burning")
[2] burning, churning, earning, learning, spurning, turning, yearning.
[3] adjourning, concerning, discerning, returning.

SURPRISING RHYMING:
[2] **Firming**, perming, squirming.
Blurring, purring, slurring, spurring, stirring, swerving, whirring.
Merging, purging, scourging, splurging, surging, urging, verging.
Blurting, flirting, hurting, shirting, skirting, spurting, squirting.
Curling, hurling, swirling, twirling, whirling.
Cursing, nursing, pursing, versing.
Lurking, networking, perking, shirking, smirking, twerking, working.
[3] **Affirming**, confirming, reaffirming.
Deterring, incurring, inferring, occurring, preferring, recurring.
Conserving, deserving, observing, preserving, reserving, unnerving.
Converging, diverging, emerging, submerging.
Alerting, asserting, averting, deserting, diverting, exerting, inserting.
Coercing, dispersing, immersing, rehearsing, reversing.

5.2.17 "--urse" (as in "curse")
[1] curse, hearse, nurse, purse, terse, verse, worse.
[2] adverse, averse, coerce, commerce, converse, disperse, diverse, immerse, perverse, rehearse, reimburse, reverse, universe.

SURPRISING RHYMING:
[1] **Blurs**, firs, furs, hers, purrs, sirs, slurs, spurs, stirs, whirrs.
Burst, cursed, first, nursed, pursed, thirst, worst.
Curves, nerves, pervs, serves, swerves.
Blurt(s), cert(s), curt, dirt, flirt(s), hurt(s), pert, shirt(s), skirt(s), spurt(s), squirt(s).
Birch, church, lurch, perch, search, smirch, wordsearch.
Dirge, merge, purge, scourge, serge, splurge, surge, urge, verge.
[2] **Chauffeurs**, defers, deters, hipsters, incurs, infers, liqueurs, liquors, lovers, masseurs, occurs, poseurs, prefers, refers, voyeurs.
Conserves, deserves, observes, preserves, reserves, unnerves.
Cloudburst, coerced, dispersed, headfirst, immersed, outburst, rehearsed, reversed, starburst, sunburst.
Advert(s), alert(s), avert(s), concert(s), convert(s), dessert(s), divert(s), exert(s), expert(s), insert(s), nightshirt(s), overt, pervert(s), sweatshirt(s), T-shirt(s), unhurt.
Converge, diverge, emerge, submerge, upsurge.
[3] **Amateurs**, bon viveurs, challengers, connoisseurs, entrepreneurs, managers, massacres, messengers, passengers, publishers, punishers, scavengers, theatres/theaters (U.S.), villagers, voyagers.

5.2.18 "--urses" (as in "nurses")
[2] curses, nurses, purses, verses.
[3] coerces, converses, disburses, disperses, immerses, rehearses, reverses, submerses, traverses, universes.

SURPRISING RHYMING:
[1] **Curse**, hearse, nurse, purse, terse, verse, worse.
[2] **Adverse**, averse, coerce, commerce, converse, disperse, diverse, immerse, perverse,

rehearse, reimburse, reverse, universe.
Churches, lurches, perches, searches, wordsearches.
Merges, purges, scourges, splurges, surges, urges, verges.
[3] **Converges**, diverges, emerges, submerges, upsurges.

5.2.19 "--ursing" (as in "nursing")
[2] cursing, nursing, pursing.
[3] coercing, conversing, dispersing, immersing, rehearsing, reversing, traversing.

SURPRISING RHYMING:
[2] **Curving**, serving, swerving.
Merging, purging, scourging, splurging, surging, urging, verging.
Blurring, purring, slurring, spurring, stirring, whirring.
Curling, hurling, swirling, twirling, whirling.
Burning, earning, learning, spurning, squirming, turning, yearning.
Flirting, hurting, lurking, shirking, skirting, squirting, twerking, working.
[3] **Conserving**, deserving, preserving, reserving, unnerving.
Converging, diverging, emerging, submerging.
Adjourning, affirming, concerning, confirming, discerning, returning.
Assertion, aversion, coercion, conversion, desertion, diversion, excursion, exertion, immersion, insertion, perversion, version.

5.2.20 "--ursion" (as in "excursion")
[3] aspersion, assertion, aversion, coercion, conversion, desertion, diversion, excursion, exertion, immersion, incursion, insertion, perversion, submersion, subversion, version.

SURPRISING RHYMING:
[2] **Cursin'** *(silent 'g')*, mergin', nursin', purgin', scourgin', searchin', surgeon, surgin', urgin', urgent, vergin', virgin.
Certain, curtain, uncertain.
Burden, person, sermon, unburden, worsen.
Blurtin' *(silent 'g')*, flirtin', hurtin', jerkin', lurkin', shirkin', smirkin', squirtin', twerkin'.
[3] **Coercin'** *(silent 'g')*, dispersing, immersing, rehearsing, reversing.
Conservin' *(silent 'g')*, deservin', observin', preservin', reservin', unnervin'.
Convergin' *(silent 'g')*, divergin', emergin', submergin'.

5.2.21 "--urst" (as in "worst")
[1] burst, cursed, first, nursed, pursed, thirst, worst.
[2] cloudburst, coerced, conversed, disbursed, dispersed, headfirst, immersed, outburst, rehearsed, reversed, starburst, sunburst.

SURPRISING RHYMING:
[1] **Curse**, hearse, nurse, purse, terse, verse, worse.
Blurt(s), cert(s), curt, dirt, flirt(s), hurt(s), shirt(s), skirt(s), squirt(s).
Birch, church, lurch, perch, search, smirch, wordsearch.
Blurs, firs, furs, hers, purrs, sirs, slurs, spurs, stirs, whirrs.
[2] **Adverse**, averse, coerce, commerce, converse, disperse, diverse, immerse, perverse, rehearse, reverse, universe.
Advert, alert, assert, avert, concert, convert, desert, dessert, divert, exert, expert, nightshirt, overt, pervert, sweatshirt, T-shirt, unhurt.

5.2.22 "--urt" (as in "hurt")
[1] blurt, cert, curt, dirt, flirt, hurt, pert, shirt, skirt, spurt, squirt.
[2] advert, alert, assert, avert, concert, convert, desert, dessert, divert, exert, expert, inert, insert, nightshirt, overt, pay dirt, pervert, revert, sweatshirt, T-shirt, unhurt.
[3] extrovert, introvert, miniskirt, undershirt, underskirt.

SURPRISING RHYMING:
[1] **Burst**, cursed, first, nursed, pursed, thirst, worst.

Lurched, perched, researched, searched.
Berk, clerk (U.S.), dirk, irk, jerk, lurk, perk, quirk, shirk, smirk, work.
Irked, jerked, lurked, perked, shirked, smirked, worked.
Bird, blurred, heard, herd, nerd, stirred, third, whirred, word.
Burned, burnt, earned, learned, learnt, spurned, turned, yearned.
[2] **Cloudburst**, coerced, dispersed, headfirst, immersed, outburst, rehearsed, reversed, starburst, sunburst.
Artwork, berserk, clockwork, firework, groundwork, guesswork, homework, housework. legwork, network, patchwork.
Absurd, backward, blackbird, bluebird, buzzword, byword, crossword, firebird, forward, homeward, jailbird, keyword, lovebird, misheard, occurred, onward, password, recurred, seabird, snowbird, songbird, unheard, unstirred, upward, watchword.

5.2.23 "--urted" (as in "flirted")
[2] blurted, flirted, skirted, spurted, squirted.
[3] alerted, asserted, averted, concerted, converted, deserted, diverted, exerted, inserted, introverted, perverted, reverted.

SURPRISING RHYMING:
[2] **Blurting**, flirting, hurting, shirking, skirting, spurting, squirting.
Certain, curtain, uncertain.
Assertive, burden, circuit, furtive, nervous, purpose, service, worded.

5.2.24 "--urting" (as in "hurting")
[2] blurting, flirting, hurting, shirking, skirting, spurting, squirting.
[3] alerting, asserting, averting, converting, deserting, diverting, exerting, inserting, reverting.

SURPRISING RHYMING:
[2] **Certain**, curtain, uncertain.
Hurtling, lurking, networking, shirking, smirking, twerking, working.
Burning, churning, earning, learning, spurning, turning, yearning.
Burden, person, sermon, unburden, urban, wording, worsen.
Bursting, cursing, nursing, pursing, versing.
Merging, searching, surgeon, surging, urging, urgent, verging, virgin.
Curling, hurling, swirling, twirling, whirling.
Blurring, purring, slurring, spurring, stirring, whirring.
[3] **Affirming**, confirming, disturbing, reaffirming.
Coercing, dispersing, immersing, rehearsing, reversing, .
Conserving, deserving, observing, preserving, reserving, unnerving.

5.2.25 "--urtin" (as in "certain")
certain, curtain, uncertain.

SURPRISING RHYMING:
[2] **Blurting**, flirting, hurting, shirting, skirting, squirting.
Hurtling, lurking, networking, shirking, smirking, twerking, working.
Bursting, cursing, nursing, pursing, versing.
Burning, churning, earning, learning, spurning, turning, yearning.
Burden, person, sermon, urban, version, wording, worsen.
Merging, searching, surgeon, surging, urging, urgent, verging, virgin.
[3] **Alerting**, asserting, averting, deserting, diverting, exerting.
Confirming, determine, disturbing, reaffirming.
Conserving, deserving, observing, preserving, reserving, unnerving.
Adjourning, concerning, discerning, returning.

5.2.26 "--urth" (as in "earth")
[1] berth, birth, dearth, earth, girth, mirth, worth.

SURPRISING RHYMING:
[1] Blurt, cert, curt, dirt, flirt, hurt, pert, shirt, skirt, squirt.
Curve, nerve, perv, serve, swerve, verve.
Dirge, merge, purge, scourge, serge, splurge, surge, urge, verge.
Bird, blurred, heard, nerd, slurred, stirred, third, whirred, word.
Curse, hearse, nurse, purse, terse, verse, worse.
[2] Conserve, deserve, observe, preserve, reserve, unnerve.
Conserved, deserved, observed, preserved, reserved, unnerved.
Advert, alert, assert, avert, concert, convert, divert, exert, expert, nightshirt, overt, pervert, sweatshirt, T-shirt, unhurt.
Absurd, backward, blackbird, bluebird, buzzword, byword, crossword, firebird, forward, homeward, jailbird, keyword, lovebird, misheard, occurred, onward, password, recurred, seabird, snowbird, songbird, unheard, unstirred, upward, watchword.
Adverse, averse, coerce, commerce, converse, disperse, diverse, immerse, perverse, rehearse, reverse, universe.
[3] Extrovert, introvert, miniskirt, undershirt, underskirt.
Hummingbird, ladybird, mockingbird, overheard, undeterred.

5.2.27 "--urve" (as in "curve")
[1] curve, nerve, perv, serve, swerve, verve.
[2] conserve, deserve, observe, preserve, reserve, unnerve.

SURPRISING RHYMING:
[1] Curved, served, swerved.
Berth, birth, dearth, earth, girth, mirth, worth.
Blur, burr, fur, her, purr, sir, slur, spur, stir, were, whirr.
Dirge, merge, purge, scourge, serge, splurge, surge, urge, verge.
Bird, blurred, heard, nerd, slurred, stirred, third, whirred, word.
[2] Conserved, deserved, observed, preserved, reserved, unnerved.
Chauffer, coiffeur, confer, defer, deter, hipster, infer, liqueur, liquor, lover, masseur, occur, poseur, prefer, recur, refer, transfer, voyeur.
Adverse, averse, coerce, commerce, converse, disperse, diverse, immerse, perverse, rehearse, reverse, universe.
Converge, diverge, emerge, submerge, upsurge.
Absurd, backward, blackbird, bluebird, buzzword, byword, crossword, firebird, forward, homeward, jailbird, keyword, lovebird, misheard, occurred, onward, password, recurred, seabird, snowbird, songbird, unheard, unstirred, upward, watchword.

5.2.28 "--urved" (as in "curved")
[1] curved, served, swerved.
[2] conserved, deserved, observed, preserved, reserved, unnerved.

SURPRISING RHYMING:
[1] Curve, nerve, perv, serve, swerve, verve.
Berth, birth, dearth, earth, girth, mirth, worth.
Merged, purged, scourged, splurged, surged, urged, verged.
Bird, blurred, heard, herd, slurred, stirred, third, whirred, word.
Curled, furled, hurled, swirled, twirled, unfurled, whirled, world.
Blurt, cert, curt, dirt, flirt, hurt, pert, shirt, skirt, spurt, squirt.
Burned, churned, earned, learned, spurned, turned, yearned.
[2] Conserve, deserve, observe, preserve, reserve, unnerve.
Absurd, backward, blackbird, bluebird, buzzword, byword, crossword, firebird, forward, homeward, jailbird, keyword, lovebird, misheard, occurred, onward, overheard, password, recurred, seabird, snowbird, songbird, unheard, unstirred, upward.
Advert, alert, assert, avert, concert, convert, desert, dessert, divert, exert, expert, nightshirt, overt, pervert, sweatshirt, T-shirt, unhurt.
Adjourned, concerned, returned, sunburned.

*

5.2.29 "--urving" (as in "curving")
[2] curving, serving, swerving.
[3] conserving, deserving, observing, preserving, reserving.

SURPRISING RHYMING:
[2] **Merging**, purging, scourging, splurging, surging, urging, verging.
Cursing, nursing, pursing, versing.
Blurting, flirting, hurting, shirting, skirting, spurting, squirting.
Curling, hurling, swirling, twirling, whirling.
Burning, churning, earning, learning, spurning, turning, yearning.
Irking, jerking, lurking, networking, perking, shirking, smirking, twerking, working.
[3] **Conferring**, deferring, deterring, incurring, inferring, occurring, preferring, recurring, referring, transferring.
Converging, diverging, emerging, submerging.
Coercing, conversing, disbursing, dispersing, immersing, rehearsing, reversing, submersing, traversing.
Adjourning, concerning, discerning, returning.
Alerting, asserting, averting, converting, deserting, diverting, exerting, inserting, reverting.

* * * *

Other books by Brian Oliver

"HOW [NOT] TO WRITE A HIT SONG! —101 COMMON MISTAKES TO AVOID IF YOU WANT SONGWRITING SUCCESS"

Written in an easy, non-technical style, this book takes a close look at the essential elements consistently found in the structure, melodies and lyrics of all hit songs. It highlights the most common errors made when these key components are built into a song—so that new songwriters can try to avoid such mistakes in their own songs.

* * *

Five-star praise for "HOW [NOT] TO WRITE A HIT SONG!" from verified purchasers*:

"The best book on song writing that I have ever read. I've been writing songs for 15 years and I was worried that I would know most of it already, but I learnt a lot of new things and it has definitely improved my song writing. It is good for both beginners and experienced song writers. I wish I had read this book when I first started out as it would have saved me a lot of time that I wasted on trial and error." —Heather

"The best songwriting book ever. This is an absolutely brilliant book for the aspiring or established songwriter. I am very impressed. It is concise, easy to read and on point. A must read if you are aiming to write a HIT song!" —Y. Vernon

"This book is just superb. I am quite new to song writing but this book has helped me immeasurably. It explains every step of the process. Really is a great motivator to get them down on paper and through to recording. Don't miss this book. I've looked at a few but this for me was easily the best." —Jan Zienkiewicz

"A very good book with many good tips in it. I would recommend anyone to read it who has an interest in songwriting." —David Park

"I highly recommend this to any serious, ready to work hard aspiring songwriter! Easily the best songwriting book I've ever come across!"

"This book was a most enjoyable read. It was uncomplicated, covered all aspects thoroughly, but never tedious to read. It gave a well-balanced view and was written in a style that I feel readers of all ages could identify with. A great tool for any aspiring writer and composer!" —JD

"Absolutely packed with great insight and wisdom. If you have written hundreds or just one song this book will have benefits for you. Seriously!" —'Gogun'

"Fantastic book. Well written, great advice for the hopeful songwriter. Spot on." —Mark Edward Purvis

"This book is a must for the aspiring songwriter. As well as detailed information about the pitfalls of a newcomer to the market, the book also highlights the tried and tested successful Verse-Chorus-Verse progressions etc. Being new to song writing myself, I revisited some old songs after reading this book and reworked them using some of the advice given and I have to say they are greatly improved...Well worth buying even if you think you have mastered the art... Recommended." —G.T.

"A fantastically useful book. This is a book that does exactly what it says on the cover, and it does it in an entertaining and practical way. No words are wasted, there isn't a rambling preface or lengthy introduction, it just gets stuck in straight away." —'A fingerstyle guitarist'

*All verified Amazon purchasers

# # # #

Printed in Great Britain
by Amazon